Mastering
Autodesk®
Maya® 2011

Mastering

Autodesk® Maya® 2011

Autodesk®
Official Training Guide

Eric Keller
with Todd Palamar and Anthony Honn

WILEY

Wiley Publishing, Inc.

Acquisitions Editor: Mariann Barsolo

Development Editor: Tom Cirtin

Technical Editor: Gael McGill

Production Editor: Elizabeth Ginns Britten

Editorial Manager: Pete Gaughan

Production Manager: Tim Tate

Vice President and Executive Group Publisher: Richard Swadley

Vice President and Publisher: Neil Edde

Media Associate Project Manager: Jenny Swisher

Media Associate Producer: Josh Frank

Media Quality Assurance: Marilyn Hummel

Book Designers: Maureen Forys, Happenstance Type-O-Rama; Judy Fung

Compositor: Chris Gillespie, Happenstance Type-O-Rama

Proofreader: Word One, New York

Indexer: Robert Swanson

Project Coordinator, Cover: Lynsey Stanford

Cover Designer: Ryan Sneed

Copyright © 2010 by Wiley Publishing, Inc., Indianapolis, Indiana

Published simultaneously in Canada

ISBN: 978-0-470-63935-1
ISBN: 978-0-470-92574-4 (ebk)
ISBN: 978-0-470-92576-8 (ebk)
ISBN: 978-0-470-92575-1 (ebk)

For general information on our other products and services or to obtain technical support, please contact our Customer Care Department within the U.S. at (877) 762-2974, outside the U.S. at (317) 572-3993 or fax (317) 572-4002.

Wiley also publishes its books in a variety of electronic formats. Some content that appears in print may not be available in electronic books.

Library of Congress Cataloging-in-Publication Data is available from the publisher.

Dear Reader,

Thank you for choosing *Mastering Autodesk Maya 2011.* This book is part of a family of premium-quality Sybex books, all of which are written by outstanding authors who combine practical experience with a gift for teaching.

Sybex was founded in 1976. More than 30 years later, we're still committed to producing consistently exceptional books. With each of our titles, we're working hard to set a new standard for the industry. From the paper we print on, to the authors we work with, our goal is to bring you the best books available.

I hope you see all that reflected in these pages. I'd be very interested to hear your comments and get your feedback on how we're doing. Feel free to let me know what you think about this or any other Sybex book by sending me an email at nedde@wiley.com. If you think you've found a technical error in this book, please visit http://sybex.custhelp.com. Customer feedback is critical to our efforts at Sybex.

Best regards,

Neil Edde
Vice President and Publisher
Sybex, an Imprint of Wiley

To my wife and best friend, Zoe.

Acknowledgments

I'd like to thank all the people who worked so hard on this project, especially the editors Thomas Cirtin, my good friend Gael McGill, and Liz Britten. I'd also like to thank Mariann Barsolo and Pete Gaughan. I thank all the folks at Autodesk who provided excellent support throughout the writing of this book.

I'd like to thank Todd Palamar for his help in writing the rigging and texturing chapters. He is an excellent and extremely knowledgeable author. Please check out his book *Maya Studio Projects: Dynamics* (Sybex, 2010).

Several of my good friends contributed artwork that is used in the book. Anthony Honn built the vehicle models used in many of the example scenes; my brother, Travis Keller, designed the kitchen and pergola models used in the lighting chapters; and Chris Sanchez provided the fantastic space suit design used in the modeling chapters. I've worked with these artists at several studios; they are examples of the best of the talent working in the design and entertainment industries today.

Special thanks go to Ara Kermankian and Scott Ulliman who provided some of the artwork in the color insert.

I'd like to thank the following artists, teachers, and authors for their inspiration over the years: Scott Spencer, Kevin Llewellyn, John Brown, Alex Alvarez, Darrin Krumweide, Dariush Derakhshani, Saty Raghavachary, Drew Berry, all my teachers and students at the Gnomon School of Visual Effects, and all my friends and colleagues on the LA Freelancers list. Naturally, all the programmers and designers who work so hard to develop this software deserve special recognition for their hard work. They are the true artists who allow the rest of us to create such fantastic things.

Extra special thanks go to Daisy and Joe who all forced me to get away from the computer for some much-needed exercise. And to Blue whose hungry little ghost still haunts the kitchen.

About the Authors

Eric Keller is a freelance visual effects artist working in Hollywood. He divides his time between the entertainment industry and scientific visualization. He teaches an introductory ZBrush class at the Gnomon School of Visual Effects and has authored numerous animation and visualization tutorials for the Harvard Medical School course Maya for Molecular Biologists, taught by Gael McGill.

Eric started out as an animator at the Howard Hughes Medical Institute, where he created animations for science education for seven years. In 2005, he and his wife moved to Los Angeles, where he could study and learn from the masters of visual effects. His goal is to bring the artistry and technology of Hollywood computer graphics to the field of scientific research in the hope that it can inspire and inform the scientific community and the general public.

Eric has worked at some of the best design studios in Los Angeles, including Prologue Films, Imaginary Forces, Yu and Company, BLT and Associates, and The Syndicate. Projects include feature-film title animations for *The Invasion*, *Enchanted*, *Sympathy for Lady Vengeance*, and *Dragon Wars*. He has also contributed to numerous commercials, television shows, and design projects.

Other books by Eric Keller include *Maya Visual Effects: The Innovator's Guide* (Sybex, 2007) and *Introducing ZBrush* (Sybex, 2008). He was a contributing author to *Mastering Maya 7* (Sybex, 2006). He authored the video series *Essential ZBrush 3.1* for Lynda.com as well as numerous tutorials and articles for industry magazines. Many of his tutorials are available online at www.highend3d.com and www.molecularmovies.org.

Todd Palamar wrote Chapter 7, "Rigging and Muscle Systems," and Chapter 11, "Texture Mapping." He began his career almost 20 years ago creating traditional special effects for low-budget horror movies. Quickly gravitating to computer animation, Todd has worked on numerous video games, dozens of military- and game-style simulations, corporate commercials, and theme park rides. He has authored four books, including *Maya Cloth for Characters* (SP Effects, 2008) and *Maya Studio Projects: Dynamics* (Sybex, 2009). Currently Todd is employed as a technical art director at Vcom3D, Inc.

Anthony Honn created the vehicle models used in the example scenes throughout this book. Anthony originally trained in industrial design and architecture. After having graduated from the Art Center College of Design, a series of fateful events resulted in a career within the film and design industries. His clients have included multiple recording artists such as Janet Jackson as well as lifestyle brands such as Nike. Arguably, the industrial designer still lurks beneath, with his continued passion for robotics, automobiles, and furniture. For more of Anthony's work, visit www.anthonyhonn.com.

Contents at a Glance

Contents

Foreword

Let me start by introducing this book and its author, like so: *Mastering Maya*, written by a veritable Maya master.

It gives me great pleasure to write this foreword for my friend, industry colleague, and student Eric Keller. (I had the pleasure of having him in my MEL class, which I teach part-time at the Gnomon School of Visual Effects in Hollywood, California.)

I have been using Maya since its early days back in 1996, and over the years I have come across a lot of books written about the subject. I will tell you that this book clearly deserves to be at the top of the heap. I highly recommend you read it, learn from it, and use it to excel at Maya. Here's why—in today's animation/visual effects/content creation industry, Maya rules as the number-one software of choice for digital artists worldwide. Being consistently at the top isn't easy, but Maya has managed to stay that way ever since it was first released. It follows that if you need to succeed in this field (or if you are just starting out and need to get your foot in the door), you need to get good—make that *really* good—at using Maya. That's why this book is called *Mastering Maya*.

As for the "master" part, Eric practices what he preaches, which lends strong credibility to the material in the book. He uses Maya, together with custom MEL code that he writes and with other pieces of software, to work with scientists in biology and chemistry to create informative, visually appealing imagery. In short, he creates awesome scientific animations using Maya. You can see his work at www.molecularmovies.com and at his personal site at www.bloopatone.com. Browsing through his site, you will discover his artistic talents and the fact that he has also authored a couple of ZBrush books.

Start reading this book now so you can get on the path to mastering Maya. I wish everyone a lot of pleasure reading this book.

—*Saty Raghavachary*

Head, Digital Training and Technical Development
DreamWorks Animation
Los Angeles, June 2010

Introduction

Maya is big. It is really, really huge. The book you hold in your hands and all the exercises within represent a mere sliver of what can be created in Maya. Mastering Maya takes years of study and practice. I have been using Maya almost every day for 12 years, and I'm still constantly faced with new challenges and making new discoveries.

Learning Maya is similar to learning a musical instrument. Both Maya and music require practice, study, patience, and determination. Just as the best musicians make playing their instruments seem effortless, the best Maya artists make visualizing the impossible seem easy. This is because the musician who masters music and the artist who masters Maya have spent years and years studying, practicing, and perfecting their skills and understanding.

This book is meant to be a guide to help you not only understand Maya but also understand how to learn about Maya. The title *Mastering Maya* implies an active engagement with the software. This book is packed with as many hands-on tutorials as I could provide to keep you actively engaged. If you're looking for a quick-reference guide that simply describes each and every button, control, and tool in the Maya interface, use the Maya documentation that comes with the software instead. This book is not a description of Maya; it is an explanation illustrated with practical examples.

The skills you acquire through the examples in this book should prepare you for using Maya in a professional environment. To that end, some features, such as lighting and rendering with mental ray, nDynamics, and Maya Muscle, have received more emphasis and attention. Features that have not changed significantly over the past few versions of the software, such as Maya Software rendering, standard Maya shaders, and older rigging techniques, receive less attention since they have been thoroughly covered elsewhere.

When you read this book and work through the exercises, do not hesitate to use the Maya help files. The authors of this book will not be insulted! The Maya documentation has a very useful search function that allows you to find complete descriptions of each control in the software. To use the help files, click the Help menu in the Maya menu interface. The documentation consists of a large library of Maya resources, which will appear in your default web browser when you access the help files. Experienced Maya artists never hesitate to use the help files to find out more information about the software; there is no shame in asking questions!

Who Should Buy This Book

This book is written for intermediate Maya users and users who are advanced in some aspects of Maya and want to learn more about other aspects. The book is intended to be used by artists who are familiar with Maya and the Maya interface or who have significant experience using similar 3D packages. If you have used older versions of Maya, this book will help you catch up on the newer features in Maya 2011.

If you have never used Maya or any other 3D software on a computer before, this book will be too challenging, and you will quickly become frustrated. You are encouraged to read *Introducing Maya 2011* (Sybex, 2010) or to read through the tutorials in the Maya documentation before attempting this book.

Here are some principles you should be familiar with before reading this book:

◆ The Maya interface.

◆ Computer image basics such as color channels, masking, resolution, and image compression.

◆ Computer animation basics such as keyframes, squash and stretch, and 3D coordinate systems.

◆ Standard Maya shaders, such as the Blinn, Phong, Lambert, Layered, and Anisotropic materials, as well as standard textures, such as Fractal, Ramp, Noise, and Checker.

◆ Lighting and rendering with standard Maya lights and the Maya Software rendering engine.

◆ The basics of working with NURBS curves, polygon surfaces, and NURBS surfaces.

◆ Your operating system. You need to be familiar with opening and saving files and the like. Basic computer networking skills are helpful as well.

What's Inside

Here is a description of the chapters in this book. The lessons in each chapter are accompanied by example scenes from the companion DVD.

Chapter 1: Working in Maya   Discusses how to work with the various nodes and the node structure that make up a scene. Using the Hypergraph, Outliner, Hypershade, Attribute Editor, and Connection Editor to build relationships between nodes is demonstrated through a series of exercises. References and the Asset Editor are also introduced. These features have been created to aid with large Maya projects that are divided between teams of artists.

Chapter 2: Virtual Filmmaking with Maya Cameras   Provides an in-depth discussion of the Maya virtual camera and its attributes. A number of exercises provide examples of standard and custom camera rigs. Stereo 3D cameras are also introduced.

Chapter 3: NURBS Modeling in Maya   Walks you through numerous approaches for modeling parts of a helmet for a space suit based on a concept drawing created by a professional artist.

Chapter 4: Polygon Modeling   Continues to build on the model started in Chapter 3 using polygon and subdivision surface techniques. Smooth mesh polygons, creasing, and soft selection are demonstrated on various parts of the model.

Chapter 5: Animation Techniques   Demonstrates basic rigging with Inverse Kinematics as well as animating with keyframes, expressions, and constraints. Animation layers are explained.

Chapter 6: Animating with Deformers   Takes you through the numerous deformation tools available in Maya. Creating a facial animation rig using blend shapes is demonstrated, along with using lattices, non-linear deformers, and the geometry cache.

Chapter 7: Rigging and Muscle Systems   Explains joints, Inverse Kinematics, smooth binding, and proper rigging techniques. Maya Muscle is introduced and demonstrated on a character's arm. This chapter was written by Todd Palamar, author of the book *Maya Studio Projects: Dynamics* (Sybex, 2010).

Chapter 8: Paint Effects and Toon Shading   Provides a step-by-step demonstration of how to create a custom Paint Effects brush as well as how to animate and render with Paint Effects. Toon shading is also explained.

Chapter 9: Lighting with mental ray   Demonstrates a variety of lighting tools and techniques that can be used when rendering scenes with mental ray. Indirect lighting using Global Illumination, Final Gathering, and the Physical Sun and Sky shader are all demonstrated.

Chapter 10: mental ray Shading Techniques   Describes the more commonly used mental ray shaders and how they can be used to add material qualities to the space helmet created in Chapter 3. Tips on how to use the shaders together as well as how to light and render them using mental ray are discussed.

Chapter 11: Texture Mapping   Demonstrates how to create UV texture coordinates for a giraffe. Applying textures painted in other software packages, such as Adobe Photoshop, is discussed as well as displacement and normal maps and subsurface scattering shaders. This chapter was written by Todd Palamar, author of the book *Maya Studio Projects: Dynamics* (Sybex, 2010).

Chapter 12: Rendering for Compositing   Introduces render layers and render passes, which can be used to split the various elements of a render into separate files that are then recombined in compositing software.

Chapter 13: Introducing nParticles   Provides numerous examples of how to use nParticles. In this chapter, you'll use fluid behavior, particle meshes, internal force fields, and other techniques to create amazing effects.

Chapter 14: Dynamic Effects   Demonstrates a variety of techniques that can be used with nCloth to create effects. Traditional rigid body dynamics are compared with nCloth, and combining nCloth and nParticles is illustrated.

Chapter 15: Fur, Hair, and Clothing   Discusses how to augment your Maya creatures and characters using Maya Fur, Maya Hair, and nCloth. Using dynamic curves to create a rig for a dragon's tail is also demonstrated.

Chapter 16: Maya Fluids   Explains how 2D and 3D fluids can be used to create smoke, cloud, and flame effects, and a demonstration of how to render using the Ocean shader is given. Using nParticles as a Fluid emitter is introduced; this is a new feature in Maya 2011.

Chapter 17: MEL Scripting   Walks you through the process of creating a time- and labor-saving MEL script, illustrating how MEL is a very useful tool for all Maya artists. The Python interface is also explained.

COMPANION DVD

The companion DVD is home to all the demo files, samples, and bonus resources mentioned in the book. See Appendix B for more details on the contents of the DVD and how to access them.

How to Contact the Author

I enjoy hearing from the readers of my books. Feedback helps me to continually improve my skills as an author. You can contact me through my website at www.bloopatone.com as well as see examples of my own artwork there.

Sybex strives to keep you supplied with the latest tools and information you need for your work. Please check the book's website at www.sybex.com/go/masteringmaya2011, where we'll post additional content and updates that supplement this book should the need arise.

Chapter 1

Working in Maya

Maya's working environment has evolved to accommodate both the individual artist as well as a team of artists working in a production pipeline. The interface in Maya 2011 has changed significantly from previous versions of the program to reflect this evolution. The interface presents tools, controls, and data in an organized fashion to easily allow you to bring your fantastic creations to life.

Understanding the way Maya organizes data about the objects, animation, textures, lights, dynamics, and all the other elements contained within the 3D environment of a scene is essential to understanding how the interface is organized. Maya uses what's known as the Dependency Graph to keep track of the various packets of data, known as *nodes*, and how they affect each other. Any single element of a Maya scene consists of multiple nodes connected in a web, and each of these nodes is dependent on another. Maya's interface consists of editing windows that allow you to connect these nodes in an intuitive way and edit the information contained within each node.

There is usually more than one way to accomplish a task in Maya. As you grow comfortable with the interface, you'll discover which editing windows best suit your working style.

This chapter is a brief overview of what professionals need to understand when working in Maya. You'll learn what types of nodes you'll be working with and how they can be created and edited in Maya. You'll also learn how to work with projects and scene data as well as the various windows, panels, and controls that make up the interface. This will help you whether you are working alone or as part of a team of artists.

If you've never used Maya before, we strongly encourage you to read the Maya documentation as well as *Introducing Maya 2011* by Dariush Derakhshani (Sybex, 2010). This chapter is about working with nodes, but it is not meant to be a comprehensive guide to each and every control within Maya. That information is contained within the Maya documentation.

In this chapter, you will learn to:

- ◆ Understand transform and shape nodes
- ◆ Create a project
- ◆ Use assets
- ◆ Create file references

Creating and Editing Maya Nodes

A Maya *scene* is a system of interconnected nodes that are packets of data about what exists within the world of a Maya scene. The nodes are the building blocks you, as the artist, put together to create the 3D scene and animation that will finally be rendered for the world to see. So if you can think of the objects in your scene, their motion, and appearance as nodes, think of the Maya interface as the tools and controls you use to connect those nodes. The relationship between these nodes is organized by the Dependency Graph, which describes the hierarchical relationship between connected nodes. The interface provides many ways to view the graph, and these methods are described in this chapter.

Any given workflow in Maya is much like a route on a city map. There are usually many ways to get to your destination, and some of these make more sense than others depending on where you're going. In Maya, the best workflow depends on what you're trying to achieve, and there is usually more than one possible ideal workflow.

There are many types of nodes in Maya that serve any number of different functions. All the nodes in Maya are considered Dependency Graph (DG) nodes. Let's say you have a simple cube and you subdivide it once, thus quadrupling the number of faces that make up the cube. The information concerning how the cube has been subdivided is contained within a DG node that is connected to the cube node.

A special type of DG node is the Directed Acyclic Graph (DAG) node. These nodes are actually made of two specific types of connected nodes: transform and shape. The arrangement of DAG nodes consists of a hierarchy in which the shape node is a child of the transform node. Most of the objects you work with in the Maya viewport, such as surface geometry (cubes, spheres, planes, and so on), are DAG nodes.

To understand the difference between the transform and shape node types, think of a transform node as describing where an object is *located* and a shape node as describing what an object *is*.

The simple polygon cube in Figure 1.1 consists of six flat squares attached at the edges to form a box. Each side of the cube is subdivided twice, creating four polygons per side. That basically describes what the object is, and the description of the object would be contained in the shape node. This simple polygon cube may be 4.174 centimeters above the grid, rotated 35 degrees on the x-axis, and scaled four times its original size based on the cube's local x- and y-axes and six times its original size in the cube's local z-axis. That description would be in the transform node (see Figure 1.1).

FIGURE 1.1
A shape node describes the shape of an object and how it has been constructed; a transform node describes where the object is located in the scene.

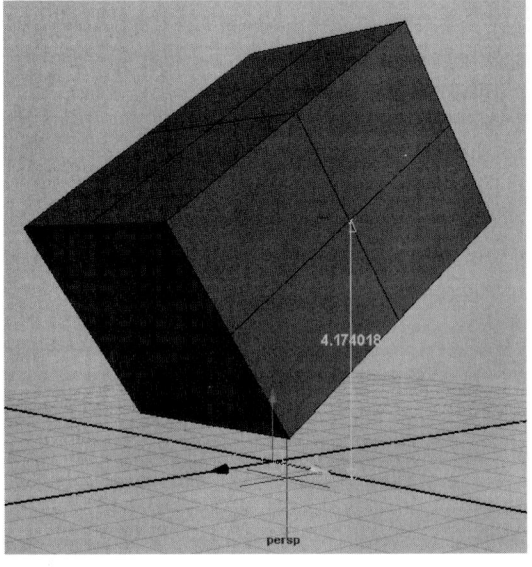

Maya has a number of workspaces that enable you to visualize and work with the nodes and their connections. The following sections describe how these workspaces work together when building a node network in a Maya scene.

Using the Hypergraph

The Hypergraph is a picture of the nodes and their connections in Maya. A complex scene can look like a very intricate web of these connections. When you really need to know how a network of nodes is connected, the Hypergraph gives you the most detailed view. There are two ways to view the Hypergraph, the hierarchy view and the connections view:

- The *hierarchy view* shows the relationships between nodes as a tree structure.

- The *connections view* shows how the nodes are connected as a web.

You can have more than one Hypergraph window open at the same time, but you are still looking at the same scene with the same nodes and connections.

This short exercise gives you a sense of how you would typically use the Hypergraph:

1. Create a new Maya scene.

2. Create a polygon cube by choosing Create ➢ Polygon Primitives ➢ Cube.

3. You will be prompted to draw a polygon on the grid by dragging on the surface. Drag a square on the grid, release the cursor, and then drag upward on the square to turn it into a three-dimensional cube (see Figure 1.2). Release the mouse button to complete the cube. At this point, feel free to make your own decisions about the size and position of the cube on the grid.

4. Select the cube in the viewport, and choose Window ➢ Hypergraph ➢ Hierarchy to open the Hypergraph in hierarchy mode. You'll see a yellow rectangle on a black field labeled pCube1. The rectangle turns gray when deselected.

FIGURE 1.2
When Interactive Creation is on, Maya prompts you to draw the object on the grid in the scene.

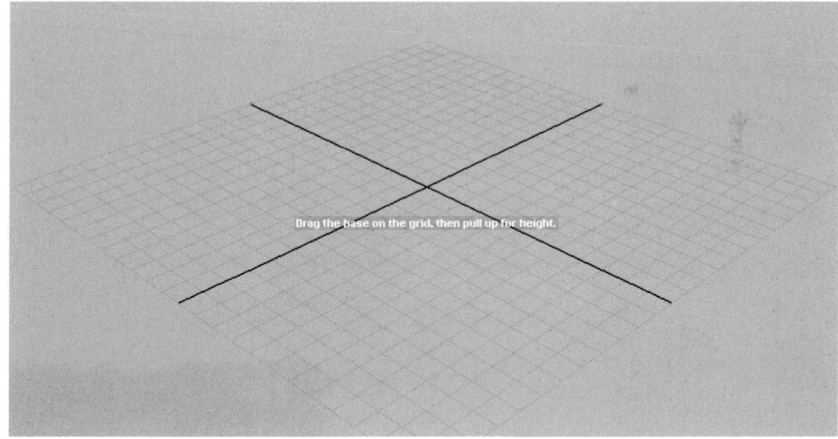

INTERACTIVE CREATION

By default Maya creates objects using the Interactive Creation method, which allows you to draw on the canvas as you create your geometry. To turn this feature off, choose the Create ➢ Polygon Primitives menu, and deselect the Interactive Creation option at the bottom of the menu.

While the Interactive Creation mode is on, you can deselect the Exit On Completion method; this means that each time you draw on the grid, you will continue to create cubes until you switch to another tool.

5. Hold the right mouse button down, and hover the cursor over the pCube rectangle. Choose Rename from the pop-up window. Rename the cube **myCube**.

6. Select myCube, and choose, from the Hypergraph menu, Graph ➢ Input And Output connections. This switches the view to the connections view just as if you had originally opened the Hypergraph by choosing Windows ➢ Hypergraph:Connections. It's the same Hypergraph, but the view mode has changed, allowing you to see more of the scene.

NAVIGATING THE HYPERGRAPH

You can navigate the Hypergraph by using the same hot key combination you use in the viewport: Alt+MMB-drag pans through the Hypergraph workspace, and Alt+RMB-drag zooms in and out. Selecting a node and pressing the **f** hot key focuses the view on the currently selected node. (MMB means clicking with the middle mouse button, and RMB means clicking with the right mouse button.)

When you graph the input and output connections, you see the connected nodes that make up an object and how the object appears in the scene. In the current view, you should see the myCube node next to a stack of connected nodes labeled polyCube1, myCubeShape, and initial-ShadingGroup, as shown in Figure 1.3. (The nodes may also be arranged in a line; the actual position of the nodes in the Hypergraph does not affect the nodes themselves.)

FIGURE 1.3
The node network appears in the Hypergraph. This shape node (myCubeShape) is connected to two other nodes, while the transform node (myCube) appears off to the side.

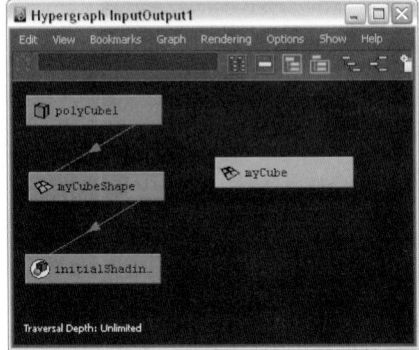

The myCube node is the transform node. The myCubeShape node is the shape node. In the Hypergraph, the shape and transform nodes are depicted as unconnected; however, there is an implied connection, as you'll see later. This is demonstrated when you rename the myCube node; the shape node is renamed as well.

In Maya, the construction history feature stores a record of the changes used to create a particular node. The polyCube1 node is the construction history node for the myCubeShape node. When you first create a piece of geometry, you can set options to the number of subdivisions, spans, width, height, depth, and many other features that are stored as a record in this history node. Additional history nodes are added as you make changes to the node. You can go back and change these settings as long as the history node still exists. Deleting a history node makes all the previous changes to the node permanent (however, deleting history is undoable).

1. Keep the Hypergraph open, but select the cube in the viewport.

2. Set the current menu to Polygons (you can change the menu set by choosing Polygons from the menu in the upper left of the Maya interface).

3. Choose Mesh ➤ Smooth. The cube will be subdivided and smoothed in the viewport.

    In the Hypergraph you'll see a new polySmoothFace1 node between the polyCube1 node and the myCubeShape node (see Figure 1.4). This new node is part of the history of the cube.

4. Select the polySmoothFace1 node, and delete it by pressing the Backspace key on the keyboard. The cube will return to its unsmoothed state.

FIGURE 1.4
Performing a smooth operation on the cube when construction history is activated causes a new polySmoothFace node to be inserted into the node network.

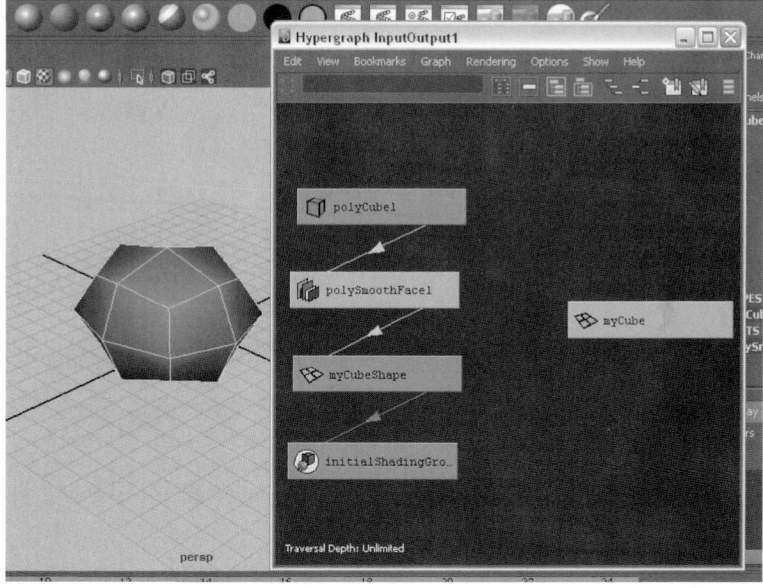

WORKING WITH HISTORY

Over the course of a modeling session, the history for any given object can become quite long and complex. This can slow down performance. It's a good idea to periodically delete history on an object by selecting the object and choosing Edit ➢ Delete By Type ➢ History. You can also choose to delete all the history in the scene by choosing Edit ➢ Delete All By Type ➢ History. Once you start animating a scene using deformers and joints, you should not delete the history or use the Delete By Type ➢ Non-Deformer History option.

You can turn off the history globally by clicking the history toggle switch on the status line, as shown here.

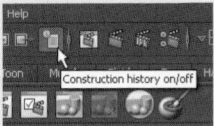

5. Select the transform node (myCube), and press the **s** hot key. This creates a keyframe on all the channels of the transform node.

   You'll see a new node icon appear for each keyframed channel with a connection to the transform node (see Figure 1.5).

6. Hold the cursor over any line that connects one node to another. A label appears describing the output and input attributes indicated by the connection line.

FIGURE 1.5
The attributes of myCube's transform node have been keyframed. The keyframe nodes appear in the Hypergraph.

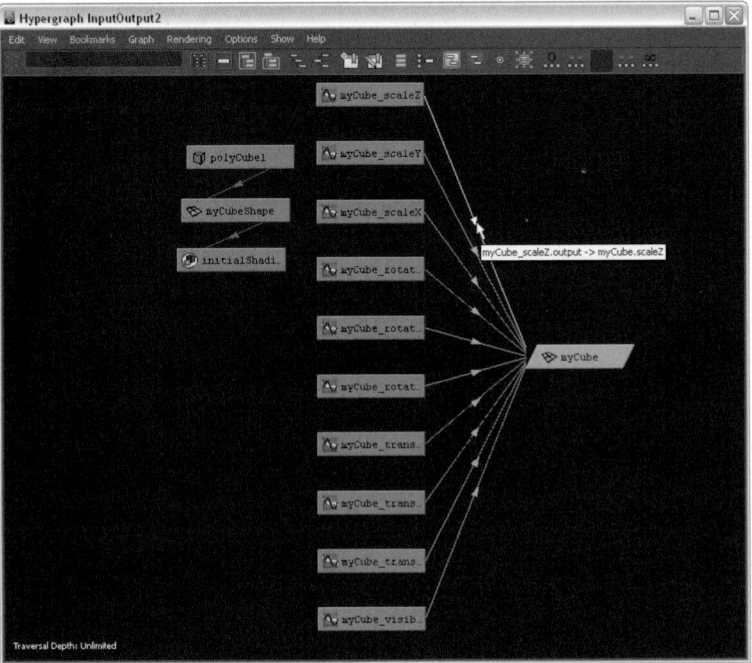

Connecting Nodes with the Connection Editor

Connections between nodes can be added, deleted, or changed using the Hypergraph and the Connection Editor.

1. Start a new Maya scene.

2. Create a locator in the scene by choosing Create ➤ Locator. A simple cross appears at the center of the grid in the viewport. This locator is a simple nonrendering null that indicates a point in space. Locators are handy tools that can be used for a wide variety of things in Maya.

3. Press the **w** hot key to switch to the Move tool; select the locator at the center of the grid, and move it out of the way.

4. Press the **g** hot key to create another locator. The **g** hot key repeats the last action you performed, in this case the creation of the locator.

5. Create a NURBS sphere in the viewport by choosing Create ➤ NURBS Primitives ➤ Sphere. If you have Interactive Creation selected, you'll be prompted to drag on the grid in the viewport to create the sphere; otherwise, the sphere will be created at the center of the grid based on its default settings.

NURBS

A Non-Uniform Rational B-Spline (NURBS) object is a type of surface that is defined by a network of editable curves. Chapter 3 introduces how to create and model NURBS surfaces.

---

6. Move the sphere away from the center of the grid so you can clearly see both locators and the sphere.

7. Use the Select tool (hot key = **q**) to drag a selection marquee around all three objects.

8. Open the Hypergraph in connections mode by choosing Window ➤ Hypergraph:Connections. You should see eight nodes in the Hypergraph (see Figure 1.6).

FIGURE 1.6
The input and output connections of the two locators and the sphere are graphed in the Hypergraph.

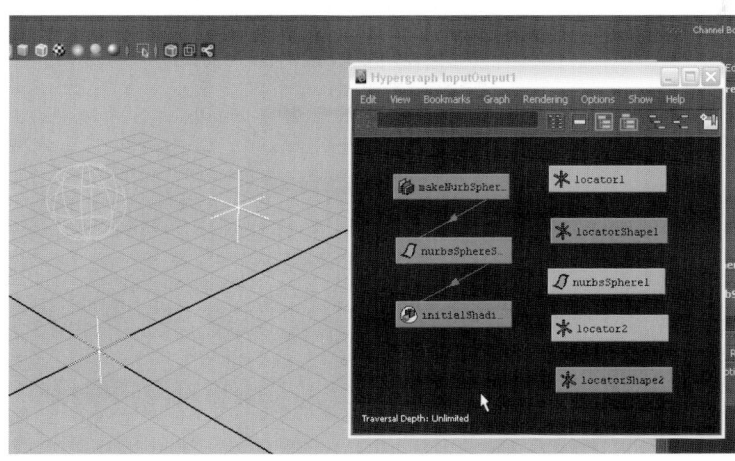

locator1 and locator2 are the two transform nodes for the locators. locatorShape1 and locatorShape2 are the two shape nodes for the locators. nurbsSphere1 is the transform node for the NURBS sphere. And nurbsSphereShape1 is the shape node for the sphere; it's connected to MakeNurbsSphere1, which is the history node, and to initialShadingGroup. The initialShadingGroup node is the default shading group that is applied to all geometry; without this node, the geometry can't be shaded or rendered. When you apply a new shader to an object, the connection to initialShadingGroup is replaced with a connection to the new shader.

9. In the Hypergraph window, use Alt+RMB to zoom out a little.

10. Select the locator1, locator2, and nurbsSphere1 nodes, and drag them away from the other nodes so you can work on them in their own space.

11. In the Hypergraph, MMB-drag the locator1 node over the nurbsSphere1 node.

12. From the pop-up menu, choose Other at the bottom (Figure 1.7). A new dialog box will open; this is the Connection Editor.

FIGURE 1.7
You can connect two nodes in the Hypergraph by MMB-dragging one on top of the other and choosing from the options in the pop-up menu.

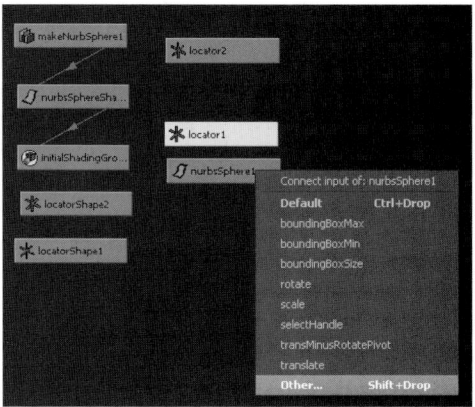

The Connection Editor is where you create and edit connections between nodes. The left side of the panel represents the output of a selected node, in this case the locator1 node. The output is the controlling node; the right side is the input, and in this case is nurbsSphere1, which will be controlled based on whatever connections you make in the list.

The list represents the attributes of each node. Any of the attributes that have a plus sign next to them can be expanded to reveal nested attributes. For instance, find the Translate attribute in the left side of the column, and expand it by clicking the plus sign. You'll see that Translate has Translate X, Translate Y, and Translate Z. This means you can choose either to select the Translate attribute, which will automatically use all three nested attributes as the output connection, or to expand Translate and choose one or more of the nested Translate X, Y, or Z attributes as the output connection. In some situations, a connection becomes grayed out, indicating that the connection between the two attributes cannot be made, usually because the connection is not appropriate for the selected attributes (see Figure 1.8).

FIGURE 1.8
The Connection Editor specifies which attributes are connected between nodes.

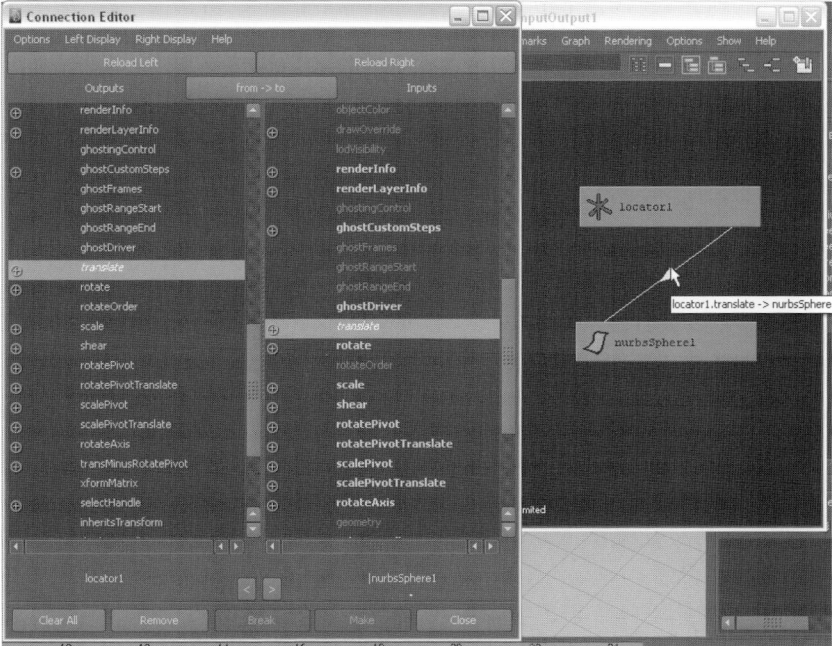

13. Select the Translate attribute on the left. You'll notice that many of the selections on the right side become grayed out, meaning that they cannot be connected to Translate. This is because Translate is a vector—it is an output consisting of three connections (Translate X, Translate Y, and Translate Z). The vector can be connected only to other vectors on the right side of the list.

14. On the right side, scroll down and select Translate. Both connections in the list are italicized, indicating that there is a connection to this attribute. If one of the other attributes on the right were italicized, it would indicate that another node is already connected to that attribute (see Figure 1.8).

15. In the viewport, switch to wireframe mode. You can do this by pressing 4 on the keyboard or clicking the wireframe icon on the icon bar at the top of the viewport window; the wireframe icon is the wireframe cube.

16. In the viewport, you'll notice that the sphere has snapped to the same position as the locator. Select the sphere, and try to move it using the Move tool (hot key = **w**). The sphere is locked to the locator, so it cannot be moved. Select the locator, and try to move it; the sphere moves with the locator. The output of the locator's Translate attributes are the input for the sphere's Translate.

INCOMING CONNECTIONS

In wireframe view, an object will be highlighted in purple if it has an incoming connection from the selected object.

---

17. Select the nurbsSphere1 node in the Hypergraph, and MMB-drag it on top of locator2.

18. From the pop-up list, choose Rotate (see Figure 1.9). The Connection Editor opens again.

FIGURE 1.9
The nurbsSphere1 node is MMB-dragged on top of the locator2 node, making the sphere the input connection for locator2.

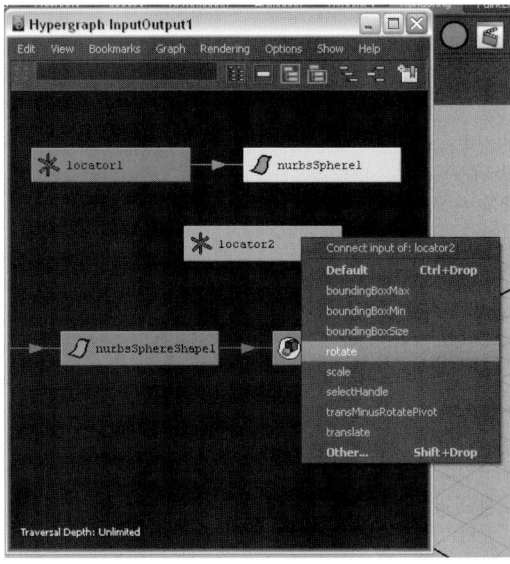

SPECIFYING CONNECTIONS

In some cases when you choose to make a connection from the pop-up window, Maya will automatically make it for you without opening the Connection Editor; however, in other cases, even when you choose what seems like an obvious connection from the list, Maya will still open the Connection Editor so you can make exactly the connection you want.

---

19. Now the nurbsSphere1 node is listed on the left, and locator2 is on the right. Find the Rotate attributes, expand the list, and choose Rotate X from the list.

20. On the right side, find the Rotate attributes, expand them, and choose Rotate Y. This causes the Rotate X of the nurbsSphere1 node to control the Rotate Y of the locator.

21. In the viewport, select the sphere, and switch to the Rotate tool (hot key = **e**).

22. Drag up and down on the red circle of the tool to rotate the sphere in X only. The locator rotates around its y-axis.

USE THE CONNECTION EDITOR TO MAKE SIMPLE CONNECTIONS

The Connection Editor is best used when you want to make a one-to-one relationship between attributes on two nodes. In other words, the value of the output connection needs to equal exactly the value of the input connection. More complex connections can be made using expressions, special nodes, or Set Driven Key. All of these options will be discussed throughout the book.

You can break a connection by reselecting the connected node on either side of the Connection Editor so that the attribute is no longer highlighted. You can also select the connecting line in the Hypergraph and press the Delete key to break the connection.

Creating Node Hierarchies in the Outliner

The Outliner shows a hierarchical list of the nodes in the scene in a form similar to the outline of a book. It is another way to view the transform and shape nodes in a scene and a way to create hierarchical relationships between nodes through parenting. The Outliner does not show the connections between nodes like the Hypergraph; rather, it shows the hierarchy of the nodes in the scene. To see how this works, try the following exercise:

1. Open the `miniGun_v01.ma` file from the `Chapter1/scenes` directory on the DVD. The scene consists of a minigun model in three parts.

2. Open the Outliner by choosing Window ➢ Outliner.

OUTLINER LAYOUT PRESETS

The Outliner can be opened as a separate panel or, like many of the panels in Maya, can be opened in a viewport. A popular window arrangement is to split the viewports into two views, with the left view set to the Outliner and the right view set to the perspective view. You can open this arrangement by going to the menu bar in a viewport window and choosing Panels ➢ Saved Layouts ➢ Persp/Outliner (as shown here). You can also click the third layout button on the left side of the interface just below the toolbox.

---

3. At the top of the Outliner is a menu bar. In the Display menu, make sure DAG Objects only is selected and Shapes is deselected (see Figure 1.10).

FIGURE 1.10
The Display menu at the top of the Outliner

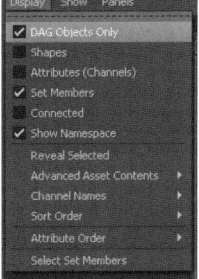

In the Outliner, you'll see three nodes listed: gunBarrels, housing, and mount in addition to the four default cameras and several set nodes (don't worry about the set nodes). These are the three transform nodes for the pieces of the minigun. Select each node, and you'll see the corresponding part highlighted in the perspective view. At the moment, each piece is completely separate and unconnected.

4. Select the housing node, and switch to the Rotate tool (hot key = **e**).

5. Rotate the objects; nothing else is affected. Try moving housing (hot key = **w**); again, nothing else is affected.

6. Hit Undo a few times until the housing node returns to its original location and orientation.

7. In the Outliner, select the gunBarrels object. Then Ctrl+click the housing object, and choose Edit ➤ Parent.

   Parenting one object to another means you have made one transform node the child of the second. When an object is a child node, it inherits its position, rotation, scale, and visibility from the parent node. In the Outliner, you'll notice that the housing node has a plus sign beside it and the gunBarrels node is not visible. The plus sign indicates that the node has a child node.

8. Click the plus sign next to the housing node to expand this two-node hierarchy. The gunBarrels node is now visible as the child of the housing node.

9. Select the housing node, and try rotating and translating it. The gunBarrels node follows the rotation and translation of the housing node (see Figure 1.11).

   Unlike the situation presented in the "Connecting Nodes with the Connection Editor" section of the chapter, the rotation and translation of the gunBarrels object are not locked to the rotation and translation of the housing node; rather, as a child, its rotation, translation, scale, and visibility are all relative to that of its parent.

FIGURE 1.11
When the gunBarrels node is made a child of the housing object, it inherits changes made to the housing object's transform node.

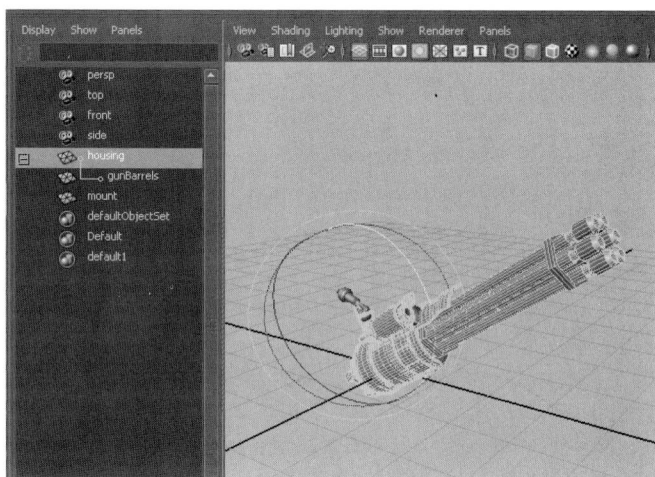

10. Select the gunBarrels node, and try rotating and translating the object; then rotate and translate the housing node. You'll see the gun barrels maintain their position relative to the housing node. You could create an animation in which the gun barrels rotate on their own z-axis to spin around while firing, while the housing node is animated, rotating on all three axes in order to aim.

11. Hit Undo a few times (hot key = **Ctrl+z**) until both the housing and gunBarrel objects are back to their original positions.

12. In the Outliner, select the housing node, and MMB-drag it on top of the mount node. This is a way to quickly parent objects in the Outliner.

13. Click the plus signs next to the mount and housing nodes in the Outliner to expand the hierarchy. The lines indicate the organization of the hierarchy; the gun barrels are parented to the housing node, which is parented to the mount node.

SHIFT+CLICK TO EXPAND THE HIERARCHY

You can expand an entire hierarchy with one click in the Outliner. Just Shift+click the arrow for the hierarchy you want to expand.

---

14. Select the mount node, and choose Edit ➢ Duplicate (hot key = **Ctrl+d**). This makes a copy of the entire hierarchy. The duplicated mount node is named mount1.

15. Select the mount1 node, and switch to the Move tool (hot key = **w**). Pull on the red arrow of the tool to move the duplicate along the x-axis about two units.

16. Select the mount node, and then Ctrl+click the mount1 node in the Outliner.

17. Choose Edit ➢ Group (hot key = **Ctrl+g**) to group these two nodes under a single parent node.

A group node is a transform node that has no shape node. It's just a location in space used to organize a hierarchy. Like a parent node, its children inherit its rotation, translation, scale, and visibility.

18. Select the group1 node, and Shift+click the plus sign next to it in the Outliner to expand the group and all its children.

19. Double-click the label for the group1 node in the Outliner to rename it; rename the group **guns**.

RENAMING NODES

You'll notice that the duplicate mount node has been renamed mount1 automatically. Nodes on the same level of the hierarchy can't have the same name. The child nodes do have the same name, and this is usually a bad idea. It can confuse Maya when more complex connections are made between nodes. Whenever you encounter this situation, you should take the time to rename the child nodes so that everything in the scene has a unique name.

---

20. Select the mount1 node in the Guns hierarchy, and choose Modify ➤ Prefix Hierarchy Names.

21. In the pop-up window, type **right_**. This renames the top node and all its children so that "right_" precedes the name. Do the same with the other mount node, but change the prefix to **left_**.

22. Select the guns group, and choose Modify ➤ Center Pivot. This places the pivot at the center of the group. Try rotating the Guns group, and you'll see both guns rotate together (see Figure 1.12).

FIGURE 1.12
The Guns group is rotated as a single unit.

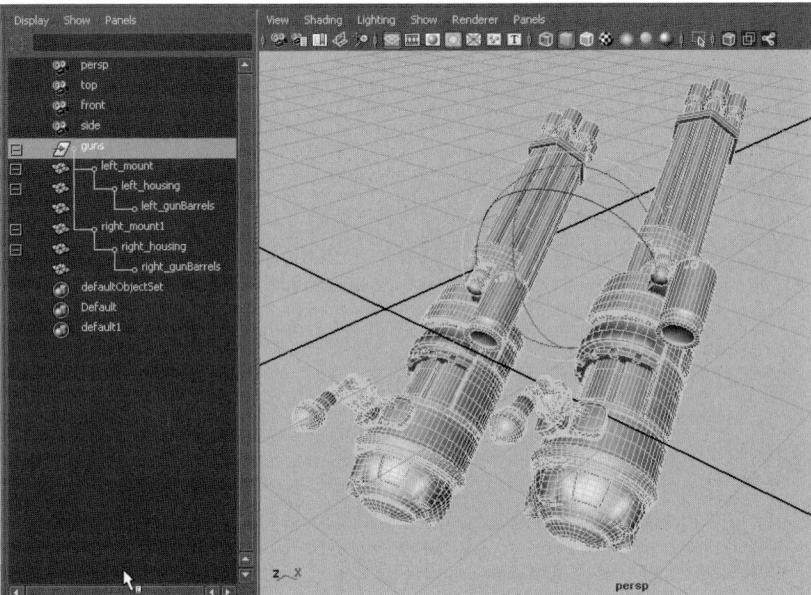

Each member of the hierarchy can have its own animation, so both gun barrels can rotate around their z-axes as they fire, the two housing nodes could be animated to aim in different directions, and the two guns could rotate as one unit, all at the same time. The entire group can be parented to another node that is part of a vehicle.

Displaying Options in the Outliner

There are several options in the Outliner for displaying nodes and their hierarchical arrangements. You can see that the default perspective, top, side, and front cameras are visible as nodes at the top of the Outliner. Also, there are a number of sets such as the defaultLightSet that appear at the bottom of the Outliner. These sets are mainly used for organization of data by Maya and are usually not directly edited or altered.

1. In the Display menu of the Outliner, select the Shapes option to display the shape nodes of the objects. The shape nodes appear parented to their respective transform node. You can select either the transform node or the shape node in the Outliner to select the object.

ACCESSING OUTLINER OPTIONS

You can right-click in the Outliner to quickly access the Outliner's display options rather than use the menu at the top of the Outliner.

---

2. In the Display menu, activate the visibility of attributes by selecting the Attributes (Channels) option. Each node now has an expandable list of attributes. Most of the time you may want this option off because it clutters the Outliner and there are other ways to get to these attributes. Ultimately, how you use these options is up to you.

3. Turn off the Attributes display, and turn off the DAG Objects Only option. This allows you to see all the nodes in the scene in the Outliner list as opposed to just the DAG nodes.

DAG stands for "Directed Acyclic Graph," and DAG objects are those objects that have both a shape and a transform node. It's not really crucial to understand exactly what Directed Acyclic Graph means as long as you understand that it is an arrangement in which a shape node is parented to a transform node. When you turn off DAG Objects Only in the Outliner, you'll see all the nodes in the Maya scene appear. Many of these are default utility nodes required to make Maya function, such as the renderLayerManager node or the dynController1 node. Many other nodes appear when you create a new node or connection. An example of this would be a keyframe or an expression node.

When you turn off DAG Objects Only, the list can get quite long. To find a node quickly, you can type the node's name in the field at the very top of the Outliner. This hides all nodes except the named node. Clearing the field restores the visibility of all nodes in the Outliner (see Figure 1.13).

FIGURE 1.13
The Outliner can display shape nodes as well as other types of nodes in the scene.

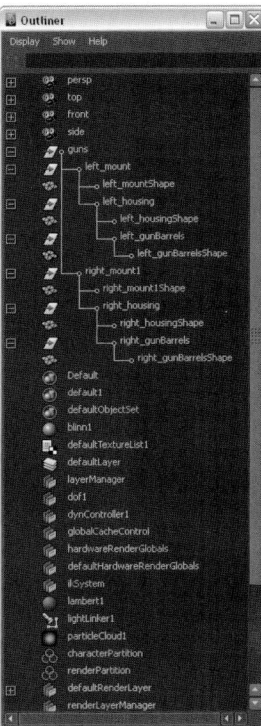

Additional viewing options are available in the Show menu, which contains options for displaying only nodes of a certain type. Throughout this book the Outliner will be used extensively, so you'll have lots of practice working with this panel.

To see a finished version of the scene, open `miniGun_v02.ma` from the `chapter1\scenes` directory on the DVD.

 **Real World Scenario**

SEARCHING FEATURES IN THE OUTLINER

A complex scene in Maya can easily have hundreds of nodes. Just one character often has associated geometry, dozens of animation controls, joints, textures, and so on. Add another character to the scene with their own set of node networks, and the Outliner can become very cluttered very quickly. Establishing an organized naming system for the nodes in your scenes has many benefits, one of which is that you can use the search feature in the Outliner to filter what is displayed, thus making it easy to access the nodes you need. In my work, I make sure that I take the time to name my nodes in such a way as to make searching easy. The following illustrates how the search feature can be used in a complex scene.

Let's say I have a scene with two complex characters, one named Larry and the other named Cecil. Both characters have similar rigs that use NURBS curves to control their animation rigs, and both have geometry, joints, shaders, and so on. When naming the nodes associated with each character, I would make sure that all larry nodes start with the name "larry." So, Larry's skin geometry might be named "larry_SKIN_GEO," while his clothes would use names like "larry_PANTS_GEO." Using capital letters in this case is purely personal preference; the important thing is that the name of each node starts with "larry." Cecil would use the same convention; his skin geometry would be "cecil_SKIN_GEO," and his pants would be "cecil_PANTS_GEO." I end the names using GEO, so I know that this is a geometry node.

The controls for the animation rig would use names like "larry_LEFT_HAND_wrist_CTRL1," "larry_SPINE_CTRl1," and "larry_NECK_CTRL1." You get the idea. You can see that each of these nodes belongs to Larry, nodes for the left side of the body are clearly identified, the associated body part is identified, and they end with the letters *CTRL*. The same goes for Cecil.

Now here's where this type of organization, or something similar, is helpful in the Outliner. At the top of the Outliner is a blank field. To filter the nodes listed in the Outliner, you need to type some text and either precede or follow the text with an asterisk (*). The asterisk tells Maya to show all nodes that use the text before or after the asterisk in the name. So if you want to see all nodes associated with larry, type **larry***. If you want to see all the control nodes for both Cecil and Larry, type ***CTRL***. In this case, there may be text before and after the CTRL letters, so use an asterisk before and after CTRL. If you want to see the controls associated with Cecil's hands, type **cecil*HAND***, and so on.

The following images show variations on how to search through the Outliner with this method. If nothing appears in the Outliner when you type some text, check to see whether the asterisk is in the right place. To find one specific node, type its full name without the asterisk.

The Channel Box

The term *channel* is, for the most part, interchangeable with *attribute*. You can think of a channel as a container that holds the attribute's value. The Channel Box is an editor that lists a node's attributes for quick access. The Channel Box displays the node's attributes, which are most frequently keyframed for animation.

The Channel Box is located on the right side of the screen at the end of the status bar when the view mode button in the upper right of the status line is set to Show The Channel Box/Layer Editor (see Figure 1.14).

FIGURE 1.14
The icon in the upper right of the interface toggles the visibility of the Channel Box.

There are two tabs on the very right side of the screen that allow you to quickly switch between the Channel Box and the Attribute Editor, as shown in Figure 1.15. (The Attribute Editor is discussed in detail later in this chapter.) These tabs are visible when both the Attribute Editor icon and the Channel Box icon are activated on the status bar in the upper-right corner of the interface.

FIGURE 1.15
The two tabs on the right of the screen allow you to quickly switch between the Channel Box and the Attribute Editor.

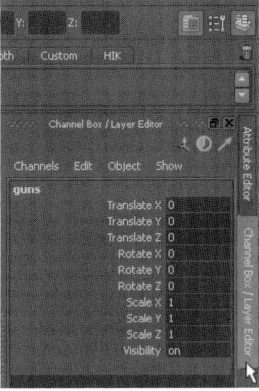

This short exercise gives a quick tour of how to work in the Channel Box:

1. Create a new scene in Maya, and create a NURBS Sphere on the grid (Create ➤ NURBS Primitives ➤ Sphere). You'll be prompted to draw the sphere on the grid if Interactive Creation mode is on; if not, the sphere will appear at the center of the grid. Either option is fine.

2. Make sure the Channel Box is visible on the right side of the screen. To do this, click the icon at the farthest right of the status bar (shown in Figure 1.14). This is a toggle to display the Channel Box. Click it until the Channel Box appears, as in Figure 1.16.

3. The Channel Box will list the currently selected object. Select the sphere, and you'll see nurbsSphere1 appear. The list below it shows the attributes for the nurbsSphere1's transform node.

FIGURE 1.16
The Channel Box displays the channels for the currently selected object.

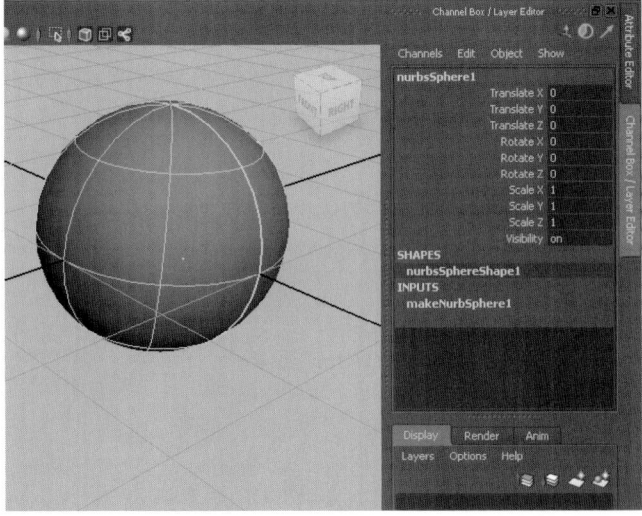

The lower half of the Channel Box lists the connections to this node. You'll see the name of the associated shape node under SHAPES, and below this a section for the inputs. In this case, the input is the history node, named makeNurbSphere1, which contains the original settings used to create the sphere. If you delete history on the sphere, these attributes will no longer be accessible.

4. In the upper section of the Channel Box, under nurbsSphere1, try selecting the fields and inputting different values for Translate, Scale, and Rotate. The sphere updates its position, orientation, and size.

5. In the Visibility channel, select the word *On* in the field, and type **0**. The sphere disappears. Input the value **1**, and it reappears. Visibility is a Boolean, meaning it is either on or off, 1 or 0.

6. Select the Translate X field so it is highlighted. Shift+click the Rotate Z value, and all the values in between are also selected.

7. Type **0** in the Translate X field while they are selected, which sets all the Translate and Rotate values to the same value, places the sphere at the center of the grid, and returns it to its original orientation (see Figure 1.17).

FIGURE 1.17
You can quickly "zero out" the Translate and Rotate channels by Shift+clicking their fields and entering 0.

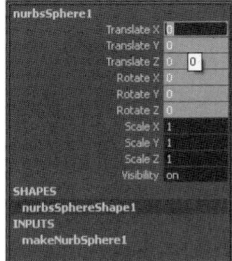

8. In the makeNurbsSphere section, highlight the Start Sweep channel. Enter a value of **90**, and the sphere opens up. You're altering the construction history of the sphere so it is no longer a closed surface.

9. Select the word *Sections* so it is highlighted in blue. MMB-drag in the viewport view back and forth. Doing this creates a virtual slider so you can change the value of the field interactively instead of numerically. This should work for all the channels (most of the time).

10. Set the timeline to frame 1, and press the **s** hot key. You'll see all the channels turn orange, indicating that they have been keyframed. The s hot key keyframes all the available channels.

11. Move the timeline to frame 24, and change some settings on both the transform node (the upper half of the Channel Box) and under makeNurbsSphere1.

12. Press the **s** hot key again to set another key. Play the animation, and you'll see the sphere update based on the keyframed changes.

The s hot key keyframes everything, even those channels you may not need to keyframe. You can use the Channel Box to keyframe specific channels.

13. Rewind the timeline, and choose Edit ➤ Keys ➤ Delete Keys to remove all the keyframes on the sphere.

14. Highlight Translate X and Shift+click Translate Z so that the translation channels are all selected.

15. Right-click these values, and choose Key Selected (see Figure 1.18).

FIGURE 1.18
Right-click the selected channels, and choose Key Selected to animate just those specific channels.

16. Move to frame 24, and enter different values in the Translate fields.

17. Right-click and choose Key Selected. This places a keyframe on just the selected channels, which is often a cleaner and more efficient way to work because you're placing keyframes only on the channels you need to animate and not on every keyable channel, which is what happens when you use the s hot key.

BE THRIFTY WITH KEYFRAMES

Creating extra, unnecessary keys leads to a lot of problems, especially when you start to refine the animation on the Graph Editor (discussed in Chapter 5). Keyframes also can increase the scene size (the amount of storage space the scene uses on disk). Be cheap with your keyframes, and use the Key Selected feature to keyframe only the channels you need. Avoid using the s hot key to create keys on everything.

---

18. To remove keys, you can highlight the channels, right-click, and choose Break Connections. This removes any inputs to those channels. The values for the current keyframe will remain in the channels.

The channels are color coded to show what kind of input drives the channel:

◆ Pink indicates a keyframe.

◆ Purple indicates an expression.

◆ Yellow indicates a connection (as in a connection from another node or channel made in the Connection Editor).

◆ Brown indicates a muted channel.

◆ Gray means the channel is locked.

LOCKING AND MUTING CHANNELS

You can mute a channel by right-clicking it and choosing Mute Selected from the pop-up menu. When you mute a channel, the keyframes on that channel are temporarily disabled; as long as the channel is muted, the animation will not update. This is useful when you want to disable the keyframes in a channel so that you can focus on other aspects of the animation. Locking a channel is another option available when you right-click selected channels in the Channel Box. A locked channel prevents you from adding keyframes to a channel regardless of whether it has been animated. Animation techniques are explored further in Chapter 5.

The Channel Box will be explored throughout the book and used frequently, particularly in the chapters concerning animation.

The Attribute Editor

The Attribute Editor is a tabbed panel that gives detailed information and access to a node's attributes. The tabs at the top of the editor allow you to move between the attributes of all the upstream (input) and downstream (output) connected nodes. This exercise gives a brief tour on how to use the Attribute Editor:

1. Create a new scene in Maya. Create a polygon cube on the grid (Create ➢ Polygon Primitives ➢ Cube).

2. Select the cube, and open its Attribute Editor. There are several ways to do this:

    ◆ Right-click the cube, and choose pCube1.

    ◆ Select the cube, and choose Windows ➢ Attribute Editor.

    ◆ Click the Show Or Hide The Attribute Editor icon in the upper right of the Maya interface (Figure 1.19).

3. With the Attribute Editor open, choose the pCube1 tab at the top (Figure 1.20). The panel that opens contains the attributes for the cube's transform node, much like the upper section of the Channel Box described in the previous section. It also contains options for setting limits on the transform attributes.

FIGURE 1.19
The Show Or Hide The Attribute Editor icon resides in the upper-right corner of the Maya interface.

FIGURE 1.20
The Attribute Editor contains tabs that allow you to move through the connected nodes of a network.

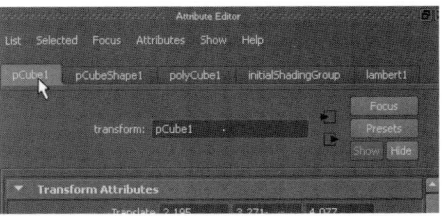

Many of the settings can be accessed through the Attribute Editor's rollout panels. These are collapsible sections of grouped settings.

4. In the Attribute Editor, on the pCube1 tab, click the triangle next to mental ray. This reveals mental ray–specific settings related to the cube. Note that there are subsections under mental ray that are also collapsible.

5. Choose the pCubeShape1 tab at the top of the Attribute Editor. This tab contains settings related to the shape node. For example, expand the Render Stats section, and you'll see a list of settings that control how the shape will appear in a render.

6. Choose the polyCube1 tab, and you'll see the construction history settings. If you delete history on the cube, this tab will no longer appear.

7. Expand the Poly Cube History rollout. If you right-click any of the fields, you get a popup menu that offers options, such as expressions, key setting, or locking, much like the fields in the Channel Box (Figure 1.21).

8. In the Subdivisions Width field, type =. The field becomes highlighted, indicating that you can add an expression.

9. Type =9*2; and press the Enter key on your keyboard's numeric keypad (see Figure 1.22). This adds an expression to this attribute that makes the Subdivisions Width value equal to 18. Note that the field turns purple, and the slider can no longer be moved.

FIGURE 1.21
Right-clicking an attribute field reveals a menu with options for animating the attribute value.

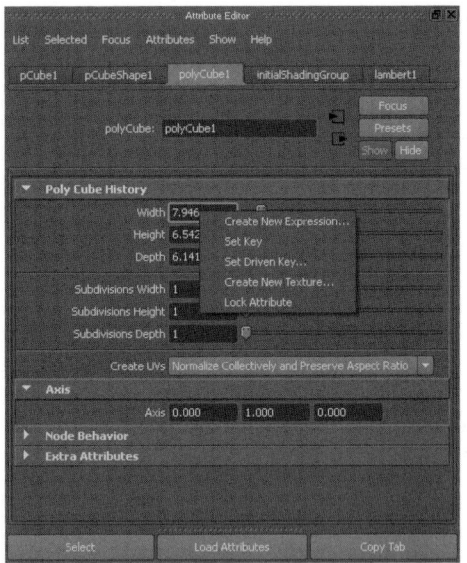

FIGURE 1.22
You can enter simple mathematical expressions directly into a field in the Attribute Editor.

Note that a new tab called Expression1 is added to the top of the Attribute Editor; this is a new expression node that is now part of the cube's node network.

If the number of connected nodes is too large to fit within the tab listing at the top, you can use the two arrow buttons to the right of the tabs to move back and forth between the tab listings. Likewise, if not all connections are visible, you can use the Go To Input and Go To Output Connections buttons to the right of the field indicating the node name.

The Notes field at the bottom is useful for typing your own notes if you need to keep track of particular settings or leave a message for yourself or other users (see Figure 1.23). You can collapse this section by dragging the bar above it downward, thus making more room for the other settings in the Attribute Editor.

FIGURE 1.23

Messages can be entered in the Notes section at the bottom of the Attribute Editor.

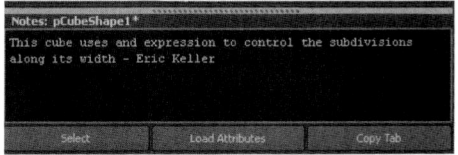

LOAD ATTRIBUTES

You can use the Load Attributes button if the attribute display needs to be refreshed. Maya automatically updates the editor when new attributes are added, but occasionally it misses an update and needs to be refreshed.

The Attribute Editor is the workhorse panel of Maya. Throughout this book we will use it constantly. Make sure you are comfortable with the core concepts of how to switch between node settings using the tabs as well as how to change the available values.

Working with Shader Nodes in the Hypershade

The Hypershade, as the name suggests, is similar in function to the Hypergraph. It gives a visual display of how nodes in a Maya scene are connected. The Hypershade is mostly concerned with shaders—nodes used to define the color and material properties of renderable objects in a scene. These include materials (also known as *shaders*), textures, lights, cameras, and shading utilities. However, it is not unusual to use the Hypershade Work Area to make connections between other types of nodes as well. In this exercise, you'll use the Hypershade to connect several types of nodes.

1. Create a new scene in Maya. Create a NURBS cone on the grid. You'll be prompted to draw the cone on the grid if Interactive Creation mode is on; if it is not, the sphere will appear at the center of the grid. Either option is fine.

2. Switch to smooth shaded mode by pressing **6** on the keyboard, or click the Smooth Shade All and Textured icons on the viewport's menu bar (Figure 1.24).

3. Press **3** on the keyboard to switch to a high-quality display of the geometry.

4. Open the Hypershade by choosing Window ➤ Rendering Editors ➤ Hypershade.

FIGURE 1.24

The Maya viewport icon bar allows you to choose between shading modes by toggling buttons.

The Hypershade comprises several frames. The format of this editor has been updated in Maya 2011. On the left side is a list and a visual menu of the nodes you can create in the Hypershade. The list is divided into sections for the Maya nodes, mental ray nodes, and a customizable list for your own favorites at the very top. Clicking a category in the list filters the node creation buttons to the right of the list, which helps to cut down on the amount of time you need to hunt for specific nodes. To add a node to the Favorites list, MMB-drag the node button from the right on top of the Favorites menu. You can also search through the nodes by typing in the field at the very top of the list. For example, typing **mia** in this field filters the node creation buttons so that all the mia (mental images architectural) nodes are displayed (see Figure 1.25).

FIGURE 1.25

The text field at the top of the Create Nodes section allows you to filter the list of buttons. MMB-dragging a button on top of the Favorites section allows you to create a custom list of your favorite shading nodes.

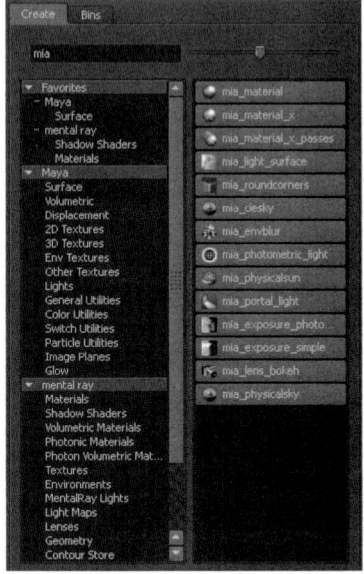

The right side of the Hypershade contains a visual display of the nodes in the scene at the top and the Work Area at the bottom (Figure 1.26). The upper section is organized by tabs named Materials, Textures, Utilities, Lights, Cameras, Shading Groups, Bake Sets, Projects, and Container Nodes. If you want to access all the file textures used in the scene, you can choose the Textures tab to see them listed with preview icons.

5. On the left side of the Hypershade, click Surface in the list of Maya nodes. Click the Blinn button to create a new Blinn material.

You can see the new blinn1 material listed on the Materials tab; it also appears in the Work Area.

FIGURE 1.26
The Hypershade
organizes render
nodes and offers a
workspace for con-
structing render
node networks.
This image shows
an example of a
shader network
graphed in the
Work Area.

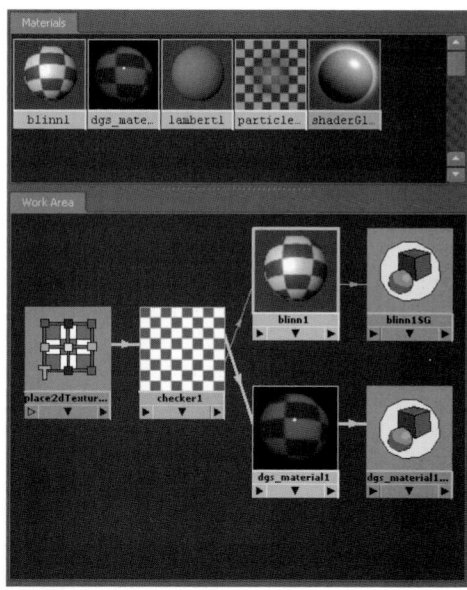

HYPERSHADE TABS

If tabs appear to be missing, you can revert to the default tab layout by choosing Tabs ➢ Revert
To Default Tabs, as shown here. This clears the current tabs and replaces them with the default
Materials, Textures, Utilities, Lights, Cameras, and other default tabs. You can use the Tabs menu
to create your own custom tabs and determine which tabs you want visible and in what order.

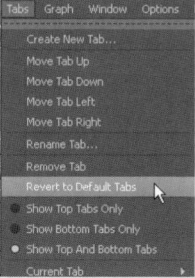

DEFAULT SCENE MATERIALS

All Maya scenes start with three materials already created: lambert1, particleCloud, and shaderGlow.
The lambert1 material is the default material applied to all newly created geometry, the particleCloud
material is a special material reserved for particle cloud objects, and the shaderGlow node sets the
glow options for all shaders in the scene.

6. Select the blinn1 material in the Work Area, and from the menu at the top of the Hypershade choose Graph ➤ Input And Output Connections. This displays all the upstream and downstream nodes connected to blinn1. Upstream nodes are nodes that plug into a node and affect its attributes; downstream nodes are ones that are affected by the node.

   The blinn1SG node is a downstream node known as a *shader group*, connected to blinn1. All materials have a shader group node connected to them. This node is a required part of the network that defines how the shader is applied to a surface and is often used when creating complex mental ray shader networks and overrides (see Figure 1.27).

FIGURE 1.27
Shaders all have shading group nodes attached, which define how the shader is applied to the geometry.

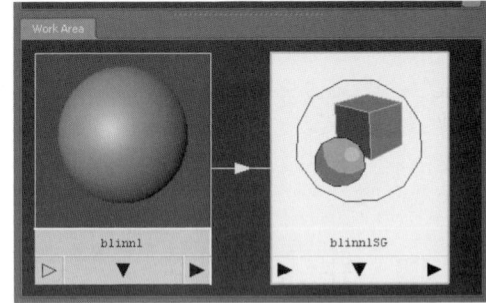

7. In the Work Area of the Hypershade, select the blinn1 node, right-click it, and choose blinn1. This opens the Attribute Editor for the Blinn shader, if it's not open already. This is where you adjust the settings that define the look of the material.

8. In the viewport, select the cone. You can apply the blinn1 material in several ways to the cone:

   ◆ MMB-drag the material icon from the Hypershade on top of the cone in the viewport window.

   ◆ Select the cone, right-click the blinn1 node in the Hypershade, and choose Assign Material To Selection (Figure 1.28).

   ◆ Right-click the surface in the viewport, and choose Assign New Shader to create a new shader or choose Assign Existing Material to assign a shader you've already created.

FIGURE 1.28
Right-click a shader, and drag upward on the marking menu to choose Assign Material To Selection.

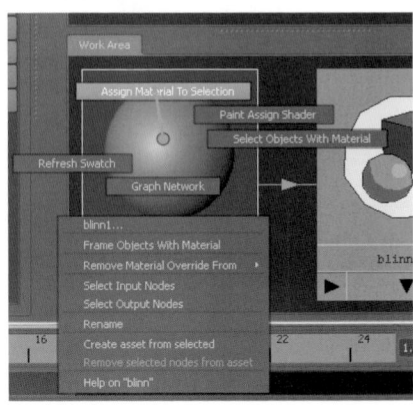

USE THE SHELF BUTTONS TO CREATE A NEW SHADER

You can assign a new material to a surface using the buttons in the rendering shelf at the top of the Maya interface (shown here). If you select an object and click one of these buttons, a new shader is created and assigned to selected objects. If no objects are selected, then it just creates a new shader, which you'll find on the Materials tab of the Hypershade.

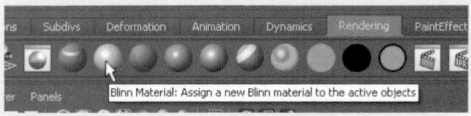

---

9. In the Attribute Editor for the blinn1 node, rename the material **coneShader** by typing in the field at the top of the editor.

10. Click the checkered box to the right of the Color slider. This opens the Create Render Node window (Figure 1.29).

FIGURE 1.29
Click the checkered box next to the Color slider to open the Create Render Node window.

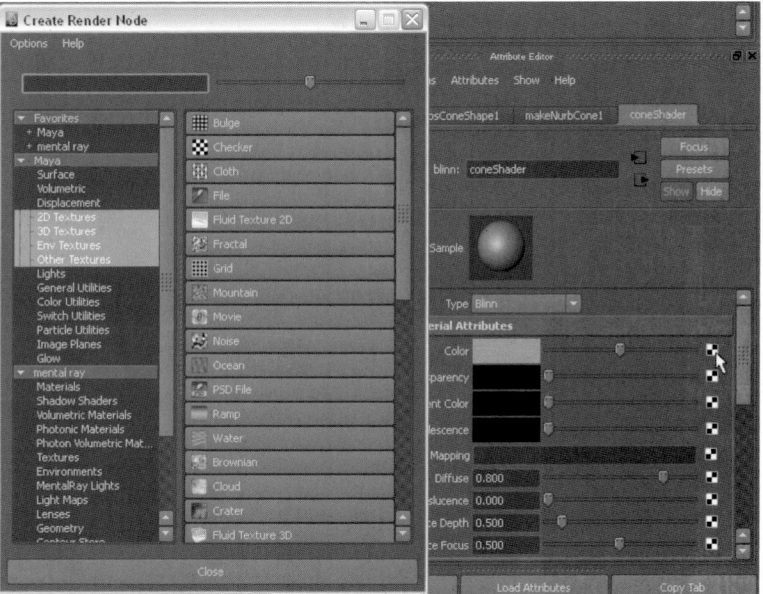

11. Select 2D Textures from the list on the left, and click the Grid button on the right side of the panel to create a grid texture; this is applied to the color channel of the cone and is visible on the cone in the viewport when textured and smooth shaded mode is on (hot key = **6**) See Figure 1.30.

12. Select coneShader in the Work Area, and right-click its icon. Choose Graph Network. You'll see that the coneShader node now has the grid1 texture node as well as the place2dTexture1 node attached (Figure 1.31).

FIGURE 1.30
The grid texture appears on the cone when the perspective view is set to shaded mode.

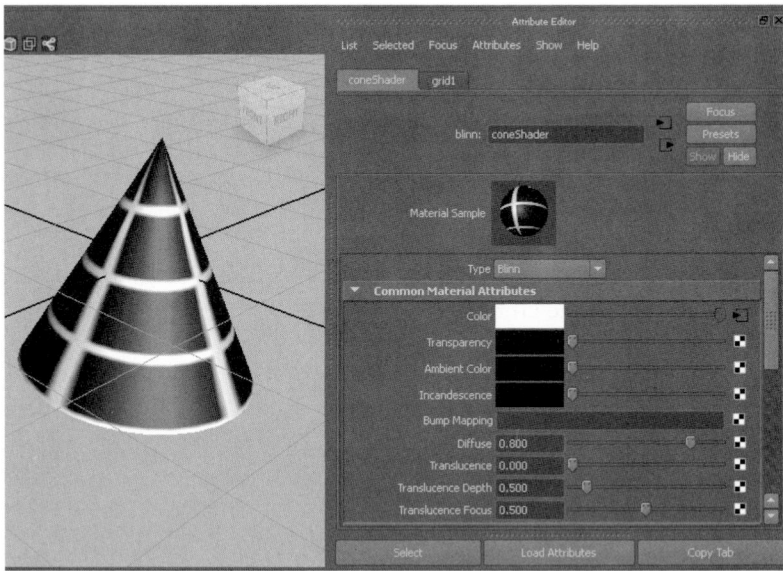

FIGURE 1.31
Applying the grid texture to the color channel of the coneShader adds two new nodes to the shader network.

13. Click the place2dTexture1 node in the Work Area, and its attributes will be displayed in the Attribute Editor.

14. Type **0.5** in the first field next to Coverage. This reduces the coverage of the grid texture in U space by one half.

NURBS UV TEXTURE COORDINATES

NURBS surfaces have their U and V texture coordinates based on the parameterization of the surface, unlike polygon meshes, which require defined UV coordinates. You can use the attributes in the place2dTexture node to position textures on NURBS surfaces. NURBS surfaces are discussed in Chapter 3, and UV coordinates are discussed in Chapter 11.

15. Select the grid1 node in the Work Area of the Hypershade to open its settings in the Attribute Editor.

16. Expand the Color Balance rollout, and click the color swatch next to Default Color. This opens the Color Chooser. Set the color to red.

DEFAULT COLOR

The default color of the texture is the color "behind" the grid texture. Any part of the surface that is not covered by the grid (based on the settings in the place2dTexture node) will use the default color.

17. In the left panel of the Hypershade, select 2D Textures in the Maya list, and click the Ramp button to create a ramp node. At the moment, it is not connected to any part of the coneShader network. This is another way to create render nodes in the Hypershade.

NAVIGATING THE HYPERSHADE WORK AREA

You can zoom out in the Work Area of the Hypershade by holding the Alt button while dragging with the right mouse button; likewise, you can pan by holding the Alt button while MMB-dragging.

18 Select the grid texture to open its settings in the Attribute Editor.

19. In the Work Area of the Hypershade, MMB-drag the ramp texture from the Work Area all the way to the color swatch next to the Filler color in the grid's Attribute Editor. Hold the middle mouse button while dragging; otherwise, you'll select the ramp texture, and the Attribute Editor will no longer display the Grid texture attributes (see Figure 1.32).

20. Select the coneShader node in the Work Area of the Hypershade, and choose Graph ➢ Input And Output Connections from the Hypershade menu. In the Work Area, you can see that the ramp texture is connected to the grid texture. The grid texture is connected to the coneShader, and the shader is connected to the blinn1SG node (see Figure 1.33).

FIGURE 1.32
A texture node can be MMB-dragged from the Hypershade into an attribute slot in the Attribute Editor.

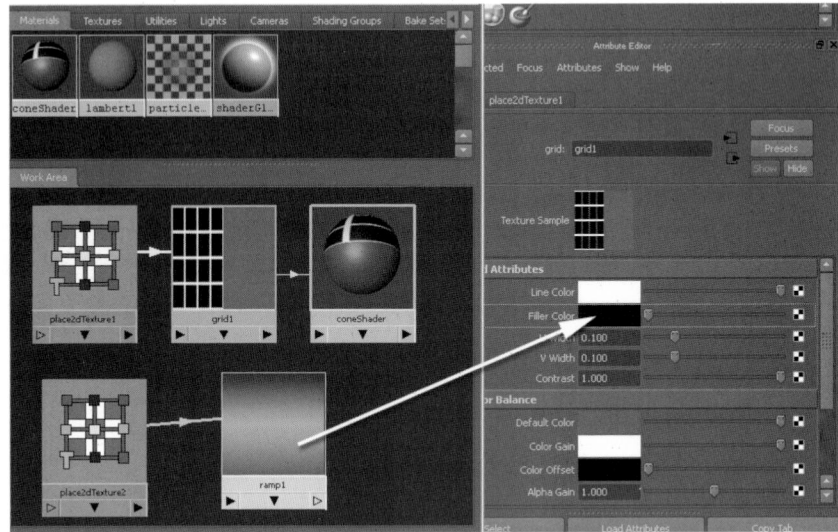

FIGURE 1.33
The coneShader network has grown with the addition of new nodes.

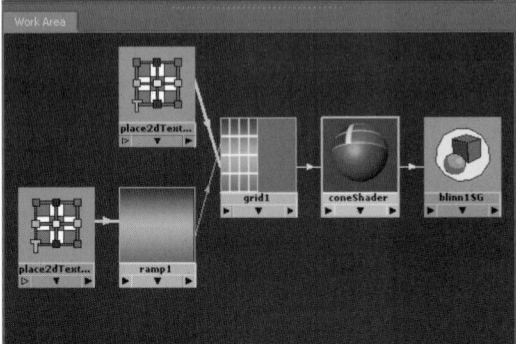

GRAPHING SHADER NETWORKS

You can graph the shader network at any time to refresh the view of the connected nodes in the Work Area. Just right-click the node you want to graph and choose Graph Network, or click the Input/Output connections button at the top of the Hypershade (shown here). More options for displaying the network are available in the Graph menu at the top of the Hypershade.

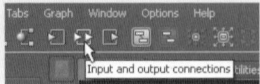

21. Select the blinn1SG node, and graph its input and output connections. The cone's shape node appears (if the bottom caps option was on in the creation options for the NURBS cone, you'll see a second shape node for the cone's bottom cap surface). The blinn1SG node is also connected to the render partition and the light linker, which defines which lights are used to light the cone (see Figure 1.34).

FIGURE 1.34
The shape nodes for the cone are included in the graph when the input and output connections of the blinn1SG node are graphed.

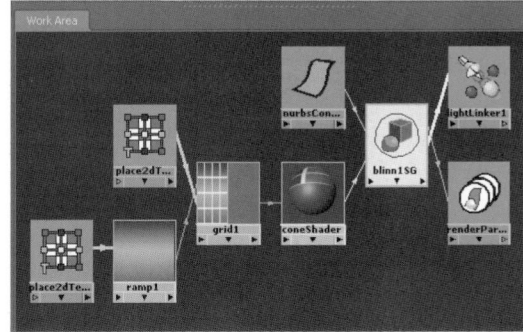

The Hypershade is a very powerful and easy-to-use editor. You can build complex networks of nodes quickly just like rearranging building blocks. You can see how nodes are connected by holding the mouse pointer over the lines that connect the nodes.

The previous sections of this chapter revealed the many ways Maya nodes can be displayed, connected, and edited in a Maya scene. You should make sure that you are comfortable with the basics of working with the editors described. You will rely on them heavily throughout the book, and through the various exercises you will gain proficiency in using them.

Creating Maya Projects

Organization is the key to creating a successful animation. Whether you are working by yourself or with others in a production pipeline, you'll want to know where to find every file related to a particular project, whether it's a scene file, a texture map, an image sequence, or a particle disk cache. To help you organize all the files you use to create an animation, Maya offers you the option of easily creating a Maya project, which is simply a directory with subfolders where each file type related to your scenes can be stored.

Creating a New Project

Creating a new project is very simple. Projects can be created on your computer's primary hard drive, a secondary drive, or a network. The scene files used for each chapter in this book are stored in their own project directories on the DVD that comes with the book. Maya uses a default project directory when one has not been specified. This is located in your My Documents\maya\projects folder in Windows or Documents\maya\projects on a Mac. As an example, you'll create a project directory structure for the examples used in this chapter.

1. Start a new Maya 2011 session. You'll note that an empty scene is created when you run Maya.

2. Choose File ➤ Project ➤ New.

3. The New Project dialog box opens. In the Name field, type **Mastering_Maya_Chapter01**.

4. In the Location field, use the Browse button to find where on your computer or network you want the project to be stored, or simply type the path to the directory. The project folder can be a subfolder of another folder if you like (see Figure 1.35).

   In the Project Locations section, you'll see a large number of labeled fields. The labels indicate the different types of files a Maya scene may or may not use. The fields indicate the path to the subdirectory where these types of files will be located.

5. At the bottom of the New Project dialog box, click the Use Defaults button. This automatically fills in all the fields (see the left side of Figure 1.36).

FIGURE 1.35
The New Project dialog box lets you set the location of a new project directory structure on your hard drive.

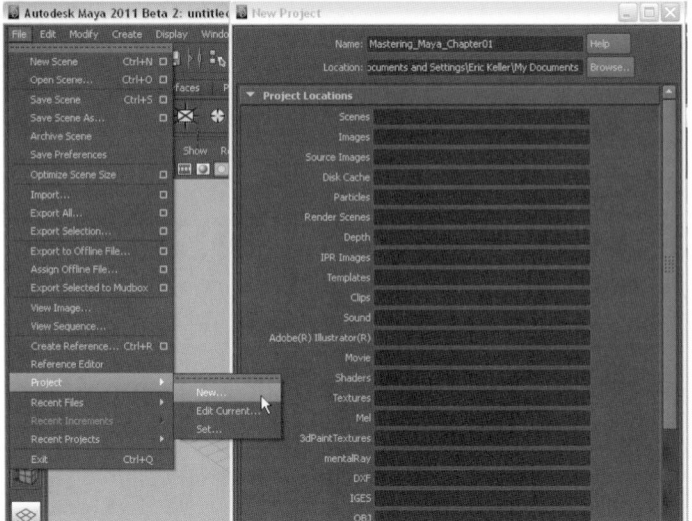

FIGURE 1.36
Clicking the Use Defaults button fills in all the fields with Maya's preferred default file structure (left side of the image). The directory structure is created on the specified drive (right side of the image).

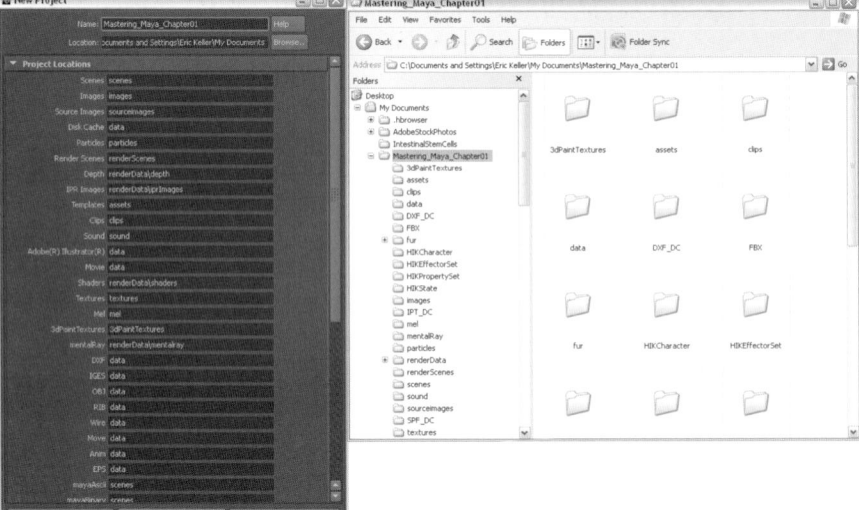

The fields contain the name of the subdirectory relative to the project file. So when you choose to use the default settings, all Maya scene files (files with the .mb or .ma file extension) will be stored in a folder labeled Scenes. The path to that folder will be, in this example, Mastering_Maya_Chapter01\Scenes.

EDITING DEFAULT FILE LOCATIONS

If you decide you want to store the scene files in a different directory, you can type the path to that directory in the field or type a name of a directory you'd like Maya to create when it makes the project.

---

6. Click Accept. Maya will take a few moments to create the project directory and all subfolders on the specified disk drive.

7. Use your computer's file browser to locate the new project; then expand the folder, and you'll see all the subfolders (see the right side of Figure 1.36).

Editing and Changing Projects

You may not need to use every folder Maya creates for you, or you may decide to change where Maya looks for elements, such as file textures. If you're working on a number of different projects, you may need to switch the current project. All of these options are available in the Maya File menu.

1. To edit the current Project, choose File ➤ Project ➤ Edit Current. The Edit Project window opens with all the paths to the project subdirectories. You can type a new directory path into any one of these fields.

RELINKING FILES AFTER CHANGING PROJECT SETTINGS

If you edit the project, Maya will look in the newly specified folders from this point on, but files used prior to editing the project will not be copied or moved. You'll need to move these files using the computer's file browser if you want Maya to easily find them after editing the project.

If you don't want a particular directory to be created when you set up a project, leave the field blank.

2. To switch Projects, you can choose File ➤ Project ➤ Set or choose a project listed in the Recent Projects menu.

When working on a project with a number of other animators, you can choose to share the same project, which is a little risky, or each animator can create their own project directory structure within a shared folder. The latter example is a little safer because it prevents two people from having the same project open or overwriting each other's work. Later in the chapter, you'll learn how multiple animators can share parts of the scene using file references.

It is possible to work on a scene file outside the current project. This happens usually when you forget to set the project using the File ➤ Project ➤ Set option. Make a habit of setting the current project each time you start to work on a scene; otherwise, linked files such as textures, dynamic caches, and file references can become broken, causing the scene to behave unpredictably (which is a nice way of saying the scene will fall apart and possibly crash Maya).

OVERRIDING PROJECT SETTINGS

You can choose to override a project setting for an individual scene element. For instance, by default, Maya looks to the source images directory for file textures. However, when you create a file texture node, you can use the Browse button to reference a file anywhere on your machine or the network. This is usually not a great idea; it defeats the purpose of organizing the files in the first place and can easily lead to broken links between the scene and the texture file. It's a better idea to move all file textures used in the scene to the sourceimages directory or whatever directory is specified in your project settings.

Organizing Complex Node Structures with Assets

A production pipeline consists of a number of artists with specialized tasks. Modelers, riggers, animators, lighting technical directors (TDs), and many others work together to create an animation from a director's vision. Organizing a complex animation sequence from all the nodes in a scene can be a daunting task. Assets are a workflow management tool designed to help a director separate the nodes in a scene and their many attributes into discrete interfaces so each team of specialized artists can concern itself only with its own part of the project.

Assets are a collection of nodes you choose to group together for the purpose of organization. An asset is not the same as a group node; assets do not have an associated transform node and do not appear in the viewport of a scene. For example, a model, its animation controls, and its shaders can all be placed in a single asset. This example demonstrates some of the ways you can create and work with assets.

Creating an Asset

In this example, you'll create an asset for the front wheels of a vehicle:

1. Open the vehicle_v01.ma file from the Chapter1\scenes directory on the DVD. You'll see a three-wheeled vehicle. In the Outliner, the vehicle is grouped.

2. Expand the vehicle group in the Outliner. The group consists of subgroups for the two front wheels, the rear wheel, the chassis, the suspension, and a NURBS curve named steering.

3. Select the steering node in the Outliner. This is the animation control for the steering. Switch to the Rotate tool (hot key = **e**), and drag the green circular handle of the Rotate tool to rotate the steering node on the y-axis. The front wheels match the arrow's orientation (see the left image in Figure 1.37).

FIGURE 1.37

The Y rotation of each front wheel is connected to the Y rotation of the steering control (left). The X rotation of each front wheel is connected to the Y translate of the steering control, giving the animator the ability to tilt the wheels if needed (right).

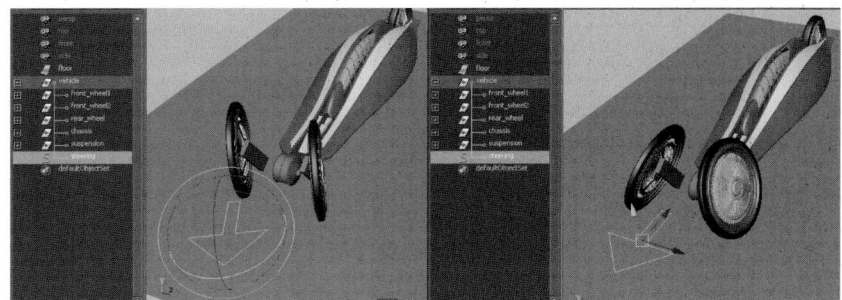

If you select one of the front_wheel groups in the Outliner, you'll see that its Rotate Y channel is colored yellow in the Channel Box, indicating it has an incoming connection. The steering curve's Y rotation is connected to both front_wheel groups' Y connection.

4. Select steering again, and switch to the Move tool (hot key = **w**).

5. Move steering up and down along the y-axis by dragging the green arrow of the Move tool. The front wheels rotate on the x-axis based on the height of the steering object, making them tilt (see the right image in Figure 1.37).

If you look in the Channel Box for either of the front_wheel groups, you'll see that the Rotate X channel is colored orange, indicating that it has been keyframed. In fact, the Rotate channels of the group use what's known as a *driven key* to determine their values. The keyframe's driver is the Y translation of the arrow group. You'll learn more about using this technique in Chapter 5.

6. Select the vehicle group node, and switch to the Move tool.

7. Drag the red arrow of the Move tool to translate the vehicle back and forth along the x-axis. All three wheels rotate as the car moves.

If you expand the front_wheel1 group in the Outliner and select the wheel1Rotate child group node, you'll see that the Rotate Z channel is colored purple in the Channel Box, indicating an expression is controlling its z-axis rotation. You can open the Attribute Editor for the front_wheel1 group and switch to the Expression4 tab to see the expression; see Figure 1.38. (The field isn't large enough to display the entire expression; you can click the field and hold down the right arrow button on the keyboard to read the whole expression.) Creating expressions will be covered in Chapter 5.

This model uses a very simple rig, but already there are a lot of nodes connected to the vehicle geometry to help the job of the animator. To simplify, you can create an asset for just the wheels and their connected nodes so the animator can focus on just this part of the model to do its job without having to hunt through all the different nodes grouped in the Outliner.

FIGURE 1.38
The Z rotation of the
wheels is controlled
by an expression
node. The expression
node is a separate
tab in the Attribute
Editor.

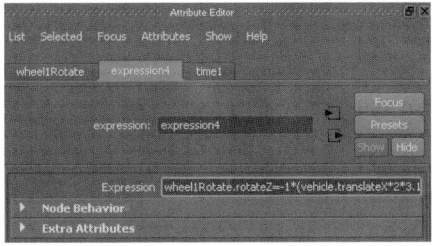

8. In the Outliner, expand the vehicle group and the two front_wheel groups.

9. Ctrl+click front_wheel1, wheel1Rotate, front_wheel2, wheel2Rotate, and the steering curve node.

10. Open the Hypergraph in connections mode (Window ➤ Hypergraph:Connections).

11. In the Hypergraph menu, choose Graph ➤ Input And Output Connections (see Figure 1.39).

12. In the Hypergraph, select the node named time1 and the vehicle node, and drag them out of the way of the other nodes.

13. Drag a selection over all the nodes except time1 and vehicle. These nodes include the group nodes, keyframe nodes, and expression nodes all related to controlling the rotation of the front wheel groups.

14. In the Hypergraph menu, choose Edit ➤ Assets ➤ Advanced Assets ➤ Create Asset ➤ Options (Options is selected by clicking the small square to the right of the command list in the menu).

FIGURE 1.39
The vehicle group
is expanded, and
several of the
nodes related to
the front wheels
are selected and
graphed on the
Hypergraph.

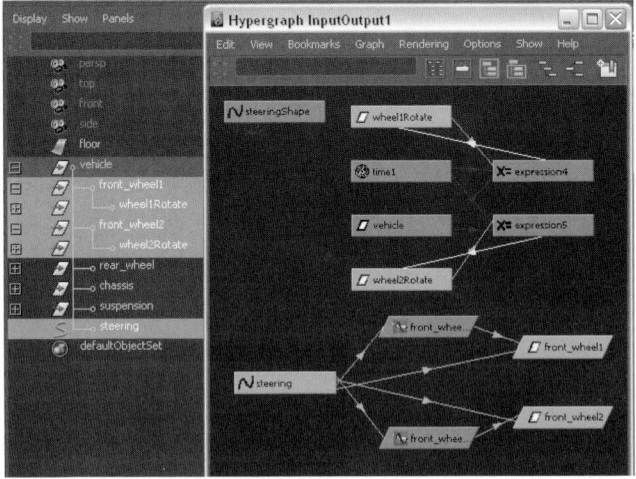

THE OPTIONS BOX

The small square to the right of a listing in the menu indicates the options. When you select just the listing in the menu, the action will be performed using the default settings. When you click the Options box to the right of the menu listing (shown here), a dialog box will open allowing you to change the options for the action. In this book, when you're asked to choose options, this means you need to click the Options box to the right of the menu listing.

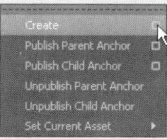

15. In the Create Advanced Assets Options dialog box, set the name of the container to **front_wheels**. Make sure all the settings under Include Options and Publish Options are deselected. All of the keyframes and expressions are applied to the rotation of the wheel groups, not the geometry nodes contained in the groups, so you needn't worry about including the contents of the groups in the asset (see Figure 1.40).

16. Choose the Create Asset option.

FIGURE 1.40
The options are set for the container that will hold all the selected nodes in the Hypergraph.

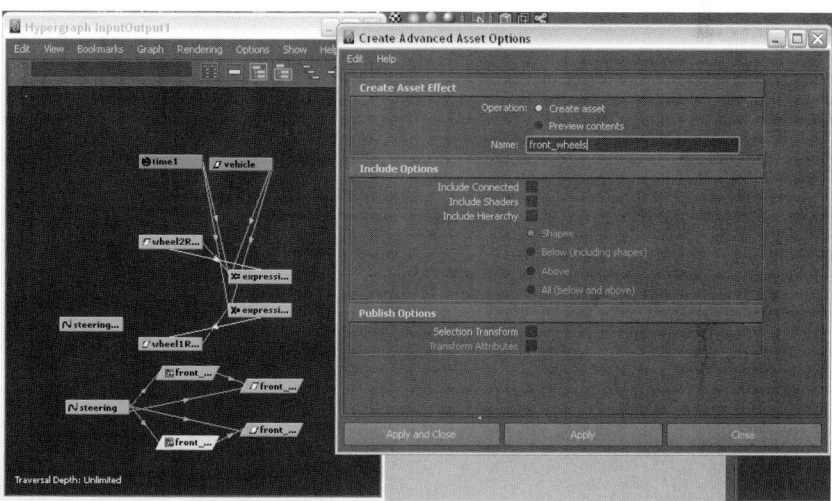

PREVIEW THE ASSET CONTENTS

The Preview Contents options selects all the nodes that will be included in the asset when you click the Apply button, but it will not actually create the asset. This is so you can verify that you have all the various nodes you want included in the Asset before creating it.

17. Click Apply and Close to create the asset.

In the Hypergraph, you'll see a gray box labeled front_wheels; this box is also visible in the Outliner. The time1 and vehicle nodes are still visible in the Hypergraph. It may appear as though they have been disconnected, but that's not actually the case.

18. Select the front_wheels asset in the Hypergraph, and graph its input and output connections (Graph ➤ Input And Output Connections). The connections to the time1 and vehicle nodes are visible again.

19. Select the front_wheels asset in the Hypergraph, and click the Expand Selected Assets(s) icon on the Hypergraph menu bar (or double-click the container). You will see the nodes within the container (see Figure 1.41).

FIGURE 1.41
Expanding the view of a container in the Hypergraph makes the connections between nodes within the container visible.

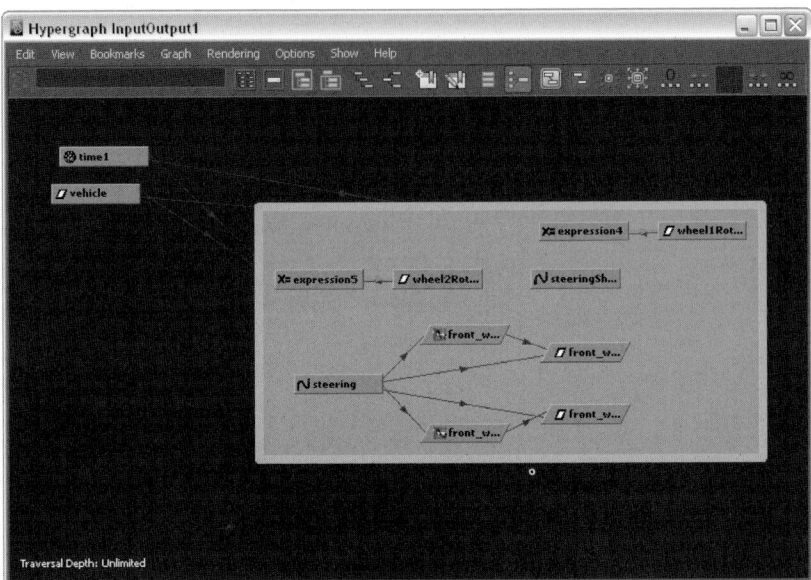

20. Double-click the thick border of the asset to collapse it, or click the Collapse Selected Assets icon at the top of the Hypergraph.

You can select a node inside the container and remove it from the container by right-clicking the node and choosing Remove From Container.

21. Save the scene as **vehicle_v02.ma**.

TIPS ON WORKING WITH ASSETS

Here are some tips for working with assets:

◆ To delete an asset, select it and choose (from the Hypergraph menu) Edit ➢ Asset ➢ Remove Asset. Don't select the asset and delete it; deleting the asset will delete the contents from the scene as well.

◆ You can remove all the assets in a scene, without deleting their contents, by choosing Edit ➢ Delete By Type ➢ Assets.

◆ In the Outliner, you can expand the asset node to reveal the contents. Note that the wheel groups are no longer shown as children of the vehicle group but are now inside the asset group. The nodes themselves still behave as children of the vehicle group. If you change the position of the vehicle, the wheels will still rotate and move with the vehicle.

◆ Assets can be created in the Hypershade as well and can contain any type of node including shaders and textures.

◆ You can create assets without going into the Hypershade. Just select the nodes in the scene, and use the options in the Assets menu.

◆ If you choose Set Current Assets from the Assets menu, all new nodes created in the scene will automatically become part of the specified asset.

◆ You can use the Create Assets With Transform option in the Assets menu to create an asset with a selectable transform handle. Translating or rotating the asset will also translate and rotate the contents of the asset.

Publishing Asset Attributes

You can publish selected attributes of the container's nodes to the top level of the container. This means that the animator can select the asset node and have all the custom controls available in the Channel Box without having to hunt around the various nodes in the network. You can also template your asset for use with similar animation rigs.

In this exercise, you'll publish the attributes of the front_steering asset:

1. Continue with the file from the previous section, or open vehicle_v02.ma from the chapter1\scenes folder on the DVD.

2. In the Outliner, select the front_wheels asset, and expand the node by clicking the plus sign to the left of the node. Select the steering node from within the asset.

3. In the Channel Box, select the Translate Y channel, and from the Edit menu in the Channel Box, choose Publish To Asset ➢ Options.

4. In the Publish Attribute Options box, choose both Selected Channel Box Attributes and Custom Name.

5. Type **wheelTilt** in the Custom String field. Click Apply and Close (see Figure 1.42).

6. Select the front_wheels container in the Outliner; you'll see the wheelTilt channel has been added in the Channel Box. If you change this value between -1 and 1, the arrow controller moves up and down, and the front wheels tilt.

FIGURE 1.42

The Translate Y attribute of the steering node is published to the container under the name wheelTilt.

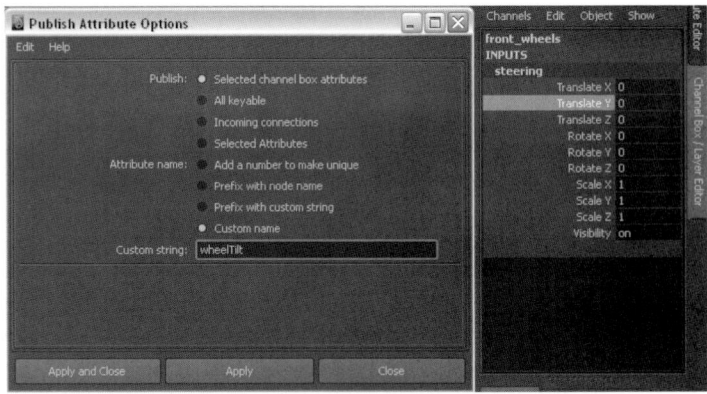

PUBLISH ATTRIBUTES FROM THE ATTRIBUTE EDITOR

If you need to publish a specific attribute that does not appear in the Channel Box, you can open the Attribute Editor for the appropriate node, right-click the attribute name, and choose the publish options from the pop-up menu.

Using the Asset Editor

The Asset Editor can help you further customize and manage your scene's assets. You can use it as another way to publish specific attributes of an asset.

1. Open the scene vehicle_v03.ma from the chapter1\scenes folder on the DVD.

   In the Outliner you'll see two containers: one for the wheels and another named carPaint, which holds the blue paint shader applied to the car.

2. To open the Asset Editor, choose Assets ➤ Asset Editor. The editor is in two panels; on the left side you'll see all the assets in the scene.

   The Asset Editor opens in view mode. In the list of assets on the left, you can click the plus sign in the square to see the nodes contained within each container. You can see the attributes of each node listed by clicking the plus sign in the circle next to each node.

3. Select the front_wheels container, and click the pushpin icon above and to the right of the asset list to switch to edit mode. On the right side of the editor, you'll see the wheelTilt attribute you created in the previous section.

4. Select the arrow next to wheelTilt on the right panel, and the wheels container expands to reveal the Translate channel of the steering node. This is the attribute originally published to the container as wheelTilt.

5. In the list on the left below the Translate channels, expand the Rotate attributes of the steering node. Select Rotate Y, and click the second icon from the top in the middle bar of the Asset Editor. This publishes the selected attribute to the container with a custom name (see Figure 1.43).

6. A dialog box will open, prompting you to name the selected attribute. Name it **steer**.

FIGURE 1.43
Attributes can be published to the container from within the Asset Editor.

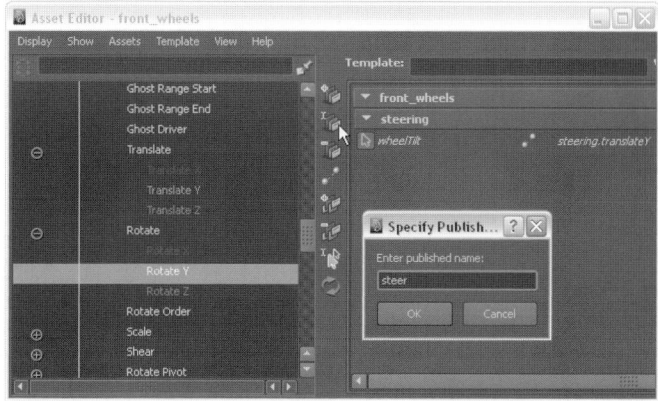

Note that steps 5 and 6 are just another way to publish an attribute; the end result is the same as when you published the wheelTilt attribute from the Channel Box in the previous section.

7. Steer now appears in the right side of the Asset Editor. The view on the right side of the Asset Editor shows the attributes grouped by node. If you want to see just the published attributes, choose View ➤ Mode ➤ Flat from the Asset Editor's menu bar.

8. Select the front_wheels asset in the Outliner, and open its Attribute Editor.

9. Expand the Asset Attributes rollout, and turn on Black Box (see Figure 1.44). When you do this, the only attributes that appear in the Channel Box are the ones that have been published to the asset (wheelTilt and steer). Likewise, in the Outliner, you can no longer expand the asset node.

The Black Box option allows you to restrict access to an asset's attributes so that other artists working on the team can focus on just the attributes they need.

The Asset Editor has a number of advanced features, including the ability to create templates of complex assets that can be saved to disk and used in other scenes for similar assets.

FIGURE 1.44
Turning on Black Box restricts access to the container's contents and their attributes.

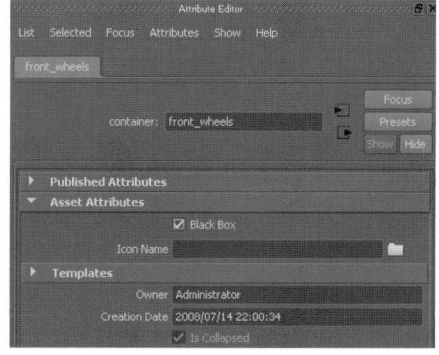

File References

File referencing is another workflow tool that can be used when a team of artists is working on the same scene. For example, by using file references, an animator can begin animating a scene while the modeler is still perfecting the model. This is also true for any of the other team members. A texture artist can work on textures for the same model at the same time. The animator and texture artist can import a reference of the model into their Maya scene, and each time the modeler saves a change, the model reference in the other scenes will update (when the animator and texture artist reload either the scene or the reference).

FILE REFERENCING VS. IMPORTING

File referencing is not the same as importing a Maya scene into another Maya scene. When you import a Maya scene, all the imported nodes become fully integrated into the new scene and have no links to any external files. On the other hand, file references maintain a link to external files regardless of whether the referenced files are open or closed. You can alter a referenced file in a scene, but it's not a great idea; it can break the link to the referenced file and defeats the purpose of file referencing in the first place.

Referencing a File

In this example, you'll reference a model into a scene, animate it, and then make changes to the original reference to get a basic idea of the file referencing workflow.

1. Find the vehicleReference_v01.ma scene and the street_v01.ma scene in the chapter1\ scenes directory of the DVD. Copy both of these files to your local hard drive. Put them in the scenes directory of your current project.

2. Open the scene street_v01.ma from the scenes directory of the current project (or wherever you placed the file on your local drive). The scene contains a simple street model. A locator named carAnimation is attached to a curve in the center of the street. If you play the animation, you'll see the locator zip along the curve.

3. To bring in a file reference, choose File ➤ Create Reference. The File Browser will open.

4. Find the vehicleReference_v01.ma scene that you copied to your local drive. Select it and choose Reference from the File dialog box. After a few moments, the car will appear in the scene (see Figure 1.45).

    In the Outliner, you'll see the vehicleReference_v01:vehicle node as well as the vehicleReference_v01:front_wheels and carPaint container nodes. The container node is an asset with both the wheelTilt and steer attributes created in the previous section.

REFERENCING MAYA SCENES

You don't need to do anything special to the scene you want to reference; it can be a standard Maya scene. When you reference a file in a scene, all of its associated nodes appear using the referenced file's scene name as a prefix. You can change this to a custom string using the options in the Create Reference command.

FIGURE 1.45
The referenced vehicle appears in the scene with its associated containers.

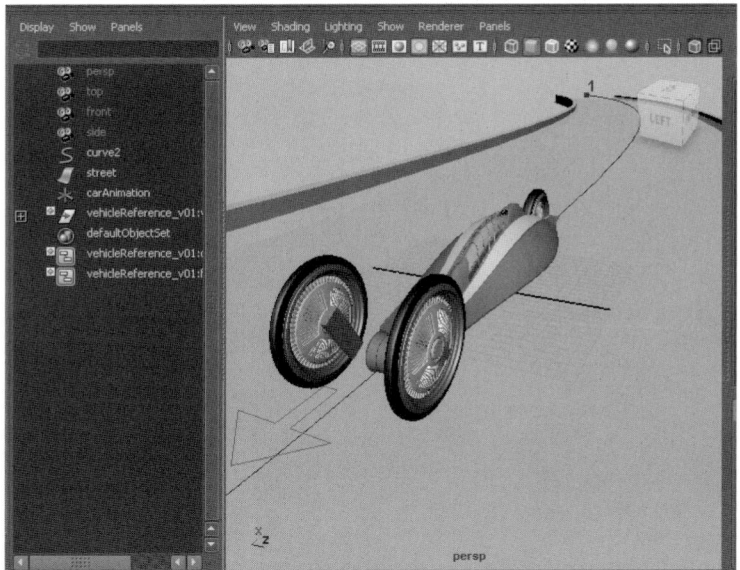

5. In the Outliner, select the carAnimation locator, and then Ctrl+click the vehicleReference_v01:vehicle node.

6. Switch to the Animation menu set, and choose Constrain ➤ Parent ➤ Options.

7. In the options for the Parent constraint, turn off Maintain Offset, make sure both Translate All and Rotate All are selected, and set the weight to **1**.

8. Click Add to make the constraint. The car is now constrained to the locator and will zip along the curve in the center of the street.

9. Try setting keyframes on the wheelTilt and steer attributes of the vehicleReference_v01:front_wheels node.

10. Save the scene to your local scenes directory as **street_v02.ma**.

11. Open the vehicleReference_v01.ma scene from the directory where you copied this file on your local drive.

12. Expand the Vehicle group and the Chassis subgroup.

13. Select the Body subgroup. Set its Scale Y attribute to **0.73** and its Scale Z attribute to **1.5**.

14. Open the Hypershade (Window ➤ Rendering Editors ➤ Hypershade), and select the bluePaint material.

15. Click the blue color swatch next to the Color channel, and use the Color Chooser to change the color to red.

16. Save the scene using the same name (vehicleReference_v01.ma).

17. Open the street_v02.ma scene. The car model has all the changes you created in the vehicleReference_v01.ma scene. It is red, and the body is much wider (see Figure 1.46).

FIGURE 1.46
The changes made to the
body shape and color in
the `vehicleReference
_v01.ma` file are reflected
in the referenced model
in the street scene.

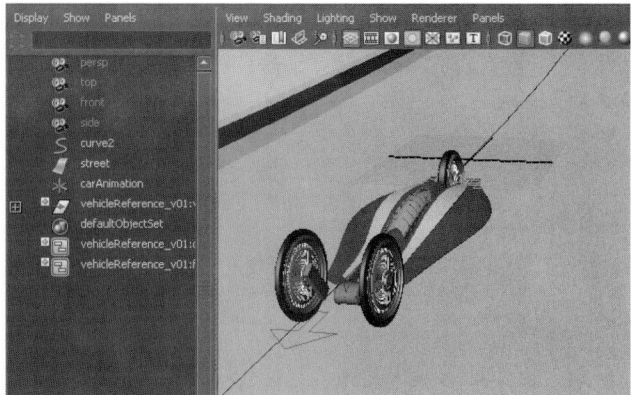

This is the basic file referencing workflow; however, a file referencing structure can be made much more complex to accommodate the needs of multiple teams. In addition, a referenced file can also use other references so that a file referencing tree can be constructed layering several levels of file references. This kind of structure is best planned out and agreed upon in the beginning in order to minimize confusion and keep a consistent workflow.

Using Reference Proxies

You can use proxy objects for your file references to temporarily substitute higher-resolution objects with lower-resolution objects. This can make animating the scene a little easier because the lower-resolution objects will improve performance and update faster in Maya as you play the animation on the timeline.

Multiple versions of the model can be created and used as proxies to facilitate different needs in the scene. A proxy should be the same size and roughly the same shape as the referenced file.

1. Open the `street_v03.ma` scene from the `chapter1\scenes` directory on the DVD. This scene has the same street as before with the same animated locator.

2. First bring in the file reference by choosing File ➢ Create Reference ➢ Options.

3. Under General Options in the Reference Options dialog box, turn on Group and Locator (see Figure 1.47). This will create a locator in the scene and a parent reference to the locator. Set File Type to Maya Ascii.

REFERENCE GROUPING

For the reference and proxy to share the same translation, rotation, and scale animation, the reference must have grouping enabled when it is brought into the scene. Otherwise, when you animate the proxy and then switch to the reference, animation placed on the transform node of the proxy will not be transferred to the reference.

---

4. Click the Reference button, and choose the `vehicleReference_v01.ma` file from the `chapter1\scenes` directory on the DVD.

   When the reference loads, you'll see that it is parented to a locator named vehicleReference_v01RNlocator in the Outliner.

FIGURE 1.47
In the file reference options, make sure Group is on if you want to animate the reference and proxies.

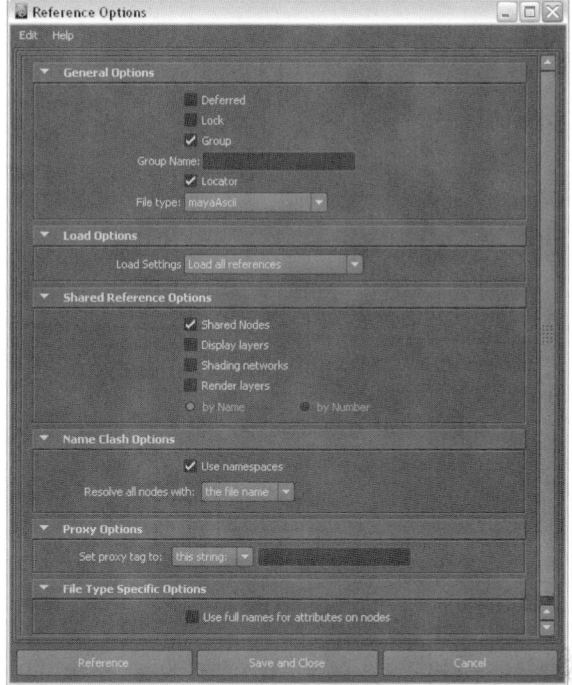

5. In the Outliner, MMB-drag the vehicleReference_v01RNlocator on top of the carAnimation locator.

6. Then select the vehicleReference_v01RNlocator, open the Channel Box, and set all of its Translate and Rotate channels to **0** (Figure 1.48).

FIGURE 1.48
The vehicle-Reference_v01RN-locator is parented to the carAnimation locator, and all of its Translate and Rotate channels are set to zero so it follows the animation of the carAnimation locator.

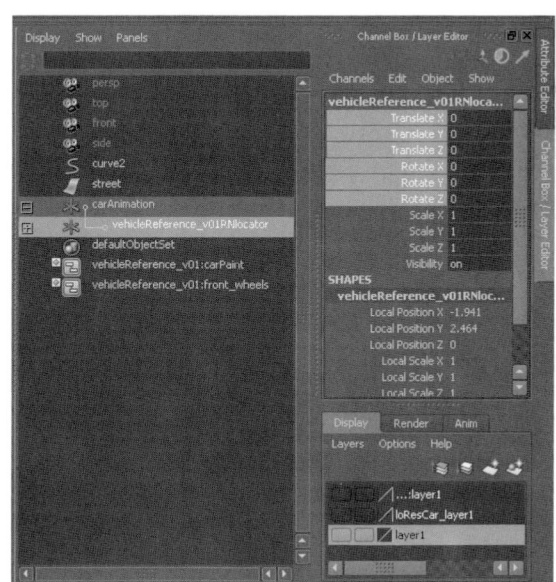

7. Choose File ➤ Reference Editor to open the Reference Editor window.

8. In the bottom half of the Reference Editor window, select the vehicleReference_v01RN node. Choose Proxy ➤ Add Proxy ➤ Options.

9. In the Proxy Options, type **loRes** into the Set Proxy Tag To field. Click the Apply button.

10. Use the File Browser dialog box to choose the loResCar_v01.ma scene from the chapter1\ scenes directory on the DVD.

11. The Proxy Options dialog box should remain open after you add the loRes proxy. Change the field so that it reads **mediumRes**, and click the Proxy button.

12. Use the File Browser to select the medResCar_v01.ma scene from the chapter1\scenes folder on the DVD.

    The Reference Editor won't look much different except that the icon next to the vehicleReference listing in the lower half has changed to the double-diamond icon, indicating that the reference has proxies available.

13. To switch to the proxy, make sure vehicleReference_v01PM is selected in the Reference Editor.

14. From the menu bar in the Reference Editor, choose Proxy ➤ Reload Proxy As ➤ loRes. After a moment, the original vehicle is replaced with the lower-resolution version.

15. Try using this menu to switch to the mediumRes version of the vehicle. The vehicle should be replaced with a slightly higher-resolution version. If you play the animation, the vehicle still moves along the animation curve (Figure 1.49).

16. To bring back the reference, select the original from the list in the Proxy ➤ Reload Proxy As menu.

The Reference Editor can be used to change proxies; remove proxies; and load, duplicate, unload, and reload references. When a reference is unloaded, it is removed from the scene.

FIGURE 1.49
The Reference Editor is used to switch between different versions of the proxy and the original referenced model.

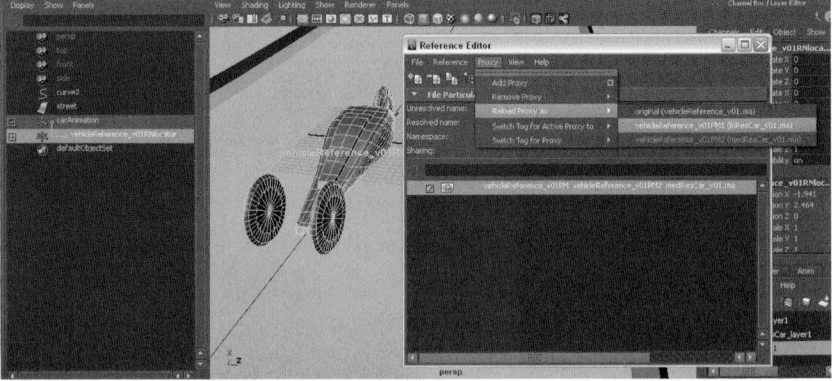

The Bottom Line

Understand transform and shape nodes   DAG nodes have both a transform node and a shape node. The transform node tells where an object is located; the shape node describes how it is made. Nodes can be parented to each other to form a hierarchy.

> **Master it**   Arrange the nodes in the miniGun_v03.ma file in a hierarchical structure so the barrels of the guns can rotate on their z-axis, the guns can be aimed independently, and the guns rotate with the turret.

Create a project   Creating a project directory structure keeps Maya scene files and connected external files organized to ensure the animation project is efficient.

> **Master it**   Create a new project named Test, but make sure the project has only the scene, source images, and data subfolders.

Use assets   An asset is a way to organize the attributes of any number of specified nodes so that their attributes are easily accessible in the Channel Box. This means that members of each team in a pipeline only need to see and edit the attributes they need to get their job done, thus streamlining production.

> **Master it**   Create an asset from the nodes in the miniGun_v04.ma scene in the chapter1\ scenes folder. Make sure that only the Y rotation of the turret, the X rotation of the guns, and the Z rotation of the gun barrels are available to the animator.

Create file references   File references can be used so that as part of the team works on a model, the other members of the team can use it in the scene. As changes to the original file are made, the referenced file in other scenes will update automatically.

> **Master it**   Create a file reference for the miniGun_v04.ma scene; create a proxy from the miniGun_loRes.ma scene.

Chapter 2

Virtual Filmmaking with Maya Cameras

Maya is a visual effects studio designed with the art of filmmaking in mind. Maya's virtual camera replicates real-world cameras as much as possible, while at the same time offering enough flexibility in the settings to allow for a wide variety of creative uses. This chapter introduces the core concepts of how to work with Maya's virtual cameras.

Although the technical aspects of using Maya's cameras are not difficult to learn, mastering the art of virtual cinematography can take years of practice. As with all filmmaking, the story is told through the camera. The camera is used to manipulate the elements of the scene, letting the viewer know what they need to focus on and how they should feel about what is going on in the scene.

Working with Maya's cameras should never be an afterthought. In fact, when you start to build a scene that you intend to render, configuring the cameras should be one of your first concerns. That is why this chapter appears early in this book. From the moment you frame the first shot in the animation, you assume the role of director. The lessons in this chapter are designed to make you feel comfortable with the technical aspects of configuring your cameras as well as give you some creative examples that demonstrate the effect your camera setup has on how the viewer will perceive the scene.

In this chapter, you'll learn to:

◆ Determine the image size and film speed of the camera

◆ Create and animate cameras

◆ Create custom camera rigs

◆ Use depth of field and motion blur

◆ Create orthographic and stereoscopic cameras

Determining the Image Size and Film Speed of the Camera

When starting a new project in Maya, you should first determine the final size of the rendered image or image sequence as well as the film speed (frames per second). These settings will affect every aspect of the project, including texture size, model tessellation, render time, how the shots are framed, and so on. You should raise this concern as soon as possible and make sure every member of the team, from the producer to the art director to the compositor to the editor, is aware of the final output of the animation. This includes the image size, the resolution, the frames per second, and any image cropping that may occur after rendering. Nothing is worse than having to redo a render or even an animation because of a miscommunication concerning details such as resolution settings or frames per second.

TAKING OVER A PROJECT

If you inherit a shot or a project from another animator, double-check that the resolution and camera settings are correct before proceeding. Never assume that the animation is set up properly. It's always possible that something has changed between the time the project started and the moment you took over someone else's scene files.

Setting the Size and Resolution of the Image

The settings for the image size and resolution are located in the Render Settings window under the Image Size rollout panel on the Common tab (shown in Figure 2.1). When you start a new scene, visit this section first to make sure these settings are what you need.

FIGURE 2.1
The Image Size rollout panel in the Render Settings window is where you establish the image size and image resolution. Visit this panel when you start a new project.

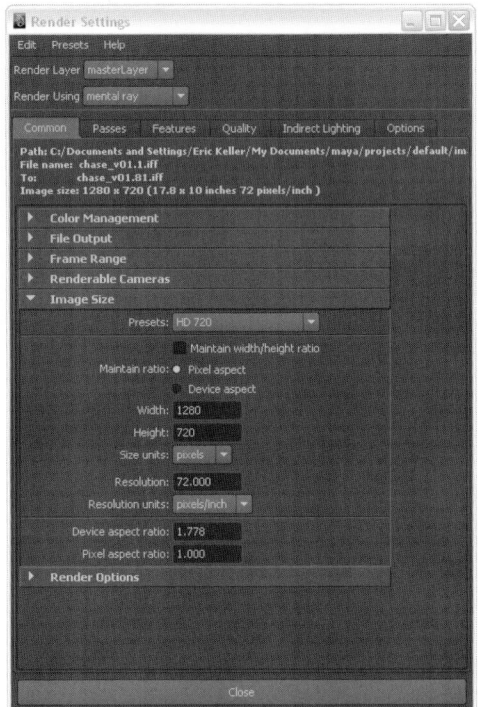

Image size refers to the number of pixels on the horizontal axis by the number of pixels on the vertical axis. So, a setting of 640 by 480 means 640 pixels wide by 480 pixels tall.

Resolution refers to how many pixels fit within an inch (or centimeter, depending on the setting). Generally you'll use a resolution of 72 pixels per inch when rendering for animations displayed on computer screens, television screens, and film. Print resolution is much higher, usually between 300 and 600 pixels per inch.

You can create any settings you'd like for the image size and resolution, or you can use one of the Maya Image Size presets. The list of presets is divided so that common film and video presets are at the top of the list and common print settings are at the bottom of the list. You can change the size and resolution units on the Common tab of the Render Settings window as well.

ADJUSTING SIZE FOR RENDER TEST PREVIEWS

If you need to create test renders at a smaller size, you can change the size of just the images you see in the Render Preview window by choosing a setting from the Render ➤ Test Resolution menu in the Rendering menu set. This option affects images only when they're displayed in the Render Preview window; it does not change the final output settings. When you render your final animation using a batch render, your images will use the size settings specified on the Common tab of the Render Settings window.

Resolution is expressed in a number of ways in Maya:

Image aspect ratio   The ratio of width over height. An image that is 720 by 540 has a ratio of 1.333.

Pixel aspect ratio   The ratio of the actual pixel size. Computer monitors use square pixels: the height of the pixel is 1, and the width of the pixel is 1; thus, the pixel aspect ratio is 1. Standard video images use nonsquare pixels that are 1 pixel high by 1.1 pixel wide, giving them a pixel aspect ratio of 0.9.

Device aspect ratio   The image aspect ratio multiplied by the pixel aspect ratio. For a video image that is 720 by 486 (1.48) using nonsquare pixels (0.9), this would be $1.48 \times 0.9 = 1.333$.

Film aspect ratio   The camera aperture attribute (found in the Attribute Editor for a camera) represented as a ratio. For a typical 35mm video image, this would be $0.816 \div 0.612 = 1.333$.

VIEWING NONSQUARE PIXELS ON A COMPUTER MONITOR

Viewing nonsquare pixels on a computer monitor makes the image look squished. Typically you would test render your animation using a pixel aspect ratio of 1.0 with an image size of 720 by 540. When you are ready for final output, you can switch your resolution to a standard video resolution using a pixel aspect ratio of 0.9 and an image size of 720 by 486.

Setting the Film Speed

The film speed (also known as *transport speed*) is specified in frames per second. You can find this setting in the Maya Preferences window (Window ➤ Settings/Preferences ➤ Preferences). Under the Categories column on the left side of the window, choose Settings. In the Working Units area, use the Time drop-down list to specify the frames per second of the scene. You can change this setting after you've started animating, but it's a good idea to set this at the start of a project to avoid confusion or mistakes. When changing this setting on a scene that already has keyframed animation, you can choose to keep the keyframes at their current frame numbers or have Maya adjust the keyframe position automatically based on the new time setting (see Figure 2.2).

FIGURE 2.2
You set the anima-
tion speed (frames
per second) in the
Preferences window.

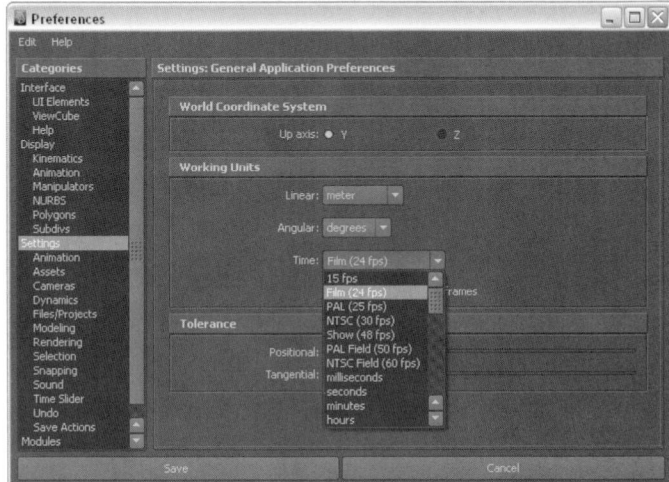

Creating and Animating Cameras

When you add a camera to a scene, you should think about how the shot will be composed and whether the camera will be animated. The composition of a shot affects the mood and tells the viewer which elements visible within the frame are most important to the story. The camera settings allow you to fine-tune the composition of the shot by controlling what is visible within the frame and how it appears.

Most of the attributes of a camera can be animated, allowing you to set the mood of a scene and create special camera effects. Three types of cameras offer different animation controls. These are the one-, two-, and three-node cameras. The controls available for each camera type are suited for different styles of camera movement. This section covers how to create different camera types for a scene and how to establish and animate the settings.

ANIMATICS

An *animatic* is a film industry term referring to a rough animation designed to help plan a shot, like a moving storyboard. Typically models in an animatic are very low resolution and untextured with simple lighting. Animatics are used to plan out both computer-generated (CG) and live-action shots. Camera work, timing, and the composition of elements within the frame are the most important aspects of an animatic.

Creating a Camera

Every new Maya scene has four preset cameras by default. These are the front, side, top, and perspective (persp) cameras. You can render using any of these cameras; however, their main purpose is to navigate and view the 3D environment shown in the viewport. It's always a good idea to create new cameras in the scene for the purpose of rendering the animation. By keeping navigation and rendering cameras separately, you can avoid confusion when rendering.

1. Open the chase_v01.ma scene from the chapter2/scenes folder on the DVD. You'll find that a simple animatic of a car racing down a track has been created.

2. Create a new camera (Create ➤ Cameras ➤ Camera). Open the Outliner, and select the new camera1 node. Double-click its transform node in the Outliner, and rename it **shotCam1** (see Figure 2.3).

FIGURE 2.3
A new camera is created and renamed in the Outliner.

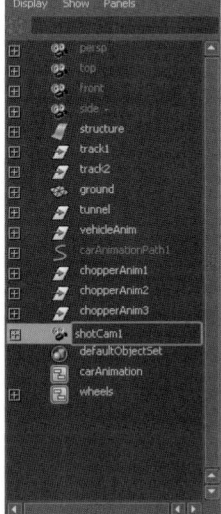

3. In the Display Layer Editor, turn off the visibility of all the layers except the street layer to hide the unnecessary geometry in the scene.

4. Select shotCam1 in the Outliner, and press the **f** hot key to focus on this camera in the viewport.

DISPLAY LAYERS

You can find display layers below the Channel Box/Layer Editor on the right side of the screen. Clicking the V button toggles the visibility of the layer.

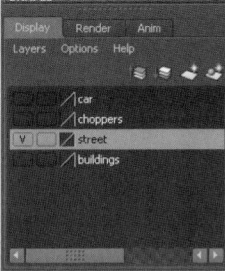

The icon for the camera looks like a movie camera. It has a transform node and a shape node. The camera attributes are located on the shape node.

5. Select shotCam1, and switch to the Move tool (hot key = w).

6. Move the camera up from the center of the grid to the level of the street. Set the Translate X, Y, and Z channels to **1.382**, **4.138**, and **-3.45**.

7. In the toolbox, click the Show Manipulators tool (the bottom icon in the toolbox). If you zoom out in the viewport, you'll see the camera has a second positional icon; this is the center of interest (see Figure 2.4). The value shown in the camera's Channel Box for the center of interest is the distance (in the scene's working units, which is meters for this scene) between the camera and the center of interest. Grab this part of the manipulator, and position it on the street so the camera is looking up the road (toward the beginning of the track where the car starts). This is one technique for aiming the camera.

FIGURE 2.4
The Show Manipulators tool allows you to aim the camera using a second transform manipulator.

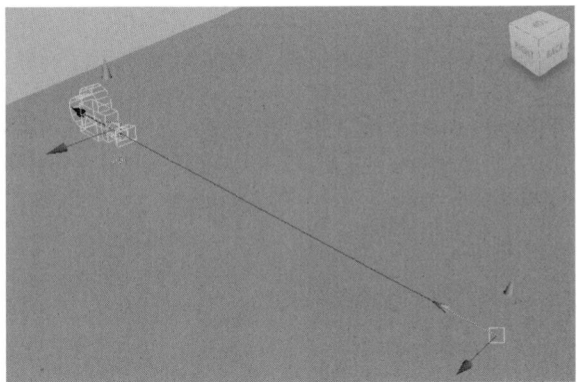

8. In the Viewport panel menu, choose Panels ➤ Look Through Selected Camera (or Panels ➤ Perspective ➤ shotCam1). This will switch the view to shotCam1.

You can use the icons at the top of the Viewport panel to quickly access common viewport settings (see Figure 2.5). The first group of icons on the left side is directly related to camera display options. Starting from the left, these are the actions associated with each icon:

Select Camera   Selects the transform node of the current viewing camera.

Camera Attributes   Opens the Attribute Editor for the current viewing camera.

Bookmark   Stores a bookmark for the current camera position. To move the camera to a bookmarked position, choose View ➤ Bookmarks, and choose the bookmark from the list.

FIGURE 2.5
The panel icon bar provides easy access to common viewport commands. The first two groups of icons on the left side are camera-related options.

CAMERA BOOKMARKS

You can name your stored bookmarks and create a shelf button for each using the Bookmark Editor (View ➤ Bookmarks ➤ Edit Bookmarks).

Image Plane   Creates an image plane for the current camera. Chapter 3 discusses image planes.

2D Pan/Zoom   Toggles between the current view and the 2D Pan/Zoom view for the current viewing camera. This is a new feature in Maya 2011. For more information, see the "2D Pan/Zoom Tool" sidebar.

Grid View   Turns the Grid display on or off.

Film Gate   Turns the Film Gate display on or off.

Resolution Gate   Turns the Resolution Gate display on or off.

Gate Mask   Turns the shaded Gate Mask display on or off when either the Resolution Gate or Film Gate display is activated.

Field Chart   Turns the Field Chart display on or off.

Safe Action   Turns the Safe Action display on or off.

Safe Title   Turns the Safe Title display on or off.

New!

2D PAN/ZOOM TOOL

The 2D Pan/Zoom tool is a new feature of Maya 2011. The purpose of this tool is to allow you to pan or zoom around the view of the current viewing camera without changing its position or rotation. This tool is designed to help you if you are working on a scene in which you are matching the animation of a model to footage projected on an image plane very closely. To do this, you may need to zoom in or move the view to get a better look without disturbing the actual position of the camera. To do this, follow these steps:

1. Switch to the camera that is viewing the scene and the footage on the image plane.

2. From the panel menu, choose View ➤ Camera Tools ➤ 2D Pan/Zoom Tool ➤ Options. The options should open in the Tool Settings. In the options you can switch between 2D Pan and 2D Zoom modes.

3. Drag around in the viewport window to pan or zoom.

4. To toggle back to the actual camera view, use the 2D Pan/Zoom button in the panel menu bar or use the \ hot key.

In the Attribute Editor for the camera's shape node, you can enable rendering for the 2D Pan/Zoom view if needed under the Display Settings rollout panel.

DISPLAY SETTINGS

You can find these same settings in the Attribute Editor for the camera's shape node under the Display Options rollout. You can use these settings to change the opacity or the color of the gate mask: Turn on both the Resolution and Film Gate displays at the same time, and change the Overscan setting, which changes the amount of space between the gate and the edge of the viewport.

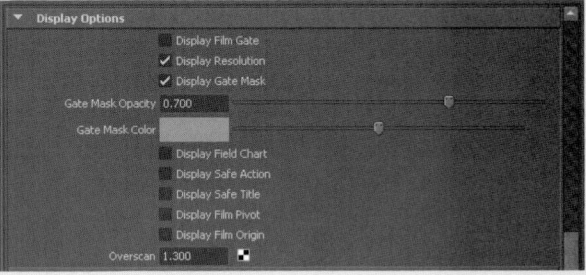

9. In the Display Layer Editor, turn on the buildings layer so the buildings are visible. Tumble around in the viewport (LMB-drag while holding down the Alt key) so you can see part of the large building to the left of the street.

10. In the panel view, turn on the Resolution Gate display. Click the Camera Attributes icon to open the Attribute Editor for shotCam1.

    The image size of this scene is set to 1280 by 720, which is the HD 720 preset. You can see the image resolution at the top of the screen when the Resolution Gate is activated. Working with the Resolution Gate on is extremely helpful when you're establishing the composition of your shots (Figure 2.6).

FIGURE 2.6
The Resolution
Gate is a helpful
tool when framing
a shot.

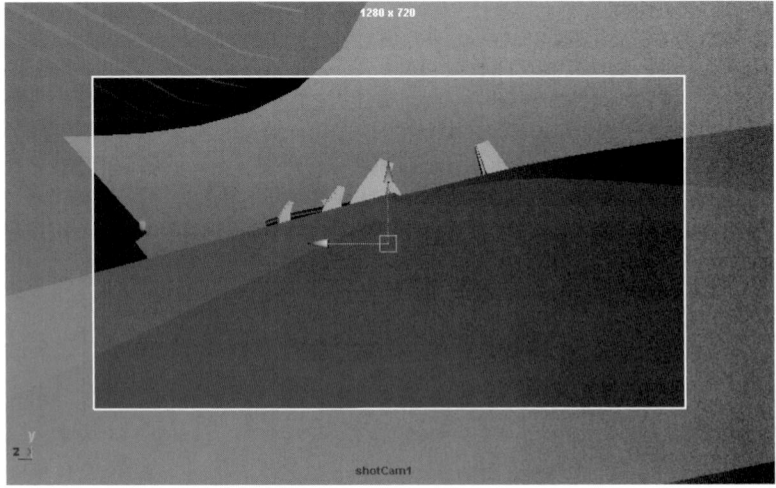

When you create a new camera to render the scene, you need to add it to the list of renderable cameras in the Render settings. You can render the scene using more than one camera.

11. Scroll down in the Attribute Editor for shotCam1, and expand the Output Settings area. Make sure the Renderable option is selected.

12. Open the Render Settings window. In the Renderable Cameras area, you'll see both the shotCam1 and persp cameras listed (see Figure 2.7). To remove the perspective camera, click the Trash Can to the right of the listing.

FIGURE 2.7
You can add cameras to the list of renderable cameras in the Render Settings window.

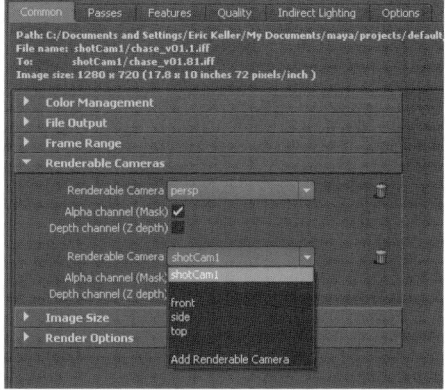

To change the renderable camera, choose a different camera from the list. To add another camera, choose Add Renderable Camera at the bottom of the list. The list shows all available cameras in the scene.

When batch rendering a scene with more than one renderable camera, Maya creates a subdirectory named after each renderable camera in the image directory of the project. You can add the camera name to the name of the image sequence by adding **%c** to the name listed in the File Name Prefix field in the Render Settings window. For example, setting the File Name Prefix to **myAnimation_%c** in a scene with two renderable cameras creates two image sequences named myAnimation_camera1.#.tif and myAnimation_camera2.#.tif. See Figure 2.8.

FIGURE 2.8
You can append the camera name to the image name in the rendered sequence by adding **%c**.

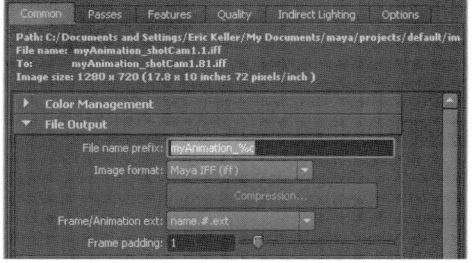

Setting Camera Attributes

At the top of the Attribute Editor for the camera's shape node, you'll find the basic settings for the camera available in the Camera Attributes rollout panel.

Single-node camera A single-node camera is just a plain camera like the perspective camera. You can change its rotation and translation by setting these channels in the Channel Box, using the Move and Rotate tools, or tumbling and tracking while looking through the camera.

MOVING THE CAMERA

You translate and rotate a camera using the standard transform tools. This is done when you are viewing the camera from another camera. When you are looking through a camera, you can use the same hot keys you use while moving around the perspective camera:

Alt+LMB = Tumble; also known as *rotating* the camera.

Alt+MMB = Track; this is the same as moving the camera on the x- and y-axes.

Alt+RMB = Dolly; this is the same as moving the camera on the z-axis. Also known as *pushing* the camera.

You can find additional camera movement controls in the panel's View menu; just choose View ➤ Camera Tools, and pick one of the tools from the list.

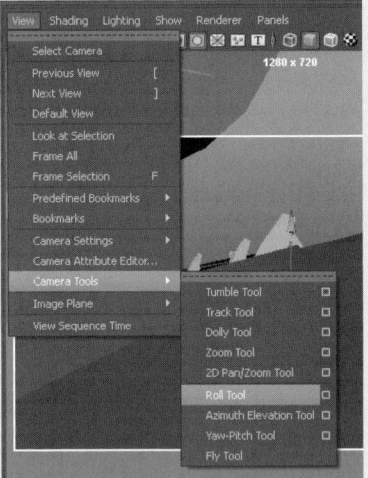

By default, each change in position that results from tumbling, tracking, or dollying a camera view is not undoable. You can change this default by activating the Undoable Movements option in the Movement Options rollout panel of the camera's Attribute Editor; however, this may add a lot to the Undo cue. Alternatively, you can use the bracket hot keys, [and], to move between previous views. Bookmarks are also a good way to store camera views. It's also common to set a keyframe on a camera's Translation and Rotation settings as a way of storing the position. The keyframe can be used as part of an animation or deleted if it's not needed in the final animation.

Two-node camera   A two-node camera is a camera that has a separate aim control. The Camera and Aim control are contained within a group. When you switch to this type of camera (or create this type of camera using the Create ≻ Cameras menu), the rotation of the camera is controlled by the position of the aim node, which is simply a locator. It works much like the Show Manipulators tool except that the locator itself has a transform node. This makes it easy to visualize where the camera is looking in the scene and makes animation easier. You can keyframe the position of the aim locator and the position of the camera separately and easily edit their animation curves on the Graph Editor.

Three-node camera   A three-node camera is created when you choose Camera, Aim, and Up from the Controls menu. This adds a third locator, which is used to control the camera's rotation around the z-axis. These controls and alternative arrangements will be explored later in the "Creating Custom Camera Rigs" section.

When working with two- or three-node cameras, resist the temptation to move or keyframe the position of the group node that contains both the camera and the aim locator. Instead, expand the group in the Outliner, and keyframe the camera and aim nodes separately. This will keep the animation simple and help avoid confusion when editing the animation. If you need to move the whole rig over a large distance, Shift+click both the camera and the aim locator, and move them together. Moving the group node separately is asking for trouble.

CAMERA TWIST

The Camera and Aim type of rig has a twist attribute on the group node above the camera and aim nodes. Twist controls the Z rotation of the camera much like the Up control on the three-node camera. This is the only control on the group node that you may want to adjust or keyframe.

For most situations, a two-node camera is a good choice since you can easily manipulate the aim node to accurately point the camera at specific scene elements, yet at the same time, it doesn't have additional nodes like the three-node camera, which can get in the way. In this example, you'll use a two-node camera to create an establishing shot for the car chase scene.

The focal length of the camera has a big impact on the mood of the scene. Adjusting the focal length can exaggerate the perspective of the scene, creating more drama.

1. Select shotCam1, and open its Attribute Editor to the shotCam1Shape tab. In the Controls drop-down list, you have the option of switching to a camera with an aim node or to a camera with an Aim and an Up control. Set the camera to Camera And Aim (Figure 2.9).

2. Expand the shotCam1_group node that now appears in the Outliner, and select the shotCam_aim node.

FIGURE 2.9
You can add other camera controls using the Controls menu in the Attribute Editor. The camera is then grouped in the Outliner with a separate Aim control.

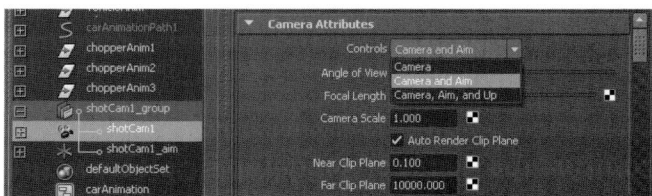

3. In the Channel Box, set its Translate X, Y, and Z settings to **-0.155**, **4.206**, **-2.884**. (The camera's node should still have its X, Y, and Z translation settings at 1.382, 4.138, and -3.45.)

4. In the Display Layer menu, turn on the car layer. Set the current frame to **60** so that the car is in view of the camera.

5. In the Attribute Editor for shotCam1, adjust the Angle Of View slider. Decreasing this setting flattens the perspective in the image and zooms in on the scene; increasing this setting exaggerates the perspective and zooms out.

6. With the camera still selected, switch to the Channel Box, and find the Focal Length setting under the shotCamShape1 node.

7. Highlight the Focal Length channel label, and MMB-drag back and forth in the viewport window. Set Focal Length to **20** (see Figure 2.10).

FIGURE 2.10
The Angle Of View slider in the Attribute Editor and Focal Length attribute in the Channel Box both adjust the zoom of the camera.

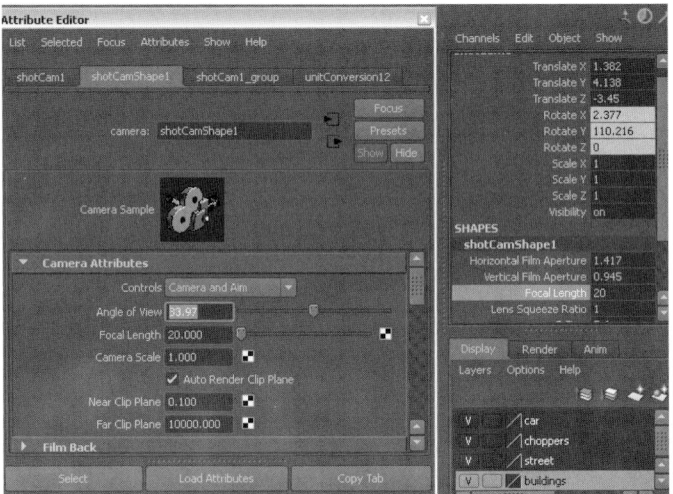

Adjusting the focal length of the camera has a similar effect on the camera as changing the angle of view; however, it is inversely related to the angle of view. Increasing the focal length zooms in on the scene, and decreasing it zooms out. The two settings are connected; they can't be set independently of each other.

In a real camera as you adjust the focal length, you are essentially repositioning the lens in the camera so that the distance between the lens and the film gate (where the film is exposed to light) is increased or decreased. As you increase the focal length, objects appear larger in frame. The camera zooms in on the subject. The viewable area also decreases—this is the angle of view. As you decrease the focal length, you move the lens back toward the film gate, increasing the viewable area in the scene and making objects in the frame appear smaller. You're essentially zooming out (see Figure 2.11).

By default, Maya cameras have a focal length of 35. Roughly speaking, the human eye has a focal length of about 50. A setting of 20 is a good way to increase drama in an action scene by exaggerating the perspective. Higher settings can flatten out the view, which creates a different type of mood; by reducing perspective distortion, you can make the elements of a scene feel very large and distant.

FIGURE 2.11
Two Maya cameras seen from above. A longer focal length produces a smaller angle of view (left camera); a shorter focal length produces a larger angle of view (right camera).

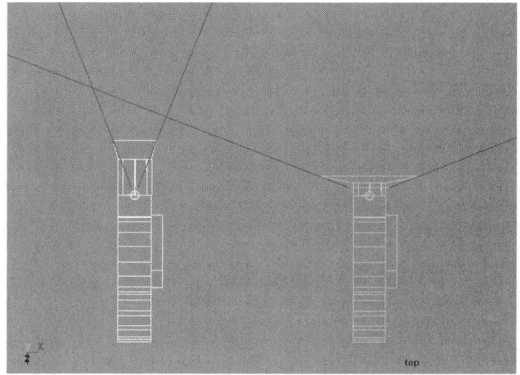

RENDERING A PORTRAIT

When you want to render a close-up of a character, a short focal length can distort the features of your character's face. To achieve the best results, you want to push the camera back in the scene and then zoom in. This flattens the depth of the scene and creates a more accurate portrayal of the character. Try these steps:

1. In the Render settings, create an image size suitable for a portrait—try something like **990 x 1220**.

2. Create a new camera, and turn on the Resolution Gate display so that you can properly frame the face.

3. Set the camera to a focal length of **50**, dolly the camera back (Alt+RMB), and frame the face.

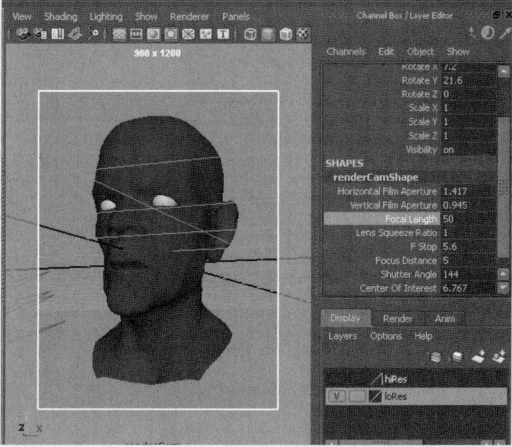

A good portrait should be slightly off-center. Divide the frame horizontally into thirds, and position the eyes at about the place where the top and middle thirds meet. You can always experiment with different camera positions relative to the subject to see how it affects the emotional impact of the image. Unless you want to create a very confrontational image, try not to put the subject dead center in the frame. When rendering characters for a portfolio, I find this setup creates a visually pleasing way to show off my work, which is not surprising since these techniques have been developed by portrait artists over the past few centuries.

Limiting the Range of Renderable Objects with Clipping Planes

Clipping planes are used to determine the range of renderable objects in a scene. Objects that lie outside the clipping planes are not visible or renderable in the current camera. Clipping planes can affect the quality of the rendered image; if the ratio between the near clipping plane and the far clipping plane is too large, image quality can suffer (if the near clipping plane is 0.1, the far clipping plane should be no more than 20,000). Keep the far image plane just slightly beyond the farthest object that needs to be rendered in the scene, and keep the detail of distant objects fairly low.

The Auto Render Clip Plane option automatically determines the position of the clipping planes when rendering with Maya software (this setting does not affect animations rendered with mental ray, Maya hardware, or vector renders). It's always a good idea to turn off this option and set the clipping plane values manually.

1. From the Panel menu, choose Panels ➤ Layouts ➤ Two Panes Side By Side. Set the left pane to the perspective view and the right pane to shotCam1.

2. Select shotCam1, and choose the Show Manipulators tool from the toolbox.

3. Zoom in on the shot cam in the perspective view, and click the blue manipulator switch (located just below the camera when the Show Manipulators tool is active; see Figure 2.12) twice to switch to the clipping plane display.

FIGURE 2.12
Clicking the blue switch below the Show Manipulators tool cycles through the various actions of the tool. Clicking twice activates the manipulators for the clipping planes.

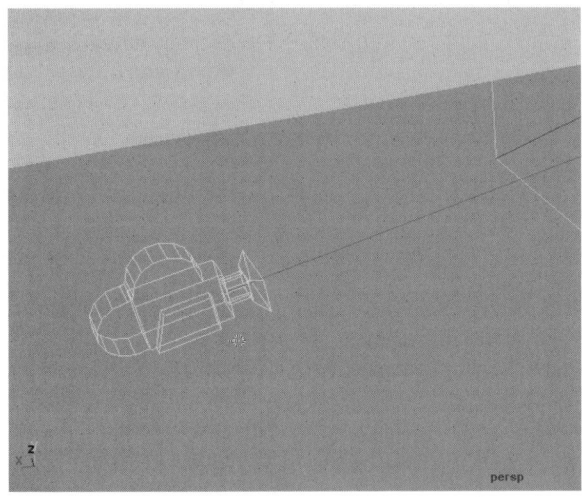

The clipping plane manipulator consists of two blue rectangles connected by lines. The near clipping plane is a small rectangle very close to the camera; the far clipping plane is very large and far from the camera.

4. Zoom in close to the shot cam, and MMB-drag the near clipping plane manipulator. You can set the position of this clipping plane interactively. Note that as you move the plane away from the camera, the geometry in the shotCam1 view is cut off. Any object between the camera and the near clipping plane will not render or will only partially render.

5. Zoom out until you can see the far clipping plane manipulator.

6. MMB-drag this to bring it in closer to the camera. Objects beyond this clipping plane will not be rendered by the camera or will appear cut off.

7. In the Attribute Editor for the shotCam1Shape node, set Near Clip Plane to **.05** and Far Clip Plane to **85** (the units for this scene are set to meters). This is a good starting place; if the positions of the planes need to change later, they can be adjusted (see Figure 2.13).

8. Save the scene as **chase_v02.ma**.

To see a version of the scene to this point, open chase_v02.ma from the chapter2/scenes directory on the DVD.

FIGURE 2.13
The positions of the clipping planes are set for shotCam1.

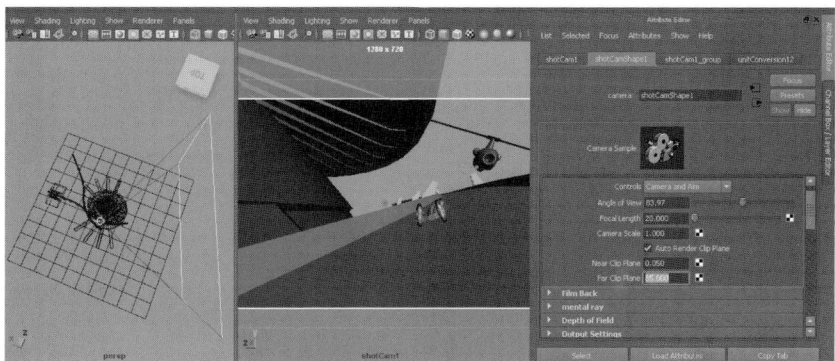

CLIPPING PLANE PROBLEMS

Sometimes you may find that everything disappears in a scene when you change the working units in the preferences or when you open a scene. This usually happens when the clipping planes have been set incorrectly or have changed. Try opening the Attribute Editor for the current viewing camera, and adjust the clipping plane values. This is true for the front, side, and top cameras as well as the perspective camera.

Composing the Shot Using the Film Back Settings

In an actual camera, the *film back* refers to the plate where the negative is placed when it is exposed to light. The size of the film determines the film back setting, so 35mm film uses a 35mm film back. The *film gate* is the gate that holds the film to the film back. Unless you are trying to match actual footage in Maya, you shouldn't need to edit these settings.

Ideally you want the Film Gate and Resolution Gate settings to be the same size. If you turn on the display of both the Film Gate and the Resolution Gate in the camera's Display Options rollout panel (toward the bottom of the Attribute Editor—you can't turn on both the Film Gate and Resolution Gate using the icons in the panel menu bar), you may see that the Film Gate is larger than the Resolution Gate. You can fix this by adjusting the Film Aspect Ratio setting. Simply divide the resolution width by the resolution height (1280 ÷ 720 = 1.777777), and put this value in the Film Aspect Ratio setting (see Figure 2.14).

FIGURE 2.14

In the top image, the Film Gate and Resolution Gate settings do not match. In the bottom image, the Film Aspect Ratio setting has been changed so that Film Gate and Resolution Gate match.

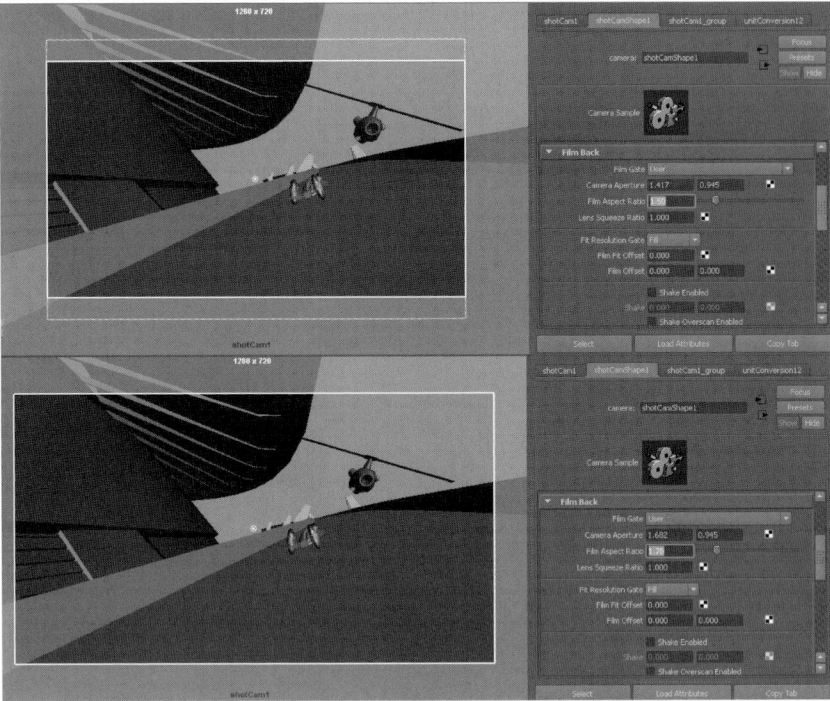

The Film Gate drop-down list has presets available that you can use to match footage if necessary. The presets will adjust the aperture, film aspect ratio, and lens squeeze ratio as needed. If you're not trying to match film, you can safely leave these settings at their defaults and concern yourself only with the Image Size and Resolution attributes in the Render Settings window.

The Film Fit Offset and Film Offset controls can be very useful in special circumstances where you need to change the center of the rendered area without altering the position of the camera. The parallax caused by the perspective of the 3D scene in the frame does not change even though the camera view has. Creating an offset in an animated camera can create a strange but very stylistic look.

The Film Fit Offset value has no effect if Fit Resolution Gate is set to Fill or Overscan. If you set Fit Resolution Gate to Horizontal or Vertical and then adjust the Film Fit Offset, the offset will be either horizontal or vertical based on the Fit Resolution Gate setting. The Film Offset values accomplish the same thing; however, they don't depend on the setting of Fit Resolution Gate.

1. Continue with the scene from the previous section, or open the chase_v02.ma scene from the chapter2/scenes directory on the DVD. Set the current camera in the viewport to shotCam1 and the timeline to frame 61.

2. In the Display Layers Editor, turn on the choppers layer so that the helicopter is visible in the shot.

3. Open the Attribute Editor for shotCam1, and switch to the shape node (shotCam1Shape) tab.

4. In the Film Back rollout panel, set Film Offset to **0.2** and **-0.05**. Notice how this change alters the composition of the frame. Even a small change can affect the emotional impact of a shot (see Figure 2.15).

FIGURE 2.15
Adjusting the
Film Offset set-
ting changes the
framing of the
shot without
actually moving
the camera or the
perspective of the
image.

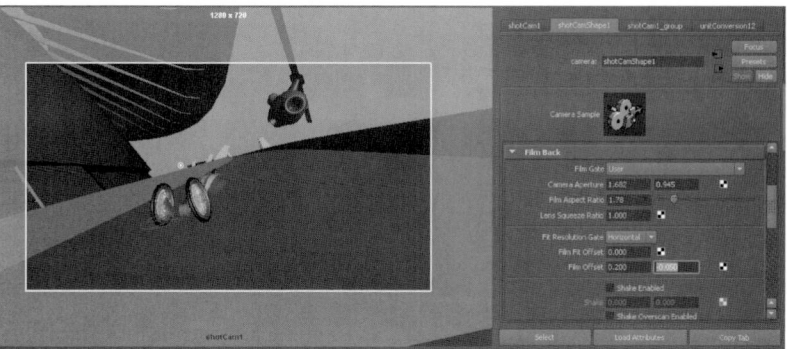

Creating a Camera Shake Effect

The Shake attribute is an easy way to add a shaky vibrating motion to a camera. The first field is the Horizontal shake, and the second field is the Vertical shake. The values you enter in the shake fields modify the current settings for Film Offset. When you are applying a shake, you're essentially shaking the film back, which is useful because this does not change how the camera itself is animated. You can apply expressions, keyframes, or animated textures to one or both of these fields. The Shake Enabled option allows you to turn the shaking on or off while working in Maya; it can't be keyframed. However, you can easily animate the amount of shaking over time.

In this example, you'll use an animated fractal texture to create the camera shaking effect. You can use an animated fractal texture any time you need to generate random noise values for an attribute. One advantage fractal textures have over mathematical expressions is that they are easier to animate over time.

1. Turn on the Shake Enabled option.

2. Right-click the first field in the Shake option, and choose Create New Texture from the pop-up window (see Figure 2.16).

FIGURE 2.16
Right-click the
attribute field,
and choose Cre-
ate New Texture.
The Create Render
Node window
will open.

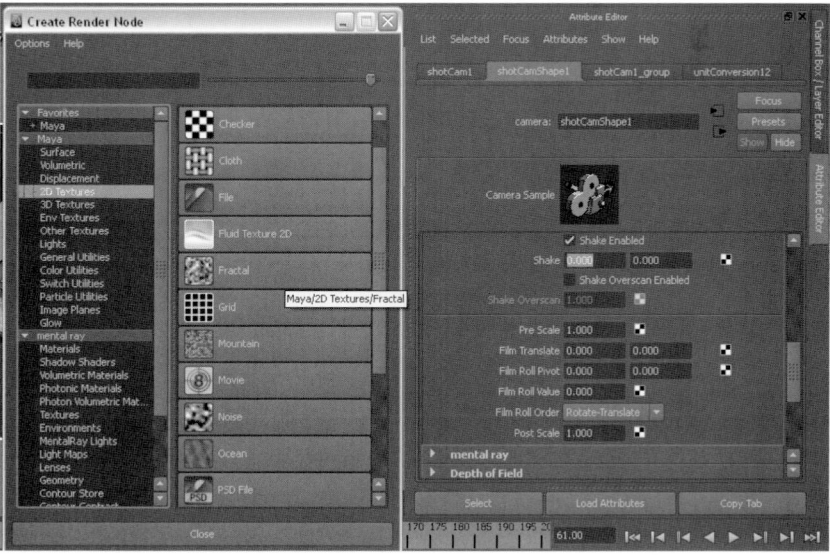

3. Under the Maya section in the node list on the left of the Hypershade, choose Fractal from the 2D Textures section. The camera view will move when you add the texture, and that's okay.

4. The attributes for the fractal texture will appear in the Attribute Editor. Set Amplitude to **0.1**.

5. Select the Animated check box to enable the animation of the texture, and rewind the animation.

6. Right-click the Time attribute, and choose Set Key (see Figure 2.17).

FIGURE 2.17
To animate a fractal texture, turn on the Animated option, and set keyframes on the time slider.

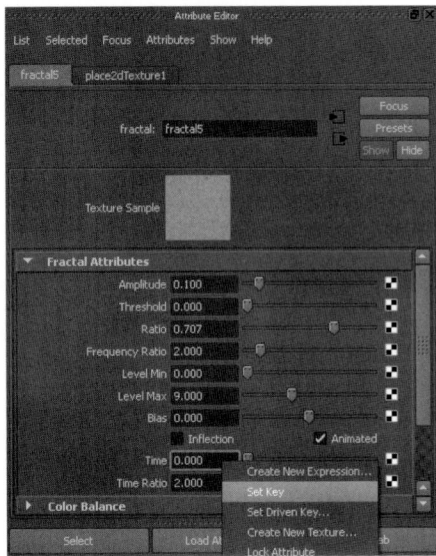

7. Set the timeline to frame 200. Set the Time attribute to **100**, and set another key.

8. Rewind and play the animation; you'll see the camera move back and forth.

9. Repeat steps 1 though 7 for the Vertical setting in Shake to add another animated fractal texture to this attribute. You want to have a different texture for each setting so that horizontal and vertical shaking of the camera are not the same value; otherwise, the camera will appear to shake diagonally.

10. Select the second fractal texture, expand its UV Coordinates rollout panel, and click the arrow to the right of it to go to the fractal texture's place2dTexture node.

11. Set the Rotate UV value to **45**. This rotates the texture so that the output of this animated texture is different from the other, ensuring a more random motion.

You may notice that the shaking is nice and strong but that you've lost the original composition of the frame. To bring it back to where it was, adjust the range of values created by each texture. The Fractal Amplitude of both textures is set to 0.1, which means each texture is adding a random value between 0 and 0.1 to the film offset. You need to equalize these values by adjusting the Alpha Offset and Alpha Gain settings of the textures.

12. Open the Hypershade by choosing Window ➤ Rendering Editors ➤ Hypershade. Click the Textures tab, and Shift+click the two fractal textures.

13. From the Hypershade menu, choose Graph ➤ Input And Output Connections. In the Work Area, you'll see the two textures connected to the camera.

14. Hold the mouse over the line connecting one of the textures to the shotCamShape1 node. The pop-up label shows that the outAlpha attribute of the texture is connected to the vertical or horizontal shake of the camera. This means you must adjust the outAlpha value to compensate for the change made to the camera's offset (see Figure 2.18).

FIGURE 2.18
The outAlpha value generated by the animated fractal texture is connected to the camera's horizontal shake.

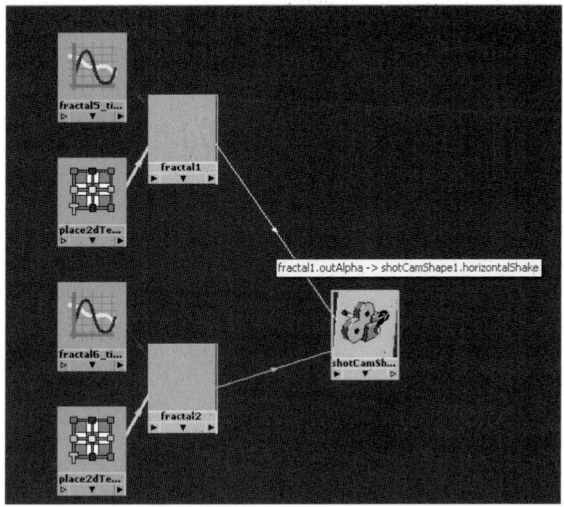

If you look at what's going on with the fractal texture, you'll see that when the Amplitude setting of the texture is 0, the outAlpha value is 0.5 (you can see this by switching to the shotCamShape1 tab and looking at the Horizontal Shake field). The fractal texture itself is a flat gray color (value = 0.5). As you increase the Amplitude setting, the variation in the texture is amplified. At an Amplitude of 1, the outAlpha attribute ranges from 0 to 1. You can see this in the values generated for the Shake attribute in the camera node. This is a very large offset and causes the shaking of the camera to be very extreme. You can set Amplitude to a very low value, but this means the outAlpha value generated will remain close to 0.5, so as the shake values are added to the film offset, the composition of the frame is changed—the view shifts up to the right.

To fix this, you can adjust the Alpha Gain and Alpha Offset attributes found in the Color Balance section of each fractal texture. Alpha Gain is a scaling factor. When Alpha Gain is set to 0.5, the outAlpha values are cut in half; when Alpha Gain is set to 0, outAlpha is also 0, and thus the Shake values are set to 0, and the camera returns to its original position. So if you want to shake the camera but keep it near its original position, it seems as though the best method is to adjust the Alpha Gain value of the fractal texture.

However, there is still one problem with this method. You want the outAlpha value of the fractal to produce both negative and positive values so that the camera shakes around its original position in all directions. If you set Alpha Gain to a positive or negative number, the values produced will be either positive or negative, which makes the view appear to shift in one direction or the other. To properly adjust the output of these values, you can use the Alpha Offset attribute to create a shift.

Set Alpha Offset to negative one-half of Alpha Gain to get a range of values that are both positive and negative; 0 will be in the middle of this range. Figure 2.19 shows how adjusting the Amplitude, Alpha Gain, and Alpha Offset attributes affect the range of values produced by the animated fractal texture.

FIGURE 2.19
You can adjust the range of values produced by the animated fractal texture using the Amplitude, Alpha Offset, and Alpha Gain attributes.

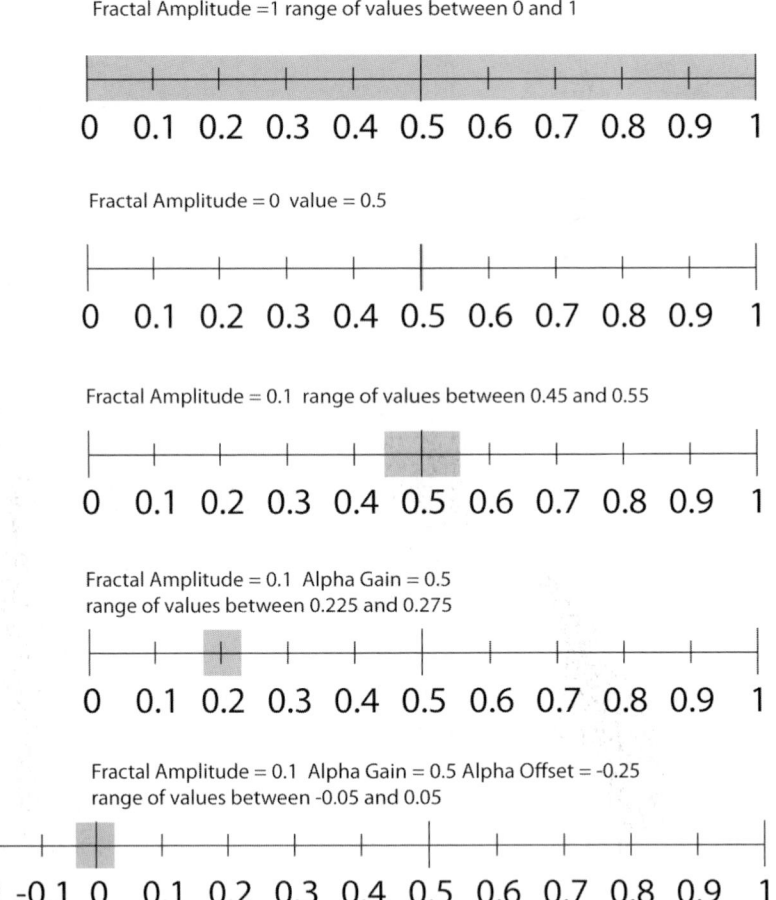

Fractal Amplitude =1 range of values between 0 and 1

0   0.1   0.2   0.3   0.4   0.5   0.6   0.7   0.8   0.9   1

Fractal Amplitude = 0 value = 0.5

0   0.1   0.2   0.3   0.4   0.5   0.6   0.7   0.8   0.9   1

Fractal Amplitude = 0.1 range of values between 0.45 and 0.55

0   0.1   0.2   0.3   0.4   0.5   0.6   0.7   0.8   0.9   1

Fractal Amplitude = 0.1 Alpha Gain = 0.5
range of values between 0.225 and 0.275

0   0.1   0.2   0.3   0.4   0.5   0.6   0.7   0.8   0.9   1

Fractal Amplitude = 0.1 Alpha Gain = 0.5 Alpha Offset = -0.25
range of values between -0.05 and 0.05

-0.2 -0.1 0   0.1   0.2   0.3   0.4   0.5   0.6   0.7   0.8   0.9   1

Using an Expression to Control Alpha Offset

You can reduce the number of controls needed to animate the camera shake by automating the Alpha Offset setting on the fractal node. The best way to set this up is to create a simple expression where Alpha Offset is multiplied by negative one-half of the Alpha Gain setting. You can use this technique any time you need to shift the range of the fractal texture's outAlpha to give both positive and negative values.

1. Select the fractal1 node, and open its attributes in the Attribute Editor. Expand the Color Balance rollout panel, and set the Alpha Gain value of fractal1 to **0.25**.

2. In the field for Alpha Offset, type **=-0.5*fractal1.alphaGain;**. Then hit the Enter key on the numeric keypad to enter the expression (Figure 2.20).

   You can create the same setup for the fractal2 node. However, it might be a better idea to create a direct connection between the attributes of fractal1 and fractal2, so you need only adjust the Alpha Gain of fractal1, and all other values will update accordingly.

FIGURE 2.20
An expression is created to automatically set the Alpha Offset value of fractal1 to negative one-half of the Alpha Gain value.

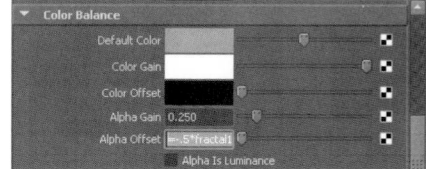

3. In the Hypershade, MMB-drag fractal1 on top of fractal2, and choose Other from the pop-up menu to open the Connection Editor.

4. Use the Connection Editor to connect the Alpha Gain and Offset settings of fractal1 to Alpha Gain and Offset of fractal2. On the left side of the Connection Editor, select alphaGain from the list; on the right side, select alphaGain to connect these two attributes. Select alphaOffset on the left side, and then select alphaOffset on the right side to connect these two attributes.

5. Select Amplitude on the left, and then select Amplitude on the right to connect these two attributes as well (see Figure 2.21).

FIGURE 2.21
The Connection Editor is used to connect the Alpha Gain, Alpha Offset, and Amplitude of fractal2 to fractal1.

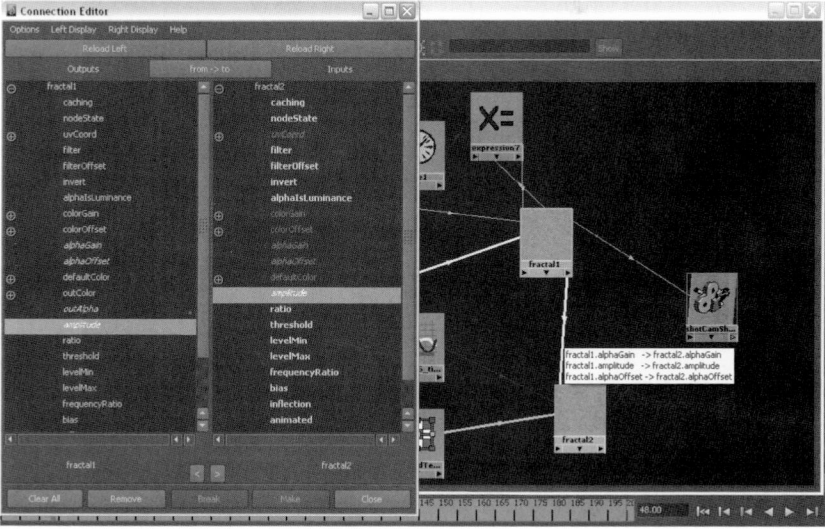

6. Play the animation, and you'll see the camera shake. To tone down the movement, reduce the Alpha Gain of fractal1.

7. Set the timeline to frame 60, and set the Alpha Gain value of fractal1 to **0**. Right-click the Alpha Gain field, and choose Set Key.

8. Set the timeline to frame 65. Set the Alpha Gain value of fractal1 to **0.5**, and set another key.

9. Set the timeline to frame 90. Set the Alpha Gain value of fractal1 to **0**, and set a third key.

10. Play back the animation, and you'll see the camera shake as the car and helicopter fly by (make sure the playback speed in the timeline preferences is set to Real-Time [24FPs]; otherwise, the shake will not appear at the proper speed in the view window as you play the animation).

11. Save the scene as **chase_v03.ma**.

To see a version of the scene to this point, open the chase_v03.ma file from the chapter2\ scenes directory.

The Shake Overscan attribute moves the film back and forth on the z-axis of the camera as opposed to the Shake settings, which move the film back and forth horizontally and vertically. Try animating the Shake Overscan setting using a fractal texture to create some dramatic horror-movie effects.

SHAKING CAMERA ASSET

This camera arrangement is a good candidate for an asset. You can create an asset from nodes that have already been connected and animated. In the Outliner, turn off DAG Objects Only in the Display menu. From the list of nodes in the Outliner, select the camera's shape node, expression, and fractal textures, and create an asset. You can then use the Asset Editor to publish the Amplitude and Alpha Gain attributes of fractal1 to the container as custom attributes (give the attributes descriptive names, such as **shakeAmplitude** and **shakeScale**). When you need to make changes to the animation of the shake, you can simply set keyframes on the published shakeScale attribute. For more information on assets, consult Chapter 1.

Creating Custom Camera Rigs

Maya's three camera types (Camera, Camera and Aim, Ccamera Aim, and Up) work well for many common animation situations. However, you'll find that sometimes a custom camera rig gives you more creative control over a shot. This section shows how to create a custom camera rig for the car chase scene. Use this example as a springboard for ideas to design your own custom camera rigs and controls.

Swivel Camera Rig

This rig involves attaching a camera to a NURBS circle so that it can easily swivel around a subject in a perfect arc.

1. Open the chase_v03.ma scene from the chapter2\scenes directory on the DVD, or continue with the scene from the previous section. In the Display layers, turn off both the choppers and buildings layers.

2. Switch to the persp camera in the viewport.

3. Create a NURBS circle by choosing Create ➤ NURBS Primitives ➤ Circle. Name the circle **swivelCamRig**.

4. Create a new camera (Create ➤ Cameras ➤ Camera), and name it **swivelCam**.

5. Open the Attribute Editor for swivelCam to the swivelCamShape tab. Set Controls to Camera and Aim.

6. Expand the new swivelCam_group node in the Outliner. Select the swivelCam, and press the **f** hot key to focus on the camera in the viewport.

7. In the Outliner, select swivelCam, and Ctrl+click the swivelCamRig circle.

8. Switch to the Animation menu set, and choose Animate ➤ Motion Paths ➤ Attach To Motion Path ➤ Options.

9. In the options, set Time Range to Start, and turn off Follow.

10. Click Attach to attach the camera to the circle (see Figure 2.22).

FIGURE 2.22
The swivelCam is attached to the NURBS circle using the Attach To Motion Path command.

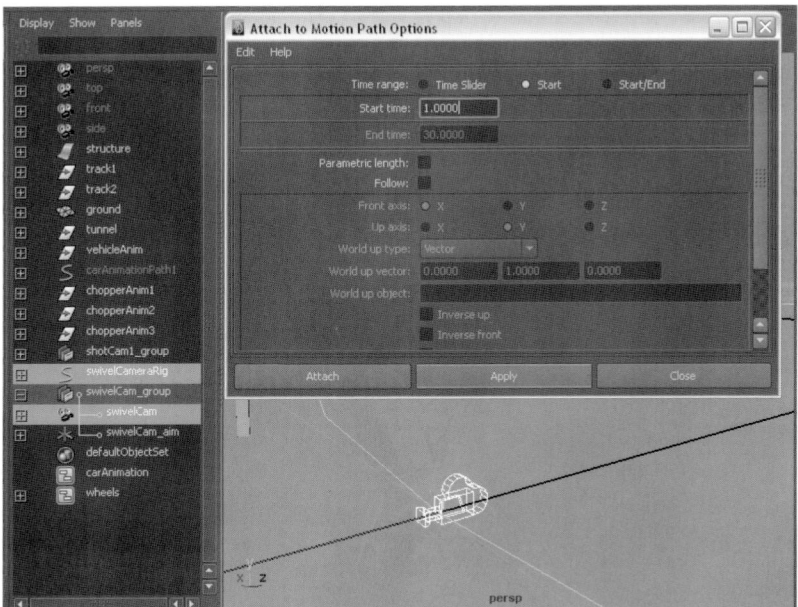

TURN OFF THE FOLLOW OPTION

The camera's rotation channels are already controlled by the Aim locator. If you leave the Follow option selected in the Attach To Motion Path options, you'll get an error message in the Script Editor bar.

The camera is now attached to the circle via the motion path; the camera will stay in a fixed position on the circle curve. This is a fast and easy way to attach any object or other type of transform node (such as a group) to a curve.

11. Make sure the visibility of the street and car display layers is on, and rewind the animation.

12. Zoom out in the perspective viewport. In the Outliner, select the swivelCamRig, and MMB-drag it up in the Outliner into the vehicleAnim group.

13. Expand the vehicleAnim group, and select the swivelCamRig.

14. Open the Channel Box, and set the Translate and Rotate channels to **0**. The circle will be repositioned around the car.

15. Select the swivelCam_aim locator from within the swivelCam_group.

16. In the Outliner, MMB-drag this up into the vehicleAnim group as well. Set its Translate and Rotate channels to **0**. This will move to the pivot point of the vehicleAnim group.

17. Select the swivelCamRig, and in the Channel Box set Translate Y to **0.4**. Set the Scale attributes to **0.5**.

18. Set the viewport to the swivelCam, and turn on the Resolution Gate display.

19. Select the swivelCam node, and set its focal length to **20**. Play the animation. You'll see the camera follow along with the car as it drives down the road.

Swivel Camera Rig Asset

The camera follows the car, but things don't get interesting until you start to animate the attributes of the rig. To cut down on the number of node attributes that you need to hunt through to animate the rig, you'll create an asset for the camera and rig and publish attributes for easy access in the Channel Box. (For more information on assets, consult Chapter 1.)

1. In the Outliner, Ctrl+click the swivelCam node, swivelCamShape, the swivelCam_aim locator, and the swivelCamRig node (Figure 2.23).

2. Choose Assets ➢ Advanced Assets ➢ Create ➢ Options.

3. Set Operation to Create Asset, and set the name to **swivelCamera**. Turn off Include Hierarchy so that only the nodes selected in the Outliner are included.

4. Click Apply and then Close to create the container (Figure 2.24).

FIGURE 2.23
The NURBS circle (swivelCamRig) and the swivel-Cam_aim have been parented to the vehicleAnim group.

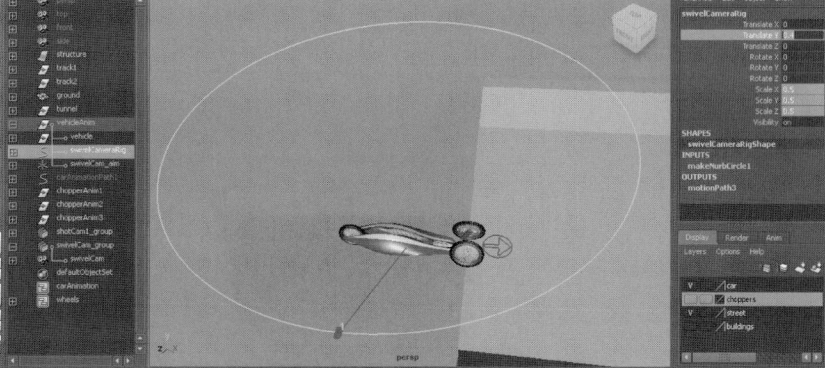

FIGURE 2.24
The advanced options for creating an Asset.

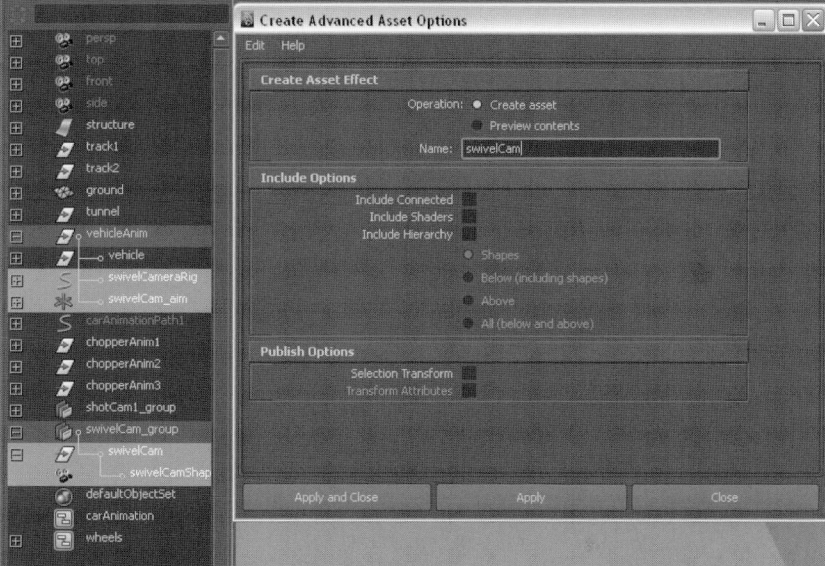

5. Choose Assets ➢ Asset Editor. On the left side of the Asset Editor, select the swivelCamera asset, and click the pushpin icon to edit the asset.

6. Click the plus sign in the square to expand the swivelCamera asset, and then expand the swivelCam rig node (click the plus sign in the circle next to swivelCamRig).

7. From the list of attributes, scroll down to find the Translate attributes. Expand the Translate group by clicking the plus sign in the circle, and select the Translate Y attribute.

8. Click the second icon from the top at the center of the Asset Editor. Set the published name to **rise**.

9. Expand the Rotate group, select the Rotate Y attribute, and publish it using the name **swivel**. Expand the Scale group, select Scale Z, and publish it using the name **push**.

10. On the left side of the editor, expand the swivelCam_aim node, and select its Translate attribute.

11. Publish it using the name **aim** (see Figure 2.25). The three attributes Aim X, Aim Y, and Aim Z will be created at once.

FIGURE 2.25
Various attributes are chosen from the nodes in the swivelCam asset and published to the Channel Box using the Asset Editor.

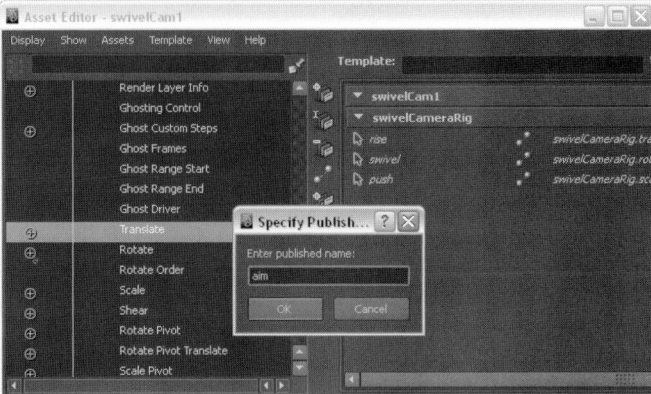

12. Expand the swivelCam (click the plus sign in the square) and the swivelCamShape nodes (click the plus sign in the circle).

13. Select the Focal Length attribute, and publish it using the name **zoom**.

14. Close the Asset Editor, and select the swivelCamera asset node in the Outliner. Try changing the values of the published attributes and playing the animation.

LOCK UNUSED ROTATION CHANNELS

To cut down on rotation problems, you'll want to lock the Rotate X and Rotate Z values of the swivelCamRig. Select the node in the INPUTS section of the Channel Box, set the values to **0**, right-click these attributes, and choose Lock Selected. This keeps the rotation nice and simple.

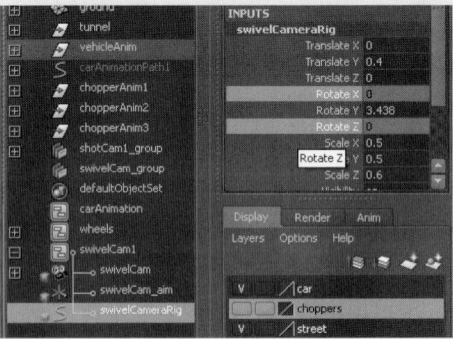

15. Open the Preferences panel (Window ➤ Settings/Preferences ➤ Preferences), and select Animation from the left column. Make sure Default In Tangent and Default Out Tangent are set to Clamped.

16. Try setting the following keyframes to create a dramatic camera move using the rig (see Figure 2.26):

FRAME	RISE	SWIVEL	PUSH	AIM X	AIM Y	AIM Z
Frame 1	3.227	48.411	6	0	0	0
Frame 41	0.06	134.265	0.3	0	0	0
Frame 92	0.06	246.507	0.3	0	0.091	0.046
Frame 145	0.13	290.819	0.8	0	0.167	-0.087
Frame 160	0	458.551	0.4	0	0.132	-0.15
Frame 200	0.093	495.166	0.4	0	0.132	-0.015

17. Set the view in the perspective window to swivelCam (Panels ➤ Perspective ➤ swivelCam).

18. Turn on all the display layers, and play the animation (Figure 2.27). Save the scene as **chase_v04.ma**.

To see a finished version of the animation, open the chase_v04.ma scene from the chapter2\ scenes directory on the DVD.

FIGURE 2.26
The attributes of the asset are selected and keyframed.

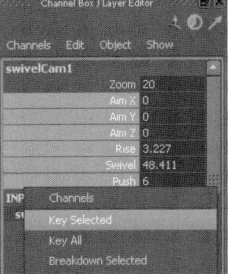

FIGURE 2.27
A custom camera rig can make exciting camera animation easy to create and edit.

CAMERA SEQUENCING

New!

Maya 2011 introduces the Camera Sequencer tool, which allows you to create a sequence of shots for scenes that use multiple cameras. You can arrange and edit the camera sequence using the non-linear camera sequence editor, which is similar to the Trax Editor. For more information on how to use this feature watch the CameraSequencer.mov movie in the BonusMovies folder on the DVD.

Applying Depth of Field and Motion Blur

Depth of field and motion blur are two effects meant to replicate real-world camera phenomena. Both of these effects can increase the realism of a scene as well as the drama. However, they can both increase render times significantly, so it's important to learn how to efficiently apply them when rendering a scene. In this section, you'll learn how to activate these effects and the basics of how to work with them. Using both effects effectively is closely tied to render-quality issues. Chapter 12 discusses render-quality issues more thoroughly.

Rendering Using Depth of Field

The depth of field (DOF) settings in Maya simulate the photographic phenomena where some areas of an image are in focus and other areas are out of focus. Artistically this can greatly increase the drama of the scene, because it forces the viewers to focus their attention on a specific element in the composition of a frame.

Depth of field is a ray-traced effect and can be created using both Maya software and mental ray; however, the mental ray DOF feature is far superior to that of the Maya software. This section describes how to render depth of field using mental ray.

DEPTH OF FIELD AND RENDER TIME

Depth of field adds a lot to render time, as you'll see from the examples in this section. When working on a project that is under time constraints, you will need to factor DOF rendering into your schedule. If a scene requires an animated depth of field, you'll most likely find yourself re-rendering the sequence a lot. As an alternative, you may want to create the DOF using compositing software after the sequence has been rendered. It may not be as physically accurate as mental ray's DOF, but it will render much faster, and you can easily animate the effect and make changes in the compositing stage. To do this, you can use the Camera Depth Render Pass preset (discussed in Chapter 12) to create a separate depth pass of the scene and then use the grayscale values of the depth pass layer in conjunction with a blur effect to create DOF in your compositing software. Not only will the render take less time to create in Maya, but you'll be able to fine-tune and animate the effect quickly and efficiently in your compositing software.

There are two ways to apply the mental ray depth of field effect to a camera in a Maya scene:

◆ Activate the Depth Of Field option in the camera's Attribute Editor

◆ Add a mental ray physical_lens_dof lens shader or the mia_lens_bokeh to the camera (mental ray has special shaders for lights and cameras, as well as surface materials)

Both methods produce the same effect. In fact, when you turn on the DOF option in the Camera Attributes settings, you're essentially applying the mental ray physical DOF lens shader to the camera. The mia_lens_bokeh lens shader is a more advanced DOF lens shader that has a few additional settings that can help improve the quality of the depth of field render. For more on lens shaders, consult Chapter 10.

The controls in the camera's Attribute Editor are easier to use than the controls in the physical DOF shader, so this example will describe only this method of applying DOF.

1. Open the `chase_v05.ma` scene from the `chapter2/scenes` directory on the DVD.

2. In the viewport, switch to the DOF_cam camera. If you play the animation (which starts at frame 100 in this scene), you'll see the camera move from street level upward as two helicopters come into view.

3. In the Panel menu bar, click the second icon from the left to open the DOF_cam's Attribute Editor.

4. Expand the Environment settings, and click the color swatch.

5. Use the Color Chooser to create a pale blue color for the background (Figure 2.28).

6. Open the Render settings, and make sure the Render Using menu is set to mental ray. If mental ray does not appear in the list, you'll need to load the `Mayatomr.mll` plug-in (`Mayatomr.bundle` on the Mac) found in the Window ➤ Settings/Preferences ➤ Plug-in Manager window.

7. Select the Quality tab in the Render settings, and set the Quality preset to Preview:Final Gather.

FIGURE 2.28
A new background color is chosen for the DOF_cam.

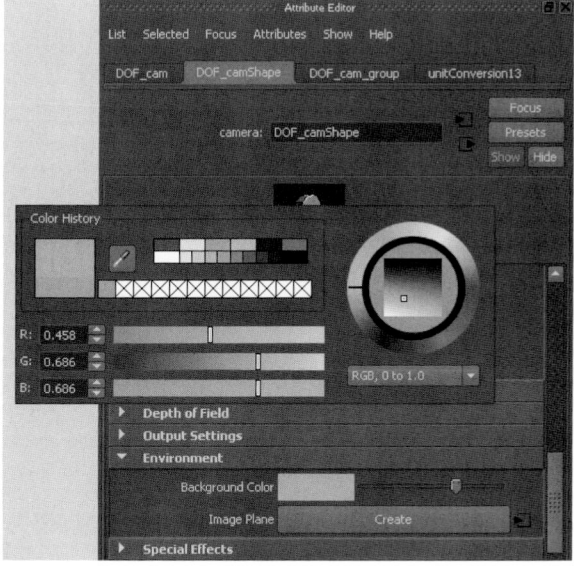

8. Switch to the Rendering menu set. Choose Render ➤ Test Resolution ➤ 50% Settings. This way, any test renders you create will be at half resolution, which will save a lot of time but will not affect the size of the batch-rendered images.

9. Set the timeline to frame 136, and Choose Render ➤ Render Current Frame to create a test render (see Figure 2.29).

FIGURE 2.29
A test render is created for frame 136.

The Render View window will open and render a frame. Even though there are no lights in the scene, even lighting is created when Final Gather is activated in the Render settings (it's activated automatically when you choose the Preview:Final Gather Quality preset). The pale blue background color in the current camera is used in the Final Gather calculations. (Chapter 10 discusses more sophisticated environmental lighting.) This particular lighting arrangement is simple to set up and works fine for an animatic.

As you can see from the test render, the composition of this frame is confusing to the eye and does not read very well. There are many conflicting shapes in the background and foreground. Using depth of field can help the eye separate background elements from foreground elements and sort out the overall composition.

10. In the Attribute Editor for the DOF_cam, expand the Depth Of Field rollout panel, and activate Depth Of Field.

11. Store the current image in the Render Preview window (from the Render Preview window menu, choose File ➤ Keep Image In Render View), and create another test render using the default DOF settings.

12. Use the scroll bar at the bottom of the Render View window to compare the images. There's almost no discernable difference. This is because the DOF settings need to be adjusted. There are only three settings:

Focus Distance This determines the area of the image that is in focus. Areas in front or behind this area will be out of focus.

F Stop This describes the relationship between the diameter of the aperture and the focal length of the lens. Essentially it is the amount of blurriness seen in the rendered image. F Stop values used in Maya are based on real-world f-stop values. The lower the value, the blurrier the areas beyond the focus distance will be. Changing the focal length of the lens will affect the amount of blur as well. If you are happy with a camera's DOF settings but then change the focal length or angle of view, you'll probably need to reset the F Stop setting. Typically values range from 2.8 to about 12.

Focus Region Scale This is a scalar value that you can use to adjust the area in the scene you want to stay in focus. Lowering this value will also increase the blurriness. Use this to fine-tune the DOF effect once you have the Focus Distance and F Stop settings.

13. Set Focus Distance to **15**, F Stop to **2.8**, and Focus Region Scale to **0.1**, and create another test render.

The blurriness in the scene is much more obvious, and the composition is a little easier to understand. The blurring is very grainy. You can improve this by adjusting the Quality settings in the Render Settings window. Increasing the Max Sample level and decreasing the Anti-Aliasing Contrast will smooth the render, but it will take much more time to render the image. For now you can leave the settings where they are as you adjust the DOF (see Figure 2.30). Chapter 12 discusses render-quality issues.

14. Save the scene as **chase_v06.ma**.

To see a version of the scene so far, open chase_v06.ma from the chapter2\scenes directory on the DVD.

FIGURE 2.30
Adding depth of field can help sort the elements of a composition by increasing the sense of depth.

Creating a Rack Focus Rig

A *rack focus* refers to a depth of field that changes over time. It's a common technique used in cinematography as a storytelling aid. By changing the focus of the scene from elements in the background to the foreground (or vice versa), you control what the viewer looks at in the frame. In this section, you'll set up a camera rig that you can use to interactively change the focus distance of the camera.

1. Continue with the scene from the previous section, or open the chase_v06.ma file from the Chapter2\scenes directory of the DVD.

2. Switch to the perspective view. Choose Create ➤ Measure Tools ➤ Distance Tool, and click two different areas on the grid to create the tool. Two locators will appear with an annotation that displays the distance between the two locators in scene units (meters for this scene).

3. In the Outliner, rename locator1 to **camPosition**, and rename locator2 to **distToCam** (see Figure 2.31).

FIGURE 2.31
A measure tool, consisting of two locators, is created on the grid.

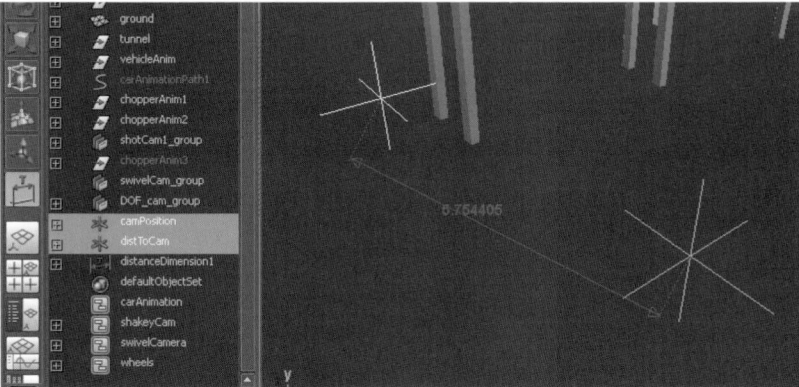

4. In the Outliner, expand the DOF_cam_group. MMB-drag camPosition on top of the DOF_cam node to parent the locator to the camera.

5. Open the Channel Box for the camPosition locator, and set all of its Translate and Rotate channels to **0**; this will snap camPosition to the center of the camera.

6. Shift-select the camPosition's Translate and Rotate channels in the Channel Box, right-click the fields, and choose Lock Selected so that the locator can no longer be moved.

7. In the Outliner, MMB-drag distToCam on top of the camPosition locator to parent distToCam to camPosition.

8. Select distToCam; in the Channel Box, set its Translate X and Y channels to **0**, and lock these two channels (see Figure 2.32). You should be able to move distToCam only along the z-axis.

9. Open the Connection Editor by choosing Window ➤ General Editors ➤ Connection Editor.

10. In the Outliner, select the distanceDimension1 node, and expand it so you can select the distanceDimensionShape1 node (make sure the Display menu in the Outliner is set so that shape nodes are visible).

FIGURE 2.32
The Translate X and Y channels of the distToCam node are locked so that it can move only along the z-axis.

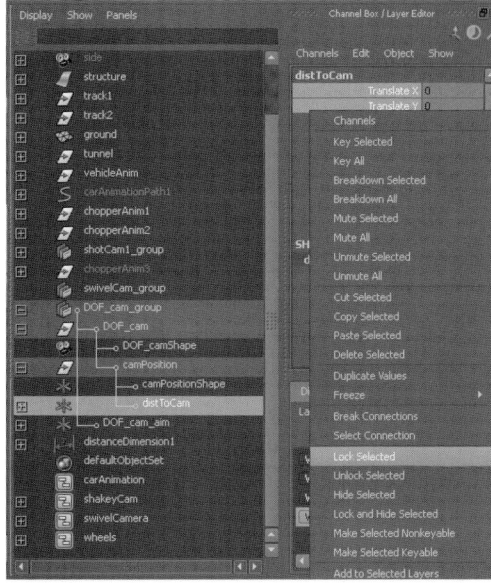

11. Click the Reload Left button at the top of the Connection Editor to load this node.

12. Expand the DOF_Cam node in the Outliner, and select DOF_camShape. Click Reload Right in the Connection Editor.

13. From the bottom of the list on the left, select Distance. On the right side, select FocusDistance (see Figure 2.33).

FIGURE 2.33
The Distance attribute of the distance DimensionShape1 node is linked to the focusDistance attribute of the DOF_camShape node using the Connection Editor.

14. Look in the perspective view at the distance measured in the scene, select the distToCam locator, and move it so that the annotation reads about 5.5 units.

15. Select the DOF_camShape node, and look at its focusDistance attribute. If it says something like 550 units, then there is a conversion problem:

    A. Select the distanceDimensionShape node in the Outliner, and open the Attribute Editor.

    B. From the menu in the Attribute Editor, click Focus, and select the node that reads unit-Conversion14. If you are having trouble finding this node, turn off DAG Objects Only in the Outliner's Display menu, and turn on Show Auxiliary Nodes in the Outliner's Show menu. You should see the unitConversion nodes at the bottom of the Outliner.

    C. Select unitConversion14 from the list to switch to the unitConversion node, and set Conversion Factor to **1**.

    Occasionally when you create this rig and the scene size is set to something other than centimeters, Maya converts the units automatically, and you end up with an incorrect number for the Focus Distance attribute of the camera. This node may not always be necessary when setting up this rig. If the value of the Focus Distance attribute of the camera matches the distance shown by the distanceDimension node, then you don't need to adjust the unitConversion's Conversion Factor setting.

16. Set the timeline to frame 138. In the Perspective window, select the distToCam locator, and move it along the z-axis until its position is near the position of the car (about -10.671).

17. In the Channel Box, right-click the Translate Z channel, and choose Key Selected (see Figure 2.34).

18. Switch to the DOF_cam in the viewport, and create a test render. The helicopters should be out of focus, and the area near the car should be in focus.

19. Set the timeline to frame 160.

FIGURE 2.34
The distToCam locator is moved to the position of the car on frame 138 and keyframed.

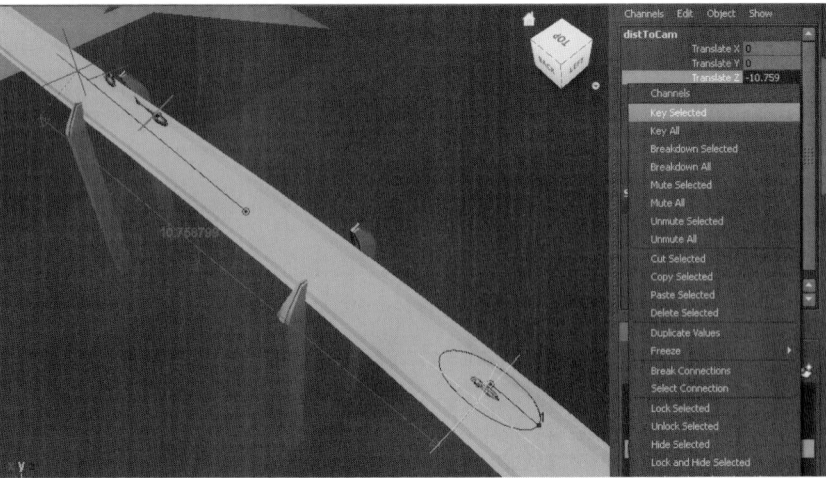

20. Move the distToCam node so it is at about the same position as the closest helicopter (around -1.026).

21. Set another keyframe on its Z translation.

22. Render another test frame.

The area around the helicopter is now in focus (see Figure 2.35).

If you render a sequence of this animation for the frame range between 120 and 180, you'll see the focus change over time. To see a finished version of the camera rig, open chase_v07.ma from the chapter2\scenes directory on the DVD.

FIGURE 2.35
The focus distance of the camera has been animated using the rig so that at frame 160 the helicopter is in focus and the back-ground is blurry.

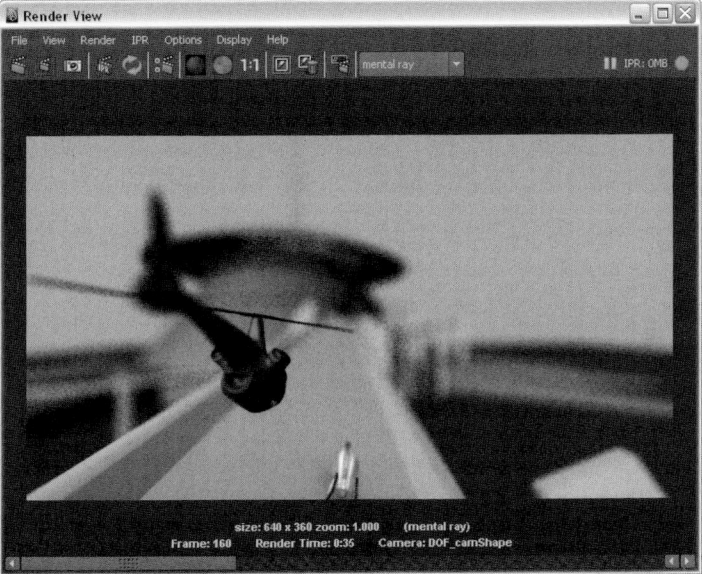

Adding Motion Blur to an Animation

If an object changes position while the shutter on a camera is open, this movement shows up as a blur. Maya cameras can simulate this effect using the Motion Blur settings found in the Render settings as well as in the camera's Attribute Editor. Not only can motion blur help make an ani-mation look more realistic, it can also help smooth the motion in the animation.

Like depth of field, motion blur is very expensive to render, meaning it can take a long time. Also much like depth of field, there are techniques for adding motion blur in the composit-ing stage after the scene has been rendered. You can render a motion vector pass using mental ray's passes (render passes are discussed in Chapter 12) and then adding the motion blur using the motion vector pass in your compositing software. For jobs that are on a short timeline and a strict budget, this is often the way to go. In this section, however, you'll learn how to create motion blur in Maya using mental ray.

There are many quality issues closely tied to rendering with motion blur. In this chapter, you'll learn the basics of how to apply the different types of motion blur. Chapter 12 discusses issues related to improving the quality of the render.

MENTAL RAY MOTION BLUR

The mental ray Motion Blur setting supports all rendering features such as textures, shadows (ray trace and depth map), reflections, refractions, and caustics.

You enable the Motion Blur setting in the Render Settings window, so unlike the Depth Of Field setting, which is activated per-camera, all cameras in the scene will render with motion blur once it has been turned on. Likewise, all objects in the scene have motion blur applied to them by default. You can, and should, turn off the Motion Blur setting for those objects that appear in the distance or do not otherwise need motion blur. If your scene involves a close-up of an asteroid whizzing by the camera while a planet looms in the distance surrounded by other slower-moving asteroids, you should disable the Motion Blur setting for those distant and slower-moving objects. Doing so will greatly reduce render time.

To disable the Motion Blur setting for a particular object, select the object, open its Attribute Editor to its shape node tab, expand the Render Stats rollout panel, and deselect the Motion Blur option. To disable the Motion Blur setting for a large number of objects at the same time, select the objects, and open the Attribute Spread Sheet (Window ➢ General Editors ➢ Attribute Spread Sheet). Switch to the Render tab, and select the Motion Blur header at the top of the column to select all the values in the column. Enter **0** to turn off the Motion Blur setting for all the selected objects (see Figure 2.36).

FIGURE 2.36
You can disable the Motion Blur setting for a single object in the Render Stats section of its Attribute Editor or for a large number of selected objects using the Attribute Spread Sheet.

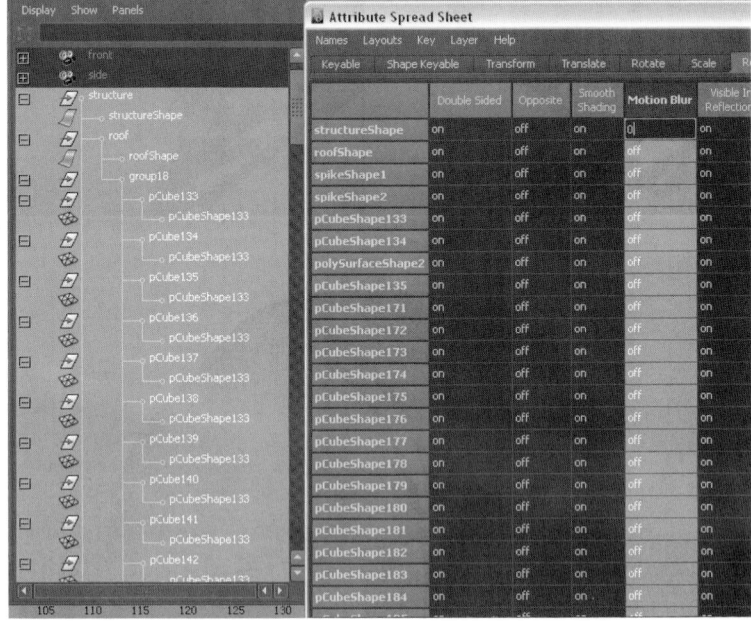

MOTION BLUR AND RENDER LAYERS

The Motion Blur setting can be active for an object on one render layer and disabled for the same object on another render layer using render layer overrides. For more information on using render layers, consult Chapter 12.

There are two types of motion blurs in mental ray for Maya: No Deformation and Full. No Deformation calculates only the blur created by an object's transformation—meaning its translation, rotation, and scale. A car moving past a camera or a helicopter blade should be rendered using No Deformation.

The Full setting calculates motion vectors for all of an object's vertices as they move over time. Full should be used when an object is being deformed, such as when a character's arm geometry is skinned to joints and animated moving past the camera. Using Full motion blur will give more accurate results for both deforming and nondeforming objects, but it will take a longer time to render than using No Deformation.

MOTION BLUR FOR MOVING CAMERAS

If a camera is moving by a stationary object, the object will be blurred just as if the object were moving by a stationary camera.

The following procedure shows how to render with motion blur:

1. Open the scene chase_v08.ma from the chapter2\scenes directory of the DVD.

2. In the Display Layer panel, right-click the buildings display layer, and choose Select Objects. This will select all the objects in the layer.

3. Open the Attribute Spread Sheet (Window ➢ General Editors ➢ Attribute Spread Sheet), and switch to the Render tab.

4. Select the Motion Blur header to select all the values in the Motion Blur column, and turn the settings to Off (shown in Figure 2.36). Do the same for the objects in the street layer.

5. Switch to the Rendering menu set. Choose Render ➢ Test Resolution ➢ Render Settings. This will set the test render in the Render View window to 1280 by 720, the same as in the Render Settings window. In the Render Settings window under the Quality tab, set Quality Preset to Preview.

6. Switch to the shotCam1 camera in the viewport.

7. Set the timeline to frame 59, and open the Render View window (Window ➢ Rendering Editors ➢ Render View).

8. Create a test render of the current view. From the Render View panel, choose Render ➢ Render ➢ ShotCam1. The scene will render. Setting Quality Preset to Preview disable Final Gathering, so the scene will render with default lighting. This is okay for the purpose of this demonstration.

9. In the Render View panel, LMB-drag a red rectangle over the blue helicopter. To save time while working with motion blur, you'll render just this small area.

10. Open the Render Settings window.

11. Switch to the Quality tab. Expand the Motion Blur rollout panel, and set Motion Blur to No Deformation. Leave the settings at their defaults.

12. In the Render View panel, click the Render Region icon (second icon from the left) to render the selected region in the scene. When it's finished, store the image in the render view. You can use the scroll bar at the bottom of the render view to compare stored images (see Figure 2.37).

FIGURE 2.37
The region around the helicopter is selected and rendered using motion blur.

In this case, the motion blur did not add a lot to the render time; however, consider that this scene has no textures, simple geometry, and default lighting. Once you start adding more complex models, textured objects, and realistic lighting, you'll find that the render times will increase dramatically.

OPTIMIZING MOTION BLUR

Clearly, optimizing Motion Blur is extremely important, and you should always consider balancing the quality of the final render with the amount of time it takes to render the sequence. Remember that if an object is moving quickly in the frame, some amount of graininess may actually be unnoticeable to the viewer.

---

13. In the Render Settings window, switch to the Features tab, and set the Primary Renderer to Rasterizer (Rapid Motion), as shown in Figure 2.38.

FIGURE 2.38

The Primary Renderer has been changed to Rasterizer (Rapid Motion); in some cases, this can reduce render time when rendering with motion blur.

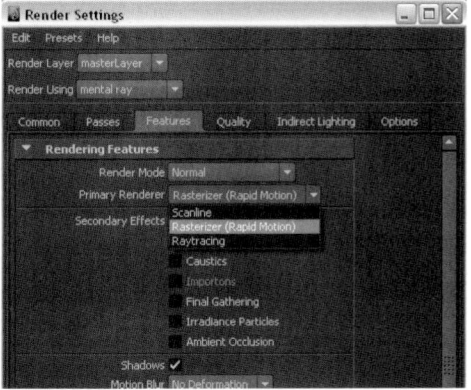

14. Click the Render Region button again to re-render the helicopter.

15. Store the image in the render view, and compare it to the previous render. Using Rapid Motion will reduce render times in more complex scenes.

The Rapid Motion setting uses a different algorithm to render motion blur, which is not quite as accurate but much faster. However, it does change the way mental ray renders the entire scene.

The shading quality produced by the Rasterizer (Rapid Motion) option is different from the Scanline option. The Rasterizer does not calculate motion blurring for ray-traced elements (such as reflections and shadows). You can solve some of the problem by using detailed shadow maps instead of ray-traced shadows (discussed in Chapter 9), but this won't solve the problem that reflections lack motion blur.

16. Switch back to the Quality tab, and take a look at the settings under Motion Blur:

Motion Blur-By This setting is a multiplier for the motion blur effect. A setting of 1 produces a realistic motion blur. Higher settings create a more stylistic or exaggerated effect.

Shutter Open and Shutter Closed These two settings establish the range within a frame where the shutter is actually opened or closed. By increasing the Shutter Open setting, you're actually creating a delay for the start of the blur; by decreasing the Shutter Close setting, you're moving the end time of the blur closer to the start of the frame.

17. Render the region around the helicopter.

18. Store the frame; then set Shutter Open to **0.25**, and render the region again.

19. Store the frame, and compare the two images. Try a Shutter Close setting of **0.75**. Figure 2.39 shows the results of different settings for Shutter Open and Shutter Close.

Setting Shutter Open and Shutter Close to the same value effectively disables motion blur. You're basically saying that the shutter opens and closes instantaneously, and therefore there's no time to calculate a blur.

FIGURE 2.39
Different settings for Shutter Open and Shutter Close affect how motion blur is calculated. From left to right, the Shutter Open and Shutter Close settings for the three images are (0, 1), (0.25, 1), and (0.25, 0.75). The length of time the shutter is open for the last image is half of the length of time for the first image.

USING THE SHUTTER ANGLE ATTRIBUTE

You can achieve results similar to the Shutter Open and Shutter Close settings by changing the Shutter Angle attribute on the camera's shape node. The default setting for Maya cameras is 144. If you set this value to 72 and render, the resulting blur would be similar to setting Shutter Angle to 144, Shutter Open to 0.25, and Shutter Close to 0.75 (effectively halving the total time the shutter is open). The Shutter Angle setting on the camera is meant to be used with Maya Software Rendering to provide the same functionality as mental ray's Shutter Open and Shutter Close settings. It's a good idea to stick to one method or the other—try not to mix the two techniques, or the math will start to get a little fuzzy.

---

20. Return the Shutter settings to **0** for Shutter Open and **1** for Shutter Closed.

21 In the Quality section below the Motion Blur settings, increase Motion Steps to **6**, and render the helicopter region again.

22. Store the image, and compare it to the previous renders. Notice that the blur on the helicopter blade is more of an arc, whereas in previous renders, the blur at the end of the blade is a straight line (Figure 2.40).

FIGURE 2.40
Increasing Motion Steps increases the number of times the motion of the objects is sampled, producing more of an accurate blur in rotating objects.

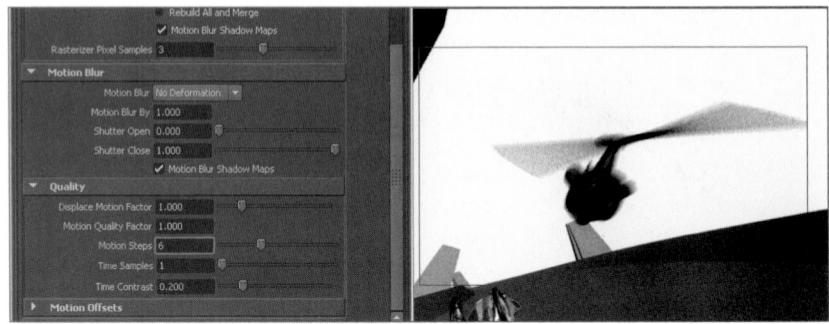

The Motion Steps attribute increases the number of times between the opening and closing of the shutter that mental ray samples the motion of the moving objects. If Motion Steps is set to 1, the motion of the object when the shutter opens is compared to the motion when the shutter is closed. The blur is calculated as a linear line between the two points. When you increase the Motion Steps setting, mental ray increases the number of times it looks at the motion of an object over the course of time in which the shutter is open and creates a blur between these samples. This produces a more accurate blur in rotating objects, such as wheels or helicopter blades.

The other settings in the Quality section include the following:

Displace Motion Factor   This setting adjusts the quality of motion-blurred objects that have been deformed by a displacement map. It effectively reduces geometry detail on those parts of the model that are moving past the camera based on the amount of detail and the amount of motion as compared to a nonmoving version of the same object. Slower-moving objects should use higher values.

Motion Quality Factor   This is used when the Primary Renderer is set to Rasterizer (Rapid Motion). Increasing this setting lowers the sampling of fast-moving objects and can help reduce render times. For most cases, a setting of 1 should work fine.

Time Samples   This controls the quality of the motion blur. Raising this setting adds to render time but increases quality. As mental ray renders a two-dimensional image from a three-dimensional scene, it takes a number of spatial samples at any given point on the two-dimensional image. The number of samples taken is determined by the anti-alias settings (discussed further in Chapter 12). For each spatial sample, a number of time samples can also be taken to determine the quality of the motion blur effect; this is determined by the Time Samples setting.

Time Contrast   Like Anti-Aliasing contrast (discussed in Chapter 12), lower Time Contrast values improve the quality of the motion blur but also increase render time. Note that the Time Samples and Time Contrast settings are linked. Moving one automatically adjusts the other in an inverse relationship.

Motion Offsets   These controls enable you to set specific time steps where you want motion blur to be calculated.

Using Orthographic and Stereo Cameras

Orthographic cameras are generally used for navigating a Maya scene and for modeling from specific views. A stereoscopic or stereo camera is actually a special rig that can be used for rendering stereoscopic 3D movies.

Orthographic Cameras

The front, top, and side cameras that are included in all Maya scenes are orthographic cameras. An orthographic view is one that lacks perspective. Think of a blueprint drawing, and you get the basic idea. There is no vanishing point in an orthographic view.

Any Maya camera can be turned into an orthographic camera. To do this, open the Attribute Editor for the camera, and in the Orthographic Views rollout panel, turn on the Orthographic option. Once a camera is in orthographic mode, it appears in the Orthographic section of the viewport's Panels menu. You can render animations using orthographic cameras; just add the camera to the list of renderable cameras in the Render Settings window. The Orthographic Width is changed when you dolly an orthographic camera in or out (see Figure 2.41).

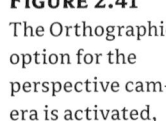

FIGURE 2.41
The Orthographic option for the perspective camera is activated, flattening the image seen in the perspective view.

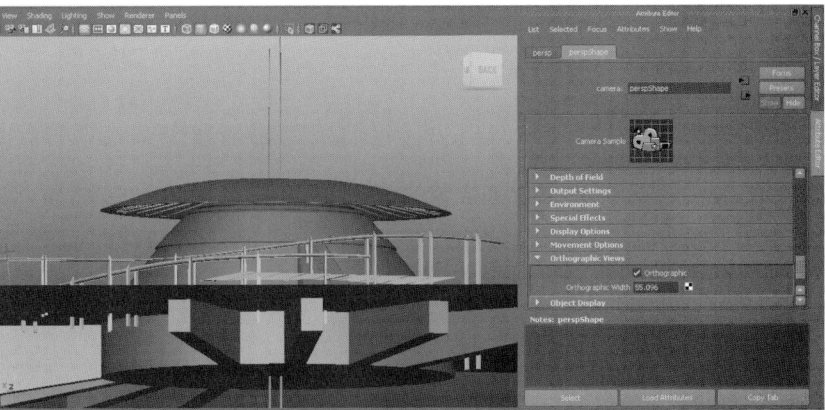

Stereo Cameras

You can use stereo cameras when rendering a movie that is meant to be seen using special 3D glasses. Follow the steps in this example to learn how to work with stereo cameras:

1. Create a new scene in Maya. From the Create menu, choose Cameras ➤ Stereo Camera. You'll see three cameras appear on the grid.

2. Switch the panel layout to Panels ➤ Saved Layouts ➤ Four View.

3. Set the upper-left panel to the perspective view and the upper right to Panels ➤ Stereo ➤ Stereo Camera.

4. Set the lower left to StereoRigLeft and the lower right to StereoRigRight.

5. Create a NURBS sphere (Create ➤ NURBS Primitives ➤ Sphere).

6. Position it in front of the center camera of the rig, and push it back in the z-axis about -10 units.

7. In the perspective view, select the center camera, and open the Attribute Editor to stereoRigCenterCamShape.

   In the Stereo settings, you can choose which type of stereo setup you want; this is dictated by how you plan to use the images in the compositing stage. The interaxial separation adjusts the distance between the left and right cameras, and the zero parallax defines the point on the z-axis (relative to the camera) at which an object directly in front of the camera appears in the same position in the left and right cameras.

8. In the Attribute Editor, under the Stereo Display Controls rollout panel, set Display Frustum to All. In the perspective view you can see the overlapping angle of view for all three cameras.

9. Turn on Display Zero Parallax Plane. A semitransparent plane appears at the point defined by the Zero Parallax setting.

10. Set the Stereo setting in the Stereo rollout panel to Converged.

11. Set the Zero Parallax attribute to **10** (see Figure 2.42).

12. In the perspective view, switch to a top view, and make sure the NURBS sphere is directly in front of the center camera and at the same position as the zero parallax plane (Translate Z = -10).

As you change the Zero Parallax value, the left and right cameras will rotate on their y-axes to adjust, and the Zero Parallax Plane will move back and forth depending on the setting.

FIGURE 2.42

A stereo camera uses three cameras to render an image for 3D movies. The zero parallax plane is positioned at the point where objects in front of the center camera appear in the same position in the left and right cameras.

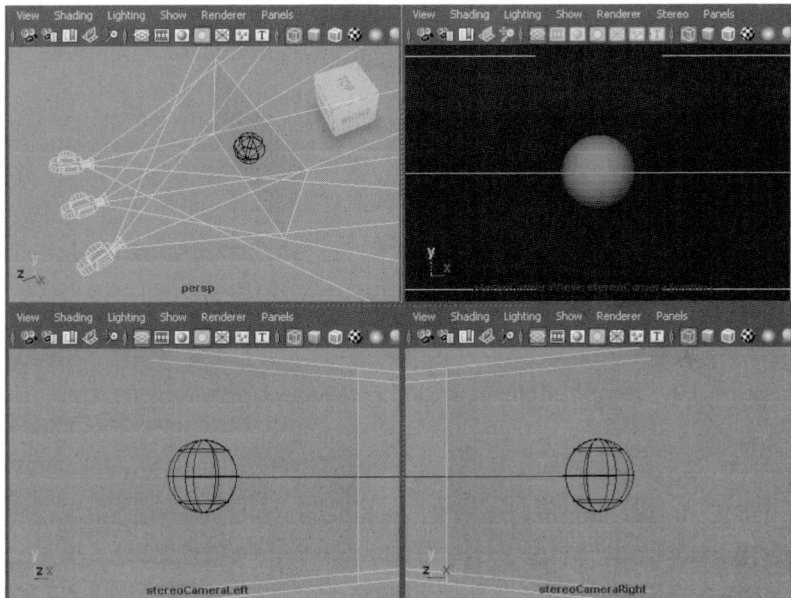

13. In the top view, move the sphere back and forth toward and away from the camera rig. Notice how the sphere appears in the same position in the frame in the left and right camera view when it is at the zero parallax plane. However, when it is in front of or behind the plane, it appears in different positions in the left and right views.

If you hold a finger up in front of your eyes and focus on the finger, the position of the finger is at the zero parallax point. Keep your eyes focused on that point, but move your finger toward and away from your face. You see two fingers when it's before or behind the zero parallax point (more obvious when it's closer to your face). When a stereo camera rig is rendered and composited, the same effect is achieved, and, with the help of 3D glasses, the image on the two-dimensional screen appears in three dimensions.

14. Turn on the Safe Viewing Volume option in the Attribute Editor. This displays the area in 3D space where the views in all three cameras overlap. Objects should remain within this volume in the animation so that they render correctly as a stereo image.

15. Open the Render settings to the Common tab.

16. Under Renderable Cameras, you can choose to render each camera of the stereo rig separately, or you can select the Stereo Pair option to add both the right and left cameras at the same time. Selecting the stereoCamera option renders the scene using the center camera in the stereo camera rig. This can be useful if you want to render a nonstereoscopic version of the animation.

The cameras will render as separate sequences, which can then be composited together in compositing software to create the final output for the stereo 3D movie.

COMPOSITING STEREO RENDERS IN ADOBE AFTER EFFECTS

Adobe After Effects has a standard plug-in called 3D Glasses (Effects ➤ Perspective ➤ 3D Glasses) that you can use to composite renders created using Maya's stereo rig. From Maya you can render the left and right camera images as separate sequences, import them into After Effects, and apply the 3D Glasses effect.

You can preview the 3D effect in the Render View window by choosing Render ➤ Stereo Camera. The Render View window will render the scene and combine the two images. You can then choose one of the options in the Display ➤ Stereo Display menu to preview the image. If you have a pair of red/green 3D glasses handy, choose the Anaglyph option, put on the glasses, and you'll be able to see how the image will look in 3D.

The upper-right viewport window has been set to Stereo Camera, which enables a Stereo menu in the panel menu bar. This menu has a number of viewing options you can choose from when working in a stereo scene, including viewing through just the left or right camera. Switch to Anaglyph mode to see the objects in the scene shaded red or green to correspond with the left or right camera (this applies to objects that are in front or behind the zero parallax plane).

The Bottom Line

Determine the image size and film speed of the camera   You should determine the final image size of your render at the earliest possible stage in a project. The size will affect everything from texture resolution to render time. Maya has a number of presets that you can use to set the image resolution.

> **Master it**   Set up an animation that will be rendered to be displayed on a high-definition progressive-scan television.

Create and animate cameras   The settings in the Attribute Editor for a camera enable you to replicate real-world cameras as well as add effects such as camera shaking.

> **Master it**   Create a camera setting where the film shakes back and forth in the camera. Set up a system where the amount of shaking can be animated over time.

Create custom camera rigs   Dramatic camera moves are easier to create and animate when you build a custom camera rig.

> **Master it**   Create a camera in the car chase scene that films from the point of view of chopperAnim3 but tracks the car as it moves along the road.

Use depth of field and motion blur   Depth of field and motion blur replicate real-world camera effects and can add a lot of drama to a scene. Both are very expensive to render and therefore should be applied with care.

Master it   Create a camera asset with a built-in focus distance control.

Create orthographic and stereoscopic cameras   Orthographic cameras are used primarily for modeling because they lack a sense of depth or a vanishing point. A stereoscopic rig uses three cameras and special parallax controls that enable you to render 3D movies from Maya.

Master it   Create a 3D movie from the point of view of the driver in the chase scene.

Chapter 3

NURBS Modeling in Maya

Creating 3D models in computer graphics is an art form and a discipline unto itself. It takes years to master and requires an understanding of form, composition, anatomy, mechanics, gesture, and so on. It's an addictive art that never stops evolving. This chapter and Chapter 4 will introduce you to the different ways the tools in Maya can be applied to various modeling tasks. With a firm understanding of how the tools work, you can master the art of creating 3D models.

Together, Chapters 3 and 4 demonstrate various techniques for modeling with NURBS, polygons, and subdivision surfaces to create a single model of a space suit. Chapter 3 begins with using NURBS surfaces to create a detailed helmet for the space suit.

In this chapter, you will learn to:

◆ Use image planes

◆ Apply NURBS curves and surfaces

◆ Model with NURBS surfaces

◆ Create realistic surfaces

◆ Adjust NURBS render tessellation

Understanding NURBS

NURBS is an acronym that stands for Non-Uniform Rational B-Spline. A NURBS surface is created by spreading a three-dimensional surface across a network of NURBS curves. The curves themselves involve a complex mathematical computation that, for the most part, is hidden from the user in the software. As a modeler, you need to understand a few concepts when working with NURBS, but the software takes care of most of the advanced mathematics so that you can concentrate on the process of modeling.

Early in the history of 3D computer graphics, NURBS were used to create organic surfaces and even characters. However, as computers have become more powerful and the software has developed more advanced tools, most character modeling is accomplished using polygons and subdivision surfaces. NURBS are more ideally suited for hard-surface modeling; objects such as vehicles, equipment, and commercial product designs benefit from the types of smooth surfacing produced by NURBS models.

All NURBS objects are automatically converted to triangular polygons at render time by the software. You can determine how the surfaces will be *tessellated* (converted into polygons) before rendering and change these settings at any time to optimize rendering. This gives NURBS the advantage that their resolution can be changed when rendering. Models that appear close to the camera can have higher tessellation settings than those farther away from the camera.

One of the downsides of NURBS is that the surfaces themselves are made of four-sided patches. You cannot create a three- or five-sided NURBS patch, which can sometimes limit the kinds of shapes you can make with NURBS. If you create a NURBS sphere and use the Move tool to pull apart the control vertices at the top of the sphere, you'll see that even the patches of the sphere that appear as triangles are actually four-sided panels (see Figure 3.1).

To understand how NURBS works a little better, let's take a quick look at the basic building block of NURBS surfaces: the curve.

FIGURE 3.1
Pulling apart the control vertices at the top of a NURBS sphere reveals that all the patches have four sides.

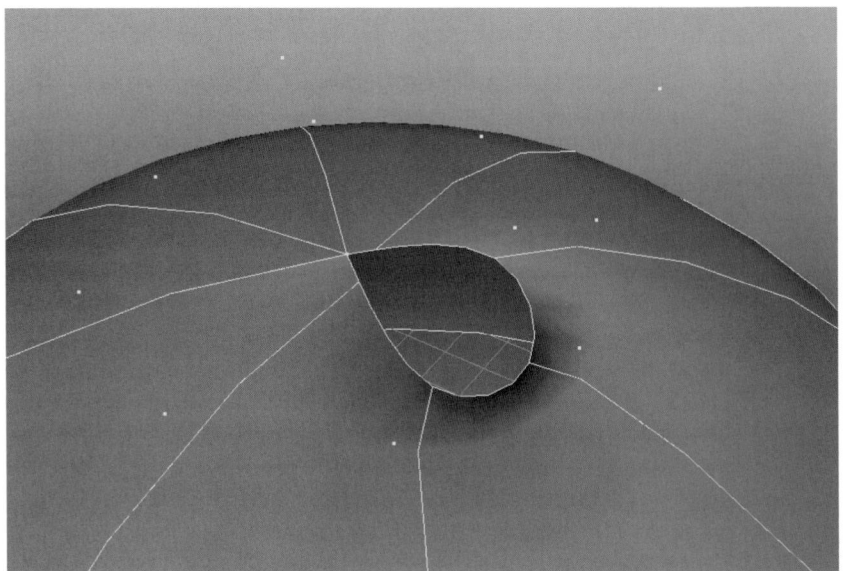

Understanding Curves

All NURBS surfaces are created based on a network of NURBS curves. Even the basic primitives, such as the sphere, are made up of circular curves with a surface stretched across them. The curves themselves can be created several ways. A *curve* is a line defined by points. The points along the curve are referred to as *curve points*. Movement along the curve in either direction is defined by its U coordinates. When you right-click a curve, you can choose to select a curve point. The curve point can be moved along the U direction of the curve, and the position of the point is defined by its U parameter.

Curves also have *edit points* that define the number of spans along a curve. A *span* is the section of the curve between two edit points. Changing the position of the edit points changes the shape of the curve; however, this can lead to unpredictable results. It is a much better idea to use a curve's control vertices to edit the curve's shape.

Control vertices (CVs) are handles used to edit the curve's shapes. Most of the time you'll want to use the control vertices to manipulate the curve. When you create a curve and display its CVs, you'll see them represented as small dots. The first CV on a curve is indicated by a small box; the second is indicated by the letter *U*.

Hulls are straight lines that connect the CVs; these act as a visual guide. Figure 3.2 displays the various components.

FIGURE 3.2
The top image shows a selected curve point on a curve, the middle image shows the curve with edit points displayed, and the bottom image shows the curve with CVs and hulls displayed.

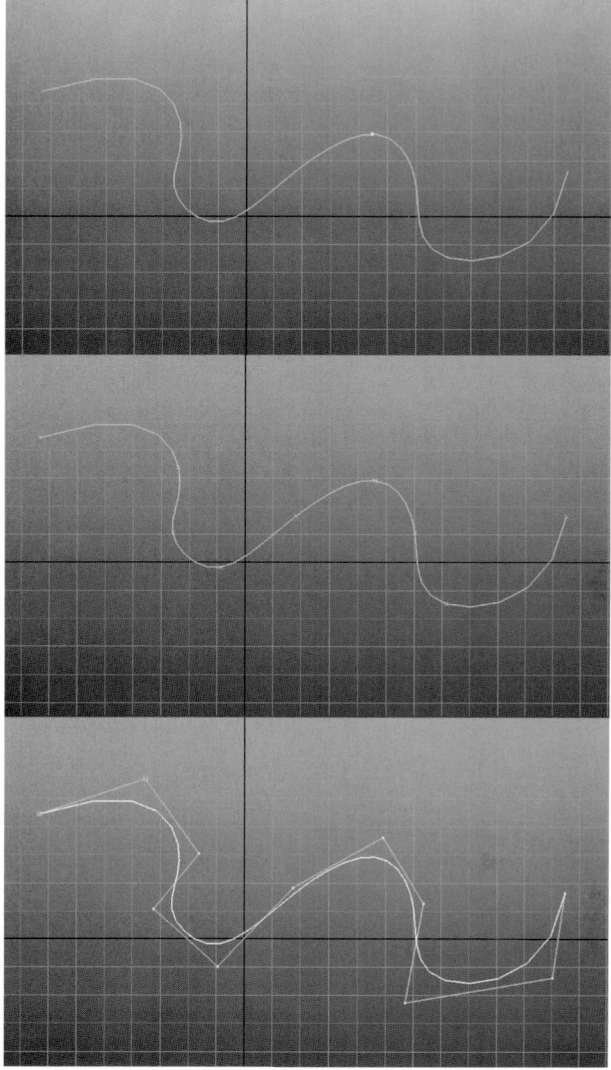

The degree of a curve is determined by the number of CVs per span minus one. In other words, a three-degree (or cubic) curve has four CVs per span. A one-degree (or linear) curve has two CVs per span (Figure 3.3). Linear curves have sharp corners where the curve changes directions; curves with two or more degrees are smooth and rounded where the curve changes direction. Most of the time you'll use either linear (one-degree) or cubic (three-degree) curves.

You can add or remove a curve's CVs and edit points, and you can also use curve points to define a location where a curve is split into two curves or joined to another curve.

FIGURE 3.3
A linear curve has sharp corners.

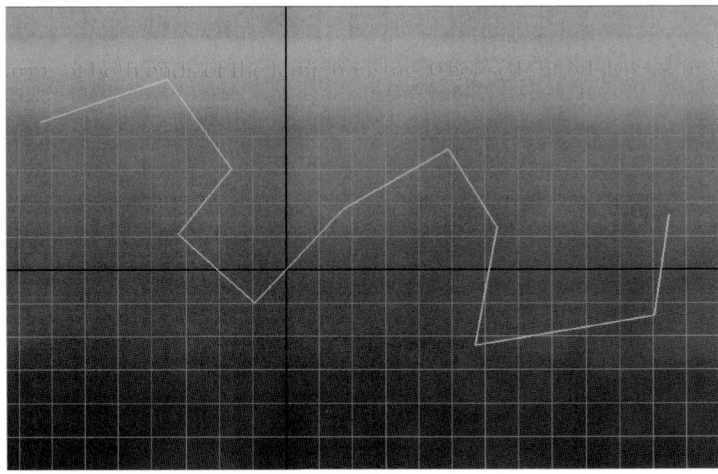

The *parameterization* of a curve refers to the way in which the points along the curve are numbered. There are two types of parameterization: *uniform* and *chord length*.

Uniform parameterization   A curve with uniform parameterization has its points evenly spaced along the curve. The parameter of the last edit point along the curve is equal to the number of spans in the curve. You also have the option of specifying the parameterization range between 0 and 1. This method is available to make Maya more compatible with other NURBS modeling programs.

Chord length parameterization   Chord length parameterization is a proportional numbering system that causes the length between edit points to be irregular. The type of parameterization you use depends on what you are trying to model. Curves can be rebuilt at any time to change their parameterization; however, this will sometimes change the shape of the curve.

You can rebuild a curve to change its parameterization (Edit Curves ➤ Rebuild Curve). It's often a good idea to do this after splitting a curve or joining two curves together or when matching the parameterization of one curve to another. By rebuilding the curve, you ensure that the resulting parameterization (Min and Max Value attributes in the curve's Attribute Editor) is based on whole-number values, which leads to more predictable results when the curve is used as a basis for a surface. When rebuilding a curve, you have the option of changing the degree of the curve so that a linear curve can be converted to a cubic curve, and vice versa.

BEZIER CURVES

New!

Maya 2011 introduces a new curve type: Bezier curves. These curves use handles for editing as opposed to CVs that are offset from the curve. To create a Bezier curve, choose Create ➤ Bezier Curve tool. Each time you click in the perspective view, a new point is added. To extend the handle, hold the mouse and drag after adding a point. The handles allow you to control to smoothness of the curve. The advantages of bezier curves are that they are easy to edit and you can quickly create curves that have both sharp corners and round curves.

IMPORTING CURVES

You can create curves in Adobe Illustrator and import them into Maya for use as projections on the model. For best results, save the curves in Illustrator 8 format. In Maya, choose File ➤ Import ➤ Options, and choose Adobe Illustrator format to bring the curves into Maya. This is often used as a method for generating logo text.

Understanding NURBS Surfaces

NURBS surfaces follow many of the same rules as NURBS curves since they are defined by a network of curves. A primitive, such as a sphere or a cylinder, is simply a NURBS surface lofted across circular curves. You can edit a NURBS surface by moving the position of the surface's CVs (see Figure 3.4). You can also select the *hulls* of a surface, which are groups of CVs that follow one of the curves that define a surface (see Figure 3.5).

FIGURE 3.4
The shape of a NURBS surface can be changed by selecting its CVs and moving them with the Move tool.

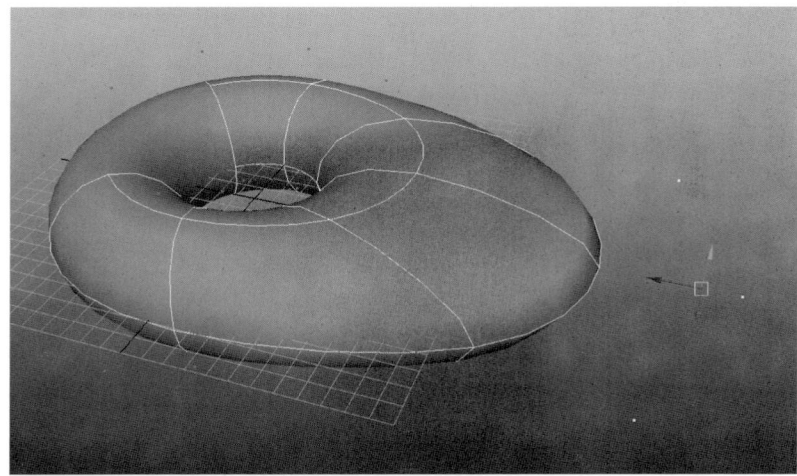

FIGURE 3.5
A hull is a group of connected CVs. Hulls can be selected and repositioned using the Move tool.

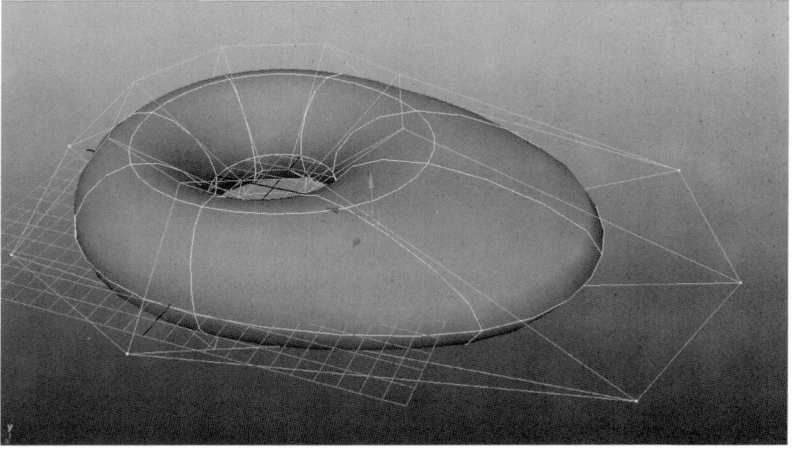

NURBS curves use the U coordinates to specify the location of a point along the length of the curve. NURBS surfaces add the V coordinate to specify the location of a point on the surface. So, a given point on a NURBS surface has a U coordinate and a V coordinate. The U coordinates of a surface are always perpendicular to the V coordinates of a surface. The UV coordinate grid on a NURBS surface is just like the lines of longitude and latitude drawn on a globe.

SURFACES MENU SET

You can find the controls for editing NURBS surfaces and curves in the Surfaces menu set. To switch menu sets, use the drop-down menu in the upper-left corner of the Maya interface.

Just like NURBS curves, surfaces have a degree setting. Linear surfaces have sharp corners, and cubic surfaces (or any surface with a degree higher than 1) are rounded and smooth (see Figure 3.6). Oftentimes a modeler will begin a model as a linear NURBS surface and then rebuild it as a cubic surface later (Edit NURBS ➢ Rebuild Surfaces ➢ Options).

FIGURE 3.6
A linear NURBS surface has sharp corners.

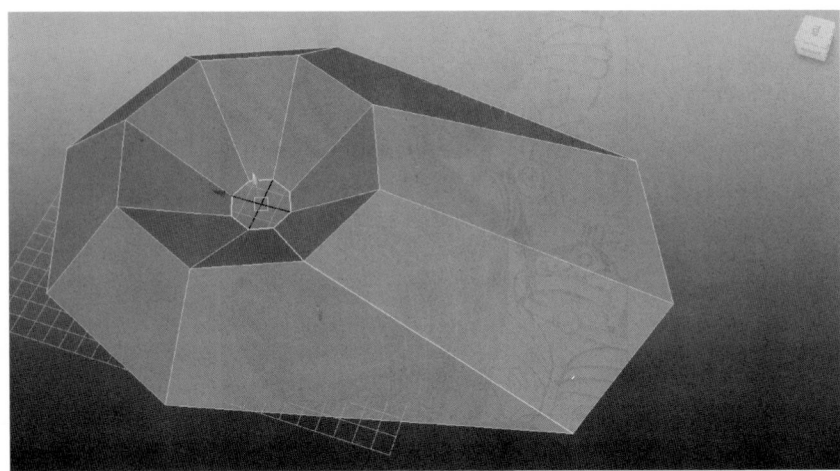

You can start a NURBS model using a primitive, such as a sphere, cone, torus, or cylinder, or you can build a network of curves and loft surfaces between the curves or any combination of the two. When you select a NURBS surface, the wireframe display shows the curves that define the surface. These curves are referred to as *isoparms*, which is short for "isoparametric" curve.

A single NURBS model may be made up of numerous NURBS patches that have been stitched together. This technique was used for years to create CG characters. When you stitch two patches together, the tangency must be consistent between the two surfaces to avoid visible seams. It's a process that often takes some practice to master (see Figure 3.7).

LINEAR AND CUBIC SURFACES

A NURBS surface can be rebuilt (Edit NURBS ➢ Rebuild Surfaces ➢ Options) so that it is a cubic surface in one direction (either the U direction or the V direction) and linear in the other (either the U direction or the V direction).

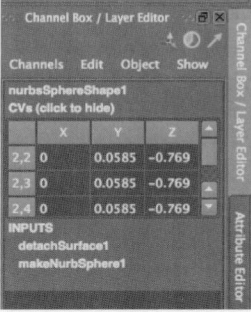

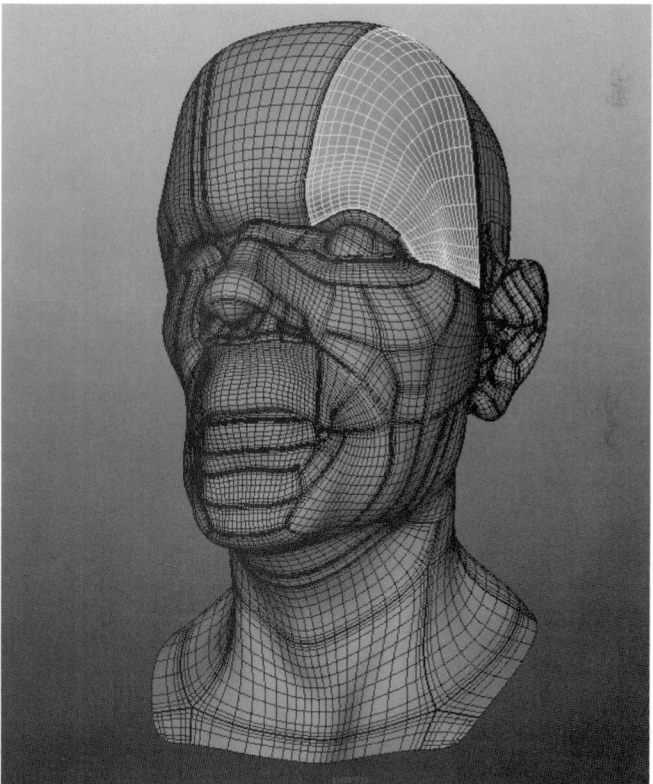

Surface Seams

Many NURBS primitives have a seam where the end of the surface meets the beginning. Imagine a piece of paper rolled into a cylinder. At the point where one end of the paper meets the other there is a seam. The same is true for many NURBS surfaces that define a shape. When you select a NURBS surface, the wireframe display on the surface shows the seam as a bold line. You can also find the seam by selecting the surface and choosing Display ➢ NURBS ➢ Surface Origins (see Figure 3.8).

FIGURE 3.8
The point on a NURBS surface where the seams meet is indicated by displaying the surface origins.

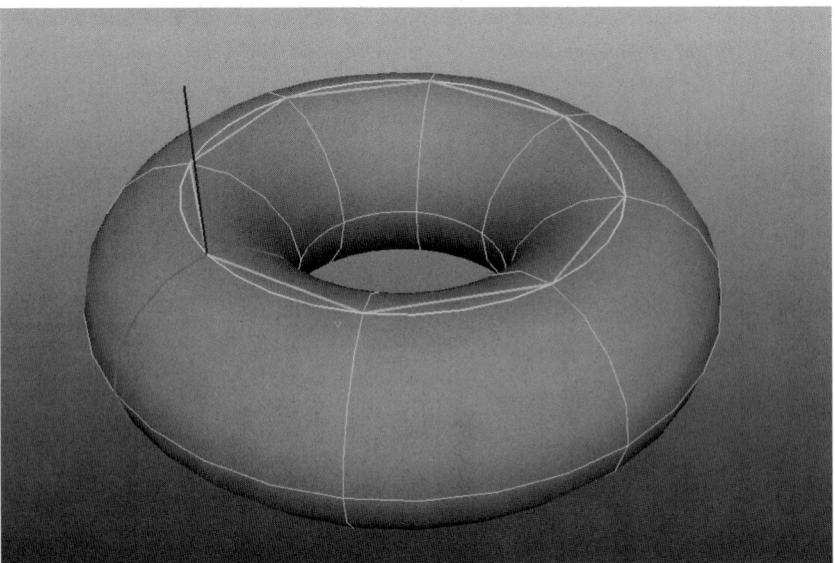

The seam can occasionally cause problems when you're working on a model. In many cases, you can change the position of the seam by selecting one of the isoparms on the surface (right-click the surface and choose Isoparms) and choosing Edit NURBS ➢ Move Seam.

NURBS Display Controls

You can change the quality of the surface display in the viewport by selecting the surface and pressing 1, 2, or 3 on the keyboard.

◆ Pressing the 1 key displays the surface at the lowest quality, which makes the angles of the surface appear as corners.

◆ Pressing the 3 key displays the surface as smooth curves.

◆ Pressing the 2 key gives a medium-quality display.

None of these display modes affects how the surface will look when rendered, but choosing a lower display quality can help improve Maya's performance in heavy scenes. The same display settings apply for NURBS curves as well. If you create a cubic curve that has sharp corners, remember to press the 3 key to make the curve appear smooth.

Employing Image Planes

Image planes refer to images attached to a Maya camera. The images themselves can be used as a guide for modeling or as a rendered backdrop. In this section, you'll learn how to create image planes for Maya cameras and how to import custom images created in Photoshop to use as guides for modeling the example subject: a futuristic space suit.

The example used in this chapter is based on a design created by Chris Sanchez. For this book we asked Chris to design a character in a futuristic space suit that is heavily detailed and stylish in the hope that as many modeling techniques as possible could be demonstrated using a single project. Figure 3.9 shows Chris's drawing.

CHRIS SANCHEZ

Chris Sanchez is Los Angeles–based concept artist/illustrator/storyboard artist. He attained his BFA in illustration from the Ringling College of Art and Design. He has foundations in traditional and digital techniques of drawing and painting. Chris has contributed designs to numerous film projects including *Spider-Man 3*, *Iron Man*, *Iron Man 2*, *Sherlock Holmes*, *The Hulk*, *Bridge to Terabithia*, *RocknRolla*, and *Tropic Thunder*. For more of Chris's work, visit www.chrissanchezart.com.

FIGURE 3.9
The concept drawing for the project, drawn by Chris Sanchez

It's not unusual in the fast-paced world of production to be faced with building a model based on a single view of the subject. You're also just as likely to be instructed to blend together several different designs. You can safely assume that the concept drawing you are given has been approved by the director. It's your responsibility to follow the spirit of that design as closely as possible, with an understanding that, at the same time, the technical aspects of animating and rendering the model may force you to make some adjustments. Some design aspects that work well in a two-dimensional drawing don't always work as well when translated into a three-dimensional model.

The best way to start is to create some orthographic drawings based on the sketch. You can use these as a guide in Maya to ensure that the placement of the model's parts and the proportions are consistent. Sometimes the concept artist creates these drawings for you; sometimes you need to create them yourself (sometimes you may be both the modeler and the concept artist). When creating the drawings, it's usually a good idea to focus on the major forms, creating bold lines and leaving out most of the details. A heavily detailed drawing can get confusing when working in Maya. You can always refer to the original concept drawing as a guide for the details. Since there is only one view of the design, some parts of the model need to be invented for the three-dimensional model. Figure 3.10 shows the orthographic drawings for this project.

After you create the orthographic drawings, your first task is to bring them into Maya and apply them to image planes.

FIGURE 3.10
Simplified drawings have been created for the side and front views of the concept.

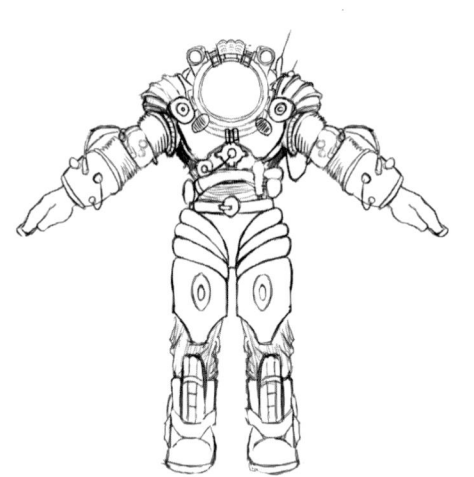

Creating Image Planes

Image planes are often used as a modeling guide. They are attached to the cameras in Maya and have a number of settings that you can adjust to fit your own preferred style.

1. Create a new scene in Maya.

2. Switch to the side view. From the View menu in the viewport panel, choose Image Plane ➢ Import Image (see Figure 3.11).

3. A dialog box will open; browse the file directory on your computer, and choose the spaceGirlSide.tif image from the chapter3\sourceimages directory on the DVD.

FIGURE 3.11
Use the View menu in the panel menu bar to add an image plane to the camera.

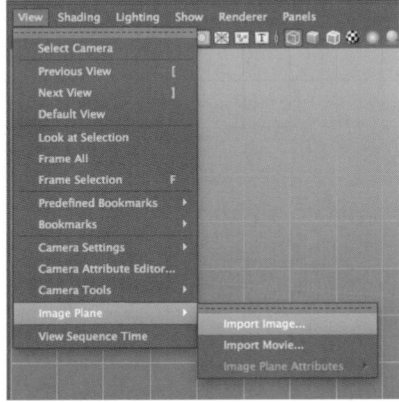

4. The side view opens and appears in the viewport. Select the side camera in the Outliner, and open the Attribute Editor.

5. Switch to the imagePlane1 tab (see Figure 3.12).

6. In the Image Plane Attributes section, you'll find controls that change the appearance of the plane in the camera view. Make sure the Display option is set to In All Views. This way, when you switch to the perspective view, the plane will still be visible.

FIGURE 3.12
The options for the image plane are displayed in the Attribute Editor.

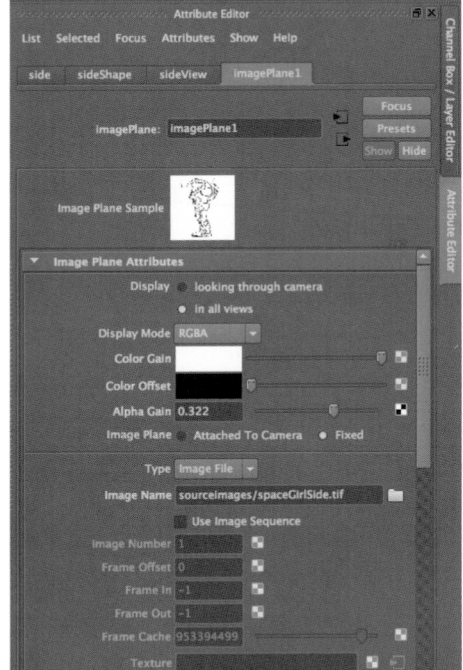

You can set the Display mode to RGB if you want just color or to RGBA to see color and alpha. The RGBA option is more useful when the image plane has an alpha channel and is intended to be used as a backdrop in a rendered image as opposed to a modeling guide. There are other options such as Luminance, Outline, and None.

The Color Gain and Color Offset sliders can be used to change the brightness and contrast. By lowering the Color Gain and raising the Color Offset, you can get a dimmer image with less contrast.

7. The Alpha Gain slider adds some transparency to the image display. Lower this slider to reduce the opacity of the plane.

8. When modeling, you'll want to set Image Plane to Fixed so the image plane does not move when you change the position of the camera. When using the image plane as a renderable backdrop, you may want to have the image attached to the camera.

ARRANGING IMAGE PLANES

In this example, the image plane is attached to Maya's side-view camera, but you may prefer to create a second side-view camera of your own and attach the image plane to that. It depends on your own preference. Image planes can be created for any type of camera. In some cases, a truly complex design may require creating orthographic cameras at different angles in the scene.

If you want to have the concept drawing or other reference images available in the Maya interface, you can create a new camera and attach an image plane using the reference image (you can use the spacegirlConcept.tif file in the chapter3\sourceimages directory on the DVD). Then set the options so the reference appears only in the viewing camera. Every time you want to refer to the reference, you can switch to this camera, which saves you the trouble of having the image open in another application.

Other options include using a texture or an image sequence. An image sequence may be useful when you are matching animated models to footage.

9. Scroll down in the Attribute Editor for the image plane. In the Placement Extras settings (see Figure 3.13), you can use the Coverage sliders to stretch the image. The Center options allow you to offset the position of the plane in X, Y, and Z. The Height and Width fields allow you to resize the plane itself. In the Center options, set the Z file to **-1.8** to slide the plane back a little.

10. Switch to the front camera, and use the View menu in the viewport to add another image plane.

11. Import the spaceGirlFront.tif image.

12. By default both image planes are placed at the center of the grid. To make modeling a little easier, move them away from the center. Use the following settings:

Center X attribute of the side-view image (imagePlane1): **-15**

Center Z attribute of the front-view image (imagePlane2): **-12**.

In the perspective view, you'll see that the image planes are no longer in the middle of the grid (see Figure 3.13).

FIGURE 3.13
The image planes are moved away from the center of the grid by adjusting the Center attributes in the Attribute Editor.

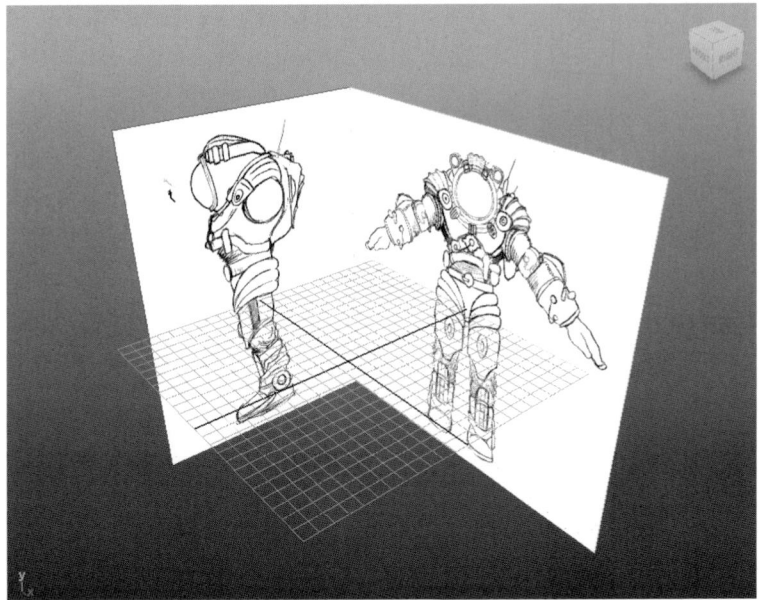

Reference Plane Display Layers

During the course of a modeling session, you may want to turn the image planes on and off quickly without taking the time to open the Attribute Editor for each and change the settings. To make things more convenient, you can put each plane on its own display layer.

1. Create a display layer in the Display Layer Editor, and name it **frontView**.

2. Select the image plane for the front view in the perspective window (drag a selection across the edge of the plane in the perspective view).

3. In the Display Layer Editor, right-click the front-view layer, and choose Add Selected Objects. You can now toggle the visibility of the front view by clicking the V button for the layer in the Display Layer Editor.

4. Repeat steps 1–3 for the side-view image plane, and then name the new layer **sideView** (see Figure 3.14).

5. Save the scene as **spaceGirl_v01.ma**.

   To see a finished version of the scene, open spaceGirl_v01.ma from the chapter3\ scenes directory.

FIGURE 3.14
The image planes are added to display layers so that their visibility can be turned on and off while working.

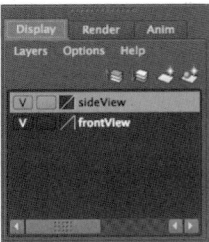

COPY REFERENCE IMAGES TO DISK

You may want to copy the orthographic images and the concept drawing from the `chapter3\` `sourceimages` directory to a directory on your local disk so Maya can find them when you open the scene files. You will need to specify the location of the images in the Attribute Editor of the image plane node after moving the images.

Modeling NURBS Surfaces

To start the model of the space girl, begin by creating the helmet from a simple NURBS sphere:

1. Continue with the scene from the previous section, or open the `spaceGirl_v01.ma` scene from the `chapter3\scenes` folder on the DVD. Make sure the images are visible on the image planes. You can find the source files for these images in the `chapter3\sourceimages` folder.

2. Choose Create ➤ NURBS Primitives ➤ Sphere to create a sphere at the origin. If you have Interactive Creation active in the NURBS Primitives menu, you will be prompted to draw the sphere on the grid (we find Interactive Creation a bit of a nuisance and usually disable it).

3. In the Channel Box for the sphere, click the makeNurbSphere1 node. If this node is not visible in the Channel Box, you need to enable the construction history and remake the sphere (click the icon that looks like a script on the status bar, as shown in Figure 3.15). The construction history needs to be on for this lesson. Make sure Sections is set to **8** and Spans is set to **4**.

FIGURE 3.15
You can turn on the construction history by clicking the script icon in the status bar at the top of the interface.

4. Switch to the side view; select the sphere; and move it up along the y-axis so it roughly matches the shape of the helmet in the side view (see Figure 3.16). Enter the following settings in the Channel Box:

   Translate X: **0**

   Translate Y: **9.76**

   Translate Z: **0.845**

   Rotate X: **102**

   Rotate Y: **0**

   Rotate Z: **0**

   Scale X: **2.547**

   Scale Y: **2.547**

   Scale Z: **2.547**

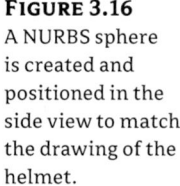

FIGURE 3.16
A NURBS sphere is created and positioned in the side view to match the drawing of the helmet.

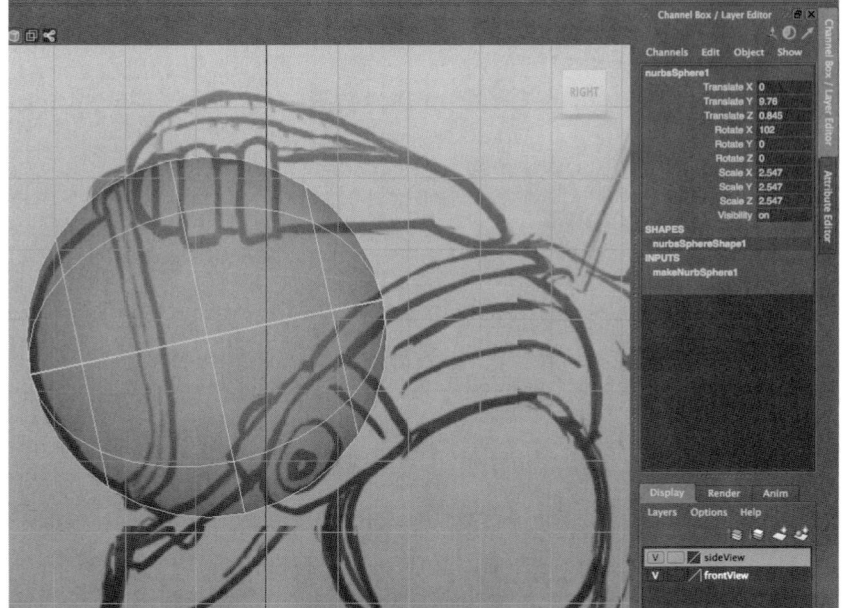

5. To see the sphere and the reference, you can enable X-Ray mode in the side view (Shading ➤ X-Ray). Also enable Wireframe On Shaded so you can see where the divisions are on the sphere.

ARTISTIC JUDGMENT

Keep in mind that the main goal of this chapter is to give you an understanding of some of the more common NURBS modeling techniques. Creating a perfect representation of the concept image or an exact duplicate of the example model is not as important as gaining an understanding of working with NURBS. In some cases, the exact settings used in the example are given; in most cases, the instructions are general.

In the real world, you would use your own artistic judgment when creating a model based on a drawing; there's no reason why you can't do the same while working through this chapter. Feel free to experiment as you work to improve your understanding of the NURBS modeling toolset. If you want to know exactly how the example model was created, take a look at the scene files used in this chapter and compare them with your own progress.

To create a separate surface for the glass shield at the front of the helmet, you can split the surface into two parts.

6. Right-click the sphere, and choose Isoparm. An isoparm is a row of vertices on the surface; sometimes it's also referred to as *knots*.

7. Select the center line that runs vertically along the middle of the sphere.

8. Drag the isoparm forward on the surface of the sphere until it matches the dividing line between the shield and the helmet in the drawing (see Figure 3.17).

FIGURE 3.17
An isoparm
is selected to
match the place
where the glass
shield meets
the rest of the
helmet.

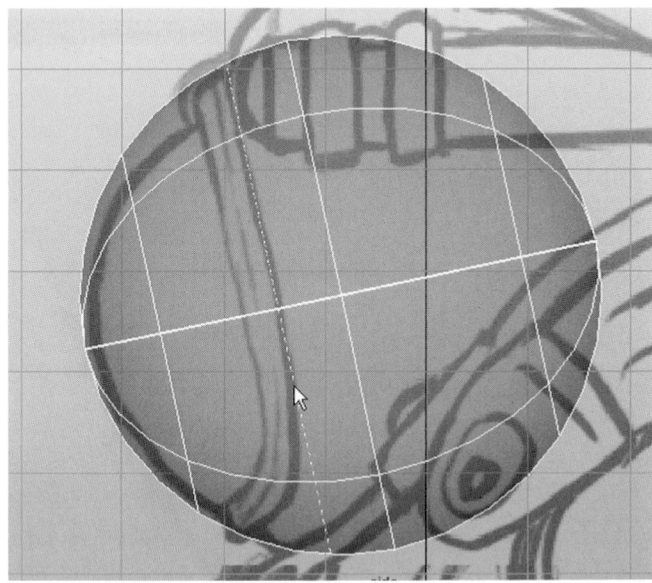

9. Choose Edit NURBS ➢ Detach Surfaces. This splits the surface into two parts along the selected isoparm. Notice the newly created node in the Outliner.

10. Rename detachedSurface1 **shield**, as shown in Figure 3.18.

FIGURE 3.18
The area of
the shield is
detached from
the rest of the
sphere, creat-
ing a new sur-
face node.

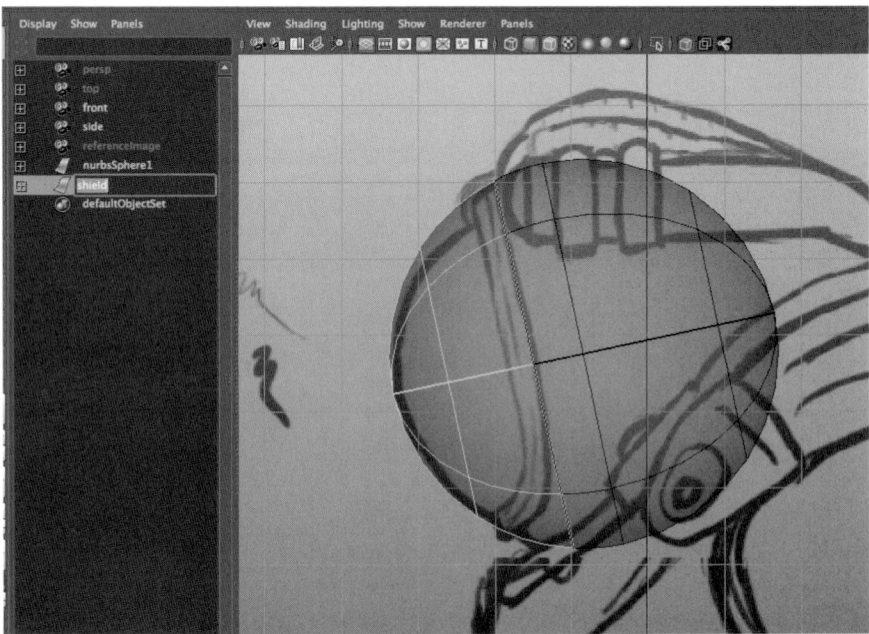

11. Select the front surface, and scale down and reposition it so that it matches the drawing. Enter the following settings in the Channel Box:

    Translate X: **0**

    Translate Y: **9.678**

    Translate Z: **1.245**

    Rotate X: **102**

    Rotate Y: **0**

    Rotate Z: **0**

    Scale X: **2.124**

    Scale Y: **2.124**

    Scale Z: **2.124**

12. Right-click the rear part of the sphere, and choose Control Vertex.

13. You'll see the CVs of the helmet highlighted. Drag a selection marquee over the vertices on the back, and switch to the Move tool (hot key = w).

14. Use the Move tool to position these vertices so they match the contour of the back of the helmet.

15. Select the Scale tool (hot key = r), and scale them down by dragging on the blue handle of the Scale tool.

16. Adjust their position with the Move tool so the back of the helmet comes to a rounded point (see the top image in Figure 3.19).

FIGURE 3.19
The CVs of the rear section of the surface are moved and scaled to roughly match the drawing.

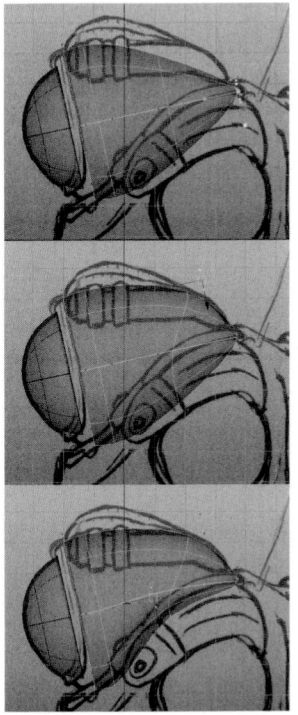

17. Select the group of vertices at the top of the helmet toward the back (the third isoparm from the left), and use the Move tool to move them upward so that they match the contour of the helmet (see the middle image in Figure 3.19).

18. Select the group of vertices at the bottom of the helmet along the same isoparm.

19. Move these upward to roughly match the drawing (see the bottom image in Figure 3.19).

NURBS COMPONENT COORDINATES

When you select CVs on a NURBS surface, you'll see a node in the Channel Box labeled CVS (Click To Show). When you click this, you'll get a small version of the Component Editor in the Channel Box that displays the position of the CVs in local space—this is now labeled CVs (Click To Hide)—relative to the rest of the sphere. The CVs are labeled by number. Notice also that moving them up in world space actually changes their position along the z-axis in local space. This makes sense when you remember that the original sphere was rotated to match the drawing.

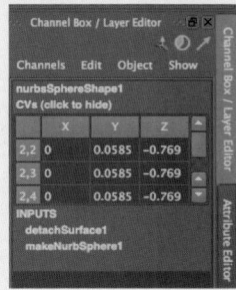

---

20. Rename the back portion **helmet**.

21. Save the scene as **helmet_v01.ma**.

To see a version of the scene to this point, open the helmet_v01.ma scene from the chapter3\scenes directory on the DVD.

Lofting Surfaces

A *loft* creates a surface across two or more selected curves. It's a great tool for filling gaps between surfaces or developing a new surface from a series of curves. In this section, you'll bridge the gap between the helmet and shield by lofting a surface.

1. Continue with the scene from the previous section, or open the helmet_v01.ma scene from the chapter3\scenes folder on the DVD.

2. Switch to the side view; right-click the helmet surface, and choose Isoparm.

3. Select the isoparm at the open edge of the surface.

SELECTING NURBS EDGES

When selecting the isoparm at the edge of a surface, it may be easier to select an isoparm on the surface and drag toward the edge until it stops. This ensures that you have the isoparm at the very edge of the surface selected.

4. Right-click the helmet's shield, and choose Isoparm.

5. Hold down the Shift key and select the isoparm at the edge of the surface so you have a total of two isoparms selected: one at the open edge of the helmet and the other at the open edge of the shield (sometimes this takes a little practice).

6. Choose Surfaces ➤ Loft ➤ Options.

7. In the options, choose Edit ➤ Reset Settings to set the options to the default settings.

8. Set Surface Degree to Linear and Section Spans to **5**.

9. Click Loft to create the surface (see Figure 3.20).

FIGURE 3.20
The options for creating a loft. The loft bridges a gap between surfaces.

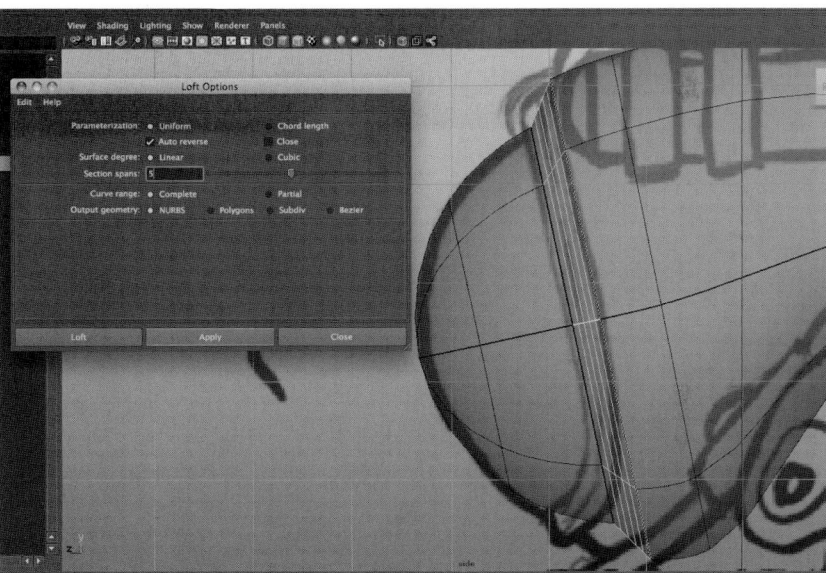

By setting Surface Degree to Linear, you can create the hard-edge ridge detail along the helmet's seal depicted in the original drawing.

10. In the side view, zoom in closely to the top half of the loft.

11. Right-click the Loft, and choose Hull.

12. Select the second hull from the left, and choose the Move tool (hot key = **w**).

13. Open the options for the Move tool, and set Move Axis to Normals Average so you can easily move the hull back and forth relative to the rotation of the helmet.

14. Move the hull forward until it meets the edge of the shield (see Figure 3.21).

FIGURE 3.21
Select the hulls of the lofted surface, and use the Move tool to shape the contour of the loft.

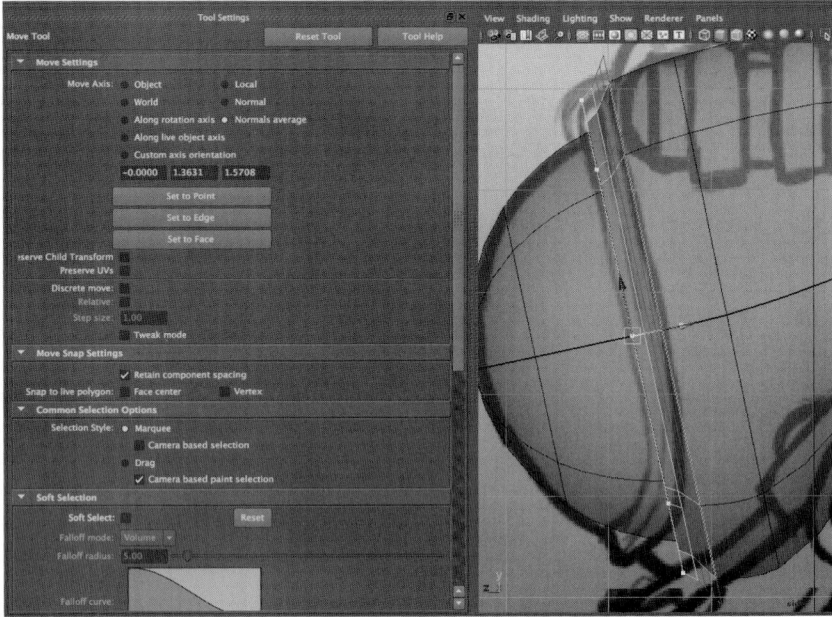

15. Using the up-arrow key, select the next hull in from the left.

16. Move this hull toward the back to form a groove in the loft.

PICK WALKING

Using the arrow keys to move between selected components or nodes is known as *pick walking*.

---

17. Use the Scale and Move tools to reposition the hulls of the loft to imitate some of the detail in the drawing.

18. Turn off the visibility of the image planes layers and disable X-Ray mode so you can see how the changes to the loft look.

19. Switch to the perspective mode, and examine the helmet (see Figure 3.22).

As long as the construction history is preserved on the loft, you can make changes to the helmet's shape, and the loft will automatically update. If you take a close look at the original concept sketch, it looks as though the front of the helmet may not be perfectly circular. By making a few small changes to the helmet's CVs, you can create a more stylish and interesting shape for the helmet's shield.

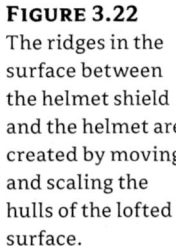

FIGURE 3.22
The ridges in the surface between the helmet shield and the helmet are created by moving and scaling the hulls of the lofted surface.

20. Select the helmet and the shield but not the loft.

21. Switch to component mode. The CVs of both the helmet and the shield should be visible.

22. Select the four CVs at the bottom center of the shield and the four CVs at the bottom of the helmet.

23. In the options for the Move tool, make sure Move Axis is still set to Normals Average.

24. Switch to the side view, and use the Move tool (hot key=**w**) to pull these forward toward the front of the helmet.

25. Switch to the Rotate tool (hot key=**e**), and drag upward on the red circle to rotate the CVs on their local x-axes.

26. Switch back to the Move tool, and push along the green arrow to move them backward slightly.

    These changes will cause some distortion in the shape of the shield and the loft. You can adjust the position of some of the CVs very slightly to return the shield to its rounded shape.

27. Select the CVs from the side view by dragging a selection marquee around the CVs so that the matching CVs on the opposite side of the x-axis of the helmet are selected as well (as opposed to just clicking the CVs).

28. Use the Move tool to adjust the position of the selected CVs.

29. Keep selecting CVs, and use the Move tool to reposition them until the distortions in the surface are minimized. Remember, you are only selecting the CVs of the helmet and shield, not the CVs of the lofted surface in between (remember to save often!).

30. Save the scene as **helmet_v02.ma**.

This is the hardest part of NURBS modeling, and it does take practice, so be patient as you work. Figure 3.23 shows the process. Figure 3.24 shows the reshaped helmet and shield from the perspective view.

FIGURE 3.23
The CVs at the bottom of the shield and helmet are selected from the side view. Using the Move and Rotate tools, they are carefully positioned to match the shape of the helmet in reference drawings.

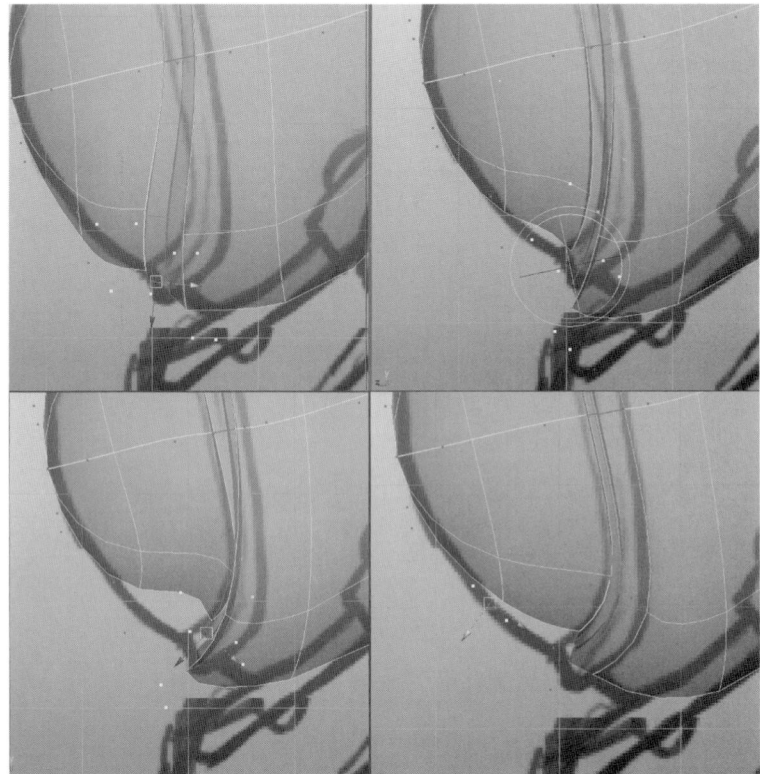

FIGURE 3.24
The reshaped helmet and shield from the perspective view

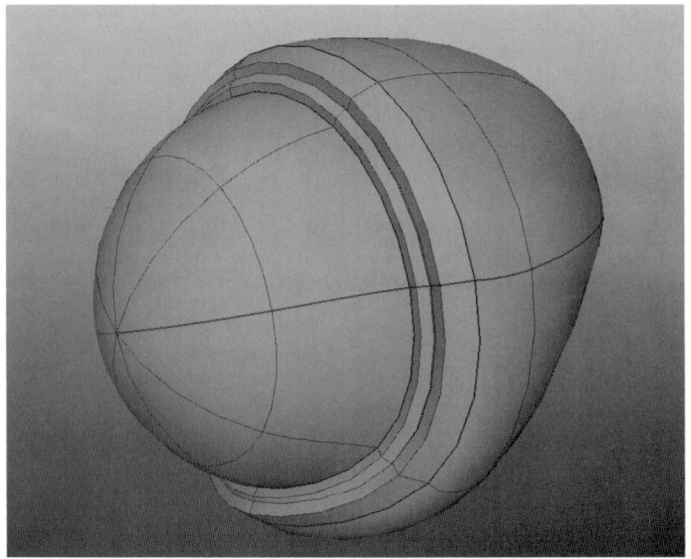

To see a version of the scene to this point, open the `helmet_v02.ma` scene from the `chapter3\` `scenes` directory.

Intersecting Surfaces

You can use one NURBS object to model another. Using a bit of ingenuity, you can find ways to create interesting shapes by carving a NURBS surface with a second surface. In this section, you'll prepare the helmet in order to create an opening at its bottom so the space girl can fit the helmet around her head.

1. Continue with the scene from the previous section, or open the `helmet_v02.ma` scene from the `chapter3\scenes` directory.

2. Create a new NURBS sphere. Position the sphere so it intersects the bottom of the helmet, and scale it in size so it covers most of the bottom of the helmet. Use the following settings in the Channel Box:

   Translate X: **0**

   Translate Y: **8.491**

   Translate Z: **-1.174**

   Scale X: **1.926**

   Scale Y: **2.671**

   Scale Z: **2.834**

3. Select the helmet, and then Shift+click the sphere.

4. Choose Edit NURBS ➤ Intersect Surfaces ➤ Options.

5. In the options, choose Edit ➤ Reset Settings to return the options to the default settings.

6. Set Create Curves For to First Surface. This creates a NURBS curve on the first selected surface.

7. Click the Intersect button to perform the operation (see Figure 3.25).

FIGURE 3.25
The options for the Intersect Surfaces operation

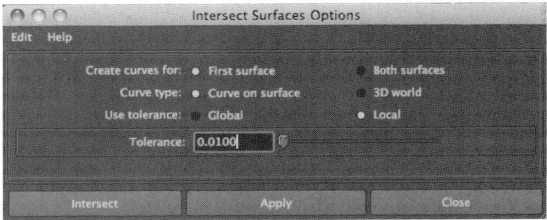

8. In the viewport you'll see a new curve created on the helmet. Select the sphere you created for the intersection, and hide it (Ctrl+h). You can see the curve drawn on the bottom of the helmet (see Figure 3.26).

FIGURE 3.26
The Intersect Surfaces operation creates a curve on the surface where the two surfaces intersect.

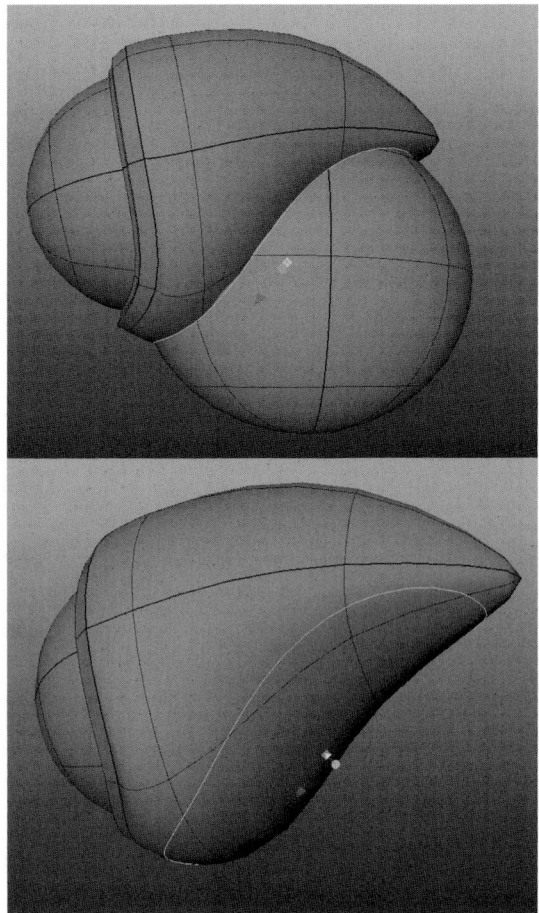

Because of the helmet's construction history, if you move either sphere of the helmet, the curve will change positions. The curve on the surface can be selected and moved as well using the Move tool. As you reposition the curve on the surface, it will remain attached to the surface.

Trim Surfaces

When you *trim* a surface, you cut a hole in it. This does not actually delete parts of the surface; rather, it makes the parts invisible as if they had been deleted. This is one way to get around the fact that NURBS surfaces must consist of only four cornered patches. To trim a surface, you must first create a curve on the surface, as demonstrated in the previous section.

1. Undo any changes made to the position of the two surfaces or the curve on the surface.

2. Select the helmet, and choose Edit NURBS ➢ Trim Tool. When the Trim tool is activated, the surface appears as a white wireframe with the edges and curves on the surface highlighted in a bold solid line.

3. The Trim tool indicates which parts of the surface you want to remain visible when the Trim operation is completed. Use the tool to click several parts of the helmet, but not within the area defined by the curve on the surface.

4. Wherever you click, a marker indicates the parts of the surface that will remain visible. When you have created five or six markers, press the Enter key to trim the helmet. A hole will appear at the bottom of the helmet. If it does not work, click Undo and try again (see Figure 3.27).

FIGURE 3.27
The Trim tool allows you to indicate which parts of the surface will remain visible when you execute the Trim operation.

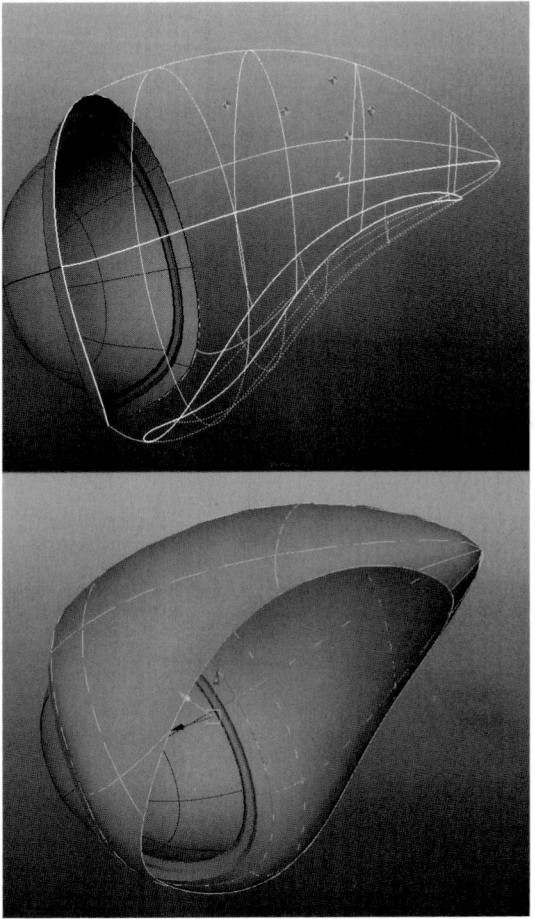

Just like with the curve on the surface, as long as the construction history is maintained for the surface, any changes you make to the intersecting spheres or the curve on the surface will change the position and shape of the hole in the helmet. You can animate the intersecting sphere to make the hole change size and shape over time; however, be aware that some changes may cause errors.

Working with Trim Edges

The edge of the trimmed surface can be used as a starting point for lofts or other NURBS surface types.

1. Right-click the helmet, and choose Trim Edge. This option appears only for trimmed surfaces (see Figure 3.28).

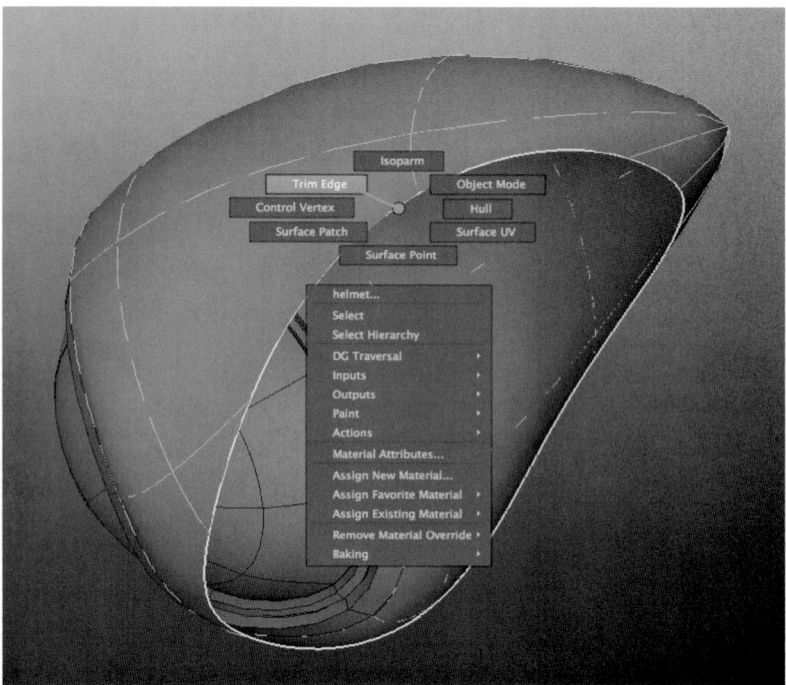

2. Select the trim edge (it should turn yellow when selected), and choose Edit Curves ➢ Duplicate Surface Curves. This creates a new curve that can be positioned away from the helmet.

3. Select the new curve and choose Modify ➢ Center Pivot so the pivot point of the new curve is at its center.

4. Use the Move tool to position duplicateCurve1 below the helmet. Scale it up in size a little as well. Use these settings:

   Translate X: **0**

   Translate Y: **-0.174**

   Translate Z: **0**

   Scale X: **1.275**

   Scale Y: **1.275**

   Scale Z: **1.275**

5. With the curve selected, tumble the view so you can clearly see the bottom of the helmet.

6. Right-click the helmet, and choose Trim Edge.

7. Shift+click the trim edge at the bottom of the helmet so both the duplicate curve and the trim edge are selected.

8. Choose Surfaces ➤ Loft to create a loft using the same settings used to close the gap between the helmet and shield (see Figure 3.29).

FIGURE 3.29
A loft surface is created between the trim edge and the duplicate curve.

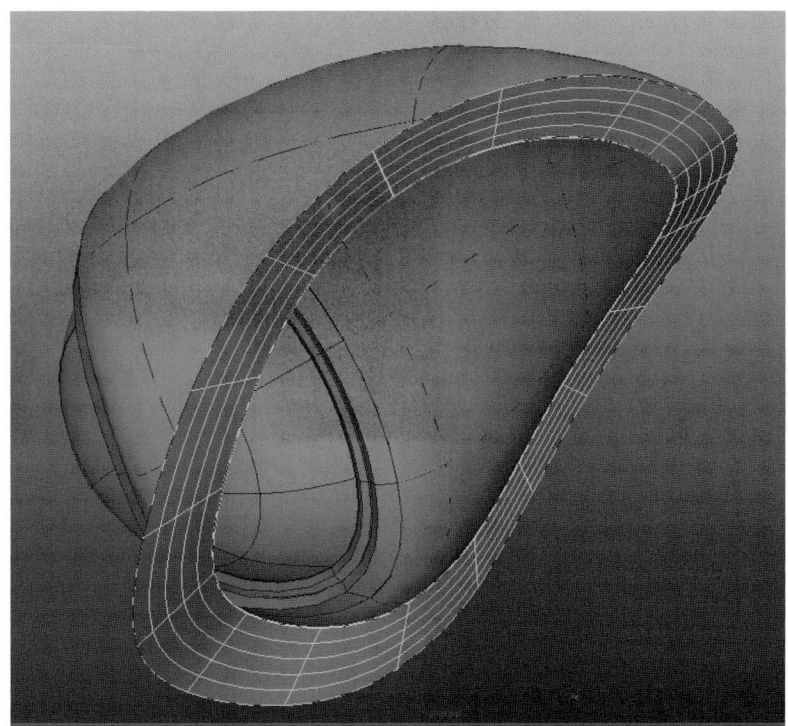

9. Right-click the new lofted surface, and choose Hull.

10. Use the Move and Scale tools to change the position and size of the hulls to create a couple grooves in the loft. This technique is similar to the one used to add detail to the loft between the helmet and the shield (see Figure 3.30).

11. Save the scene as **helmet_v03.ma**.

To see a version of the scene to this point, open the helmet_v03.ma scene from the chapter3\ scenes folder on the DVD.

FIGURE 3.30
By repositioning the hulls of the loft, the surface around the helmet is shaped to resemble the concept drawing.

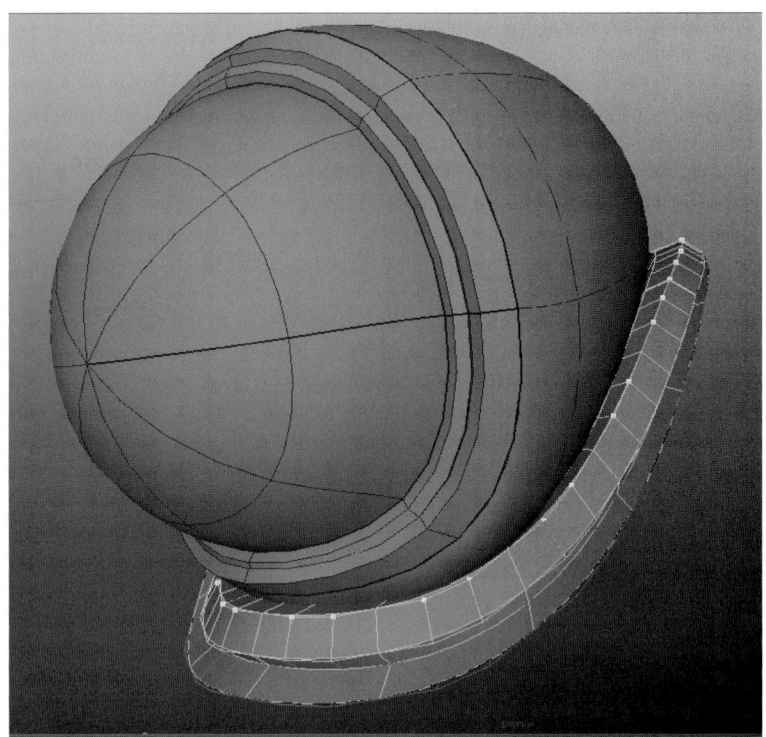

ORGANIZING SURFACES

When you're working with NURBS surfaces, the Outliner can quickly fill up with oddly named objects, such as detachedSurface23. When the scene gets big, this can get confusing. It's usually a good idea to occasionally take the time to rename the surfaces as you're working to help reduce clutter and confusion.

DUPLICATING TRIM EDGES OVER SEAMS

Sometimes you'll run into a situation where you want to create a curve from the edge of a trimmed surface. If the trim edge overlaps a seam in the model, you may find that the trim edge is broken into segments. This becomes apparent when you right-click the opening in the surface and choose Trim Edge.

To make a single curve from the trim edges, use the following steps:

1. Shift+click each part of the trim edge until all the segments are highlighted.

2. Choose Edit Curves ➢ Duplicate Surface Curves.

3. Hide the NURBS surfaces so you can clearly see the curves.

4. Select two of the curves, and choose Edit Curves ➢ Attach Curves ➢ Options.

5. In the options, set Attach Method to Connect and set Multiple Knots to Remove. Turn off Keep Originals.

6. Click Apply to attach the curves. When attaching curves, you may want to specify which end to attach by selecting a curve point at the end of the curve.

7. Repeat this process until you have a single curve.

8. Rebuild the curve by choosing Edit Curves ➢ Rebuild Curve. You may also want to delete the construction history on the curve.

Extrude Surfaces: Distance Extrude

There are several ways to create NURBS surfaces by extruding from a curve. In this section, you'll see how these methods can be applied to create the lamps on the helmet and some of the other details.

1. Continue with the scene from the previous section, or open the helmet_v03.ma scene from the chapter3\scenes directory.

2. Create a NURBS sphere. Switch to the front view.

3. Select the sphere, and use the Move and Scale tools to translate and scale the sphere so that it matches the lamp on the right side of the helmet. Use the following settings:

    Translate X: **2.175**

    Translate Y: **11.785**

    Translate Z: **1.621**

    Rotate X: **90**

    Rotate Y: **0**

    Rotate Z: **0**

    Scale X: **0.518**

    Scale Y: **0.176**

    Scale Z: **0.518**

4. From the side view, select the center isoparm, and choose Edit NURBS ➢ Detach Surfaces. The front section of the sphere will be the glass casing of the lamp; the rear section will be the reflector inside the lamp.

5. Select the rear part of the sphere, and name it **reflector**.

6. Scale it up slightly, and move it forward (see Figure 3.31).

FIGURE 3.31
The sphere is
divided into two
sections to create
the lamp on the
helmet. The rear
section is scaled
up and moved
forward.

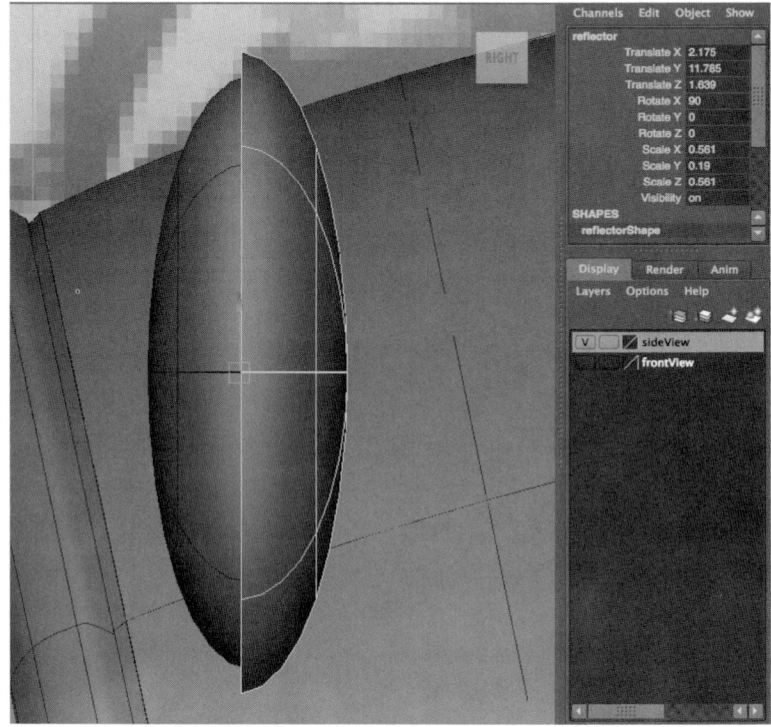

7. Select the front of the sphere, and name it **lamp**.

8. Create a loft to fill the gap between the lamp and the reflector.

9. In the Loft Options, set Number Of Spans to **1**.

10. Select the isoparm at the edge of the reflector, and choose Edit Curves ➢ Duplicate Surface Curves.

11. Select the curve, and center its pivot (Modify ➢ Center Pivot).

12. Move the curve back along the z-axis a little, and scale it up. Figure 3.32 shows the duplicated curve at its new position.

13. Select the curve, and choose Surfaces ➢ Extrude ➢ Options. Choose Edit ➢ Reset Settings to reset the options.

14. Set Style to Distance and Extrude Length to **2**. Direction should be left at Profile Normal.

15. Click the Extrude button to create the surface. Name the extruded surface **lampHousing** (see Figure 3.33).

FIGURE 3.32
A curve is created by duplicating the edge of the reflector. The curve is scaled up and moved back a little.

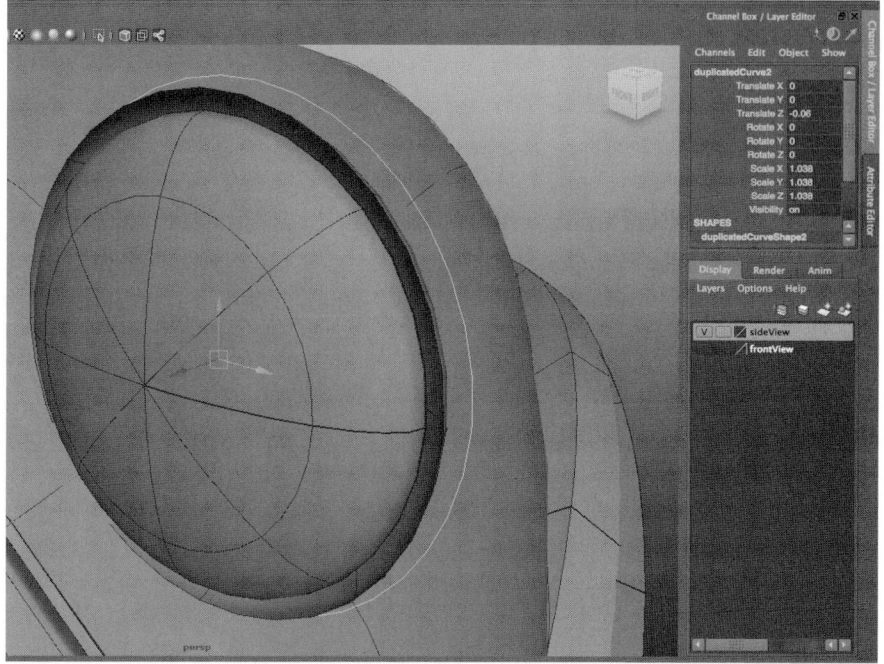

FIGURE 3.33
The housing for the lamp is created by extruding the duplicated curve.

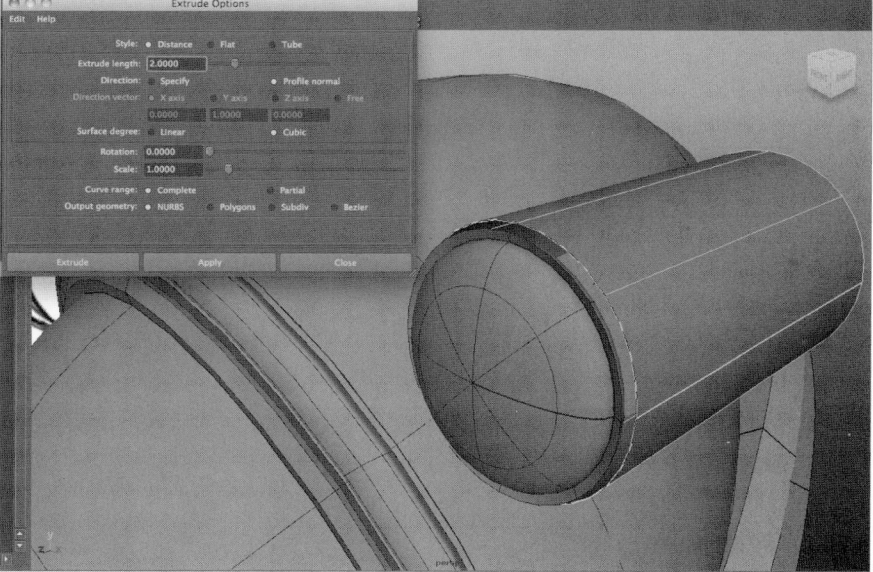

Extruding Surfaces: Profile Extrude

The distance extrude is the simplest type of extrusion you can create and requires only a single profile curve. To create the rounded surface between the helmet and the shield, you can use a profile curve extrusion. This requires two curves.

1. Right-click the loft between the helmet, and choose Isoparm.

2. Select one of the isoparms that run around the loft at the edge, and drag it back toward the center of the loft.

3. Choose Edit Curves ➤ Duplicate Surface Curves to create a new curve that runs around the helmet's shield.

4. With the curve selected, choose Modify ➤ Center Pivot to center the pivot point on the curve (see Figure 3.34).

5. Switch to the top view, and turn on Wireframe.

6. To get a clear view of the grid, choose (from the viewport menu) Show ➤ NURBS Surfaces to temporarily hide the surfaces.

7. Turn on Grid Snapping, and create a NURBS curve (Create ➤ CV Curve Tool).

FIGURE 3.34
A curve is created by duplicating a selected isoparm on the shieldSeal.

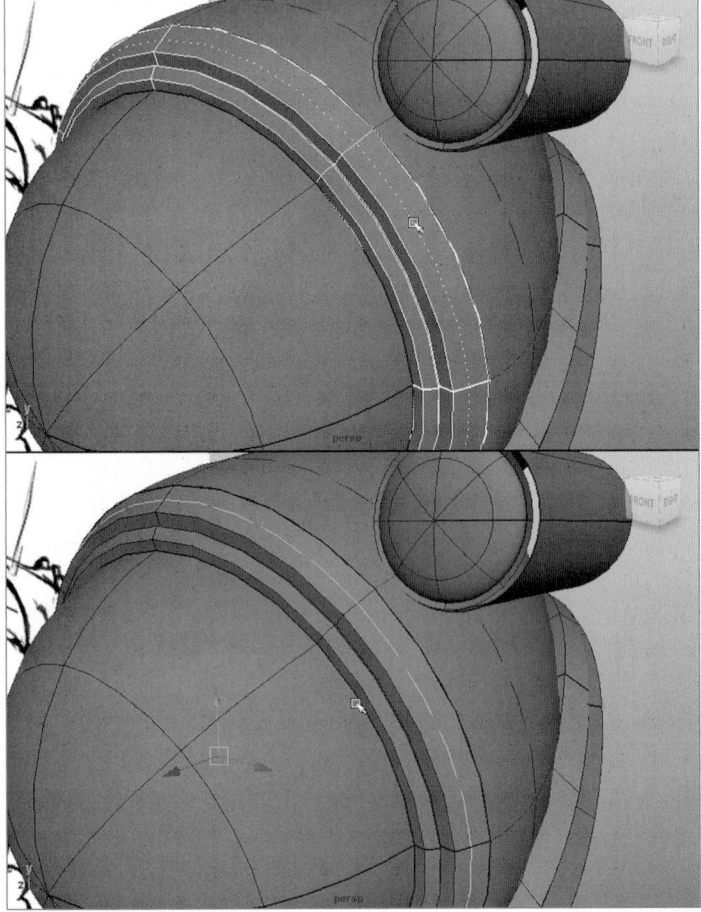

8. To create the curve, click once on the grid point two units to the left of center; then, moving down one unit, click twice on the grid point. This will give a harder edge to the curve while still retaining some roundness.

9. Click the grid point one unit below the center; then click twice on the grid point one unit down and two units to the right of center.

10. Finish the curve by clicking the grid point two units to the right of center. Press the Enter key to complete the curve (see the top image in Figure 3.35).

11. Scale the curve down to **0.12** units in X, Y, and Z.

12. Turn off Grid Snapping, and right-click the curve.

13. Select Control Vertex. Select the CV at the center of the line, and pull it down slightly to create a small arch in the curve (see the bottom image in Figure 3.35).

14. In the Outliner, select the newly created curve, and Ctrl+click the curve created from the loft (make sure you Ctrl+click the second curve; Shift+click may produce different results).

15. Choose Surfaces ➤ Extrude ➤ Options.

FIGURE 3.35
A curve is drawn on the grid from the top view using Grid Snapping. It's then scaled down and shaped by pulling a CV.

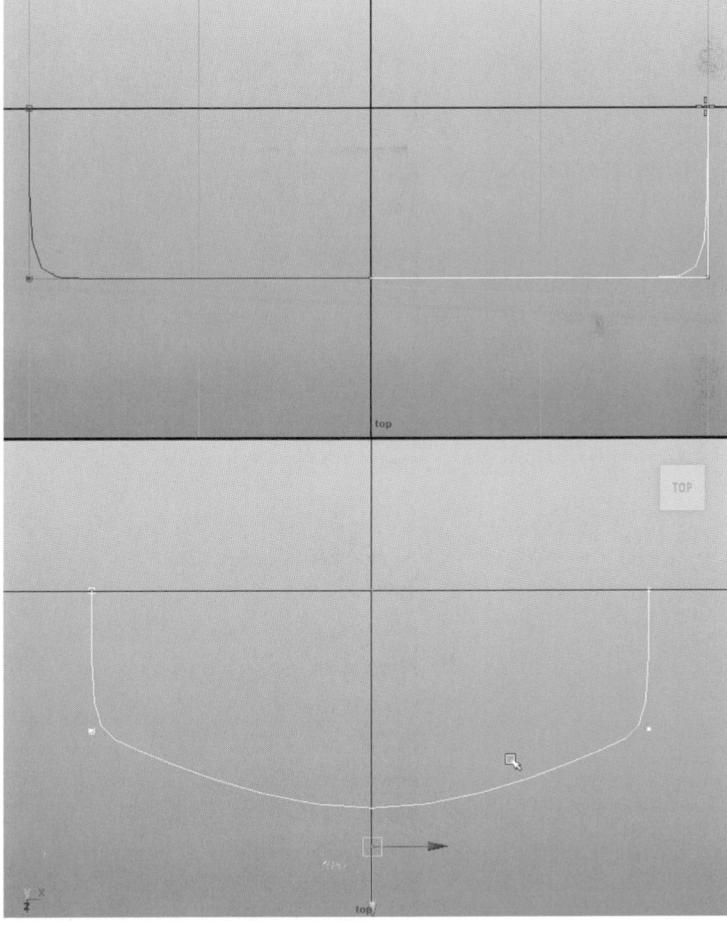

16. In the Extrude Options, set the following:

Set Style to Tube.

Set Result Position to At Path.

Set Pivot to Component.

Set Orientation to Path Direction.

Make sure Curve Range is set to Complete and Output Geometry is set to NURBS.

17. Click Extrude to make the extrude (Figure 3.36).

At the front of the helmet, you'll see a rounded tube surrounding the border of the hel-met's shield. You can adjust the position of the duplicate curve and the position and shape of the profile curve to refine the shape of the extrusion.

18. To refine the shape of the extruded surface, you can scale and reposition duplicateCurve3 (the path curve) and also scale and rotate curve1 (the profile curve you drew on the grid) along its y-axis about 45 degrees. Name the new surface **shieldSeal2**.

19. Save the scene as **helmet_v04.ma**.

FIGURE 3.36
A surface is cre-
ated by extruding a
profile curve along a
path that surrounds
the seal between the
glass shield and the
helmet.

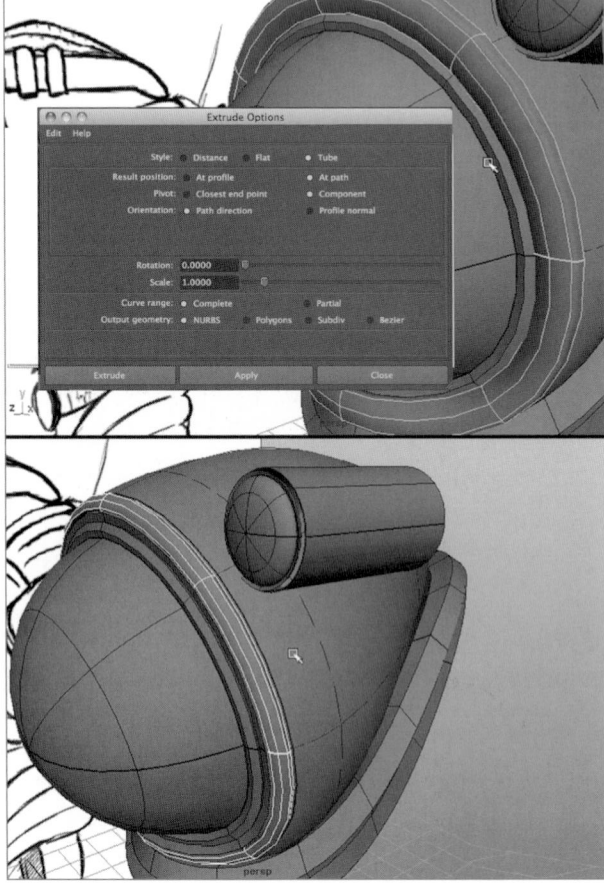

EXTRUSION SETTINGS

Often when creating an extrusion, you'll find that once you create it you need to adjust the options under the extrude node in the Channel Box to get the proper direction of the extrusion.

If you choose the Partial option under Curve Range, you'll find the subCurve1 and subCurve2 nodes in the Channel Box. By setting keyframes on the Min and Max values under these nodes, you can animate the surface extruding along the curve. This is a popular technique for animating tubes moving through space.

To see a version of the helmet to this point, open the helmet_v04.ma scene from the chapter3\ scenes directory on the DVD.

Fillet Surfaces

A fillet surface is another method for bridging gaps between surfaces. You can create one to bridge the gap between the lamp and its housing.

1. Continue with the scene from the previous section, or open the helmet_v04.ma scene from the chapter3\scenes directory on the DVD.

2. Select the isoparms at the edge of the reflector and the lamp housing.

3. From the Surfaces menu, choose Edit NURBS ➤ Surface Fillet ➤ Freeform Fillet.

4. The freeform fillet creates a smooth, rounded surface between the two surfaces. Select the freeformFilletSurface1 node, and open the Channel Box.

5. Set Depth to **0.8** and Bias to **-0.8**. The Depth setting adjusts the curvature of the surface, and the Bias setting moves the influence of the curvature toward one end or the other of the fillet (see Figure 3.37).

FIGURE 3.37
A free-form fillet surface bridges the gap between the lamp and the lampHousing.

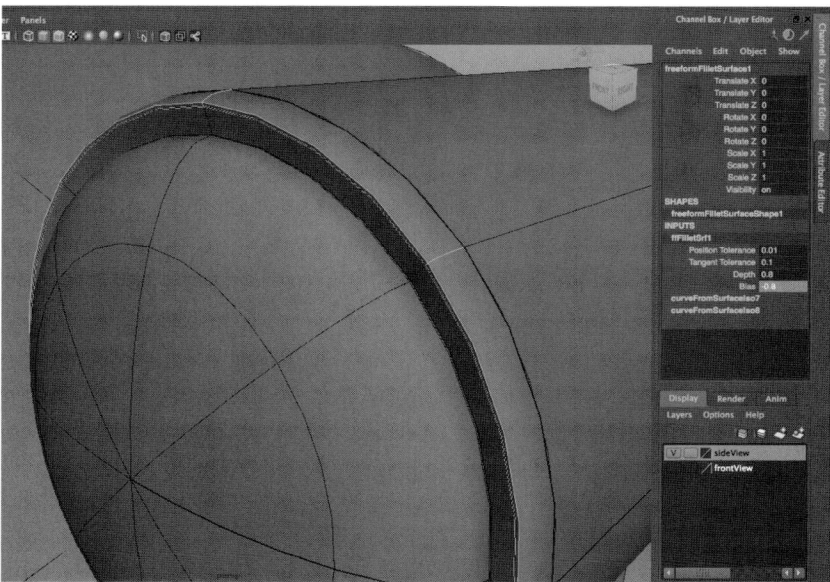

Next you'll add some additional fillets to the lamp housing to create more detail.

6. Select the isoparms at both ends of the lamp housing. Choose Edit NURBS ➤ Insert Isoparms ➤ Options.

7. In the options, set Insert Location to Between Selections, and set # Isoparms To Insert to **4**.

8. Click the Insert button to make the change. This creates four new isoparms evenly spaced along the housing (see Figure 3.38).

FIGURE 3.38
Four isoparms are added to the lamp-Housing surface.

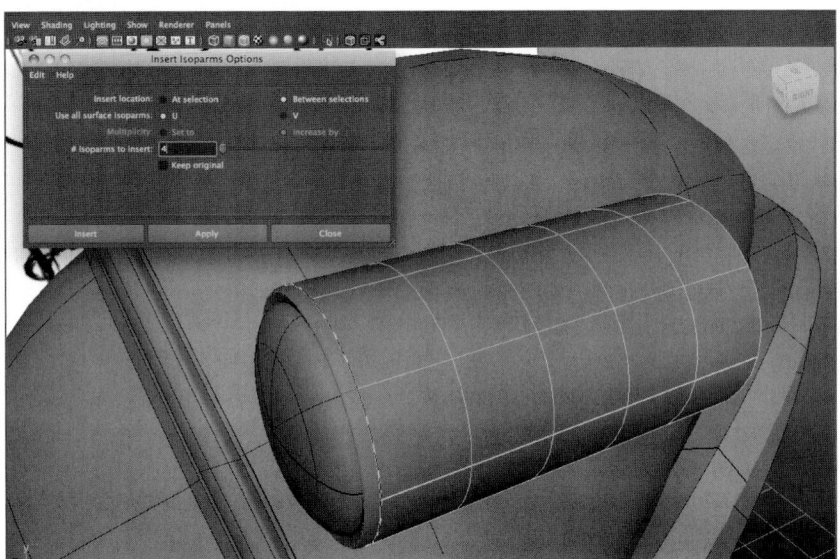

9. Select the four newly created isoparms, and choose Edit Curves ➤ Duplicate Surface Curves.

10. Select the four curves, and center their pivots (Modify ➤ Center Pivot).

11. Scale the curves up to **1.5** on the x-axis and y-axis.

12. Create two lofts between the two pairs of curves. Make sure the lofts are cubic, and give them both two section spans.

13. Create a free-form fillet by choosing an isoparm at the front edge of the front loft and an isoparm on the lamp housing just ahead of the loft.

14. Choose Edit NURBS ➤ Surface Fillet ➤ Freeform Fillet.

15. Perform steps 13 and 14 three more times to create fillets between the other edges of the two lofts and the lamp housing (see Figure 3.39).

16. Right-click each loft, and choose Hulls. Shift+click the outside hulls on the top of both lofts, and use the Move tool to pull them upward.

17. Switch to the Scale tool, and scale them along the x-axis to flatten the tops of the lofts.

FIGURE 3.39
Four isoparms on
the lamp housing are
duplicated, scaled,
lofted, and then con-
nected to the lamp
housing using a free-
form fillet.

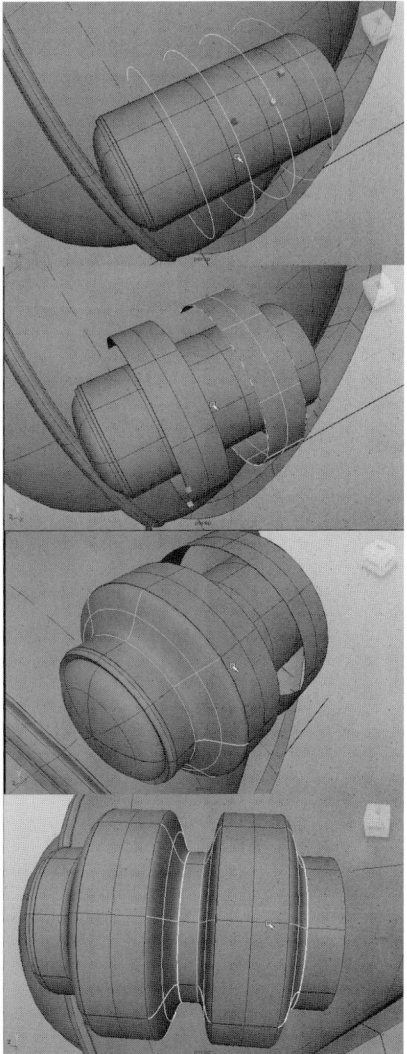

18. Shift+click the top-center hull on both lofts, and use the Move tool to pull them all down, closer to the housing.

19. Switch to the Rotate tool.

20. Rotate the hulls along the x-axis to give them a slight angle.

21. Experiment with the shape of these surfaces by continuing to translate, rotate, and scale the hulls of the lofted surfaces. Because of construction history, the free-form fillet surfaces will update. You can also make changes by editing the curves duplicated from the lamp housing isoparms in step 5.

SELECTING AND MOVING HULLS

For some surfaces, selecting hulls can be tricky. If you're having trouble selecting a specific hull, try selecting a nearby hull that is more exposed, and then use the arrow keys to pick walk your way to the hull you need to select.

22. Select all the surfaces that make up the lamp and housing, the lofts, and the fillets.

23. Delete history on these surfaces, and group them. Name the group **leftLamp** (it's on the character's left).

24. Delete all the associated curves (see Figure 3.40).

FIGURE 3.40
The hulls of the lofted surface on the lamps are selected, moved, and scaled to shape the surfaces of the lamp casing.

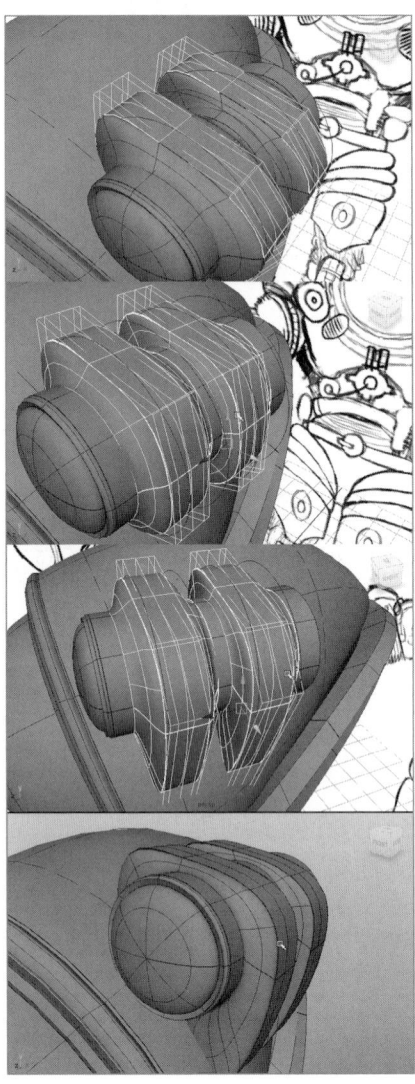

25. Select the leftLamp group, and choose Edit ➤ Duplicate Special ➤ Options.

26. In the options, set the X scale to **-1**.

27. Click the Duplicate button. This creates a copy of the lamp on the opposite side of the helmet. Name the duplicate lamp **rightLamp** (see Figure 3.41).

28. Save the scene as `helmet_v05.ma`.

To see the scene up to this point, open the `helmet_v05.ma` scene from the `chapter3\scenes` directory on the DVD.

FIGURE 3.41
The surfaces that make up the lamp are grouped. The group is mirrored to the right side by duplicating with a -1 setting in the Scale X attribute.

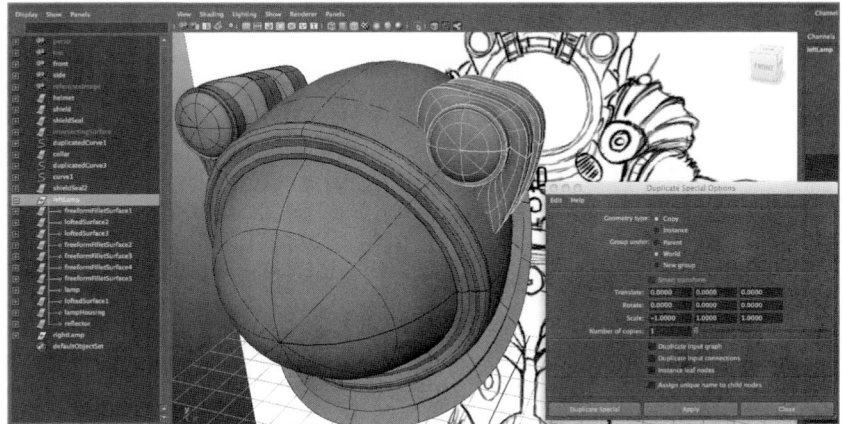

Creating Rail Surfaces

A rail surface uses at least one profile curve and two rail curves to create a surface.

1. Continue with the scene from the previous section, or open the `helmet_v05.ma` scene from the `chapter3\scenes` directory on the DVD.

2. Select the leftLamp and rightLamp groups, and hide them (hot key = **Ctrl+h**).

3. Switch to the side-view camera.

4. Switch to wireframe mode (hot key = **4**).

5. Choose Create ➤ CV Curve tool make sure you are in the side view).

6. Place the first point of the curve near the front/top of the helmet.

7. Create a curve as shown in Figure 3.42.

8. Switch to the front view.

9. Select the curve, and choose Modify ➤ Center pivot.

10. Select the Move tool.

11. Press the **d** key on the keyboard to switch to pivot mode.

12. Pull down on the y-axis of the Move tool.

FIGURE 3.42
A curve is drawn in the side view.

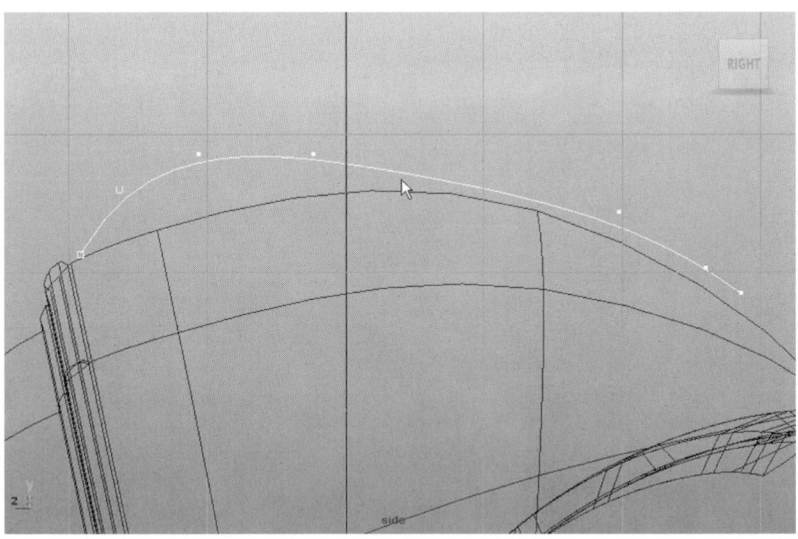

13. Reposition the pivot so that, from the front view, it is aligned with the center of the helmet's shield (see Figure 3.43).

14. Switch to the Rotate tool (hot key = **e**).

15. Rotate the curve -14 degrees on the z-axis.

16. Duplicate the curve (hot key = **Ctrl+d**), and rotate the duplicate -29 degrees on the z-axis.

FIGURE 3.43
The pivot point of the new curve is placed at the center of the helmet's shield in the front view.

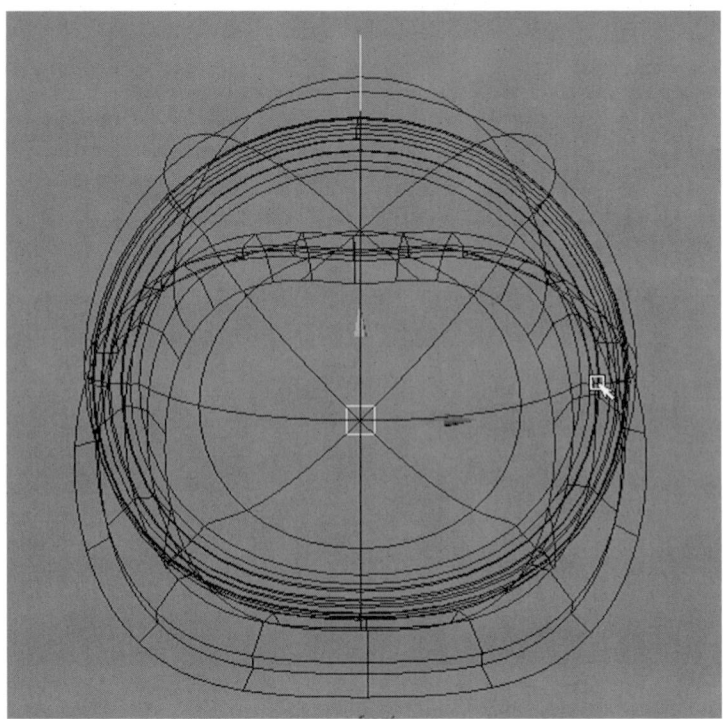

17. Scale the duplicate curve to 0.95 on the y-axis. These two curves will become the rails for the birail surface.

18. Switch to the perspective view, and turn shading mode back on.

19. Turn on Curve Snapping, and select the EP Curve tool (Create ➢ EP Curve Tool). This will allow you to create a curve by clicking just twice.

20. Click the first rail curve, and drag toward the end to make the first point of the curve.

21. Click the second rail curve and drag toward its end (toward the back of the helmet) to make the second point of the curve. This might be easier to do if you rotate the view so the curves are not overlapping the surfaces. This helps avoid a situation in which Curve Snapping places one of the points of the EP curve on one of the isoparms of a visible surface (see Figure 3.44).

22. Select the curve between the two rails, and choose Edit Curves ➢ Rebuild Curve ➢ Options.

23. In the options, reset the settings. Set the following:

Number Of Spans: **8**

Degree: 1 Linear

24. Click Rebuild to rebuild the curve (see Figure 3.45).

FIGURE 3.44
With Curve Snapping enabled, each end point of an EP curve can be placed at the end of the two rail curves.

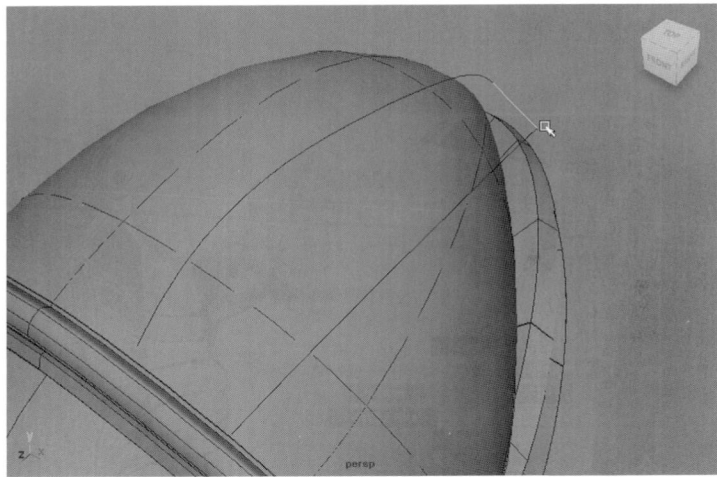

FIGURE 3.45
The options for the rebuilt curve

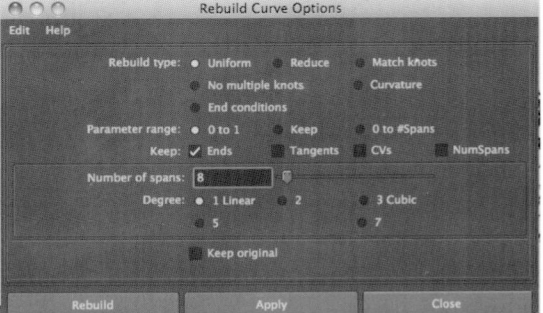

25. Select the new curve, and switch to component mode.

26. Turn Curve Snapping off. Use the Move tool to drag some of the CVs to shape the profile. The profile will be swept along the curves to create grooves, similar to the detail on the top of the helmet in the drawing. You can keep it simple for now and add detail later.

MOVING CVS AND OTHER COMPONENTS

While using the Move tool to edit the position of CVs, experiment with the different axis settings in the Move tool options. Sometimes it's easier to use object mode, sometimes another mode. You can even use the position of a specific CV (or edge or face) to set the axis of the Move tool. To do this, switch the object to component mode, open the Move Tool Options box, click the Set To Point button, and then select a CV. The axis of the Move tool will be oriented to face the CV.

---

27. To create the birail, choose Surfaces ➢ Birail ➢ Birail1 Tool. (The options may open automatically; if they do, click the Birail 1 Tool button to start using the tool.)

28. In the viewport, select the profile curve first, and hit the Enter key.

29. Select the first and then the second rail curves. Hit the Enter key (see Figure 3.46).

FIGURE 3.46
The birail surface is created with the Birail 1 Tool. Select the profile first, hit Enter, and then select both rail curves.

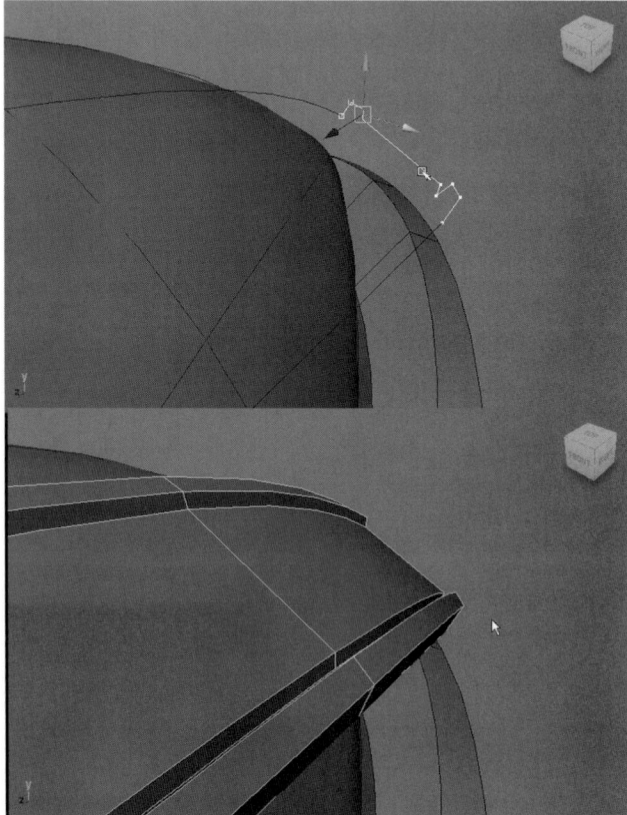

You can change the shape of the surface by editing the position of the CVs on the profile curve. Be careful not to change the position of the rail curves. If the three curves no longer touch, the surface will disappear.

30. To make changes to the surface, select it, delete the history, and then edit the surface by selecting the hulls and moving them with the Move tool.

31. When you're happy with the basic shape of the birail, select it and choose Edit ➤ Duplicate Special ➤ Options.

32. In the options, set Scale X to **-1**.

33. Click Duplicate. This makes a copy of the surface on the opposite side of the helmet (see Figure 3.47).

FIGURE 3.47
The birail surface is adjusted by manipulating its hulls using the Move and Rotate tools. The surface is then mirrored to the opposite side of the helmet using Duplicate Special.

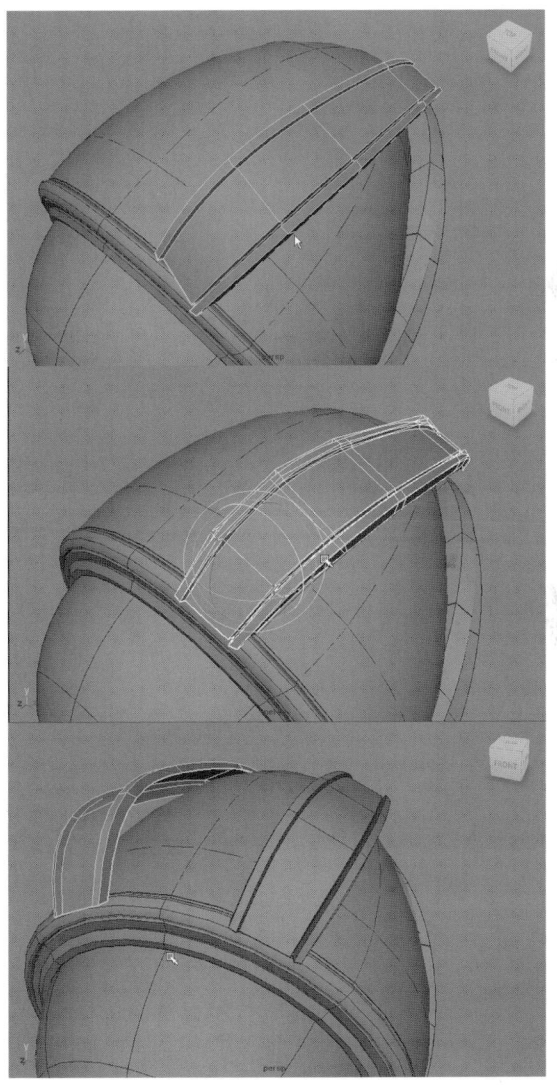

34. Create a loft between the two inside edges of the birail surface. The loft should have nine divisions.

35. Use the Move tool to position the hulls of the loft to create the three curving bumps, as shown in the concept sketch (see Figure 3.48).

FIGURE 3.48
A loft is created between the two inner edges of the birail surfaces. The hulls are moved and scaled to match the concept drawing.

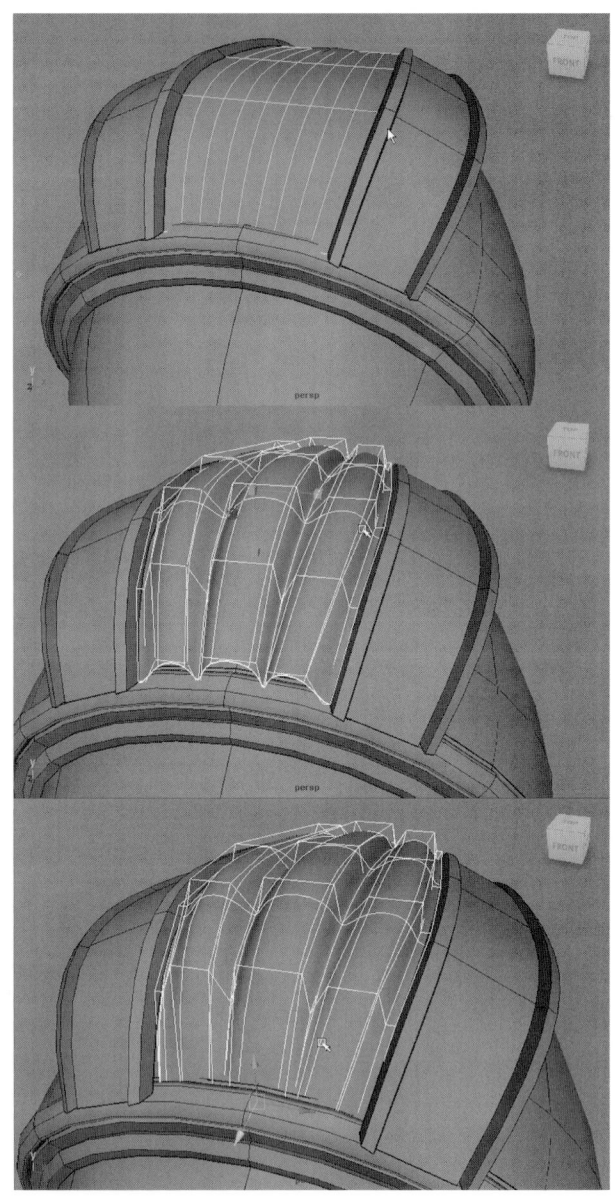

36. Select the surface, and choose Edit ➢ Delete By Type ➢ History to remove the construction history from the object.

37. Save the scene as `helmet_v06.ma`.

Lofting Across Multiple Curves

To create the back of the helmet, you can loft a surface across multiple profile curves:

1. Continue with the scene from the previous section or open the `helmet_v06.ma` scene from the `chapter3\scenes` directory on the DVD.

2. Right-click the rear of the housing for the leftLamp; select Isoparms. Select the isoparm at the very back end of the housing.

3. Choose Edit Curves ➢ Duplicate Surface Curves to create a curve based on the selected isoparm.

4. Choose Edit ➢ Duplicate Special ➢ Options, and set Scale X to **-1**.

5. Click the Duplicate button to make a mirror copy of the curve on the other side.

6. Select the first duplicate curve and choose Edit ➢ Duplicate (hot key = **Ctrl+d**) to make a standard duplicate of the curve.

7. Set the rotation of this curve to 50 degrees in Y.

8. Select the curve on the opposite side, and duplicate it as well. Set the Y rotation to **-50** degrees.

9. Starting from the helmet's left side, Shift+click each of the duplicate curves (this may be easier to do if you hide the NURBS surfaces using the Show menu in the panel menu bar).

10. Choose Surfaces ➢ Loft ➢ Options. In the options, make sure the degree of the loft is set to Cubic. Set the spans to **2**.

11. Click the Loft button.

12. When the loft is created (turn the visibility of NURBS surfaces back on to see the loft), right-click the new surface, and choose Control Vertex to switch to component mode.

13. Select pairs of CVSs at the back of the surface, and use the Move tool to reposition them to create a more interesting shape to the surface (Figure 3.49).

14. Name the new surface **helmetRear**. When you're happy with the result, save the model as `helmet_v07.ma`.

To see a version of the scene to this point, open the `helmet_v07.ma` scene from the `chapter3\scenes` directory on the DVD.

FIGURE 3.49
The duplicated curves are selected in order from left to right, and then a loft surface is created. The CVs of the loft are selected and repositioned to match the reference images.

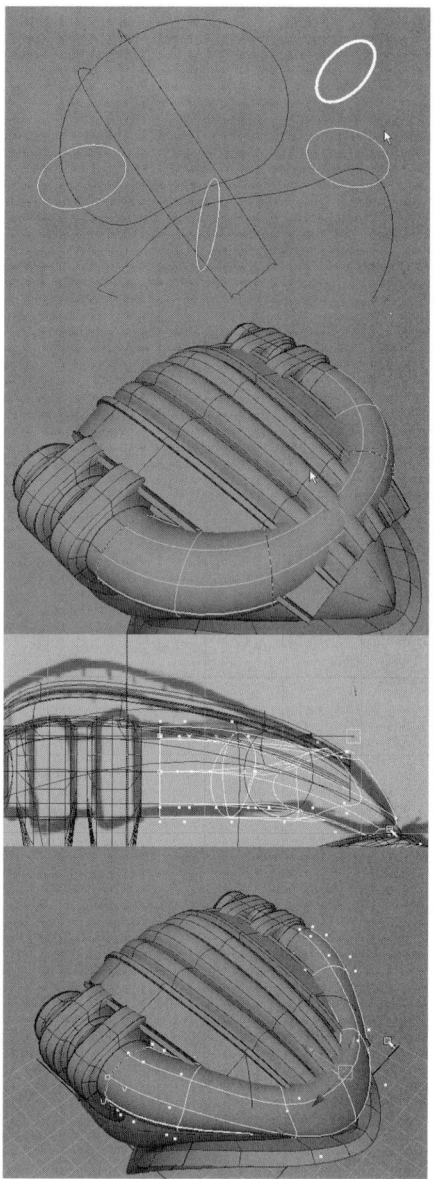

Live Surfaces

When you make a NURBS surface "live," you put it into a temporary state that allows you to draw curves directly on it. This is a great way to add detail that conforms to the shape of the object.

1. Continue with the scene from the previous section, or open the helmet_v07.ma scene from the chapter3\scenes directory on the DVD.

2. Make sure that Wireframe On Shaded is enabled, and zoom into the model so you can see the birail surface you created in the previous section.

    You're going to add some isoparms to the surface so that drawing clean curves on the surface will be a little easier. The isoparms will act as a guide for the curves that you draw.

3. Right-click the birail surface, and choose Isoparms.

4. Add two isoparms that run along the length of the birail surface (in the options for Insert Isoparm, make sure Location is set to At Selection).

5. Add two additional isoparms just outside the isoparms created in step 4.

6. Add two additional isoparms that run across the surface, as shown in the bottom image in Figure 3.50.

FIGURE 3.50
Four isoparms are added to the birail surface that runs along the length, and four isoparms are added that run across the surface. These will be used as guides for adding curves to the surface.

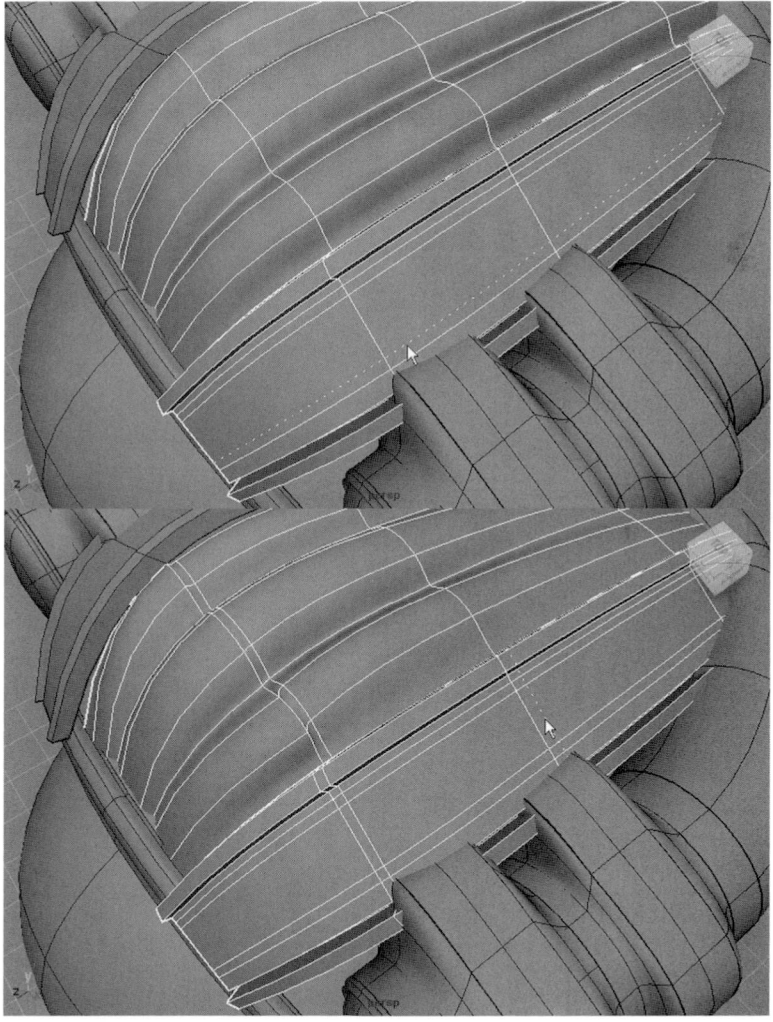

7. With the birail surface selected, choose Modify ➤ Make Live to make the surface live. You'll see the wireframe lines now appear green on the surface.

8. Enable Grid Snapping, and choose Create ➤ CV Curve Tool ➤ Options.

9. In the options, make sure Curve is set to Linear.

10. With Grid Snapping enabled, the points of the curve will be snapped to the isoparms on the surface. Follow the guide in Figure 3.51 to add points to the curve.

FIGURE 3.51
Two linear curves are drawn on the live birail surface using the added isoparms as a guide. When Grid Snapping is enabled, a new curve will snap to the isoparms of a live surface.

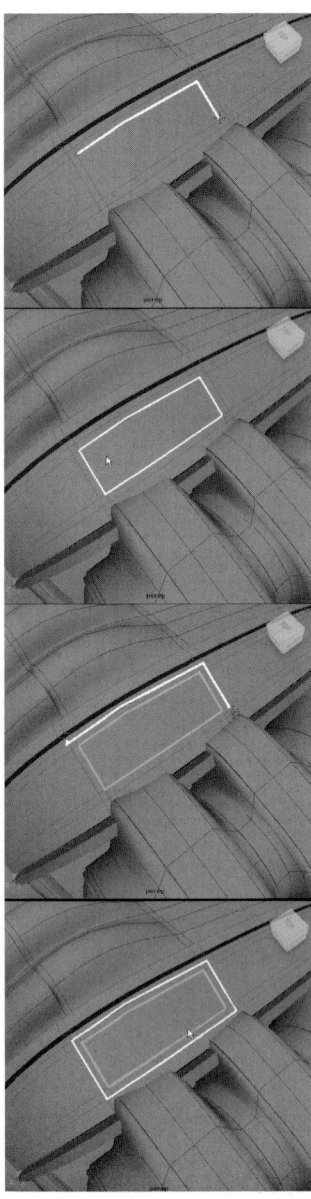

11. Finish the curve by clicking one more time at the point where you started the curve. When you are finished, press the Enter key.

12. Repeat steps 10 and 11 to add another curve that surrounds the first. Make sure you add the same number of points in the same order and that you close the curve when finished.

13. To select curves on a surface, turn off Surface Selection in the Selection Mask Options, and select the curves drawn on the surface.

14. Select the outside curve, and then Shift+click the inside curve.

15. Choose Surfaces ➢ Loft ➢ Options.

16. In the options, make sure the degree of the loft is Cubic and the number of spans is set to **2**.

17. Click Loft to make the loft.

18. When the loft is created, right-click it, and choose Hulls.

19. Turn off Grid Snapping, select the three central hulls of the loft. Switch to the Move tool.

20. In the options, set the Axis to Normals Average, and pull the hull up to create a raised surface (see Figure 3.52).

21. To make the birail surface "unlive," you can select it in the Outliner and choose Modify ➢ Live (alternatively, you can select the shape node of the birail surface in the Outliner).

CONSTRUCTION HISTORY

As long as the Construction History option for the loft surface is enabled, you can experiment with the position of the loft by selecting the curves on the surface and moving them around using the Move tool.

FIGURE 3.52
The hulls of the loft are selected and moved upward to create surface detail.

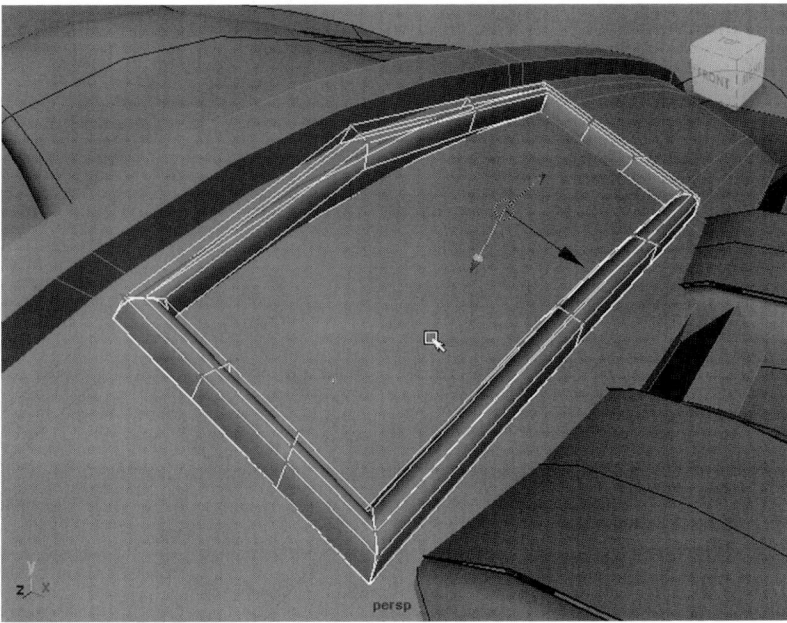

Project Curves on the Surface

You can project a curve onto the surface as a way of devising interesting shapes. These shapes can be used for creating details, such as parting lines and seams on the surface.

1. Switch to the side view, and turn on Grid Snapping.

2. Choose Create ➤ CV Curve Tool ➤ Options, and make sure Curve Degree is set to Linear.

3. Draw a simple square off to the side of the helmet using the grid as a guide. Use five points to make a complete square.

4. With the square curve selected, choose Edit Curves ➤ Open/Close Curves. This will close the curve so it is a loop.

5. Choose Modify ➤ Center Pivot to center the pivot on the square.

6. Turn off Grid Snapping, and switch to the perspective view.

7. Use the Move tool to position the square on the helmet's left, as shown in Figure 3.53.

FIGURE 3.53
A square-shaped curve is created and positioned to the helmet's left side.

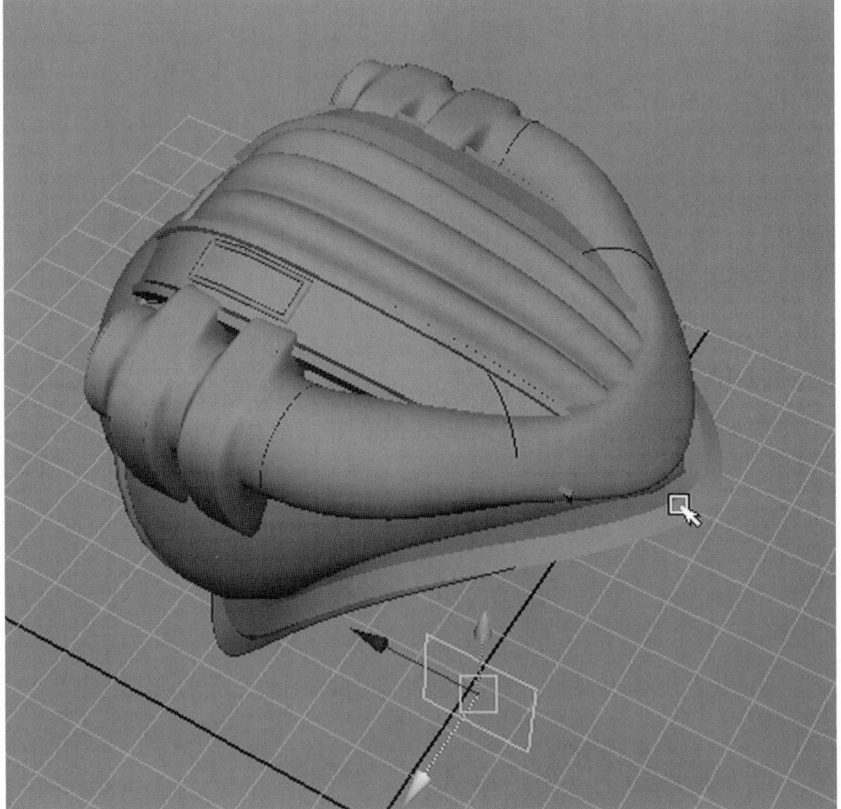

8. Switch back to the side view. Make sure the square curve is overlapping the helmetRear surface.

9. Select the curve and the helmetRear surface.

10. Choose Edit NURBS ➤ Project Curve On Surface ➤ Options, and choose Edit ➤ Reset to reset the settings. You want to project the curve from the active view, which is currently the side-view camera.

11. Click Project to make the projection.

12. Switch to the perspective view again. You'll see the curve projected onto the back part of the helmet; it wraps around the surface. Any change you make to the square curve will change the shape of the curve on the surface.

13. Select the square projection curve, and use the Move, Rotate, and Scale tools to reposition the curve until the projection resembles something like the projection shown in Figure 3.54.

To create a raised panel from the curve on the surface, you'll trim the surface. You'll need two copies of the surface: one that has the hole and the other that has the raised portion of the surface.

14. Select the helmetRear surface, choose Edit ➤ Duplicate Special ➤ Options, and choose Duplicate Input Connections. This creates a duplicate of the surface with the same projected curve on the surface.

15. Click Duplicate to make the copy.

FIGURE 3.54
The projected square curve is moved, scaled, and rotated. This changes the shape of the projected curve on the surface.

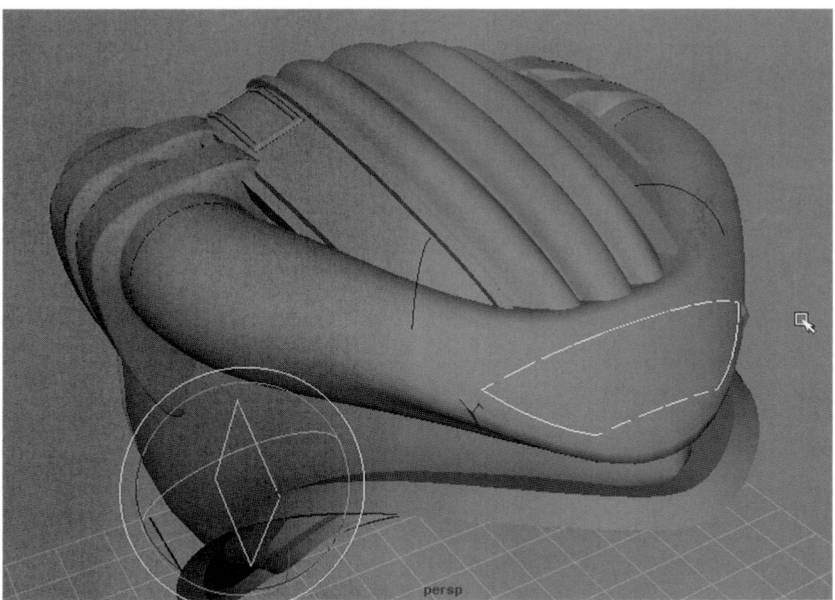

16. In the perspective view, move the duplicate surface in X about -5 units. There is still a history connection between the curve and the curve on the surface for both copies of the surface, so try not to move the duplicate along any axis but X.

17. Select the original surface, and choose Edit NURBS ➢ Trim Tool.

18. Use the Trim tool to place markers in a few positions on the surface; don't place any markers in the area defined by the projected curve.

19. Press the Enter key to make the trim.

20. Repeat step 17 for the duplicate surface; however, place the trim markers only in the area defined by the projected curve. You should be left with just the piece defined by the projected curve (Figure 3.55).

FIGURE 3.55
Both the original helmetRear surface and the helmetRear1 surface are trimmed based on the projected curve. However, one trim leaves a hole in the surface, and the other leaves the surface defined by the projected curve.

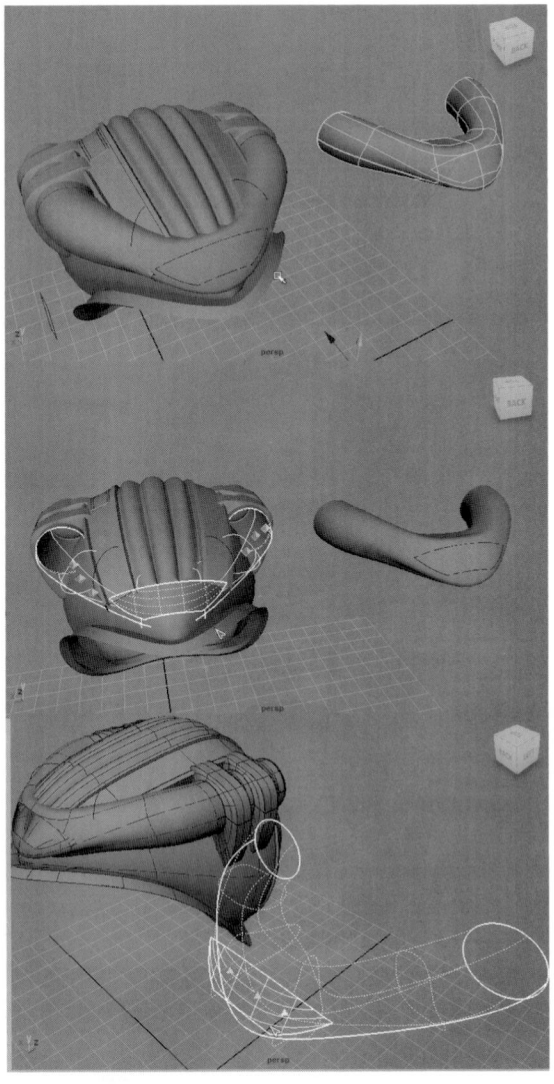

21. Select both copies of the helmetRear surfaces, and choose Edit ➤ Delete By Type ➤ History. Now you can move the surfaces without worrying about changing the shape of the opening.

22. Change the name of helmetRear1to **panelTop**.

23. Center the pivot of panelTop. Set its Translate X back to **0,** and position it just above the opening in the helmetRear surface. Scale it down just slightly (see Figure 3.56).

24. To fill the gaps between the opening and the top of the panel, right-click the original surface, and choose Trim Edge.

25. Select the edge, right-click over the panel top, choose Trim Edge, and then Shift+click the second trim edge. You can then use a free-form fillet to close the gap (Edit NURBS ➤ Surface Fillet ➤ Freeform Fillet). Repeat this step for all the edges around the panel (see Figure 3.57).

FIGURE 3.56
The panelTop surface is moved above the opening in the helmetRear surface and scaled down slightly.

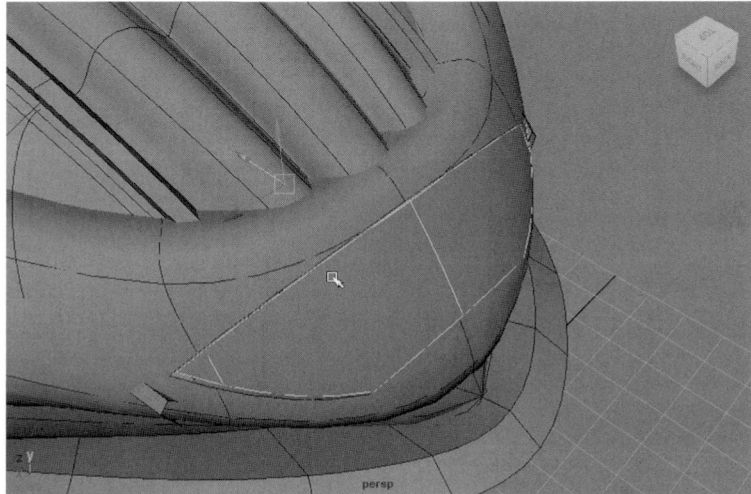

FIGURE 3.57
Free-form fillet surfaces are created to fill the gaps between the four sides of the panelTop and the opening in the helmetRear surface.

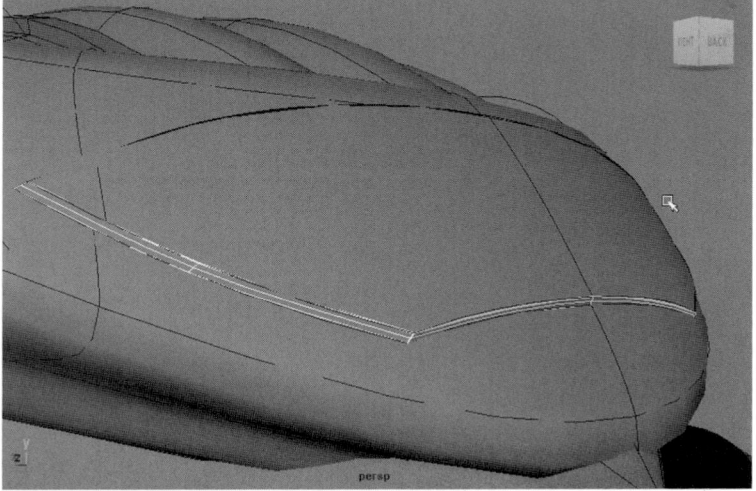

26. Take a few minutes to rename the surfaces in the Outliner with descriptive names.

27. Group the surfaces accordingly, and delete the history.

28. Delete all the curves created while modeling. Figure 3.58 shows how we have organized the surfaces in our version of the scene.

29. Save the scene as `helmet_v08.ma`.

To see a version of the helmet to this point, open the `helmet_v08.ma` scene from the `chapter3\scenes` directory on the DVD.

FIGURE 3.58
The surfaces have been renamed and organized using grouping. The history has been deleted, and the curves have been removed.

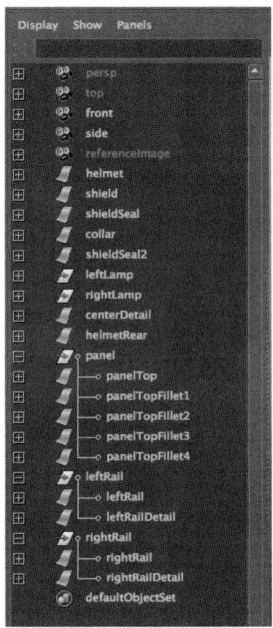

Revolve

A *revolve* sweeps a surface generated by a curve around an axis. It's a very versatile modeling technique. In this section, you'll add a sensor to the lamp housing using a revolve operation.

1. Continue with the scene from the previous section, or open the `helmet_v08.ma` scene from the `chapter3\scenes` directory on the DVD.

2. Switch to a front view, and turn on Grid Snapping.

3. Choose Create ➢ CV Curve Tool ➢ Options. In the options, set Curve Degree to Linear.

You'll start by roughing out the curve on the grid. Using Grid Snapping is a good way to ensure that lines are straight. After the points of the curve are laid out on the grid, you'll turn Grid Snapping off and change their positions to refine the shape of the curve.

4. Starting from the center line, create a curve that looks like half of a blocky Y shape. Use Figure 3.59 as a reference.

MODELING NURBS SURFACES 149

FIGURE 3.59
A revolve surface
is created from
a linear curve.
By adjusting the
points of the curve,
the revolve surface
is shaped into a
mechanical scope.

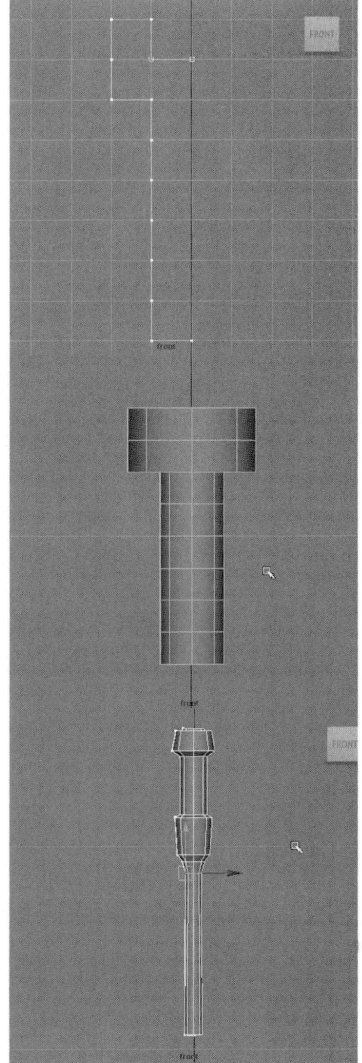

5. In total, click 14 times to create a 14-point curve.

6. Press the Enter key when you have finished adding points to the curve.

7. Select the curve, and choose Modify ➤ Center Pivot. This brings the pivot point up from the origin.

8. Select the Move tool, hold the **d** key, and move the pivot so it snaps to the center line of the grid.

9. Turn off Grid Snapping, and use the Scale tool to scale the curve down to **0.15** in X, Y, and Z.

10. With the curve selected, choose Surfaces ➤ Revolve. By default, the revolve will sweep around the y-axis.

11. Zoom in on the surface, and turn off Surface Selection in the Selection Mask Options on the status line.

12. Select the curve, and switch to component mode.

13. Use the Move tool to reposition the CVs of the Curve tool. You want to create a long, thin, mechanical-looking scope.

14. When you have a basic shape that you like, rename the surface **Sensor**.

15. Select the revolved surface, center its pivot, and use the Move, Scale, and Rotate tools to position it next to the lamp on the spacesuit's left side; use Figure 3.60 as a guide.

FIGURE 3.60
The sensor is moved, scaled, and rotated to fit next to the lamp on the left side of the helmet.

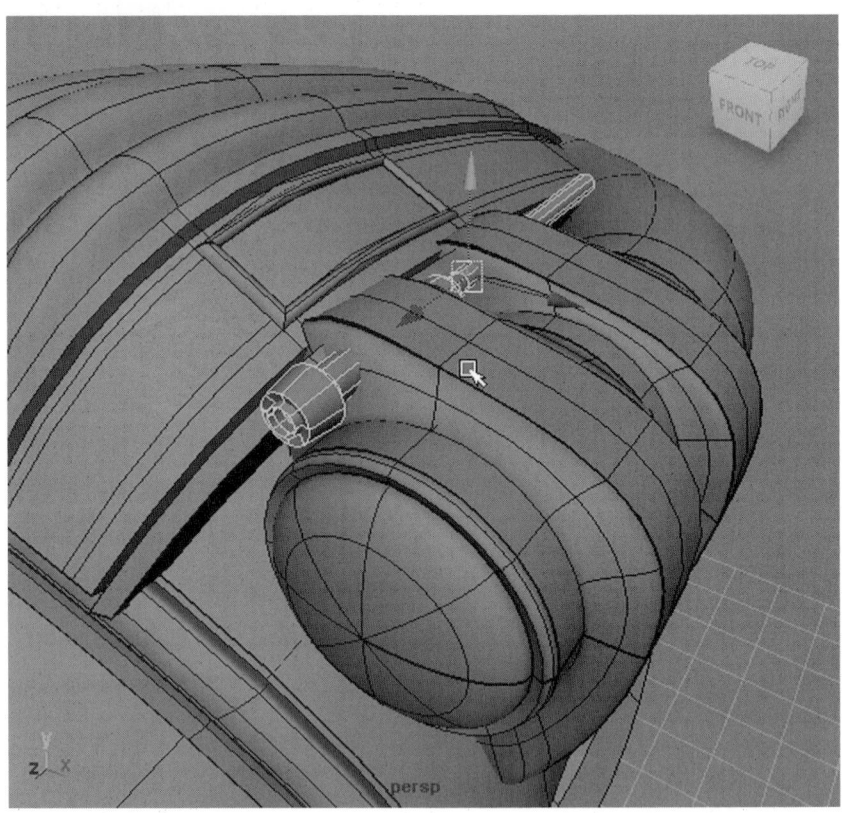

Once you have it roughly in position, you can continue to edit the position of points on the original curve to change its shape. It may be easier to split the Maya interface into two windows. Use a front-view camera to make changes in the curve, and use the perspective camera to see the results of the changes.

16. Make the sensor extend a fair way toward the back of the helmet, as shown in Figure 3.61.

FIGURE 3.61
By editing the points of the original revolved curve, you can continue to change the shape of the sensor after it has been positioned.

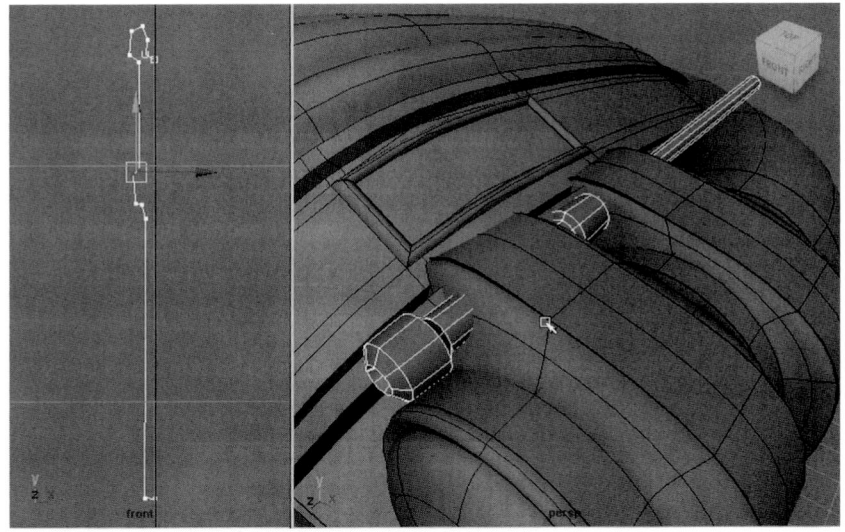

Using the Bend Deformer

Deformers are found under the Animation menu set, but they can be very useful as modeling tools. In this section, you'll add a slight bend to the end of the sensor created in the previous section. Small bends and curves created in mechanical parts can add a lot of style and realism to your model.

1. Select the sensor created in the previous section.

2. Select an isoparm near the end of the tube, and Shift+click an isoparm about halfway down the back of the sensor.

3. To create a smooth bend at the end of the sensor, add additional isoparms to the surface:

    A. Choose Edit NURBS ➤ Insert Isoparms ➤ Options.

    B. In the options, set Location to Between Selection.

    C. Set the Number Of Isoparms To Insert to **6**.

    You should see six new isoparms added to the back of the sensor (see Figure 3.62).

4. Switch to the Animation menu set.

5. Select the sensor, and choose Create Deformers ➤ Nonlinear ➤ Bend.

6. Select the bend1Handle in the Outliner.

7. In the Channel Box, select the Bend1 node under INPUTS, and set Curvature to **1**.

8. To restrict the bend to the back portion of the sensor, set High Bound to **0**. The Bounds determine the length of the bend deform.

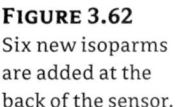

FIGURE 3.62
Six new isoparms
are added at the
back of the sensor.

9. In the Channel Box, set Rotate Z to **-90** so the sensor bends downward.

10. Use the Move tool to move the Bend tool back along its y-axis (see Figure 3.63).

FIGURE 3.63
Using the settings
in the Channel
Box, edit the bend
deformer to add a
slight bend at the
end of the sensor.

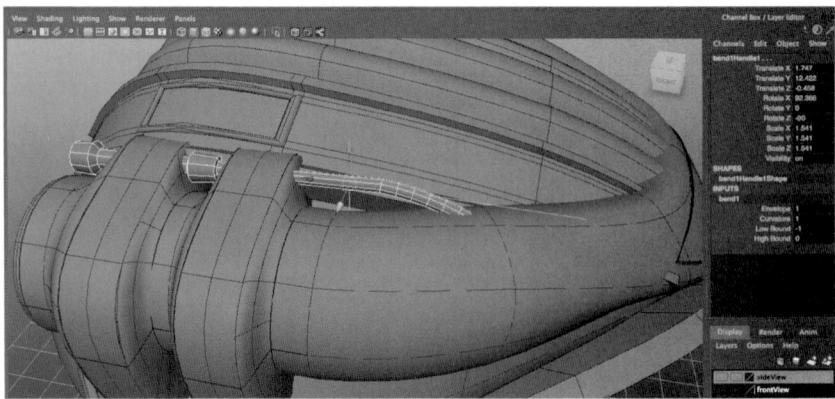

11. Select the sensor, and choose Edit ≻ Delete By Type ≻ History to make the changes to the sensor permanent. This removes the bend handle from the scene.

12. Group all the objects in the scene, and name the group **Helmet**.

13. Delete history and any unused curves and surfaces.

14. Save the scene as `helmet_v09.ma`.

To see a version of the scene up to this point, open the `helmet_v09.ma` scene from the `chapter3\scenes` directory on the DVD.

MIRROR OBJECTS

When you've completed changes on one side of the model, you can mirror them to the other side:

1. Create a group for the parts you want to mirror; by default the pivot for the new group will be at the center of the grid.

2. Select the group, and choose Edit ≻ Duplicate Special.

3. Set Scale X of the duplicate to -1.

When you create the duplicate, you can freeze transformations on the objects and ungroup them if you like.

Creating Realism

The key to realistic modeling is in the details. Real, manufactured objects have seams, bolts, screws, weather stripping, and rubber gaskets. In any place two surfaces meet, try to create a believable transition using a surface fillet or a loft. By building from curves created on the surface, you can quickly add believable detail. In production, sometimes these details are modeled as part of the surface; sometimes they are created as part of the texture. In this example, the details are modeled for the purpose of instruction.

Think about the possible use of the objects you model. In the case of the helmet, think about what parts of the object need to form a tight seal to protect the wearer from the harsh environment of space. Also think about which parts of the helmet may need to be manipulated by a person wearing heavy gloves. Think about things like servos and handles for the mechanical parts on the helmet.

Figure 3.64 shows the completed NURBS helmet from different views. Open the `NURBShelmet.ma` scene from the `chapter3\scene` directory on the DVD, and examine the model to see whether you can figure out the techniques that were used to make it. All of the techniques used are just variations of the ones described in this section.

FIGURE 3.64
The completed
NURBS helmet.
Details were
created using
a combination
of techniques
described in the
chapter.

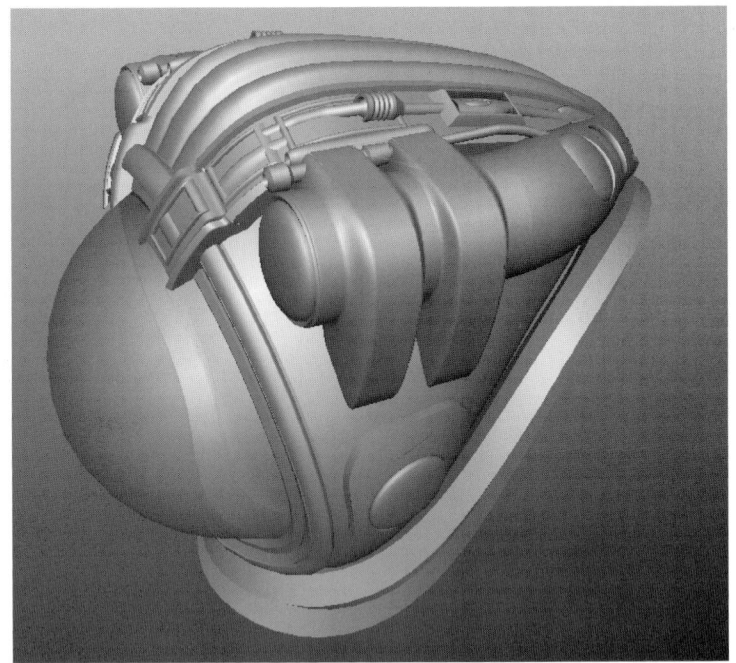

NURBS Tessellation

While working with NURBS surfaces, you may see small gaps or areas around the trim edge
that do not precisely follow the curve. This is due to the settings found in the NURBS Display
section of the surface's Attribute Editor. These settings adjust how the NURBS surfaces appear
while working in Maya. They do not necessarily represent how the object will look when rendered. By increasing the precision of the NURBS surface display, you may find that the performance of Maya on your machine suffers. It depends on the amount of RAM and your machine's
processor speed. The main thing to keep in mind is that changing these settings will not affect
how the surface looks when rendered.

To preview how the surface will look in the render, you can enable Display Render
Tessellation in the Tessellation rollout of the surface's Attribute Editor. A wireframe will appear
on the surface, which represents the arrangement of triangles that will be used when the surface
is converted to polygons by the renderer (note that the surface will remain as NURBS in the
scene when you render).

Using the Tessellation settings found in the Simple or Advanced Tessellation Options, you
can determine how the surface will look when rendered (see Figure 3.65). Keep in mind that
increasing the precision of the tessellation will increase your render time. You can adjust the
settings based on how close an object is to the rendering camera. The triangle count gives you
precise numeric feedback on how many triangles a surface will contain based on its tessellation settings. Take a look at the NURBSdisplay.ma scene in the chapter3\scenes directory on
the DVD.

FIGURE 3.65
You can change the accuracy of the NURBS surface display and change the quality of the render tessellation in the Attribute Editor for the NURBS shape node. Three identical trimmed NURBS spheres have different settings applied.

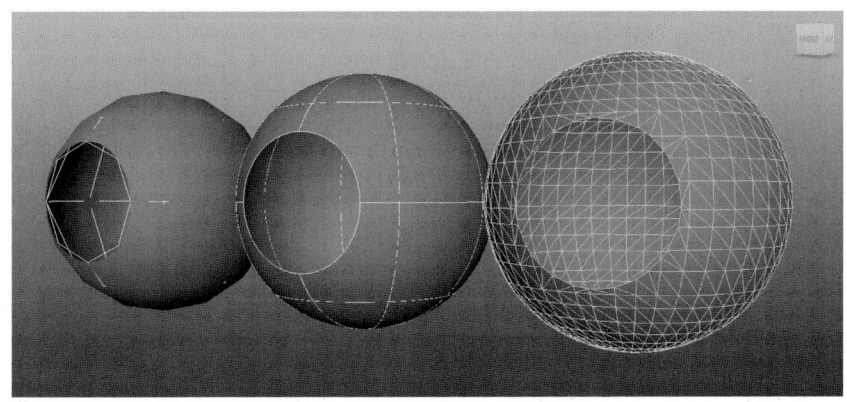

The Advanced Tessellation settings give you even more control over how the object will be tessellated. Keep in mind that Advanced is not always better or appropriate. In some circumstances, you may get better results using Simple Tessellation rather than Advanced. It depends on the model and the scene. If you're having problems with the scene, you can experiment using the two methods.

The Bottom Line

Use image planes   Image planes can be used to position images for use as a modeling guide.

> **Master it**   Create image planes for side, front, and top views for use as a model guide.

Apply NURBS curves and surfaces   NURBS surfaces are created by lofting a surface across a series of curves. The curve and surface degree and parameterization affect the shape of the resulting surface.

> **Master it**   What is the difference between a one-degree (linear) surface, a three-degree (cubic) surface, and a five-degree surface?

Model with NURBS surfaces   A variety of tools and techniques can be used to model surfaces with NURBS. Hard-surface/mechanical objects are well-suited subjects for NURBS surfaces.

> **Master it**   Create a NURBS model of a common object you own such as a cell phone, a computer monitor, or a particle accelerator.

Create realistic surfaces   Manufactured objects usually have visible seams and parting lines that reveal how they are put together. Adding these details to your surfaces greatly increases the realism of your objects.

> **Master it**   Examine a manufactured object closely, and pay attention to the seams and parting lines. Look at weather stripping on the windows of vehicles; look at the trim around tail lights and openings in the surface. Look at the panels on the underside of

electronic products such as a cell phone. Try to imitate these in your models even if the object does not exist in the real world.

Adjust NURBS render tessellation   You can change how the rendering engine converts a NURBS surface into triangles at render time by adjusting the tessellation of the objects. This can impact render times and increase efficiency in heavy scenes.

Master it   Test the tessellation settings on a row of NURBS columns. Compare render times and image quality using different tessellation settings.

Chapter 4

Polygon Modeling

Modeling with polygons in Maya is quite different from the NURBS techniques you learned in Chapter 3. In some cases, it may feel a bit more intuitive. Rather than lofting surfaces across curves, polygon models are constructed by attaching flat geometric shapes together to form a volume. There are fewer restrictions when working with polygons, and for this reason they are more popular as a modeling tool than NURBS. However, NURBS and polygons are not mutually exclusive. As an artist, you can combine the two types of surfaces and take advantage of the strengths of both, as you'll see in this chapter.

This chapter continues the project started in Chapter 3. Using the space suit concept as a subject, you'll learn various techniques for working with polygons. You'll also learn how to convert the NURBS models you started in Chapter 3. Additional techniques such as using Paint Effects as a modeling tool will be explored, and you'll be introduced to subdivision surfaces. Subdivision surfaces are like a hybrid of NURBS and polygon surfaces.

In this chapter, you will learn to

- ◆ Understand polygon geometry
- ◆ Work with smooth mesh polygons
- ◆ Model using deformers
- ◆ Combine meshes
- ◆ Model polygons with Paint Effects
- ◆ Convert NURBS surfaces to polygons
- ◆ Sculpt polygons using Artisan
- ◆ Use subdivision surfaces

Understanding Polygon Geometry

Polygon geometry refers to a surface made up of polygon faces that share edges and vertices. A polygon face is a geometric shape consisting of three or more edges. Vertices are points along the edges of polygon faces, usually at the intersection of two or more edges.

Polygons are simpler to understand and work with than NURBS surfaces. Polygon geometry is not restricted to four-sided patches as are NURBS surfaces. The many tools available allow you to make more arbitrary changes (such as splitting, removing, and extruding) to polygon faces. They are also versatile. They can be used to create hard-surface models, such as vehicles, armor, and other mechanical objects, as well as organic surfaces, such as characters, creatures, and other natural objects.

Modeling polygons generally means pushing and pulling the components (vertices, edges, and faces) of the geometry as well as extruding surfaces and edges, welding pieces together, and bridging gaps and holes with polygon faces.

In this chapter, you'll continue to use the space suit design as an example as you tour the various polygon-modeling tools and techniques Maya has to offer. The chapter focuses on how various polygon tools and techniques can be used to create the model.

Before you get started working on the space suit, it's a good idea to get an understanding of the basic components of a polygon surface.

Polygon Vertices

A polygon is a surface constructed using three or more points known as *vertices*. The surface between these vertices is a *face*. A *mesh* is a series of faces that share two or more vertices. The most common way to create a polygon surface is to start with a primitive (such as a plane, sphere, or cube) and then use the numerous editing tools to gradually shape the primitive into the object that you want to create. Here's a quick demonstration:

1. Open a new scene in Maya.

2. Choose Create ➤ Polygon Primitives ➤ Plane.

   At this point, you will be prompted to drag on the grid if Interactive Creation is on in the Polygon Primitives menu (see Figure 4.1).

3. Drag on the surface to create the plane; you'll see a green square appear.

4. Press **5** to switch to shaded mode.

   The polygon plane consists of a shaded square with four corners. The vertices are at each corner.

5. Right-click the plane, and choose Vertex. You'll see the vertices appear as a pink dot at each corner.

FIGURE 4.1
The Interactive Creation feature is found in the Polygon Primitives menu and is on by default.

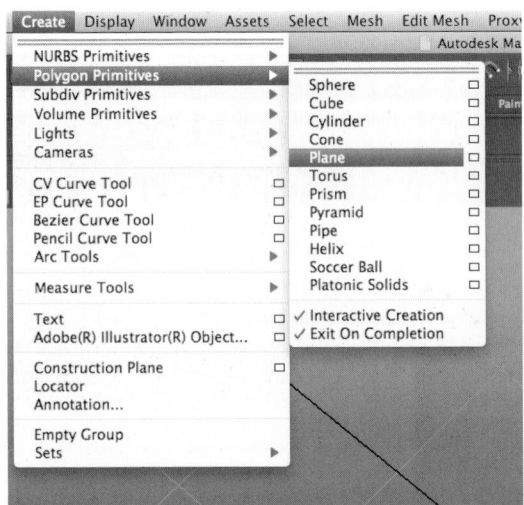

6. Drag a selection over one of the vertices to select it.

7. Choose the Move tool from the toolbox (hot key = **w**), and move the vertex around (see Figure 4.2).

8. As you move the vertex around, the shape changes. Tilt the view, and try pulling the vertex upward. This creates a fold in the surface (see Figure 4.3).

FIGURE 4.2
Use the Move tool to move a vertex.

FIGURE 4.3
Moving one of the vertices upward creates a fold in the surface.

When all the vertices of a polygon are along a single plane, the surface is referred to as *planar*. When the vertices are moved to create a fold in the surface, as shown in step 8, the surface is referred to as *nonplanar*. It's usually best to keep your polygon surfaces as planar as possible. This avoids possible render problems, especially if the model is to be used in a video game. As you'll see in this chapter, you can use a number of tools to cut and slice the polygon to reduce nonplanar surfaces.

POLYGON MENU SET

Many of the tools used in this chapter are found in the Polygon menu set. Use the drop-down menu in the upper left of the Maya interface to switch to this menu set.

Polygon Edges

The line between two polygon vertices is an edge. You can select one or more edges and use the Move, Rotate, and Scale tools as another way to edit a polygon surface.

1. Undo the changes to the position of the vertex so that the polygon is planar again.

2. Right-click the polygon, and choose Edge.

3. Hold the mouse pointer over one of the edges; it will turn red. Click an edge, and it will turn orange when selected.

4. Use the Move tool to move the edge around (see Figure 4.4). You can also rotate the edge (the hot key for the rotate tool is **e**), although this may result in a nonplanar surface.

5. Double-click an edge to extend the selection so that all the border edges are selected.

   When you double-click an edge, Maya will try to select all the edges along a continuous path. This is extremely helpful when editing complex surfaces.

6. Undo the changes to the position of the edge.

7. Select a single edge, and choose Edit Mesh ➤ Extrude. The manipulator will appear.

FIGURE 4.4
Use the Move tool to manipulate the polygon edge. The edge can also be rotated and scaled.

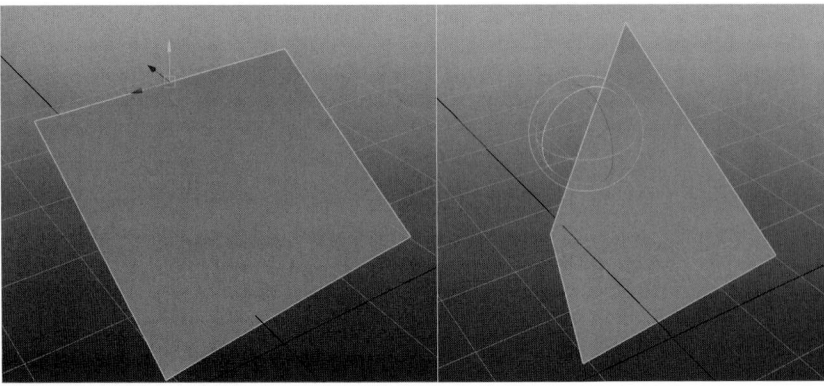

8. Drag upward to extrude the edge. This adds a second polygon to the initial edge (see Figure 4.5).

9. Select the edge that you originally extruded in step 6.

10. Create another extrusion and pull it out so that three polygons share the same edge (see Figure 4.6).

FIGURE 4.5
A second polygon is created by extruding the edge.

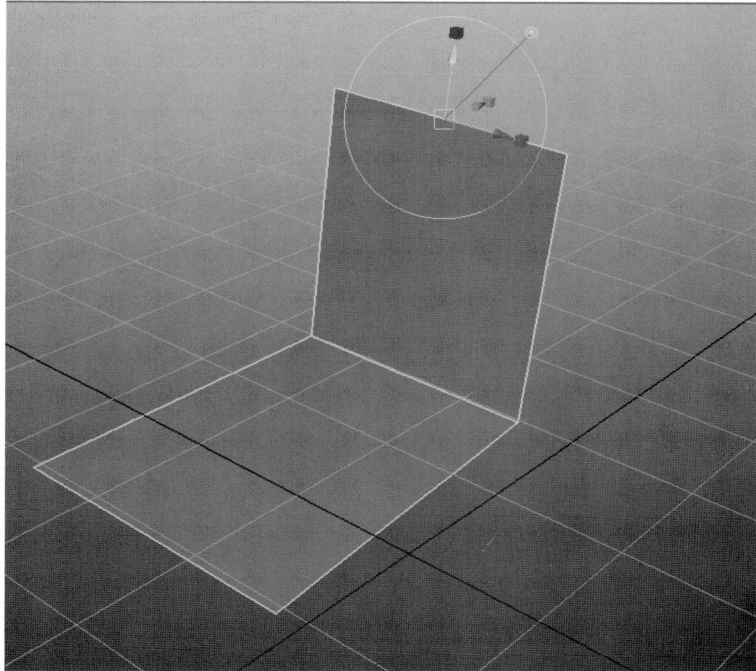

FIGURE 4.6
A third polygon is extruded from the same edge.

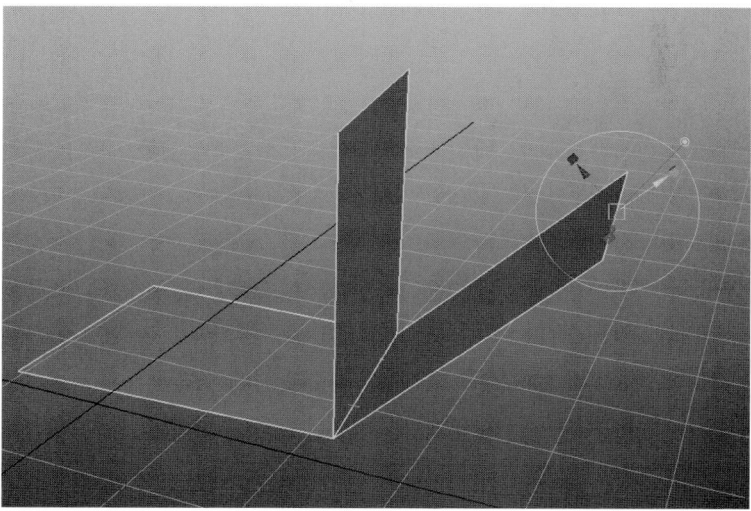

This configuration is known as a *nonmanifold* surface, and it's another situation to avoid. Some polygon-editing tools in Maya do not work well with nonmanifold surfaces, and it can lead to render and animation problems. Another example of a nonmanifold surface is a situation where two polygons share a single vertex but not a complete edge, creating a bow-tie shape (see Figure 4.7).

FIGURE 4.7
Another type of nonmanifold surface is created when two polygons share a single vertex.

Polygon Faces

The actual surface of a polygon is known as a *face*. Faces are what appear in the final render of a model or animation. There are numerous tools for editing and shaping faces, which will be explored throughout this chapter.

1. Right-click the surface, and choose Face. As you hold your mouse pointer over the faces of the surface, they are shaded in red indicating which polygon will be selected.

2. Select the face created from the last extrusion operation; it will turn orange when selected.

3. Press the Delete key, and it disappears. This is how you remove polygons from a surface.

4. Right-click the remaining polygons, and choose Select to select the whole model.

5. Choose Display ➢ Polygons ➢ Face Normals.

   You'll see two green lines poking out of the center of each polygon face (see Figure 4.8). This line indicates the direction of the face normal; essentially it's where the face is pointing. The direction of the face normal affects how the surface is rendered; how effects such as dynamics, hair, and fur are calculated; and other polygon functions. Many times when you are experiencing strange behavior when working with a polygon model, it's because there is a problem with the normals. This is usually easily fixed.

FIGURE 4.8
The face normals are indicated by green lines pointing from the center of the polygon face.

6. Right-click one of the faces, and select it.

7. Choose Normals ➤ Reverse. You'll see the green line now flips over to the other side (see Figure 4.9).

FIGURE 4.9
The normal of the second polygon is flipped to the other side.

This is a third type of nonmanifold surface; it is caused by a situation in which two adjacent polygons have their normals pointing in opposite directions. Try to avoid this configuration.

8. Right-click the polygons, and choose Select to select the whole surface.

9. Choose Normals ➤ Conform. This corrects the problem and restores the surface so that all the normals face in the same direction.

Working with Smooth Polygons

There are two ways to smooth a polygon surface: you can use the Smooth operation (from the Polygon menu set, choose Mesh ➤ Smooth), or you can use the Smooth Mesh Preview command (select a polygon object and press the **3** key).

When you select a polygon object and use the Smooth operation in the Mesh menu, the geometry is subdivided. Each level of subdivision quadruples the number of polygon faces in the geometry and rounds the edges of the geometry. This also increases the number of polygon vertices available for manipulation when shaping the geometry (Figure 4.10).

FIGURE 4.10
From left to right, a polygon cube is smoothed two times. Each smoothing operation quadruples the number of faces, increasing the number of vertices available for modeling.

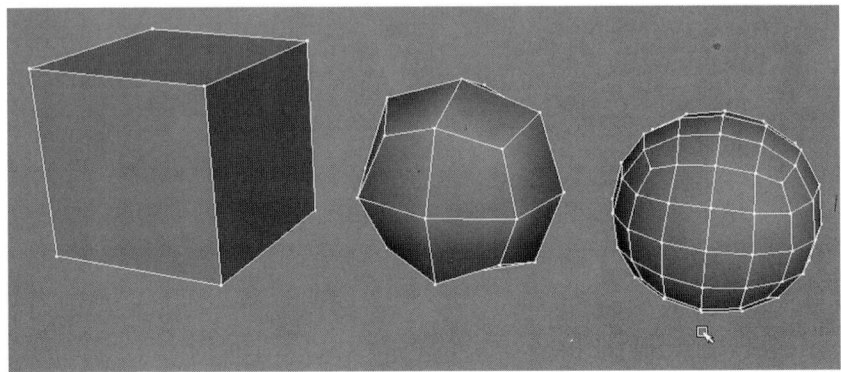

When you use the smooth mesh preview, the polygon object appears smooth; however, it is not subdivided. Think of this as a mode where you can preview the polygon surface as if you had used the smooth option in the mesh menu (which is why it's called *smooth mesh preview*).

When a polygon surface is in smooth mesh preview mode, the number of vertices available for manipulation remains the same as the original unsmoothed geometry; this simplifies the modeling process.

◆ To create a smooth mesh preview, select the polygon geometry, and press the **3** key.

◆ To return to the original polygon mesh, press the **1** key.

◆ To see a wireframe of the original mesh overlaid on the smooth mesh preview, press the **2** key (Figure 4.11).

The terms *smooth mesh preview* and *smooth mesh polygons* are interchangeable; you see both used in this book and in the Maya interface.

FIGURE 4.11
This image shows the original cube, the smooth mesh preview with wireframe, and the smooth mesh preview.

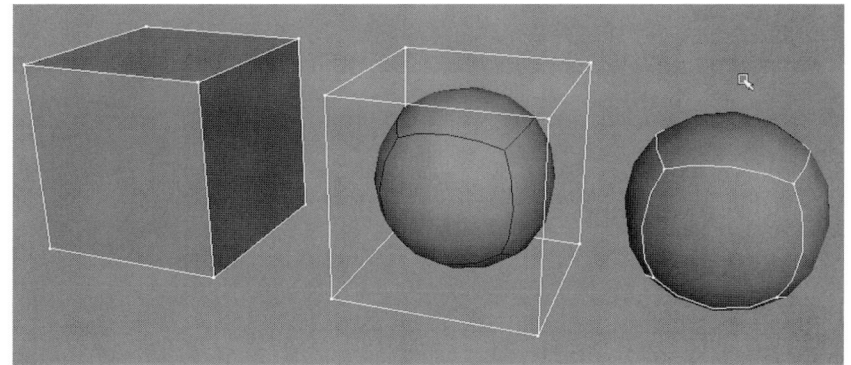

When you render polygon geometry as a smooth mesh preview using mental ray, the geometry appears smoothed in the render without the need to convert the smooth mesh to standard polygons or change it in any way. This makes modeling and rendering smooth and organic geometry with polygons much easier.

Using Smooth Mesh Polygons

In this section, you'll create the basic shape of the torso for the space suit character introduced in Chapter 3 using smooth mesh polygon geometry:

1. Open the `torso_v01.ma` scene from the `chapter4\scenes` directory on the DVD.

   In this scene, you'll see the NURBS helmet created in Chapter 3 as well as the image planes that display the reference images. If the reference images are not displaying correctly, select each image plane, open its Attribute Editor, and click the folder icon next to the Image Name field. The reference images are found in the `source images` subdirectory of the `chapter4` folder on the DVD.

   To make the torso, you'll use a technique known as *box modeling*. This uses the polygon-modeling tools to shape a basic cube into a more complex object.

2. Choose Create ➢ Polygon Primitives ➢ Cube.

3. Switch to a side view and turn on X-Ray mode (Shading ➢ X-Ray) so you can see the reference images through the geometry.

4. Select the cube, and name it **torso**.

5. Position and scale the torso so it roughly matches the position of the torso in the side view.

6. Set the channels as follows:

   Translate X: **0**

   Translate Y: **6.375**

   Translate Z: **-1.2**

   Scale X: **8.189**

   Scale Y: **6.962**

   Scale Z: **6.752**

7. In the Channel Box, click the polyCube1 heading in the INPUTS section.

8. Under the polyCube1 settings, set Subdivisions Width to **4** and Subdivisions Height and Depth to **3**, as shown in Figure 4.12.

9. With the torso selected, press the **3** key to switch to smooth mesh preview. The edges of the cube become rounded.

FIGURE 4.12
Place a polygon cube roughly in the position of the torso.

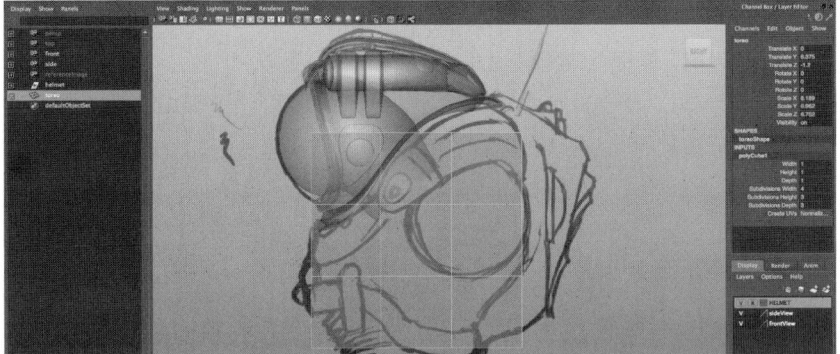

SMOOTH MESH PREVIEW SETTINGS

By default, the smooth mesh preview displays the smoothing at two divisions, as if you had applied a smoothing operation to the geometry twice. You can change the display settings on a particular piece of polygon geometry by selecting the object and choosing Display ➤ Polygons ➤ Custom Polygon Display. At the bottom of the options you'll find the Smooth Mesh Preview settings. Changing the value of the Division Levels slider sets the number of subdivisions for the smooth mesh preview. You can also enable the Show Subdivisions option to see the subdivisions on the preview displayed as dotted lines. The options are applied to the selected object when you click the Apply button. Be aware that a high Division Levels setting slows down the performance of playback in Maya scenes.

Additional controls are available under the Extra Controls rollout. Lowering the Continuity slider decreases the roundness of the edges on the preview. You can also choose to smooth the UV Texture coordinates and preserve Hard Edges and Geometry Borders.

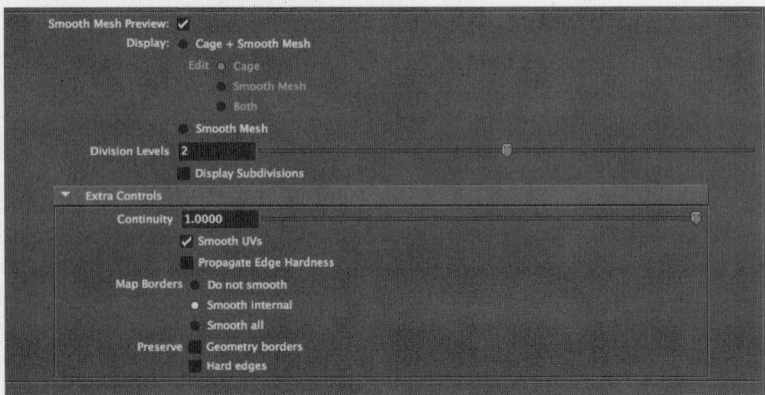

Editing Polygon Components

Polygon objects are shaped by selecting their components and editing them with the Select, Move, Rotate, and Scale tools. Using the settings available in the Tool options box, you can fine-tune how each of these tools work to make editing much easier and more accurate.

In the following exercise, you'll learn how to use the options available for the tools and how to use them to shape the torso of the space suit.

Using Soft Selection

The Soft Selection option lets you determine a range for selection and editing. This range is color coded, which gives you a visual indication of the number of vertices that will be affected as well as the falloff. *Falloff* refers to the area where the effect of the editing tool decreases as the distance from the center of the selection increases. This exercise demonstrates how to activate and edit these options.

1. Switch to the perspective view and turn off X-Ray shading so you can see the geometry more clearly.

2. Choose the Select tool (hot key = **q**), and open the Tool Options box.

3. Right-click the torso, and choose Face from the marking menu. As you hover the mouse pointer over the torso, the face nearest the mouse pointer is highlighted in red. If you switch to edge or vertex selection, the edges or vertices become highlighted as you hover over them.

4. Right-click the torso, and choose Multi from the marking menu. In this mode, you can select any combination of faces, edges, or vertices (see Figure 4.13).

FIGURE 4.13
The Multi selection mode allows you to select multiple types of components at the same time.

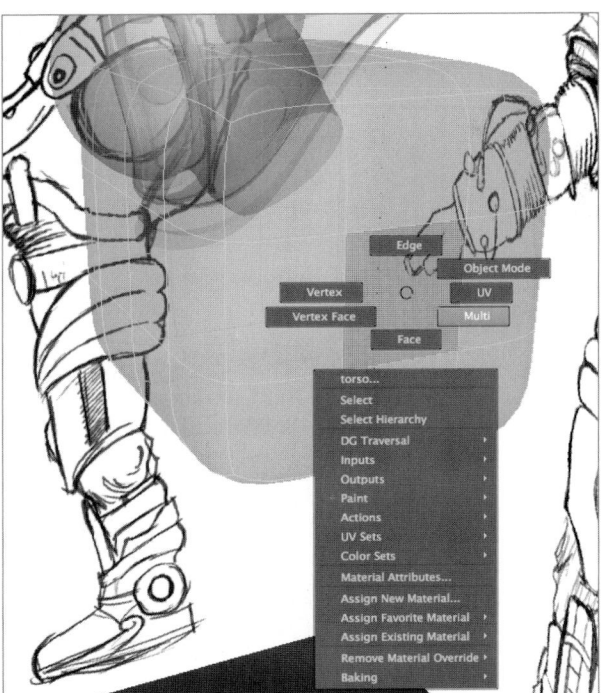

5. Select one of the vertices on the side of the torso.

6. Double-click the Select tool in the toolbox to open the Tool Options box.

7. In the options for the Select tool, enable Soft Select. The wireframe display of the torso becomes colored. The coloring indicates the radius of the soft selection.

8. In the options for the Select tool, look at the Soft Selection section.

   The colored ramp sets the coloring for the Soft Select option. By default, components that are 100 percent selected are yellow. As the strength of the selection diminishes, the color coding of the components moves to orange and then to black. Areas beyond the black part of the radius are not selected.

9. Increase Falloff Radius to 8. The radius of the color coding increases on the torso model (see Figure 4.14).

FIGURE 4.14
Increasing Falloff Radius expands the number of vertices that are selected on the model.

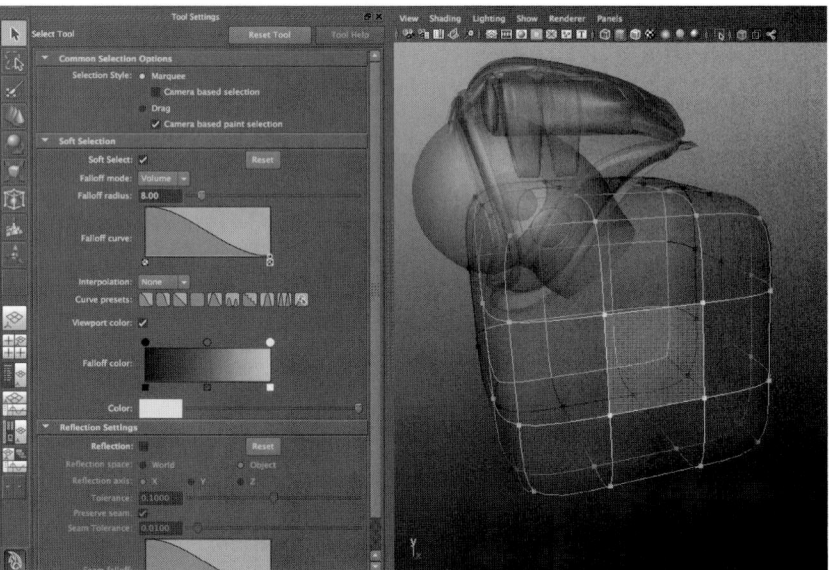

You can set Falloff Mode to Surface, Volume, Global, or Object. In surface mode, the Soft Select radius selects components based on their position on the surface. If you selected a vertex on the upper lip of a character with a closed mouth, the vertices on the lower lip would not be selected, even if they are close to the center of the falloff radius in world space.

When you set Falloff Mode to Volume, any vertex within the falloff radius is selected. So if you select a vertex on the upper lip of the same character, vertices on the lower lip would also be selected if they fall within the falloff radius. Global mode works very similarly to Volume (Figure 4.15).

You can further refine the falloff using Falloff Curve. By adding points to the curve and changing their position, you can create selection shapes. A number of preset curve shapes are available. You can access these by clicking any of the preset icons below Falloff Curve.

Soft Selection is available for the Select, Paint Select, Move, Scale, and Rotate tools.

FIGURE 4.15
Falloff Mode
determines how
the falloff radius
is applied to the
components of a
surface.

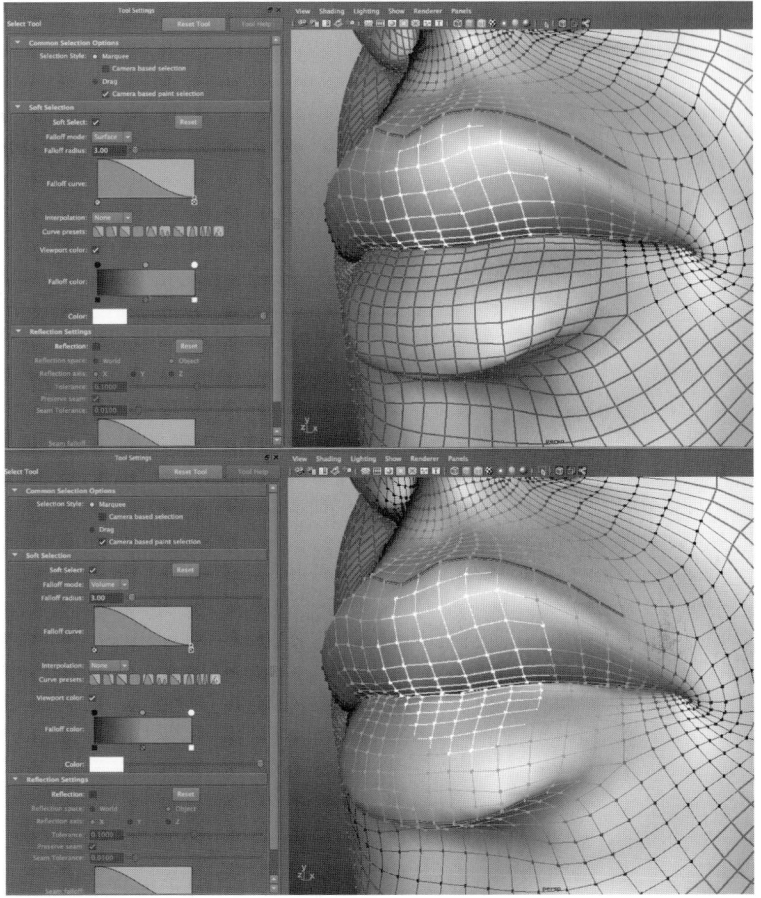

ADDITIONAL SELECTION SETTINGS

Many options are available for customizing selection. These include Reflection, Preserve Seam, Marquee selection, Drag mode, and Camera Based Selection.

Reflection option The Reflection option lets you work on two sides of a model at the same time, thus making it easier to create symmetrical surfaces such as a face. When this is enabled, component selection is mirrored across a specified axis. By default this is set to the x-axis.

Preserve Seam option The Preserve Seam option protects components along the center of the reflection axis from being moved away from the center. This ensures that the symmetry of the model is preserved.

Marquee selection option The Marquee selection option lets you select a component by dragging a rectangular selection box over the components you want to select.

Drag mode In Drag mode, you can paint over the surface to select the components you want. This works similarly to the Paint Selection tool.

Both Marquee selection and Drag selection have a Camera Based Selection option. When this is on, only the components facing the current viewing camera will be selected. When this option is off, any components within the selected area will be selected, including those on the opposite side of the model.

USE SOFT SELECT IN OBJECT MODE

New!

New to Maya 2011, you can now use Soft Select in Object mode. Use this mode when you want to select a large number of unconnected polygon objects. In this case, the falloff radius determines how the influence of the selection diminishes as the distance from the initial selected object increases.

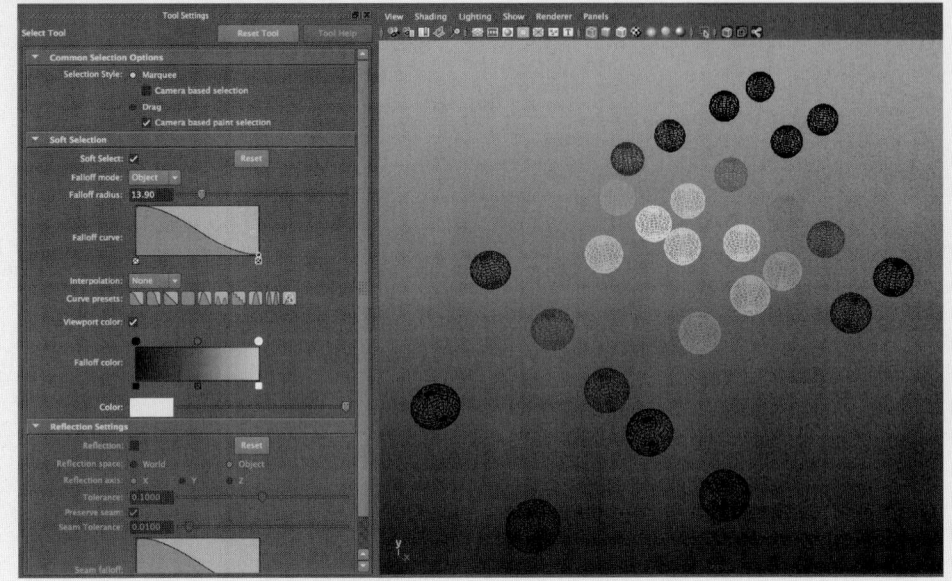

Create the Shape for the Torso

The Move tool has many of the same options as the Select tool. When you change the settings for the Select tool, the same settings are applied to the Move tool, and vice versa.

1. Continue with the space suit model from the previous section.

2. Turn X-Ray mode back on, and switch to a side view of the model.

3. Open the options for the Move tool, and use the following settings:

   Set Move Axis to Local.

   Set Selection Style to Marquee mode.

   Turn off Camera Based Selection.

   Enable Soft Select.

   Set Falloff Mode to Surface.

   Set Falloff Radius to **3**.

   Enable Reflection; the default Reflection setting should work.

4. From the side view, select vertices, and use the Move tool to reposition the vertices of the torso to roughly match the sketch. The torso surface will serve as frame for the upper part of the space suit. At this time you want to keep the amount of detail fairly low.

5. Adjust the selection settings as you work. Align the four corners of one of the faces toward the rear with the arm socket opening in the sketch, as shown in Figure 4.16.

FIGURE 4.16
Use the Move tool to position the vertices of the torso to match the sketches on the image planes.

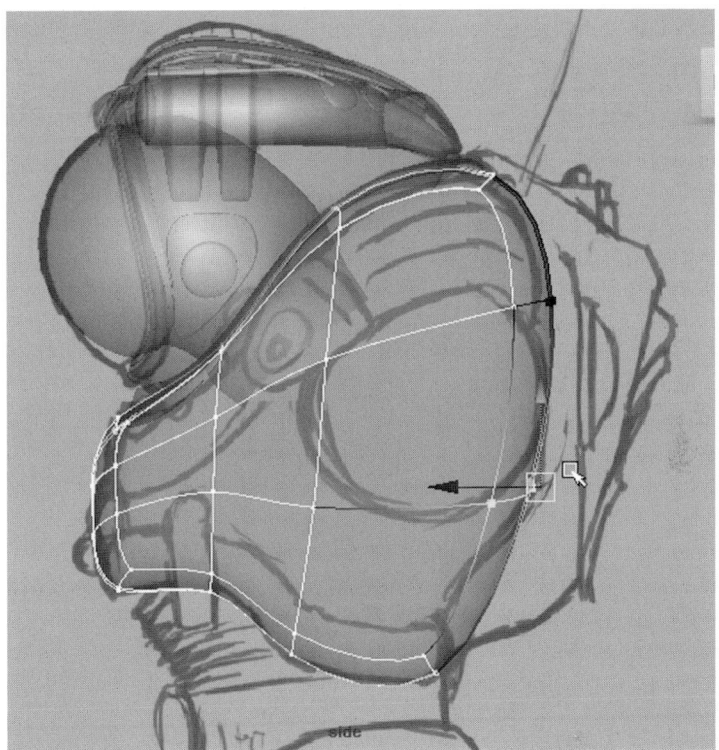

SMOOTH MESH VERTEX DISPLAY

As you select vertices using the Move tool, you'll notice that the handle of the Move tool is offset from the selected vertices. If you find this confusing, press the **2** key to see a wireframe cage of the original mesh. Then you'll see the actual positions of the vertices on the unsmoothed version of the surface.

---

6. Switch to the front view, and continue to shape the cube to roughly match the drawing. Remember, your goal is to create a rough shape at this point. Most of the details will be added as additional sections of armor later (see Figure 4.17).

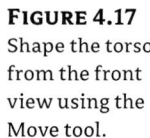

FIGURE 4.17
Shape the torso from the front view using the Move tool.

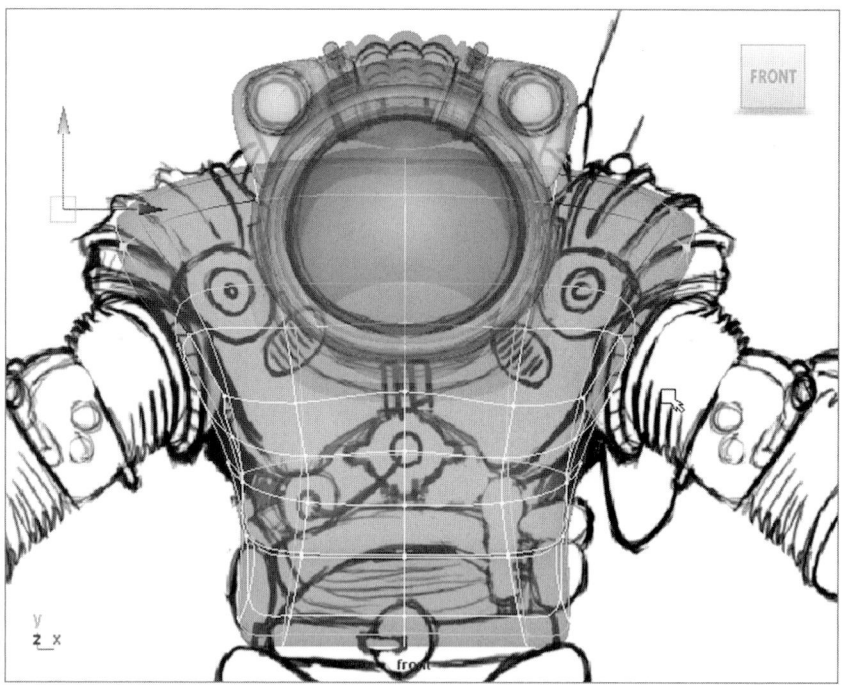

Since you've already shaped much of the profile in the side view, restrict the changes you make in the front view to movements along the x-axis.

7. Finally, switch to the perspective view, and shape the torso further. This requires some imagination and artistic judgment as to how the shape of the space suit looks in perspective. It may be easier to do this if you turn off X-Ray mode and set the helmet display layer to Template mode.

   Don't forget to refer to the original sketch; if you switch to the referenceImage camera, you'll see the sketch on an image plane. Also remember to adjust your Move tool selection settings as needed. Always keep things as simple as possible, and avoid getting lost in the details.

8. Save the scene as **torso_v02.ma**.

To see a version of the scene to this point, open the `torso_v02.ma` scene from the `chapter4\` `scenes` directory on the DVD.

TWEAK MODE

You can activate tweak mode for the Move tool in the Move tool options. When this is on, any component you touch is nudged in the direction of the mouse pointer movement. Combined with Soft Select, the Move tool feels much more like a sculpting tool, and changes are more intuitive. Note that the Move tool manipulator is not displayed when tweak mode is activated.

Adding Components

Polygon components such as vertices, edges, and faces can be added to a model as you work. This is how a simple cube can eventually be shaped into a car or a space suit. Adding components is achieved using the tools in the Edit Mesh menu of the Polygon menu set.

Insert Edge Loops

An edge loop is an unbroken ring of edges that traverses polygon geometry, similar to an isoparm in NURBS geometry. Think of the circular area around your lips and eyes. In 3D modeling, these areas are often defined using edge loops. You can insert edge loops into a model interactively using the Insert Edge Loops tool.

1. Continue with the scene from the previous section, or open the `torso_v02.ma` scene from the `chapter4\scenes` directory on the DVD.

2. Select the Polygons menu set from the upper-left menu in the interface.

3. Switch to the side view.

4. Select the torso object, and choose Edit Mesh ➢ Insert Edge Loop Tool. The wireframe cage appears around the torso while the tool is active.

5. Click one of the cage's edges at the bottom row of the torso, as shown in Figure 4.18.

FIGURE 4.18
Add an edge loop at the base of the torso.

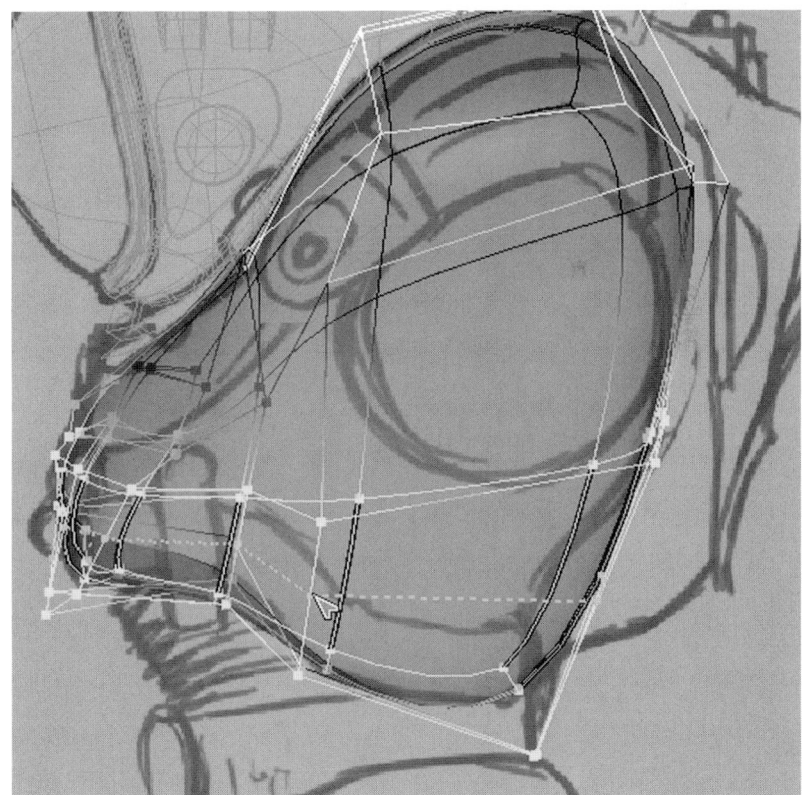

Edge loops are always added perpendicular to the selected edge. The loop continues to divide polygons along the path of faces until it encounters a three-sided or *n*-sided (more than four-sided) polygon (Figure 4.19).

6. Once you have inserted the edge loop, press **q** to drop the tool (as long as the tool is active, you can continue to insert edge loops in a surface).

7. Select the vertices created by the new edge loop path, and continue to shape the torso using the Move tool (Figure 4.20).

8. Save the scene as **torso_v03.ma**.

To see a version of the scene to this point, open the torso_v03.ma scene from the chapter4\ scenes directory on the DVD.

FIGURE 4.19
The Edge Loop tool divides along a path of four-sided polygons (left image). The path of the edge loop stops when a three-sided or *n*-sided polygon is encountered (right image).

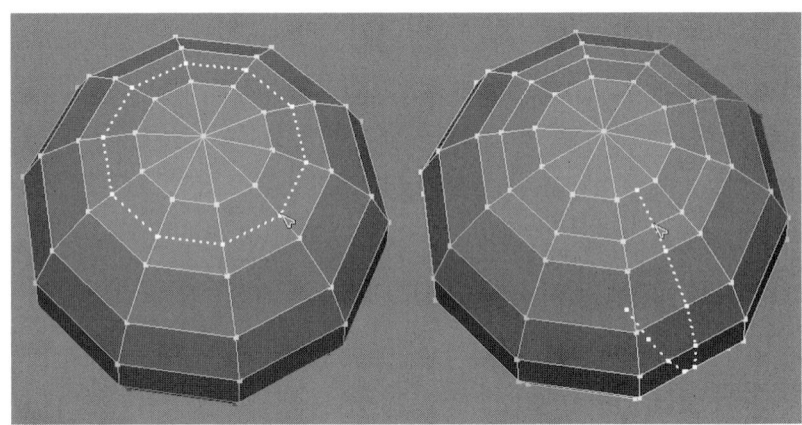

FIGURE 4.20
Shape the torso using the new vertices added with the inserted edge loop.

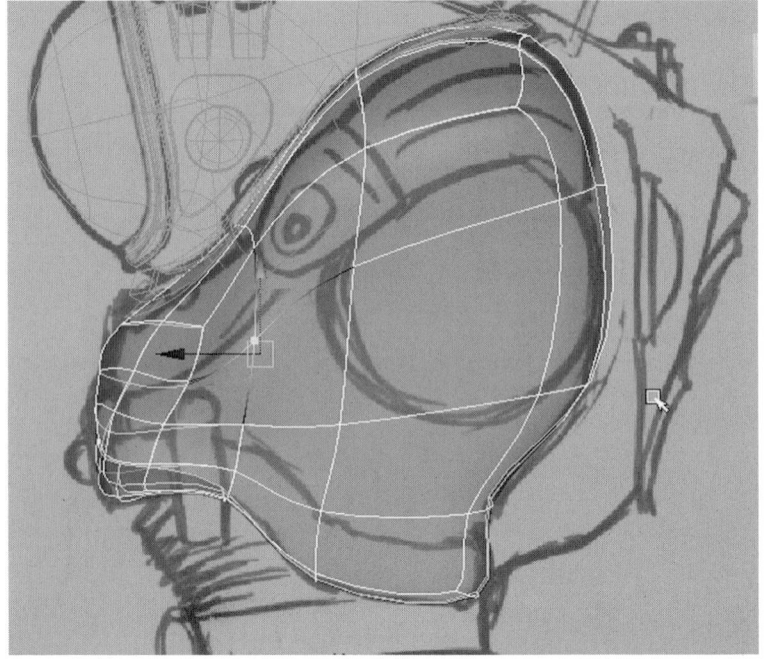

BE STINGY WITH YOUR EDGE LOOPS

It's always tempting to add a lot of divisions to a surface to have more vertices available for sculpting detail. However, this often leads to a very confusing and disorganized modeling process. Keep the number of vertices in your meshes as low as possible. Add only exactly what you need, when you need it. If you are disciplined about keeping your models simple, you'll find the modeling process much easier and more enjoyable. Too many vertices too early in the process will make you feel like you're sculpting with bubblegum.

Extruding Polygons

Extruding a polygon face adds geometry to a surface by creating an offset between the extruded edge or face. New polygon faces are then automatically added to fill the gap between the extruded edge or face. In this section, you'll see a couple of the ways to use extrusions to shape the torso of the space suit.

1. Continue with the scene from the previous section, or open the `torso_v03.ma` scene from the `chapter4\scenes` directory on the DVD.

2. Switch to the perspective view, and turn off X-Ray shading.

3. Right-click the model, and choose Face to switch to face selection mode.

4. Select the face on the side that corresponds with the placement of the arm socket. Shift+click the matching face on the opposite side.

5. Choose Edit Mesh ➤ Extrude. A manipulator appears at the position of the new extruded face.

6. Click and drag on the blue arrow of the manipulator to move the extruded face toward the center of the torso. The extruded face on the opposite side should move into the center as well.

7. Open the Channel Box.

8. Under the channels for the polyExtrudeFace1 node, scroll toward the bottom, and set Divisions to **2**. This increases the number of polygons used to bridge the gap between the extruded face at the torso (Figure 4.21).

9. Select the six faces on the top of the torso that are directly beneath the NURBS helmet. It's a good idea to turn on Camera Based Selection in the Select Tool options. This prevents you from accidentally selecting faces on the opposite side of the torso. You can also turn off Soft Select.

FIGURE 4.21
Extrude the face at the side of the torso inward. Set the divisions of the extruded faces to **2**.

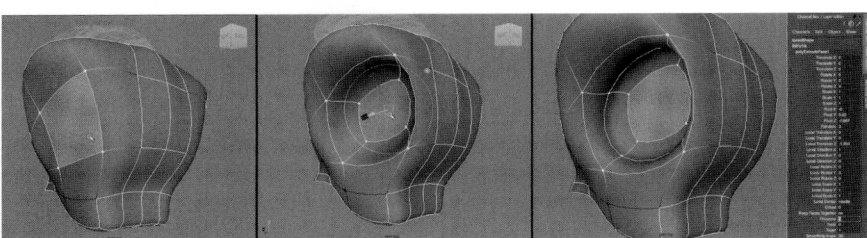

10. Choose Edit Mesh ➢ Extrude.

11. Click one of the scale cubes at the end of the manipulator handle (at the tip of one of the arrows). This switches the manipulator to Scale mode.

12. Drag to the left on the light blue cube at the center of the manipulator to scale down the extruded faces.

13. Set the Divisions value of the polyExtrudeFace2 node to **2**.

14. Drag the blue arrow of the extrude manipulator downward to create a depression at the top of the torso (Figure 4.22).

15. Turn Soft Select back on, and use the Move tool to shape the torso so it matches the design on the image planes. It may be helpful to set the HELMET display layer to Reference so you can close the gap between the neck opening and the bottom of the helmet. The base of the helmet should stay on top of the torso (Figure 4.23).

16. Save the scene as **torso_v04.ma**.

To see a version of the scene to this point, open the torso_v04.ma scene from the chapter4\ scenes directory on the DVD.

FIGURE 4.22
Create a depression at the top of the torso using an extrude operation.

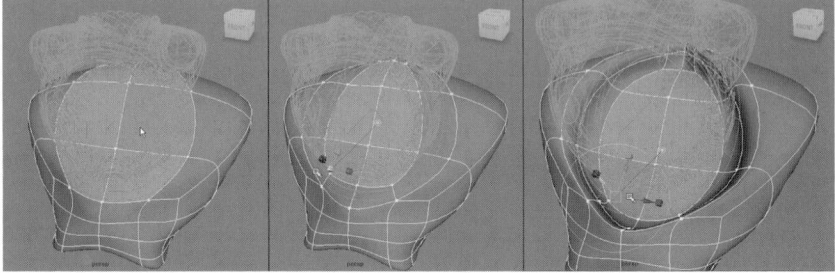

FIGURE 4.23
Shape the top of the torso with the HELMET layer visible. The NURBS helmet acts as a guide while modeling the torso.

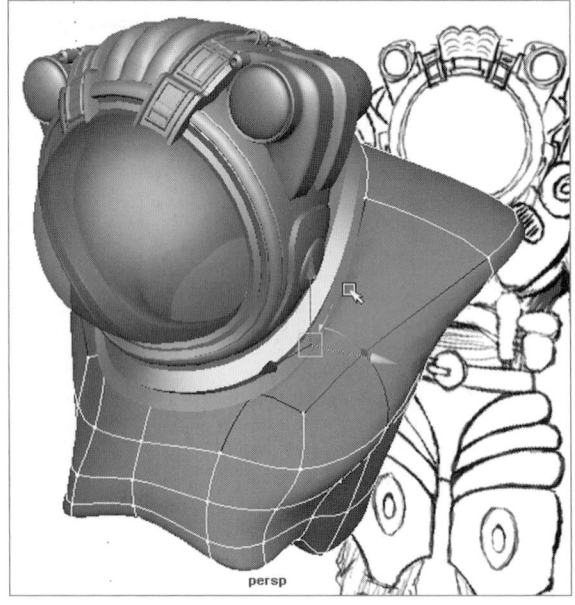

Edge Creasing

One drawback to using the smooth mesh preview on polygon objects is that surfaces can look too smooth and almost pillowy. To add hardness to the edges of a smoothed object, you can use creasing.

In this section, you'll create the arm socket detail so you have a place to insert the arms into the torso (Figure 4.24).

1. Continue with the scene from the previous section, or open the `torso_v04.ma` scene from the `chapter4\scenes` directory on the DVD.

2. Create a polygon sphere (Create ➤ Polygon Primitives ➤ Sphere).

3. In the INPUTS section of the Channel Box, set Subdivisions Axis to **24** and Subdivisions Height to **12**.

4. Switch to a side view, and zoom in on the sphere.

5. Right-click the sphere, and choose Face.

6. In the Select Tool options, set Selection Style to Marquee, and turn off Camera Based Selection.

7. Select the top four rows on the sphere and delete them.

8. Select the bottom three rows on the sphere and delete them as well.

FIGURE 4.24
The arm socket detail on the original sketch

9. Switch to the perspective view. Select the sphere, and name it **socket**.

10. With socket selected, choose Edit Mesh ➤ Extrude. This extrudes all the faces at the same time.

11. Push in on the blue arrow of the extrude manipulator to add some thickness to the socket.

12. Use the Insert Edge Loop tool to insert edge loops on the upper side of the socket, as shown in the third image of Figure 4.25.

FIGURE 4.25
Add thickness to the sphere using the Extrude operation.

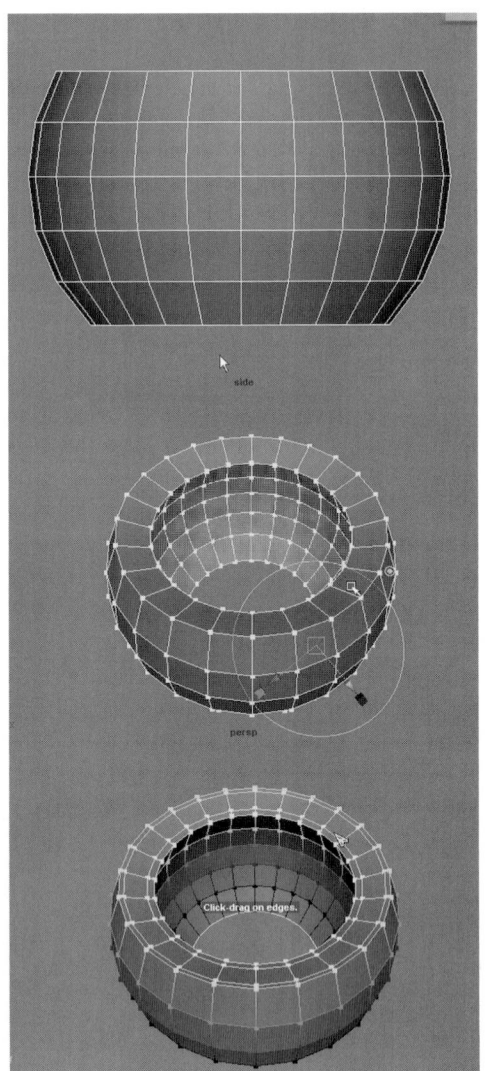

13. Rotate the view so you can clearly see the top of the socket.

14. In the Select Tool options, set Selection Style to Drag, and turn on Camera Based Paint Selection. The mouse pointer turns into a paintbrush icon.

15. Paint a selection around the top of the socket.

16. Select the middle row of polygon faces around the top.

DESELECTING POLYGONS

If you select extra polygons by accident, you can hold the Ctrl key and paint on them to deselect them. To add to the current selection, hold the Shift key while painting the selection.

---

17. With the faces selected, choose Edit Mesh ➤ Extrude.

18. Open the Channel Box for the polyExtrudeFace4 node.

19. Toward the bottom, set Keep Faces Together to off.

20. Click one of the scale cubes at the tip of the arrows on the extrude manipulator to switch to scale mode.

21. Drag on the light blue cube at the center of the manipulator to scale down the extruded faces. Note that with Keep Faces Together turned off, each face is extruded individually.

22. With faces selected, create another extrusion (the **g** hot key repeats the last action).

23. Push up on the blue manipulator to move the extruded faces upward.

24. When you have finished creating the extrusion, press the **q** hot key, or choose another tool to drop the Extrusion tool.

25. Select the socket object, and press the **3** key to switch to smooth mesh preview. The extrusions at the top look like rounded bumps (Figure 4.26).

26. Use the Select tool to select each of the faces at the top of the rounded bumps. Hold the Shift key as you select each face.

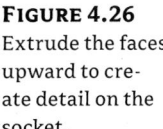
FIGURE 4.26
Extrude the faces upward to create detail on the socket.

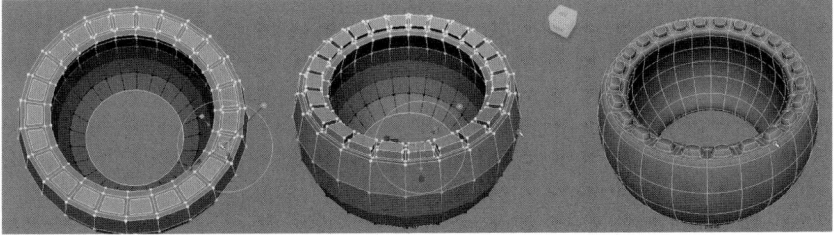

27. Once you have all the faces selected, press Shift+> to expand the selection one time. The faces around each bump are now selected as well.

28. Choose Select ➤ Convert Selection ➤ To Edges. Now the edges are selected instead of the faces.

29. Choose Edit Mesh ➤ Crease Tool.

30. Drag to the right while holding the MMB. The edges become less round as you drag to the right and more round as you drag to the left. Set the creasing so the edges of the bumps are just slightly rounded.

31. Select the socket object, and switch to edge selection mode.

32. Double-click the first edge loop outside the extruded bumps. Double-clicking an edge selects the entire edge loop.

33. Use the Crease tool to create a crease on the selected edge loop.

34. Repeat steps 31–33 for the first edge on the inside the socket just beyond the extruded bumps (Figure 4.27).

FIGURE 4.27
Crease the edges of the extruded bumps to create a more mechanical look.

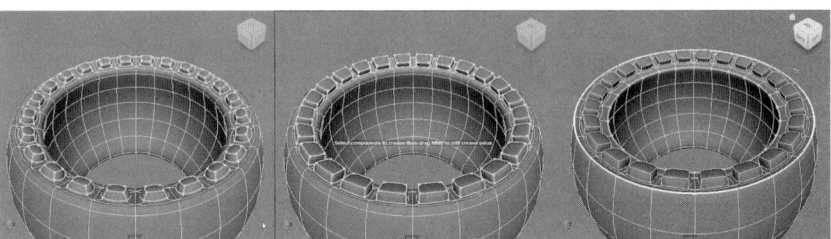

35. Select the socket, and switch to the Move tool.

36. Move, scale, and rotate the socket so it fits into the space on the side of the torso (Figure 4.28).

37. Set these values in the Channel Box:

Translate X: **3.712**

Translate Y: **7.5**

Translate Z: **-2.706**

Rotate X: **11.832**

Rotate Y: **5.385**

Rotate Z: **-116.95**

Scale X: **1.91**

Scale Y: **1.91**

Scale Z: **1.91**

FIGURE 4.28
Position the socket
in the opening
at the side of the
torso.

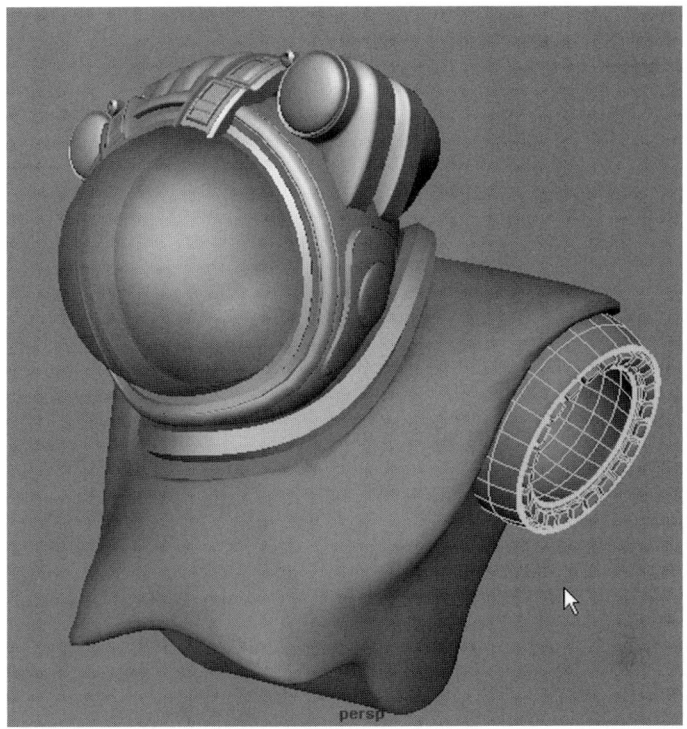

38. After placing the socket, spend a few minutes editing the position of the points on the torso so the socket fits more naturally.

39. Save the scene as **torso_v05.ma**.

To see a version of the scene to this point, open the torso_v05.ma scene from the chapter4\ scenes directory on the DVD.

CREASE SETS

If you create a crease for a number of selected edges that you will later readjust, you can create a crease set. A crease set saves the currently selected creased edges under a descriptive name. To create a crease set, follow these steps:

1. Select some edges that you want to crease or that already have a crease.

2. Choose Edit Mesh ➤ Create Sets ➤ Create Crease Set ➤ Options.

3. In the options, enter a descriptive name for the set.

Any time you want to select the edges again to apply a crease, follow these steps:

1. Choose Edit Mesh ➤ Crease Sets.

2. Choose the name of the set from the list.

The edges will then be selected, and you can apply or adjust the creasing as needed.

Mirror Cut

The Mirror Cut tool creates symmetry in a model across a specified axis. The tool creates a cutting plane. Any geometry on one side of the plane is duplicated onto the other side and simultaneously merged with the original geometry.

The back side of the shoulder armor is not visible in the image (Figure 4.29), so we're going to assume that it's a mirror image of the geometry on the front side. You'll model the front side first and then use Mirror Cut for the geometry across the z-axis to make the back.

FIGURE 4.29
The shoulder armor is the next object to model.

In this section, you'll model the geometry for the space suit's shoulder armor. You'll start by modeling the armor as a flat piece and then bend it into shape later.

In the options for Mirror Cut, you can raise the Tolerance, which will help prevent extra vertices from being created along the centerline of the model. If you raise it too high, the vertices near the center may be collapsed. You may have to experiment to find the right setting.

1. Continue with the scene from the previous section, or open the `torso_v05.ma` scene from the `chapter4\scenes` directory on the DVD.

2. Create a new display layer named **TORSO**.

3. Add the torso and the socket geometry to this layer, and turn off the visibility of the layer.

4. Turn off the visibility of the other layers as well so you have a clear view of the grid.

5. Create a polygon pipe by choosing Create ➢ Polygon Primitives ➢ Pipe.

6. In the polyPipe1 node (under the INPUTS section of the Channel Box), use the following settings:

   Height: **1**

   Subdivisions Axis: **24**

   Subdivisions Caps: **2**

7. Switch to the top view.

8. Choose the Move tool.

9. In the Options box, set Selection Style to Marquee, and turn off Camera Based Selection. This way you can select vertices on the top and bottom of the geometry from the top view.

10. Turn off Soft Select, and turn on Reflection. Make sure Reflection Axis is set to the x-axis.

11. Right-click the pipe, and choose Vertex.

12. Select the vertices on the outer edge of the pipe in the top half of the screen.

13. Use the Scale and Move tools to move them away from the pipe.

14. Scale them up so the upper edge of the pipe has a shallow arc, as shown in the top image of Figure 4.30.

FIGURE 4.30
Select, move, and scale the vertices at one end of the pipe.

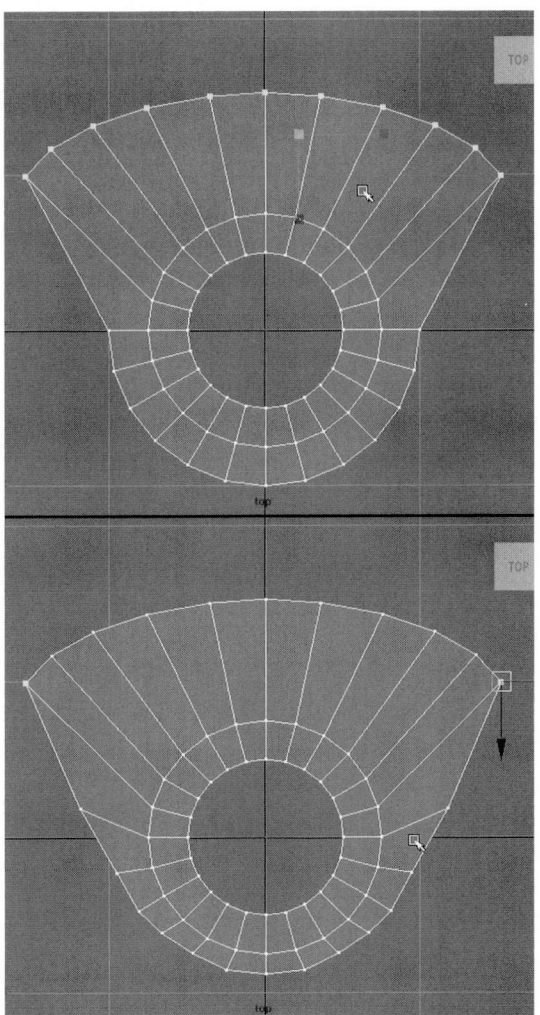

15. Select the vertices on the outer edge of the pipe at the bottom of the screen.

16. Use the Move tool to shape these vertices so they are slightly closer to the center. Use the bottom image in Figure 4.30 as a reference.

17. Switch to the perspective view.

18. Turn on Marquee and Camera Based Selection in the Select Tool options.

19. Select the faces at the wide end of the pipe, shown in the first image in Figure 4.31.

FIGURE 4.31
Extrude and scale the faces at the long side of the pipe.

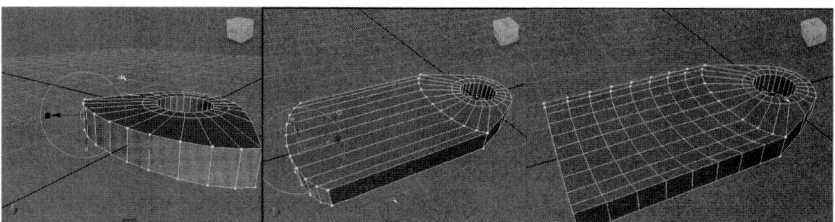

20. Choose Edit Mesh ➤ Extrude to perform an extrusion on these faces. Before you move the extrusion with the manipulator, click the blue circle switch on the manipulator to switch to extrude in world space (the second image in Figure 4.31).

21. Pull on the blue arrow of the manipulator to extend the face about three and a half units.

22. Use the blue scale handle of the extrude manipulator to flatten the arc in these extruded faces.

23. In the INPUTS section of the Channel Box, set Divisions for the polyExtrudeFace6 node to **8**.

24. Select the pipe, and choose Mesh ➤ Mirror Cut. A plane appears at the center of the pipe.

25. In the Channel Box, set the Y rotation of mirrorCutPlane1 to **0**. The pipe is now mirrored across the z-axis.

26. Set the Translate Z channel of mirrorCutPlane1 to **-3.42**. The mirrored geometry is extended. If you see extra triangular polygons appear near the cutting plane, try moving the plane back and forth a little until they disappear.

DISAPPEARING POLYGONS

It may look as though polygons disappear when you use the Mirror Cut tool. It might just be that Maya is not displaying them correctly. If this happens to you, select the object and apply a Lambert shader to it (just switch to the Rendering shelf and click the Lambert material icon). This should fix the problem.

In the Outliner, several new nodes have been created. These include the mirrorCutPlane1 and the mirroredCutMesh1 group. The pipe has been renamed polySurface1 (Figure 4.32).

FIGURE 4.32
Mirror the pipe across the z-axis using the Mirror Cut tool.

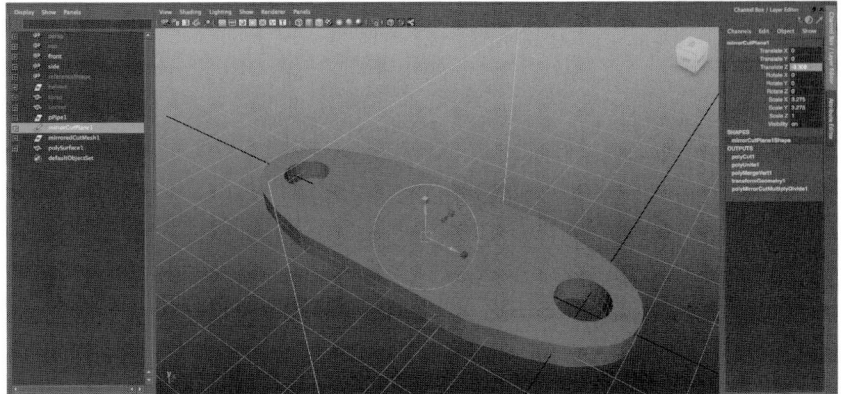

27. Select the polySurface1 node, and choose Edit ➤ Delete By Type ➤ History. This removes the group nodes that were created. Select the mirrorCutPlane1 node, and delete it.

28. Name the polySurface1 node **shoulderArmor1**.

    Figure 4.33 shows some of the changes that were made to the shoulderArmor1 object to make it match the shoulder armor in the image using the Insert Edge Loop tool and the Extrude operation.

29. Save the scene as `torso_v06.ma`.

    To see a version of the scene to this point, open the `torso_v06.ma` scene from the `chapter4\scenes` directory on the DVD.

FIGURE 4.33
Additional changes are made to the shoulderArmor1 object.

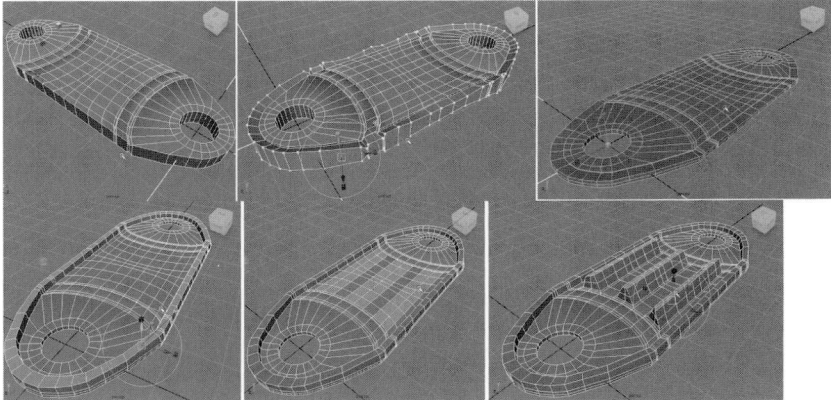

Modeling with Deformers

Deformers are used to bend, twist, and otherwise warp geometry. They are often used as Animation and Rigging tools but are quite helpful when modeling as well.

In this section, you'll use several deformers to bend the shoulder armor into a shape that matches the design in the original concept sketch.

Using a Lattice

The lattice creates a rectangular cage around a selected surface. You can move, scale, and rotate the points of the lattice to deform the selected object.

1. Continue using the scene from the previous section, or open the `torso_v06.ma` scene from the `chapter4\scenes` directory on the DVD.

2. Select the shoulderArmor1 object.

3. Choose Modify ➢ Center Pivot to place the pivot point at the center of the surface.

4. Turn on the TORSO and HELMET display layers so you can see the other parts of the model.

5. Move the shoulderArmor1 object roughly above the shoulder of the torso. Try the following settings (see Figure 4.34):

   Translate X: **4.327**

   Translate Y: **10.364**

   Translate Z: **0.21**

   Scale X: **0.783**

   Scale Y: **0.177**

   Scale Z: **0.783**

6. With the shoulderArmor1 object selected, press the **3** key to switch to smooth mesh preview.

7. Switch to the Animation menu set, and choose Create Deformers ➢ Lattice.

FIGURE 4.34
Position the armor above the shoulder.

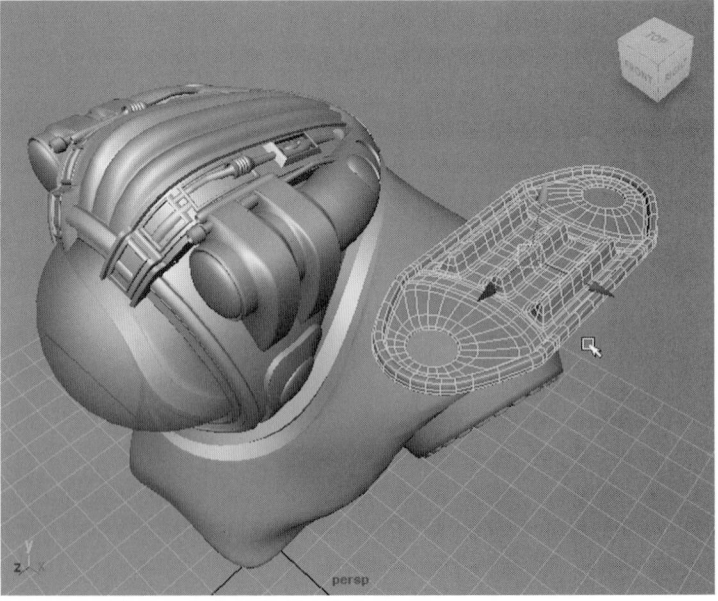

LATTICE NODES

There are two nodes created when you make a lattice: ffd1Lattice node and ffd1Base node. The letters *ffd* stand for "free-form deformer." The changes you make to the lattice are made to the ffd1Lattice node. The changes in the shape of the ffd1Lattice cage are compared with the shape of the ffd1Base node, and the difference in the shape is transferred to the deformed object. If you need to move, scale, or rotate a lattice to match the position, size, and orientation of the object you want to deform, make sure you apply the transformations to both the ffd1Lattice and ffd1Base nodes. You can group them together and apply transformations to the group.

Before you edit the points of the lattice, you need to change the settings on the lattice so it's set up to deform the object correctly.

8. Select the ffd1Lattice node in the Outliner, and open its Attribute Editor.

9. Switch to the ffd1 tab, and turn off the Local option. This makes the deformation of the object smoother.

   When Local is on, changes to the lattice points affect only the object nearest the selected lattice point. When Local is off, changes made to the lattice points are applied more evenly to the entire object, resulting in a smoother deformation.

10. Switch to the ffd1LatticeShape tab, and enter the following settings:

    S Divisions: **9**

    T Divisions: **2**

    U Divisions: **15**

    This changes the way the lattice is divided.

11. Open the options for the Move tool.

12. Turn off Soft Select, and turn on Reflection.

13. Set Reflection Space to Object and Reflection Axis to Z.

14. Right-click the lattice, and choose Lattice Point. (Sometimes this is tricky if you are right-clicking both the lattice and the surface. Right-click a corner of the lattice that has empty space behind it.)

15. Drag a marquee selection over the lattice points at the front of the lattice.

16. Select the first six rows of lattice points, as shown in Figure 4.35. The points in the back of the lattice will be selected as well because of the Move tool's Reflection settings.

17. Switch to the Rotate tool, and drag on the red circle at the center of the tool to rotate the lattice points along the x-axis.

18. Use both the Rotate tool and the Move tool to position the lattice points so the shoulder armor has a bend at the front and back (see Figure 4.36).

FIGURE 4.35
Select the first
six rows of lattice
points.

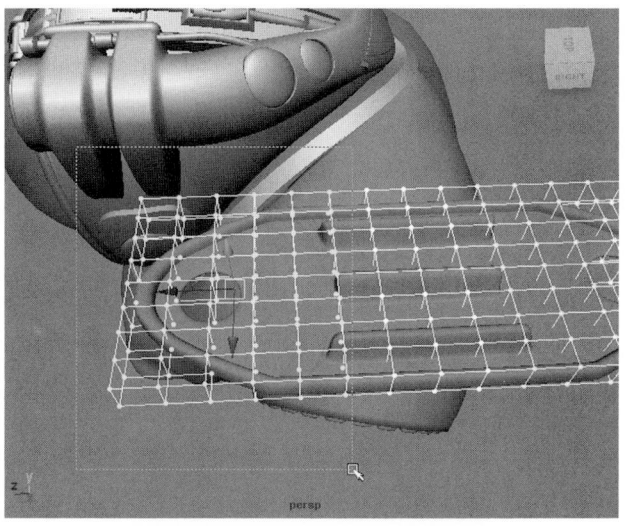

FIGURE 4.36
Rotate the selected
lattice points and
move them into posi-
tion to create a bend
in the surface.

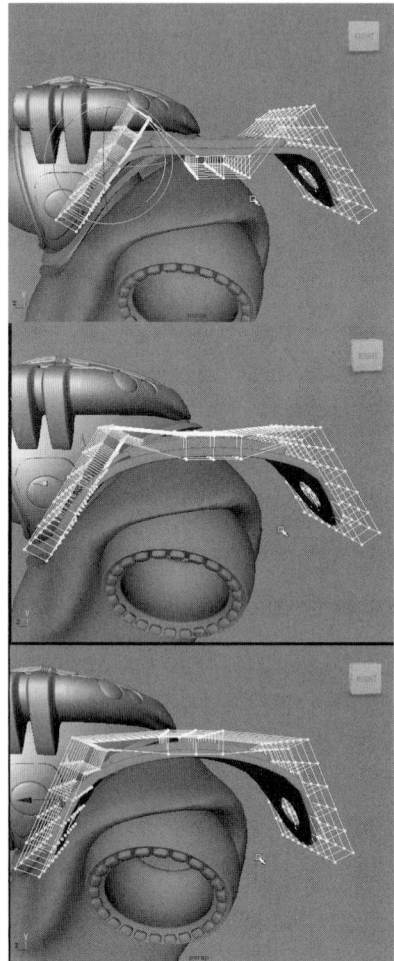

19. When you are happy with the bend created in the shoulderArmor1 object, select the object in the Outliner, and choose Edit ➤ Delete By Type ➤ History. This deletes the lattice nodes and makes the changes to the object permanent.

20. Save the scene as **torso_v07.ma**.

To see a version of the scene up to this point, open the torso_v07.ma scene from the chapter4\ scenes directory on the DVD.

Soft Modification Tool

The Soft Modification tool is a special deformer designed to help you sculpt objects. Using it is similar to activating the Soft Select option in the Move tool. In fact, the Soft Modification tool was the predecessor to the Soft Select option.

1. Continue with the scene from the previous section, or open the torso_v07.ma scene from the chapter4\scenes directory on the DVD.

2. Select shoulderArmor1 in the Outliner, and select the Soft Modification icon in the toolbox. It's the icon that shows a red arrow pulling up the vertices of a blue surface.

When you activate the Soft Modification tool, the surface turns orange and yellow. The colors indicate the strength of the tool's falloff, similar to the color coding used by the Soft Select option on the Move tool.

When you activate the Soft Modification tool, you'll see options in the toolbox to edit the tool's falloff. However, when you edit the settings, you'll see no change in the tool that is currently active in the viewport window. What's happening is that these settings will be applied to the tool the next time you use it.

3. To edit the settings for the currently active Soft Modification tool, open the Attribute Editor, and select the softMod1 tab.

4. Set Falloff Radius to **3.3**.

5. Pull up on the green arrow of the Soft Modification tool to add a rounded warp to the surface. Use the scale handles to shape the surface of the armor.

6. Switch to the Channel Box for the softMod1Handle, and enter these settings (the result is shown in Figure 4.37):

Translate Y: **1.526**

Scale X: **1.513**

Scale Z: **1.472**

7. In the toolbox, choose the Select tool. The Soft Modification handle and node disappear, and the changes are committed to the surface.

FIGURE 4.37
The Soft Modifi-
cation tool adds
a slight spherical
bend to the
surface.

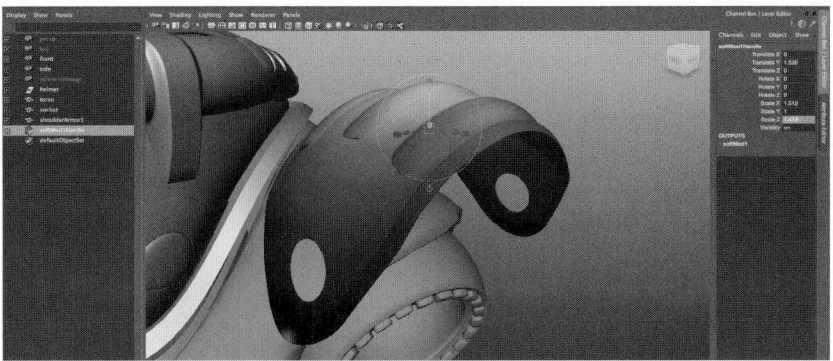

8. Select the shoulderArmor1 object, and use the Move, Rotate, and Scale tools to position it over the shoulder of the torso to match the concept sketch. Try these settings:

   Translate X: **4.327**

   Translate Y: **9**

   Translate Z: **0.775**

   Rotate X: **-3.379**

   Rotate Y: **4.324**

   Rotate Z: **-38.9**

   Scale X: **0.778**

   Scale Y: **0.176**

   Scale Z: **0.778**

9. Use the Move tool with Soft Select activated to move the vertices, and continue to shape the shoulderArmor1 object. Try using the Crease tool to add creases to some of the edges (see Figure 4.38).

10. Save the scene as **torso_v08.ma**.

To see a version of the scene to this point, open torso_v08.ma from the chapter4\scenes directory on the DVD.

FIGURE 4.38
Shape the
shoulderArmor1
object using the
Move tool and the
Crease tool.

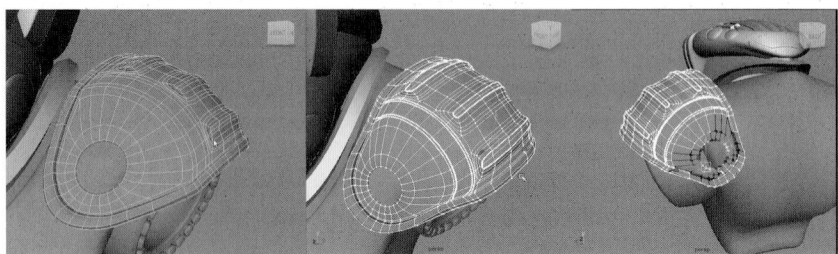

Combining Meshes

The Combine operation places two or more polygon meshes under a single transform node. Once they are combined, you can then use polygon-editing tools to merge edges and vertices.

Creating the Bolt Detail

To create the large bolt detail on the shoulder armor, you'll combine several simple polygon primitives.

1. Continue with the scene from the previous section, or open the torso_v08.ma scene from the chapter4\scenes directory on the DVD.

2. Choose Create ➤ Polygon Primitives ➤ Torus.

3. In the polyTorus1 node (under the INPUTS section of the Channel Box), set Subdivisions Axis to **20** and Subdivisions Height to **4**.

4. In the options for the Select tool, turn off Reflection and Soft Select.

5. Right-click the torus, and choose Edge.

6. Double-click one of the edges on the top of the torus to select the edge loop.

7. Scale these edges inward, and move them down toward the center of the torus to create a beveled edge on the inner ring of the torus. See the upper-left image of Figure 4.39.

8. Use the Insert Edge Loop tool to create two new edge loops, one just outside the hole and one halfway down the top of the torus, as shown in the upper-right image of Figure 4.39.

9. Select the torus and press **3** to switch to smooth mesh preview.

FIGURE 4.39
Create the bolt detail using a torus and a sphere. Create the groove in the sphere with an Extrude operation.

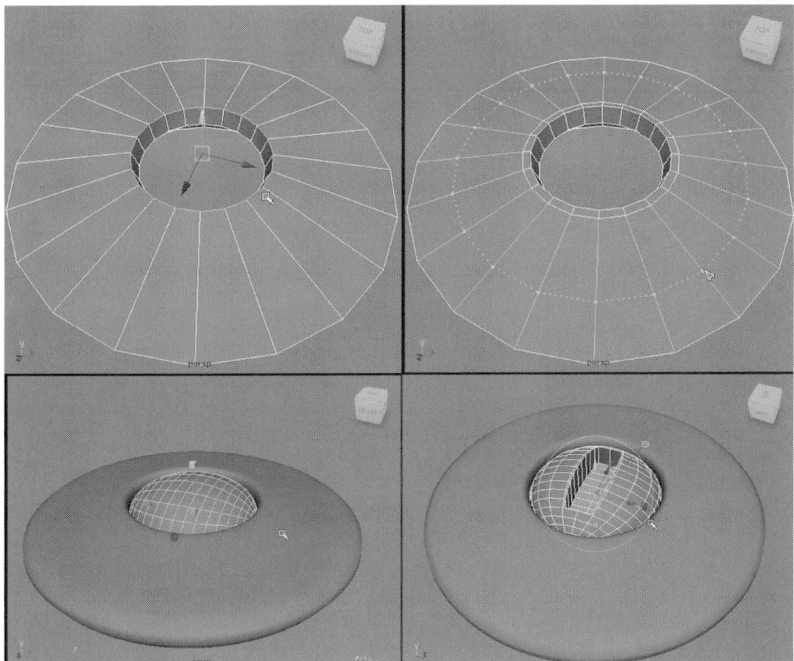

10. Create a polygon sphere, and place it at the center on the torus.

11. Rotate it 90 degrees on the z-axis, and use the Scale tool to flatten the sphere, as shown in the lower-left image of Figure 4.39.

12. To create the groove in the bolt, select two rows of faces at the top of the sphere.

13. Extrude the selected faces once and scale the extrusion slightly inward; extrude again and push the faces of the second extrusion down into the sphere. This is shown in the lower-right image of Figure 4.39.

14. A smooth mesh preview surface can't be combined with a normal polygon object. Select the sphere, and press **3** to switch to the smooth mesh preview.

15. Shift+click the sphere and the torus, and choose Mesh ➤ Combine. The two surfaces now share the same transform and shape nodes.

16. In the Outliner, the combined surface is renamed polySurface1. Select this surface, and choose Edit ➤ Delete By Type ➤ History.

    When the surfaces are combined, you'll see the original surface nodes appear as groups in the Outliner. Deleting the history on the surface removes these groups. If you decide that you need to move a surface after combining it with another surface, you can select the transform node parented to these groups and use the Move tool to reposition the surface. Once you delete history, this is no longer possible.

17. Use the Crease tool to add creasing to the edges around the center ring of the torus and to the edges around the groove in the bolt.

18. Use the Move tool to tweak the position of the edge loops (see Figure 4.40).

FIGURE 4.40
Refine the shape of the bolt by creasing and moving some of the edge loops on the surfaces.

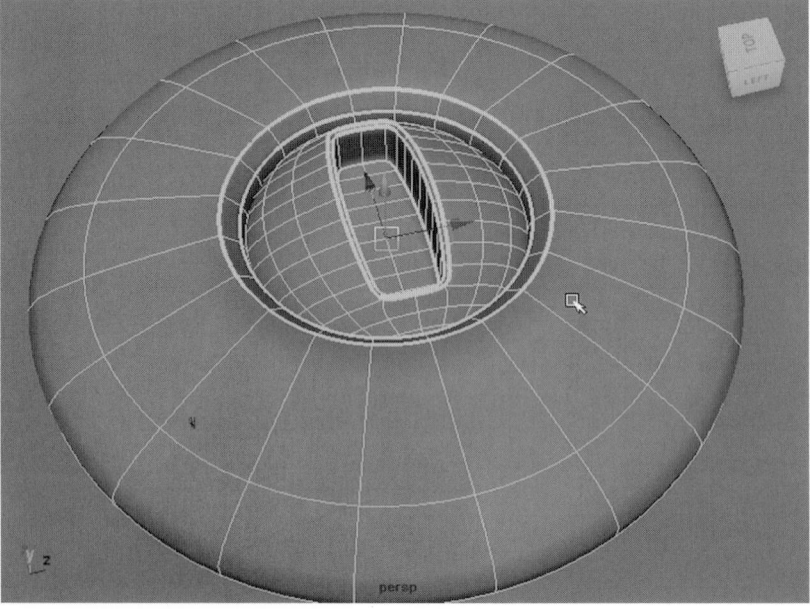

SELECTING PARTS OF COMBINED SURFACES

Double-click a face to select all the connected faces in a mesh. This is one way to select one of the parts of a combined mesh after you've deleted history on the object. You can then use the Move tool to reposition the selected faces.

19. Select the polySurface1 object, and use the Move, Rotate, and Scale tools to position it in the hole in the front of the shoulderArmor1 object.

20. Try these settings in the Channel Box:

    Translate X: **3.806**

    Translate Y: **8.237**

    Translate Z: **-.034**

    Rotate X: **84.726**

    Rotate Y: **13.881**

    Rotate Z: **11.096**

    Scale X: **0.291**

    Scale Y: **0.291**

    Scale Z: **0.291**

21. Duplicate polySurface1, and position the duplicate in the hole on the back side of the armor.

22. Shift+click the shoulderArmor1 and both polySurface objects, and choose Mesh ➢ Combine.

23. Delete history on the new combined surface, and rename it **shoulderArmor1**.

24. Select the vertices of the shoulderArmor1 object, and use the Move tool to close any gaps between the combined surfaces.

25. Use the Crease Edges tool to create a crease in the edges around the bolts (see Figure 4.41).

26. Save the scene as **torso_v09.ma**.

To see a version of the scene to this point, open the torso_v09.ma scene from the chapter4\ scenes directory on the DVD.

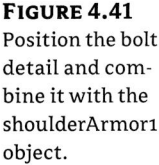

FIGURE 4.41
Position the bolt detail and combine it with the shoulderArmor1 object.

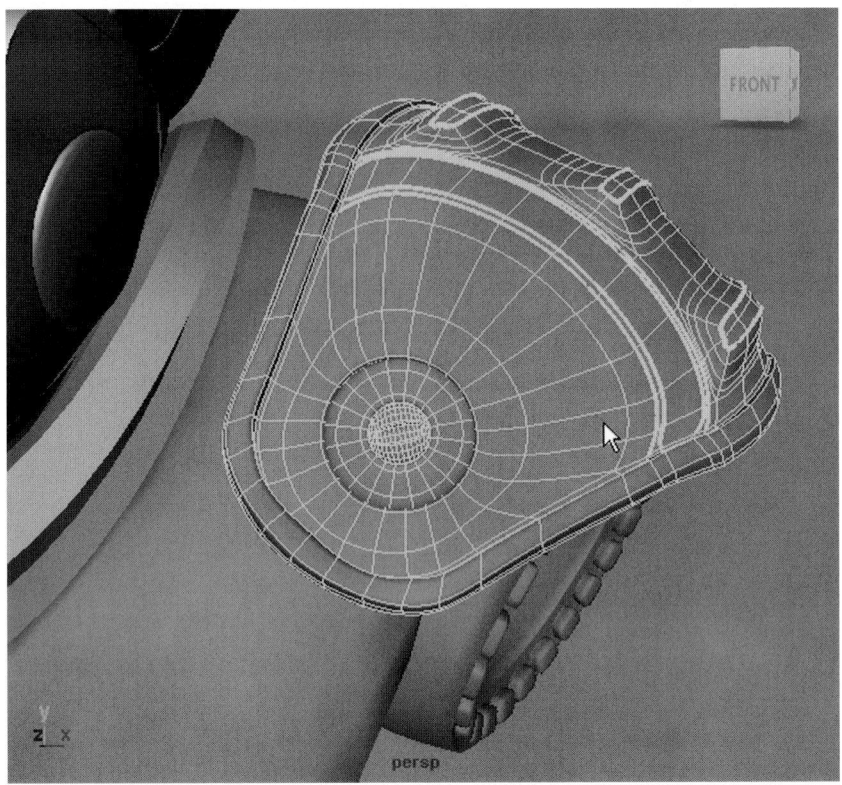

Using Bevel Plus and Bevel Edges

The Bevel Plus tool is normally used to create 3D text for logos, but it is actually very useful as a way to extrude shapes made with curves. In this section, you'll use Bevel Plus to create the design on the chest plate of the space suit.

Creating the Curves

To start the design, you'll create curve outlines that follow the pattern on the chest armor shown in Figure 4.42.

1. Open the chestDetail_v01.ma scene from the chapter4\scenes directory on the DVD. The chest armor has already been started in this scene using techniques described in previous parts of the chapter.

2. Switch to the front camera. Turn on Grid Snapping, and make sure the grid is visible.

3. Choose Create ➢ CV Curve Tool ➢ Options.

FIGURE 4.42
You'll create the
curves to match
the design on the
chest armor in the
sketch.

ANNOTATED GUIDES

Many of the steps used to create the space suit involve variations on the techniques already covered in the previous sections of the chapter. Because of the space limitations of the book, I can't describe every step used to create the suit in the text. However, I have included annotated files that briefly describe the steps left out of the text. Take a look at the `chestarmorStart.ma` file in the `chapter4\ scenes` directory to see how the chest armor plate was created for this section.

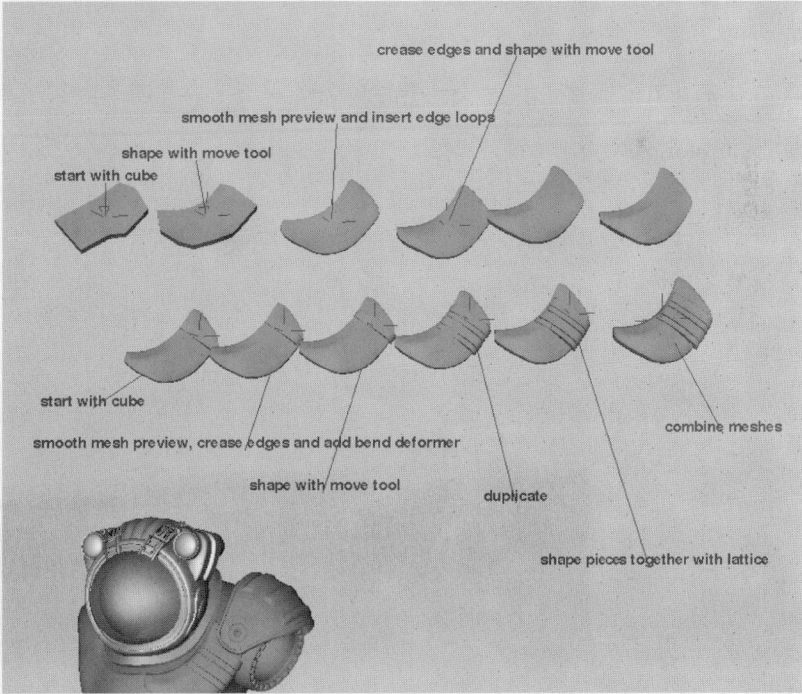

4. In the options, make sure Curve Degree is set to Cubic (see the upper-left panel of Figure 4.43).

5. Draw an S curve, as shown in the upper right of Figure 4.43. Snap each point to the grid as you go. The curve should have about 14 CVs total (resulting in 11 spans).

6. Turn Grid Snapping off, and use the Move tool to rearrange the points on the curve so that the spiral shapes are smoother (see the upper-right panel of Figure 4.43).

7. Select the curve, and switch to the Surfaces menu set.

8. Choose Edit Curves ➤ Offset ➤ Offset Curve. This creates a second curve offset from the first.

9. Select the second curve, and delete its history (Edit ➤ Delete By Type ➤ History).

10. Select the offset curve, and choose Edit Curves ➤ Rebuild Curve ➤ Options.

11. In the options, set Number Of Spans to **11**. Click Rebuild.

12. Use the Move tool to shape the CVs of the second curve.

13. Shift+click both curves, and choose Edit Curves ➤ Attach Curves ➤ Options.

14. In the options, set Attach Method to Blend and disable Keep Originals. Click Attach to perform the operation. One end of the two curves will be joined (see the lower-left panel of Figure 4.43).

FIGURE 4.43
Draw a curve in the front view (upper images). Create a duplicate curve using the Curve Offset operation (lower left). Join the duplicate to the original, and shape it with the Move tool (lower right).

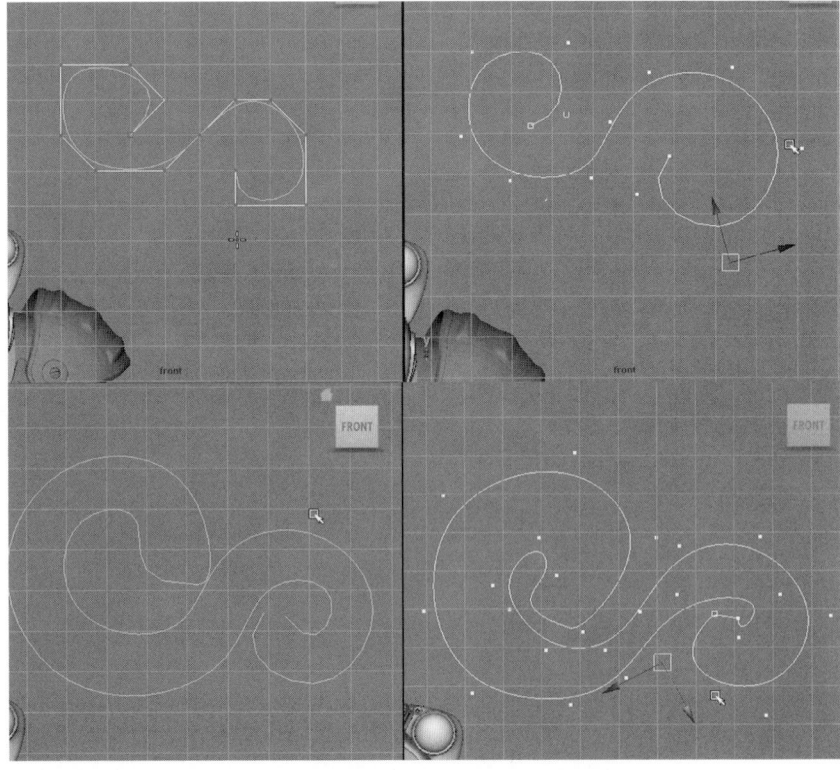

15. Select the curves, and choose Edit Curves ➤ Open/Close Curves. This closes the other end of the curves.

16. Delete the history on the curve.

17. Press the **3** key to smooth the display of the curve.

18. Use the Move tool to reposition the points of the curve to create the spiral S curve design (see the lower-right panel of Figure 4.43).

19. Save the scene as **chestDetail_v02.ma**.

To see a version of the scene to this point, open the chestDetail_v02.ma scene from the chapter4\scenes directory on the DVD.

Bevel Plus

The Bevel Plus tool extrudes a curve and adds a bevel to the extrusion. The bevel can be shaped using the options in the Bevel Plus tool.

1. Continue with the scene from the previous section, or open the chestDetail_v02.ma scene from the chapter4\scenes directory on the DVD.

2. Select the curve, and switch to the Surfaces menu set.

3. Choose Surfaces ➤ Bevel Plus ➤ Options.

Most of the options can be changed after the surface is created using the settings in the Attribute Editor. But you can specify the type of geometry Bevel Plus will create in the Output Options of the Options box.

4. Switch to the Output Options tab in the Bevel Plus Options dialog box (Figure 4.44):

◆ Make sure Output Geometry is set to Polygons.

◆ Tessellation Method should be set to Sampling.

You can change the default Sampling Controls after you create the surface.

5. Click Bevel to make the surface.

FIGURE 4.44
The Output
Options tab for the
Bevel Plus tool

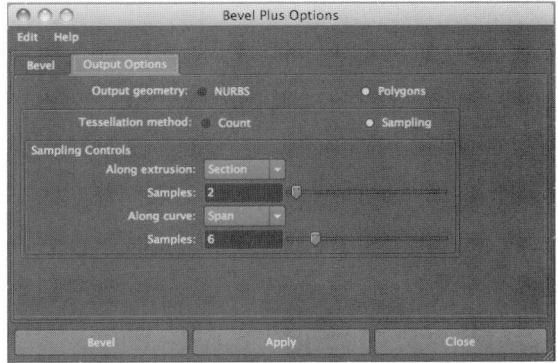

6. Switch to the perspective view, and select the bevelPolygon1 node in the Outliner.

7. Open the Attribute Editor, and select the bevelPlus1 tab.

8. Only the front side of the surface is visible, so you can economize the geometry of the surface by turning off the Bevel At Start and Caps At Start options.

9. Enter the following settings:

   Bevel Width: **0.124**

   Bevel Depth: **0.091**

   Extrude Distance: **1**

10. Activate Bevel Inside Curves so the outside edge of the surface is defined by the shape of the curve.

11. To change the bevel style, click the arrow to the right of Outer Style Curve (or click the outerStyleCurve1 tab in the Outliner). You can choose a style from the style list. Choose Convex Out.

12. In the Polygon Output Options section in the bevelPlus1 tab, make sure Sampling is set to Extrusion Section in the top menu and Curve Span in the bottom menu. You can use these controls to edit the resolution of the surface. Set Curve Span to **9** (see Figure 4.45).

FIGURE 4.45
Edit the bevel surface using the controls in the Attribute Editor.

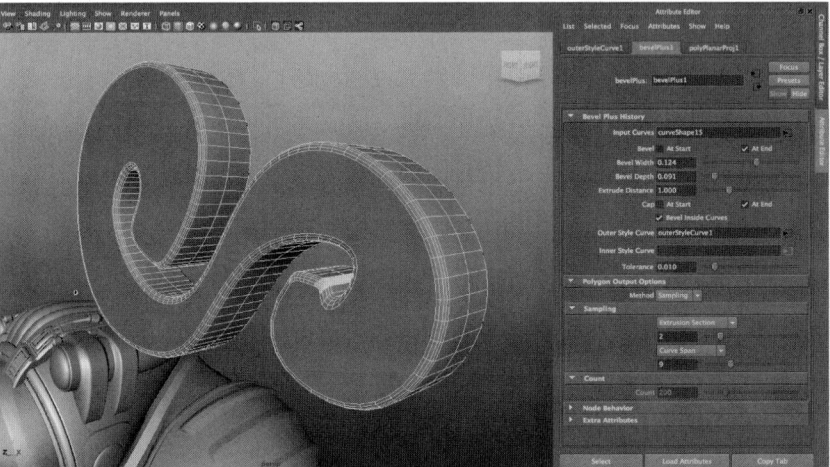

BEVEL PLUS TOOL TIPS

It's a good idea to create your own Bevel Plus presets when you establish a style that you know you'll use again. To create a preset, follow these steps:

1. Click the Presets button in the upper-right corner of the bevelPlus1 tab.

2. Select Save bevelPlus Preset.

3. Give your preset a descriptive name.

When you create a similar surface using the Bevel Plus tool, you can apply the preset by clicking the Presets button. This will save you a lot of time and work.

If you are creating a number of bevels from several different curves and some of the surfaces push out while others push in, try reversing the curve direction on the original curve used for the bevel operation. Select the curve, and choose (from the Surfaces menu set) Edit Curves ➢ Reverse Curve Direction.

To create a hole in the beveled surface, select the outer curve first, and then Shift+click the inner curve and apply Bevel Plus.

If surfaces are behaving strangely when you apply Bevel Plus, make sure there are no loops in the curves, and try deactivating Bevel Inside Curves to fix the problem. Sometimes it's just a matter of repositioning the CVs of the original curve.

Once you have the bevel style that you like, you can refine the shape of the object by moving the CVs of the original curve. The bevelPlus1 surface has a construction history connection to the original curve.

13. Select bevelPolygon1 in the Outliner, and rename it **armorDetail1**.

14. Center its pivot by choosing Modify ➢ Center Pivot.

15. Position the surface roughly above the chest armor plate. Try the following settings (your results may be different depending on the shape and size of your original curve):

    Translate X: **-4.797**

    Translate Y: **-8.926**

    Translate Z: **0.782**

    Rotate X: **-36.883**

    Rotate Y: **19.96**

    Rotate Z: **-15.679**

    Scale X: **.08**

    Scale Y: **.08**

    Scale Z: **.08**

16. Once you have armorDetail1 roughly in position, switch to a front view, and use the Move tool to shape the CVs of the original curve some more. The armorDetail1 object will update as you edit the curve.

    It's a good idea to split the layout into two views while you work. Use the front view to edit the curve, and use the perspective view to observe the changes in the armorDetail1 surface as you work (Figure 4.46).

17. Switch to the Animation menu set.

FIGURE 4.46
When you edit the curve in the front view (right), you can observe changes to the armorDetail1 objects simultaneously in the perspective view (left).

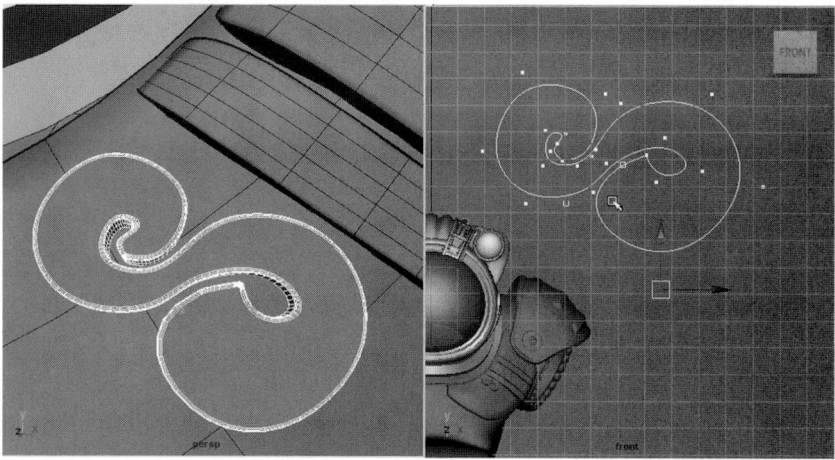

18. Select the armorDetail1 surface, and choose Create Deformers ➤ Lattice. Use the following settings:

    S Divisions: **5**

    T Divisions: **5**

    U Divisions: **2**

    In the Attribute Editor, turn off Local on the ffd1 tab.

19. Use the Move tool to edit the lattice points so the armorDetail1 object conforms to the surface of the chest armor.

20. Save the scene as **chestDetail_v03.ma**.

To see a version of the scene to this point, open the chestDetail_v03.ma scene from the chapter4\scenes directory on the DVD.

KEEP YOUR HISTORY

You can build the other parts of the chest armor detail using the same techniques in this section. Don't delete history on your bevel objects until you have all the pieces in place. As long as you keep your construction history, you can easily edit the bevels using the CVs of the original curves. You may also find it easier to make the beveled objects conform to the surface of the armor if you deform all the bevel surfaces using a single lattice. To see a finished version of the armor design, open the chestDetail_v04.ma scene from the chapter4\scenes directory on the DVD.

Bevel Edges

Adding a slight bevel to the edges of a surface makes an object look much more realistic in the final render. Perfectly sharp corners on an object make it look computer generated, which of course it is. For most manufactured objects, the smooth mesh preview is overkill. All you really need is the Bevel tool. In this section you'll create the detail at the center of the chest, as shown in Figure 4.47.

1. Open the `chestDetail_v05.ma` scene from the `chapter4\scenes` directory on the DVD. This scene has the completed chest armor plates (see Figure 4.48).

2. Turn off the display of the TORSO and HELMET layers in the Display Layer Editor.

FIGURE 4.47
Create the detail at the center of the chest using the Bevel tool.

FIGURE 4.48
The armor has been mirrored to the opposite side of the suit.

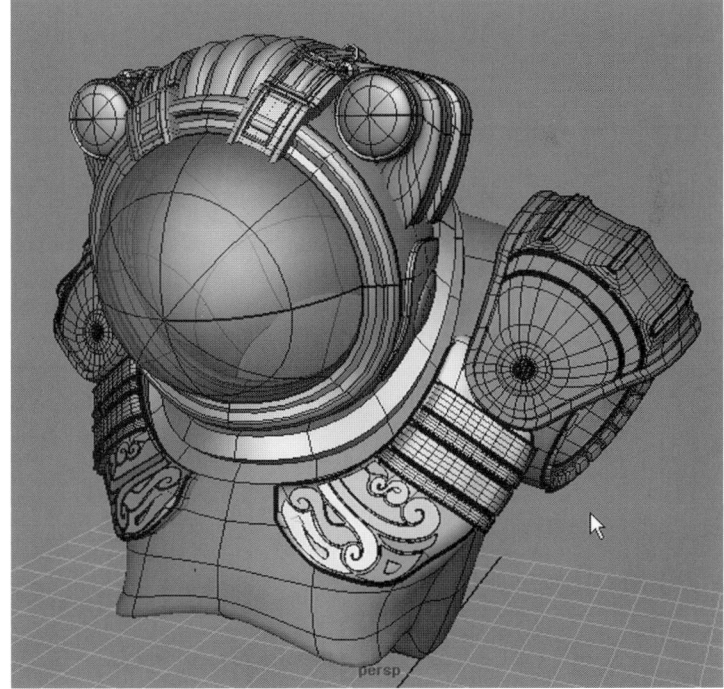

MIRROR OBJECTS

The shoulder armor, arm sockets, and chest armor have been mirrored to the opposite side of the model. To do this quickly, group the object so the pivot is at the center of the grid; choose Edit ➤ Duplicate Special ➤ Options. In the options, set the Scale X value to **-1**. After the object has been duplicated, you can freeze the transformations on the object and unparent it from the group.

3. Create a polygon cube at the center of the grid (Create ➤ Polygon Primitives ➤ Cube). The cube should be scaled to **1** unit in the x-, y-, and z-axes.

4. Right-click the cube, and select Edges to switch to edge selection mode.

5. Select the four edges that run vertically on each side of the cube.

6. Choose Edit Mesh ➤ Bevel. The edges are now beveled.

7. Open the Channel Box, and expand the polyBevel1 node in the INPUTS section.

8. Set Offset to **0.4** to decrease the size of the bevel.

9. Rotate the view to the bottom of the cube.

10. Select the face at the bottom, and delete it.

11. Select the cube, and create another bevel (Edit Mesh ➤ Bevel). When the object is selected, the bevel is applied to all the edges (see the top panel of Figure 4.49).

12. Select the polyBevel2 node in the Channel Box, and use the following settings:

    Segments: **3**

    Offset: **0.3**

    Increasing the segments can make the bevel appear rounded. You can also control the roundness using the Roundness attribute.

13. Choose Create ➤ Polygon Primitives ➤ Cylinder to create a cylinder.

14. Set the Translate Y channel to **0.344**, and set the Scale X, Scale Y, and Scale Z channels to **0.265**.

15. In the Channel Box under the polyCylinder1 node, type **1** in the Round Cap channel to add a rounded cap to the cylinder. Set Subdivisions Caps to **5**. Set Subdivisions Axis to **12**.

16. Set Scale Y to **0.157** and Translate Y to **0.448** (see the middle panel of Figure 4.49).

17. Switch to a side view, and turn on Wireframe.

18. Right-click the cylinder, and choose Faces to switch to face selection mode.

19. Select all the faces on the rounded bottom of the cylinder, and delete them (select the faces and press the Delete key).

20. In the perspective view, select each face on the side of the cylinder that points toward the beveled corners of the cube, and extrude them as shown in the lower panel of Figure 4.49.

FIGURE 4.49
Create the centerpiece from two polygon meshes that have been beveled and combined.

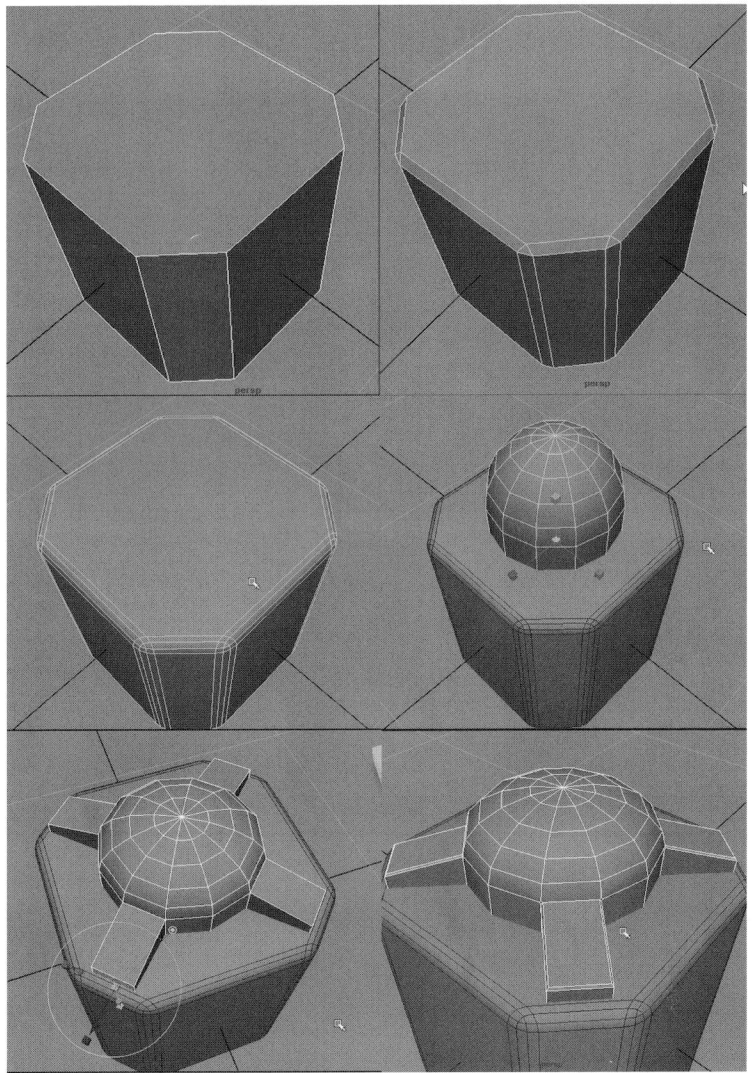

21. Use the extrude manipulator to scale the extruded faces down along their y-axes.

22. Switch to edge selection mode.

23. Shift+click the edges that run along the top edge of each extruded section, and choose Edit Mesh ➢ Bevel to bevel these edges.

24. In the options for the bevel node, set Offset to **0.1** (see the bottom-right panel of Figure 4.49).

25. Select both meshes, and choose Mesh ➢ Combine.

26. Delete history on the combined mesh, and name it **centerpiece**.

27. Move, rotate, and scale the centerpiece so it is positioned at the front of the torso, as shown in Figure 4.50. Try these settings:

Translate X: **0**

Translate Y: **5.667**

Translate Z: **2.061**

Rotate X: **80.678**

Rotate Y: **13.293**

Rotate Z: **42.411**

Scale X: **1**

Scale Y: **0.608**

Scale Z: **1**

28. Save the scene as **chestDetail_v06.ma**.

To see a version of the scene, open the chestDetail_v06.ma scene from the chapter4\ scenes directory on the DVD.

FIGURE 4.50
Place the center-piece at the center of the front of the torso.

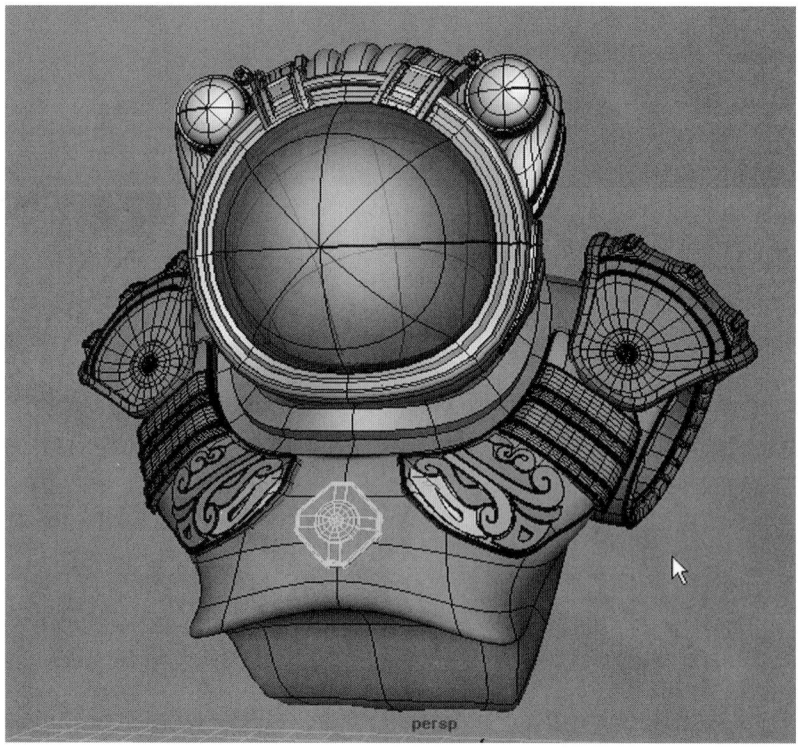

Polygon Modeling with Paint Effects

Paint Effects is most often used for creating large plants, trees, and other natural and organic objects. However, Paint Effects is not limited to these types of objects by any means. You can easily adapt the procedural approach used to create Paint Effects strokes to create details, such as wires and hoses used for mechanical objects. You can convert the strokes into NURBS surfaces or polygons and incorporate them into your models.

Typically, modeling details, such as wires or hoses, involves extruding a circle along a path curve. The resulting NURBS surface can be used as is or converted to polygons.

One problem encountered with a typical extrusion is that the extruded tube can appear flattened or kinked if the extrusion path has sharp corners. When you apply a Paint Effects stroke to a curve and then convert the stroke to a NURBS surface or polygons, you'll encounter fewer problems at the corners of the curve. Figure 4.51 shows a typical NURBS extrusion at the top. The middle and bottom surfaces were created using a Paint Effects curve converted into a NURBS surface (middle) and polygons (bottom). Notice that the surface does not flatten out as it moves around the corners of the curve.

FIGURE 4.51
A typical NURBS extrusion (top) produces kinks at the corners of the path. A Paint Effects stroke is converted to a NURBS surface (middle) and to polygons (bottom). There are fewer kinks in the converted surface.

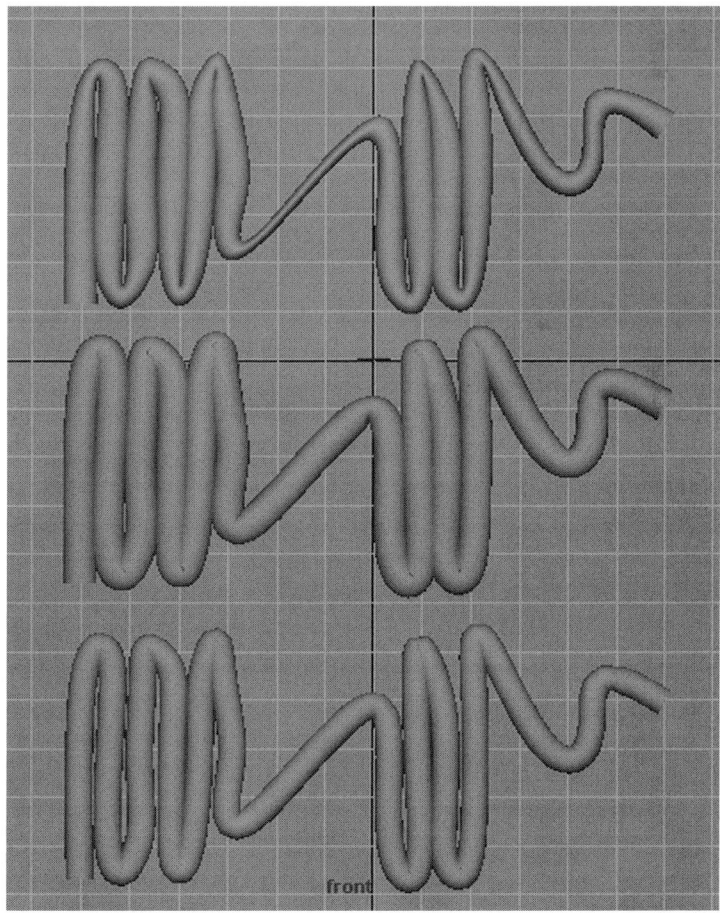

In addition, since the converted surface created from the Paint Effects stroke still has a connection to the original stroke, you can use the Paint Effects controls to add detail and even animate the surface (Figure 4.52).

FIGURE 4.52
You can add details
to the extrusion
using the controls
in the Paint Effects
brush attributes.

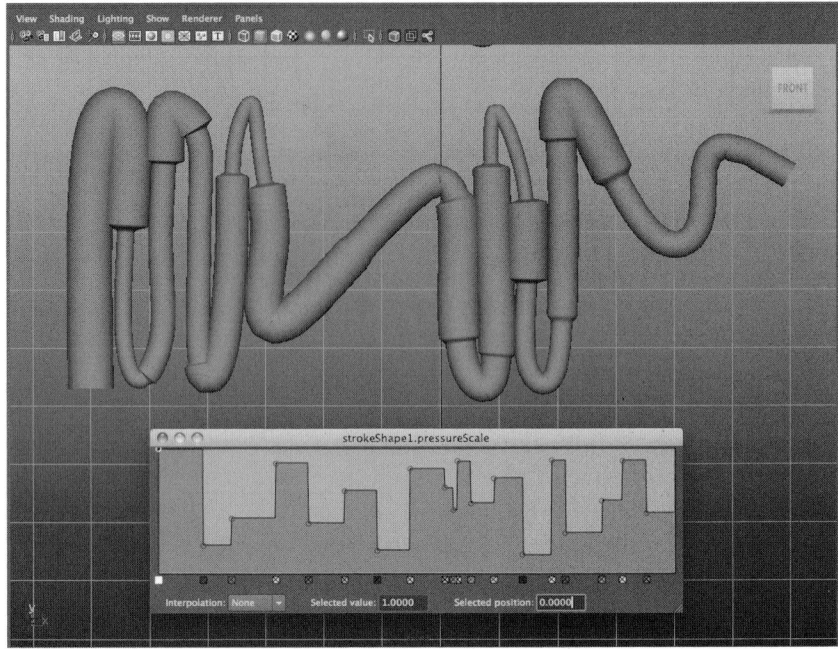

Attaching Strokes to Curves

Paint Effects is covered in detail in Chapter 8. In this section, you'll use some basic Paint Effects techniques to create some of the hoses and wires on the space suit.

1. Open the `paintEffectsHose_v01.ma` scene from the `chapter4\scenes` directory on the DVD.

   This scene contains the torso and helmet as well as the armor created in previous sections. Two small connectors have been added to the space suit. These were created by extruding selected faces on a sphere and pipe primitive.

2. Switch to the front view, and turn on wireframe display (hot key = **4**).

3. Choose Create ➢ CV Curve Tool. Make sure Curve Degree is set to Cubic.

4. Create a short six-point curve that connects the two connector objects.

5. Switch to the perspective view.

6. Select the curve, and center its pivot (Modify ➢ Center Pivot).

7. Use the Move tool to position the curve closer to the connectors on the suit.

8. Right-click the curve, and choose Control Vertex.

9. Move the points of the curve. The curve should be shaped to look like a hose connecting parts of the suit (Figure 4.53).

FIGURE 4.53
Create a curve
between the two
connector objects.

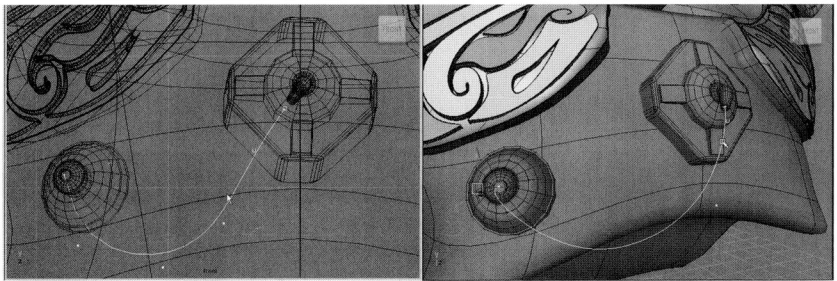

10. Switch to the Rendering menu set, and choose Paint Effects ➤ Curve Utilities ➤ Attach Brush To Curves.

    Step 10 attaches the currently selected stroke to a selected curve. Unless you have selected a stroke from the presets in the Visor, the default stroke is used for the curve. The default stroke works very well for simple hoses, although you'll notice that its default size is a little big.

11. In the Outliner, select the stroke1 node, and choose Modify ➤ Convert ➤ Paint Effects To Polygons (see Figure 4.54).

12. In the Outliner, select stroke1, and hide it (Ctrl+h).

13. Select the Brush2MeshGroup, and choose Edit ➤ Ungroup.

14. Rename brush2Main as **hose1**.

15. Select hose1, choose Lighting/Shading ➤ Assign New Material, and select Lambert from the panel that opens.

16. Save the scene as `paintEffectsHose_v02.ma`.

To see a version of the scene to this point, open the `paintEffectsHose_v02.ma` scene from the `chapter4\scenes` directory on the DVD.

FIGURE 4.54
Attach a stroke
to the curve, and
convert it into
polygons.

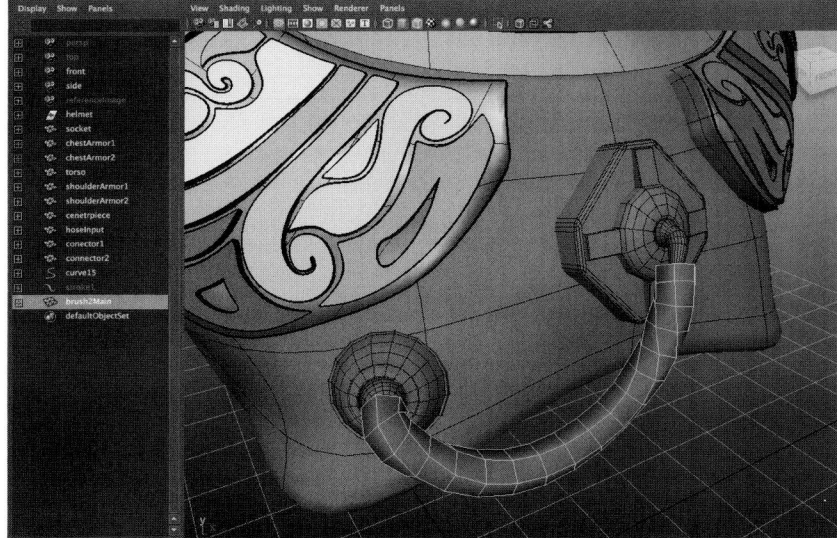

Modifying the Converted Stroke

Now you are set to edit the stroke itself to define the shape of the hose. The settings required to do this are spread out between two tabs in the Attribute Editor. Paint Effects requires a bit of bouncing around between settings, which can be a little disconcerting at first. With some practice you'll get the hang of it. It helps to understand how Paint Effects brushes work. Creating and designing Paint Effects brushes is discussed in detail in Chapter 8.

1. Continue with the scene from the previous section, or open the paintEffectsHose_v02.ma scene from the chapter4\scenes directory on the DVD.

2. Select the stroke1 node in the Outliner, and open the Attribute Editor.

3. Switch to the brush2 tab. Set Global Scale to **1**.

4. In the Twist section, activate Forward Twist. This setting automatically rotates leaves on Paint Effects plants so they continually face the camera. In some cases, it can also remove unwanted twisting and other problems when creating simple hoses from strokes.

5. Switch to the strokeShape1 tab in the Attribute Editor.

6. Set Sample Density to **4** (if the slider won't go beyond 1, type the number **4** in the field). This increases the divisions in the curve and makes it smoother.

7. Set Smoothing to **10**. This relaxes the shape of the hose somewhat.

8. Scroll down and expand the Pressure Scale settings in the Pressure Mappings rollout.

   The Pressure Scale settings translate the recorded pressure applied while painting a Paint Effects stroke using a digital tablet into values applied to specified stroke attributes. Since you simply applied the stroke to a curve, no pressure was recorded; however, you can still use these settings to modify the shape of the hose.

9. Set Pressure Map 1 to Width.

10. Click the arrow to the right of the pressure scale curve. This expands the pressure scale curve into its own window.

    Since Pressure Map 1 is set to Width, changes made to the scale curve affect the width of the hose. You can add additional attributes using the Pressure Map 2 and Pressure Map 3 settings. This stroke does not use tubes, so settings like Tube Width and Tube Length have no effect on the shape of the hose.

11. Click the curve in the curve editing window to add points. Observe the changes in the hose shape.

12. Drag the points down to make the hose thinner (see Figure 4.55).

13. When you're happy with the shape of the curve, refine the shape of the hose by editing the CVs of the original curve.

14. Save the scene as **paintEffectsHose_v03.ma**.

To see a version of the scene up to this point, open the paintEffectsHose_v03.ma scene from the chapter4\scenes directory on the DVD.

FIGURE 4.55
Create the shape of the hose by editing the settings of the Paint Effects brush.

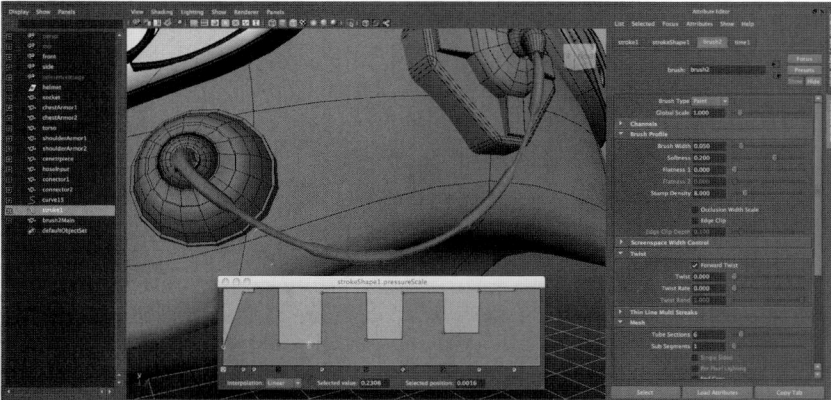

INTERPOLATION

Interpolation sets the out tangent style of the selected point on the curve:

◆ Setting this to None creates a hard edge.

◆ Setting this to Linear creates an angle.

◆ Setting this to Smooth and Spline creates curved tangents.

If you want to add a lot of detail, you'll need to increase the Sample Density value of the stroke. You can force the points of the curve to go beyond the range displayed in the Curve Editor by typing a value greater than 1 in the Selected Value field.

Drawing Curves on a Live Surface

Creating curves on a live surface is a quick way to create wires and hoses that conform to the shape of the object.

1. Continue with the scene from the previous section, or open the `paintEffectsHose_v03.ma` scene from the `chapter4\scenes` directory on the DVD.

2. The TORSO display layer is set to Reference; click the R next to the label of the layer to set the display layer to normal editing mode.

3. Select the torso object, and choose Modify ➢ Make Live.

4. Choose Create ➢ CV Curve Tool. Make sure Curve Degree is set to Cubic in the options.

5. Click the surface to start drawing curves. Create a few short curves like the ones shown in Figure 4.56, and press the Enter key when you finish drawing each one. (In some cases, you may have to switch to wireframe view to see the curve as you draw it on the surface.)

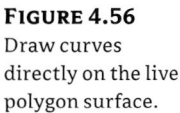

FIGURE 4.56
Draw curves directly on the live polygon surface.

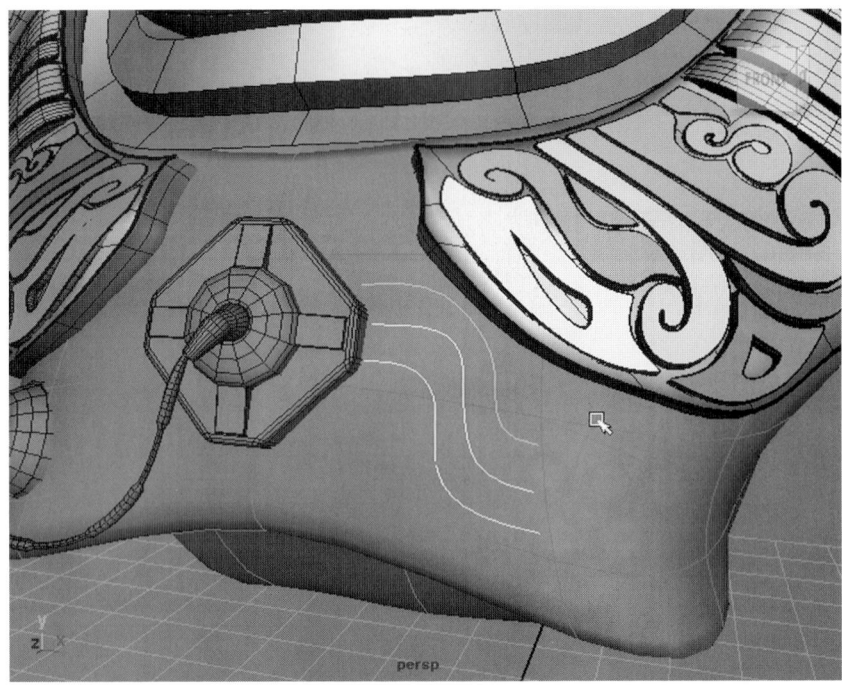

The curves may appear to float above or beneath the smooth mesh polygons. This is normal behavior when drawing curves on polygons. You can adjust the CVs of the curves later if necessary.

6. Select the stroke1 brush in the Outliner.

7. Switch to the Rendering menu set, and choose Paint Effects ➤ Get Settings From Selected Stroke. This grabs the settings used for the stroke so they can be applied to the curves.

8. Select the curves drawn on the surface, and choose Paint Effects ➤ Curve Utilities ➤ Attach Brush To Curves.

9. Convert the strokes into polygons, and use the techniques described in the earlier "Modifying the Converted Stroke" section to shape the curves into hoses and wires.

10. To get the torso geometry out of the "live" state, select it in the Outliner, and choose Modify ➤ Make Live. This will toggle the surface back to its normal state (see Figure 4.57).

11. Save the scene as **paintEffectsHoses_v04.ma**.

To see a version of the scene to this point, open the paintEffectsHoses_v04.ma scene from the chapter4\scenes folder on the DVD.

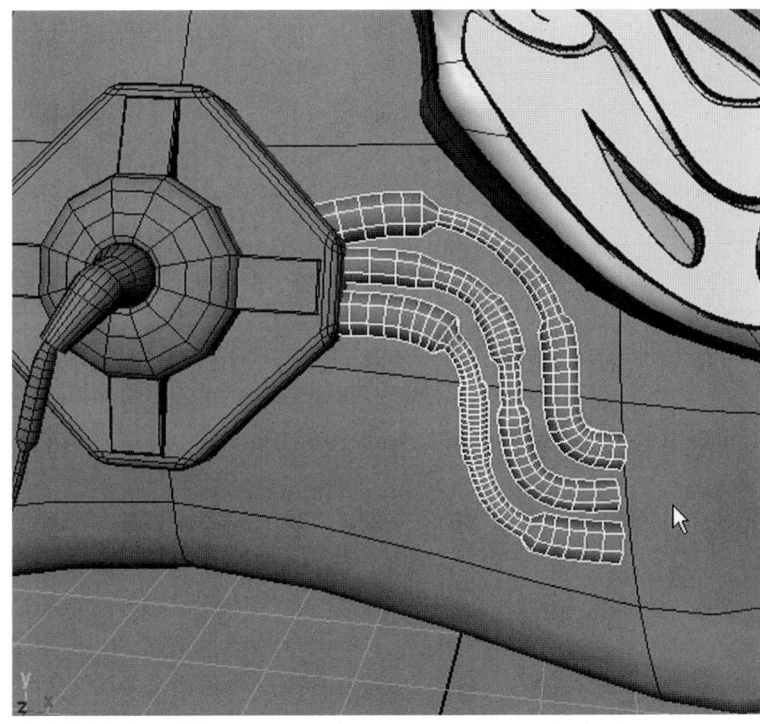

Convert NURBS Surfaces to Polygons

You can use a NURBS surface to start a polygon model. Using NURBS primitives and extruded and revolved surfaces, you can combine the strengths of both NURBS and polygon-modeling tools and techniques in your projects.

To convert NURBS objects to polygons, follow these steps:

1. Choose Modify ➤ Convert ➤ NURBS To Polygons ➤ Options.

2. Set the options to determine how the polygon mesh will be constructed from the NURBS surface.

If you are not familiar with NURBS modeling, review Chapter 3 before attempting the exercises in this section.

Employing Revolved Surfaces

In the concept sketch by Chris Sanchez, a number of parts of the suit look like a pleated material. The arm sections and the area around the waist look like a good opportunity to use a revolved surface as a starting place for the model. In this exercise, you'll create the area below the torso. You can apply the same techniques to the arms (see Figure 4.58).

1. Open the `belly_v01.ma` scene from the `chapter4\scenes` directory on the DVD.

2. Switch to a front view.

FIGURE 4.58
The area of the waist on the sketch looks like a good place to use a NURBS revolve.

3. Turn on Grid Snapping, and choose Create ➤ CV Curve Tool ➤ Options.

4. In the options, set Curve Degree to Linear.

5. Use the Curve tool to create a sawtooth pattern running down the y-axis of the grid.

6. Draw the curve four units away from the center line.

7. Make the sawtooth pattern using six angles, as shown in Figure 4.59.

8. Switch to the Surfaces menu set, and choose Surfaces ➤ Revolve. A new surface is created that looks like a pleated cylinder.

9. In the Channel Box, set the Sections of the revolve1 node to **12**.

10. Turn Grid Snapping off.

FIGURE 4.59
Create the pleated surface by revolving a jagged curve.

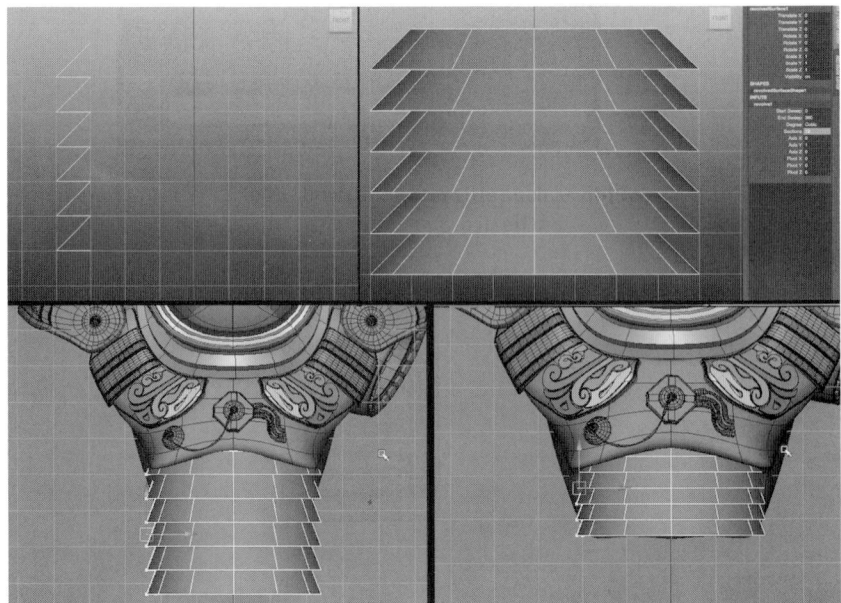

11. Select the curve, and use the Move and Scale tools to position it beneath the torso. The surface moves with the curve because of the construction history.

12. Select the curve, and switch to component mode.

13. Select the CVs at the points of the curve, and move them inward to make the pleating less extreme.

14. Continue to move and shape the curve until the surface resembles the concept sketch.

15. Select revolvedSurface1, and choose Modify ➤ Convert ➤ NURBS To Polygons ➤ Options.

16. In the options, set Type to Quads and Tessellation Method to General. This method works very well for making the polygon surface closely match the isoparms of the original surface.

17. Set U Type and V Type to Per Span # Of Iso Params.

18. Set Number U and Number V to **1** (see Figure 4.60).

FIGURE 4.60
The options for converting NURBS to polygons

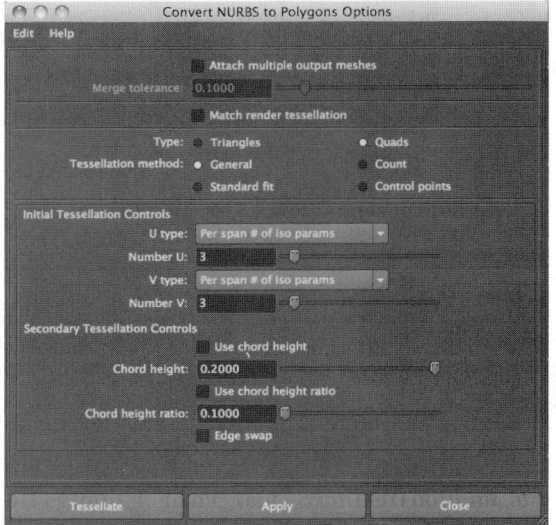

19. Click Tessellate to apply.

20. In the Outliner, hide the original NURBS surface (Ctrl+h).

21. Select the new nurbsToPoly1 node, and rename it **bellyPleats**.

22. Select bellyPleats, and press the **3** key to switch to smooth mesh polygons.

23. Right-click the surface, and choose Vertex.

24. Use the Move tool with Soft Select activated to move around the vertices of the pleated surface (see Figure 4.61).

FIGURE 4.61
You can model irregularity into the pleats using the Move and Crease tools.

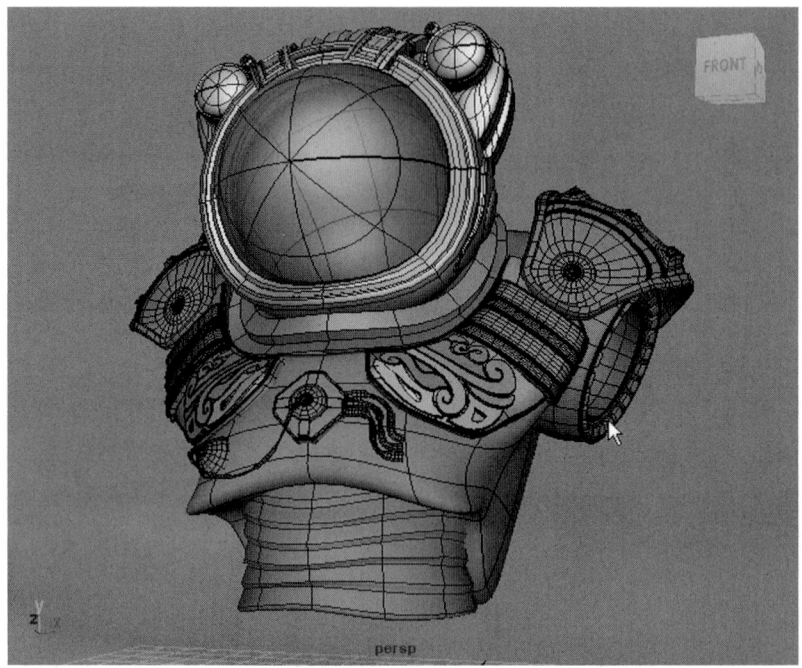

25. Create some irregularity in the pleated surface so it looks less perfect and more like a flexible material that has been used a lot. Use the Crease tool on a few of the edges.

26. When you are happy with the way the surface looks, delete history for the bellyPleats node, and delete the revolvedSurface1 node and the curve.

27. Save the scene as **belly_v02.ma**.

NURBS Extrusions

To create the rounded surface that surrounds the bottom of the torso, a NURBS extrusion converted to polygons may work better than a Paint Effects stroke. This is because the shape does not appear perfectly round. It might be easier to extrude an oval along a path curve to create this particular shape.

1. Continue with the scene from the previous section, or open the belly_v02.ma scene from the chapter4\scenes directory on the DVD.

2. Make sure the TORSO display layer is not in reference mode.

3. Right-click the torso, and choose Edge to switch to edge selection mode.

4. Double-click one of the edges toward the bottom of the torso. The entire edge loop is selected when you double-click an edge.

5. Choose Modify ➤ Convert ➤ Polygon Edges To Curve to create a curve based on these edges.

6. Select the newly created curve, and delete its construction history.

7. The curve does not perfectly match the surface. Use the Move tool with Reflection on to reposition the CVs of the curve so they more closely resemble the shape of the torso.

8. Choose Create ➢ NURBS Primitives ➢ Circle, and rotate the circle 90 degrees on the x-axis.

9. Set the following values in the Scale channels:

   Scale X: **0.12**

   Scale Y: **0.725**

   Scale Z: **0.378**

10. Select the circle, and Ctrl+click polyToCurve1.

11. From the Surfaces menu, choose Surfaces ➢ Extrude ➢ Options.

12. In the options, set the following:

    Style: Tube

    Result Position: At Path

    Pivot: Component

    Orientation: Path Direction

    Click the Extrude button to make the extrusion.

13. Select the new extrudedSurface1 node, and choose Modify ➢ Convert ➢ NURBS To Polygons.

14. Use the same settings from the earlier "Employing Revolved Surfaces" section (see Figure 4.62).

FIGURE 4.62
Create a curve from the polygon edges. Extrude a circle along the curve.

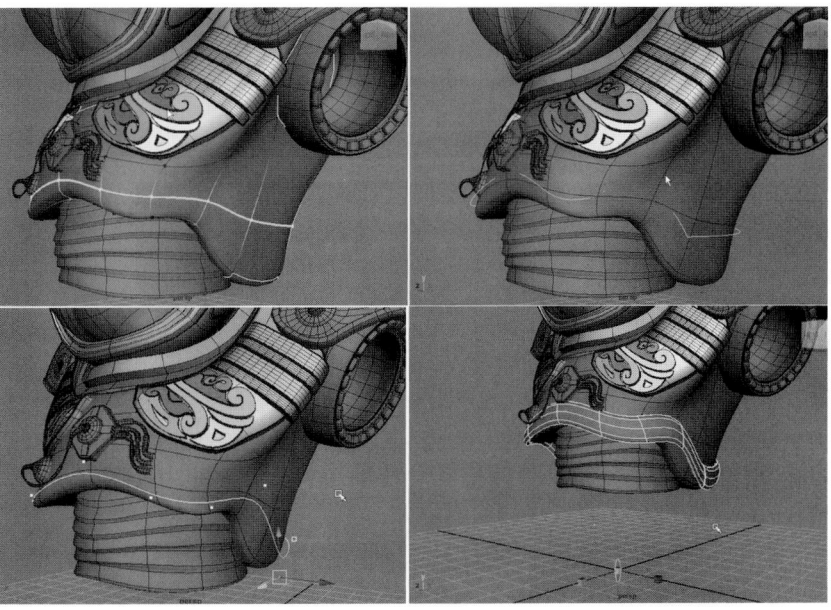

15. Hide the NURBS surface.

16. Select the nurbsToPoly1 object, and name it **torsoTrim**.

17. Press the **3** key to switch to smooth mesh preview mode.

18. Select the polyToCurve1 curve, and use the Move tool to position its CVs so the torsoTrim surface fits snugly against the base of the torso.

19. When you are happy with the overall shape of the surface, delete history on torsoTrim, and delete the extruded surfaces and the curves.

20. Use the Move tool to further refine the vertices of the trim surface (see Figure 4.63).

21. Save the scene as **belly_v03.ma**.

To see a version of the scene to this point, open the belly_v03.ma scene from the chapter4\scenes directory on the DVD.

FIGURE 4.63
Use the Move tool to refine the shape of the torsoTrim object.

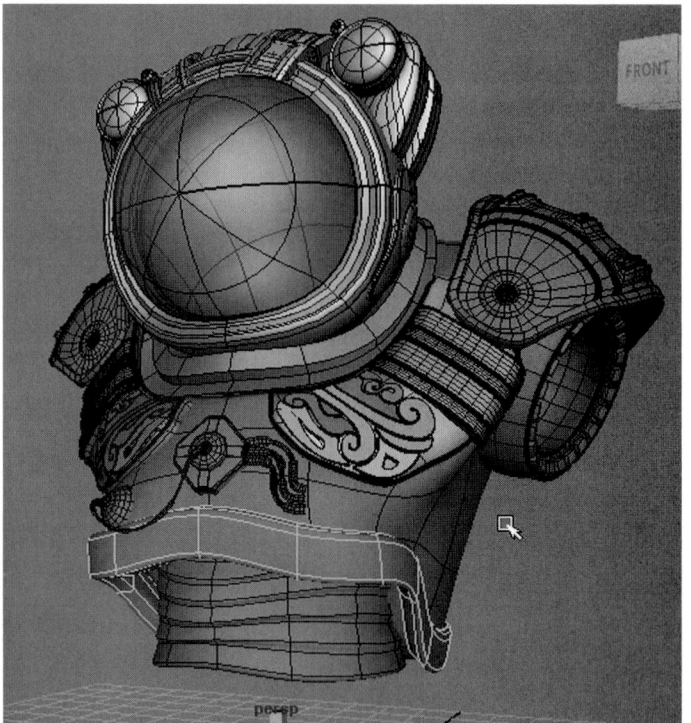

Boolean Operations

A Boolean operation in the context of polygon modeling creates a new surface by adding two surfaces together (union), subtracting one surface from the other (difference), or creating a surface from the overlapping parts of two surfaces (intersection). Figure 4.64 shows the results of the three types of Boolean operations applied to a polygon torus and cube.

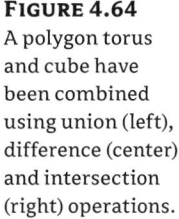

FIGURE 4.64
A polygon torus and cube have been combined using union (left), difference (center), and intersection (right) operations.

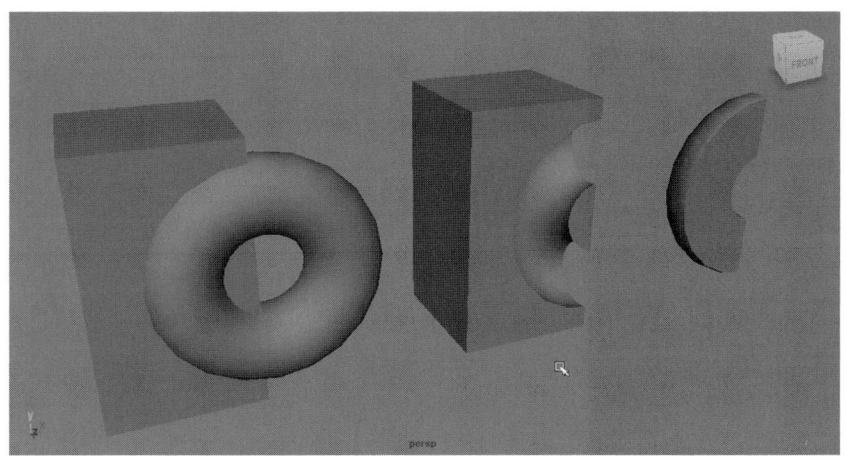

The difference between using Combine to create a single mesh from two meshes and using a Boolean Union is that a Boolean Union operation removes all interior faces when the two surfaces are added together.

The geometry created using Booleans can sometimes produce artifacts in renders, so it's best to keep the geometry as simple as possible.

Using Booleans

In this section, you'll use Boolean operations to create detail for the space suit's torso:

1. Open the `torsoDetail_v01.ma` scene from the `chapter4/scenes` directory on the DVD.

2. Select the torsoTrim object in the Outliner.

   Booleans don't always work well on smooth mesh preview objects, so it's a good idea to convert the smooth mesh preview to polygons.

3. Choose Modify ➤ Convert ➤ Smooth Mesh Preview To Polygons.

CONVERTING SMOOTH MESH PREVIEW TO POLYGONS

Converting a smooth mesh preview to polygons produces the same result as selecting the object, pressing the **1** key to deactivate smooth mesh preview, and then performing a Smooth operation (Mesh Smooth). However, if you have a creased edge on a smooth mesh preview surface, the crease will be carried over to the converted polygon model. The same is not true when you use the Smooth operation.

---

4. Create a polygon cylinder.

5. Scale the polygon down to **0.5** in the x-, y-, and z-axes.

6. In the Channel Box, set Subdivisions Height to **3**. Make sure Subdivisions Axis is set to **20**.

7. Switch to a side view, and do the following:

A. Turn on face selection mode.

B. Select all the polygons on the lowest subdivision.

C. Scale them down, as shown in Figure 4.65.

FIGURE 4.65
Scale down the
faces of the bottom
row of the cylinder.

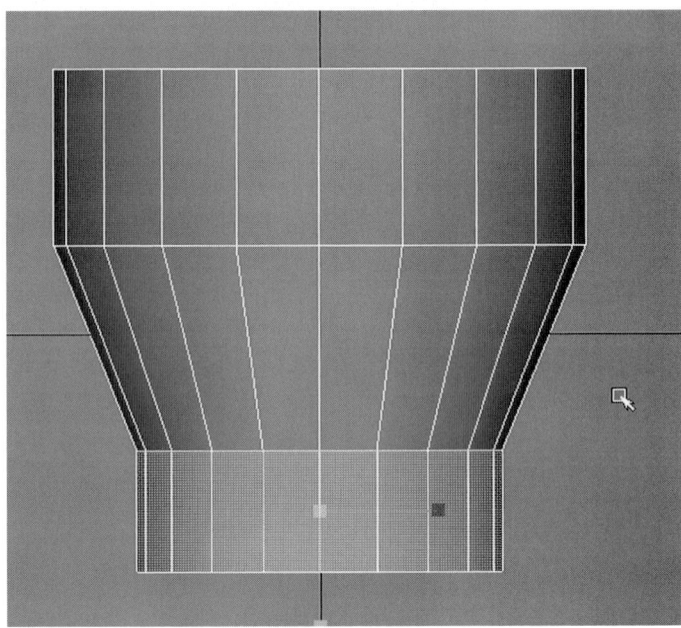

8. Select the cylinder, and set its Scale Y to **0.165**.

9. Position the cylinder so it intersects with the front of the torsoTrim object. Try these settings in the Channel Box:

Translate X: **0.418**

Translate Y: **4.607**

Translate Z: **2.575**

Rotate X: **90.2**

Rotate Y: **1.776**

Rotate Z: **0.318**

Scale X: **0.316**

Scale Y: **0.104**

Scale Z: **0.316**

10. Select the torsoTrim object, and Shift+click the cylinder. Choose Mesh ➤ Booleans ➤ Difference. The cylinder disappears, and a hole is now cut into the torsoTrim object (see Figure 4.66).

FIGURE 4.66
Cut a hole into the
torsoTrim object
using a cylinder.

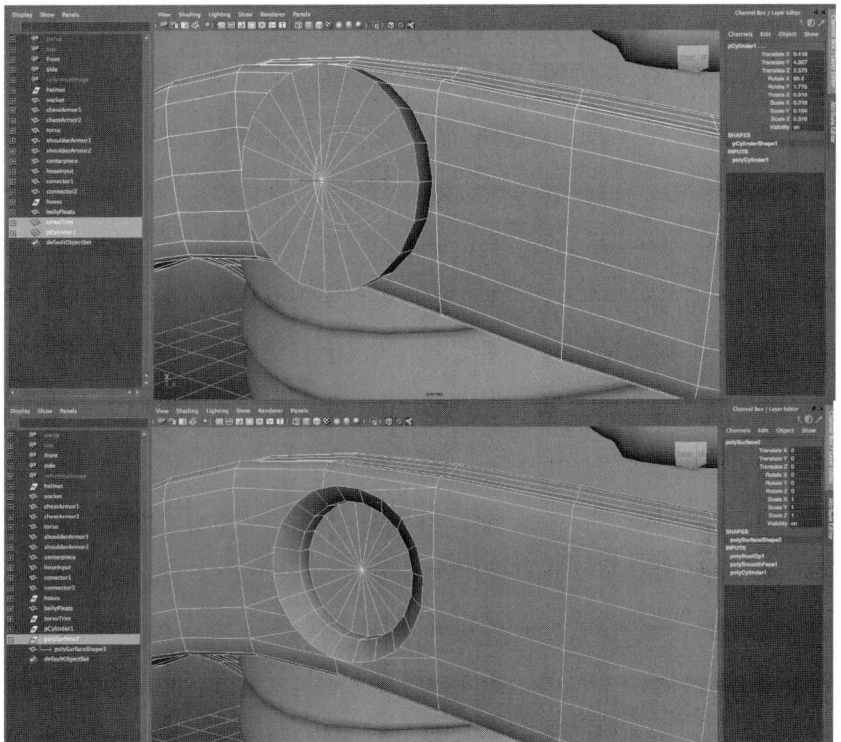

When using the Boolean ➤ Difference operation, Shift+click the object you want to cut into first and the cutting object second.

11. In the Outliner the pCylinder node is now a group. The mesh object no longer appears. You can adjust the position of the hole in the torsoTrim object by moving the pCylinder1 group (Figure 4.67). Once you delete history on the object, the position of the hole is permanent.

BEVEL THE CUTTING OBJECT

Applying a bevel to the edges created using a Boolean doesn't always work. Sometimes it's easier to create the bevel in the cutting object first. You did this when you scaled down the bottom section of the cylinder. You can then adjust the position of the cutting object after the Boolean operation to create the bevel in the edges.

12. Create a polygon sphere:

   A. Make sure the Subdivisions Axis and Height are set to **20**.

   B. Set the Scale X, Y, and Z of the sphere to **0.2**.

   The sphere will be placed inside the hole created by the cylinder and then merged with the torsoTrim object using a Union.

FIGURE 4.67
You can change the position of the hole by moving the pCylinder1 group.

13. To keep the geometry produced by the Booleans as clean as possible, match the edges of the sphere with the edges of the hole created by the cylinder. One way to align the sphere involves creating a parent constraint between the pCylinder group node and the sphere.

14. In the Outliner, select the pCylinder1 group.

15. Ctrl+click the sphere.

16. Switch to the Animation menu set, and choose Constrain ➤ Parent Options.

17. In the options, turn off Maintain Offset. Turn on All for both Translate and Rotate (see Figure 4.68).

FIGURE 4.68
Constrain the polygon sphere to the position of the cylinder.

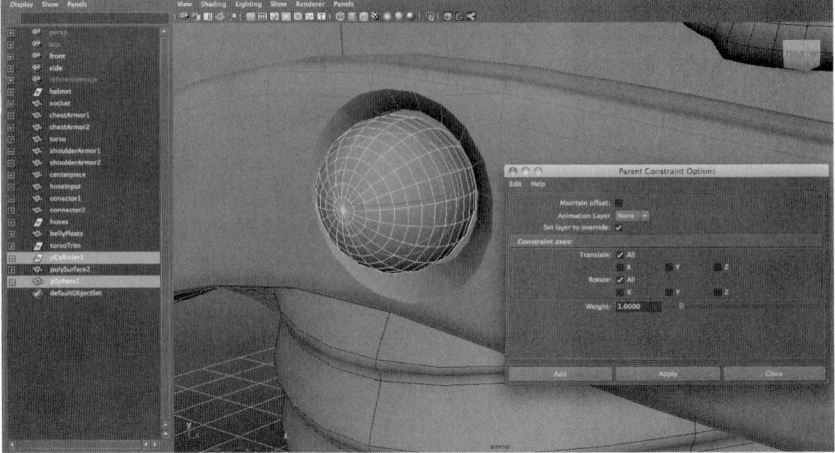

18. Once the sphere is constrained to the pCylinder1 group, it should appear in the hole. Expand the pSphere1 object in the Outliner, select the pSphere1_parentConstraint1 node, and delete it.

19. Select the pSphere1 node and the polySurface2 node in the Outliner, and choose Mesh ➢ Booleans ➢ Union. The objects are now merged into a single mesh.

20. Zoom in on the sphere (hot key = **f**). You'll see that the edges that wrap around the sphere match the position of the edges of the hole cut by the cylinder (see Figure 4.69). This is not always required when using Boolean operations, but it keeps the polygon geometry clean and reduces render artifacts.

FIGURE 4.69
Merge the sphere with the rest of the surface using a Union operation.

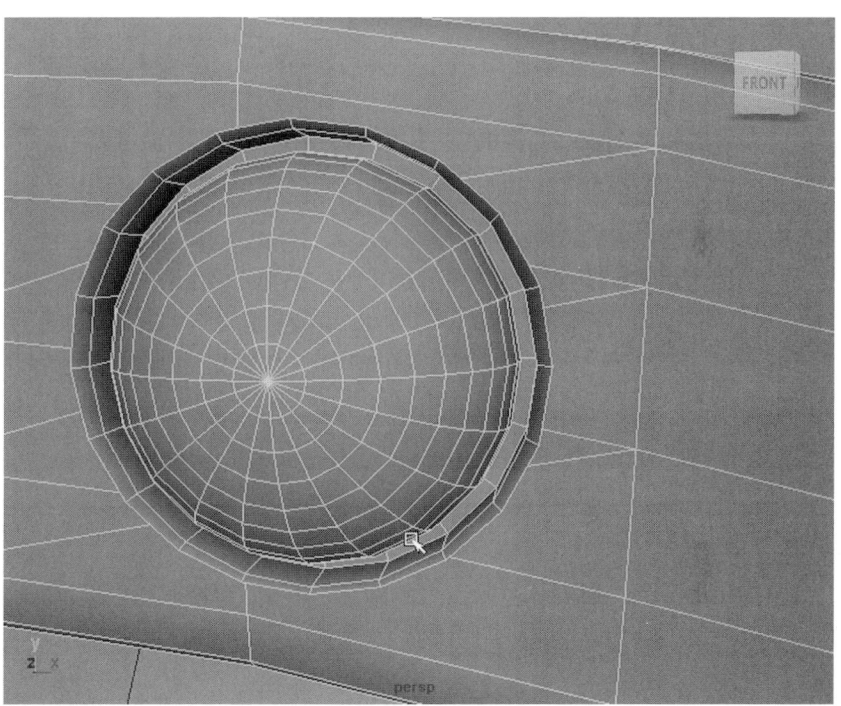

21. Select the pSphere1 group in the Outliner.

22. Scale it down on the y-axis a little.

23. In the options for the Move tool, set Move Axis to Local, and push the sphere back in the hole a little (shown in Figure 4.69).

24. Delete history on polySurface3, and rename it **torsoTrim**.

25. Save the scene as **torsoDetail_v02.ma**.

To see a version of the scene to this point, open torsoDetail_v02.ma from the chapter4\ scenes directory on the DVD.

Sculpting Polygons Using Artisan

The Artisan interface is a Maya editing system that simulates using a brush to sculpt surfaces and paint attribute values. Artisan works best when used with a digital tablet and stylus, but it will also work with a standard mouse.

When used in modeling mode, Artisan can be used to sculpt polygon, NURBS, and subdivision surface geometry. In other parts of this book, you'll see how Artisan can also be used to paint weights for deformers, edit texture maps, and paint the strength of nParticle force fields emitted by surfaces.

For the most part, the Artisan modeling controls are the same whether you are working with polygons, NURBS surfaces, or subdivision surfaces. In this section, you'll be introduced to Artisan as you sculpt the fabric parts of the pants on the space suit.

Sculpting Polygons

The Artisan sculpting brushes work very well for creating details such as folds in fabric. In this section, you'll create the fabric portion of the legs between the armor plates and the thigh and the shin guards (see Figure 4.70).

FIGURE 4.70
You'll use the Artisan sculpting brushes to create the folds in the cloth parts of the pants shown in the drawing.

ANNOTATED LEG MODEL

In this section, the basic parts of the leg armor have already been modeled using the same techniques described in this chapter. To see a scene with an annotated guide describing the steps used to create these leg parts, open `legStart.ma` from the `chapter4\scenes` directory on the DVD.

1. Open the `pants_v01.ma` scene from the `chapter4\scenes` directory on the DVD. You'll see the helmet, torso, and parts of the legs have been modeled already.

2. Open the Outliner, select the rightBoot and rightThighGuard groups, and hide them (Ctrl+h). These groups are named based on the character's right side.

3. Create a polygon cube.

4. Position the cube between the leftBoot and leftThighGuard groups. Try these settings in the Channel Box:

   Translate X: **2.018**

   Translate Y: **-6.384**

   Translate Z: **-1.689**

   Scale X: **2.3**

   Scale Y: **5**

   Scale Z: **2.4**

   Subdivisions Width: **3**

   Subdivisions Height: **6**

   Subdivisions Depth: **3**

5. Select the cube, and press the **3** key to switch to smooth mesh preview.

6. Right-click the cube, and choose Vertex to switch to vertex editing mode.

7. Switch to the Move tool.

8. In the options for the Move tool, turn on Soft Select.

9. Use the Move tool to shape the cube into a loose cylinder. The upper part should fit inside the opening at the bottom of the leftThighGuard. The bottom of the cube should fit over the top of the leftBoot (Figure 4.71).

   There's no need to be overly precise at this point; just try to imagine this surface as bulky, insulated fabric. It has to be flexible enough to bend but durable enough to protect the wearer in harsh environments, such as outer space. You'll refine the shape using Artisan.

10. Select the cube, and name it **leftPants**.

11. Choose Modify ➤ Convert ➤ Smooth Mesh Preview To Polygons.

12. Select leftPants, and choose Mesh ➤ Sculpt Geometry Tool. Make sure the Tool Options window is open.

FIGURE 4.71
Place a cube in the open area of the leg. Use the Move tool to roughly shape the vertices of the cube.

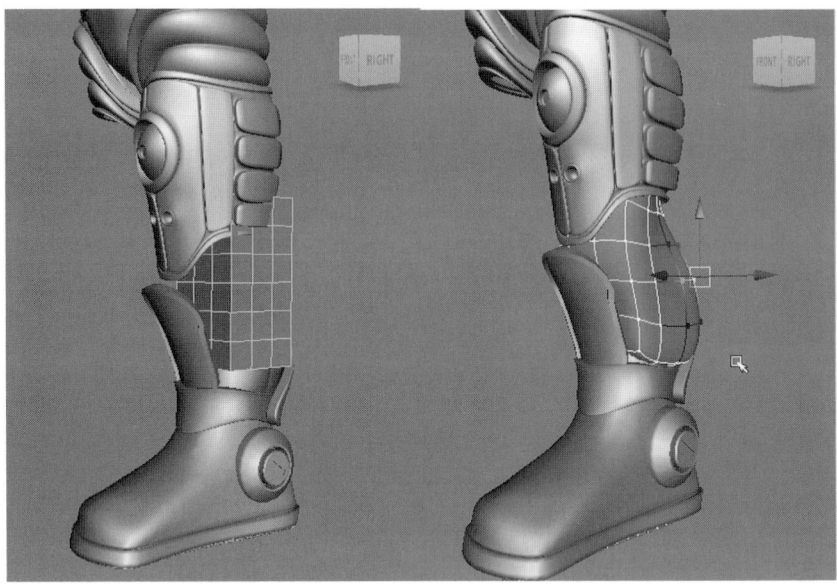

Choosing the Sculpt Geometry Tool activates the Artisan brush-based interface. The settings in the Options box control how the brush works as you sculpt the surface. At the top of the Options box are the basic controls:

Radius(U) and Radius(L)   These settings define the range for the radius of the brush. If you are using a digital tablet and stylus, you can actually change the radius based on the amount of pressure you apply to the brush. The Radius(U) setting is the upper limit of the radius; Radius(L) is the lower limit of the radius. If you are using a mouse, only the Radius(U) value is used. You can also set the Radius(U) value interactively by holding the **b** key while dragging left or right on the surface in the viewport. The radius of the brush is represented by a red circle (Figure 4.72).

FIGURE 4.72
The settings for the Artisan brush-based sculpting tool. The circle represents the radius of the brush.

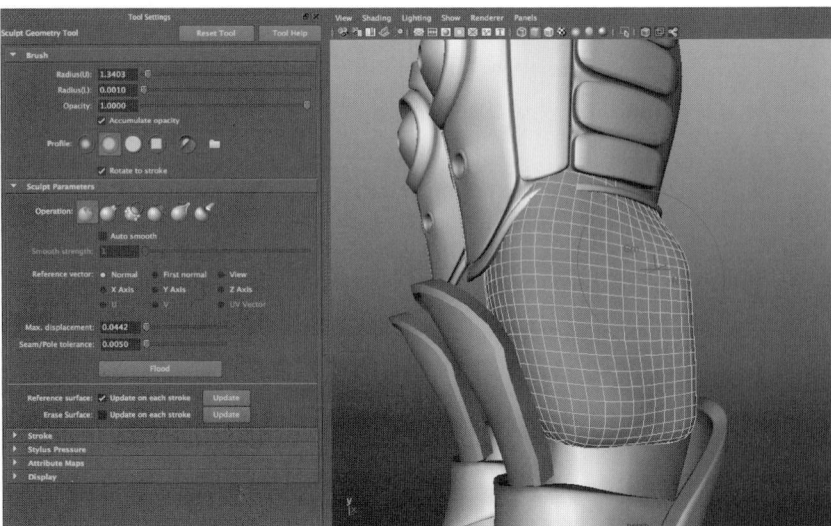

By default, the pressure you apply to the brush affects only the opacity of the stroke. If you want the pressure to control the radius of the brush, or both the radius and the opacity at the same time, scroll down to the Stylus Pressure settings and select from the choices in the Pressure Mapping menu.

Opacity   This setting determines the strength of the change created by the brush. When using Artisan to sculpt geometry, Opacity modifies the Max Displacement setting found in the Sculpt Parameters section. If Max Displacement is set to 1 unit and Opacity is set to 0.1, each stroke displaces the surface 0.1 units. If Accumulate Opacity is activated, each time a single stroke passes over itself, the surface is displaced further. Setting Opacity to 0 means that the stroke has no effect on the surface.

Profile   This setting determines the shape of the brush tip. The first two icons on the left create a soft edge to the brush. This is more apparent when the geometry is very dense and has a lot of points that can be displaced. The second two icons produce a hard edge to the brush: one is circular, the other is square. By clicking the Browse button, you can load a grayscale image to use as the brush shape. The Rotate To Stroke option rotates the image as you draw, so it always points in the direction of the stroke.

Sculpt Parameters   This section contains the settings for how the surface will react to the brush strokes. The Operation buttons cause the brush to push down, push up, smooth, relax, pinch, or erase the stroke. Smooth and relax are very similar. Smooth averages the position of the vertices on the surface. Relax averages the bumpiest areas of the surface while maintaining the overall shape of the surface.

New!

PINCH

The Pinch operation is new to Maya 2011. It can be used to further refine wrinkles on clothing or skin.

Reference Vector   This setting determines the direction of the change sculpted on the surface. When set to Normal, the vertices are displaced in the direction of their normal. When set to First Normal, all the vertices are displaced in the direction of the normal of the first vertex affected by the stroke. View displaces the vertices based on the current view, and the X, Y, and Z Axis options restrict displacement to the specified axis.

Flood   This button fills the entire object based on the Operation, Reference Vector, Opacity, and Max. Displacement settings. You can use it to smooth or relax the whole object after making changes or to inflate or shrink the entire object.

Reflection   These options, found in the Stroke section, are similar to the Reflection options found in the Move tool and are useful when sculpting symmetrical objects.

13. In the Sculpt Geometry Tool options, set Radius(U) to **0.25** and Opacity to **0.1**.

14. Click the first icon in the Profile section and the first icon in the Operation section.

15. Set Reference Vector to Normal and Max. Displacement to **0.5**.

16. If you are using a digital tablet and a stylus, activate Stylus Pressure, and set Pressure Mapping to Both.

17. In the Display section, turn on Draw Brush While Painting and Draw Brush Feedback so you can see how the brush changes based on the amount of pressure applied to the pen on the tablet. You may also want to turn off Show Wireframe so the wireframe display does not obscure your view of the changes made on the brush.

18. Paint some strokes on the leftPants object. Create folds in the clothing like the ones shown in the original sketch. You can hold the Ctrl key while you paint on the surface to invert the direction of the displacement. When you hold the Shift key while painting, the brush mode switches to smooth.

As you paint, experiment with the options for the Artisan brush settings. You can also activate smooth mesh preview on the surface by pressing the **3** key.

19. After you have created some folds, set Operation to Relax, and click the Flood button a few times to even out the lumps and bumps. Then switch to the Pinch operation to help define the edges of the wrinkles.

20. When you are happy with the surface, unhide the rightThighGuard and rightBoot groups.

21. Create a mirror duplicate of the leftPants surface and rename it **rightPants**.

22. Use the Artisan brushes to sculpt changes into this surface so it does not look like a copy of leftPants (see Figure 4.73). Remember to select the surface and choose Mesh ➢ Sculpt Geometry Tool.

23. Save the scene as **pants_v02.ma**.

To see a version of the scene to this point, open the pants_v02.ma scene from the chapter4\ scenes directory on the DVD.

FIGURE 4.73
Sculpt the fabric portions of the pants using the Artisan brush interface.

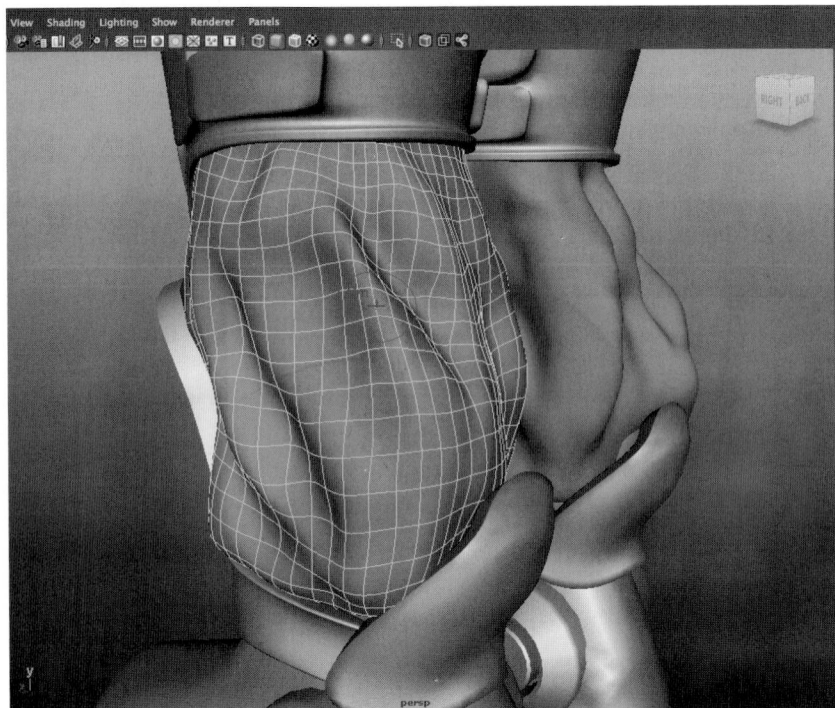

Advanced Polygon Editing Tools

The Edit Mesh menu in the Polygon menu set has a number of advanced editing tools that will aid you when you need to model detailed objects. This section demonstrates techniques for using some of these tools.

Append a Polygon

The Append operation is used to fill in a gap between two or more polygon surfaces. To use this, any surfaces must first be combined before the tool will work. An example of this tool would be connecting the bottom part of a human face to the top.

1. Open the `face1.ma` scene from the `chapter4\scenes` folder on the DVD. This scene has two parts of a face made up of polygons.

2. Shift-select both pieces, and choose Mesh ➢ Combine.

3. Choose Edit Mesh ➢ Append To Polygon Tool.

4. Click the border edge of the top surface, and then click the border edge of the bottom surface. A pink polygon appears (figure 4.74).

5. Press the Enter key to complete the operation.

FIGURE 4.74
A polygon is appended to connect two surfaces.

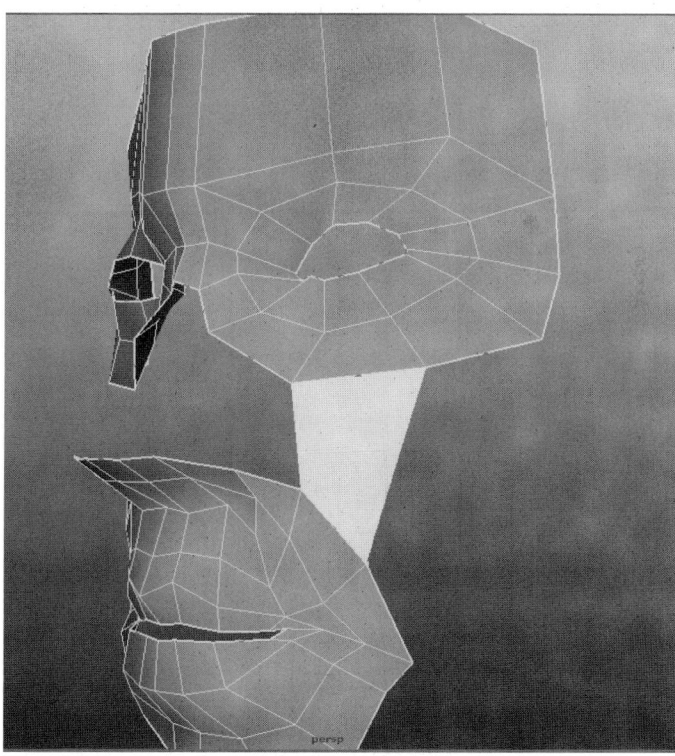

BOWTIES

The term *bowtie* refers to a situation in which the Append Polygon tool creates a twisted polygon that resembles a bowtie. This happens when you combine two meshes that have opposing normals and then connect the meshes using the Append Polygon tool. To fix this, follow these steps:

1. Select the polygon meshes.

2. Use the Separate command to break them into two meshes (Mesh ➤ Separate).

3. Select one of the meshes.

4. Choose Normals ➤ Reverse.

5. Combine the meshes again, and then try the Append Polygon tool.

The resulting polygons should no longer be twisted.

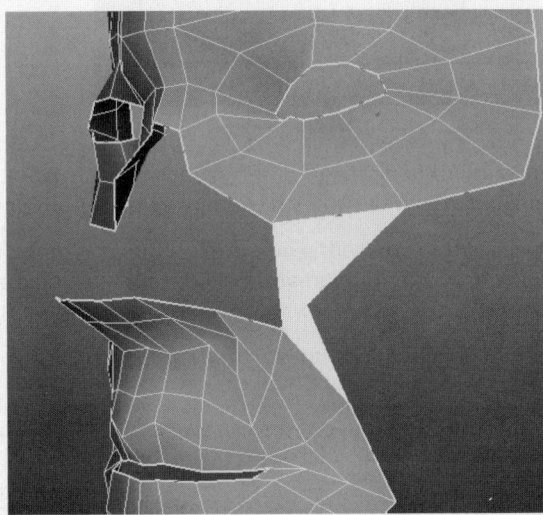

Split a Polygon

The Split Polygon tool allows you to divide a polygon face arbitrarily so that you can add vertices at specific points.

1. Continuing with the example from the previous section, zoom in closely on the face's left eye.

2. Select the object, and choose Edit Mesh ➤ Split Polygon Tool.

3. Click the edge at the corner of the eye opening, where the tear duct would be.

4. Click again on the edge on the opposite side.

5. Click a third time on the corner vertex at the bridge of the nose (see Figure 4.75).

6. Hit the Enter key to complete the operation.

FIGURE 4.75
The Split Polygon tool is used to divide polygon faces.

Spin a Polygon Edge

You can spin the edge of a polygon to alter the arrangement of polygons on a surface.

1. Continuing with the example from the previous section, zoom in closely on the face's left eye.

2. Right-click the surface, and choose Edge.

3. Select the edge added in the previous section that goes down to the bridge of the nose. This edge has divided the polygon into a four-sided and three-sided polygon.

4. Choose Edit Mesh ➤ Spin Edge Backwards.

The edge is spun around, changing the configuration of the polygons on the surface (Figure 4.76). This can be helpful when you need to alter the arrangement of the edges on the surface to allow the Insert Edge Loop tool to function properly or so that the *topology* of the surface is easier to control.

FIGURE 4.76
The Polygon edge has been spun, thus changing the topology of the surface.

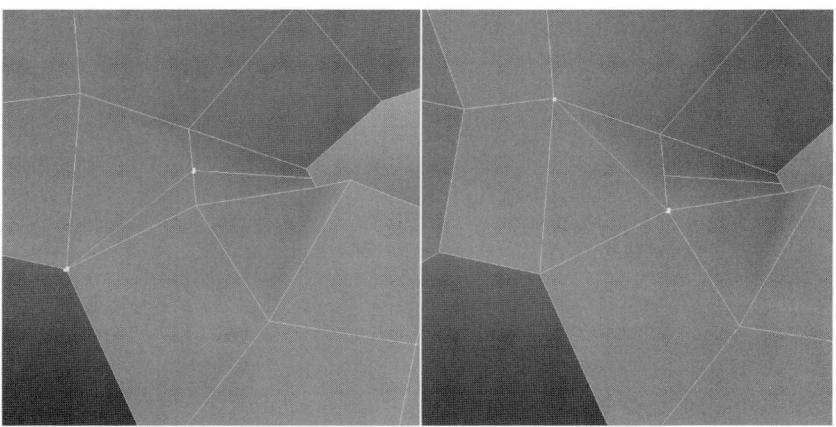

Bridge Polygons

The Bridge tool appends a series of polygons between two surfaces. Just like with the Append tool, the two surfaces must be combined before the Bridge tool will work.

1. Continuing with the example from the previous section.

2. Right-click the surface, and choose Edge.

3. Shift-select the four edges on the bridge of the nose.

4. Shift-select the corresponding edges on the top of the bottom section of the face.

5. Choose Edit Mesh ➢ Bridge. The gap is filled with several polygons.

6. You can control the number of divisions in the polygons created by the Bridge tool by selecting the surface and choosing the polyBridge1 node in the INPUTS section of the channel box. Set Divisions to **3** (see Figure 4.77).

You can use the Bridge tool on polygon faces as well. You can use this to create a pipelike surface between two faces that are opposed to each other.

To see some examples of how these techniques were used to create a simple head, open the faceModel.ma scene from the chapter4\scenes folder on the DVD.

FIGURE 4.77
The Polygon edge has been spun, thus changing the topology of the surface.

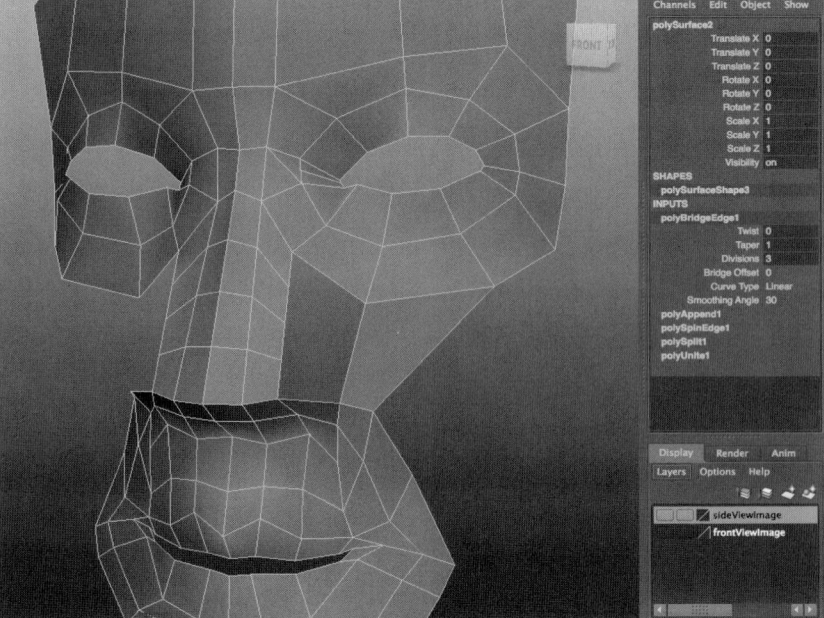

IMPORTING AND EXPORTING POLYGON GEOMETRY

These days, character models are rarely created in Maya anymore. Digital sculpting programs such as Autodesk's Mudbox and Pixologic's ZBrush are becoming a very important part of the character-creation pipeline. Because of their intuitive digital-sculpting tools and capacity for working with very dense meshes, they're often used to add changes and detail to models started in Maya. For more information, take a look at *Introducing ZBrush* by Eric Keller (Sybex, 2008) and *Introducing Mudbox 2011* by Ara Kermanikian (Sybex 2011).

As your modeling skills improve, you may decide to branch out and try using other software programs for creating character detail and texturing. It's important to understand the best way to move geometry in and out of Maya so you can use other 3D programs successfully. The most common file format supported by most 3D applications is the .obj format.

When importing and exporting .obj files from Maya, make sure that the point order does not change in the model. This ensures that the UVs are consistent and that you can use blend shapes correctly and subdivide the model in other programs successfully.

To export a model in the .obj format from Maya, use the following steps:

1. Make sure the objExport.mll plug-in is loaded in the Plug-in Manager.

2. Choose Window ➤ Settings/Preferences ➤ Plug-In Manager, and select the Loaded box next to objExport.mll (on the Mac it will be listed as objExport.bundle).

3. Select the polygon mesh you want to export, and choose File ➤ Export Selected ➤ Options.

4. In the options, choose the obj format from the File Type menu. It's usually a good idea to set all the File Type options to Off.

5. Click the Export Selection button in the options, and use the dialog box to choose a location for the file on your hard drive.

To import a file back into Maya after editing it in another program, use the following steps:

1. In Maya, choose File ➤ Import ➤ Options.

2. In the options, set File Type to obj. You should not need to worry about the Reference options if the file is not meant to be a reference (references are discussed in Chapter 1).

   The Name Clash options help you avoid problems that may occur when an object is imported into a scene that has another node that uses the same name. You can choose to append the filename to the imported object or a custom string using the options in the Resolve menus.

3. Under the File Specific options, set the File Type Specific Options to Single Object. This prevents Maya from changing the point order in the imported object. This is the most important option in the Import options. If you remember to turn this option off, then you should be able to move the file back and forth between your other 3D editors without any problems.

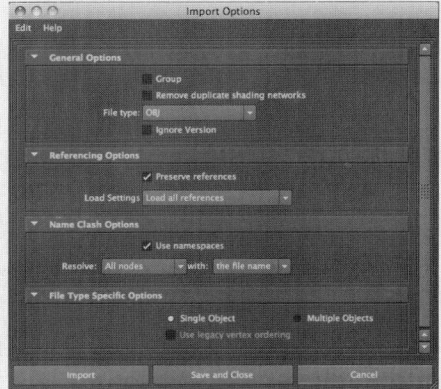

Using Subdivision Surfaces

Maya's subdivision surfaces are very similar to the polygon smooth mesh preview that you have been working with throughout the chapter. The primary distinction between smooth mesh preview and subdivision surfaces (aka subDs) is that subdivision surfaces allow you to subdivide a mesh to add detail only where you need it. For instance, if you want to sculpt a fingernail at the end of a finger, using subDs you can select just the tip of the finger and increase the subdivisions. Then you have more vertices to work with just at the fingertip, and you can sculpt the fingernail.

Most subD models start out as polygons and are converted to subDs only toward the end of the modeling process. You should create UV texture coordinates while the model is still made of polygons. They are carried over to the subDs when the model is converted.

So, why are subDs and smooth mesh preview polygons so similar, and which should you use? SubDs have been part of Maya for many versions. Smooth mesh preview polygons have only recently been added to Maya; thus, the polygon tools have evolved to become very similar to subDs. You can use either type of geometry for many of the same tasks; it's really up to you to decide when to use one versus the other.

When you convert a polygon mesh to a subdivision surface, you should keep in mind the following:

◆ Keep the polygon mesh as simple as possible; converting a dense polygon mesh to a subD significantly slows down Maya's performance.

◆ You can convert three-sided or *n*-sided (more than four-sided) polygons into subDs, but you will get better results and fewer bumps in the subD model if you stick to four-sided polygons as much as possible.

Working with SubDs

In this section, you'll build gloves for the space suit. These gloves will start as polygon models, and then they will be converted to subDs.

Each stage in the construction of the glove has been saved as a separate model so you can see the process involved. Since this is intended to be a big, bulky glove, there does not need to be a lot of detail.

1. Open the `gloveStart.ma` scene from the `chapter4\scenes` directory on the DVD. You'll see that one of the gloves has been created using standard polygon-modeling techniques (see Figure 4.78).

2. Turn off the visibility of the GLOVE_CONSTRUCT display layer so the earlier versions of the glove are not visible.

3. Select glove10, and zoom in on the model (hot key = **f**).

4. With glove10 selected, choose Modify ➤ Convert ➤ Polygons To Subdiv.

5. Press the **3** key to switch to smooth display of the model.

6. Right-click the model, and choose Vertex to display the vertices.

   The vertices of a subD object behave very similarly to the CVs of a NURBS object. The vertices are offset from the surface much like NURBS CVs (Figure 4.79).

FIGURE 4.78
The glove has been created using standard polygon-modeling techniques.

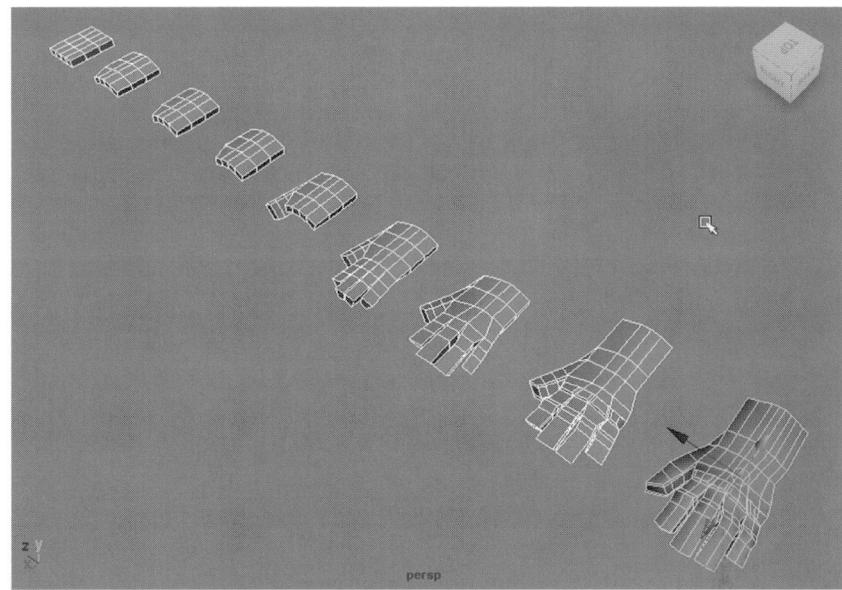

FIGURE 4.79
Convert the glove into a subdivision surface. Display the vertices of the model.

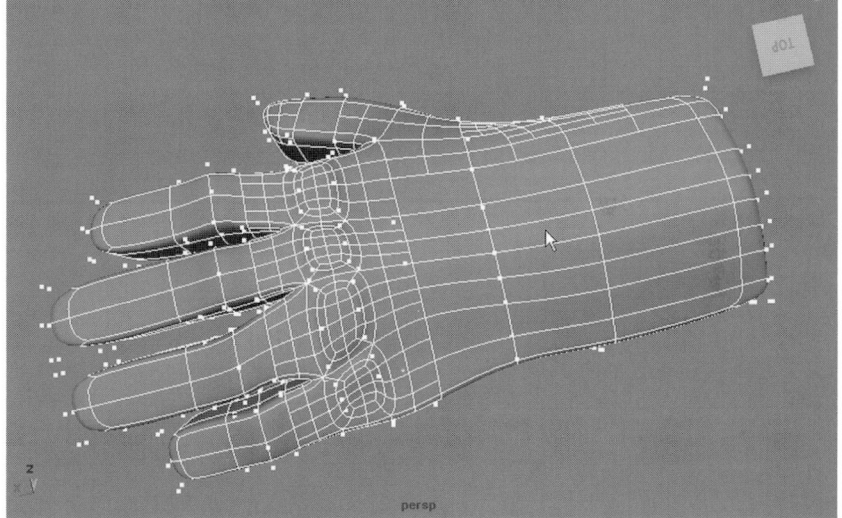

7. Right-click the model, and choose Edge. The edges appear as a cage around the object.

   You can move the edges, vertices, or faces of the model. To add a crease to an edge, follow these steps:

   A. Switch to the Surfaces menu set.

   B. Expand the Subdivision Surfaces menu.

   C. At the top of the menu are options for adding a full crease, adding a partial crease, or removing a crease (Figure 4.80).

FIGURE 4.80
The creasing options appear at the top of the Subdivision Surfaces menu.

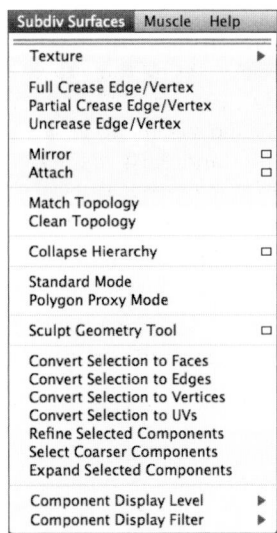

8. Select the polyToSubd1 object in the Outliner.

9. Choose Subdivision Surfaces ➤ Polygon Proxy Mode. The edge appears as a cage around the model.

10. In the Outliner, expand the polyToSubd1 object.

    Under the transform node, you'll see two shape nodes:

    ◆ polyToSubdShape1 node

    ◆ polyToSubdShape1HistPoly node

    Maya has created a duplicate polygon version of the model and placed it under the polyToSubd1 node. You can edit the polygon cage (by editing the polyToSubdShape1Hist-Poly node) using many of the polygon-editing tools, and the changes will be transferred to the subD version of the model (Figure 4.81).

11. To turn off the polygon proxy, select the model, and choose Subdivision Surfaces ➤ Standard Mode.

12. Save the scene as **glove_v01.ma**.

    To see a version of the scene, open the glove_v01.ma scene from the chapter4\scenes directory on the DVD.

FIGURE 4.81
A polygon version of the model appears in the Outliner under the polyToSubd1 node when polygon proxy mode is activated.

SubD Levels

If you take a look at the area of the knuckles on the glove, you'll see that these parts of the model appear to have a higher number of divisions than the rest of the model. Subdivision surfaces have multiple levels of division. You can see this in the wireframe display when the object is selected. The knuckles and parts of the thumb have a higher level of subdivision than the rest of the glove. The different levels of subdivision are edited separately. So even though you can see that there are more divisions around the area of the knuckle, you need to switch to a higher subdivision level before you can edit these points directly. This exercise will show you how to do this.

1. Continue with the scene from the previous section, or open the glove_v01.ma scene from the chapter4\scenes directory on the DVD.

2. Right-click the glove, and choose Vertex. The vertices are displayed for the model; notice that the top of each knuckle has six vertices.

3. Select the Move tool, and open the Tool options.

4. Activate Tweak Mode.

5. Spend a few minutes shaping the glove using the Move tool. In tweak mode, you can select each vertex and nudge it with the Move tool. The standard Move tool manipulator is not visible when you have tweak mode activated.

6. Right-click the model, and choose Display Finer (Figure 4.82). This moves you to the next higher level of subdivision. The knuckles have more vertices available for editing.

   The lowest level of subdivision is labeled level 0 or the base level. The next level is 1, then 2, and so on.

7. Use the Move tool to reposition the vertices of the knuckle. If you are having trouble moving the vertices at the higher levels, try disabling Soft Select in the Move tool options. To switch back to level 0, right-click the model, and choose Display Coarser.

FIGURE 4.82
At the finer display level, more vertices are available for editing the knuckles of the glove.

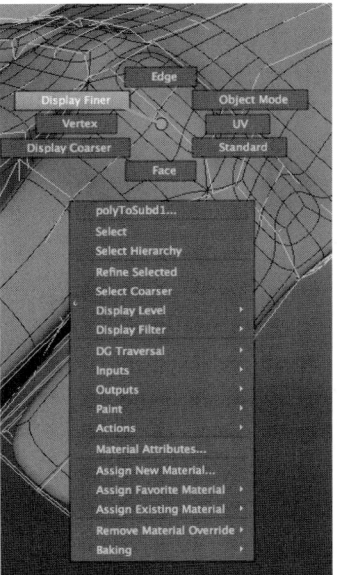

8. To add a level of subdivision to a specific area of the model, select a component, and right-click the model.

9. Choose Refine Selected from the marking menu.

   Notice that when you are working in level 1, if you change the position of a vertex that lies on the border of a level 0 region, the area near the edited vertex is subdivided automatically.

   The glove has three levels of subdivision, 0 through 2. The level 2 area is found where the thumb meets the glove. Changes made at level 2 are best suited for details such as wrinkles and small folds. You can add up to 13 levels of subdivision to a model.

10. Select the Glove model, and choose Subdivision Surfaces ➢ Sculpt Geometry Tool.

11. You can use the Artisan brush interface to reshape the model. The Smooth operation is helpful for rounding the edges near the wrist.

12. When you are happy with the model, save the glove as **glove_v02.ma**.

To see a version of the finished glove, open the glove_v02.ma scene from the chapter4\ scenes directory on the DVD.

You can import the glove into your version of the space suit scene and scale, rotate, and position it to fit at the end of the arm:

1. Make a mirror copy of the glove.

2. Position it at the end of the other arm (see Figure 4.83).

   You can also use the armStart.ma scene from the chapter4\scenes directory on the DVD.

To see a finished version of the space suit character, open the space suitFinished.ma scene on the chapter4\scenes directory of the DVD (see Figure 4.84).

FIGURE 4.83
Import the gloves into the space suit scene and add them to the model.

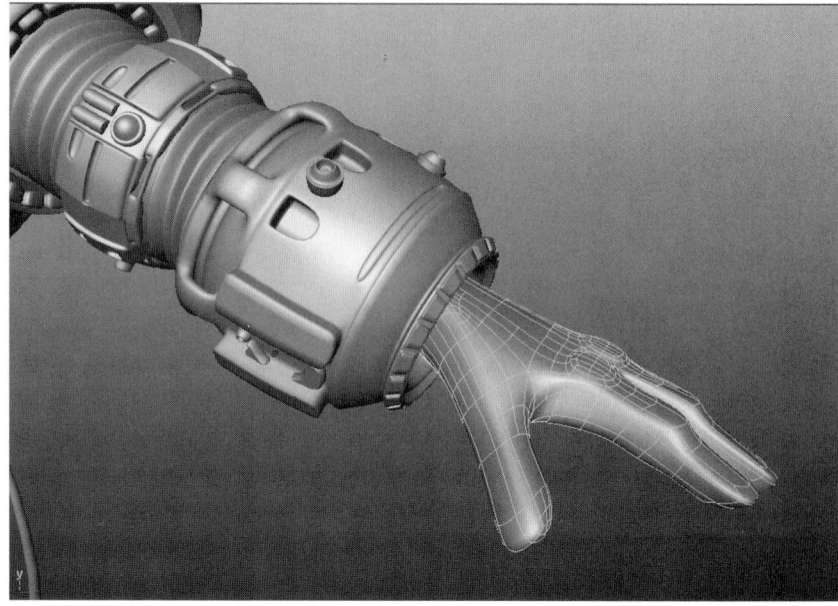

FIGURE 4.84
The completed space suit model

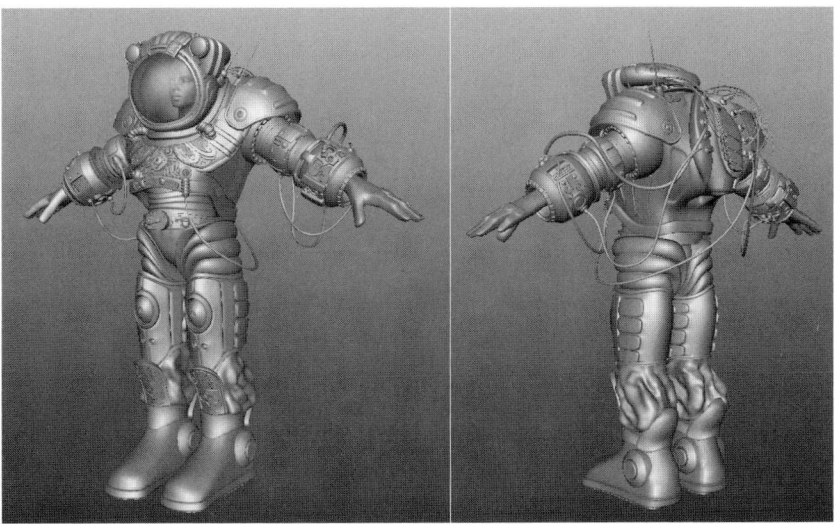

ARMS

If you'd like to see how the arms were created, open the `armStart.ma` scene in the `chapter4\` `scenes` directory on the DVD.

The Bottom Line

Understand polygon geometry Polygon geometry consists of flat faces connected and shaped to form three-dimensional objects. You can edit the geometry by transforming the vertices, edges, and faces that make up the surface of the model.

Master it Examine the polygon primitives in the Create ➢ Polygon Primitives menu.

Work with smooth mesh polygons The smooth mesh preview display allows you to work on a smoothed version of the polygon model while limiting the number of components needed to shape the model. You can use creasing to create hard edges in selected areas.

Master it Create a backpack for the space suit.

Model using deformers Deformers such as the lattice, nonlinear deformers, and the Soft Modification tool can be used to help shape geometry and groups of objects.

Master it Create a number of small-detail objects for the belt of the space suit. Shape the details so that they conform to the belt.

Combine meshes Multiple meshes can be combined under a single shape node. When this is done, you can edit the components of the combined meshes as a single mesh.

Master it Combine two polygon spheres, and use the polygon-editing tools to join the faces of the spheres.

Model polygons with Paint Effects   Paint Effects strokes can be converted to NURBS and Polygon geometry. Using the default brush, you can quickly create hoses and wires. Because construction history connects the converted objects to the strokes, you can use the stroke settings to edit the shape of the converted objects.

Master it   Add additional hoses and wires to the space suit.

Convert NURBS surfaces to polygons   NURBS surfaces are frequently used as a starting place to create polygon objects, giving you the power of both types of models.

Master it   Convert the helmet object into polygons.

Sculpt polygons using Artisan   The Artisan toolset is a brush-based modeling and editing tool. Using Artisan, you can sculpt directly on the surface of geometry.

Master it   Use Artisan to sculpt dents into a surface.

Use subdivision surfaces   Subdivision surfaces are similar to smooth mesh preview polygons except that specific parts of the model can be subdivided and edited as needed. You can traverse the subdivision levels while you work.

Master it   Add wrinkles, seams, and other details to the glove model.

Chapter 5

Animation Techniques

Computer animation has revolutionized the way stories are told. Whether the animation is used for entertainment, to advertise a product, or to demonstrate a complex scientific principle, the ability to construct virtual three-dimensional objects and then manipulate their movements over time has given the artist an unprecedented amount of power. A creative Maya user will find that there are few limits to what they can accomplish through animation.

Animation in Maya is accomplished through a wide variety of tools and techniques. The goal of this chapter is to show you how to use the tools in Maya to animate the attributes of various nodes. Gaining an understanding of how you can solve problems in Maya is essential to telling your story through computer animation.

In this chapter, you will learn to:

◆   Use Inverse Kinematics

◆   Animate with keyframes

◆   Use the Graph Editor

◆   Preview animations with a playblast

◆   Animate with expressions

◆   Animate with motion paths

◆   Use animation layers

Using Joints and Constraints

Most of this chapter is devoted to exercises that animate a simple mechanical bug model. Animation and rigging are closely related skills. *Rigging* is the process where controls are created to allow you to manipulate the three-dimensional objects you create in order to create animation. Even if you don't intend to do much of your own rigging, you'll have an easier time understanding how to animate if you know what goes into creating a rig. Chapter 7 delves into more advanced rigging concepts; in this chapter, you'll learn some basic tools and techniques for rigging to get you started.

Joint Basics

A *joint* is the basic animation control. It is essentially a point in space connected by a virtual bone, symbolized by an elongated pyramid. The geometry is bound to the joints in a process known as *skinning*. The skinned geometry is then deformed when the joints are moved to create such effects as the bend in an elbow or a knee.

When rigging mechanical objects and robots, it's not always necessary to use joints; you can parent the parts of the object together in an organized fashion and then set keyframes directly on the geometry (this is demonstrated in Chapter 1). However, because of the built-in hierarchy of joints as well as the many animation controls available, using joints can make rigging and animating mechanical objects easier, even if you don't intend to bind or skin the geometry so that it is deformed by the joints.

You create joints using the Joint tool (from the Animation menu set, choose Skeleton ➢ Joint Tool). A joint is represented by a simple wire sphere. As noted before, when one joint is connected to another, the space between the two joints is bridged with a wireframe pyramid shape referred to as a *bone*. The broad end of the bone is placed next to the parent joint, and the pointed end of the bone is pointed toward the child joint (see Figure 5.1).

Joints are most often animated by rotating the parent joint or using *Inverse Kinematics*, which orients the joints based on the position of a goal called an *End Effector*. This is discussed later in this chapter. Joints can also be animated by placing keyframes on Translate or Scale channels; however, this is slightly less common.

Joints are usually placed in a hierarchical relationship known as a *joint chain*. Joint chains can have many branches and numerous controls depending on the complexity of the model. A series of joint chains is known as a *skeleton*.

A joint is a type of deformer that typically influences the shape of nearby components depending on how the components of the geometry are bound, or skinned, to the joints. Since the bug in these examples is mechanical, the joints do not need to deform the geometry of the model. You can simply parent the pieces of the leg geometry to the individual joints. Skinning geometry to joints is explored further in Chapter 7.

FIGURE 5.1
Two joints are
placed on the grid.

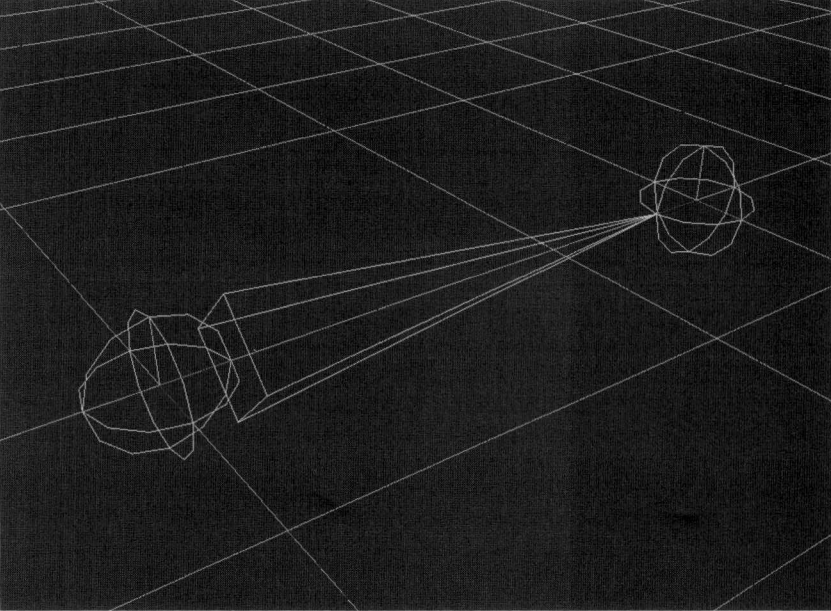

Point Constraints

A point constraint uses the world space position of one object to control the world space position of another object. World space coordinates tell exactly where an object is in relation to the rest of the scene. This is different from object space coordinates, which are relative to the object's initial position.

For instance, if you move an object on the grid, the Translate channels in the Channel Box indicate where an object is in object space. If you freeze the transformations on an object (Modify ➢ Freeze Transformations) after moving the object, its Translate (and Rotate) channels become 0 in X, Y, and Z (Scale channels become 1 in X, Y, and Z), and its current position is now its starting position in object space.

If you create a joint in a scene and then reposition it and freeze transformations, you'll notice that the Rotate channels all become zero for its new orientation; however, the Translate channels are not affected by freeze transformations. If you want to place a joint exactly at the position of another object, you can't rely on the object's Translate channels as an accurate description of the object's location in world space. One way to get around this is to use a point constraint to position the joint according to the object's world space coordinates.

You'll use point constraints to place joints precisely at the pivot points of the leg parts. Once the joints are positioned, you can delete the constraints.

The bug model, which is used in this exercise, is a combination of NURBS and polygon geometry. The bug's parts have already been parented in the Outliner to form a basic hierarchy (see Figure 5.2).

FIGURE 5.2
The mechanical bug is created from NURBS and polygon surfaces. Its various parts are organized in the Outliner.

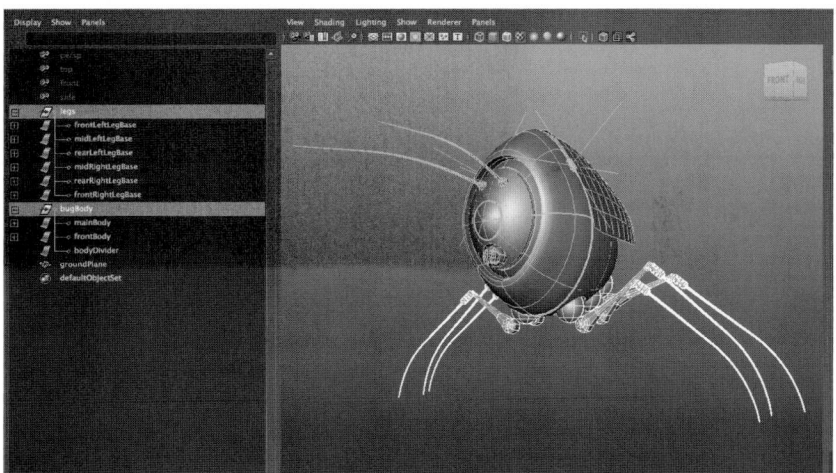

The model consists of two main groups: the legs and the bugBody. At the moment, these two groups are separate. The legs and body are placed on two different display layers so their visibility can be turned off easily while working.

1. Open the mechBugRig_v01.ma scene from the chapter5\scenes directory on the DVD.

2. In the Layer Editor, turn off the BODY display layer so only the legs are visible.

3. Make sure the grid is visible in the perspective view. Switch to the Animation menu set, and turn on Grid Snapping.

4. Choose Skeleton ➤ Joint Tool. Draw three joints evenly spaced on the grid starting at the center. It doesn't matter in which direction you place the joints; they will be repositioned in a moment (see Figure 5.3).

FIGURE 5.3
Place three joints on the grid.

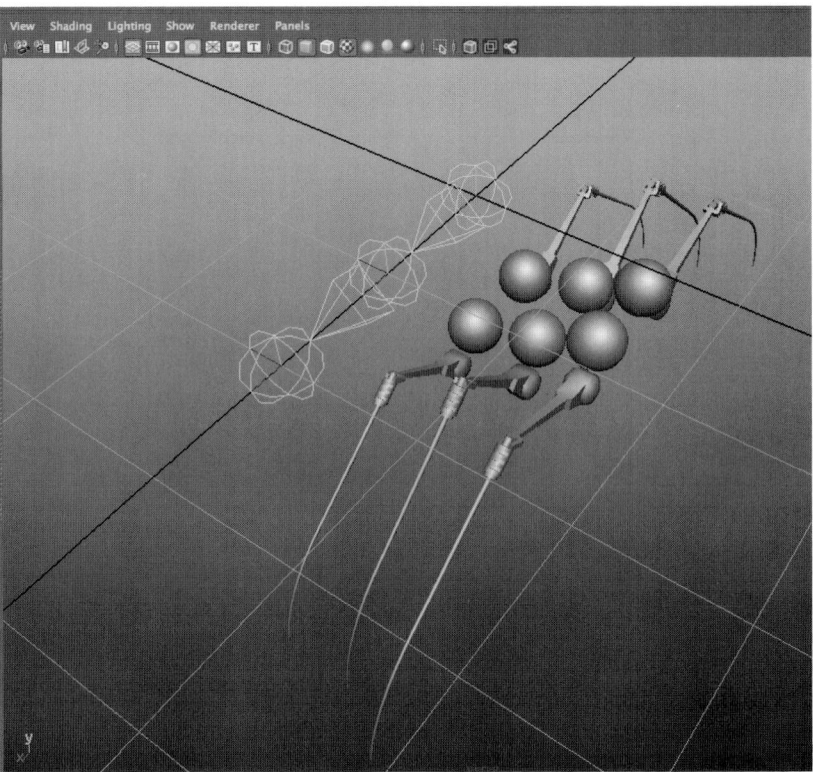

5. In the Outliner, expand the legs group.

6. Select the frontleftLegBase object, Ctrl+click joint1, and choose Constrain ➤ Point ➤ Options.

7. In the Options box, make sure Maintain Offset is off and Constrain Axes is set to All (see Figure 5.4). Click Apply to create the constraint; the joints will snap to the position of the leg's base sphere.

When you create a constraint node, it appears in the Outliner parented to the constrained object. The icon looks like an exclamation point (see Figure 5.5). In this particular situation, you're only using the constraint to quickly position the joint at the same spot as the geometry, so once the joint is repositioned, you can remove the constraint. This technique is a fast and easy way to make one object snap to the world space position of another. Using constraints as an animation tool is discussed later in the chapter.

FIGURE 5.4
The options for the point constraint

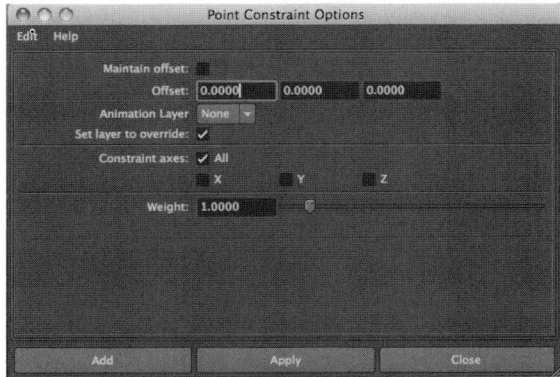

FIGURE 5.5
The point constraint appears as an exclamation point parented to the constrained object in the Outliner.

8. In the Outliner, expand joint1.

9. Select joint1_pointConstraint1, and press the Delete key to remove the constraint.

MEL IN ACTION: QUICK OBJECT-REPOSITION SCRIPT

You may find yourself frequently using a point constraint to snap one object to another. You can create a shelf button using a short MEL script so that, instead of repeating the same three steps over and over again, you can simply click a shelf button to instantly snap one object to another. This is an example of how learning just a little bit of MEL can make your workflow faster and easier.

Open a text editor such as Notepad (on Windows) or TextEdit (on the Mac). Type the following line:

```
string $mySelection[] = `ls -sl`;
```

This creates a variable array that holds a list of the currently selected objects. The list is numbered starting with zero, so once the list has been created from one or more selected objects, the first selected object is referred to as $mySelection[0], the second selected object is referred to as $mySelection[1], and so on.

The ls command stands for "list," and the -sl flag modifies the list command so it creates its list from the currently selected objects. The variable actually holds the result of the list command, so the list command is contained within the backtick marks (`). The backtick key is the one below the Esc key on standard keyboards (not the apostrophe key). All commands in MEL must end in a semicolon.

Hit Enter (or Return) to start a new line. In this line, type the following:

```
delete `pointConstraint $mySelection[0] $mySelection[1]`;
```

(CONTINUES)

MEL IN ACTION: QUICK OBJECT-REPOSITION SCRIPT *(CONTINUED)*

This command is actually two commands in a single line. The command within the accent marks creates a point constraint. The second object in the list, $mySelection[1], is constrained to the first, $mySelection[0]. When you create a constraint, you select the constraining object first and then the object that is constrained. The delete command then deletes the constraint immediately after it has been created, so that when you run the script, the second object snaps to the first, and you don't need to delete the constraint in the Outliner.

It may seem confusing to nest the point constraint command within the delete command and place them on a single line, but there's a good reason for using this convention. Let's say you wrote the script so that the point constraint command on one line creates the constraint—thus snapping one object to another—and then a second delete command deletes the constraint on another line. The delete command needs to know which point constraint it should delete. If you assume that the new point constraint will be named pointConstraint1, you run the risk of deleting a point constraint that already exists in the scene. You need a scripting strategy that creates a constraint, retrieves the correct name of the new constraint, and then deletes this new constraint. This involves many more lines of code. Hence, it is much easier, and simpler, to nest the point constraint command within the delete command. Everything is taken care of within a single line of code.

1. Select both lines in the text editor and copy them.

2. In Maya, paste the script into the bottom half of the Script Editor (you can open the Script Editor by choosing Window ➤ General Editors ➤ Script Editor).

3. In the Shelf tab, switch to the Custom shelf.

4. Select both lines in the Script Editor, and choose File ➤ Save Script To Shelf.

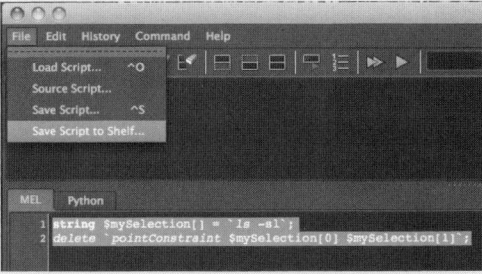

5. In the pop-up menu, give the script a short, six-letter title such as **objSnp** (coming up with a descriptive six-letter title for a script is an art form unto itself).

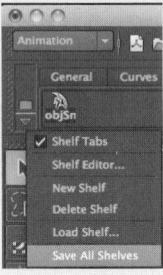

6. To the left of the shelf, click the down-arrow button and choose Save All Shelves so this shelf button is available in future Maya sessions.

7. Create two objects in a Maya scene.

8. Select the constraining object first.

9. Shift+click the object to be constrained.

10. Click the objSnp button in the Custom tab of the shelf to test the script. If you get an error, you can edit the command in the Shelf Editor.

11. Click the down-arrow button to the left of the shelf, and choose Shelf Editor.

12. Select the Custom shelf in the Shelves tab.

13. In the right side of the Shelf Contents tab, select the objSnap script.

14. Click the Commands tab, and you'll see the script in the edit area.

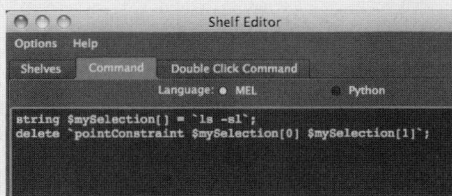

15. Correct any typos, and save the shelf.

To see a version of the script, open the objSnp.mel script in a text editor. The script is located in the chapter5\mel directory on the DVD.

10. Repeat steps 5 and 6 (or use the shelf button created in the "MEL in Action: Quick Object-Reposition Script" sidebar) to reposition joint2 to the frontLeftFoot object.

11. Turn on Point Snapping (turn off Grid Snapping), and position joint3 at the very tip of the frontLeftFoot.

12. Rename joint1 **frontLeftLegJoint**. Rename joint2 **frontLeftFootJoint**, and rename joint3 **frontLeftEndJoint**.

13. Make sure all point constraints on the joints have been deleted. Parent the frontLeftLegBase object to the frontLeftLegJoint, and parent the frontLeftFoot to the frontLeftFootJoint (see Figure 5.6).

14. Create similar joint systems for the remaining five legs. Remember to rename your joints in a descriptive manner (see step 8) to avoid confusion when animating.

15. When you have finished creating all the joints, place them in the legs group. To do this, MMB-drag each of the top joints in the chain into the legs group in the Outliner (see Figure 5.7).

16. Save the scene as **mechBugRig_v02.ma**.

To see a version of the scene to this point, open the mechBugRig_v02.ma scene from the chapter5\scenes directory.

FIGURE 5.6
Parent the parts of
the leg to the leg
joints.

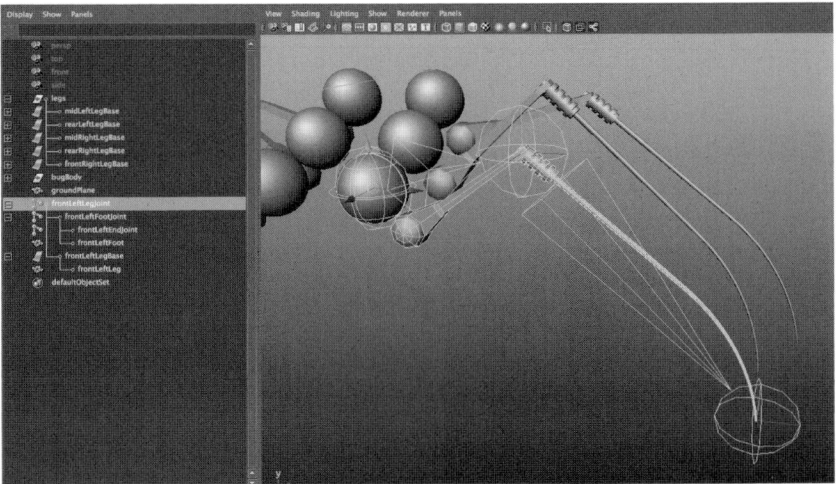

FIGURE 5.7
Create joint chains
for each of the legs.

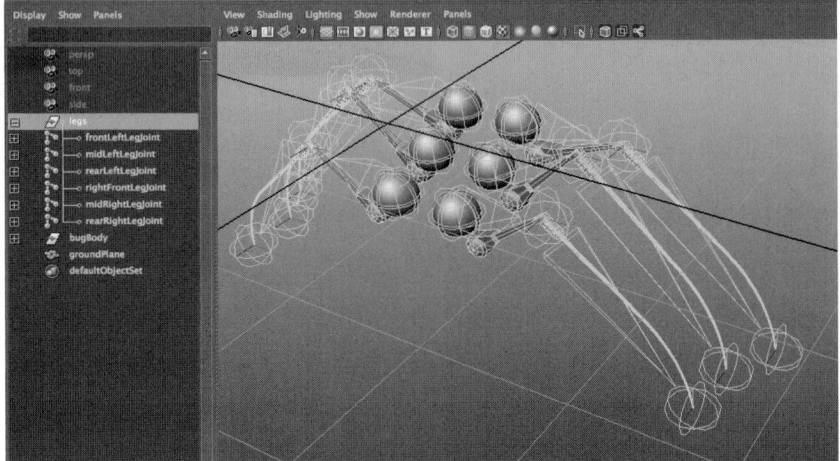

Aim Constraints

An *aim constraint* constrains the orientation of an object relative to the position of one or more other objects.

1. Continue with the scene from the previous section, or open the mechBugRig_v02.ma scene from the chapter5\scenes directory on the DVD.

2. Turn on the display layer for BODY; turn off the LEGS layer so the legs are hidden and the body is displayed.

3. Create a locator (Create ➢ Locator), and name it **eyeAimLoc**.

4. Set the eyeAimLoc's Translate X, Y, and Z channels to **0**, **0**, and **2**, respectively.

5. In the Outliner, expand the bugBodyGroup.

6. MMB-drag eyeAimLoc into the bugBody group.

7. Select the eyeAimLoc, and choose Modify ➤ Freeze Transformations so the Translate channels become 0, 0, and 0.

8. Expand the frontBody group, the head group, and the face group.

9. Select the eyeAimLoc, and Ctrl+click the eyeBase group (see Figure 5.8).

10. From the Animation menu set, choose Constrain ➤ Aim ➤ Options.

11. In the options, choose Edit ➤ Reset to return the settings to the default.

12. Set the Aim Vector fields to **0**, **0**, and **1** so that the aim vector is set to the z-axis (see Figure 5.9).

FIGURE 5.8
Select the eyeAim-
Loc locator and the
eyeBase object in
the Outliner.

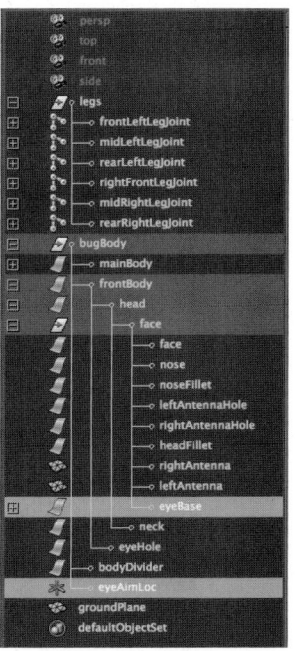

FIGURE 5.9
The Aim Con-
straint Options
window

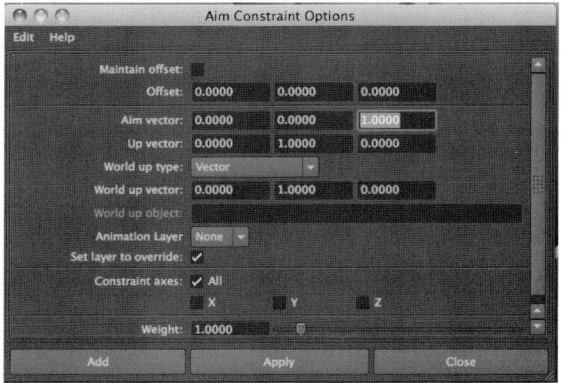

13. Apply to create the constraint.

14. Move the locator around in the scene, and you'll see that the eyes follow it (see Figure 5.10). Because the locator is parented to the bug body, when you animate the bug, the locator will move with it.

FIGURE 5.10
The eyes follow the position of the eye-AimLoc locator.

15. Create two new locators named **leftAntennaAimLoc** and **rightAntennaAimLoc**.

16. Set leftAntennaAimLoc's Translate X, Y, and Z to **1**, **0**, and **3**, respectively, and set rightAntennaAimLoc's Translate X, Y, and Z to **-1**, **0**, and **3**.

17. Freeze transformations for both locators.

18. Shift+click both locators, and group them together. Name the group **antennaAim**. Leave the pivot point for the group at the center of the grid.

19. In the Outliner, MMB-drag antennaAim into the bugBody group.

20. Expand the antennaAim group, and expand the face group (in the bugBody/frontBody/head group).

21. Aim constrain the leftAntenna to the leftAntennaAimLoc locator and the rightAntenna to the rightAntennaAimLoc locator.

When you move each antennaAimLoc locator, the antennae follow; when you rotate the antennaAim group, the locators move and the antennae follow. This gives you a way to animate the antennae separately and together (see Figure 5.11).

22. Save the scene as **mechBugRig_v03.ma**.

FIGURE 5.11
You can animate the antennae separately or together based on the grouping of the antennaAimLoc locators.

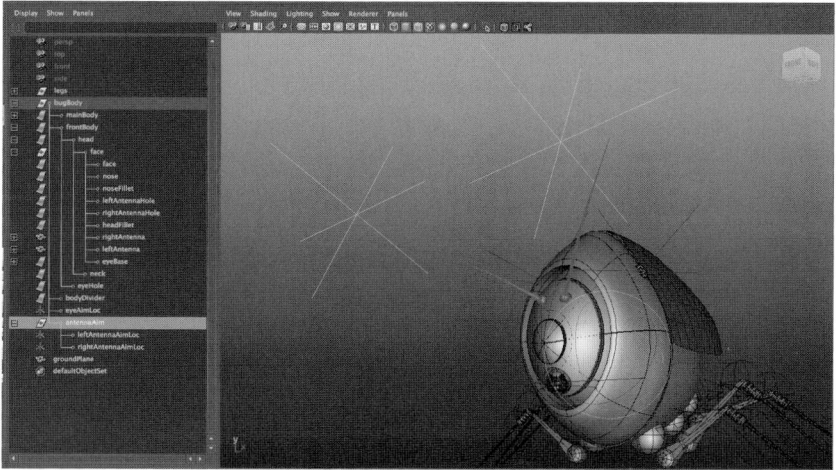

To see a version of the scene to this point, open the `mechBugRig_v03.ma` scene from the `chapter5\scenes` directory on the DVD.

Inverse Kinematics

Kinematics is the study of the motion of objects. This is related to but distinguished from dynamics in that kinematics does not study the cause of the objects' motion, only the way in which the objects move. In 3D computer graphics, the term *kinematics* describes how joints can be moved to animate objects and characters. There are two main types of kinematics: Forward Kinematics and Inverse Kinematics.

Forward Kinematics refers to a situation in which each joint in the chain inherits the motion of its parent joint. So if you have four joints in a chain, when you rotate the root, the three child joints move based on the rotation of the root. When you rotate the second joint, the third and fourth joints inherit the motion of the second (see Figure 5.12).

Forward Kinematics can be useful in many situations; for instance, it is often used for basic arm animation for characters. However, it can be tedious and difficult to work with for other types of animation, particularly when animating the legs of a character walking or jumping. Constant adjustments have to be made to ensure that as the root joints are animated, the limbs of the character do not penetrate the floor or slide during a walk cycle.

FIGURE 5.12
When using Forward Kinematics, each joint inherits the rotation of its parent.

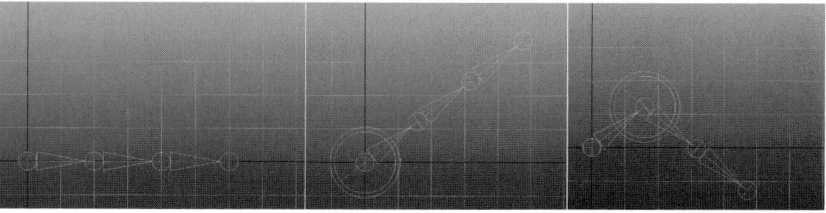

Inverse Kinematics (IK) causes the joints in a chain to orient themselves based on the position of a goal known as the *End Effector* (see Figure 5.13). Inverse Kinematics can be a more intuitive technique in many situations. When used on legs, the Sticky option for Inverse Kinematics can prevent joints from penetrating the floor or sliding during a walk cycle. When animating an IK chain, you can simply change the position of the End Effector using the Inverse Kinematics (IK) Handle, and all the joints in the chain will orient themselves based on the position of the End Effector. The End Effector itself is positioned using the IK Handle; the End Effector is not actually visible or selectable in the viewport (it can be selected in the Hypergraph window).

FIGURE 5.13
Inverse Kinematics cause the joints in a chain to rotate based on the position of a goal.

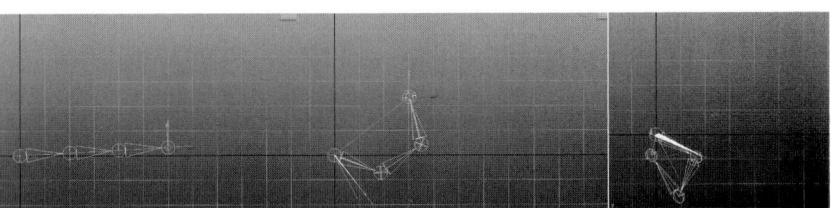

There are controls for blending between Forward and Inverse Kinematics known as FK/IK Blend. You can switch between Forward and Inverse Kinematics and even blend between the two. This is covered in more detail in Chapter 7.

Maya's kinematic controls work very well for many standard situations. Most professional riggers prefer to create their own custom controls and solutions. Creating custom controls is discussed in Chapters 6 and 7. In this section, a very basic, simple IK technique is used on the legs of the mechanical bug. This makes animating the legs easier and more intuitive because you need only worry about the position of a single goal when animating all the parts of one of the legs.

IK Handle Tool

In this section, you'll add Inverse Kinematics to each of the legs on the mechanical bug:

1. Continue with the scene from the previous section, or open the `mechBugRig_v03.ma` scene from the `chapter5\scenes` directory on the DVD.

2. In the Layer menu, turn off Visibility for the BODY layer.

3. From the Animation menu set, choose Skeleton ➢ IK Handle Tool ➢ Options.

4. In the options, set the Current solver to ikSCsolver. This is the Single Chain solver that works well for simple joint chains, such as the legs in this bug.

   The other option is the Rotate Plane solver (RPsolver). This solver has extra controls that can be used to solve joint-flipping problems, which can occur with more complex joint arrangements. If you create an IK Handle using the ikSCsolver and your joints behave unpredictably, try switching to the RPsolver (you can do this after creating the handle using the menu options in the IK Handle's Attribute Editor). The various types of IK solvers are discussed in Chapter 7.

   In general, when adding Inverse Kinematics to a joint chain using the IK Handle tool, you don't want the joints to be aligned in a straight line. There should be at least a small bend in the joint chain. This helps the solver figure out how the joints should bend as they attempt to rotate based on the position of the End Effector. It's also a good idea to freeze transformations on the joints so their X, Y, and Z rotation channels are set to zero before adding the IK Handle (in the mechBug_v03.ma scene this has already been done).

5. Turn on Solver Enable, and turn off Snap Enable.

    Snap Enable causes the IK Handle to snap back to the position of the end joint when you release it. You'll create a custom handle using a curve, so this option should be off.

6. Turn on Sticky.

    Sticky keeps the IK Handle's position constant as you pose the rest of the skeleton. This is very useful for keeping feet from moving through the floor when animating the other parts of the skeleton (see Figure 5.14).

7. The other settings can be left at the default. With the IK Handle tool activated, click the frontLeftLeg joint (the joint at the root of the front left leg); then click the joint at the end of the frontLeftLeg chain. The IK Handle appears at the end of the joint chain (see Figure 5.15).

FIGURE 5.14
The options for
the IK Handle tool

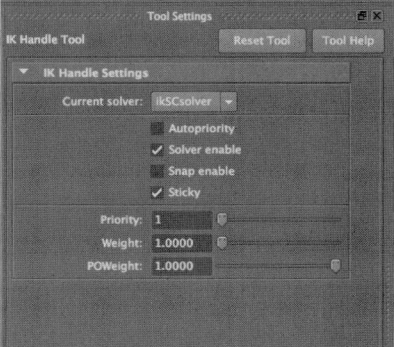

FIGURE 5.15
The IK Handle
tool creates an
IK solver for the
front left leg.

8. Try moving the IK Handle; you'll see the rest of the joint rotate based on the position of the handle.

9. Click Undo until the IK Handle returns to its original location.

It's usually a good idea to use a curve or another easily selectable object as a control for the IK Handle. This makes it easy to select the handle directly in the scene without having to hunt around in the Outliner.

10. Create a NURBS circle (Create ➢ NURBS Primitives ➢ Circle).

11. In the Channel Box for the NURBS circle, expand the makeNurbCircle 1 section under INPUTS. This gives you access to the shape node settings for the circle. Set the radius to 0.4.

12. Use the objSnp shelf button created earlier in the chapter (see the "MEL in Action: Quick Object-Reposition Script" sidebar) to position the circle at the location of the IK Handle.

    A. Select the ikHandle1 object.

    B. Ctrl+click the nurbsCircle1.

    C. Click the objSnp button in the Custom shelf.

13. Select the nurbsCircle1, and rename it **frontLeftFootCtrl**.

14. Choose Modify ➢ Freeze Transformations so the current position of the curve becomes its home position.

15. Select the frontLeftFootCtrl, and Ctrl+click the ikHandle.

16. Create a point constraint so the handle is constrained to the frontLeftFoot circle (Constrain ➢ Point).

17. You can turn off visibility of the ikHandle1 object. To move the leg, select the frontleftLegCtrl circle and move it around. To reset its position, set its Translate X, Y, and Z channels to **0**.

18. Repeat steps 2 through 17 to create controls for the other five legs (the options for the IK Handle tool should already be stored, so you can just activate the tool and use it to add IK to the other legs).

19. When you have finished making the controls for the other legs, select the control circles, and group them. Name the group **legsControlGroup**.

20. Select the legsControlGroup group, and choose Modify ➢ Center Pivot. This places the pivot of the group at the center of the controls.

21. Make another NURBS circle; name the circle **legsCtrl**.

22. Use the objSnp button to place the circle at the position of the legControlGroup's pivot.

23. Freeze transformations on the legsCtrl.

24. Select the legsCtrl circle, and Ctrl+click the legsControlGroup.

25. Choose Constrain ➢ Parent ➢ Options.

26. In the options, make sure Maintain Offset is on and both Translate and Rotate are set to All.

27. Click Apply to create the constraint. The Parent constraint constrains both the translation and the rotation of one object to another.

Now you have a selectable control for moving all the legs as well as each individual leg. This will mean less time hunting around in the Outliner.

COLOR-CODING CONTROLS

You can create different colors for the NURBS curve you use as a control. To do this, open the Attribute Editor for the curve, and expand the Object Display rollout and then the Drawing Overrides rollout. Click Enable Overrides, and use the Color slider to choose a new color for the circles. This helps them stand out in the scene.

---

28. Finally, you can straighten up the Outliner by grouping the IK Handles. Name the group **feetIkhandles**.

29. Group the legs and bugBody together, and name this group **bug**.

30. Save the scene as **mechBugRig_v04.ma**.

To see a version of the scene to this point, open the mechBugRig_v04.ma scene from the chapter5\scenes directory on the DVD.

Create a Master Control

To finish the rig, you can create a selectable control to animate the position and the rotation of the bug body and then group all the parts of the bug together so that it can be easily moved or scaled in the scene.

1. Continue with the scene from the previous section, or open the mechBugRig_v04.ma scene from the chapter5\scenes directory on the DVD.

2. Create a new display layer named **CONTROLS**.

3. Turn off the visibility of the LEGS and BODY display layers.

4. Select the NURBS circles, and add them to the CONTROLS layer.

5. Turn off the visibility of the CONTROLS layer so the scene is blank.

6. Turn on the visibility of the grid, and turn on Grid Snapping.

7. Choose Create ➤ CV Curve Tool ➤ Options. Set Curve Degree to Linear.

8. Switch to the top view, and use the curve to draw a shape like the one in Figure 5.16. The shape should be a cross with an arrowhead at each end of the cross.

9. Press Enter to complete the curve.

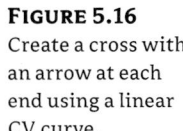

FIGURE 5.16
Create a cross with an arrow at each end using a linear CV curve.

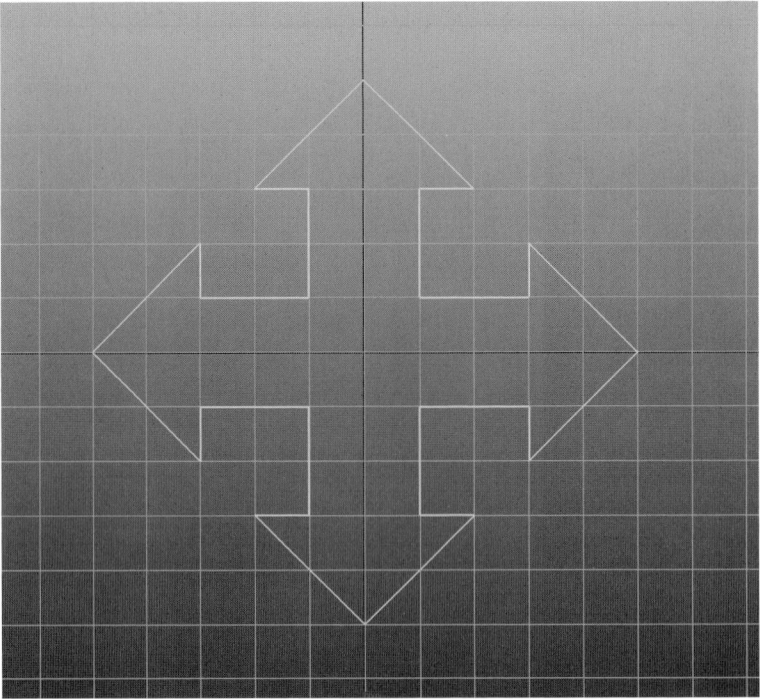

10. Center the pivot of the curve and name it **bodyCtrl**.

11. Scale the bodyCtrl curve in X, Y, and Z to **0.35**.

12. Freeze transformations on the curve.

    Next, you want to move the curve above the body so you can easily select it. This curve controls the translation and rotation of the bugBody. However, you want to keep the pivot point of the control at the center of the bug body. Since you snapped the curve to the center of the bugBody, the pivot point of the curve is at the same position as the bugBody. So, how do you move the curve without moving the pivot point? Simple—you move all of the CVs of the curve above the bug body. This moves the curve without changing its pivot point.

13. Select the bodyCtrl curve, and switch to CV selection mode (right-click the curve, and choose Control Vertex).

14. Drag a selection marquee over all the CVs of the curve.

15. Turn the visibility of the body back on. Switch to the Move tool, and drag up on the y-axis to position the CVs of the curve above the body. Since the pivot point has not changed, it doesn't matter how high you place the curve above the bug; it just has to be easily select-able (see Figure 5.17).

16. Select the bodyCtrl curve in the Outliner, and Ctrl+click the bug group.

FIGURE 5.17
Move the CVs of the bodyCtrl curve above the bugBody; the pivot point of the curve remains at the center of the bugBody.

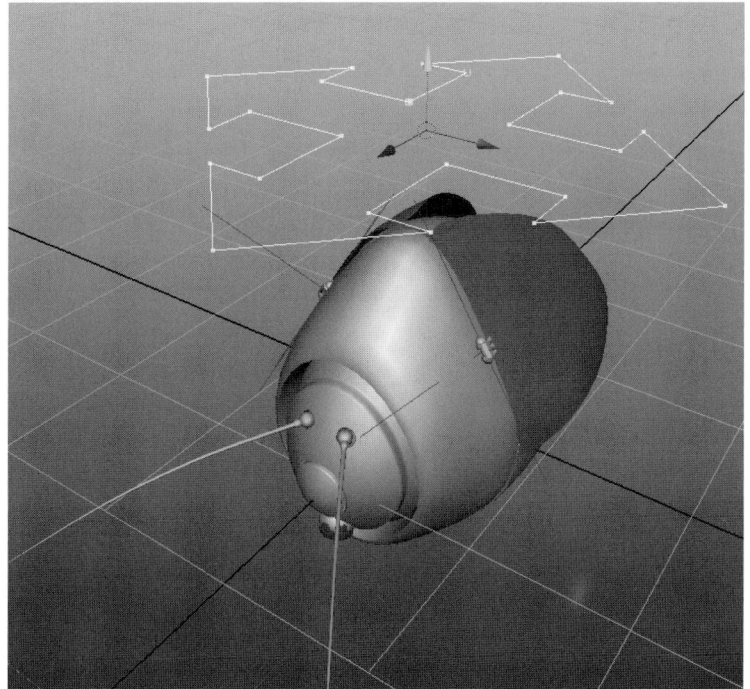

17. Choose Constrain ➤ Parent ➤ Options. In the options, make sure Maintain Offset is selected and Translate and Rotate are set to All. Create the constraint.

    The parent constraint constrains both the translation and rotation of one object to another object.

18. Turn on the LEGS layer.

19. Select the bodyCtrl curve, and try moving and rotating it. The legs stay on the ground (within a certain range).

    At this point, you should have a nice set of simple controls for both the body and the legs of the bug. All this work will make animating the bug a much more pleasant experience.

20. Finally, select everything in the Outliner except the ground plane, and group them together. Name the group **mechanicalBug**.

21. Add the bodyCtrl curve and the three locators for the eyes and antenna controls to the CONTROLS layer.

22. Save the scene as `mechBugRig_v05.ma`.

To see a version of the scene to this point, open the `mechBugRig_v05.ma` scene from the `chapter5\scenes` directory of the DVD (see Figure 5.18).

FIGURE 5.18
The completed
bug rig is ready
for animation.

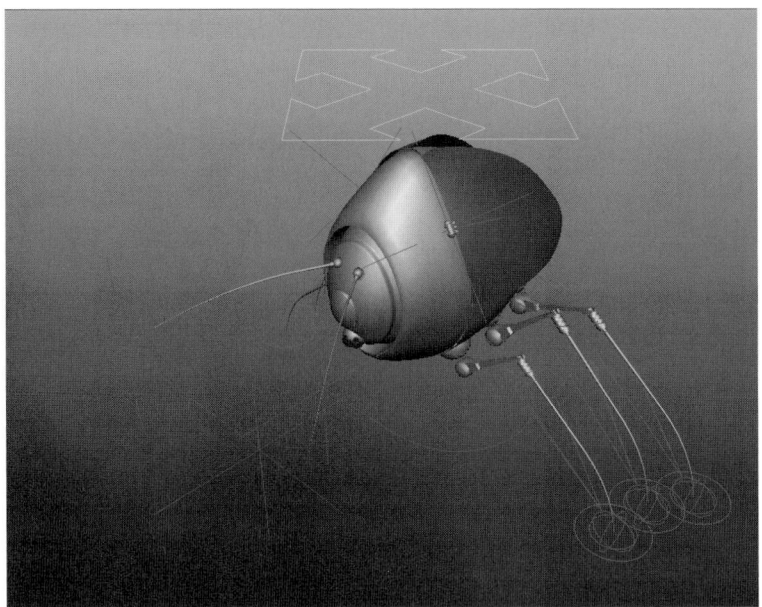

One last control you can add to the bug is a selectable rotational control for the antennaAim group. Use the same techniques used to create the bodyCtrl curve. The `mechBug_v01.ma` scene has an example of this control.

Keyframe Animation

The simplest way to animate an object in Maya is to use keyframes. A keyframe records the value of an attribute at a point in time on the timeline. When two keyframes are set for an attribute at different points in time, Maya interpolates the value between the two keyframes on the timeline, and the result is an animation.

Keyframes can be set on almost any attribute in Maya. You can use keyframes to animate an object's position, the color of the shader applied to the object, the visibility of the object, whether the object becomes dynamic, and so on.

Now that you have a rig for the mechanical bug that can be animated, you can get to work bringing him to life.

Creating Keyframes

In this exercise, you'll see the various ways you can set and manipulate keyframes in the Maya interface.

The mechanical bug in this scene has been rigged using the techniques discussed in the first part of the chapter. The major difference is that a circle has been added between the two antenna controls that you can select and animate to control both antennae at the same time.

The controls are color coded so they are more organized visually. The visibility of the joints is turned off in the Show menu of the perspective view; however, they are still present in the scene.

Keyframes can be placed on the individual channels of an object using the Channel Box. It's usually a good idea to keyframe on the channels that need to be animated rather than all of the channels and attributes of an object. To keyframe individual channels, follow these steps:

1. Open the mechBug_v01.ma scene in the chapter5\scenes directory on the DVD.

2. In the perspective view, select the blue bodyCtrl curve above the bug (the curve that looks like a cross with an arrow on each end).

3. Move the current frame in the timeline to frame 20 by clicking and dragging the timeline until the marker is at frame 20. Alternatively, type **20** into the box to the far right of the timeline.

4. With the bodyCtrl selected, highlight the Translate Y channel in the Channel Box by clicking it; then right-click and choose Key Selected from the pop-up menu (see Figure 5.19).

5. Set the timeline to frame 48.

6. Use the Move tool to pull the bodyCtrl curve up to about two units, and set another keyframe on the Translate Y channel. The keys are represented on the timeline by a thin red vertical line (see Figure 5.20).

7. Rewind and play the animation; you'll see the bug start moving upward on frame 20 and stop on frame 48.

FIGURE 5.19
Set a keyframe on the Translate Y channel of the bodyCtrl.

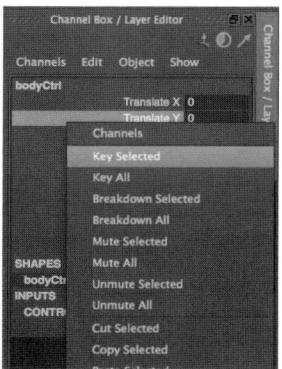

FIGURE 5.20
Keyframes are represented on the timeline by a thin red vertical line.

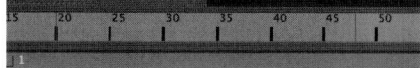

For the most part, setting keyframes is pretty straightforward. If you want to set a keyframe on all the Translate channels at the same time, the hot key is **W**. To set a keyframe on all Rotate channels at once, use **E**. To set a keyframe on all the Scale channels at once use, use **R**.

PLAYBACK SPEED

You can change the playback speed of the animation in Maya in the timeline Preferences window (you can also access these options quickly by right-clicking the timeline and choosing a playback speed option from the pop-up menu). Open the options by choosing Window ➤ Settings/Preferences ➤ Preferences. Choose Time Slider from the list of categories. The Playback Speed menu allows you to choose the playback speed.

You can choose Play Every Frame, Real-Time (24 frames per second), Half-Time (12 frames per second), or Twice (48 frames per second), or you can set a custom playback speed. Generally, the most useful speeds are Play Every Frame and Real-Time. If there are dynamics in the scene (such as particles, nCloth, rigid bodies, and so on), set this option to Play Every Frame so the dynamics calculate correctly. You can set the Max Playback speed as well so the animation speed cannot exceed a certain rate. Setting Max Playback to Free means the animation will play back as fast as your processor allows, which can be faster than the final rendered animation.

Auto Keyframe

The Auto Keyframe feature automatically places keyframes on an object when a change is made to one of its attributes. For Auto Keyframe to work, the attribute must already have an existing keyframe. To turn Auto Keyframe on, click the key icon to the right of the timeline. This exercise shows you how to use Auto Keyframe:

1. On the timeline for the mechBug_v01.ma scene, set the current frame to **20**.

   An easy way to do this is to use the Step Back One Key or Step Forward One Key button to the right of the timeline. The hot keys for moving back and forth one key are **Alt+comma** and **Alt+period**.

2. Shift+click all six of the small purple leg control circles below the bug's feet (see Figure 5.21).

FIGURE 5.21
Select the leg control circles.

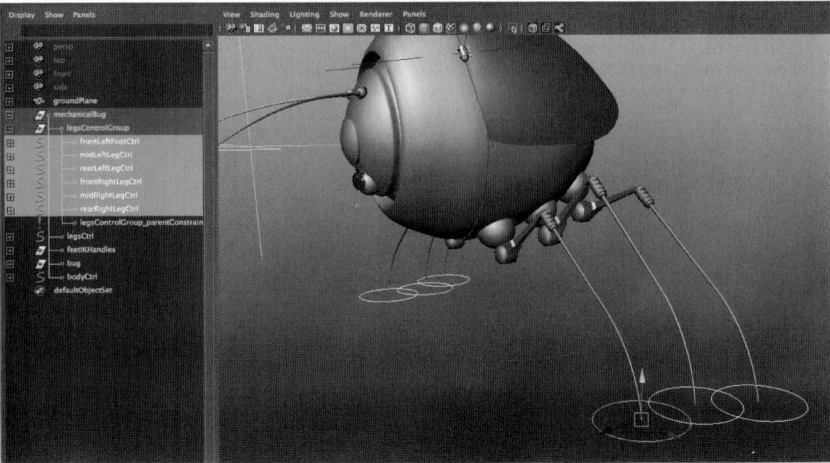

3. With the control circles selected, press the **W** hot key to place a keyframe on the Translate channels for all the selected curves.

4. Click the Key icon to the far right of the timeline to turn on Auto Keyframe.

5. Set the timeline to frame 40.

6. Select each of the circles, and move them in toward the center (see Figure 5.22).

7. When you play the animation, you'll see that the legs move inward without you having to set a keyframe in the Channel Box.

8. Save the scene as **mechBug_v02.ma**.

To see a version of the scene to this point, open the mechBug_v02.ma scene from the chapter5\scenes directory on the DVD.

FIGURE 5.22
Move the leg control circles in toward the center of the bug.

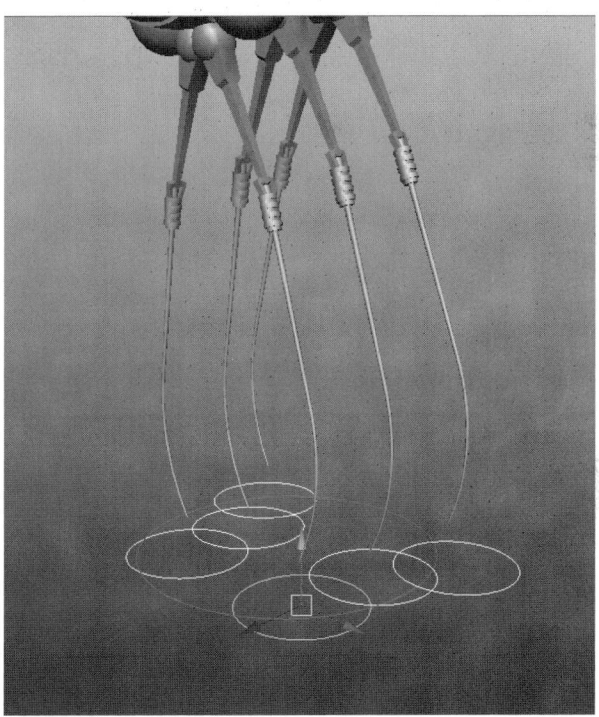

HANDLE WITH CARE

Using Auto Keyframe is certainly a matter of personal preference. You can easily set unwanted keys on an object by mistake using this feature, so remember to use it with caution.

Move and Scale Keyframes on the Timeline

You can reposition keys on the timeline interactively by selecting the key markers and sliding them back and forth.

1. Continue with the scene from the previous section, or open the mechBug_v02.ma scene from the chapter5\scenes directory on the DVD.

2. In the Perspective window, select the blue bodyCtrl curve.

3. Hold the Shift key, and drag a selection directly on the timeline. You'll see a red area appear as you drag. Keep dragging this area so it covers both keyframes set on the bodyCtrl curve (see Figure 5.23).

FIGURE 5.23
Hold the Shift key, and drag on the timeline to select a range of keys.

4. To move the keys forward or backward in time, drag on the two arrows at the center of the selection. Drag these arrows to move the keys so the first key is on frame 10.

   To scale the keys, drag one of the arrows on either side of the selection. The other end of the selection acts as the pivot for the scaling operation; you may need to reposition the keys on the timeline again after scaling.

5. Scale the keys down by dragging the arrow on the right side of the selection toward the left.

6. After scaling the keys, drag the arrows at the center to reposition the keys so the animation starts on frame 10.

7. Save the scene as **mechBug_v03.ma**.

SNAP KEYS

As you scale and move keys, you'll notice that a keyframe can be positioned on the fraction of a key. In other words, a key might end up on frame 26.68. You can fix this by choosing Edit ➤ Keys ➤ Snap Keys. In the options, set the value for Snap To to a multiple of 1 and set Snap Operation to Time. You can apply this to selected objects—or all objects, selected channels, or all channels—and define the time range. You can also right-click selected keyframes on the timeline and choose Snap. This automatically snaps keyframes to the nearest integer value.

You can move an individual key by Shift+clicking the key marker on the timeline and then dragging the arrows to move the key.

Repositioning and scaling keys directly on the timeline is usually good for simple changes. To make more sophisticated edits to the animation, you can use the Graph Editor discussed later in the chapter.

When you play the animation, you'll see that the bug jumps up fairly quickly and much sooner than before. You'll also notice that the animation of the legs has not changed.

Spend a few minutes practicing these techniques on each of the legBase objects. Changes made to the position of the keyframes affect selected objects. You can edit each legCtrl circle separately or all of them at the same time.

To see a version of the scene to this point, open the mechBug_v03.ma scene from the chapter5\ scenes directory on the DVD.

Copy, Paste, and Cut Keyframes

There are a number of ways you can quickly copy, paste, and cut keyframes on the timeline and in the Channel Box.

1. Continue with the scene from the previous section, or open the mechBug_v03.ma scene from the chapter5\scenes directory on the DVD.

2. Select the bodyCtrl curve in the perspective view.

3. On the timeline, Shift-drag a selection over both of the keyframes.

4. Right-click the selection, and choose Copy (see Figure 5.24).

FIGURE 5.24
You can copy keyframes directly onto the timeline.

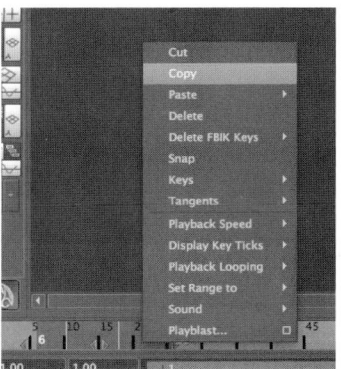

5. Deselect the keys by clicking the timeline, move to frame 70, right-click the timeline, and choose Paste ➢ Paste.

   The keys for the Translate Y channel are pasted on the timeline at frame 70. If you play the animation, you'll see that the bug jumps up, moves back down, and then jumps up again.

   Other options include the following:

   Paste Connect   Pastes the copied key with an offset starting at the value of the previous key.

   Cut   Removes the keyframes from the timeline but copies their values to the clipboard so they can be pasted anywhere on the timeline.

   Delete   Removes the keys.

   Delete FBIK   Deletes the Full Body IK keys.

   You can copy and paste keys from two different channels by using the options in the Channel Box.

6. Select the bodyCtrl curve in the perspective view.

7. In the Channel Box, right-click the Translate Y channel.

8. Choose Copy Selected (see Figure 5.25).

9. Highlight the Translate Z channel, right-click, and choose Paste Selected.

FIGURE 5.25
You can copy key-frames using the menu options in the Channel Box.

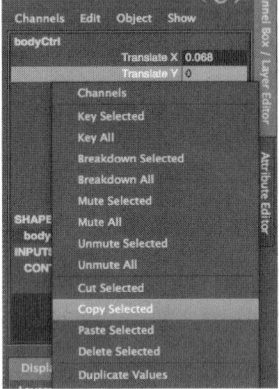

This pastes the values (including keyframes) copied from the Translate Y channel to the Translate Z channel. The starting point of the pasted keyframes is based on the current time in the timeline. When you play the animation, the bug moves forward as it moves up. The forward motion will be offset (in time) depending on the current frame in the timeline.

You can also cut and delete keyframes in the Channel Box. The Duplicate keyframe operation allows you to copy keyframes from one object to another:

1. Create a NURBS sphere, and set its Translate X to **5**.

2. Select the sphere, and then Shift+click the bodyCtrl curve.

3. Right-click the Translate Y channel, and choose Duplicate Values.

   This connects the keyframes on the Translate Y channel of the bodyCtrl curve to the NURBS sphere. If you change the values of these keys, both the bodyCtrl curve and the sphere will reflect the changes made to the keys.

When duplicating keyframes, the order in which you select the objects is important. Select the object you want to use as the source of the duplicate keyframes last. If you graph the objects on the Hypergraph, you'll see that the same keyframe nodes are attached to both objects.

The Graph Editor

The timeline and the Channel Box offer a few basic controls for creating and editing keyframes. However, when you're refining an animation, the controls in the Graph Editor offer greater flexibility as well as visual feedback on the interpolation between keyframes. To open the Graph Editor, choose Window ➢ Animation Editors ➢ Graph Editor. You can also set a viewport to the Graph Editor view.

THE GRAPH EDITOR AXES

The Graph Editor is a two-dimensional display of the animation in a scene (shown here). The Graph Editor has two axes: x and y. The x, or horizontal, axis typically displays the time of the scene in frames. As you move from left to right on the graph, time moves forward. Moving from right to left means going backward. It is possible to go into negative keyframe values if you create keys to the left of the zero marker.

The y, or vertical, axis displays the values of the keys in units for translation and scale and in degrees (or radians depending on the setting in the rotation settings in the preferences) for rotation. The higher you go on the y-axis, the higher the value of the key. Of course, anything below the zero line indicates negative values.

Animation Curves

Animation curves visually describe how the values between two keyframes are interpolated over time. A keyframe is represented by a point on the curve. The portion of the curve on the graph to the left of a keyframe represents the animation before the key, and the line and the portion on the right represent the animation after the key. The keys themselves have handles that can be used to fine-tune the shape of the curve and thus the behavior of the animation both before and after the key. The shape of the curve to the left of the key is known as the *incoming tangent* (or in tangent), and the shape of the curve to the right of the key is known as the *outgoing tangent* (or out tangent); this is shown in Figure 5.26.

Each animated channel has its own curve on the graph. You can use the menu in the Graph Editor to edit the keys and change the way the curves are displayed on the Graph Editor.

In this exercise, you'll use the Graph Editor to refine a simple animation for the mechanical bug. In this animation, the bug will leap in the air, hover for two seconds, lean forward, and then fly off the screen in a gentle arc. You'll start by setting keys on the Translate channels of the bug. To make things easier, you'll use Auto Keyframe.

The setting applied to the tangents of the curves sets the overall shape of the curve before and after each key. You can apply a tangent setting to one or more selected keys on the graph, and the in and out tangents can also have their own setting.

FIGURE 5.26
The curves on the Graph Editor represent the interpolation of values between keyframes for a selected object.

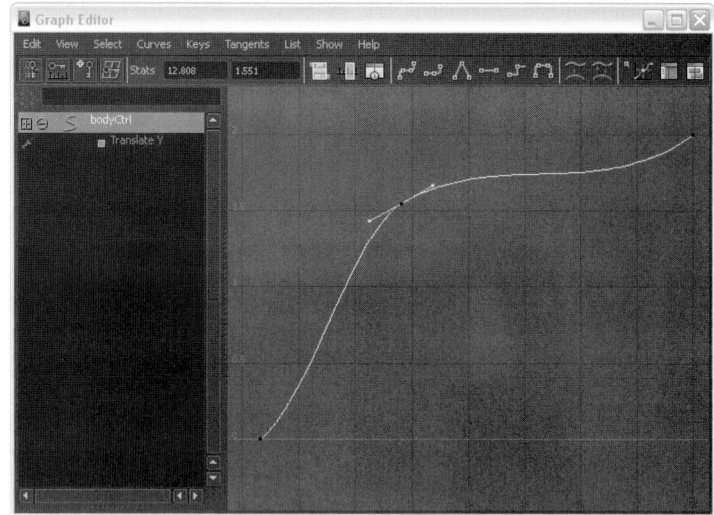

The settings are listed in the Tangents menu in the Graph Editor and are also represented visually by the icons at the top of the Graph Editor. Clicking one of these buttons or applying a setting from the Tangents menu changes the interpolation of the selected key(s) or tangent handles (see Figure 5.27).

FIGURE 5.27
The icons for the tangent settings at the top of the Graph Editor

When blocking out an animation, it's common to use the Stepped tangent setting. The Stepped tangent setting creates no interpolation between keys, so an object's animated values do not change between keyframes; instead, the animation appears to pop instantly from key to key. Using stepped keys when you block out the animation gives you a clear idea of how the object will move without the additional motion that can be added by curved tangents. Once you're happy with the blocking, you can switch to another tangent type and then refine the animation.

1. Open the mechBug_v01.ma scene from the chapter5\scenes directory on the DVD. This is the original rigged bug without the keyframes you added in the previous sections.

2. Open the Preferences window by choosing Window ➤ Settings/Preferences ➤ Preferences.

3. Click the Animation category under Settings.

4. Set Default In Tangent to Flat and Default Out Tangent to Stepped. You can't set Default In Tangent to Stepped in the Preferences window.

5. Make sure Auto Keyframe is enabled. Click Save to save the preferences (see Figure 5.28).

FIGURE 5.28
The animation preferences are established in the Preferences window.

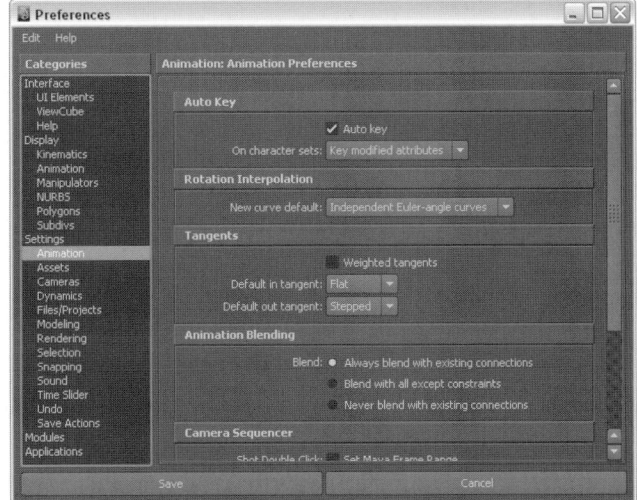

6. Set the length of the timeline to 120.

7. Set the current frame to 20.

8. Select the blue bodyCtrl curve in the perspective view.

9. Press **W** and **E** to set keyframes on the Translate and Rotate channels.

   When blocking out the animation, the only object that needs to be keyframed at this point is the bodyCtrl curve.

10. Set the timeline to frame 25, and move the bodyCtrl curve down so the Translate Y channel is about -0.78.

11. Set the timeline to frame 35.

12. Drag up on the bodyCtrl curve until the Translate Y channel is around 7 units.

13. Set the timeline to 45.

14. Rotate the bodyCtrl slightly, and move the bug a little forward and to the side. This gives the bug a slight wobble as he hovers. Try these settings:

    Translate X: **-0.68**

    Translate Y: **4.968**

    Translate Z: **0.532**

    Rotate X: **-11**

    Rotate Y: **7**

    Rotate Z: **10**

    Many of these values were arrived at by simply moving and rotating the bodyCtrl curve in the scene. You can use these exact values or something that's fairly close. Most of the time when blocking in the animation you'll move the objects in the scene rather than type in precise values, but the keyframe values are included here as a rough guide. Remember, right now the only object being keyframed is the bodyCtrl curve.

15. Set the frame to 60. The bug is starting to turn as he decides which way to fly. Rotate him to his left a little and add a bit more variation to his position. Try these settings:

    Translate X: **-.057**

    Translate Y: **4.677**

    Translate Z: **-1.283**

    Rotate X: **-18**

    Rotate Y: **20**

    Rotate Z: **-13**

16. Move the time slider to frame 79. Now the bug is starting to fly away. Rotate him so he is facing downward slightly. Try these settings:

    Translate X: **1.463**

    Translate Y: **3.664**

    Translate Z: **-.064**

    Rotate X: **31**

    Rotate Y: **35**

    Rotate Z: **1.5**

17. Set the time slider to frame 95. The bug is beginning his flight, so he turns more to the left and dips down a little. Try these settings:

    Translate X: **4.421**

    Translate Y: **3.581**

    Translate Z: **1.19**

    Rotate X: **1.5**

    Rotate Y: **46**

    Rotate Z: **2**

18. In the final keyframe on frame 120, the bug is flying away. Try these settings:

    Translate X: **11.923**

    Translate Y: **9.653**

    Translate Z: **6.794**

    Rotate X: **49**

    Rotate Y: **62**

    Rotate Z: **24**

19. Play back the animation a few times. You'll see the bug pop from one position to another. Make changes if you like, but try not to add any more keys just yet. It's best to use as few keys as possible; you'll let the curves do all the work in a moment.

20. Select the red legsCtrl circle, and keyframe its Translate channels so it follows the flight of the bug. To keep it interesting, place the keys at different frames than the bodyCtrl curve. Remember to set an initial keyframe before using Auto Keyframe.

    You can set keys on the individual foot controls, but at this point let's keep things simple and focus on just the bodyCtrl curve and the translation of the legsCtrl curve.

21. In the Perspective View menu, choose Panels ➤ Saved Layouts ➤ Persp/Graph/Outliner so the interfaces are split between the perspective in the Outliner and the Graph Editor.

22. Select the bodyCtrl curve, and hold the cursor over the Graph Editor.

23. Press the **f** hot key so you can see all the animation curves for the bodyCtrl object. Since the tangents are set to Stepped, they look like straight lines in a stepped pattern (Figure 5.29).

24. Save the scene as **mechBug_v04.ma**.

To see a version of the scene to this point, open the mechBug_v04.ma scene on the chapter5\ scenes folder of the DVD.

FIGURE 5.29
The Graph Editor is in its own panel in the interface; the keys for the bodyCtrl curve appear as straight lines.

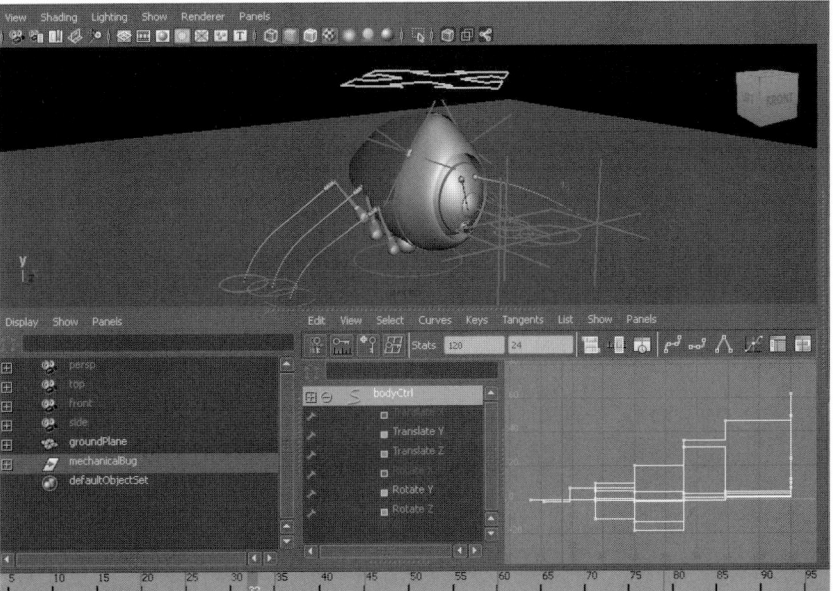

GHOSTING

Ghosting is a way to visualize how an object changes over time in space, as shown here. It is analogous to "onion skinning" in traditional animation, where you can see how the object looks in the animation several steps before and/or after the current frame.

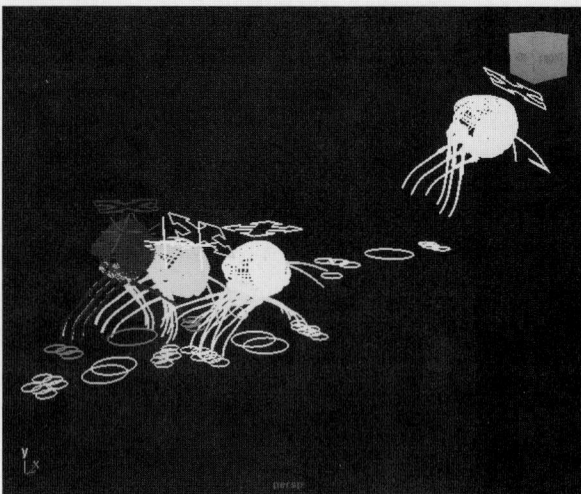

To activate ghosting, select an animated object and choose Animate ➤ Ghost Selected ➤ Options. In the options, you can specify the number of frames to display before and/or after the current frame. You can also choose to display specific frames. To remove the ghosting, select the object, and choose Animate ➤ Unghost Selected or Animate ➤ Unghost All.

Editing Animation Curves

At this point you're ready to start refining the animation curves using the tangent tools. Keep things simple and add keys only when absolutely necessary.

1. Continue with the scene from the previous section, or open the mechBug_v04.ma scene from the chapter5\scenes directory on the DVD.

2. In the Display Layers menu, turn off the visibility of the LEGS layer so you can just focus on the animation of the body.

3. Select the bodyCtrl curve, and in the Graph Editor drag a selection marquee over all the translation and rotation keys.

4. Test how the animation looks when different tangent types are applied to the keys.

5. On the menu bar of the Graph Editor, click the first tangent icon, or choose Tangents ➤ Spline. This changes all the selected key tangents to spline.

6. Play the animation, and observe how the bug moves as it jumps, hovers, and flies away.

7. In the Graph Editor, zoom in closely to the selected keys (MMB+Alt-drag).

You'll notice that spline tangents add a bit of overshoot to some of the keys, as shown in Figure 5.30, which results in a smooth, natural motion. However, in some cases this may add extra motion where you don't want it. It depends on how much precise control you want over the animation.

8. Try switching to the clamped-type tangent (the second tangent icon, or choose Tangents ➢ Clamped).

Clamped tangents are very similar to spline tangents; in fact, you'll notice a difference between spline and clamped tangents only when two values in a curve are very close together. Clamped tangents remove any overshoot that may cause sliding or slipping in an object. In the current animation example, you won't see much a difference at all except for a couple keyframes (see Figure 5.31).

FIGURE 5.30
Switching to spline tangents adds a slight overshoot to the animation curves. Notice how the curve dips below the lowest value of some of the keyframes.

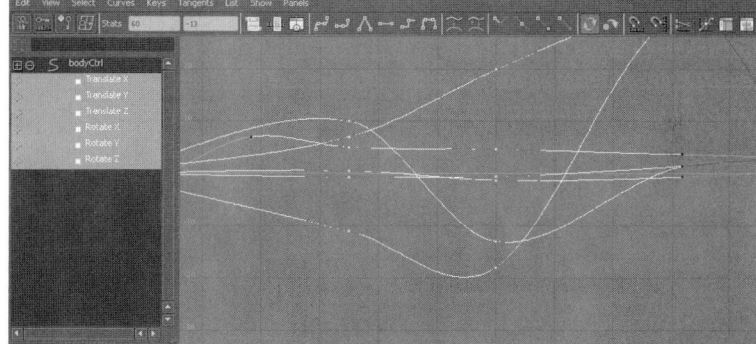

FIGURE 5.31
Clamped tangents are very similar to spline tangents except for values that are very close. In this figure spline tangents (top image) are converted to clamped tangents (bottom image).

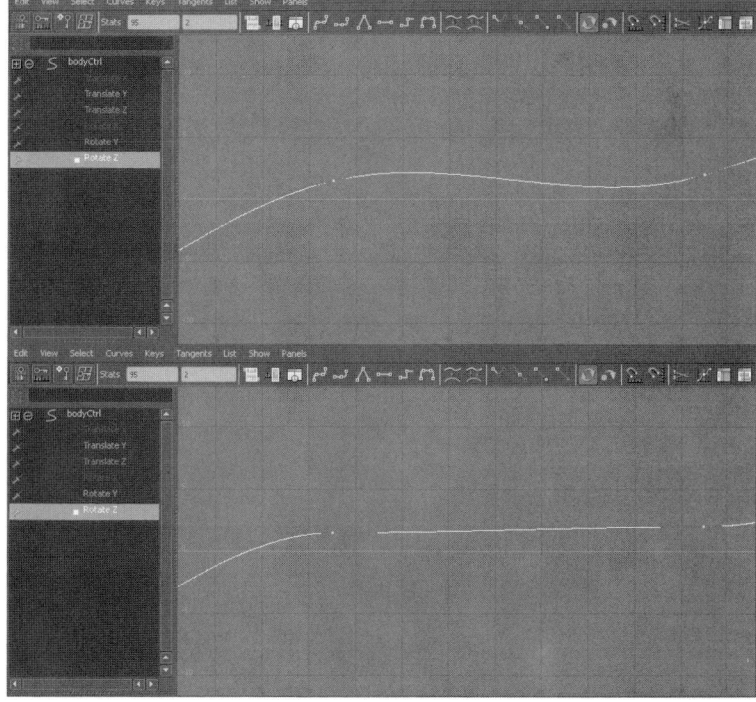

Aside from spline, clamped, and stepped tangents, you can also try using one of these tangent types. A single curve can use any combination of tangent types as well.

Linear tangents   Create straight lines between keyframes, resulting in a very sharp and direct motion.

Flat tangents   Make the tangents completely horizontal. Flat keyframes are very useful when you want to create a slow ramping effect to the values, known as *easing in* or *easing out*. Easing in means that the animation curve starts out flat and then gradually becomes steeper; easing out is the opposite.

Plateau tangents   Create smooth curves between keyframes. However, the overshoot that occurs with spline and clamped tangents is eliminated, so the peaks of each curve do not go beyond the values you set when you create the keyframes. Plateau tangents offer a good balance between smooth motion and control.

9. With all the keys selected in the Graph Editor, click the last tangent icon, or choose Tangents ➢ Plateau to switch to plateau-type tangents. Once an overall tangent type is established, you can edit the tangents and values of individual keys.

    A good place to start editing the animation is the initial leap that occurs at frame 20.

10. Make sure you can see both the Graph Editor and the body of the bug in the perspective view. The bugCtrl object should be selected so you can see its animation curves.

11. In the left column of the Graph Editor, highlight Translate Y to focus on just this individual curve.

    The leap has a slight anticipation where the bug moves down slightly before jumping in the air. At the moment, the motion is uniform, making it look a little uninteresting. You can edit the curve so the bug leaps up a little faster and sooner. Start by moving the third keyframe closer to the second.

12. Select the third keyframe, and click the move key icon (first icon on the far left of the menu bar) or use the **w** hot key. To move the key, MMB-drag to the left (see Figure 5.32). To constrain the movement horizontally so its value is not changed (only its time), hold the Shift key while dragging with the MMB.

    You can enter numeric values into the Stats field for precise control. The first field is the keyframe's time in frames; the second field is the value for the keyframe.

FIGURE 5.32
Move the third keyframe on the bodyCtrl's Translate Y channel to the left, closer to the second keyframe.

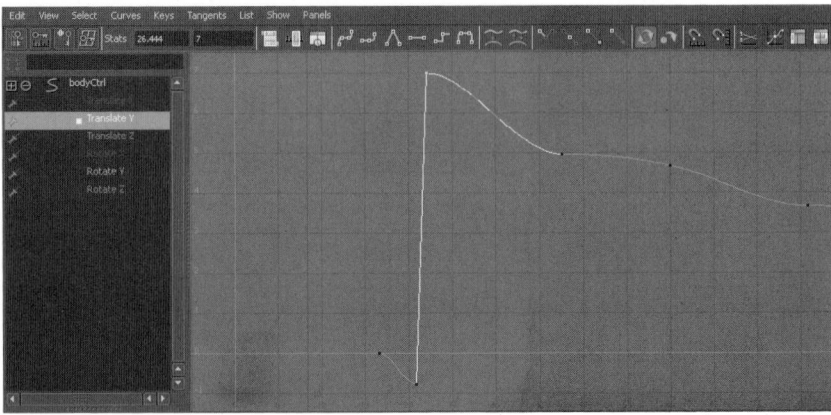

13. Slide the keyframe to the left so it is close to the second keyframe; the curve in between should become more of a straight line. If you want the keys to snap to whole values, select the key and choose Edit ➢ Snap.

There are two magnet icons on the menu bar of the Graph Editor (these may be visible only when the Graph Editor is maximized). These icons turn on horizontal and vertical snapping, respectively. The keyframes are then snapped to the grid in the Graph Editor (see Figure 5.33).

14. You can change the shape of the curves by editing the tangents directly:

A. Drag a selection box around the handle to the right of the third key.

B. Press the **w** hot key to switch to the Move tool.

C. MMB-drag upward to add overshoot to the out tangent (see Figure 5.34).

FIGURE 5.33
The magnet icons turn on horizontal and vertical snapping.

FIGURE 5.34
MMB-drag the tangent handles to directly edit the curve shape.

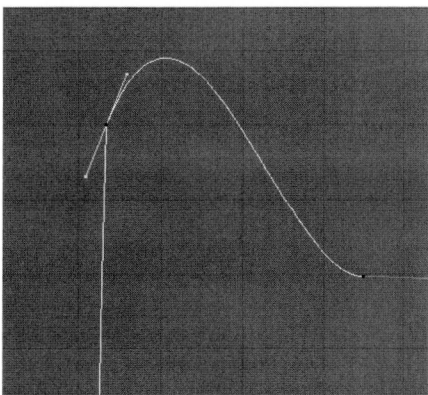

15. You'll notice that as you drag upward on the tangent handle, the handle on the opposite side of the key moves downward, maintaining the shape of the curve through the key. You can break the tangency of the curve handles if you want a different interpolation for the in and out tangents:

A. Drag a selection around both handles of the second key on the Translate Y channel.

B. Choose Keys ➢ Break Tangents to break the tangency of the handles. The in tangent is now colored gray, and the out tangent is colored brown.

C. Drag a selection handle around the in tangent, and MMB-drag it upward so there is a slight bump and then a sharp dip in the curve (Figure 5.35).

When you play the animation, the bug moves up slightly, moves down quickly, and then leaps into the air. You can unify the tangents by choosing Keys ➢ Unify Tangents. The angle of the tangents will not change, but you won't be able to edit the in and out tangents independently until you break the tangents again.

16. Save the scene as **mechBug_v05.ma**.

To see a version of the scene to this point, open the mechBug_v05.ma scene from the chapter5\scenes directory on the DVD.

FIGURE 5.35
When you break the tangency of the handles, you can move the tangent handles on either side of the keyframe independently of each other.

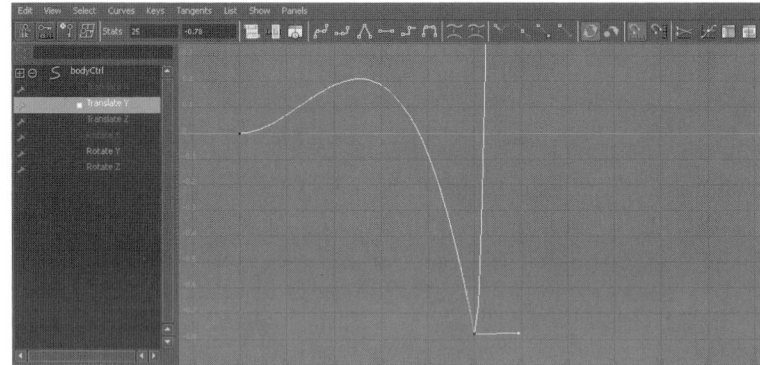

Weighted Tangents

You can convert the tangents to weighted tangents, which means you can further refine the in and out tangents by pulling on the tangent handles.

1. Continue with the scene from the previous section, or open the mechBug_v05.ma scene from the chapter5\scenes directory on the DVD.

2. Select the bodyCtrl curve, and in the Graph Editor select the Translate Y channel to isolate the curve.

3. Press the **f** hot key so the entire curve fits in the Graph Editor.

4. Drag a selection around the fourth key, and use the MMB to drag it down a little to create a slight dip in the curve (the upper left of Figure 5.36).

FIGURE 5.36
Weighted tangents allow you to edit the curves by pulling and pushing the tangent handles.

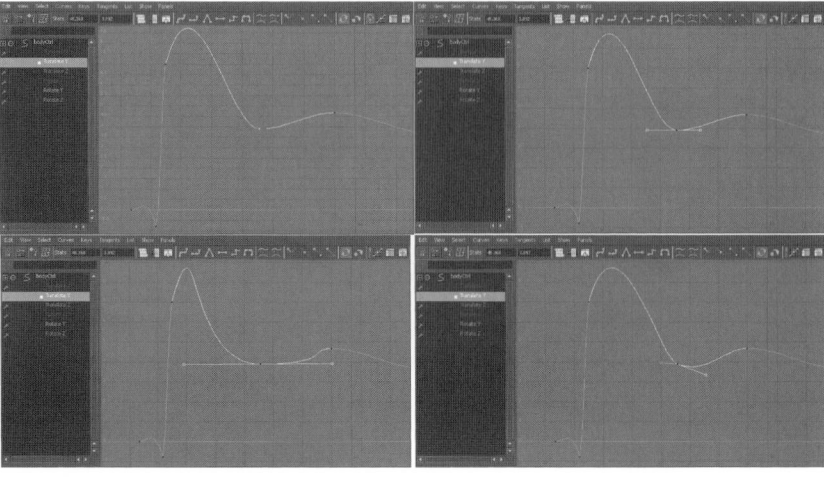

5. With the key selected, choose Curves ➤ Weighted Tangents. The ends of the handles are extended. When a key is converted to a weighted tangent, all the keys on the curve also become weighted tangents.

6. Select the handles, and choose Keys ➤ Free Tangent Weight. The handles turn to small squares, indicating that the tangents can be pulled (the upper-right image of Figure 5.36).

7. MMB-drag the handles left or right to extend the length of the handles; notice the change in the shape of the curve (the lower-left image of Figure 5.36).

8. Break the tangents on the selected handles (Keys ➤ Break Tangents).

9. Push the handle on the left of the fourth key toward the right to shorten the incoming tangent.

10. Pull the outcoming tangent of the fourth keyframe down and to the right (the lower-right image of Figure 5.36).

11. Play the animation, and see how changing the length of the handles affects the way the bug jumps.

12. Save the scene as `mechBug_v06.ma`.

To see a version of the scene to this point, open the `mechBug_v06.ma` scene from the `chapter5\scenes` folder on the DVD.

Additional Editing Tools

In addition to moving keyframes and tangents, you can also use the Scale tool to stretch and shrink a number of selected keys at once.

1. Continue with the scene from the previous section, or open the `mechBug_v06.ma` scene from the `chapter5\scenes` directory on the DVD.

2. Select the bodyCtrl curve in the perspective view, and open the Graph Editor.

3. Press the **f** hot key so all the curves are visible on the editor.

4. Drag a selection marquee over all the keys to the right of the third key.

5. From the Graph Editor menu bar, choose Edit ➤ Transformation Tools ➤ Scale Keys Tool ➤ Options.

6. In the options, turn on Manipulator. A box is drawn around the keys. You can stretch or shrink the box to change the distance between selected keys.

   When the Scale Keys tool option is set to Gestural, the position of the cursor on the graph is the pivot for the scaling operation.

7. Increasing the scale horizontally slows down the animation; decreasing the horizontal scale speeds up the animation (see Figure 5.37). Drag the lower-left corner of the Scale Keys tool to the right a little to extend the animation and slow it down after the fourth keyframe.

   If you want to scale just the values, you can drag up or down. Small changes made with the Scale Key tool can have a large effect, so use this tool with caution.

FIGURE 5.37
The Scale Keys tool stretches or shrinks the distances between selected keys on the graph.

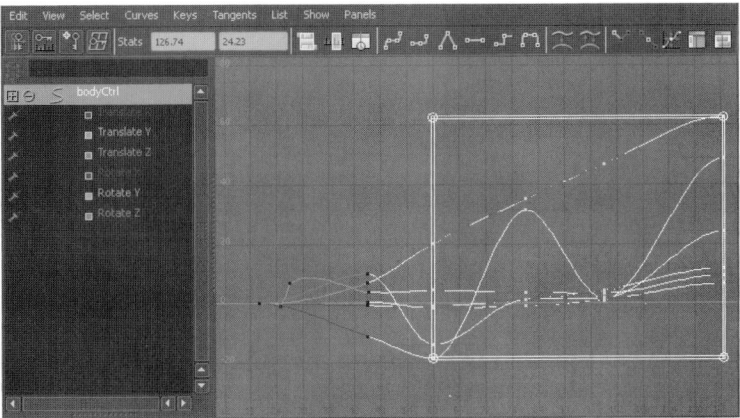

Another way to edit the keys is to use the Lattice Deform Keys tool.

8. With the keys still selected, choose Edit ➤ Transformation Tools ➤ Lattice Deform Keys Tool. This creates a lattice deformer around the selected keys.

9. Click and drag on the points and lines of the lattice to change the shape of the lattice (see Figure 5.38). This is a good way to add a little variation to the animation.

FIGURE 5.38
The Lattice Deform Keys tool creates a lattice around selected keys to manipulate groups of selected keys.

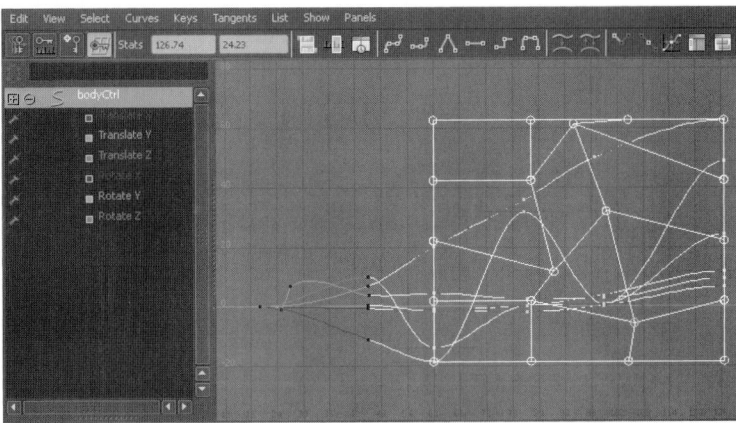

To change the number of rows and columns in the lattice, open the Tool Options box while the Lattice Deform Keys tool is active. If the lattice does not update properly when you change the settings in the Tool Options box, try reselecting the keys in the Graph Editor.

The Insert Keys tool inserts a key in one or more animation curves. To use this tool, follow these steps:

1. Select one or more animation curves in the Graph Editor.

2. Click the Insert Key icon in the Graph Editor toolbar.

3. MMB-click the curve.

The Add Key tool is similar to the Insert Keys tool except that wherever you click in the Graph Editor will be used as the value for the added key. Both tools require that you MMB-click in the Graph Editor (see Figure 5.39).

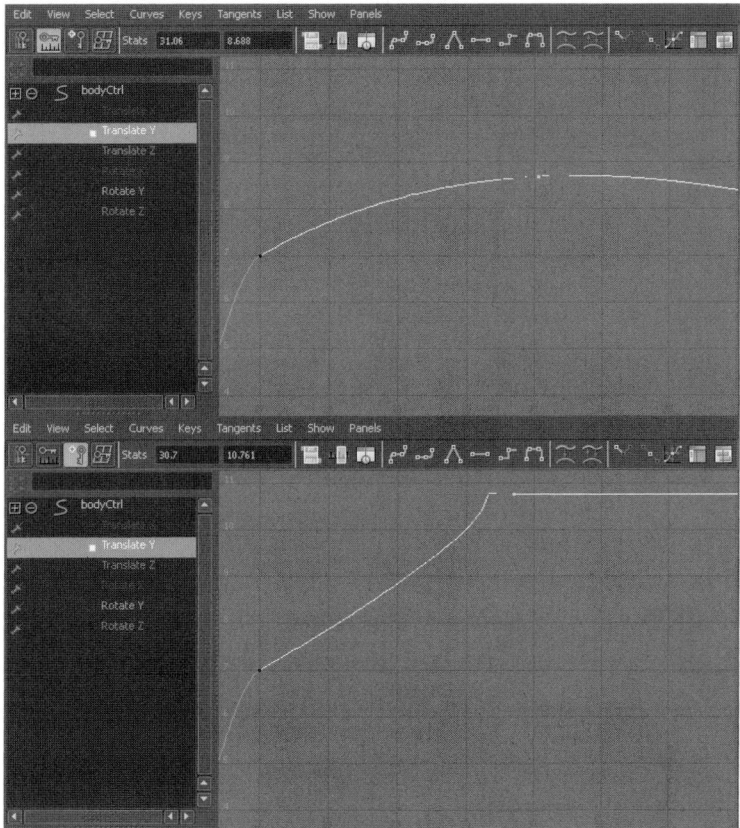

You can copy and paste keys on the graph; pasted keys are placed at the current location on the timeline. This means that if you select a group of keys that start at frame 40 and then move the timeline to frame 60 and paste, the keys will be pasted at frame 60. For more precise copying and pasting, use the Copy and Paste options in the Graph Editor's Edit menu.

Practice editing the keys on the Graph Editor for the bodyCtrl curve (both Translate and Rotate channels). When you're happy with the animation, make the legs visible, and edit the keys set on the legCtrl circle.

If you decide to use Auto Keyframe when refining the animation for other parts of the robot, switch the default in and out tangents to spline, clamped, or plateau in the preferences. Otherwise, Maya inserts stepped keyframes while Auto Keyframe is on, which can be frustrating to work with at this point.

You can add natural-looking motion to the way the bug hovers by simply shifting the keys placed on the different channels back and forth in time so they don't occur on the same frame (see Figure 5.40).

FIGURE 5.40
Shift the keys for the various channels back and forth in time so they don't occur on the same frame. This creates a more natural motion.

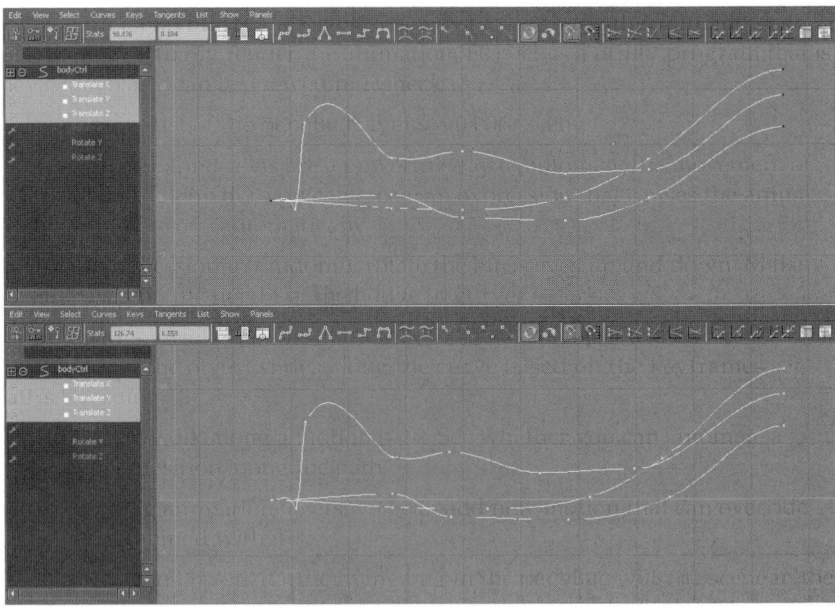

To see a version of the scene where the keys have been edited, open the mechBug_v07.ma scene in the chapter5\scenes directory on the DVD.

Breakdowns and In-Betweens

A *breakdown* is a special type of helper keyframe. The breakdown itself is just like a keyframe; what makes it special is how the breakdown affects the other keys on the curve. When you insert a breakdown and then move keys before or after the breakdown, the position of the breakdown moves as well to maintain a proportional relationship with the other keys on the curve. Normally when you move a keyframe, the other keys are not adjusted.

Try this short exercise to understand how breakdowns work:

1. Open the mechBug_v07.ma scene from the chapter5\scenes directory on the DVD.

2. Turn off the visibility of the LEGS layer so you can focus on just the bug body.

3. Select the blue bodyCtrl curve, and open the Graph Editor.

4. Select the Translate Y channel so it is isolated on the graph.

5. Drag a selection around the third key on the graph.

6. Switch to the Move tool (hot key = **w**). Hold the Shift key, and MMB-drag back and forth on the graph. The other keys on the graph do not move; this is the normal behavior for keys.

7. Drag a selection around the second and fourth keys on the graph.

8. From the menu in the Graph Editor, choose Keys ➢ Convert To Breakdown.

You won't notice any difference in the key itself or its tangent handles. The color of the key tick mark on the graph changes to green, but other than that, it looks and acts the same.

9. Drag a selection around the third key on the graph, and try moving it back and forth.

This time you'll notice that the second and fourth keys adjust their position to maintain a proportional relationship in the shape of the curve with the changes made to the third key. The same behavior occurs if you change the first key (see Figure 5.41).

You can convert any key to a breakdown using the Edit menu. To insert a breakdown, set the timeline to the frame where you want the breakdown, right-click one or more channels in the Channel Box, and choose Breakdown Selected. You can add a breakdown to all the channels by choosing Breakdown All.

FIGURE 5.41
Breakdowns are special keys that maintain the proportions of the curve when neighboring keys are edited.

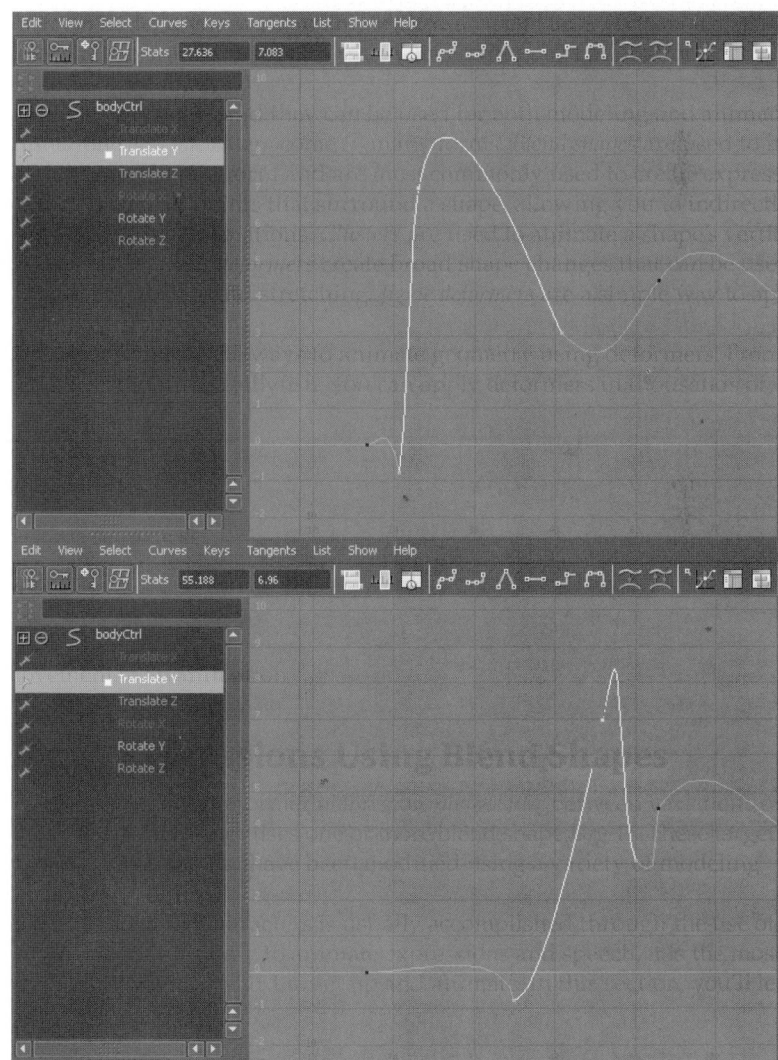

Breakdowns are useful for adding very precise animation to an object's channels without affecting the tangents of the surrounding keys. This can be important if you have perfected an animation but need to make a small change to a single key.

An *in-between* is a point on the curve that does not have a keyframe. In other words, each frame between two keys is known as an in-between. When you add an in-between, you shift all the keys to the right of the current point in the timeline one frame to the right. When you remove an in-between, you shift all the keys to the left.

BUFFER CURVES

Buffer curves are a Graph Editor tool designed to let you experiment with variations of animation curves without losing any of the work you've done. To use a buffer curve, follow these steps:

1. Select the animated object, and open the Graph Editor.

2. In the Graph Editor, choose View ➤ Show Buffer Curves to enable the visibility of these curves.

3. Select the curve you want to edit, and choose Curves ➤ Buffer Curve Snapshot. This places a copy of the selected curve into memory.

4. Make changes to the curve.

   The Buffer Curve appears in a faint gray color of the Graph Editor, which is visible as you edit the curve. The default color scheme Maya uses for the Graph Editor can make the gray color of the buffer curve very difficult to see. You can change the color of the Graph Editor:

   A. Choose Window ➤ Settings/Preferences ➤ Color Settings.

   B. In the Colors editor, select Animation Editors.

   C. Adjust the Graph Editor Background setting so that it is light gray.

   This should allow you to see the buffer curve more easily.

5. To swap between the edited curve and the buffer curve, choose Curves ➤ Swap Buffer Curve.

6. To turn off Buffer Curves when you have finished editing, go to the View menu in the Graph Editor, and turn off Buffer Curves.

Pre- and Post-Infinity

The Pre- and Post-Infinity settings can be used to quickly create simple repeating motions. To animate the flapping wings, you can set three keyframes and then set the Post-Infinity settings to Cycle.

1. Open the mechBug_v07.ma scene from the chapter5\scenes directory on the DVD.

2. Set the timeline to frame 10.

3. In the perspective view, zoom in closely to the body of the bug; on its left side, select the small piece of geometry that holds the wing to the body. The object is called leftWingMotor (see Figure 5.42).

4. Right-click the Rotate X channel in the Channel Box, and choose Key Selected.

FIGURE 5.42
Select the
leftWingMotor on
the side of the bug.

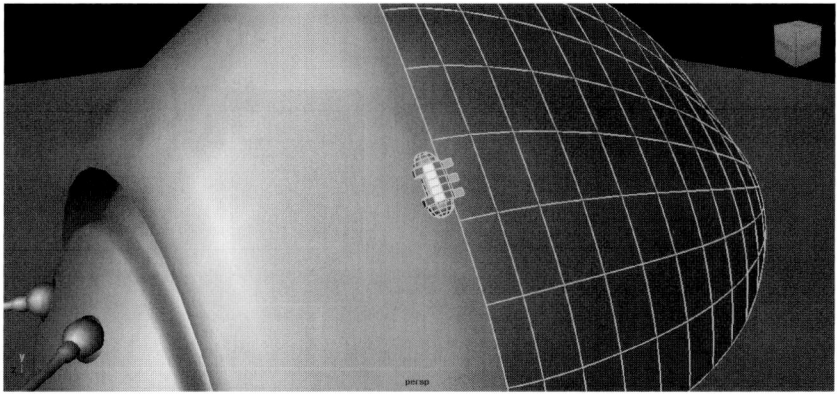

5. Set the frame in the timeline to frame 12. Set Rotate X to **60**, and create another keyframe.

6. Set the timeline to frame 14, set Rotate X to **0**, and create another keyframe.

7. With the leftWingMotor selected, open the Graph Editor.

8. Select Rotate X in the column on the left, and press the **f** key so the editor focuses on the animation curve for this channel.

9. Select all the keys, and choose Tangents ➢ Linear to convert the curve to linear tangents.

10. Zoom out a little in the Graph Editor (drag using Alt+RMB on the editor).

11. With the curve selected, choose Curves ➢ Post Infinity ➢ Cycle.

12. Choose View ➢ Infinity in the Graph Editor. The cycling keyframes are shown as a dotted line on the graph (see Figure 5.43).

13. Play the animation in the perspective view. The wing starts flapping in frame 10; it continues to flap at the same rate for the rest of the animation.

    To make the wing flap faster, simply scale the keyframes.

14. Repeat steps 7 through 12 for the rightWingMotor.

15. Save the animation as **mechBug_v08.ma**.

FIGURE 5.43
You can view how
the keyframes will
cycle by choosing
View ➢ Infinity.
The animation
curve after the last
keyframe is shown
as a dotted line.

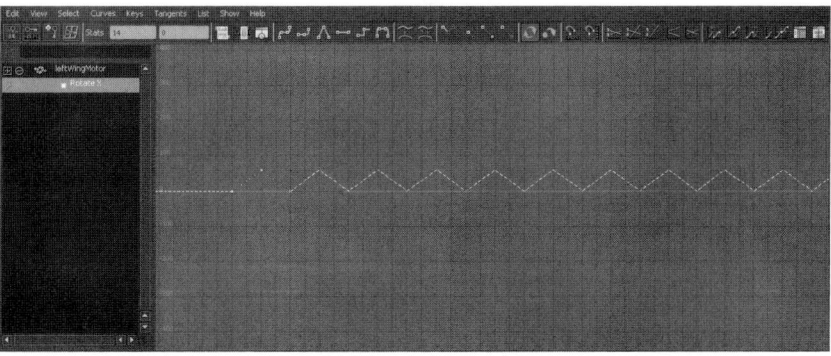

To see a version of the animation to this point, open the mechBug_v08.ma scene from the chapter5\scenes directory on the DVD.

The Pre-Infinity options work just like the Post-Infinity options, except the cycling occurs before the first keyframe. The Oscillate option cycles the keyframes backward and forward.

Cycle With Offset cycles the animation curve with an offset added to the cycle based on the value of the last keyframe (see Figure 5.44).

FIGURE 5.44
Cycle With Offset adds an offset to the cycle based on the value of the last keyframe.

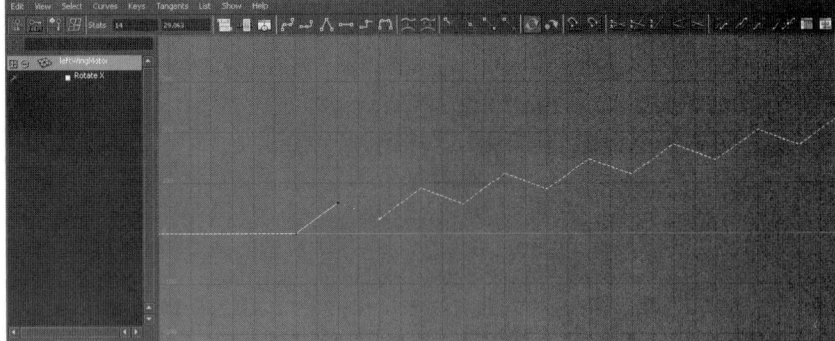

The Linear option extends the curve, based on the tangency of the final keyframe, into infinity. So if you wanted the bug to continue to fly upward forever, you can select the Translate Y channel and set Post Infinity to Linear.

GRAPH EDITOR VIEWING OPTIONS

New!

New to Maya 2011 are several options that can make working in the Graph Editor a bit easier:

Stacked Curve   The Stacked Curve option in the view menu separates the view of each curve of the selected object and stacks them vertically (as shown here). This may make it easier to see what's going on with each curve rather than in the default view, which overlays the curves in a single view.

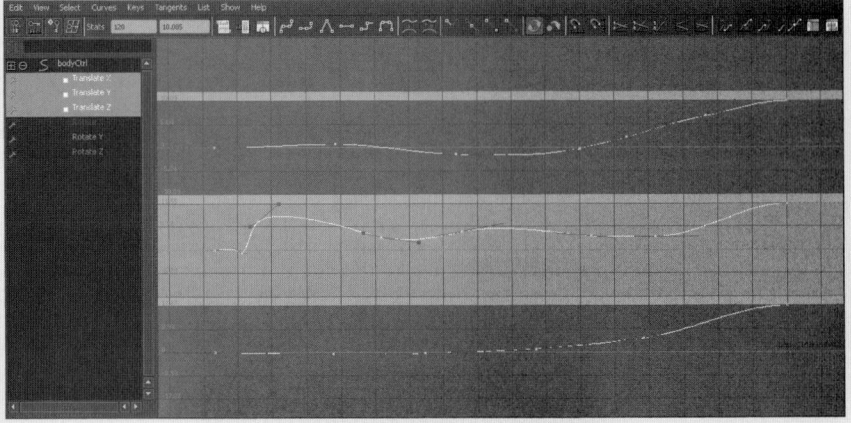

Pin Channel   The Pin Channel option in the Curves menu keeps the animation curve of a selected channel in the Graph Editor. Normally the curves displayed in the Graph Editor update as you select different objects in the scene. When you pin a channel, it stays visible regardless of what else is selected. You can activate this by pressing the pin icon in the list of channels on the left side of the Graph Editor.

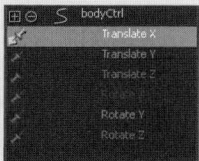

Display Normalized   The Display Normalized Option in the View menu fits the selected animation curve within a range between -1 and 1. This does not affect the actual values of the animation, just how they're displayed. In some cases, you may want to think of an animation curve's values in terms of a percentage; by normalizing the curve, you can think of the values between 0 and 1 as 0 to 100 percent.

You can now also change the color of selected animation curves by choosing Edit ➤ Change Curve Color ➤ Options. A color swatch appears in the options enabling you to pick a custom color.

Playblast and FCheck

A *playblast* is a way to create an unrendered preview of an animation. When you create a playblast, Maya captures each frame of the animation. The frames can be stored temporarily or saved to disk. You should always use playblasts to get a sense of the timing of the animation. What you see in the Maya viewport window is not always an accurate representation of how the final animation will look.

FCheck (or Frame Check) is a utility program that ships with Maya. This program plays back a sequence of images with some very simple controls. When you create a playblast, you have the option of viewing the sequence in your operating system's media player or in FCheck. FCheck is usually the better choice because of its simplicity and support for a variety of image formats.

Creating and Viewing a Playblast

This exercise will show you how to preview an animation using a playblast and FCheck:

1. Open the mechBug_v08.ma scene from the chapter5\scenes directory on the DVD.

2. Switch to the shotCam camera in the perspective view.

3. Choose Window ➤ Playblast ➤ Options.

4. In the options, set Time Range to Time Slider. Set Format to iff (this option specifies FCheck; the qt and avi options use the default movie viewer for your operating system).

5. Set Display Size to From Window, and set Scale to **0.75** (see Figure 5.45).

6. Click Playblast to record the image sequence. In the case of the bug animation, this should take only a few seconds. A scene that has a lot of dynamics or a lot of geometry may take longer.

FIGURE 5.45
The options for
a playblast

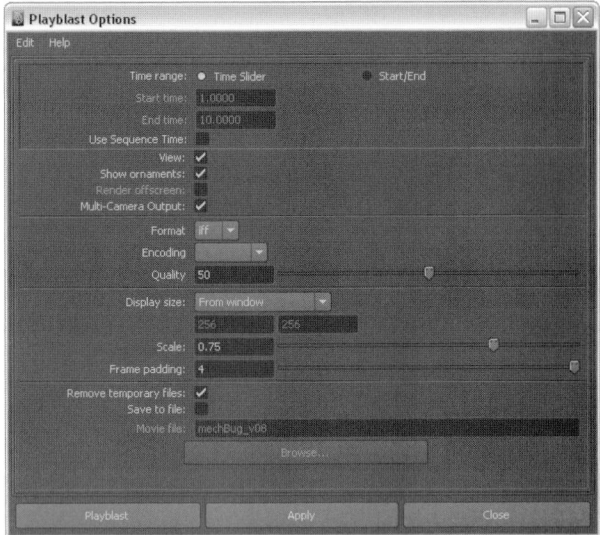

Once the playblast is complete, FCheck should open automatically and play the sequence. You can also open a sequence in FCheck by choosing (from the main Maya menu bar) File ➤ View Sequence.

In the FCheck window, the movie-viewing controls are at the top of the menu bar. The Alpha and Z Depth display options work only for rendered sequences that have alpha or Z Depth channels included.

In Windows, you can scrub back and forth in the animation by clicking and dragging directly on the image in FCheck. You can also RMB-drag on the image to draw quick notes and annotations. The notes remain on the frame as long as FCheck is open (see Figure 5.46). You can use FCheck's File menu to save and load animation sequences.

FIGURE 5.46
FCheck is a utility program that plays back image sequences. In Windows, you can draw on the frames displayed in FCheck using the RMB.

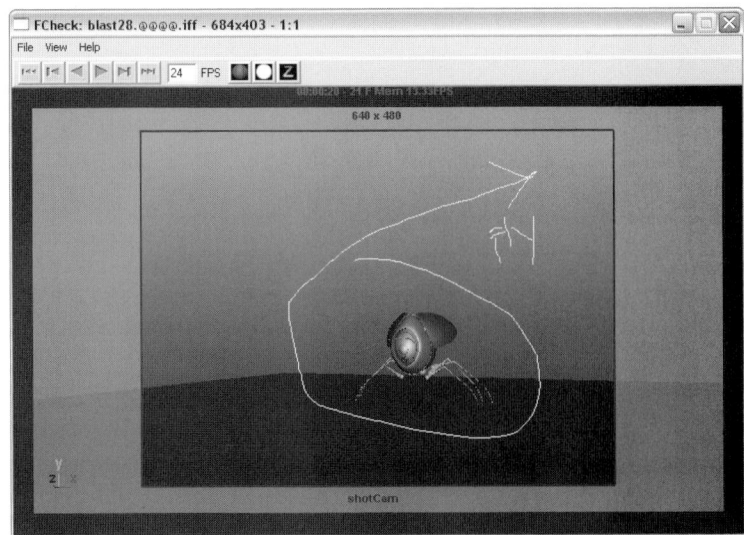

The Mac version of FCheck uses a separate control panel called Fcheck Info. You can scrub through the movie by dragging left or right in the window. In the Mac version, you cannot draw on the images as you can with the Windows version. The Mac version may also display a blank image for a minute or so while it loads the sequence into memory. Once it has loaded, press the **t** hot key to see the sequence play at the correct frame rate; otherwise, the sequence may play too quickly.

Driven Keys

Driven keys are keyframes that are driven by the attributes of another object rather than time. Standard keyframes describe a change for an object's attribute at two different points in time. For example, a cube may have a Translate Y value of 0 at frame 10 and a Translate Y value of 30 at frame 50. When the animation is played, the cube moves up 30 units between frames 10 and 50. When you create driven keys, you create a relationship between any two attributes. For example, you could have the Rotate X channel of a cone control the Translate Y channel of a cube. So when the cone's Rotate X is at 0 degrees, the Translate Y channel of the cube is at 0. When the Rotate X channel of the cone is 90 degrees, the Translate Y channel of the cube is at 50. The cone is referred to as the *driving object*, and the cube becomes the *driven object*. You can even have the attribute of one object drive one or more attributes on the same object.

Driven keys are often used in rigging to automate the animation of parts of the model, which saves a lot of time and tedious keyframing when animating the rest of the model.

Creating a Driven Key

In this section, you'll create driven keys to automate the walking motion of the mechanical bug's legs so that when the bug moves forward or backward on its z-axis, the legs automatically move.

1. Open the mechBugWalk_v01.ma scene from the chapter5\scenes directory on the DVD.

2. In the perspective view, use the Show menu to turn off the visibility of the joints so it's easier to select the leg controls. Make sure the Tangents settings in the Animation Preferences are set to Flat for both Default In and Default Out tangents.

   Driven keys are set through a separate interface. You'll set up the walk cycle for one leg and then copy and paste the keys to the others.

3. From the Animation menu set, choose Animate ➤ Set Driven Keys ➤ Set. The Set Driven Key window opens.

   The upper part of the Set Driven Key window lists the driving object (there can be only one at a time) and its attributes. The bottom part of the window lists the driven objects (there can be more than one at a time) and their attributes. The first step is to load the driving and driven objects. Figure 5.47 shows the Set Driven Key window with objects loaded already; you'll load the objects and attributes in the next few steps.

4. Select the bodyCtrl curve, and click the Load Driver button.

5. Select the frontLeftFootCtrl curve, and click Load Driven.

   To create the walk cycle for the front left leg, the Z translation of the bodyCtrl curve will drive the Z translation of the front left foot (making it move forward) and the Y translation of the front left foot (making it move up as it moves forward). You need to create the first key to establish the starting position of the front left leg.

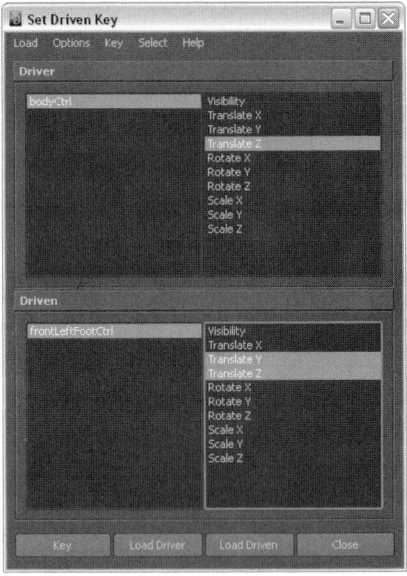

FIGURE 5.47
The Set Driven Key interface lists the driver objects at the top and the driven objects on the bottom.

6. Select the frontLeftFootCtrl curve, and set its Translate Z channel to **-1**.

7. In the Set Driven Key window, select Translate Z in the upper-right corner (this indicates the Translate Z of the bodyCtrl curve as selected in the upper left of the box).

8. Shift+click the Translate Y and Translate Z channels in the lower right; this indicates the Translate Z and Translate Y of the frontLeftFootCtrl curve (see Figure 5.47).

9. Click the Key button at the bottom of the Set Driven Key window.

   When you click the Key button, the current value for the channel selected in the upper right is the driver for the values of the channels in the lower left.

   ◆ The Translate Z of bodyCtrl is set to 0.

   ◆ The Translate Z of frontLeftFootCtrl is set to -1.

   ◆ The Translate Y of frontLeftFootCtrl is set to 0.

   A keyframe relationship is set up between the Translate Z of bodyCtrl and the Translate Z and Translate Y of frontLeftFootCtrl. When frontLeftFootCtrl is selected, its Translate Y and Translate Z channels are colored pink in the Channel Box, indicating a keyframe has been set on these channels.

10. Select the bodyCtrl curve again, and set its Translate Z to **1**.

11. Select the frontLeftFootCtrl curve, and set its Translate Z to **1** and its Translate Y to **0.8**.

12. Make sure that in the Set Driven Key window the Translate Z channel is selected in the upper right, and both the Translate Y and Translate Z channels are selected in the lower right.

13. Click the Key button again to set another key. Enter the following settings:

Translate Z of bodyCtrl: **2**.

Translate Z of frontLeftFootCtrl: **3**

Translate Y: **0**

14. Click the Key button again.

15. Set the Translate Z of bodyCtrl to **4**. Don't change either setting for Translate Z or Translate Y of frontLeftFootCtrl. Set another key.

The IK applied to the front left leg keeps it stuck in place, which makes the walk cycle easy to animate.

16. In the perspective view, try moving the bodyCtrl rig back and forth on the y-axis. You'll see the front left foot take a step.

17. Save the scene as **mechBugWalk_v02.ma**.

To see a version of the scene to this point, open the mechBugWalk_v02.ma scene from the chapter5\scenes directory on the DVD.

Looping Driven Keys

To make the foot cycle, you can simply use the Pre- and Post-Infinity settings in the Graph Editor:

1. Continue with the scene from the previous section, or open the mechBugWalk_v02.ma scene from the chapter5\scenes directory on the DVD.

2. Select the frontLeftFootCtrl, and open the Graph Editor (Window ➢ Animation Editors ➢ Graph Editor).

3. In the left column, select the Translate Y and Translate Z channels.

You'll see the animation curves appear on the graph. Since these are driven keys, the horizontal axis does not represent time; rather, it is the Translate Z channel of the bodyCtrl curve. So, as the graph moves from left to right, the value of the bodyCtrl's Translate Z channel increases. Moving from right to left, the value decreases.

4. In the Graph Editor menu, choose View ➢ Infinity. You can now see the Pre- and Post-Infinity values for the curves.

5. Select the green Translate Y curve. Choose Curves ➢ Pre Infinity ➢ Cycle. Then choose Curves ➢ Post Infinity ➢ Cycle.

By doing this, you create a repeating cycle for Translate Y. The foot moves up and down in the same pattern as the bodyCtrl curve moves back and forth. The Translate Z channel is a little different. Since it is moving along the z-axis in space, you need to offset the value for each step so the foot continues to step forward.

6. Select the blue Translate Z curve, and choose Curves ➢ Pre Infinity ➢ Cycle With Offset. Then choose Curves ➢ Post Infinity ➢ Cycle With Offset. The dotted line on the graph shows how the Translate Z channel moves up in value with each cycle (see Figure 5.48).

FIGURE 5.48
The Pre- and Post-Infinity values of the Translate Z channel are set to Cycle With Offset so it continually steps as the bug is moved back and forth.

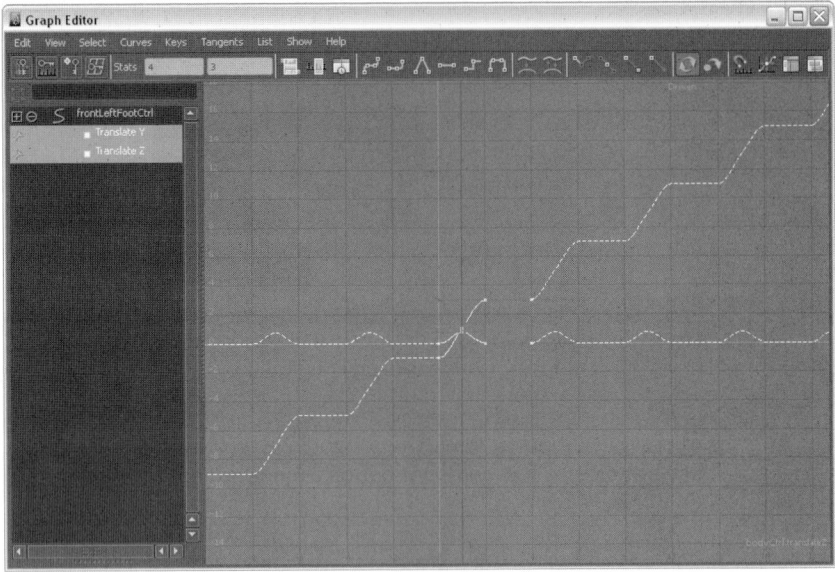

7. Move the bodyCtrl curve back and forth on the z-axis, and you'll see that the front left leg now walks with the bug.

8. Save the scene as **mechBugWalk_v03.ma**.

To see a version of the scene to this point, open the mechBugWalk_v03.ma scene from the chapter5\scenes directory on the DVD.

Copying and Pasting Driven Keys

The trick at this point is to create the same driven key arrangement for the other five legs in the easiest way possible. You can achieve this using Copy and Paste. The important thing to remember is that to paste driven keys from a channel on one object to another, you should have one driven key already created for the target objects.

1. Continue with the scene from the previous section, or open the mechBug_v03.ma scene from the chapter5\scenes directory on the DVD.

2. From the Animation menu set, choose Animate ➢ Set Driven Key ➢ Set to open the Set Driven Key window.

3. Select the bodyCtrl curve, and load it as the driver.

4. Select all the leg control curves except the frontLeftLegCtrl.

5. Click the Load Driven button.

6. Make sure the Translate Z channel of the bodyCtrl curve is at **0**. Set the Translate Z of the five leg control curves to **-1**.

7. Select the Translate Z channel in the upper right of the Set Driven Key window. In the lower left, make sure all the leg control curves are selected.

8. Select the Translate Y and Translate Z channels in the lower right (see Figure 5.49).

FIGURE 5.49

Set an initial
driven key on the
Translate Y and
Translate Z chan-
nels of the five
remaining legs.

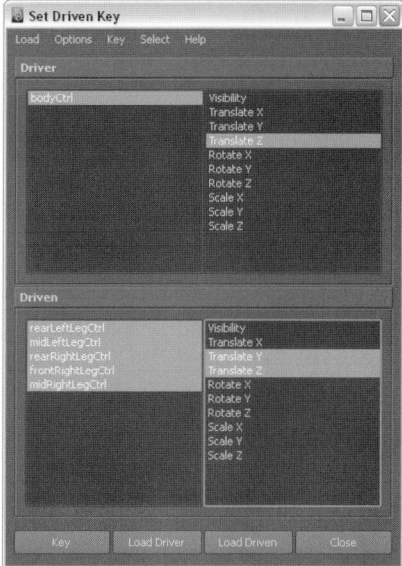

9. Click the Key button to create an initial key for the five legs. You can close the Set Driven Key window.

10. Make sure the bodyCtrl curve's Translate Z channel is at **0**. Select the frontLeftFootCtrl curve. In the Channel Box, highlight the Translate Y and Translate Z channels. Right-click, and choose Copy Selected.

11. Deselect frontLeftFootCtrl curve. Shift+click the five other leg control curves.

12. Highlight the Translate Y and Translate Z channels, right-click, and choose Paste Selected.

    When you move the bodyCtrl curve back and forth, the other legs take one step. You need to loop the driven keys of the other legs in the Graph Editor.

13. Select the leg control circles for the five remaining legs, and open the Graph Editor.

14. Ctrl+click the Translate Y channels of all the leg controls in the left column of the editor.

15. Drag a selection over the keys on the graph, and choose Curves ➤ Pre Infinity ➤ Cycle and then Curves ➤ Post Infinity ➤ Cycle.

16. Ctrl+click the Translate Z channel for each of the leg controls in the Graph Editor.

17. Drag a selection around the keys on the graph, and choose Curves ➤ Pre Infinity ➤ Cycle With Offset and then Curves ➤ Post Infinity ➤ Cycle With Offset.

18. Drag the bodyCtrl curve back and forth on the Graph Editor. All the legs take a step; however, they all do so at the same time, which looks a little silly.

19. To create a more convincing walk cycle for the bug, select each leg control, and open the Graph Editor.

20. Select the keys on the graph and use the Move tool to slide them a little backward or forward in time so each leg has its own timing. See Figure 5.50.

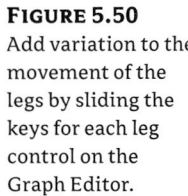

FIGURE 5.50
Add variation to the
movement of the
legs by sliding the
keys for each leg
control on the
Graph Editor.

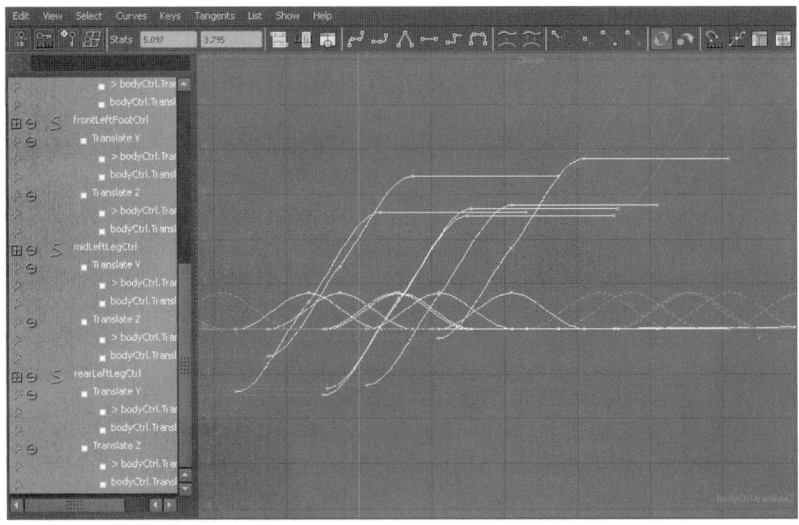

As you change the position of the Translate Z keys on the Graph Editor, you may need to also slide the curves up or down a little to make sure that they remain within the proper leg length range as they step. You can generally figure out the proper setting through experimentation.

21. Save the scene as **mechBugWalk_v04.ma**.

Creating a walk cycle this way is a little tricky and will take some practice. You can set keyframes on the Translate Z channel of the bodyCtrl curve so the bug walks forward and then adjust the position of the legCtrl curves as the animation plays. You can also change the position for the keyframes on the Graph Editor for pairs of legs so the midLeftLegCtrl, frontRightLegCtrl, and rearRightLegCtrl all move together, alternating with the remaining leg controls. Study the mechBugWalk_v04.ma scene in the chapter5\scenes directory on the DVD to see how this walk cycle was accomplished.

To see a finished version of the walking bug, open the mechBugWalk_v04.ma scene from the chapter5\scenes directory on the DVD.

Animation Using Expressions

Mathematical expressions can be used to automate animation of an object's attributes. Expressions can be very simple or quite complex. There is almost an infinite variety of expression types and applications. In this section, you'll see how to add a few simple and common expressions to animate the bug's antennae.

1. Open the mechBugExpressions_v01.ma scene from the chapter5\scenes directory on the DVD. This scene has an animation of the mechanical bug walking.

2. Select the yellow circle in front of the bug. This is the antennaCtrl, which controls the rotation of the antenna control group.

3. In the menu above the Channel Box, select the Rotate Y channel so that it is highlighted.

4. Choose Edit ➢ Expressions. This opens the Expression Editor.

5. In the Expression section, type **rotateY=sin(time);**.

6. Click the Create button to add the expression to the antennaCtrl object (see Figure 5.51).

FIGURE 5.51
Enter an expression for the antennaCtrl curve in the Expression Editor.

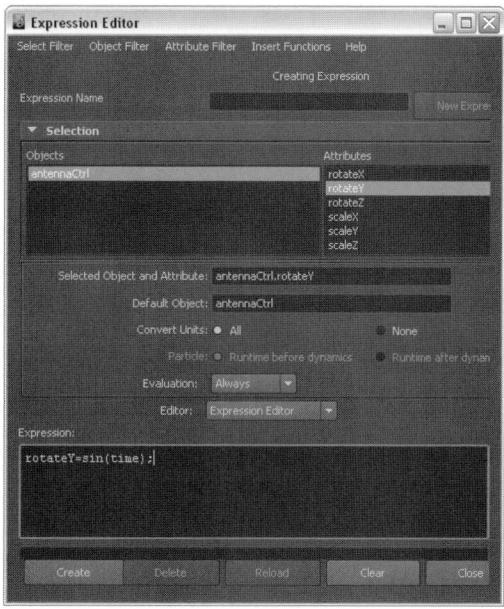

This expression creates a relationship where the rotation of the antennaCtrl group moves back and forth over time. The `sin` function creates a smooth curve using time as the input. The value of `sin` moves between -1 and 1. The value of the Rotate Y channel is expressed in degrees, so this expression does not create a very visible motion. It oscillates between -1 and 1 degrees. To fix this, you can add a multiplier to the expression.

When you click the Create button, Maya fills in the detailed path to the antennaCtrl channel. The original expression is replaced with `antennaCtrl.rotateY=sin(time)`. As long as an object is selected when you open the Expression Editor, you can type the name of the channel, and Maya will understand that the channel is connected to the selected object. Otherwise, you must specify the path to the channel by typing **objectName.channelName**. Each statement in the expression should end with a semicolon.

7. In the Expression Editor, change the expression to read **antennaCtrl.rotateY=30*(sin(time));**.

8. Click the Edit button to change the expression.

9. Rewind and play the animation. The antennae swing back and forth.

If you want the motion to move faster, create a multiplier for `time`. Change the expression so that it reads **antennaCtrl.rotateY=30*(sin(time*2));**. This makes the rotation occur twice as fast.

If you want to slow down the motion, multiply the time by a fraction. `time*0.5` makes the rotation move at half the original speed.

You can add an expression to the Translate Y of the antennaCtrl group to make the antenna move up and down:

1. Select the antennaCtrl, and open the Expression Editor (if it's not still open).

2. In the Expression section, type **translateY=cos(time);** below the first expression (see Figure 5.52).

FIGURE 5.52
Add the expression for the Y translation as a second line in the Expression Editor.

3. Click the Edit button to create the expression.

   This moves the antennaCtrl group up and down, making the antennae rotate upward and downward (recall that the locators in the antennaCtrl group are aim locators for the antennae geometry). The cos function (cosine) works like the sin function (sine) except the cosine is the opposite of sine, so when sine is at -1, cosine is at 1, and vice versa.

   To make the motion more interesting, you can add a noise function to each of the locators in the antenna control group. The noise function creates a continuous random pattern that moves between -1 and 1 (as opposed to the rand function, which creates a discontinuous random motion between -1 and 1).

4. Select one of the yellow locators in the perspective view.

5. In the Channel Box, highlight the Translate Y channel, and choose Edit ➤ Expressions to open the Expression Editor for the locator.

6. In the Expression section, type **translateY=noise(time*4);**. Then click the Create button to make the expression.

7. Play the animation; you'll see the antenna move somewhat randomly.

8. Add a similar expression to the Translate Y of the other yellow locator. To make the motion slightly different, try **translate=noise(time*5);**.

9. Save the scene as **mechBugExpressions_v02.ma**.

To see a version of the scene, open the mechBugExpressions_v02.ma scene from the chapter5\ scenes directory on the DVD.

Conditional Statements in Expressions

You can make expressions even more sophisticated by adding variables and conditional statements. A simple conditional statement looks like this in the Expression Editor:

```
if (x is true){
      Perform action;
}
else
{
      Perform a different action;
}
```

There are other ways to state conditionals, but this is the most common and simplest way to do it. To make the motion of the antennae more interesting, you'll make the antennae move faster when they are closer to the ground.

1. Continue with the scene from the previous section, or open the mechBugExpressions_v02.ma scene from the chapter5\scenes directory on the DVD.

2. Select one of the yellow locators in front of the bug, and open the Expression Editor using the Edit menu in the Channel Box.

    To create a condition, you'll make a variable that can hold a value. The value will be different depending on the outcome of the test performed by the conditional statement. In this case, the variable can hold a value, which will be a multiplier for time in the noise(time) statement applied to the locator's Translate Y channel. Before you can use the variable, you should declare it at the start of the expression. This lets Maya know what type of data the variable will hold. In this case, the variable can be an integer (a number without a decimal). The variable you will create is called $antSpeed, for antenna speed. All variables must be preceded by a dollar sign.

3. In the Expression Editor, select the text, and press the Backspace or Delete key to clear the Expression field. Type **int $antSpeed;** in the field.

4. Press the Return key (the Return key on the keyboard, *not* the Enter key on the numeric keypad), and enter the following lines:

```
if (antennaCtrl.translateY<0){
     $antSpeed = 10;
}
else
{
     $antSpeed=2;
}
translateY = noise(time*$antSpeed);
```

    Since the expression is testing to see the height of the antennaCtrl group, you need to specify the path to the antennaCtrl group's Translate Y channel. Expressions for channels are self-contained, so unless you specify the path to another object's channel, Maya won't understand what you're talking about. Figure 5.53 shows the expression in the Expression Editor.

5. Add the same expression to the other locator in the group. Use different values for the $antSpeed variable so that the two antennae move in different ways.

6. Save the scene as **mechBugExpressions_v03.ma**.

To see a finished version of the scene, open the mechBugExpressions_v03.ma scene from the chapter5\scenes directory on the DVD.

FIGURE 5.53
Create a conditional statement as an expression to make the antenna move faster when it's closer to the ground.

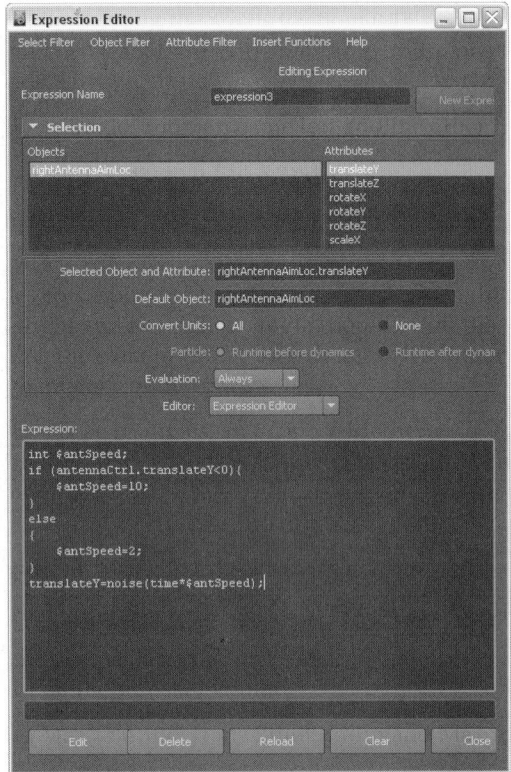

Motion Path Animation

You can animate the movement of an object by attaching the object to a curve and then sliding down the length of the curve over time. This is known as *motion path animation*. To create a Motion Path, perform the following steps:

1. Open the `mechBugPath_v01.ma` scene from the `chapter5\scenes` directory on the DVD.

2. Turn on the grid display, and choose Create ➢ CV Curve Tool ➢ Options.

3. In the options, make sure Curve Degree is set to Cubic.

4. Draw a curve on the grid using any number of points; make sure the curve has some nice twisty bends in it.

5. Right-click the curve, and choose Control Vertex.

6. Use the Move tool to move the CVs of the curve up and down so the curve is three-dimensional (see Figure 5.54).

7. In the Outliner, select the mechanicalBug group, and Ctrl+click the curve.

8. From the Animation menu set, choose Animate ➢ Motion Paths ➢ Attach To Motion Path ➢ Options.

FIGURE 5.54
Draw and shape a
curve in the scene.

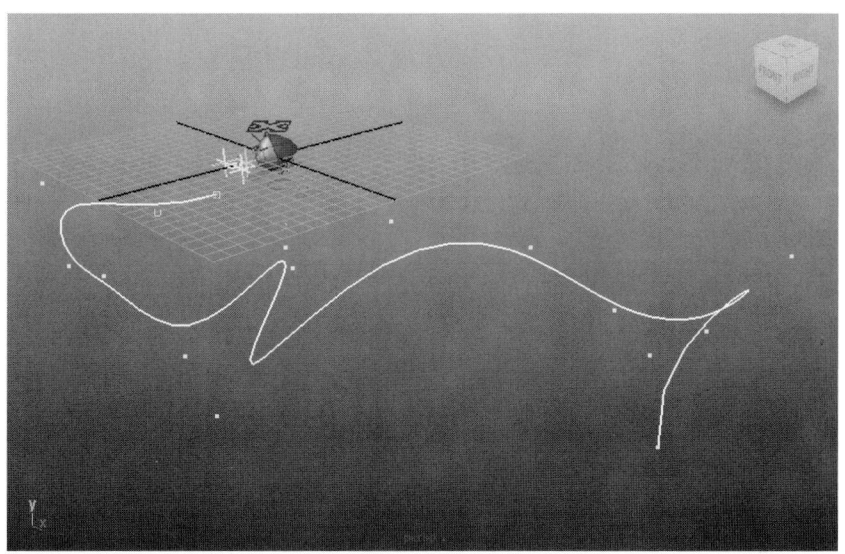

9. In the options, choose Edit ➤ Reset to reset the options. Enter the following:

   Set Front Axis to Z.

   Turn on Follow.

   Enable Bank.

   Set Bank Limit to **30**.

10. Click Attach to attach the bug to the curve (see Figure 5.55).

FIGURE 5.55
The options for Attach
To Motion Path

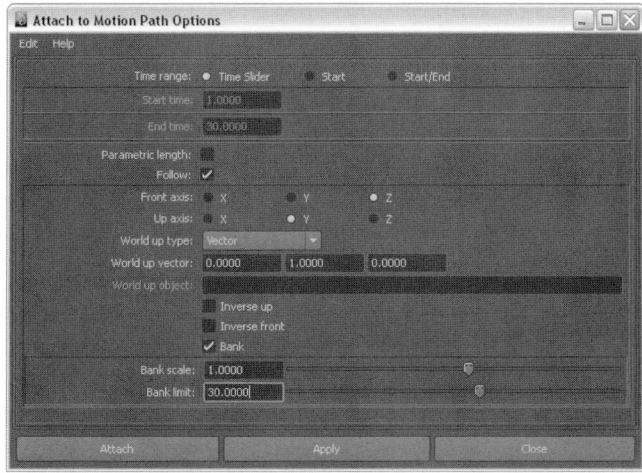

The default Time Range is set to Time Slider so the bug will travel the length of the curve based on the current length of the time slider (200 frames in this scene). You can change this after the motion path is created.

The Follow option orients the animated object so the front axis follows the bends in the curve. The Bank option adds a rotation on the z-axis around bends in the curve to simulate banking.

11. Play the animation. The bug follows the path (see Figure 5.56).

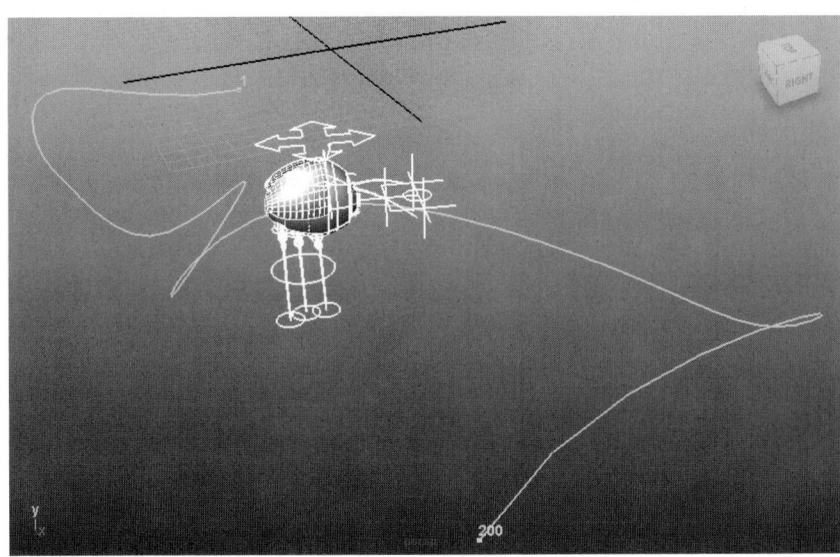

FIGURE 5.56
The bug is attached to the motion path curve. As the animation plays, the bug travels along the length of the curve.

At this point, the animation looks a little silly; the other parts of the bug need to be animated, which you can do using the techniques described in the chapter. By attaching the mechanicalBug group as opposed to the bodyCtrl group, you now have the option of adding animation to the bodyCtrl curve to provide variation in the movement of the bug as it flies along the curve.

You can change the rate at which the bug flies along the curve by editing the motionPath1 node's U Value attribute on the Graph Editor:

1. In the Outliner, select the mechanicalBug group.

2. In the Channel Box under Inputs, select motionPath1.

3. Choose Window ➤ Animation Editors ➤ Graph Editor to open the Graph Editor.

4. In the left column, select the motionPath1 U Value attribute, and press the **f** hot key to focus the graph on its animation curve.

5. Use the graph-editing tools to edit the curve.

6. Save the scene as **mechBugPath_v02.ma**.

To see a version of the scene to this point, open the mechBug_v02.ma scene in the chapter5\ scenes directory on the DVD.

Animating Constraints

You can constrain an object to more than one node. The weighting of the constraint strength can be blended between the two nodes and even animated. This is a great technique for solving difficult animation problems, such as a character picking up and putting down an object.

Dynamic Parenting

Dynamic parenting refers to a technique in which the parenting of an object is keyframed. In this exercise, you'll animate the mechanical bug sitting on a moving object for a few moments before flying off along a motion path.

This scene has the bug rigged and sitting at the origin of the grid. A cattail is bobbing up and down in the breeze. Above the cattail, a curve defines a motion path (see Figure 5.57).

FIGURE 5.57
The scene contains an animated cattail and a motion path.

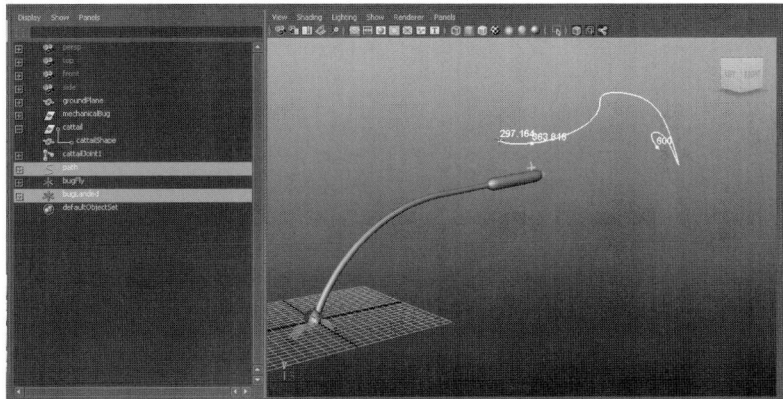

A locator named bugLanded is constrained to one of the joints of the cattail using a parent constraint. On the motion path is another locator named bugFly. To make the bug sit on the moving cattail, you'll create a parent constraint between the bug and the bugLanded locator.

1. Open the `mechBugConstrain_v01.ma` scene from the `chapter5\scenes` directory on the DVD.

2. In the Outliner, select the bugLanded locator, and Ctrl+click the mechanicalBug group.

3. From the Animation menu set, choose Constrain ➢ Parent ➢ Options.

4. In the options, turn off Maintain Offset. Leave Translate and Rotate set to All.

5. Click Add to make the constraint (see Figure 5.58).

FIGURE 5.58
The options for the parent constraint

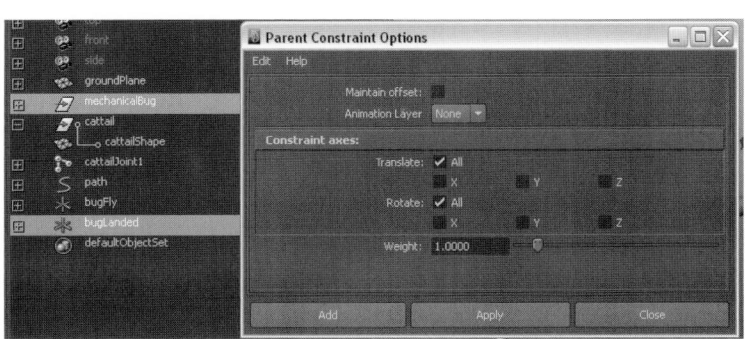

The mechanical bug now appears on the end of the cattail. You can reposition the bug on the cattail using the bodyCtrl and legCtrl curves.

6. In the Display Layers window, turn on the CONTROLS layer.

7. Select the blue bodyCtrl curve, and pull it upward to move the bug up above the end of the cattail.

8. Turn on Wireframe view.

9. Select the red legCtrl circle, and move it upward with the Move tool so the legs are positioned on the end of the cattail. (Use the Show menu in the viewport to turn off the visibility of Joints so that you can easily see the geometry.)

10. Position each of the small purple leg control circles so the bug's legs are posed on the end of the cattail geometry (see Figure 5.59).

FIGURE 5.59
Pose the legs using the legCtrl curves so the bug is standing on the cattail.

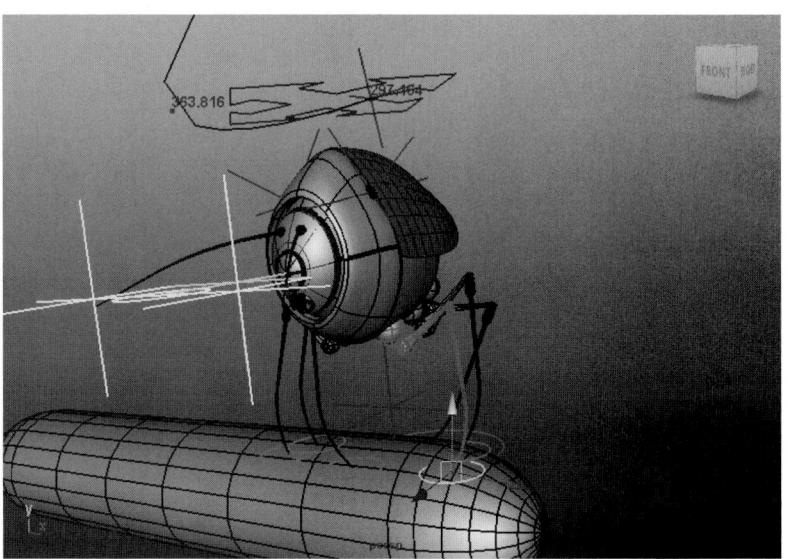

11. Play the animation. You'll see the bug sticking to the cattail as it moves up and down.

12. Set the timeline to frame 320.

13. In the Outliner, select the bugFly locator, and Ctrl+click the mechanicalBug.

14. Create another parent constraint; the same options should be applied automatically when you create the constraint.

   When you play the animation, you'll see that the bug is floating between the two locators, thus inheriting a blend of their animation. This is because the strength of both constraints is at 1 (or full strength).

15. Set the timeline to frame 353. This is a point where the two locators are very close and a good time for the bug to start to fly off.

16. In the Outliner, expand the mechanicalBug group. Select the mechanicalBug_parent-Constraint1 node.

17. In the Channel Box, set Bug Fly W1 to **1** and Bug Landed W0 to **0**. The bug reorients itself to match the orientation of the bugFly locator.

18. Shift+click both the Bug Landed W0 channel and the Bug Fly W1 channel in the Channel Box (see Figure 5.60). Right-click, and choose Key Selected.

FIGURE 5.60
Set the weights of the parent constraint and key it at frame 353.

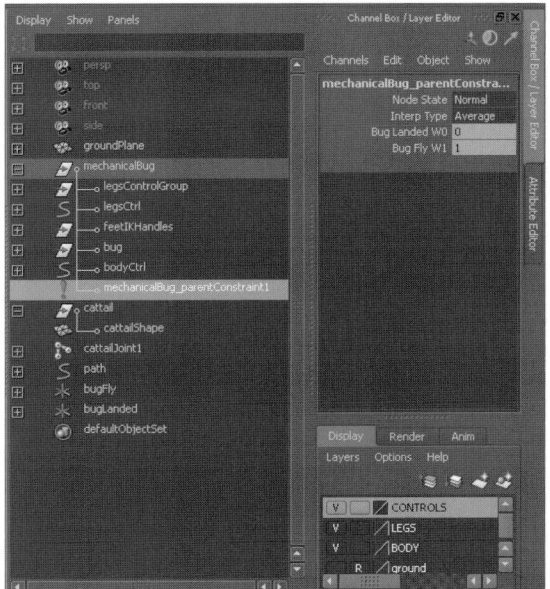

19. Set the timeline to 347.

20. Reverse the values of the two weights so Bug Landed W0 is at **1** and Bug Fly W1 is at **0**.

21. Set another keyframe.

22. Rewind and play the animation. You'll see the bug sitting on the cattail as it bobs up and down. At frame 347, the bug switches to the motion path and flies off.

23. With the mechanicalBug parentConstraint1 node selected, open the Graph Editor.

24. Select the Bug Landed W0 and Bug Fly W1 channels on the left column of the Graph Editor, and press the **f** hot key to focus on their animation curves.

25. Use the curve-editing tools to fine-tune the animation so the transition between the cattail and the motion path is smoother. This usually takes a fair amount of experimentation (Figure 5.61).

26. Save the scene as **mechBugConstrain_v02.ma**.

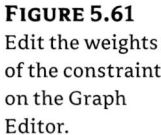

FIGURE 5.61
Edit the weights
of the constraint
on the Graph
Editor.

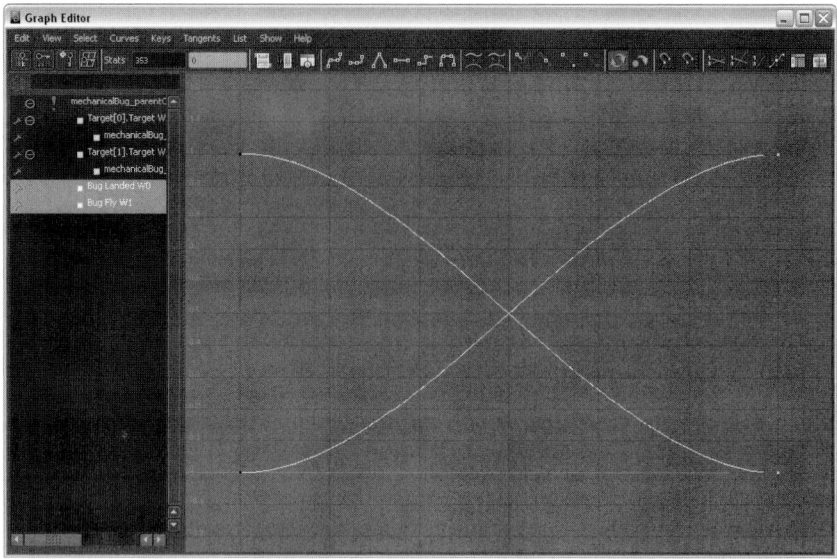

In some cases, you can create a smoother transition by extending the length of time between the keyframed weight values. It depends on what type of motion you are trying to achieve and your own personal taste.

As shown in the mechBugConstrain_v02.ma scene from the chapter5\scenes directory on the DVD, you can also animate the bodyCtrl curve and the leg controls to create a more believable motion to the bug as he takes flight.

Animation Layers

Animation layers separate the keyframe data applied to objects in the scene so you can create variations of animation for approval from a director, blend different versions of an animation together for a higher level of control, or organize the animated parts of an animation. This section is a tour of how animation layers work and some of the ways they can be applied in a scene. There is a great amount of flexibility in how animation layers can be used; no doubt you will create your own preferred animation layer workflow after a little bit of practice.

Creating an Animation Layer

In this section, you'll create a simple dancing motion for the mechanical bug. Animation layers take some getting used to, so you'll start with a very simple animation.

1. Open the mechBugLayers_v01.ma scene from the chapter5\scenes directory on the DVD.

2. Set the current frame on the timeline to 1.

3. Select the blue bodyCtrl curve above the bug, and set its Translate Y channel to **-0.5**.

4. Create a keyframe for this channel.

5. Set the current frame to 20, set Translate Y to **0.5**, and create another keyframe.

6. Create three more keyframes for the bodyCtrl curve:

Frame 40 Translate Y: **-0.5**

Frame 60 Translate Y: **0.5**

Frame 80 Translate Y: **-0.5**

When you play the animation, the bug bobs up and down.

7. In the Layer panel in the lower-right corner of the screen below the Channel Box, set Mode to Anim. This switches the Layer Editor to Animation layers as opposed to Display or Render layers.

8. Choose Layers ➤ Create Empty Layer. Two layers appear. The new layer is AnimLayer1, and the default Base Animation layer is at the bottom.

In the perspective view, nothing has changed regardless of which layer is selected.

9. Double-click AnimLayer1, and rename it **bounce** (see Figure 5.62).

FIGURE 5.62
Create a new animation layer in the scene, and rename it **bounce**.

10. Select the bodyCtrl curve.

11. In the Animation Layer panel, select the bounce layer, RMB+click it, and choose Add Selected Objects. This adds just the bodyCtrl curve.

Notice that all the channels in the Channel Box are now yellow. You'll also notice that in the INPUT section under the Channel Box for the bodyCtrl curve, bounce has been added to the list of inputs.

When creating an animation layer, you have the option of creating the layer from selected objects in the scene or copying an existing layer (using the options in the Layers menu). When you copy a layer, the keyframes are also copied to the new layer. The Layers menu has a lot of options you'll explore as you go through the next few exercises.

12. Select the bounce layer, and a green circle appears on the right. This indicates that the layer is active.

13. Play the animation. It looks the same as before. Notice that there are no keyframe tick marks on the timeline.

14. Select the BaseAnimation layer; the tick marks reappear. So, what does this mean?

Each layer has its own set of keyframes for the objects in that particular layer. The bounce layer has no keyframes yet, so what you're seeing when you play the animation is the keyframes set on the BaseAnimation layer. The way in which the keyframes on one layer interact with the keys on another depends on the layer's Mode and Accumulation settings.

You can also choose Layers ➢ Selected Objects to create a new layer based on the selected objects. The keyframes set on the object are removed from the current selected layer and added to the new layer created from the Extract operation.

Layer Mode

The mode of a layer can be either Additive or Override. Additive layers blend the values of the keys together so the resulting animation is a combination of the two layers. Using the Additive mode, you can add changes to the animation without affecting the original keyframes on the BaseAnimation layer.

When a layer is set to Override mode, the animation on that layer overrides the animation on the layers below it. Override mode is a good way to create different "takes" or versions of an animation without affecting the original BaseAnimation layer.

Follow the next steps to see how these modes work:

1. In the Layer Editor, select the bounce layer.

2. Choose (from the menu in the Layer Editor) Layers ➢ Layer Mode ➢ Override. When you play the animation, the bug no longer moves.

   If you switch to the BaseAnimation layer, you can see the keyframes on the timeline, but the bug still doesn't move. This is because even though the bounce layer is not selected, it is overriding the BaseAnimation layer.

3. In the Layer Editor, click the Mute Layer button to the left of the ghosting icon (the ghost icon looks like a little man on a red background) button on the Bounce layer (see Figure 5.63). The Mute Layer button temporarily disables the layer; when you click Play, you'll see the bug move up and down again.

4. Turn the Mute Layer button off, and then play the animation. The bug should stop moving.

5. Select the bounce layer, and drag the Weight slider slowly to the left as the animation plays (see Figure 5.64).

   As you drag the Weight slider down, the influence of the overriding layer decreases, and you can see the bug start to move up and down again. When the weight is at zero, the overriding layer has no more influence. The K button to the right of the Weight slider sets a keyframe on the Weight value so you can animate the strength of the weight over time.

FIGURE 5.63
The Mute Layer button temporarily disables a layer.

FIGURE 5.64
The Weight slider determines the amount of influence the layer has over the animation.

6. Select the bounce layer.

7. Set the Weight for the bounce Layer to **1**, and make sure the layer is not muted. When you play the animation, you should see no motion.

8. Select the bodyCtrl curve, and set the following keyframes on the Translate Y channel.

   Frame 1 Translate Y: **-0.05**

   Frame 10 Translate Y: **0.5**

9. With the bodyCtrl curve selected, open the Graph Editor, and select the Translate Y channel.

10. Drag a selection around the keys, and choose Curves ➢ Post Infinity ➢ Oscillate.

    When you play the animation, the bug bounces a little faster. As you lower the Weight setting for the layer, you'll see the slower bouncing motion of the BaseAnimation layer.

    If you turn off the Passthrough option in the Layers ➢ Layer Mode menu, the animation of the lower layers does not pass through the upper layers, so as you lower the Strength value, you'll see the bouncing stop as the Weight value approaches 0.

11. Set Layer Mode to Additive, as shown in Figure 5.65.

FIGURE 5.65
When Layer Mode is set to Additive, the animation of the two layers is combined.

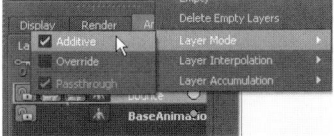

12. Set the Weight setting of the bounce layer to **1**, and play the animation.

    You can see that the resulting animation is now a combination of the keyframe values on the bounce and BaseAnimation layers (the Passthrough option has no effect on additive layers).

    When the mode is set to Additive, the keyframe values from the top layer are added to the layers below; in this case, the values of the Bounce layer are added to the values in the Base Animation layer. As you alter the weight slider for additive layers, this decreases the layer's keyframe values. Keep in mind that the layer only affects the keyframe values of the objects that it contains.

13. In the Options menu of the Layer Editor, choose the Turn On Ghosts Manually option.

14. Click the ghosting icon (looks like a little man on a red background) in the Base Animation layer. This creates a ghost of the animated objects on this layer so you can compare it with the animation on other layers. In this case, you'll see a red copy of the bodyCtrl curve moving according to the keyframes set on the BaseAnimation layer. The icon switches so that you'll see two men on the button. One represents the ghost of the other.

15. Rewind the animation, and select the bodyCtrl curve.

16. In the Layer Editor, choose Create Layer From Selected. Name the new layer **rock**, and set its mode to Override.

17. Select the rock layer. In the Channel Box, highlight the Rotate X, Y, and Z channels, and set a keyframe on these channels.

18. Turn on the Auto Keyframe feature by clicking the key icon to the right of the timeline.

19. Set the timeline to various points in the animation, and use the Rotate tool to rotate the bug, making him do a happy little dance.

20. Rewind and play the animation. You'll see him move around.

Experiment with the weight of the rock layer; try setting its mode to Additive, and observe the result.

By varying the weight, you get a pretty good dancing action (for a mechanical bug) fairly easily.

21. Save the scene as **mechBugLayers_v02.ma**.

To see a version of the scene to this point, open the mechBugLayers_v02.ma scene from the chapter5\scenes folder on the DVD.

USE ANIMATION LAYERS FOR DRIVEN KEYS

Layers can be created for other types of keyframe animation such as driven keys. For instance, you can create a layer where driven keys make the legs of the bug appear to crawl forward as the bodyCtrl moves along the z-axis and then a second layer where a new set of driven keys makes the bug appear to crawl sideways as the bodyCtrl moves along the x-axis.

Other Options in the Layer Editor

The Layer Editor includes other options as well:

Lock Layer   Click the padlock icon to the left of the layer. When this is active, you cannot add keyframes to the layer. This is helpful if you use Auto Keyframe because it prevents you from accidentally changing the animation on a layer.

Solo Layer   Click the horizontal bar icon to left of the layer. This temporarily disables the animation of other layers so you can focus on just the soloed layer (more than one layer can be in solo mode).

Mute Layer   This button disables animation on the selected layer.

Ghost Layer   This button creates a ghost of the animated objects on the layer. You can change the color of the ghost by right-clicking the ghosting button and choosing a color from the pop-up window.

Zero Key Layer   The Zero Key Layer is a way to edit a small portion of an animation using an animation layer. Select an object in the layer, and click the Zero Key icon in the upper left of the Layer Editor to create a starting point on the timeline for the edit. Then move the Time slider to a later point in the animation, and click the Zero Key icon again. Any keyframes you set on the object between these two points in time will not be offset from the original animation.

You can change the order of layers by clicking the up and down arrows in the upper right of the Layer Editor window. The order of layers affects how the animation behaves. For instance, an override layer overrides animation on the layers below it but not above it. You can stack additive layers above, and Override Layer adjusts their weighting and rearranges their order to create different variations on the animation.

The Layer Accumulation settings under Layers ➤ Scale Accumulation determine how scaling and rotation are calculated when two or more layers that have animated scaling and rotation are combined.

The animated scaling on two layers can be added or multiplied depending on the Layer Accumulation setting.

Euler and quanternion are two different methods for calculating rotation. Euler is the standard method used in Maya. If the combination of rotation animation on two different layers leads to an unexpected result, try switching to quanternion in the Layer Accumulation settings.

EULER VS. QUANTERNION ROTATION

Euler rotation is calculated based on three angle values (X, Y, and Z) plus the order in which the angles are calculated. This is the standard method for calculating rotation in Maya, and it works in most cases. Euler rotation is prone to the problem of Gimbal Lock, where two of the axes overlap and lead to the same result.

Quanternion rotation uses a more complex algorithm that helps it avoid Gimbal Lock problems. When Rotation is set to Quanternion, Maya calculates the animation of rotation by using the X, Y, Z animation curves to create a fourth curve (W), which represents the rotation in quanternion units.

Layer Hierarchy

You can create a hierarchical relationship between animation layers. This is useful as an organizational tool and can speed up your workflow as you animate. Creating a hierarchy means parenting one or more animation layers to another. When you mute or solo the parent layer, all the child layers are also muted or soloed. Likewise, the Weight and Mode settings of the parent can affect the child layers. When animation layering becomes complex, you can use the hierarchy to quickly enable, disable, and rearrange the layers.

1. Continue with the scene from the previous section, or open the `mechBugLayer_v02.ma` scene from the `chapter5\scenes` folder on the DVD.

2. In the Animation Layer Editor, mute the rock and bounce layers. You'll notice that the bug still bounces. This is because of the keyframes set on the BaseAnimation layer.

3. Before creating a hierarchy for the layers, you can quickly move the animation on the BaseAnimation layer to its own new layer.

   A. Select the bodyCtrl curve and the BaseAnimation layer.

   B. Right-click the BaseAnimation layer.

   C. Choose Extract Selected Objects.

Extracting the bodyCtrl object from the BaseAnimation layer creates a new animation layer that contains the bodyCtrl curve and its animation. At the same time, the keyframes from the bodyCtrl curve are removed from the BaseAnimation layer. If you mute all the layers except BaseAnimation, the bug no longer moves when you play the animation.

4. Name the new layer **bounce1**, and rename bounce as **bounce2**.

5. Make sure bounce1 is below bounce2. Mute all the layers (see Figure 5.66).

6. In the Layer Editor, choose Layers ➤ Create Empty Layer. Name the new layer **legAnim**.

7. Select the circle under the front left leg.

8. In the Layer Editor, choose Layers ➤ Create From Selected. Name the new layer **FLeftLegAnim**.

9. MMB-drag FLeftLegAnim on top of the legAnim layer to make it a child of this layer. A small black triangle appears, and the FLeftLegAnim layer is indented above the legAnim layer (see Figure 5.67).

FIGURE 5.66
Copy the Base-Animation layer, renamed it bounce1, and move it below the other layers. Mute all layers.

FIGURE 5.67
The FLeftLegAnim layer is parented to the legAnim layer.

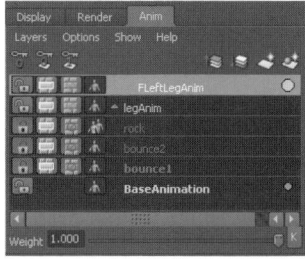

10. Repeat steps 7 through 9 for the front right leg circle. Name the new layer **FRightLegAnim**.

11. Select the FLeftLegAnim layer, and in the perspective view, select the circle under the front left leg.

12. In the Channel Box, Shift+click all the channels except the Translate channels.

13. Right-click, and choose Remove From Selected Layers (see Figure 5.68).

14. With the FLeftLegAnim layer selected, set a keyframe on the left leg control circle's Translate channels. Then use the Auto Keyframe feature to create an animation of the leg moving up and down as if it's tapping out a little beat.

FIGURE 5.68
Remove the Rotate and Scale channels from the animation layer.

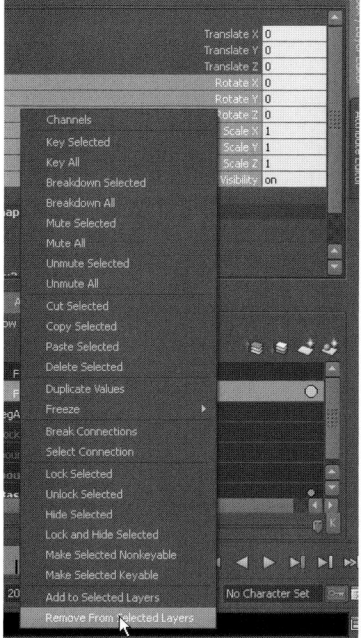

15. Switch to the FRightLegAnim layer, and create a similar animation for the front right leg.

16. When you have a nice animation going for both layers, unmute the other layers, and play the animation.

17. Click the black triangle on the legAnim layer to collapse the layer.

    Experiment with the Weight setting of the legAnim layer. The Weight value of the parent layer applies to both child layers as well. This is also true for the Layer Mode, Mute, and Solo settings.

18. Save the scene as **mechBugLayers_v03.ma**.

You can create further nested layers within the hierarchy. Each child layer can have its own Mode setting. To keep things simple, you can use empty layers as parent layers. The empty parent layers can be used to set the Weight and Mode operations of the child layers. If the parent layer is empty, you don't have to worry about how the animation in a parent layer is blended with the child layers.

To see a version of the scene to this point, open the mechBugLayers_v03.ma scene from the chapter5\scenes folder on the DVD.

Merging Layers

You can merge the animation of two layers into a single animation layer.

1. Continue with the scene from the previous section, or open the mechBugLayers_v03.ma scene from the chapter5\scenes folder on the DVD.

2. In the Animation Layers Editor, Shift-select the bounce2 and bounce1 layers.

3. Choose Layers ➢ Merge Layers ➢ Options.

4. In the options, set the Merge To option to Bottom Selected Layer.

5. Set Layers Hierarchy to Selected and Result Layer Mode to Additive.

6. Turn on the Smart Bake option.

   When you merge two or more layers, the animation of the objects on the layers is baked. You can choose to sample the baked keyframes based on the Sample By value. For instance, if you set Sample By to 1, then the object on the resulting baked layer will have a keyframe placed on the animated channels for every frame of the animation. A setting of 2 creates a key on every other frame. The Smart Bake option creates a curve from the combined animation layers with fewer keyframes. The Increase Fidelity setting increases the accuracy of the resulting animation curve to better represent the combined animation of the two layers. The Sample By option is more accurate but creates a lot of keyframes, which can be hard to edit. The Smart Bake option works very well when there are fewer layers or the animation is simple.

   You can bake a parent layer and all its child layers into a single layer. You can also choose to delete the original layers or keep them. Figure 5.69 shows the options for merging layers.

FIGURE 5.69
The options for
merging layers

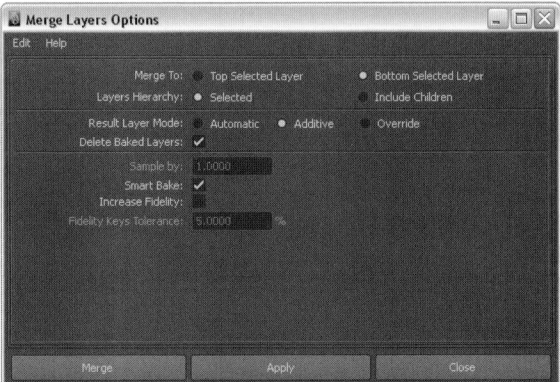

7. Click Apply to merge the layers. A new layer named Merged Layer is created. Rename the new layer **bounce**.

8. Select the bounce layer.

9. In the perspective view, select the bodyCtrl, and open the Graph Editor. You'll see the merged animation curve in the Graph Editor (see Figure 5.70).

10. Save the scene as **mechBugLayers_v04.ma**.

   To see a version of the scene, open the mechBugLayers_v04.ma scene in the chapter5\scenes folder on the DVD.

FIGURE 5.70
The merged animation curve is displayed in the Graph Editor.

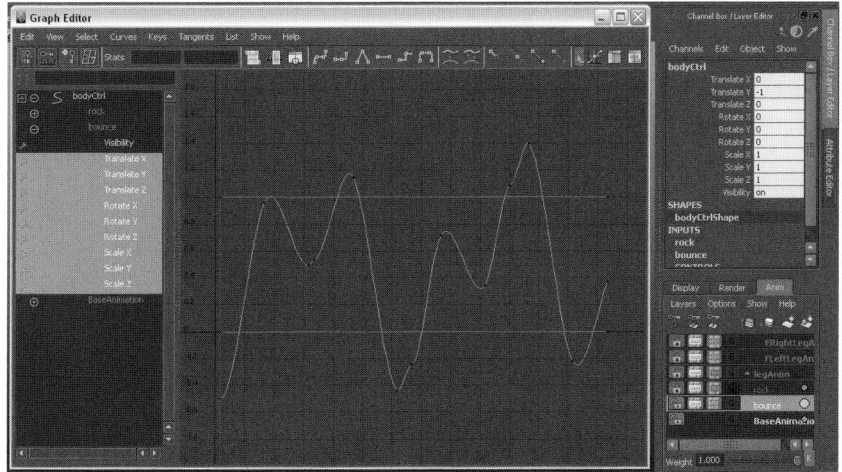

CAMERA SEQUENCING

New!

Maya 2011 introduces the Camera Sequencer, which gives you the ability to plan and test your shots before you render. For more information on these tools, refer to the CameraSequencer.mov movie file included in the BonusMovies folder on the DVD.

The Bottom Line

Use Inverse Kinematics   Inverse Kinematics creates a goal object, known as an End Effector, for joints in a chain. The joints in the chain orient themselves based on the translation of the goal. The IK Handle tool is used to position the End Effector.

Master it   Create an Inverse Kinematic control for a simple arm.

Animate with keyframes   A keyframe marks the state of a particular attribute at a point in time on the timeline. When a second keyframe is added to the attribute at a different point in time, Maya interpolates the values between the two keyframes, creating animation. There are a number of ways to edit keyframes using the timeline and the Channel Box.

Master it   Create a number of keyframes for the Translate channels of a simple object. Copy the keyframes to a different point in time for the object. Try copying the keyframes to the Scale channels. Try copying the keys to the Translate channels of another object.

Use the Graph Editor   More sophisticated animation editing is available using the animation curve editing tools on the Graph Editor.

Master it   Create a looping animation for the mechanical bug model using as few keys as possible. The bug should leap up repeatedly and move forward with each leap.

Preview animations with a playblast   A playblast is a tool for viewing the animation as a flip book without having to actually render the animation. FCheck is a utility program that is included with Maya. Playblasts can be viewed in FCheck.

Master it   Create a playblast of the mechBugLayers_v04.ma scene.

Animate with expressions   Expressions are a powerful way to automate the movement of an object. Using conditional statements, you can create an expression that causes the animation to react to changes in the scene automatically.

Master it   Create an expression to randomly rotate the bug's eyes up and down. Make the rotation faster based on the height of the bodyCtrl curve.

Animate with motion paths   Motion paths allow you to attach an object to a curve. Over the course of the animation, the object slides along the curve based on the keyframes set on the motion path's U Value.

Master it   Make the bug walk along a motion path. See whether you can automate a walk cycle based on the position along the path.

Use animation layers   Using animation layers, you can add new motion that can override existing animation or be combined with it.

Master it   Create animation layers for the flying bug in the mechBug_v08.ma scene in the chapter5\scenes directory on the DVD. Create two layers: one for the bodyCtrl curve and one for the legsCtrl curve. Use layers to make the animation of the wings start with small movements and then flap at full strength.

Chapter 6

Animating with Deformers

As you learned in Chapter 1, objects in a Maya scene have both a transform node and a shape node. The transform node contains data concerning where the object is in a scene, its orientation, and its scale. The shape node contains data about the form of the object. If you want to animate an object moving around in a scene, usually you'll keyframe the translation, rotation, and scale of the transform node. If you want to animate the shape of an object, such as the facial expressions of a character, you want to use a *deformer*, which is a type of animation control applied to the shape node of an object.

Deformers are extremely versatile, and they can be used for both modeling and animation and as part of an animation rig. Deformers come in many forms. *Blend shapes* are used to interpolate between variations of a shape's form and are most commonly used to create expressions for characters. *Lattices* are a cage of points that surround a shape, allowing you to indirectly reshape a form to create smooth deformations. *Clusters* are used to animate a shape's vertices or groups of vertices easily. *Nonlinear deformers* create broad shape changes that can be used for cartoonish effects such as squashing and stretching. *Jiggle deformers* are a simple way to apply secondary jiggling effects to a shape.

In this chapter, you'll see some of the ways to animate geometry using deformers. From creating facial expressions to animating a jellyfish, you can apply deformers in thousands of ways to bring your creations to life.

In this chapter, you will learn to:

◆ Animate facial expressions

◆ Create blend shape sequences

◆ Deform a 3D object

◆ Animate nonlinear deformers

◆ Add jiggle movement to an animation

Animating Facial Expressions Using Blend Shapes

As the name suggests, a blend shape deformer blends, or *interpolates*, between variations of a geometric form. A blend shape deformer uses one or more blend shape *targets*. These targets are duplicates of the original model that have been modified using a variety of modeling techniques.

Animating facial expressions for characters is usually accomplished through the use of blend shapes. Although this is not the only way to animate expressions and speech, it is the most common because it is relatively straightforward to set up and animate. In this section, you'll learn how to create blend shape targets, paint blend shape weights, create a blend shape deformer, and build a simple facial animation rig.

You create the blend shape deformer by selecting the targets and the original model and choosing Create Deformers ➢ Blend Shape. The deformer controls consist of sliders—one for each blend shape target. The original model is animated by moving and keyframing the sliders. As the value of a slider moves between 0 and 1, Maya interpolates the change, blending between the original shape and the target shape. The duplicate model is known as the *blend shape target*, and the original model is known as the *base mesh*.

You should understand a few things about how blend shapes work before you set up a facial animation rig. First, blend shapes always move in a straight line when interpolating the change between the original model and the blend shape target. Think of how your eyelids move when you blink. Your eyelid is a flap of skin that moves over the spherical shape of your eyeball. If you make a dot on the edge of your eyelid with a marker (don't do this—just imagine it) and then follow the path of that dot from a side view, the dot moves in an arc as your eyelid closes.

If you have a model of a face with the eyes open and a blend shape target with the eyes closed, when you create the blend shape deformer and then animate the eyes closing, instead of moving in an arc, the eyelids will move in a straight line from the open position to the closed position. Most likely the eyelid geometry will pass through the eyeball geometry, creating a less-than-convincing blinking behavior (see Figure 6.1). Understanding that the blend shape deformer moves in a linear direction from one state to the next is important if you are to develop a solution for this problem.

Second, a blend shape target should have the same number of vertices and the same point order as the original geometry. Vertices on polygons and control vertices (CVs) on NURBS geometry are numbered in a specific order. You can see the numbers listed in the Script Editor when the vertices are selected. If the number of points and the order of the points on a blend shape target do not match the original, the deformer will not be created, or it will behave strangely (see Figure 6.2). It is possible to use a blend shape target that has a different number of vertices than the base mesh; however, this can lead to some unpredictable results.

FIGURE 6.1
Blend shape deformations move in a straight line, which can cause problems for certain types of facial movements, such as blinking eyelids.

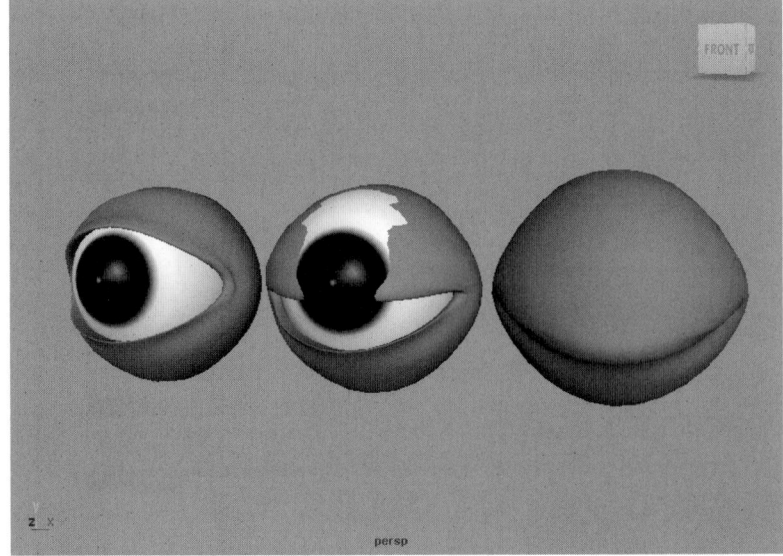

FIGURE 6.2
When the point order of the base mesh and the blend shape target do not match, strange results can occur when the deformer is applied.

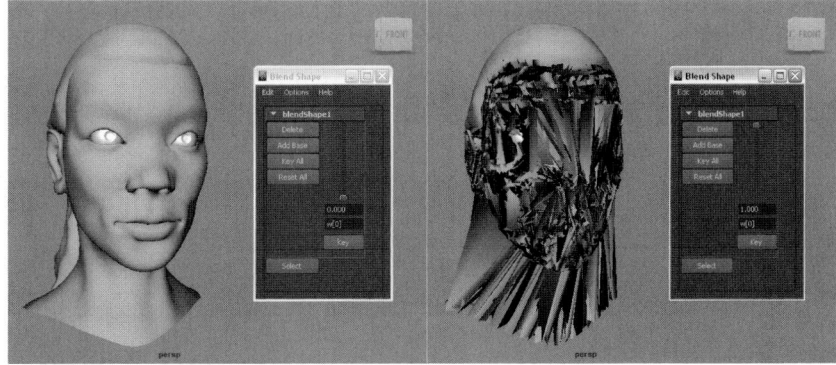

POINT ORDER CHANGES ON IMPORT

It is a fairly common practice to export a polygon model from Maya as an .obj format file for editing in another 3D program such as Mudbox or ZBrush. When the edited object is imported back into Maya, the vertex order can change if the options are not set correctly in Maya's Import Options box. The model may have exactly the same number of points as the original, but when you use the imported model as a blend shape target and animate the deformer, the model suddenly becomes mangled.

When you import an .obj format model into Maya, always remember to check the Single Object option or make sure Use Legacy Vertex Ordering is *off* when importing an .obj file made up of multiple objects (these options are available when File Type is set to OBJ). If the option is set to Multiple Objects and Use Legacy Vertex Ordering is selected, the point order of the model can change, which would cause major problems when using the imported model as a blend shape target.

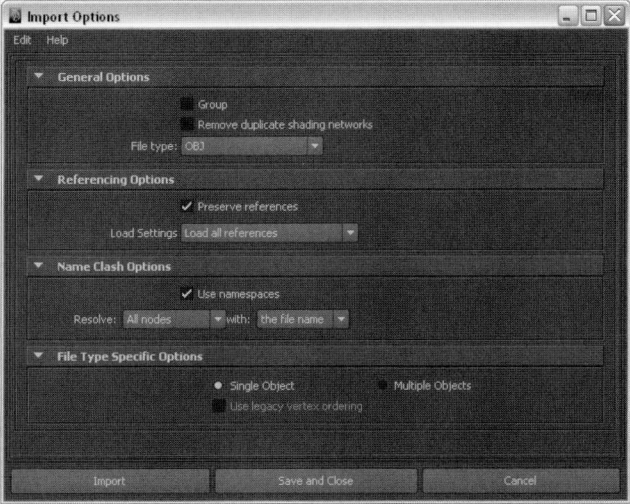

Third, when deforming a model with more than one blend shape target, the changes created by the targets are added together. So if you have one blend shape target in which a face is smiling and a second target in which the face is frowning, you may think that one target cancels the other. In fact, setting both blend shape targets to full strength creates a strange result on the base mesh because the smile and the frown will be added together (see Figure 6.3).

FIGURE 6.3
A smile shape and a frown shape are added together to create a very strange expression.

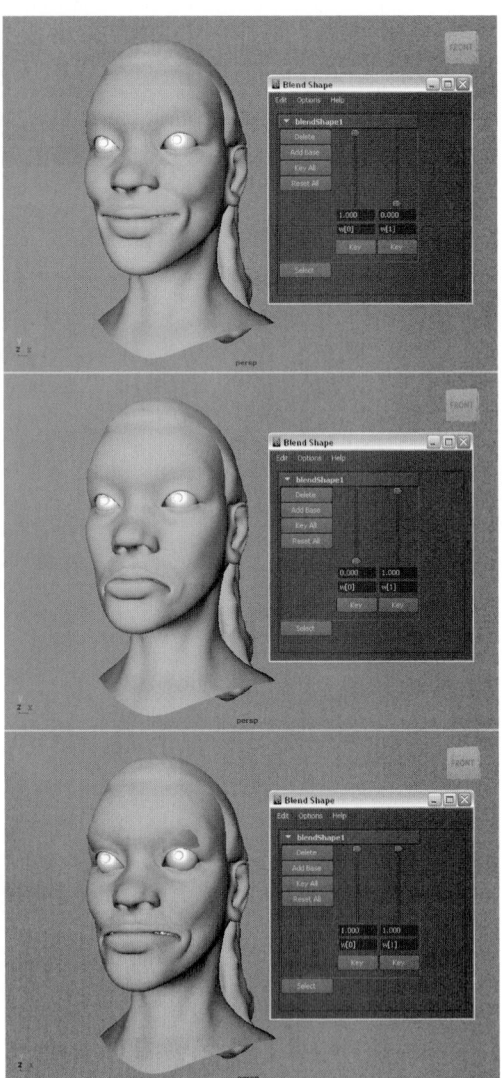

Creating Blend Shape Targets

The first step in setting up a blend shape facial animation rig is to model the actual blend shapes based on the base mesh. The final rig works something like the controls for a puppet. Rather than animate blend shape targets using a happy face model and a sad face model, you really want the blend shape target models built so that they allow you to isolate individual muscle movements. This will give you the most control when animating. When animating a smile, you'll have controls for the mouth, eyelids, eyebrows, cheeks, and more, so you have the option of animating a smile with brows up for a happy character and a smile with brows down for a menacing character. In addition, you want to isolate the sides of the face so the corner of one side of the mouth can be animated separately from the corner of the other side of the mouth.

When creating blend shape targets, it's best to think in terms of what the muscle is doing rather than a particular expression. The same targets are used to animate speech and emotion. So, rather than creating a blend shape target for a smile and a blend shape target for the "eeeee" sound, you want to make a single blend shape target that pulls a corner of the mouth back. Then this blend shape target combined with muscle movements created for other targets can be used for smiling, saying "cheeeese," or doing both at the same time.

In this exercise, you'll create blend shape targets for a character's mouth that can be used for widening the lips as in a smile as well as narrowing the lips as in a kiss. These two shapes (mouthWide and mouthNarrow) will then be separated into four shapes (leftMouthWide, left-MouthNarrow, rightMouthWide, and rightMouthNarrow).

1. Open the nancy_v01.ma scene from the chapter6\scenes directory on the DVD. This scene shows a very basic polygon head. Simple shapes for the eyes, tongue, teeth, and hair are included.

Using Standard Facial Features

It's a good idea to have models of the teeth and hair included in the scene when creating blend shape targets even if they are just temporary versions. It makes modeling the shape changes easier. Teeth play a big role in the way the mouth is shaped when moving, so it's good to have some kind of guide available while making blend shape targets. A simple hair shape is useful as a visual indicator for where the hairline starts when working on shapes for the brow.

---

2. Select the nancy model, and duplicate it (Ctrl+d). Move the duplicate to the side, as shown in Figure 6.4. Name the duplicate **mouthWide**.

FIGURE 6.4
A duplicate of the original head model is created.

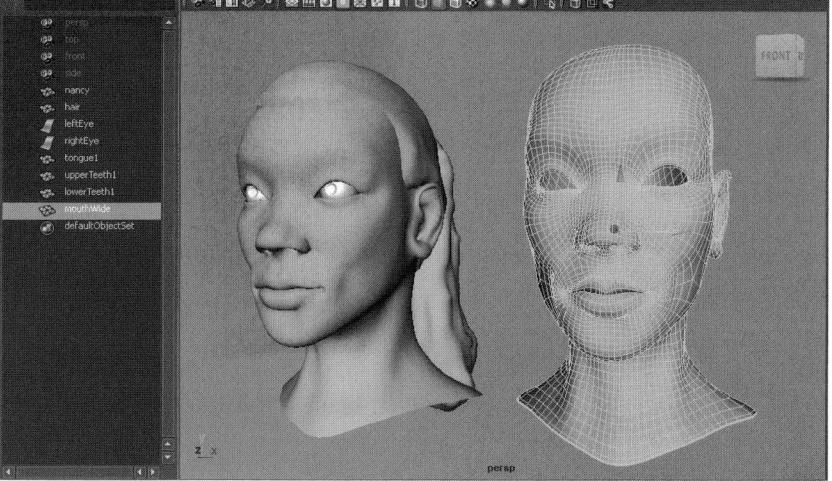

By default, blend shape deformers calculate only shape node–level changes. In other words, only changes made on the vertex level are considered. You can move, rotate, and scale the targets without affecting the base mesh—unless you specify otherwise in the deformer options (this will be discussed further later in the chapter).

3. Select the Move tool, and open the Options box for the tool. Under the Reflection Settings, activate Reflection, and set Reflection Axis to X.

4. Turn on Soft Select, and set Falloff Mode to Surface. Set Falloff Radius to **0.80**, and add a point to the Falloff Curve. Set Interpolation to Spline, and adjust the curve to look like Figure 6.5. You'll be changing these options a lot, so keep the Tool Settings window open while you work.

5. Right-click the mouthWide geometry, and choose Vertex to switch to vertex selection mode.

6. Select a vertex at the corner of the mouth, as shown in Figure 6.6. You'll see the vertices colored, indicating the Soft Selection radius and falloff. Carefully start moving the corner to the side and back toward the ear.

The muscles in the face work in concert to create facial expressions. Most of the face muscles are designed to convey emotion, aid with speech, and keep food in your mouth while you eat. Muscles work in groups to pull parts of the face in various directions like a system of pulleys. When you smile or grimace, the corners of your mouth are pulled back toward the ears by several muscles working together.

FIGURE 6.5
The options for the
Move tool

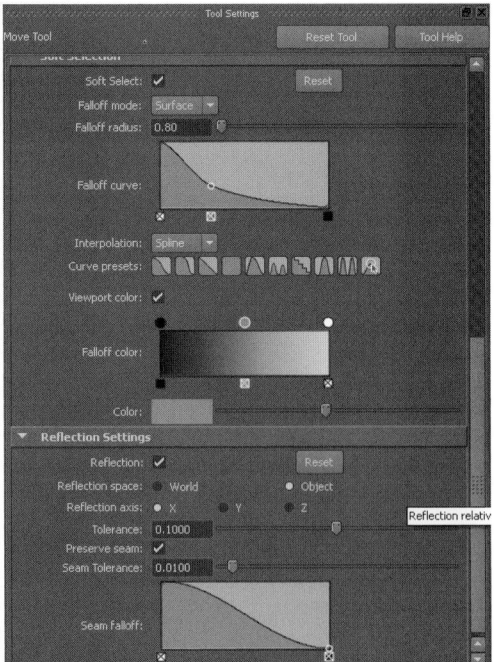

FIGURE 6.6
The vertices are color coded to indicate the falloff strength and radius of the Move tool when Soft Selection is enabled.

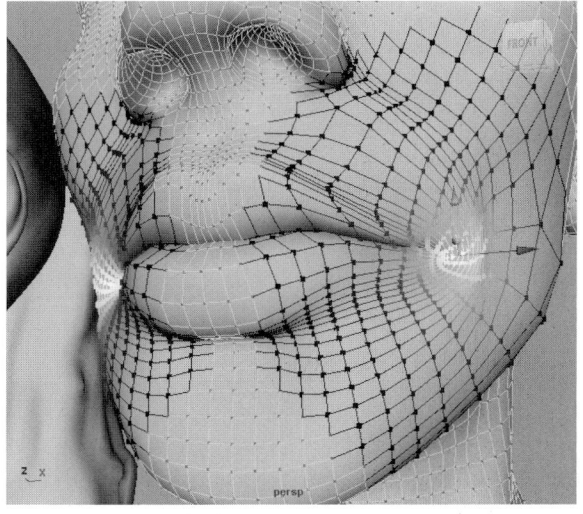

Cartoons often simplify the smile by drawing the corners of the mouth upward into a U shape. However, in reality the corners of the mouth actually move upward only a very small degree. The illusion of perspective makes it look as though the mouth is forming a U. The smile shape is not really a U shape, but rather the lips are stretched in a nearly straight line across the teeth. Perform the following procedure to refine the smile:

1. It will take a little work to form the smile shape on the face. Use a mirror for reference. Keep in mind that as the lips are pulled across the teeth, they are stretched and lose volume, giving them a thinner appearance (see Figure 6.7).

   As you work, make adjustments to the settings on the Move tool, and change the Falloff Radius and Falloff Curve values as needed.

2. When the corners of the mouth are pulled back, adjust other parts of the face near the corners and on the lips, but don't go too far beyond the area of the mouth. Remember, you are making an isolated change in the shape of the mouth, not a complete facial expression.

3. In addition to the Move tool, the Artisan Brush is very useful for sculpting changes in the model. To activate this tool, select the mouthWide model, and choose (from the Polygon menu set) Mesh ➢ Sculpt Geometry. To ensure that the changes you make are mirrored across the x-axis in the Options box, make sure the Reflection option is activated in the Stroke section.

FIGURE 6.7
Moving left to right, these images show some of the steps involved in creating a smile using the Move tool and the Artisan Brush tool.

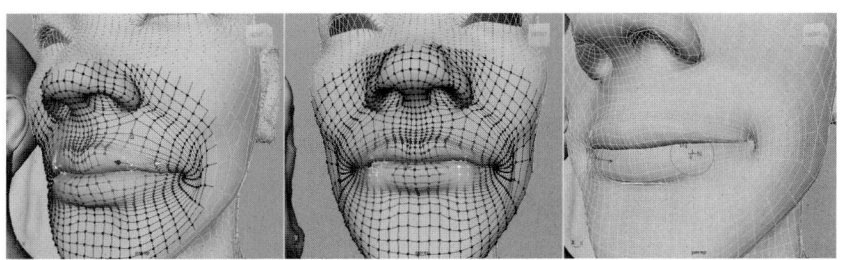

The final wide mouth shape should look like a fake smile because there are no changes in the other parts of the face. I tend to build a little overshoot into my blend shape targets so I have wider range to work with when animating (see Figure 6.8).

FIGURE 6.8
The base model (left) and the completed smile blend shape target (right)

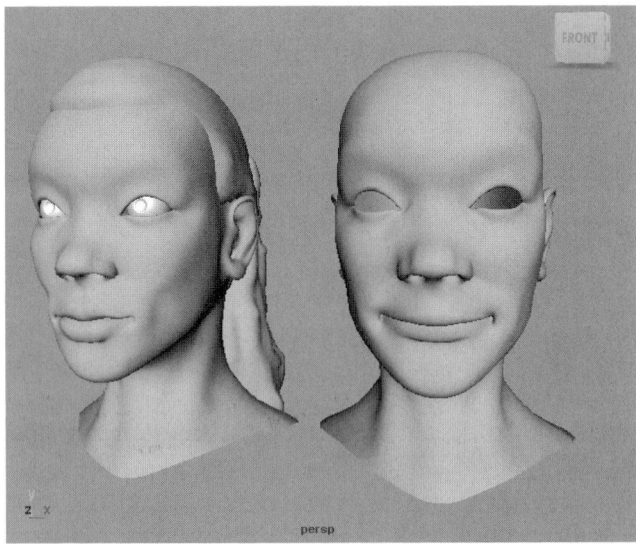

4. Save the scene as **nancy_v02.ma**.

5. Create another duplicate of the nancy model. Name the duplicate **mouthNarrow**. Move it to the model's right side. You may want to move the teeth with the model so you can use them as a guide.

6. Use the Move tool and the Artisan Brush to push the sides of the mouth toward the center of the face. The lips should bulge up in the center.

   As the lips push together and bulge at the center, there is a slight curling outward. Those parts of the upper and lower lips that touch in the neutral pose become exposed, and the flesh of the lips rolls outward (but just very slightly).

7. Use the Rotate tool to help create this rolling outward effect (see Figure 6.9). Figure 6.10 shows the finished narrow mouth blend shape target, the base mesh, and the smile blend shape target, respectively.

8. Once you are satisfied with the two mouth shapes, save the scene as **nancy_v02.ma**.

FIGURE 6.9
Moving left to right, the images show some of the steps involved in shaping the narrow lips using the Move tool, the Rotate tool, and the Artisan Brush tool.

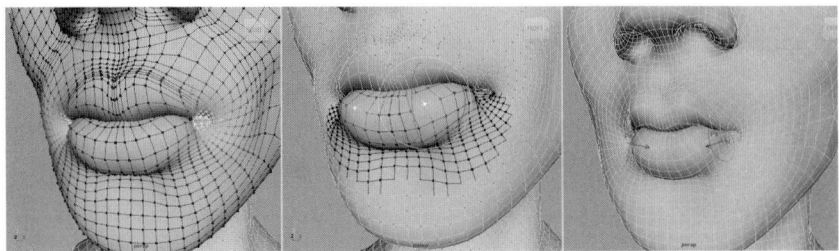

FIGURE 6.10
The completed narrow mouth blend shape target is on the left of the base mesh and smile blend shape targets.

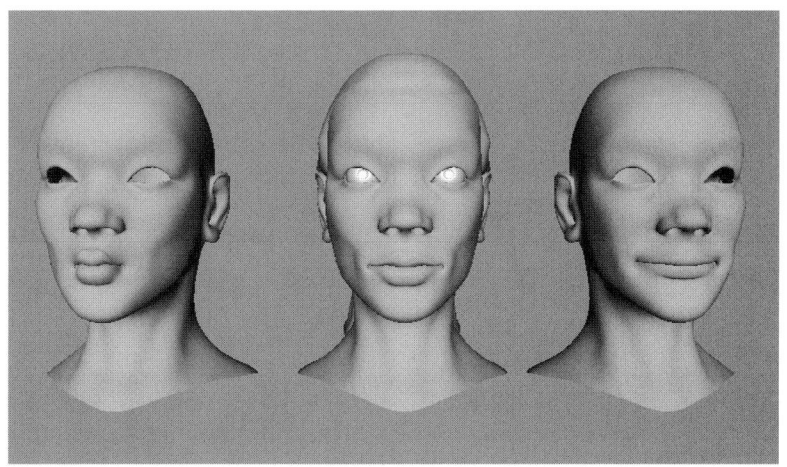

SURFACE VS. VOLUME SOFT SELECT

To move the vertices of the lips separately, use Soft Selection in surface mode. To move parts of the lips together, use Soft Selection in volume mode.

To see a version of the scene up to this point, open the nancy_v02.ma scene from the chapter6\ scenes folder on the DVD.

Creating Blend Shapes

To create the blend shape deformer, select all the targets first and then the base mesh. Next choose the Blend Shape deformer from the Deformers menu in the Animation menu set. In this section, you'll create the deformer using the mouthWide and mouthNarrow shapes.

1. Continue with the scene from the previous section, or open the nancy_v02.ma scene from the chapter6\scenes folder on the DVD.

2. Shift+click the mouthWide model and the mouthNarrow model; then Shift+click the nancy model.

3. Switch to the Animation menu set, and choose Create Deformers ➢ Blend Shape ➢ Options. In the Options box, choose Reset to set the options to the default settings. You want Origin set to Local; this means that only shape node–level changes will be used on the deformer. If target can be moved, scaled, or rotated, it will not affect how the deformer is applied.

4. Name the blend shape deformer **nancyFace** (see Figure 6.11). Click Create to make the deformer.

FIGURE 6.11
The options for the
blend shape deformer

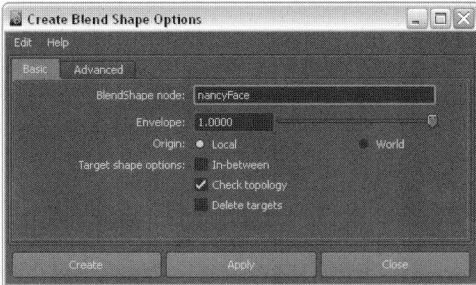

5. To test the deformer, choose Window ➤ Animation Editors ➤ Blend Shape. A small pop-up window appears with two sliders. These are the controls for the blend shape deformers.

6. Move the sliders up and down, and see how they affect the model (see Figure 6.12). Try putting both sliders at 1 to see the shapes added together. Try setting the values to negative values or values beyond 1.

7. Save the scene as **nancy_v03.ma**.

To see a version of the scene to this point, open the nancy_v03.ma scene from the chapter6\ scenes directory on the DVD.

FIGURE 6.12
The blend shapes
are controlled
using the blend
shape sliders.

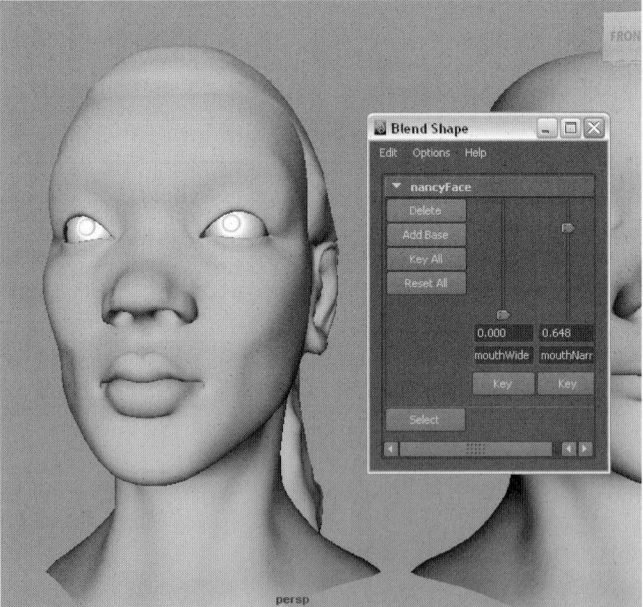

Painting Blend Shape Weights

At this point, you have two blend shapes available for animating, mouthWide and mouthNarrow. You may decide you want additional blend shape targets for the same mouth shape but restricted to just one side of the mouth. This gives you more options for animating a wider variety of facial movement. One easy way to create these additional targets is to use blend shape weighting as a shortcut for making additional blend shape target models from the symmetrical facial poses you've already created.

1. Continue with the scene from the previous section, or open the `nancy_v03.ma` scene from the `chapter6\scenes` directory on the DVD.

2. Select the nancy model, and choose Edit Deformers ➤ Paint Blend Shape Weights Tool ➤ Options.

3. The model turns completely white, and the options open in the Tool Options box on the right side of the screen.

   In the Target box is the list of all the current blend shapes applied to the model. The white color on the model indicates that the blend shape weight is at full strength.

4. Open the blend shape control window by choosing Window ➤ Animation Editors ➤ Blend Shapes. Set the mouthWide slider to 1 so you can see the deformer applied to the model (see Figure 6.13).

FIGURE 6.13
Activating the Paint Blend Shape Weights tool turns the model white, indicating that the selected target in the options is applied at full strength to all the model's vertices.

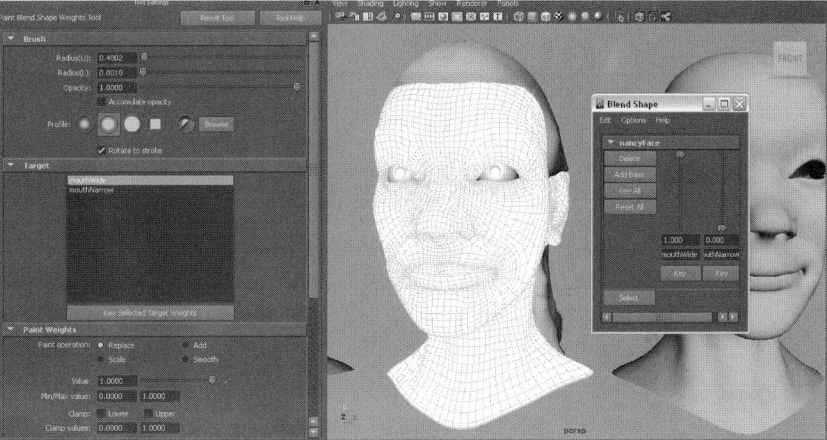

5. In the Paint Blend Shape Weights Tool options, set Paint Operation to Replace and Value to **0**. Click the Flood button. This floods the model with a zero-weight value. The model turns black, and the effect of the mouthWide deformation disappears.

6. Set Value to **1**, and paint the area around the mouth on the model's left side. As you paint, you'll see the left side move into the mouthWide shape within the area painted white (see Figure 6.14).

EMPLOYING THE USE COLOR RAMP OPTION

You can receive even more detailed visual feedback by activating the Use Color Ramp option. This assigns a gradient of colors to the values painted on the vertices. You can customize these colors by changing the colors in the Weight Color option, or you can use one of the preset gradients.

FIGURE 6.14
As the weights are painted, the side of the mouth moves into the mouth-Wide shape.

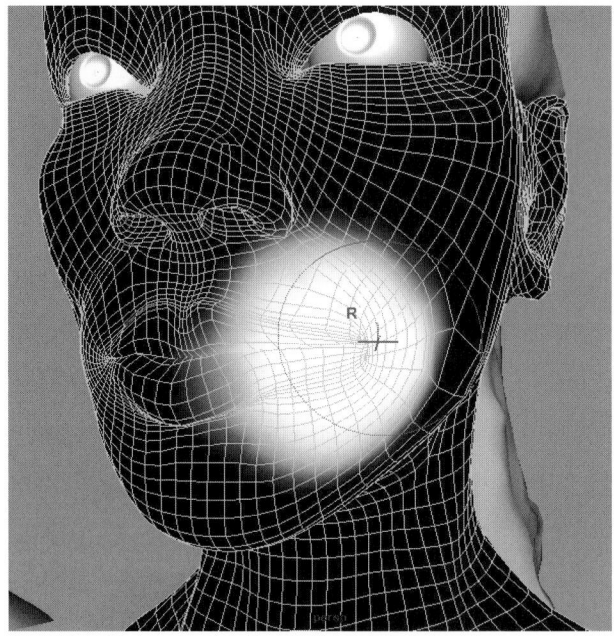

7. When you think you have painted enough of one side of the mouth, select the nancy model, and duplicate it (Ctrl+d). Move the duplicate up and off to the side, and name it **mouthLeftWide** (remember to name the deformers based on the character's left or right side, not your left or right).

8. Select the nancy model again, and choose Edit Deformers ➤ Paint Blend Shape Weights.

9. Flood the model with a zero value again, set Value to **1**, and this time paint the mouth area on the model's right side.

10. Duplicate the model again, and move the duplicate model up and away from the nancy model. Name this duplicate **mouthRightWide**.

11. Select the nancy model again, and choose Edit Deformers ➤ Paint Blend Shape Weights. Set Value to **1**, and flood the model to return the weight for the mouthWide shape to 1.

    The two duplicate models will look somewhat strange; this is a very unusual expression (see Figure 6.15). You can use the Artisan Brush and the Move tool to make the mouth look more natural, but try to restrict your edits to one side of the mouth or the other. Remember that this particular mouth movement will most likely be accompanied by other shape changes during animation, which will make it look more natural. Most likely these shapes will not be used at their full strength, but it's good to model a little over-shoot into the shape to expand the range of possible movements.

12. Open the Blend Shape control window (Window ➤ Animation Editors ➤ Blend Shapes). Set the mouthWide slider to **0** and the mouthNarrow slider to **1**.

13. Select the nancy model, and choose Edit Deformers ➤ Paint Blend Shape Weights. Select the mouthNarrow shape in the Target options, and repeat steps 5 through 11 to create two more blend shape targets based on the mouthNarrow shape, one for each side of the mouth.

FIGURE 6.15
Two new blend shape targets have been created using the Paint Blend Shape Weights tool.

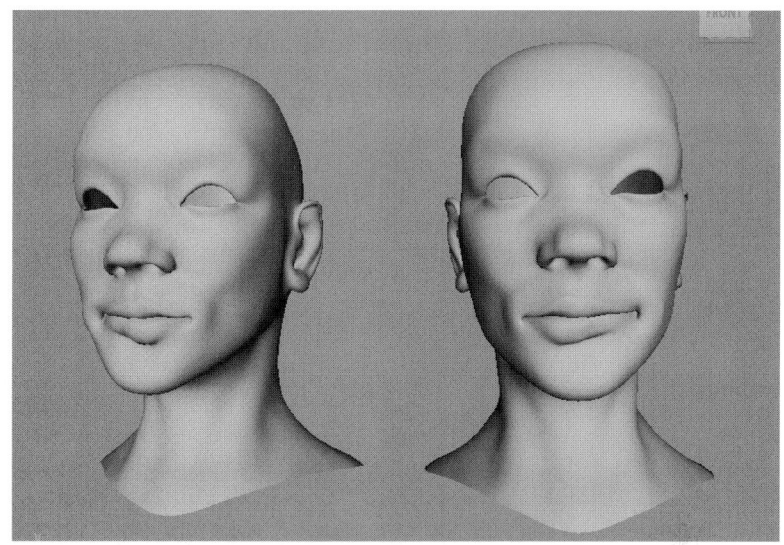

14. Name the two new targets **mouthRightNarrow** and **mouthLeftNarrow**. At this point, you should have a total of six blend shape targets (see Figure 6.16).

15. Save the scene as **nancy_v04.ma**.

To see a version of the scene to this point, open the nancy_v04.ma scene from the chapter6\ scenes directory on the DVD.

FIGURE 6.16
The scene is starting to fill up with blend shape targets.

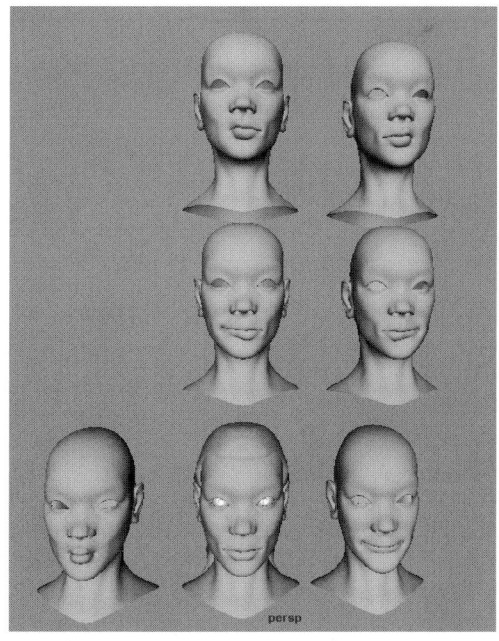

Adding Targets

You can add the new targets to the existing blend shape deformer, as follows:

1. Continue with the scene from the previous section, or open the nancy_v04.ma scene from the chapter6\scenes directory on the DVD.

2. Select the nancy model, and choose Window ➢ Animation Editors ➢ Blend Shape to open the blend shape controls.

3. Choose the mouthRightWide target, and Shift+click the nancy model. Choose Edit Deformers ➢ Blend Shapes ➢ Add. You'll see a new slider appear in the blend shape controls.

4. Repeat step 3 for the mouthLeftWide, mouthRightNarrow, and mouthLeftNarrow targets (see Figure 6.17).

5. Save the scene as **nancy_v05.ma**.

FIGURE 6.17
Sliders are added to the blend shape control window as the additional targets are added to the deformer.

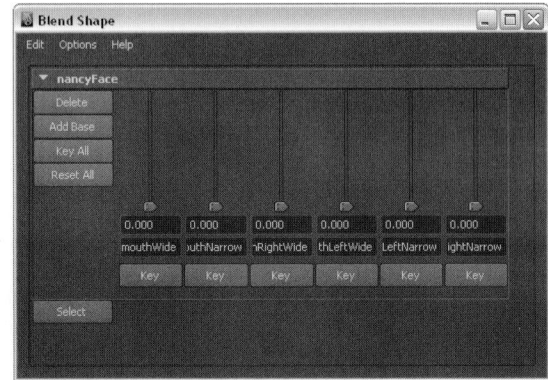

To see a version of the scene to this point, open the nancy_v05.ma scene from the chapter6\scenes directory on the DVD.

Test the slider controls in the Blend Shape window. You can continue to edit the blend shape targets after they have been added to the deformer. You may want to make additional changes to improve the expressions and the movement between shapes. Remember that at this point it's fine to have some strange-looking expressions. The final rig may have dozens of blend shape targets that all work together to create various expressions and facial movements. As long as you have the blend shape targets available, you can continue to refine the expressions by editing the targets.

You can quickly create new blend shape targets from existing targets. This can be helpful when making targets that represent small or subtle muscle movements. To do this, make an expression by experimenting with the values in the Blend Shape control panel, use the Paint Blend Shape Weights tool to fine-tune, and then duplicate the deformed base mesh to create a new target. You can then add the target to the blend shape node, giving you more sliders and more targets to work with. In a production situation, a realistic blend shape may consist of hundreds of targets.

ADDING JOINTS

Some facial movements, such as opening and closing the jaw, blinking the eyes, and moving the tongue, are better suited for joint rigs than for blend shape targets. In the end, the final rig will use a combination of deformers to create the full range of facial movements.

Creating a Custom Mouth Control Slider

You can animate the facial expressions by moving the sliders in the Blend Shape window and clicking the Key button beneath each slider. You can then use the Graph Editor to edit the animation curves. It is possible to animate this way, but you may find that as opposing shapes are animated, their animation curves start to overlap and create strange and unwanted facial movement.

There's a much better way to handle facial animation: create a set of intuitive interactive controls that you can move in the perspective view itself. These controls can be connected to the blend shape deformer using set driven keys. Animating the character will feel like moving a puppet, which will make your work easier and more enjoyable.

In this section, you'll see how to set up a basic interactive control to animate the blend shapes created in the previous section.

1. Continue with the scene from the previous section, or open the nancy_v05.ma scene from the chapter6\scenes directory on the DVD.

2. Once you have the blend shape deformer set up, you can safely delete the blend shape targets. Save a version of the scene with the targets just in case you need to go back and make a change. Then select the target models, and delete them.

3. Switch to a front view, and turn on Grid Snapping. Choose Create ➢ CV Curve Tool ➢ Options. In the options, set Curve Degree to Linear. In the front view, create a rectangle that is 1 unit high and 4 units long.

4. Name the curve **wideNarrowCtrl**. Select it, and choose Modify ➢ Center Pivot.

5. Use the Curve tool to create a triangle below the rectangle. Name the triangle **wideNarrow**. Center the pivot on the wideNarrow triangle (see Figure 6.18).

FIGURE 6.18
A rectangle and a triangle are created using a linear curve.

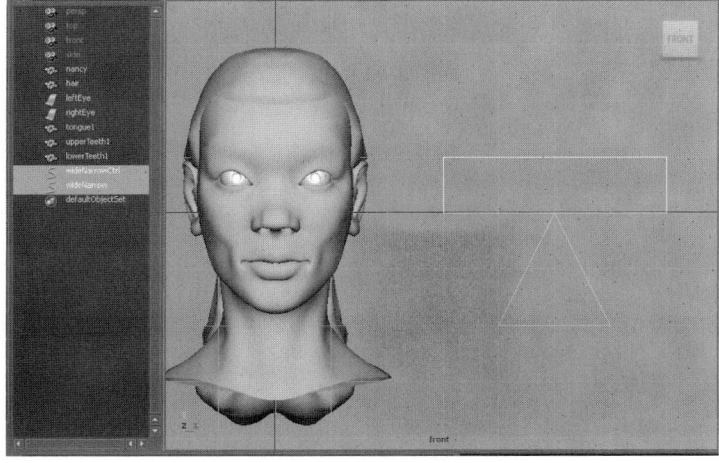

6. Scale the wideNarrowCtrl down along the y-axis to about **0.15**. Scale the wideNarrow triangle down to **0.3** in X and Y. Deactivate grid snapping, and place the wideNarrow triangle just below the wideNarrowCtrl rectangle.

7. Make two duplicates of the triangle, and name one **left** and the other **right**.

8. Scale the left and right triangles down to **0.1** in X and Y.

9. Arrange the left and right triangles so they fit in the bottom half of the wideNarrow triangle.

   The left and right triangles correspond to the character's left and right sides, so the left triangle should be on the right and the right triangle should be on the left. This may seem confusing, but in a 3D scene the camera can be anywhere, so it's important to keep left and right relative to the character's point of view.

10. Select the rectangle and the three triangles, and choose Modify ➤ Freeze Transformations. This will return them to this arrangement when their Translate and Rotate channels are set to 0.

11. Parent the left and right triangles to the wideNarrow triangle, and parent the wideNarrow triangle to the wideNarrowCtrl rectangle.

12. Select the wideNarrow triangle, and open its Attribute Editor to the wideNarrow tab.

13. In the Limit Information rollout, expand the Translate controls. Select the boxes next to each Limit channel to turn on the translate limits.

14. Set Trans Limit Y Min and Max to **0** and Trans Limit Z Min and Max to **0**. Set Trans Limit X Min to **-2** and Trans Limit X Max to **2**.

15. Move the wideNarrow triangle back and forth along the x-axis. It can travel the length of the wideNarrowCtrl rectangle but not beyond.

   This is one way to create a custom slider in Maya. When the Translate X channel of the triangle is set to 0, the triangle should be in the middle of the rectangle. Figure 6.19 shows the arrangement of the slider controls.

16. Use the same technique to set limits on the translation of both the left and right triangles. They should be restricted so they can move only between -1 and 1 on the x-axis. Their y- and z-axis limits Min and Max should be set to **0**.

17. Save the scene as **nancy_v06.ma**.

To see a version of the scene to this point, open the nancy_v06.ma scene from the chapter6\ scenes directory on the DVD.

FIGURE 6.19
Limits are set on the movement of the slider controls.

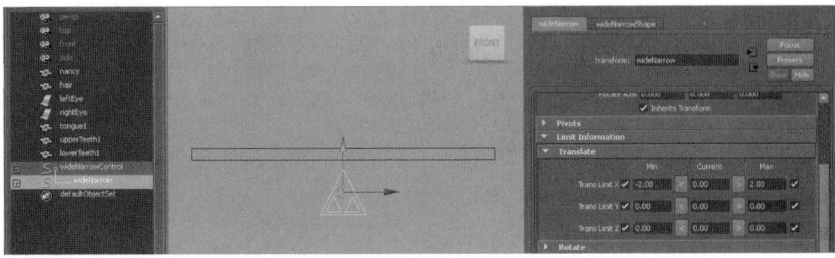

Connecting the Slider to the Blend Shape

To make the slider functional, it will be connected to the blend shape using driven keys. The theory behind this arrangement is that you want to have opposing shapes on the opposite ends of a slider control. The mouthWide and mouthNarrow shapes are connected to the X translation of the wideNarrow triangle, so the mouth is either wide or narrow but not both at the same time.

However, you also want to have enough freedom to control the sides of the mouth independently, so you'll connect the left and right triangles to the blend shapes for each side of the mouth. This way you still have the freedom to mix the blend shapes together to create a wide variety of possible mouth movements. This example uses only the wide and narrow controls. When you create similar controls for other mouth shapes, such as mouth corners down, lower lip curl, upper lip sneer, and so on, you end up with a very intuitive way to control the face by moving the sliders directly on the screen.

The next step in the process is creating the driven keys:

1. Continue with the scene from the previous section, or open the nancy_v06.ma scene from the chapter6\scenes directory on the DVD.

2. Make sure the Translate X channels for all the triangles are set to **0**. Make sure all the Blend Shape controls are set to **0** as well so the face is in a neutral pose.

3. From the Animation menu set, choose Animate ➢ Set Driven Key ➢ Set to open the Set Driven Key window (see Figure 6.20).

4. Select the wideNarrow triangle, and click the Load Driver button in the Set Driven Key window. In the upper left of the Set Driven Key window, select wideNarrow. Its animation channels will appear in the upper right.

5. From the Display menu in the Outliner, turn off the DAG Objects Only option so all the nodes in the scene are visible.

6. Select the nancyFace blend shape node, and click the Load Driven button in the Set Driven Key window.

    You need to set a keyframe so that when the wideNarrow triangle's Translate X channel is at 0, the mouthWide Blend Shape setting is also at 0.

FIGURE 6.20
Open the Set Driven Key window.

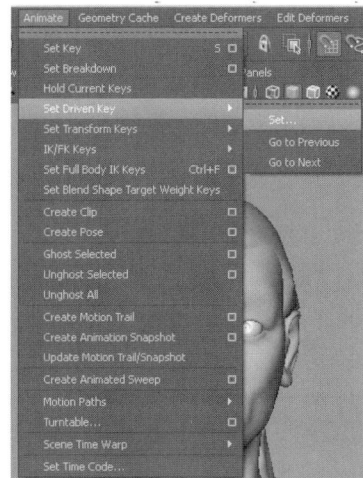

7. Select Translate X in the upper right of the Set Driven Key window and mouthWide in the lower right of the window, and click the Key button at the bottom of the Set Driven Key window (Figure 6.21).

FIGURE 6.21
The Set Driven Key window creates a keyframe relationship between the Translate X of wideNarrow and the mouthWide of nancyFace.

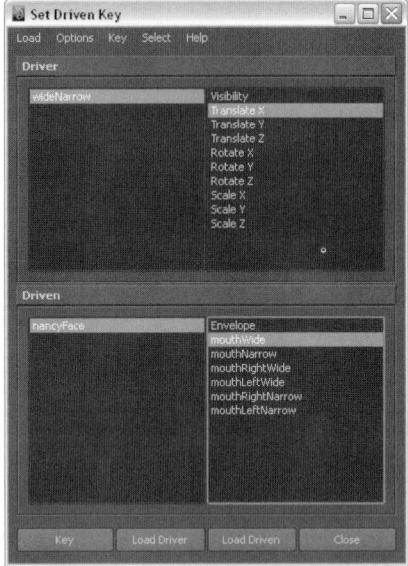

8. Click the wideNarrow label in the upper left of the Set Driven Key window.

9. Open the Channel Box, and set Translate X to **-2**.

10. Select the nancyFace label in the lower left of the Set Driven Key window.

11. In the Channel Box, set mouthWide to **1**. Click the Key button at the bottom of the Set Driven Key window.

12. Zoom out in the front view so you can see the control and the nancy character.

13. Move the wideNarrow triangle back and forth along the slider. You should see the mouth move between the neutral pose (when wideNarrow is at the center of the slider) and the mouthWide shape (when wideNarrow is moved all the way to the left of the wideNarrowCtrl slider).

14. Set wideNarrow back to **0** in the Translate X channel of the Channel Box.

15. In the lower right of the Set Driven Key window, select mouthNarrow, and click the Key button.

16. Select wideNarrow in the upper left of the Set Driven Key window. In the Channel Box, set Translate X to **2**.

17. Select the nancyFace label in the lower left of the Set Driven Key window.

18. In the Channel Box, set mouthNarrow to **1**. In the Set Driven Key window, click the Key button.

19. In the viewport, move the wideNarrow slider back and forth along the length of the wideNarrowCtrl. You'll see the face move between the mouthNarrow shape when the triangle is on the left side and the mouthWide shape when it's on the right side. Now the control is functional, and you can move between the two opposing mouth shapes using a single control.

20. Create set-driven keys for the small triangles named left and right. Use the following settings:

right Translate X = 0	mouthRightWide = 0
right Translate X = -1	mouthRightWide = 1
right Translate X = 0	mouthRightNarrow = 0
right Translate X = 1	mouthRightNarrow = 1
left Translate X = 0	mouthLeftWide = 0
left Translate X = 1	mouthleftWide = 1
left Translate X = 0	mouthLeftNarrow = 0
left Translate X = -1	mouthLeftNarrow = 1

It seems a little tedious at first to create this kind of rig, but when you have the whole rig working, it's the easiest way to animate the face using blend shapes. Once you have all the driven keys created, spend some time moving the sliders back and forth. See how many mouth shapes you can create just by moving the sliders (see Figure 6.22).

21. Save the scene as **nancy_v07.ma**.

To see a finished version of the scene, open the nancy_v07.ma scene from the chapter6\ scenes directory on the DVD.

There are many different ways to set up these types of controls. For a complex facial rig, try using curves to make controls that resemble a simplified face. This way, you have a visual representation of how moving the controls affects the facial movements.

FIGURE 6.22
A variety of mouth shapes can be created by moving the triangle controls.

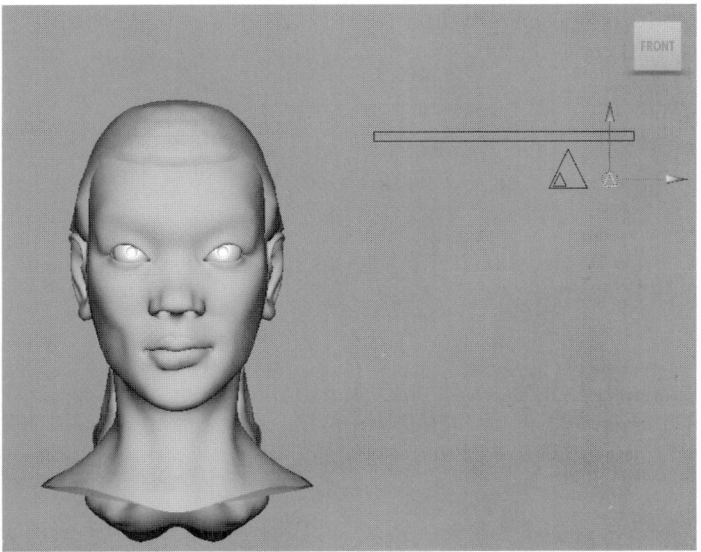

Open the nancy_rig.ma scene from the chapter6\scenes directory to see a more functional face and head rig. Play the animation to see the controls in action. Try moving various parts of the controls to see the resulting expressions (see Figure 6.23).

This rig uses a combination of blend shapes, joints, and a dynamic hair curve connected to a spline IK handle (spline IK is covered in Chapter 7) to create the various movements. A total of 49 blend shape targets were created for this rig. A more complete rig may use 100 or more blend shape targets.

FIGURE 6.23
A more complete facial animation rig. The controls are positioned to give visual clues to the parts of the face they control.

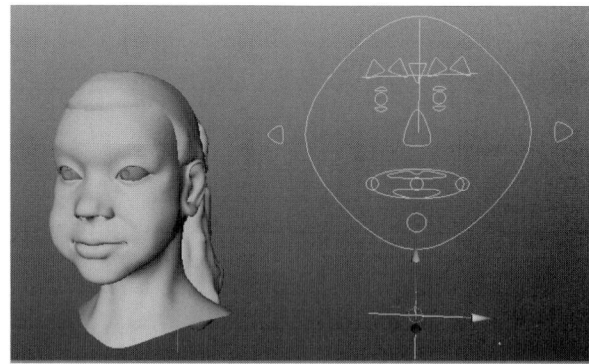

DEFORMER ORDER

When using blend shapes with joints or other deformers, you may have to change the position of the deformer in the deformer order. If you're getting strange results when you animate blend shapes, you may need to rearrange the deformer in the list of inputs. To do this, right-click the base mesh, and choose Inputs ➤ All Inputs from the marking menu. In the list of input operations, you can MMB-drag any of the deformers up and down the list to change its position. You also have the option of setting the blend shape order on the Advanced tab of the options when you create the blend shape deformer.

Animating Blend Shapes Sequentially

When you choose the In Between setting in the Blend Shape options, the blend shape deformer deforms the base mesh based on a sequence created from the selected targets. The order in which you select the targets determines the sequence of the animation created when you move the blend shape slider.

This feature is very useful for creating certain types of animation, for example when you want to make an object grow and change over time. The key to creating a successful blend shape sequence is planning. The targets used in the sequence should have the same number of vertices and the same vertex order. This means that you'll need to create the model that represents the end of the sequence first and then derive all the in-between targets from the final model. This way, when you create the blend shape sequence, the deformation behaves as you would expect, and the geometry is not mangled or distorted during animation.

To understand this better, try the following exercise, which uses a blend shape sequence to animate the growth of a snowflake crystal. You'll take advantage of using construction history as the model of the fully formed snowflake is created so that you can easily create the in-between snowflake shapes for the blend shape sequence.

Creating the Base Mesh

You'll start by creating the base mesh snowflake from a polygon prism using a series of polygon extrusions. It's important to name each extrude node as you create it so you can keep track of how it affects the shape of the snowflake.

1. Create a new scene in Maya. Make sure Construction History is enabled.

2. Switch to the Polygon menu set, and choose Create ➤ Polygon Primitives ➤ Prism.

3. Open the Channel Box, and select the polyPrism1 node from the INPUTS section. Set Number Of Sides to 5 and Length and Side Length to 1 (see Figure 6.24).

4. Right-click the prism, and choose Faces. Shift+click the five faces on the sides of the prism, but not the faces on the top or bottom.

5. From the Polygon menu set, choose Edit Mesh ➤ Extrude. For the moment, do not pull on the extrude manipulator; you'll use the Channel Box to extrude the faces in the next steps.

FIGURE 6.24
Create a five-sided prism.

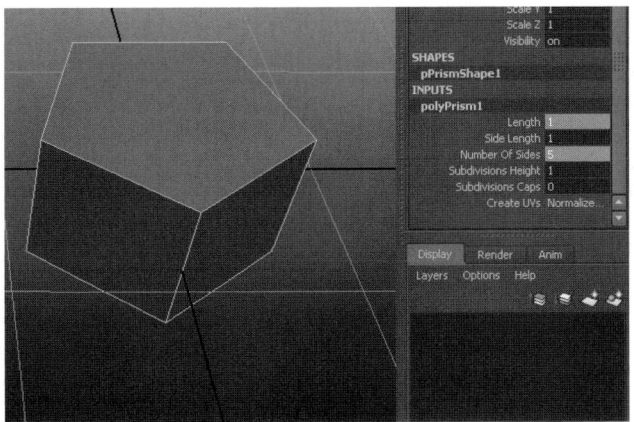

6. In the options for the polyExtrudeFace1 node in the Channel Box, set Keep Faces Together to Off.

7. Click the polyExtrudeFace1 label in the Channel Box, and rename the node to **armRoot**. Since you'll be editing a number of extrude nodes later in the process, it's good to give them descriptive names so you can keep track of each of the extrusions.

8. In the Channel Box, in the channels under the armRoot node, set Local Translate Z to **1.7** and Local Scale X and Local Scale Y to **0.5** (see Figure 6.25).

FIGURE 6.25
Extrude the faces on the sides of the prism, and rename the extrusion node to **armRoot**.

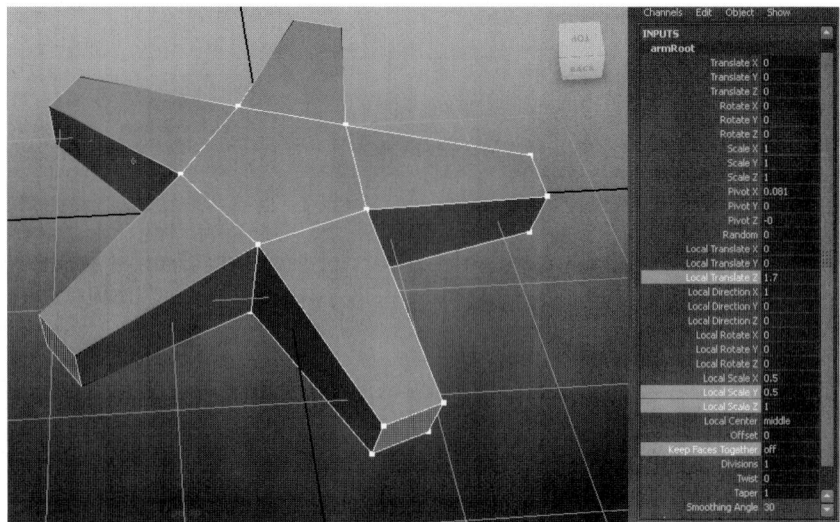

9. With the faces on the end of each extrusion still selected, press the **g** hot key to repeat the last action, which creates another extrusion.

10. Rename the new polyExtrudeFace1 node to **firstArmSection**. Set its Local Translate Z channel to **1.5**. Set all the Local Scale channels to **0.5**. Set Divisions to **2**.

11. Shift+click the inside faces of the upper division on each of the arms of the snowflake, as shown in Figure 6.26. Press the **g** hot key to make another extrusion. Name this extrusion **firstBranch**.

12. Set the Local Translate Z channel of the firstBranch node to **1**. Set the Local Scale channels to **0.5**.

13. Select the face at the tip of each arm. Press the **g** hot key to create another extrusion. Name the extrusion **firstTipSection**. Set the Local Scale of firstTipSection to **2**.

14. Press the **g** hot key to make one last extrusion. Name the extrusion **secondTipSection**. Set the Local Translate Z channels of secondTipSection to **0.4** and the Local Scale channels to **0.4**. Figure 6.27 shows the final snowflake.

15. Select and rename the prism to **snowflakeFinal**.

16. Save the scene as **snowflake_v01.ma**.

FIGURE 6.26
Using a series of extrude operations, form the arms of the snowflake.

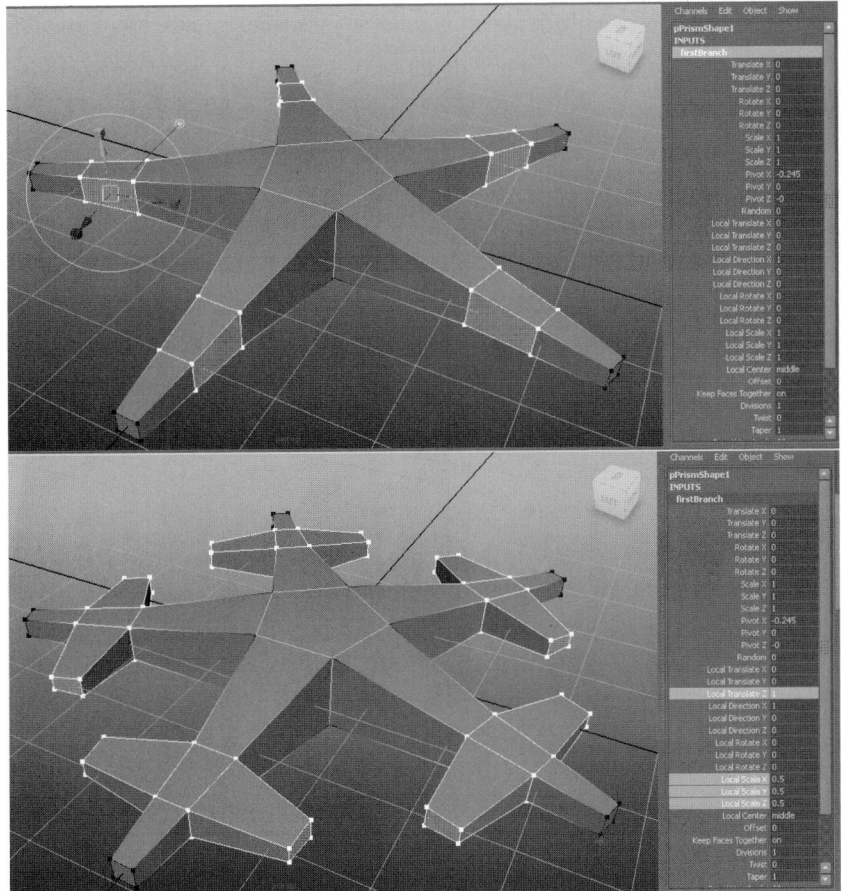

FIGURE 6.27
The final shape of the snowflake after the extrusions have been applied

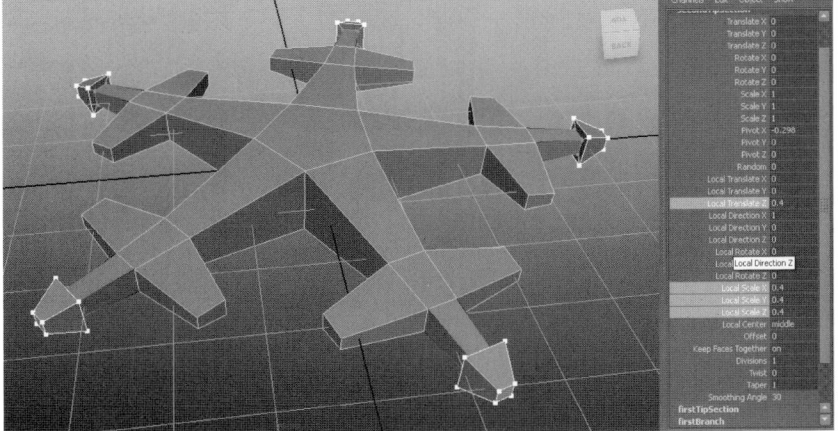

Creating the Blend Shape Targets

The sequence of blend shapes will be created using duplicates of the snowflake. You'll make a duplicate for each growth stage in the sequence, working backward from the final snowflake shape.

1. Continue with the scene from the previous section, or open the snowflake_v01.ma scene from the chapter6\scenes directory on the DVD.

2. Select snowflakeFinal, and choose Edit ➤ Duplicate Special ➤ Options. In the options, enable Duplicate Input Graph, and set Group Under to World. This makes a copy of the snowflake model, including all the extrusion nodes (see Figure 6.28).

FIGURE 6.28
The options for
Duplicate Special

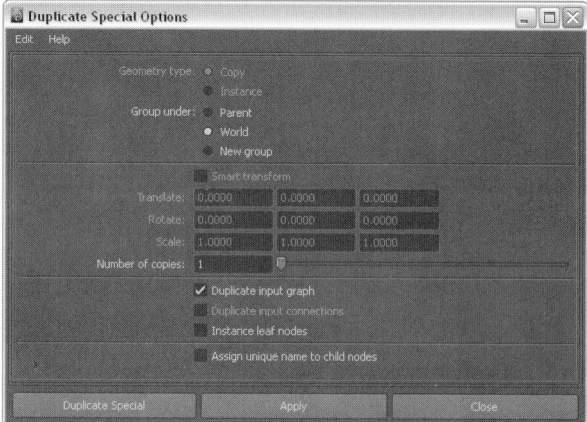

3. Name the duplicate **snowflakeTips**, and move it off to the side.

4. Select snowflakeTips, and open the Channel Box. Select the secondTipSection1 node, and set the Local Scale channels to **1** and Local Translate Z to **0** so the tips disappear. Do the same for the firstTipSection1 node.

5. Select snowflakeTips, and choose Edit ➤ Duplicate Special to make another copy. Name this copy **snowflakeBranches**, and move it off to the side.

6. In the Channel Box for snowflakeBranches, select the firstBranch2 node, and set its Local Scale channels to **1** and its Local Translate Z to **0**.

7. Repeat this process until there are five duplicates of the snowflake. Each duplicate is a stage in the growth of the snowflake (see Figure 6.29). Name the last duplicate **snowflakeStart**. It should look just like the original five-sided prism.

8. Save the scene as **snowflake_v02.ma**.

To see a version of the scene to this point, open the snowflake_v02.ma scene from the chapter6\scenes directory.

FIGURE 6.29
Create a duplicate
for each stage of
the snowflake's
growth.

FIGURE 6.29
Create a duplicate
for each stage of
the snowflake's
growth.

Creating the Blend Shape Sequence

This process may seem a little strange, but it's important to remember that for the blend shape deformer to work correctly, the number of vertices and the point order of each model used in the blend shape deformer have to match. Therefore, it's best to work backward from the finished model. You should be able to see at this point why naming each extrusion node is helpful. If the nodes do not have descriptive names, it's very hard to know which node corresponds to which part of a duplicate of the original snowflake, especially if you decide to make a more complex crystalline structure.

At this point, the hard work is done; creating the blend shape sequence is very easy:

1. Shift+click the snowflake models in the order of their stage of growth, but don't select the snowflakeStart model.

2. With all the models selected in the order of their growth stage, Shift+click the snowflake-Start model, and switch to the Animation menu set.

3. Choose Create Deformers ➢ Blend Shape ➢ Options. In the options, enable In-between. Click Create to make the blend shape (see Figure 6.30).

FIGURE 6.30
Enable the In-
between option in
Create Blend Shape
Options.

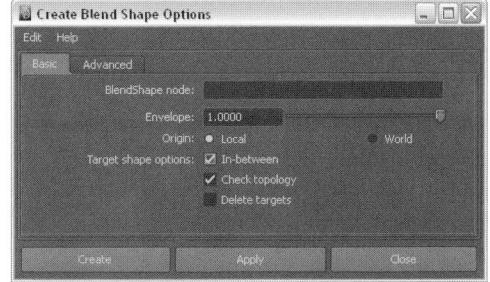

4. Choose Window ➤ Animation Editors ➤ Blend Shape to open the blend shape controls. Move the slider up and down, and the snowflakeStart model should grow into a snow-flake as you move the slider up.

5. Save the scene as **snowflake_v03.ma**.

To see a finished version of the scene, open snowflake_v03.ma.
If you decide to change the order of the sequence, swap targets:

1. Select two of the blend shape targets, and choose Edit Deformers ➤ Blend Shapes ➤ Swap. This swaps the order of the selected targets in the blend shape sequence.

2. If you're happy with the final animation, delete all the targets. Don't delete the snowflake-Start model.

3. Save the scene as **snowflake_v04.ma**.

To see a finished version of the scene, open the snowflake_v04.ma scene from the chapter6\ scenes directory on the DVD.

LAYER BLEND SHAPES

A blend shape target can also be deformed using another blend shape deformer with a completely separate set of blend shape targets. You can create very complex effects by applying additional blend shape deformers (as well as other types of deformers) to your blend shape targets. These deformations can be animated, and that animation will carry on through to the base mesh.

Animating with Lattices

Lattices are the most versatile deformers available in Maya. A lattice is a cube-shaped cage that surrounds the object. When the points of the lattice are moved, the surface of the object becomes deformed. Chapter 4 shows how a lattice can be used as a modeling tool. In this chapter, you'll animate a lattice to add cartoonish movement to a simple character.

Lattices can deform all types of geometry, groups, particles, and even other lattices. When you create a lattice, two nodes are added to the scene: lattice node, which is labeled ffd1Lattice (the number 1 changes depending on how many lattices are in the scene), and ffd1Base. The letters *ffd* stand for free-form deformer. When you edit the shape of the ffd1Lattice, Maya compares the differences in the shapes of the ffd1Lattice and the ffd1Base and makes changes to the deformed object relative to the differences between these two nodes.

ENVELOPE

All deformers have an Envelope control that adjusts the overall strength of the deformer.

Creating a Lattice

To create a lattice for a surface or a group of surfaces, simply select the surface and choose Lattice from the Deformers menu. In this section, the relationship between the lattice deformer and its base affects a group of surfaces.

1. Open the mushroom_v01.ma scene from the chapter6\scenes directory on the DVD. This scene shows three cartoon mushrooms on a hill.

2. Select mushroom1Group in the Outliner, and choose Create Deformers ➤ Lattice. A cage appears around the pink mushroom. In the Outliner, there are two new nodes named ffd1Lattice and ffd1Base (Figure 6.31).

   The lattice is automatically sized and scaled to surround the deformed object.

3. Select the ffd1Lattice node, and switch to the Move tool. Try moving the lattice; the entire mushroom1Group moves with it because the lattice surrounds the entire group. The same is true as you scale or rotate the lattice.

   If you move the ffd1Base node, the mushroom character moves in the opposite direction and becomes mangled in the process. In most cases, you want to avoid moving the base node by itself (Figure 6.32).

FIGURE 6.31
The lattice deformer appears as a cage over the mushroom1Group.

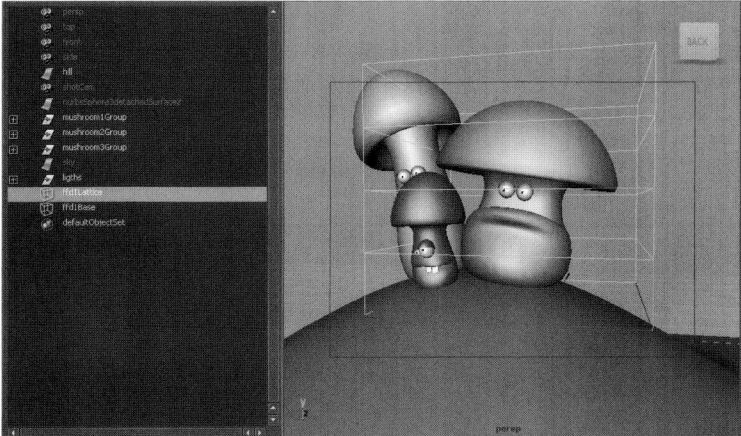

FIGURE 6.32
Moving the ffd-1Base node badly distorts the mushroom1Group.

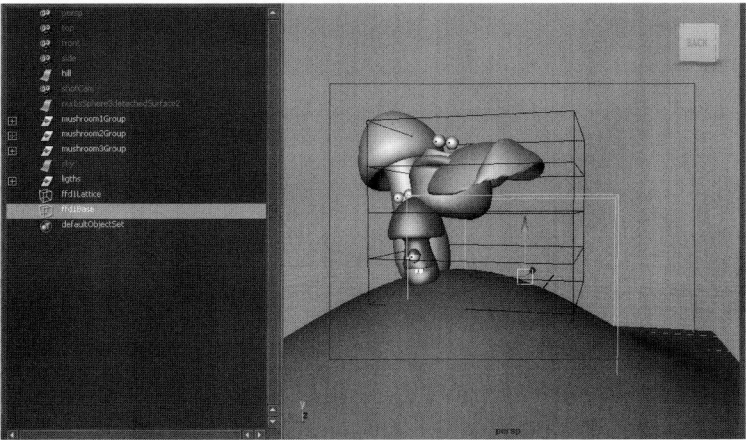

4. Undo any changes made to the ffd1Lattice and ffd1Base nodes. Shift+click both the ffd1Lattice and ffd1Base nodes, and move them together. When you move the nodes together, there's no change in the deformed object.

   If you need to reposition a lattice over part of a model or scale it so it engulfs a larger portion of the scene, remember to select both the ffd1Base and ffd1Lattice nodes together and make the changes while both nodes are selected. You can even group the nodes if that makes it easier.

5. Right-click the lattice, and choose Lattice Point from the marking menu.

6. Drag a selection marquee over some of the points, and move them. The mushroom-1Group becomes distorted again but in a more controllable manner (see Figure 6.33).

FIGURE 6.33
Moving selected lattice points deforms the mushroom.

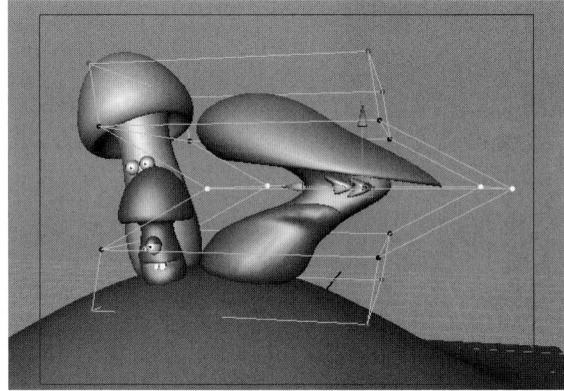

7. Select the ffd1Lattice node, and open its Attribute Editor to the ffd1 tab. Disable the Local option. This makes the lattice deformations much smoother.

8. Choose Edit Deformers ➤ Remove Lattice Tweaks to reset the lattice to its original state.

9. Switch to the ffd1LatticeShape tab in the Attribute Editor, and experiment with changing the settings in the sliders for the S, T, and U divisions. These control how many divisions are along each axis of the lattice.

The axes of the lattice are specified using the letters S, T, and U, kind of like the x-, y-, and z-axes of an object. A lattice point is placed at the intersection of each division. Each point has a certain amount of influence over the deformed object. When the Local option is enabled in the ffd1 tab, each point can deform only the parts of the object that are nearby. When Local is off, any changes to a lattice point's position affect the entire object, resulting in a smoother deforma-tion. When local mode is enabled, you can set the strength of the local influence using the Local S, T, and U sliders.

The Outside settings on the ffd1 tab specify the amount of influence the lattice has over parts of the deformed object that lie outside the lattice cage. When Outside Lattice is set to Inside, changes to the lattice affect only the parts of the model inside the lattice. When this is set to All, changes to the lattice affect the entire object regardless of whether the parts are inside or outside the lattice.

The Falloff setting specifies a range of distance. Parts of the object that fall within this distance are affected by changes to the lattice, but the strength of influence diminishes as the space between the object and the lattice increases. Figure 6.34 shows the settings available on the ffd1Lattice-Shape and ffd1 tabs of the Attribute Editor.

FIGURE 6.34
You can set options for the lattice on the tabs of the lattice's Attribute Editor.

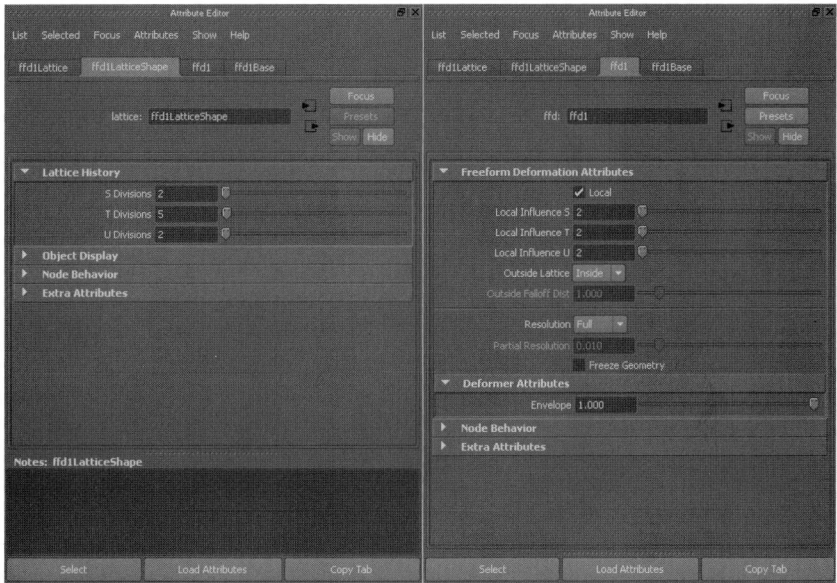

Using the Lattice Membership Tool

The Lattice Membership tool allows you to add or remove vertices from a lattice (as well as other deformers).

1. Right-click the lattice applied to mushroom1Group, and select Lattice Points. Use the Move tool to move the lattice points and deform the mushroom.

2. Choose Edit Deformers ➢ Edit Membership Tool. With the tool active, select the lattice; you'll see the points of the geometry in the mushroom1Group appear.

3. To remove points from the lattice, Ctrl+drag over the vertices. To add points, Shift+drag over the vertices.

PRUNE MEMBERSHIP

The Prune Membership tool is meant to help you optimize animations that rely on deformers by removing objects or components that are not affected by the selected deformer. This works on Lattice, Cluster, Wire, and Wrap deformers. Be careful when using this tool: The tool prunes parts of the model from the deformer based on the current frame, so it's possible to accidentally remove parts of the model from the deformer that should be part of the deformer later in the animation. To use the tool, select the lattice, and choose Edit Deformers ➢ Prune Membership Tool.

Adding an Object to an Existing Lattice

You can add an object to an existing lattice in a scene using the Relationship Editor.

1. Continue with the `mushroom_v01.ma` scene. Select the ffd1Lattice object in the Outliner.

2. Choose Windows ➢ Relationship Editors ➢ Deformer Sets.

3. On the left side of the Relationship Editor, choose the ffd1Set. On the right side, select mushroom2Group (see Figure 6.35). The gold mushroom will be added to the existing lattice.

FIGURE 6.35
The Relationship Editor allows you to add and remove objects from existing lattices.

Animating Lattices

There are lots of ways to animate lattices. You can animate the transform node of the lattice or the individual points of the lattice; you can also apply deformers to the lattice and even bind a lattice to joints. In this example, you'll create a very simple animation by animating the transform node of the lattice:

1. Continue with the `mushroom_v01.ma` scene. Delete the ffd1Lattice node in the Outliner. The ffd1Base node will also be deleted.

2. Select mushroomGroup1, and choose Deformers ➢ Create Lattice to create a new lattice.

3. Select the ffd1Lattice and ffd1Base nodes, and group them (hot key = **Ctrl+g**). Select the group, name it **lattice**, and center its pivot (Modify ➢ Center Pivot).

4. Select the lattice group, and in the Channel Box, set Scale Y to **5**.

5. Expand the lattice group in the Outliner; then select the ffd1Lattice node. In the Channel Box, set the T Divisions to **20**.

6. Hide the Sky object. Switch to a side view, right-click the lattice, and choose Lattice Point.

7. Hold the Shift key, and drag a selection marquee over every other row of points on the lattice.

8. Switch to the Scale tool, and push in the blue handle of the Scale tool to scale the lattice points along the z-axis. This creates an accordion shape in the lattice points (see Figure 6.36).

9. Switch to the front view, and push in the red handle of the Scale tool to scale the points along the x-axis.

10. Select the lattice group, open the Channel Box, and highlight the Translate Y attribute.

11. From the Channel Box menu, choose Edit ➤ Expressions.

12. In the Expression field, type `lattice.translateY=4*(sin(time));`.

    This expression moves the lattice group up and down along the y-axis, using the sin of the current time multiplied by 4.

13. Click the Create button to make the expression.

14. Set the length of the timeline to **200,** and play the animation (see Figure 6.37).

FIGURE 6.36
A very tall lattice is created around the mushroom; the points of the lattice are scaled to create an accordion shape.

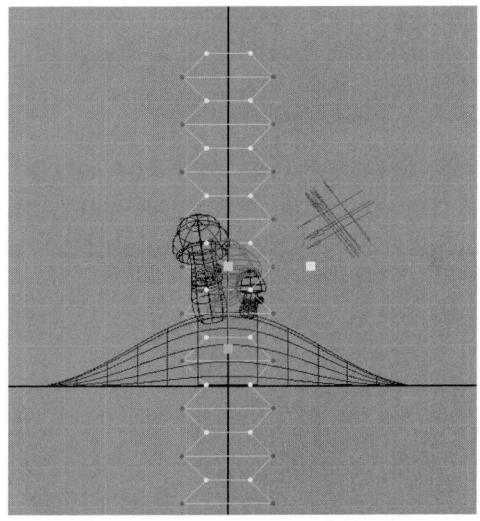

FIGURE 6.37
Create an expression to automatically move the lattice up and down over time.

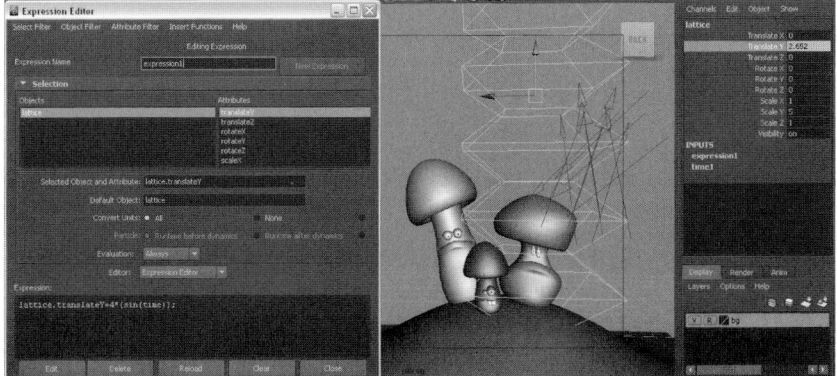

The movement of the lattice group causes a wave-type distortion in the mushroom. This is an extremely simple application of the lattice deformer, but it gives you a good idea of how it works. Lattices become even more powerful when you combine them with other deformers and techniques.

15. Save the file as `mushroom_v02.ma`.

To see a finished version of the scene, open the `mushroom_v02.ma` scene from the `chapter6\` `scenes` folder of the DVD.

FLOW PATH OBJECTS

You can make an object that has been attached to a motion path conform to the shape of the path using a Flow Path object. This automatically generates a lattice that matches the shape of the path. To create this effect, select an object that has been attached to a motion path, and choose (from the Animation menu set) Animate ➢ Motion Path ➢ Flow Path Object. You can specify in the options whether the lattice covers the entire curve or just the selected object.

If you apply the lattice to the entire curve, you can then edit the lattice points to add deformations to the object as it moves along the path. You can achieve similar results by rigging a lattice to a joint chain that is controlled by an IK spline. However, even though the Flow Path object offers less control than an IK spline, it is much easier and faster to set up. To see an example, open the `FlowPathObject.ma` scene in the `chapter6\scenes` folder on the DVD.

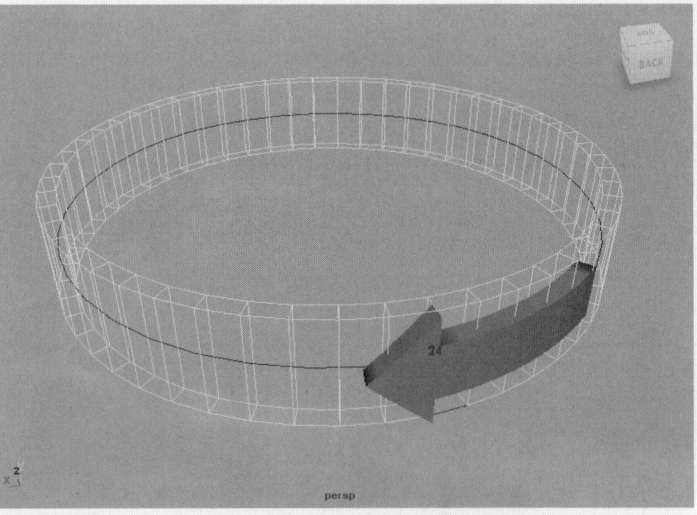

Animating Object Components with Clusters

As deformers go, none is simpler or more useful than a cluster. A *cluster* is a handle that can be applied to objects or components. Most often, a cluster is applied to the vertices of an object. Think of a cluster as a way to group the vertices of one or more objects. You can then apply keyframes to the cluster to animate the vertices.

In this section, you'll see a few ways to create, edit, and animate clusters.

KEYFRAMING COMPONENTS

It is possible to set keyframes on the components of geometry, such as the CVs of a curve or the points of a lattice. However, it's a better idea to create a cluster deformer for the component and then set keyframes on the cluster. Clusters are easier to work within the viewport and on the Graph Editor, and you can return a cluster to its original position by setting all of its Translate and Rotate channels to 0.

Adding Cluster Objects

You'll start by placing a cluster on a group:

1. Open the `tree_v01.ma` scene from the `chapter6\scenes` directory on the DVD. This scene consists of a polygon palm tree model created by converting a Paint Effects stroke into polygons.

2. Select the palmTree group in the Outliner, and switch to the Animation menu set.

3. Choose Create Deformers ➢ Cluster. A small *c* appears in the viewport, and you'll see the cluster1Handle node in the Outliner (see Figure 6.38).

4. Select the Move tool, and move the cluster around. The palmTree group moves with the cluster.

5. In the Outliner, select the cluster, and Ctrl+click the palmTree group. Use the Move tool to move both objects.

   The movement created using the Move tool is doubled for the tree. This is an example of a *double transform*. This occurs when you move the object and the deformer; the translation of the deformer is added to the translation of the cluster.

6. Undo all the changes you made with the Move tool. Try selecting the palmTree group and moving it. The cluster stays in its original position.

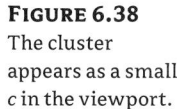

FIGURE 6.38
The cluster appears as a small *c* in the viewport.

If you move the cluster now, it still works, but it has been offset from the deformed object. This is another situation you don't want. Once you cluster an object or part of an object, move the cluster by itself.

RELATIVE CLUSTERS

When you create a cluster deformer, in the Options box you can choose the Relative option. This option is also available in the Attribute Editor for the cluster node and can be turned on and off after you create the cluster deformer.

In a situation where you need to group a number of clusters with the object they deform and then translate the group node, you should turn on Relative. Otherwise, moving the group will create a double transform, which leads to unexpected results.

Painting Cluster Weights

The strength of cluster weights can be painted directly on an object, which means you can use the Artisan Brush tool to establish the amount of influence a cluster has over parts of the geometry. As you paint across the surface, you'll get visual feedback, making the process very intuitive.

1. Continue with the previous scene, and return the cluster and the objects to their original positions.

2. Select the palmTree group, and choose Edit Deformers ➤ Paint Cluster Weights Tool. The palm tree turns white, indicating that the strength of the weight is at 1 (100 percent).

3. Reduce the radius of the brush by holding the **b** hot key while dragging to the left in the viewport. In the Tool Options box, set Paint Operation to Replace. Set Value to **0**.

4. Paint around the area of the trunk; it should turn black as you paint. The black color indicates that the strength values of the cluster at the trunk are now set to 0 (see Figure 6.39).

FIGURE 6.39
The cluster weights at the bottom of the tree are reduced using the Paint Attributes tool.

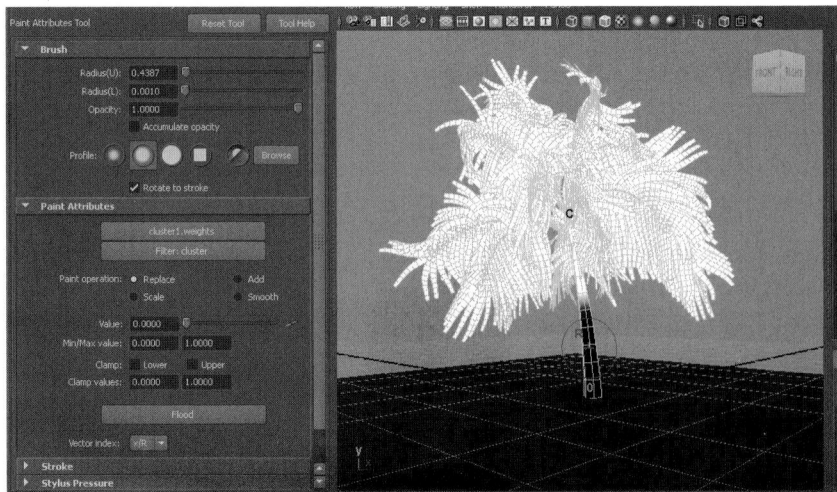

5. Set Paint Operation to Smooth, and click the Flood button a few times to smooth the transition between the white and black areas.

6. Select the cluster in the Outliner, and use the Move and Rotate tools to move it around. The trunk stays firmly planted in the ground (see Figure 6.40).

7. Save the scene as **tree_v02.ma**.

To see a version of the scene to this point, open the `tree_v02.ma` scene from the `chapter6\` `scenes` directory on the DVD.

FIGURE 6.40
After you paint the weights of the cluster, the trunk stays in the ground when the cluster is moved.

Applying Cluster Components

The most common use for clusters is to directly deform components of an object. Clusters are a great way to attach CVs of a curve to another object.

1. Create a new scene in Maya.

2. Turn on Grid Snapping, and choose Create ➤ EP Curve Tool.

3. Click twice on two different parts of the grid, 10 units apart to make a curve about 10 units in length. Hit the Enter key to complete the Curve tool.

4. Right-click the curve, and choose Control Vertex so you can select the control vertices of the curve.

5. Select one of the CVs at the end of the curve, and then Shift+click the other two CVs at the center of the curve.

6. Choose Create Deformers ➤ Cluster. The cluster will be named cluster1Handle.

7. Repeat steps 3 and 4, but this time select the CV at the opposite end of the curve as well as the two CVs in the middle. This is named cluster2Handle (be careful not to select cluster1Handle while you're selecting the middle CVs).

You should end up with two clusters. The two CVs in the middle of the curve are deformed by both clusters.

You can adjust the amount of influence each cluster has on the vertices using the Component Editor:

1. Select the middle CV closest to cluster1Handle, and choose Window ➢ General Editors ➢ Component Editor.

2. In the Component Editor, switch to the Weighted Deformer tab.

3. Set the weight for cluster1 to **0.75** and the weight for cluster2 to **0.25**. Together the weights add up to 1 (Figure 6.41).

4. Select the middle CV closest to cluster2Handle. In the Component Editor, set the weight for cluster1 to **0.25** and the weight for cluster2 to **0.75**.

5. Close the Component Editor.

6. In the perspective view, switch to the Move tool.

7. Select cluster1Handle, hold the **d** key on the keyboard to switch to pivot point editing mode. While holding the **d** key, snap the pivot point for cluster1Handle to the CV at the closest end (see Figure 6.42).

8. Repeat steps 5–7 for cluster2Handle; snap its pivot point to the opposite end of the curve (closest to the cluster2Handle).

FIGURE 6.41
The weight for each cluster of the selected CV is entered numerically in the Component Editor.

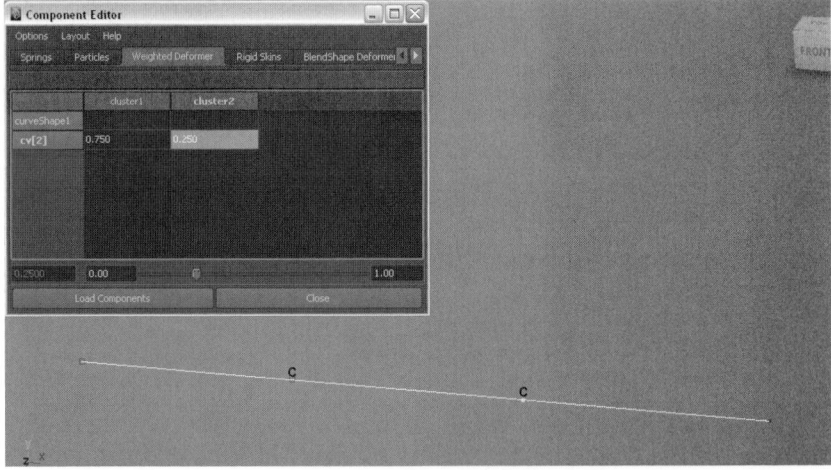

FIGURE 6.42
The pivot point for the cluster handle is moved to the end of the curve.

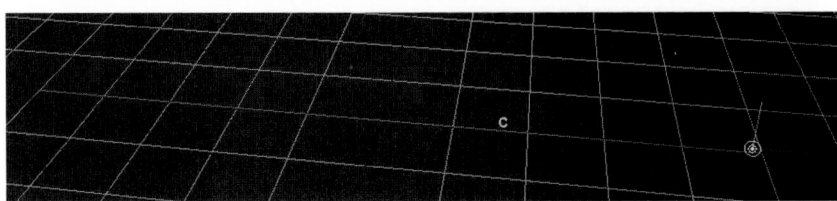

9. Select cluster1Handle, and move it around. You can now easily move one end of the curve, and there is a built-in falloff in strength down the length of the curve (Figure 6.43).

It may look like the cluster is offset from the curve, but in fact the C in the viewport is placed an average distance away from the deformed CVs. The display of the deformer handle is not important at this point because the actual handle has been snapped to the end of the curve. You can see this in the position of the Move tool manipulator.

10. Save the scene as **clusterCurve_v01.ma**.

To see a version of the scene to this point, open the clusterCurve_v01.ma scene from the chapter6\scenes directory on the DVD.

FIGURE 6.43
Moving the cluster moves the end of the curve. The CVs in the middle of the curve are weighted to create a falloff in the strength of the clusters at either end.

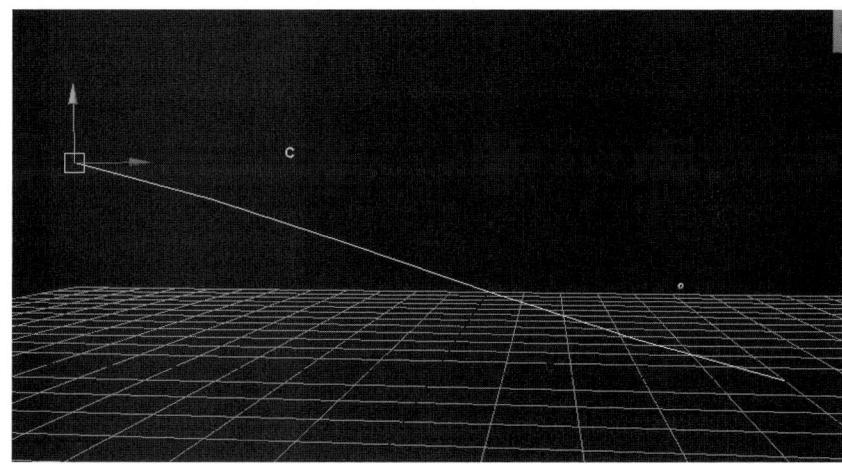

Constraining Clusters

Clusters can be parented to other objects, but I actually prefer using *constraints*. Using a constraint means that you don't have to worry about whether the cluster is set to Relative, and it reduces the chance of accidentally creating a double transformation. As long as you animate only the constraining objects and not the clusters themselves, you should be fine.

1. Continue with the scene from the previous section, or open the clusterCurve_v01.ma scene from the chapter6\scenes directory on the DVD.

2. Select both cluster handles, and make sure all of their Translate and Rotate channels are set to **0** in the Channel Box.

3. Create a NURBS sphere. Move the sphere so its surface is placed at the edge of the curve closest to cluster1Handle. If the sphere radius is 1 unit and Grid Snapping is enabled, the surface of the sphere should touch the edge of the curve when the sphere is placed 1 unit beyond the end of the curve.

4. In the Outliner, select the nurbsSphere1 node, and Ctrl+click cluster1Handle.

5. From the Animation menu set, choose Constrain ➢ Parent ➢ Options.

6. In the options, make sure that you enable Maintain Offset, and set the axes for Translate and Rotate to All (see Figure 6.44).

   When you move or rotate the sphere, the curve travels with it.

7. Repeat steps 3 through 6, and create a sphere for the opposite end of the curve. Constrain cluster2Handle to this sphere (Figure 6.45).

8. Try extruding a circle along the length of the curve, or attach a Paint Effects stroke to the curve (consult Chapter 3 for information on extruding along paths).

9. Save the scene as **clusterCurve_v02.ma**.

FIGURE 6.44
A sphere is placed at one end of the curve. cluster1Handle is constrained to the sphere.

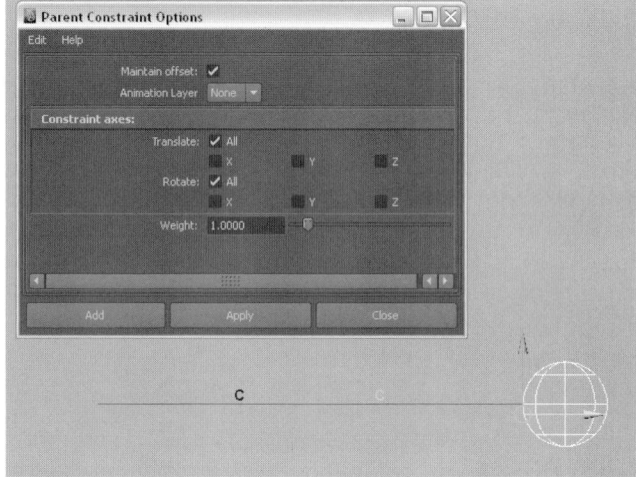

FIGURE 6.45
The clusters are constrained to the spheres. A hose is created along the length of the curve using a Paint Effects curve that has been converted to polygons.

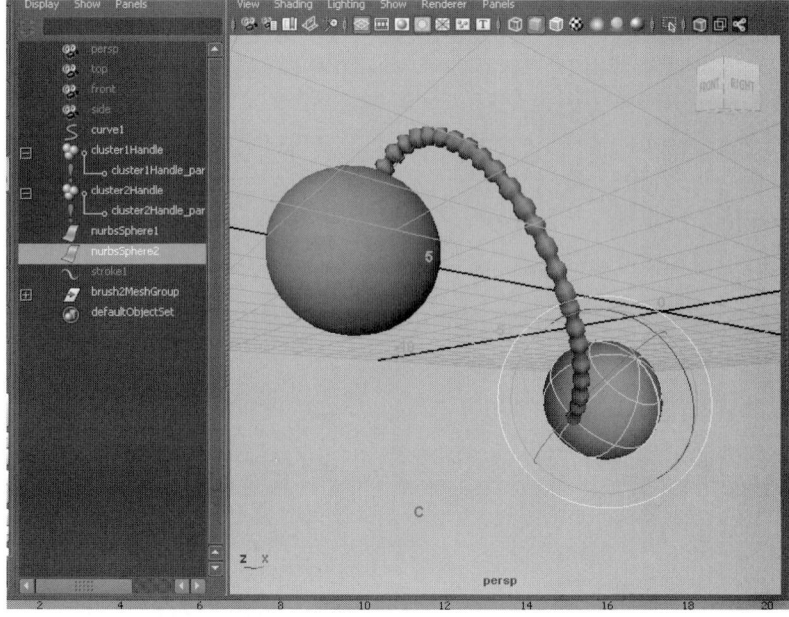

MODELING WITH PAINT EFFECTS

Chapter 4 demonstrates how to model using Paint Effects. This is a great way to create a simple hose that connects two pieces of geometry. This technique works pretty well for many situations; however, you may experience some flipping of the curve when the spheres are rotated.

To see a version of the scene to this point, open the clusterCurve_v02.ma scene from the chapter6\scenes directory on the DVD.

Animating a Scene Using Nonlinear Deformers

The nonlinear deformers include the bend, flare, sine, twist, squash, and wave deformers. The names of the deformers give a pretty good indication of what they do. They work well for creating cartoonish effects and even do a decent job of faking dynamic effects, saving you from the extensive setup many dynamic simulations require. All the nonlinear deformers work the same way. The deformer is applied to a surface, a lattice, components, or a group of surfaces, and then parameters are edited to achieve the desired effect. The parameters can be animated as well. You can use nonlinear deformers in combination with each other and with other deformers.

In this section, you'll use nonlinear deformers to animate a jellyfish bobbing in the ocean. You'll use just a few of the deformers to create the scene, but since they all work the same way, you can apply what you've learned to the other nonlinear deformers in your own scenes.

Creating a Wave Deformer

The wave deformer creates a ring of sine waves like a circular ripple in a puddle. To create the gentle bobbing up and down of a jellyfish, you'll animate the parameters of a wave deformer.

1. Open the jellyfish_v01.ma scene from the chapter6\scenes directory on the DVD.

   This scene contains a very simple jellyfish model. The model consists of the body of the jellyfish and its tendrils. All the surfaces are NURBS. The tendrils, which were created by converting Paint Effects strokes to NURBS surfaces, are grouped together and then grouped again with the body (see Figure 6.46).

FIGURE 6.46
The jellyfish model is created from groups of NURBS surfaces.

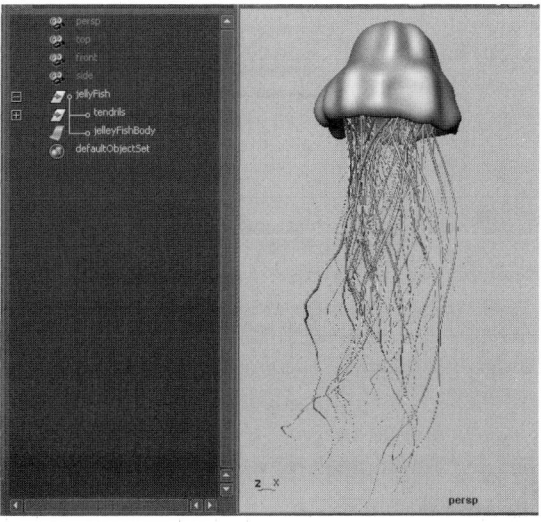

2. Select the jellyFish group in the Outliner. Switch to the Animation menu set, and choose Create Deformers ➢ Nonlinear ➢ Wave. The deformer appears as a wireframe wave. In the Outliner, you'll see that a new wave1Handle node has been created.

3. Select wave1Handle, and open its Attribute Editor. Click the wave1 tab. The tab contains the parameters for the deformer.

4. Set Amplitude to **0.041**. The Amplitude increases the height of the sinusoidal wave. This is displayed in the wireframe deformer handle in the viewport. Notice that the jellyfish is now distorted.

5. Set Wavelength to **0.755**; this decreases the distance between the peaks and valleys of the sine wave, creating a long, smooth type of distortion (see Figure 6.47).

6. Select the wave1Handle node, and use the Move tool to position it at the center of the jellyfish body. Set the Translate coordinates as follows:

   Translate X: **0**

   Translate Y: **0.787**

   Translate Z: **-0.394**

7. Set all three Scale channels to **30**.

8. To animate the bobbing motion, create a simple expression that connects the Offset value to the current time. Open the Attribute Editor for wave1Handle to the wave1 tab. In the field next to Offset, type **=time;** (see Figure 6.48), and press the Enter key.

9. Set Min Radius to **0.1**. If you switch to wireframe display, you'll see that a gap has appeared at the center of the deformer handle.

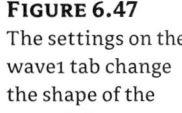

FIGURE 6.47
The settings on the wave1 tab change the shape of the wave deformer.

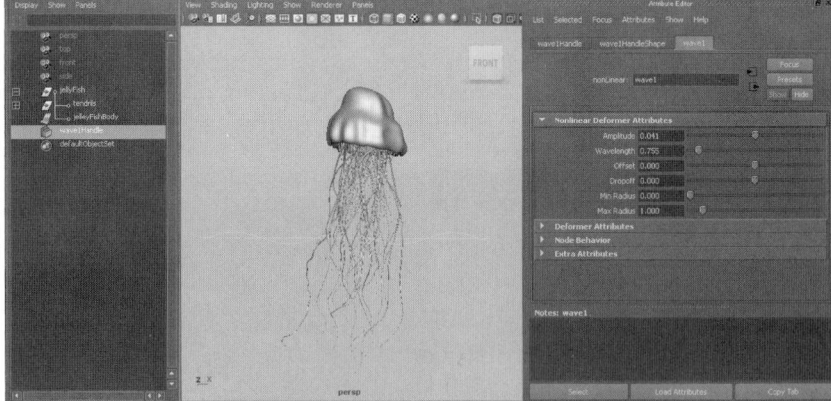

FIGURE 6.48
The Offset attribute is connected to time.

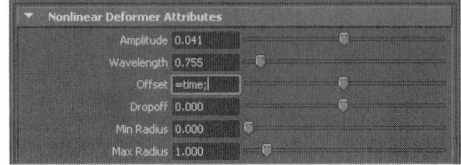

The deformer now affects only the areas between the edge of the min radius and the outer edge of the deformer. You can set a range of deformation by adjusting the Min and Max Radius sliders. Dropoff reduces the amplitude of the deformer at the outer edges of the range. Setting Dropoff to **-1** reduces the amplitude at the center of the deformer.

10. Save the scene as `jellyfish_v02.ma`.

To see a version of the scene up to this point, open the `jellyfish_v02.ma` scene from the `chaper6\scenes` directory on the DVD.

Squashing and Stretching Objects

The squash deformer can actually both squash and stretch objects. It works well for cartoony effects. In this section, you'll add it to the jellyfish to enhance the bobbing motion created by the wave deformer.

1. Continue with the scene from the previous section, or open the `jellyfish_v02.ma` scene from the `chapter6\scenes` directory on the DVD.

2. Switch to the Animation menu set.

3. Select the jellyFish group in the Outliner, and choose Create Deformers ➤ NonLinear ➤ Squash. A node named squash1Handle appears in the Outliner. In the perspective view, the squash handle appears as a long line with a cross at either end.

4. Select squash1Handle in the Outliner, and use the Move tool to position the handle at the center of the jellyfish.

5. Set the Translate channels to the following:

   Translate X: **0**

   Translate Y: **1.586**

   Translate Z: **0**

6. Select the squash1Handle, and open the Attribute Editor to the squash1 tab. The Low and High Bound sliders set the overall range of the deformer. Leave Low Bound at -1, and set High Bound to **0.5** (see Figure 6.49).

FIGURE 6.49
The squash deformer settings appear in the Attribute Editor.

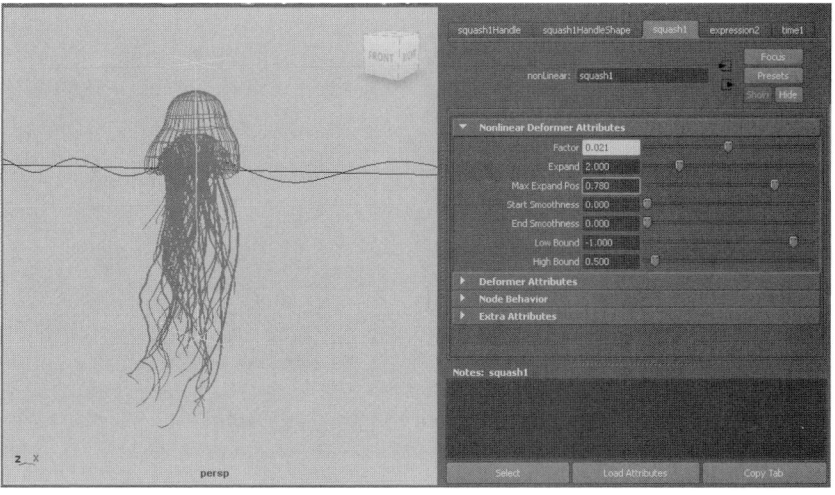

You can animate any of the settings to add motion to the jellyfish. In this case, you'll add an expression to the Factor setting of squash1. Setting Factor to a positive value stretches the object; setting Factor to a negative value squashes the object. For the jellyfish, animating between squash and stretch helps make the model appear as though it's floating in water. You can use a sin function as part of an expression that smoothly animates the Factor value between positive and negative values:

1. In the field next to Factor, type `=0.25*(sin(time*2));` and hit the Enter key.

   Multiplying `time` by 2 speeds up the animation of the values. Multiplying the entire expression by 0.25 keeps the range of values between -0.25 and 0.25. Going beyond this range deforms the jellyfish a bit too much.

   Factor controls the vertical displacement created by the squash deformer; the Expand setting controls the horizontal displacement created by the effect.

2. Set Expand to 2. Set Max Expand Pos to **0.78**. This places the vertical position of the center of the effect along the length of the deformer.

3. Save the scene as `jellyfish_v03.ma`.

To see a version of the scene to this point, open the `jellyfish_v03.ma` scene from the `chapter6\scenes` directory on the DVD.

Twisting Objects

The twist deformer twists an object around a central axis. You'll add this to the jellyfish to create some additional motion for the tendrils.

1. Continue with the scene from the previous section, or open the `jellyfish_v03.ma` scene from the `chapter6\scenes` directory on the DVD.

2. In the Outliner, expand the jellyFish group, and select the tendrils group.

3. Choose Create Deformers ➤ Nonlinear ➤ Twist. A new twist1Handle node will appear in the Outliner.

4. Select twist1Handle in the Outliner, and set the Translation channels to the following:

   Translate X: **0**

   Translate Y: **-18**

   Translate Z: **0**

5. Open the Attribute Editor for twist1Handle to the twist1 tab.

Just like for the squash deformer, you can specify the range of the effect of the deformer using the Low Bound and High Bound sliders:

1. Set Low Bound to **-1** and High Bound to **0.825**.

   The Start Angle and End Angle values define the amount of twist created along the object. If you move the End Angle slider, the top of the tendrils spin around even if they are outside the High Bound range. Moving the Start Angle slider twists the tendrils at their ends, which is more like the effect you want. You can use a simple noise expression to create a smooth type of random oscillation between values. Since the Start Angle is specified in degrees, you can multiply the noise expression by 360 to get a full range of twisting motion.

2. In the Start Angle field, type `=360*(noise(time*0.1));`. Multiplying `time` by 0.1 slows down the motion of the twisting.

3. Rewind and play the animation. You're on your way to creating an interesting jellyfish motion (see Figure 6.50).

4. Save the scene as `jellyfish_v04.ma`.

To see a version of the scene to this point, open the `jellyfish_v04.ma` scene from the `chapter6\scenes` directory on the DVD.

Try adding nonlinear deformers to the jellyfish.

FIGURE 6.50
The jellyfish is animated using a number of nonlinear deformers.

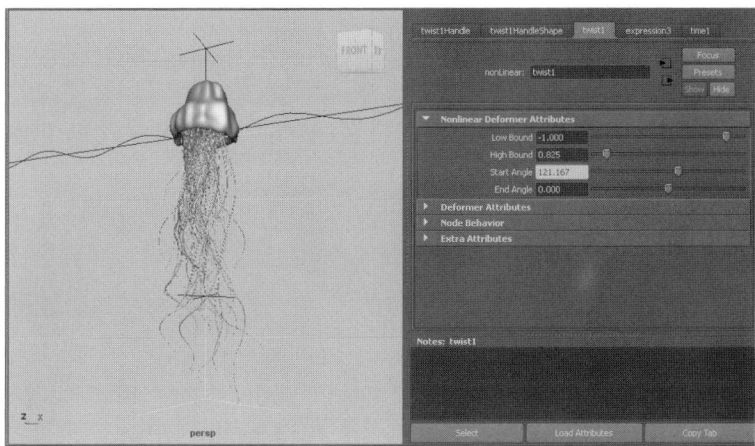

UNDULATING BACTERIA

While working on a creepy animation sequence for the closing titles of a feature film, I was asked to create hairy microbes floating in a cellular environment. The art director wanted the bacteria encased in an undulating membrane. To do this, I combined nonlinear deformers and a blend shape. Using a blend shape, I transferred the animation of the undulating membrane from a copy of the bacteria to the animated version of the bacteria. You can try this yourself using the following steps:

1. Create a model of a bacterium. Usually a rounded elongated cube with a lot of divisions does a good job.

2. Create a duplicate of the bacterium geometry.

3. Animate the original geometry floating in an environment or slinking along an animation path.

4. Apply a series of deformers to the duplicate geometry to make the surface undulate and throb.

5. Select the deformed duplicate and the animated original, and choose Create Deformers ➢ Blend Shape. Set the Value of the Blend Shape on the animated bacterium to **1**. The deformations applied to the duplicate are now transferred to the original.

Using this setup, you won't need to worry about grouping the nonlinear deformers or parenting them to the animated original. You can move the duplicate and its deformers out of camera view and continue to edit the animation by changing the settings on the duplicate's deformers.

Creating a Jiggle Effect

A jiggle deformer is a very simple way to add a jiggling motion to deformed objects. Jiggle deformers do not have the same level of control as dynamic systems such as nucleus, fluids, or hair. Jiggle deformers are best used as a substitute for dynamics when the situation requires just a little jiggly motion.

Applying Jiggle Deformers

There aren't very many options for creating jiggle deformers. To apply a jiggle deformer, select the object you want to jiggle, and create the deformer. In this section, you'll add the jiggle to the jellyfish:

1. Continue with the scene from the previous section, or open the `jellyfish_v04.ma` scene from the `chapter6\scenes` directory on the DVD.

2. Select the jellyFish group in the Outliner. Choose Create Deformers ➢ Jiggle Deformer ➢ Options.

3. In the options, set Stiffness to **0.1** and Damping to **0.8**. A higher Stiffness setting creates more of a vibrating type of jiggle; lowering the Stiffness value makes the jiggle more jellylike.

4. Click Create to make the deformer. You won't see any new nodes appear in the Outliner because the Display option is set to DAG Objects Only.

   If you turn off the DAG Objects Only option in the Outliner, you'll see that a jiggle deformer is created for each surface. A jiggle cache is created to aid in the calculation and playback of the scene (Figure 6.51).

5. Rewind and play the scene; you'll see that the jellyfish has a jiggling motion, especially in the tendrils.

FIGURE 6.51
A node for each jiggle deformer applied to the surfaces appears in the Outliner.

If you want to edit the settings of all the jiggle deformers at once (since there are so many tendrils, a lot of deformer nodes were created), disable the DAG Objects Only option in the Outliner's Display menu, Shift+click all the jiggle nodes, and then edit the settings in the Channel Box. When you have multiple objects selected, editing the settings in the Channel Box applies the settings to all the selected objects. This is not true when working in the Attribute Editor.

Painting Jiggle Weights

The jiggle effect looks good in the area of the tendrils, but it's a little too strong on the top of the jellyfish body. You can edit the weights of the deformer interactively using the Paint Jiggle Weights tool.

1. Select the jellyFishBody node in the Outliner, and choose Edit Deformers ➢ Paint Jiggle Weights Tool.

2. In the Options box, set Paint Operation to Replace and Value to **0**. Paint the area at the top of the jellyfish body.

3. Set Paint Operation to Smooth, and click the Flood button a few times to smooth the overall weighting (see Figure 6.52).

FIGURE 6.52
Paint the weights of the jiggle deformer on the top of the jellyfish body, and then smooth them using the Flood button.

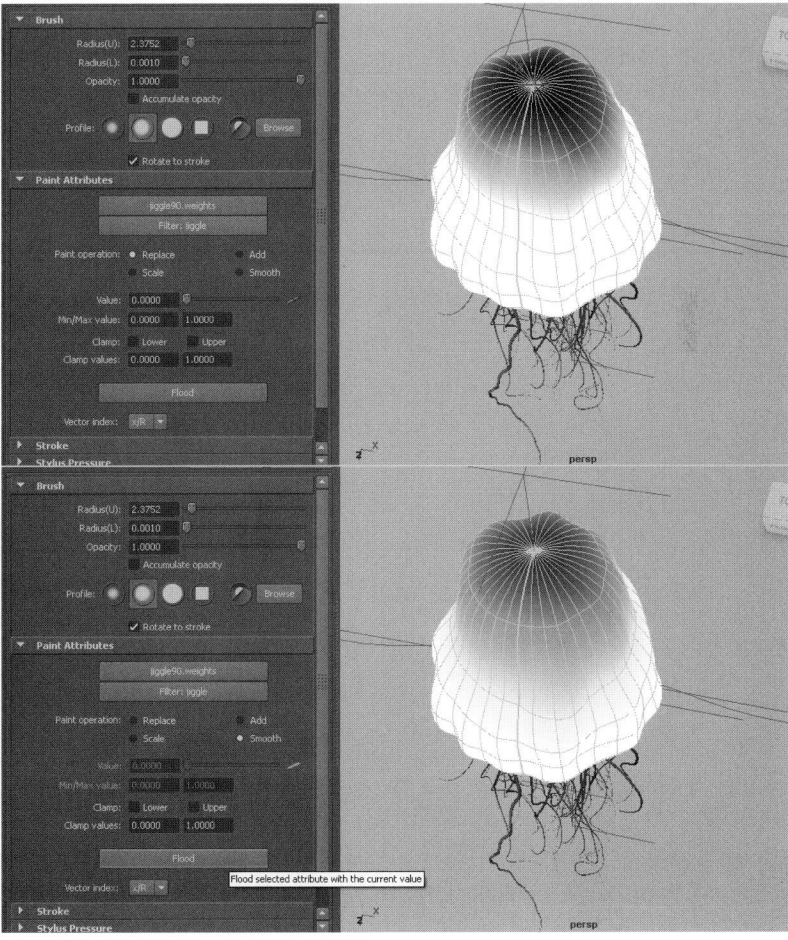

4. Rewind and play the animation. The jiggling is not quite as strong on the top of the jellyfish.

5. Save the scene as **jellyfish_v05.ma**.

To see a version of the scene to this point, open the jellyfish_v05.ma scene from the chapter6\scenes directory on the DVD.

SETTING THE PLAYBACK SPEED

If the jellyfish seems to explode during playback, it is probably because you have the timeline play-back preferences set to Real Time. Change the playback speed to Play Every Frame. You can access these settings by clicking the icon next to the key at the bottom-right corner of the interface or through the preferences (Windows ➤ Settings/Preferences ➤ TimeSlider).

Optimizing Animations with the Geometry Cache

When you create a geometry cache for animated geometry, a series of files are written to your computer's hard drive that store the position of each of the points of the specified geometry over time. Geometry caches are used to optimize the performance of an animation. As your scenes become filled with complex animated characters that interact with environments and effects, Maya's playback performance can get bogged down, making the scene frustrating to work with. By using geometry caches, you can store that animation data on the hard drive as a separate file, thus freeing up resources so your computer can more easily play the animation and ensuring that you'll have a much easier time working on other aspects of the scene such as lighting, effects, or other animated elements.

Once you create a geometry cache, you can add more deformers and animation to the cached geometry and even alter the playback speed of the cached geometry.

In this section, you'll get a sense of how you can use a geometry cache by creating one for the jellyfish animated in the previous section. Then you'll see how you can use the geometry cache settings to slow the playback of the jellyfish so the floating motion looks more natural. This is just one example of a creative use of the geometry cache.

Creating a Geometry Cache

The motion-deformed jellyfish looks pretty good as a simple animation. However, after all the deformers have been combined and the jiggle has been added, the motion looks a little too fast for a convincing deep-sea environment. Obviously, you can continue to edit the expressions used on the deformers, but in this section you'll take a shortcut by using a geometry cache.

1. Continue with the scene from the previous section, or open the jellyfish_v05.ma scene from the chapter6\scenes directory on the DVD.

   Unless you have a very powerful computer, most likely the playback of the jellyfish is not quite in real time. It may look okay in the scene view, but when you create a playblast, you'll see that the overall motion is too fast.

2. In the viewport panel menu, disable the display of deformers in the Show menu so you can clearly see the jellyfish.

3. Choose Window ➢ Playblast ➢ Options to open Playblast Options.

4. Set Time Range to Time Slider. Set Format to iff to see the animation playback in FCheck. You can also choose AVI or QT to see the movie play back using your computer's default media player.

5. Set Display Size to From Window, and use the Scale slider to determine the size of the movie.

6. Click the Playblast button in the options. Maya will play through the animation and take a screenshot of each frame as it plays. When it's finished, you can watch the movie play back in the default media viewer or in FCheck (see Figure 6.53).

FIGURE 6.53
The options for creating a playblast

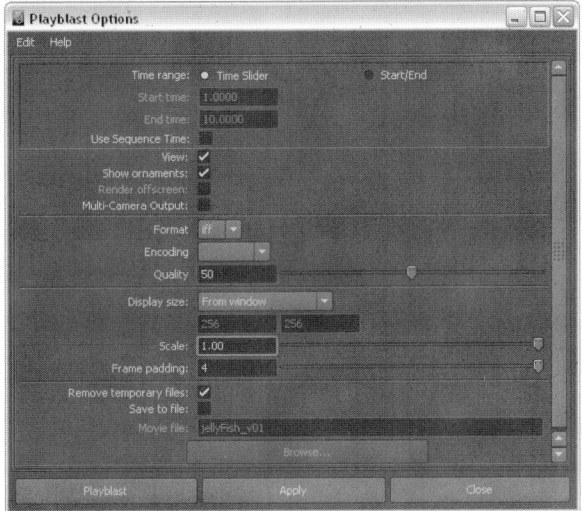

To create a geometry cache, you need to select the geometry nodes; selecting group nodes or parents of the geometry nodes won't work.

1. In the Outliner, hold the Shift key and click the plus sign next to the jellyfish group to expand the group and the tendrils group at the same time.

2. Shift+click all the tendril objects and the jellyFishBody surface.

3. From the Animation menu set, choose Geometry Cache ➢ Create New Cache ➢ Options.

4. In the options, use the Base Directory field to specify a directory for the cache. By default the cache is created in the Data folder for the current project. If you will be rendering across computers on a network, make sure all the computers have access to the directory that contains the cache.

5. Name the cache **jellyfish**. Set File Distribution to 1 file and Cache Time Range to Time Slider.

6. Click Create to make the cache. Maya will play through the animation and write the cache files to disk.

7. When Maya has completed the cache, it should automatically be applied to the jellyfish. To prove this, you can select the deformers in the scene, delete them, and then play back the animation. The jellyfish should still bob up and down.

Editing the Cache Playback

Once the cache has been created, you can use the settings in the cache node to change the speed of the playback. This will create a more believable motion for the jellyfish.

1. Select any of the surfaces in the jellyfish (not the jellyfish group node), and open the Attribute Editor.

2. Switch to the jellyfishCache1 tab. Set the Scale attribute to **5**. This scales the length of the animation to be five times its original length, thus slowing down the speed of playback (see Figure 6.54).

FIGURE 6.54
The options for the geometry cache playback

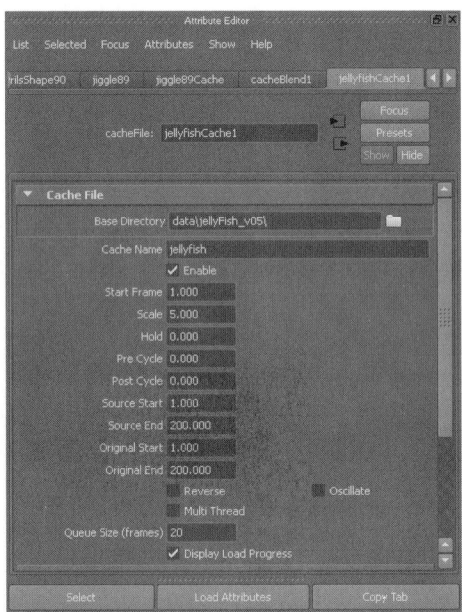

3. Set the length of the timeline to **1000**. The original 200-frame animation has been scaled to 1,000 frames.

4. Create a playblast. You'll see that the jellyfish is now much slower and looks more like an undersea creature.

   Once you have created a cache, you can add other deformers, animate the movement of the jellyfish group, and even make animated copies.

5. Select the jellyFish group, and choose Edit ➢ Duplicate Special ➢ Options.

6. In the options, set Geometry Type to Instance. Click Duplicate Special to create the copy.

7. Move the copy away from the original, and rotate it on its y-axis so it does not look exactly like the original.

8. Make a few more copies like this to create a small jellyfish army. Play back the animation to see the army in action (see Figure 6.55).

To create variations among the jellyfish, you can create three or four original jellyfish animations that have differences in their deformer settings and create a different cache for each. Then create several sets of instances for each jellyfish. Position them strategically in the camera view, and vary their Y rotations.

FIGURE 6.55
Duplicates of the original jellyfish are created to make a small jellyfish army.

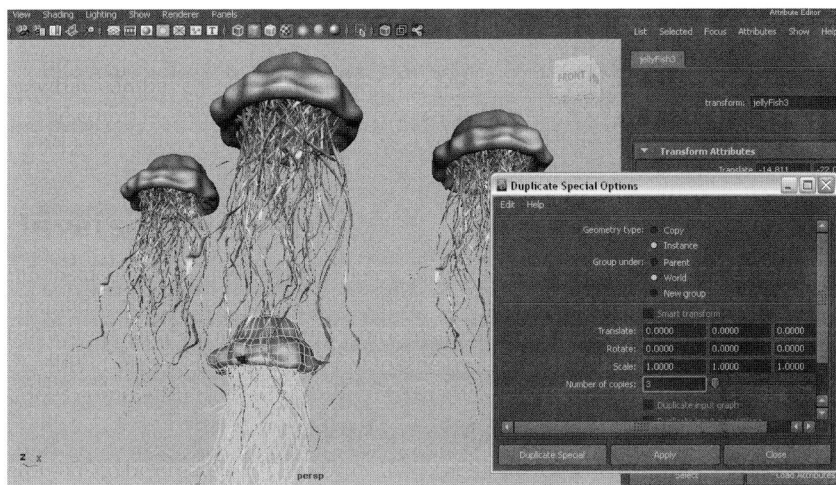

The Bottom Line

Animate facial expressions   Animated facial expressions are a big part of character animation. It's common practice to use a blend shape deformer to create expressions from a large number of blend shape targets. The changes created in the targets can be mixed and matched by the deformer to create the expressions and speech for a character.

> **Master it**   Create blend shape targets for the nancy character. Make an expression where the brows are up and the brows are down. Create a rig that animates each brow independently.

Create blend shape sequences   Blend shapes can be applied in a sequential order to animate a sequence of changes over time.

> **Master it**   Create a blend shape sequence of a mushroom growing.

Deform a 3D object   Lattices are free-form deformers that create a 3D cage around an object. The differences between the lattice and the lattice base are used to deform geometry.

> **Master it**   Animate a cube of jelly squishing along a path.

Animate nonlinear deformers   Nonlinear deformers apply simple changes to geometry. The deformers are controlled by animating the attributes of the deformer.

> **Master it**   Animate an eel swimming past the jellyfish you created in this chapter.

Add jiggle movement to an animation   Jiggle deformers add a simple jiggling motion to animated objects.

> **Master it**   Add a jiggling motion to the belly of a character.

Chapter 7

Rigging and Muscle Systems

Rigging is the process of creating an organized system of deformers, expressions, and controls applied to an object so it can be easily and efficiently animated. A good *rig* should intuitively allow an animator to concentrate on the art of animation without the technical aspects of rigging getting in the way. In addition, a good rig should be well organized so it can easily be changed, repurposed, or fixed if there is a problem.

Rigging as a practice is continually evolving in the industry. New technologies, concepts, and approaches emerge every day and are widely debated and discussed among professional technical directors throughout the world. Although this chapter offers advice on how to best approach creating part of a character rig in Maya, its main purpose is to help you understand how the tools work so that you can approach creating your own rigs and adapting rigging practices from others.

The first half of this chapter explores techniques for creating efficient character rigs. There are many approaches to rigging characters; the main focuses of these lessons are to build an understanding of how the Maya toolset works so you can adapt it to your preferred rigging workflow. The lessons provide additional tips and tricks that can help you avoid common rigging pitfalls.

The second half of the chapter is devoted to Maya Muscle, which is a plug-in designed to create realistic deformations for character rigs. The muscle system works with skeletons to simulate the qualities of flesh and skin.

The focus of this chapter is to rig and weight a giraffe. You will create controls to operate its legs and spine. Regardless of the character, in this case a giraffe, the concepts are the same. The typical pipeline is to build a skeleton, create the rig, and then weight the geometry.

In this chapter, you will learn to:

- ◆ Create and organize joint hierarchies
- ◆ Use Inverse Kinematics rigs
- ◆ Apply skin geometry
- ◆ Use Maya Muscle

Understanding Rigging

Today's characters are more complex than ever. Even the simplest are expected to have a full range of motion and perform as if they actually existed. To achieve this level of realism, numerous tools and techniques are applied. In this chapter, you'll build a realistic giraffe.

The most common types of rigs are created using joint deformers. In character animation, a skeletal system is created from joints to match the basic shape of the character. A joint is represented by a simple wireframe sphere. Joints are connected by bones, which are represented by a wireframe pyramid. When one joint is parented to another joint, the bone is aligned so the pointed end of the pyramid points to the child joint (see Figure 7.1).

FIGURE 7.1
Joints are positioned based on the shape of the object they are meant to deform.

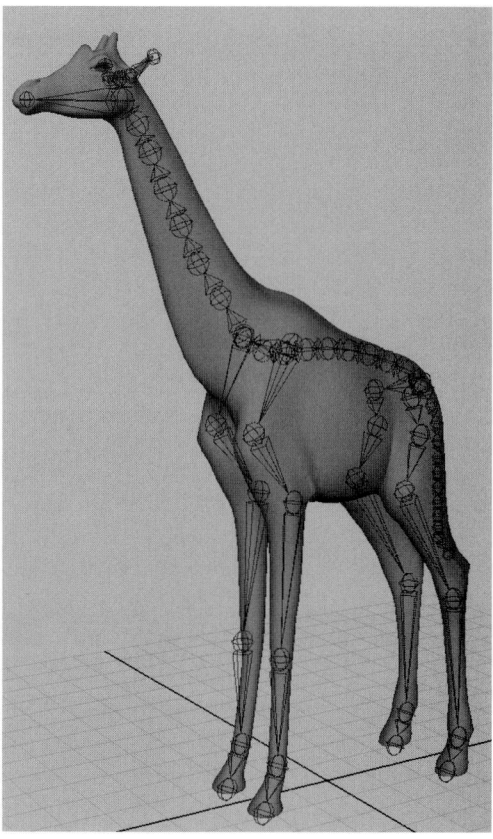

The geometry of the character is bound or skinned to the joints so the joints deform the geometry, making knees bend, wrists twist, fingers clench, and so on. Each joint in a hierarchy exerts influence over each vertex of the geometry, pushing or pulling it in one direction or another. The amount of influence exerted on a vertex by a joint is controlled through weighting.

Once geometry has been skinned to a skeleton of joints, a system of controls is created to make animating the joints as simple as possible. Controls can be created from locators or curves or any other node that can be selected in the viewport. These nodes then control the movement of joints via expressions, utility nodes, constraints, or driven keys. You used a simple control system in Chapter 5 to rig a mechanical bug model.

In addition, other types of deformers are often applied to the geometry to compensate for the shortcomings of simple joint deformations. Influence objects, lattice deformers, Maya Muscle, and other tools and techniques are often used to create believable motion and simulate the properties of flesh and tissue for characters.

Creating and Organizing Joint Hierarchies

The Joint tool creates a joint each time you click the scene. As long as the Joint tool is active, each time you click the scene, a new joint is added and parented to the previous joint, forming a simple hierarchy known as a *joint chain*. To exit the Joint tool, press the Enter key on the keyboard. This is useful if you need to finish one joint chain and then start another.

You can create branches of joints by parenting joint chains to intermediate joints in the initial chain. By parenting the branches and groups of joint chains, very sophisticated joint hierarchies, known as *skeletons*, can be created quickly.

Because many skeletons can become quite complex, they should be properly organized and named so animators and other riggers (referred to as *technical directors* in some instances) can easily access and understand the skeleton and all of its various parts.

The orientation of joints relative to their parent joints must be consistent throughout the skeleton to achieve proper functionality. The default orientation of a joint, established when the joint is added to a chain, is often incorrect and can lead to problems such as Gimbal Lock.

GIMBAL LOCK

Gimbal Lock is a situation in which a joint or object achieves a rotation that causes two of the rotation axes to overlap. When this occurs, the rotations for the overlapping axes are the same, which prevents the joint from rotating in three dimensions. Two of the rotational axes are so close that, when rotated along either axis, the resulting motion is the same.

Skeletons are built by using the Joint tool. The goal is to create joints to mimic the functionality of a real skeleton. It is not always necessary to replicate every single bone in your character. Often you can create the same effect of the real thing through a reduced number of joints. Some other cases require the addition of joints that don't exist at all to achieve the effect you are after. Either way, it's important to remember the goal of a skeleton is to provide the necessary structure for a character to move, or in other words, to provide whatever it takes in the most efficient manner possible.

1. Open the `giraffe_v01.ma` scene from the `chapter7\scenes` folder on the DVD. The scene contains a polygon giraffe.

2. Switch to the side view. The first part of the skeleton to draw is the giraffe's front leg.

DRAWING JOINTS

Although joints can be drawn in any view, it is best to use an orthographic view. When joints are started in the perspective, their origin is unpredictable. You can, however, draw joints onto an existing skeleton. The origin of the new joints resides in the same plane as the joint to which it is being connected.

---

3. Switch to the Animation menu set, and choose Skeleton ➤ Joint Tool.

4. To keep the joints visible through the geometry, choose Shading ➤ X-Ray Joints from the viewport's menu.

5. Starting just below the neck, begin drawing five joints down the length of the leg. You can reposition the joints as you go. If you hold the left mouse button instead of clicking, you can move the joint to better position it. After you release the button, use the middle mouse button to make other alterations. Continue clicking with the LMB until all five joints are drawn. When you're done, press Enter to complete the operation. Use Figure 7.2 as a reference.

FIGURE 7.2
Draw five joints for
the giraffe's front leg.

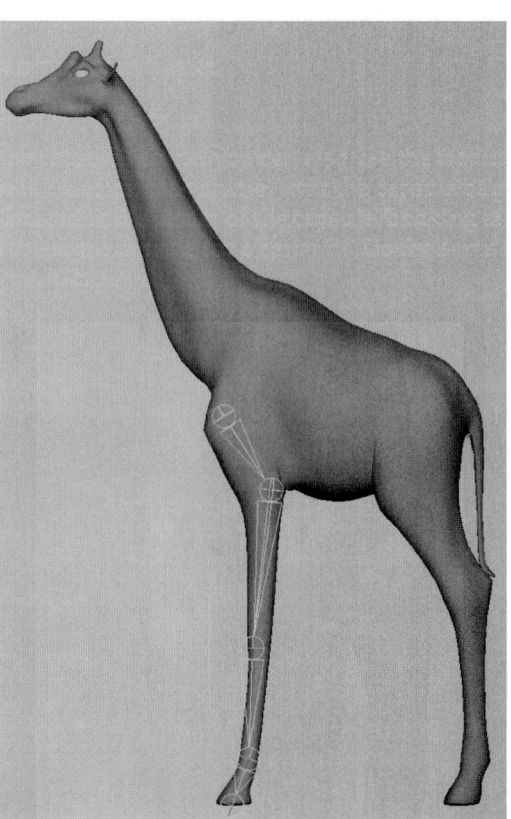

It's important to have a slight rotation for the knee if you decide to use Inverse Kinematics later. Inverse Kinematics is a special type of control mechanism for animating the joints; this will be discussed later in the chapter.

When you create Inverse Kinematics, Maya needs a hint as to how you want the joint to bend when the IK Handle is moved. For now, make sure there is an angle in the joint chain at the location of the knee (joint3).

6. The joints are located properly in the side view, but they must be positioned from the front view as well. Switch to the front view.

7. Translate the root joint to move the entire skeleton inside the left leg:

 A. Using the down-arrow key, pick walk through the skeleton's hierarchy to reposition the rest of the joints. This method of moving the joints works fine as long as you move the joints in order.

 B. If you go back up the hierarchy, any changes made to a joint affects all the joints underneath it. To avoid this, with a joint selected, press Insert or Home on the keyboard to activate the joint's pivot point. You can now move the joint independently.

Holding the **d** key also activates the joints pivot point. Figure 7.3 shows the joint's final position in the front view.

FIGURE 7.3
Move the joints in
the front view.

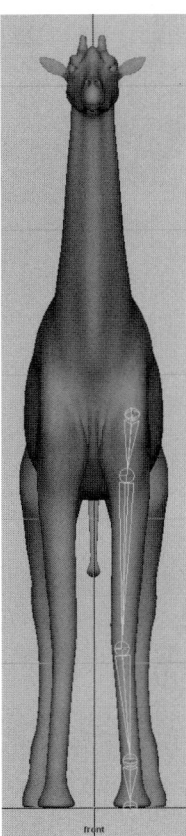

8. Repeat the procedure for the left hind leg. Use Figure 7.4 for reference.

9. Next is the giraffe's spine. Switch to the side view.

10. You want the spine joints to be evenly spaced. This ensures the geometry receives an even distribution of influence from the joints. Move off into empty space, and snap nine joints to the grid.

FIGURE 7.4
Draw the bones for
the left hind leg.

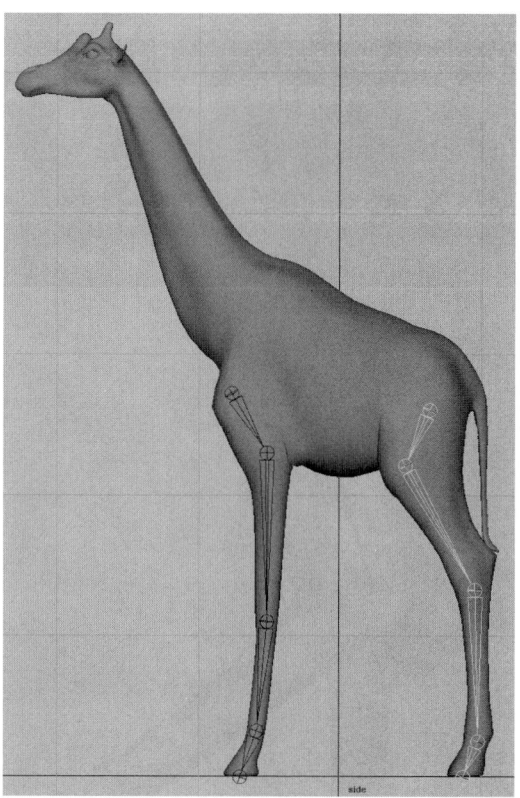

JOINT DISPLAY SIZE

You can change the display size of the joints in the viewport window by choosing Display ➤ Animation ➤ Joint Size.

---

11. Translate the root of the snapped joints just above the giraffe's tail. The spine is much longer than the giraffe's geometry.

    A. To maintain its uniform size, Shift-select each joint, starting with the tip and ending with the root.

    B. Select the Scale tool. The manipulator is displayed at the location of the last joint selected.

    C. Scale the skeleton in the z-axis until the tip is above the front leg's second joint.

12. Rotate each joint to get the proper curve in the spine. Use Figure 7.5 as a guide.

13. The joints for the neck and tail are created in a similar fashion. Repeat the procedure, placing 11 joints in the tail and 8 in the neck. Figure 7.6 shows the finished skeleton parts.

FIGURE 7.5
Rotate the joints to give curvature to the spine.

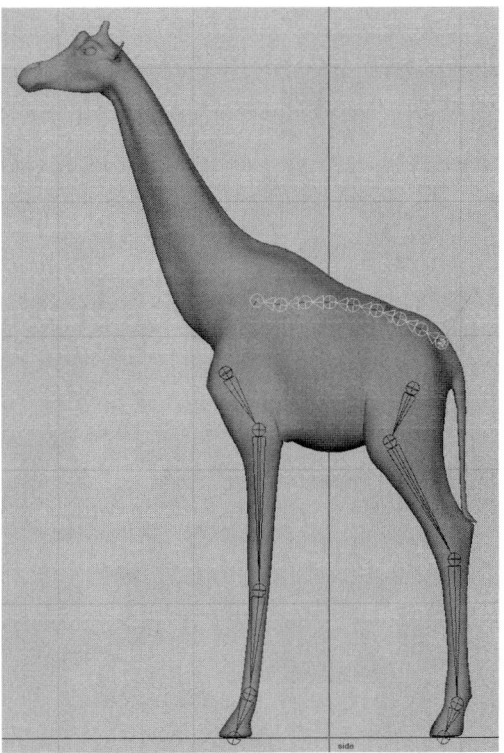

FIGURE 7.6
Create the neck and tail.

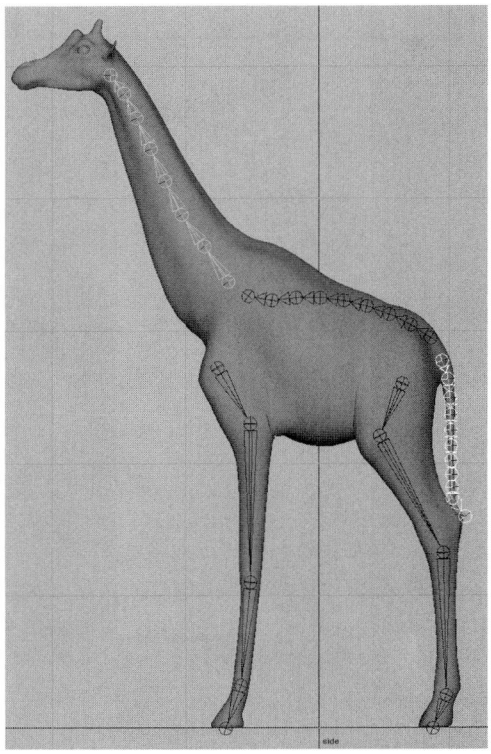

14. The only remaining joints are in the head. Choose Skeleton ➤ Joint Tool.

15. With the Joint tool active, click the last neck joint.

16. Next, click the end of the head. The head joint is automatically connected to the neck.

17. Finish up the head by adding ears (see Figure 7.7).

FIGURE 7.7
The head is finished by adding two more joints for the ears.

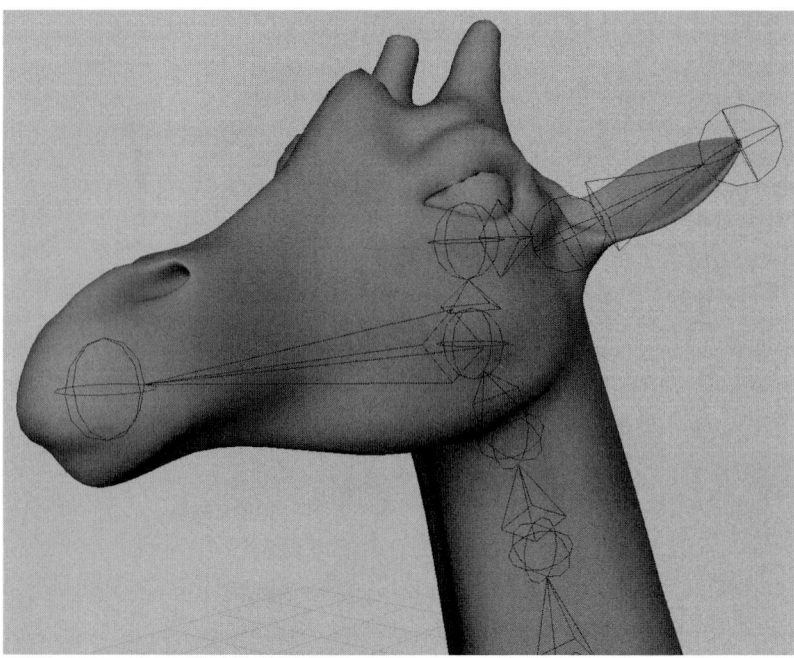

18. It's now time to attach the front leg to the spine. You need to add one more joint, which would be the human equivalent of the clavicle, in between the spine and front leg. Create and position a single joint above the left leg, equal in height to the spine. Position it using Figure 7.8 as a guide.

19. Select the root of the left leg. Hold Shift, and choose the newly created clavicle joint.

20. Press the **p** key to parent the joints.

21. Select the clavicle joint, and parent it to the second to the last spine joint.

22. Repeat steps 18–21 for the hind leg. Instead of a clavicle, create a hip bone. Use Figure 7.9 as reference.

23. Finish up by parenting the tail to the root of the spine.

24. Save the scene as `giraffe_v02.ma`.

To see a version of the scene to this point, open the `giraffe_v02.ma` scene from the `chapter7\ scenes` directory on the DVD.

FIGURE 7.8
Create a
clavicle joint.

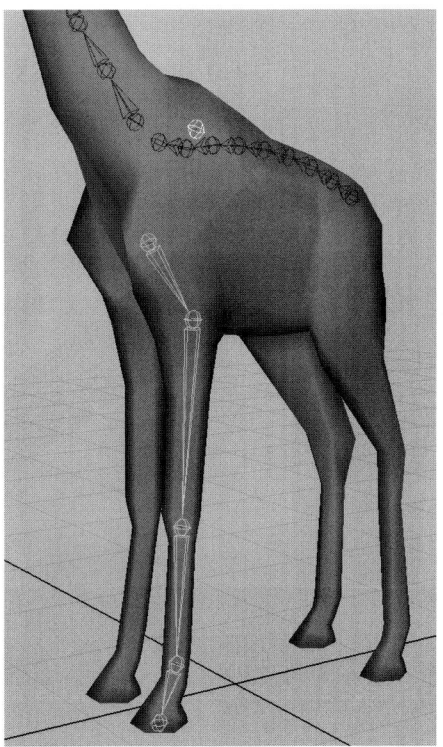

FIGURE 7.9
Create a hip joint,
and parent the
joints together.

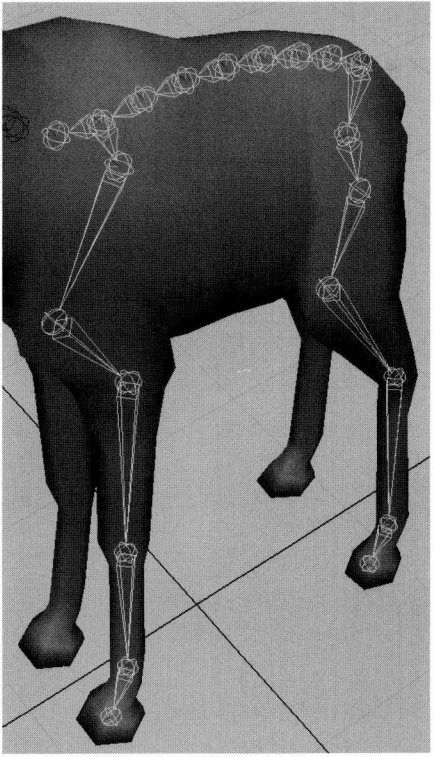

Orienting Joints

Like with most nodes in Maya, you can alter the way a joint rotates. This is done for numerous reasons:

◆ To make sure the orientation of the joint is aligned with its bone. Often when re-positioning, a joint's orientation diverges from the direction of its bone, thus causing a skewed rotation.

◆ To help avoid Gimbal Lock.

◆ To change the orientation for effect or specific control. For instance, you can have the left leg rotate in unison with the right leg when both are rotated simultaneously. By altering the right leg's orientation, you can have them rotate opposite one another, in a scissorlike fashion, when rotated simultaneously.

Typically orientation is done prior to binding your geometry to the skeleton. This is to prevent your geometry from inheriting any transformations. However, Maya does provide tools to orient joints after they have been attached to geometry such as the Move Skinned Joints tool.

Typically, each joint is oriented so the x-axis of its rotation is aimed along the length of the joint. The axis points down toward the child joint.

1. Continue with the scene from the previous section, or open the `giraffe_v02.ma` scene from the `chapter7\scenes` directory on the DVD.

2. Select the skeleton's root, and freeze transformations on Translate, Rotate, and Scale. You want to make sure all the joints have a rotation of 0 and a scale of 1. The translation cannot be zeroed, therefore it doesn't matter if it is included in the operation.

3. With the root still selected, open the tool options by choosing Skeleton ➤ Orient Joint. By default the Orient Joint tool affects child joints when applied to a parent. Since you are starting at the root of the skeleton and working your way down, you can leave this selected.

4. Keep all the default settings, and choose Orient (see Figure 7.10).

   The rotation axis of each joint should be consistent throughout the skeleton to ensure predictable behavior. Ideally, the red x-axis should be pointing down the length of the joint, and the rotation of the green y-axis and blue z-axis should match throughout the skeleton as much as possible. There will be exceptions to this based on the requirements of the skeleton or your own personal preference. For the most part, consistency is the most important aspect to watch out for.

FIGURE 7.10
Use the Orient Joint tool to force the x-axis down the length of the bone.

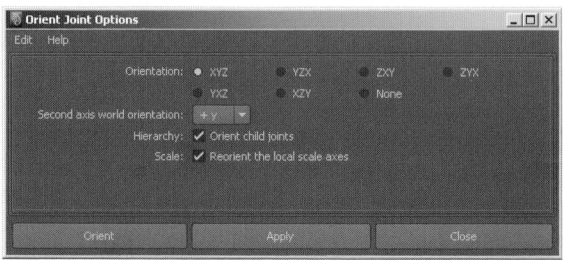

NONZERO ROTATIONS

The Freeze Transformations command should zero out all your joint rotations. However, Maya sometimes retains a miniscule amount of rotation, resulting in the following error:

```
// Warning: Skipping joint33: It has non-zero rotations. //
```

If this happens, select the joint and manually type 0 for all the rotation values. You can then apply the Orient Joint command.

5. Check all the joints for consistency. Some of the joints may not have oriented properly based on their position in the world. If so, re-orient the joint by deselecting Orient Child Joints in the Orient Joint tool options.

6. Save the scene as **giraffe_v03.ma**.

   To see a version of the scene to this point, open the leftArm_v03.ma scene from the chapter7\scenes directory on the DVD.

Naming Joints

When creating a skeleton, you need to be extremely conscientious about how you name the joints. Clear, concise naming helps everyone involved in the animation understand how the rig is set up and how each joint is supposed to function. When naming joints, use a prefix such as L_ to indicate the left side and R_ to indicate the right side. If a joint is meant to be used as a control, use a suffix such as _CTRL. The advantage of being consistent with prefixes and suffixes is that you can easily search and replace the prefix or suffix if it needs to be changed on a large number of joints.

1. Continue with the scene from the previous section, or open the giraffe_v03.ma scene from the chapter7\scenes folder on the DVD.

2. Open the Outliner, and select each of the joints making up the spine, starting with the root joint.

3. Click the icon next to the input field on the status line.

4. Choose Rename. Type **spine** and press Enter. Maya changes the name and automatically increments the numbering.

5. Rename the neck and tail the same way.

NAMING THE LAST JOINT

It is a good idea to name the last joint of a hierarchy something different. For instance, rename the last joint on the tail to **tailtip**. These joints are typically not weighted; therefore, it's good practice to differentiate them from the rest of the skeleton.

6. Naming the legs is more of a manual process since each joint should be named differently.

Starting from the top of the front leg, name the joints as follows:

Name the hind leg:

clavicle_	hip_
shoulder_	thigh_
upperarm_	upperleg_
forearm_	lowerleg_
forefoot_	hindfoot_
forefoottip_	hindfoottip_

Make sure to include the underscore.

7. To prevent the leg names from having a conflict from left to right and to better organize your naming structure, add a prefix to all the names. Select the root joint of both legs. Choose Modify ➤ Prefix Hierarchy Names. In the input field, enter **L_**.

It is also a good idea to add a suffix to the joints to further prevent confusion further into the rigging process.

8. Select all the joints to the legs.

9. Choose Modify ➤ Search And Replace Names.

10. In the Search for field, enter _.

11. In the Replace field, enter **_jnt**.

12. Click Replace.

The underscore you added to the names is swapped out, and the names are now complete.

You could have easily typed **_jnt** as you were creating each of the names. The main point of the preceding step was to familiarize you with the Search And Replace tool. In addition, if you are renaming numerous nodes or are unsure of your naming convention, you can add an underscore to make altering the name of multiple objects easier.

Figure 7.11 shows the final hierarchy and names.

AUTOMATING RENAMING

Michael Comet has bottled these tools' functionalities to take them a step further. He offers an easy-to-use script called cometRename that can handle all of your renaming needs. You can download it at www.comet-cartoons.com/melscript.php.

---

13. Save the scene as **giraffe_v04.ma**.

To see a version of the scene to this point, open the giraffe_v04.ma scene from the chapter7\ scenes directory on the DVD.

FIGURE 7.11
Name each of the joints to make its purpose clear and to keep it organized.

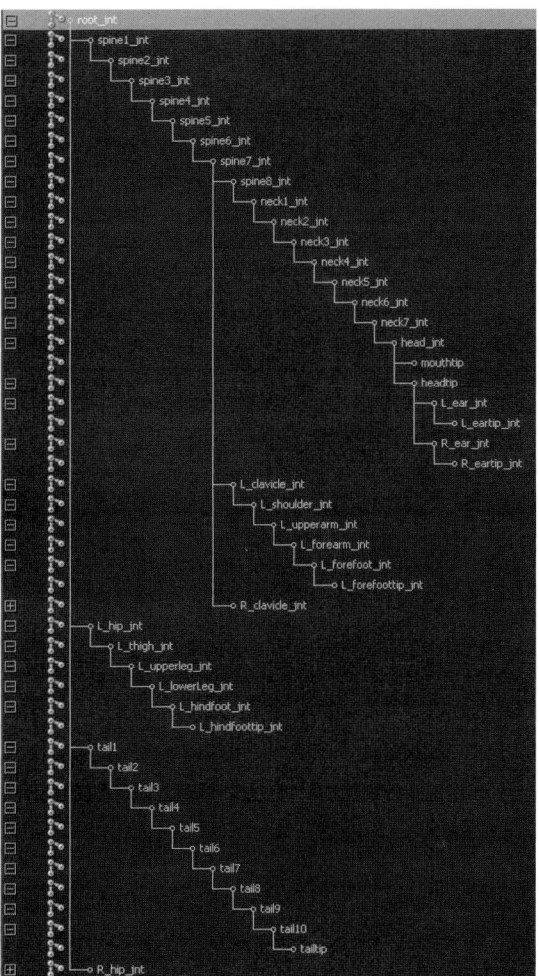

Mirroring Joints

The Mirror Joint command is used to instantly duplicate part of the skeleton across a specified axis. It's a timesaving device when creating symmetrical character skeletons. For example, if a joint chain is parented to part of the skeleton or the collar bone is connected to the spine, the mirrored joint chain is parented to the same joint in the spine.

1. Continue with the scene from the previous section, or open the `giraffe_v04.ma` scene from the `chapter7\scenes` directory on the DVD.

2. Select L_clavicle_jnt.

3. Choose Skeleton ➤ Mirror Joint ➤ Options.

4. In the options, set Mirror Across Axis to YZ, and set Mirror Function to Behavior.

   Behavior is usually the best option when building character skeletons. When this option is enabled, corresponding joints on either side of the central axis rotate the same way. So if both shoulder joints are selected and rotated, both arms will rotate forward toward the chest, producing a mirror image across the central axis. The Orientation option means that when corresponding joints are rotated the same amount on the same axis, one of the arms will have the opposite behavior of the other.

5. In the Replacement Names For Duplicate Joints section, set Search For to L_ and Replace With to R_. This automatically renames the joint chains based on what you put in these fields. In this case, the front leg on the giraffe's right side uses the prefix R_ instead of L_ (see Figure 7.12).

FIGURE 7.12
Name each of the joints to make its purpose clear and to keep it organized.

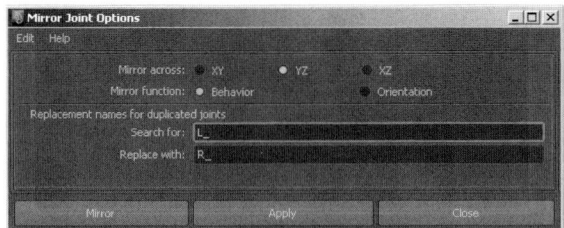

6. Click the Apply button to mirror the leg.

7. Repeat the process for the hind leg and the ear.

8. Save the scene as **giraffe_v05.ma**.

To see a version of the scene, open the giraffe_v05.ma scene from the chapter7\scenes directory on the DVD.

Rigging the Giraffe

As mentioned at the beginning of the chapter, today's rigs must be robust. Many different tools and aspects of Maya come together when character rigging. Inverse Kinematics (IK) was introduced in Chapter 5, where you created a very simple mechanical bug using IK Handles and basic techniques. In this section, you'll explore Inverse Kinematics a little further as well as some of the specialized IK rigging tools Maya offers.

As discussed in Chapter 5, *kinematics* is the study of the motion of objects. There are two main types of kinematics:

Forward Kinematics   This refers to a situation in which each joint in the chain inherits the motion of its parent joint.

Inverse Kinematics   This causes the joints in a chain to orient themselves based on the position of a goal known as the *End Effector*.

In this section, you'll learn about how to set up and use Inverse Kinematics in more detail.

IK Legs

Maya uses several types of solvers to calculate how the bones orient themselves based on the position of the End Effector. In Chapter 5, you used the Single Chain solver (ikSCsolver), which is a very simple solver with a few controls.

1. Open the `giraffe_v05.ma` scene from the `chapter7\scenes` directory on the DVD.

2. From the Animation menu set, choose Skeleton ➤ IK Handle Tool ➤ Options.

3. In the options, set Current Solver to ikRPsolver, and leave the other settings at the defaults (see Figure 7.13).

4. With the IK Handle tool active, click the L_upperarm_jnt, and then click L_forefoot_jnt. You'll see a line drawn between the first joint you clicked and the second joint. The line is known as the *IK Handle Vector*. You can also see a line that runs through the joint chain (see Figure 7.14).

FIGURE 7.13
Choose the ikRPsolver in the IK Handle Settings options.

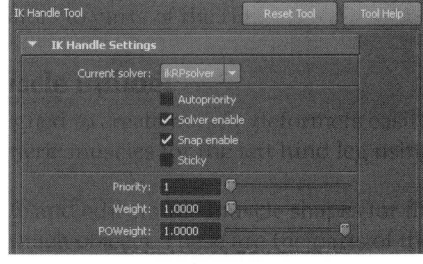

FIGURE 7.14
Attach the IK Handle to the joint chain by clicking the two end joints in the chain. Inverse Kinematics is indicated by a line between the two selected joints.

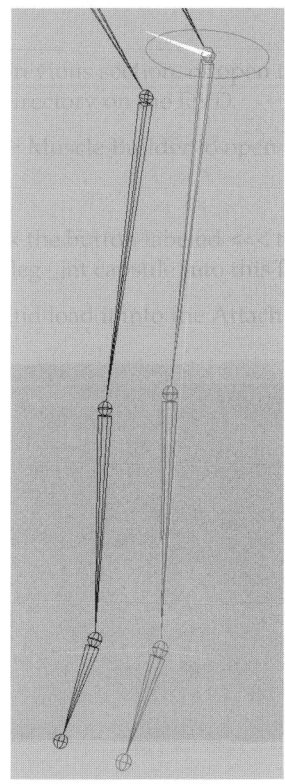

Inverse Kinematics controls can be applied to any joints in the chain, not just between the root and the end joint.

In the Outliner, you'll see that a node named effector1 has been added at the end of the chain. Also, a node named ikHandle1 appears in the Outliner.

5. Switch to the perspective view, select ikHandle1 in the Outliner, and move it around. Notice how the joint chain reacts. Notice also that in some positions the joints flip around to try to match the position of the IK Handle.

The two main settings for the IK Handle are Sticky and Snap Enable:

◆ When Snap Enable is on, the IK Handle snaps back to the end joint.

◆ The Sticky setting keeps the joints oriented toward the goal when the root joint is moved. This is very useful for legs, because it keeps the feet from sliding on the floor.

The difference is obvious:

A. Move the L_upperarm_jnt while Sticky is off.

B. Use undo to return the joint to its original position.

C. Select the ikHandle1 node, and open its Attribute Editor.

D. Set the Stickiness setting to Sticky.

E. In the Outliner, select L_shoulder_jnt, and move the joint around; note how the chain remains oriented toward the IK Handle.

F. Set Stickiness back to off before continuing.

To animate a joint chain with Inverse Kinematics, you set keyframes on the IK Handle, not the joints. In most situations, you'll want to constrain the IK Handle to another type of control object, such as a curve. The control is keyframed, and the IK Handle is constrained to the control so that it inherits the animation of the control. Constraining the IK Handle to another node produces the same effect as the Stickiness option. Let's add a simple control handle to the front leg.

An ideal animation rig should be easy to understand and animate. This means the controls should be clearly labeled and easy to select directly in the viewport window. With any handle, the animator should be able to enter 0 in all the translation channels for the controls to return the rig to the start position if needed. IK Handles use world space coordinates, so setting their translation channels to 0 moves a handle to the origin. One common solution to this problem is to constrain the handle to a locator, which can then be used to animate the handle. You can set a start position for the control and then freeze transformations on it so that when the translation channels are set to 0, the control moves to the start position and brings the IK Handle along.

1. Choose File ➤ Import. Import `sphereHandle.ma` from the `chapter7\scenes` directory on the DVD.

The imported sphere was created by duplicating the surface curves of a low-resolution NURBS sphere. The multiple curves were cut and reattached into a single continuous curve. When designing your own control handle, you can always overlap the curve onto itself. You will not notice a performance hit by using a few extra control vertices.

2. Snap the sphere to the center of L_forefoot_jnt.

3. Freeze the transforms, and rename it to L_FrontLeg_CTRL.

4. With the sphere selected, Shift-select the IK Handle.

5. Choose Constrain ➤ Point Tool Options.

6. Reset the tool settings from the Edit menu to make sure you are using the defaults.

7. Add the constraint (see Figure 7.15).

FIGURE 7.15
Use the Point con-
straint defaults
to connect the
IK Handle to the
sphere control

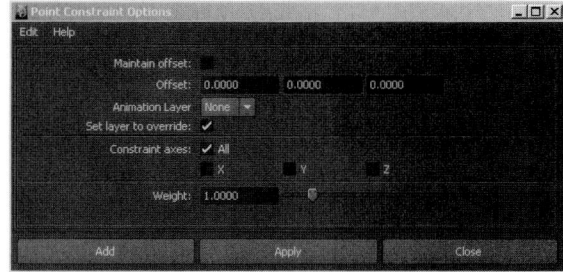

8. Add an SC handle from the L_forefoot_jnt to the L_forefoottip_jnt. The SC handle functions differently and is not affected like the RP handles are when they are constrained.

9. Turn on Sticky to keep the handle fixed.

10 Parent the SC handle to the sphere.

11. Save the scene as **giraffe_v06.ma**.

To see a version of the scene, open the giraffe_v06.ma scene from the chapter7\scenes directory on the DVD.

FK Blending

Once the constraint is added, new joints appear over the leg. These joints are a representation of a Forward Kinematics chain. Maya automatically applies FK to any IK chain. Figure 7.16 shows a combination of joints.

The FK joints are displayed larger than the IK joints to help differentiate between the two. You can control how both are displayed by choosing Window ➤ Settings/Preferences ➤ Preferences and then selecting Kinematics under the Display category. Essentially the two joints are the same. They do not have separate nodes, but they can be controlled independently.

The IK Handle inherently has an IK Blend attribute. When it is set to 1, the IK solver is 100 percent active. When set to 0, FK is 100 percent active. It is possible to blend the effects of both by using any value in between. As with the IK Handle, you do not want to keyframe the FK joints directly. Instead, you can assign handles to each joint. Let's do that next:

1 Open the giraffe_v06.ma scene from the chapter7\scenes directory on the DVD.

2. Choose Create ➤ NURBS Primitives ➤ Circle.

FIGURE 7.16
The FK joints are
drawn larger than
the IK joints.

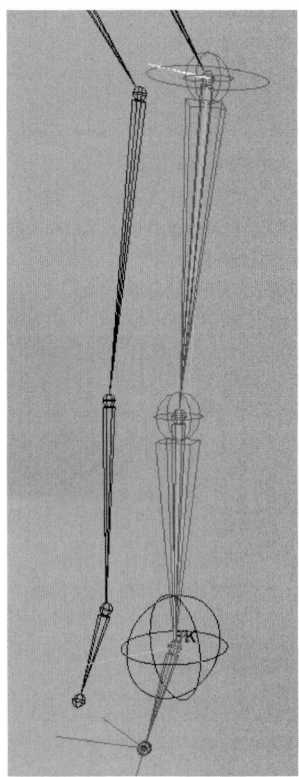

3. Snap the circle to L_forearm_jnt.

4. Scale the circle uniformly to .25.

5. Freeze the transforms, and delete its history.

6. Change the name of the circle to **L_forearm_FK**.

7. With the circle selected, Shift-select L_forearm_jnt.

8. Choose Constrain ➢ Orient Tool Options.

9. In the Orient tool options, select Maintain Offset. Make sure all the axes are constrained, and choose Add.

    Rotating L_forearm_FK won't do anything yet. To see the effects of the handle, set the IK Blend attribute to 0 and then rotate the handle. After testing it, be sure to return the handle's rotate values to 0.

10. Duplicate L_forearm_FK, and rename it to **L_upperarm_FK**.

11. With L_upperarm_FK selected, Shift-select L_upperarm_jnt.

12. Choose Constrain ➢ Orient using the same options from step 9 (see Figure 7.17).

    When you rotate L_upperarm_FK, with IK Blending set to 0, you will notice that L_forearm_FK is left behind. A point constraint will fix this.

FIGURE 7.17
Use primitive
NURBS circles for
FK Handles.

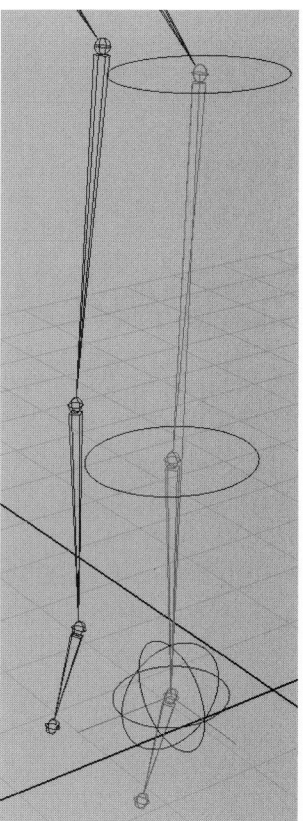

13. Select L_forearm_jnt.

14. Shift-select L_forearm_FK.

15. Choose Constrain ➤ Point Tool Options. Make sure the options are set to default, and click Add.

16. Save the scene as `giraffe_v07.ma`.

   To see a version of the scene, open the `giraffe_v07.ma` scene from the `chapter7\scenes` directory on the DVD.

Rotate Plane Solvers

The Rotate Plane solver (RP solver) differs from the Single Chain solver in that the End Effector matches the position of the IK Handle but not the rotation. Instead, the rotation of the chain is controlled using a special disc-shaped manipulator that can be keyframed if needed. The RP solver is more predictable and used most often, especially when creating skeletons for characters. The RP solver is similar to the SC solver except that an additional circular icon appears indicating the pole vector for the chain. The pole vector determines the direction of rotation for the joints as they attempt to reach the IK Handle (see Figure 7.18).

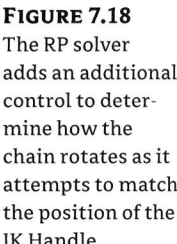

FIGURE 7.18
The RP solver adds an additional control to determine how the chain rotates as it attempts to match the position of the IK Handle.

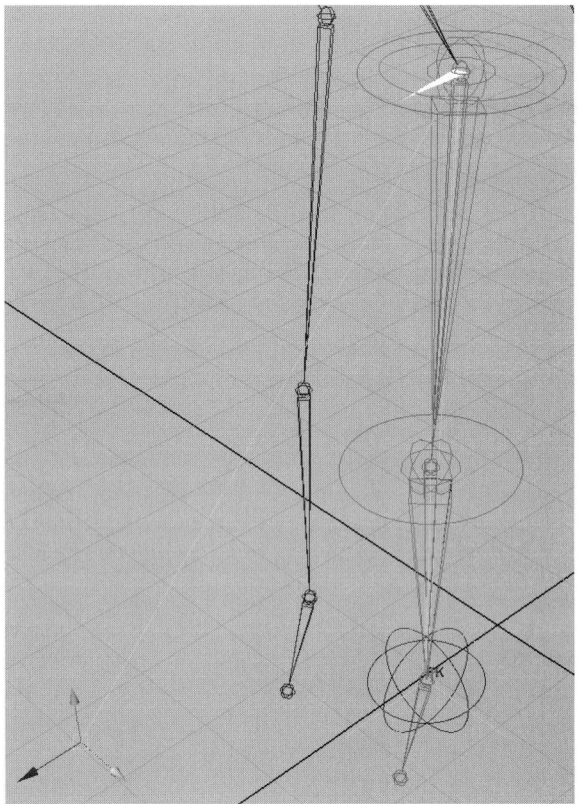

You can select the IK Handle (ikHandle2 in the example) and turn on the Show Manipulators tool. Using the tool, you can do the following:

◆ Rotate the blue disc to adjust the rotation of the chain

◆ Change the numeric values in the Channel Box using the Twist channel

The pole vector of the chain is indicated by the white triangle in the rotate plane indicator at the start point of the IK chain. Changing the pole vector also changes the orientation of the chain. The pole vector determines the angle of the rotate plane for the RP solver. This can be used to control unwanted flipping while animating the IK Handle.

The Twist attribute is directly related to the pole vector. In general, you'll want to adjust the pole vector to properly orient the chain and then use the Twist attribute to solve any flipping problems you may encounter while animating.

The pole vector of an IK Handle can be constrained to another node just like the IK Handle. Controlling the pole vector through a separate node allows you to zero out the transforms and gives you a visual representation in the viewport. Let's add one to the front leg:

1. Open the `giraffe_v07.ma` scene from the `chapter7\scenes` directory on the DVD.

2. The pole vector can be controlled just like the IK Handle. Choose File ➤ Import and select `poleVectorHandle.ma` from the `chapter7\scenes` directory on the DVD. Rename the imported handle to **L_Leg_PV**.

3. Open the IK Handle's Attribute Editor.

4. Choose Copy Tab at the bottom of the window.

5. From the copied window, open the IK Solvers Attributes tab, and find the Pole Vector XYZ coordinates (see Figure 7.19).

FIGURE 7.19
Find the Pole Vector attributes in the Attribute Editor.

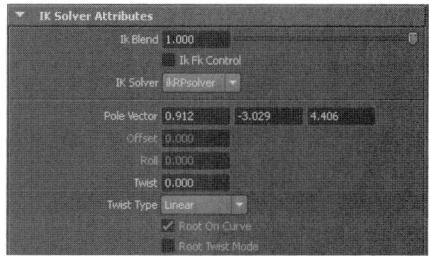

6. Copy the Pole Vector's XYZ coordinates to the L_Leg_PV Translate XYZ. The values of the pole vector place the handle along the same vector. This prevents the pole vector from shifting or being altered from its vector when it will eventually be constrained to the handle.

By adding an Aim constraint, you force the pole vector handle to always orient in the same direction of the forearm joint. This does not provide any necessary functionality, only a better visual representation.

7. Select L_forearm_jnt.

8. Shift-select L_leg_PV. Choose Constrain ➤ Aim Tool Options.

9. Change the options to match those in Figure 7.20, and click Add.

FIGURE 7.20
Set the Aim constraint options.

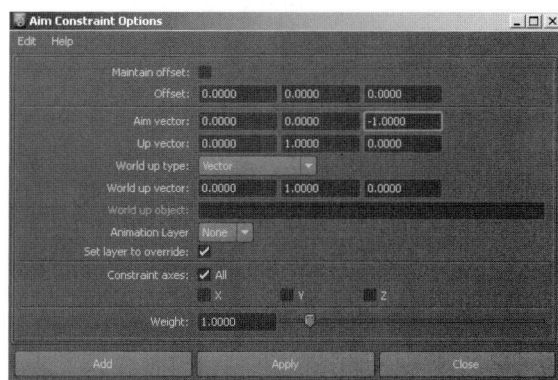

The pole vector handle is too close to the joints. This will cause the joint chain to flip a lot when the IK Handle is moved around.

10. Select L_FrontLeg_PV, and translate it in the Z to about 4.0 units.

11. Find L_FrontLeg_PV in the Outliner or Hypergraph.

12. Attached to it is the Aim constraint. Select it and delete it.

13. Select L_FrontLeg_PV, and freeze the transforms.

14. With it still selected, choose the leg's IK Handle.

15. Add a pole vector constraint by choosing Constrain ➤ Pole Vector. You can see the connection, as shown in Figure 7.21, if you select the IK Handle.

16. Save the scene as `giraffe_v08.ma`.

To see a version of the scene, open the `giraffe _v08.ma` scene from the `chapter7\scenes` directory on the DVD.

FIGURE 7.21
Use a Pole Vector constraint to control the pole vector of the front leg's IK Handle.

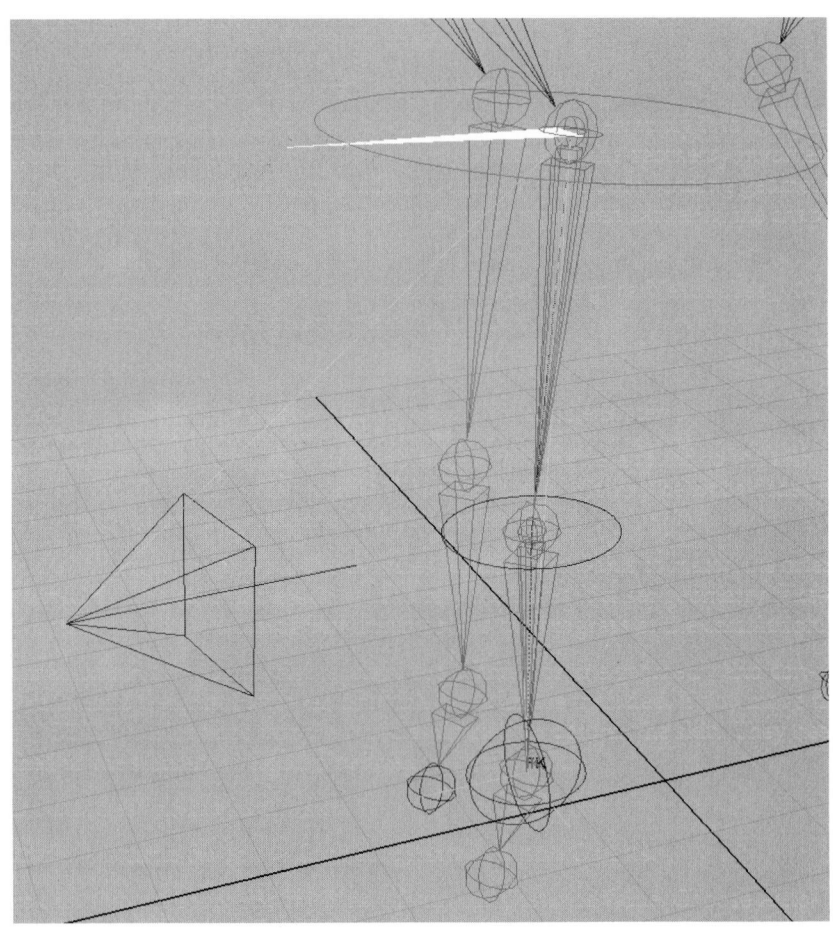

Creating Custom Attributes

You have added several control handles to the leg. The IK and FK Handles have overlapping functionality. When the leg is under full control of the IK, there is no need to see the FK controls; likewise, when the FK is in full control, there is no need to see the IK controls. You can add an attribute that will toggle between the two without any direct input from the user. Using utility nodes and custom attributes can add a tremendous amount of flexibility and power to your rig. The next exercise creates a custom attribute and based on its value turns off or on the visibility of your controls:

1. Open the `giraffe_v08.ma` scene from the `chapter7\scenes` directory on the DVD. The scene picks up where the previous exercise left off.

2. Select L_FrontLeg_CTRL.

3. Choose Modify ➢ Add Attribute. The Add Attribute window is displayed. Change the settings to match those in Figure 7.22. Make sure the Make Attribute option is set to Keyable and the Data Type option is Float.

4. Click OK to add the attribute.

   You can also access the Add Attribute window through the Channel Box by choosing Edit ➢ Add Attribute.

5. Look in the Channel Box with L_FrontLeg_CTRL selected, and you'll see the new channel named Ik Blend. The attribute exists but has no functionality.

6. Select L_FrontLeg_CTRL and L_Forearm_FK, and choose Window ➢ Hypergraph:Connections (see Figure 7.23).

7. In the Hypergraph window, choose Rendering ➢ Create Render Node.

FIGURE 7.22
Add an IKblend attribute to the L_FrontLeg_CTRL.

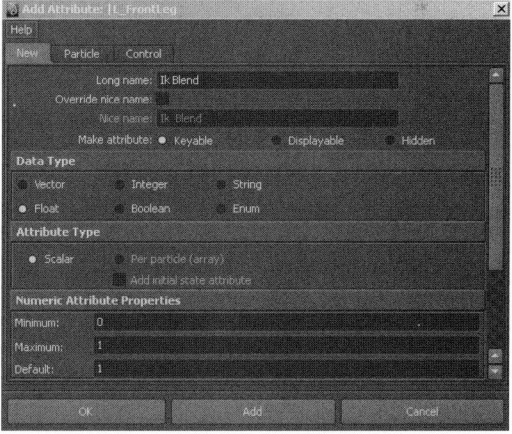

FIGURE 7.23
The node's up and downstream connections are displayed in the Hypergraph.

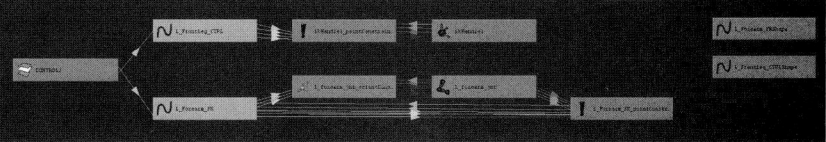

8. With the Create Render Node window open, choose Utilities from the Favorites menu.

9. After the window updates, select Condition. A condition node is created in the Hypergraph.

A condition node sets up an if...else statement. In this exercise, you want the condition to state that if Ik Blend is 1, then the visibility of the FK Handles is off. Furthermore, if Ik Blend is less than 1, then the FK Handles visibility is on.

10. MMB on L_FrontLeg_CTRL, and drag it onto Condition1. Notice when you drag the mouse, a plus sign is displayed. This lets you know you are performing an action.

11. After you release the MMB, choose Other from the pop-up menu. The Connection Editor opens with the first and second nodes preloaded (see Figure 7.24).

FIGURE 7.24
The Connection Editor shows attributes of the two nodes to be connected.

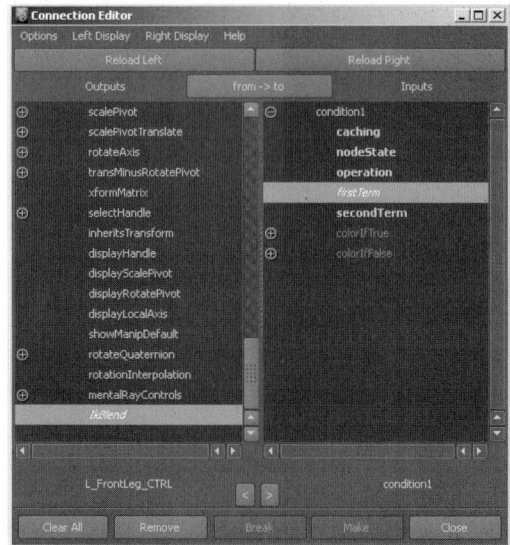

12. Choose IkBlend from the bottom of the left-side list (L_FrontLeg_CTRL).

13. In the right side list (Condition1), select firstTerm. The two attributes are now connected, with IkBlend driving the values of the firstTerm attribute. Leave the Connection Editor open.

14. Open condition1's Attribute Editor. Use Figure 7.25 for the rest of the settings.

◆ The First Term setting is the variable; its value determines if and what action needs to be taken.

◆ The Second Term setting is what the First Term is compared against. The Operation is how comparison should be executed.

◆ The True and False are what should happen based on the condition. In this case, if the condition is true and Ik Blend is less than 1, the resulting value will be 1. If it is greater than 1 or false, the resulting value will be 0.

FIGURE 7.25
Change the values of
the Condition node.

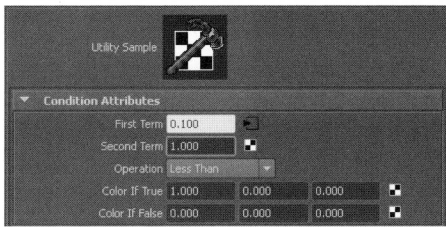

You need only one channel to make this operation work. Use the first attribute, which is defined as Color Red. The other two channels, blue and green, have been set to 0 simply to avoid confusion.

15. With Condition1 selected, choose Reload Left in the Connection Editor.

16. Next, select L_forearm_FK, and choose Reload Right.

17. Select OutColorR from Condition1 and Visibility from L_forearm_FK.

The connection is complete. You can test it by opening L_FrontLeg_CTRL in the Channel Box and setting the Ik Blend attribute to anything less than 1.

18. Connect the same OutColorR of Condition1 to the visibility of L_upperarm_FK. Now they both turn on or off simultaneously. Figure 7.26 shows the connected nodes in the Hypergraph.

19. Save the scene as **giraffe_v09.ma**.

To see a version of the scene, open the giraffe_v09.ma scene from the chapter7\scenes directory on the DVD.

FIGURE 7.26
The connections
are displayed in
the Hypergraph.

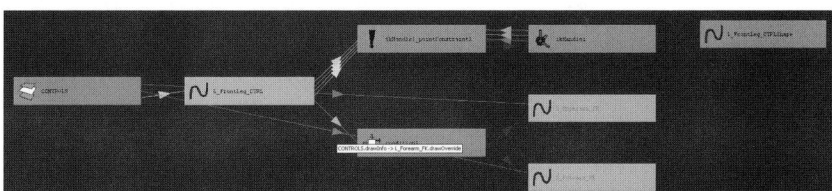

SET DRIVEN KEYS

Set Driven Keys are an invaluable assets to character rigging. Controlling the leg of the giraffe can be furthered by driving the rotation of L_clavicle_jnt and L_shoulder_jnt with Z rotation from L_upperarm_jnt. These bones have a limited specific amount of movement and therefore can be automated with the motion of the leg.

Spline IK

IK Spline Solver uses a curve to control the rotation of the joints. This is ideal for long snaking chains and tails. The solver can generate a curve or use an existing curve. The CVs of the curve become the manipulators for the joint chain. Usually it's a good idea to create clusters for the CVs of the curve and animate CVs of the curve indirectly using the clusters. In the next example, you'll use a spline IK to control the giraffe's spine:

1. Open the `giraffe_v10.ma` scene from the `chapter7\scenes` directory on the DVD. The scene has been continued from the previous exercise; all of the legs have been rigged.

2. Choose Skeleton ➢ IK Spline Handle Tool Options.

3. Deselect Auto Simplify Curve to prevent Maya from reducing the number of control vertices in the spline. Use Figure 7.27 to confirm your settings.

4. With the Spline IK Handle tool active, choose root_jnt and then spine8_jnt. The tool auto-completes and connects the spine chain to a curve. If you grab a CV and move it, you can see the spine's motion. Figure 7.28 demonstrates.

FIGURE 7.27
Create an IK Spline
Handle with these
options.

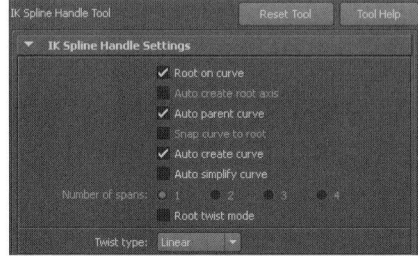

FIGURE 7.28
The CVs of the
spline are used to
manipulate the
spine's joints.

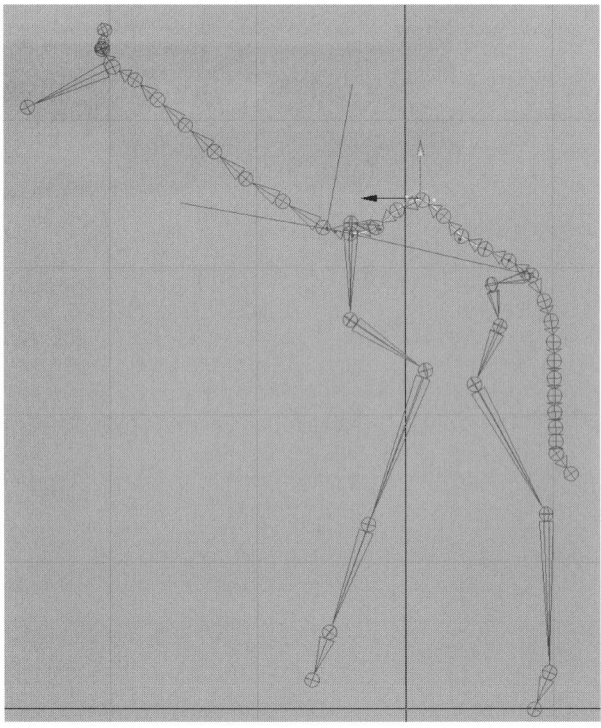

5. Select the curve, and switch to the Surfaces menu set.

6. Choose Edit Curves ➤ Selection ➤ Cluster Curve. This automatically places clusters on each CV of the curve (see Figure 7.29). When animating the curve, you should keyframe the clusters and not the CVs of the curve. For more information on clusters, consult Chapter 6.

FIGURE 7.29
Each CV of the spline is now attached to a cluster handle.

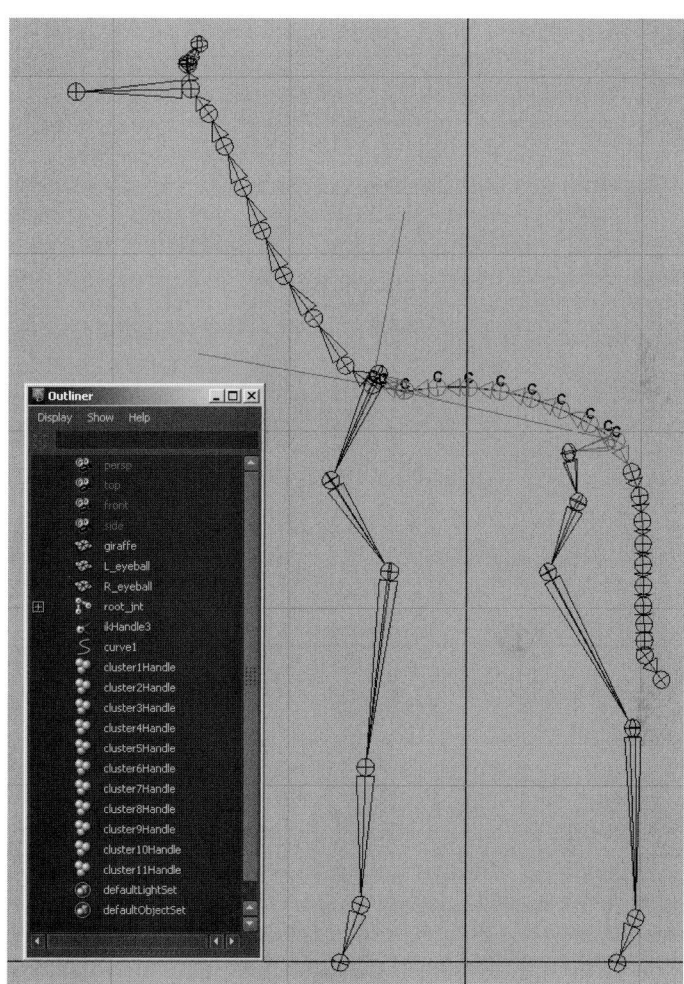

The cluster handles are created with their translates and rotates set to 0, which is perfect for animating. However, cluster handles have a low selection priority, making them difficult to deal with, especially in a complex rig. As with the other handles, it is best to create a custom controller to operate the clusters.

7. Choose Create ➤ NURBS Primitive ➤ Circle.

8. Rename the handle to **shoulder_CTRL**, and snap it to spine7_jnt.

9. Scale the handle uniformly to .7.

10. Duplicate shoulder_CTRL, and rename it to **torso_CTRL**.

11. Translate torso_CTRL to be centered between spine5_jnt and spine4_jnt. Scale it uniformly to .5.

12. Duplicate torso_CTRL, and rename it to **hip_CTRL**.

13. Snap hip_CTRL to spine1_jnt. Figure 7.30 shows the position of the three circles.

    The cluster handles will not react through a parent-child relationship because the Relative feature is selected. In addition, parenting the cluster handles and getting them to move with the character results in unwanted deformations and double transformations on the spline curve. Instead, the cluster handles are constrained to the NURBS curves.

14. Select hip_CTRL, and Shift-select cluster1Handle.

15. Choose Constrain ➤ Parent Options.

FIGURE 7.30
Position three
NURBS circles
along the giraffe's
spine.

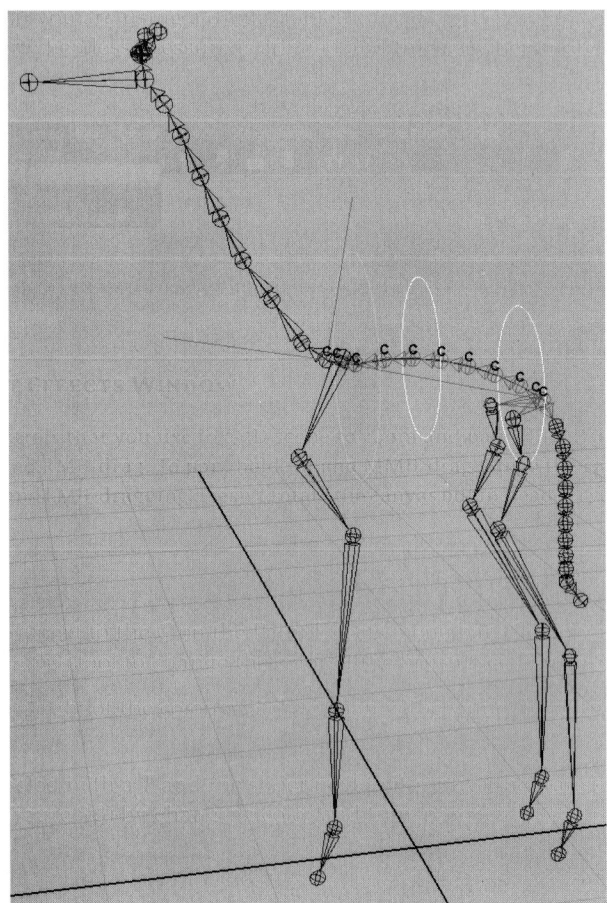

16. Select Maintain Offset, and make sure All is selected for Translate and Rotate. Figure 7.31 shows the settings. Repeat this step for the next three cluster handles.

17. Select torso_CTRL, and add the same Parent constraint from step 14 to clusterHandle 5, 6, 7, and 8.

18. Select shoulder_CTRL, and add the same Parent constraint from step 14 to clusterHandle 9, 10, and 11.

19. Grab hip_CTRL, and move it around. Notice how joints pull away from the curve and the other control handles. Figure 7.32 shows an example.

FIGURE 7.31
Add a Parent constraint to the first four cluster handles.

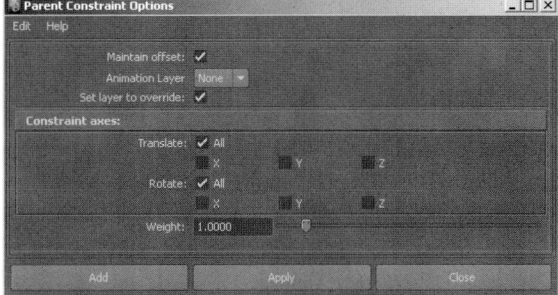

FIGURE 7.32
The joints pull away from the curve, causing undesirable effects.

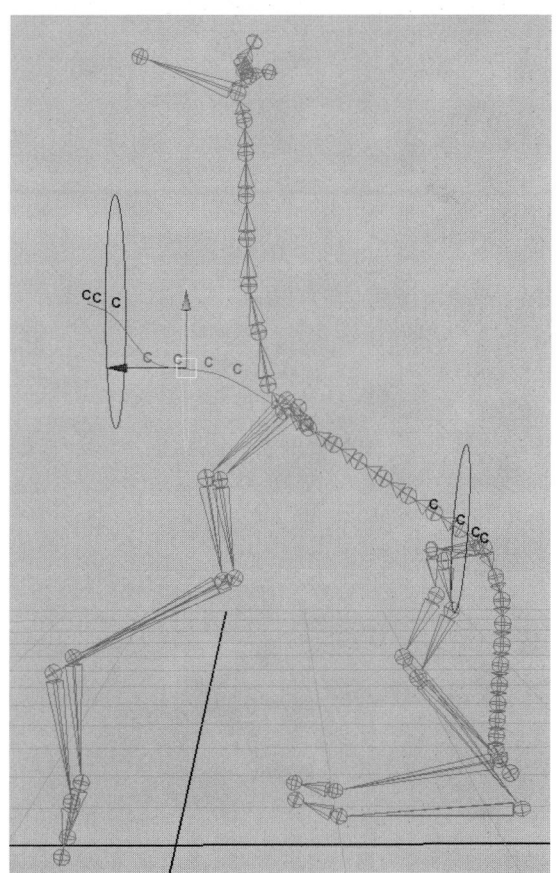

This is undesirable and causes major problems while animating. The fix is to point constrain each control to the one before it. However, constraining a handle directly would lock out the translation and prevent you from keyframing it. Empty group nodes are used instead, and the control handles are parented to them.

20. Choose Create ➤ Empty Group. null1 is created. Change its name to **torso_GRP**.

21. Snap torso_GRP to spine4_jnt. Freeze the transforms.

22. Select hip_CTRL and then torso_GRP.

23. Choose Constrain ➤ Point Options.

24. Check Maintain offset, and make sure all axes are being constrained. Click Apply.

25. Select torso_CTRL, and make it a child of torso_GRP.

26. Choose Create ➤ Empty Group.

27. Change the null's name to **shoulder_GRP**.

28. Snap shoulder _GRP to spine7_jnt. Freeze the transforms.

29. Select torso_CTRL and then shoulder _GRP.

30. Choose Constrain ➤ Point Options.

31. Select Maintain Offset, and make sure all axes are being constrained. Click Apply.

32. Move the hip_CTRL again and look at the differences the groups and constraints have made. Figure 7.33 shows the results.

33. Save the scene as `giraffe_v11.ma`.

FIGURE 7.33
Add a Parent constraint to the first four cluster handles.

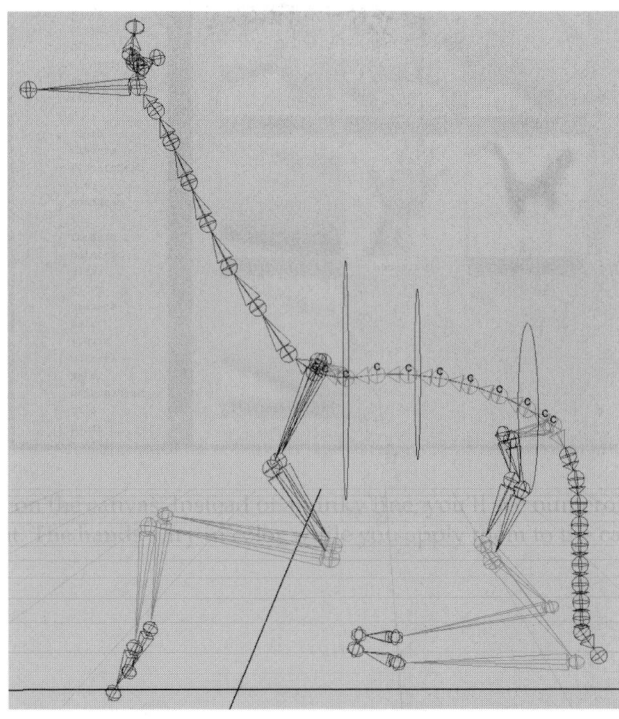

To see a version of the scene, open the `giraffe_v11.ma` scene from the `chapter7\scenes` directory on the DVD.

Spline IK Handles come with an extra feature called Twist. Although this attribute shows up on other types of IK Handles, it affects only Spline IK. Ultimately, the giraffe's final rig will not have any IK Handles visible, since all their control is being passed to a custom handle. Keeping in line with this, you can add the twist of the Spline IK to a custom attribute on the shoulder control.

You can apply what you have learned to complete the rest of the giraffe. If you get stuck, you can take a look at the complete giraffe in the scene `giraffe_v11.ma` in the `chapter7\scenes` directory on the DVD.

Full Body Inverse Kinematics

Full Body IK (FBIK) is used for Full Body IK skeletons. This system creates IK Handles that control an entire biped or quadruped skeleton rather than using multiple IK chains on individual limbs. It is a very powerful system capable of producing smooth animations quickly. In addition, the time it takes to set up a Full Body IK skeleton is a fraction of the time of creating your own rig.

Full Body IK does come with drawbacks, though, that keep it from becoming a staple in the industry:

◆ The skeleton has to be created in a certain way, which is a deal breaker in an industry where customization is key.

◆ Another downfall is fine-tuning your animation. It is very difficult to modify the animation curves in this system. Doing so usually results in the altered joint losing its synchronization with the rest of the skeleton. Autodesk's Motionbuilder is better suited for animating Full Body IK rigs.

Maya has two examples of full rigged FBIK skeletons available in the Visor. Open the Visor window (Window ➢ General Editors ➢ Visor), and switch to the FBIK Examples tab. To load an example into a scene, right-click the icon and choose to import the example.

Skinning Geometry

Skinning geometry is the process in which geometry is bound to joints so that as the joints are rotated or translated, the geometry is deformed. The terms *skinning* and *binding* are interchangeable. There are three types of skinning: smooth binding, interactive skin binding (an extension of smooth binding), and rigid binding. Although rigid binding is available as an option, it is rarely used, so this section focuses on smooth binding.

Polygon and NURBS geometry can be bound to skeletons; however, polygon geometry often produces more predictable results. In this section, you will continue with the giraffe, which is polygon geometry.

When geometry is smooth bound to a skeleton, each vertex of the geometry receives a certain amount of influence from the joints in the skeleton. The amount of weight value of the joints determines the amount of influence each vertex receives from a joint. By default the values are normalized, ranging from 0 to 1, where 0 is no influence and 1 is full (or 100 percent) influence. Weight values can be normalized in two different ways, Post (the default method) or Interactive. Post weights are only calculated when the bound mesh is deformed, preventing previously weighted vertices from being changed. Interactive normalization sets the weight value exactly as you enter it, forcing the weights to always total 1.0. When you bind geometry to a skeleton, the vertex weights are set automatically based on the options you specify in the Smooth Bind command. In most situations, the weights of the geometry require further editing after executing the Smooth Bind command.

When binding geometry to the skeleton, make sure the rotations of the joints in the skeleton are all at 0. This means that if an IK Handle has been added to the skeleton, you should select and disable the handle (choose Skeleton ➢ Disable Selected IK Handles) and then set the joint rotation channels to 0. Bind the skin to the joints and reenable the IK Handle (choose Skeleton ➢ Enable Selected IK Handles).

The pose the skeleton is in when you bind the geometry is known as the *bind pose*. If you need at some point to detach and reattach the geometry to edit the geometry, you will need to be able to easily return to the bind pose. Do this by selecting the skeleton's root joint and choosing Skin ➢ Go To Bind Pose.

Editing the skin weights is usually accomplished through several tools:

Interactive Skin Binding tool   First, this tool enables you to rapidly alter the area of influence by each joint.

Paint Skin Weights   Next, you can refine your weights further with this tool. It employs the Artisan brush interface to interactively set weights.

Component Editor   You can also edit the weight values directly for selected vertices using the Component Editor. The Component Editor gives you precise control over each vertex and the exact amount of weight it receives.

Editing skin weights can be a difficult and occasionally frustrating process. In the following exercise, you'll learn a few tips that can help make the process a little easier and faster.

Interactive/Smooth Binding

Maya automatically assigns skin weights to each vertex of the geometry as it is bound to the joints. There are options for assigning these weights based on the vertices' proximity to the joints and the number of joints that can influence any particular vertex. Even so, after binding, you'll need to edit the weights using the Paint Skin Weights tool. If the geometry is very dense, meaning it has a lot of vertices, this process can take a while.

Interactive skin binding uses an adjustable volume to define smooth skin weights. The volumes can be moved and shaped to fit your character's geometry, all the while giving you instant feedback on how the vertices are being influenced.

Weighting the Giraffe

There isn't only one tool used in weighting a character. Numerous tools and techniques are applied to achieve maximum performance. In this exercise, you will weight the giraffe with an interactive skin bind:

1. Open the giraffe_v11.ma scene from the chapter7\scenes directory on the DVD. The scene has a complete version of the giraffe's rig.

2. Select root_jnt and the giraffe's mesh.

3. Choose Skin ➢ Bind Skin ➢ Interactive Skin Bind Options.

    Notice that you can choose to bind the entire joint hierarchy or just selected joints. In this example, you'll bind the entire hierarchy.

BROKEN-JOINT SKELETONS

Keep in mind that you also have the option of binding only selected joints. In some circumstances, this can be quite useful. For example, if you set up what is known as a *broken-joint* skeleton, which uses additional bones outside the main skeleton hierarchy as deformers, these additional joints are usually constrained to the main hierarchy using parent constraints. By using parent constraints, the joints "float" outside the main hierarchy, giving them a level of freedom of movement to create special deformation effects. (Sometimes floating joints are used for facial animation instead of or in addition to blendshape deformers.) When skinning a broken rig to the skeleton, select the floating joints along with the joints in the main hierarchy when the smooth bind operation is performed.

The following are the relevant settings:

Bind method The bind method determines how joints influence vertices, by either following the skeleton's hierarchy or simply using whichever joint is the closest. The hierarchy of the giraffe is complete and calls for every bone to be weighted; however, for the tips, use Closest In Hierarchy.

Include method The include method dictates which vertices are included in the initial volumes. Your options are Closest Volume and Minimum Weight. Choosing Minimum Weight opens an additional option to set the length of the volume. By default this is .25, causing each volume to be 25 percent longer than the bone to which it is attached. Most characters will have a different area of influence based on its location. For instance, the giraffe's knee needs to have a smaller falloff compared to the torso. Choose Closest Volume.

There are two types of volumes you can use, a cylinder or a capsule:

◆ A cylinder will deliver a hard edge.

◆ The capsule is rounded at its ends, providing a smoother falloff.

Keep the capsule turned on.

Skinning method The skinning method has the greatest impact on your bind. You can use Classic Linear, Dual Quaternion, or a blend of both.

◆ Dual Quaternion provides the most suitable deformations for realistic characters. It preserves the volume of a mesh when a joint is twisted or rotated.

◆ Classic Linear does not preserve volume and produces a visible shrinking of the geometry.

Take a look at Figure 7.34 to see the differences between the two.

The last two settings relate to how many influences a single vertex can have. It is important to remember that joints are not the only nodes that can be bound to geometry. Other geometry can also be used and is therefore considered an influence as well. Most weighted objects do not require more than four influences per vertex, which is Maya's default. In addition, a lot of game engines have a hard limit of four influences on a single vertex. After binding, you can keep the influences locked to four by selecting Maintain Max Influences.

This is particularly useful when weighting geometry for an environment outside of Maya, such as a game engine. Keep the default settings for the giraffe (see Figure 7.35).

4. Choose Bind Skin.

Keep in mind that all the weighting can be altered after the bind has been applied. These settings merely give you a place to start and typically require a lot of fine tuning. Furthermore, you can change these settings through the skinCluster node that is attached to the bound geometry (see Figure 7.36).

FIGURE 7.34
The Classic Linear skinning method is applied to the joints on the left and Dual Quaternion on the right.

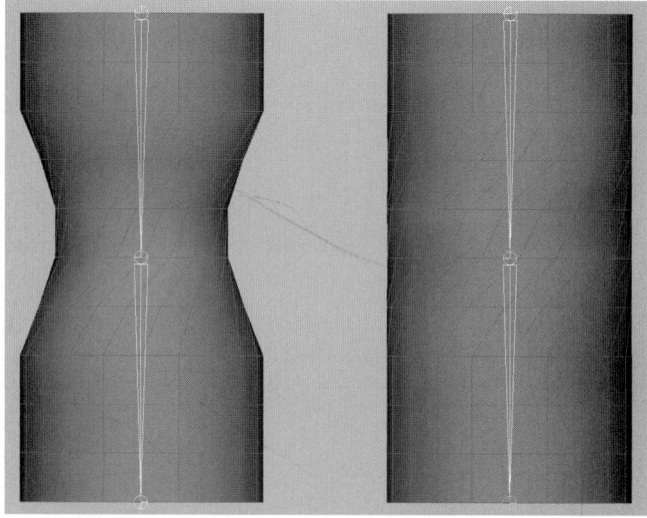

FIGURE 7.35
Bind the giraffe geometry to its skeleton.

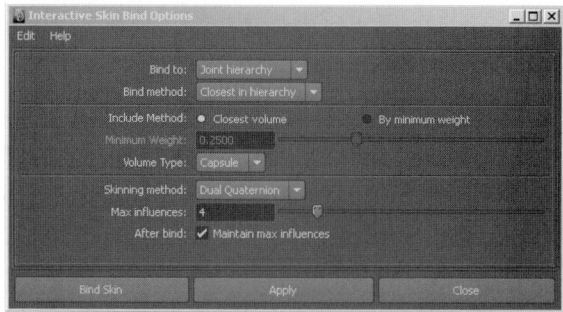

FIGURE 7.36
The skinCluster node holds all the settings from the initial binding options.

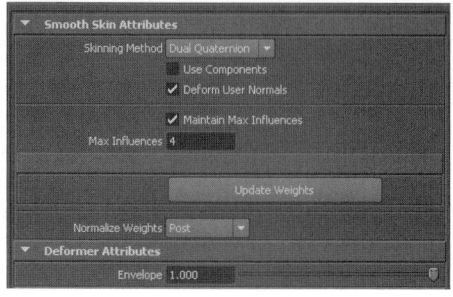

The giraffe's initial bind is established; now it's time to finetune its weighting. Traditionally, modifying weighted geometry has been like feeling your way around in the dark. Maya's interactive skin tool not only sheds light on each and every vertex but does so with precision and ease of use. The Interactive Skin Bind tool allows you to quickly massage the weights to an acceptable level.

5. Start with the giraffe's front legs to get used to the controls. Select L_upperarm_jnt. If it isn't active already, choose Skin ➢ Edit Smooth Skin ➢ Interactive Skin Bind Tool. By default two volumes are displayed. The only interactive one is the volume on the selected joint. The second volume is a reflection that is attached to r_upperarm_jnt. The reflection is displayed based on the reflection tool settings and operates the same way as it does with the transformation tools (see Figure 7.37).

FIGURE 7.37
The interactive volumes are reflected by default.

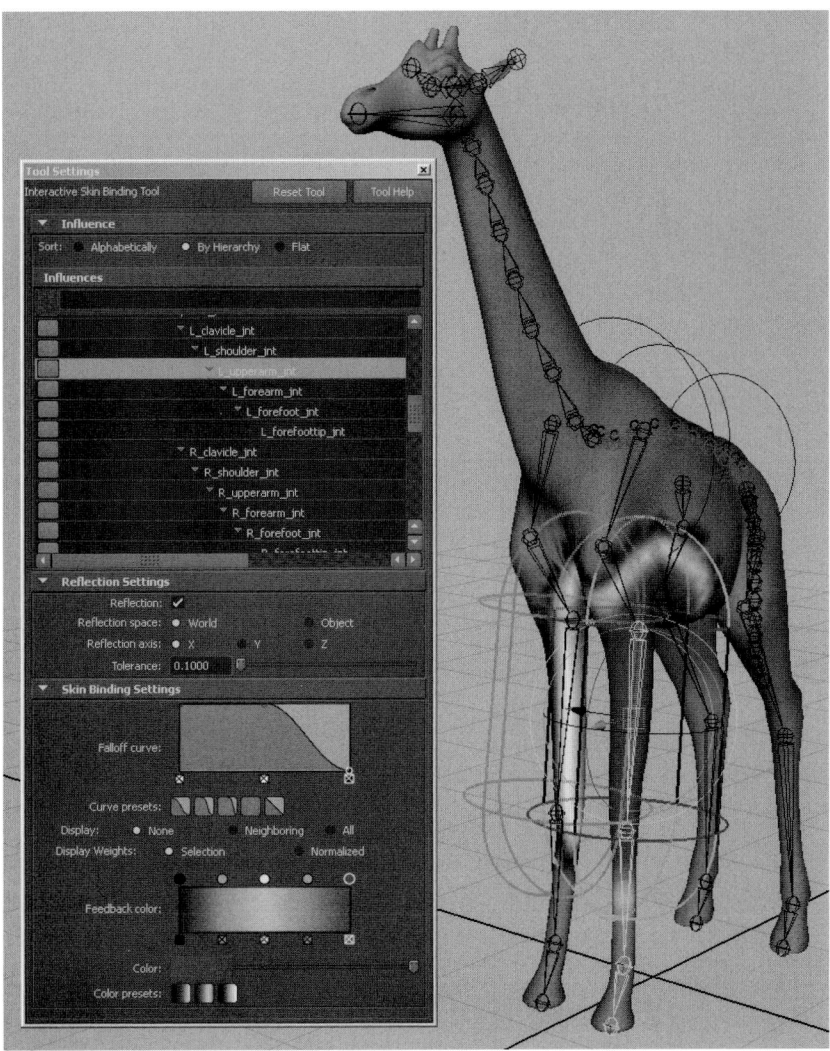

Each volume can be translated, rotated, and shaped. A heat-style color graph is used to illustrate the joint's influence, with red being the highest amount of influence and blue being the least. A few color presets are provided along with the ability to change the color graph any way you would like.

The capsule's manipulator is also color coded. Red, green, and blue are used to represent the three axes, respectively. Depending on which part of the manipulator you grab, the shape of the capsule is altered. For the most part, each axis scales the selected ring uniformly.

6. Use the LMB and grab the top, red, horizontal ring.

7. Resize it to decrease the amount of influence.

8. Repeat this operation for the lower ring.

9. In addition to changing the capsule's shape, you can also use the traditional Move And Rotate manipulator (scale is based on the volume) to fit the capsule better to the geometry. The manipulator is located in the center of the capsule. Looking at the front of the giraffe, translate and rotate the capsule for a better fit. Do the same for its profile. Figure 7.38 shows the adjusted capsule.

FIGURE 7.38
Translate and rotate the capsule to encompass the leg geometry.

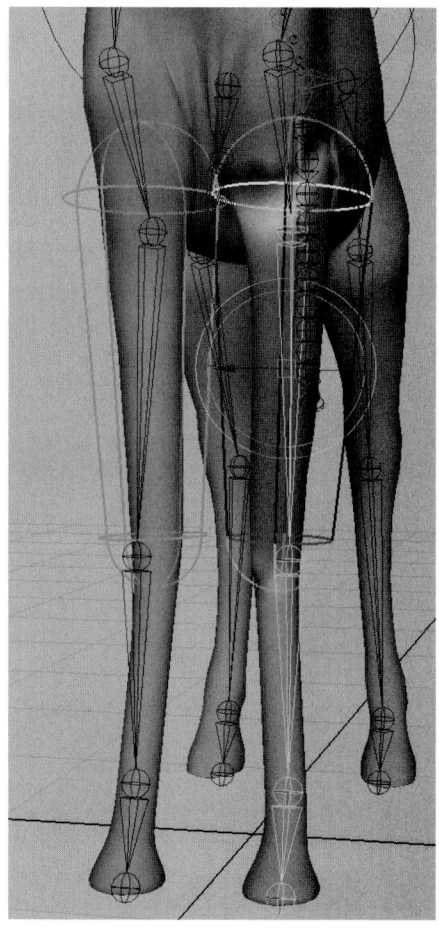

10. Visible interactivity has been limited so far because the giraffe is in its original bind pose position. Translate the leg 1.0 in the Z and 0.5 in the Y.

11. Select l_upperarm_jnt. Notice that the geometry in the middle of the bone appears to be sagging (Figure 7.39). This is an indication that the geometry is not weighted to 1 at those particular vertices. However, the heat map shows full influence. Use the up arrow to go to the preceding joint, L_shoulder_jnt.

FIGURE 7.39
The geometry in the middle of the bone is sagging even though the volume shows the hottest influence.

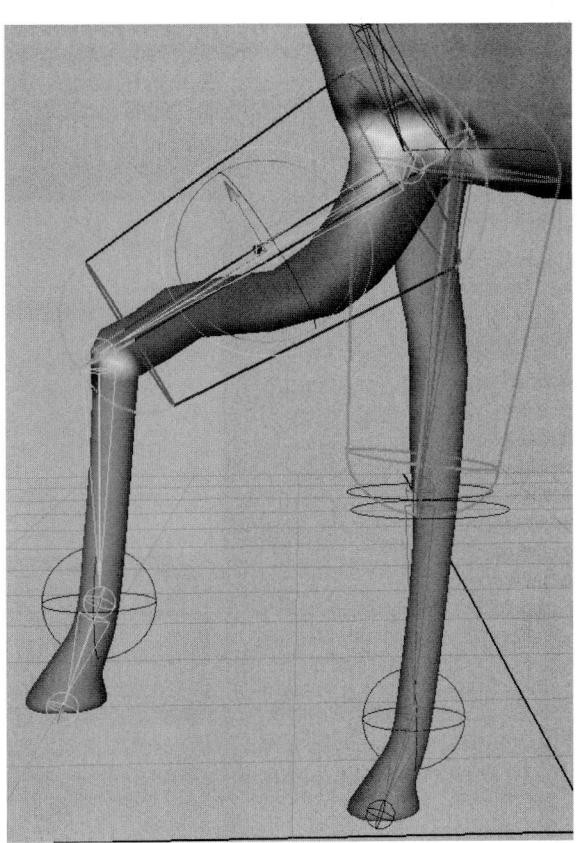

12. L_shoulder_jnt overlaps the L_upperarm_jnt, obviously causing the problem. Use the down arrow to return to L_shoulder_jnt.

    Maya is displaying the non-normalized weight of the joint; therefore, the color displayed is red. What you are actually seeing is the combined weight value of both joints.

13. In the tool settings for Interactive Skin Bind, find Display Weights. It is located above the color graph. Change it to Normalized. You can now see the true weight value of the joint.

14. Use the up arrow to go back to L_shoulder_jnt.

15. Modify the volume to fit its bone better. You can hold Shift while moving the red rings to uniformly scale the entire volume. If you hold Shift while adjusting the green or blue rings, the effects are local to that ring. Figure 7.40 shows the results of the new volume shape.

16. Save the scene as `giraffe_v12.ma`.

To see a version of the scene, open the `giraffe_v12.ma` scene from the `chapter7\scenes` directory on the DVD.

FIGURE 7.40
Modifying the L_shoulder_jnt's volume fixes the upper arm.

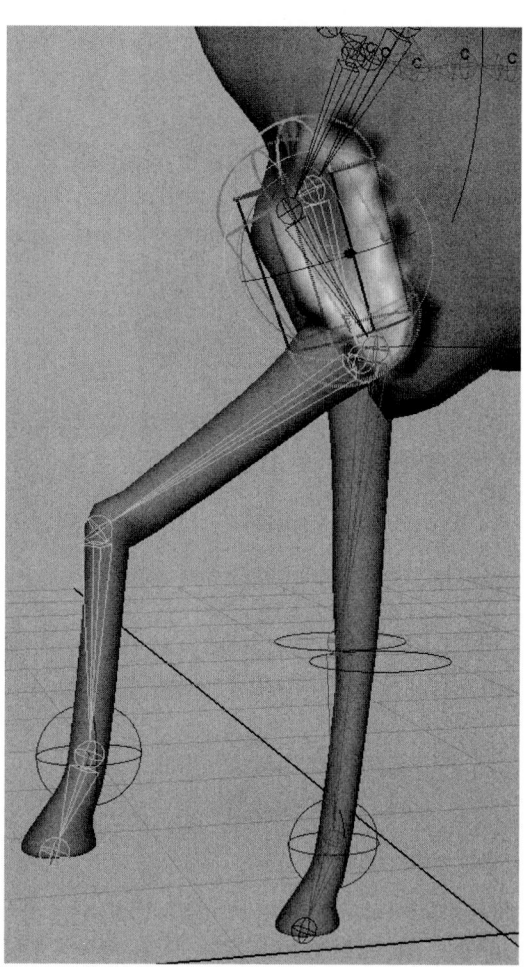

Painting Skin Weights

The Interactive Skin Bind tool takes you really far into the weighting process. However, the weights still need work. To make the skin move properly, you need to edit the weight values of the vertices; this can be done with the Paint Weights tool. To maximize the benefits of painting weights, your geometry should have good UVs. These are explained in Chapter 11. This exercise demonstrates techniques for painting weights on various parts of the giraffe:

1. Continue with the scene from the previous section, or open the giraffe_v12.ma scene from the chapter7\scenes directory on the DVD.

2. Move the giraffe leg up again to interactively see the effects of painting weights.

3. Translate the leg 1.0 in the Z and 0.5 in the Y.2.

4. In the viewport, switch to smooth-shaded mode (hot key = **6**).

5. Select the giraffe geometry, and choose Skin ➤ Edit Smooth Skin ➤ Paint Skin Weights Tool. Make sure the Tool Options window is open.

   The geometry turns black except for the area around the joint listed in the Influence section of the Paint Skin Weights Tool window. The geometry is color coded.

   ◆ White indicates a joint weight value of 1 (100 percent).

   ◆ Black indicates a joint weight value of 0.

   ◆ Shades of gray indicate values between 0 and 1 (see Figure 7.41).

   You can also switch to use the same gradient color ramp used in the Interactive Skin Bind tool.

FIGURE 7.41
The Paint Skin Weights tool color codes the geometry based on the amount of weight influence each joint has for each vertex of the skinned geometry.

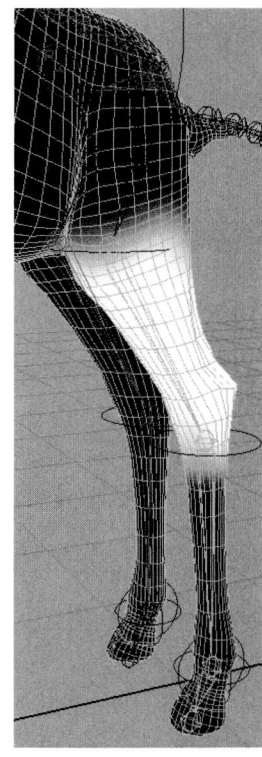

The Paint Skin Weights tool uses the Artisan brush interface. As you paint on the model, the operation selected in the Paint Weights section determines how the brush edits the weights. You can replace, add, smooth, or scale weights in the areas you paint on the model. The easiest way to approach weight painting is to stick to only the Add and Smooth operations.

Each vertex on the model receives up to a value of 1 from all the joints on the model. The total weight values must equal 1, so if a selected vertex receives a value of 0.8 from a particular joint, the remaining weight value (0.2) must come from another joint in the chain. Usually this remaining weight value comes from a joint close by the vertex as determined by Maya. This is where things can get tricky. If you paint on a vertex using the Replace operation with a value of 0.5 for a particular joint, the remaining 0.5 weight value is distributed among the other joints in the chain, which can lead to some strange and unpredictable results. If instead you use the Add operation with very low values, you can carefully increase a joint's influence over a vertex without worrying about Maya assigning the remaining weight values to other joints in the chain.

6. The area you want to paint is the armpit of the front left leg. To expedite the process, force the Paint Weights tool to only display the joints you want to paint influence for. To do this, hold Ctrl and pick each joint you want to work with in the Influences section of the Paint Weights tool. You can also use Shift to select the first and last joints to highlight a group.

7. With your joints selected, click the tack icon in the upper-right corner of the Influences section (see Figure 7.42).

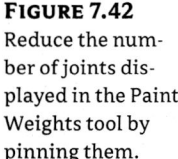

FIGURE 7.42
Reduce the number of joints displayed in the Paint Weights tool by pinning them.

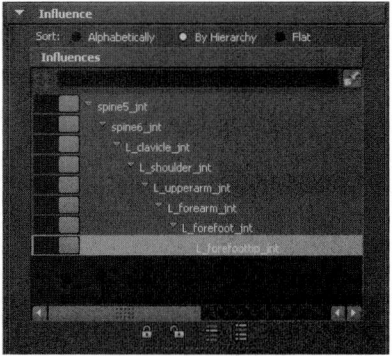

8. Choose L_upperarm_jnt from the influences.

9. Set Paint Operation to Replace and Value to 0.0.

10. Paint the area being pulled by the arm that belongs to the torso. To resize your brush, use the **b** key. Use Figure 7.43 for reference.

11. Once you have separated the torso skin from arm skin, use the Smooth operation to clean the weights.

The giraffe has a bone jutting out in this location. A lot of the weights are still being used by the torso.

FIGURE 7.43
Paint a weight of 0 to remove the influence of the arm.

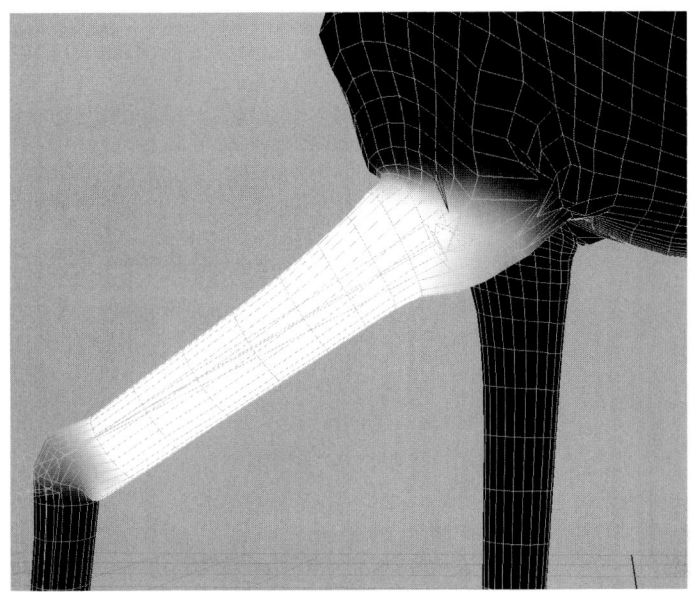

12. Set the paint value to 0.1.

13. Use the Add operation to move the weights more onto the upper arm.

14. When finished, go back over it with the Smooth operation again. Figure 7.44 shows the progress so far.

FIGURE 7.44
The skin weighting has been smoothed.

There are still a few vertices that are being unruly.

15. Change Paint Tool Mode to Select, and choose two or three of the worst vertices. You can also choose Paint Select.

Toward the top of the Paint Skin Weights window is a Tools section. The middle icon is the Weight Hammer tool. This tool assigns an average of the weights around the selected vertices. Figure 7.45 shows the same area from Figure 7.44 after the Weight Hammer tool was applied.

FIGURE 7.45
The skin weights have been cleaned up with the Weight Hammer tool.

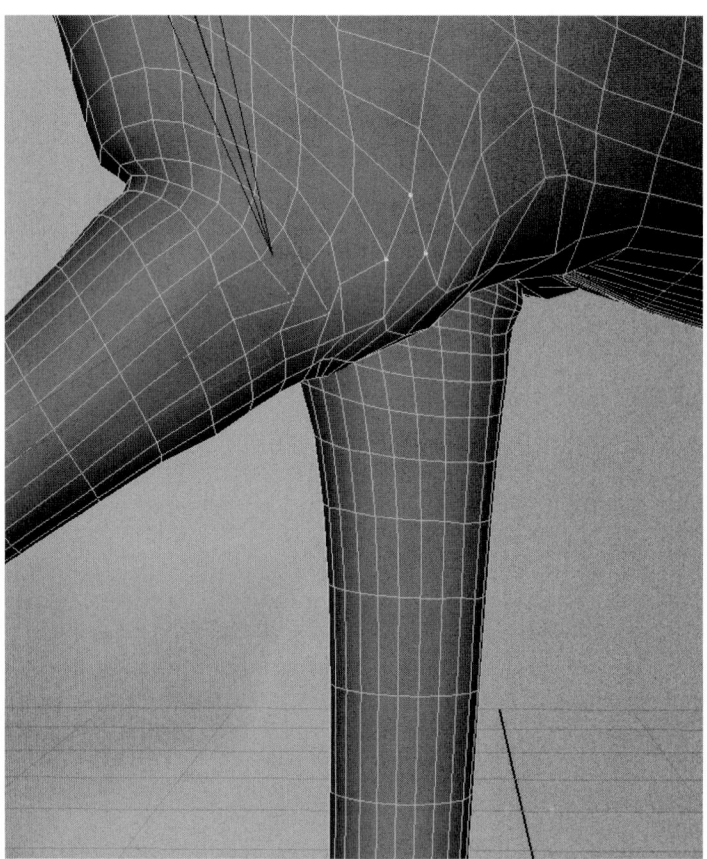

16. You can continue to paint the skin weights with the joints posed. This is an excellent way to get visual feedback as you edit the weights.

17. Save the scene as **giraffe_v13.ma**.

To see a version of the scene to this point, open the giraffe_v13.ma scene from the chapter7\ scenes directory on the DVD.

Editing Skin Weights in the Component Editor

In some cases, you may want to edit the skin weights by entering a precise numeric value. To do this, follow these steps:

1. Switch to component mode, and select the vertices you need to edit directly.

2. Choose Window ➤ General Editors ➤ Component Editor.

3. On the Smooth Skins tab, you'll see a spreadsheet that lists each joint's influence for each of the selected vertices (Figure 7.46). You can change these values by directly entering numbers into the spreadsheet.

FIGURE 7.46
You can use the Component Editor to enter numeric weight values for the joints.

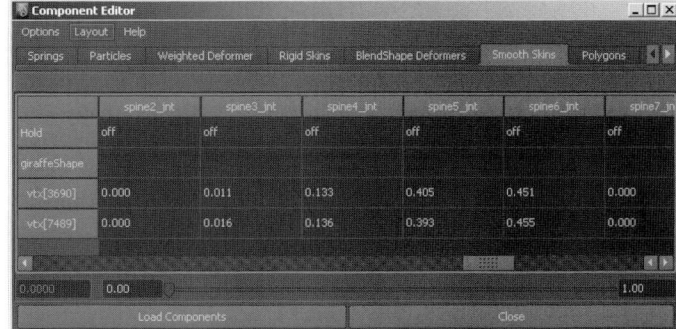

Remember that each vertex must have a total weight value of 1, so if you set a value lower than 1, the remaining value will be assigned to a different joint. You can turn on the Hold option to lock a vertex's weight value so Maya will not change the value automatically.

Copying Skin Weights

You can copy the weights from the low-resolution model to the high-resolution model. It does not matter that the vertices do not perfectly match because the overall weighting can easily be transferred. This reduces the difficulty of editing the initial weights on the high-resolution model.

Copying weights is extremely useful when you have a lot of characters to weight. Once you are happy with one character, you can copy its weights onto another character, even if the dimensions are not the same. The Copy Weights tool copies weighting information based on proximity. As long as the vertices are close to one another, the weights are transferred regardless of vertex density or geometry shape. It is even possible to move the bones of the weighted objects to match the new object more closely. The source does not matter. Of course, the closer the two are in shape and size, the better the end results.

COPYING SKIN WEIGHTS

We have worked on several projects that require numerous characters to be weighted. The characters' geometries are always different, and most of the time so are their skeletons. However, when copying skin weights none of that matters. You can copy weights from an adult-sized character to a child-sized character with decent precision. Here is what to do:

1. After completing the weights on one character, import the character into another scene with an existing bound character. The weights on this character have not been touched.

2. Take the character with good weights and snap or move its joints to match the character with no weighting.

3. If the skinned character's geometry still doesn't match up well, go into the Hypergraph: Connections and find its original shape node. This node is connected to the skinCluster node and is set to the Intermediate object in its Attribute Editor.

4. Turning off the Intermediate object reveals the geometry's original bind pose. Alter the geometry of this node to better match the character you want to copy weights to.

5. Once finished, change the original shape node back to Intermediate. All of the changes you made are transferred to the bound geometry.

6. Copy the weights over.

It never copies perfectly, but it comes real close and is significantly better than starting from scratch.

Mirroring Skin Weights

You can copy weight values from one side of a symmetrical character to another using the Mirror Skin Weights command. This greatly reduces the amount of time spent painting weights and ensures consistency in weighting for both sides of a character. To do this, select the mesh and choose Skin ➤ Edit Smooth Skin ➤ Mirror Skin Weights ➤ Options. In the options, you can choose which axis the weights are mirrored across.

The Maya Muscle System

Maya Muscle tools deform the surface of geometry much like other types of deformers. They simulate the behavior of actual muscles and can be driven by the rotation of joints or expressions. Muscles are similar to Maya's influence objects, but they offer better control for deforming the skinned geometry surface. Much of the purpose and functionality of influence objects are replaced by Maya Muscle, so this edition of *Mastering Maya* does not discuss influence objects.

The Maya Muscle deformer is actually a surface that can be manipulated while connected to the deformed geometry. The muscle objects can create complex deformation by allowing for multiple end shapes per muscle.

Muscle objects can slide beneath the deformed geometry to create special effects, and muscles also have properties that allow movement such as jiggle, force, and collision.

Understanding the Maya Muscle System

The Maya Muscle system is a collection of deformation tools that can work independently or in concert to deform geometry so it looks like muscles are bulging and stretching beneath skin. The primary system has three main deformer types: capsules, bones, and muscles.

Capsules   Capsules are very simple skin deformers used as replacements for Maya's joints. It is necessary to use capsules because standard Maya joints cannot work directly with the muscle deformer. Capsules are shaped like a simple pill. The basic capsule shape cannot be changed. However, it can be scaled to simulate the basic shape of muscles.

Bones   Bones are skin deformers that have been converted from regular polygon geometry. Because of this, bones can be almost any shape you need. The term *bones* in this sense should not be confused with Maya's standard bones, which are the shapes that connect joints. The reason the Maya Muscle system uses the term *bones* is because these deformers are useful for simulating the movement of specially shaped bones—such as the scapula—beneath skin.

Muscles   Muscles are skin deformers created from NURBS surfaces. The muscle deformers are designed to replicate the behavior of real-life muscles. To achieve this, they have two connection points at either end, which are attached to the character's rig. So, for example, when the character moves/bends his arm, the connection points move closer together, creating a bulging/squashing effect. When the character extends his arm, the connection points move farther apart, creating a stretching effect. The transition between squashing and stretching is automatically eased in and out, so the deformer's movements are very smooth.

Any of these muscle deformers can be bound to the character's skin geometry using one of the various types of weighting available. Weighting muscle deformers to geometry is similar to using smooth binding to connect geometry to Maya joints. The weighting types include Sticky, Sliding, Displacement, Force, Jiggle, Relax, and Smooth. The following sections demonstrate using muscle deformers with Sticky weighting, which is very similar to smooth binding, discussed earlier in the chapter.

To use a muscle system, you must first create the muscle objects (capsule, bone, or muscle), apply the muscle deformer to the character's skin, connect the specific muscle objects (capsule, bone, or muscle) to the deformer, and then use a weighting type to bind it to determine how the deformer affects the character's skin using one of the available weighting types.

It is important to understand that when you use the Maya Muscle system, the character's skin geometry must be bound to objects that have the cMuscleObject shape node. In other words, you must either replace or convert any existing joints with capsules or Maya Muscle bones. You can also transfer any existing skin weights created for Maya joints to the muscle system.

In the following exercises, you'll add the Maya Muscle system to the giraffe.

Using Capsules

Capsules are very similar to Maya joints except their shape can be used to influence the deformation of the character's skin geometry. It's also necessary to replace existing joints with capsules or polygon bones to use the Maya Muscle deformer.

This scene picks up where the painting weights exercise left off. The geometry is smooth bound to the rig, and the weights for the joints have been cleaned up.

The Maya Muscle plug-in may not be loaded. If you do not see the Muscle menu in the Animation menu set, then you'll need to load the plug-in using the Plug-in Manager.

1. Open the `giraffe_v13.ma` scene from the `chapter7\scenes` directory on the DVD.

2. Choose Window ➢ Settings/Preferences ➢ Plug-in Manager.

3. In the Plug-in Manager window, select the Loaded and Auto Load options next to `MayaMuscle.mll` (see Figure 7.47).

FIGURE 7.47
Load the Maya Muscle plug-in using the Plug-in Manager.

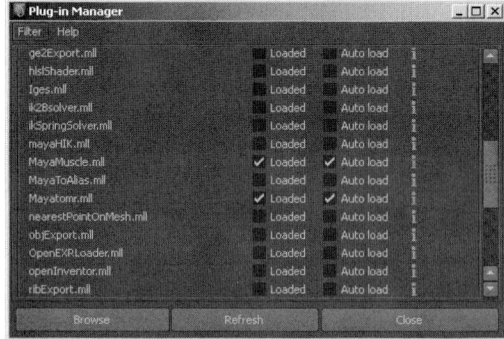

Once the plug-in is loaded, you should see the Muscle menu in the Animation menu set (the Muscle menu actually appears in all the menu sets; for the moment, though, you should be using the Animation menu set).

4. Choose Edit ➢ Select All By Type ➢ Joints.

5. Go through the selection, and deselect all the tip joints.

6. With only the joints selected, choose Muscle ➢ Muscle/Bones ➢ Convert Surface To Muscle/Bone. The joints automatically convert to capsules, and polygon geometry automatically converts to polygon bones. In this case, you should not have any polygon geometry selected.

It is important to make sure that the joints are oriented properly. We discussed this earlier in the chapter in the "Orienting Joints" section. In the example scene, the joints have been oriented so the x-axis points along the length of the bone toward the child joint.

7. When you execute the conversion command, you'll be asked to specify which axis points down the length of the joints. This is used to orient the capsules. Since the joint rig is set up to use the x-axis, choose X-Axis from the pop-up window (see Figure 7.48).

8. The capsules on the right side of the skeleton are flipped. This is a result of mirroring the skeleton. The joints have the proper orientation, but the capsules do not. To change this, select each capsule of the legs, and change its capsule axis in the Channel Box to Neg X-Axis.

FIGURE 7.48
Maya asks you to specify the axis that points down the length of the joint.

You can edit the attributes of the capsule in the SHAPES section of the capsule's Channel Box. At the bottom of the Channel Box, you can determine the display quality of the capsule. The NSegs and NSides settings change the number of divisions in the capsule, but these settings do not affect how the capsule deforms the skin. NSegs sets the number of radial segments in the capsule; NSides sets the number of divisions around the radius of the capsule.

9. Spend a few minutes editing the size of capsules. Use a small radius size for the capsules.

10. Save the scene as `giraffeMuscles_v01.ma`.

To see a version of the scene, open `giraffeMuscles_v01.ma` from the `chapter7\scenes` directory on the DVD.

Converting joints to capsules is the easiest way to prepare an existing rig for use with Maya Muscle. The Convert Surface To Muscle/Bone command works only on selected joints and surfaces. You can also create individual capsules using the Muscle/Bones ➤ Make Capsule and Muscle/Bones ➤ Make Capsule With End Locator commands. You can add a capsule to a rig by parenting the capsule or its end locators to parts of the rig.

Creating a Muscle Using Muscle Builder

The Muscle Builder interface is designed to create muscle deformers easily and quickly. In this section, you'll create several generic muscles for the left hind leg using the Muscle Builder window.

This interface allows you to create and edit simple muscle shapes for the skeleton. To make the muscle, you'll first specify the Attach objects. These are the parts of the skeleton where each end of the muscle will be attached. Once you create the muscle, you can edit its shape using the controls in the Muscle Builder interface:

1. Continue with the scene from the previous section, or open the `giraffeMuscles_v01.ma` scene from the `chapter7\scenes` directory on the DVD.

2. Choose Muscle ➤ Simple Muscles ➤ Muscle Builder to open the Muscle Builder interface.

3. Select the L_upperleg_jnt.

4. In the Muscle Builder window, click the button labeled <<< to the right of the Attach Obj 1 field. This loads the L_ upperleg _jnt capsule into this field.

5. Select the L_lowerleg_jnt capsule, and load it into the Attach Obj 2 field (see Figure 7.49).

FIGURE 7.49
Specify the two Attach objects in the Muscle Builder window.

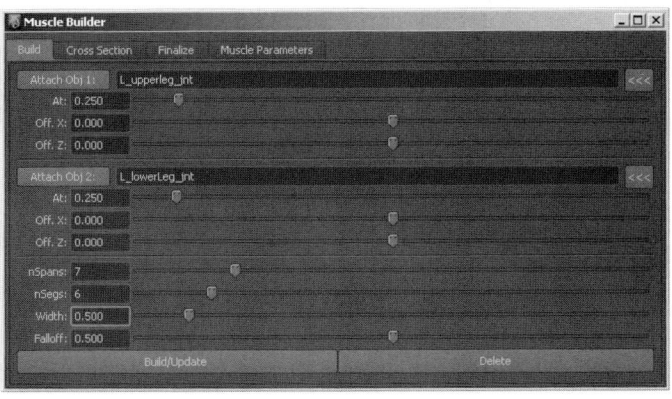

6. Click the Build/Update button to create the muscle.

The nSpans, nSegs, Width, and Falloff sliders determine the shape of the muscle's surface. NSpans and nSegs determine the number of spans and segments that the NURBS muscle surface will use. Falloff determines how the ends of the muscle taper at each end; a lower setting creates less of a taper. Width determines the overall width of the muscle shape. As long as the AttachObj fields are still filled out, you can interactively adjust the muscle.

7. Use the settings from Figure 7.49 to size the muscle to the leg.

If you can't achieve the position you are after with the sliders, you can click the AttachObj1 or AttachObj2 button. This selects the appropriate node for manual positioning using the normal transform tools. The Muscle object appears in the perspective view attached to the skeleton, as shown in Figure 7.50. You'll see that a new NURBS surface named cMuscle-Builder_surf1 has been created along with two new cameras named MuscleBuilderCamera and MuscleBuilderCameraSide. The cameras are used in the Muscle Builder interface.

8. Save the scene as `giraffeMuscles_v02.ma`.

To see a version of the scene, open the `giraffeMuscles_v02.ma` scene from the `chapter7\` `scenes` directory on the DVD.

FIGURE 7.50
The muscle surface appears attached to the skeleton.

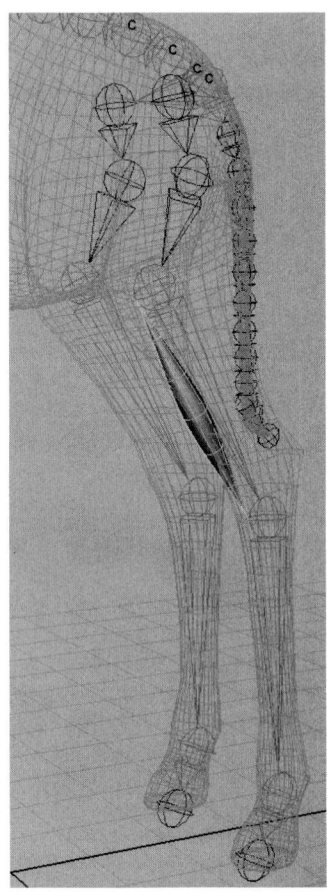

To properly place the muscles, you should check an anatomy reference. Some experimentation is required to place the muscle and achieve realistic motion and deformation. The settings applied to the muscle may look exaggerated in Maya, but this may be necessary to create a realistic deformation.

1. Switch to the Cross Section tab in the Muscle Builder. In this section of the interface, the curves that control the shape of the muscle surface are listed on the left. (If you have loaded the saved scene or reloaded your own, it's necessary to choose Update from the Build section of the Muscle Builder. You must enter the same information from Figure 7.49 to keep the muscle from changing.) Two camera views allow you to select the curves and move them to shape the overall muscle.

2. To edit the position of one of the circles, select one or more of the curves listed on the left and then use the Move tool to reposition the curve. Movements of each control circle are limited to the x- and y-axes.

   You can move the circles in the perspective view as well as in the cross-section view of the Muscle Builder interface (see Figure 7.51).

FIGURE 7.51
You can use the cross-section views to edit the shape of the muscle.

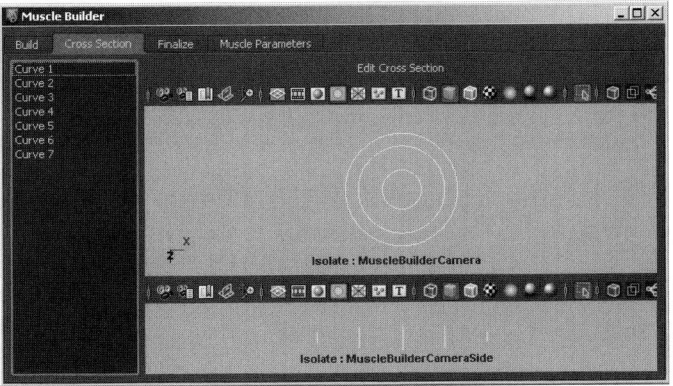

At this point, you may also find that the initial placement needs adjusting. You can go back and forth between the Cross Section tab and Build tab to finalize the muscle's position.

MUSCLE SHAPE

Even though you have complete control over the shape of the muscle, it is best to keep it close to its original shape. Altering the muscle too much can result in awkward deformations. Muscles deform the skin they're attached to, based on the position of their control vertices, making muscle shape very important. However, you can paint influence on the skin to minimize the shape's impact.

When you have finished editing the basic shape of the muscle, you are ready to convert it to a muscle deformer. This action is performed on the Finalize tab of the Muscle Builder window.

3. Leave Num Controls set to 3, and set Type to Cube (you can choose Curve or Null as well—whichever you prefer).

   If you need to mirror the muscle to the opposite side of the body, you can choose a mirror axis from the Create Mirror Muscle options. You can use the Search and Replace fields to replace prefixes such as L (for left) with R (for right) on the mirrored objects.

4. Click the Convert To Muscle button to create the deformer.

5. In the pop-up box, you will be warned that further changes cannot be made to the muscle using the interface controls. You'll also be prompted to name the muscle. Name it **L_legbicep** (see Figure 7.52).

FIGURE 7.52
You are prompted to name the muscle when you click the Convert To Muscle button.

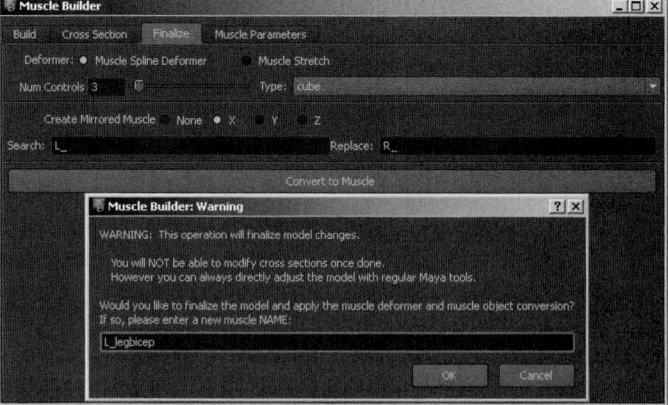

CHANGING MUSCLES

You can still change the shape of a muscle after you finalize it by altering the muscle surface's controls vertices. All the normal components used with NURBS, such as hulls and CVs, can be modified.

When you finalize the muscle, the original surface is grouped with its controls. Control cubes appear at either end of the muscle and in the center. These can be used to fix position and rotation problems.

6. Add several more generic muscle shapes to fill in the leg and gluteus maximus areas. Figure 7.53 shows the addition of six more muscles.

7. Save the scene as `giraffeMuscles_v03.ma`.

To see a version of the scene to this point, open the `giraffeMuscles_v03.ma` scene from the `chapter7\scenes` directory on the DVD.

FIGURE 7.53
Add six more muscles to the hind end of the giraffe.

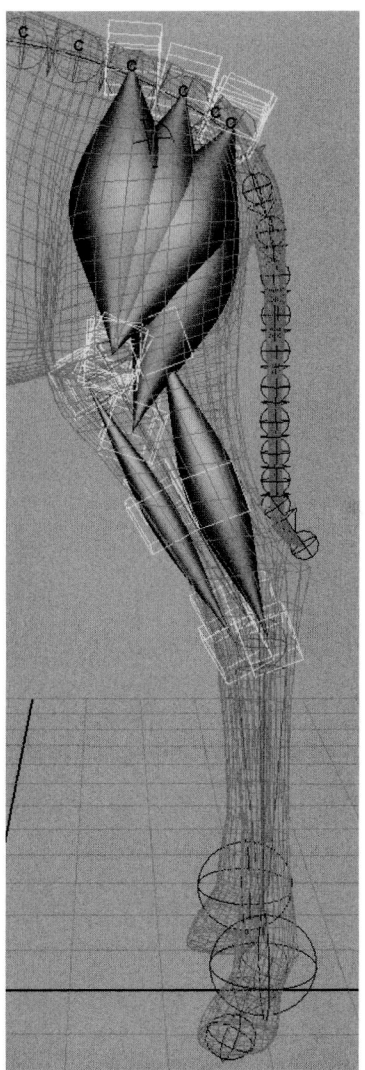

Editing Muscle Parameters

Muscle parameters determine how the muscle behaves as the joints are animated. If you select the L_HindLeg_CTRL and move it around, you'll see that the muscles stretch and squash.

Many of the settings in the Muscle Parameters section can be changed in the Channel Box or Attribute Editor. To refine how the muscle reacts to motion, you need to have the Muscle Builder window open.

1. Continue with the scene from the previous section, or open the `giraffeMuscles_v03.ma` scene from the `chapter7\scenes` folder on the DVD. If it is not open already, choose Muscle ➤ Simple Muscles ➤ Muscle Builder to open the Muscle Builder interface.

2. In the Muscle Parameters Settings section, set Draw to Muscle. If this is set to Off, you'll see the deformer, but changes made to the Squash and Stretch settings will not be displayed.

   The first step toward editing the muscle's behavior is to establish its default stretch and squash shapes based on the movement of the leg.

   The giraffe's leg is positioned in the animal's default stance and default pose in Maya. You can use this pose to establish the default shape of the bicep muscle. Since the giraffe is standing, you would assume that the muscle is engaged and slightly flexed.

3. In the Spline Length Settings section, click the Set Current As Default button.

4. In the perspective view, select L_HindLeg_CTRL, and translate it to 2.0 in the Y and -3.2 in the Z. This stretches the L_bicep muscle to its extreme pose.

5. Click the Set Current as Stretch button.

6. Set the L_HindLeg_CTRL to 2.0 in the Translate Y and 4.0 in the Translate Z to push the leg toward the chest.

7. Click the Set Current As Squash button.

8. Proceed with the rest of the leg muscles. You can move the leg forward and set all the squash positions for those muscles that would be flexed. You do not have to do one muscle at a time. Muscle Builder affects whichever muscle is selected. Figure 7.54 shows the combination of squashed and stretched muscles.

   The settings in the Stretch Volume Presets section determine how the shape muscle deformer transitions between extreme poses. To set this properly, animate the leg so you can adjust the settings and see the results as the leg moves.

9. Set the Time slider to 100 frames.

10. Select the L_HindLeg_CTRL, and create a short animation where the locator moves back and forth, causing the leg to bend and straighten. Use the same values from steps 4 and 6 as your in-between frames.

11. Select the bicep muscle in the viewport.

12. Play the animation, and make sure the Muscle Builder window is still open. As the leg moves, you may see some jiggling in the muscle; that's part of the Jiggle settings, which you'll edit in the next few steps.

FIGURE 7.54
Set the squash and
stretch of each
muscle.

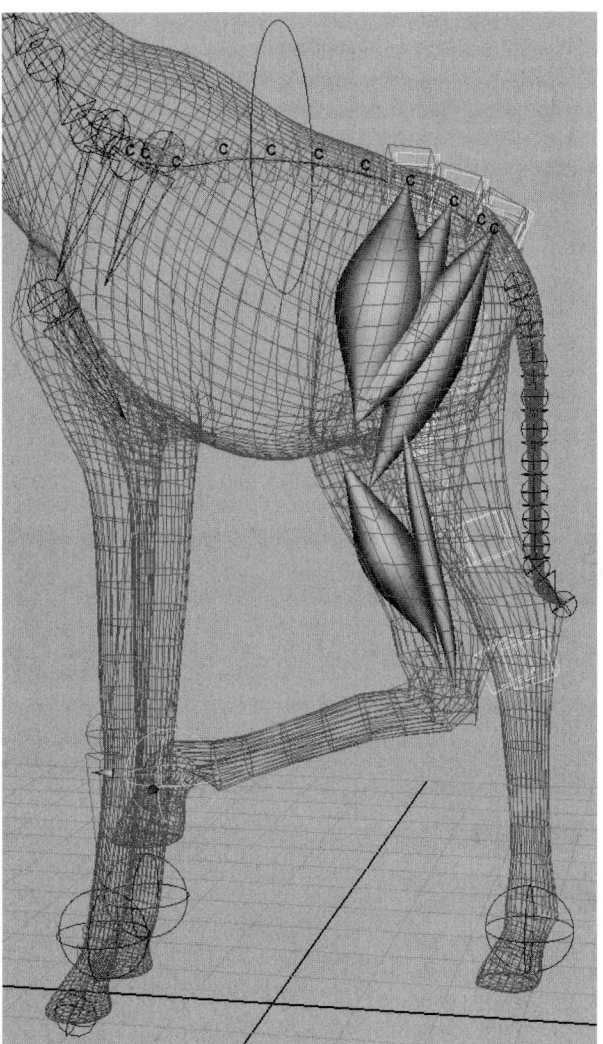

13. As the leg moves back and forth, click the Small, Medium, and Large buttons. Notice the change in the muscle's size and behavior as you switch between presets.

14. You can edit the numeric values in the START, MID, and END fields to fine-tune the behavior. It's usually easiest to start by loading one of the presets and then make small changes to the values.

   When you're happy with how the muscle is shaped as it moves, you can move on to editing the Jiggle motion.

15. While the animation plays, click the Default, Light, Medium, Heavy, and OFF buttons in the Jiggle Presets section. Observe the difference in behavior as each preset is applied.

16. You can fine-tune the behavior of the jiggling by editing the numeric values in the START, MID, and END fields for Jiggle, Cycle, and Rest:

♦ Jiggle is the intensity of jiggle.

♦ Cycle is the frequency of jiggle oscillation.

♦ Rest is the time it takes for the muscle to come to a stop.

The Dampen settings add a damping effect as the muscle reaches extreme poses.

17. Make sure to remove any animation applied to the controls.

18. Save the scene as `giraffeMuscles_v04.ma`.

To see a version of the scene to this point, open the `giraffeMuscles_v04.ma` scene from the `chapter7\scenes` directory on the DVD.

Converting the Smooth Skin to a Muscle System

Now that the muscles have been set up and are working properly, you can apply it to the giraffe geometry so it deforms the character's skin. Applying the deformer to the geometry involves weighting the skin to the muscles. This is very similar in concept to smooth binding geometry to Maya's joints. In fact, you can actually convert the skin weights painted earlier in the chapter to the muscle system.

1. Continue with the scene from the previous section, or open the `giraffeMuscles_v04.ma` scene from the `chapter7\scenes` directory on the DVD.

2. Select the giraffe geometry.

3. Choose Muscle ➢ Skin Setup ➢ Convert Smooth Skin To Muscle System.

4. Maya asks whether you want to delete or disable the skin weights applied to the arm. Choose Disable. (You can delete the weights if you want to, but it may be a good idea to keep the weights in the scene in case they are needed later.)

5. Maya asks you to choose the axis for the capsules. Choose the x-axis to match the orientation of the capsules. Converting the skin takes a few moments (denser geometry takes longer to process); you'll see a dialog box that displays the progress of the calculation.

This takes the smooth skin joint weights that were painted on the geometry and converts them to muscle weights. However, only the capsules are included. If you move the L_HindLeg_CTRL, you'll notice that the muscles do not yet deform the skin. They need to be attached to the skin and weighted before they will work.

6. Select all the muscles and the giraffe skin.

7. Choose Muscle ➢ Muscle Objects ➢ Connect Selected Muscle Objects.

8. A dialog box asks you to set the Sticky Bind Maximum Distance value. Choose Auto-Calculate. Each muscle is calculated.

The muscles are now connected to the skin geometry. However, it still will not affect the geometry until the weights are painted for each muscle.

9. Switch to shaded view.

10. Select the giraffe mesh, and choose Muscle ➤ Paint Muscle Weights.

11. The geometry becomes color coded to indicate the weight strength of each muscle listed in the Muscle Paint window. Make sure the Weight type is set to Sticky.

12. Scroll to the bottom of the list in the Muscle Paint window, and select L_glute1. The geometry turns black, indicating there is no weight for this muscle.

13. Use the L_HindLeg_CTRL to pose the arm as you paint weight values for the glutes.

14. Set Weight to **0.1** and Operation to Add.

15. Paint over the area of the glute to start adding weights.

   ◆ Low-weight values are blue.

   ◆ Higher-weight values are green, orange, and red.

   You can also set the Paint Skin Weights tool to paint in Gray.

16. Paint L_glute2 as well. Figure 7.55 shows the results of painting the weights.

FIGURE 7.55
Paint weight values for the glute muscles.

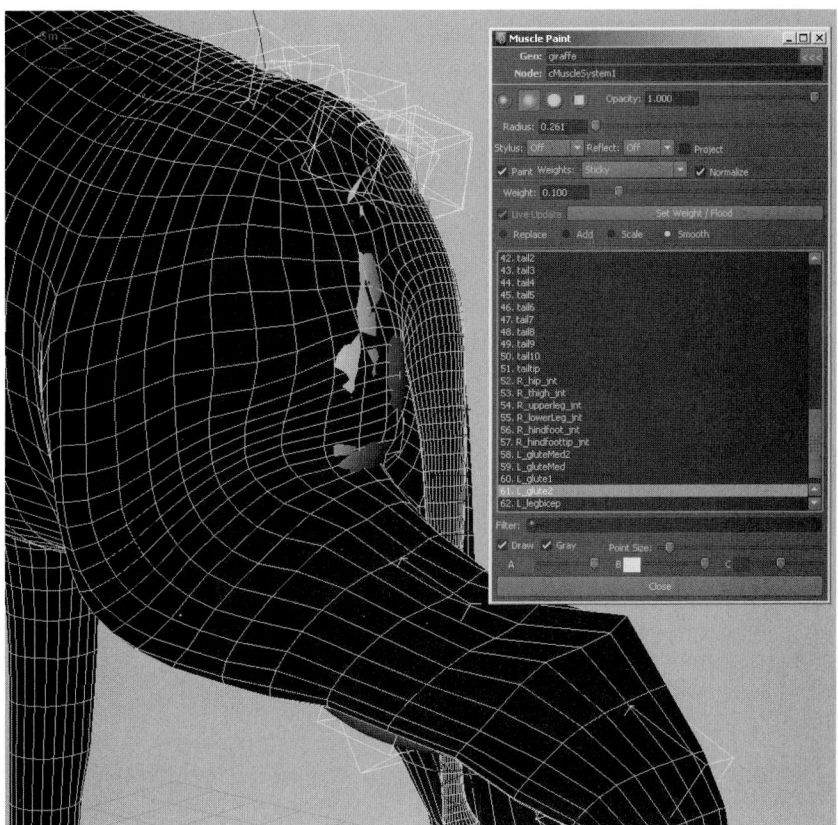

Keep in mind that the muscles do not have to fit perfectly under the skin. They are not rendered with the character, so penetration is OK. The important part is how the skin looks and reacts.

17. When you have finished painting the weights, close the window.

18. Create another animation for L_HindLeg_CTRL so you can see the muscle in action as it deforms the skin.

19. If you need to change muscle parameters, such as the Jiggle attributes, select the muscle and choose Muscle ≻ Simple Muscle ≻ Set Muscle Parameters. Use the settings in the Muscle Parameters tab to adjust the muscle quality.

20. Save the scene as `giraffeMuscles_v05.ma`.

To see a version of the scene, open the `giraffeMuscles_v05.ma` scene from the `chapter7\scenes` directory on the DVD.

Sliding Weights

Sliding weights are used to create the effect of skin sliding over bones and muscle. In this example, you'll make the skin at the top of the hind leg a little loose by painting sliding weights.

1. Continue with the scene from the previous section, or open the `giraffeMuscles_v05.ma` scene from the `chapter7\scenes` directory on the DVD.

2. Select the giraffe mesh.

3. In the Channel Box, select the cMuscleSystem1 node under INPUTS.

4. Set Enable Sliding to On. This is an easy step to forget, but if you don't enable sliding weights on the character's skin, you won't see the sliding effects.

5. With the giraffe mesh selected, choose Muscle ≻ Paint Muscle Weights.

6. Choose the L_glute1 from the list of muscle objects.

7. Set Weights to Sliding and the operation to Add. Set Weight to **0.5**.

8. Paint the muscle area.

9. Switch to L_glute2, and paint its sliding weight also.

10. Select the L_HindLeg_CTRL, and move the control handle back and forth to see the effects of the sliding weights.

11. Save the scene as `giraffeMuscles_v06.ma`.

To see a version of the scene to this point, open the `giraffeMuscles_v06.ma` scene from the `chapter7\scenes` directory on the DVD.

Creating the anatomy for an entire character takes good research and a lot of time. The muscle system is versatile enough to only add muscles where needed. You can add them gradually to the skin and test them as you go. It is not necessary to fill the skin with muscles. To learn more, check out the book *Maya Feature Creature Creations* (Charles River Media, 2002).

The Bottom Line

Create and organize joint hierarchies   A joint hierarchy is a series of joint chains. Each joint in a chain is parented to another joint, back to the root of the chain. Each joint inherits the motion of its parent joint. Organizing the joint chains is accomplished through naming and labeling the joints. Proper orientation of the joints is essential for the joints to work properly.

Master it   Create a joint hierarchy for a giraffe character. Orient the joints so the x-axis points down the length of the joints.

Use Inverse Kinematics rigs   A joint chain that uses Inverse Kinematics uses a goal called an End Effector to orient the joints in the chain. A number of solvers are available in Maya.

Master it   Create an Inverse Kinematic rig for a character's leg. Use a separate control to position the knee of the character.

Apply skin geometry   Skinning geometry refers to the process in which geometry is bound to joints so that it deforms as the joints are moved and rotated. Each vertex of the geometry receives a certain amount of influence from the joints in the hierarchy. This can be controlled by painting the weights of the geometry on the skin.

Master it   Paint weights on the giraffe model to get smooth-looking deformations on one side of the model. Mirror the weights to the other side.

Use Maya Muscle   Maya Muscle is a series of tools designed to create more believable deformations and movement for objects skinned to joints. Capsules are used to replace Maya joints. Muscles are NURBS surfaces that squash, stretch, and jiggle as they deform geometry.

Master it   Use Maya Muscle to create muscles for the hind leg of the giraffe. Use the muscle system to cause skin bulging and sliding.

Chapter 8

Paint Effects and Toon Shading

Paint Effects is a special Maya module designed to allow artists to quickly build, animate, and render large amounts of organic and natural detail. Trees, grass, flowers, clouds, blood vessels, vines, rocks, and even small towns can be interactively painted into a scene in three dimensions. Paint Effects is both a dynamic particle-based system and a procedural modeling tool. There are many options for rendering the objects that you create using Paint Effects, giving you an astonishing amount of creative flexibility when incorporating natural elements into your projects.

Paint Effects is also part of Maya's Toon Shading system, which is used to simulate the look of hand-drawn cartoons when rendering 3D animations. This chapter looks at how Paint Effects works through several short, experimental projects. By the end of the chapter, you'll understand how to design and apply your own custom Paint Effects objects in a scene.

In this chapter, you'll learn to:

◆ Use the Paint Effects canvas

◆ Paint on 3D objects

◆ Design a brush

◆ Shape strokes with behaviors

◆ Animate strokes

◆ Render Paint Effects strokes

◆ Use Toon Shading

Using the Paint Effects Canvas

Maya actually contains a 2D paint program that can be used to paint illustrations, create textures, or experiment with Paint Effects brushes. The Paint Effects canvas works like a simplified version of a digital paint program such as Corel Painter. You can paint on the canvas using any of the Paint Effects brushes; it's a great way to test a brush before applying it in a 3D scene.

USING A TABLET

You don't have to use a digital tablet and pen to work with Paint Effects, but it makes things much easier. In this chapter, we assume that you'll be using a digital tablet. If you are using a mouse, understand that to paint with Paint Effects you can left-click and drag to apply a stroke. If you're using a digital tablet, you can drag the pen across the tablet to apply a stroke to the Paint Effects canvas or to a 3D scene.

The Paint Effects Window

The Paint Effects window is like a mini digital paint program inside Maya. In this section, you'll experiment with some basic controls to create simple images on the canvas.

1. Create a new scene in Maya.

2. In the view panel, choose Panels ➢ Panel ➢ Paint Effects to open the Paint Effects window.

OPENING THE PAINT EFFECTS WINDOW

You can open Paint Effects in a number of ways. You can use the panel menu in a viewport, you can choose Window ➢ Paint Effects, or you can press **8** on the numeric keypad of your keyboard.

The viewport now appears white with some icons at the top. This white area is the Paint Effects canvas. If you see a 3D scene instead, choose Paint ➢ Canvas (Figure 8.1).

3. Click and drag on the canvas; you'll see a black line resembling ink appear wherever you paint on the canvas. If you are using a digital tablet, vary the pressure as you paint: the line becomes thinner when less pressure is applied and thicker when more pressure is applied.

FIGURE 8.1
Choosing Paint Canvas from the Paint menu switches Paint Effects to 2D paint mode.

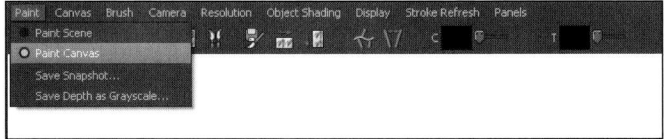

NAVIGATING THE PAINT EFFECTS WINDOW

You can use the same controls that you use in a 3D scene to zoom and pan while Paint Effects is open. To zoom, hold Alt and RMB-drag. To pan, hold Alt and MMB-drag. Since the canvas is two-dimensional, holding Alt and LMB-dragging doesn't rotate the canvas but instead serves as another way to pan.

---

4. Click the color swatch next to the C on the Paint Effects menu bar. This opens the Color Chooser. You can use this tool to change the color of the brush (see Figure 8.2).

5. Move the slider to the right of the color swatch to change the value (brightness) of the paintbrush color.

6. The color swatch labeled with a *T* and the slider next to it control the transparency of the current stroke (see Figure 8.3) by changing color and transparency as you paint on the canvas.

FIGURE 8.2
The Paint Effects canvas is a 2D paint program within Maya. Clicking the C color swatch opens the Color Chooser, allowing you to change the brush color.

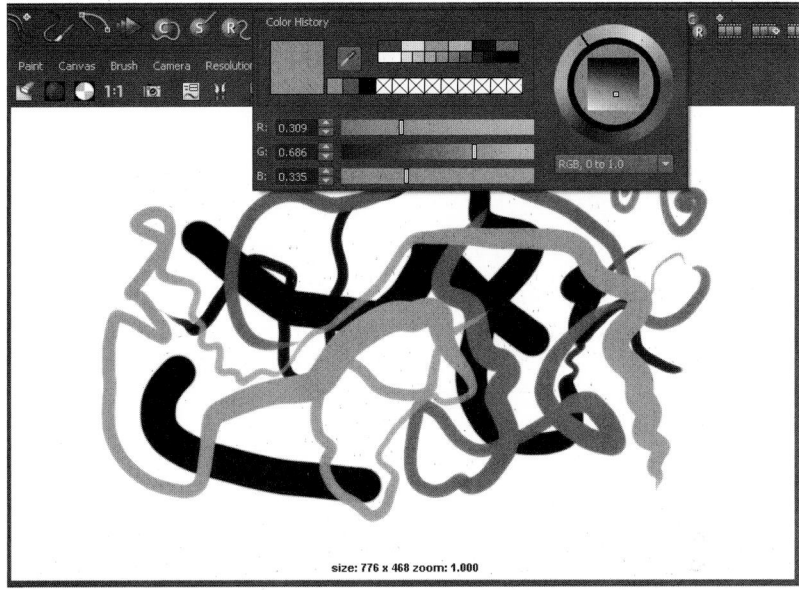

FIGURE 8.3
The icons on the menu bar of the Paint Effects window

These are the other icons on the panel, from left to right, as shown in Figure 8.3:

◆ The eraser icon clears the canvas.

◆ The color icon displays the RGB channels (color) of the canvas.

◆ The white circle icon displays the alpha channel of the strokes on the canvas.

◆ The 1:1 icon displays the actual size of the canvas.

◆ The camera icon takes a snapshot of the canvas.

◆ The editor icon opens the Attribute Editor for the current brush settings.

◆ The double paintbrush icon opens the Visor, which displays the available Brush presets.

◆ The computer disk and brush icon opens the `sourceimages` folder. When this button is active, every time you make a change to the canvas, the image will be automatically saved. The first time you activate the button, you'll be prompted to choose a location on disk to save the image.

◆ The sideways arrow allows horizontal tiling. As you paint off one side of the canvas, this stroke is continued on the opposite side. This is useful when you want to create seamless tiling textures.

◆ The down arrow enables vertical tiling. Strokes that you paint off the top or bottom of the canvas are continued on the opposite side.

◆ The branching stroke icon enables tube painting. This will be discussed in more detail later in the chapter.

◆ The diagonally split icon flips the tube direction. This will be discussed along with tubes.

7. Click the eraser icon to clear the canvas.

8. Click the double brush icon to open the Visor (or choose Window ➣ General Editors ➣ Visor).

9. In the Visor, make sure the Paint Effects tab is selected at the top. From the list of folders on the left side, open the flesh folder, and select hands.mel. This switches the current brush to the hands brush—you'll see the current brush highlighted in yellow in the Visor (Figure 8.4).

THE VISOR

The Visor is a central library within Maya that allows you to access presets, example files, and other assets. The tabs at the top of the Visor allow you to browse and then choose the various types of assets. Much of the time you'll use the Visor to select a Paint Effects brush.

FIGURE 8.4
Select the hands.mel brush from the Visor.

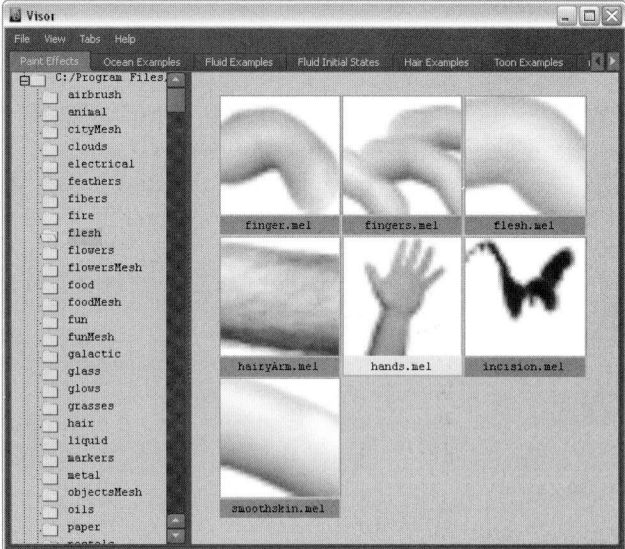

10. Paint some strokes on the canvas. Instead of an inky line, you'll see numerous hands appear as you paint. The hands vary in color while you apply them to the canvas (Figure 8.5).

To interactively change the size of the hands as you paint, hold the B key, and drag left or right on the canvas; you'll see the circular brush icon grow as you drag to the right and shrink as you drag to the left.

FIGURE 8.5
When the hands.mel brush is selected, painting on the canvas produces a number of images of human hands.

If you want to change the background color of the canvas, choose Canvas ➤ Clear ➤ Options, and change the Clear color. Clear the canvas. This removes strokes painted on the canvas and changes the background color at the same time.

11. Open the Visor, select some other brushes, and make a mess on the canvas. Try the defaultSmear.mel brush found in the airbrush folder. When you paint on the canvas, the brush smears the strokes already painted.

Some Paint Effects brushes create colors and images, while others alter the colors and images painted on the canvas. And some, such as the smearColor.mel brush, smear the strokes and apply color at the same time (see Figure 8.6).

FIGURE 8.6
Some brushes, such as the smear brush, alter the strokes painted on the canvas.

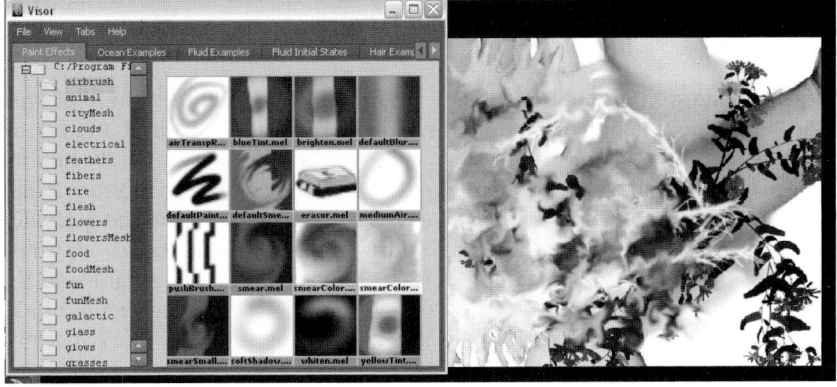

Painting in Scene Mode

You can use Paint Effects brushes to paint in 3D. The strokes actually produce three-dimensional images that are incorporated into the scene. While in the Paint Effects window, you can preview what strokes will look like in a 3D scene.

1. In the Paint Effects window, choose Paint ➤ Paint Scene. You'll be prompted by Maya to save or discard the current image on the canvas. You can click No to discard the image or Yes if you're really proud of it.

    The Paint Effects window now displays a perspective view, but notice that the Paint Effects menu is still at the top of the canvas. You are now in scene mode of the Paint Effects window. You can switch cameras using the Panels menu in the Paint Effects menu bar.

2. Open the Visor, and choose the hands.mel brush from the flesh folder. Paint some strokes on the grid.

3. The grid quickly becomes littered with dismembered hands (see Figure 8.7). Rotate the view of the scene. The hands switch to wireframe mode to help improve performance while you are changing the view. If you'd like the hands to remain visible, choose Stroke Refresh ➤ Rendered. Whenever you stop moving the camera, the strokes on the grid will reappear.

Notice that the brush icon appears as a 3D wireframe sphere. You can change its size interactively by holding the **B** key and dragging left or right in the perspective view.

FIGURE 8.7
Painting in scene mode allows you to paint strokes directly in a 3D scene.

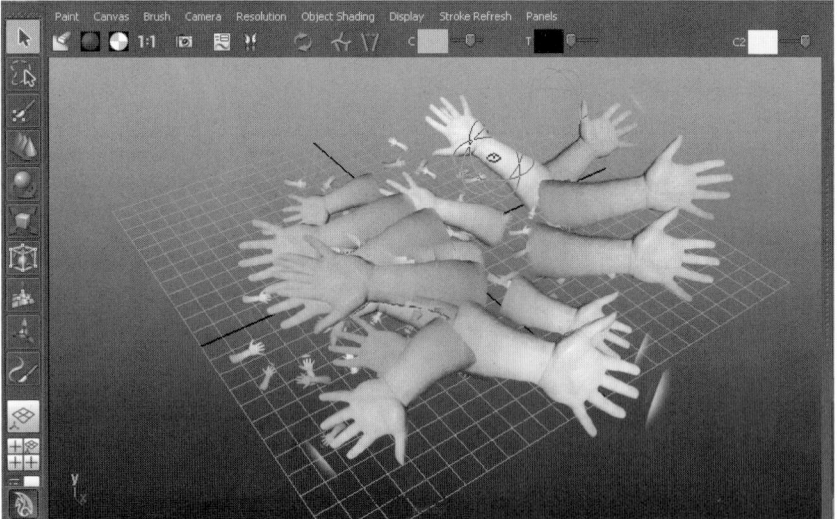

Painting on 3D Objects

Once you are comfortable selecting and applying Paint Effects brushes, you're ready to actually paint on some 3D objects. Both NURBS and polygon objects can be painted on the canvas using Paint Effects. You can add grass and flowers to rolling fields, clouds in the sky, and whiskers on an old man's chin.

You're not limited to using the Paint Effects window when adding Paint Effects strokes to a scene. You can apply Paint Effects while working in any camera view in a standard Maya scene. However, if you'd like to see a more accurate preview of what the stroke will look like when rendered, then use the Paint Effects window in scene mode. For these exercises, you'll paint strokes in a scene using the standard Maya viewports.

In this scene, there is a simple NURBS plane named waterSurface, which was created by lofting a surface between two dynamic hair curves. The hair system provides a gentle fluid-like motion. There's also a rock created from a polygon mesh (see Figure 8.8).

FIGURE 8.8
The waterPlant_
v01.ma scene
contains a NURBS
plane and a poly-
gon rock.

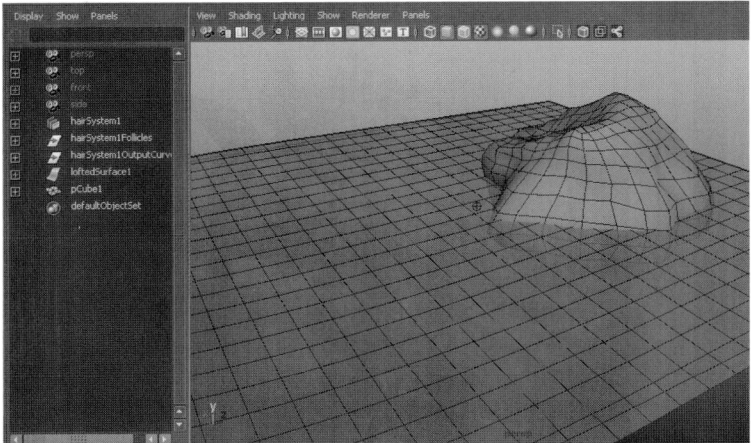

To paint on 3D objects, they must be made "paintable." Otherwise, any strokes you paint will appear on the grid and not on the objects. Furthermore, polygon objects must have UV texture coordinates that are nonoverlapping and lie within the 0 to 1 range in the UV texture editor (for more information on creating UV coordinates, consult Chapter 11).

1. Open the waterPlant_v01.ma scene from the chapter8\scenes directory on the DVD.

2. Select the waterSurface, and Shift+click the rock mesh.

3. Switch to the Rendering menu set, and choose Paint Effects ➤ Make Paintable.

4. Choose Paint Effects ➤ Paint Effects Tool. Draw a stroke that starts on the rock and moves across the waterSurface, as shown in Figure 8.9.

FIGURE 8.9
A Paint Effects
stroke is painted
across two objects.

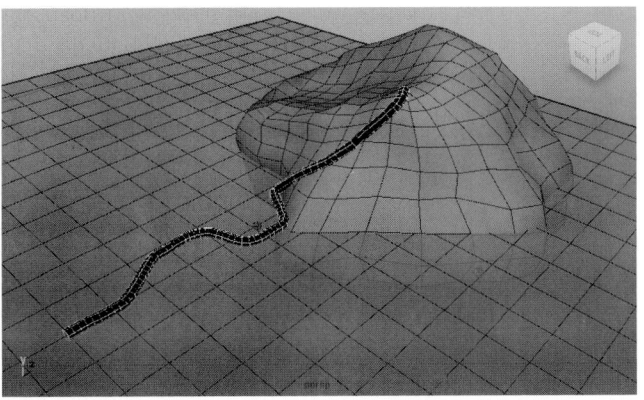

5. Rewind and play the scene. The part of the stroke that is on the water surface moves with the surface.

6. Save the scene as **paintOnObjects.ma**. To see a version of the scene, open the paintOnObjects.ma scene in the chapter8\scenes folder on the DVD.

CORRECTING UNUSUAL BEHAVIOR

A single stroke can be painted across multiple objects as long as they are paintable. If you experience unusual behavior when painting on objects, double-check the UVs on any polygon surfaces; also, check to see which way the normals of the object are facing; this can affect how some strokes behave. As you paint on the surfaces, be mindful of your viewing angle in the viewport window. Some angles will confuse Maya and cause strokes to become misplaced and stretched.

ATTACH TO A CURVE

Another way to add a stroke to a 3D object is to attach the stroke to a preexisting NURBS curve. To do this, select the stroke you want in the Visor to load it as the current stroke. Then select the curve and choose Paint Effects ➤ Curve Utilities ➤ Attach To Curve. The stroke appears on the curve without the need to paint it in the scene. Multiple strokes can be attached to the same curve.

Understanding Strokes

When you create a Paint Effects stroke in a scene, several nodes are automatically created and connected. Some of the nodes are visible, and some are not. These nodes work together to produce the strokes you see in the scene.

The Anatomy of a Paint Effects Stroke

In this section, you'll look at the nodes created when you add a Paint Effects stroke to a scene. Some of these nodes you will most likely ignore; some of the nodes you will use to edit and animate the strokes.

1. Open the waterPlant_v01.ma scene from the chapter8\scenes directory on the DVD.

2. Switch to the Rendering menu set. Select the rock object, and choose Paint Effects ➤ Make Paintable.

3. Choose Window ➤ General Editors ➤ Visor to open the Visor.

4. Choose the Grasses folder, and select the astroturf.mel brush; the icon turns yellow in the Visor.

5. Zoom in to the rock, and start painting grass on it. Paint exactly three strokes. Each time you release the mouse button (or the pen from the tablet), a stroke node is added in the Outliner (see Figure 8.10).

6. Once you have three strokes applied, look in the Outliner. You'll see that a stroke node was created each time you painted on a paintable surface.

FIGURE 8.10

FIGURE 8.10
Astroturf is
painted on the
surface of
the rock.

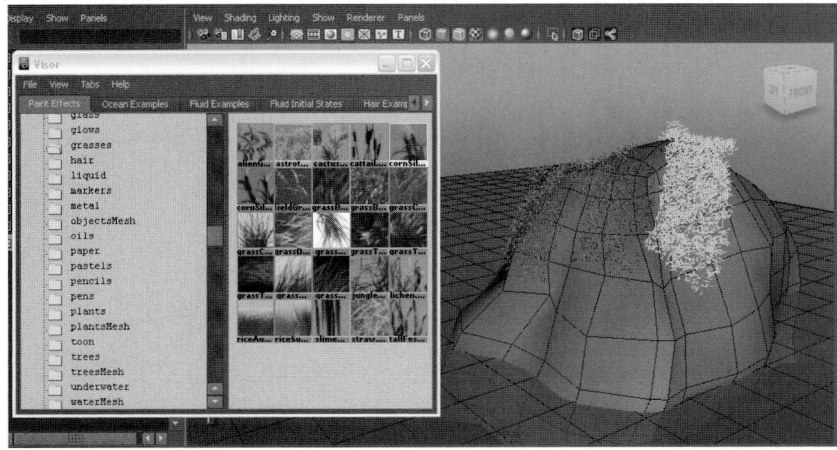

MAKING AN OBJECT PAINTABLE

The rock does not have to be selected to paint on it, but it must be made paintable: choose Paint
Effects ➢ Make Paintable, as you did in step 2 in this exercise.

Each stroke has a transform node and a shape node. Figure 8.11 shows the Outliner with
one of the stroke nodes expanded so you can see that the stroke's shape node is parented to the
stroke's transform node (for more about transform and shape nodes, consult Chapter 1).

The transform node contains information about the stroke's position, scale, and rotation.
Most likely you'll almost never edit the transform node's attributes except maybe to hide the
node by changing its Visibility attribute.

FIGURE 8.11
The Astroturf
nodes appear in the
Outliner for each
stroke painted
on the rock. Each
stroke has a trans-
form node and a
shape node.

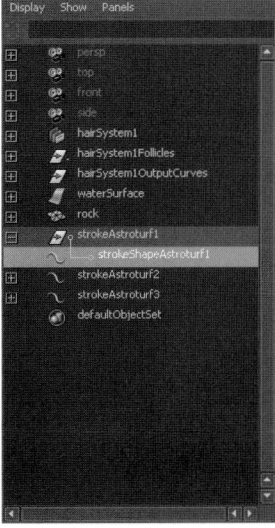

The shape node has a number of attributes specific to how the node appears and behaves:

1. Select the strokeAstroturf1 node, and open the Attribute Editor. You'll see a tab for the transform node labeled strokeAstroturf1.

2. Open the Attribute Editor for the shape node by clicking the strokeShapeAstroturf1 tab in the Attribute Editor.

   The strokeShapeAstroturf1 node has attributes that control how the stroke is displayed in the scene, how it renders, the pressure settings, and other settings specific to the individual stroke (see Figure 8.12).

3. In the Attribute Editor, switch to the astroturf1 tab. This tab contains settings for the astroturf1 brush. Editing these settings also changes the way the stroke appears in the scene.

FIGURE 8.12
The strokeShape-
Astroturf1 tab con-
tains settings that
control the stroke
in the scene.

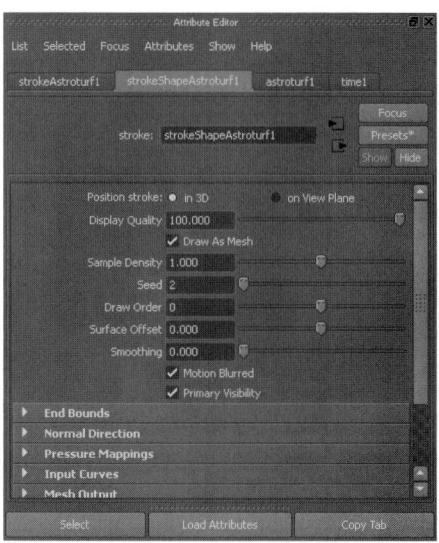

UNDERSTANDING THE CONNECTION BETWEEN THE SHAPE NODE AND THE BRUSH NODE

The relationship between the shape node (strokeShapeAstroturf1) and the brush node (astroturf1) can be a little confusing at first. Think of it this way: if you draw on a wall with a crayon, the mark on the wall is the stroke, and the shape node controls the appearance of that particular stroke. The crayon you used to make the mark on the wall is the brush (using Paint Effects terminology). Changing the settings on the brush would be like changing the crayon itself, which would affect the appearance and behavior of the strokes themselves. However, unlike in the real world where changing the crayon affects only each subsequent mark made by the crayon, there is a construction history connection between the stroke and the brush that made the stroke. Changing the settings on the brush causes a change in the strokes already created by that brush in the scene.

---

4. In the astroturf1 tab of the Attribute Editor, set Global Scale to **0.1**. The size of stroke Astroturf1 shrinks. Notice that the other strokes are not affected (Figure 8.13).

FIGURE 8.13
Changing the
Global Scale
setting in the
astroturf1 brush
node affects only
the size of one of
the strokes painted
on the rock.

FIGURE 8.13
Changing the
Global Scale
setting in the
astroturf1 brush
node affects only
the size of one of
the strokes painted
on the rock.

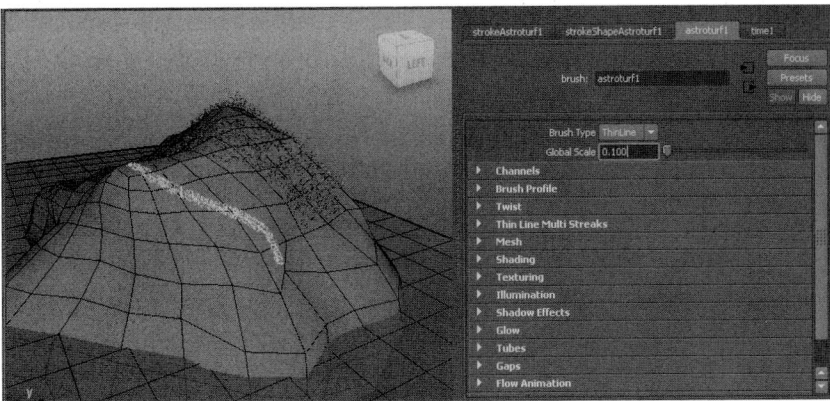

Brush Sharing

Another aspect of the relationship between the brush node (astroturf1) and the shape node (strokeShapeAstroturf1) is that even though you have the same brush selected when you create multiple astroturf strokes on an object, Maya creates a new brush node for each stroke. It's as if you had a box of identical crayons, and each time you make a mark on the wall, you switch to a new crayon. This is confusing at first, but it means you have more options for varying strokes in a Maya scene. To understand this relationship further, let's take a closer look at the nodes in the scene.

1. In the Outliner, expand the Display menu, and turn off DAG Objects Only. This causes the Outliner to display all the nodes in the scene (for more on DAG nodes, consult Chapter 1).

   In the Outliner, you'll see several astroturf brush nodes (the nodes with the brush icon; in some cases, one of the nodes may be listed with the other astroturf nodes). These nodes are labeled astroturf, astroturf1, astroturf2, and astroturf3.

   The first astroturf node is really an instance of the currently selected brush. If you change your current brush selection to a different brush, the node changes to match the name of the new brush. Think of this as a placeholder for the current brush settings. Each time a stroke is created in the scene, a copy of this node is created and associated with the stroke. Figure 8.14 shows how the node name changes when the grass ornamental brush is selected in the Visor (middle image); if the scene is reloaded in Maya, the brush is relabeled brush1.

2. Select astroturf2, and open the Attribute Editor to the astroturf2 node. Making a change to the settings—such as the Global Scale—affects only the associated stroke (in this case strokeAstroTurf2).

FIGURE 8.14
The name of the first
brush node changes
depending on the
brush currently
selected in the Visor.

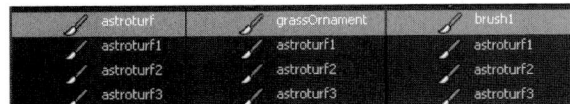

The ability to change the brush settings associated with each stroke means that you can easily create variations of the brushes within the scene. However, let's say you have 200 brush strokes that all use the same brush and you need to change a setting, such as the Global Scale for all of them or maybe even just 99 of them. Instead of changing each brush stroke individually, you can enable brush sharing so that the same brush node affects all the associated strokes.

3. In the Outliner, Shift+click strokeAstroturf1, strokeAstroturf2, and strokeAstroturf3.

4. Choose Paint Effects ➢ Share One Brush. After a couple seconds, all of the brushes adopt the same Global Scale settings.

  If you look in the Outliner, only one brush node is labeled astroturf3. The strokes adopt the brush settings of the last selected brush.

5. Select the astroturf3 node in the Outliner, and change its Global Scale slider. All three strokes update as you make the change.

6. Select the three strokeAstroturf nodes in the Outliner, and choose Paint Effects ➢ Remove Brush Sharing. At the bottom of the Outliner, you'll see the three astroturf brush nodes reappear (the numbering of the brushes may change when you remove brush sharing). Now you can return to editing each brush individually.

7. Save the scene as **grassOnRock.ma**. To see a version of the scene, open the grassOnRock.ma file from the chapter8\scenes folder on the DVD.

Note that turning on brush sharing applies only to changes made to the settings in the brush node. Each individual brush still has its own shape node. The settings in the shape node can't be shared among multiple brushes. We'll discuss this further in the "Designing Brushes" section.

Understanding Brush Curve Nodes

When you paint a Paint Effects stroke in a scene, the stroke is attached to a curve that determines the overall shape of the stroke. The curve node itself may be visible or not depending on how the stroke is created. If you paint directly on the grid (Paint Effects ➢ Paint On View Plane), Maya creates a curve in the scene. The curve node is visible in the Outliner.

If you select a NURBS object, choose Paint Effects ➢ Make Paintable, and then paint on the surface, Maya creates a curveOnSurface node. You can see the curve on surface if you hide or delete the stroke node after creating it. The curveOnSurface node is parented to the shape node of the NURBS surface, and you can also see the connection to this node by selecting the stroke and graphing it in the Hypergraph (Windows ➢ Hypergraph Connections), as shown in Figure 8.15.

When you paint on a polygon surface, Maya creates a curveFromMeshCom node, which allows Maya to draw a curve on a polygon surface. When you graph a stroke painted on a polygon, you can see both the curve node and the curveFromMeshCom node. You can also see the curves parented to the shape node of the polygon geometry in the Outliner (see Figure 8.16).

You may not be immediately concerned with the curve nodes Maya creates when you paint a stroke on a surface; however, a situation may arise in which you need to access the curve nodes to make some kind of change to the connection (for instance, if you decide you want to transfer a stroke from a regular curve to a dynamic hair curve). In these situations, it's good to have a basic understanding of how the paintbrushes are actually applied to 3D objects.

FIGURE 8.15
A stroke painted on the NURBS waterSurface is graphed in the Hypergraph. The node named curveBrush-Shape111 is the curveOnSurface node.

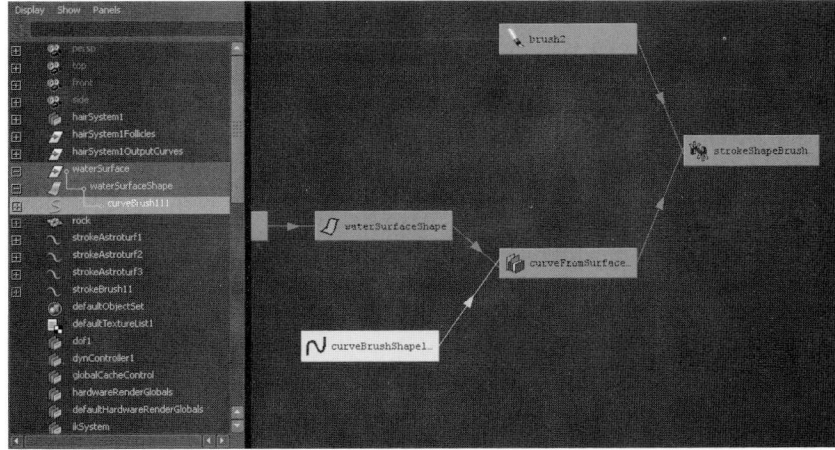

FIGURE 8.16
A stroke painted on a polygon surface creates a curve node and a curveFrom-MeshCom node.

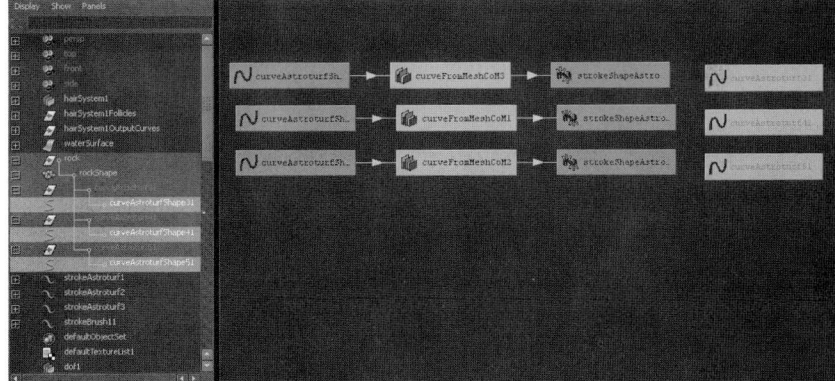

Designing Brushes

There's no better way to learn how to use Paint Effects than to get some hands-on training designing a custom brush. Once you have practical experience working with the many settings available for Paint Effects brushes, you'll have a much easier time working with the brushes listed in the Visor.

When you create your own brushes, most of the time you'll start with one of existing brushes available in the Visor and then edit its settings until you get the look and the behavior you want. For instance, if you want to create a creepy nerve growing in a test tube, you may start with a brush preset that looks similar to what you want, such as a tree branch, and then experiment with the settings in the Attribute Editor until the branch looks and acts like a creepy nerve.

Paint Effects is a procedural modeling and animation workflow—meaning that the objects created by Paint Effects and the animation applied to the models are derived from mathematical algorithms (as opposed to pushing and pulling vertices). The math involved is beneath the hood, so you don't need to worry about breaking out the slide rule. However, this does mean that you'll be working with a lot of interconnected sliders, settings, and controls. It's a very experimental process. Changing one setting affects a number of others. There's no particular order in how you edit the settings either; in fact, you'll find yourself bouncing around among the various controls and nodes in the Attribute Editor. Although this may seem overwhelming at first, after some practice you'll see that there's a lot to discover in Paint Effects, and you can create many very unusual and unexpected things, which is always a lot of fun.

Paint Effects is most famous for creating plant life. The underlying technology that drives Paint Effects is based on L-systems, which are mathematical algorithms often used to simulate living systems such as plants. Most recently Paint Effects was used to create large parts of the alien jungles of Pandora in the movie *Avatar*. In the next few sections of this chapter, the exercises will show you how you can design your own alien plant life and have it react to elements within a scene.

L-SYSTEMS

L-systems were developed by the 20th century Hungarian biologist Aristid Lindenmayer as a way to mathematically describe the growth patterns of organisms such as yeast and algae. L-systems are comprised of simple rules that determine branching growth patterns. More complex L-systems lead to fractal-like patterns. L-systems have been a strong influence in the development of computer graphics and artificial life.

Starting from Scratch

You'll start by painting with the default paintbrush on the surface of the water in the waterPlant scene. Gradually you'll develop the look of the brush until it resembles an alien plant that floats on the surface like a water lily or lotus flower. The only reason you'll be starting with the default stroke, as opposed to one of the presets in the Visor, is so that you can get some practice designing a stroke from the beginning. This is the best way to learn how Paint Effects works.

1. Open the waterPlant_v01.ma scene from the chapter8\scenes directory on the DVD.

2. In the Outliner, select waterSurface. Switch to the Rendering menu set, and choose Paint Effects ➤ Make Paintable.

3. To make sure you are starting with the default brush, choose Paint Effects ➤ Reset Template Brush.

4. Choose Paint Effects ➤ Paint Effects Tool.

5. Paint a meandering line across the waterSurface, as shown in Figure 8.17.

6. Select the newly painted brush stroke in the Outliner, and open the Attribute Editor.

7. Switch to the tab labeled brush (it may have a number such as brush1 or brush 2, depending on how many strokes have been painted in the scene).

   The first setting is the Brush Type, which determines how the brush will render and affect other rendered objects in the scene:

   Paint type brush   The Paint type brush creates strokes that are a series of dots stamped along the path of the stroke. The strokes look much smoother when a higher number of dots is used.

FIGURE 8.17
The default stroke is painted on the surface of the water.

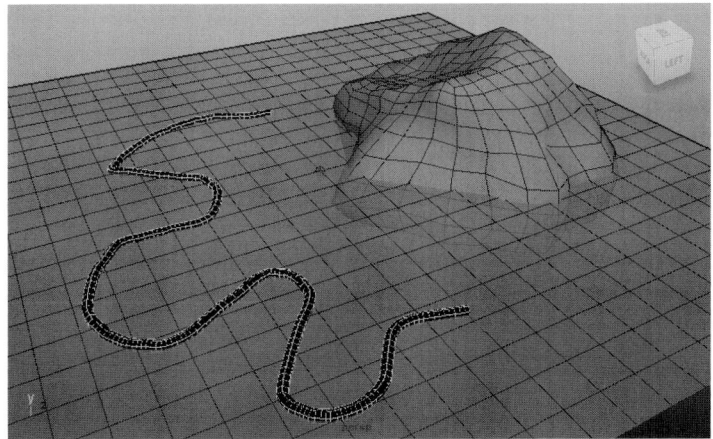

Smear and Blur type brushes   Smear and Blur type brushes distort or soften (respectively) the appearance of paint strokes applied to the canvas or objects in the scene. You can use this to create some interesting effects. For instance, objects behind the strokes in 3D space will appear smeared when rendered (Figure 8.18). To see an example of this, open the smearBrush.ma scene from the chapter8/scenes folder on the DVD.

ThinLine/MultiStreak type brushes   ThinLine/MultiStreak type brushes render strokes as groups of thin lines. This works well for hair and whisker effects.

Erase type brush   The Erase type brush creates a black hole in the alpha channel of a scene. It can be used to paint holes in the rendered image.

Mesh type brush   The Mesh type brush actually creates geometry from the stroke. This type of brush works well for hard-edge objects that appear close to the camera, such as trees or buildings. There are several folders in the Visor that contain mesh type brush strokes. Using the mesh type stroke is not the same as converting a stroke to polygons. Mesh type strokes, like all the other types, will not render in mental ray.

8. Save the scene as **waterPlant_v02.ma**.

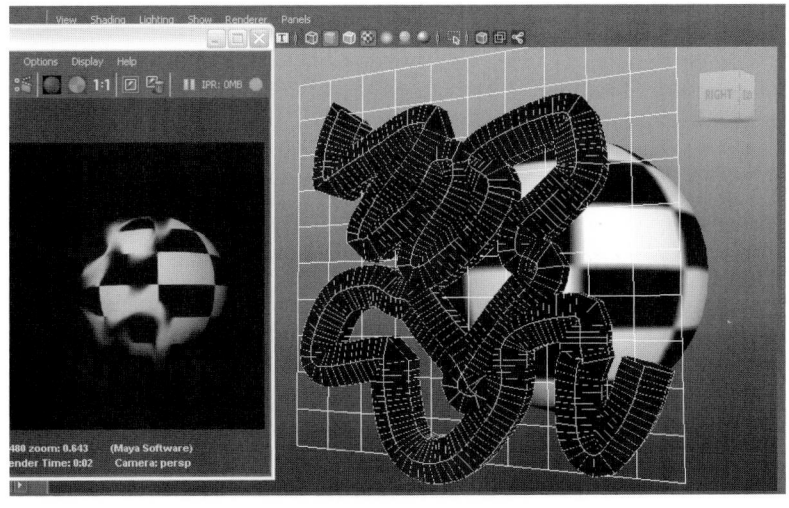

RENDERING BRUSH TYPES

Paint Effects brush strokes render only in the Maya Software Renderer. There are some workarounds that allow you to render Paint Effects in mental ray. These include converting the strokes to geometry (polygons or NURBS). However, this won't work for all brush types. For instance, the smear brush type will not smear pixels when converted to geometry.

The Global Scale slider adjusts the overall size of the stroke relative to other objects and strokes in the scene.

Adjusting the Brush Width value changes the size of the area covered by the brush stroke. For simple strokes, such as the default stroke, it appears as though changing the Brush Width value is similar to changing the Global Scale value. However, with more complex brushes that use tubes (described in the following section), changing the Brush Width changes the amount of area covered by the tubes. For instance, paint a stroke using the astroturf brush; the Brush Width changes the width of the area covered by the grass. Changing the Global Scale changes the overall size of the stroke, including the size of each blade of grass, as shown in Figure 8.19.

FIGURE 8.19
Three strokes are painted on the grid using the astroturf brush. The two strokes on the left have different Brush Width values; the stroke on the right has a larger Global Scale.

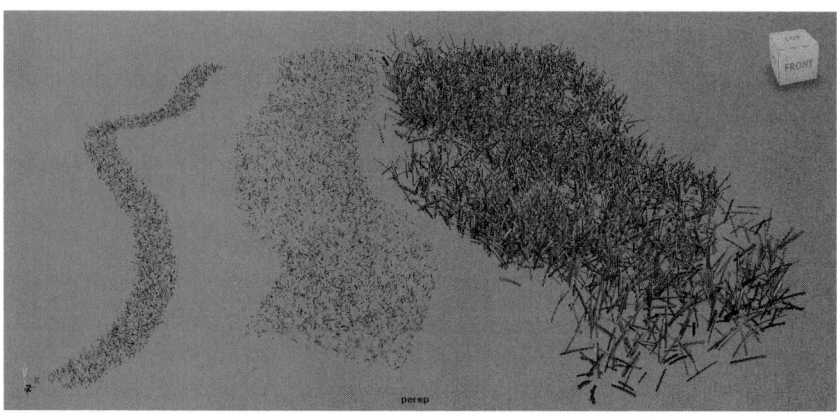

Increasing the brush's Softness value creates a fuzzy edge to the rendered stroke. Negative Softness values create a very unusual-looking brush.

The default Paint brush is a rounded tube. Increasing the Flatness1 setting makes the brush appear as a flat strip. You can then use the Twist controls (under the Twist rollout panel a little further down in the Attribute Editor) to rotate the stroke around its path curve. Increasing Twist Rate twists the stroke like a ribbon. Flatness2 is available only for strokes that use tubes (tubes are discussed later in the chapter).

Stamp Density controls how many dots are used to create the stroke when Type is set to Paint. Increasing this setting creates a smoother stroke; decreasing the setting breaks the stroke into visible dots.

If you want the brush size to remain constant regardless of how close the camera is to the stroke, you can use the Screen Space Width controls. These controls are very useful when working with toon lines. They will be discussed in more detail in the "Using Toon Shading" section later in the chapter.

Tubes

So, how do you get a flowering plant from a simple black line drawn on a surface? The answer is *tubes*. Tubes are smaller brush strokes that radiate from the center of the area defined by the brush width. Using tubes, you can create a series of crawling vines as opposed to the long singular strands created by brushes that don't use tubes (like the default brush). The tubes themselves can grow branches, twigs, leaves, and flowers. A complex brush can create a row of trees. Each tree can have its own branches and leaves.

Tubes have a lot of controls. Rather than describe what every control does, this section uses hands-on exercises to get you used to using the controls. The Maya documentation has descriptions for every control available for Paint Effects. Go to the help files and enter **Paint Effects** into the Search field. The page listed as Paint Effects Brush Settings provides you with brief descriptions of all the controls found in the brush node for a Paint Effects stroke.

1. Continue with the scene from the previous section, or open the `waterPlant_v02.ma` scene from the `chapter8\scenes` folder on the DVD.

2. In the Outliner, select the strokeBrush11 node, and open the Attribute Editor.

3. Switch to the brush2 tab. Scroll down to the Tubes rollout panel. Expand it, and turn on the Tubes check box.

   The snaking black line now becomes a series of lines that shoot out from the original Paint Effects stroke (see Figure 8.20). The Tubes Completion setting adjusts how the tubes behave toward the end of the painted stroke. When Tube Completion is off, tubes near the end of a Paint Effect stroke are not complete, just as younger branches at the top of a tree may be shorter than older branches toward the bottom.

4. Leave Tubes Completion on. Expand the Creation rollout panel, and set Tubes Per Step to **0.1**. This determines how many tubes will be created along the length of the stroke.

   The brush you are creating will have a series of flowers along the length of the stroke. Each flower will grow on a tube. So, at this point, you're establishing the placement of the flowers along the stroke using the settings in the Creation rollout panel.

5. Set Tubes Rand to **0.5** and Start Tubes to **0**.

FIGURE 8.20
When Tubes are turned on, the snaking black line becomes a series of spikes.

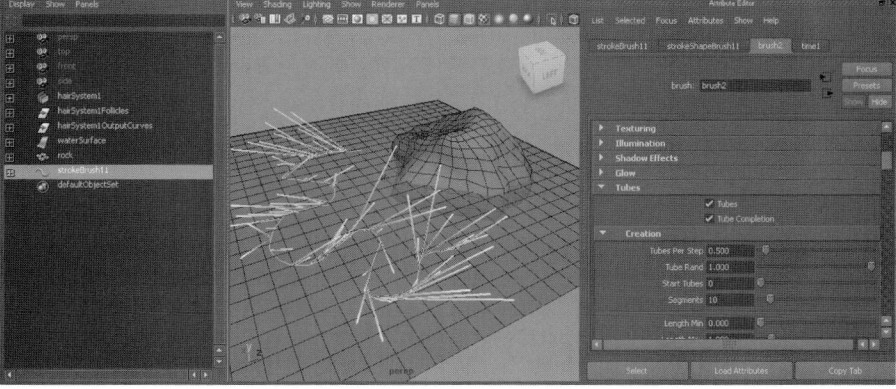

Tubes Rand randomizes the placement of tubes along the stroke. Start Tubes is useful if you want a single tube or a clump of tubes to appear at the start of the stroke. The value determines the number of tubes placed at the start of the stroke. If you wanted to create a starburst effect, you can set Tubes Per Step to **0** and increase the Start Tubes value.

It will be easier to see how the other settings in the Creation rollout panel work once you have some flowers growing along the stroke.

REVERSED TUBES

If you encounter a situation where you have painted a single stroke across multiple surfaces and the tubes on one surface seem to face the opposite direction compared to the tubes on the other surface, you need to reverse the normals of one of the surfaces. This means going to the Polygon menu set and choosing Normals ➤ Reverse. If a NURBS surface is causing the problem, then go to the Surfaces menu set and choose Edit NURBS ➤ Reverse Surface. Unfortunately, this may adversely affect your painted strokes. You may need to delete the strokes and repaint them across the reversed surfaces.

Growing Flowers

The controls in the Growth section of the brush settings allow you to add flowers, leaves, branches, and buds to your strokes.

1. Expand the Growth rollout panel, and turn on Flowers. You'll see flowers appear at the end of the tubes.

   At this point, it would be nice if the flowers were resting on the surface of the water, more or less pointing upward; right now the flowers are pointing in the direction of the tubes. There are a few ways to fix this. The easiest way is to adjust the Tube Direction sliders back in the Creation Settings.

   The sliders in the Tube Direction section control the overall direction in which the tubes point. As you develop your own custom brushes, you're likely to return to this section a lot because changes further in the process may require you to tweak the tube direction.

   You're likely to constantly experiment with these controls as you work, but it's good to have an understanding of what the controls actually do:

   Tube Direction to Along Normal   Setting Tube Direction to Along Normal makes the tubes point in a direction based on the normal of the path curve. Usually this means perpendicular to the curve itself.

   Tube Direction to Along Path   Setting Tube Direction to Along Path means the tubes point in the direction of the path.

   Elevation   Elevation refers to the direction the tubes point up and down, relative to the path. If you were lifting a flagpole to position it in the ground, the elevation of the pole at 0 would mean the flagpole is lying on the ground, and an elevation of 1 would mean the flagpole is sticking straight up out of the ground. Values greater than 1 push the flagpole over in the opposite direction.

Azimuth   Azimuth refers to the direction the tubes point as they rotate around their origin on the path. If you pointed a flashlight straight in front of you, the azimuth of the light beam would be 1. If you pointed it 90 degrees to the side, the azimuth would be 0.5. At 1.5 the flashlight would point in the opposite direction from 0.5 (see Figure 8.21).

Together the sliders can be used to define a range of elevation and azimuth for the tubes. How these sliders work is affected by the setting used in Tube Direction. Keep in mind that if Elevation Min and Elevation Max are both set to 1, changing the azimuth will have no effect.

FIGURE 8.21
The top image demonstrates changes in the elevation of a 3D arrow. The bottom image demonstrates changes in the azimuth of a 3D arrow.

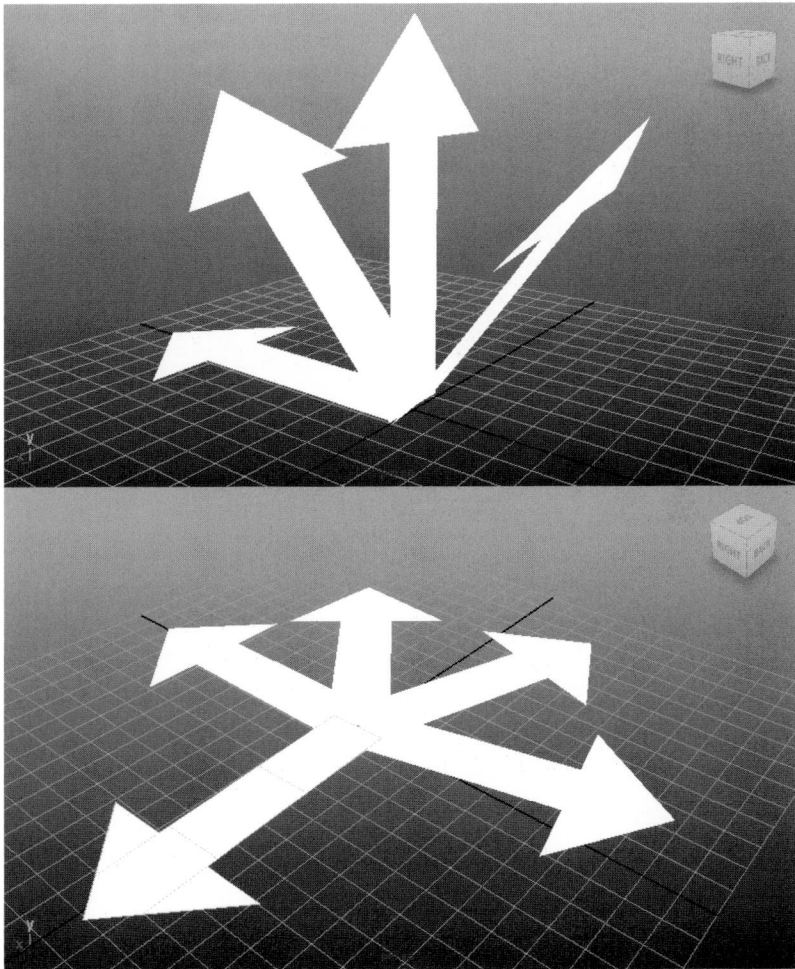

2. Scroll up to the Creation settings in the Attribute Editor, and enter the following settings:

   Tube Direction: **Along Path**

   Elevation Min: **0**

   Elevation Max: **0.15**

   Azimuth Min: **-0.086**

   Azimuth Max: **0.15**

3. Scroll up to Length Max in the Creation settings. Set this value to **0.01** so the flowers rest on the water (see Figure 8.22).

   At this point, you can focus on changing the look of the flowers.

FIGURE 8.22
After adjusting the Tube Direction and Tube Length settings, the flowers now rest on the surface of the water.

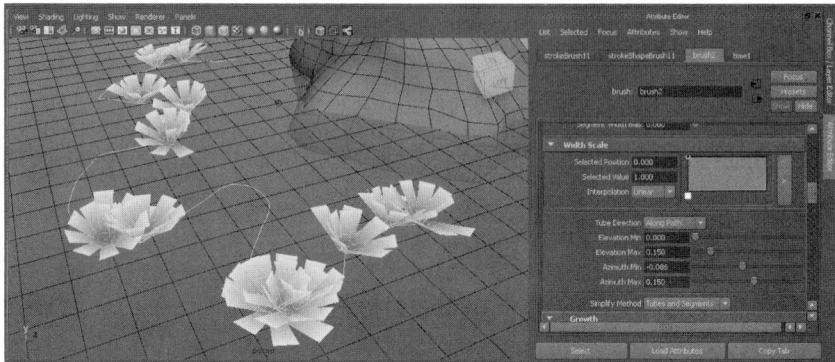

4. In the Attribute Editor, scroll back down to the Flowers rollout panel in the Growth section, and enter the following settings:

   Petals In Flowers: **6**

   Num Flowers : **1**

   Petal Dropout: **0.17**

   Petals In Flowers determines how many petals each flower has. Num Flowers determines how many flowers exist along the tube. Since the tubes in this stroke are very short, increasing this value would appear to add more petals to the flowers; in actuality, what is happening is that several flowers are stacked up on top each other because the tubes length is very short. You can use this to your advantage to customize the look of the flower.

   Petal Dropout prunes petals from the flowers to help randomize the look of each flower. If this setting is at 0, every flower has exactly the same number of petals. If the setting is at 1, then all petals are pruned.

5. Enter additional settings:

   Set Petal Length: **0.18**

   Petal Base Width: **0.17**

   Petal Tip Width: **0**

These settings help you establish a general shape for the flower petals. Making the Petal Tip Width value smaller than the Petal Base Width creates a tapered end to the petals.

6. Using the Petal Tip Width scale ramp, you can further refine the shape of the petals. Try adding points to the ramp. Set the Interpolation menu to Spline for each point that you add. This helps round the shape of the petals.

Think of the Petal Width Scale ramp as a cross section of the petal (see Figure 8.23). Click the arrow to the right of the ramp to open a larger view in a pop-up window.

FIGURE 8.23
The Petal Width Scale ramp can be used to shape the flower petals.

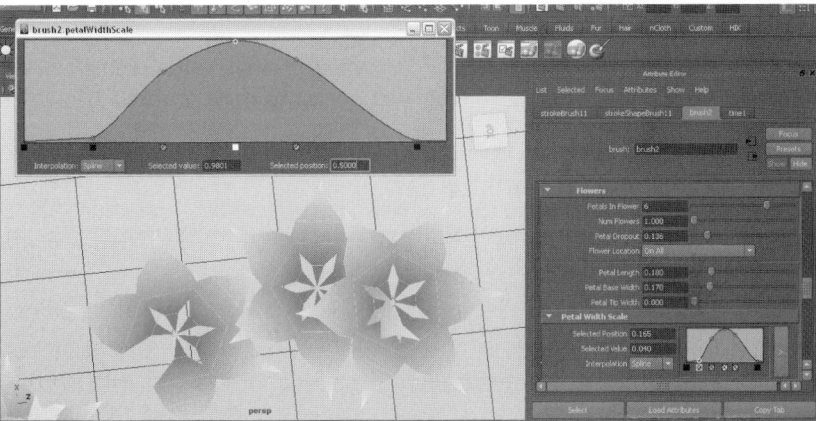

Flower Start is much like Tubes Start; it sets the location along the length of the tube where the first flowers appear. Flower Angle 1 and 2 determine a range for the angle of the flowers as they tilt inward from the tube. If you move Flower Angle 1, you'll see the petals tilt, but Flower Angle 2 appears to do nothing. This is because at the moment there is just a single flower coming out of the end of each tube. If you had a longer tube with a series of flowers growing along it, you'd see that Flower Angle 1 sets the angle for the first flower on the branch and Flower Angle 2 sets the angle for the last flower (see Figure 8.24). Flowers in between use angles in between the two settings. But you want to use these settings in a creative way to design a unique flower. To do this, you can overlap multiple flowers to create a more complex-looking plant.

1. Scroll back up to the top of the Flowers settings, and set Num Flowers to 6.

FIGURE 8.24
Flower Angle 1 and Flower Angle 2 set a range of angles for the flower petals along the length of the tube.

2. Go back down below Petal Width Scale, and enter the following settings:

   Flower Start: **1**

   Flower Angle 1: **70**

   Flower Angle 2: **2**

3. Set Flower Twist to **0.6**. Flower Twist will rotate the flowers along the length of the tube.

4. Set Petal Bend to **-0.34**. Petal Bend bends the petals toward or away from the center (see Figure 8.25).

   At this point you should have a nice-looking flower developing.

5. Save the scene as `waterPlant_v03.ma`.

   To see a version of the scene, open the `waterPlant_v03.ma` scene from the `chapter8\` `scenes` folder on the DVD.

FIGURE 8.25
The flower shape is further refined using the angle, twist, and bend settings.

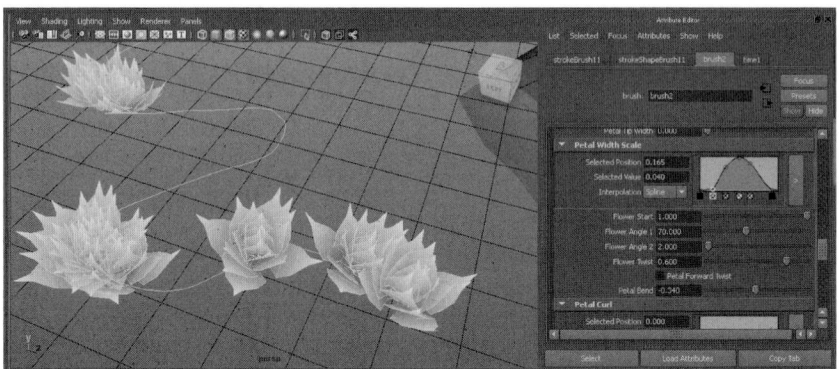

You can use the settings in the Petal Twirl section to give the petals more volume. To best see how this works, you can add geometry resolution to the petals by increasing the Petal Segments setting.

1. Set Petal Segments to **12**.

   Petal Twirl rotates the petals around their base. Decreasing Petal Flatness adds volume to the petals, making them more three-dimensional. Decreasing Petal Size Decay decreases the size of the petals toward the end of the tubes. When this is at 1, all petals are the same size. Moving this beyond 1 inverts the effect so petals toward the end of the tubes are larger than those at the bottom.

2. To create a more alien-looking flower, try these settings:

   Petal Twirl: **0.156**

   Petal Flatness: **0.7**

   Flower Size Decay: **1.7**

New!

> ## UNDERSTANDING THE FLOWER FACES SUN SETTING
>
> New to Maya 2011, some aspects of Paint Effects strokes can be made to simulate what's known in botany as *phototropism*: the tendency for a plant to face a light source. The Flower Faces Sun setting sets the strength of this force:
>
> ◆ A value of 1 causes the flower petals to face the Sun Direction.
>
> ◆ A value of 0 has no effect.
>
> The Sun Direction setting is a vector value found in the Growth rollout panel. A similar setting can also be used to control the direction of leaves. The Sun Direction vector can be animated.

Before moving on to leaves, you can set the color for the petals of the flowers. We'll return to the Flower Translucence and Flower Specular settings when we discuss illuminating strokes later in the chapter.

3. Set Petal Color **1** to a pinkish red color and Petal Color **2** to a pale purple.

4. The Flower Hue Rand, Sat Rand, and Val Rand settings add variation to the color by randomizing hue, saturation, and value, respectively. Enter the following settings:

Flower Hue Rand: **0.027**

Flower Sat: **0.095**

Flower Val Rand: **0.034**

5. Save the scene as `waterPlant_v04.ma`.

To see a version of the scene, open the `waterPlant_v04.ma` scene from the `chapter8\scenes` folder on the DVD.

Adding Leaves

The process for adding leaves to Paint Effects is very similar to adding flowers. One way you can add realism to Paint Effects strokes is to use a texture to shade the leaf geometry.

1. Continue with the scene from the previous section, or open the `waterPlant_v04.ma` scene from the `chapter8\scenes` folder on the DVD.

2. Select the stroke in the Outliner, and open the Attribute Editor to the brush2 tab.

3. Under the Tubes rollout, expand Growth, and turn on the Leaves option.

4. Expand the Leaves rollout panel in the Growth section, and use the following settings:

Leaves in Cluster: **4**

Num Leaf Clusters: **3**

Leaf Drop Out: **0.415**

Leaf Length: **0.17**

Leaf Base Width: **0.1**

Leaf Tip Width: **0.1**

Leaf Start: **1**

Leaf Angle 1: **90**

Leaf Angle 2: **80**

Leaf Twist: **0.65**

Leaf Bend: **-0.068**

Leaf Twirl: **-1**

Leaf Segments: **14**

Leaf Flatness: **1**

Leaf Size Decay: **0.5**

5. You can add a curl to the tip of the leaves by adjusting the Leaf Curl ramp. The default setting is 0.5; by raising or lowering points on the ramp, the leaves will curl in one direction or the other. The right side corresponds to the tip of the leaf, and the left side corresponds to the base. Try adjusting the ramp as shown in Figure 8.26.

FIGURE 8.26
The Leaf Curl ramp
adds curl to the
ends of the leaves.

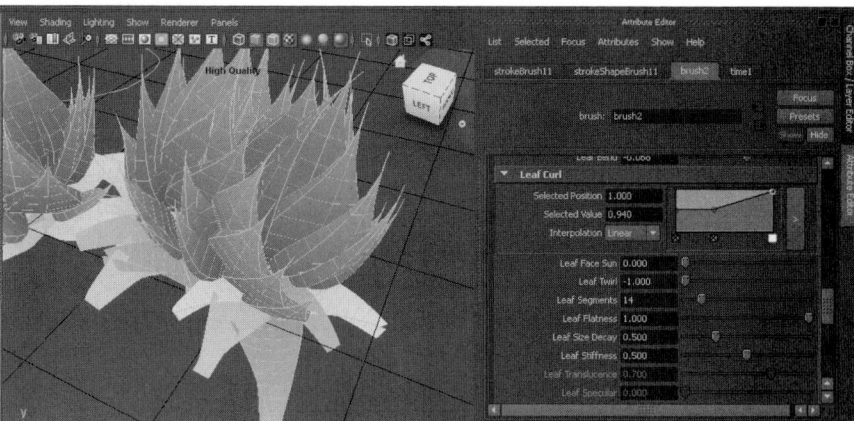

6. Set Leaf Color 1 and Leaf Color 2 to light greenish/yellow colors.

7. Enter the following settings:

Leaf Hue Rand: **0.034**

Leaf Sat Rand: **0.061**

Leaf Val Rand: **0.259**

8. Turn off the Leaf Use Branch Tex option; this makes the Image Name field available.

9. Click the folder to the right of the field, and choose the `leaf.tif` image from the `chapter8\sourceimages` folder.

The leaf image will be visible when the scene is rendered using Maya Software.

10. Choose Window ➢ Rendering Editors ➢ Render View.

11. Set the Renderer option to Maya Software using the menu in the top bar of the Render View window.

12. Zoom in to one of the flowers in the perspective view. In the Render View window, choose Render ➢ Render ➢ Persp. In the rendered image, you can see how the leaf texture has been applied to the leaves (see Figure 8.27).

13. Save the scene as **`waterPlant_v05.ma`**.

FIGURE 8.27
A file texture can add realism to the leaves of Paint Effects strokes.

File textures can also be used for flower petals. Strategic use of file textures can create very realistic plants and other objects with Paint Effects.

To see a version of the scene, open the `waterPlant_v05.ma` scene from the `chapter8\scenes` folder on the DVD.

LEAF RENDER QUALITY

If you notice that the edges of the leaf image look a little jagged, you can improve the render quality by opening the Render Settings window. On the Maya Software tab, you can scroll to the bottom, expand the Paint Effects Rendering options, and enable the Oversample check box.

PAINT EFFECTS CARDS

You may be required, at some point in your career, to create a very dense forest or a crowd of people that will fill the background of a scene. To maximize rendering efficiency, it's common practice to map images to flat pieces of geometry. These *flats* (also known as *billboards*) can be placed in the background to fill in spaces in the render. If they are far from the camera, in most cases no one will notice that they are not actually 3D objects. You can use Paint Effects to quickly paint these flats into the scene. Here are the steps to accomplish this:

1. Create a stroke in the scene. Paint it in the area where you want the flats to appear.

2. Turn on Tubes and Tube Completion for the stroke.

3. In the Stroke Profile section, set Flatness1 and Flatness2 to a value of **1**.

4. In the Creation section, set Segments to **1**.

5. Lower the Tubes Per Step to increase the amount of space between flats.

6. Set the Tube Direction to Along Normal. Set Elevation Min and Max and Azimuth Min and Max to **1**.

7. Make the tubes match the proportions of the image you want to map to the flats. Set Length Min and Length Max to the height value and TubeWidth1 and TubeWidth2 to the same value.

8. In the Texturing options, activate Map Color and Map Opacity.

9. Set Texture Type to File, and use the Image Name field to select the image file. Use a file texture that has an alpha channel.

10. In the Twist controls, activate Forward Twist. This ensures that the tubes rotate to face the camera. Note that the automatic rotation occurs around only a single axis of the flats.

11. In the Shading section, you can add a slight randomization to the Hue, Saturation, and Value of the images to increase variety. Create several similar brushes that use different images, and overlap brush strokes to create a dense forest or thick crowd.

Open the pfxFlatForest.ma scene from the chapter8\scenes folder on the DVD to see an example of this technique.

Create Complexity by Adding Strokes to a Curve

You can increase the complexity of your plant life by attaching different strokes to the same curve.

Now you can try adding tendrils that drop below the surface of the water beneath each flower. A simple way to do this is to add a stroke to the same control curve and then manipulate its settings in order to achieve the effect. Branches can be used to split the tubes into dense thickets.

1. Continue with the scene from the previous section, or open the waterPlant_v05.ma scene from the chapter8 folder on the DVD.

   To add a stroke to the original control curve, duplicate the flower stroke and its input connections.

2. Select the strokeBrush11 stroke in the Outliner, and choose Edit ➢ Duplicate Special ➢ Options.

3. In the options, set Group Under to World, and turn on Duplicate Input Connections; make sure Number of Copies is set to 1.

4. Click Apply to duplicate the stroke.

   The duplicate stroke looks exactly like the original, which is fine; you'll change that in a second.

5. Select strokeBrush11, and rename it **flowers**; select the new stroke, and rename it **tendrils**.

6. In the Outliner window, use the Display menu to turn on the visibility of the shape nodes (Display ➢ Shapes).

7. Expand the flower node, and rename its shape node **flowerShape**. Rename the shape node for the tendril stroke to **tendrilShape**. Taking the time to do this will help avoid confusion when working in the Attribute Editor.

8. Select the tendrils stroke, open its Attribute Editor, and switch to the brush3 tab.

9. Scroll down to the Growth section under Tubes, turn off Flowers and Leaves, and turn on Branches.

10. Scroll up to the Creation settings, and set Length Min to **0.53** and Length Max to **1**. The flowers and leaves have disappeared, and now each flower has what appear to be sticks coming out of the top. These sticks will become the tendrils (see Figure 8.28).

    By duplicating the original stroke, we've ensured that the tubes of the second stroke are placed at the same position as the original; of course now we need to find a way to get them to point downward into the water. The reason we're duplicating the stroke rather than just activating branches on the original is because doing so would change the number of flowers and thus mess up our carefully constructed plant so far.

FIGURE 8.28
The duplicated stroke appears as sticks coming out of the top of each flower.

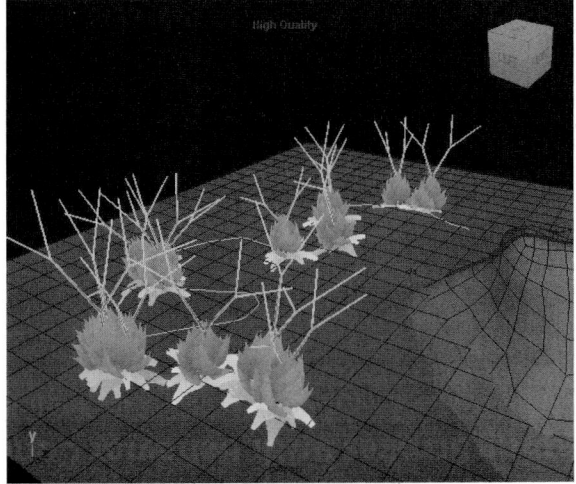

11. In the Attribute Editor, switch to the tendrilShape tab. Expand the Normal Direction roll-out panel, and turn on Use Normal.

12. Set the Normal fields to **0, -1, 0**. This points the tubes downward along the negative y-axis (see Figure 8.29).

FIGURE 8.29
Use the Normal Direction settings on the stroke's Shape tab to control the direction of the tubes.

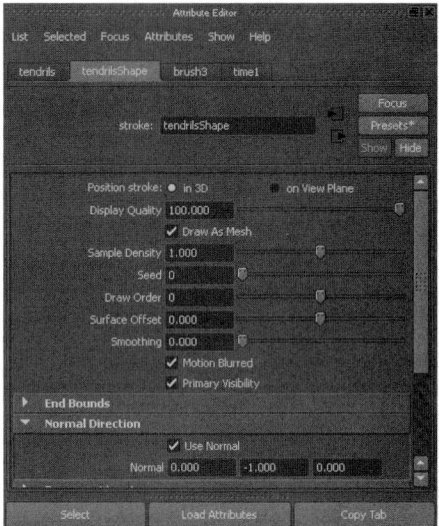

13. Switch back to the brush3 tab, and use the following settings to make the tubes look more like twisted tendrils:

UNDER CREATION	UNDER BRANCHES
Tubes per Step: **0.1**	Start Branches: **0**
Segments: **20**	Num Branches: **3**
Tube Width 1: **0.025**	Split Max Depth: **2**
Tube Width 2: **0.005**	Branch Dropout: **0**
Tube Direction: **Along Path**	Split Rand: **0.204**
Elevation Min: **0.172**	Split Angle: **19.5**
Elevation Max: **0.119**	Split Twist: **0.1**
Azimuth Min: **0.073**	Split Size Decay: **0.602**
Azimuth Max: **-0.007**	Split Bias: **-0.633**

These settings were arrived at through an experimental process and certainly not in the order in which they are listed. Once you become more comfortable with working with Paint Effects, you'll be able to design your own brushes through experimentation as well (see Figure 8.30).

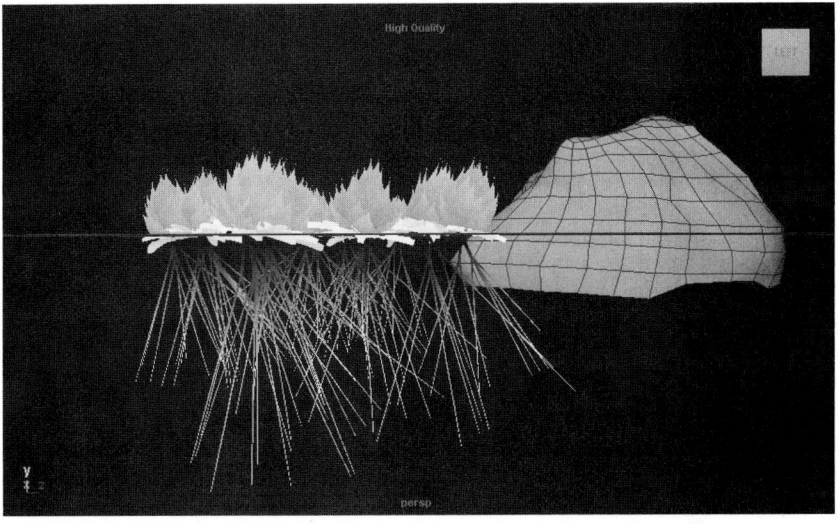

Middle Branch adds a branch at the center of each branch split.

Twigs are very similar in concept to branches, and their controls are similar to those used in the Creation section of the Attribute Editor. Experiment using twigs with and without branches. Sometimes they can be used to extend branches; sometimes they work well as an alternative to branches.

Buds are tiny tubes that are placed at the ends of branches and leaves.

14. Save the scene as **waterPlant_v06.ma**.

To see a version of the scene open the waterPlant_v06.ma scene from the chapter8\scenes folder on the DVD.

PAINT EFFECTS DISPLAY CONTROLS

As you add more elements to the scene, it may slow down the performance of Maya. You can reduce the display quality of the strokes in the scene or disable Display As Mesh. This makes working in the scene much more responsive.

You can find the display quality controls on the shape node of each stroke—not in the brush controls. So, you need to set each one individually. However, if you have a lot of strokes in the scene, you can Shift+click them all in the Outliner and then change the display settings in the SHAPES section of the Channel Box.

Reducing the Display Percent makes it look as though parts of the stroke are being removed, but this will not actually affect how the stroke looks when rendered. Turning off Draw As Mesh makes the brush appear as a curve in the scene.

Shaping Strokes with Behavior Controls

The controls found in the Behavior section of the brush attributes are similar to deformers that you apply to models. You can use behaviors to shape the strokes and control how they appear in the scene.

Applying Forces

The order in which these settings are placed in the Attribute Editor is not exactly intuitive. Displacements are listed above Forces, but you may find that it's easier to work with the Forces settings first to establish a shape to the strokes and then use the Displacement settings to add detail to the shape of the strokes.

The various controls in the Forces rollout panel offer different ways of pushing and pulling the strokes. They can be used separately or in combination. Once again, applying these settings is an experimental process.

Path Follow Path Follow causes the strokes to grow along the length of the path used to define the stroke. A setting of 1 causes the strokes to cling to the original path. A negative value makes the strokes grow in the opposite direction. This can be used to make tangled vines or twisted rope grow along the length of a stroke.

Path Attract Path Attract causes the original stroke to influence the growth of the tubes and branches. Increasing this value makes the tubes bend toward the path; decreasing this value makes the tubes bend away.

Curve Follow and Curve Attract The Curve Follow and Curve Attract settings work the same way as Path Follow and Path Attract; however, they use a separate control curve rather than the original path curve. If there is no control curve present, these settings have no effect.

To add a control curve, follow these steps:

1. Draw a curve in the scene.

2. Select the strokes in the Outliner and the curve.

3. Choose Paint Effects ➤ Curve Utilities ➤ Set Control Curves.

More than one curve can be used. The Max Distance slider sets a maximum distance for the influence the control curve has on the stroke. A control curve can be attached to an animated object or character so that when the character comes close to the strokes, they bend away from or toward the character. Control curves can be used to more precisely define the overall shape of the strokes. For instance, if you need ivy to grow in a very specific way over the arched doorway of a building, you can use multiple control curves to shape the ivy strokes.

In the case of our waterPlant scene, a simple Gravity force can be used to make the tendrils droop in the water.

1. Continue with the scene from the previous section, or open the waterPlant_v06.ma scene from the chapter8\scenes folder on the DVD.

2. Select the tendrils stroke, and open the Attribute Editor.

3. Switch to the brush3 tab. Toward the bottom, you'll find the Behavior section.

4. Expand Behaviors and then the Forces rollout panel. Set Gravity to **0.5**.

The Uniform Force and Gravity controls apply a force to the strokes along a specified axis. You can define the axis of influence by entering numeric values in the Uniform Force fields. By increasing the Gravity slider, the force is applied in the negative Y direction.

5. To add a more root-like appearance, set Random to **0.42**.

Deflection is used to keep strokes from going through the surface they are painted on. In this case, it's not needed, but it can be useful if you find that your strokes are penetrating surfaces.

The Length Flex setting allows the tubes to stretch in response to forces like gravity. Momentum is used when stroke animation is enabled; stroke animation is discussed a little later in the Animating Strokes section of this chapter.

Displacement, Spiral, and Bend

You can add details to the stroke shape using the sliders in the Displacement section. It is sometimes easier to add displacements after adding forces.

Displacement Delay causes the changes made with the Displacement controls to be stronger toward the ends of the tubes. Setting this to 0 means that displacements are applied along the length of the tube.

The Noise, Wiggle, and Curl sliders add tiny bends to the tubes and branches to create randomness. A larger Frequency value adds more detail to the changes. The Offset sliders are used when animating these attributes. Keyframing the offset over time will make the strokes appear to wiggle, curl, or move randomly, which can be great when creating animated creatures using Paint Effects. The following example shows how you can change the shape of the strokes using Displacement, Spiral, and Bend:

1. Try the following settings on the tendrils stroke:

Displacement Delay: **0.2**

Noise: **0.5**

Noise Frequency: **0.1**

Wiggle: **0.3**

Wiggle Frequency: **8**

Curl: **0.5**

Curl Frequency: **2**

Figure 8.31 shows the result.

FIGURE 8.31
Displacement settings are used to add detail to the strokes.

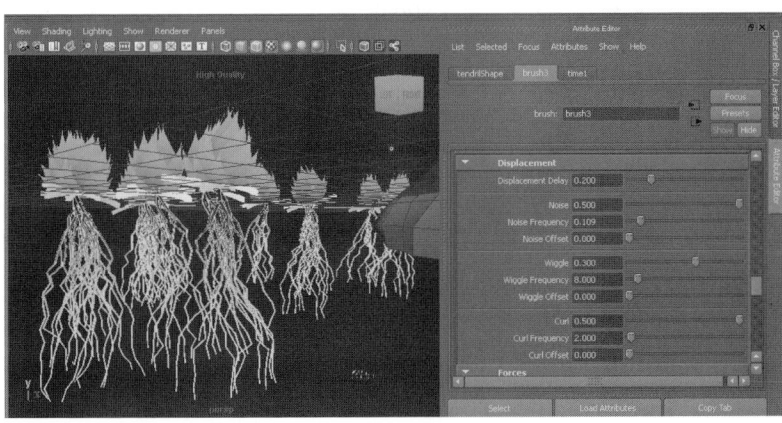

Spiral and Bend are similar to each other except that increasing the Spiral attribute creates a curve in the tubes, leaves, and flowers that bends the stroke around the stroke normal, whereas increasing the Bend attribute curves the stroke bend along the direction of the path. Once again, the best way to understand these behaviors is through experimentation.

2. Now try these settings:

Spiral Min: **-0.741**

Spiral Max: **0.510**

Spiral Decay: **0.027**

Positive Spiral Decay values create tighter spirals; negative values create looser spirals.

3. Set Bend to **-1.156** and Bend Bias to **0.197**. This spreads out the ends of the tendrils (Figure 8.32).

FIGURE 8.32
The tendrils are bent and twisted around after the Spiral and Bend settings are applied.

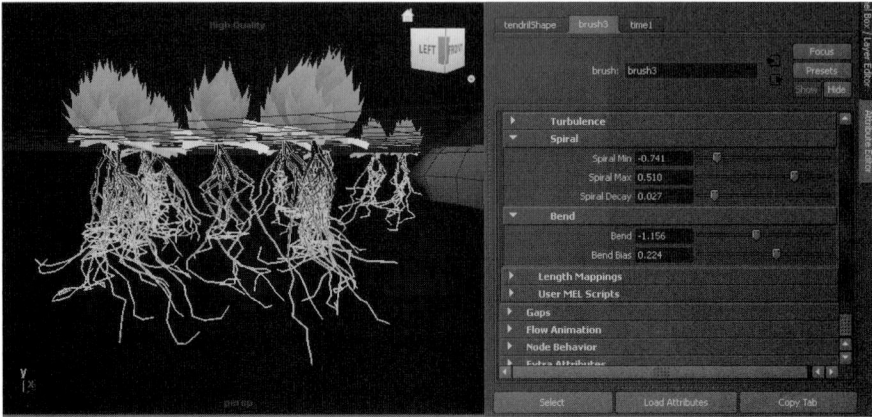

Bend Bias determines where, along the length of the tube, the bend starts. A Bias value of 0 makes the bend start at the base. Higher values cause the bend to be closer to the tip.

LEAF STIFFNESS

If you find that the Displacement settings distort the shape of the leaves, you can increase the Leaf Stiffness setting in the Leaf controls to force the leaves back into their original shapes.

---

4. Save the scene as **waterPlant_v07.ma**.

To see a version of the scene, open the waterPlant_v07.ma scene from the chapter8\scenes folder on the DVD.

Animating Strokes

Paint Effects strokes can be animated in a number of ways. Animation creates the sense that the strokes are alive and organic. Even a small amount of animation can have a major impact on the mood of a scene. In this section, you'll learn some of the techniques available for animating Paint Effects.

PRESSURE MAPPINGS

When you paint strokes in a scene using a digital tablet as an input device, variations in pressure are recorded as you paint the stroke. You can actually edit these recorded pressure values in the Attribute Editor for each stroke's shape node and change which attributes are affected by pressure after the stroke has been painted.

In the shape node for a Paint Effects stroke, the recorded pressure values are listed in a table found under Pressure Mappings ➤ Pressure in the Attribute Editor. When you expand this list, you can select values and change them by typing in new values. To scroll down the list, select the lowest displayed value, and press the down-arrow key on the keyboard.

You can select up to three stroke attributes that can be controlled by the recorded pressure values. Select the stroke attribute you want pressure to affect from the menu next to Pressure Map 1, 2, and 3.

The Pressure Scale section provides you with a ramp curve that can be used to fine-tune how the pressure modifies the stroke attribute values.

You can use the Pressure Mappings to further refine the shape and the animation of a brush stroke. Note that since the Pressure Mappings are part of the stroke shape node, they are not included when Brush Sharing is enabled.

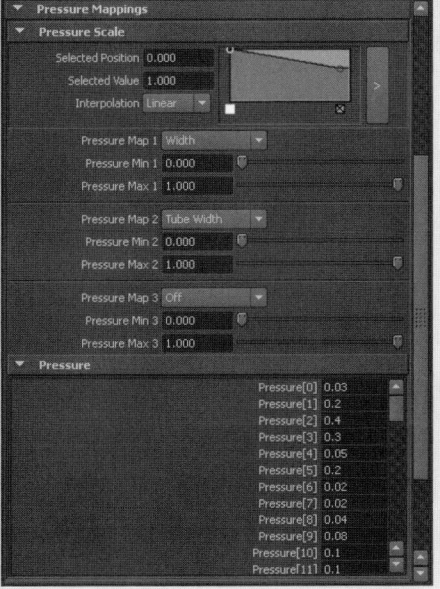

Animating Attribute Values

As you have no doubt noticed, a Paint Effects brush has a large number of attributes. Almost every single one of these can be animated using keyframes, expressions, driven keys, and textures. There's almost no limit to the number of wild effects that you can achieve by animating attribute values. This section demonstrates just a couple creative ways to keyframe the attributes.

1. Continue with the scene from the previous section, or open the waterPlant_v07.ma scene from the chapter8\scenes directory on the DVD.

2. Select the tendrils stroke in the Outliner, and open the Attribute Editor to the brush3 tab.

3. Scroll down to the bottom of the Attributes section, and expand the Behavior controls in the Tubes rollout.

4. In the Displacement rollout, in the field next to Wiggle Offset, type **=time;**. This creates a very simple expression that sets the Wiggle Offset value equal to the current time (in seconds), as shown in Figure 8.33.

5. Set the timeline to **200**, and play the animation. The tendrils wiggle as a sinusoidal pattern moves along the length of the stroke.

FIGURE 8.33
Add a simple expression to the Wiggle Offset attribute.

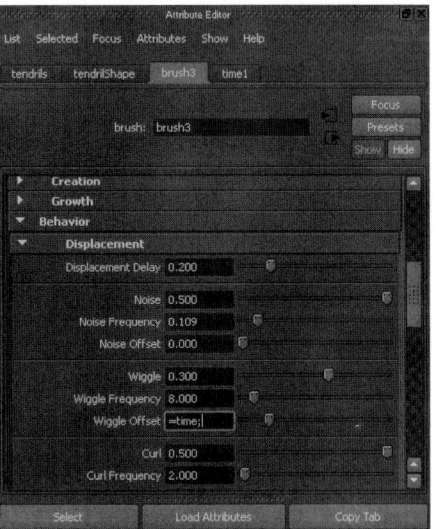

Adding Turbulence

Paint Effects strokes have built-in Turbulence controls that are similar to the fields used with a dynamic system, such as nCloth and nParticles. You can choose among several types of turbulence.

Turbulence as a *force* causes the ends of the tubes to move back and forth as though the turbulence is moving laterally through a field of tubes. Turbulence as a *displacement* causes the tubes to bob up and down so the strokes are being displaced based on the normal of the stroke.

The Turbulence options are Off, Local Force, World Force, Local Displacement, World Displacement, Grass Wind, and Tree Wind, as shown in Figure 8.34. You can choose to have the turbulence force or displacement applied in local or world space. World space is generally a better option if you want a number of separate strokes to appear as though they are all affected by the same turbulence.

FIGURE 8.34
You can choose from a number of different types of turbulence.

Grass Wind and Tree Wind are similar in that the turbulence affects the ends of the tubes more than the roots so it appears as though the strokes are blowing in the wind. Grass Wind affects the tips of the tubes; Tree Wind affects the tips of branches. Both forces are applied using world space coordinates.

The interpolation (see Figure 8.34) adjusts the quality of the turbulence. A linear setting causes a jerkier, random motion; Smooth Over Time and Smooth Over Time And Space create a more natural motion. Smooth Over Time And Space offers the highest quality, while Linear and Smooth Over Time work better for higher turbulence speeds.

Adding turbulence is very simple:

1. Select the tendrils stroke in the Outliner, and open the Attribute Editor to the brush3 tab.

2. In the Displacement section under Behavior, right-click the Wiggle Offset field, choose Delete Expression, and set this value to **1**.

3. Expand the Turbulence rollout panel underneath Forces. Take a look at the options in the Turbulence Type menu.

4. Set Turbulence Type to Grass Wind and Interpolation to Smooth Over Time and Space.

5. Further, enter the following settings:

   Turbulence: **1**

   Frequency: **0.884**

   Turbulence Speed: **0.809**

6. Play the animation. To get a sense of how the branches behave, create a playblast.

7. Save the scene as `waterPlant_v08.ma`.

Animating Growth

The most interesting way to animate a stroke is to animate its growth using the Flow Animation controls. Flow animation animates the growth of tubes, branches, leaves, twigs, and flowers along the path of the stroke.

1. Continue with the scene from the previous section, or open the `waterPlant_v08.ma` scene from the `chapter8\scenes` directory on the DVD.

2. Select the tendrils stroke in the Outliner, and open the Attribute Editor to the brush3 tab.

3. In the Turbulence settings, set turbulence to 0.1. Reducing the turbulence will allow you to see how the flow animation affects the tendril stroke better.

4. Scroll to the bottom of the attribute list, and expand the Flow Animation controls. Set Flow Speed to **1**.

5. Turn on the options for Stroke Time and Time Clip.

6. Turn off Texture flow.

ABOUT TIME CLIP

When Time Clip is enabled, the display of the strokes automatically converts to wireframe; this does not affect how the strokes appear in the render.

- If Stroke Time is on, the tubes at the start of the stroke will grow first, and the tubes at the end of the stroke will grow last so that the growth moves along the path of the stroke. If Stroke Time is off, all the tubes grow at the same time.

- Time Clip enables the growth animation. If this option is off, the strokes will not grow. However, if Texture Flow is on and Time Clip is off, textures applied in the Texturing section appear to move along the tubes. Applying Textures to tubes is covered later in the chapter.

- Time Clip uses the Start and Time values to establish the beginning and end of the animation. These values refer to seconds. So if your animation is set to 24 frames per second and you enter **2** for the start time, the growth will not begin until frame 48 (24 × 2).

- The End time is usually set to a high value, but you can create very interesting effects by lowering this setting. If the End time is within the range of the animation, the strokes will appear to fly off the path as they disappear from the root of each tube. This is great for creating the look of fireworks or solar flares.

7. Select the flowers stroke in the Outliner.

8. Switch to the brush2 tab in the Attribute Editor, and apply the same settings to its Flow Animation.

9. Create a playblast of the animation to see the tendrils grow and the flowers bloom. They will be represented as wireframes during the animation.

10. Try setting the End time to **1** for both strokes, and create another playblast.

11. Save the scene as `waterPlant_v09.ma`.

To see a version of the scene, open the `waterPlant_v09.ma` scene from the `chapter8\scenes` folder on the DVD.

Color Gallery

On the following pages, you will find color versions of some of the renders created from the example scenes in this book. In addition, you'll find examples of work by Maya users.

This image demonstrates how translucency can be applied to the mental ray mia material to simulate light passing through leaves. This is discussed in Chapter 10.

The Physical Sun and Sky network is used to generate realistic outdoor lighting. Rotating the sunDirection light changes the time of day. This technique is explained in Chapter 9. **TOP:** The pergola model from Chapter 9 at midday. **BOTTOM:** The same model viewed at dusk. Model created by Travis Keller (`www.silverhammerdesign.com`).

TOP: Anthony Honn's car model is rendered using a studio lighting rig. **BOTTOM:** The same car is rendered in the same scene on a different render layer using outdoor lighting and different textures. This technique is explained in Chapter 12.

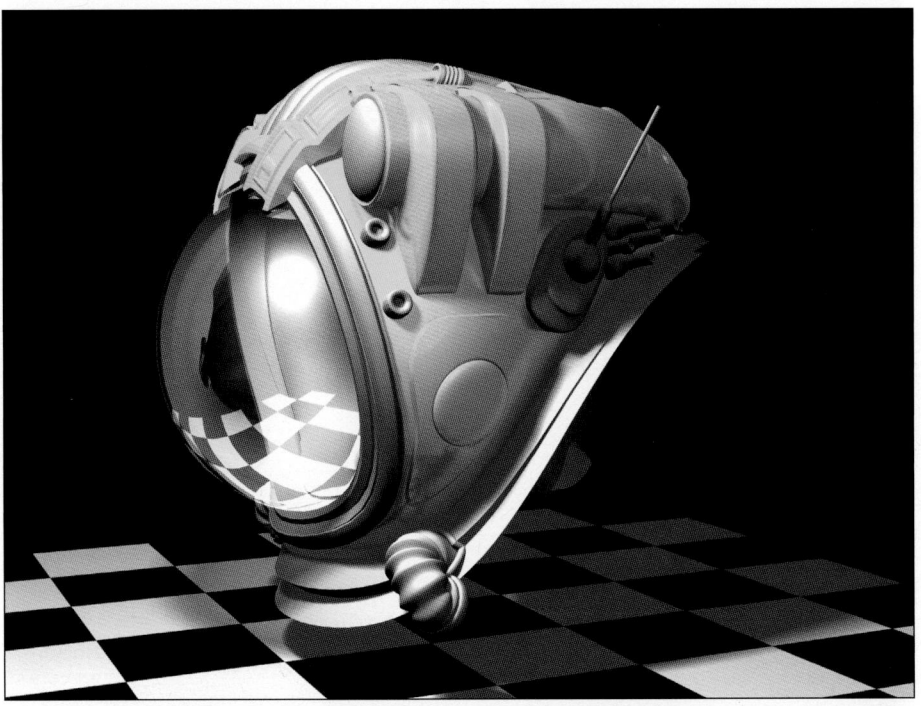

TOP: mental ray base shaders can be used to create realistic painted metal for the space helmet. These techniques are discussed in Chapter 10. **BOTTOM:** mental ray architectural shaders are used to create realistic materials for the helmet. These techniques are discussed in Chapter 10.

A vehicle designed, modeled, and textured by Anthony Honn (www.anthonyhonn.com).

This kitchen model was created by Travis Keller (www.silverhammerdesign.com) and rendered using a combination of direct and indirect lighting techniques.

Creations by Scott Ulliman (www.scottulliman.com). **TOP:** "Octopus Ahoy."
BOTTOM: "Birds and Bolts."

TOP: "MRV" wireframe model by Ara Kermanikian (www.kermaco.com). **BOTTOM:** "MRV2 and MRV17 Exhibit" by Ara Kermanikian (www.kermaco.com).

END BOUNDS

You can also animate the growth of strokes by keyframing the Min and Max Clip attributes found in the End Bounds controls in the Attribute Editor of the stroke's shape node.

Modifiers

Modifiers can be used to affect specified regions of a stroke. A modifier appears as a sphere or a cube. The modifier's position, rotation, and scale can be animated. You can use this when an object or character moves past Paint Effects strokes and you'd like the strokes to react to the object or character's movement. The modifier can be attached to the object or character.

To add a modifier, follow these steps:

1. Select one or more strokes.

2. Choose Paint Effects ➤ Create Modifier.

3. In the Attribute Editor for the modifier, set the range and falloff for the modifier as well as which stroke attributes are affected by the modifier.

Rendering Paint Effects

When Maya renders Paint Effects strokes, they are added to the image after the rest of the image has been created. This is known as *post-process*. Because the strokes are rendered after the rest of the scene elements have been rendered, very complex Paint Effects objects can render very quickly. However, it takes a little work to smoothly integrate Paint Effects into a realistic rendering.

Paint Effects are rendered normally using Maya Software. At the bottom of the Maya Software tab in the Render Settings window are a number of options specific to Paint Effects. Strokes will not render unless Stroke Rendering is enabled. You can improve the quality of rendered strokes by enabling Oversampling, and you can also choose to render only the strokes by themselves.

Illumination

There are two ways to light Paint Effects strokes in the scene. You can use the scene lights or a default Paint Effects light. In the Illumination section of the Brush attributes, you'll find the controls for these options.

If the Illumination option is not selected, the strokes render as a flat color using the color specified in the Shading options of the Brush attributes. If the Real Lights option is not selected, then you can specify the direction of the default Paint Effects lights numerically using the Light Direction fields. If Real Lights is selected, then the strokes will be lit using the lights in the scene, which can add to render time.

The Lighting Based Width option alters the width of the tubes based on the amount of light they receive.

There are a number of options, including Translucence and Specular, that affect the shading of the strokes and tubes when they are lit (see Figure 8.35).

FIGURE 8.35
The Illumination options determine how strokes react to lighting.

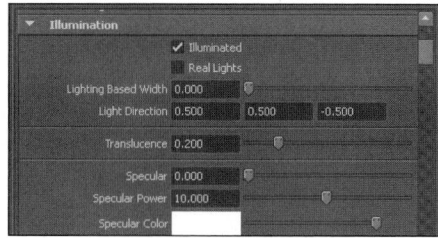

Shadow Effects

Paint Effects strokes can cast shadows in a number of ways. The options are set in the Shadow Effects controls in the Brush attributes.

If you want the shadows to be cast based on the actual lights in the scene, activate Real Lights in the Illumination options, set the Fake Shadow option to None, and activate the Cast Shadows option at the bottom of the Shadow Effects section. To change the quality of the shadows, you should use the Shadow controls for the lights in the scene (see Figure 8.36). The other options in the Shadowing section of the Brush attributes will have no effect on the render. Make sure shadows are enabled for the shadow casting light. Paint Effects works only with Depth Map shadows (shadows are covered in Chapter 9).

FIGURE 8.36
To cast shadows from scene lights, activate the Real Lights and Cast Shadows options in the Brush attributes.

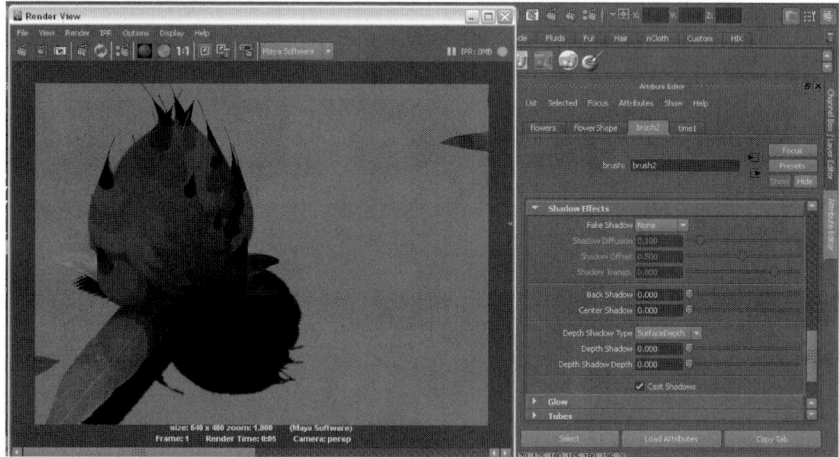

LIGHT LINKING AND PAINT EFFECTS

Light Linking will not work with Paint Effects. If you want only specific lights to illuminate Paint Effects strokes, use render layers to separate the strokes and shadows from the other scene elements, and then use compositing software to merge the passes. Render Layer techniques are discussed further in Chapter 12.

Paint Effects also has a number of controls for creating fake shadows. You can use 2D Offset to create a simple drop shadow, much like a drop-shadow effect created in a paint program such as Adobe Photoshop. You can also create fake 3D cast shadows. When you select 3D Cast in the Fake Shadows menu, Paint Effects creates an invisible plane beneath the surface of the stroke. Shadows are cast onto this plane and rendered in the scene (see Figure 8.37).

FIGURE 8.37
These two strokes demonstrate the difference between the two types of fake shadows. The top stroke uses 2D Offset; the bottom uses 3D Cast.

Some of the options available include the following:

Shadow Diffusion   Increasing this setting softens the edge of the shadows.

Shadow Offset   This determines the distance between the stroke and the 2D Offset fake shadow type. This option is not available for 3D cast shadows.

Shadow Transparency   Increasing this value makes the fake shadow more transparent.

Back Shadow   This darkens the areas of the stroke that face away from the light source.

Center Shadow   This is useful when painting a clump of strokes, such as tall grass. The areas inside the clump are shaded darker than the areas that are more exposed to light. This makes a clump of strokes look more realistic.

Depth Shadow   This darkens the tube based on its distance from the surface or path. When you increase this setting, you can fine-tune the look by choosing Path Dist or Surface Depth from the Depth Shadow Type menu. Path Dist darkens the parts of the stroke that are closer to the path; Surface Depth darkens parts of the stroke that are close to the surface.

Depth Shadow Depth   If the distance between the stroke and the shadow-receiving surface is greater than this setting, the shadow will not appear.

Shading Strokes and Tubes

The controls in the Shading section of a brush's Attribute Editor control how colors and textures are applied to strokes and tubes. As we discussed earlier in the chapter, flower petals and leaves are shaded separately using controls in the Growth section.

1. Open the `waterPlant_v09.ma` scene from the `chapter8\scenes` folder. Rewind the scene.

   In this version of the scene, the strokes are animated using the Flow Animation controls, so most likely they are not visible at the start of the animation.

2. Open the Attribute Editor for each stroke, switch to its brush tab, and deactivate Stroke Time and Time Clip in the Flow Animation section to make the strokes visible again.

3. Select the Tendrils stroke, and open its Attribute Editor.

4. Switch to the brush3 tab. Scroll to the shading section, and expand the Shading rollout panel.

   There are two sets of controls: the Shading controls for the stroke and the Tube Shading controls that affect tubes and branches.

   Shading controls The Shading controls are very simple. The Color 1 slider applies a flat color to the stroke. This color is mixed with the color chosen in the Incandescence control. When the Transparency slider is increased, the incandescence has a stronger influence on the shading of the stroke. A transparent stroke with a bright incandescence setting creates a nice neon glow or laser beam effect.

   Tube Shading controls The controls in the Tube Shading section are listed as Color 2, Incandescence 2, and Transparency 2. When you adjust these controls for a stroke that has tubes, it will shade the tips of tubes and branches. So, a gradient between the Color 1 color and the Color 2 color is created along the length of the tube (see Figure 8.38). The same goes for Incandescence and Transparency.

   Just for fun we'll see what happens when glow is applied to the plant tendrils toward the tips.

FIGURE 8.38
Setting different colors for the Shading and Tube shading controls creates a gradient along the length of the tubes.

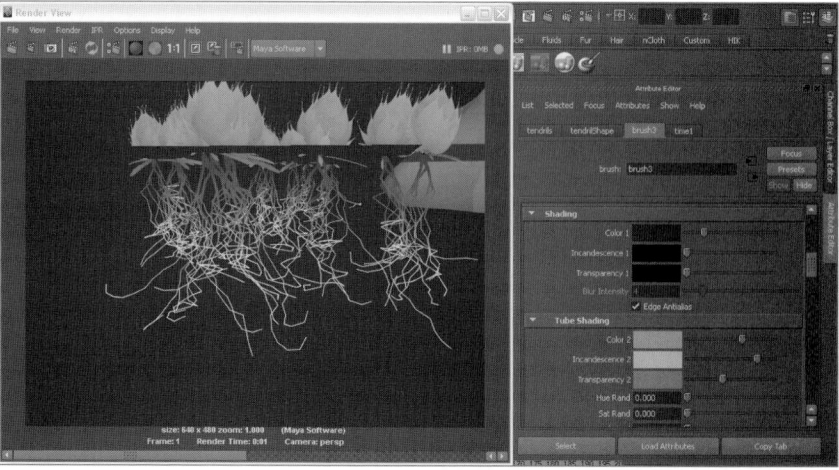

5. In the Shading section, enter the following settings:

Color 1: **Dark green**

Incandescence1: **Black**

Transparency 1: **Black**

6. In the Tube Shading section, enter the following settings:

Color 2: **Light green**

Incandescence 2: **Bright green**

Transparency 2: **Dark gray**

7. Create a test render of the scene in the Render Preview window using Maya Software.

The Hue, Sat, Val, and Brightness rand sliders can be used to add random variation to the tube shading. Root Fade and Tip Fade will make the ends transparent.

8. Scroll down to the Glow section below Shadow Effects, and enter the following settings:

Glow: **0.318**

Glow color: **Pale yellow**

Glow Spread: **1.7**

Shader Glow: **0.2**

9. Create a test render.

The Glow settings are useful when you want to create effects such as lightning or neon tubes. Glow is applied to the whole stroke including leaves and flower petals (see Figure 8.39).

FIGURE 8.39
The Glow settings can add glowing effects to strokes and tubes.

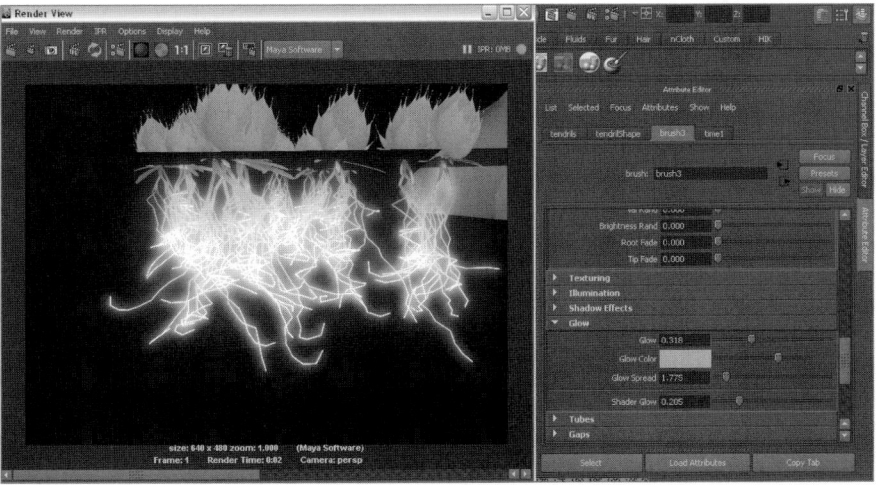

WORKING WITH THE SHADER GLOW NODE

To fine-tune the look of a glowing stroke, set the value for the Shader Glow slider above zero, and select the shader glow node in the Hypershade. The shader glow node is a global control for all glowing shaders and strokes in the scene. You can spend a fair amount of time working with these settings to produce glowing effects. Be aware that when you render an animation that has glowing shaders, you may see a noticeable flickering. To remove the flickering, turn off the Auto Exposure setting. When you do this, the glows will appear blown out. You can lower the Glow Intensity slider in the Glow Attributes to eliminate the blown-out look in the render.

Texturing Strokes

To create variation in the surface of a stroke, you can apply textures to the color, opacity, and even the displacement of the strokes.

1. Continuing with the settings on the brush3 tab of the Attribute Editor, in the Glow section set Glow to **0** and Shader Glow to **0** to turn off the glow.

2. In the Tube Shading section, set Incandescence 2 to black.

3. Scroll down to the Texturing section. Turn on Map Color.

4. Set Tex Color Scale to **0** and Tex Color Offset to **0**.

5. Scroll down and set Texture Type to Fractal and Map Method to Full View. Set Repeat U and Repeat V to **2**.

6. Toward the bottom of the section, set Fractal Amplitude to **1**.

7. Create a test render in the Render View window using Maya Software (see Figure 8.40).

8. To bring back the green color of the tubes, increase the Tex Color Scale slider. Tex Color Offset can be used to brighten the fractal texture. You can also use the Tex Color 1 and Tex Color 2 sliders to adjust the colors used in the fractal texture.

FIGURE 8.40
A fractal texture is applied to the tubes.

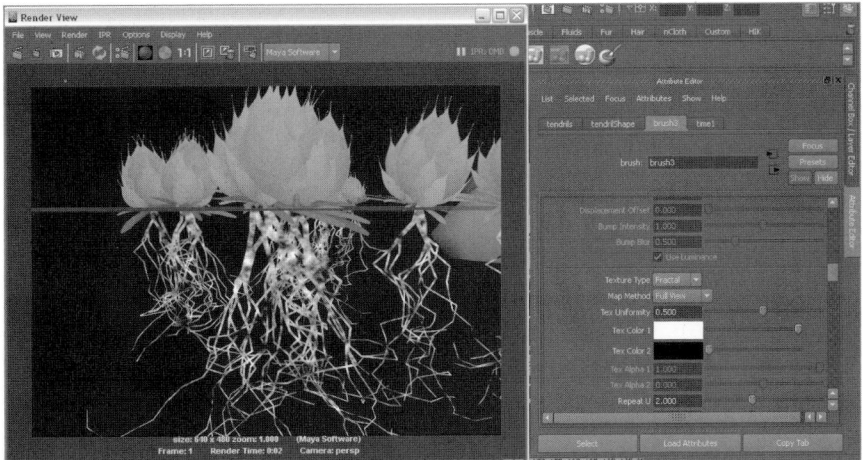

The Map Method setting controls how the texture is applied to the strokes. Both the Tube 2D and Tube 3D methods wrap the texture around the stroke. However, when Map 2D is used, the texture is always centered on the stroke. This eliminates any visible seam as the texture wraps around the stroke. Using the Map 3D method may give better results if the view of the stroke is animated.

Using Full View maps the texture across the entire view scene in the viewport.

9. Set Texture Type to File.

10. Scroll down and click the folder next to Image Name.

11. Use the File Browser dialog box to select the `metalPlate.tif` file from the `chapter8\sourceimages` directory on the DVD. Figure 8.41 shows the image.

FIGURE 8.41
The metal plate texture that will be applied to the stroke

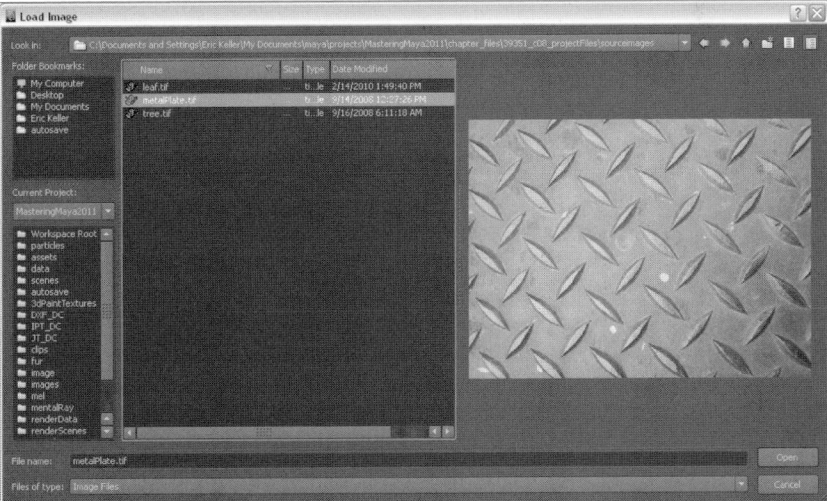

12. Set Map Method to Full View and Tex Color Scale to **0**.

13. Create a test render. The image is revealed by the stroke. The image fills the viewable area. If this stroke covered most of the screen, you would see the entire metalPlate image (see Figure 8.42).

FIGURE 8.42
Full View maps the texture to the stroke based on the viewable area of the scene.

ANIMATING A LOGO

One possible use for this mapping method would be to animate a logo reveal by mapping an image file of a logo to the stroke using the Full View method. The stroke could then be animated by drawing on the screen to reveal the logo.

The Brush Start method works similarly to the Full View method. However, the image is scaled to fit within the viewable area defined by the stroke.

You can map a texture to the opacity of the stroke and use a texture as a displacement. When using a displacement, Stroke Type should be set to Mesh, and you may need to increase the Tube Sections and Sub Sections settings in the Mesh controls. Setting Softness to 0 helps make the displacement more obvious. At this point, you can see how designing strokes involves a lot of moving back and forth among settings in the Attribute Editor.

14. Disable Map Color, enable Map Displacement.

15. Scroll up to the top of the Attribute Editor, and set Brush Type to Mesh in the Brush Profile rollout. Set Softness to **0**.

16. In the Mesh rollout panel, set Tube Sections to **30** and Sub Sections to **20**.

17. Scroll back down to the Texturing section, and enter the following settings:

Texture Type: **Fractal**

Repeat U: **4**

Repeat V: **4**

18. At the bottom of the Texturing rollout panel, set Fractal Amplitude to **1**.

19. Expand the Illumination settings just below the Texturing rollout panel, and enable Illuminated and Real Lights.

20. Set Lighting Based Width to **0.68**. This causes lighter areas of the stroke to become thinner.

21. Create a test render. You can see that the fractal texture displaces the stroke, making it appear lumpy (see Figure 8.43).

22. Save the scene as `waterPlant_v10.ma`.

To see a version of the scene, open the `waterPlant_v10.ma` scene from the `chapter8\scenes` directory on the DVD.

FIGURE 8.43
Applying a fractal texture as a displacement makes the surface of the stroke appear lumpy.

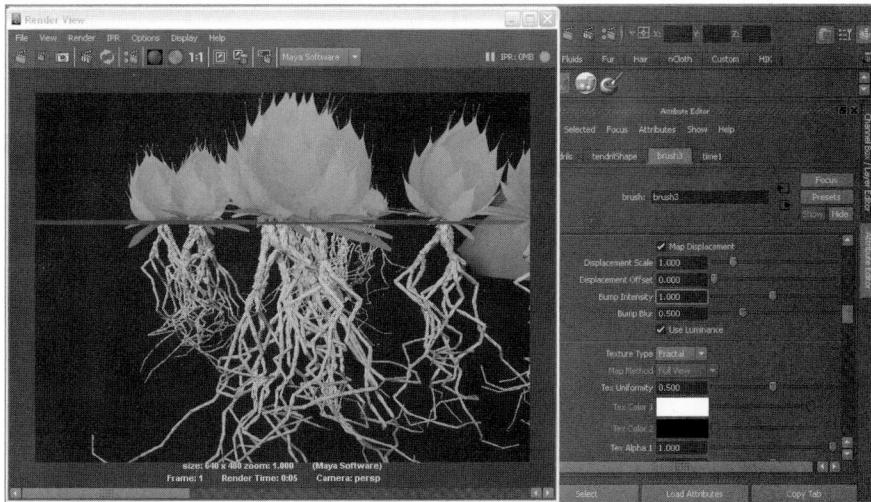

CONVERTING DISPLACED STROKES TO POLYGONS

The displacement created by the texture persists even when you convert the Paint Effects stroke to polygons (Modify ➤ Convert Paint Effects To Polygons). Converting strokes is covered later in the chapter.

Converting Strokes to Geometry

If you need to render Paint Effects strokes using mental ray, the best way to accomplish this is to convert the Paint Effects strokes into geometry. You can convert strokes into polygons or NURBS geometry. When you do this, Maya automatically creates a shader and applies it to the converted surface. The shader attempts to replicate any shading and texturing applied to the stroke in the Brush panel. File textures used for leaves and petals will be transferred to the newly created shaders. However, you'll most likely need to tweak the shader a little (or replace the shader with one of your own) to get the best results. A new shader is created for each stroke, so if you have a grass lawn made up of 30 strokes, Maya creates 30 identical shaders. You may want to apply one shader to all the strokes and then delete the unused shaders.

When you convert strokes to polygons, there is a limit to the number of polygons that Maya can generate. This limit can be adjusted in the options for Convert Paint Effects To Polygons. If the conversion exceeds the polygon limit, you'll see a warning, and the resulting geometry will be incomplete.

To convert the stroke to NURBS, select the stroke, and choose Modify ➤ Convert Paint Effects To NURBS. The resulting geometry will be created from a group of NURBS surfaces.

When converting Paint Effects to geometry, you can choose to hide the original strokes in the scene; this option is on by default. There is a history connection between the converted stroke and the geometry, so any animation applied to the stroke will be carried over to the geometry.

If you convert a stroke that uses flow animation into polygons, you may find that at some point during the growth of the stroke the polygon limit is exceeded. To avoid this, set the timeline to the end of the stroke's growth when it has reached its full length, and then convert the Paint Effects to polygons. You'll get a warning if the limit is exceeded. You can then take measures such as reducing the number of tubes or re-creating the animation using a number of shorter strokes.

1. Continue with the scene from the previous section, or open the `waterPlant_v10.ma` scene from the `chapter8\scenes` folder on the DVD.

2. Select the Flowers stroke in the Outliner, and choose Modify ➤ Convert Paint Effects To Polygons. After a few moments, the flower petals and leaves will be converted to polygons. You'll notice that the leaf texture now appears in the viewport window applied to the leaves.

3. In the Outliner, expand the brush2MainGroup node, and you'll see separate nodes created from brush2Main, brush2Leaf, and brush2Flower.

   If you select any of these nodes and open the Attribute Editor, you'll find a tab for brush2. The settings here will affect the polygon geometry as long as history is not deleted on any of the geometry nodes.

4. Select the tendrils node, and open its Attribute Editor to the brush3 tab.

5. In the Mesh section, set Tube Segments to **8** and subSegments to **2**. If these settings are too high, you may encounter problems when converting to geometry.

6. Select Tendrils in the Outliner, and choose Modify ➤ Convert Paint Effects To NURBS. In the Outliner, you'll see a new group node named tendrilsShapeSurfaces; parented to this node is another group containing all the NURBS surfaces for the tendrils.

CONVERTING PAINT EFFECTS TO GEOMETRY

There are many advantages to converting Paint Effects to geometry. You can apply complex shaders to the converted strokes and take advantage of mental ray shaders, which can be much more realistic than May Software render. You can also use modeling techniques to further refine the converted geometry, thus using Paint Effects as a way to start organic models such as trees and grass.

Be mindful that the geometry you create with Paint Effects can be quite heavy, which can lead to a slowdown in performance and longer render times. Many artists choose to create complex scenes using a combination of Paint Effects strokes and strokes that have been converted to geometry.

7. In the Outliner, expand the brush2Mesh group, and select the brush2Flower node.

8. Switch to the Polygon menu set, and choose Mesh ➢ Smooth. After a few moments, you'll see the geometry has been subdivided and smoothed.

9. Open the Render View window, set the render menu to mental ray, and create a test render (see Figure 8.44).

10. Save the scene as `waterPlant_v11.ma`.

To see a finished version of the scene, open the `waterPlant_v11.ma` scene from the `chapter8\scenes` folder on the DVD.

FIGURE 8.44
After converting strokes to geometry, you can render the Paint Effects strokes using mental ray.

Using Toon Shading

You can make your 3D objects and characters look as though they are hand-drawn cartoons using Toon Shading. Toon Shading is simple to apply and use, and it generally renders very quickly.

Toon Fills

A toon fill is simply a ramp shader that you apply to the objects in a scene. There are several Fill presets you can apply from the Maya Rendering menu set. Each one is a ramp shader with different settings designed to give you a starting point from which you can design your own custom look.

The scene consists of several cartoon mushrooms on a hill. There is also a directional light in the scene:

1. Open the toon_v01.ma scene from the chapter8\scenes folder on the DVD.

2. In the perspective view, switch to the shotCam camera.

3. Switch to the Rendering menu set, and choose Toon ➤ Set Camera Background Color ➤ Shot Cam (Figure 8.45). The Color Chooser appears; choose a sky blue color.

4. To use the preset fills, select an object, and choose Toon ➤ Assign Fill Shader; then choose one of the presets from the list.

FIGURE 8.45
Choose a background color for the scene.

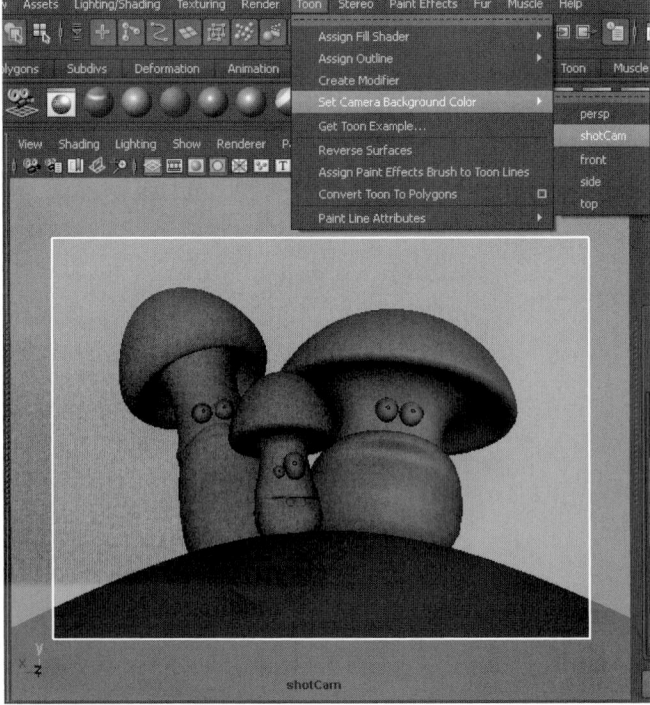

5. Apply the following:

   Apply a solid color fill to the hill.

   Set Light Angle Two Tone to mushroomGroup1.

   Set Shaded Brightness Two Tone to mushroomGroup2.

   Set Shaded Brightness Three Tone to mushroomGroup3.

6. Create a test render using Maya software (choose Production Quality from the Quality presets). Compare the look of the different shaders (see Figure 8.46).

7. Open the Hypershade to see the newly created shaders. Select one of the shaders, and change its settings in the Attribute Editor.

8. Click the Presets button in the upper right of the shader. Try some of the other presets available in the Assign Fill Shader menu, such as Dark Profile and Rim Light.

FIGURE 8.46
You can apply fills to objects using the presets in the Toon menu.

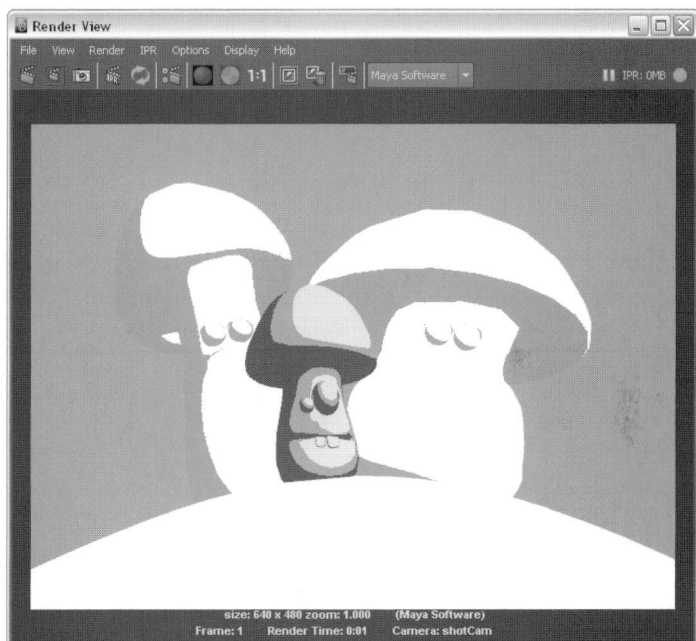

All of the Fill presets are created from ramp shaders. Ramp shaders use ramps to apply a color to the surface based on an input, such as light angle, facing angle, or brightness. You can add or remove colors from the various ramps by clicking them in the Attribute Editor. The Interpolation option determines the smoothness of the transition between each color in the ramp (see Figure 8.47).

FIGURE 8.47
Toon fills are created from ramp shaders. The settings can be adjusted in the Attribute Editor to customize the look of the fill.

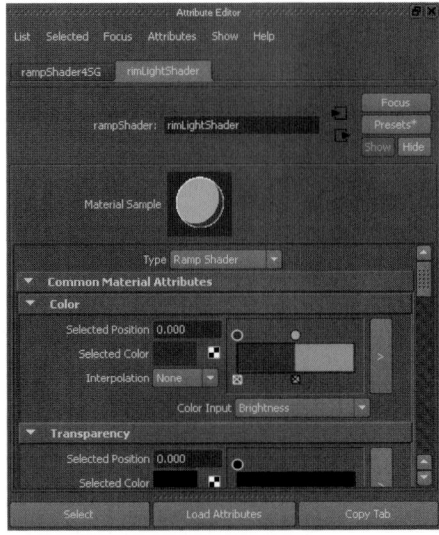

RAMP SHADER PRESETS

A number of additional presets can be applied and even blended together. In the Attribute Editor for any of the ramp shaders, click the Preset button in the upper-right corner, select a preset from the list, and choose to replace the current shader settings using the presets or blend the current settings with one of the presets.

Toon Outlines

Toon outlines are a special type of Paint Effects stroke. When you add a Paint Effects toon outline to an object and then rotate the object or the camera, the outline adjusts its position automatically so that it always remains on the contour of the object regardless of the viewing angle.

1. Open the `toon_v02.ma` scene from the `chapter8\scenes` directory on the DVD. This version of the scene has the same mushrooms as toon_v01.ma. In this case, fill shaders have already been applied to the mushroom characters.

2. In the Outliner, Shift+click the hill and each mushroom group.

3. Choose Toon ➤ Assign Outline ➤ Add New Toon Outline. In the Outliner, you'll see a new pfxToon1 node.

4. Select the pfxToon1 node in the Outliner, and open the Attribute Editor.

5. Select the pfxToonShape1 tab. This is where you'll find all the settings for tuning the look of toon lines. The toon lines are visible in the viewport window as well.

6. Expand the Common Toon Attributes, and set Line Width to **0.025**.

7. Create a test render in the render view from the shotCam camera.

8. Save the scene as **toon_v03.ma**.

To see a version of the scene to this point, open the `toon_v03.ma` scene from the `chapter8\` `scenes` directory (see Figure 8.48).

FIGURE 8.48
Toon lines are applied to the contours of the mushroom characters.

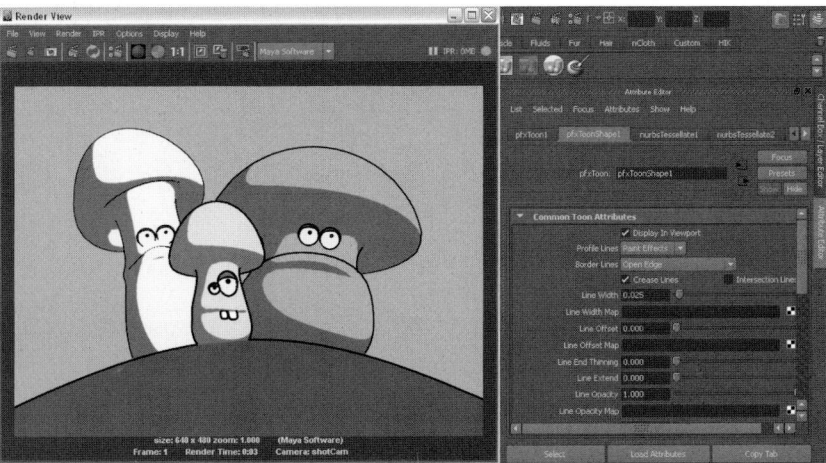

There are a large number of settings you can use to control the look of the toon lines. Some of the more important settings are listed here:

Profile Lines   A profile line is the line that is attached to the contours of the geometry. If you draw an apple on a piece of paper, the line that describes the outside edge of the apple is the profile line. Profile lines can be Paint Effects strokes or an offset mesh. An offset mesh is a copy of the surface that is scaled slightly larger than the original. The faces of the offset mesh are inverted to create the look of toon lines. This technique can be used when rendering with mental ray.

Border Lines   These lines can be set to appear at the open edge of geometry, such as the lip of a cup. They can also appear at the border between two shaders that have been applied to the geometry or both.

Crease Lines   These lines appear at the hard edges of geometry, such as the corner edge of a cube.

Intersection Lines   These appear at the intersection of two pieces of geometry. In the mushroom scene, the base of each mushroom character intersects with the geometry of the hill. If intersection lines are activated, a line will appear where these two surfaces meet.

In the lower section of the Attribute Editor are settings to control how each of these types of lines appears. You can edit their color, width, and specific attributes that apply to these types of lines.

CREATING A TOON WIREFRAME

You can create the look of a wireframe object in a render by turning on crease lines. In the Crease Lines settings, turn on Hard Creases Only, and lower the Crease Angle Min slider until you get the look that you want.

Using Paint Effects Presets for Toon Lines

You can replace the toon lines assigned to a model with a Paint Effects preset. You can use any brush available in the Visor or any brush that you create. The process for doing this is very simple:

1. Continue with the scene from the previous section, or open the toon_v03.ma scene from the chapter8\scenes directory on the DVD.

2. Choose Window ➤ General Editors ➤ Visor. Select the Toon folder from the Visor.

3. Choose the brokenWiggle.mel brush from the Toon presets. The icon should turn yellow when it's selected, indicating that it's the currently loaded brush.

4. Select the pfxToon1 node in the Outliner, and choose Toon ➤ Assign Paint Effects Brush To Toon Line.

5. Create a test render of the scene. You may want to increase the Line Width setting in the pfxToon1 node to see the line more clearly.

The brokenWiggle brush now replaces the original toon lines (see Figure 8.49). You can edit the settings on the pfxToon1 node to change how the toon lines behave. You also now have the brokenWiggle1 brush attributes available. These attributes work just like any other Paint Effects brush.

To edit the settings for the brokenWiggle brush, select the pfxToon1 brush, and open the Attribute Editor. You may need to click the right arrow in the upper-right corner of the Attribute Editor about a dozen or so times to find the brokenWiggle1 tab. Alternatively, you can turn off the DAG Objects Only option in the Display menu of the Outliner and select the brokenWiggle1 node.

FIGURE 8.49
The toon lines are replaced by the brokenWiggle Paint Effects stroke.

The Bottom Line

Use the Paint Effects canvas   The Paint Effects canvas can be used to test Paint Effects strokes or as a 2D paint program for creating images.

Master it   Create a tiling texture map using the Paint Effects canvas.

Paint on 3D objects   Paint Effects brushes can be used to paint directly on 3D objects as long as the objects are either NURBS or polygon geometry. Paint Effects brushes require that all polygon geometry have mapped UV texture coordinates.

Master it   Create a small garden or jungle using Paint Effects brushes.

Design a brush   Custom Paint Effects brushes can be created by using a preset brush as a starting place. You can alter the settings on the brush node to produce the desired look for the brush.

Master it   Design a brush to look like a laser beam.

Shape strokes with behaviors   Behaviors are settings that can be used to shape strokes and tubes, giving them wiggling, curling, and spiraling qualities. You can animate behaviors to bring strokes to life.

Master it   Add tendrils to a squashed sphere to create a simple jellyfish.

Animate strokes   Paint Effects strokes can be animated by applying keyframes, expressions, or animated textures directly to stroke attributes. You can animate the growth of strokes by using the Time Clip settings in the Flow Animation section of the Brush attributes.

Master it   Animate blood vessels growing across a surface. Animate the movement of blood within the vessels.

Render Paint Effects strokes   Paint Effects strokes are rendered as a post process using Maya software. To render with mental ray, you should convert the strokes to geometry.

Master it   Render an animated Paint Effects tree in mental ray.

Use Toon Shading   Toon Shading uses Paint Effects to create lines around the contours of an object and a ramp shader to color the surface of the object to replicate the look of a hand-drawn cartoon.

Master it   Add glowing contour lines to a futuristic vehicle to imitate the look of a vector-style rendering in a computer display.

Chapter 9

Lighting with mental ray

To achieve professional-quality, realistic renders in Maya, you need to master the mental ray render plug-in that comes with Maya. mental ray is a complex rendering system that is incorporated through the Maya interface. Learning how to use it properly and efficiently takes time, study, and practice. Chapters 9 through 12 discuss various aspects of working with mental ray. This chapter is concerned with using mental ray lighting tools and techniques to create realistic renders.

There are a lot of options within mental ray that allow you to achieve a wide variety of techniques. You won't need to use them all in every case, but a good understanding of what is available will help you make better decisions when approaching a lighting problem in a scene. In this chapter you will learn to:

◆ Use shadow-casting lights

◆ Render with Global Illumination

◆ Render with Final Gathering

◆ Use Image-Based Lighting

◆ Render using the Physical Sun and Sky network

◆ Understand mental ray area lights

Shadow-Casting Lights

There are two types of shadows that can be created in mental ray, cast shadows and ambient occlusion, and several methods for creating them. Any combination of cast shadows and ambient occlusion can be used in a mental ray scene.

Cast shadows   Cast shadows are created when an object blocks the rays of light coming from a light source from reaching one or more other surfaces. Cast shadows are the most familiar type of shadow, and they are often a good indication of the type, location, and orientation of the light source casting the shadow.

Ambient occlusion   Ambient occlusion occurs when indirect light rays are prevented from reaching a surface. Ambient occlusion is a soft and subtle type of shadowing. It's usually found in the cracks and crevices of 3D objects and scenes.

In this section, you'll create and tune cast shadows using lights in mental ray. Ambient occlusion is discussed later in the chapter in the sections titled "Indirect Lighting: Global Illumination" and "Indirect Lighting: Final Gathering," as well as in Chapter 12.

REVIEW MAYA LIGHTS

Before starting this chapter, you should be familiar with the basics of using lights in Maya. You should understand how to create, position, and edit standard Maya lights (spotlight, directional light, point light, area light). Using Maya Software as a renderer is not covered in this book. Maya Software settings have not changed significantly in several years, while mental ray's implementation in Maya continues to develop and to expand. In a professional setting, you will be expected to understand how to render with mental ray, so this book is devoted to helping you achieve the necessary understanding of and skill with mental ray.

A light source in a Maya scene casts either ray trace or depth map shadows. When you create a light in Maya, its shadows are turned off by default. To activate shadow casting, you can open the Attribute Editor for the light's shape node and activate either depth map or ray trace shadows. You can use both depth map and ray trace shadows together in the same scene, but each light can cast only one or the other type of cast shadow.

Shadow Preview

When you create a shadow-casting light in a Maya scene, you can preview the position of the shadow in the viewport window.

This scene shows a futuristic tractor vehicle designed by Anthony Honn on a simple, flat plane. The shaders used for the vehicle are very simple standard Maya Blinn materials. When setting up lights for a scene, it's usually a good idea to use simple shaders as you work. This makes test rendering faster and also keeps the focus on how the lighting will work within the composition. Later, as you refine the lighting of the scene, you can add more complex shaders and textures.

1. Open the tractorDroid_v01.ma scene from the chapter9\scenes directory on the DVD.

2. Create a spotlight by choosing Create ➤ Lights ➤ Spot Light.

   To position the spotlight, use the Move and Rotate tools. You can also look through the light as if it were a camera, which is often a faster and easier way to place the light in the scene.

3. Select the spotlight, and from the panels menu choose Panels ➤ Look Through Selected Camera. Use the Alt+MMB and the Alt+RMB key combinations to move the view so you can see the model from above (Figure 9.1).

4. The green circle at the center of the view represents the cone angle of the spotlight. Open the Attribute Editor for the spotLight1 object, and click the spotLightShape1 tab. Set the cone angle to **90**. The light from the spotlight now covers more area in the scene.

5. Switch to the renderCam view in the viewport (from the viewport Panels menu, choose Panels ➤ Perspective ➤ renderCam).

6. In the viewport Panels menu, choose Renderer ➤ High Quality Rendering.

7. In the Panels menu, choose Lighting ➤ Shadows; this option is available only when Use All Lights has been activated.

   You won't see any shadows until you activate shadows for the lights in the scene.

FIGURE 9.1
View the scene
from the position
of the spotlight.

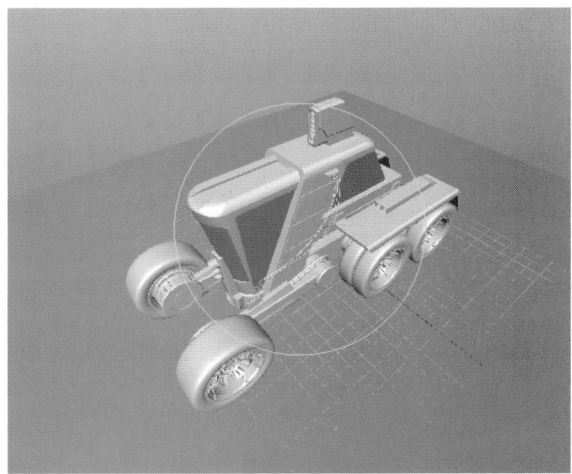

8. Select the spotLight1 object, open its Attribute Editor, and click the spotLightShape1 tab.

9. Expand the Shadows section, and activate Use Depth Map Shadows. A preview of the shadow appears on the ground plane (Figure 9.2).

10. Select the spotlight, and use the Move and Rotate tools to change its position and rotation. Observe the changes in the preview. The preview will most likely slow down the performance of Maya, so use this feature only when you are positioning lights.

11. Scroll to the top of the spotlight attributes, and set Type to Directional. Notice the difference in the shape of the shadow.

The shadow preview works only for spotlights and directional-type lights.

FIGURE 9.2
Activate a preview
of the spotlight's
shadow in the
scene.

12. Switch Type back to Spotlight, and set the cone angle back to 90.

13. Save the scene as **tractorDroid_v02.ma**.

To see a version of the scene, open the tractorDroid_v02.ma file from the chapter9\scenes folder on the DVD.

Depth Map Shadows

Depth map shadows (also known as *shadow maps*) are created from data stored in a file that is generated at render time. The file stores information about the distance between the shadow-casting light and the objects in the scene from the light's point of view. Depth map shadows usually take less time to render than ray trace shadows and produce excellent results in many situations.

When using mental ray, you can choose to use Maya's native depth map shadows or to use mental ray's own depth map format. In this exercise, you will compare the results produced using various depth map shadow settings.

USING THE MENTAL RAY PLUG-IN

The implementation of mental ray in the Maya interface is admittedly not intuitive. Remember that mental ray is a separate program that is integrated into Maya, which is why it seems very scattered. Understanding this can help you cope with the strangeness of mental ray's Maya integration. Be prepared for some convoluted workflow practices as well as a certain level of redundancy, because mental ray has its own version of many common Maya nodes.

---

1. Open the pergola_v01.ma scene from the chapter9\scenes directory on the DVD. This scene shows the back of a house and a pergola (which is a lattice of wooden beams used to provide shade).

Using a simple flat shader speeds up the render and allows you to focus on how the shadows look on the surfaces without the distraction of reflections and specular highlights.

2. Open the Render Settings window (Window ➢ Rendering Editors ➢ Render Settings), and make sure mental ray is the selected option in the Render Using menu.

3. Switch to the Quality tab, and set the Quality Presets drop-down to Production (see Figure 9.3).

4. Open the Attribute Editor for spotLight1, and click the spotLightShape1 tab.

5. Scroll down to the Shadows section; Depth Map Shadows should be activated. Turn this option on whenever you want to use depth map shadows.

LOADING MENTAL RAY

If mental ray does not appear in the Render Using list, you'll need to load the plug-in listed in the preferences; this happens from time to time. Choose Window ➢ Settings/Preferences ➢ Plug-in Manager. In the list of plug-ins, make sure there's a check mark in the box next to Mayatomr.dll (or Mayatomr.bundle on the Mac) in the Loaded And AutoLoad column. You'll see that mental ray now appears in the Render Using drop-down menu.

FIGURE 9.3
Choose the Production preset on the mental ray Quality tab.

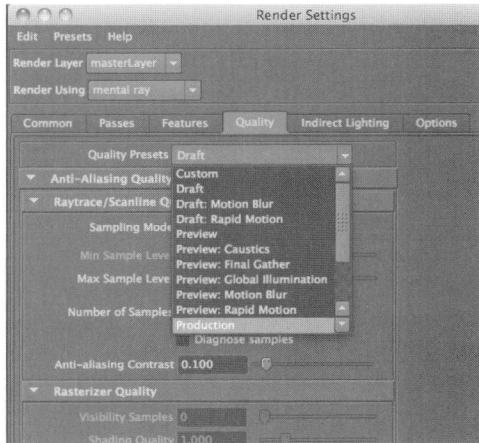

6. Choose Window ➤ Rendering Editors ➤ Render View to open the Render View window.

   The Render View window is where you can preview your renders as you work. As you create renders, you can store the images and compare them with previous renders.

7. From the Render View menu, choose Render ➤ renderCam.

You'll see the render appear in the window after a few seconds. By default, the quality of depth map shadows is pretty poor. With some tweaking, you can greatly improve the look of the shadows.

The shadow is generated using a special depth file, which is an image. As such, the image has a resolution that is controlled by the Resolution slider. When the resolution is low, you can see a visible grainy quality in the shadows, as shown in Figure 9.4.

FIGURE 9.4
The default depth map shadows have a grainy quality.

VIEW DEPTH MAP FILES

Using Maya on Windows, you can view the depth map files created by the lights in the scene using FCheck. However, this works only for depth map files generated when rendering with Maya Software. Follow these steps to view a depth map file:

1. Create a scene using a light with Use Depth Map Shadows activated.

2. Set Renderer to Maya Software.

3. In the Attribute Editor for the light's shape node, set the Disk Based Dmaps menu to Overwrite Existing Dmap(s). In the field, type a name for the file, and use the `.iff` extension.

4. Create a render of the scene using Maya Software in the Render View window.

5. Open FCheck (you can choose File ➢ View Image in Maya to do this).

6. In FCheck, use the File menu to browse to the `renderData\Depth` folder in the current project. Open the file labeled `depthmaptest.iff_spotLightShape1.SM.iff`. FCheck will appear blank until you enable the Z Depth setting.

7. In FCheck, click the Z button to enable a preview of the Z Depth file.

You'll see the scene from the point of view of the shadow-casting light, as shown here. The resolution of the image should match the resolution setting in the light's Attribute Editor.

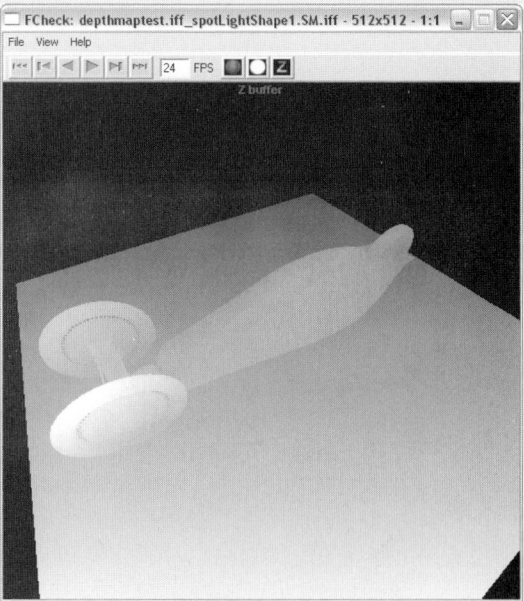

To improve the look of the shadow, you can balance the resolution with the filter size:

1. Set Resolution to **2048** and Filter Size to **0**.

2. Create a test render in the render view, and store the image in the Render View window (in the Render View menu, choose File ➢ Keep Image In Render View). The shadow is improved and relatively free from artifacts.

3. Set Resolution to **512** and Filter Size to **2**.

4. Create a test render, store the render in the Render View window, and use the scroll bar at the bottom of the render view to compare the two images (Figure 9.5).

FIGURE 9.5
Two renders using depth map shadows. The left side uses a high-resolution map with no filtering; the right side uses a low-resolution map with high filtering.

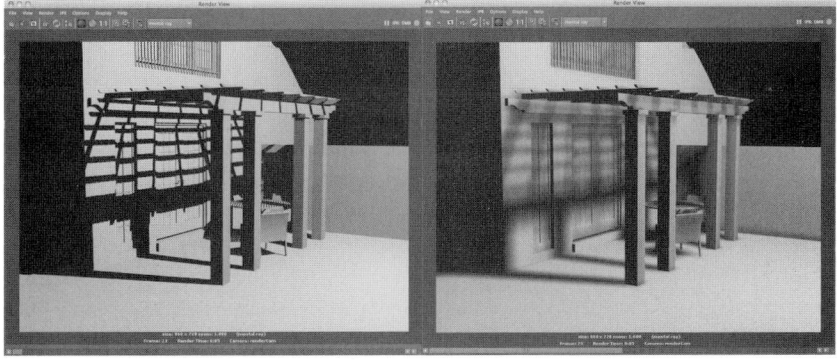

Using a low resolution (such as 512) and a high filter size (such as 2) creates soft shadows, the kind you might expect on an overcast day. One weakness in using a high filter size is that the blurring is applied to the entire shadow. In reality, shadows become gradually softer as the distance increases between the cast shadow and the shadow-casting object.

The Use Mid Dist feature is enabled by default. This option corrects banding artifacts that can occur on curved and angled surfaces, like on the side of the vehicle shown in Figure 9.6. The Mid Dist Map is a second image file that records the points midway between the first surface encountered by the light and the second surface encountered by the light. The second image is used to modify the depth information of the original depth map file to help eliminate banding artifacts.

FIGURE 9.6
When Use Mid Dist is disabled, artifacts can appear on the surface.

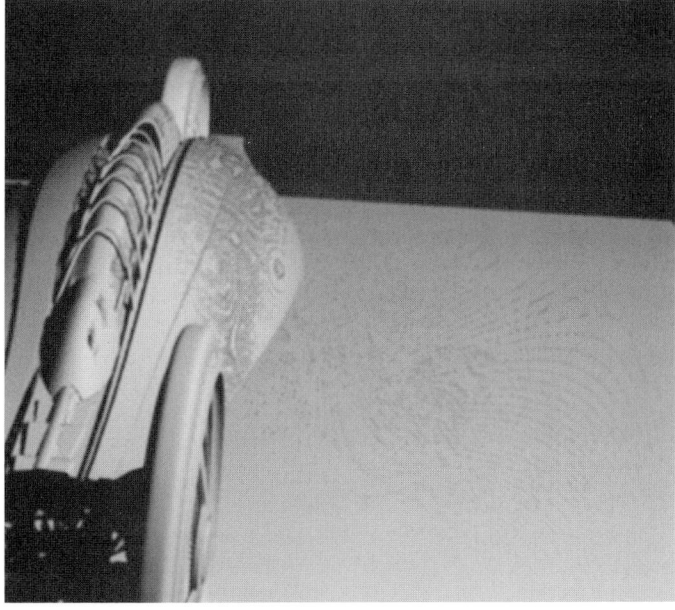

The Bias slider provides a similar function for eliminating artifacts. The slider adjusts the depth information in the depth map file. Increasing the bias pushes surface points closer to the shadow-casting light to help eliminate artifacts. This transformation of surface points occurs in the depth map file, not in the actual geometry of the scene.

If you are encountering artifacts on the surface of objects and Use Mid Dist is enabled, you can use the Bias slider to reduce the artifacts. Change the bias values in small increments as you create test renders. If the bias is too high, you'll see a gap between the shadow-casting object and the shadow.

The Use Auto Focus setting automatically adjusts the objects within the field of the light's viewable area to the maximum size of the shadow map resolution. So if, from the light's point of view, an object is surrounded by empty space, the light will zoom into the object in the depth map image. This helps optimize the use of the pixels within the depth map image so that none are wasted. It's usually a good idea to leave this setting enabled when using spotlights; however, you may encounter a different situation with other types of lights.

Now try this:

1. Set Resolution of the depth map to **512** and Filter Size to **0**.

2. Scroll up in the Attribute Editor, and set Light Type to Directional.

3. Create a test render, and store the image.

4. Create a polygon plane object (Create ➤ Polygon Primitives ➤ Plane), and set its Scale X and Scale Z values to **50**.

5. Create another test render, and compare it to the last render created.

The shadow is very blocky when the size of the ground plane is increased (see Figure 9.7).

FIGURE 9.7
When the size of the ground plane is increased, depth map shadows cast by directional lights appear very blocky.

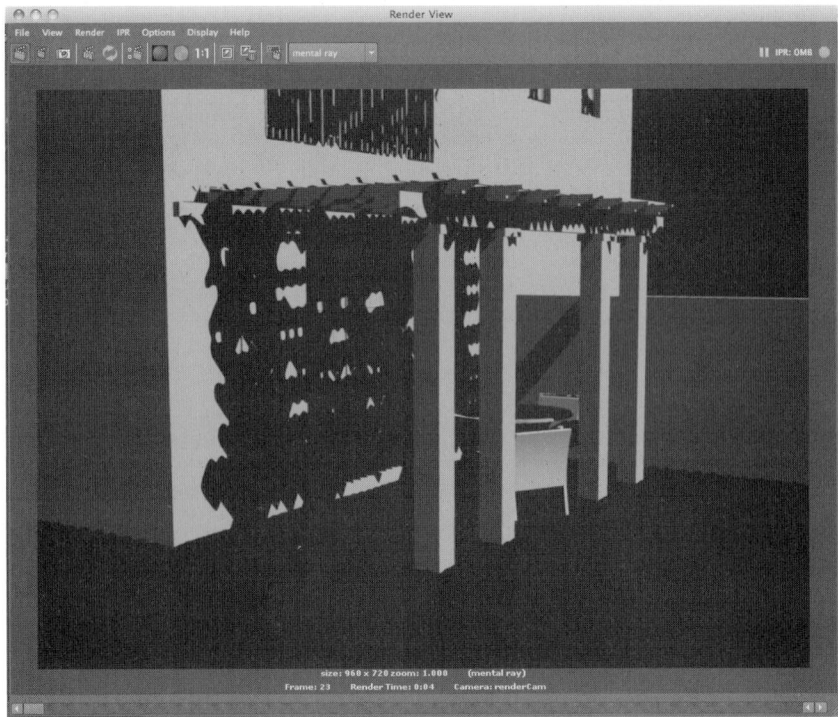

When using spotlights, the size of the viewable area from the light's point of view is restricted by the cone angle and the distance between the light and the subject. When using directional lights, the size of the viewable area is always adjusted to fit all the objects in the scene. This is because directional lights do not factor in their position in the scene when calculating shadows, only their orientation.

In this situation, you can use the new Shadow Map Camera feature described in the "mental ray Shadow Map Overrides" section.

VIEWPORT 2.0

New to Maya 2011 is a mode for viewing your scenes in the viewport window. This is known as Viewport 2.0, and you can select this option from the Renderer menu at the top of the viewport. This mode's main advantage is that the performance is improved when viewing scenes with a great deal of complex geometry. It's also possible to view bump and normal maps (covered in Chapter 11) as well as other textures applied to your models. You can also preview depth map shadows cast by the lights in the scene but not ray trace shadows. Ray trace shadows are covered later in the chapter.

---

mental ray Shadow Map Overrides

The mental ray overrides offer settings that are similar to the standard Maya shadow maps. In addition to the Resolution setting, there are also Samples and Softness settings. The Softness setting is similar to the Filter Size attribute for Maya shadow maps. You can click the Take Settings From Maya button to automatically load the settings created for standard Maya shadow maps into the mental ray attributes.

1. Open the `pergola_v02.ma` scene from the `chapter9\scenes` directory on the DVD. In the Render Settings window, make sure Render Using is set to mental ray. On the Quality tab, make sure the Quality Presets drop-down is set to Production.

2. Select the spotlight, and open the Attribute Editor to the spotlightShape1 tab. In the Shadows section, make sure Use Depth Map Shadows is on.

3. Scroll down to the Attribute Editor, expand the mental ray rollout, and expand the Shadows section under mental ray.

4. Check the Use mental ray Shadow Map Overrides box. This activates the Shadow Map Overrides section, giving you access to mental ray controls for shadow maps.

5. Set Resolution to **2048** and Softness to **0.025**.

6. Create a test render. Store the image in the Render View window. The render is similar to the results seen before—in other words, it's very grainy.

7. Set Samples to **64**, and create another test render. The graininess is reduced without significantly impacting the render time. Store the image in the render view.

   Detail shadow maps are a more advanced type of shadow map that stores additional information about the surface properties of shadow-casting objects. This information includes surface properties such as transparency. The render takes longer, but the shadows are improved.

New!

USE SHADOW MAP CAMERA FOR DIRECTIONAL LIGHTS

The Use Shadow Map Camera feature is new to Maya 2011 and is designed to solve the problem of rendering shadow maps with directional lights in scenes with large areas of geometry such as a ground plane that stretches off into the distance. To use this feature, follow these steps:

1. Enable Shadow Map Overrides in the mental ray section of the directional light's Attribute Editor.

2. Press the Take Settings From Maya button. Doing this will automatically copy the settings from the Maya Depth Map Shadows settings. It will also automatically fill in the name for the Shadow Map camera settings.

3. Decrease the Camera Aperture setting, and increase the Camera Resolution setting. Test the render, and adjust the settings until the desired result is achieved.

---

8. Set Shadow Map Format to Detail Shadow Map, and create another render (see Figure 9.8).

9. Use the scroll bar at the bottom of the render view to compare this render with the previous two renders (Figure 9.9).

10. Save the scene as **pergola_v03.ma**.

FIGURE 9.8
Enable Detail Shadow Map in the mental ray Shadows settings.

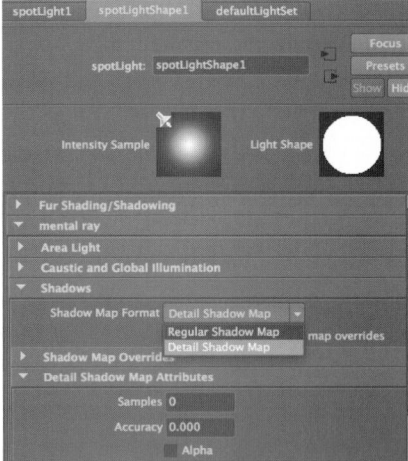

FIGURE 9.9
The pergola is rendered with Samples set to 1 (left image), Samples set to 64 (middle image), and Detail Shadow Map enabled (right image).

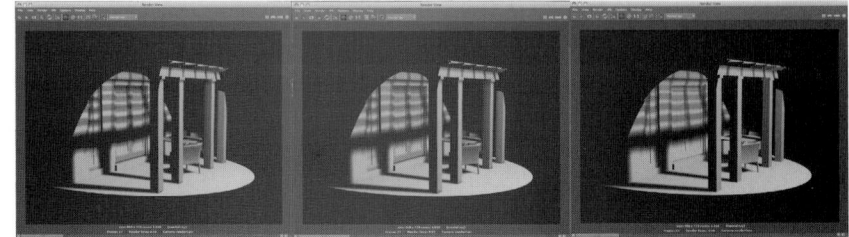

Rendering with Detail Shadow Maps enabled will take more time, but the quality is improved. Detail shadow maps are more sensitive to changes in the Softness setting in the Shadow Map Overrides rollout. There are also additional Samples and Accuracy settings in the Detail Shadow Maps rollout that can be used to tune the quality of the maps. You can use the Shadow Map File Name field to set a name for saved shadow maps and then reuse the shadow maps to improve render time as long as the lights are not animated. The settings for saving shadow maps are found in the Shadows section of the Render Settings window on the Quality tab.

The bottom line is when using depth map shadows, you can use a number of options to improve the quality of the shadows. The goal is to strike a balance between render time and quality.

To see a version of the scene to this point, open the `pergola_v03.ma` scene from the `chapter9\` `scenes` directory on the DVD.

Ray Trace Shadows

Ray trace shadows are created by tracing the path of light rays from the light source to the rendering camera. Using ray trace shadows produces more accurate results but often takes a little more time and processor power to calculate (although this has become less of an issue in recent years because of improvements to computer processor speed).

These are some advantages ray trace shadows have over shadow maps:

◆ Ray trace shadows created with area lights become softer and lighter as the distance increases between the shadow and the shadow-casting object.

◆ Ray trace shadows can be accurately cast from transparent, refractive, and colored objects.

To activate ray trace shadows, make sure Raytracing is enabled on the Quality tab of the mental ray Render Settings window, and enable Use Ray Trace Shadows for the light. When you choose the Production quality preset for mental ray, Raytracing is enabled by default (see Figure 9.10).

FIGURE 9.10
Raytracing is enabled in the mental ray Render Settings window, and Use Ray Trace Shadows is enabled for the light.

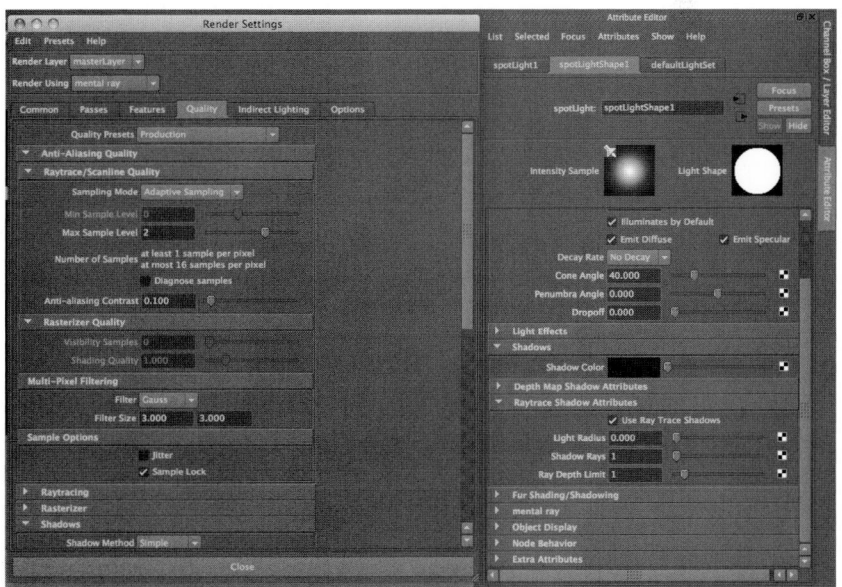

Ray trace shadows are typically very crisp when enabled. To add softness to the shadow, increase the Shadow Rays and Light Radius values in the Ray Trace Shadow Attributes section. In Figure 9.11, you can see how increasing the Light Radius and Shadow Rays values adds softness to the shadow. The render in the left image uses a Light Radius of 0 and a Shadow Rays setting of 1. The render in the right image has a Light Radius of 1, and Shadow Rays is set to 40. Notice that the blurring on the shadow increases as the distance between the shadow and the shadow-casting object increases.

Increase the Ray Depth Limit value when you need a shadow to be visible in reflections. Each level of the Ray Depth Limit corresponds to the number of transparent surfaces between the light and the shadow (Figure 9.12).

FIGURE 9.11
Add softness to ray trace shadows by increasing the Light Radius and Shadow Rays settings.

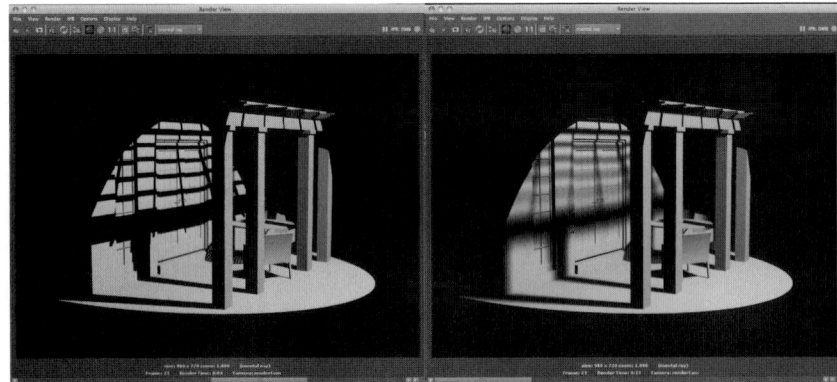

FIGURE 9.12
When Ray Depth Limit is set to 1, the shadow is not visible in the reflection (left image). When it is set to 2, the shadow is visible (right image).

UMBRA AND PENUMBRA

The *umbra* of a shadow is the area that is completely blocked from the light source. The *penumbra* is the transition from a lighted area to the umbra. Crisp shadows have a very small penumbra; soft shadows have a large penumbra.

Indirect Lighting: Global Illumination

In reality, when a ray of light hits an opaque surface, it is either absorbed or reflected (or a little of both) by the surface. If the light ray is reflected, it reenters the environment and continues to bounce off reflected surfaces until it is absorbed by another surface. Objects illuminated by reflected light are thus lit indirectly.

As light rays bounce around in an environment, fewer light rays reach the parts that are hidden in corners, cracks, and crevices. The lack of light in these areas creates a type of shadowing known as *ambient occlusion*. You can see ambient occlusion shadowing in the crevices of the photograph in Figure 9.13.

FIGURE 9.13
Ambient occlusion refers to the shadowing effect seen in the crevices of this photograph

mental ray has several methods for simulating indirect lighting and ambient occlusion shadowing: the Global Illumination, Final Gathering, and Ambient Occlusion shaders. You can use them separately or together depending on what you are trying to achieve in your render.

In this section, you'll get some hands-on experience working with the Global Illumination and Final Gathering shaders. Using ambient occlusion will be discussed along with ambient occlusion render passes in Chapter 12.

Global Illumination

Global illumination simulates photons of light bouncing off geometry in a Maya scene. It is actually a two-step process. The photon-emitting light shoots out photons into a scene. A photon map is created that records the position of the photons and their intensities in three-dimensional space. Then the area is searched for surfaces that intersect the photons, the surfaces are illuminated based on the intensities of the intersecting photons, and the diffuse value of the shader is applied to the surface.

Glossy, black, or reflective surfaces with no diffuse value will not be affected by global illumination; a diffuse value must be present. The second part of the process is the actual rendering of the image. The photon map is stored in a data structure known as a *Kd-Tree*. During rendering, the energy values are averaged over a given radius in the Kd-Tree, and these values are interpolated to create the look of light bouncing off the diffuse surfaces. The great thing about this method is that once you have perfected the look of the global illumination, if the elements of the scene are fairly static, you can save the photon map and reuse it in the scene, cutting down on the amount of time required to render each frame.

In this exercise, you'll use global illumination to light a simple kitchen scene. There are no textures or color in the scene, so you can focus specifically on how global illumination reacts with surfaces.

1. Open the `kitchen_v01.ma` scene from the `chapter9\scenes` directory on the DVD. In the scene, a camera named renderCam has already been created and positioned.

SILVER HAMMER DESIGN AND CONSTRUCTION

The pergola and kitchen models used in this chapter were created by my brother Travis Keller for his design company Silver Hammer Design and Construction. The models were created in Google's free 3D modeling program SketchUp.

It's interesting to note that SketchUp is quickly gaining popularity, not only with design and architectural companies but with production designers working in the entertainment industry. SketchUp has been used for set design on TV shows such as ABC's *V* and for robot design for feature films such as *Avatar*. Because it is fast and easy to use, a designer can quickly create a 3D concept that can then be turned over to artists working in Maya who can make adjustments, create textures, and light the model. To export a model from SketchUp, you will need to use the Professional edition of SketchUp. You can learn more about SketchUp at `sketchup.google.com`.

---

2. Create a directional light, and place it outside the window.

3. Rotate the light so it's shining in the window (the position of a directional light does not affect how it casts light—only the rotation does—but it's convenient to have it outside the window). Use these settings in the Channel Box:

   Rotate X: **-54.914**

   Rotate Y: **64.041**

   Rotate Z: **-34.095**

4. In the Attribute Editor, switch to the directionalLightShape1 tab.

5. In the Shadows rollout, turn on Use Ray Traced Shadows.

6. Make sure the Quality Preset drop-down menu in the Render Settings is set to Production. Create a test render in the render view using the renderCam camera. The image should look very dark except for parts of the window frame at the sink.

7. Open the Render Settings window, and switch to the Indirect Lighting tab.

8. Expand the Global Illumination rollout, turn on Global Illumination, and use the default settings (see Figure 9.14).

FIGURE 9.14
Activate Global Illumination in the Render Settings window, and use the default settings for the light.

9. In the Attribute Editor settings for directionalLightShape1, expand the mental ray rollout and, under Caustic and Global Illumination, activate Emit Photons.

10. Create another test render. The resulting render should look pretty horrible.

Using a directional light is a perfectly reasonable choice for creating the look of light coming through a window. The light rays cast by a directional light are parallel, which simulates the way light from a distant source, such as the sun, behaves. However, directional lights tend to have an overexposed quality when used as photon-casting lights (see Figure 9.15). This is because the photons cast from a photon-emitting light need to have both a direction and a position. Directional lights have only a direction (based on the rotation of the light), so the light often casts too many photons, and artifacts can result. It's a good practice to avoid directional lights altogether as photon-casting light. The best types of lights to use are area, spot, and point. Area lights tend to work best since they cast light from a sizeable area as opposed to a point in space.

The photon-casting properties of a light are completely separate and unrelated to the light's intensity. In practice, it's often a good idea to use one light to cast direct light, as well as to create cast shadows, and another light to create the indirect light.

FIGURE 9.15
When a directional-
type light is used
to cast photons,
the result is a
blown-out image.

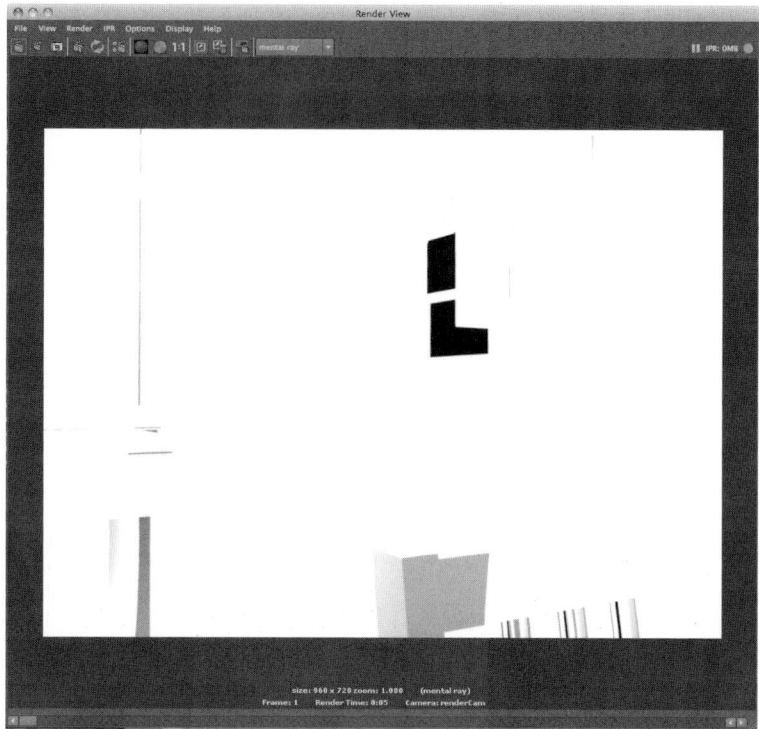

If you are in a situation where the same light is casting direct and indirect illumination, raising the intensity can cause the area around the light to become overexposed. In this situation,
you may want to use two lights placed near each other. One light should cast only direct light
(that is, Cast Photons is disabled), and the other light should have 0 Intensity, but Cast Photons
should be enabled, as follows:

1. In the Attribute Editor for the directional light, turn off Emit Photons in the Caustic And
   Global Illumination settings. Rename the light **Sun**.

2. Create an area light (Create ➢ Lights ➢ Area Light).

3. Place the light near the wall opposite the window. Name the light **Bounce**. You can use
   these settings in the Channel Box:

   Translate X: **5.323**

   Translate Y: **12.614**

   Translate Z: **-39.104**

   Rotate Y: **-90**

   Scale X: **11.119**

   Scale Y: **10.476**

   Scale Z: **1**

4. Open the Attribute Editor for Bounce. Turn off Emit Diffuse and Emit Specular. Set Intensity to **0**.

5. In the mental ray rollout, turn on Emit Photons.

6. Create a test render of the scene, and store the image in the Render View window.

The render is a big improvement, although clearly the default settings are not adequate and require some tuning, but it looks less like a nuclear blast.

GLOBAL ILLUMINATION AND SCALE

Global Illumination is sensitive to the scale of the objects in a scene. If you continue to get blown-out results using other types of lights as photon emitters, try uniformly increasing the scale of the objects in the scene.

---

7. The image looks a little weird because there is sunlight coming through a black window. To create a quick fix for this, select renderCam, and open its Attribute Editor.

8. In the Environment tab, set the background color to white. Create another test render (Figure 9.16).

9. Save the scene as **kitchen_v02.ma**.

To see a version of the scene to this point, open the kitchen_v02.ma scene from the chapter9\ scenes directory on the DVD.

FIGURE 9.16
Photons are cast from an area light placed opposite the window in the kitchen. When the background color for the camera is set to white, the area outside the window is white.

Tuning Global Illumination

Adjusting the look of the global illumination requires editing the settings in the area light's Attribute Editor and in the Render Settings window. The settings work together to create the effect. Often you'll tune the lighting of the scene by adjusting and readjusting the various settings until you get the best result you can.

1. Continue with the scene from the previous section, or open the `kitchen_v02.ma` file from the `chapter9\scenes` directory on the DVD.

2. Take a look at the area light's settings under Caustic And Global Illumination:

   Emit Photons   Turns on the photon-casting property of the light.

   Photon Color   Adds color to the actual photons.

   Photon Intensity   Controls the energy of the photons as they are shot into the room and how they are reflected from various sources.

   Exponent   Controls the photon decay rate. A setting of 2 is consistent with the inverse square law, which states that the intensity of light is inversely proportional to the square of the distance from the source. A setting of 2 would be analogous to setting a light's Decay rate to Quadratic. This simulates how light actually works in the real world. Setting Exponent to 1 is analogous to setting a light's Decay setting to Linear, which is closer to how light from distant bright sources, such as the sun, decays.

   Global Illum Photons   The number of photons cast into the room by the photon-casting light. Increasing this value often aids in the look of the effect. The more photons you add, the longer the render can take in some cases.

3. The indirect lighting looks a little blown out. Lower Photon Intensity to **5000**.

   The blotchy quality on the wall is caused because there are not enough photons being cast by the light. Increasing the number of photons creates more overlapping and thus smoothes the look of the light as it reflects from the surface.

4. Set Global Illum Photons to **25000**. Create a test render (Figure 9.17).

> **MORE IS NOT ALWAYS BETTER**
>
> Each situation demands its own settings to create the ideal look of indirect lighting. Sometimes increasing Global Illum Photons beyond a certain level will make the renders look just as blotchy as a low setting. It's best to experiment to find the right setting for your scene.

5. Open the Render Settings window, and click the Indirect Lighting tab. Take a look at the Global Illumination settings:

   Global Illumination   Turns on global illumination calculations. Some mental ray presets, such as Preview Global Illumination, activate this option when chosen. Notice the Caustics check box above. This activates the caustics calculations, which are separate from Global Illumination; this will be explained later in the chapter.

   Accuracy   Sets an overall level of accuracy in the global illumination calculations. If this is set to 1, the photons are not blended together at all, and you can see the individual photons (Figure 9.18). Generally it's a good idea to keep Accuracy between 250 and 800 for most situations.

FIGURE 9.17
By decreasing
Photon Intensity
and increasing
Global Illum
Photons, the
lighting is
improved.

FIGURE 9.18
Lowering the Accu-
racy setting in the
Render Settings
window reveals
the individual
photons as they
are reflected on
surfaces.

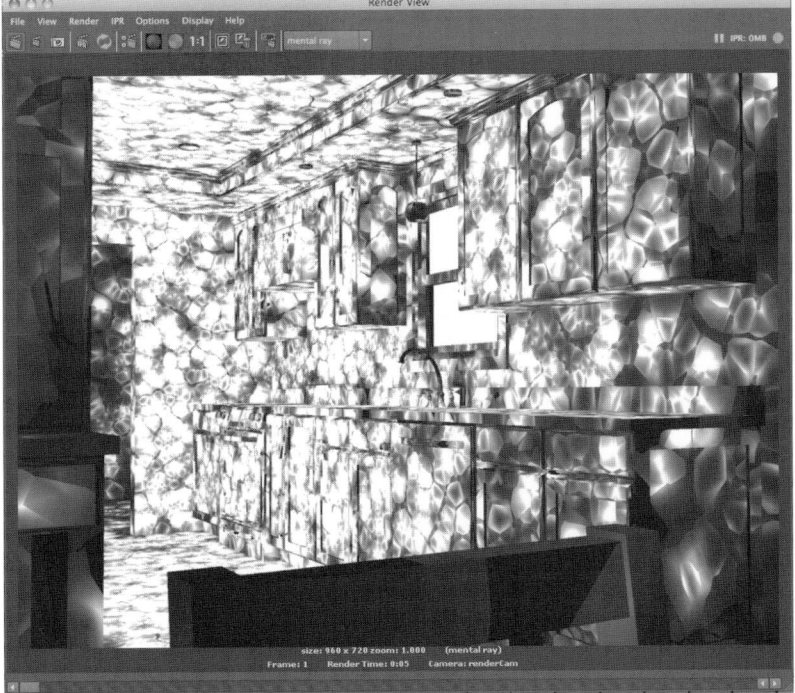

Scale   Can act as a global brightness control for the global illumination effect.

Radius   Controls the radius of the actual photons. When this is set to 0, mental ray determines the radius of the photons based on the requirements of the scene. The radius is not actually 0. Increasing the radius can smooth the photons; however, too large an area can cause a loss of detail in the shadows and color bleeding, which leads to a blurry, undefined sort of look.

Merge Distance   Specifies a distance in world space within which overlapping photons are merged. This is used to reduce the size of photon maps and decrease render times. You should raise this setting by very small increments. It can increase the blotchy look of the render.

6. Click the color swatch next to Scale to open the Color Chooser.

7. Set the mode of the Color Chooser to HSV. Set the value (V) to **1.2**, and create another test render (Figure 9.19). This is a good way to brighten the overall global illumination effect without raising the Photon Intensity value on one or more lights.

8. Save the scene as `kitchen_v03.ma`.

To see a version of the scene to this point, open the `kitchen_v03.ma` scene from the `chapter9\ scenes` directory on the DVD.

Rendering with global illumination requires a lot of testing and tuning. At a certain point, you'll need to combine the techniques with other indirect lighting tools such as Final Gathering to perfect the look.

FIGURE 9.19
Raising the Scale value brightens the overall effect of global illumination.

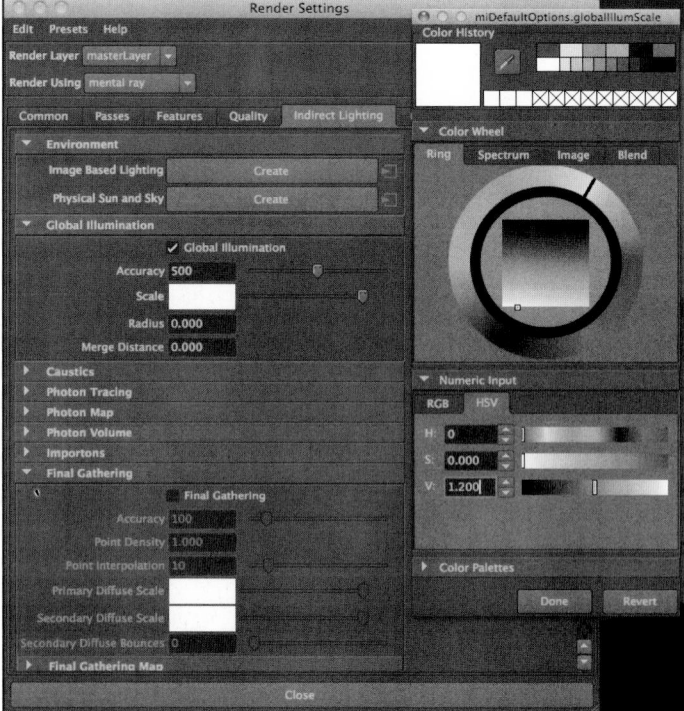

Working with Photon Maps

Photon maps are generated during a mental ray render using Global Illumination. They store the position, energy, color, and other data associated with the photons cast during render. The map can be saved to disk and reused to cut down on render time. This, in fact, eliminates the first stage of rendering with Global Illumination on subsequent renders.

Of course, if there is a lot of animation in the scene, reusing the same map will not always work, but in a scene such as the current one, it can be quite helpful.

To save a photon map, type a name for the map in the Photon Map File field (found in the Photon Map section on the Indirect Lighting tab of the Render Settings window), and create a render (do not add a file extension to the name). When you want to reuse the same map, deselect Rebuild Photon Map. The map is stored in the `renderData\mentalRay\photonMap` directory with the `.pmap` extension. When you want to overwrite the map, simply select Rebuild Photon Map.

Remember to turn on Rebuild Photon Map when you make changes to the scene. Otherwise, the scene will not update correctly as you create test renders.

The Enable Map Visualizer option is a way to visualize how the photons are cast in the scene. When you enable this and create a Global Illumination render, you'll see dots spread around the scene in Maya's camera view, representing the distribution of photons cast by the light.

1. Type **test** into the Photon Map File field in the Photon Map section of the Indirect Lighting tab in the Render Settings window.

2. Select Rebuild Photon Map and Enable Map Visualizer.

3. Open the render view, and create a test render from the renderCam.

4. Close the render view when the render is complete. Look at the perspective view in Maya. You should see the geometry covered in dots representing the distribution of photons created by the bounce light.

5. Choose Window ➢ Rendering Editors ➢ mental ray ➢ Map Visualizer. The options in the box allow you to customize the look of the Visualizer in the perspective window (see Figure 9.20).

6. To remove the dots, select the mapViz1 node in the Outliner, and delete it. This will not affect the render or the saved photon map.

FIGURE 9.20
The map Visualizer allows you to see how the photons are cast in the scene.

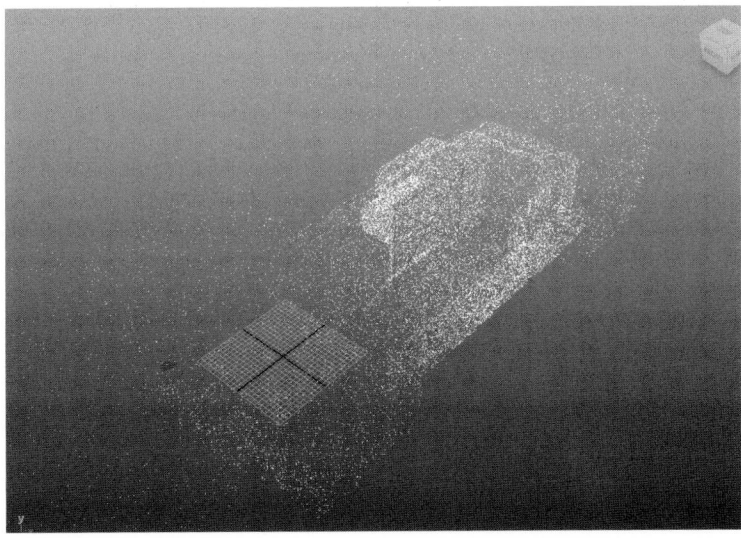

The dots in the scene can be colored based on the Photon Color setting of the light; you can use this to diagnose how each photon-casting light is affecting the scene. Also, if you save more than one photon map, you can load and view them using the Enable Map Visualizer option. Use the Map File Name dialog box to load saved maps.

CONSERVING PHOTONS

You can see in Figure 9.20 that a lot of photons are cast into areas of the model outside the render view. You can conserve photons by creating a simple polygon cube that encompasses the photons that are visible within the render, as shown here. Turn off the primary visibility of the cube, and delete any polygons that may block the outside light. In some cases, this can improve the look of your render.

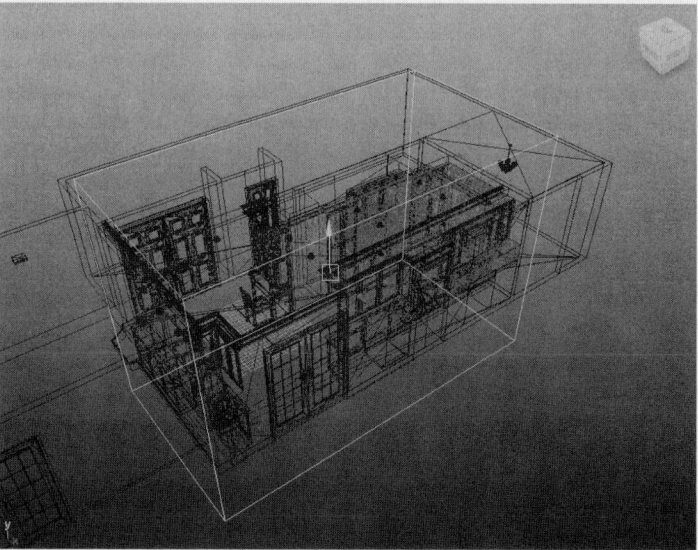

Another way to visualize the photons in the scene is to use the Diagnose Photon menu. When you choose a setting from this menu and create a render, the shaders in the scene are replaced with a single shader colored to indicate either the photon density or the irradiance of surfaces in the scene (irradiance is discussed a little later in this chapter).

Color Bleeding

When light is reflected from a colored surface, the color can mix with the indirect light. mental ray's Global Illumination can simulate this property.

1. Open the kitchen_v04.ma scene from the chapter9\scenes directory on the DVD. This scene has a bucket added close to where the sunlight strikes the floor.

2. The model has a Lambert shader applied with bright red set for the color. Create a test render. You'll see the red color bleed onto the surrounding area of the temple.

Color bleeding is a part of Global Illumination and occurs automatically when colored objects are near the photon-emitting lights.

IRRADIANCE

You can find the Irradiance controls in the mental ray rollout in standard Maya shaders applied to objects. The slider is a multiplier used to adjust how a particular surface responds to the total amount of incoming light energy (or radiant power) from the surroundings.

By raising the value of Irradiance, the surface is affected by the color in the Irradiance Color slider. You can lower the value of the Irradiance Color slider to eliminate any areas on the shader that may appear too bright or blown out. You can also change the hue of the irradiance color to change the color of the indirect lighting on all surfaces that have the shader applied. Remember to keep these settings as consistent as possible between shaders in a given scene to avoid incoherence in the lighting.

Importons

Importons are very similar to photons. Importons are emitted from the camera and bounce toward the light. Photons, on the other hand, are emitted from the lights and bounce toward the camera, so importons actually move in the opposite direction of photons. You can use importons to improve the quality of global illumination maps.

You can find the Importons controls on the Indirect Illumination tab in the Global Illumination Controls of the Render Settings window. Importons are available only when Global Illumination is enabled.

When you render using importons, mental ray first calculates the importon emission and then renders the scene. The importons are discarded when the render is completed.

The Density value of the importons controls how many importons are emitted from the camera per pixel. Generally, this value does not need to be higher than 1. The Merge setting works very similarly to the Merge setting used for photons. The Traverse feature maximizes the number of importons in the scene; it's generally a good idea to leave this option on.

You can improve the quality of Global Illumination renders by activating the Importons option. The option must be turned on in the Indirect Lighting tab in the Render Settings window and also in the Features tab of the Render Settings window.

Caustics

Global Illumination simulates light reflected from diffuse surfaces. Caustics simulate light reflected from glossy and reflective surfaces as well as light that passes through refractive transparent materials. Caustics are calculated completely independently from Global Illumination; however, the workflow is very similar.

This exercise will show you how to set up and render using Caustics. The scene contains a globe with crystalline structures emanating from the top. The globe is set on top of a metal stand. At the moment, all the objects in the scene use a simple Lambert shader.

1. Open the `crystalGlobe_v01.ma` scene from the `chapter9\scenes` directory on the DVD.

2. In the Outliner, expand the Globe group, and select the crystal object.

3. Assign a Blinn shader to the crystal (from the Rendering menu set, choose Lighting/Shading ➢ Assign Favorite Material ➢ Blinn).

4. Open the Attribute Editor for the Blinn material, and name it **crystalShade**.

5. Set the Color option of crystalShade to red and Transparency to a very light gray—almost white.

6. In the Specular Shading section of the Attribute Editor, use the following settings:

   Eccentricity: **0.05**

   Specular Roll Off: **1**

   Specular Color: white

   Reflectivity: **0.25**

7. Expand the Raytrace Options rollout, and activate Refractions; set Refractive Index to **1.2** (Figure 9.21).

FIGURE 9.21
The settings for the crystalShade shader

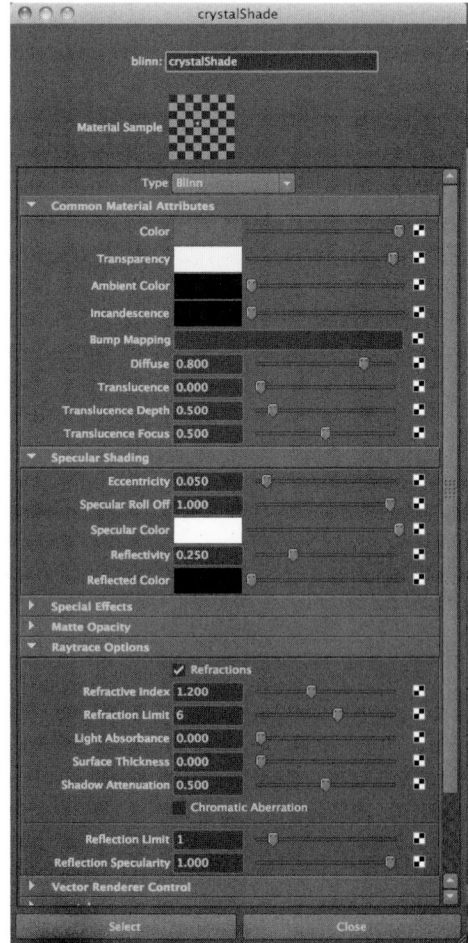

8. Create a spotlight. Select the spotlight, and choose Look Through Selected Camera.

9. Aim the spotlight so it's looking down at the globe and stand. Position the light so the globe fits inside the cone angle radius (the circle at the center of the screen), as shown in Figure 9.22.

FIGURE 9.22
The scene is viewed from the spotlight. Position the light so the cone angle fits around the globe and stand.

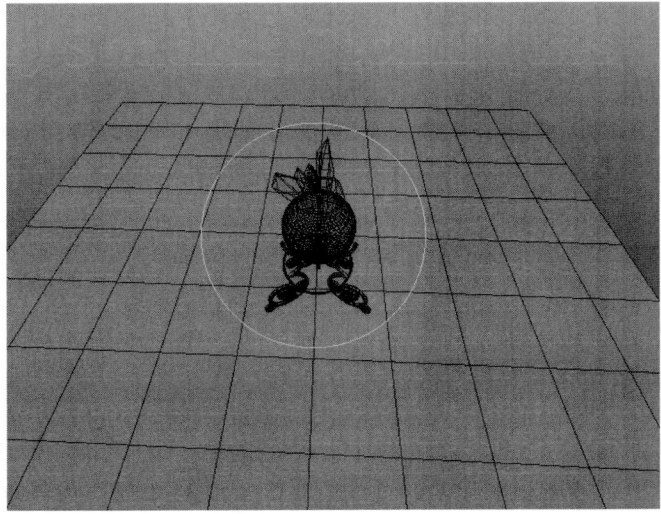

10. Switch to the perspective view. Open the Render Settings window, and set Render Using to mental ray.

11. On the Quality tab, set Quality Presets to Production.

12. In the Attribute Editor for the spotlight, turn on Use Ray Trace Shadows.

13. Create a test render of the scene using the renderCam camera.

At the moment, Caustics have not been activated. Keep this image in the render view so you can compare it with the Caustics render.

14. Open the Render Settings window, and switch to the Indirect Lighting tab.

15. Under Global Illumination, turn on Caustics. Leave Global Illumination deselected.

16. Select the spotlight. In the Attribute Editor for the spotlight, scroll down to the mental ray section. Under Caustics And Global Illumination, turn on Emit Photons.

17. Create another test render in the render view. Immediately you can see a dramatic difference in the two renders (Figure 9.23).

The light passing through the refractive surface produces a white highlight in the shadow on the floor. You can also see some of the red color of the globe reflected on the floor in a few spots. Notice, however, that the shadow is no longer transparent. The light that passes through the transparent globe is bent by the globe's refractive properties. This results in the hot spot seen at the center of the shadow. mental ray adds the bright spot on top of an opaque shadow.

FIGURE 9.23
The image on the
left is rendered
without Caustics
enabled; the image
on the right has
Caustics enabled.

FIGURE 9.23
The image on the
left is rendered
without Caustics
enabled; the image
on the right has
Caustics enabled.

18. The Caustics settings are similar to the Global Illumination settings. In the spotlight's Attribute Editor, lower Photon Intensity to **3000**. Set Caustic Photons to **80000**.

    You can adjust the color of the caustic highlight by changing the caustic photon color or by changing the color of the transparency on the crystal shader. It's probably a better idea to change the transparency color on the shader; that way, if one light is creating Caustics on two different objects that are shaded with different colors, the color of the caustic photons won't clash with the color of the objects.

    The Exponent setting for Caustics works just like the Exponent setting for Global Illumination.

19. Select the crystal object, and open the Attribute Editor.

20. Click the Crystal Shade tab. Set the Transparency color to a light pink.

21. Open the Render Settings window, and click the Indirect Lighting tab. Set Accuracy of the Caustics to **32**.

22. Create a test render of the scene (Figure 9.24).

FIGURE 9.24
The scene is ren-
dered after lower-
ing the Accuracy
and the Photon
Intensity settings.

A lower Accuracy value produces sharper caustic highlights at the risk of some graininess. A higher value removes the grainy quality but softens the look of the caustics. You can also soften the look a little by setting Filter to Cone.

The Radius value can be left at 0 if you want Maya to determine the proper radius at render time. Settings less than 1 make individual photons more visible. The Merge Distance setting merges all photons within the specified distance, which can decrease render times but remove the detail in the caustic patterns.

Caustic Light Setup

In practice, spotlights are usually the best choice for creating Caustics. Area lights don't work nearly as well. The cone angle of the spotlight is reduced, so no photons are wasted; they are concentrated on the globe and stand. However, you may not want the visible edge of the spotlight cone on the floor. To fix this, you can use two spotlights—one to create the caustic photons and the other to light the scene.

1. Select the spotlight, and duplicate it (Ctrl+d).

2. Open the Attribute Editor for spotlight1:

    A. Under Spotlight Attributes, turn off Emit Diffuse.

    B. Under Shadows, turn off Use Ray Trace Shadows.

3. Select spotlight2, and open its Attribute Editor. Under Spotlight Attributes, turn off Emit Specular.

4. Set Cone Angle to 90.

5. Turn off Emit Photons under Caustics And Global Illumination.

6. Create a test render of the scene. The scene looks pretty much the same, but the area of light cast by the spotlight has been widened.

7. In the Outliner, select the Stand group, and apply a Blinn shader. Name the shader **standShader**.

8. Open the Attribute Editor for the standShader:

    A. Set Color to a light, bright yellow.

    B. Set Diffuse to **0.25**.

9. Under Specular Shading, apply the following settings:

    Eccentricity: **0.1**

    Specular Roll Off: **1**

    Specular Color: white

    Reflectivity: **0.85**.

10. Create another test render. You can clearly see the light reflected off the stand and onto the floor (see Figure 9.25).

11. Save the scene as **crystalGlobe_v02.ma**.

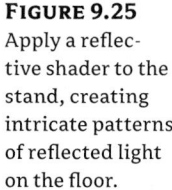

FIGURE 9.25
Apply a reflective shader to the stand, creating intricate patterns of reflected light on the floor.

When working with Caustics, you'll get more interesting results when the caustic light patterns are created from complex objects. You'll also find that the patterns created by transparent objects vary greatly when you change the Refractive Index value of the transparent shader.

To see a version of the scene to this point, open the `crystalGlobe_v02.ma` scene from the `chapter9\scenes` directory on the DVD.

Indirect Illumination: Final Gathering

Final Gathering is another method for calculating indirect lighting. It can be used on its own or in conjunction with Global Illumination. Final Gathering uses irradiance sampling and ambient occlusion to create the look of ambient and indirect lighting. When Final Gathering is enabled, rays are cast from the camera into the scene. When a ray intersects with a surface, a Final Gathering point is created that samples the irradiance value of the surface and how it is affected by other scene elements, such as nearby objects, lights, and light-emitting surfaces.

Final Gathering uses ray tracing rather than photon casting. Each Final Gathering point that the camera shoots into the scene lands on a surface and then emits a number of Final Gathering primary rays, which gather information about the irradiance values and proximity of other scene elements. The information gathered by the rays is used to determine the shading of the surface shading normal at the location of the Final Gathering point. Imagine a hemispherical dome of rays that are emitted from a point on a surface; the rays gather information about other surfaces in the scene. Like Global Illumination, this allows it to simulate color bleeding from nearby surfaces.

Light-Emitting Objects

One of the most interesting aspects of Final Gathering is that you can use objects as lights in a scene. An object that has a shader with a bright incandescent or ambient color value actually casts light in a scene. This works particularly well for situations in which geometry needs to cast light in a scene. For example, a cylinder can be used as a fluorescent lightbulb (Figure 9.26). When a shader is assigned to the cylinder with a bright incandescent value and Final Gathering is enabled, the result is a very convincing lighting scheme.

FIGURE 9.26
A cylinder with an incandescent shader actually casts light in the scene when Final Gathering is enabled.

In this exercise, you'll light a three-wheeled car designed by Anthony Honn using only objects with incandescent shaders. Polygon planes will be used as so-called light cards to simulate the look of diffuse studio lighting. You'll find that it's easy to get a great-looking result from Final Gathering rendering while still using very simple, standard Maya shaders.

1. Open the car_v01.ma scene from the chapter9\scenes directory on the DVD.

2. Open the Render Settings window, and click the Common tab.

3. Scroll to the bottom of the window, and expand the Render Options rollout. Make sure the Enable Default Light option is not checked.

   The Enable Default Light option is normally on so that when you create a test render in a scene with no lights, you can still see your objects. When you add a light to the scene, the default light is overridden and should no longer illuminate the objects in the scene. However, since you won't be using actual lights in this scene, you need to deselect Enable Default Light.

4. Click the Quality tab, and set Quality Presets to Production.

5. Create a quick test render using the renderCam camera. The scene should appear completely black, confirming that no lights are on in the scene.

6. Switch to the Indirect Lighting tab, scroll down, and activate Final Gathering.

7. Do another test render. The scene should still be black.

8. Select the renderCam camera in the Outliner, and open its Attribute Editor.

9. Switch to the renderCamShape tab, scroll down to the Environment section, and set Background Color to white.

10. Create another test render. Make sure the renderCam is chosen as the rendering camera.

You'll see the car appear as the scene renders. There are no lights in the scene. However, the white color of the background is used in the Final Gathering calculations. You'll notice that the scene renders twice.

The Final Gathering render takes place in two stages:

A. In the first pass, Final Gathering projects rays from the camera through a hexagonal grid that looks like a low-resolution version of the image.

B. In the second stage, the Final Gathering points calculate irradiance values, and the image is actually rendered and appears at its proper quality.

You'll often notice that the first pass appears brighter than the final render.

The car has a simple white Lambert shader applied. The shadowing seen under the car and in the details is an example of ambient occlusion that occurs as part of a Final Gathering render (Figure 9.27).

11. Set Background Color of the renderCam to black.

12. Create a polygon plane, and apply a Lambert shader to the plane.

13. Set the Incandescence of the plane's Lambert shader to white.

FIGURE 9.27
The car is rendered with no lights in the scene. The background color is used to calculate the Final Gathering points.

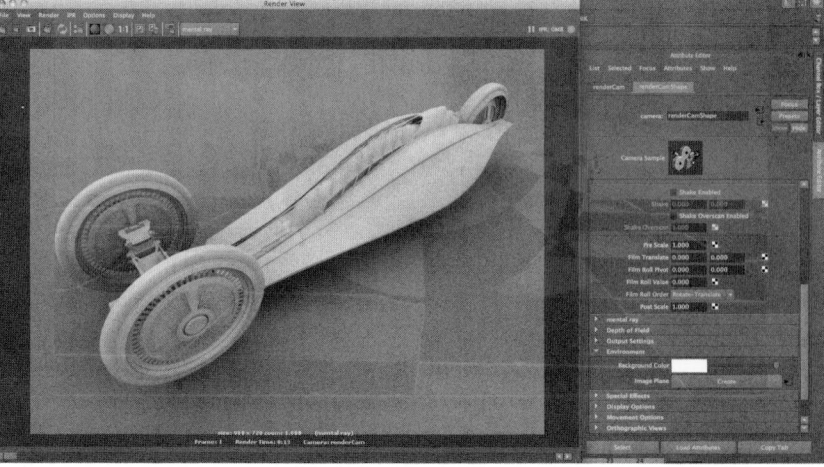

14. Use the Move and Rotate tools to position the plane above the car at about a 45-degree angle. Use the following settings in the Channel Box for the plane:

Translate X: **-.431**

Translate Y: **25.793**

Translate Z: **14.072**

Rotate X: **45**

Rotate Y: **0**

Rotate Z: **0**

Scale X: **40**

Scale Y: **20**

Scale Z: **20**

15. Select the plane, and open the Attribute Editor to the pPlaneShape2 tab.

16. Expand the Render Stats rollout, and turn off Primary Visibility. This means that the plane still influences the lighting in the scene and can still be seen in reflections and refractions, but the plane itself is not seen by the rendering camera.

17. Create another test render from the renderCam. The car appears much darker this time.

18. Select the pPlane2 shape, and open the Attribute Editor.

19. Select the tab for the plane's Lambert shader, and click the swatch next to Incandescence to open the Color Chooser.

20. Set the slider mode to HSV using the menu below the Color Chooser. Set the value slider (V) to 4.

21. Create another test render. The car should be more visible now (Figure 9.28).

FIGURE 9.28
Raising the value of the incandescence on the shader's plane makes the car more visible.

Using incandescent objects is a great way to simulate the diffuse light boxes used by photographers. You can easily simulate the lighting used in a studio by strategically placing incandescent planes around the car. However, you'll notice that the lighting is somewhat blotchy. You can fix this using the Final Gathering settings on the Indirect Lighting tab of the Render Settings window.

The Final Gathering options in the render settings set the global quality of the Final Gathering render. Here is a brief description of what these settings do:

Accuracy This value determines the number of Final Gathering rays shot from the camera. Higher values increase render time. A value of 100 is fine for testing; a high-quality render typically uses 500 to 800 rays.

Point Density This setting determines the number of Final Gathering points generated by the rays. Increasing this value also increases quality and render time.

Point Interpolation This setting smoothes out the point calculation. Increasing this value improves the quality of the result without adding too much to render time. However, as with any smoothing operation, detail can be lost at higher values.

Primary Diffuse Scale Just like with Global Illumination and Caustics, this scale brightens the resulting Final Gathering render.

Secondary Diffuse Bounces Enabling this option allows Final Gathering rays to bounce off a second diffuse surface before terminating. This increases realism as well as render time. Final Gathering rays do most of their work on the first or second bounce; beyond that, the calculations don't yield a significant difference.

Secondary Diffuse Scale Increasing the value of Secondary Diffuse Scale increases the influence of the Secondary Diffuse Bounces.

PER-SURFACE FINAL GATHERING SETTINGS

Individual surfaces can have their own Final Gathering settings located in the mental ray rollout in the surface's shape node. These settings will override the render settings and can be used as needed for optimizing renders.

---

22. Set Accuracy to **400**, Point Density to **2**, and Secondary Diffuse Bounces to **1**.

23. In the Outliner, expand the Car group. Select the leftBody, and Ctrl+click the rightBody.

24. Open the Hypershade, and assign the metal shader to these two groups.

25. Create another test render (Figure 9.29).

    The white polygon is reflected in the surface of the car. The shader that is applied to the body is a very simple Phong-type shader, and it looks pretty good.

26. Save the scene as **car_v02.ma**.

To see a version of the scene to this point, open the car_v02.ma scene from the chapter9\ scenes directory on the DVD.

FIGURE 9.29
Apply a reflective material to the body, enhancing the realism of the lighting.

Final Gathering Maps

Setting the Rebuild option to Off causes mental ray to reuse any saved Final Gathering maps generated from previous renders. This saves a great deal of time when creating a final render. However, if the camera is moving and Final Gathering requires additional points for interpolation, new points are generated and appended to the saved map.

When Rebuild is set to Freeze, the scene is rendered with no changes to the Final Gathering map regardless of whether the scene requires additional points. This reduces flickering in animated sequences, but you need to make sure the scene has enough Final Gathering points generated before using the Freeze option.

NEON LIGHTS

For several commercial projects I have created convincing neon lights using light-emitting objects; an example is shown here. By adding a glow effect to my incandescent shaders and rendering with Final Gathering, the neon lights can look very realistic.

This is my technique for creating this effect:

1. Create a series of curves to build the neon light geometry. Shape them into letters or decorative elements.

2. Apply a Paint Effects brush to the curves to build the neon tubes.

(CONTINUES)

NEON LIGHTS *(CONTINUED)*

3. Convert the brush strokes into NURBS or polygon geometry.

4. Apply a Blinn shader to the neon tube geometry. In the incandescence channel of the shader, add a ramp texture.

5. To make the center of the tube brighter than the edges, connect a Sampler Info node to the ramp. Use the Connection Editor to connect the Facing Ratio attribute of the Sampler Info node to the V Coordinate attribute of the ramp. Make sure the ramp is set to V Ramp.

6. Edit the ramp so the top of the ramp (which corresponds to the center of the neon tube) is brighter than the bottom of the ramp (which corresponds to the edges of the neon tube).

7. In the Special Effects rollout of the shader, increase the Glow Intensity setting. A value of 0.1 should be sufficient.

8. In the Hypershade, select the shaderGlow1 node, and open its Attribute Editor. Turn off Auto Exposure. This eliminates flickering problems that may occur if the scene is animated.

9. Turning off Auto Exposure causes the glow effect to be overly bright. In the Glow Attributes section of the shaderGlow node, lower the Glow Intensity setting. Finding the proper value takes some experimentation on a number of test renders.

   There is only one shaderGlow node for each Maya scene. This node applies the same settings to all the glowing objects within a scene. The glow effect is a post-process effect, so you won't see the glow applied in the render until all the other parts of the image have been rendered.

10. In the Render Settings window, make sure Renderer is set to mental ray.

11. In the Indirect Lighting tab, turn on Final Gathering.

12. Click the swatch next to Primary Diffuse Scale to open the Color Chooser. Raise the Value above 1. A setting between 2 and 4 should be sufficient.

Surfaces near the neon tubes should have a high diffuse value so they reflect the light emitted by the tubes. To see an example of neon lighting using Final Gathering, open the vegas.ma scene from the chapter9\scenes directory on the DVD.

If a scene has an animated camera, you can generate the Final Gathering map by rendering an initial frame with Rebuild set to On, moving the Time slider until the camera is in a new position, and then setting Rebuild to Off and rendering again. Repeat this procedure until the path visible from the camera has been sufficiently covered with Final Gathering points. Then create the final render sequence with Rebuild set to Freeze. This short exercise demonstrates this technique.

1. Open the `car_v03.ma` scene from the `chapter9\scenes` directory on the DVD. In this scene, a camera named FGCam is animated around the car.

   The first 10 frames of the animation have been rendered using Final Gathering. In the Final Gathering Map section of the Render Settings window, the Rebuild attribute is set to On, so new Final Gathering points are calculated with each frame.

2. View the rendered sequence by choosing File ➢ View Sequence. The 10-frame sequence is found in the `chapter9\images` directory on the DVD. The sequence is labeled carFG_test1. You can clearly see flickering in this version of the animation.

3. In the Final Gathering Map section, turn on Enable Map Visualizer. Set the timeline to frame 1, and create a test render using the FGCam camera.

4. When the render is complete, switch to the perspective view. In the viewport window, disable NURBS Surfaces, and disable Polygons in the Show menu. You can clearly see the Final Gathering points outlining the surface of the car.

   Notice there are no points on the surfaces that have the metal texture applied. This is because they are reflective surfaces with a very low diffuse value—remember that Final Gathering is used for rendering diffuse surfaces, such as the surfaces with the white Lambert shader applied (see Figure 9.30).

5. In the Render Settings window, set Rebuild to Off. Set the timeline to **4**, and create another test render using the FGCam camera.

   You'll notice it takes less time to render, and the display of the Final Gathering points in the perspective view is updated. More points have been added to correspond with the FGCam's location on frame 4. The Final Gathering points are saved in a file named `default.fgmap`.

FIGURE 9.30
The Final Gathering points are visible in the scene after creating a test render.

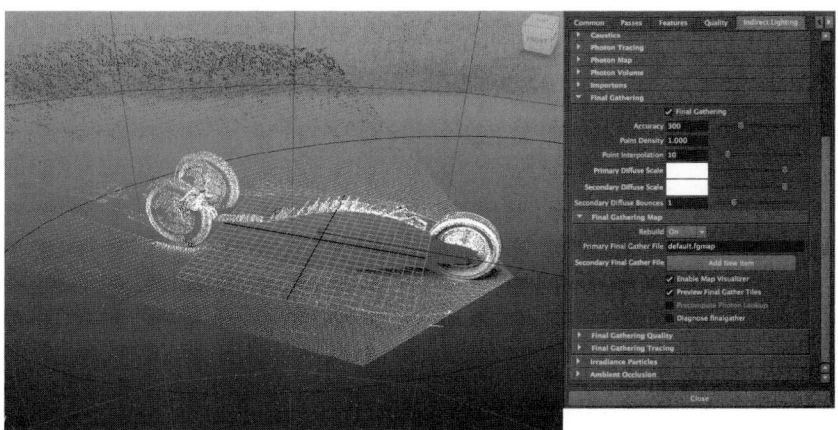

6. Make three more test renders from frames 6, 8, and 10.

7. Render a sequence of the first 10 frames of the animation, and compare this to the carFG_test1 sequence. You can also view the carFG_test2 sequence in the chapter9\ images directory on the DVD.

The flickering in the new sequence is greatly reduced using this technique.

8. Save the scene as **car_v04.ma**.

To see a version of the sequence, open the car_v04.ma scene from the chapter9\scenes directory on the DVD (see Figure 9.31).

This system does not work if there are animated objects in the scene. If the Final Gathering map is generated and saved while an object is in one position, the same irradiance values are used on a subsequent frame after the object has moved to a new position. This can lead to a strange result. You can enable the Optimize For Animations option in the Final Gathering Tracing section to help reduce Final Gathering flickering in scenes with animated objects.

The Diagnose Final Gathering option color codes the Final Gathering points so you can easily distinguish the initial points created with the first render from points added during subsequent renders.

FIGURE 9.31
Additional Final Gathering points are added to the existing map file each time a test render is created.

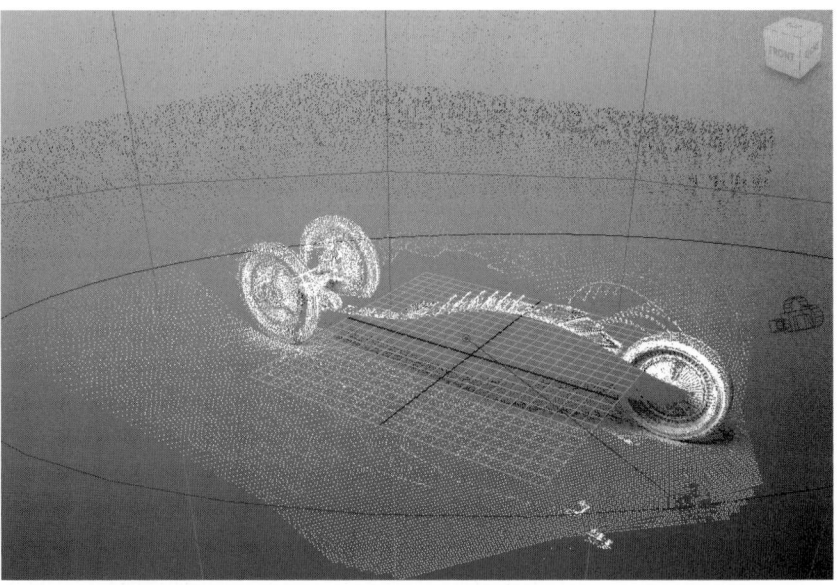

FINAL GATHERING PASS

You can render a special Final Gathering map render pass to automate the process described in the previous section. The purpose of this pass is to create a Final Gathering map for the entire scene before rendering the images. This can save time on subsequent renders if you do not need to change the lighting or if you need to recompute Final Gathering points for a specific set of frames or render layers. Once the Final Gathering Map pass is created, you can specify the files generated by the pass in the Final Gathering Map section in the Indirect Lighting section of the Render Settings window. For more information on creating render passes, consult Chapter 12.

Other Final Gathering quality controls are found in the Final Gathering Quality and Final Gathering Tracing sections in the Indirect Lighting tab of the Render Settings window.

Optimize For Animations This option essentially automates the system described previously. It reduces flickering but at the expense of accuracy.

Use Radius Quality Control This setting has been largely replaced by the Point Interpolation setting. However, it can still be used if you prefer. If this option is enabled, the Point Interpolation setting is automatically disabled, and vice versa. Use Radius Quality Control corresponds to the Accuracy setting. It basically sets the sampling range for Final Gathering rays to search for irradiance information from nearby surfaces. The typical practice is to set Max Radius to 10 percent of the overall scene size and Min Radius to 10 percent of Max Radius. You also have the option of specifying the radius in terms of pixel size. These settings help to reduce artifacts.

Filter This attribute relates to using High Dynamic Range (HDR) images and will be discussed later in this chapter.

Falloff Start and Stop These settings limit the distance Final Gathering rays can travel. This is especially important in a large scene where objects may be far apart. You can optimize render time by setting a range for these values. When a Final Gathering ray has reached its maximum distance as set by Falloff Max, it samples any further irradiance and color values from the environment and uses them to shade the surface. The falloff start begins a linear transition to the environment sampling, and the falloff stop is the end point for this transition as well as the farthest point a Final Gathering ray can travel. Think of the start and stop points as the beginning and end of a gradient. At the start portion of the gradient, surface sampling is at 100 percent, and the environment sampling is at 0 percent. At the stop point of the gradient, the surface sampling is at 0 percent, and the environment sampling is at 100 percent.

This can reduce render times even in an indoor scene. By default the scene background color is black. If you set Falloff Start to 15 and Falloff Stop to 20 and render, the frame takes less time to render but comes out very dark in shadowed areas that are 15 to 20 units from a Final Gathering point. This is because the default black background is being blended into the surface color. If you feel too much detail is lost to the darkness, you can create an environment dome with a constant color or an HDR image, or you can simply set the render camera's background to a value greater than 0. Setting the value too high reduces contrast in the scene, similar to adding an ambient light. A low value between 0.25 and 0.5 should work well.

Reflections, Refractions, and Max Trace These sliders set the maximum number of times a Final Gathering ray can be reflected (create a secondary ray) or refracted from reflective, glossy, or transparent surfaces. The default values are usually sufficient for most scenes.

MIDEFAULTOPTIONS NODE

You can access even more options for Global Illumination and Final Gathering settings by selecting the miDefaultOptions node. To find this node, open the Outliner, and under the Display menu, deselect DAG Options Only. Scroll down and select the miDefaultOptions node from the list, and open the Attribute Editor. You'll see the options described earlier as well as some options not otherwise available, such as the FG Diffuse Bounces field, which you can use to set the number of diffuse bounces to more than 2 (which of course you rarely need to do).

Using Lights with Final Gathering

The previous exercises demonstrated how Final Gathering can render a scene without lights by using only incandescent objects. However, for many situations, you'll want to combine Final Gathering with lights so that specular highlights and clear shadows are visible in the render. If you take a look outside on a sunny day, you'll see examples of direct lighting, cast shadows, indirect lighting, and ambient occlusion working together. Likewise, a typical photographer's studio combines bright lights, flashbulbs, and diffuse lights to create a harmonious composition. You'll also find that combining lights and Final Gathering produces a higher-quality render. In the `car_v05.ma` scene found in the `chapter9\scenes` directory on the DVD, light-emitting planes are used as fill lights in conjunction with a shadow-casting spotlight (Figure 9.32).

FIGURE 9.32
A spotlight is combined with light-emitting planes and rendered using Final Gathering.

FINAL GATHERING AND GLOBAL ILLUMINATION

In many cases, the look of indirect lighting can be improved and rendering times can be reduced by using Final Gathering and Global Illumination at the same time. Final Gathering usually works fairly well on its own, but Global Illumination almost always needs a little help from Final Gathering to create a good-looking render. When Global Illumination and Final Gathering are enabled together, the Final Gathering secondary diffuse bounce feature no longer affects the scene; all secondary diffuse light bounces are handled by Global Illumination.

Image-Based Lighting

Image-Based Lighting (IBL) uses the color values of an image to light a scene. This can often be done without the help of additional lights in the scene. When you enable IBL, you have the choice of rendering the scene using Final Gathering, IBL with Global Illumination, or IBL with the mental ray Light Shader. This section will describe all three methods.

You can use both High Dynamic Range (HDR) images and Low Dynamic Range (LDR) images with IBL. HDR differs from LDR in the number of exposure levels stored in the format. An LDR image is typically a standard 8-bit or 16-bit image file, such as a TIFF. An HDR image is a 32-bit floating-point format image that stores multiple levels of exposure within a single image. Both 8-bit and 16-bit image formats store their color values as integers (whole numbers), while a 32-bit floating-point file can store colors as fractional values (numbers with a decimal). This means that the 8-bit and 16-bit formats cannot display a full range of luminance values, whereas the 32-bit floating-point images can. Multiple levels of exposure are available in HDR 32-bit floating-point images, which can be used to create more dynamic and realistic lighting in your renders when you use IBL.

HDR images come in several formats including .hdr, OpenEXR (.exr), Floating Point TIFFs, and Direct Draw Surface (DDS). Most often you'll use the .hdr and .exr image formats when working with IBL.

OpenEXRLoader

To view and use OpenEXR images in Maya, you'll need to enable the openEXRLoader.mll plug-in. It should be on by default, but occasionally it does not load when you start Maya. To load this plug-in, choose Window ➤ Settings/Preferences ➤ Plug-in Manager. From the list of plug-ins, select the Loaded and Auto Load boxes next to the openEXRLoader.mll plug-in (openEXRLoader.bundle on the Mac).

When an HDR image is used with IBL, the lighting in the scene looks much more realistic, utilizing the full dynamic range of lighting available in the real world. When integrating CG into live-action shots, a production team often takes multiple HDR images of the set and then uses these images with IBL when rendering the CG elements. This helps the CG elements match perfectly with the live-action shots.

The downside of HDR images is that they require a lot of setup to create. However, you can download and use HDR images from several websites, including Paul Debevec's website (www.debevec.org/Probes/). Debevec is a pioneer in the field of computer graphics and virtual lighting. He is currently a researcher at the University of Southern California's Institute for Creative Technologies.

Several companies, such as Dosch Design (www.doschdesign.com/), sell packages of HDRI images on DVD, which are very high quality.

HDR images are available in several styles including angular (light probe), longitude/latitude (spherical), and vertical cubic cross. mental ray supports angular and spherical. You can convert one style to another using a program such as HDRShop.

Enabling IBL

To use IBL in a scene, open the Render Settings window, and make sure mental ray is chosen as the renderer. Switch to the Indirect Lighting tab, and click the Image Based Lighting Create button at the top of the window. This creates all the nodes you need in the scene to use IBL.

You can have more than one IBL node in a scene, but only one can be used to create the lighting.

IBL and Final Gathering

Using IBL with Final Gathering is similar to the concept of using light-emitting objects. When you enable IBL, a sphere is created, and you can map either an HDR or an LDR image to the sphere (HDR is the most common choice). The scene is rendered with Final Gathering enabled, and the luminance values of the image mapped to the sphere are used to create the lighting in the scene. You can use additional lights to create cast shadows and specular highlights or use IBL by itself. The following exercise takes you through the process of setting up this scenario.

You'll need a High Dynamic Range image (HDRI) to use for the mentalrayibl node. You can download a number of these images free of charge from Debevec's website at www.debevec.org/ Probes/. Download the all_probes.zip file, and unzip it; place the files in the sourceimages folder of your current project.

1. Open the car_v06.ma scene from the chapter9\scenes directory on the DVD.

2. Open the Render Settings window, and make sure the Render Using option is set to mental ray.

3. Switch to the Indirect Lighting tab, and click the Create button next to Image Based Lighting. This creates the mentalrayIbl1 node, which is a sphere scaled to fit the contents of the scene.

4. Select the mentalrayIbl1 node in the Outliner, and open its Attribute Editor.

5. Click the folder icon next to the Image Name field. Choose the building_probe.hdr image from the images you downloaded from www.debevec.org/Probes/.

6. Connect this image to the mentalrayIbl node in the scene.

7. The image is in the Angular mapping style, so set Mapping to Angular.

8. In the Render Settings window, enable Final Gathering.

9. Create a test render using the renderCam camera.

   In this case, you'll see that the image is blown out. You can also see the HDR image in the background of the scene.

10. In the Attribute Editor for the mentalrayIblShape1 node, scroll down to Render Stats, and turn off Primary Visibility.

11. Enable Adjust Final Gathering Color Effects. This enables the Color Gain and Color Offset sliders. Set the Color Gain slider to a light gray.

12. Create another test render (Figure 9.33).

13. Save the scene as **car_v10IBL_FG.ma**.

FIGURE 9.33
The settings on the mentalray-IblShape1 node are adjusted in the Attribute Editor. The scene is lit using the HDR image and Final Gathering.

To see a version of the scene, open the `car_v7IBL_FG.ma` scene in the `chapter9\scenes` folder on the DVD. Note that you will need to connect the IBL node to the `building_probe.hdr` image in order for this scene to render correctly.

You can see the car is now lit entirely by the HDR image. The HDR image is also visible in the reflection on the surface of the car. If you want to disable the visibility of the reflections, turn off Visible As Environment.

If you need to adjust the size and position of the IBL sphere, turn off the Infinite option at the top of the node's Attribute Editor.

You can adjust the quality of the lighting using the Final Gathering controls in the Render Settings window.

ADDITIONAL IBL TECHNIQUES

The IBL node can be used to emit photons into the scene, both Global Illumination and Caustics. This can be used in conjunction with Final Gathering or with Global Illumination alone.

You'll get better results combining Global Illumination with either Final Gathering or the IBL Light Shader. You can also turn on Caustics in the Render Settings window if you want create caustic light effects from a surface reflecting the IBL.

You can use the Global Illumination settings in the Render Settings window as well as the Photon Emission settings in the mentalrayIbl1 node to tune the look of the photons. By default, photons emitted from the IBL node are stored in the map at the moment they hit a surface. This makes the Global Illumination render fast and work well if Global Illumination is used by itself.

When the Emit Light option is enabled in the mentalrayIbl1 node, the image used for the IBL node emits light as if the image itself were made up of directional lights. Each directional light gets a color value based on a sampling taken from the image mapped to the sphere. This technique tends to work best with images that have large areas of dark colors.

To see examples of these techniques, open the `car_v7IBL_GI.ma` and the `car_v7IBL_FG.ma` files from the `chapter9/scenes` folder on the DVD. Note that you will need to connect the IBL node to the `building_probe.hdr` image in order for this scene to render correctly.

Physical Sun and Sky

mental ray provides a special network of lights and shaders that can accurately emulate the look of sunlight for outdoor scenes. Using the Physical Sun and Sky network requires rendering with Final Gathering. It's very easy to set up and use.

Enabling Physical Sun and Sky

To create the Physical Sun and Sky network, use the controls in the Indirect Lighting tab of the Render Settings window.

1. Open the `pergola_v04.ma` scene from the `chapter9\scenes` directory on the DVD.

2. Open the Render Settings window, and make sure Render Using is set to mental ray.

3. Switch to the Indirect Lighting tab in the Render Settings window, and click the Create button for Physical Sun And Sky.

   Clicking the Create button creates a network of nodes that generates the look of sunlight. These include the mia_physicalsun, mia_physicalsky, and mia_exposure simple nodes. You'll notice that there is a directional light named sunDirection that has been added to the scene. To control the lighting of the scene, you'll change the orientation of the light. The other light attributes (position, scale, intensity, color, and so on) will not affect the lighting of the scene. To change the lighting, you need to edit the mia_physicalsky node in the Attribute Editor.

4. Select the sunDirection light in the Outliner, and use the Move tool to raise it up in the scene so you can see it clearly. The position of the sun will not change the lighting in the scene.

5. In the Render Settings window, make sure Final Gathering is enabled. It should be turned on by default when you create the physical sun nodes.

6. Open the Render View window, and create a test render from the renderCam camera.

7. Store the rendered image in the Render View window.

   The rendered image includes cast shadows from the sun, ambient occlusion created by Final Gathering, and a sky gradient in the background that is reflected in the windows of the building.

8. Select the sunDirection light, and set its Rotate X value to **negative 150**.

9. Create another test render, and compare it with the first.

   When you change the orientation of the sunDirection light, it affects the color of the lighting as well to accurately simulate the lighting you see at different times of day.

10. Select the sunDirection node, and use the following settings:

    Rotate X: **-156.337**

    Rotate Y: **37.115**

    Rotate Z: **11.934**

11. Select the sunDirection node in the Outliner, and open its Attribute Editor.

12. Select the mia_physicalsky1 tab. In the Shading rollout, use the following settings:

Sun Disk Intensity: **0.5**

Sun Disk Scale: **1**

Sun Glow Intensity: **0.5**.

13. Create another test render. With these settings, the sun is actually visible in the sky (see the bottom image of Figure 9.34).

14. Save the scene as **pergola_v05.ma**.

To see a finished version of the scene, open the pergola_v05.ma scene from the chapter9\ scenes directory on the DVD.

FIGURE 9.34
Changing the rotation of the sunDirection light changes the lighting to emulate different times of the day.

PHYSICAL SUN AND SKY BACKGROUND

Note that the sky in the background of the rendered images will not appear when importing into compositing software unless you choose to ignore the alpha channel.

Editing the Sky Settings

To change the look of the sky in the scene, use the settings found on the mia_physicalsky node.

A number of settings in the Attribute Editor for the sunDirection node help define the color and quality of the sky and the sun in the render. Here is a brief description of some of these settings (Figure 9.35):

Multiplier   This setting adjusts the overall brightness of the sky.

R, G, and B Unit Conversions   These setting adjust the coloring of the sky in the R (red), G (green), and B (blue) channels when these values are changed incrementally.

Haze   This setting adds haziness to the sky.

Red/Blue Shift   Use this option to shift between warm and cool lighting in a scene. Negative numbers shift colors toward blue; positive numbers shift colors toward red. The value range should be kept between -1 and 1.

Horizon Height and Blur   These settings change the position and blurriness of the horizon line visible in the renders behind the geometry.

Ground Color   This option changes the color of the area below the horizon. Note that the horizon does appear in reflective shaders applied to the geometry in the scene.

Night Color   This option affects the color of the sky when the sun is rotated close to 180 degrees.

Sun Direction   This setting rotates the sunDirection light in the scene to change the sun direction. Fields should be left at 0.

Sun   This option connects the sun settings to a different light in the scene.

Sun Disk Intensity, Sun Disk Scale, and Sun Glow Intensity   These settings affect the look of the sun when it is visible in the render.

Use Background   This option adds a texture for the environment background. Use this setting as opposed to the standard Maya environment shaders.

Update Camera Connections   This button adds a new renderable camera to the scene after you create the Physical Sun and Sky network. The network applies specific shaders to all of the renderable cameras in the scene when it is first created. Any new cameras added to the scene will not have these connections enabled by default. Click this button each time you add a new camera to the scene.

Remove Camera Connections   This option removes all cameras from the Physical Sun and Sky network.

If you need to delete the Physical Sun and Sky network from the scene, open the Render Settings window, and click the Delete button for the Physical Sun and Sky attribute.

FIGURE 9.35
The settings for
changing the look
of the physical sky
in the render

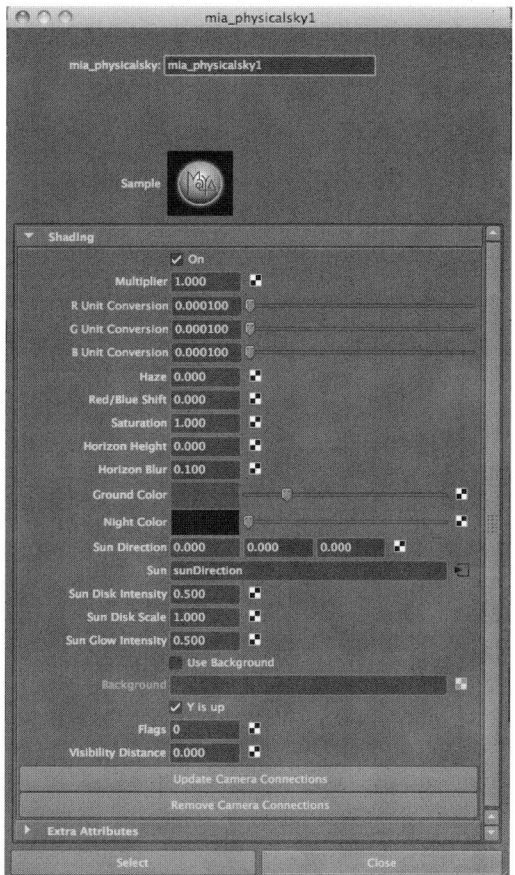

mental ray Area Lights

mental ray area lights are designed to create a simulation of light sources in the real world. Most lights in Maya emit light rays from an infinitely small point in space. In the real world, light sources are three-dimensional objects, such as a lightbulb or a window, that have a defined size.

Lighting a scene using standard lights, such as the point and spot lights, often require additional fill lighting to compensate for the fact that these lights do not behave like real-world light sources. Area lights are designed as an alternative to this approach. A mental ray area light is essentially an array of spot lights. The array creates a 3D light source, which results in more realistic light behaviors, especially with regard to shadow casting. The downside is that area lights often take longer to render, so they are not always ideal for every situation.

Using Area Lights

Follow the steps in this exercise to understand how to use area lights in mental ray:

1. Open the `kitchen_v05.ma` scene from the `chapter9\scenes` directory on the DVD.

2. Create an area light (Create ➤ Lights ➤ Area Light). Position the light using the following settings:

   Translate X: **14.386**

   Translate Y: **30.286**

   Translate Z: **-27.862**

   Rotate X: **-90**

   Scale X: **6.718**

   Scale Y: **9.095**

   Scale Z: **4.639**

3. In the Attribute Editor under the areaLightShape1 heading, turn Enable Ray Traced Shadows to On.

4. Open the Render Settings window, and set Render Using to mental ray.

5. On the Quality tab, set the Quality Presets option to Production.

6. Open the Render View window, and create a test render from the renderCam camera.

7. Store the image in the render view.

   The render looks very blown out and grainy. You can reduce the grainy quality by increasing the shadow rays used on the light. However, there is something important and potentially confusing about using a standard Maya area light with mental ray that you should know. The light as it stands right now is not actually taking advantage of mental ray area light properties. To make the light a true mental ray area light, you need to enable the Use Light Shape attribute in the Attribute Editor. Until you enable this attribute, you'll have a hard time getting the area light to look realistic.

8. Open the Attribute Editor for areaLight1. Switch to the AreaLightShape1 tab.

9. In the mental ray ➤ Area Light rollout, activate Use Light Shape, and create another test render (See Figure 9.36).

FIGURE 9.36
The mental ray area light is enabled when Use Light Shape is activated in the Attribute Editor.

The new render is less blown out, and the shadows are much softer (although still grainy).

Unlike standard Maya area lights, the intensity of mental ray area lights is not affected by the scale of the light. To change the intensity, use the Intensity slider at the top of the Attribute Editor. The shape of the shadows cast by mental ray area lights is affected by the shape chosen in the Type menu and the scale of the light.

To improve the quality of the shadows, increase the High Samples setting. The High Samples and Low Samples settings control the quality of the shadow in reflected surfaces. These can be left at a low value to improve render efficiency.

10. Set Light Shape Type to Sphere, and increase High Samples to **32**.

11. Scale the light down to **2** in X, Y, and Z, and turn on the Visible option.

12. Move the light down along the y-axis so that it is visible within the camera view.

13. Create a test render, and compare the render to the previous versions (Figure 9.37).

The Sphere type area light is similar to a point light, but instead of emitting light from an infinitely small point in space, it emits from a spherical volume, making it ideal for simulating light cast from things such as lightbulbs.

You can also create an area light that behaves like a spotlight.

14. Scroll up in the Attribute Editor for areaLight1, and set the light Type setting to Spotlight. Set Cone Angle to **70**, and set Intensity to **2**.

15. Scroll down to the mental ray section. Notice that Area Light is still activated. In the scene you can see that the area light is attached to the spotlight. It may be still set to the sphere type.

16. There are now two fields available: High Samples and Low Samples. These represent the distribution of samples in U and V space within the area light shape. Set both High Samples to **8**.

FIGURE 9.37
The area light is visible in the render.

17. Turn off the visible option.

18. Place the light within one of the recessed light fixtures in the ceiling. Try these settings in the Channel Box:

Translate X: **17.775**

Translate Y: **30.854**

Translate Z: **-24.856**

19. Create another test render (Figure 9.38).

20. Save the scene as `kitchen_v06.ma`.

The light quality and shadow shape remain the same as in the previous renders. However, switching the light Type setting to Spotlight adds the penumbra shape you expect from a spotlight. This allows you to combine the properties of spotlights and mental ray area lights. The Visible option in the mental ray settings does not work when using a spotlight as the original light.

To see a version of the scene, open the `kitchen_v06.ma` scene from the `chapter9\scenes` directory on the DVD.

FIGURE 9.38
The shape of the spotlight creates shadows based on the area light settings.

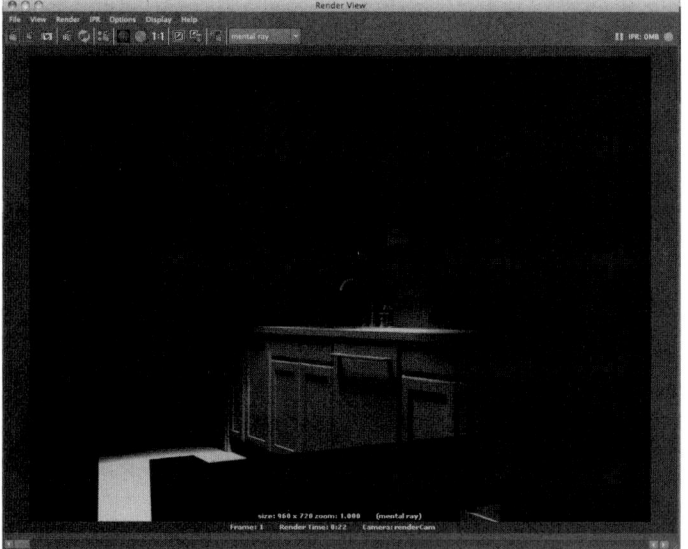

Light Shaders

mental ray has a number of light shaders that can be applied to lights in a scene. The purpose of these shaders is to extend the capabilities of Maya lights to allow for more lighting options. When a mental ray shader is applied to a Maya light, specific attributes on the original light node are overridden. The light's attributes can then be set using the controls on the light shader node.

Some shaders, such as the Mib_blackbody and Mib_cie_d shaders, are very simple. These two shaders translate the color of the light as a temperature specified in Kelvin. Other shaders are more complex, providing a number of attributes that can be used in special circumstances.

This section will discuss some of the light shaders and how you can use them in Maya scenes.

Physical Light Shader

The Physical Light shader is a type of shadow-casting light that is used in combination with indirect lighting (Final Gathering, Global Illumination) to create more physically accurate light behavior. There are also certain materials, such as the mental ray Architectural materials (mia), that are designed to work with physical lights (these materials are discussed in Chapter 10).

Physical lights always cast ray trace shadows, and the falloff rate for the light obeys the inverse square law just like lights in the real world. This law states that the intensity of light is inversely proportional to the square of the distance from the source. So, the light intensity decreases rapidly as the light travels from the source.

Physical lights are easy to set up and use. Once you are comfortable with them, consider using them whenever you use indirect lighting, such as Global Illumination and Final Gathering. This exercise will show you how to create a physical light. The scene has a number of standard Maya spotlights positioned to match the recessed lighting fixtures in the ceiling; six of these lights are currently hidden so that you can focus on just two of the lights. Final Gathering has been enabled for the scene.

1. Open the kitchen_v07.ma scene from the chapter9\scenes directory on the DVD.

2. Open the Render View window, and create a test render from the renderCam camera.

3. Store the render in the render view window so that you can compare it with other renders as you make changes (see Figure 9.39).

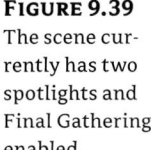
FIGURE 9.39
The scene currently has two spotlights and Final Gathering enabled.

4. Select spotLight1, and open its Attribute Editor.

5. Expand the Custom Shaders rollout, and click the checkered box to the right of the Light Shader field.

6. From the Create Render Node pop-up, select the mental ray lights heading under the mental ray section.

7. Click the physical_light button to create a light shader. This connects it to spotLight1 (see Figure 9.40).

FIGURE 9.40
Apply the Physical Light shader to the point light.

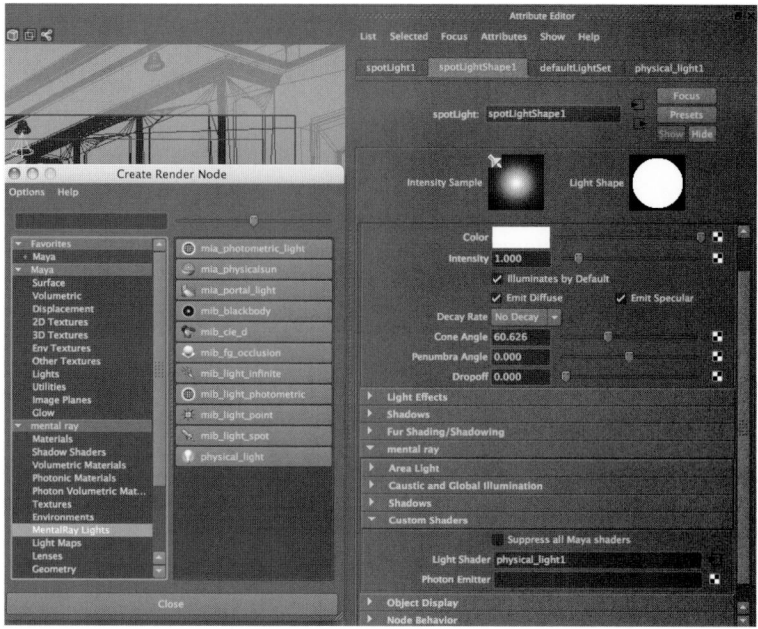

The attributes for the physical_light shader will open in the Attribute Editor. You'll see the settings for the shader:

Color   The Color setting controls the color and intensity of the light by adjusting the color values in the color swatch.

Cone   The Cone setting is used when the Physical Light shader is applied to mental ray spot and area spotlights to define the cone angle and penumbra. Higher values create a softer penumbra.

Threshold   The Threshold setting defines a minimum illumination value. When you increase the threshold, the lighting in the scene is contracted around the brighter areas, giving you more control over the precise areas of light in the scene. This can cause hard edges to appear around the edges of light cast by spotlight even after adjusting the Cone value.

Cosine Exponent   The Cosine Exponent attribute is similar to the Cone setting and works only when the shader is applied to mental ray area lights. It contracts the area of light cast when this shader is applied to mental ray area lights. As value of Cosine Exponent increases, the light cast by the area light becomes more focused.

8. Open the Hypershade editor.

9. Switch to the Utilities tab. (If the tabs do not appear at the top of the Hypershade, choose Tabs ➤ Revert To Default Tabs, and click OK on any warning windows that pop-up.)

10. Select the spotlight2 node in the Outliner, and open its Attribute Editor.

11. MMB drag the physicalLight1 shader from the Utilities section of the Hypershade to the Light Shader field in the mental ray section of spotlight2's Attribute Editor. This means that both spotlights are connected to the same physical light shader.

12. Create a test render from the renderCam camera (see Figure 9.41).

FIGURE 9.41
Render the scene using a physical light.

13. Store the render in the Render View window.

    The lighting looks extremely dark. The reason for this is because a physically accurate falloff of the light requires a much higher intensity setting. To fix this, you'll use the Color swatch value in the physical_light1's Attribute Editor. The default value for the light is 1,000. You can see this by clicking the color swatch to open the Color Chooser; the RGB values are all 1,000.

14. Create a new test render. The lighting looks a bit blown out, and it does not look as though the lights are accurately lighting the room (Figure 9.42). You can fix this by applying a tone-mapping lens shader to the renderCam camera.

15. Save the scene as `kitchen_v08.ma`.

    To see a version of this scene, open the `kitchen_v08.ma` from the `chapter9\scenes` folder on the DVD.

FIGURE 9.42
The physical light shader creates a blown-out look to the render.

COLOR CHOOSER BUG

Maya's new Color Chooser suffers from a bug that was not present in previous versions of the software. At the time of this writing, it is impossible to set values greater than 1,000 for the color sliders in the Color Chooser. To get around this, you can use a simple line of MEL scripting:

1. Open the Script Editor (Windows ➤ General Editors ➤ Script Editor).

2. On the MEL tab of the lower half of the Script Editor, type the following:

    ```
    setAttr "physical_light1.color" -type double3 4000 4000 4000;
    ```

3. Select the text in the Script Editor, and press the Enter key on the numeric keypad of your computer (not the Return key). Writing MEL scripts is explored in detail in Chapter 17.

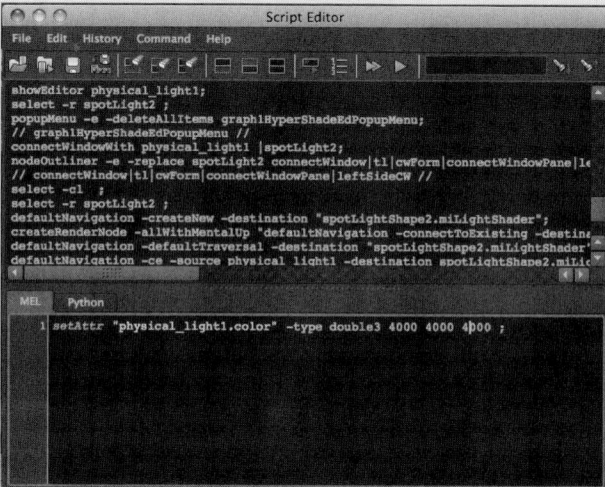

This sets the value of the light to greater than 1,000. Be aware that if you open the Color Chooser for the Color attribute of the physical light shader again, you'll have to repeat these steps. Let's hope the bug will be resolved in a future release of the software.

Tone Mapping

Rendering using physical lights often results in a very blown-out image. This is because computer monitors are unable to display the full range of luminance values created by physical lights. To correct this, you may need to apply a tone-mapping lens shader to the rendering camera (mia_exposure_photographic or mia_exposure_simple).

1. Continue with the scene from the previous section, or open the kitchen_v08.ma scene from the chapter9\scenes folder on the DVD.

2. Select the renderCam camera in the Outliner, and open its Attribute Editor.

3. Scroll down to the mental ray rollout, and click the checker icon next to the lens shader.

4. In the Create Render Node window, select Lenses from the mental ray section.

5. Click the mia_exposure_simple button to attach a lens shader to the camera. (Lens shaders are explored further in Chapter 10.)

6. Create a test render using the renderCam camera. You'll see that the bounced light created by the Final Gathering is more visible and the lights look less blown out (see Figure 9.43).

7. To soften the edges of the light cast by the spotlight, open the Attribute Editor for the physical_light1 light shader. Set Cone Attribute to 1.5.

8. Unhide the other spot lights in the scene.

9. Attach the physical_light1 light shader to each of these lights, and create another test render (Figure 9.44).

FIGURE 9.43
Applying a lens shader to the camera corrects the tonal values of the image so that it appears correct on your computer monitor.

FIGURE 9.44
The light shader is applied to all the lights in the scene.

The room is starting to look more properly lit. Use the MEL script mentioned in the earlier sidebar "Color Chooser Bug" to adjust the light values. The three values at the end of the line of code correspond to the red, green, and blue channels of the light color. By raising or lowering these values, you can add color to the light. For example, to give the light a yellow tint, make the red and green values higher like so:

```
setAttr "physical_light1.color" -type double3 5000 5000 4000;
```

To see a version of the scene, open the `kitchen_v09.ma` scene from the `chapter9\scenes` folder on the DVD.

Photometric Lights and Profiles

Photometric lights allow you to attach light profiles created by light manufacturers so you can simulate specific lights in your scenes. These profiles are often available on light manufacturers' websites. The profile itself is a text file in the `.ies` format.

The profiles simulate the qualities of the light, such as falloff, and the influence of the light fixture. A light profile can include the sconces and fixtures attached to the light itself. This is most helpful in creating accurate architectural renderings.

To use a photometric light, you can attach the Pmib_light_photometric shader to a point light and then attach the profile to the light using the Profile field in the shader's attributes. You can also skip using the shader altogether and attach the `.ies` profile directly to the point light in the Light Profile field available in point lights.

In many cases, you'll need to adjust the shadows cast by lights using a profile to make them more realistic. Use ray trace shadows and adjust the Shadow Rays and Light Radius values to improve the look of the shadows.

If you'd like to experiment using light profiles, you can download `.ies` format light profiles from www.lsi-industries.com/products.asp.

BONUS MOVIES

You'll find some movies on the book's companion DVD that cover the use of additional mental ray lighting nodes such as the portal light and participating media. You can find them in the bonus-Movies directory on the DVD.

The Bottom Line

Use shadow-casting lights Lights can cast either depth map or ray trace shadows. Depth map shadows are created from an image projected from the shadow-casting light, which reads the depth information of the scene. Ray trace shadows are calculated by tracing rays from the light source to the rendering camera.

Master it Compare mental ray depth map shadows to ray trace shadows. Render the `crystalGlobe.ma` scene using soft ray trace shadows.

Render with Global Illumination Global Illumination simulates indirect lighting by emitting photons into a scene. Global Illumination photons react with surfaces that have diffuse shaders. Caustics use photons that react to surfaces with reflective shaders. Global Illumination works particularly well in indoor lighting situations.

Master it Render the `rotunda_v01.ma` scene using Global Illumination.

Render with Final Gathering Final Gathering is another method for creating indirect lighting. Final Gathering points are shot into the scene from the rendering camera. Final Gathering includes color bleeding and ambient occlusion shadowing as part of the indirect lighting. Final Gathering can be used on its own or in combination with Global Illumination.

Master it Create a fluorescent lightbulb from geometry that can light a room.

Use Image-Based Lighting Image-Based Lighting (IBL) uses an image to create lighting in a scene. High Dynamic Range Images (HDRI) are usually the most effective source for IBL. There are three ways to render with IBL: Final Gathering, Global Illumination, and with the light shader. These can also be combined if needed.

Master it Render the car scene using the Uffizi Gallery probe HDR image available at www.debevec.org/Probes/.

Render using the Physical Sun and Sky network The Physical Sun and Sky network creates realistic sunlight that's ideal for outdoor rendering.

Master it Render a short animation showing the car at different times of day.

Understand mental ray area lights mental ray area lights are activated in the mental ray section of an area light's shape node when the Use Light Shape option is enabled. mental ray area lights render realistic, soft ray trace shadows. The light created from mental ray area lights is emitted from a three-dimensional array of lights as opposed to an infinitely small point in space.

Master it Build a lamp model that realistically lights a scene using an area light.

Chapter 10

mental ray Shading Techniques

A *shader* is a rendering node that defines the material qualities of a surface. When you apply a shading node to your modeled geometry, you use the shader's settings to determine how the surface will look when it's rendered. Will it appear as shiny plastic? Rusted metal? Human skin? The shader is the starting point for answering these questions. Shading networks are created when one or more nodes are connected to the channels of the shader node. These networks can range from simple to extremely complex. The nodes that are connected to shaders are referred to as *textures*. They can be image files created in other software packages or procedural (computer-generated) patterns, or they can be special nodes designed to create a particular effect.

Maya comes with a number of shader nodes that act as starting points for creating various material qualities. The mental ray plug-in also comes with its own special shader nodes that expand the library of available materials. Since the mental ray rendering plug-in is most often used to create professional images and animations, this book will emphasize mental ray techniques as much as possible. You'll learn how to use mental ray shaders to create realistic images.

In this chapter, you will learn to:

- ◆ Understand shading concepts
- ◆ Apply reflection and refraction blur
- ◆ Use basic mental ray shaders
- ◆ Apply the car paint shader
- ◆ Use the MIA materials
- ◆ Render contours

Shading Concepts

Shaders are sets of specified properties that define how a surface reacts to lighting in a scene. A mental ray material is actually a text file that contains a description of those properties organized in a way that the software understands. In Maya, the Hypershade provides you with a graphical user interface so you can edit and connect shaders without writing or editing the text files themselves.

The terms *shader* and *material* are synonymous; you'll see them used interchangeably through the book and the Maya interface. mental ray also uses shaders to determine properties for lights, cameras, and other types of render nodes. For example, special lens shaders are applied to cameras to create effects such as depth of field.

THE MENTAL RAY PLUG-IN

mental ray is a rendering plug-in that is included with Maya. It is a professional-quality photorealistic renderer used throughout the industry in film, television, architectural visualization, and anywhere photorealism is required.

Learning mental ray takes time and practice. Even though it's a plug-in, you'll find that it is as deep and extensive as Maya itself. mental ray includes a library of custom shading nodes that work together to extend the capabilities of mental ray. There are a lot of these nodes, many more than can be covered in this book.

When approaching mental ray as a rendering option, you can become quickly overwhelmed by the number of shading nodes in the mental ray section of the Hypershade. When these shading nodes are coupled with the mental ray–specific attributes found on standard Maya nodes, it can be very difficult to know what to use in a particular situation. Think of mental ray as a large toolkit filled with a variety of tools that can be used in any number of ways. Some tools you'll use all the time, some you'll need only for very specific situations, and some you may almost never use. You'll also find that over time, as your understanding and experience with mental ray grows, you may change your working style and use particular nodes more often. As you work with mental ray, expand your knowledge and experience through study and experimentation.

In this chapter, you'll be introduced to the more commonly used nodes, which will make you more comfortable using them in professional situations. There should be enough information in this chapter to give the everyday Maya user a variety of options for shading and rendering using mental ray. If you decide that you'd like to delve deeper into more advanced techniques, we recommend reading the mental ray shading guide that is part of the Maya documentation, as well as Boaz Livny's excellent book *mental ray for Maya, 3ds Max, and XSI* (Sybex, 2008).

Before starting this chapter, make sure you are familiar with using and applying standard Maya shaders, such as the Lambert, Blinn, Phong, Ramp, Surface, and Anisotropic shaders. You should be comfortable making basic connections in the Hypershade and creating renders in the Render View window. You should understand how to use Maya 2D and 3D textures, such as Fractal, Ramp, and Checker. Review Chapter 9 for background on lighting with mental ray. Many of the issues discussed in this chapter are directly related to lighting and mental ray lighting nodes.

This section focuses on shaders applied to geometry to determine surface quality. Three key concepts that determine how a shader makes a surface react to light are diffusion, reflection, and refraction. Generally speaking, light rays are reflected or absorbed or pass through a surface. Diffusion and reflection are two ways in which light rays bounce off a surface and back into the environment. Refraction refers to how a light ray is bent as it passes through a transparent surface. This section reviews these three concepts as well as other fundamentals that are important to understand before you start working with the shaders in a scene.

MAYA STANDARD SHADERS AND MENTAL RAY MATERIALS

The Maya standard shaders are found in the left list in the Hypershade window when you click the Surface heading under Maya (as shown here). The most often used standard shaders are Blinn, Lambert, Phong, Phong E, and Anisotropic. You can use any of these shaders when rendering with mental ray.

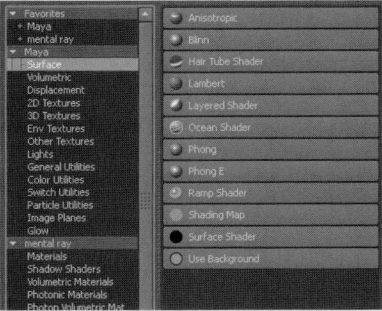

The mental ray materials (also referred to as *shaders*) are found in the left list in the Hypershade window when you click Materials under mental ray (as shown here). The shaders will work only when rendering with mental ray.

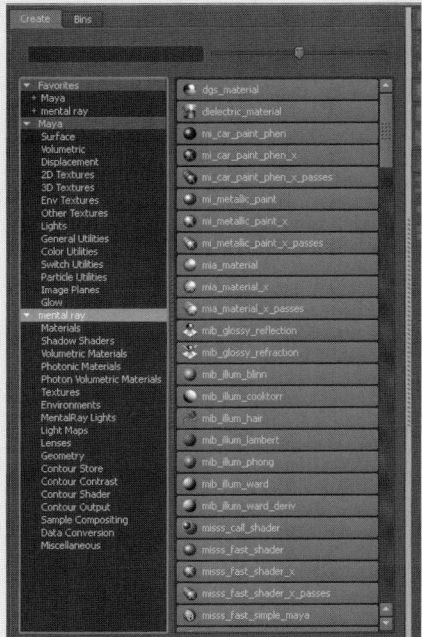

This chapter will discuss some aspects of working with the standard Maya shaders, but for the most part it will focus on the most often used mental ray shaders. If you are unfamiliar with the standard shaders, we recommend you review the Maya documentation or read *Introducing Maya 2011* by Dariush Derakshani (Sybex, 2010).

Diffusion

Diffusion describes how a light ray is reflected off a rough surface. Think of light rays striking concrete. Concrete is a rough surface covered in tiny bumps and crevices. As a light ray hits the bumpy surface, it is reflected back into the environment at different angles, which diffuse the reflection of light across the surface (see Figure 10.1).

FIGURE 10.1
Light rays that hit a rough surface are reflected back into the environment at different angles, diffusing light across the surface.

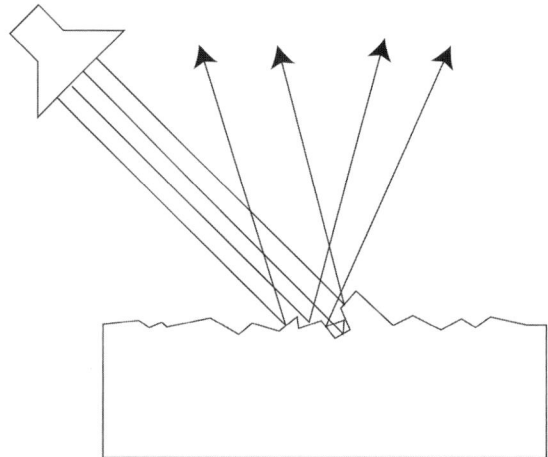

You see the surface color of the concrete mixed with the color of the lighting, but you generally don't see the reflected image of nearby objects. A sheet of paper, a painted wall, and clothing are examples of diffuse surfaces.

In standard Maya shaders, the amount of diffusion is controlled using the Diffuse slider. As the value of the Diffuse shader is increased, the surface appears brighter because it is reflecting more light back into the environment.

Reflection

When a surface is perfectly smooth, light rays bounce off the surface and back into the environment. The angle at which they bounce off the surface is equivalent to the angle in which they strike the surface—this is the *incidence angle*. This type of reflection is known as a *specular* reflection. You can see the reflected image of surrounding objects on the surface of smooth, reflective objects. Mirrors, polished wood, and opaque liquids are examples of reflective surfaces. A specular highlight is a reflection of the light source on the surface of the object (see Figure 10.2).

Logically, smoother surfaces, or surfaces that have a specular reflectivity, are less diffuse. However, many surfaces are composed of layers (think of glossy paper) that have both diffuse and specular reflectivity.

A glossy reflection occurs when the surface is not perfectly smooth but not so rough as to completely diffuse the light rays. The reflected image on a surface is blurry and bumpy and otherwise imperfect. Glossy surfaces can represent those surfaces that fit between diffuse reflectivity and specular reflectivity.

FIGURE 10.2
Light rays that hit
a smooth surface
and are reflected
back into the
environment at an
angle equivalent
to the incidence of
the light angle

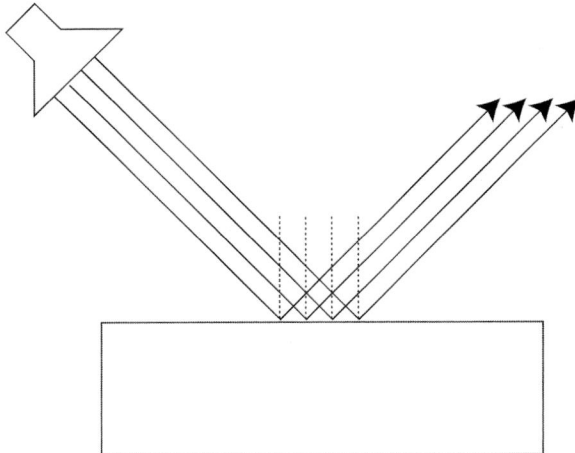

Refraction

A transparent surface can change the direction of the light rays as they pass through the surface
(Figure 10.3). The bending of light rays can distort the image of objects on the other side of the
surface. Think of an object placed behind a glass of water. The image of the object as you look
through the glass of water is distorted relative to an unobstructed view of the object. Both the
glass and the water in the glass bend the light rays as they pass through.

FIGURE 10.3
Refraction changes
the direction of light
rays as they pass
through a transpar-
ent surface.

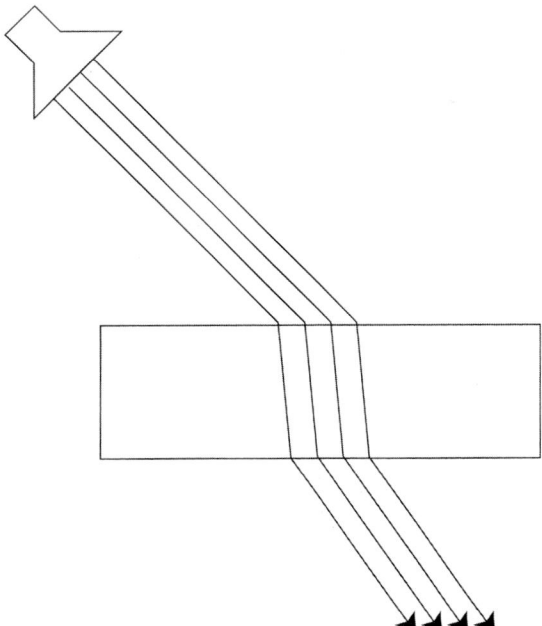

Shaders use a refractive index value to determine how refractions will be calculated. The refraction index is a value that describes the amount in which the speed of the light rays is reduced as it travels through a transparent medium, as compared to the speed of light as it travels through a vacuum. The reduction in speed is related to the angle in which the light rays are bent as they move through the material. A refraction index of 1 means the light rays are not bent. Glass typically has a refraction index between 1.5 and 1.6; water has a refraction index of 1.33.

If the refracting surface has imperfections, this can further scatter the light rays as they pass through the surface. This creates a blurry refraction.

Refraction in Maya is available only when ray tracing is enabled (mental ray uses ray tracing by default). The controls for refraction are found in the Raytrace section of the Attribute Editor of standard Maya shaders. A shader must have some amount of transparency before refraction has any visible effect.

The Fresnel Effect

The *Fresnel effect* is named for the nineteenth-century French physicist Jean Augustin Fresnel (pronounced with a silent *s*). This effect describes the amount of reflection and refraction that occurs on a surface as the viewing angle changes. The glancing angle is the angle at which you view a surface. If you are standing in front of a wall, the wall is perpendicular, and thus the glancing angle is 0. If you are looking across the ocean, the glancing angle of the surface of the water is very high. The Fresnel effect states that as the glancing angle increases, the surface becomes more reflective than refractive. It's easy to see objects in water as you stare straight down into water (low glancing angle); however, as you stare across the surface of water, the reflectivity increases, and the reflection of the sky and the environment makes it increasingly difficult to see objects in the water.

Opaque, reflective objects also demonstrate this effect. As you look at a billiard ball, the environment is more easily seen reflected on the edges of the ball as they turn away from you than on the parts of the ball that are perpendicular to your view (see Figure 10.4).

FIGURE 10.4
A demonstration of the Fresnel effect on reflective surfaces: the reflectivity increases on the parts of the sphere that turn away from the camera.

Anisotropy

Anisotropic reflections appear on surfaces that have directionality to their roughness. When you look at the surface of a compact disc, the tiny grooves that are created when data is written to the disc to create the satin-like anisotropic reflections. Brushed metal, hair, and satin are all examples of materials that have anisotropic specular reflections.

Creating Blurred Reflections and Refractions Using Standard Maya Shaders

Standard Maya shaders, such as the Blinn and Phong shaders, take advantage of mental ray reflection and refraction blurring to simulate realistic material behaviors. These options are available in the mental ray section of the shader's Attribute Editor. As you may have guessed, since these attributes appear in the mental rollout of the shader's Attribute Editor, the effect created by these settings will appear only when rendering with mental ray. They do not work when using other rendering options such as Maya Software.

Reflection Blur

Reflection blur is easy to use and is available for any of the standard Maya shaders that have reflective properties, such as Blinn, Phong, Anisotropic, and Ramp. This exercise demonstrates how to add reflection blur to a Blinn shader. This scene contains a space helmet model above a checkered ground plane.

1. Open the `reflectionBlur.ma` file from the `chapter10\scenes` directory on the DVD.

2. In the Outliner, select the shield surface. This is the glass shield at the front of the helmet. Assign a Blinn shader to the shield, and name the shader **shieldShader**.

QUICKLY ASSIGN A SHADER TO A SURFACE

There are several ways to quickly assign a shader to a surface:

◆ Many standard Maya shaders are available in the Rendering Shelf. You can select an object in a scene and simply click one of the shader icons on the shelf. This creates a new shader and applies it to the selected object at the same time. The names of the shaders appear in the help line in the lower left of the Maya interface.

◆ Another way to apply a shader is to select the object in the viewport window, right-click it, and choose Assign New Material from the bottom end of the marking menu. This will open the Hypershade window to the Materials section.

◆ You can select the object, switch to the Rendering menu set, and choose Lighting/Shading ➢ Assign New Material.

---

3. In the Common Material attributes rollout of the shieldShader, set Diffuse to 0, and set Transparency to white so that you can see inside the helmet.

4. In the Specular Shading rollout, set Specular Color to white and set Reflectivity to 1.

5. Render the scene in the Render View window from the renderCam camera (the left side of Figure 10.5).

6. Store the image in the Render View window.

7. Scroll down in the Attribute Editor for shieldShader, expand the mental ray rollout, and increase Mi Reflection Blur to **8** (Figure 10.6).

8. Create another test render, and compare this to the render in the previous step (the right side of Figure 10.5).

FIGURE 10.5
The reflection on the shield is blurred in the right image.

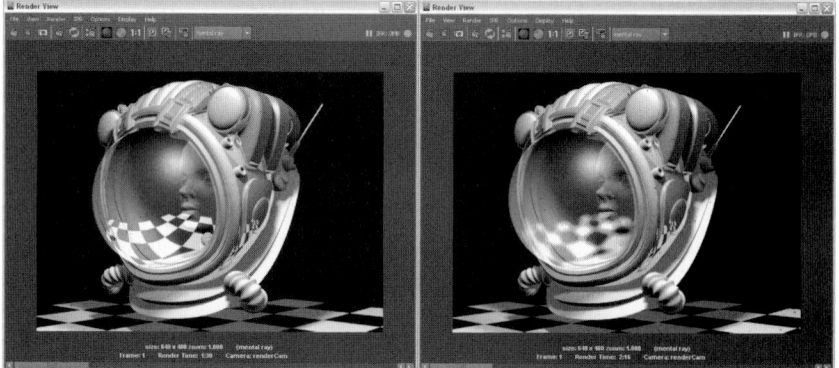

FIGURE 10.6
The Reflection Blur settings are in the mental ray rollout of the shader's Attribute Editor.

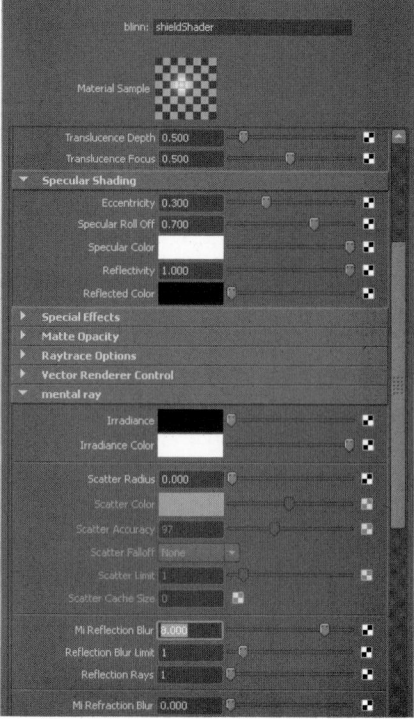

You can see how the reflection of the checkered pattern on the shield now appears blurred.

Reflection Blur Limit sets the number of times the reflection blur itself is seen in other reflective surfaces. Increasing the Reflection Rays value increases the quality of the blurring, making it appear finer. Notice that the reflection becomes increasingly blurry as the distance between the reflective surface and the reflected object increases.

Many surfaces are more reflective than you may realize. A wooden tabletop or even asphalt can have a small amount of reflection. Adding a low reflectivity value plus reflection blurring to many surfaces increases the realism of the scene.

Refraction Blur

Refraction blur is similar to reflection blur. It blurs the objects that appear behind a transparent surface that uses refraction. This gives a translucent quality to the object.

1. Continue with the scene from the previous section.

2. Set the Mi Reflection Blur of the reflectionBlurShader back to 0. Set Reflectivity to 0 as well. This way, you'll clearly be able to see how refraction blur affects the shader.

3. In the Attribute Editor for the shieldShader, expand the Raytrace Options rollout, and activate the Refractions option. Set Refractive Index to **1.2**.

4. Render the scene from the renderCam camera, and store the image in the Render View window (see the left image in Figure 10.7). The image of the face appears distorted behind the shield object because of the refraction of light as it passes through the glass.

FIGURE 10.7
The image of the face is refracted in the surface of the shield (left image). The refracted image is then blurred (right image).

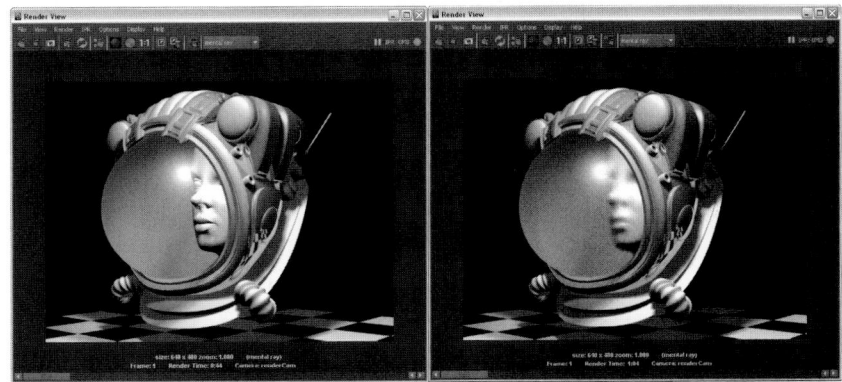

5. Expand the mental ray section in the shieldShader's Attribute Editor. Set Mi Refraction Blur to **2**, and create another test render (see the right image in Figure 10.7).

6. Save the scene as **reflectionBlur_v02.ma**.

To see a version of the scene, open the reflectionBlur_v02.ma file from the chapter10\ scenes directory on the DVD.

Refraction Blur Limit sets the number of times the refraction blur itself will be seen in refractive surfaces. Increasing the value of Refraction Rays increases the quality of the blurring, making it appear finer.

INTERACTIVE PHOTOREALISTIC RENDER PREVIEW

Interactive Photorealistic Render (IPR) preview is a mode that can be used in the Render View window. When you create a render preview using the special IPR mode, any change you make to a shader or the lighting, or even some modeling changes in the scene, automatically updates the Render View window, allowing you to see a preview of how the change will look interactively. IPR works very well with mental ray; in fact, it supports more rendering features for mental ray than for Maya Software. The workflow for creating an IPR render in mental ray is slightly different from the one for creating a Maya Software IPR. To create an IPR render, follow these steps:

1. Open the Render View window.

2. Set the current camera for the Render View window (Choose Render ➢ Snapshot ➢ *camera name*).

3. Click the IPR button at the top of the Render View window. The image will not actually render, but a message tells you to select a region to start tuning. Information about the scene is collected by mental ray. This may take a few seconds for complex scenes.

4. Select a region in the Render View window by drawing a rectangle over the parts of the image you want to tune; you'll see this part of the image update.

5. Make changes to the materials and the lighting; you'll see the image in the selected area update as you make the changes.

Most, but not all, mental ray features are supported by IPR. Occasionally you'll need to click the IPR button to update the render if IPR gets out of sync (or choose IPR ➢ Refresh IPR Image from the menu in the Render View window). The IPR render is a close approximation of the final render; be aware that what you see in the IPR render may look slightly different in the final render.

Basic mental ray Shaders

mental ray has a number of shaders designed to maximize your options when creating reflections and refractions, as well as blurring these properties. Choosing a shader should be based on a balance between the type of the material you want to create and the amount of time and processing power you want to devote to rendering the scene.

This section looks at a few of the shaders available for creating various types of reflections and refractions. These shaders are by no means the only way to create reflections and refractions. As discussed in previous sections, standard Maya shaders also have a number of mental ray–specific options for controlling reflection and refraction.

Once again, remember to think of mental ray as a big toolbox with lots of options. The more you understand how these shaders work, the easier it will be for you to decide which shaders and techniques you want to use for your renders.

DGS Shaders

Diffuse Glossy Specular (DGS) shaders have very simple controls for creating different reflective qualities for a surface as well as additional controls for transparency and refraction. The reflections and refractions created by this shader are physically accurate, meaning that at render time, mental ray simulates real-world light physics as much as possible to create the look seen in the render.

The scene has a very simple light setup. The key lighting is provided by a mental ray area light, which can be seen as a specular highlight on the orange metal of the helmet and on the glass face shield. The fill lighting is supplied by two directional lights; these lights have their specularity turned off so they are not seen as reflections on the surface of the helmet (see Figure 10.8).

The helmet uses standard Maya shaders. The metal of the helmet uses an orange Blinn, the face shield uses a transparent Blinn, and the helmet details and the woman's head use Lambert shaders. The grainy quality of the shadows results from the low sampling level set for the area light. By keeping the samples low, the image renders in a fairly short amount of time (less than a minute on my machine). The reflection of the checkerboard plane beneath the helmet is clearly seen in the metal of the helmet and on the face shield.

1. Open the helmet_v01.ma scene from the chapter10\scenes directory on the DVD.

2. Open the render view, and create a render using the renderCam camera.

3. Store the render in the Render View window.

4. Open the Hypershade editor. In the list on the left side of the Hypershade editor, select Materials under the mental ray heading.

5. Click the dgs_material button at the top of the material list twice to create two DGS material nodes.

6. Name the first one **helmet_dgs** and the second **shield_dgs**.

7. In the Outliner, select the group labeled helmetSurfaces.

8. In Hypershade, right-click the helmet_dgs shader, and choose Assign Material To Selection from the marking menu. This assigns the material to all the objects in the group.

9. In the Outliner, select the shield surface. In Hypershade, right-click the shield_dgs material, and choose Assign Material To Selection from the marking menu.

10. In the Hypershade, select the helmet_dgs material, and open its Attribute Editor.

11. Set the Diffuse color to bright orange. Set Glossy to black and Specular to white.

12. In the Hypershade, select the shield_dgs material.

13. Set Transparency to **0.8**. Set Glossy to black and Specular to white.

14. In the render view, render the scene from the renderCam camera. Compare this render to the previous render. Immediately you'll notice a lot of strange things going on with the materials you just applied (see Figure 10.9).

If you compare Figure 10.9 with Figure 10.8, you should notice a few details:

◆ The surfaces are reflective; however, there is no specular highlight (reflection of the light source) on either the helmet surfaces or the glass shield.

◆ The shadow of the face shield that falls on the checkered floor is not transparent in Figure 10.9, but it is transparent in Figure 10.8.

FIGURE 10.9
The helmet and face shield surfaces have DGS shaders applied.

Let's look at how to solve these problems. The shader is meant to be physically accurate. The Specular attribute refers to the reflectivity of the shader. In standard Maya shaders, reflectivity and specularity are separated (however, increasing one affects the intensity of the other). But in the DGS shader attributes, the Specular channel controls the reflection of visible objects, so a light source must be visible to be seen in the specular reflections.

1. Select the area light in the Hypershade, and open its Attribute Editor.

2. In the areaLightShape1 tab, expand the mental ray attributes, and activate the Visible option.

3. Render the scene again. This time you can see a reflection of the light in the surfaces. You can clearly see that the light is square shaped.

Glossy reflections, on the other hand, automatically render the reflection of a light source regardless of whether the light source is set to visible. The Glossy attribute on the DGS shader controls how reflections are scattered across the surface of an object. The term *specular highlight* with regard to shading models implies a certain amount of glossiness. Understandably, it's confusing when talking about specular reflections and specular highlights as two different things. The bottom line is this: to make a specular highlight appear in a DGS shader, either the light has to be visible when the Specular attribute is greater than zero and Glossy is set to zero *or* the Glossy setting must be greater than zero (that is, not black).

Glossy reflections can be blurry or sharp. To control the blurriness of a glossy reflection, you need to adjust the Shiny setting. Lower Shiny values create blurry reflections; higher Shiny values create sharp reflections.

1. Select the helmet_dgs shader, and open its Attribute Editor. Enter the following settings:

   Glossy: A medium gray

   Specular color: Black

   Shiny: **10**

2. Create another render. This time the surface of the helmet appears more like painted metal and less like a mirror (the upper-left image in Figure 10.10).

   The Shiny U and Shiny V settings control the blurriness of the glossy reflection when Shiny is set to 0. Using these settings, you can create an anisotropic type of reflection.

3. The U and V values control the direction of the anisotropic reflections across the surface. For best results, set one value higher than the other:

   Shiny: **0**

   Shiny U value: **3**

   Shiny V value: **10**

4. Create another render; the helmet now appears more like brushed metal (the upper-right image in Figure 10.10).

The Shiny U and Shiny V settings simulate the anisotropic reflections on the material by stretching the reflection along the U or V direction. In this case, this is not physically accurate and does not simulate how tiny grooves in the surface affect the reflection.

FIGURE 10.10
Rendering using different settings for the DGS materials applied to the helmet metal and face shield

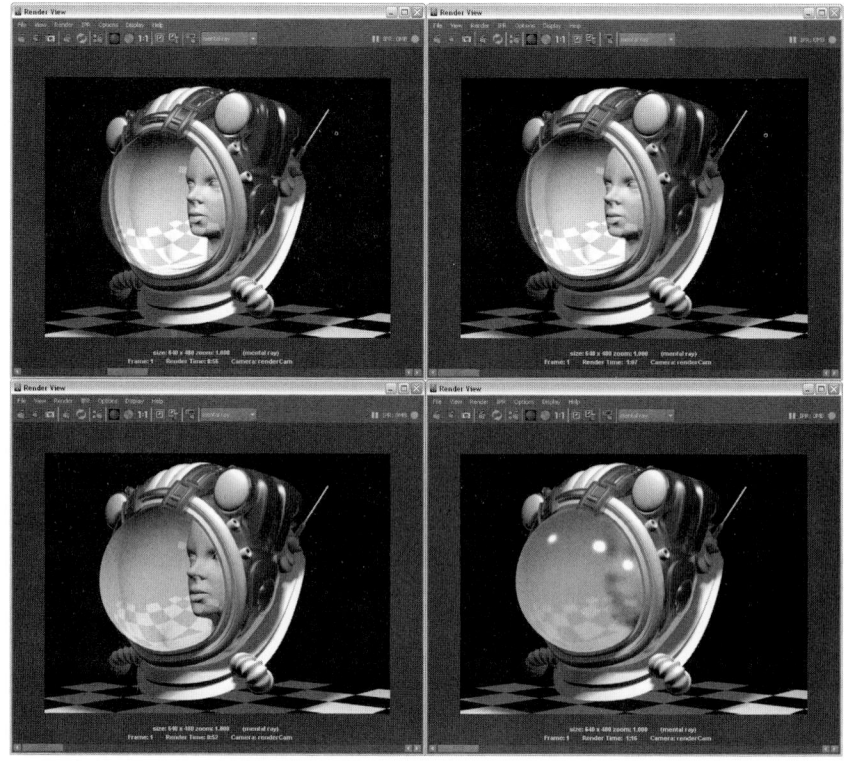

ISOTROPIC AND ANISOTROPIC SPECULAR REFLECTIONS

Isotropic and *anisotropic* both refer to a glossy specular highlight caused by microfacets on a surface. These tiny imperfections scatter reflected highlights, giving a glossy or blurry edge to highlights. Isotropic surfaces have a random order to the direction of the microfacets on the surface; anisotropic surfaces have microfacets that all run in a similar direction, which spread the specular highlights in a particular direction.

When rendering transparent surfaces using the DGS shader, the Specular, Glossy, Transparency, and Refraction settings all work together to create the effect. For transparency to work, the shader must have a Transparency setting higher than zero and either a Specular or a Glossy setting greater than zero. If Transparency is set to 1 and both Specular and Glossy are set to black, the surface will render as opaque, the same as if Transparency were set to 0.

The Specular color can be used to color the transparent surface, and the Glossy setting can be used (along with the Shiny settings) to create the look of a translucent material, such as plastic, ice, or frosted glass:

1. Select the shield_dgs material. Set the Specular color to a light green, and set Transparency to **0.8**.

2. Set Index Of Refraction to **1.1**. This makes the glass appear thicker because the light rays are bent as they pass through the glass.

3. Create another test render. Notice that the green specular color tints both the objects behind the glass as well as the reflections on the surface (see the lower-left image in Figure 10.10; the image is in black and white, but you can clearly see the effect of the refraction setting).

4. To create the look of frosted glass, enter these settings:

   Diffuse: Light gray

   Specular: Black

   Glossy: Light gray

   Shiny: **20**

   Transparency: **0.8**

   Index Of Refraction: **1.2**

5. Create another test render to see the result (the lower-right image in Figure 10.10).

6. Save the scene as **helmet_v02.ma**.

A few details are worth noting about using the Glossy settings:

◆ Specular reflections of all the lights in the scene are visible on the surface when Glossy is greater than zero. Notice that the highlights of the two directional lights are visible in the glass even though the Specularity option for both lights is disabled. To avoid this, consider using Global Illumination or Final Gathering to create fill lighting in the scene (see Chapter 9 for information on these techniques).

◆ Glossy reflections and refractions are physically accurate in that objects close to the refractive or reflective surface will appear less blurry than objects that are farther away.

◆ To make an object look more metallic, tint the Glossy color similar to the Diffuse color.

◆ Try using textures in the Glossy and Specular channels to create more interesting materials.

◆ When using the shader on scenes that employ Global Illumination, you need to create a dgs_material_photon node (found in the Photonic Materials section of the mental ray render nodes of the Hypershade). Attach this shader to the shading group of the original DGS material in the Photon Shader slot, and then use the settings on the dgs_material_photon to control the shader.

◆ You can increase realism further by rendering a separate reflection occlusion pass to use in a composite or plug occlusion textures into the specular and glossy attributes (enable Reflection on the occlusion textures).

To see a finished version of the scene, open the helmet_v02.ma scene from the chapter10\ scenes directory on the DVD.

Dielectric Material

The purpose of the Dielectric material is to accurately simulate the refraction of light as it passes through transparent materials. The Dielectric material is designed to accurately simulate the refractive qualities of glass, water, and other fluids. The term *Dielectric* refers to a surface that transmits light through multiple layers, redirecting the light waves as they pass through each layer.

If you observe a fish in a glass bowl, the light rays that illuminate the fish in the bowl transition from air to glass, then from glass to water, then again from water back to glass, and finally from glass out into the air on the other side. Each time a light ray makes a transition from one surface to another, the direction of the light ray changes. The index of refraction describes the change in the light ray's direction.

Most standard materials in Maya use a single index of refraction value to simulate the change of direction of the light ray as it is transmitted through the surface. This is not accurate, but it's usually good enough to create a believable effect. However, if you need to create a more physically accurate refractive surface, the Dielectric material is your best choice. This is because it has two settings for the index of refraction that describes the change of the light ray's direction as it makes a transition from one refractive surface to the next.

In this exercise, you'll create a physically accurate rendering of a glass of blue liquid using the Dielectric material. Light will move from the air into glass and then from the glass into the water. The glass is open at the top, so you'll also need to simulate the transition from air to water. This means you'll need to use three dielectric materials: one for air to glass, one for glass to water, and one for air to water. This tutorial is based on Boaz Livny's discussion of the Dielectric material in *mental ray for Maya, 3ds Max, and XSI* by Boaz Livny (Sybex, 2008).

In this scene, a simple glass has been modeled and split into four surfaces, named air_glass1, air_glass2, liquid_glass1, and liquid_air1. Each surface represents one of the three transitions that will be simulated using the Dielectric material. To make this easier to visualize, each surface has a colored Lambert shader applied. The scene is lit using a single spotlight that casts ray trace shadows.

1. Open glass_v01.ma from the chapter10\scenes directory on the DVD.

2. Open the Hypershade window. Select the Materials heading under the mental ray section from the list on the left side of the Hypershade window.

3. In the Materials section, click the dielectric_material button.

4. Name the new dielectric_material1 node **air2GlassShader**.

5. Create two more dielectric materials, and name one **glass2LiquidShader** and the other **liquid2AirShader**.

6. Apply the air2GlassShader to both the airGlass1 and airGlass2 objects. Apply glass2Liquid-Shader to the liquid_glass1 object and liquid2AirShader to liquid_air1.

7. Select the air2glassShader, and open its Attribute Editor.

   The index of refraction (IOR) for glass is typically 1.5, and the IOR for air is 1. Look at the settings for the air2Glass shader. The Index Of Refraction setting defines the IOR for the material; the Outside Index Of Refraction setting defines the IOR for the medium outside the material. The default settings for the Dielectric material are already set to the proper glass-to-air transition. Index Of Refraction should be set to **1.5**, and Outside Index Of Refraction should be set to **1**.

8. Set Phong Coefficient to **100**, and turn on Ignore Normals.

The Phong Coefficient creates a specular reflection on the glass. The Dielectric material uses the surface normals of the object to create the refraction effect. If you activate the Ignore Normals option, the shader bases the normal direction on the camera view. For a basic glass model such as this one, you can safely use the Ignore Normals feature.

9. Select the glass2LiquidShader; open its Attribute Editor; and enter the following settings:

Index Of Refraction: **1.33** (the IOR of water is 1.33)

Outside Index Of Refraction: **1.5**

Phong Coefficient: **100**

Turn on Ignore Normals.

10. Click the color swatch next to the Col attribute. This determines the color of the shader. (Why spell out Index Of Refraction in the interface but at the same time abbreviate Color? It's one of the many mysteries of Maya.)

11. In the Color Chooser, use the menu below the color wheel to set the mode to HSV (Hue, Saturation, Value), as shown in Figure 10.11. This is just another way to determine color as opposed to setting RGB (red, green, blue) values. Set the following:

Hue (H): **180**

Sat (S): **0.45**

Value (V): **1**

FIGURE 10.11
Use the menu in the Color Chooser to set the mode to HSV.

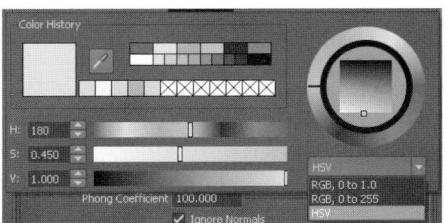

12. Select the liquid2AirShader. Set Index Of Refraction to **1.33**, and leave Outside Index Of Refraction at 1. Set Phong Coefficient to **100**, and turn on Ignore Normals.

13. Select the Col swatch, and use the same HSV values in the Color Chooser that you set in step 11.

14. Open the Render View window, and create a test render from the renderCam camera (see Figure 10.12).

15. Save the scene as **glass_v02.ma**.

FIGURE 10.12
Render the glass using the Dielectric material (left image). Add transparent shadows by rendering with caustics (right image).

To see a version of the scene, open the `glass_v02.ma` scene from the `chapter10\scenes` folder on the DVD.

You can see that there are differences between the refractions of the various surfaces that make up the glass and the water. Just like the DGS shader, the Dielectric material fails to cast transparent shadows (the left image of Figure 10.12). The best solution for this problem is to enable Caustics. When enabling Caustics with the Dielectric shader, you need to connect a dielectric_material_photon material to the Photon Shader slot of the Shading Group node and enable Caustics. The settings for the dielectric_material_photon material should be the same as the settings for the Dielectric material.

To see an example of this setup, open the `dielectricCaustics.ma` scene in the `chapter10\scenes` directory of the DVD. The image on the right of Figure 10.12 shows the glass rendered with Caustics enabled. Using Caustics is explained in Chapter 9.

mental ray Base Shaders

A number of shaders available in the Hypershade are listed with the prefix *mib* (mental images base): mib_illum_cooktor, mib_illum_blinn, and so on. These are the mental ray base shaders. You can think of these nodes as building blocks; you can combine them to create custom mental ray shaders to create any number of looks for a surface. There are far too many to describe in this chapter, so it's more important that you understand how to work with them. Descriptions of each node are available in the mental ray user guide that is part of the Maya documentation.

In this exercise, you'll see how a few of these shaders can be combined to create a custom material for the helmet:

1. Open the `helmet_v03.ma` scene from the `chapter10\scenes` folder on the DVD. This scene currently uses standard Maya shaders applied to the geometry.

2. Open the Hypershade window, and select the Materials heading under the mental ray section in the list on the left side. Scroll down the list, and you'll see a number of mib materials toward the bottom (see Figure 10.13).

3. Click the mib_illum_cooktorr button to create a Cook-Torrance material, and open its Attribute Editor.

FIGURE 10.13
The mental ray base
shaders are available in the Materials section of the
Create mental ray
Nodes menu.

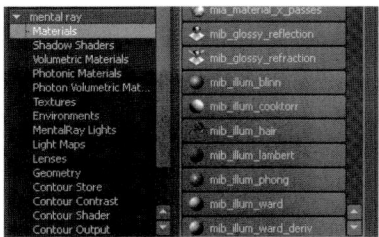

The Cook-Torrance shader creates physically accurate isotropic specular highlighting, meaning that the specular highlights on surfaces are scattered as if the surface was covered with tiny microfacets arranged randomly.

The look of the highlight is created by setting the Specular color to a value greater than zero. The Roughness slider determines the spread of the highlight. The shader has three separate controls to determine the index of refraction for each color channel (red, green, and blue). When light is reflected from the tiny bumps on an isotropic surface, the directionality of each light wave changes. The three IOR sliders allow you to specify this directional change for each color channel. This gives the specular highlight the appearance of *color fringing*—a slight tint on the edge of the highlight (this appears as blue fringe in the shader's preview). The color fringing around the highlight makes this shader very useful for creating realistic-looking metals.

The Ward (mib_illum_ward) material is similar to the Cook-Torrance but offers more options for creating realistic anisotropic specularity. The Ward material works best on NURBS surfaces; the mib_illum_ward_deriv shader is a little easier to use, giving you two simple sliders to control the direction of the anisotropy along the U and V coordinates of the surface.

4. In the Outliner, select the helmetSurfaces group.

5. In the Hypershade, right-click the mib_illum_cooktorr1 shader, and choose Assign Material To Selection from the marking menu.

6. In the Attribute Editor, use the following settings:

   Diffuse color of the shader: Light orange

   Specular channel: Light gray

   Roughness: **0.19**

7. To create an orange fringe around the highlight, set the following:

   Index Of Refraction, Red: **80**

   Index Of Refraction, Green: **10**

   Index Of Refraction, Blue: **8**

8. In the Render View window, create a test render using the renderCam camera (Figure 10.14).

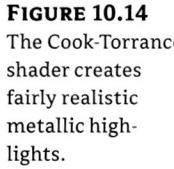

FIGURE 10.14
The Cook-Torrance shader creates fairly realistic metallic high-lights.

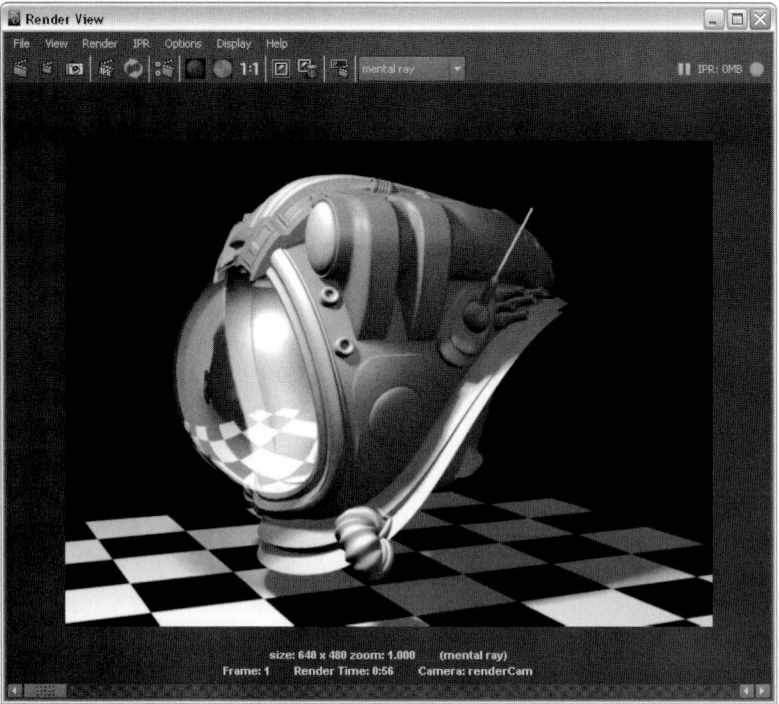

The helmet has a very convincing metallic look, but you'll notice there are no reflections. To add reflections, you can combine the Cook-Torrance shader with a glossy reflection node.

1. From the list of matrials on the left side of the Hypershade editor, click the mib_glossy_reflection button.

2. Assign the new mib_glossy_reflection1 node to the helmet surfaces group. This over-writes the Cook-Torrance shader that has been applied.

3. Open the Attribute Editor for the mib_glossy_reflection1 node.

4. From the Hypershade window, MMB-drag the mib_cook_torr1 node from the Hypershade to the Base Material slot of the mib_glossy_reflection1 node (see Figure 10.15).

5. Set Reflection Color to white (white sets the shader to maximum reflectivity; darker shades create a less-reflective material), and create another render in the Render View window (Figure 10.16).

6. The default settings create a blurry reflection in the helmet surfaces. To adjust the quality and blurriness of the reflections, increase the Samples value to **32**.

The U Spread and V Spread sliders control the glossiness of the reflections, much like the Shiny U and Shiny V settings on the DGS shader. Higher values produce glossier reflections.

Using a different value for U than V creates anisotropic specular highlights. Ideally, you want to match the glossiness of the reflections on the mib_glossy_reflection1 shader with the glossiness of the highlight on the mib_cooktorr shader.

FIGURE 10.15
Connect the Cook-Torrance shader to the Base Material slot of the mib_glossy_reflection1 node.

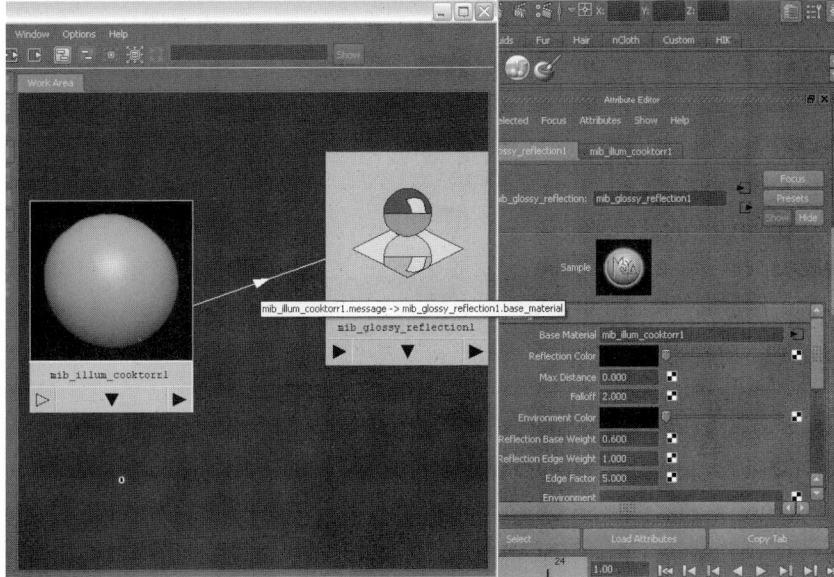

FIGURE 10.16
The combination of the two materials creates a reflective metal for the helmet.

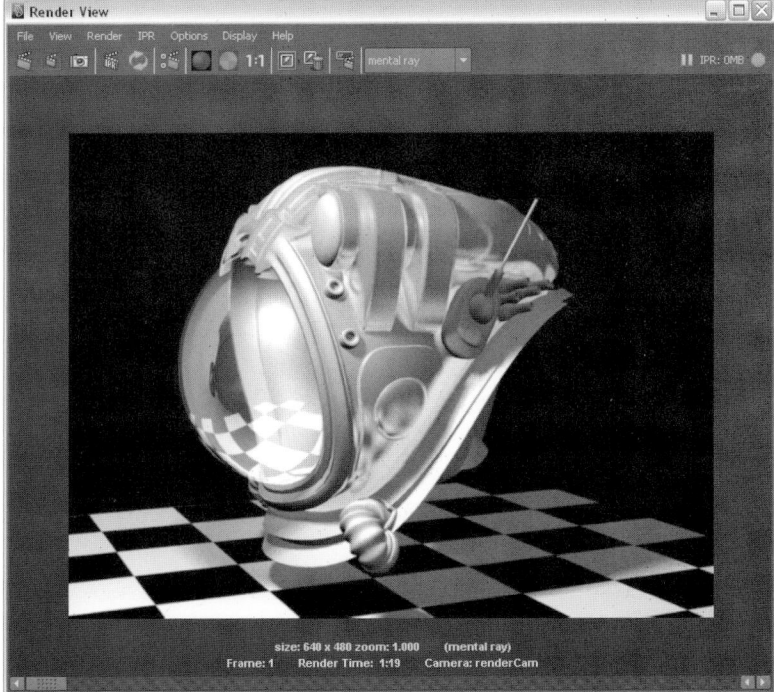

You can blend between a reflection of the objects in the scene and an environment reflection. To do this, you first need to create an environment reflection node:

1. Select the Environments heading under mental ray in the left side of the Hypershade window.

2. Click the mib_lookup_background button to create an mib_lookup_background node.

3. Open the Attribute Editor for the mib_glossy_reflection1 node.

4. From the work area of the Hypershade, MMB-drag the mib_lookup_background1 node to the Environment field in the Attribute Editor of the mib_glossy_reflection1 node (Figure 10.17).

FIGURE 10.17
The mib_lookup_
background1 node
is connected to the
Environment field
of the mib_glossy_
reflection1 node.

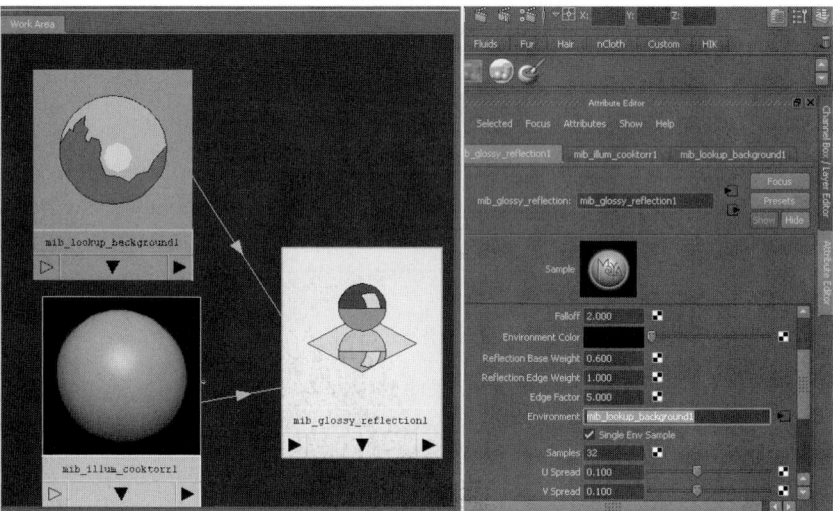

This connects a mib_lookup_background node to the Environment slot of the mib_glossy_reflection1 node. You can use any of the environment nodes to map an image to the reflection of the environment. The mib_lookup_background node works with standard rectangular images. The node sizes the background image to fit the resolution of the rendering camera.

5. Open the Attribute Editor for the mib_lookup_background1 node.

6. Click the checkered box next to the Texture tab to add a mental ray texture node. This allows you to map an image to the background.

7. In the Attribute Editor for the mentalRayTexture1 node, click the folder next to Image Name (see Figure 10.18).

8. Load the desert.jpg image found in the sourceimages directory in the Chapter10 folder on the DVD.

9. Select the mib_glossy_reflection1 node, and in its Attribute Editor, set Environment Color to a medium gray. This sets the strength of the reflectivity of the environment.

FIGURE 10.18
Select the
desert.jpg
image to use in
the mentalray-
Texture1 node.
This image will
appear reflected
in the metal of
the helmet.

The shader can create a smooth transition from the reflections of objects in the scene and the environment reflections. The Max Distance attribute sets a limit in the scene for tracing reflections. When reflection rays reach this limit, they stop sampling reflections of objects in the scene and start sampling the image mapped to the environment. The Falloff value determines the smoothness of the transition. The Falloff value is a rate of change. A setting of 1 creates a linear falloff; higher values create a sharper transition.

10. Set Max Distance to **5** and Falloff to **2**.

11. Turn off Single Env Sample, and create another test render. You can see the blue sky of the desert image reflected in the metal of the helmet (see Figure 10.19; you can find a color version of this image in the color insert of this book).

FIGURE 10.19
The blue sky of the
desert image colors
the reflections
on the metal of the
helmet.

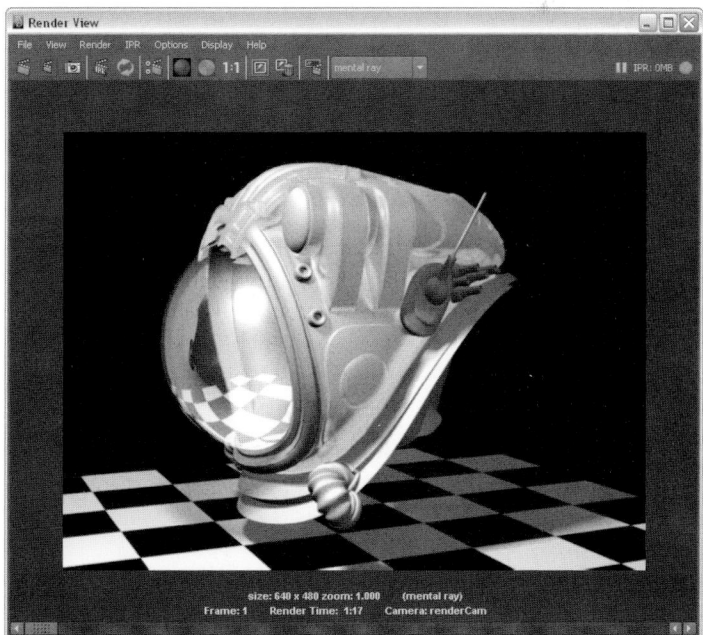

To increase the realism of the reflections, you can add an ambient occlusion node to decrease the intensity of the reflections in the crevices of the model. Using ambient occlusion is discussed in Chapter 9; in this example, the mib_ambient_occlusion node is used as part of the helmet shader network:

1. Open the Attribute Editor of the mib_glossy_reflection node.

2. Click the checkered box next to Reflection Color. From the Create Render Node pop-up, select the Textures heading under mental ray in the list.

3. Click the Mib_amb_occlusion node button on the right of the Create Render Nodes window.

4. Open the Attribute Editor for the mib_amb_occlusion node, and enter the following settings:

   Samples: **32**

   Bright Color: Medium gray

   Dark Color: Very dark gray (but not black)

   Max Distance: **5**

   Turn on Reflective.

5. Create another test render of the scene. Now the reflections on the model look much more believable because the areas of the model within the crevices are not reflecting as much light as the areas that are fully exposed (see Figure 10.20).

6. Save the scene as **helmet_v04.ma**.

FIGURE 10.20
Adding an ambient occlusion node to control the reflectivity on the surface of the helmet helps to add realism to the render.

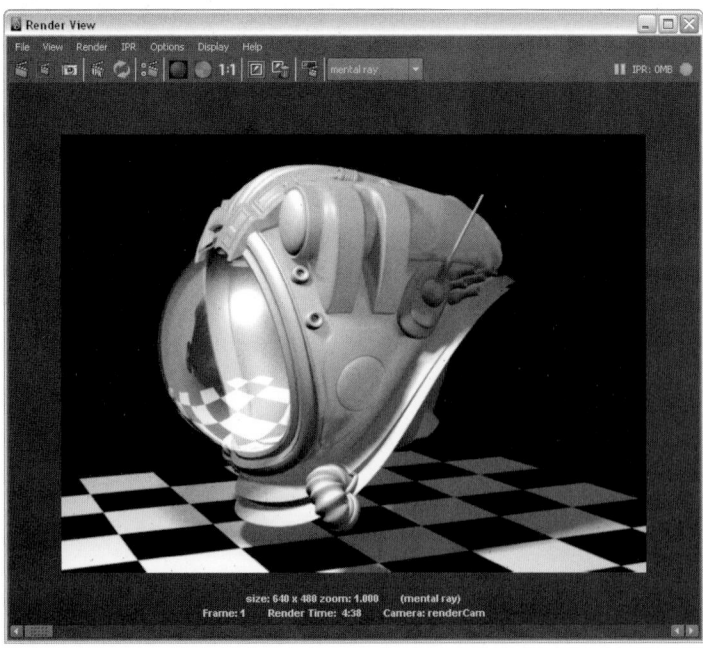

Figure 10.21 shows the shader network for this material.

This gives you an idea of how to work with the mental ray base materials. Of course, you can make many more complex connections between nodes to create even more realistic and interesting surface materials. Experimentation is a good way to learn which connections work best for any particular situation.

To see a version of the scene to this point, open the `helmet_v04.ma` scene from the `chapter10\ scenes` directory on the DVD.

FIGURE 10.21
The mental ray base shaders are connected to create a realistic painted metal surface for the helmet.

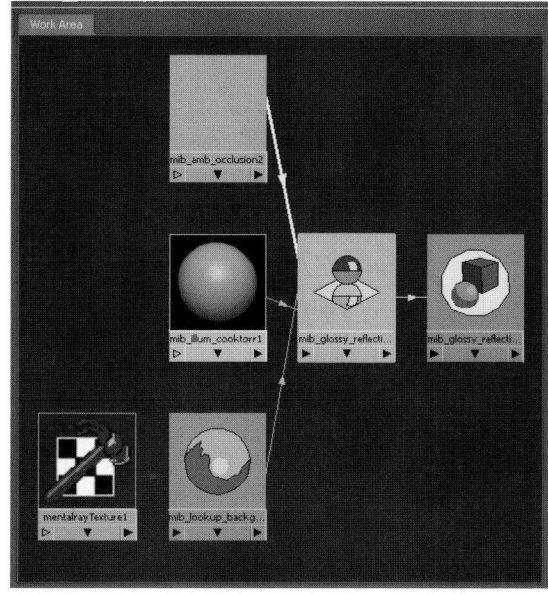

Car Paint Materials

Simulating the properties of car paint and colored metallic surfaces is made considerably easier thanks to the special car paint phenomenon and metallic paint mental ray materials.

In reality, car paint consists of several layers; together these layers combine to give the body of a car its special, sparkling quality. Car paint uses a base-color pigment, and the color of this pigment actually changes hue depending on the viewing angle. This color layer also has thousands of tiny flakes of metal suspended within it. When the sun reflects off these metallic flakes, you see a noticeable sparkling quality. Above these layers is a reflective clear coat, which is usually highly reflective (especially for new cars) and occasionally glossy. The clear coat itself is a perfect study in Fresnel reflections. As the surfaces of the car turn away from the viewing angle, the reflectivity of the surface increases.

The metallic paint material is very similar to the car paint phenomenon material. In fact, you can re-create the car paint material by combining the mi_metallic_paint node with the mi_glossy_reflection node and the mi_bump_flakes node.

In this section, you'll learn how to use the car paint material by applying it to the tractorDroid model created for this book by designer Anthony Honn.

1. Open the `tractorDroid_v01.ma` scene from the `chapter10\scenes` directory on the DVD. This scene uses the Physical Sun and Sky network for lighting.

PHYSICAL SUN AND SKY

When setting out to texture a model, sometimes I like to start by using the Physical Sun and Sky lighting model that was introduced in Chapter 9. As I develop the materials for the model, it's helpful to see how they react to physically accurate lighting. This light setup uses Final Gathering, which can add a little extra time to the rendering because the image must go through two passes: one to calculate the Final Gathering and a second to render the image. All of this is explained in detail in Chapter 9.

2. Open the Hypershade window, and select the Materials heading in the mental ray section on the left side of the Hypershade window.

3. Click the mi_car_paint_phen_x shader button (see Figure 10.22).

FIGURE 10.22
The car paint materials are in the Materials section of the mental ray Nodes section in Hypershade.

MENTAL RAY EXTENDED MATERIALS

The mental ray nodes that use the *x* suffix are more advanced (extended) versions of the original shader. Most of the advancements are in the back end; the interface and attributes of mi_car_paint_phen and mi_car_paint_phen_x are the same. It's safe to use either version. You can upgrade the mi_car_paint_phen material by clicking the buttons in the Upgrade Shader section of the material's Attribute Editor. The x_passes materials are meant to be used with render passes. For the most part, I always use the materials with the *x* suffix and later upgrade the material if I decide I need to use render passes. Render passes are covered in Chapter 12.

4. The body of the tractor droid already has two shaders applied. In the Materials tab on the right side of Hypershade, right-click the body_shader icon, and choose Select Objects with Material; this will select all the polygons on the model that use this shader (see Figure 10.23).

5. Right-click the mi_car_paint_phen_x shader created in step 3, and choose Assign Material to Selection. This applies the car paint material to the selected polygons. Parts of the tractor body should now appear red (see Figure 10.24).

6. Open the Attribute Editor for the mi_car_paint_phen_x shader. Rename the shader **carPaint**.

FIGURE 10.23
Use the Hyper-shade marking menu to select the parts of the model that use the body_ shader material.

FIGURE 10.24
Assign the car paint material to the selected poly-gons of the model.

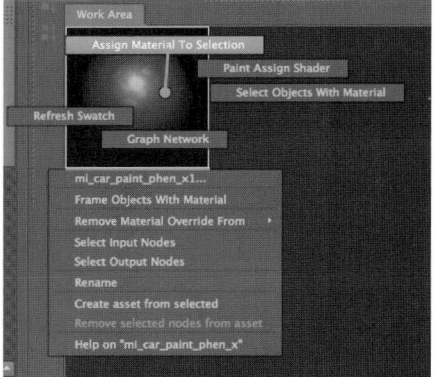

Diffuse Parameters

At the top of the attributes you'll find the Diffuse Parameters rollout. The settings here determine the color properties of the base pigment layer. As the color of this layer changes depending on the viewing angle, the various settings determine all the colors that contribute to this layer.

1. Set Base Color to dark navy blue; this is the main color of the base layer. If you wanted to add a texture map to apply decals to the car, you would use this channel.

2. Set Edge Color to a similar shade of blue, but lower the value so it is almost black. The Edge Color is apparent on the edges that face away from the camera. Newer cars and sports cars benefit from a dark Edge Color.

Edge Color Bias sets the amount of spread seen in the Edge Color. Lower values (0.1 to 3) create a wider spread; higher values (4 to 10) create a narrower band of Edge Color.

3. Lit Color is the color seen in the surface areas that face the light source. Set this color to a bright purplish blue.

Lit Color Bias works on the same principle as Edge Color Bias. Lower values (above zero) create a wider spread in the Lit Color.

4. Diffuse Weight and Diffuse Bias set the overall strength of the Diffuse colors. Set Diffuse Bias to **2**.

A lower Diffuse Bias value (0 to 1) flattens the color; higher values (1 to 2) increase intensity toward the lit areas.

Specular Parameters

The Specular Parameters settings define the look of the specular highlight on the surface. In this particular shader, these settings are separate from the Reflection Parameters settings. By adjusting the settings in Specular Parameters, you can make the car paint look brand new or old and dull. The following describes how the settings work.

When rendered, the specular highlight has two components: a bright center highlight and a surrounding secondary highlight. Spec Weight and Spec Sec Weight are multipliers for the primary specular and secondary specular colors (respectively).

Spec Exp and Spec Sec Exp determine the tightness of the highlight; higher values (30 and greater) produce tighter highlights. Generally, Spec Sec Exp should be less than Spec Exp.

The Spec Glazing check box at the bottom of the Specular Parameters section adds a polished shiny quality to the highlight, which works well on new cars. Turn this feature off when you want to create the look of an older car with a duller finish.

For this exercise, you can leave the specular parameters at their default settings.

Flake Parameters

The Flake Parameters settings are the most interesting components of the shader. These determine the look and intensity of the metallic flakes in the pigment layer of the car paint:

Flake Color   Flake Color should usually be white for new cars.

Flake Weight   Flake Weight is a multiplier for Flake Color. Higher values intensify the look of the flakes; usually 1 is a good setting for most situations.

Flake Reflect   Flake Reflect adds ray-tracing reflectivity to the flakes. This means that the flakes contribute to reflections of objects in the scene. For most situations, a value of 0.1 is sufficient.

Flake Exp   Flake Exp is the specular exponent for the flakes. Much like Spec Exp, higher values create a tighter highlight.

Flake Density   Flake Density determines the number of flakes visible in the paint. The values range from 0.1 to 10. In many situations, a high value actually means that the individual flakes are harder to see.

Flake Decay   Flake Decay optimizes rendering times by setting a limit to the visibility of the flakes. Beyond the distance specified by this value, the flakes are no longer rendered, which can keep render times down and reduce render artifacts, especially if Flake Density is set to a high value.

Flake Strength   Flake Strength varies the orientation of the flakes in the paint. Setting this to 0 makes all the flakes parallel to the surface; a setting of 1 causes the flakes to be oriented randomly, making the flakes more reflective at different viewing angles.

Flake Scale   Flake Scale sets the size of the flakes. It's important to understand that the size of the flakes is connected to the scale of the object. If you notice that the size of the flakes is different on one part of the car than another part of the car, select the surface geometry and freeze the transformations so that the Scale X, Y, and Z values are all set to 1. This will correct the problem and ensure that the flakes are a consistent size across all the parts of the car.

For this exercise, use the following settings:

Flake Reflect: **0.1**

Flake Density: **1.5**

Flake Strength: **1**

Flake Scale: **0.008**

Reflection Parameters

The Reflection Parameters settings are similar to those for the reflection parameters on the glossy reflection material. The reflectivity of the surface is at its maximum when Reflection Color is set to white. When this is set to black, reflections are turned off.

Edge Factor   Edge Factor determines the transition between the reflection strength at glancing angles and the reflection strength at facing angles.

Reflection Edge Weight   Reflection Edge Weight sets the strength of reflectivity at glancing angles, and Reflection Base Weight sets the reflectivity at facing angles. Generally the base weight should be lower than the edge weight to create a proper Fresnel reflection effect.

Samples   Samples sets the sampling for glossy reflections. Unless you want to create blurry reflections, which are best used for older, duller cars, you can leave Samples at 0.

Glossy Spread   Glossy Spread defines the glossiness of the reflections. Max Distance sets the point where reflection rays start sampling environment shaders and stop sampling the geometry in the scene.

Dirt Parameters   The Dirt Parameters settings allow you to add a layer of dirt to the surface of the car. Dirt Weight specifies the visibility strength of the dirt. For best results, you can connect a painted texture map to Dirt Color if you want to add splashes of mud and grime.

1. Set Edge Factor to **4**, and leave the other settings at their defaults (see Figure 10.25).

2. In the Render View window, create a test render from the renderCam camera (Figure 10.26).

FIGURE 10.25
The settings for the car paint shader

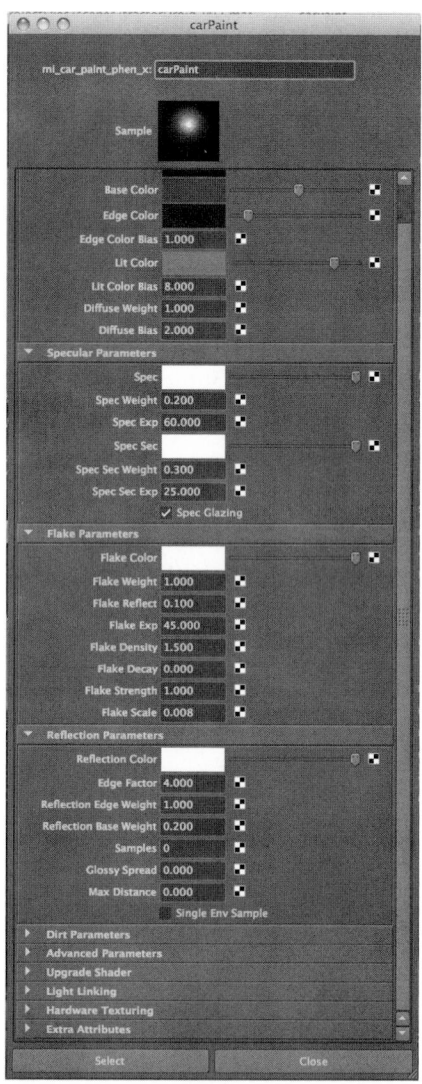

FIGURE 10.26
The car paint material is applied to the body of the car and rendered with the physical sun and sky lighting.

3. Store the image in the render view, and create a second test render from the closeUp camera.

4. Save the scene as **tractorDroid_v02.ma**.

To see a finished version of the scene, open the tractorDroid_v02.ma file from the chapter10\scenes directory on the DVD.

The MIA Material

The MIA material is the Swiss Army knife of mental ray shaders. It is a monolithic material, meaning that it has all the functionality needed for creating a variety of materials built into a single interface. You don't need to connect additional shader nodes into a specific network to create glossy reflections, transparency, and the like.

MIA stands for mental image architectural, and the shaders (mia_material, mia_material_x, mia_material_passes) and other lighting and lens shader nodes (mia_physicalsun, mia_portal, mia_exposure_simple, and so on) are all part of the mental images architectural library. The shaders in this library are primarily used for creating materials used in photorealistic architectural renderings; however, you can take advantage of the power of these materials to create almost anything you need.

The MIA material has a large number of attributes that at first can be overwhelming. However, there are also presets available for the material. You can quickly define the look you need for any given surface by applying a preset. Then you can tune specific attributes of the material to get the look you need.

Using the MIA Material Presets

The presets that come with the MIA material are the easiest way to establish the initial look of a material. Presets can also be blended to create novel materials. Furthermore, once you create something you like, you can save your own presets for future use in other projects. You'll work on defining materials for the space helmet. Just like the example in the previous section, this version of the scene uses the mia_physicalsunsky lighting network and Final Gathering to light the scene.

1. Open the helmet_v05.ma scene from the chapter10\scenes directory on the DVD. The surfaces in the model have been grouped by material type to make it easier to apply shaders.

2. Open the Hypershade window, and select Materials under the mental ray section of the list on the left of the editor.

3. Click the mia_material_x button to create a material, and name it **metalShader**.

4. In the Outliner, select the helmetMetalSurfaces group, and apply the metalShader material to this group (right-click the material in the Hypershade, and choose Assign Material To Selection).

5. Open the Attribute Editor for the metalShader.

6. Click the Presets button in the upper right, and choose Copper ➤ Replace.

7. Open the Render View window, and create a render from the renderCam camera. It really looks like copper. Save the render in the render view.

8. The material could use a little tweaking to make it look less like a kitchen pot. Click the Presets button again, and choose SatinedMetal ➤ Blend 50%. This will add some anisotropy to the highlights on the helmet.

9. In the Attribute Editor, scroll to the Diffuse rollout at the top.

10. Set Color to a medium grayish-blue (the color should be fairly unsaturated; otherwise, the helmet will look very disco!).

11. Just below the Diffuse rollout, in the Reflection section, set Color to a light blue, and turn on Metal Material—this adds a bluish tint to the reflections.

12. Create another test render, and compare it with the previous render (Figure 10.27).

FIGURE 10.27
The MIA material comes with a number of presets that can be blended together to create novel materials.

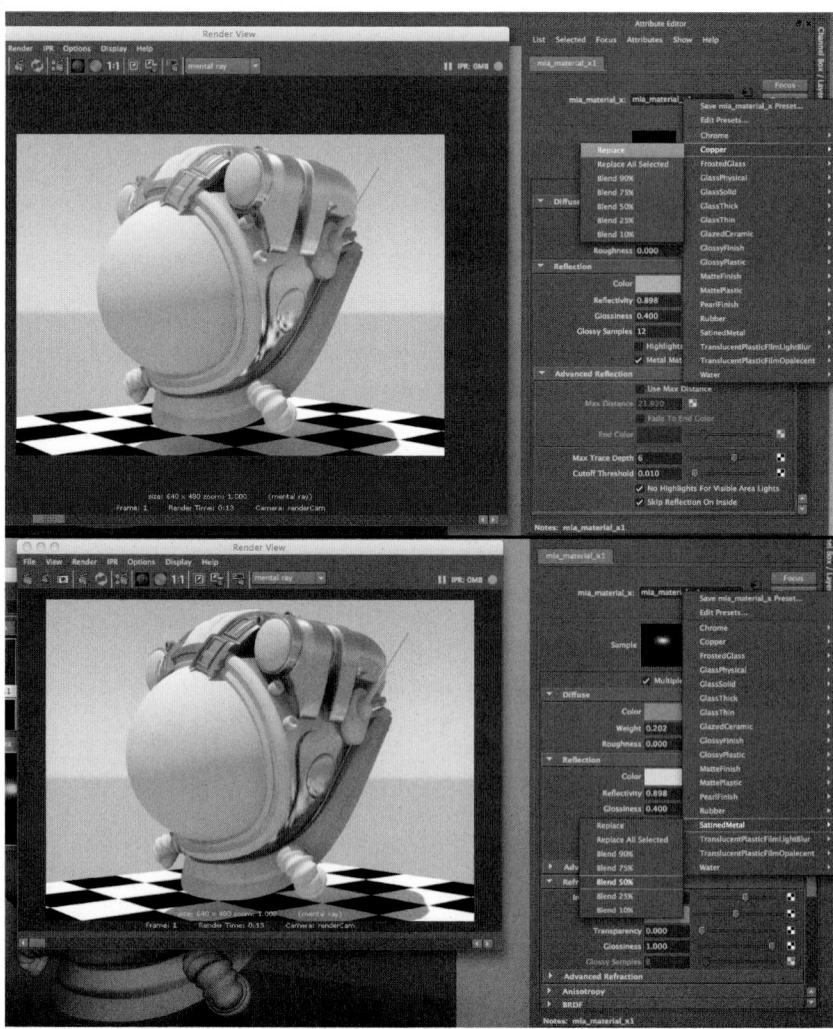

You can tweak many of the settings to create your own custom metal, and already it looks pretty good. Like the other materials in this chapter, the Glossiness setting adds blur to the reflections. Turning on Highlights Only creates a more plastic-like material—with this option activated, the Reflection settings apply only to specular highlights.

Next you can add chrome to the helmet:

1. Create a new mia_material_x shader, and name it **chromeShader**.

2. Select the chromeParts group in the Outliner, and apply the chromeShader to the group.

3. Open the Attribute Editor for the chromeShader material.

4. Click the Presets button, and apply the Chrome preset to the shader.

5. Create another mia_material_x shader, and name it **rubberShader**. Apply this shader to the rubberParts group. Use the Presets button to apply the rubber preset.

6. Create another test render, and compare it to the previous renders.

Add Bump to the Rubber Shader

The rubber shader can use a little tweaking. A slight bump can increase the realism. The mia_ material has two slots for bump textures; they're labeled Standard Bump and Overall Bump. Standard Bump works much like the bump channel on a standard Maya shader (Blinn, Lambert, Phong, and so on). The Overall bump is used primarily for the special mia_roundcorners texture node, which is explained in the next section.

When using a texture to create a bump effect, connect the texture to the Standard Bump slot, as demonstrated in this exercise:

1. Scroll down in the Attribute Editor for the rubberShader, and click the checkered box next to Standard Bump.

2. In the Create Render Nodes pop-up, select the 3D Textures heading under Maya in the list on the left, and click Leather to create a Leather texture node (Figure 10.28).

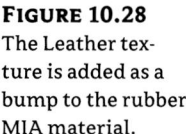

FIGURE 10.28
The Leather texture is added as a bump to the rubber MIA material.

3. Open the Attribute Editor for the leather1 node. (It should open automatically when you create the node.) Use the following settings:

Cell Color: Light gray

Crease Color: Dark gray

Cell Size: **0.074**

4. In the Hypershade work area, select the rubber shader, and choose Graph ➤ Input And Output connections from the Hypershade menu.

5. Select the bump3d1 node, and open its Attribute Editor. Set the Bump Depth value to 0.1. This makes the bump effect less prominent and creates a more realistic look for the rubber. Bump maps are covered in greater detail in Chapter 11.

6. Create a test render of the helmet using the closeUp camera (Figure 10.29).

FIGURE 10.29
The bump adds realism to the rubber parts of the helmet.

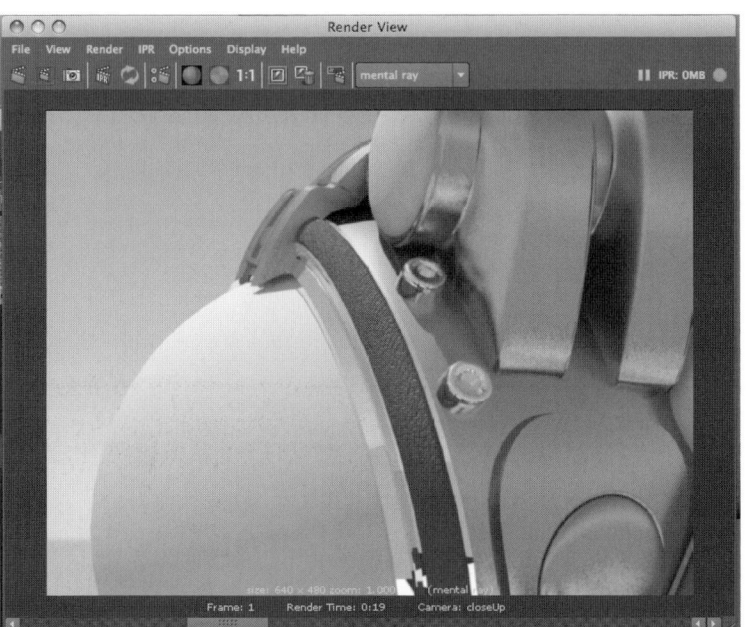

You'll notice that in the Bump rollout there is a No Diffuse Bump check box. When a texture is connected to the Standard Bump field and No Diffuse Bump is activated, the bump appears only in the specular and reflective parts of the material, which can be useful for creating the look of a lacquered surface.

Create Beveled Edges Using mia_roundcorners

A very slight edge bevel on the corners of the model can improve the realism of the model (sharp edges on surface are often a telltale sign that the object is computer generated). Usually this bevel is created in the geometry, which can add a lot of extra vertices and polygons. The mia_roundcorners texture adds a slight bevel to the edges of a surface that appears only in the render, which means you do not need to create beveled edges directly in the geometry.

The mia_roundcorners texture is attached to the Overall Bump channel of the mia_material. The reason the mia_material has two bump slots is so that you can apply the roundcorners texture to the Overall Bump shader and another texture to the Standard Bump shader to create a separate bumpy effect.

Let's take a look at the roundcorners texture in action by applying it to the chrome material:

1. First create a render in the Render View window from the closeUp camera, and store the image so you can compare it after the changes are made to the shader.

2. In the Hypershade, select the chromeShader, and open its Attribute Editor.

3. Scroll down to the Bump section, and click the checkered box to the right of Overall Bump.

4. In the Create Render Nodes pop-up, select the Textures heading from the list on the left, and click the Mia_roundcorners button on the right side to create this node.

5. In the Attribute Editor for the mia_roundcorners1 node, set Radius to **0.1**.

6. Create another test render, and compare it to the previous renders. You'll see that the chrome trim around the helmet has a slight roundness to it, making it look a little more believable.

7. Try adding and mia_roundcorners node to the metalShader and see how it affects the render. Use a Radius value of 0.05 (see the right image of Figure 10.30).

To see a version of the scene, open the `helmet_v06.ma` scene from the `chapter10\scenes` folder on the DVD.

FIGURE 10.30
Adding the mia_roundcorners texture to the chromeShader's Overall Bump channel creates a slight beveled edge to the geometry in the render. The circles in the right images highlight the beveling created by the texture. Compare these areas of the image to the left image, which does not have this beveled effect applied.

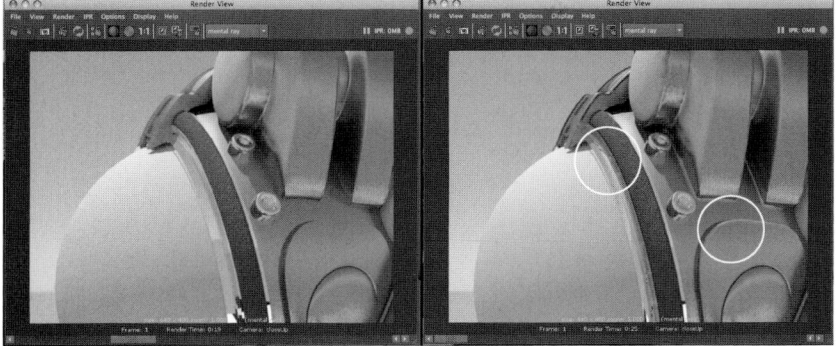

Creating Thick and Thin Glass and Plastic

Another feature of the mia_material shader is the ability to simulate thickness and thinness in the material itself without creating extra geometry. This can be very useful, especially for glass surfaces.

1. Continue with the scene from the previous section, or open the `helmet_v06.ma` file from the `chapter10\scenes` folder on the DVD.

2. In the Hypershade, create two new mia_material_x nodes. Name one **thinGlass** and the other **thickGlass**.

3. Apply the thinGlass shader to the glassShield object in the Outliner.

4. Apply the thickGlass material to the lampShields group in the Outliner.

5. In the Attribute Editor for the thinGlass material, use the Preset button to apply the glassThin preset.

6. In the Attribute Editor for the thickGlass shader, apply the glassThick preset.

7. Create another test render from the renderCam camera.

The lamps at the top of the helmet have a chrome reflector behind the thick glass, which adds to the reflectivity of the material. The settings to control thickness are found under the Advanced Refractions controls. Along with the standard Index Of Refraction setting, there is an option for making the material either thin walled or solid. You also have the option of choosing between a transparent shadow and a refractive caustic that is built into the material (the caustics render when caustic photons are enabled and the light source emits caustic photons; for more information on caustics, consult Chapter 9).

1. Open the Hypershade window, and create another mia_material_x node. Name this one **plastic**. Apply this shader to the plasticParts in the Outliner.

2. Open the Attribute Editor for the plastic shader, and apply the translucentPlasticFilm-LightBlur preset.

3. Create another test render.

   This preset creates very translucent plastic using glossy refractions. In this situation, it seems a little too transparent. Use the following settings to make the plastic look a little more substantial:

   A. In the Diffuse section, set Color to a dim pale blue.

   B. In the Reflection section, set Color to a dark gray, and set Glossiness to **0.35**.

   C. In the Refraction section, set Color to a dark blue and Glossiness to **0.52**.

   D. Scroll down to the Ambient Occlusion section, and activate Ambient Occlusion.

   E. Set Ambient Light Color to a light gray.

4. Create another test render (see Figure 10.31).

5. Save the scene as `helmet_v07.ma`.

To see a finished version of the scene, open the `helmet_v07.ma` scene from the `chapter10\scenes` directory on the DVD.

FIGURE 10.31
Apply the glass and
plastic presets to
parts of the helmet.

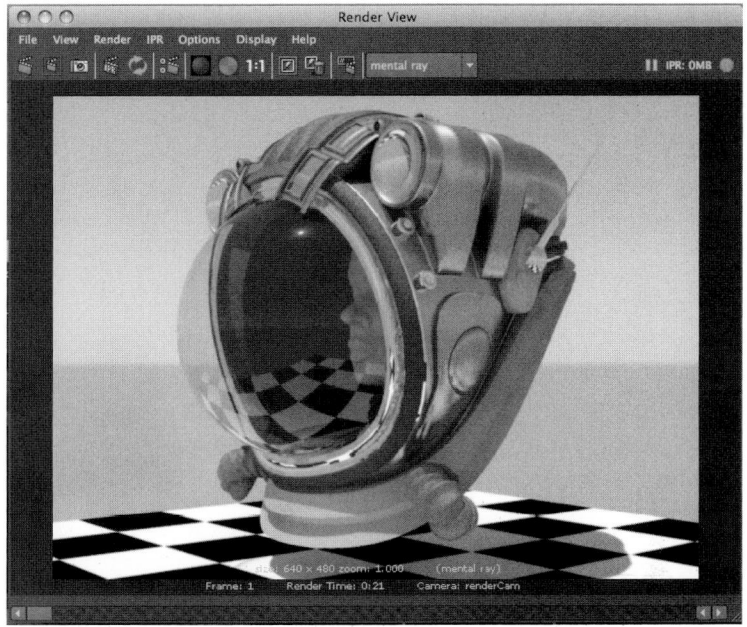

Other MIA Material Attributes

The mia_material has a lot of settings that can take some practice to master. It's a good idea to take a look at the settings used for each preset and take note of how they affect the rendered image. Over time you'll pick up some good tricks using the presets as a starting point for creating your own shaders. The following sections give a little background on how some of the other settings work.

BUILT-IN AMBIENT OCCLUSION

The Ambient Occlusion option on the material acts as a multiplier for existing ambient occlusion created by the indirect lighting (Final Gathering/Global Illumination). The Use Detail Distance option in the Ambient Occlusion section can be used to enhance fine detailing when set to On. When Use Detail Distance is set to With Color Bleed, the ambient occlusion built into the mia_ material factors the reflected colors from surrounding objects into the calculation.

TRANSLUCENCY

The Translucency setting is useful for simulating thin objects, such as paper. This option works only when the material has some amount of transparency. The Translucency Weight setting determines how much of the Transparency setting is used for transparency and how much is used for translucency. So if Transparency is 1 (and the transparency color is white) and Translucency Weight is 0, the object is fully transparent (the left of Figure 10.32). When Translucency Weight is at 0.5, the material splits the Transparency value between transparency and translucency (the center of Figure 10.32). When Translucency Weight is set to 1, the object is fully translucent (the right of Figure 10.32).

FIGURE 10.32
Three planes with
varying degrees
of translucency
applied

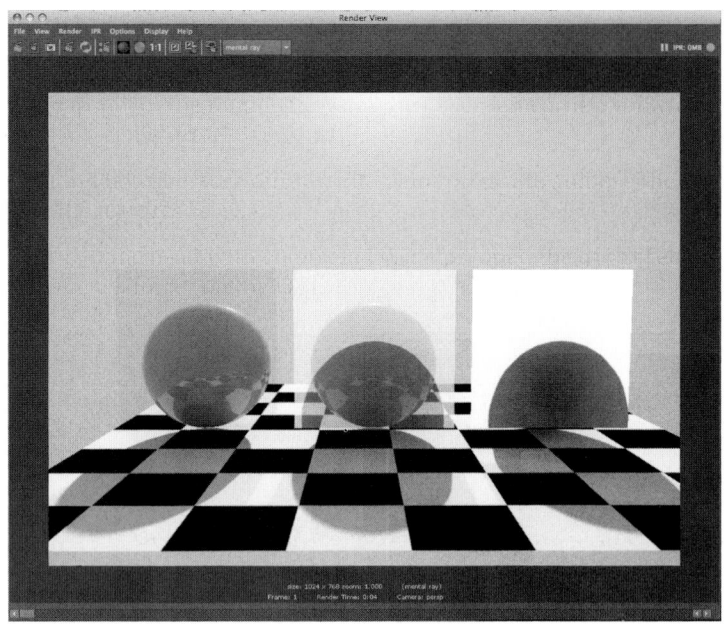

Notice that you can also create translucent objects by experimenting with the glossiness in the Refraction settings. This can be used with or without activating the Use Translucency option. If you find that the translucency setting does not seem to work or make any difference in the shading, try reversing the normals on your geometry (in the Polygons menu set, choose Normals ➤ Reverse). The MIA materials have a wide variety of uses beyond metal and plastic. The materials offer an excellent opportunity for exploration. For more detailed descriptions of the settings, read the *mental ray for Maya Architectural Guide* in the Maya documentation.

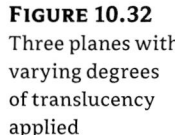 **Real World Scenario**

USING THE MIA_MATERIAL TO SHADE ORGANIC OBJECTS

The many settings of the mia_material can be used to create material properties well beyond what is listed in the Presets menu. In fact, the mia_material is by far my favorite shader available in Maya because of its versatility. The Translucency attributes make it ideal for shading things like leaves in a close-up, insect wings, and clothing. I've even used the material to create the look of flakes of skin as seen on a microscopic scale.

I usually create these effects by mapping file textures to various channels of the mia_material. Mapping file textures is covered in depth in Chapter 11, but this example should be simple enough to follow even if you have not worked with texture maps very much.

The mia_shader has an advanced attribute called Cut Out Opacity. This is like a second transparency channel that is used to map a texture to define the silhouette of an object. Here's how you can use this channel:

1. Open the `leaves_v01.ma` scene from the `chapter10\scenes` folder on the DVD.

2. In the Hypershade editor, create a new mia_material_x shader.

3. Apply this shader to the leaf1 and leaf2 objects in the scene.

4. Create a new file texture node (select 2D Textures from under the Maya heading in the list on the left), and click the File button.

5. Open the Attribute Editor for the file1 node.

6. Click the Image Name field. Browse your computer, and find the `leaf.tif` file located in the `chapter10\sourceimages` directory.

7. MMB-drag the file1 node from the Hypershade to the color swatch in the Diffuse rollout of the mia_material_x1 node's Attribute Editor.

8. Repeat step 7, but this time connect the file1 node to the Color swatch in the Refraction node. This will use the file1 image, which is a picture of a leaf, to color the transparency of the leaf objects.

9. In the Reflection rollout, set Reflectivity to **0.18** and Glossiness to **0.2**.

10. In the Refraction rollout, set Transparency to **0.15**.

11. In the Translucency rollout, turn on Use Translucency. Set Color to a light gray and Weight to 0.8.

12. Create a test render.

    Well, these are some nice-looking translucent leaves, but there is an ugly black box appearing around the leaf image in the texture. This is where Cutout Opacity is useful. You can easily use this channel to create the edges of the leaves based on the alpha channel stored in the original `leaf.tif` file.

13. Expand the Advanced rollout toward the bottom of the mia_material_x1 shader's Attribute Editor.

14. MMB-drag the file1 node from the Hypershade window onto the Cutout Opacity slider. This will automatically connect the alpha channel of the file1 texture to the Cutout Opacity setting.

15. Create another test render. *Et voila!* Translucent leaves!

This technique is useful because the shader can be applied to very simple geometry. The planes used for the leaves can be turned into nCloth objects and have dynamic forces create their movement (nCloth and Dynamics are covered in Chapters 14 and 15).

There are several things you may need to remember, to check whether this technique is not working in your own scenes:

◆ Make sure the normals of your polygon objects are facing the correct direction.

◆ Make sure the file texture you use for the Cutout Opacity has an alpha channel.

◆ Make sure that the Transparency setting is above 0 in order for the translucency to work.

(CONTINUES)

Real World Scenario

USING THE MIA_MATERIAL TO SHADE ORGANIC OBJECTS *(CONTINUED)*

The many settings of the mia_material can be used to create material properties well beyond what is listed in the Presets menu. In fact, the mia_material is by far my favorite shader available in Maya because of its versatility. The Translucency attributes make it ideal for shading things like leaves in a close-up, insect wings, and clothing. I've even used the material to create the look of flakes of skin as seen on a microscopic scale.

I usually create these effects by mapping file textures to various channels of the mia_material. Mapping file textures is covered in depth in Chapter 11, but this example should be simple enough to follow even if you have not worked with texture maps very much.

You may notice that the texture was connected to the refraction color and not the translucency color. This is so that the shadows cast by the leaves are semi-transparent. You can map a texture to the translucency color, but your shadows may appear black.

One other useful setting is the Additional Color channel in the advanced rollout. This can be used to create incandescent effects similar to the incandescence channel on standard Maya shaders (Blinn, Phong, Lambert, and so on).

Controlling Exposure with Tone Mapping

Tone mapping refers to a process in which color values are remapped to fit within a given range. Computer monitors lack the ability to display the entire range of values created by physically accurate lights and shaders. This becomes apparent when using HDRI lighting, MIA materials, and the physical light shader. Using tone mapping, you can correct the values to make the image look visually pleasing when displayed on a computer monitor.

Lens shaders are applied to rendering cameras in a scene. Most often they are used for color and exposure correction. You've already been using the mia_physicalsky lens shader, which is created automatically when you create the Physical Sun and Sky network using the controls in the Indirect Lighting section of the Render Settings window.

ADDING CAMERAS TO PHYSICAL SUN AND SKY NETWORK

When you add a new camera to a scene that already has the Physical Sun and Sky network, you may find that the images rendered with this camera look all wrong. To fix this, you need to add the camera to the Physical Sun and Sky network. To do this, follow these steps:

1. Select the sunDirection node in the Outliner.

2. Open its Attribute Editor, and switch to the mia_physicalsky tab.

3. Click the Update Camera Connections at the bottom of the Attribute Editor.

Doing this ensures that the correct lens shaders are applied to the camera. The Physical Sun and Sky network is discussed in detail in Chapter 9.

Using Exposure Shaders

The mia_exposure_photographic and mia_exposure_simple shaders are used to correct exposure levels when rendering with physically based lights and shaders. The mia_exposure_photographic lens shader has a lot of photography-based controls that can help you correct the exposure of an image. The mia_exposure_simple lens shader is meant to accomplish the same task; however, it has fewer controls and is easier to set up and use. In this exercise, you'll use the mia_exposure_simple lens shader to fix problems in a render.

The scene you'll use is the space helmet scene. This version of the scene uses the same mia_materials as the previous section. In the previous section, the problems with the exposure were not noticeable because lens shaders were already applied to all the cameras when the Physical Sun and Sky network was created. In this section, you'll learn how to apply the lens shader manually.

1. Open the helmet_v08.ma scene from the chapter10\scenes directory in the DVD. Currently this scene has no lighting. All the materials on the helmet are the same MIA materials described in the previous section.

2. Open the Render Settings window, and switch to the Indirect Lighting tab.

3. Click the Create button next to Image Based Lighting. (Image Based Lighting is covered in detail in Chapter 9.)

4. In the Attribute Editor for the mentalrayIbl1 node, click the folder next to Image Name.

5. You'll need a High Dynamic Range (HDRI) image to use for the mentalrayibl node. You can download a number of these images free of charge from Paul Debevc's website at www.debevec.org/Probes:

   A. Follow the link in the text to download the all_probes.zip file.

   B. Unzip these files, and place them in the sourceimages folder of your current project.

6. Choose the building_probe.hdr image from the all_probes folder.

7. Set Mapping to Angular.

8. In the Render Stats section, turn off Primary Visibility so that the IBL sphere is not visible in the render.

9. Enable Final Gathering on the Indirect Lighting tab of the Render View window, and set Accuracy to **200**.

10. Create a test render in the Render View window using the renderCam camera, and store the image in the Render View window.

    The rendered image looks very underexposed; the dark parts are very dark (see the left image in Figure 10.33).

FIGURE 10.33
The image on the left appears under-exposed; adding a lens shader to control exposure fixes the problem, as shown in the image on the right.

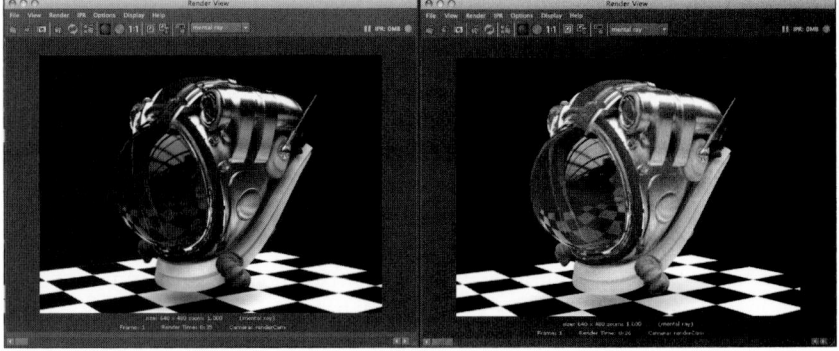

11. In the Outliner, select the renderCam camera, and open its Attribute Editor.

12. Expand the mental ray section, and click the checkered box to the right of Lens Shader.

13. In the Create Render Nodes window, select the Lenses heading in the mental ray section.

14. Click the mia_exposure_simple button.

    This applies the mia_exposure_simple lens shader to the rendering camera. You need to remember to apply this shader to any of the cameras you'll use for rendering the scene.

15. Create another test render from the renderCam camera. You'll see a big improvement in the image using the default settings of the mia_exposure_simple lens shader (see the right image in Figure 10.33).

16. Save the scene as **helmet_v09.ma**.

To see a finished version of the scene, open the helmet_v09.ma scene from the chapter10\ scenes directory on the DVD. The HDRI probe images are not included on the DVD; you will need to reconnect the building_probe.hdr image you downloaded in order for the example scene to work correctly.

The following is a brief description of the mia_exposure_simple shader's attributes:

Pedestal Adds lightness to the black areas of the image; a negative value will "crush the blacks" by adding contrast to the image.

Gain Increases the brightness of the lighter areas in the image.

Knee value Sets the point where overbright values (values that go beyond the 0–1 range) are brought down within the normal range.

Compression setting Applies compression to the overbright values as defined by the Knee setting.

Gamma Applies the overall color correction to the image so it appears correct on the computer monitor. A typical value for Windows displays is 2.2. It's important to make sure that if you set the Gamma value in the lens shader, additional gamma correction does not take place in the rendering and compositing pipeline.

For a more in-depth discussion of tone mapping, consult the *mental ray for Maya Architectural Guide* included in the Maya documentation.

Rendering Contours

mental ray has a special contour rendering mode that enables you to render outlines of 3D objects. This is a great feature for nonphotorealistic rendering. You can use it to make your 3D animations appear like drawings or futuristic computer displays. The end title sequence of the film *Iron Man* is a great example of this style of rendering.

Enable Contour Rendering

Rendering contours is easy to set up, but it requires activating settings in several different places.

1. Open the tractorDroidContour_v01.ma scene from the chapter10\scenes directory on the DVD. This scene shows the vehicle modeled by Anthony Honn. A standard Maya Lambert material is applied to the tractor.

2. Open the Render Settings window, and select the Features tab.

3. Expand the Contours section, and click Enable Contour Rendering. This makes contour rendering possible, but you won't see any results until you activate a few more options.

4. Expand the Draw By Property Difference section. These settings define how the contours will be drawn. One of these options must be activated, or contour rendering will not take place. Click Between Different Instances. This means lines will be drawn around each piece of geometry in the scene (see Figure 10.34).

FIGURE 10.34
To render contour lines, you must select Enable Contour Rendering and choose a Draw By Property Difference option.

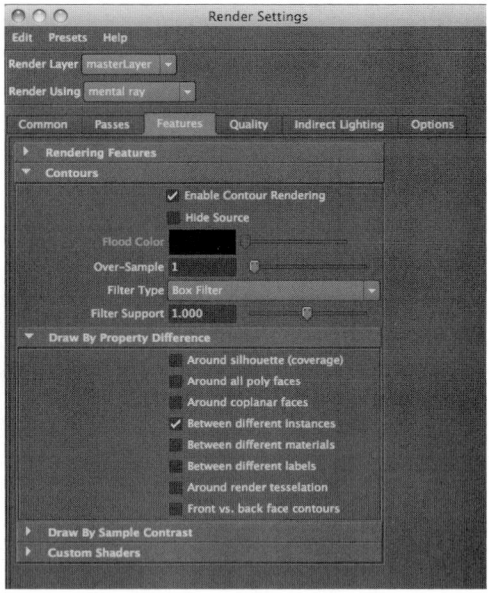

5. Open the Hypershade window, select the whiteLambert material, and graph its input and output connections.

6. In the work area of the Hypershade, select the whiteLambert4SG node that is attached to the whiteLambert shader, and open its Attribute Editor. Switch to the whiteLambert4SG tab.

7. In the Contours section of the mental ray rollout in the Attribute Editor, select the Enable Contour Rendering option. Set Color to red (Figure 10.35).

FIGURE 10.35
Contour Rendering also needs to be enabled in the shader's shading group node settings.

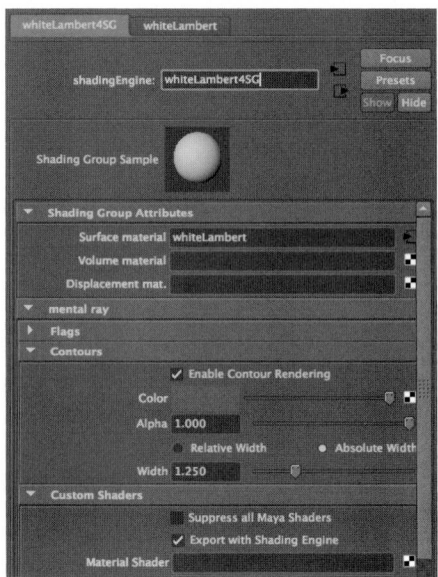

8. Create a test render in the Render View window from the renderCam camera. The contours are added after the scene renders, on top of the shaded view of the geometry.

9. Open the Render Settings window.

10. In the Features tab, in the Contours section, activate Hide Source, and set Flood Color to a dark blue.

11. Create another test render (see Figure 10.36).

FIGURE 10.36
Contour rendering creates lines on top of the rendered surface. In the bottom image, the source has been hidden, so only the lines render.

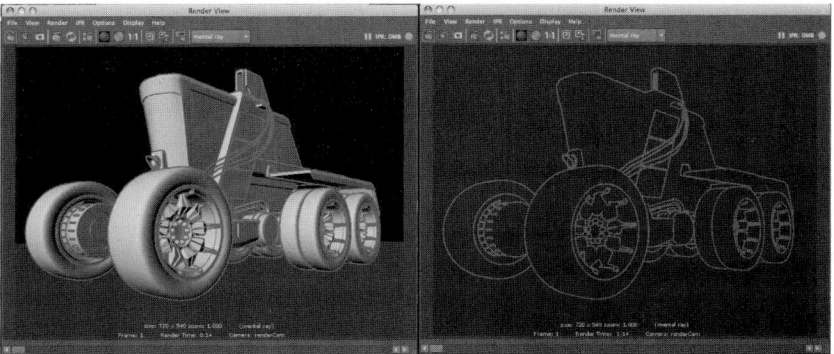

This time the original geometry is hidden, and only the contours are rendered. Flood Color determines the background color when Hide Source is activated. Oversampling sets the quality and anti-aliasing of the contour lines. To see a finished version of the scene, open the tractorDroidContour_v02.ma scene from the chapter10\scenes folder on the DVD.

You can adjust the width of the contours using the controls in the Contours section of the shading group. Absolute Width ensures that the contours are the same width; Relative Width makes the width of the contours relative to the size of the rendered image.

Since each shading group node has its own contour settings, you can create lines of differing thickness and color for all the parts of an object. Just apply different materials to the different parts, and adjust the settings in each material's shading group node accordingly.

Experiment using different settings in the Draw By Property Difference section of the Render Settings window. More complex contour effects can be created by plugging one of the contour shaders available in the Create mental ray Node section of the Hypershade into the Contour Shader slot under the Custom Shaders section of the shading group node.

The Bottom Line

Understand shading concepts Light rays are reflected, absorbed by, or transmitted through a surface. A rough surface diffuses the reflection of light by bouncing light rays in nearly random directions. Specular reflections occur on smooth surfaces; the angle at which rays bounce off a smooth surface is equivalent to the angle at which they strike the surface. Refraction occurs when light rays are bent as they are transmitted through the surface. A specular highlight is the reflection of a light source on a surface. In CG rendering, this effect is often controlled separately from reflection; in the real world, specular reflection and highlights are intrinsically related.

Master it Make a standard Blinn shader appear like glass refracting light in the `jellybeans_v01.ma` scene in the `chapter10\scenes` folder of the DVD.

Apply reflection and refraction blur Reflection and Refraction Blur are special mental ray options available on many standard Maya shading nodes. You can use these settings to create glossy reflections when rendering standard Maya shading nodes with mental ray.

Master it Create the look of translucent plastic using a standard Maya Blinn shader.

Use basic mental ray shaders The DGS and Dielectric shaders offer numerous options for creating realistic reflections and transparency. The mib (mental images base) shader library has a number of shaders that can be combined to create realistic materials.

Master it Create a realistic CD surface using the mib shaders.

Apply the car paint shader Car paint consists of several layers, which creates the special quality seen in the reflections on car paint. The mi_carpaint_phen shader can realistically simulate the interaction of light on the surface of a car model. The diffuse, reflection, and metallic flakes layers all work together to create a convincing render.

Master it Design a shader for a new and an old car finish.

Use the MIA materials The MIA materials and nodes can be used together to create realistic materials that are always physically accurate. The MIA materials come with a number of presets that can be used as a starting point for your own materials.

Master it Create a realistic polished-wood material.

Render contours mental ray has the ability to render contours of your models to create a cartoon drawing look for your animations. Rendering contours requires that options in the Render Settings window and in the shading group for the object are activated.

Master it Render the space suit helmet using contours.

Chapter 11

Texture Mapping

The use of two-dimensional images to add color and detail to three-dimensional objects has been a big part of computer modeling and animation from the very start. This is known as *texture mapping*, and it is practically an art form all its own. A well-painted texture map can add an astonishing degree of realism, especially when combined with good lighting and a well-constructed 3D model. In this chapter, you'll see how to use texture mapping to create a photorealistic giraffe.

Texture mapping has many different levels. On one end, you add as much as you can to the map, light, reflections, and shadow. On the other end, you rely on shaders and rendering techniques and have maps that provide nothing more than shades of color.

In this chapter, you will learn to:

- ◆ Create UV texture coordinates
- ◆ Create bump and normal maps
- ◆ Create a misss_fast_skin shader

UV Texture Layout

UV texture mapping is a necessary part of completing a model. UVs provide space for painted images to be placed on your model. In Maya, using UVs goes beyond texture mapping. Having good UVs also provides you with a surface to paint skin weight maps, fur attributes, and simulation parameters. UV mapping has been simplified in Maya to a couple of tools and can be done very rapidly.

UVs are often looked at as tedious and difficult but a necessary evil. There is a lot of truth to this; however, UV mapping has a strong purpose and should be looked at as an important part of the process. UV mapping is a lot like wrapping a present, where you have a flat sheet of paper that needs to go around an awkwardly shaped object with as few seams as possible.

LINKING TEXTURE FILES

The project files in this chapter are linked to texture files found in the chapter11\sourceimages directory on the DVD. It's possible that these links may break when working with the scenes on the DVD. You may want to copy the Chapter 11 project to your local hard drive and make sure that the current project is set to Chapter 11. This way, when you load a premade scene and render it, the scenes should render properly.

What Are UV Texture Coordinates?

Just as x-, y-, and z-coordinates tell you where an object is located in space, u- and v-coordinates tell you where a point exists on a surface. Imagine a dot drawn on a cardboard box. The u- and v-coordinates specify the location of that dot on the surface of the box. If you unfold the box and then place a grid over the flattened box, you can plot the position of the dot using the grid. One axis of the grid is the u-coordinate; the other axis is the v-coordinate. 3D software uses u- and v-coordinates to determine how textures should be applied to 3D objects. *UV mapping* refers to the process of determining these coordinates for polygon objects. *UV layout* is a term that refers to the 2D configuration of the UVs on a surface, such as a picture of the unfolded box on a grid taken from above (see Figure 11.1). In the UV Texture Editor, u-coordinates are plotted along the horizontal axis, and v-coordinates are plotted along the vertical axis.

FIGURE 11.1
UV coordinates appear as an unfolded version of the model. They determine how textures are applied to 3D models. In this image, the coordinates tell Maya where to place the word *hello* on the cube.

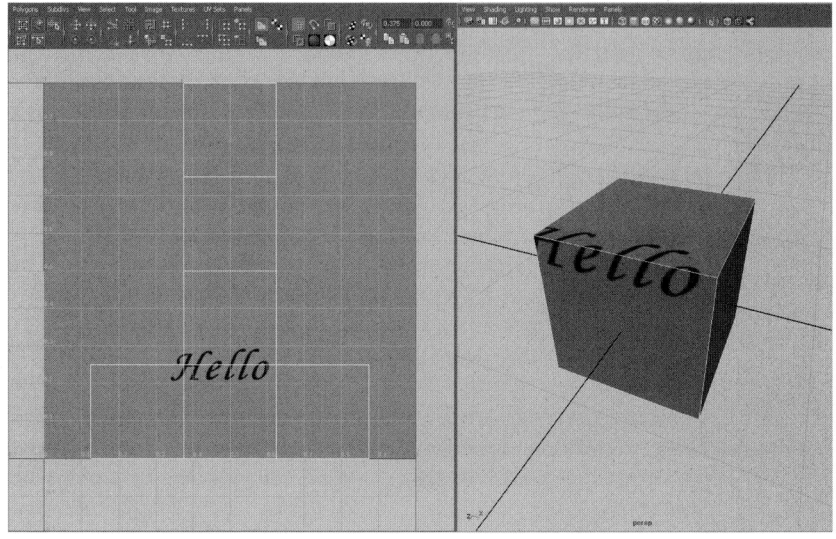

NURBS surfaces have implicit UVs; this means that the coordinates are built into the parameterization of the surface. UV texture coordinates do not have to be created for NURBS surfaces; only polygon and subdivision surfaces require mapped UVs. With regard to subdivision surfaces, it's usually best to map the UVs on a polygon version of the model and then convert that model to subdivision surfaces. The mapped UV coordinates are converted along with the polygon object.

UV maps act as a guide for the placement of images. Images can be painted in Maya on a flat canvas in 2D space or in 3D space directly on the model. Other third-party software is usually employed to do the bulk of the texture work, like Photoshop, Mudbox, and ZBrush. Figure 11.2 shows a typical Photoshop texture-painting session using a snapshot of the UVs, created in Maya, as a guide.

FIGURE 11.2

UV coordinates are used as a guide for painting 3D model textures in digital paint programs such as Photoshop.

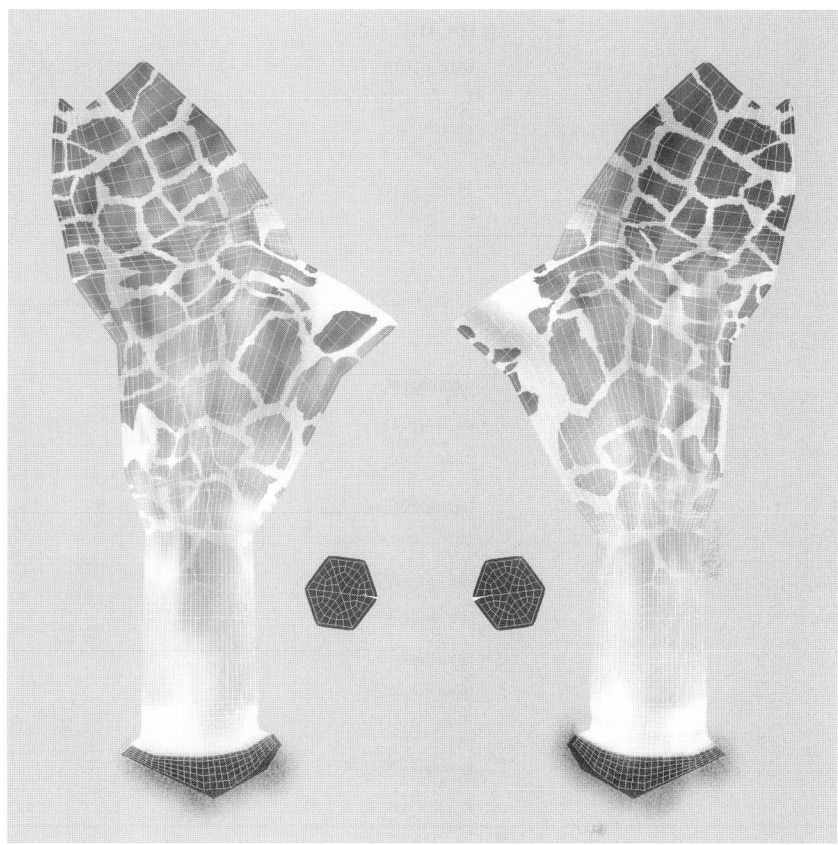

A good UV layout will also minimize stretching, warping, and the appearance of seams between the parts of the UV map. For a character's head, a good UV layout may look a little strange, but you should be able to make out where the eyes, nose, mouth, ears, and other features are located. This is often referred to as a *human-readable* UV layout as opposed to an automatically tiled layout that functions just fine but is impossible to decipher when trying to paint a 2D map in Photoshop (see Figure 11.3).

Even if you intend to create texture maps in a program such as Mudbox, BodyPaint 3D, or ZBrush, which allow you to paint directly on a 3D model, it's a good idea to make sure you have human-readable UVs. This is especially true when working in a production pipeline. The textures you create in ZBrush or BodyPaint may need to be mapped or enhanced in Photoshop. If the UVs are not human-readable, the process becomes extremely difficult.

FIGURE 11.3
Human-readable UVs bear some resemblance to the original 3D object so that an artist can easily paint textures (top). Automatically tiled UVs (bottom) will function but are impossible for artists to decipher.

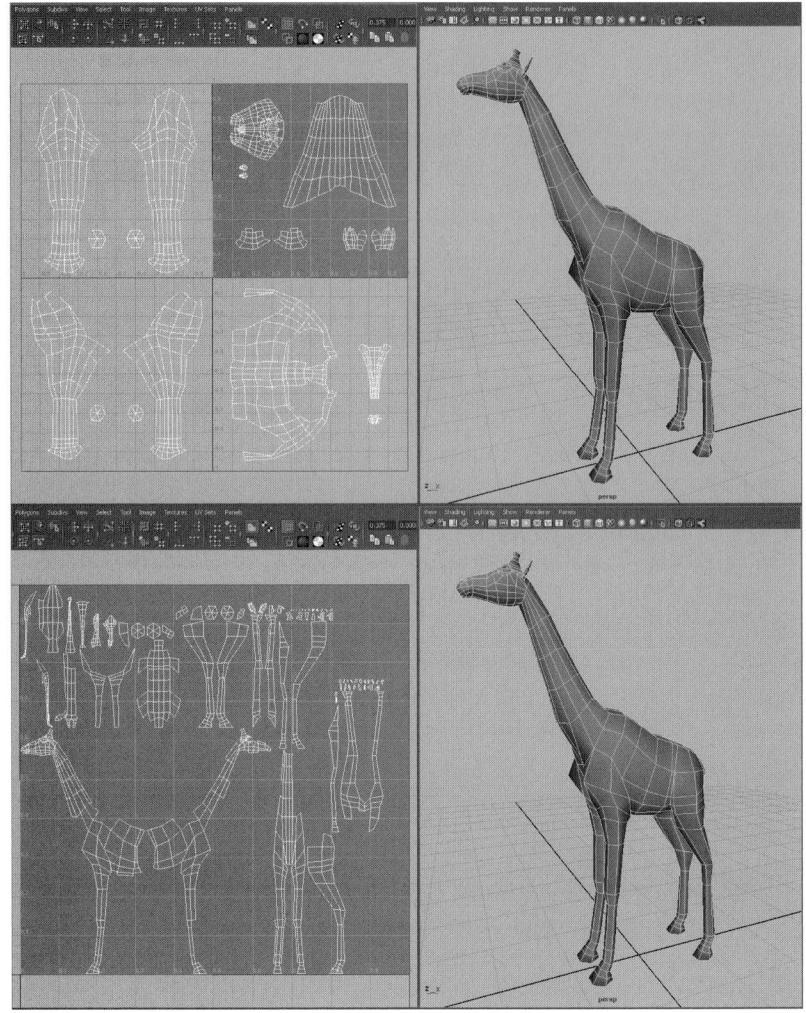

The process of mapping UVs is typically done with a viewport and the UV Texture Editor. The interface of the UV Texture Editor is a 2D graph with menus and an icon bar at the top (see Figure 11.4). Many of the icon commands are duplicated in the menu selections in the editor window. You can also find the same tools in the Polygon menu set under Create UVs and Edit UVs. The UV Texture Editor graph is divided into four quadrants. The upper-right quadrant (shaded darker gray) is typically where you'll keep your texture coordinates. Notice the numbers on the graph; the upper-right quadrant has the positive U and V values. The values range from 0 to 1. It is possible to have coordinates existing outside this range, which is useful when creating photorealistic models, but most of the time you want to keep the coordinates within this range.

The best time to create UV coordinates for a model is when you've finished editing the model. Inserting edges, subdividing, and extruding will alter the coordinate layout and produce undesirable effects. However, to save time, if the model is symmetrical, the UVs can be laid out when the model is half finished.

FIGURE 11.4
UV Texture Editor

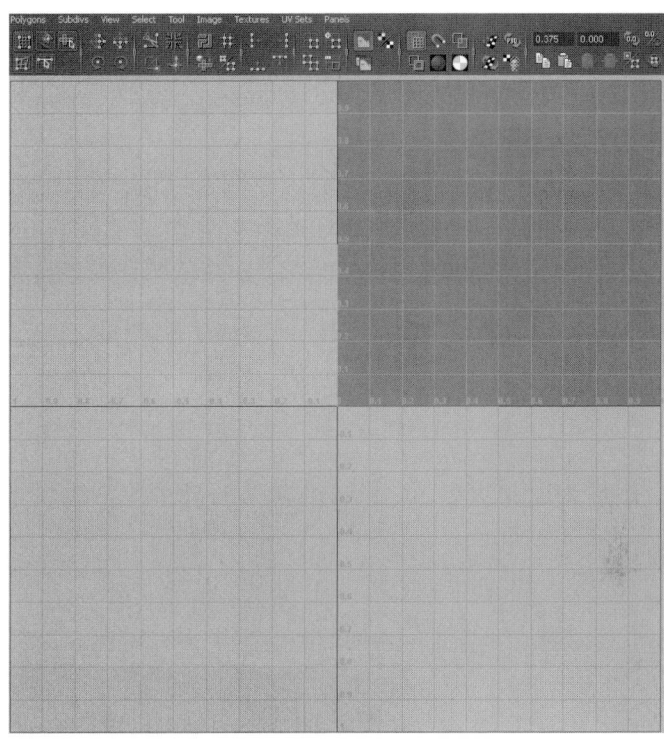

Take a look at Figure 11.5. The giraffe has been cut in half. UVs are part of the geometry. Mirroring the geometry also mirrors the UVs. Therefore, it is necessary to lay out the UVs for only half the model. When you're done, the geometry can be mirrored over, and the UVs can be finished.

FIGURE 11.5
The giraffe has been cut in half in preparation for UV mapping.

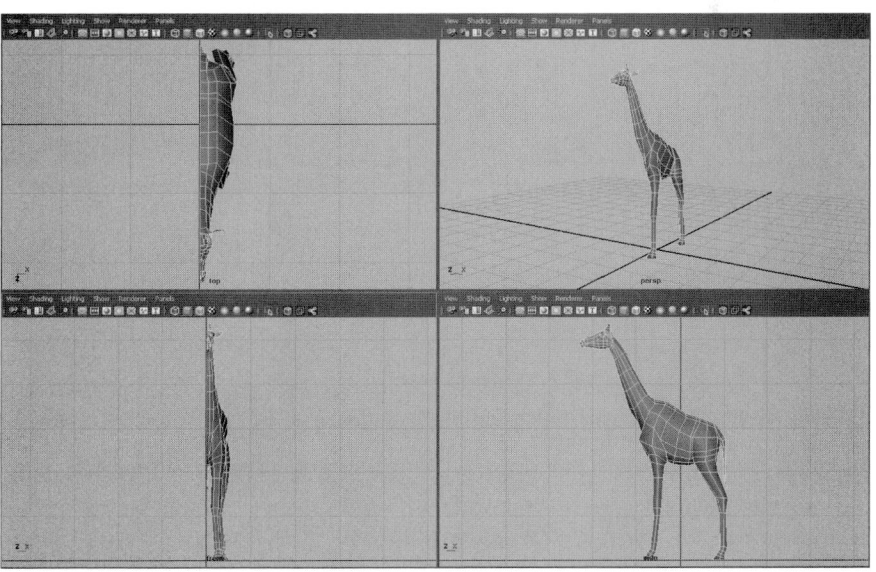

UVs are created by selecting polygon faces and projecting coordinates onto your selection. Maya has several different projection methods to facilitate UV mapping. The trick is to match your projection to your selection, and vice versa. To familiarize yourself with the process, take the giraffe from Chapter 7 and lay out the UVs for its front leg, body, and head. The following exercises walk you through the process.

Mapping the Giraffe Leg

Using the giraffe model from Chapter 7, begin laying out its UVs, starting with its front leg. The model has been cut in half to allow mirroring later in the chapter.

1. Open the scene file `giraffeUV_01.ma` from the `chapter11\scenes` folder on the DVD.

2. Select the model, and choose Panels ➢ Saved Layouts ➢ Persp/UV Texture Editor.

3. Legs are simple to UV map because they match the cylindrical projection tool. Choose a group of faces on the lower half of the giraffe's front leg. Hold Shift+> to grow your selection. Continue up the leg until you achieve the selection shown in Figure 11.6 (make sure you do not select the underside of the foot).

   You want the top to be roughly the same width as the bottom, just like a cylinder. As long as the middle retains the basic shape, its dimensions are not a concern.

FIGURE 11.6
Select the faces on the front leg.

4. In the Polygons menu set, choose Create UVs ➢ Cylindrical Mapping. UVs are created; however, they don't look pretty (see Figure 11.7).

FIGURE 11.7
The cylindrically mapped UVs

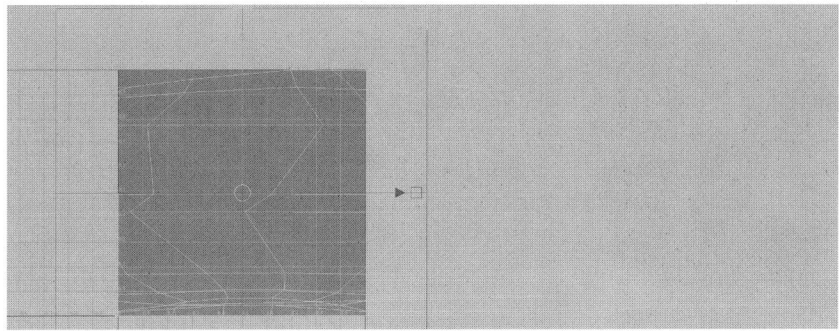

NAVIGATION IN THE UV TEXTURE EDITOR

You can move around in the UV Texture Editor just as you can in the perspective view, except that you can't tumble around, since by its nature UV texturing is a 2D process. Use Alt+right-click to zoom and Alt+middle-click to pan.

---

5. You need to fit the manipulator to the geometry in order to improve the quality of the UVs. It needs to be translated and rotated. To do this, find the red T at the bottom of the manipulator.

6. Click it to activate the combined Move/Rotate/Scale tool.

7. Translate the cylinder first in the Z and then rotate it. Use Figure 11.8 as reference.

FIGURE 11.8
Fit the manipulator to the leg.

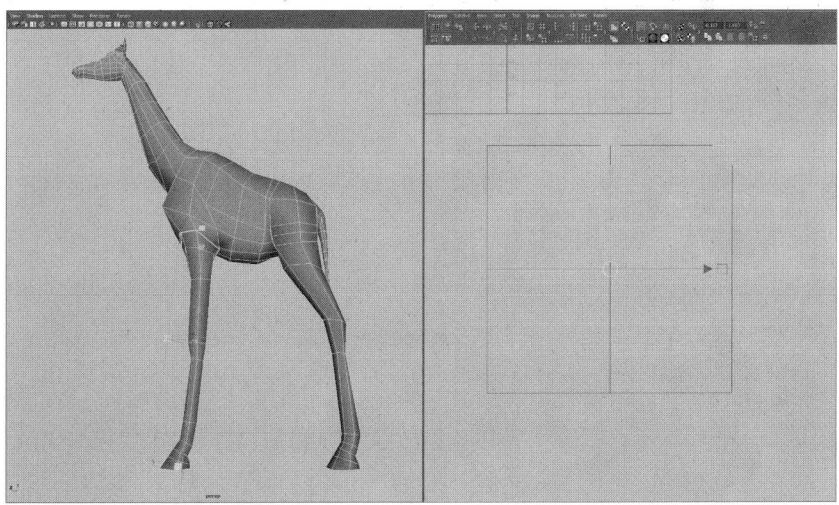

SELECTING THE PROJECTION MANIPULATOR

If you accidentally deselect the manipulator, click the polyCylProj node from the Channel Box. Next, choose the manipulator icon from the toolbar.

8. While the faces are still selected, change them to UVs by choosing Select ➤ Convert Selection To UVs.

   When faces are selected, only those faces are shown in the UV Texture Editor. When you select UVs in whole or in part, all the mapped UVs are displayed. Moving your UV shells into empty space keeps them from overlapping.

9. Move the UV selection away from the texture space into solid gray space. You can use the Move tool from the toolbar. Moving the *UV shell* into empty space is done to give you more space to work in.

10. Go back to the giraffe model, and select the last two rows of polygons on the upper leg (see Figure 11.9).

FIGURE 11.9
Select the rest of the leg.

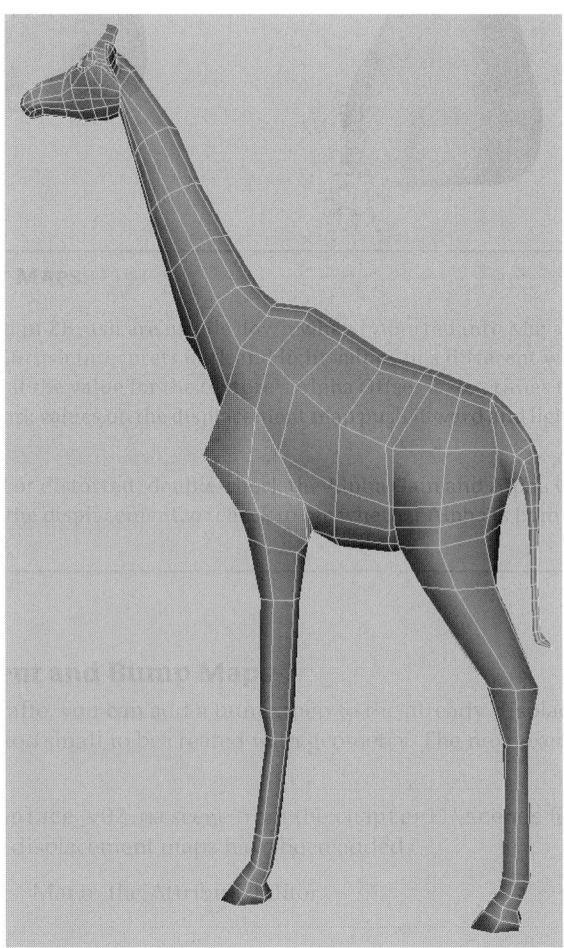

11. Choose Create UVs ➤ Cylindrical Mapping. The UVs lay out nicely, so there is no need to alter the manipulator.

12. The leg is in two pieces. By selecting shared edges, you can sew the pieces together. Start by moving the two UV shells so that the upper leg sits above the lower leg. You should have something similar to Figure 11.10.

FIGURE 11.10
Arrange the
two UV shells.

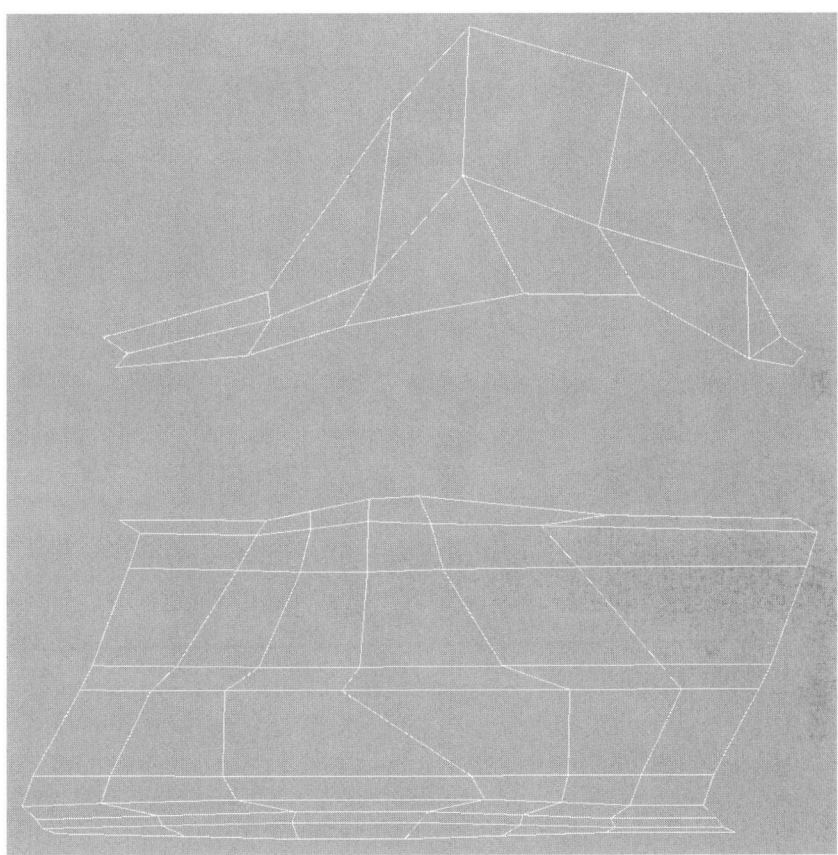

13. Choose the bottom-left corner edge of the top UV shell. Notice how its corresponding edge on the lower UV shell is also highlighted. Continuing selecting the entire row (see Figure 11.11).

14. From the menu bar in the UV Texture Editor, choose Polygons ➤ Move And Sew UV Edges. The two pieces are sewn together. The smaller UV shell is always moved to the larger UV shell.

15. Select a single UV, and then choose Select ➤ Select Shell.

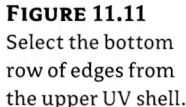

FIGURE 11.11
Select the bottom
row of edges from
the upper UV shell.

16. Next convert the selection to faces by choosing Select ➤ Convert Selection To Faces.

After some experience, you will be able to look at a UV shell and determine whether it is good or needs improvement. However, to see the smallest defects, it's necessary to assign a textured pattern to the faces.

17. With the shell selected, in the perspective viewport right-click a face and choose Assign a New Material from the marking menu.

18. Choose a Lambert material, and assign a checker pattern to the Color channel.

19. Press **6** to see the texture in the viewport (see Figure 11.12).

20. Save the scene as **giraffeUV_v02.ma**.

Notice that when you move the UV coordinates around the UV Texture Editor, the checker pattern moves but does not disappear. This is because the pattern repeats infinitely beyond the 0 to 1 range of the grid (where the image preview is seen when the Display Image button is activated). Eventually you'll move the leg back to the grid, but for now you just want to move it out of the way while you work on other parts of the giraffe.

To see a version of the scene to this point, open the giraffeUV_v02.ma scene from the chapter11\scenes directory on the DVD.

FIGURE 11.12
The UVs stretch and warp the checkered pattern.

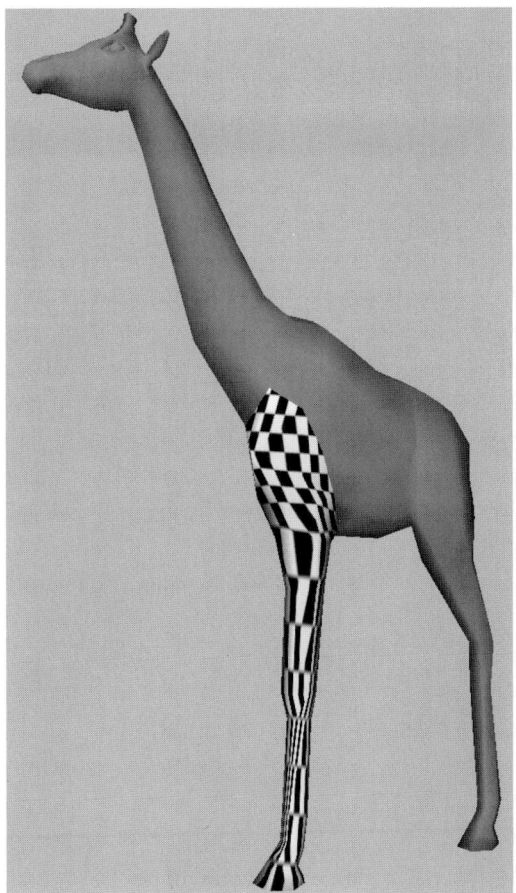

Unfolding UVs

Once you have the basic UV layout created for the model, you can use Maya's UV Unfold command to remove any remaining overlapping UVs as well as to reduce distortion on the model. Unfold UVs can be used at any time during the process on entire shells or just selected UVs. The Unfold command tries to make the UVs conform to the three-dimensional shape of the object.

1. Open the giraffeUV2.ma scene from the chapter11\scenes folder on the DVD. The scene picks up where the previous exercise left off.

2. Select the UV shell for the leg. Remember, you can do this quickly by selecting a single UV and choosing Select ➤ UV Shell.

3. Choose the options for Polygons ➤ Unfold.

4. In the options, leave Weight Solver set to 0. There are two types of solvers, Local and Global. The slider determines a bias setting toward one or the other. A setting of 0 means the Local solver will be used, a setting of 1 means the Global solver will be used, and any setting in between blends the two solvers.

LOCAL VS. GLOBAL UNFOLD SOLVER

The Local Unfold solver is faster than the Global solver, and in most cases, such as with this model, it works just fine. If you experience an undesirable tapering effect on parts of a UV layout when using UV Unfold, try raising the slider value to increase the bias toward the Global solver. It will take longer to solve but may help with problem areas.

5. Deselect Pin UV Border. Check Pin UVs and Pin Unselected UVs so that the entire shell can be unfolded without pins. If you want to unfold only part of the shell, you can use the Pinning settings to constrain the unselected UVs or the UV border so that they remain unaltered while the selected UVs are unfolded.

6. Set Unfold Constraint to None so the UVs can be moved in both U and V.

   The Unfold calculations are iterative. The unfolding process will continue until the maximum iterations have been reached or the stopping threshold has been met. Maya makes its calculations based on a comparison between the original model and the unfolded result.

7. The Rescale feature is useful when you are unfolding multiple shells that need to have a consistent size. Select this option so the face and neck shells have a consistent size when the unfold operation is performed. Set Scale Factor to **1** so the shells remain about the same size. Figure 11.13 shows the final settings.

8. Click the Apply button, and observe the results in the perspective view. Figure 11.14 shows the results.

   The checkered pattern looks good but can still be improved on. You can smooth out the overlapping UVs interactively using the Smooth UV tool.

9. From the menu bar in the UV Texture Editor, choose Tool ➤ Smooth UV Tool ➤ Options. Make sure you are using the default settings shown in Figure 11.15.

FIGURE 11.13
The settings for the Unfold tool

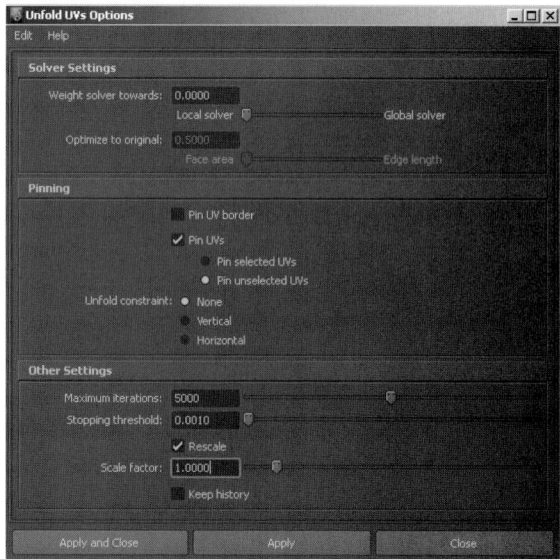

FIGURE 11.14
The results of
unfolding the
leg UVs

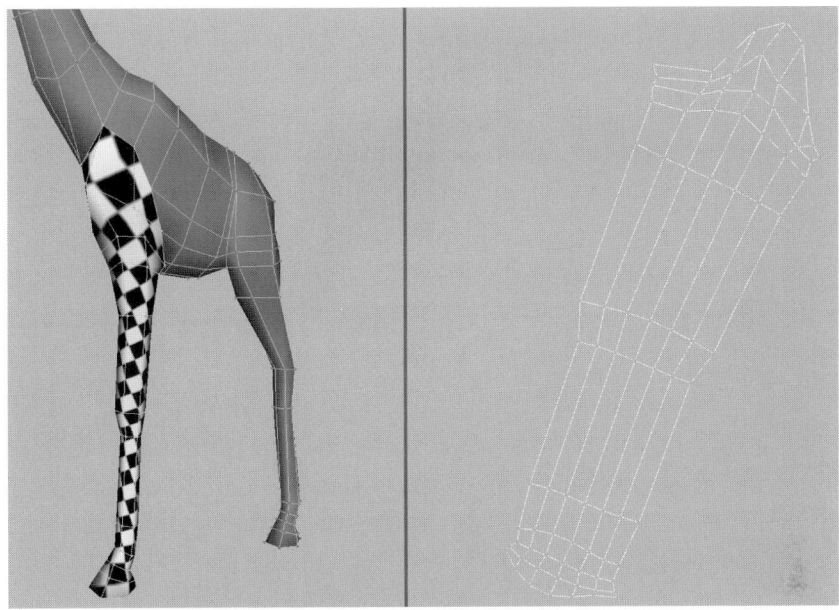

FIGURE 11.15
Use the default
settings of the
UV Smooth tool.

10. In the UV Texture Editor, you'll see a handle with two text boxes: one labeled Unfold, the other labeled Relax. The position of the tool in the UV Texture Editor does not affect its operation. Click and drag over the word *Relax* (drag back and forth). This smoothes the UVs by averaging their distances.

    By dragging back and forth, you can interactively set the level of relaxation. Keep an eye on the model in the perspective view to see how relaxing the UVs affects the texture mapping.

11. Use Undo to return the UVs to their state prior to using Relax.

12. Drag over the word *Unfold*. The Unfold operation untangles the UVs while trying to match the shape of the 3D surface. This works like the Unfold tool except on an interactive level.

13. Drag Unfold to the right until the UVs stop moving. Figure 11.16 shows the final outcome.

14. Save the scene as **giraffeUV_v03.ma**.

FIGURE 11.16
The UVs for the leg
are unfolded and
look good.

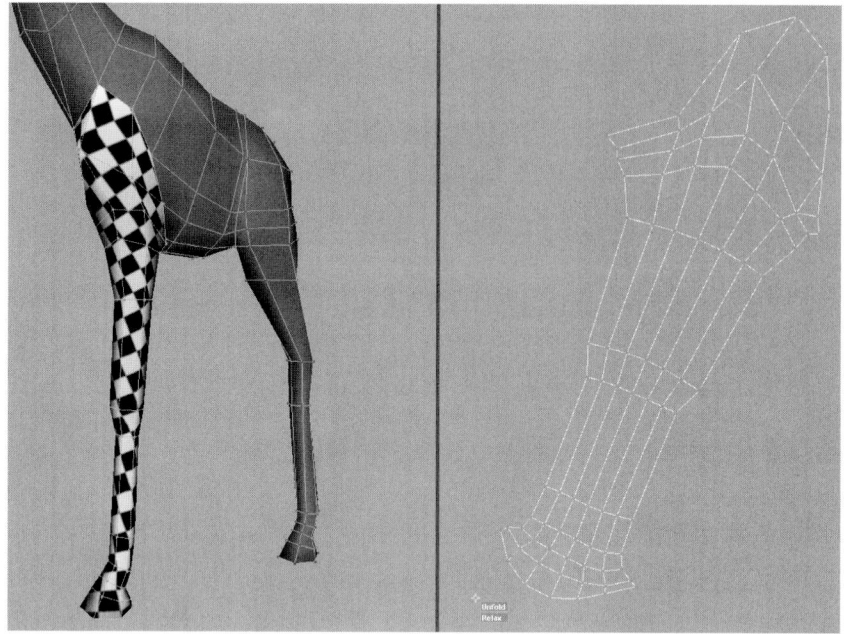

To see a version of the scene to this point, open the `giraffeUV_v03.ma` scene from the `chapter11\scenes` directory on the DVD.

Most of the UVs can be flattened nicely with the default settings of the Unfold tool. However, the further the shape is from the projected method, the more you will need to play with the solver settings.

If your checkered pattern is blurry in the viewport, you can turn on High Quality Rendering under the Renderer menu. If your graphics card does not support this, you can also increase the displayed resolution. This is located on each material under the Hardware Texturing rollout. Use Figure 11.17 for the proper settings. Using the Material hardware options causes the texture to be clipped based on the UV shells. If you move the shells after settings these attributes, you will need to redo the attributes to force the texture to be updated.

FIGURE 11.17
Change the set-
tings in the mate-
rial's Hardware
Texture rollout to
improve the dis-
played texture in
the viewport.

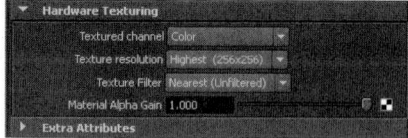

Mapping the Giraffe Head

Whether a human or an animal, generating UVs for the face is the hardest part, primarily because this is where the majority of the visible detail is. You want to minimize warped or stretched UVs as much as possible, especially around the nose and eyes, where defining lines can become stretched, making the model appear less believable. The following exercise is one approach to mapping the head:

1. Open the `giraffeUV_v03.ma` scene from the `chapter11\scenes` folder on the DVD. The scene picks up where the previous exercise left off.

2. Similar to the leg, you want to establish a good selection. Use the Select Lasso tool, and select all the head faces (see Figure 11.18).

3. Use the Paint Select tool to deselect the ears, nose interior, eye socket, and horns (see Figure 11.19). By default, the Paint Select tool is set to select. By holding Ctrl, you can reverse the operation. You also may have to change your selection to faces, which can be done by right-clicking and choosing Face from the marking menu.

FIGURE 11.18
Select the giraffe's head.

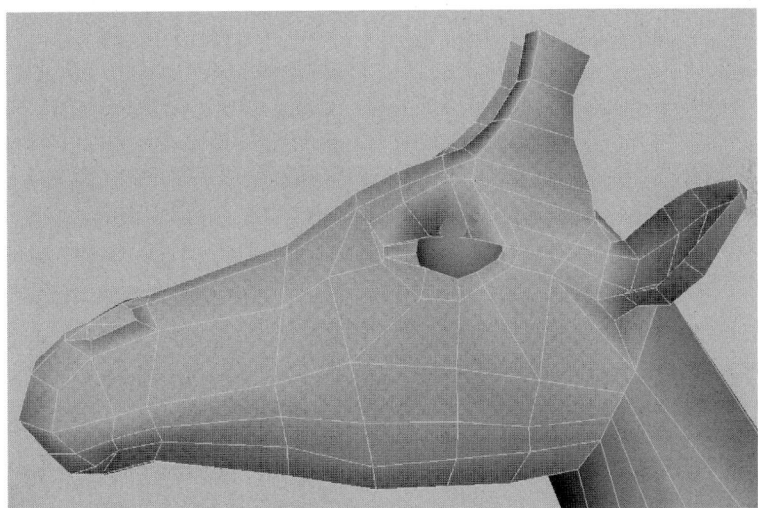

FIGURE 11.19
Deselect the ears, nose, eye socket, and horn parts of the giraffe's head.

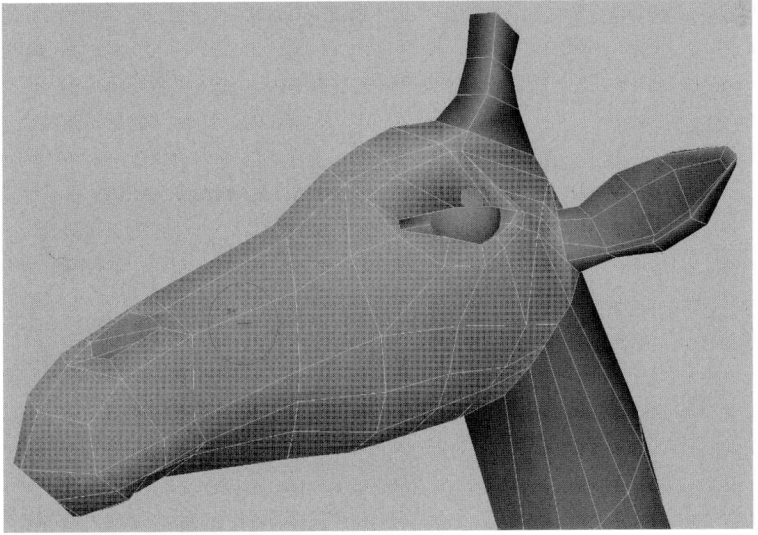

4. Choose Create UVs ➤ Cylindrical Mapping (see Figure 11.20).

5. Rotate the cylindrical projection to -90.0 in the X and Z axes.

6. Using the z-axis, translate the manipulator closer to the geometry.

Notice in the Channel Box it is the Projection Center X that is updated. These are the manipulator's world coordinate values. The UVs should now resemble the geometry (see Figure 11.21).

FIGURE 11.20
Use a cylindrical projection to project the UVs.

FIGURE 11.21
Translate the manipulator to correct the head UVs.

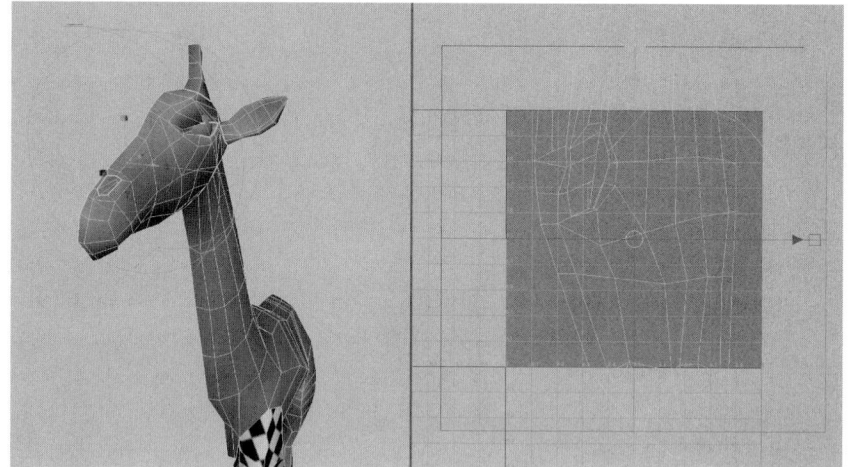

7. With the faces still selected, assign a new material with a checker pattern for the color channel. (If you need help, refer to steps 11 and 12 in the "Mapping the Giraffe Leg" section's exercise.)

8. Select the shell, and translate it into empty space.

9. Choose the Smooth tool by clicking its icon or by choosing Tool ➤ Smooth UV tool.

10. Drag the Unfold tool until the UVs stop moving (see Figure 11.22).

FIGURE 11.22
Drag the Unfold
tool to correct the
head UVs.

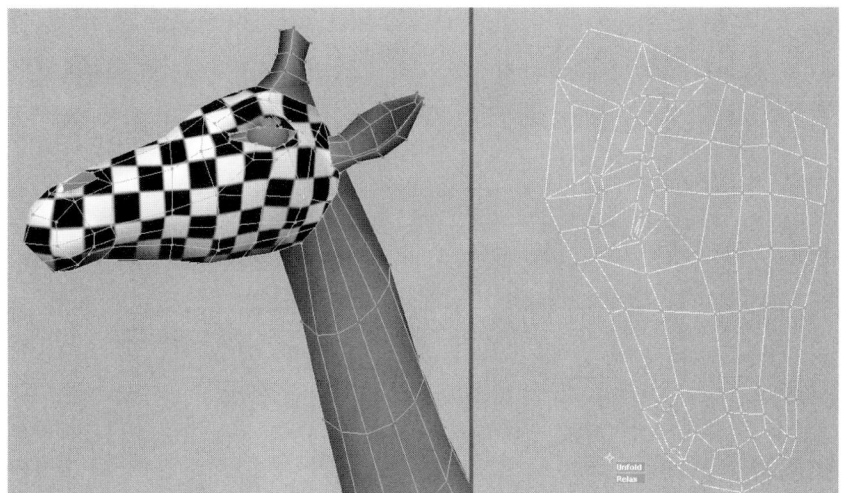

FIGURE 11.22
Drag the Unfold
tool to correct the
head UVs.

11. Save the scene as **giraffeUV_v04.ma**.

The head UVs are laid out nicely; however, including the other half does change things. The next exercise on mirroring geometry continues with the head UVs.

To see a version of the scene to this point, open the giraffeUV_v04.ma scene from the chapter11\scenes directory on the DVD.

Mirroring UVs

There is no way to mirror UVs only. You must mirror the geometry. The basic workflow for a symmetrical model is to lay out the UVs for one side of the model and then mirror the geometry.

1. Open the giraffeUV_v05.ma scene from the chapter11\scenes folder on the DVD. The scene has been continued from the previous exercise. All the UVs have been laid out in preparation for mirroring the geometry.

2. Select the giraffe. Choose Mesh ➢ Mirror Geometry ➢ Options. Make sure you are mirroring across the -X (see Figure 11.23).

3. Click polyMirror1 in the Channel Box, and set Merge Threshold to **0.005**.

4. Open the UV Texture Editor.

   It appears that none of the UVs has been mirrored. However, the mirrored UVs are sitting on top of the preexisting UVs.

FIGURE 11.23
Set the options for
the Mirror Geom-
etry tool.

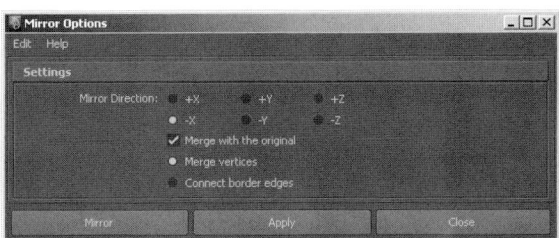

5. Select a single UV from the viewport on the right side of the giraffe's head.

6. Choose Select ➤ Select Shell from the UV Texture Editor.

7. Choose Image ➤ Display Image (deselect this option in the UV Texture Editor's menu bar) to turn off the texture preview. The checkerboard disappears in the UV Texture Editor.

DIM IMAGE

You can use the Dim Image button just below the Display Image button to lower the opacity of the image in the UV Texture Editor.

---

8. Translate the UVs in the Y direction to separate the right side from the left (see Figure 11.24).

FIGURE 11.24
Separate the left side of the head from the right.

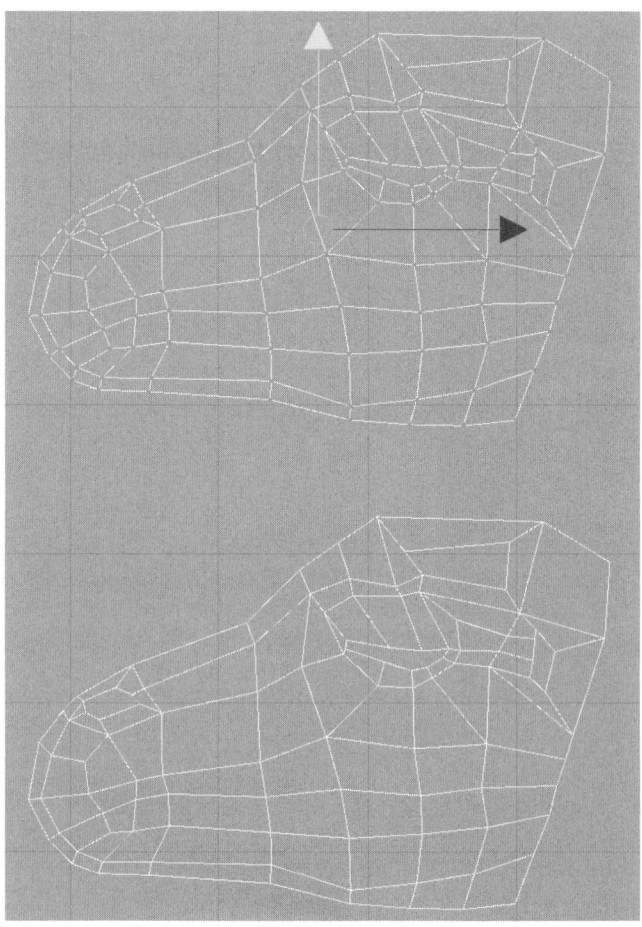

FLIPPED UVS

When creating UV texture coordinates, you need to make sure that the direction is consistent among all of the UVs; otherwise, strange artifacts can appear when the model is textured and rendered. Maya color codes the shells to differentiate between their directions; one of the side-of-the-face shells is blue, and the other is red. You can view this by choosing Image ➤ Shade UVs.

9. The goal is to sew the halves of the head back together. To do this, the UVs must be flipped so the edges align properly. With the right-side UVs still selected, choose the icon to flip the UVs in the V direction. You can also choose Polygons ➤ Flip.

ICON HELP

Remember that if you hover over an icon with the mouse, the name of the tool will appear in the help line at the lower left of the screen. This is useful when the icon for the tool is less than intuitive.

10. Select the edges along the top of the head. Start at one edge in front of the nose, and go all the way back to the neck. Use Figure 11.25 for reference.

FIGURE 11.25
Select edges to be sewn together.

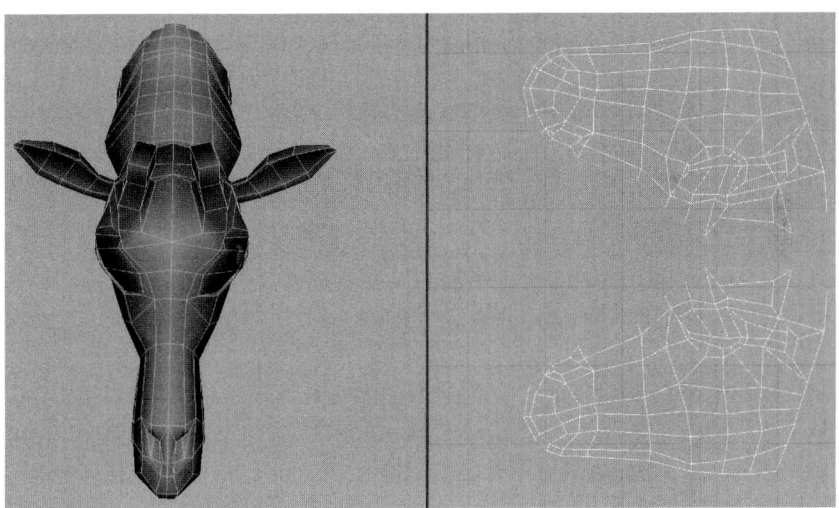

11. Choose Move And Sew. The two halves of the head come together.

12. Select the shell, and use the Smooth tool to unfold the UVs. The UVs should look like Figure 11.26 when finished.

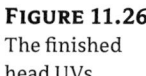

FIGURE 11.26
The finished
head UVs

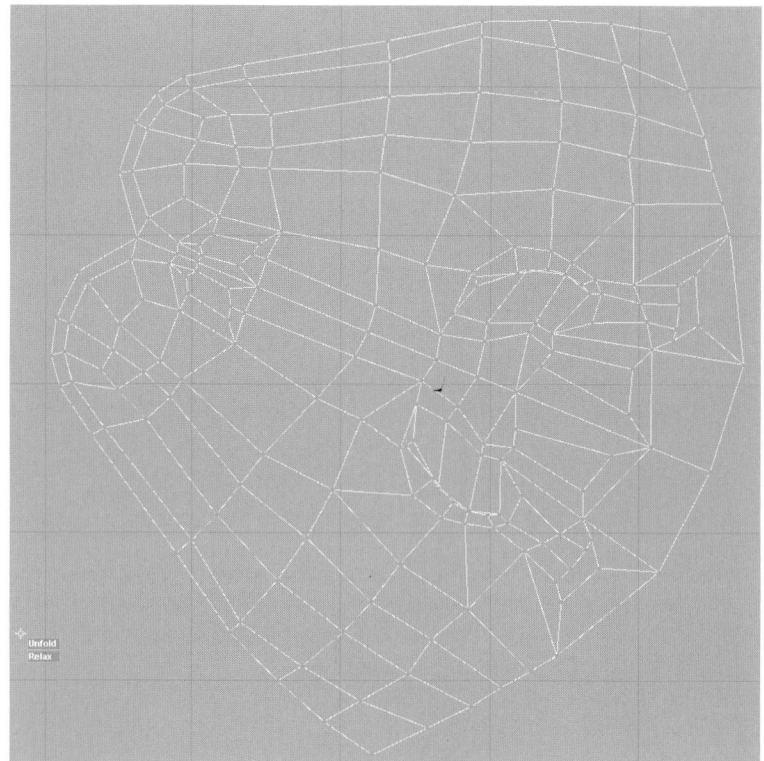

13. Do the rest of the UVs in the same way.

14. Save the scene as **giraffeUV_v06.ma**.

To see a version of the scene to this point, open the giraffeUV_v06.ma scene from the chapter11\scenes directory on the DVD.

More UV Tools

Often, UVs don't go where you want them to, leading to overlap and warping issues. Other situations call for the UVs to match existing ones or be placed precisely according to production specifications. Maya comes with several tools to assist in manipulating UVs manually.

The first is the UV Lattice tool. It creates a 2D structure with a definable set of control points, allowing you to make broad changes to groups of UVs. Figure 11.27 shows an example. You can move the lattice by its points or move an edge. It is located under the Tools menu in the UV Texture Editor.

Next is the UV Smudge tool. It works with selected UVs, making it a great choice for moving any that are overlapping. It has a similar effect as the UV Lattice tool; however, it uses a brush instead of handles. You can scale the brush size by holding the **b** key and dragging the mouse. It is also located under the Tools menu in the UV Texture Editor. Figure 11.28 shows the tool in action.

FIGURE 11.27
You can use the UV Lattice tool to make broad changes to groups of UVs.

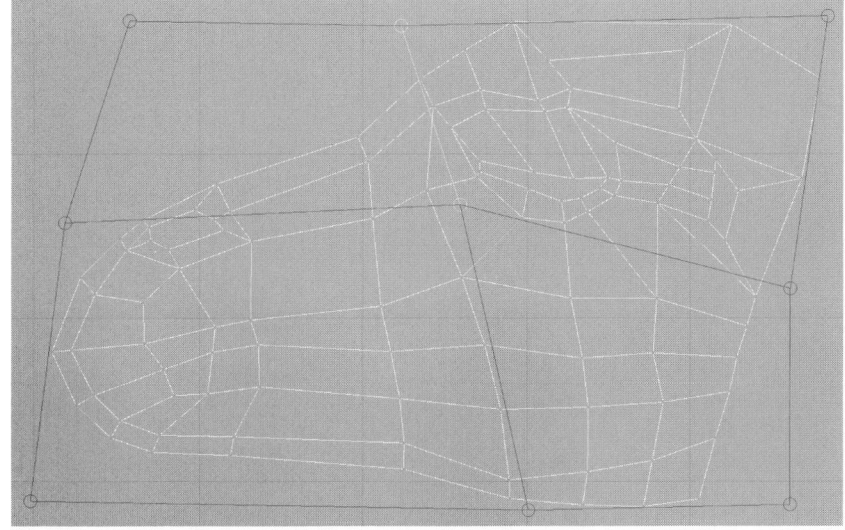

FIGURE 11.28
The UV Smudge tool moves selected UVs with a brush.

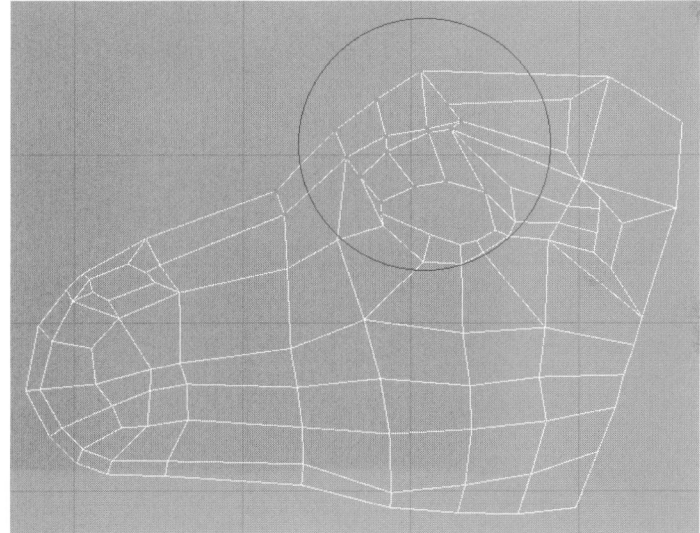

Another great tool is Automatic Mapping. It is another projection method for mapping UVs. You can use it to quickly generate UVs for hard-to-reach areas, such as the inside of a mouth or ear canal. It is also great for handling small parts like teeth. Automatic mapping typically does not give you good UVs, but it saves a lot that would otherwise be spent selecting faces and moving manipulators. Automatic mapping is located in the main Polygons interface under Create UVs.

Arranging UV Shells

Depending on your project or model, its purpose will dictate how you arrange your UV shells. If you are using your model in a game, your UVs should be condensed to the fewest maps possible. The goal is to put as many of the UV shells onto a single material. Most games support multiple maps and therefore allow you to split up groups of UV shells onto multiple materials. Figure 11.29 shows the arrangement of UVs for the giraffe if it was going to use a single map in a game environment.

FIGURE 11.29
The UV shells are arranged into the 0 to 1 texture space in preparation for a game environment.

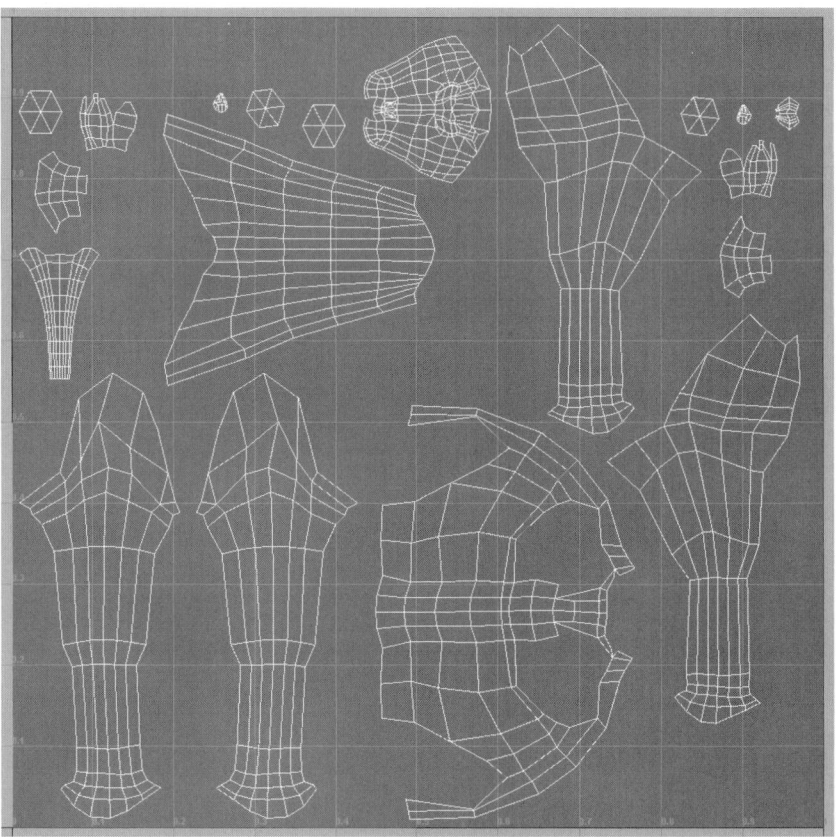

For film and other projects without real-time game restrictions, you can arrange your UVs to maximize texture space. This means a single UV shell can fill all the 0 to 1 texture space if needed. Textures are automatically repeated inside the UV Texture Editor; therefore, your UVs can be positioned outside the normalized texture space (see Figure 11.30). This makes viewing and modifying UVs easier. They can also sit on top of one another, as long as they are assigned to separate materials.

FIGURE 11.30
The UV groups are spread out and assigned to multiple materials to utilize more texture space.

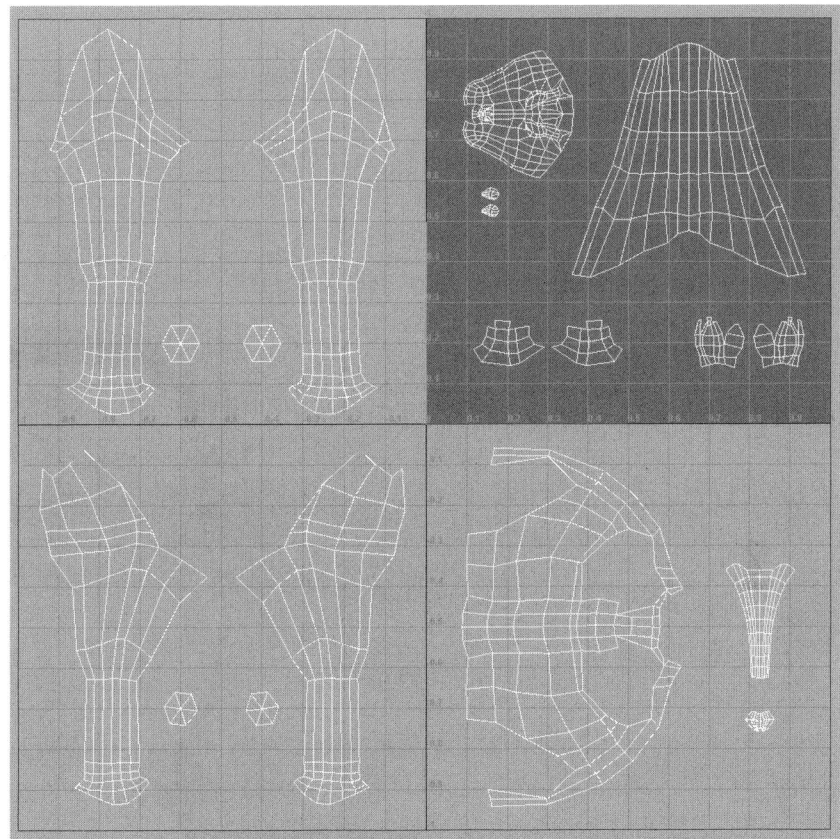

You can generate a snapshot of the UVs that will serve as a guide for painting the textures in Photoshop.

1. In the UV Texture Editor window, choose Polygons ➢ UV Snapshot.

2. In the options, use the Browse button to choose the directory where you want to save the file.

3. Set the size of the texture file. In this case, choose 2048.

    You can resize the document in Photoshop if you decide you need higher or lower resolution for the texture. Since this is a single-head model that will be seen close up, you may eventually want to increase the resolution as high as 4096. It's usually best to keep these dimensions the same size in X and Y so the texture is square.

4. Keep Color Value white so the UV texture guide appears as white lines on a dark background.

    In Photoshop, you can set the UV texture snapshot on a separate layer above all the other layers and set the blend mode to Screen so that the UV texture lines appear on top of the painted textures.

5. Set the image format to `.tiff`, and click OK to generate the snapshot.

6. You can also set the UV range to grab an area other than the 0 to 1 texture space. For instance, to get a snapshot of the hind leg UVs in the lower-left corner, you would use a -1.0 for the U and V (see Figure 11.31).

7. Open the snapshot in Photoshop or your favorite paint program, and use the UVs as a guide for painting the textures.

To see a finished version of the head with complete UV maps, open the `giraffeUV_v07.ma` file from the `chapter11\scenes` folder on the DVD.

FIGURE 11.31
The options for taking a UV snapshot

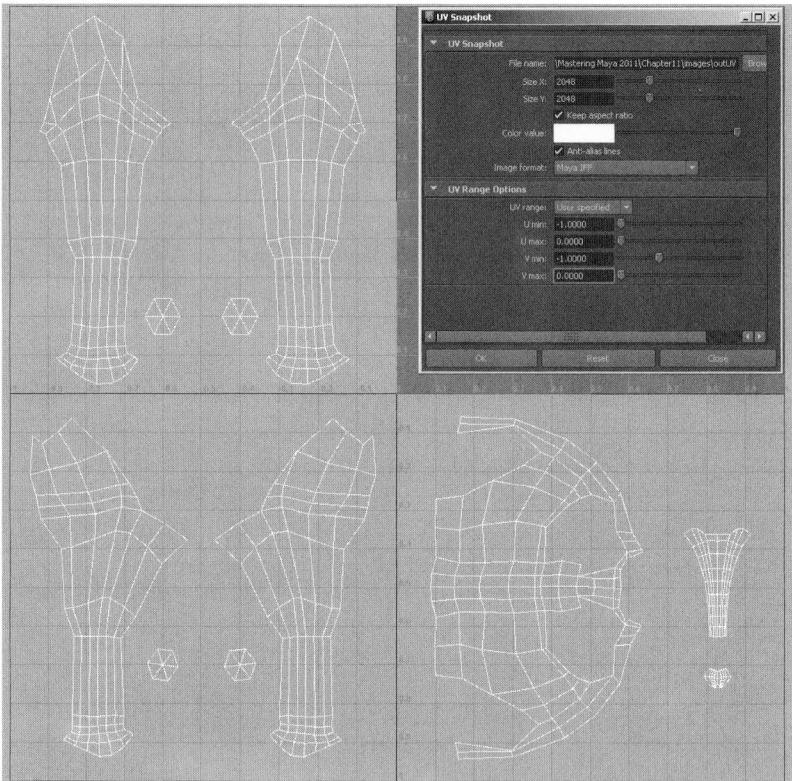

Additional UV Mapping Considerations

Proper UV mapping is essential for creating and applying painted textures to your polygon and subdivision surface models. However, UV mapping can also affect how your models work with other aspects of Maya. Since displacement maps are essentially textures that deform geometry, it's important that UV coordinates are properly created in order for the displacements to deform the geometry properly.

2D procedural nodes, such as ramps, fractals, and (obviously) checker patterns, are affected by UV mapping. When you apply a fractal to a polygon model, the seams between UV coordinates can be very obvious if the UVs are not carefully mapped. Likewise, paint effects, hair, skin weighting, and fur all rely on UV coordinates to function properly.

UVs can also be animated using keyframes. You can use this to create some interesting effects, especially in games where it may be more efficient to create a repeating animated loop of UV texture coordinates than to create an animated sequence of images. To animate UVs, select the UVs in the UV Texture Editor, press the **s** hot key to create a keyframe, change their positions, and set another keyframe by pressing the **s** hot key again. You can refine the animation using the Graph Editor.

Transferring UVs

UVs can be transferred from one object to another. This is usually done between two versions of the same object and can be useful as a tool for quickly creating UVs on a complex object. The workflow might go something like this:

1. Create a duplicate of a complex object.

2. Smooth the duplicate using an operation such as Average Vertices or the sculpting brush.

3. Generate UV coordinates for the smoothed version using any combination of methods. Smoothing out the detail makes applying UV coordinates a little easier.

4. Select the smoothed version; then Shift+click the original, and choose Mesh ➤ Transfer Attributes ➤ Options.

5. Set the options so the UVs are copied from the smoothed version to the original.

Multiple UV Sets

An object can actually have more than one version of the UV coordinates. These are known as *UV sets*. For instance, for a character's head you may use one UV set to control how color information is applied to the face and another set to control how the hair or fur is applied to the head. To create multiple sets, you can use the UV Set Editor (Create UVs ➤ UV Set Editor). You can copy UVs from one set to another and link textures to different sets using the Relationship Editor (Window ➤ Relationship Editors ➤ UV Linking).

Optimizing Textures

Maya offers an optimized format that is used at render time. Textures using standard image file formats such as `.tif` are loaded into memory before rendering begins, which can slow down the rendering and lead to instability. Maya can convert the file texture to an optimized, uncompressed, OpenEXR format that allows Maya/mental ray to load the texture as needed during render, which not only increases stability but also allows for the use of much larger textures.

The original file textures, such as the `.tif`, are still used in the scene and stored in the `sourceimages` directory be referenced when you work in the scene. The conversion takes place automatically, and the converted files are stored in the `sourceimages/cache` directory by default. When you render the scene, you'll see your file textures listed there with the `.map` extension. In versions of Maya prior to 2008, you had to convert file texture images to the `.map` format manually using the `imf_copy` utility.

To enable this feature, follow these steps:

1. Choose Window ➤ Settings/Preferences ➤ Preferences.

2. In the Rendering section, select Use Optimized Textures (Auto-conversion), as shown in Figure 11.32.

FIGURE 11.32
Enable the Use
Optimized Tex-
tures feature in
the Preferences
window.

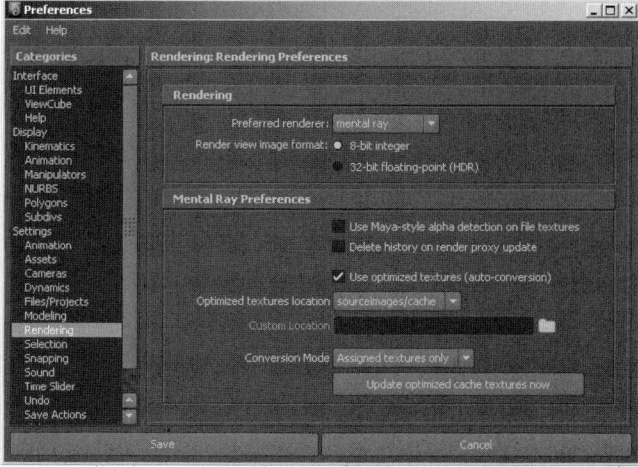

3. You can choose to use the default source images/cache directory for the current project or specify a custom location. If you are rendering on a network, make sure that all render nodes on the farm can see the directory where you store the optimized file.

4. You can also choose to convert all textures or just the ones that have been assigned to shaders. To update the files, click the Update Optimize Cache Textures Now button. The files should update automatically at render time, but just in case they don't for some reason, you can use this button to force a refresh.

Bump and Normal Mapping

Bump maps, normal maps, and displacement maps are three ways to add surface detail to a model using textures. In this section, you'll learn about bump and normal maps. A discussion concerning displacement maps appears later in the chapter.

Bump maps and normal maps are similar in that they both create the impression of surface detail by using color information, stored in a 2D texture map, to alter the surface normal of an object. When the light in a scene hits the surface of an object, the color values in the texture tell the rendering engine to alter the surface normal so the light creates a highlight or shading/shadowing. The surface geometry itself is not changed; however, the altered normal makes it look as though the geometry has more detail than it actually does. This saves the modeler the trouble of sculpting every single wrinkle, fold, bump, screw, or scratch into a model, as well as keeps the geometry resolution of the model down to a level the computer's processor can handle.

Bump and normal maps do not actually alter the surface geometry. This means that the part of the surface that faces the camera will appear as though it has bumps and depressions, but as the surface of the geometry turns away from the camera, it becomes apparent that the silhouette of the geometry has not actually been changed by the bump or normal map. Figure 11.33 demonstrates this principle.

FIGURE 11.33
This sphere has a noise texture applied as a bump map. It looks lumpy from the front, but the silhouette of the sphere is not altered by the bump map.

Bump Maps

Bump maps are simply grayscale textures, usually painted in a 2D paint program such as Photoshop. Bump maps are best used for fine detail, such as tiny wrinkles, pores, small rivets, scratches, small dents, wood grain, and so on. When texturing highly detailed characters, you can best use bump maps with displacement maps.

Any texture can be used as a bump map, including the 2D and 3D procedural textures such as Fractal, Ramp, Grid, Crater, Water, Brownian, and so on. When you place a texture in the Bump Mapping channel of a standard Maya shader, a connection is made between the outAlpha attribute on the texture and the Bump value of the shader. These are especially useful since a lot of textures in the real world have patterns: burlap, concrete, and so on.

HIGH-QUALITY RENDER PREVIEW

To preview the bump map on the model in the perspective view, select High Quality Rendering from the Renderer menu in the camera view, as shown here, and press **6** on the keyboard to switch to shaded view. If your graphics card supports it, you should see the bump applied to the model. Note that the bump in the perspective view is not quite as strong as in the rendered version.

Normal Maps

A bump map displaces a surface normal either up or down (relative to the surface normal) based on the value of the texture. Normal maps, on the other hand, replace the normal direction with a vector stored in the RGB colors of the map. In other words, rather than pulling out a bump or pushing in a depression, the colors of the normal map change the X, Y, Z of the normal based on the RGB color of the map (see Figure 11.34).

When viewed as a 2D texture in a paint program, normal maps have a psychedelic rainbow color. These colors tell Maya how the normal on the surface of the geometry should be bent at render time. It's very difficult for an artist to paint a normal map because the RGB values are not intuitively applied.

FIGURE 11.34
The diagram shows how bump maps and normal maps affect the surface normals of a polygon in different ways.

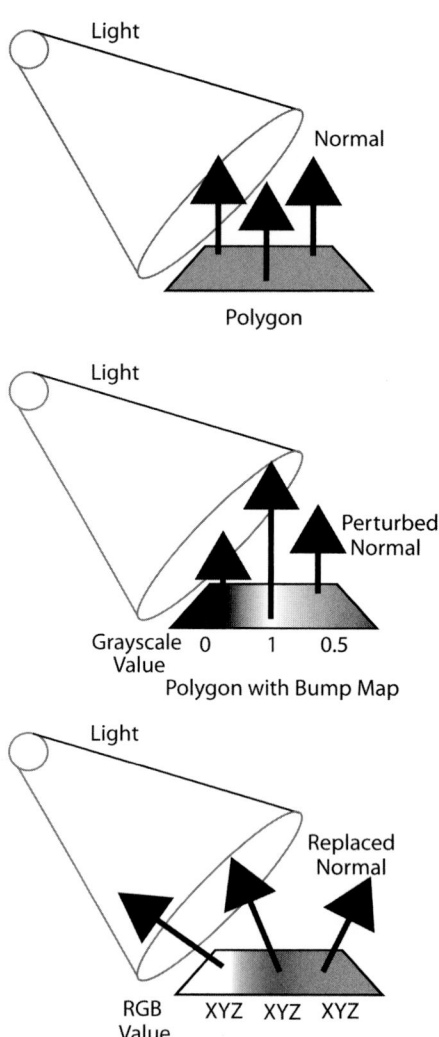

There are two types of normal maps, object space and tangent space:

Object space maps   These are used for nondeforming objects, such as walls, spaceships, trash cans, and the like. They are calculated based on the local object space of the object. *Up* in object space means toward the top of the object. If the object is rotated upside down in world space, the top is still the top—so a robot's head is still the top of the object in object space even if it's hanging upside down.

Tangent space maps   These are used for deforming objects, such as characters. Tangent space maps record the normal's vector relative to the object's surface. In tangent space, *up* means up away from the surface of the object. Tangent space maps appear more blue and purple since the direction in which the normal is being bent is always relative to the surface along the tangent space z-axis. The z-axis corresponds with the blue channel (XYZ = RGB). Object space maps, on the other hand, have more variation in color.

In practice, most artists use tangent space maps for everything. In fact, prior to Maya 2008, tangent space maps were the only type of normal maps that Maya supported. Tangent space maps actually work well for both deforming and nondeforming objects.

The most common way to create a normal map is to use a high-resolution, detailed version of the model as the source of the normal map and a low-resolution version of the model as the target for the map. The difference between the two surfaces is recorded in the colors of the map, which is then used to alter the appearance of the low-resolution model. This is a typical process when creating models for games where low-resolution models are required by the real-time rendering engine but the audience demands realistically detailed objects.

Creating Normal Maps

In this exercise, you'll create a normal map for the giraffe. A high-resolution version of the model will be used as the source of the map. To create a normal map in Maya, you'll use the Transfer Maps tool. This tool can be used to create a number of different texture map types, including normal maps.

1. Open the giraffeTransferMaps_v01.ma file from the chapter11\scenes folder of the DVD.

2. In the Display Layer panel, you'll see two layers: one labeled LORES, the other HIRES. Turn off the LORES layer, and turn on the HIRES layer. You'll see a higher-resolution detailed version of the giraffe, as shown in Figure 11.35.

3. Turn off the HIRES layer. The geometry does not need to be visible in order to extract maps, so if the high-resolution geometry is slowing down your computer, you can hide it.

4. Right-click the LORES layer, and choose Select Objects.

5. Under the Rendering menu set, choose Lighting/Shading ➢ Transfer Maps to open the Transfer Maps interface (see Figure 11.36).

6. Expand the Target Meshes rollout. The loresGiraffe object is listed since it was selected when you opened the interface. If it does not appear, select it and click the Add Selected button. No other objects should be listed; if they are, select them in the list, and click the Remove Selected button.

FIGURE 11.35
The high-resolution
giraffe

FIGURE 11.36
The Transfer
Maps interface

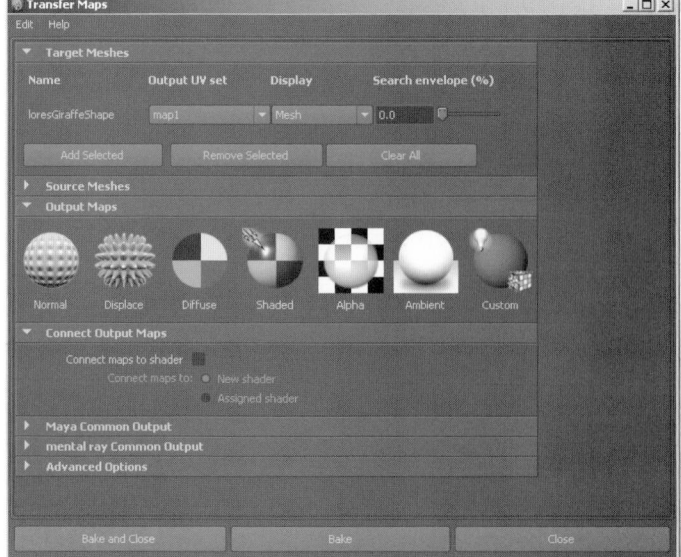

7. Expand the Source Meshes rollout, right-click the HIRES layer, and choose Select Objects.

8. Click the Add Selected button to add it to the list.

9. Expand the Output Maps section; you'll see icons representing all the different types of maps that can be created.

10. Click the Normal button to add *normal map* to the list. If other types of maps are listed, click the Remove Map button in the section for the map you want to remove.

11. Click the folder next to the Normal Map field, and set the location and filename for the location of the map that will be created.

12. Choose the `sourceimages` directory of the current project, and name the file `giraffeHead_Nrml`.

    There are a number of file format options to choose from. The two best choices are Maya IFF and EXR. Both are 32-bit formats that will ensure a detailed smooth map.

13. Choose EXR; this way you can open the map in Photoshop (CS1 and higher) for viewing if you need to. If the file format in the name of the file is something other than `.exr`, it will be automatically updated.

OPEN EXR LOADER PLUG-IN

When using the EXR format in Maya, you'll need to make sure the OpenEXRLoader plug-in is currently loaded; otherwise, you'll get an error when you try to connect the file to a shader. Choose Window ➤ Settings And Plug-ins ➤ Plug-in Manager. In the list of plug-ins, make sure `OpenEXRLoader.mll` is currently selected.

---

14. The Include Materials check box is extremely useful if you want to include a bump map as part of the normal map. For now, deselect it since there is no bump map applied to the high-resolution mesh material.

    However, make a note of this option—you can add more detail to your normal map, such as pores and fine wrinkles, by applying a bump texture to the shader for the high-resolution mesh object and then activating this option when using the Transfer Maps tool.

BAKING BUMP MAPS

When baking a bump map into the normal map using the Include Materials option, the Bump Depth setting on the shader of the source mesh will determine the intensity of the bump as it's baked into the normal map. If you need to change this later, you'll need to adjust Bump Depth on the source mesh and rebake the normal map.

---

15. Set Map Space to Tangent Space. You should always use tangent space maps for characters. Actually, as stated before, you can use them for any type of object.

16. The Use Maya Common Settings check box makes the tool use the settings specified in the Maya Common Output. If this is deselected, sliders will appear that will allow you to set the size of the map in this section. For now, keep this box selected.

17. In the Connect Output Maps settings, you can connect the map to a shader automatically. Deselect the Connect Maps To Shader option for now.

Later you'll learn how to make the connection manually. Once you understand how the connection is made, you can use the Connect Maps To Shader option in the future to make things more convenient.

18. In the Maya Common Output settings, enter the following:

   A. Set the size of the map to **2048** in width and height.

   B. Set Transfer In to Object Space, and set Sampling Quality to High.

   C. Set Filter Size to **3**.

   D. Set Filter Type to Gaussian.

   Leave Fill Texture Seams at 1 and the remaining three check boxes (Ignore Mirrored Faces, Flip U, and Flip V) deselected. Select Bake and Close to complete the tool. The settings are shown in Figure 11.37.

FIGURE 11.37
The transfer map's options

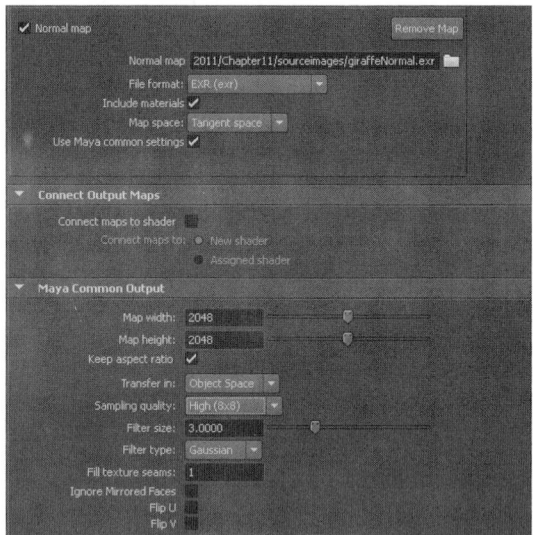

Sometimes maps do not transfer properly. Errors usually look like solid pools of color. Often this is caused by the geometry not matching properly. To fix this, you can adjust the search envelope Maya uses to extract the differences between the models. The search envelope specifies the volume of space that Maya uses to search when creating the transfer map. Maya compares the target geometry (the low-resolution map) with the source geometry (the high-resolution map) and records the difference between the two as color values in the normal map. The search envelope sets the limits of the distance Maya will search when creating the map. The envelope itself is a duplicate of the target geometry that's offset from the original. The offset distance is specified by the Search Envelope slider in the Target Meshes section of the Transfer Maps tool. What's more, you can edit the Target Mesh geometry itself to improve the results of the final map.

USE LOW-QUALITY SETTINGS WHEN TESTING

Normal maps can take a while to calculate, so it's a good idea to create a few test maps at lower quality and then raise the quality settings once you're happy that the map is free of errors.

You can bake out the rest of the UV shells by selecting each group and swapping their placement into the 0 to 1 texture space. Each group of shells is centered so you can snap the group to 0.5 and 0.5. Extending the grid helps keep things situated (see Figure 11.38).

FIGURE 11.38
Extend the grid to keep the UV shell groups organized.

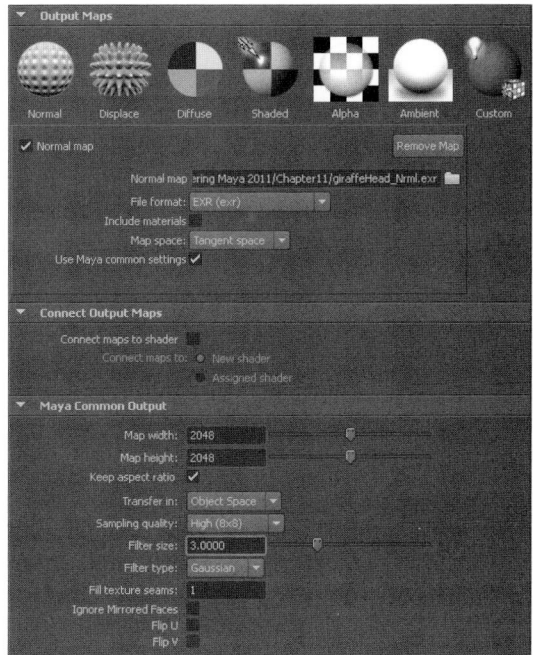

Some third-party applications like Mudbox read outside the 0 to 1 texture space and can transfer all the maps in one operation, instead of having to move the UV shell groups.

When the maps are finished, you can close the scene without saving, since no adjustments were made. The next exercise takes you through the process of applying the normal maps.

The Transfer In option has three choices: World Space, Object Space, and UV Space. These specify how the map will be calculated and transferred from the high-resolution version to the low-resolution version. If the models were different sizes, then the World Space option would be appropriate, and the models would need to be directly on top of each other. The objects used in this tutorial are the same size and very similar except for their resolutions and level of detail, so the Object Space option is more appropriate. The UV Space option works best for objects of fairly similar but not exactly the same shape, such as a female human character and a male human character.

Applying Normal Maps

Normal maps are applied to an object's shader in the Bump channel, and they can be viewed in the perspective window. In this section, you'll see how the map looks when it's applied to the model as well as a few suggestions for fixing problems.

1. Open the `giraffeUV_v07.ma` file from the `chapter11\scenes` folder of the DVD.

2. Open the Hypershade window (Window ≻ Rendering Editors ≻ Hypershade).

3. Select the giraffe Head_Mat shader, and open its Attribute Editor.

4. Click the checkered box next to the Bump Mapping channel, and choose a file from the Create Render Node pop-up.

5. When you add the file node, the Attribute Editor will open to the bump2D node. Set the Use As option to Tangent Space Normals. This tells Maya the texture you're applying is a normal map and not a bump map. You can leave the Bump Depth at 1; it has no effect on the strength of the normal map.

6. Switch to the file1 node, and click the folder next to the Image Name field.

7. Browse your computer's file directory, and find the `giraffeHead_Nrml.exr` file; it should be in the `sourceimages` directory (if you get an error when loading the image, make sure the openEXRLoader plug-in is selected in the preferences).

   Once the file is loaded, you should see a preview in the texture sample icon. The texture should appear mostly blue and purple. If it is completely flat blue, then there was an error during the creation process—most likely the source mesh was not selected in the Transfer Maps options, so you'll need to remake the map.

8. In the perspective view, choose High Quality Rendering from the Renderer menu at the top of the panel. After a few seconds, you should see a preview of the normal map in the perspective view. (Make sure you have Texture Shaded activated; press the **6** key to switch to this mode.)

   The normal map should make the low-resolution model look very similar to the high-resolution model. You can see in the silhouette of the geometry that the blockiness of the profile indicates that geometry is still low resolution, but those areas facing the camera look highly detailed. This workflow is very popular when creating models for games. The models end up looking much more realistic and detailed without taxing the processor of the game console.

9. Apply the rest of the maps in the same manner. Figure 11.39 shows the giraffe with all of its normal maps applied.

10. Inspect the model for errors in the texture.

    Most likely you'll find some errors around the lips, ears, and eyes. If large portions of the model look wrong, you'll need to try creating the map again. Sometimes just editing the geometry of the search envelope can fix the errors when you regenerate the map. Other times you may need to change the actual generation settings such as the Search Method and Max Search Depth values in the Advanced settings.

FIGURE 11.39
The low-resolution
model with all of
its normal maps.

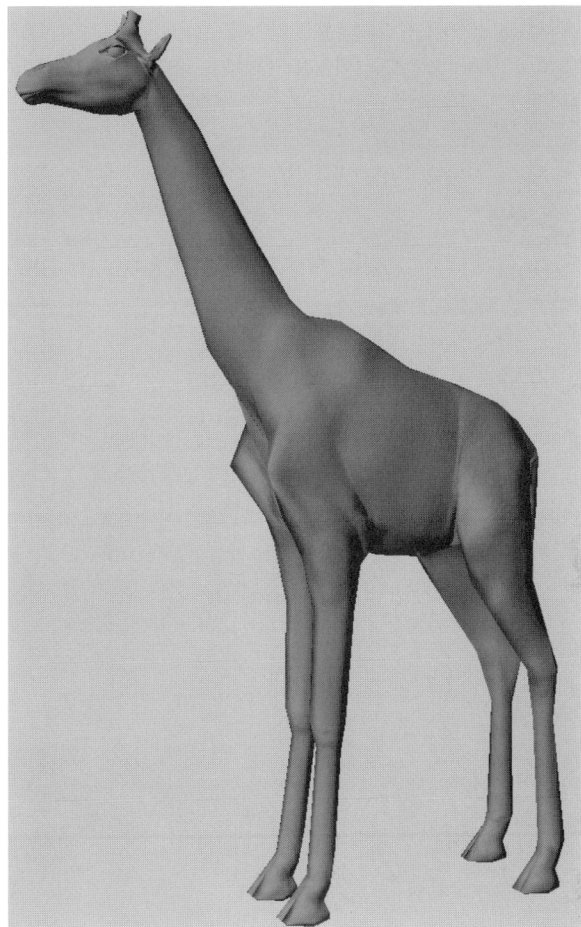

Normal maps are difficult but not impossible to edit in a 2D paint program such as Photoshop. If the normal map has just a few small glitches, you can open them in Photoshop and paint each color channel (Red, Green, and Blue) separately to clean up the maps. This can be faster than trying to regenerate a whole new map just to fix a tiny spot.

For a completed version of the scene, open the giraffeNormalMaps_v01.ma file from the chapter11\scenes folder on the DVD.

Displacement Mapping

Displacement maps are like bump maps in that they use a grayscale texture to add detail to a model. However, rather than just perturb the normal of the surface, displacement maps actually alter the geometry at render time. Unlike normal and bump maps, the silhouette of the geometry reflects the detail in the map. Displacement maps can be used with NURBS, polygon, and subdivision surfaces and can be rendered in both mental ray and Maya Software. The best results are usually achieved by rendering displacement maps on a polygon surface in mental ray using mental ray's Approximation Editor to subdivide the surface appropriately during render.

VIEWING DISPLACEMENTS

Displacement maps can be viewed only in a software render; they can't be previewed in the perspective window.

Displacement maps are tricky to use and require some practice to master; however, the results are often worth the time invested. Recent advances in digital sculpting programs such as ZBrush and Mudbox have enabled modelers to bring an unprecedented amount of realism and detail to digital characters. The detail created in these high-density meshes is often brought into Maya in the form of displacement maps (and normal maps as well).

In addition to aiding in creating detail on creatures, displacement maps have a wide variety of creative applications and innovations. You can use animated displacements to simulate rolling waves on an ocean surface, fissures opening in the earth, or veins crawling beneath the skin. In this section, you will apply displacement maps to the giraffe.

Converting Displacement to Polygons

If you decide you want actual geometry to be created from the displacement, you can convert the displacement to a polygon object. This might be helpful as a stand-in object if you need to position objects in the scene near the displaced plane or if you want to model terrain using a procedural texture.

1. Select the plane, and choose Modify ➤ Convert ➤ Displacement To Polygons. There are no options for this action. A second object will be created based on the original displaced plane. Any animation of the texture will not be reflected in the converted object; it derives its displacement from the current state of the displacing texture.

2. To increase the resolution of the converted object, increase the subdivisions in Height and Width on the original plane. The conversion will take longer to calculate, and the resulting geometry will be denser.

Displacement Maps for Characters

Using displacement maps to add detail to characters is becoming increasingly common. This allows a low-resolution version of the model to be rigged and animated and then converted into a highly detailed mesh at render time. The end result can be quite spectacular. The render time involved, however, makes this workflow usable only for film and television; game engines are beginning to use displacements in real time but in a very limited capacity.

Since a displacement map is a grayscale texture, it can be painted much like a bump map. A displacement map should be used for larger details that need to be seen in the silhouette of the geometry, such as large folds and wrinkles in the flesh, bumps on the nose, and large veins. Smaller details, such as pores, should be reserved for bump or normal maps that can be used in conjunction with displacement maps. Furthermore, with characters and complex objects, the geometry to be displaced should be fairly close in shape to the displaced version and have just enough subdivisions to allow for the additional detail.

Maya's Transfer Maps tool also allows for the creation of displacement maps. Generating a workable displacement map using this tool takes a little more work than if you used a third-party application, and it generally falls short of their precision. Through trial and error, you need to establish the proper displacement height. Second, the low-resolution geometry needs to be smoothed to avoid low-resolution shading (see Figure 11.40). In addition, do not use the `.exr` format to transfer the maps. The best format to use for transferring displacement maps is Maya's native `.iff` format.

The only difference between the settings in transferring normal maps and displacements is the Maximum Value attribute. This controls the range of values the displacement is gauged on. With the giraffe, a smaller value increases the contrast between low and high areas (see Figure 11.41).

FIGURE 11.40
This map was transferred without first smoothing the surface on the low-polygon version.

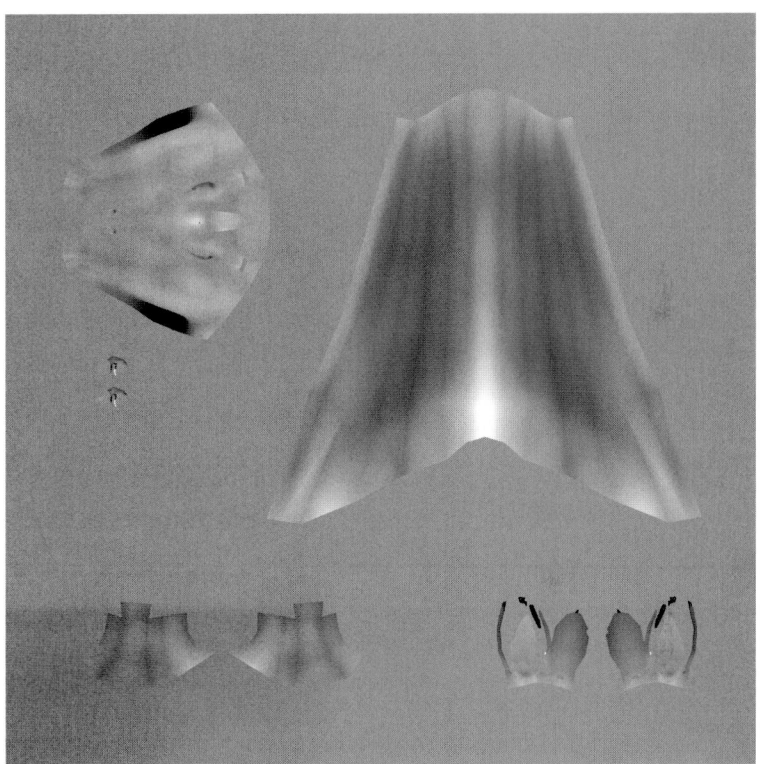

FIGURE 11.41
The options used for transferring displacement

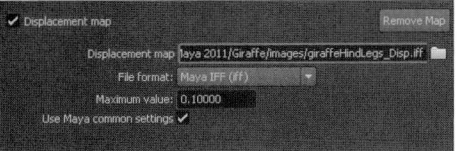

The best possible way to generate a displacement map for a character or creature is to use a digital sculpting program such as ZBrush or Mudbox. Although it involves learning another application, the results are excellent. This is becoming the workflow of choice for many major studios. When generating maps in a third-party application, it's always best to create 32-bit floating-point maps. This will ensure that the displacement is smooth and free of the stair-stepping artifacts that can appear in 16-bit maps. In this exercise, mental ray's Approximation Editor is used to tessellate the geometry of the giraffe's hind legs.

1. Open the `giraffeDisp_v01.ma` scene from the `chapter11\scenes` folder on the DVD.

   The giraffe has all of its UV texture coordinates set for applying the displacement maps. It is the same file used in applying normal maps except the materials have been changed to Blinns.

2. Select the giraffe, and create an approximation node. Choose Window ➤ Rendering Editors ➤ mental ray ➤ Approximation Editor (if mental ray does not appear in the list, you'll need to load the `Mayatomr.mll` plug-in using the Plug-in Manager).

3. In the Approximation Editor, click the Create button in the Subdivisions (Polygon And Subd. Surfaces) section. You do not need to create a displacement approximation node; the subdivision approximation provides enough geometry for displacement and smoothes the surface.

4. In the Attribute Editor for the mentalRaySubdivApprox1 node, do the following:

   A. Change the Approx Method set to Length/Distance/Angle.

   B. Set Max Subdivisions to **3**.

   C. Set the Length to **0.01**.

   This subdivides the model so the detail created by the displacement texture is more refined. Higher values allow more of the detail in the map to come through but also add more triangles. The Length/Distance/Angle efficiently adds triangles where they are needed the most. Figure 11.42 shows the settings.

FIGURE 11.42
The settings used for the subdivision approximation node

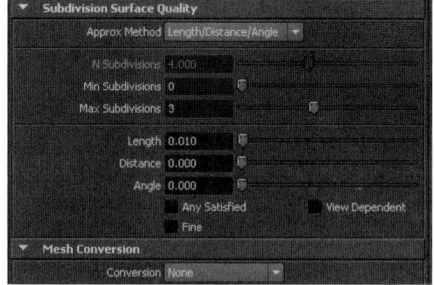

5. Set the renderer to mental ray. Create a test render of the giraffe's hind legs. It should look nice and smooth (see Figure 11.43).

6. In the Hypershade, select giraffeHindLegs_Mat, and choose Graph ➤ Input And Output Connections, or click its icon.

7. Open Blinn2SG in the Attribute Editor.

8. Click the checkered box next to Displacement Mat.

FIGURE 11.43
A close-up of the giraffe's hind legs rendered with a subdivision approximation node.

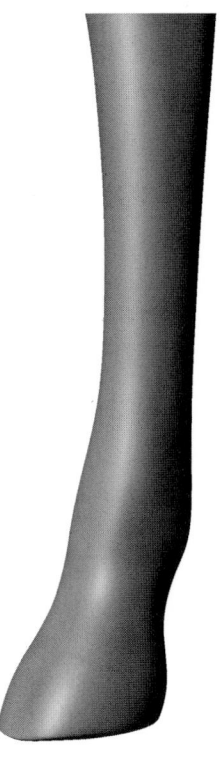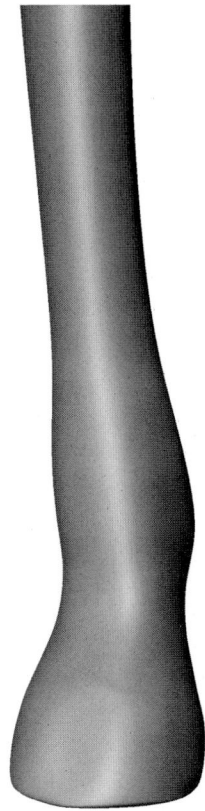

9. Choose File from the Create Render Node pop-up. An empty file node and connected Displacement node shows up in the Hypershade.

10. Open the new file node, and name it **giraffeHindLegsDisp_Text**.

11. Click the folder next to the Image Name field, and use the computer's browser to locate the giraffeHindLegs_Disp.exr file from the sourceimages directory in the chapter11\ scenes folder on the DVD.

12. Expand the Color Balance section of the giraffeHindLegsDispFile node, and set Alpha Gain to **0.5**.

13. Turn on Alpha Is Luminance, and create a test render. The giraffe should look nice and detailed (see Figure 11.44).

To see a finished version of the giraffe with all of its displacement maps connected, open the giraffeDisplace_v02.ma file from the chapter11\scenes folder on the DVD.

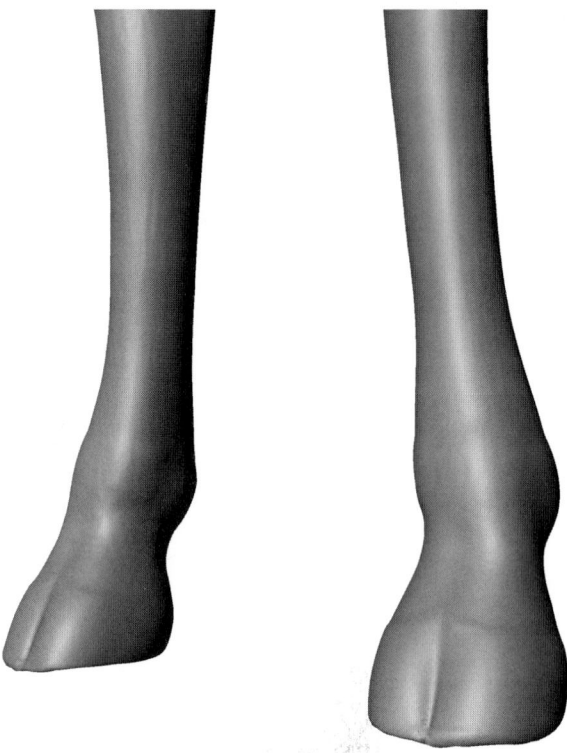

FIGURE 11.44
The displacement map adds very realistic detail to the rendered character.

ZBRUSH DISPLACEMENT MAPS

By default, textures created in ZBrush are upside down when imported into Maya and therefore must be flipped. Because ZBrush interprets dark and light values in a different way than Maya, you'll need to make sure that the value for the texture's Alpha Offset is -0.5 times the Alpha Gain setting. This ensures that dark values on the displacement map push inward and lighter areas push outward.

If your object looks bloated or distorted, double-check the Alpha Gain and Alpha Offset settings for the file texture used for the displacement, or check to see whether Alpha Is Luminance has not been selected.

Combined Displacement and Bump Maps

To add more detail to the giraffe, you can add a bump map to the already displaced geometry. This is useful for fine detail too small to be created with geometry. The next exercise takes you through the process.

1. Open the `giraffeDisplace_v02.ma` scene from the `chapter11\scenes` folder on the DVD. All the giraffe's displacement maps have been added.

2. Open giraffeHindLegs_Mat in the Attribute Editor.

3. Add a file node to the Bump Mapping channel by clicking the checkered box.

4. Set the Bump2d1 Use As option to Bump Map. Set Bump Depth to **0.02**.

5. Rename the connected file node giraffeHindLegs_Bump. Use the Image Name field to open the File Browser dialog box. Add the `giraffeHindLegs_Bump.iff` file from the `sourceimages` directory in the `chapter11\scenes` folder on the DVD.

6. For testing purposes, disconnect any color maps attached to the material. Create a test render. Figure 11.45 shows the results.

FIGURE 11.45
A close-up of the giraffe's hind legs rendered with displacement and bump mapping

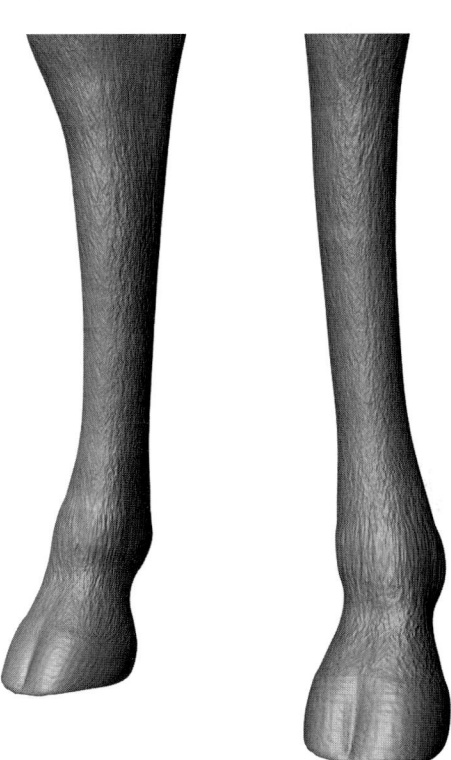

To see a completed version of the model with displacement and bumps, open the `giraffeDisplace_v03.ma` scene from the `chapter11\scenes` folder on the DVD. Figure 11.46 shows a rendered version.

FILTER

Textures have an attribute called Filter, which is found in the Special Effects rollout in the file texture node. The Filter is a blur that Maya adds to the texture to reduce artifacts in the render. Oftentimes this blur can reduce detail that is carefully painted into the map or can even create new artifacts. If you find your texture maps are not rendering correctly, try setting both the Filter and Filter Offset sliders to 0.01 as a possible solution. Setting the value to 0 may cause artifacts in some situations.

FIGURE 11.46
The displacement
and bump maps
are used together
to create realistic
detail in the model.

Subsurface Scattering

Subsurface scattering refers to the phenomenon of light rays bouncing around just beneath the surface of a material before being reflected back into the environment. It's the translucent quality seen in objects such as jade, candle wax, and human skin (actually almost every material except metal has some amount of subsurface scattering). Subsurface scattering adds an amazing level of realism to CG objects and characters. It takes practice to master, but the results are worth it.

Fast, Simple Skin Shader Setup

In Maya there are several ways to create the look of subsurface scattering ranging from simple to complex. The Translucence, Translucence Depth, and Translucence Focus sliders included on standard Maya shaders offer the simplest way to create translucency. These sliders work fine for an object made of a single material, such as candle wax. Likewise, the Scatter Radius slider and related attributes in the mental ray section of Maya shaders add a quick-and-dirty subsurface quality to simple objects. However, these options fall far short when you're trying to create a complex material such as human skin.

Since Maya 2008, the mental ray simple subsurface scattering shaders have become much easier to set up and use. Many of the connections that needed to be created manually in previous versions of Maya are now set up automatically when you create the shader.

There are several subsurface scattering shaders:

misss_call_shader

misss_fast_shader

misss_fast_shader_x

misss_fast_shader_x_passes

misss_fast_simple_maya

misss_fast_skin_maya

misss_physical

misss_set_normal

misss_skin_specular

With the exception of misss_physical, these shaders are all similar and use the same basic technique for creating the effect of subsurface scattering. Some of the misss shaders are really combined versions of others. For instance, misss_fast_skin_maya is actually a combination of misss_fast_shader and misss_skin_specular with an extra layer of subsurface scattering. In this chapter, you'll focus on using the misss_fast_skin_maya shader.

MISSS SHADERS

The prefix *misss* stands for Mental Images Subsurface Scattering.

The misss_physical shader is a more complex, physically accurate shader meant to be used with photon casting lights. For complete information on this shader, refer to *mental ray for Maya, 3ds Max, and XSI* by Boaz Livny (Sybex, 2008). This shader also works best for objects that require a deep level of scattering, such as thick candles and marble.

1. Open the giraffeSSS_v01.ma scene from the chapter11\scenes folder on the DVD. You'll see the giraffe with mental ray's Physical Sun and Sky shader applied.

2. Switch to the persp camera, and do a quick test render.

3. Store the image in the render view so you can compare it with the subsurface scattering renders.

   You'll see that the character has a Blinn texture applied along with the skin, bump, and displacement textures used in the previous section. These same file textures (along with a few others) will be plugged into the skin shader (see Figure 11.47).

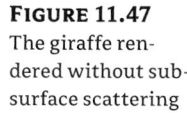

FIGURE 11.47
The giraffe rendered without subsurface scattering

4. Open the Hypershade, and, on the left side, switch to the Create mental ray Nodes section.

5. From the Materials section, create a misss_fast_skin shader. Name the shader **giraffeHeadSSS_Mat**.

6. Right-click giraffeHead_Mat, and choose Select Objects With Material from the marking menu. All the assigned faces are selected.

7. Right-click giraffeHeadSSS_Mat, and choose Assign Material To Selection from the marking menu. The parts of the giraffe assigned to the SSS shader turn a solid color in the perspective view (depending on your graphics card, the color will vary), and that's OK. Maya just can't preview some of the mental ray nodes using hardware rendering.

8. Right-click giraffeHeadSSS_Mat again, and choose Graph Network.

You'll see that Maya has automatically created the necessary light map and texture nodes (misss_fast_Imap_maya and mentalRayTexture1). If you select the mentalrayTexture1 node, you'll see that the File Size Width and File Size Texture attributes are both highlighted in purple, indicating an expression is controlling their values. The expression is tied to the render size automatically, so you don't have to set these as you did in versions of Maya before 2008.

LIGHT MAPS

A light map (lmap) is a special mental ray node used to calculate the influence of light across the surface based on the camera's position in the scene. Light maps are used to emulate the subsurface effect without having to perform physically based calculations. They render quickly and do a pretty good job of faking the subsurface scattering phenomena.

---

9. Select giraffeHeadSSS_Mat, and open its Attribute Editor. At the top you'll see the diffuse layer. This layer controls the basic color of the object, much like the Color and Diffuse settings in a standard shader but with a couple of differences.

   Diffuse Weight controls the overall contribution, or lightness, of the combined diffuse channels. The Overall Color channel is a multiplier for the Diffuse Color channel, so you'll want to put your color textures in the Diffuse Color channel and then modify it using the Overall slider. That said, you can actually do the reverse in some cases; you may want to experiment by putting a color texture map in the Overall Color channel.

10. In the Hypershade, switch to the Textures tab, and find the giraffeHeadDiffuse_Text (`giraffeHead_diffuse.iff`) node. MMB-drag it down to the Attribute Editor on top of the Diffuse Color channel.

    The Overall Color channel is also a good place for dirt or cavity maps. In addition to adding some dirt on the giraffe, it is also being used to break up the consistency of the diffuse color.

11. Add a file node to the Overall color channel. Browse your computer's file directory, and add `giraffeHead_Overall.iff`.

12. Set Diffuse Weight to **0.5**; you'll probably want to adjust this more later.

13. In the Textures area of the Hypershade, find the giraffeHeadBump_Text node (this is the texture used to create the bump texture), and MMB-drag it to the work area.

14. Expand the Bump Shader rollout in the giraffeHeadSSS_Mat, and MMB-drag the giraffeHeadBump_Text (`giraffeHead_Bump.iff`) texture on top of this channel.

15. Select the bump2d node, and set Bump Depth to **0.05**.

16. In the Materials tab of the Hypershade, find the giraffeHead_Disp shader. MMB-drag this shader on top of the shading group labeled misss_fast_skin_maya3SG node, and choose Default. These are the same displacement node, file texture, and settings created earlier in the chapter (see Figure 11.48).

FIGURE 11.48
The shading
network for the
misss_fast_skin
shader has several
file textures con-
nected to it.

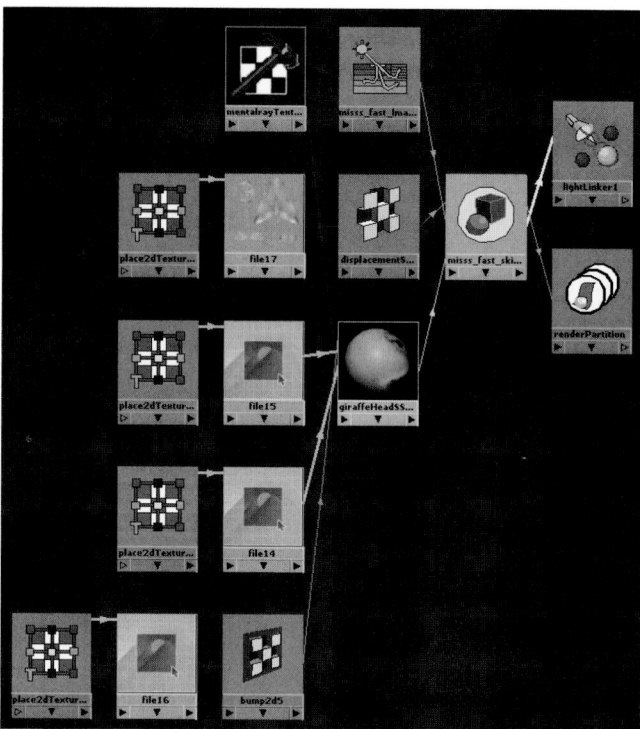

17. The scale of the giraffe is that 1 centimeter is equal to 1 meter. Subsurface scattering is calculated based on meters. Therefore, you must convert the scale of the giraffe. This can be done easily within the shader:

   A. Open the Algorithm Control rollout.

   B. Change Scale Conversion to 100 to multiply 1 centimeter by 100, effectively converting it to meters.

18. Subsurface scattering does not render normally when the Physical Sun and Sky shader is being used. There are two settings that must be changed to get it to render properly:

   A. The first, Screen Composite, is on the SSS shader located in the Algorithm Control rollout below the Scale Conversions. Deselect Screen Composite (see Figure 11.49).

   B. Next, you need to tell the shader to accept indirect lighting. This attribute is located on the misss_fast_lmap node that was automatically generated by Maya when the SSS shader was first created. Select Include Indirect Lighting (see Figure 11.50).

FIGURE 11.49
Deselect Screen
Composite on the
SSS shader.

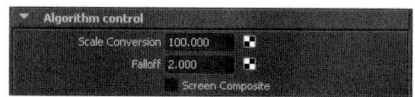

FIGURE 11.50
Select Include Indi-
rect Lighting on
the light map.

19. Create a test render to see how the giraffe looks so far.

The giraffe has a very interesting look, kind of like a plastic doll. Compare the render with the previously stored version; notice how the color texture is not nearly as strong. The subsurface settings need to be tuned to create a more realistic-looking skin.

20. Save your scene.

To see a version of the scene so far, open the giraffeSSS_v02.ma file from the chapter11\ scenes folder on the DVD. Figure 11.51 shows the render.

FIGURE 11.51
At this point, a render of the character looks grainy and plastic.

Subsurface Scattering Layers

The three channels listed under the Subsurface Scattering Layers control three different levels of subsurface scattering. Their controls are the same except for one additional attribute slider in the back scattering layer.

The Scatter Weight slider for each channel controls its overall contribution to the shader. Scatter Radius controls how light scatters across the surface of the object, and Scatter Depth (found only on Back Scatter Color in the misss_fast_skin_maya shader) controls how deeply light penetrates into the object. The Color value for each controls the color of the subsurface scattering; you can apply textures to all these values.

The Epidermal layer is the topmost layer, where you'll find freckles and moles; the Subdermal layer is just beneath the skin, where you'll find veins and capillaries; and the back scatter color is the deepest layer, where bone and cartilage allow different amounts of backlighting to show through the skin.

1. Open the giraffeSSS_v02.ma scene from the chapter11\scenes folder on the DVD. The scene picks up where the last exercise left off.

2. If you experience a grainy quality, you can remove it by expanding the Lightmap rollout in the SSS shader and increasing Samples to **256**. Raising this value does not actually increase render times much, but it will remove the graininess. The giraffe shaders are doing good at the default of 64.

3. Select the giraffeHeadSSS_Mat, and connect the giraffeHead_Epidermal.iff texture to the Epidermal Scatter Color channel. It's common practice to use the same texture for both the diffuse color and the uppermost layer of subsurface scattering.

4. In the Textures tab of the Hypershade, drag the subdermalScatterColor and backScatterColor file texture nodes down into the work area.

5. Set the following values for the Subsurface Scattering Layer channels:

    Epidermal Scatter Weight: **0.5**

    Epidermal Scatter Radius: **4.0**

    Subdermal Scatter Weight: **0.4**

    Subdermal Scatter Radius: **15.0**

    Back Scatter Weight: **.2**

    Back Scatter Radius: **25.0**

    Back Scatter Depth: **25.0**

    These values are often arrived at through experimentation. The lighting, size of the scene, and objects, along with the desired look, all affect how these values are set. In general, when working with them, you'll want to set all the weight values to 0 to turn them off and then raise the weight value of each one, starting with the back scattering layer, and set their values by tweaking and test rendering. If you arrive at settings you like, save the preset for reuse in other scenes. You can use the Scale Conversion attribute under the Algorithm Control rollout as a global scale adjuster for scenes and objects of different sizes.

6. Save your scene file as giraffeSSS_v03.ma.

To see a version of the scene so far, open the giraffeSSS_v03.ma file from the chapter11\ scenes folder on the DVD.

If you are dealing with a human head, it generally has cooler colors around the mouth and eyes and in the recesses of the neck and ears (for both male and female and across races). Warmer colors appear on the nose, cheeks, and forehead, and some yellows are seen in places where bone is close to the surface of the skin, such as in the temples and cheekbones. These colors would be represented in the subdermal and back scatter maps.

Subsurface Specularity

The Subsurface Specularity attributes provide a number of ways to control how the skin of your character reflects the lights in the scene. The giraffe is covered in fur. It still has specularity, but it reacts very differently than bare skin. The giraffe's specularity needs to be muted.

1. Open the `giraffeSSS_v03.ma` scene from the `chapter11\scenes` folder on the DVD. The scene picks up where the last exercise left off.

2. In the Specularity rollout, Overall Weight adjusts how much the combined specularity settings affect the object. Setting this to 0 turns off the specularity altogether. Set this value to **0.3**.

3. Edge Factor controls the Fresnel effect of the specular reflection. Areas of the surface that turn away from the camera reflect more light than those that face the camera. This value controls the width of this effect. A higher value creates a thinner edge for the highlight on the skin. Set this value to **2**.

   The specularity for the skin shader has two layers to simulate the broad, overall specularity of the skin as well as the shiny quality of oily or wet skin. The Primary specularity controls the broad specular reflection and should usually have lower values than the Secondary specularity values. The sliders themselves work the same way. Weight controls the overall contribution; Color controls the color or texture. Edge Weight is a multiplier for the edge of the highlight, and Shininess controls the size and intensity of the highlight (lips will have a higher shininess than the cheeks).

4. Click the checkered box next to Primary Specular Color, and add a file node.

5. Browse your computer's file directory, and add `giraffeHead_PrimSpec.iff`. Use the following settings:

   Primary Weight: **0.2**

   Primary Edge Weight: **0.8**

   Primary Shininess: **3**

   Secondary Weight: **0.3**

   Secondary Edge Weight: **0.0**

   Secondary Shininess: **40**

   The reflection settings work much like the specular values. If Reflect Environment Only is selected, only environment maps will be used for reflection, and no reflection rays will be generated for the object. Fur tends to break up light instead of reflecting it, so for this scene, Reflect Weight is set to 0.0.

6. Create a test render of the scene.

To see a completed version, open the `giraffeSSS_v04.ma` scene from the `chapter11\scenes` folder on the DVD. Compare the image (shown in Figure 11.52) with the render from Figure 11.47. Subsurface scattering does a great deal toward adding realism to a character.

FIGURE 11.52
The final render of the giraffe with displacement, bump, painted skin textures, and sub-surface scattering

 Real World Scenario

BAKING SUBSURFACE SCATTERING

Making characters look photorealistic for real-time environments is extremely difficult. While building characters for a new game engine, we wanted to improve their overall look. Our resources were limited. We could support only a few texture maps and could not implement any fancy shaders. In addition to normal maps, we wanted to have some type of subsurface scattering on the characters. Since shaders were not an option, we decided to bake the rendered look of the misss_fast_skin shader into the character's color or diffuse maps. Here is the process:

1. Create a misss_fast_skin shader along with all the appropriate maps, and assign it to the character.

2. In the Transfer Maps options window, choose Custom for the output map.

3. Enter the exact name of the misss_fast_skin shader into the Custom Shader text field. Upon entering the correct name, the Create button at the end of the field changes to Edit.

4. Set the rest of the standard output options, and choose Bake and Close.

5. The baked map looks good only from the camera's perspective, so you can bake multiple angles and piece them together in Photoshop to get a complete subsurface scattered texture map.

TEXTURE MAPPING NURBS SURFACES

NURBS surfaces use their own parameterization to determine texture coordinates. In other words, you don't need to map u- and v-coordinates using the UV layout tools. This makes NURBS easier to work with but less flexible. NURBS take a bit more planning than polygons to texture, because you must take into account the surface dimensions to paint a map properly. For instance, if the surface is 10 units long by 5 units wide, you would want your texture to be twice as long as it is wide. You can also use a projection node to place a texture onto a NURBS surface. The projection node can then be moved in order to position the texture.

The Bottom Line

Create UV texture coordinates   UV texture coordinates are a crucial element of any polygon or subdivision surface model. If a model has well-organized UVs, painting texture and displacement maps is easy and error free.

Master it   Map UV texture coordinates on a giraffe's leg; then try a complete figure.

Create bump and normal maps   Bump and normal maps are two ways to add detail to a model. Bump maps are great for fine detail, such as pores; normal maps allow you to transfer detail from a high-resolution mesh to a low-resolution version of the same model as well as offer superior shading and faster rendering than bump maps.

Master it   Create high-resolution and low-resolution versions of the model, and try creating a normal map using the Transfer Maps tool. See whether you can bake the bump map into the normal map.

Create a misss_fast_skin shader   The misss_fast_skin shader can create extremely realistic-looking skin. The secret is using painted texture maps for the Subsurface and Specularity channels.

Master it   Change the look of the giraffe by going from Blinn shaders to Subsurface scattering.

Chapter 12

Rendering for Compositing

Maya offers a number of options for dividing the individual elements of a render into separate passes. These passes can then be reassembled and processed with additional effects using compositing software, such as Adobe After Effects or Autodesk Composite. In this chapter, you'll learn how to use Maya's render layers and mental ray's render passes to split rendered images into elements that can then be used in your compositing software.

For best results when working on the project files in this chapter, you should copy the Chapter 12 project to your local drive and make sure it is the current project using the File ➢ Project ➢ Set option. This will ensure that links to textures and Final Gathering maps remain intact and that the scenes render correctly.

In this chapter, you will learn to:

◆ Use render layers

◆ Use render passes

◆ Perform batch renders

◆ Use mental ray quality settings

Render Layers

Render layers are best used to isolate geometry, shaders, and lighting to create different versions of the same animation. Render layers can be used to create a balance between efficiency and flexibility. There is an enormous amount of creative flexibility when using render layers. This chapter explains the more typical workflow; however, you may develop your own way of using render layers over time.

You can create and manage render layers using the Layer Editor in Render mode (called the Render Layer Editor). You can access the Layer Editor in the lower-right corner of the default interface layout, just below the Channel Box.

Besides Render mode, the Layer Editor has Display and Animation modes. These three modes are the three types of layers you can create in Maya. You change the mode by clicking one of the tabs at the top of the Layer Editor. Figure 12.1 shows the Render Layer Editor, with a scene that has two custom render layers and the default render layer.

FIGURE 12.1

The Render Layer Editor is a mode of the Layer Editor, which is found below the Channel Box on the lower right of the default interface.

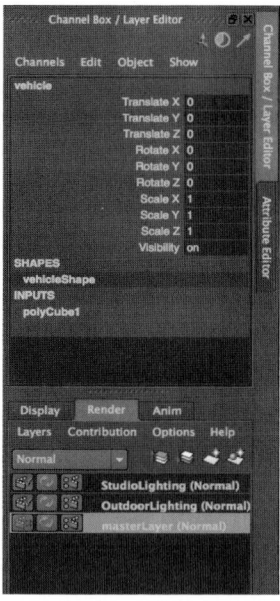

By default, every Maya scene has at least one render layer labeled masterLayer. All the lights and geometry of the scene are included in the masterLayer. When you create a new render layer, you can specify precisely which lights and objects are included in that layer. As you add render layers, you can create alternate lights for each layer, use different shaders on each piece of geometry, render one layer using mental ray and another using Maya Software, use indirect lighting effects on one layer and not on another, and so on. A render layer can be rendered using any camera, or you can specify which camera renders which layer. In this section, you'll use many of these techniques to render different versions of the same scene.

Creating Render Layers

In this exercise, you'll render Anthony Honn's vehicle model in a studio environment and in an outdoor setting. Furthermore, the car is rendered using a different shader on the body for each layer.

The scene is set up in a studio environment. The lighting consists of two point lights that have mental ray Physical Light shaders applied. These lights create the shadows and are reflected in the body of the car. An Area light and a Directional light are used as simple fill lights.

The car itself uses several mia materials for the metallic, glass, chrome, and rubber parts. The body uses a shading network that combines the mib_glossy_reflection shader and the mi_metallic_paint_x shader.

The shader used for the car body is named blueCarBody. You can select it in the Hypershade and graph the input and output connections in the Work Area to see how the shader is arranged (select the shader in the Hypershade and choose Graph ➢ Input And Output Connections from the Hypershade menu bar). Figure 12.2 shows the graphed network.

The renderCam camera has a lens shader applied to correct the exposure of the image. As you learned in Chapter 10, mia materials and physical lights are physically accurate, which means their range of values does not always look correct when displayed on a computer screen. The mia_exposure_simple lens shader is applied to the camera to make sure the scene looks acceptable when rendered.

FIGURE 12.2
The blueCarBody shader is graphed in the Work Area of the Hypershade.

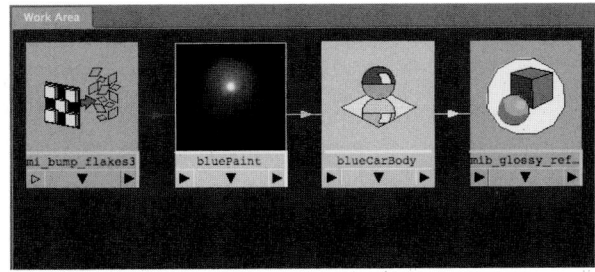

To create two alternative versions of the scene, you'll want to use two separate render layers:

◆ The first render layer will look exactly like the current scene.

◆ The second render layer will use a different shader for the car body and the Physical Sky and Sun network to create the look of outdoor lighting.

Generally when you start to add render layers, the master layer is not rendered; only the layers that you add to the scene are used for rendering.

The first step is to create a new render layer for the scene:

1. Open the carComposite_v01.ma scene from the chapter12\scenes directory on the DVD. Open the Render View window, and create a test render using the renderCam camera. It may take a minute or so to create the render (Figure 12.3).

2. Set the Layer Editor mode to Render.

FIGURE 12.3
The carComposite _v01.ma scene shows a typical studio lighting and shading arrangement for the car.

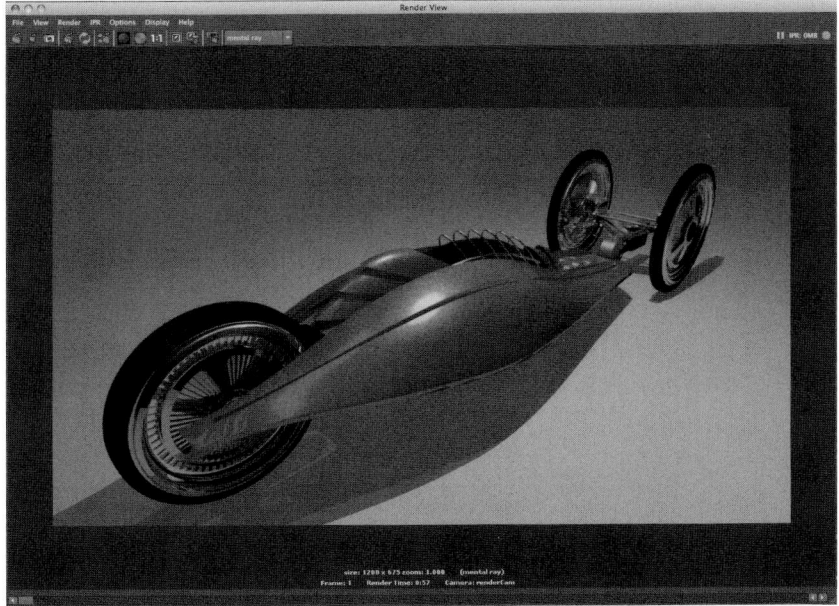

3. You can quickly add all the scene elements to a new layer by simply copying the layer:

    A. Select the masterLayer label in the Layer Editor.

    B. Right-click, and choose Copy Layer.

    This creates a duplicate of the layer in the editor using all the same settings. See the left image of Figure 12.4.

FIGURE 12.4
Copy masterLayer (top-left image) and rename it studioLighting (top right). Deactivate the Render All Layers option (bottom left), and turn off the masterLayer render option (bottom right).

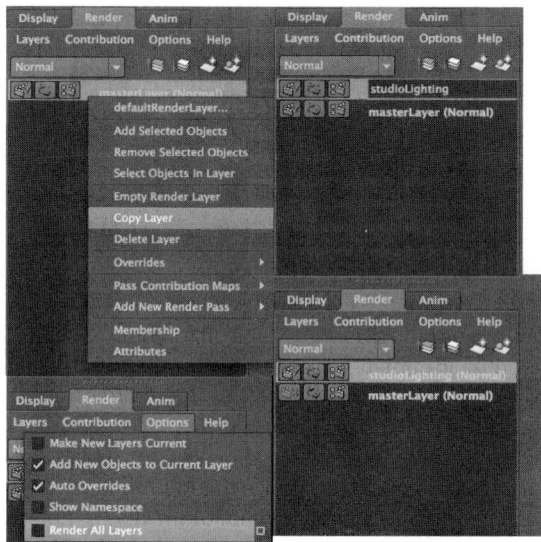

4. In the Layer Editor, double-click the label for the new layer, and rename it **studioLighting**. This is shown in the top-right image in Figure 12.4.

5. In the menu bar for the Render Layer Editor, select Options, and make sure Render All Layers is not activated (click this option until the check mark disappears). This is shown in the bottom-left image in Figure 12.4.

Right now you're interested in rendering only a single layer at a time. If this option is on, Maya will render all the layers each time you create a test render in the render view.

6. Click the clapboard icon (of the three icons, it's the one that is farthest to the left) label so a red *X* appears. This deactivates this render layer so it is not renderable. This is shown in the bottom-right image in Figure 12.4.

7. Select the studioLighting layer in the Layer Editor so it is highlighted in blue.

8. Open the Render View window, and create a test render using the renderCam camera. It should look exactly the same as the render from step 1.

9. Save the scene as **carComposite_v02.ma**.

Copying a layer is a fast and easy way to create a render layer. You can also create an empty layer as follows:

1. Choose Create Empty Layer from the Layers menu in the Layer Editor when in Render mode.

2. Select objects in the scene.

3. Right-click the new layer.

4. Choose Add Selected Objects from the pop-up menu.

Another way to create a new layer is to select objects in the scene and choose Create Layer From Selected from the layer's menu. A new render layer containing all the selected objects is created.

You can add new objects at any time by right-clicking the render layer and choosing Add Selected Objects. Likewise, you can remove objects by selecting the objects and choosing Remove Selected Objects. You can delete a render layer by right-clicking the layer and choosing Delete Layer. This does not delete the objects, lights, or shaders in the scene, just the layer itself.

To see a version of the scene to this point, open the `carComposite_v02.ma` scene from the `chapter12\scenes` directory on the DVD.

An object's visibility can be on for one render layer and off for another. Likewise, if an object is on a display layer and a render layer, the display layer's visibility affects whether the object is visible in the render layer. This is easy to forget, and you may find yourself unable to figure out why an object that has been added to a render layer is not visible. Remember to double-check the settings in the Layer Editor's Display mode if you can't see a particular object.

You can use the Relationship Editor to see which layers an object belongs to. Choose Window ➢ Relationship Editors ➢ Render Layers.

Render Layer Overrides

To create a different lighting and shading setup for a second layer, you'll use render layer overrides. An override changes an attribute for a specific layer. So, for example, if you wanted Final Gathering to calculate on one layer but not another, you would create an override in the Render Settings window from the Final Gathering attribute. To create an override, right-click next to an attribute, and choose Create Layer Override. As long as you are working in a particular layer that has an override enabled for an attribute, you'll see the label of the attribute highlighted in orange. Settings created in the master layer apply to all other layers unless there is an override.

This next exercise shows how to use overrides as you create a new layer for the outdoor lighting of the car:

1. Continue with the scene from the previous section, or open the `carComposite_v02.ma` scene from the `chapter12\scenes` directory on the DVD.

2. In the Outliner, select the Vehicle group.

3. Shift+click the ground object.

4. In the Render Layer Editor, choose Layers ➢ Create Layer From Selected.

5. Select the new layer so it is highlighted in blue, and rename it **outDoorLighting**.

If a group such as the Vehicle group is added to a render layer, all of its children are part of that layer. If you want to add just a part, such as the wheels, select the geometry (or subgroup) and add that to the render layer rather than the entire group.

Currently this layer has no lighting, so if you render it, the layer will appear dark (the default light in the render settings is off). That's fine because at this point you want to create a Physical Sky and Sun network for this layer.

6. Make sure the outDoorLighting layer is selected in the Render Layer Editor. This ensures that you are currently in this layer and that any changes you make to the lighting or shading will appear in this layer.

7. In the Render Layer Editor, click the Render Settings icon (of the three icons, it's the farthest to the right), which opens the render settings for the current layer.

    In the Render Settings window, you'll notice outDoorLighting is selected in the Render Layer menu at the top. You can use this menu to switch between settings for the different layers.

8. Switch to the Indirect Lighting tab, and click the Create button for the Physical Sun and Sky.

    This button creates a series of nodes including the Sun Direction light, the Physical Sky node, and the mia_exposure lens shader for all the lights in the scene. It also enables Final Gathering in the Render Settings window.

9. In the Render Settings window, RMB-click the label Final Gathering, and choose Create Layer Override (Figure 12.5). You'll see that Final Gathering turns orange, letting you know this setting has an override for the current layer (outDoorLighting).

FIGURE 12.5
Create a layer override for Final Gathering in the Render Settings window for the out-DoorLighting layer.

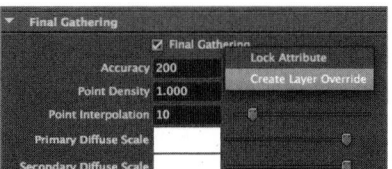

10. You want Final Gathering only for the outDoorLighting layer. In the Render Settings window, select masterLayer from the Render Layer drop-down menu. Turn off Final Gathering while this layer is selected.

11. Select the studioLighting layer from the Render Layer menu in the Render Settings window. Final Gathering should now be off for this layer as well.

12. Select outDoorLighting, and you'll see that Final Gathering is enabled and the label is still orange.

    This is the basic workflow for creating a render layer override. How do you know which settings can be overridden? Most attributes related to lighting and shading can be overridden on most nodes. You can always right-click next to the attribute layer and see whether the Create Layer Override setting is available.

13. In the Render View window, create a test render, but make sure outDoorLighting is still the selected render layer. The render will take four or five minutes (depending on your computer's speed and available RAM).

The render is obviously quite different from the render created for the studioLighting layer (Figure 12.6).

FIGURE 12.6
The lighting in the outDoorLighting layer is very different from the lighting in the studioLighting layer.

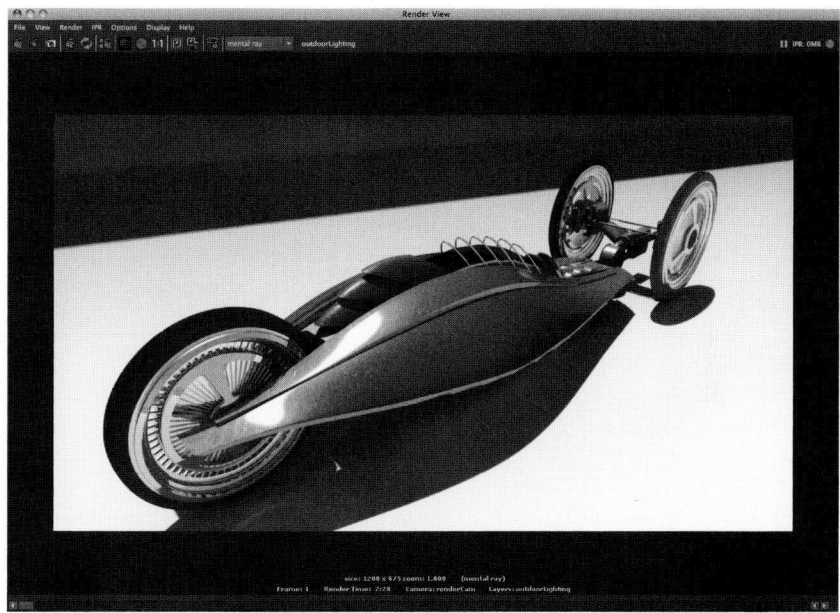

14. Store the render in the Render View window (from the File menu in the Render View window, choose Keep Image In Render View).

15. In Render mode of the Layer Editor, select the studioLighting layer, and create another test render.

Something has gone wrong because the lighting has changed for this layer. Final Gathering is not calculating, but you'll see that the render takes a long time and the lighting no longer matches the original studioLighting render. The reason for this is not because of render layers *per se* but because of the Physical Sun and Sky network that was added to the scene. Remember from Chapter 9 that when you add a Physical Sun and Sky network, a number of nodes are added to the scene and attached to the renderable cameras. Normally this feature saves time and work, but in this case it's working against the scene.

The easiest way to fix the problem is to create a duplicate render camera. One camera can be used to render the studioLighting layer; the other can be used to render the outDoorLighting layer. You can make sure that the correct lens shaders are applied to both cameras. You can use overrides to specify which camera is available from which layer.

1. Select the renderCam camera in the Outliner. Rename it **outdoorCam**.

2. Duplicate outdoorCam, and rename the duplicate **studioCam**.

3. Open the Attribute Editor for studioCam.

4. Switch to the studioCamShape tab, and expand the mental ray section.

   You'll see there are no lens or environment shaders attached to the studioCam camera. If you switch to the outdoorCam camera, you'll see the mia_physicalsky1 shader in the Environment Shader slot and the mia_exposure_simple2 shader in the Lens Shader slot. The original renderCam camera had a mia_exposure_simple1 node in the Lens Shader slot, but this was replaced by mia_exposure_simple2 when the Physical Sun and Sky network was added to the scene. The solution here is to reattach the mia_exposure_simple1 node to the lens shader of studioCam.

5. Open the Hypershade window, and switch to the Utilities tab.

6. MMB-drag mia_exposure_simple1 (you can see the full name if you hold the mouse pointer over the icon) down to the Lens Shader slot for studioCam (Figure 12.7).

FIGURE 12.7
Attach the mia_exposure_simple1 node to the Lens Shader slot of studioCam.

7. In the Hypershade, select the mia_physicalsky1 node on the Utilities tab, and open its Attribute Editor to the mia_physicalsky1 tab.

8. Right-click next to the On attribute, and choose Create Layer Override. The attribute label should turn orange.

9. After adding the override, deselect the check box for this attribute to turn it off for this layer.

10. Create a test render in the Render View window, and make sure that studioCam is chosen as the rendering camera. The render now looks like it did at the start of the section.

11. Save the scene as **carComposite_v03.ma**.

To see a version of the scene to this point, open the carComposite_v03.ma scene from the chapter12\scenes directory on the DVD.

Creating Overrides for Rendering Cameras

Notice that you do not need to add cameras to render layers when you add them to a scene. You can if you want, but it makes no difference. The cameras that render the scene are listed on the Common tab of the Render Settings window.

If you're rendering an animated sequence using two cameras with different settings as in the carComposite example, you'll want to use overrides so you don't render more images than you need.

1. Continue with the scene from the previous section, or open the carComposite_v03.ma scene from the chapter12\scenes directory on the DVD.

2. Open the Render Settings window.

3. Make sure the Render Layer menu at the top of the Render Settings window is set to studioLighting.

4. Switch to the Common tab, and expand the Renderable Cameras rollout.

5. Use the Renderable Camera menu to choose the studioCam camera.

6. Right-click next to the menu, and choose Create Layer Override (Figure 12.8).

7. Set the Render Layer drop-down at the top of the Render Settings window to outDoorLighting.

FIGURE 12.8
Create a layer override for the rendering camera on the studioLighting layer.

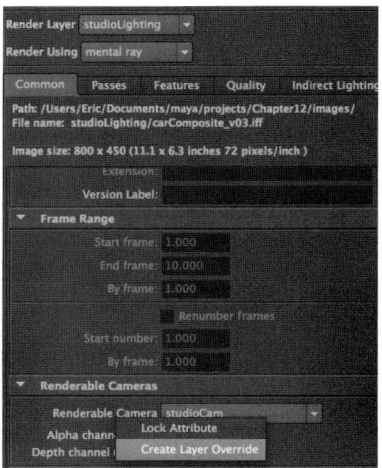

8. From the Renderable Camera menu, choose outdoorCam.

9. Right-click next to the menu, and choose Create Layer Override (in some cases Maya creates the override for you if you already have an override for the same setting on another layer).

10. Switch between the studioLighting layer and the outDoorLighting layer, and make sure the correct camera is selected for each layer.

    Maya may add the outdoorCam as a renderable camera to the studioLighting layer. If this happens, click the trash can icon next to the outdoorCam to remove it from this layer as a renderable camera.

    It is important to take these steps to ensure the right camera will render the correct layer; otherwise, you may waste time rendering images from the wrong camera.

11. Save the scene as **carComposite_v04.ma**.

To see a version of the scene to this point, open the `carComposite_v04.ma` scene from the `chapter12\scenes` directory on the DVD.

After creating the overrides for the cameras, it is still possible to render with either camera in the render view. The overrides ensure the correct camera is used for each layer during a batch render.

Using Different Shaders on Render Layers

The flexibility of render layers becomes even more apparent when you apply different shaders to the same object on different layers. This allows you to render alternate versions of the same animation.

1. Continue with the scene from the previous section, or open the `carComposite_v04.ma` scene from the `chapter12\scenes` directory on the DVD.

2. In the Render Layer Editor, select the outDoorLighting layer. Open the Hypershade.

3. In the Outliner, expand the Vehicle group, and select the carBody subgroup (Figure 12.9).

4. In the Hypershade, find the stripedCarBody shader (its icon is the same as for the mib_glossy_reflection shader). Right-click the shader, and choose Assign Material To Selection.

    This shader uses a projected texture map to color the surfaces in the carBody group. The projection node is already placed in the carBody group.

5. With the outDoorLighting render layer selected, create a test render in the Render View window. Make sure the outdoorCam camera is selected as the rendering camera (Figure 12.10).

6. Save the scene as **carComposite_v05.ma**.

FIXING BROKEN TEXTURE LINKS

If textures do not appear on the rendered models, you'll need to double-check to make sure they are linked properly. Links can break fairly easily if the scene files are moved or if the project is not set correctly. To fix the link, open the Hypershade window, switch to the Textures tab, and select the broken texture. Open its Attribute Editor, and look at the path to the texture in the Image Name field. Click the folder to open the file browser. Files for this project are found in the sourceimages directory.

FIGURE 12.9
Apply the stripedCarBody shader to the carBody group.

FIGURE 12.10
The outDoorLighting layer uses a different shader to color the body of the car.

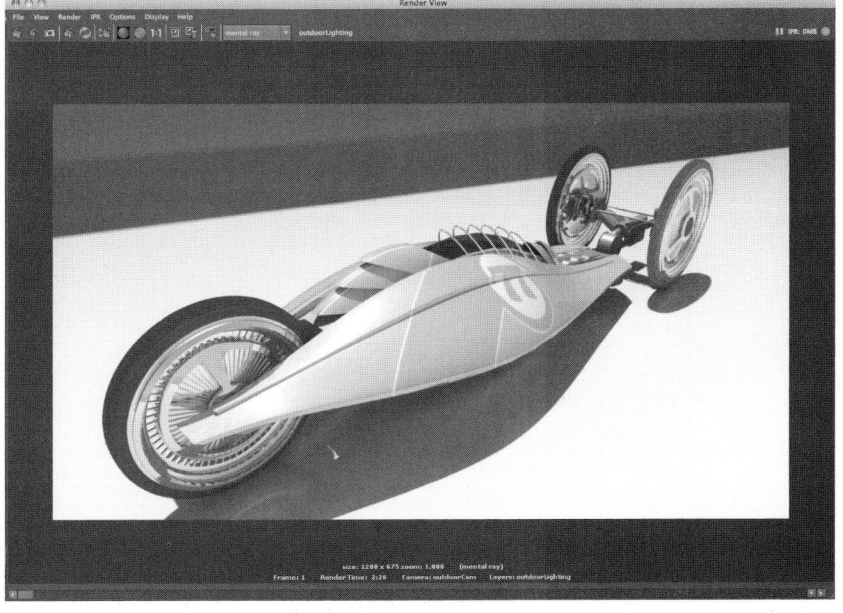

The car renders with a different material applied to the body. If you render the studioLighting layer (using the studioCam camera), you'll see the car is still blue. The new shader appears only when the outDoorLighting layer is rendered.

You don't need to create overrides to apply different materials on different render layers; however, you can create overrides for the attributes of render nodes used on different layers (for instance, one shader could have different transparency values on different render layers).

Shaders applied to the components of a surface, such as selected polygon faces, can differ from one render layer to the next.

To see a finished version of the scene, open the `carComposite_v05.ma` scene from the `chapter12\scenes` directory on the DVD.

Material Overrides

A material override applies a material to all of the objects within a particular layer. To create a material override, right-click one of the layers in the Render Layer Editor, and choose Overrides ➤ Create New Material Override. You can then select a material from the list.

Render Layer Blend Modes

Render layers can use blend modes, which combine the results of the render to form a composite. You can preview the composite in the Render View window. Typically you render each layer separately, import the render sequences into compositing software (such as Adobe After Effects or Autodesk Composite), and then apply the blend modes using the controls in the compositing software. Maya gives you the option of creating a very simple composite using render layers, which you can view in the Render View window.

Blend modes use simple algorithms to combine the numeric color values of each pixel to create a composite. A composite is created by layering two or more images on top of each other. The image on top is blended with the image below. If both images are rendered as Normal, then the top image covers the bottom image completely. If the blend mode is set to Multiply, then the light pixels in the top image are transparent, and the darker pixels of the top image darken the pixels in the bottom image. This technique is often used to add shadowing to a composite. If the blend mode of the top image is set to Screen, then the darker pixels are transparent, and the lighter pixels brighten the pixels of the lower image. You can use this to composite glowing effects.

The blend modes available in Maya are Lighten, Darken, Multiply, Screen, and Overlay:

Lighten This mode compares the layered images and uses the lightest pixel value of the two layers to determine the resulting color. For example, the lower image has a pixel in a particular spot with an RGB value of 0, 125, 255, and the pixel at the same location in the top image has an RGB value of 0, 115, 235. The resulting RGB value for that pixel will be 0, 125, 255.

Darken This is the opposite of Lighten, and the darker value is used. In the example cited previously, the resulting RGB value for the pixel would be 0, 115, 235.

Multiply The pixel values of the top image are multiplied by the pixel values of the bottom image and then divided by 255 to keep the values within the range of 0 to 255. The lighter pixels in the top image are semitransparent, and the darker values of the top image result in a darkening of the lower image.

Screen A slightly more complex algorithm is used for this mode. The formula is 255-[(255-top color RGB pixel value)*(255-bottom color RGB pixel value)/255]= blended RGB pixel value. This has the effect of making darker pixels in the top image semitransparent and lighter, resulting in a lightening of the lower image.

Overlay This combines Multiply and Screen modes so the lighter pixels of the top image brighten the bottom image and the darker pixels of the top image darken the bottom image.

In this exercise, you'll use blending modes to create soft shadows for the render of the car in the studio lighting scenario.

This scene shows the car in the studio lighting scenario. A single render layer exists already. Using the technique in this exercise, you'll eliminate the harsh cast shadows that appear on the ground in the rendered image (shown earlier in the chapter in Figure 12.2) and replace them with soft shadows created using an ambient occlusion shader. First you'll remove the shadows cast on the ground by the physical lights in the scene (note that physical lights always cast shadows; there is no option for turning shadows off when you use these lights).

1. Open the carComposite_v06.ma scene from the chapter12\scenes directory on the DVD.

2. Select the ground object in the Outliner.

3. Open its Attribute Editor, and switch to the groundShape tab.

4. Expand the Render Stats section in the Attribute Editor, and deactivate Receive Shadows (see Figure 12.11).

   Note that, for some attributes, changing a setting on a render layer automatically creates a layer override.

FIGURE 12.11
Disable Receive Shadows for the ground surface.

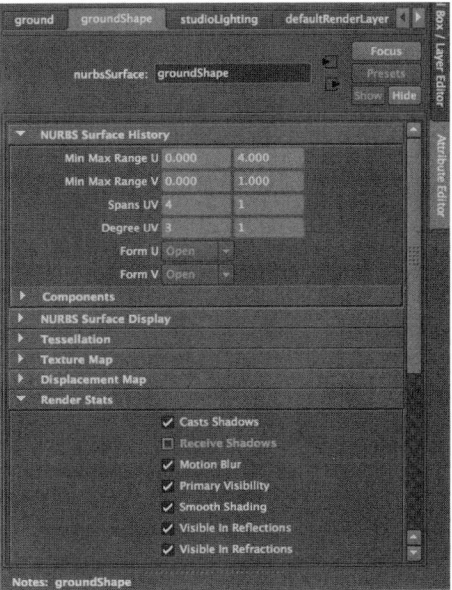

5. Select the studioLighting layer, and create a test render in the Render View window using the renderCam camera (see Figure 12.12).

6. In the Outliner, Shift+click the vehicle group and the ground surface.

7. In the Render Layer Editor, choose Layers ➢ Create Layer From Selected. Name the new layer **AOShadow**.

8. Open the Hypershade window. Make sure the AOShadow layer is selected in the Render Layer Editor.

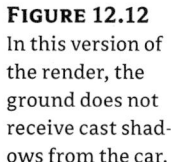

FIGURE 12.12
In this version of
the render, the
ground does not
receive cast shad-
ows from the car.

9. Create two new surface shaders in the Hypershade (from the Hypershade menu bar, choose Create ➢ Materials ➢ Surface Shader).

10. Name one of the surface shaders **shadowShader** and the other **whiteMask**.

11. In the Outliner, select the vehicle group, and apply the whiteMask shader to this group.

12. Select the ground object, and apply the shadowShader to this surface.

13. Open the Attribute Editor for the whiteMask node, and set Out Color to white.

14. Open the Attribute Editor for the shadowShader.

15. Click the checkered box to the right of Out Color. In the Create Render Nodes window, select Textures under mental ray. Choose the mib_amb_occlusion texture from the node list (Figure 12.13).

16. Open the Attribute Editor for the mib_amb_occlusion1 node, and set Samples to **64**.

17. Make sure the AOShadow is selected in the Render Layer Editor; then create a test render using the renderCam camera.

    The car appears as flat white, but you can see the soft shadows created on the ground by the ambient occlusion node (Figure 12.14). Later in this chapter you'll learn more about how ambient occlusion textures create shadows.

18. Now you are ready to preview the composite in the Render View window. In the Render Layer Editor, set the mode of the AOShadow layer to Multiply (see Figure 12.15).

    Because the car in this render layer is flat white, when the pixels of the AOShadow layer are multiplied by the pixels of the studioLight layer, only the soft shadows appear in the composite.

FIGURE 12.13
Create an ambient
occlusion texture,
and connect it to
the shadowShader's
Out Color channel.

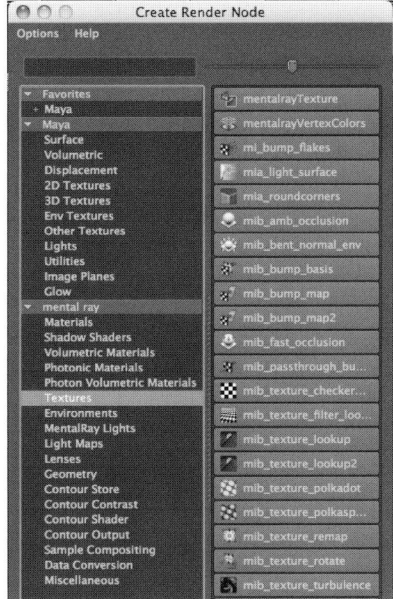

FIGURE 12.14
The soft shadows
created by the
ambient occlusion
texture appear
on the ground
while the car is
masked in flat
white.

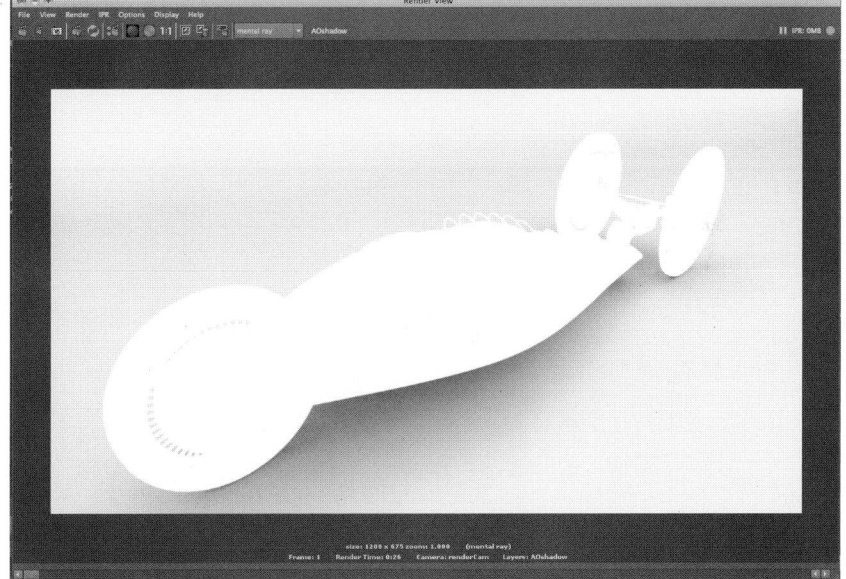

FIGURE 12.15
Set the blend mode
of the AOShadow
layer to Multiply.

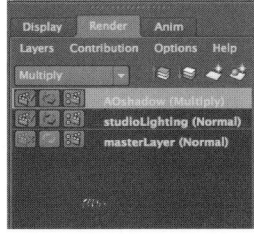

19. In the Render Layer Editor, choose Options ➢ Render All Layers ➢ Options. In the Options box, set Keep Image Mode to Composite Layers.

There are three choices in the Render All Layers Options dialog box: Composite Layers, Composite and Keep Layers, and Keep Layers.

Choosing "Composite" renders both layers and then composites them in the Render View window.

Choosing "Composite And Keep Layers" creates the composite, but it also keeps the rendered image of each individual layer available in the Render View window.

Choosing Keep Layers" will not composite the layers; instead, it renders all renderable layers and keeps them as individual images in the Render View window.

20. After choosing the Composite Layers option, click Apply and Close.

21. Make sure that Render All Layers is now selected in the Options menu of the Render Layer Editor (Figure 12.16).

22. In the Render Layer Editor, make sure the red *X* appears on the clapboard icon of master-Layer, indicating that this layer will not render. A green check box should appear next to the studioLighting and AOshadow layers, indicating that they will be rendered.

23. Open the Render View window, and create a test render using the renderCam camera. You'll see the studioLighting layer render first, and then the AOShadow layer will render on top of it. Figure 12.17 shows the composited image.

24. Save the scene as **carComposite_v07.ma**.

FIGURE 12.16
Select the Render All Layers option in the Options menu.

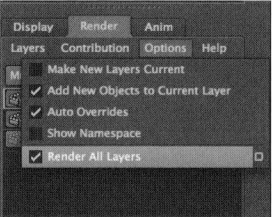

FIGURE 12.17
The two images are composited in the Render View window.

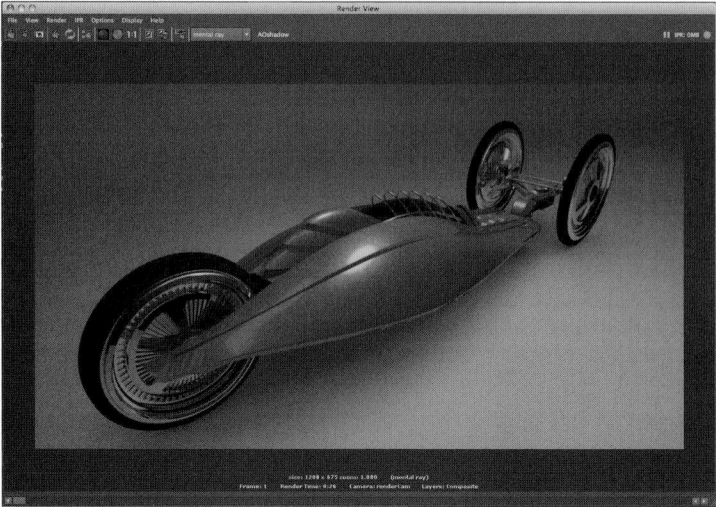

To see a finished version of the scene, open the `carComposite_v07.ma` scene from the `chapter12\scenes` directory on the DVD.

This is a good way to preview basic composites; however, in practice you will most likely want more control over how the layers are composited. To do this, you should use more advanced compositing software such as Adobe Photoshop (for still images) or Adobe After Effects or Autodesk Composite (for animations).

 Real World Scenario

COMPOSITE HARDWARE PARTICLES USING RENDER LAYERS

If you have a scene that involves a large number of nParticles, you may want to use hardware rendering to reduce the render time. If the scene also contains geometry that you want to render with Maya Software or mental ray, you can use render layers to composite the hardware-rendered nParticles with the software-rendered geometry in Maya.

1. In your scene, create a new render layer, and add the geometry to this new layer. Name the layer **geometryRL**.

2. Create a second render layer above the geometry layer; then add the nParticles and the geometry to this layer. Name the layer **nParticleRL**.

3. Open the Render Settings window for geometryRL, and set Render Using to mental ray.

4. Open the Render Settings window for nParticlesRL.

5. Right-click Render Using, and choose Create Layer Override.

6. Set the Render Using menu to Maya Hardware.

7. In the Maya Hardware tab of the Render Settings window, turn on Enable Geometry Mask.

8. In the Render Layer Editor, make sure both the nParticlesRL and geometryRL layers are set to Renderable.

9. In the Options menu, turn on Render All Layers.

10. Set the mode of the nParticlesRL layer to Screen.

11. Create a test render of a frame in which nParticles and the geometry are visible.

I use this workflow all the time in much of my scientific visualization work. Using particle sprites (covered in Chapter 17) requires hardware rendering, so it's great to have a render layer set up that allows me to render all of my detailed geometry and particles within a single scene file using two different rendering engines (mental ray and Maya Hardware).

Render Passes

Render passes divide the output created by a render layer into separate images or image sequences. Using render passes, you can separate the reflections, shadows, diffuse color, ambient occlusion, specular highlights, and so on, into images or image sequences, which can then be reassembled in compositing software. By separating things such as the reflections from the diffuse color, you can then exert maximum creative control over how the different images work together in the composite. This also allows you to easily make changes or variations or fix problems in individual elements rather than re-rendering the entire image or sequence every time you make a change.

Render passes replace the technique of using multiple render layers to separate things like reflections and shadows in older versions of Maya. (Render passes also replaces the layer presets; more on this in a moment.) Each layer can be split into any number of render passes. When render passes are created, each layer is rendered once, and the passes are taken from data stored in the Frame Buffer. This means each layer needs to render only once to create all the necessary passes. Render time for each layer increases as you add more passes.

THE FRAME BUFFER

When Maya renders an image, it collects data from the scene and stores it in a temporary image known as the Frame Buffer. When rendering is complete, the data from the Frame Buffer is written to disk as the rendered image. The images created by render passes are extracted from the render buffer, which is why the layer needs to render only once to create a number of render passes.

A typical workflow using passes is to separate the scene into one or more render layers, as demonstrated in the first part of this chapter, and then assign any number of render passes to each render layer. When you create a batch render, the passes are stored in subfolders in the Images directory of the current project. You can then import the images created by render passes into compositing software and assemble them into layers to create the final composite.

Render passes work only with mental ray; they are not available for any other renderer (Maya Software or Maya Hardware). It's also crucial to understand that at this point not all materials will work with render passes. If you find that objects in your scene are not rendering correctly, double-check that you are using a material compliant with render passes.

The materials that work with render passes are as follows:

Anisotropic	Ramp Shader
Blinn	Hair
Lambert	Fur
Phong	Image Plane
Phong E	Layered Shader
Environment Fog	Shading Map
Fluid Shape	Surface Shader
Light Fog	Use Background
Particle Cloud	mi_metallic_paint_x_passes
Volume Fog	mi_car_phen_x_passes
Volume Shader	mia_material_x_passes
Hair Tube Shader	misss_fast_shader_x_passes
Ocean Shader	

Also, each shader does not necessarily work with every type of render pass listed in the render pass interface. For more information about specific shaders, consult the Maya documentation.

Note that the mental ray DGS, Dielectric, mib_glossy_reflection, and mib_glossy_refraction shaders, as well as the other mib shaders, are not supported by render passes. Even if you use a supported shader (such as mi_metallic_paint_x_passes) as a base material for these shaders, it will not render correctly. When using these shaders, you may need to devise an alternate workflow involving render layers and material overrides.

Upgrade Materials for Rendering Passes

The decision to render a scene in passes for compositing is going to affect what type of lighting and materials you use on the surfaces in your scene. As noted earlier, not all materials work with render passes. In addition, light shaders, such as the mia-physical light shader, can behave unpredictably with certain types of passes.

Generally speaking, any of the mental ray shaders that end with the "_passes" suffix are a good choice to use when rendering passes. If you have already applied the mia_material or mia_material_x shader to objects in the scene, you can easily upgrade these shaders to the mia_material_x_passes shader. The same is true for the mi_car_paint, mi_metallic_paint, and misss_fast_shader materials.

BE CONSISTENT WITH MATERIALS

The best way to minimize errors and confusion when rendering is to keep consistent with your material types: avoid using combinations of mia materials and standard Maya shaders whenever possible within a single render layer.

The following example illustrates how to upgrade the mia_material_x shader to the mia_material_x_passes shader in order to prepare for the creation of render passes.

This scene uses an HDRI image to create reflections on the surface of the metal. To render the scene correctly, you'll need to download the `building_probe.hdr` image from Paul Debevec's website at www.debevec.org/Probes. This image should be connected to the mentalrayIbl1 node in the `helmetComposite_v01.ma` scene. Select this node in the Outliner, open its Attribute Editor, and use the Image Name field to link to the image on your disk. For more information on using the mentalrayIbl node, consult Chapter 10.

1. Open the `helmetComposite_v01.ma` scene from the `chapter12\scenes` folder on the DVD.

2. Open the Hypershade window, and select the chromeShader. This is a mia_material_x. Open the Attribute Editor, and scroll down to the Upgrade Shader rollout toward the bottom.

3. Click the Upgrade Shader To mia_material_x_passes button (Figure 12.18).

4. Repeat this process to upgrade groundShader, metalShader, plasticShader, rubberShader, thickGlass, and thinGlass.

5. Save the scene as **helmetComposite_v02.ma**.

To see a version of the scene, open the `helmetComposite_v02.ma` scene from the `chapter12\scenes` folder on the DVD.

FIGURE 12.18
Upgrade the
shader to
mia_material_x_
passes.

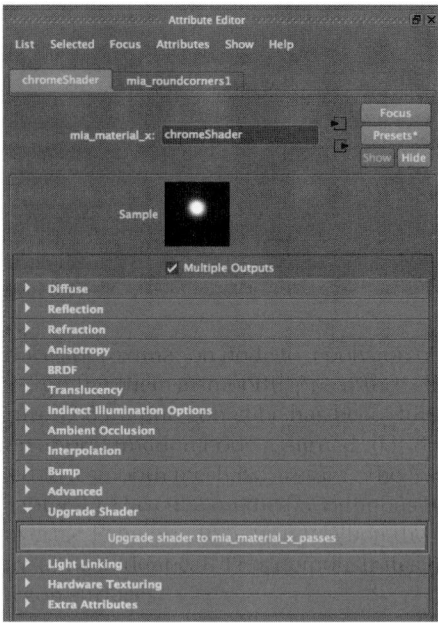

Render Multiple Passes from a Single Render Layer

In this example, you'll create multiple passes for reflection, specular, depth, and shadow using the space helmet scene.

USE DEPTH PASSES TO CREATE DEPTH OF FIELD

Depth passes are particularly helpful in compositing. They can be used to add, among other things, camera depth of field in the composite. For example, using Adobe After Effects' Lens Blur filter, you can apply a depth pass to control the focal region of the render based on the luminance of the depth pass.

There are also plug-ins available for After Effects, such as Lens Care by Frischluft, that create realistic lens effects far superior to the standard After Effects blurs. Using a depth pass for depth of field in After Effects dramatically reduces Maya render times, because mental ray's depth of field can take a long time to calculate.

Furthermore, any changes you make to the depth of field, such as the focal region, are done in After Effects and do not require re-rendering the entire scene. The same is true for motion blur. You can create a 2D or 3D motion vector pass and then use a plug-in such as Reel Smart Motion Blur to add motion blur in the composite rather than in the initial render. This is a huge time-saver.

---

1. Continue with the scene from the previous section, or open the helmetComposite_v02.ma scene from the chapter12\scenes directory on the DVD.

2. In the Render Layer Editor, select the helmet layer.

3. Click the Render Settings icon in the Render Layer Editor to open the Render Settings window, and choose the Passes tab.

4. Click the icon at the top of the stack of icons in the upper right. This opens the Create Render Passes window.

5. From the Pass list, select the Camera Depth pass, and click the Create button at the top of the window.

6. Use the same steps to create Reflection, Shadow, and Specular passes (Figure 12.19).

FIGURE 12.19
Render passes are created and listed in the Scene Passes section on the Passes tab for the Helmet render layer.

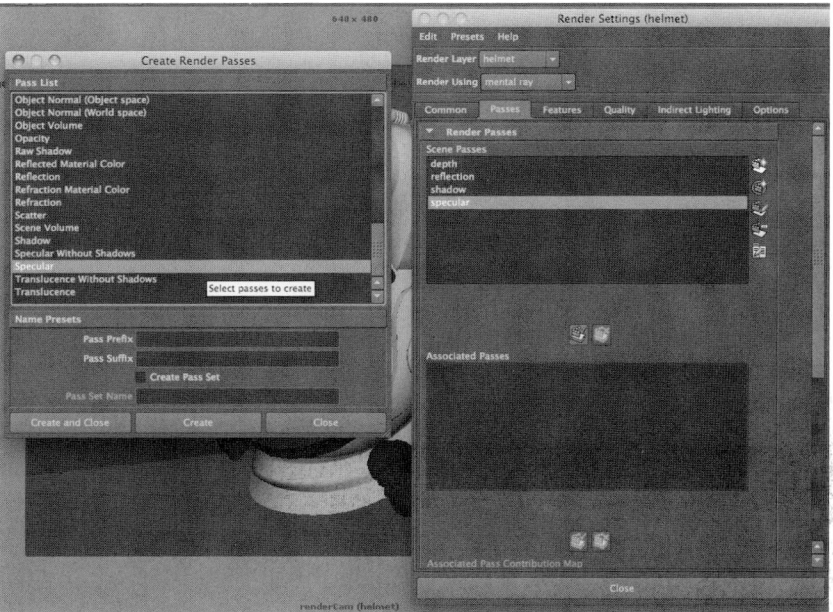

The passes have been created, but at the moment they are not associated with a render layer. You can create as many render passes as you like and then associate them with any combination of render layers in the scene—as long as those render layers are rendered using mental ray.

Once the pass is associated with the current layer, it is included in the Frame Buffer when the scene renders and saved as a separate image after rendering is complete. The Scene Passes and Associated Passes interface is a little confusing at first; just remember that only the passes listed in the Associated Passes section will be rendered for the current render layer. If you switch to another render layer, you'll see all the passes listed in the Scene Passes section. To disassociate a pass from a render layer, follow these steps:

A. Select the pass in the Associated Passes section.

B. Click the icon with the red *X* between the two sections.

This moves the pass back to the Scene Passes section. To delete a pass from either section, follow these steps:

A. Select the pass.

B. Press the Backspace key.

7. Close the Create Render Pass window.

8. In the Passes tab of the Render Settings window, Shift-select the depth, reflection, shadow, and specular passes in the Scene Passes section.

9. Make sure that the Render Layer menu at the top of the Passes section of the Render Settings window is set to helmet.

10. Click the clapboard icon with the green check mark (between the Scene Passes and Associated passes sections). This moves the selected scene passes to the Associated Passes section, meaning that the helmet render layer will now render the passes you've created.

11. Double-click the Depth pass in the Associated Passes list; this will cause its Attribute Editor to open.

12. Turn on Remap Depth Values, and set Far Clipping Plane to **20** (see Figure 12.20).

    The scene size for this scene is 20 units in Z; by setting Far Clipping Plane to 20, any parts of a surface beyond 20 units are clipped to a luminance value of 1 (meaning they are white).

FIGURE 12.20
Edit the settings for the Depth pass in the Attribute Editor.

13. Double-click Reflection to open its settings in the Attribute Editor.

14. Raise Maximum Reflection Level to **10**.

15. Create another test render from the Render View window using the renderCam camera.

You won't notice anything special about the render; the render passes have already been saved to disk in a subfolder of the project's Images directory, but they are not visible in the Render View window.

16. In the Render View window, choose File ➢ Load Render Pass ➢ Reflection (Figure 12.21). This will open the IMF_Display application.

Sometimes this opens behind the Maya interface, so you may need to minimize Maya to see it. On the Mac, the IMF_display icon appears as three colored squares on the Dock.

17. Save the scene as **helmetComposite_v03.ma**.

The reflection pass shows only the reflections on the surface of the objects; the other parts of the image are dark. Thus, the reflections are isolated. You can view the other passes using the File menu in the Render View window. Figure 12.22 shows each pass.

FIGURE 12.21
Use the File menu in the Render View window to open the render pass images in IMF_Display.

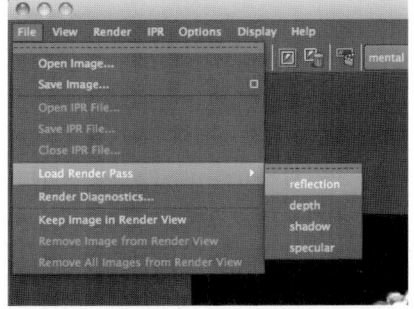

FIGURE 12.22
Clockwise from the upper left: Reflection, Shadow, Depth, and Specular render passes as seen in IMF_display. The elements of the passes appear dark because they have been separated and rendered against black.

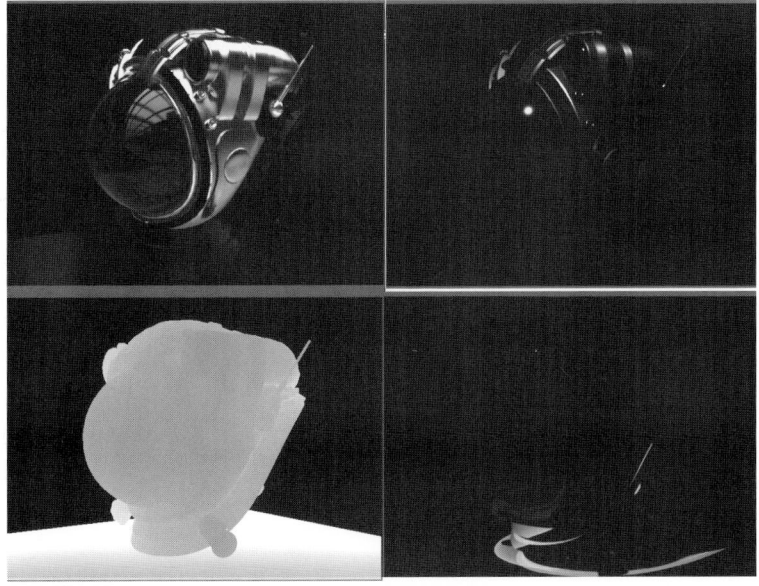

TONE MAPPING

Note that render passes are not tone mapped; in other words, lens shaders applied to adjust the exposure of the image in the render view are not applied to the passes. IMF_display allows you to view the tone-mapped image by choosing the Tone Map option in the View menu. For more about tone mapping and lens shaders, consult Chapters 9 and 10.

The shadow pass will appear inverted in IMF_display. When you import this image into your compositing program, you can invert the colors and adjust as needed to create the effect you need.

To see a finished version of the scene, open the `helmetComposite_v03.ma` scene from the `chapter12\scenes` directory on the DVD.

You can add render passes to a render layer in the Render Layer Editor. To do this, follow these steps:

1. Right-click the layer.

2. Choose Add New Render Pass.

3. Choose the type of pass from the pop-up list (Figure 12.23).

   The pass then automatically appears in the Associated Passes section in the Passes tab of the Render Settings window.

FIGURE 12.23
You can add render passes to a render layer by right-clicking the layer in the Render Layer Editor.

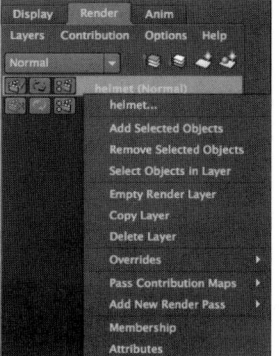

To remove a pass from a render layer, follow these steps:

1. Open the Render Settings window.

2. Switch to the Passes tab for the selected render layer.

3. Click the clapboard icon with the red *X* between the Scene Passes and the Associated Passes sections.

WRANGLING RENDER PASSES

In some situations, a certain combination of materials, lights, and lens shaders will cause render passes to misbehave, giving you results you don't expect or want. There are some workarounds you can use to try to solve these problems.

The mental ray passes materials have an Output Maya 2009 Passes option in the Advanced rollout of the materials' Attribute Editor. Activating this might solve some problems such as physical lights rendering shadow passes incorrectly.

If this doesn't work, another solution is to follow these steps:

1. Create a new render layer.

2. Use standard Maya shaders (such as Blinn, Lambert, Phong, and so on) on the surfaces.

3. Use this render layer to generate shadow passes or alternate reflection passes depending on what you need.

A third option is to fall back on the render layer presets that were used in versions of Maya before render passes were introduced in version 2009. To find these presets, follow these steps:

1. Select your render layer in the Outliner (it appears in the Outliner when the DAG Objects Only option is deselected in the Display menu).

2. Open its Attribute Editor.

3. Click the Presets button.

Here you'll find the older Luminance Depth, Occlusion, Diffuse, Specular, and other presets. The advantage of these render layer presets is that they are easy to use. The disadvantage is that these are render layers and not render passes, so Maya has to render an entirely separate sequence for the render layer instead of extracting the necessary information from the render buffer. This can mean longer render times.

Creating an Ambient Occlusion Pass

The mental ray renderer has a built-in ambient occlusion pass, which creates ambient occlusion shadowing in a render pass without the use of a custom shader network. Prior to the introduction of render passes in version 2009, the standard practice was to use a shader network to create the look of ambient occlusion, and a separate render layer used this shader as a material override. This can still be done, but in many cases using a render pass is faster and easier.

As explained in Chapter 9, ambient occlusion is a type of shadowing that occurs when indirect light rays are prevented from reaching a surface. Ambient occlusion is a soft and subtle type of shadowing. It's usually found in the cracks and crevices of objects in diffuse lighting.

To create ambient occlusion shadowing, mental ray uses ray tracing to determine how the shading of a surface is colored. When a ray from the camera intersects with geometry, a number of secondary rays are shot from the point of intersection on the surface back into the scene. Imagine all the secondary rays as a hemisphere above each point on the surface that receives an initial ray from the camera. If the secondary ray detects another object (or part of the same object) within a given distance from the original surface, that point on the original surface has a dark color applied. If no other nearby surfaces are detected, then a light color is applied. The level of dark or light color is determined by the proximity of nearby surfaces.

In this section, you'll practice creating an ambient occlusion pass for the space helmet scene. The scene has a single render layer named helmet. This layer is a duplicate of the master-Layer. You can create render passes for the masterLayer, but for the sake of simulating a production workflow, you'll use a render layer in this demonstration.

1. Open the `helmetComposite_v03.ma` scene from the `chapter12\scenes` directory on the DVD.

2. Open the Render Settings window, and choose the Passes tab. At the top of the Render Settings window, make sure Render Layer is set to Helmet.

3. Click the top icon to the right of the Scene Passes section to open the Create Render Passes window.

4. From Pass List, select Ambient Occlusion (AO) (Figure 12.24).

FIGURE 12.24
Select the Ambient Occlusion preset from the list of available render pass presets.

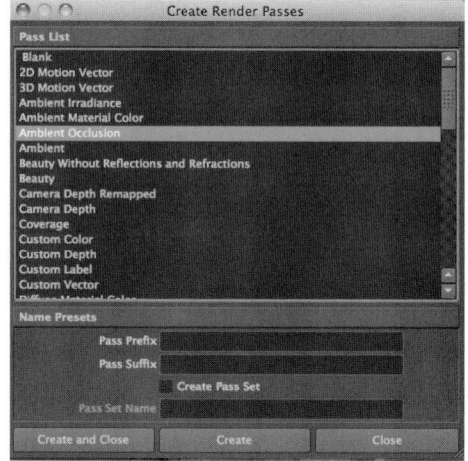

5. Click Create And Close to add the pass to the Scene Passes section.

6. You'll now see the Ambient Occlusion pass listed in the Scene Passes section as AO. Select the AO pass, and open the Attribute Editor. (If the pass settings don't appear in the Attribute Editor, double-click AO on the Passes tab of the Render Settings window.)

   The settings for the pass are listed in the Attribute Editor. These include the following:

   ◆ The number of channels used for the pass

   ◆ The bit depth

   The available settings may differ depending on the selected pass preset:

   ◆ When Channels is set to 3, the pass will contain the red, green, and blue (RGB) channels.

   ◆ When Channels is set to 4, an alpha channel is also included along with the red, green, and blue channels.

7. Set the number of channels to 4 so that the alpha channel is included in the rendered image.

GLOBAL AMBIENT OCCLUSION SETTINGS

In the Indirect Lighting tab of the Render Settings Window there is an Ambient Occlusion rollout that controls the global settings for creating ambient occlusion passes. These settings are bypassed when you activate the Use Local Settings in the Ambient Occlusion render pass attributes. Leave the Ambient Occlusion check box selected regardless of whether you are using local or global settings.

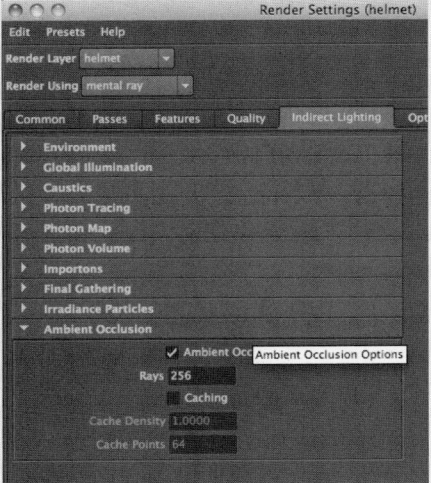

New!

8. Maya 2011 now introduces local settings for tuning the look of the ambient occlusion pass. Scroll down to the lower section of the Attribute Editor, and activate the Use Local AO Settings feature.

9. The Rays attribute adjusts the overall quality of the ambient occlusion shading. Increasing this setting improves quality but also increases render times. Leave this at 64, which is a good setting for testing.

   Bright and dark colors   The bright and dark colors determine how a surface is shaded based on the proximity of other surfaces or parts of the same surface. If you reverse these colors, you'll see the negative image of the ambient occlusion shadowing. For most compositions, it's fine to leave these as black and white. The values can easily be edited in compositing software after rendering.

   Spread   Spread determines the distance of the shading effect across the surface. Think of this as the size of the shadow. Higher values produce tighter areas of shadowing on the surface; lower values produce broader, softer shadows.

   Maximum Distance   The Maximum Distance attribute determines how much of the scene is sampled. Think of this as the distance the secondary rays travel in the scene as they search out nearby surfaces. If a nearby object is beyond the Maximum Distance, then it will not affect how ambient occlusion is calculated because the secondary rays will never reach it. When Maximum Distance is set to 0, the entire scene is sampled; the Max Distance is essentially infinite.

One of the best ways to increase efficiency in the scene is to establish a value for Maximum Distance. This decreases the render time and improves the look of the image. Determining the proper value for Maximum Distance often takes a little experimentation and a few test renders. You want to find the value that offers the type of shadowing you need within a reasonable render time.

10. Set Maximum Distance to 4. Leave Spread at 0 (see Figure 12.25).

FIGURE 12.25
The Use Local AO Settings feature allows you to adjust how the ambient occlusion will look when the AO render pass for the Helmet layer is created.

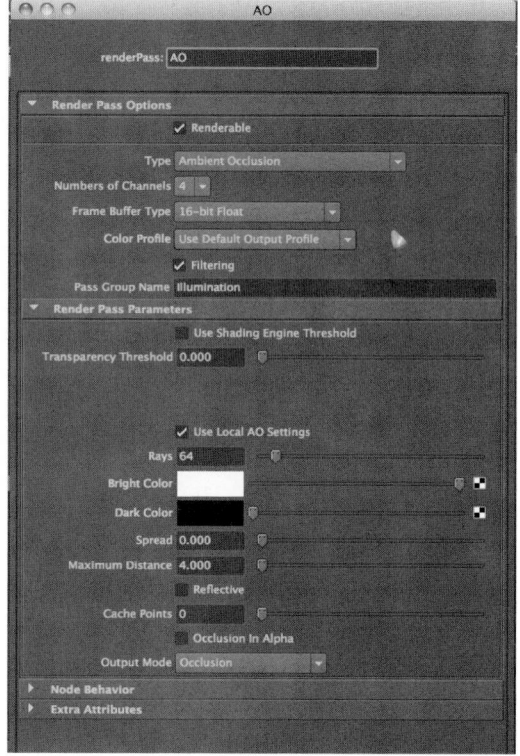

At this point, these settings should produce a nice-looking ambient occlusion pass for this scene. Now you need to associate this pass with the helmet render layer. To save some render time for this exercise, the other render passes created earlier in the chapter can be deassociated.

11. On the Passes tab of the Render Settings window for the Helmet layer, select AO in the Scene Passes section, and click the icon with the green check mark to move it down to the Associated Passes section.

12. Shift-select the depth, diffuse, reflection, shadow, and specular passes in the Associated Passes section so that they are highlighted in blue.

13. Click the icon with the red *X* to move them back to the Scene Passes section. This means that they will not be calculated when the Helmet render layer is rendered (see Figure 12.26).

FIGURE 12.26
FIGURE 12.26
Calculation of the
other render passes
is disabled by mov-
ing them from the
Associated Render
Pass section up to
the Scene Passes
section.

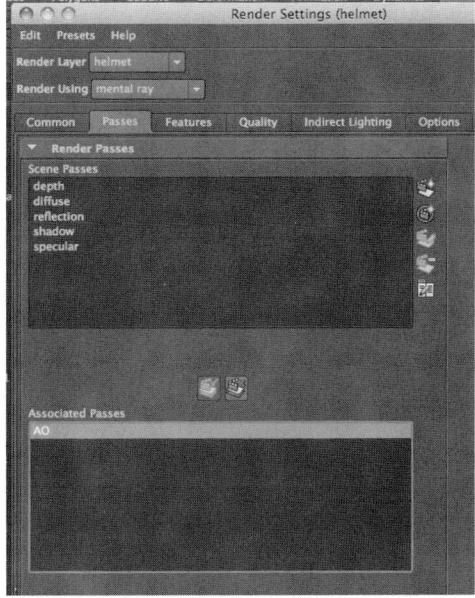

Even though you have set up the AO layer and associated it with the Helmet render layer,
the ambient occlusion will not calculate correctly until you enable Ambient Occlusion in the
Features section of the Render Settings window. This is an easy thing to forget!

14. Click the Features tab of the Render Settings window.

15. Under Secondary Effects, select the Ambient Occlusion option (see Figure 12.27).

16. Open the Render View window, and create a render using the renderCam camera. You
won't see any ambient occlusion in this render; however, it is being calculated and stored
as a separate image.

The pass is stored in a temporary folder in the project's Images directory. If the scene uses
layers, each layer has its own subfolder where the passes are stored.

FIGURE 12.27
Turn on Ambient
Occlusion on the
Features tab of the
render settings.

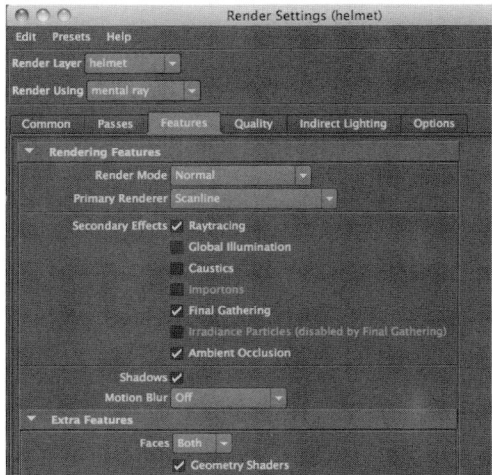

17. To see the Ambient Occlusion pass, use the File menu in the Render View window. Choose File ➢ Load Render Pass ➢ AO. The image opens in a separate image view window (see Figure 12.28).

18. Save the scene as **helmetComposite_v04.ma**.

To see a finished version of the scene, open the helmetComposite_v04.ma scene from the chapter12\scenes directory on the DVD.

FIGURE 12.28
The ambient occlusion pass as it appears in IMF_display

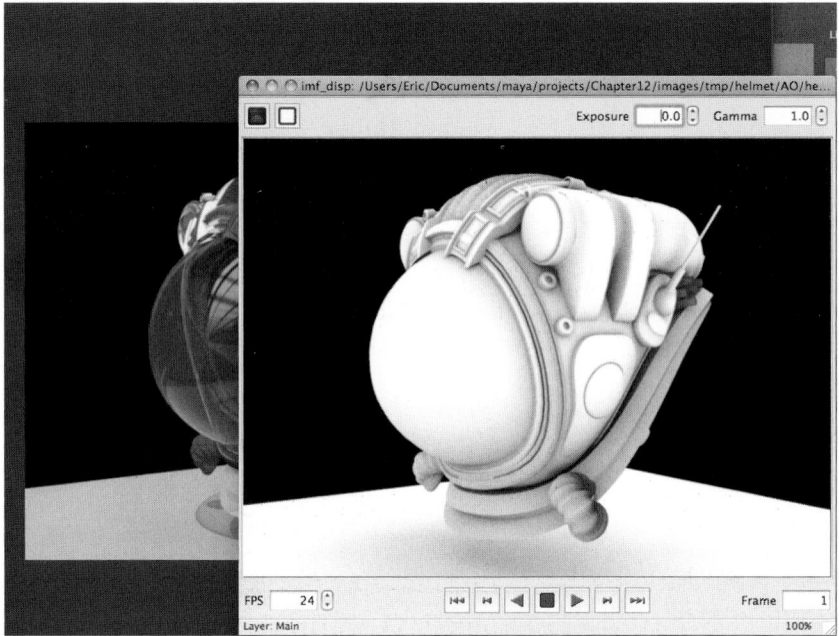

AMBIENT OCCLUSION PASSES AND BUMP/DISPLACEMENT TEXTURES

Displacement maps applied to objects via shaders will be included in the ambient occlusion render pass regardless of the type of shader that is applied to the object. However, this is not true for bump maps. The details you create using a texture connected to the object's shader may not appear in the ambient occlusion pass if you're using a standard Maya material such as a Blinn or Lambert. If you're using the mental ray mia_material_x_passes shader and a bump texture is connected to the shader's Standard Bump channel, then you'll see the details of the bump texture in the ambient occlusion pass.

In the images shown here, you can see that the two cubes at the top have a fractal texture applied to the bump channel of a standard Lambert shader. These details do not appear in the ambient occlusion pass (on the top right). The cubes at the bottom use an mia_material_x_passes shader, and you can clearly see the bump texture in the ambient occlusion pass (on the bottom right).

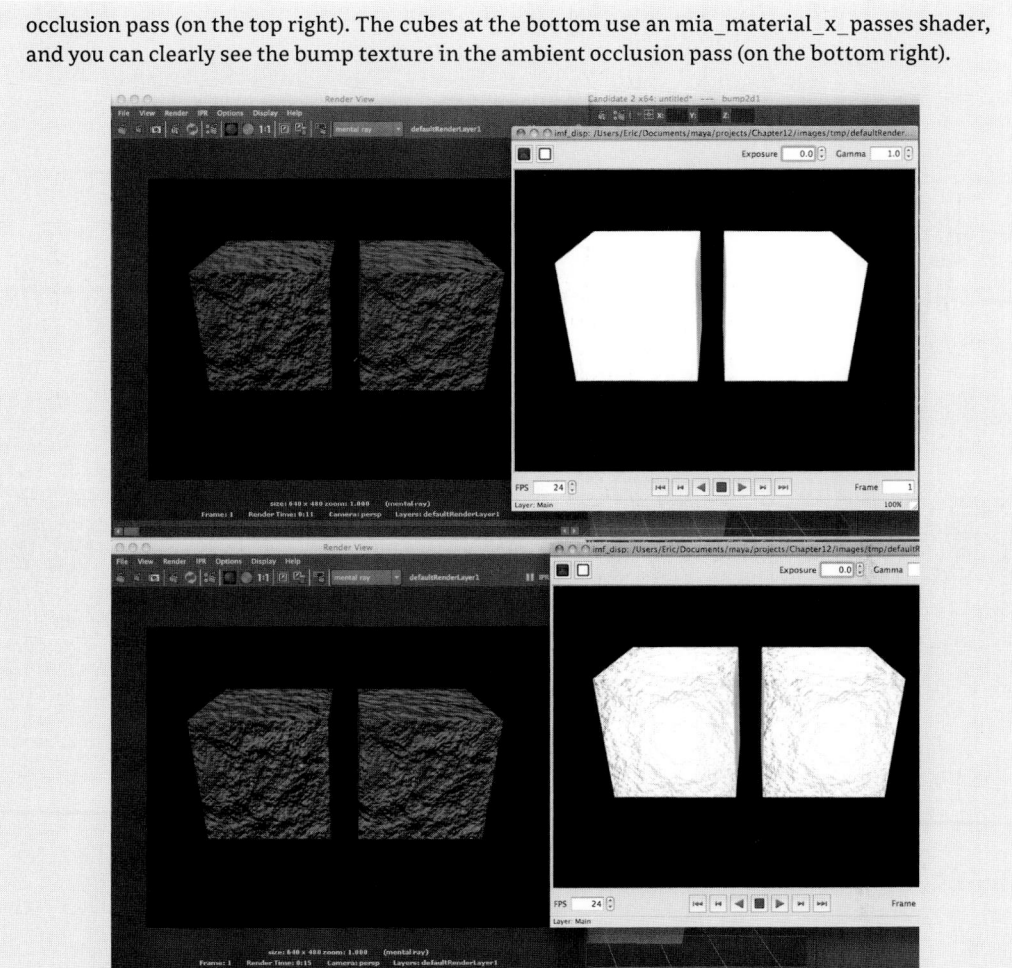

Render Pass Contribution Maps

Render pass contribution maps can be used to further customize the render passes for each layer. A contribution map specifies which objects and lights are included in a render pass. By default when you create a render pass and associate it with a particular render layer, all the objects on the layer are included in the pass. Using a contribution map, you can add only certain lights and objects to the render pass. The whole point is to give you even more flexibility when rendering for compositing. This exercise demonstrates how to set up contribution maps.

This scene uses an HDRI image to create reflections on the surface of the metal. To render the scene correctly, you'll need to download the `building_probe.hdr` image from Paul Debevec's website at www.debevec.org/Probes/. This image should be connected to the mentalrayIbl1 node in the `minigunComposite_v01.ma` scene. Select this node in the Outliner, open its Attribute Editor, and use the Image Name field to link to the image on your disk. For more information on using the mentalrayIbl node, consult Chapter 10.

1. Open the `minigunComposite_v01.ma` scene from the `chapter12\scenes` directory on the DVD. This scene contains a model of a minigun, a simple backdrop, some directional lights, and the surfaces in the scene.

2. In the Outliner, expand the turret object.

3. Select the right_mount1 node.

4. In the Render Layer Editor, right-click the miniGun layer, and choose Pass Contribution Maps ➤ Create Pass Contribution Map And Add Selected (see Figure 12.29).

5. A small arrow is added to the miniGun render layer label. Click this label to expand the layer.

6. You'll see the contribution map listed as passContributionMap1. Double-click this, and change the name to **rightGun** (see Figure 12.30).

7. Repeat steps 2–5 for the left_mount group. Name the new contribution map **leftGun**.

8. Select the miniGun render layer, open the Render Settings window, and switch to the Passes tab.

FIGURE 12.29
Create a render pass contribution map from the selected objects in the Outliner.

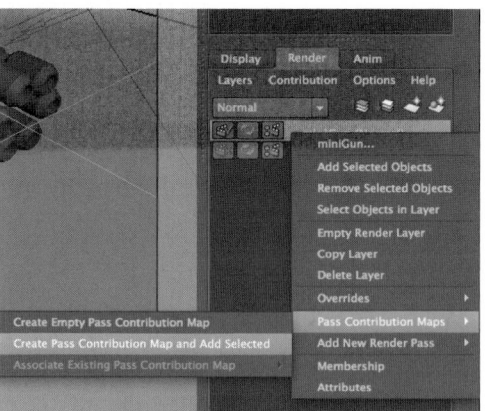

FIGURE 12.30
Rename the new map rightGun.

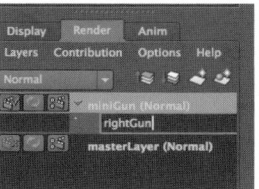

RENDER PASS CONTRIBUTION MAPS | **657**

9. Click the Create New Render Pass icon to the right of the Scene Passes section, and add Reflection and Specular passes.

10. Select both the Reflection and Specular passes in the Scene Passes section.

11. Click the green check mark icon to move them to the Associated Passes section.

12. Below the Associated Passes section, you'll see the Associated Pass Contribution Map section. Set the Associated Pass Contribution Map drop-down menu to rightGun.

13. Select the Reflection pass in the Associated Passes section, and click the green check mark icon below this section to move the Reflection pass preset to the associated pass contribution map.

    This means that only the objects in the rightGun contribution map (the right_mount1 group) appear in the Reflection pass created for the miniGun layer.

14. Repeat steps 10–13, but this time set the Associated Pass Contribution Map drop-down menu to leftGun, and move the Specular pass down to the Passes Used By Contribution Map section (Figure 12.31).

15. Open the Render View window, and create a render using the renderCam camera. Once again, the render looks the same as if you had not added any render passes.

FIGURE 12.31
Associate the Specular pass with the leftGun contribution map.

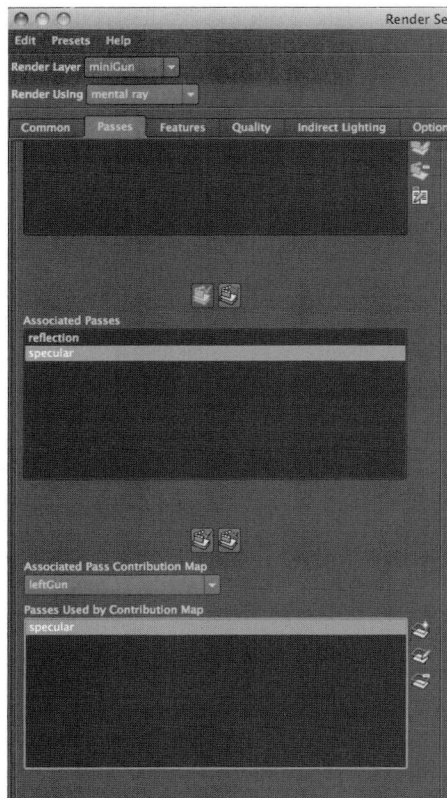

16. When the image has finished rendering, use the File menu in the Render View window to load the Specular and Reflection passes.

Notice that in these passes, only one part of the gun appears. In the Specular pass, the left_mount group appears; in the Reflection pass, the right_mount1 group appears (Figure 12.32). The rest of the gun and the backdrop are absent from each pass. Although this is not a practical application of contribution maps, it demonstrates clearly that the point of a contribution map is to specify exactly which objects appear in a render pass.

17. Save the scene as `minigunComposite_v02.ma`.

To see a version of the scene to this point, open the `minigunComposite_v02.ma` scene from the `chapter12\scenes` directory on the DVD.

FIGURE 12.32
After you render the image, the Reflection and Specular passes show only the objects added to the contribution map for each pass.

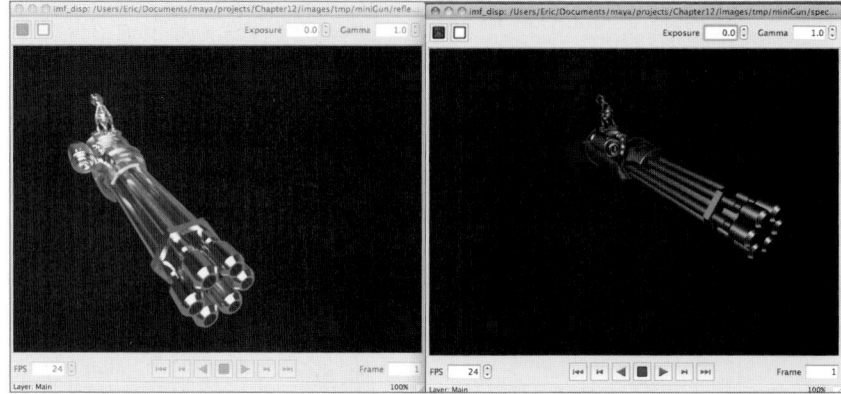

Lights and Contribution Maps

Lights can also be included in contribution maps. If no lights are specified, all the scene lights are added. In the minigun scene, the directional light is the only light that casts shadows; the other two lights have shadow casting turned off. You can use pass contribution maps to create a shadow pass just for this light.

1. Continue with the scene from the previous section, or open the `minigunComposite_v02.ma` scene from the `chapter12/scenes` directory on the DVD.

2. In the Outliner, Shift+click ground and directionalLight1.

3. In the Render Layer Editor, right-click the miniGun render layer, and choose Pass Contribution Maps ➤ Create Pass Contribution Map And Add Selected.

4. Double-click passContributionMap1, and rename it **groundShadow**.

5. Open the Render Settings window, and switch to the Passes tab.

6. Select Reflection and Specular in the Associated Passes section, and click the red *X* icon to move them to the Scene Passes section. Doing this prevents the passes from being included in the render.

7. Click the Create New Render Pass button, and add a Raw Shadow pass to the Scene Passes section.

8. Move shadowRaw from the Scene Passes section to the Associated Passes section. (Make sure miniGun is the currently selected render layer when you do this.)

9. Set Associated Pass Contribution Map to groundShadow. Use the green check mark icon below the Associated Passes to move shadowRaw into the Passes Used By Contribution Map section (see Figure 12.33).

FIGURE 12.33
Associate the shadowRaw preset with the groundShadow contribution map.

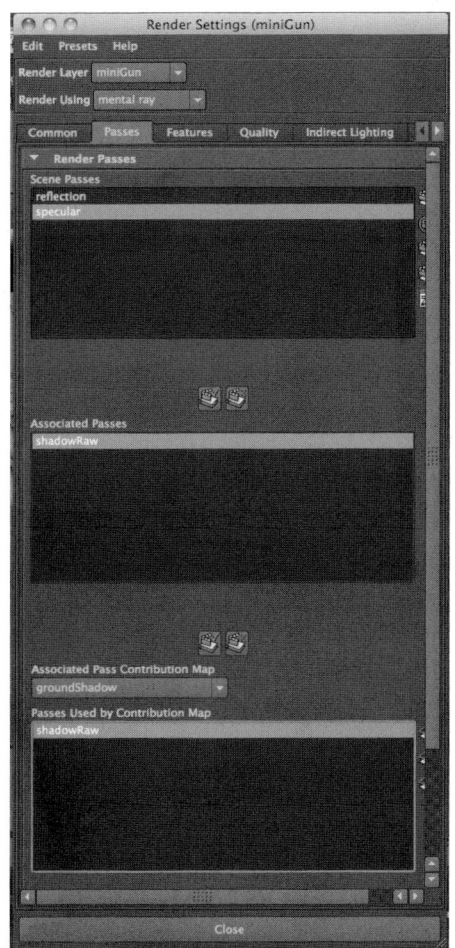

10. Double-click the shadowRaw pass to open its Attribute Editor.

11. In the Attribute Editor, disable Hold-Out (see Figure 12.34).

    The Hold-Out setting creates a geometry mask for geometry that is not included in the render pass. By disabling this, you'll see only the ground surface and the cast shadow in the render.

FIGURE 12.34
In the settings for shadowRaw, disable the Hold-Out option.

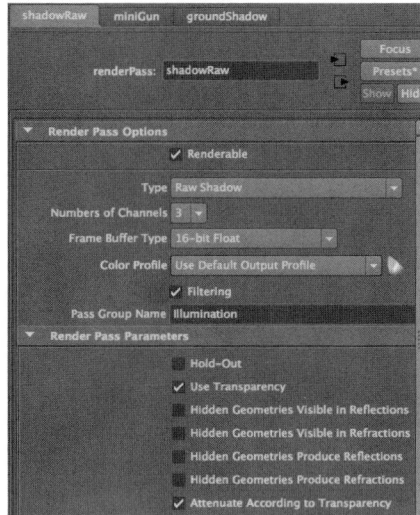

12. Open the Render View window, and create a test render from the renderCam camera (see Figure 12.35). As before, you can then view the pass by using the Render View's File ➤ Load Render Pass menu command.

13. Save the scene as `miniGun_v03.ma`.

In the composite, the shadow pass should be inverted and color corrected. When creating a shadow pass contribution map, you may want to include just the shadow-casting lights. In some cases, including all the lights can produce strange results.

To see a finished version of the scene, open the `miniGun_v03.ma` scene from the `chapter12\scenes` directory on the DVD.

FIGURE 12.35
The ground-Shadow contribution map shows only the directionalLight, the ground, and the shadow cast by the gun geometry.

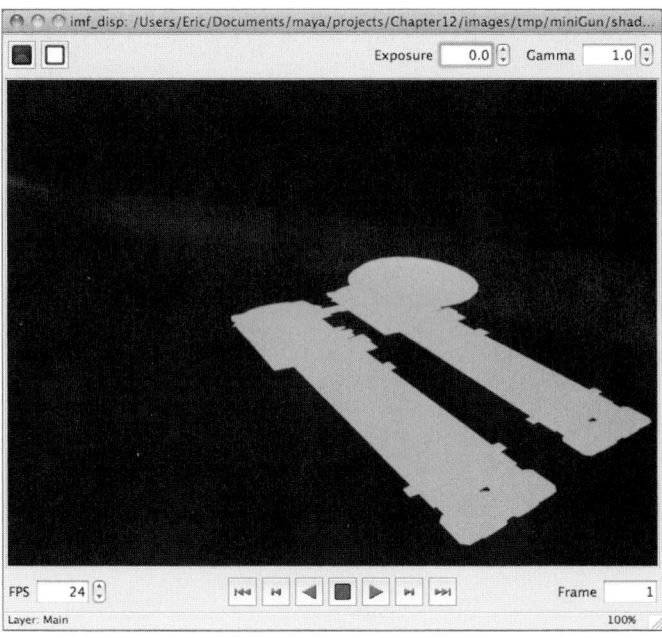

Render Pass Sets

Render pass sets are simply a way to organize large lists of render passes on the Passes tab of the Render Settings window. You can create different groupings of the passes listed in the Scene Passes section, give them descriptive names, and then associate the set with the render layer or the associated contribution maps. If you have a complex scene that has a large number of passes, you'll find it's easier to work with the pass sets rather than all the individual passes.

You can create a render pass set as you create the render passes or add them to the set later. In the Create Render Passes window, select the Create Pass Set box, and give the pass set a descriptive name (Figure 12.36). The new pass set appears in the Scene Passes section in the Render Settings window along with all the newly created passes (Figure 12.36). To associate a render layer with the new pass set, you only have to move the pass set to the Associated Passes section. All the passes included with the set will be associated with the layer even though they do not appear in the Associated Passes section.

FIGURE 12.36
You can create a pass set in the Create Render Passes window using the options at the bottom.

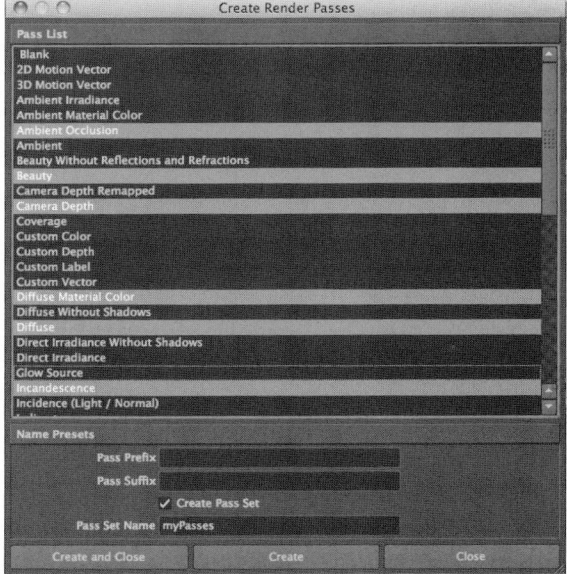

To verify which passes are included in the set, open the Relationship Editor for render passes (Window ➢ Relationship Editors ➢ Render Pass Sets). When you highlight the pass set on the left, the passes in the set are highlighted on the right. You can add or remove passes from the set by selecting them from the list on the right of the Relationship Editor (Figure 12.37).

You can add a new set on the Passes tab of the Render Settings window by clicking the Create New Render Pass Set icon. You can then use the Relationship Editor to add the passes to the set. A render pass can be a member of more than one set.

FIGURE 12.37
Associating the set with the current render layer associates all of its contained passes with the layer. You can use the Relationship Editor to add and remove passes from the set.

Setting Up a Render with mental ray

Rendering is the process of translating a Maya animation into a sequence of images. The images are processed and saved to disk. The rendered image sequences can then be brought into compositing software, where they can be layered together, edited, color corrected, combined with live footage, and have additional effects applied. The composite can then be converted to a movie file or a sequence of images for distribution or imported to editing software for further processing.

Generally you want to render a sequence of images from Maya. You can render directly to a movie file, but this usually is not a good idea. If the render stops while rendering directly to a movie file, it may corrupt the movie, and you will need to restart the whole render. When you render a sequence of images and the render stops, you can easily restart the render without recreating any of the images that have already been saved to disk.

When you set up a batch render, you can specify how the image sequence will be labeled and numbered. You also set the image format of the final render, which render layers and passes will be included and where they will be stored, and other aspects related to the rendered sequences. You can use Maya's Render Settings window to determine these properties or perform a command-line render using your operating system's terminal. In this section, you'll learn important features of both methods.

Batch rendering is also accomplished using render farm software, which distributes the render across multiple computers. This subject is beyond the scope of this book.

New!

COLOR PROFILE MANAGEMENT

New to Maya 2011, you can now specify a color profile if you need to match a specific color space in your compositing software or if you need to match footage that requires a specific setting. A color profile can be assigned to individual textures and render passes. Many nodes throughout Maya now support the assignment of color profiles. For example, when you create a file texture node for use in a shader, you'll see a drop-down menu that gives you options for assigning a color profile (underneath the File Name field in the File node's Attribute Editor).

It is crucial to understand that unless you enable Color Management on the Common tab of the Render Settings window, any color profiles you assign to textures or render passes will not work.

File Tokens

File tokens are a way to automate the organization of your renders. If your scene has a lot of layers, cameras, and passes, you can use tokens to specify where all the image sequences will be placed on your computer's hard drive, as well as how they are named.

The image sequences created with a batch render are placed in the Images folder of the current project or whichever folder is specified in the Project Settings window (see Chapter 1 for information regarding project settings). Tokens are placed in the File Name Prefix field found on the Common tab of the Render Settings window. If this field is left blank, the scene name is used to label the rendered images (Figure 12.38).

FIGURE 12.38

The File Name Prefix field on the Common tab of the Render Settings window is where you specify the image name and tokens.

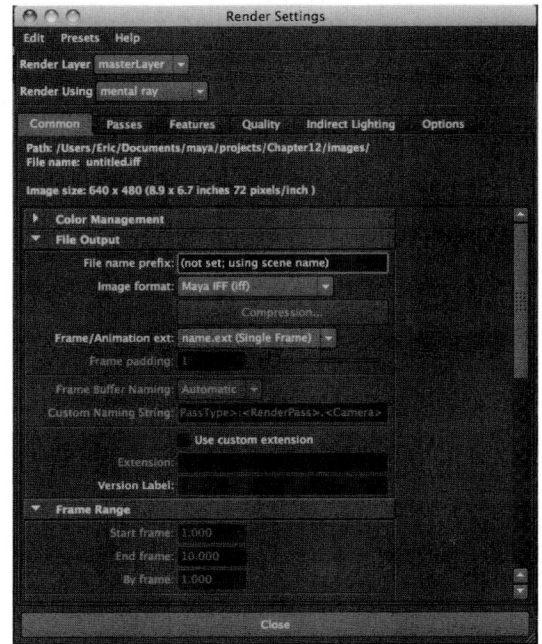

By default, if the scene has more than one render layer, Maya creates a subfolder for each layer. If the scene has more than one camera, a subfolder is created for each camera. For scenes with multiple render layers and multiple cameras, Maya creates a subfolder for each camera within the subfolder for each layer.

You can specify any directory you want by typing the folder names into the File Name Prefix field. For example, if you want your image sequences to be named marshmallow and placed in a folder named chocolateSauce, you can type **chocolateSauce/marshmallow** into the File Name Prefix field. However, explicitly naming a file sequence lacks the flexibility of using tokens and runs the risk of allowing you to overwrite file sequences by mistake when rendering. You can see a preview of how the images will be named in the upper portion of the Render Settings window (Figure 12.39).

The whole point of tokens is to allow you to change the default behavior and specify how subfolders will be created dynamically for a scene. To use a token to specify a directory, place a slash after the token name. For example, to create a subfolder named after each camera, type **<camera>/** into the File Name Prefix field. To use a token to name the images, omit the slash. For example, typing **<scene>/<camera>** results in a folder named after the scene containing a sequence of images named camera.iff.

FIGURE 12.39
A preview of the image name appears at the top of the Common tab of the Render Settings window.

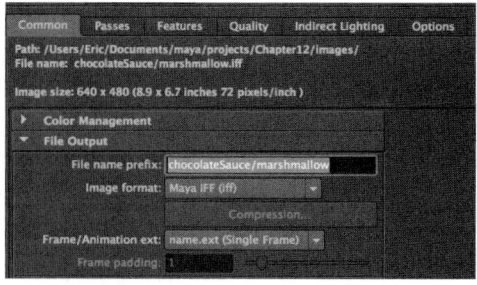

Here are some of the more common tokens:

<Scene>   This token names the images or subfolder after the scene name.

<Camera>   This token names the images or subfolders after the camera. For example, in a scene with two cameras named renderCam1 and renderCam2, <Scene>/<Camera>/<Camera> creates a single folder named after the scene, within which are two subfolders named renderCam1 and renderCam2. In each of these folders is a sequence named renderCam1.ext and renderCam2.ext.

<RenderLayer>   This token creates a subfolder or sequence named after each render layer. If there are passes associated with the layer, then the pass names are appended to the layer name. For example, if you have a layer named spurtsOfBlood and an associated specular pass, the folder or image sequence would automatically be named spurtsOfBlood_specular.

<RenderPass>   This token creates a subfolder or sequence named after the render pass. Since render passes are available only for mental ray renders, this token applies only when using mental ray.

<RenderPassType>   This token is similar to <RenderPass> except it abbreviates the name of the render pass. A reflection pass, for example, would be abbreviated as REFL.

<RenderPassFileGroup>   This adds the name of the render pass file group. The file group name is set in the Attribute Editor of the render pass node (see Figure 12.40). Render pass file groups are assigned by mental ray, but you can create your own name for the group by typing it in the Pass Group Name field of the render pass node.

<Extension>   This adds the file format extension. It is usually added to the end of the filename automatically, but you can also use this token to label a directory based on the image format.

<Version>   This adds a custom label specified by the Version Label field in the Render Settings window (Figure 12.41).

FIGURE 12.40
You can set the render pass group name in the Attribute Editor of the render pass node.

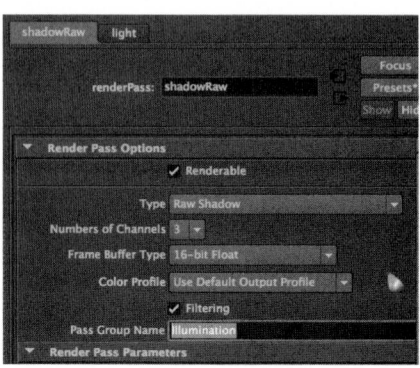

FIGURE 12.41
The `<Version>` token adds the label specified in the Version Label field in the Render Settings window.

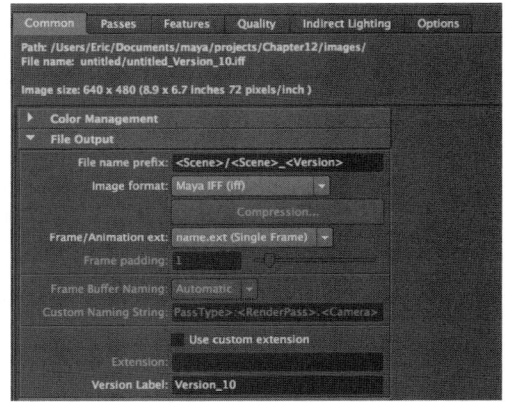

Note that the capitalization of the token name does matter. If you had a scene named choco-lateSauce that has a render layer named banana that uses a specular and diffuse pass with two cameras named shot1 and shot2 and you wanted to add the version label v05, the following tokens specified in the File Name Prefix field

`<Scene>/<RenderLayer>/<Camera>/<RenderPass>/<RenderPass>_<Version>`

would create a file structure that looks like this:

```
chocolateSauce/banana/shot1/specular/specular_v05.#.ext
chocolateSauce/banana/shot1/diffuse/diffuse_v05.#.ext
chocolateSauce/banana/shot2/specular/specular_v05.#.ext
chocolateSauce/banana/shot2/diffuse/diffuse_v05.#.ext
```

Use underscores or hyphens when combining tokens in the directory or image name. Avoid using periods.

You can right-click the File Name Prefix field to access a list of commonly used token keywords. This is a handy way to save a little typing.

TOKENS FOR OPENEXR FILES

The OpenEXR format can create multiple additional channels within a single image. Each channel can contain an image created from a render pass. If a scene has one or more render passes and you choose the OpenEXR image format, you can use the Frame Buffer Naming field to specify the name of each pass. This feature is available only when OpenEXR is chosen as the file format and the scene has one or more render passes. You can use the automatic naming setting or enable the Custom option in the Frame Buffer Naming drop-down menu. You can then use the Custom Naming String field to choose the token you want to use.

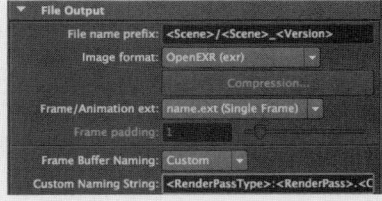

Specifying Frame Range

For multiframe animations, you have a number of options for specifying the frame range and the syntax for the filenames in the sequence. These settings are found on the Common tab of the Render Settings window. To enable multiframe rendering, choose one of the presets from the Frame/Animation Ext menu. When rendering animation sequences, the safest choice is usually the name.#.ext option. This names the images in the sequence by placing a dot between the image name and the image number and another dot between the image number and the file extension. The Frame Padding option allows you to specify a number of zeros between the image number and the extension. So, a sequence named marshmallow using the Maya IFF format with a Frame Padding of 4 would look like `marshmallow.0001.iff`.

The Frame Range settings specify which frames in the animation will be rendered. The By Frame setting allows you to render each frame (using a setting of 1), skip frames (using a setting higher than 1), or render twice as many frames (using a setting of 0.5, which renders essentially at half speed).

It is possible to render backward by specifying a higher frame number for the Start Frame value than the End Frame value and using a negative number for By Frame. You would then want to use the Renumber Frames option so the frame numbers move upward incrementally.

The Renumber Frames option allows you to customize the labeling of the image sequence numbers.

Renderable Cameras

The rendering cameras are specified in the Renderable Camera list. To add a camera, expand the Renderable Camera menu, and choose Add Renderable Camera (see Figure 12.42). To remove a rendering camera, click the trash can icon next to the renderable camera. As noted earlier in the chapter, you can use a layer override to include a specific camera with a render layer.

FIGURE 12.42
You can add and remove renderable cameras using the Renderable Camera menu.

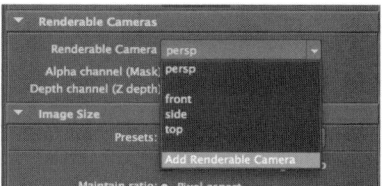

Each camera has the option of rendering alpha and Z depth channels. The Z depth channel stores information about the depth in the scene. This is included as an extra channel in the image (only a few formats such as Maya IFF support this extra channel). Not all compositing software supports Maya's Z depth channel. You may find it easier to create a camera depth pass using the custom passes (passes are described earlier in this chapter). The render depth pass can be imported into your compositing software and used with a filter to create depth-of-field effects.

File Formats and the Frame Buffer

When Maya renders a scene, the data stored in the Frame Buffer is converted into the native IFF format and then translated to the file type specified in the Image Format menu. So if you specify the SGI format, for example, Maya translates the SGI image from the native IFF format.

Most popular compositing packages (such as Adobe After Effects and Autodesk Composite) support the IFF format, so it's usually safe to render to this file format. The IFF format uses four 8-bit channels by default, which is usually adequate for most viewing purposes. If you need to change the file to a different bit depth or a different number of channels, you can choose one of the options from the Data Type menu in the Framebuffer section of the Quality tab. This is where you will also find the output options, such as Premultiply (see Figure 12.43).

FIGURE 12.43
Specify bit depth
and other output
options using
the Framebuffer
settings on the
Quality tab of the
Render Settings
window.

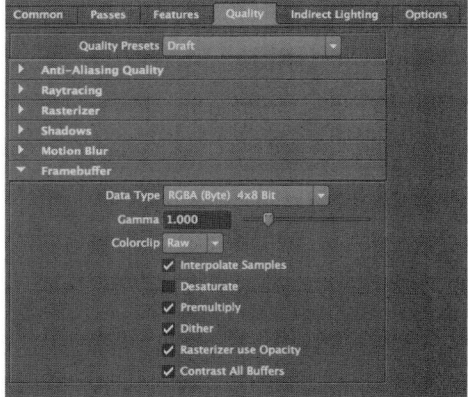

Render passes use the secondary Frame Buffer to store the image data. You can specify the bit depth of this secondary buffer in the Attribute Editor for each render pass.

A complete list of supported image formats is available in the Maya documentation. Note that Maya Software and mental ray may support different file formats.

IMAGE SIZE SETTINGS

The Image Size settings are discussed in Chapter 2.

Starting a Batch Render

When you are satisfied that your animation is ready to render and all the settings have been specified in the Render Settings window, you're ready to start a batch render. To start a batch render, set the main Maya menu set to Rendering and choose Render ➤ Batch Render ➤ Options. In the options, you can specify memory limits and multithreading, as well as local and network rendering.

One of the most useful options is Verbosity Level. This refers to the level of detail of the messages displayed in the Maya Output window as the render takes place. (This works only when using Maya with Windows.) You can use these messages to monitor the progress of the render as well as diagnose problems that may occur while rendering. The Progress Messages setting is the most useful option in most situations (Figure 12.44).

To start the render, click the Batch Render (or the Batch Render And Close) button. As the batch render takes place, you'll see the Script Editor update (Figure 12.45). For detailed information on the progress of each frame, you can monitor the progress in the Output Window.

FIGURE 12.44
Detailed progress messages for each frame can be displayed in the Output Window.

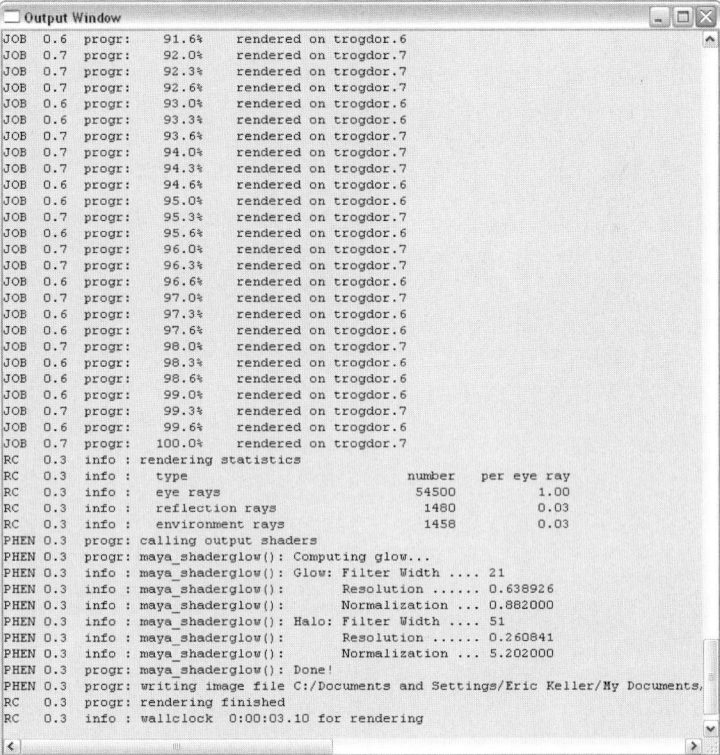

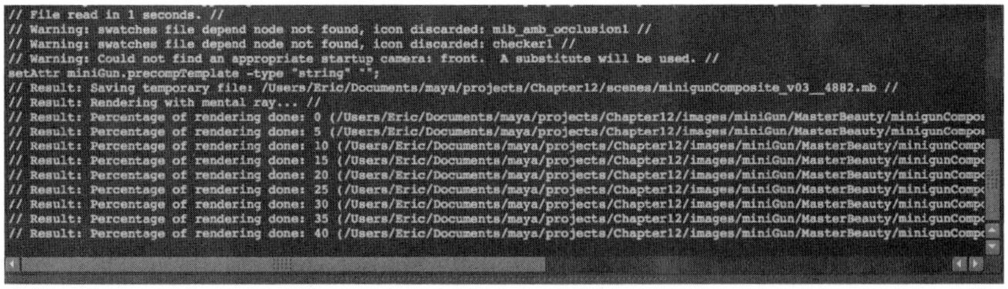

FIGURE 12.45
The Script Editor shows the progress of the batch render.

To stop a batch render, choose Render ➤ Cancel Batch Render. To see how the current frame in the batch render looks, choose Render ➤ Show Batch Render.

When the render is complete, you'll see a message in the Script Editor that says Rendering Completed. You can then use FCheck to view the sequence (File ➤ View Sequence) or import the sequence into your compositing software.

MONITORING A RENDER IN THE SCRIPT EDITOR

The Script Editor is not always completely reliable when it comes to monitoring the progress of a render. If the messages stop updating as the render progresses, it may or may not indicate that the render has stopped. Before assuming the render has stopped, use your computer's operating system to browse to the current image directory, and double-check to see whether images are still being written to disk. This is especially true when using Maya on a Mac.

Command-Line Rendering

A batch render can be initiated using your operating system's command prompt or terminal window. This is known as a *command-line render*. A command-line render takes the form of a series of commands typed into the command prompt. These commands include information about the location of the Maya scene to be rendered, the location of the rendered image sequence, the rendering cameras, the image size, the frame range, and many other options similar to the settings found in the Render Settings window.

Command-line renders tend to be more stable than batch renders initiated from the Maya interface. This is because when the Maya application is closed, more of your computer's RAM is available for the render. You can start a command-line render regardless of whether Maya is running. In fact, to maximize system resources, it's best to close Maya when starting a command-line render. In this example, you can keep Maya open.

In this exercise, you'll see how you can start a batch render on both a Windows computer and a Mac. You'll use the solarSystem_v01.ma scene, which is a very simple animation showing two planets orbiting a glowing sun.

1. From the DVD, copy the solarSystem_v01.ma scene to the scenes directory of your current project on your computer's hard drive.

2. Open the scene in Maya.

This scene has a masterLayer render layer, which should not be rendered, and two additional layers:

◆ The solarSystem layer contains the sun and planets, which have been shaded. It uses the mental ray renderer. If you open the Render Settings window to the Passes tab, you'll see this scene uses two render passes: diffuse and incandescence.

◆ The second layer is named orbitPaths. It contains Paint Effects strokes that illustrate the orbit paths of the two planets (Figure 12.46).

On the Common tab of the Render Settings window, no filename prefix has been specified, and a frame range has not been set. Maya will use the default file structure when rendering the scene, and the frame range will be set in the options for the command line.

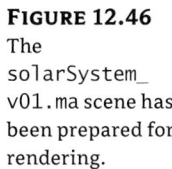

FIGURE 12.46
The solarSystem_v01.ma scene has been prepared for rendering.

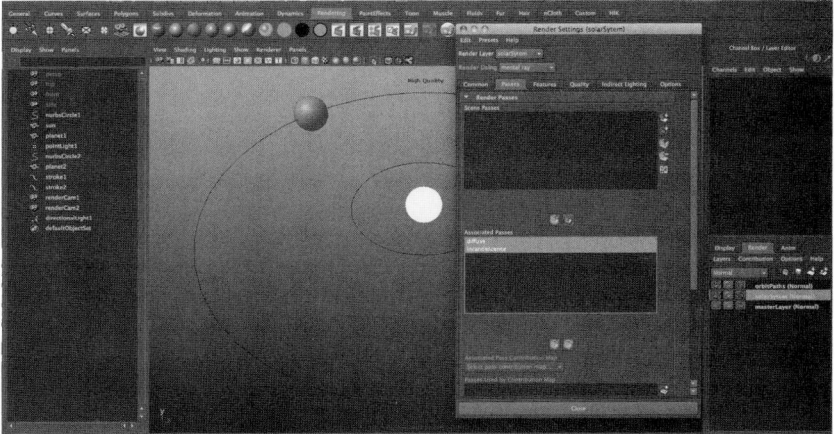

WINDOWS COMMAND-LINE RENDER

The first example starts a command-line render using Windows:

1. Go to the Windows Start menu, and choose Start ➤ All Programs ➤ Accessories ➤ Command Prompt to open the Command Prompt shell.

2. Use Windows Explorer to browse your computer's directory: right-click the Start button, and choose Explore to open Windows Explorer.

3. Open the scenes folder in your current project where you placed the solarSystem_v01.ma scene.

4. Select the Address line at the top of Windows Explorer, and choose Edit ➤ Copy to copy the path to the scenes directory to the clipboard.

5. At the command prompt, type **cd ..\..** and hit Enter. This sets the command prompt to the root directory.

6. Type **cd** and then a space; next right-click the command line and select Paste. This pastes the path to the scenes directory in the command prompt.

7. Press the Enter key to set the current directory to the scenes directory (Figure 12.47).

FIGURE 12.47
Set the command prompt to the current directory where the solarSystem_v01.ma scene is stored (the exact directory path will look different on your machine).

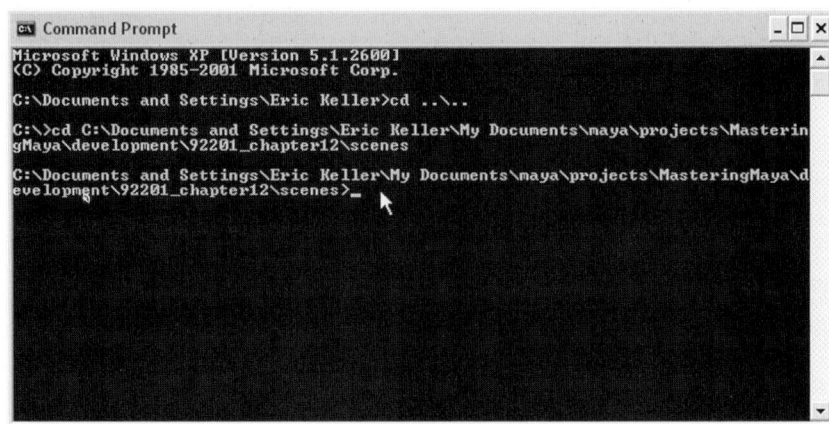

When starting a batch render, you can either specify the path to the scenes directory in the command-line options or set the command prompt to the directory that contains the scene.

To start a batch render, use the render command in the command prompt followed by option flags and the name of the scene you want to render. The option flags are preceded by a hyphen. The flags are followed by a space and then the flag setting. For example, to start a scene using the mental ray renderer, you would type **render -r mr myscene.ma**. The render command starts the batch renderer, the -r flag specifies the renderer, and mr sets the -r flag to mental ray. The command ends with the name of the scene (or the directory path to the scene if you're not already in the directory with the scene).

There are a large number of options, but you don't need to use them, except if you want to specify an option that's different from what is used in the scene. If you want all the layers to render using mental ray regardless of the layer setting in the scene, then you specify mental ray using the -r mr flag. If you omit the -r flag, then Maya uses the default renderer, which is Maya

Software. If you have a scene with several layers that use different renderers (as in the case of the solarSystem_v01.ma scene), then you would type **-r file**. This sets the renderer to whatever is specified in the file, including what is specified for each layer.

Other common flags include the following:

-s <float> sets the start frame. (It replaces <float> with the starting frame; for example, -s 120 would set the start frame to 120. A float is a number with a decimal point.)

-e <float> sets the end frame.

-x <int> sets the X resolution of the image. (An integer is a whole number without a decimal point.)

-y <int> sets the Y resolution of the image.

- cam <name> sets the camera.

-rd <path> specifies the directory for the images. (If this is not used, the directory in the project settings is used.)

-im <filename> sets the name of the rendered image.

-of <format> sets the image format.

There is a complete list of the flags in the Maya documentation. You can also print a description of commands by typing **render -help**. To see mental ray-specific commands, type **render -help -r mr**.

For example, if you want to render the scene using renderCam1, starting on frame1 and ending on frame 24, type the following in the command prompt (Figure 12.48):

```
render -r file -s 1 -e 24 -cam renderCam1solarSystem_v01.ma
```

You'll see the render execute in the command prompt. When it's finished, you can use FCheck to view each sequence. In the Images folder, you'll see two directories named after the layers in the scene. The orbitPath directory has the Paint Effects orbit paths rendered with Maya Software. The solarSystem directory has the rendered sequence of the planets and sun as well as subdirectories for the diffuse, incandescence, and MasterBeauty passes (the MasterBeauty pass is created by default when you add passes to a scene).

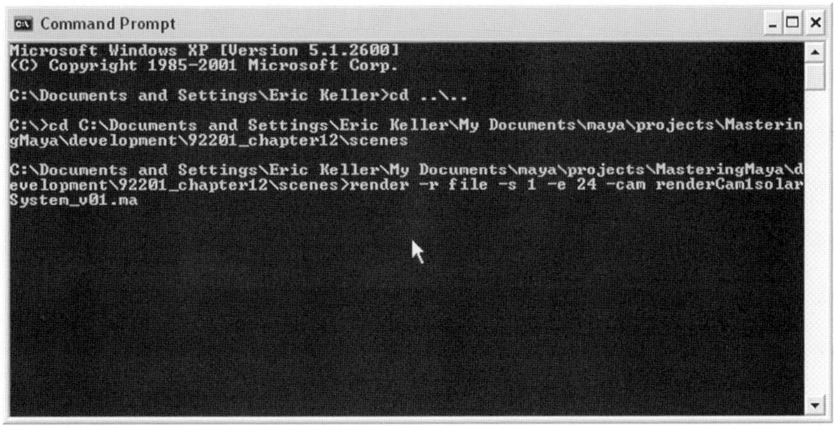

FIGURE 12.48
Enter the render command with options and the scene name in the Command Prompt window.

Let's say you want to render only the orbitPaths layer using renderCam2 for the frame range 16 to 48. You want to specify Maya Software as the renderer. You may want to name the sequence after the camera as well. Type the following into the command prompt (use a single line with no returns):

```
render -r sw -s 16 -e 48 -rl orbitPaths -cam renderCam2 -im solarSystemCam2
solarSystem_v01.ma
```

MAC COMMAND-LINE RENDER

For a Mac, the Maya command-line render workflow is similar except that instead of the command prompt, you use a special Terminal window that is included when you install Maya. This is an application called Maya Terminal.term, and it's found in the Applications\ Autodesk\ Maya 2011 folder (Figure 12.49). It's probably a good idea to add this application to the Dock so you can easily open it whenever you need to run a batch render.

FIGURE 12.49
The Maya Terminal window is installed with Maya in the Maya 2011 folder.

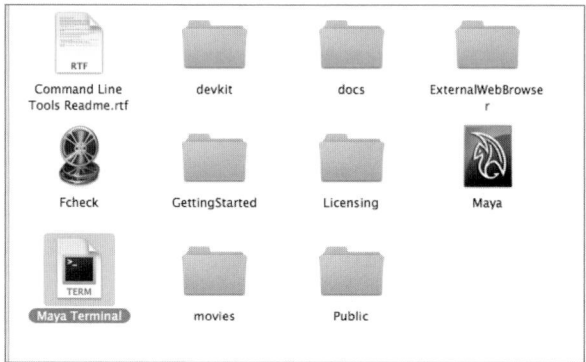

You need to navigate in the terminal to the scenes directory that contains the scene you want to render:

1. Copy the solarSystem_v01.ma scene from the DVD to the scenes directory of your current project on your computer's hard drive.

2. In the Finder, open the current project directory.

3. Start the Maya Terminal application, and type **cd** at the prompt.

4. In the Finder, drag the scenes folder from the current project on top of the Maya Terminal. This places the path to the scenes directory in the Terminal.

5. Press the Enter button. The Terminal window is now set to the project's scenes folder, which contains the solarSytem_v01.ma scene.

The commands for rendering on a Mac are the same as they are for Windows. You can continue starting with step 6 in the previous exercise.

Creating a Batch Script

It's possible to create a text file that can initiate a series of batch renders for a number of different scenes. This can be useful when you need a machine to perform several renders overnight or over a long weekend. This can save you the trouble of starting every batch render manually. This section describes how to create a batch script for Windows and Mac.

WINDOWS BATCH RENDER SCRIPT

To create a batch script for Windows, follow these steps:

1. Move the scenes you want to render into the `renderScenes` directory of the current project. Give them a name that distinguishes them from the original scenes in the `scenes` directory just to avoid confusion.

2. Create a new plain-text file using Notepad.

3. In the text file, type the render commands exactly the same way you would initiate a batch render. Use a new line for each render. For example:

```
render -r file -s 20 -e 120 -cam renderCam1 myScene.mb
render -r file -s 121 -e 150 -cam renderCam2 myScene.mb
render -r file -s 1-e 120 -cam renderCam1 myScene_part2.mb
```

4. Save the scene as a `.bat` file, and save it in the same directory as the scenes you want to render, usually the `renderScenes` directory. The file can be named anything, but it should end in `.bat`. Make sure the format is plain text, for example `weekendRender.bat`.

5. When you are ready to render, double-click the batch script (for example, `weekendRender.bat`), as shown in Figure 12.50.

FIGURE 12.50
An example of a batch script file

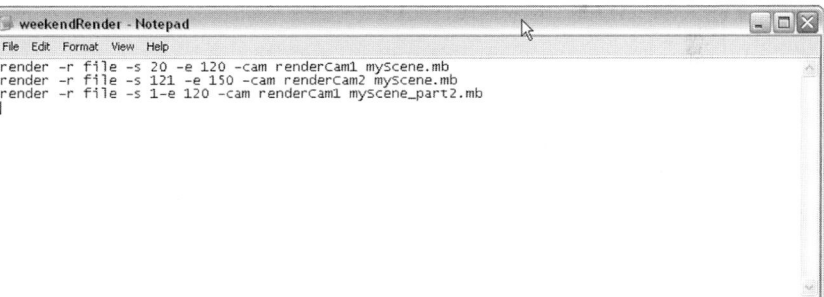

You'll probably want to close Maya to maximize system resources for the render. Maya will render each scene in the order it is listed in the batch file. Be very careful when naming the files and the image sequences so one render does not overwrite a previous render. For example, if you render overlapping frame sequences from the same file, use the `-im` flag in each batch render line to give the image sequences different names.

MAC BATCH RENDER SCRIPT

A few extra steps are involved in creating a Mac batch render script, but for the most part the process is similar to the Windows workflow.

1. Move the scenes you want to render into the `renderScenes` directory of the current project. It's a good idea to give the scenes a name that distinguishes them from the original scenes in the `scenes` directory just to avoid confusion.

2. Create a new plain-text file using TextEdit.

3. In the text file, type the render commands exactly the same way you would initiate a batch render. Use a new line for each render. For example:

```
render -r file -s 20 -e 120 -cam renderCam1 myScene.mb
render -r file -s 121 -e 150 -cam renderCam2 myScene.mb
render -r file -s 1-e 120 -cam renderCam1 myScene_part2.mb
```

4. Save the scene as a `.batch` file, and save it in the same directory as the scenes you want to render, usually the `renderScenes` directory. The file can be named anything, but it should end in `.batch`. Make sure the format is plain text, for example `weekendRender.batch`.

5. In the Maya Terminal window, navigate to the location of the batch file (in the `renderScenes` folder of the current project).

6. Convert the batch file to an executable by typing **chmod 777 weekendRender.batch**.

7. In the Maya Terminal window, navigate to the location of the batch file, and type **./weekendRender.batch**.

The scenes will render in the order in which they are listed in the batch file.

mental ray Quality Settings

The quality of your render is determined by a number of related settings, some of which appear in the Render Settings window and some of which appear in the Attribute Editor of nodes within the scene. Tessellation, anti-aliasing, sampling, and filtering all play a part in how good the final render looks. You will always have to strike a balance between render quality and render time. As you raise the level of quality, you should test your renders and make a note of how long they take. Five minutes to render a single frame may not seem like much until you're dealing with a multilayered animation that is several thousand frames long. Remember that you will almost always have to render a sequence more than once as changes are requested by the director or client (even when you are sure it is the absolute final render!).

In this section, you'll learn how to use the settings on the Quality tab as well as other settings to improve the look of the final render.

ALWAYS TEST SHORT SEQUENCES

A single rendered frame may not reveal all of the quality problems in a scene. Remember to test a short sequence of rendered frames for problems such as flickering or crawling textures before starting a full batch render.

Tessellation and Approximation Nodes

At render time, all the geometry in the scene, regardless of whether it is NURBS, polygons, or subdivision surfaces, is converted to polygon triangles by the renderer. *Tessellation* refers to the number and placement of the triangles on the surface when the scene is rendered. Objects that have a low tessellation will look blocky compared to those with a high tessellation. However, lower-tessellation objects take less time to render than high-tessellation objects (Figure 12.51). Tessellation settings can be found in the shape nodes of surfaces. In Chapter 3, the settings for NURBS surface tessellation are discussed. The easiest way to set tessellation for NURBS surfaces is to use the Tessellation controls in the shape node of the surface. You can also set tessellation for multiple surfaces at the same time by opening the Attribute Spreadsheet (Window ➤ General Editors ➤ Attribute Spread Sheet) to the Tessellation tab.

FIGURE 12.51
The sphere on the left has a low tessellation setting. The sphere on the right has a high tessellation setting.

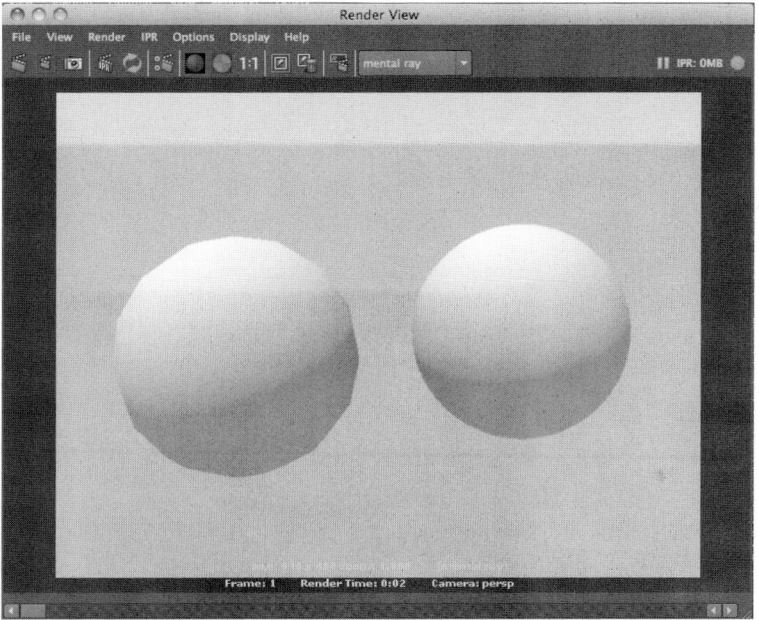

You can also create an approximation node that can set the tessellation for various types of surfaces. To create an approximation node, select the surface and choose Window ➤ Rendering Editors ➤ mental ray ➤ Approximation Editor.

The editor allows you to create approximation nodes for NURBS surfaces, displacements (when using a texture for geometry displacement), and subdivision surfaces.

To create a node, click the Create button. To assign the node to a surface, select the surface, and select the node from the drop-down menu in the Approximation Editor; then click the Assign button. The Unassign button allows you to break the connection between the node and the surface. The Edit button allows you to edit the node's settings in the Attribute Editor, and the Delete button removes the node from the scene (see Figure 12.52).

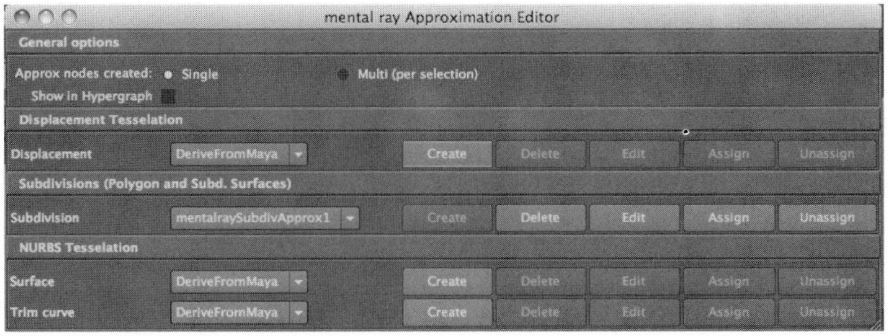

FIGURE 12.52
The Approxima-
tion Editor allows
you to create and
assign approxima-
tion nodes.

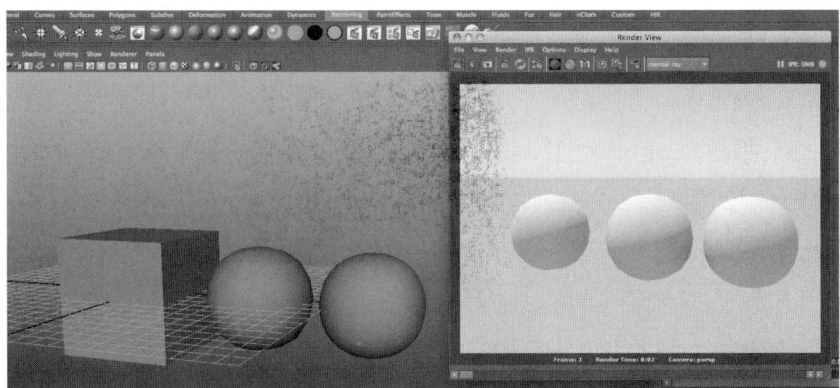

You can assign a subdivision surface approximation node to a polygon object so the polygons
are rendered as subdivision surfaces, giving them a smooth appearance similar to a smooth
mesh or subdivision surface. In Figure 12.53, a polygon cube has been duplicated twice. The
cube on the far left has a subdivision approximation node assigned to it. The center cube is a
smooth mesh. (The cube is converted to a smooth mesh by pressing the **3** key. Smooth mesh
polygon surfaces are covered in Chapter 4.) The cube on the far right has been converted to a
subdivision surface (Modify ➤ Convert ➤ Polygons To Subdiv). When the scene is rendered
using mental ray, the three cubes are almost identical. This demonstrates the various options
available for rendering smooth polygon surfaces.

FIGURE 12.53
Three duplicate
cubes are rendered
as smooth surfaces
using an approxi-
mation node, a
smooth mesh,
and a subdivision
surface.

When editing the settings for the subdivision approximation node, the Parametric Method
option is the simplest to use. You can use the N Subdivisions setting to set the smoothness of the
render. Each time you increase the number of subdivisions, the polygons are multiplied by a factor of four. A setting of 3 means that each polygon face on the original object is divided 12 times.

Anti-aliasing and Sampling

The anti-aliasing settings on the Quality tab of the Render Settings window are used to control
and reduce flickering and artifacts that can appear along the edges of 3D objects or within the
details of high-contrast or detailed textures applied to surfaces. Flickering in high-contrast textures is not noticeable in still frames, only when a sequence of frames is rendered and played
back. This is why it's often important to test short sequences of your animations when adjusting
the quality.

To minimize flickering and artifacts, you can adjust the settings found in the Anti-Aliasing
Quality section of the Render Settings window (see Figure 12.54).

FIGURE 12.54
You can control the anti-aliasing quality in the Anti-Aliasing Quality section of the Quality tab in the Render Settings window.

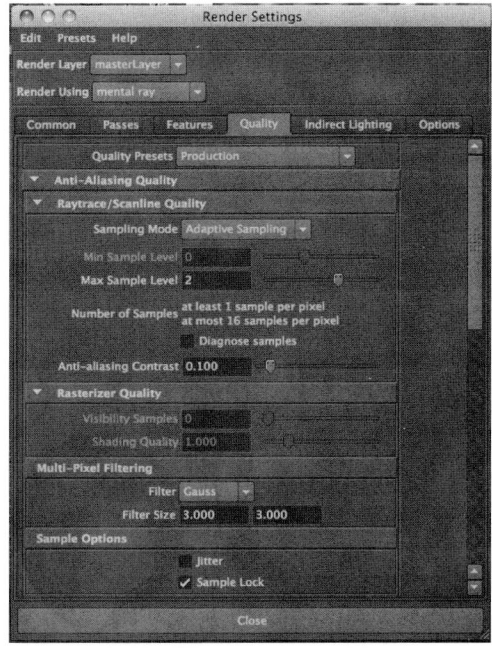

The two main controls are the Sample Levels and Anti-Aliasing Contrast. When adjusting the sampling level, you can choose among Fixed, Adaptive, and Custom sampling modes.

Sampling refers to how mental ray determines the color of a pixel in a rendered image of a 3D scene. A camera emits a number of rays into the scene (known as Primary Eye Rays) to determine the initial color value that will be created for the individual pixels in the final image. After sampling occurs, filters are applied to average the color values for each pixel in the final image. Secondary rays may be cast into the scene to determine raytracing effects such as reflections and refractions.

The type of Primary Eye Ray is determined by the Primary Renderer setting on the Features tab of the Render Settings window. Usually this is set to Scanline for most renders. Secondary rays are specified by the options in the Secondary Effects section of the Features tab (see Figure 12.55).

FIGURE 12.55
The settings on the Features tab determine the type of Primary Eye Ray cast by the rendering cameras to sample a 3D scene.

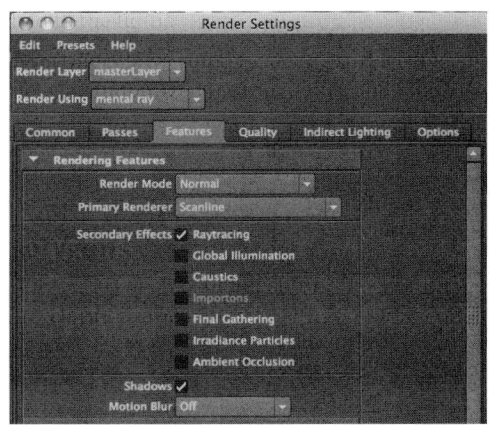

mental ray evaluates the render using tiles. A *tile* is a square section of what will become the rendered image. As mental ray renders the image, it stores the samples for each tile in the sampling Frame Buffer. Once the samples have been collected for a tile, filters are applied to average the colors. The filtered samples are translated into color values and then stored in the image buffer. A tile defines a region of samples that will become pixels in the final image.

The Min and Max Sample Levels determine the sampling range; mental ray uses the Min Sample Level as a starting point and then evaluates the scene and determines whether any parts of the scene require additional samples. If so, more samples are taken. The number of additional samples is determined by the Max Sample Level setting.

Sample levels increase by a factor of 4. A Sample Level setting of 0 means that each pixel in the image receives one sample. A sample level of 1 means four samples per pixel. A sample level of 2 means 16 samples per pixel, and so on.

Negative values mean that each sample contains a number of pixels. A sample level of -2 means that one sample is used for an area of 16 pixels in the rendered image. Again, the number of pixels in negative sampling increases by a factor of 4. As you change the sampling, the number of samples that will be used is displayed in the Render Settings window under Number Of Samples (see Figure 12.56).

FIGURE 12.56

As you adjust the Min Sample Level and Max Sample Level settings, the range of samples is displayed next to Number Of Samples.

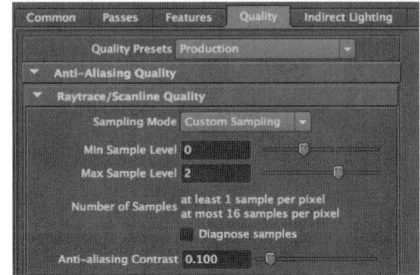

As the sampling rate is increased, the render time increases significantly. The Sampling Mode option can be used to increase the efficiency of the sampling process:

◆ When Sampling Mode is set to Fixed, mental ray uses the sampling level specified by Max Sample Level. This is often useful for rendering with Motion Blur.

◆ When Sampling Mode is set to Adaptive Sampling, mental ray uses one level below the Max Sampling Level setting as the minimum and one level above the Max Sampling Level setting as the maximum. In other words, when Max Sampling Level is set to 2, the minimum becomes 1 sample per pixel, and the maximum becomes 16 samples per pixel.

◆ When Sampling Mode is set to Custom Sampling, you can enter your own values for Min Sample Level and Max Sample Level.

So, how does mental ray know when a pixel requires more sampling? mental ray uses the Anti-Aliasing Contrast value to determine whether a pixel requires more sampling. Lower Anti-Aliasing Contrast values increase the likelihood that addition sampling will be required.

The best approach to take when setting the sampling level is to adjust Anti-Aliasing Contrast gradually before increasing the Min Sampling Level and Max Sampling Level settings. You'll notice that the Production Quality preset uses Adaptive Sampling with a Max Sampling Level of 2 and an Anti-Aliasing Contrast setting of 0.1. If you find this is not sufficient, try lowering the Anti-Aliasing Contrast setting. Try a setting of 0.05. If your image still has artifacts, you may then consider raising the Max Sample Level setting.

If your image has large blank areas and only small portions of detail, try setting a Min Sampling Level of 0 or -1 and a Max Sampling Level of 2. This way, sampling is not wasted in areas where it is not needed.

Other options include the following:

◆ Adjusting the textures

◆ Applying filtering to the textures

◆ Using the mental ray overrides on individual surface shape nodes to adjust the sampling for whichever surface is causing problems

You can get a sense of how the sampling is being applied in a render by activating the Diagnose Samples option (found in the Raytrace/Scanline Quality section on the Quality tab of the Render Settings window) and performing a test render. The rendered image will show areas of higher sampling in white and lower sampled areas in black (Figure 12.57).

FIGURE 12.57
You can visualize areas of high sampling in a test render when Diagnose Samples is activated.

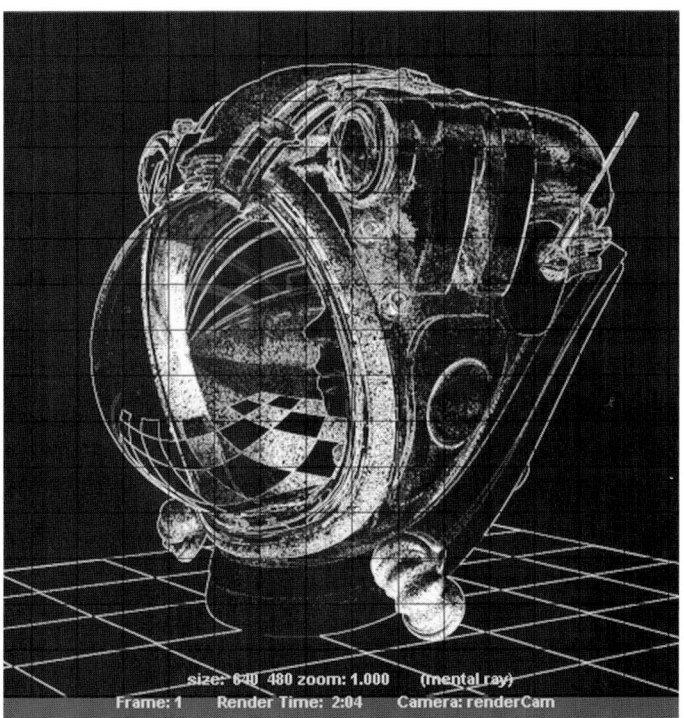

MENTAL RAY DEFAULT OPTIONS

If you'd like more control over each channel of the anti-aliasing contrast (RGB and alpha), open the miDefaultOptions node in the Attribute Editor, and use the settings in the Sampling Quality section. To access this node, turn off DAG Objects Only in the Display menu of the Outliner, and select the miDefaultOptions node. The settings will become available in the Attribute Editor.

Filtering

Filtering occurs after sampling as the image is translated in the Frame Buffer. You can apply a number of filters, found in the menu in the Multi-Pixel Filtering section of the Render Settings window's Quality tab. Some filters blur the image, while others sharpen the image. The Filter Size fields determine the height and width of the filter as it expands from the center of the sample across neighboring pixels. A setting of 1 1 covers a single pixel, and a setting of 2 2 covers four pixels. Most of the time the default setting for each filter type is the best one to use.

Box filter   Applies the filter evenly across the image's height and width.

Triangle and Gauss filters   Add a small amount of blurring to the pixels, while Mitchel and Lanczos both sharpen the image.

Jitter option   Reduces flickering or banding artifacts. Jittering offsets the sample location for a given sample block in a random fashion.

Sample Lock option   Locks the sampling pattern. This reduces flickering by forcing mental ray to sample the scene the same way for each frame. It can be useful in animated sequences and when using motion blur. If Sample Lock does not reduce flickering, try Jitter as an alternative.

Rasterizer

The Rasterizer is an alternative to the Scanline and Raytrace renderers that uses a different sampling algorithm. You can choose the Rasterizer as your primary renderer on the Features tab of the Render Settings window. The Rasterizer is most often used for scenes with motion blur or scenes with hair. It handles large amounts of overlapping thin surfaces (such as hair) quite well.

When Rasterizer is chosen as the Primary Renderer setting, the options for Raytrace/Scanline Quality sampling on the Quality tab become unavailable. Instead, you can use the Visibility Samples and Shading Quality settings in the Rasterizer Quality section of the Quality tab.

Visibility Samples works much like the Max Sample Level setting in the Raytrace/Scanline Quality options; however, the Rasterizer is not adaptive. The default setting of 0 means that one sample is used for anti-aliasing. Shading Quality sets the number of shading samples per pixel. The Rasterizer caches the samples with the geometry in the scene, so sampling actually travels with moving geometry. This is why it is an ideal algorithm for use with motion blur. Motion blur is discussed in Chapter 2.

Raytrace Acceleration

Raytrace Acceleration settings are found in the Raytrace settings on the Render Settings window's Quality tab. The purpose of these settings is to improve the speed of your renders when raytracing is enabled. Changing the settings does not affect how the image looks, only how fast it renders.

Raytracing is a process where rays are shot into a 3D scene from the rendering camera. When Raytracing is used as the primary renderer (this is set on the Features tab), each ray shot from the camera is compared with every triangle face of every piece of geometry in the scene to determine whether additional rays are required for reflection or refraction (recall that all geometry is tessellated into polygon triangles when the scene is rendered).

To reduce the number of comparisons made between each ray and each triangle, mental ray offers several versions of the Binary Space Partition (BSP) algorithm (see Figure 12.58), which is meant to accelerate the process. The BSP algorithm divides the scene into sections; each section is a 3D container known as a *voxel*. The number of calculations required for each ray is limited to the number of triangles within a section of the scene as defined by the algorithm. In the Acceleration Method menu, you'll find Regular BSP, Large BSP, and BSP2. The Large BSP method is meant for use with large scenes; it does a better job of managing memory through disk swapping than Regular BSP. The BSP2 method does not allow you to set the Size and Depth options. BSP2 is also useful for large scenes and whenever a large number of instances are present.

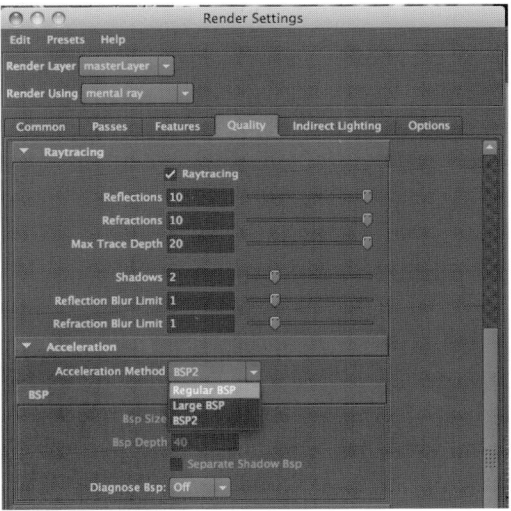

FIGURE 12.58
mental ray offers three versions of the BSP acceleration method for improving the speed of raytrace calculations.

The voxels created by the BSP method are adaptive. If needed, a voxel can be subdivided into smaller voxels. The lowest level of division is a voxel that contains only triangles; such voxels are known as *leaf nodes*.

You can set Bsp Size and Bsp Depth. Bsp Size refers to the maximum number of triangles a voxel can contain before it is subdivided. Bsp Depth sets a limit on the number of times a voxel can be subdivided. When tuning the performance of raytrace acceleration, you want to balance the size of the voxels against the voxel depth. A large voxel size means that each ray must make a large number of comparisons as it enters a voxel. A large depth value requires more memory to store the calculations for each voxel as well as more time for determining the placement and division of the voxels. Voxel depth has a larger impact on render time than voxel size.

You can use a separate BSP tree (a *BSP tree* is the hierarchy of voxels created in the scene) to calculate raytraced shadows. This is activated by turning on Separate Shadow Bsp.

Diagnose BSP

Tuning BSP settings often takes a fair amount of testing, trial, and error. You can create a visual representation of how BSP is calculated by activating the Diagnose Bsp setting. This allows you to see a color-coded version of the scene based on the BSP size or depth.

1. Open the carSceneBSP_v01.ma scene from the chapter12\scenes directory on the DVD.

   This scene uses very simple, standard Maya shaders to create reflective materials on the car and the structure behind it.

   When diagnosing acceleration, you can speed up the process by lowering the sampling in the scene and, in the case of this scene, turning off Final Gathering.

2. On the Indirect Lighting tab, deactivate Final Gathering.

3. On the Quality tab, set Sampling Mode to Fixed Sampling, and set Max Sample Level to **-3**.

4. In the Acceleration rollout within the Raytracing rollout, set Diagnose Bsp to Depth.

5. Set Acceleration Method to Regular BSP (see Figure 12.59).

6. Open the render view, and create a test render using the renderCam camera.

   The scene renders in a very low quality, but this is perfectly fine; you want to pay attention to the colors in the image. Areas that are red indicate that the maximum number of subdivisions for the voxels that contain those triangles has been reached. You'll see this around the detailed wheel section and on parts of the structure. Ideally, you want to see orange and yellow in these areas and less red. To fix this, raise the Bsp Depth setting.

7. Set Bsp Depth to **45**, and create another test render (Figure 12.60).

8. Set the Diagnose Bsp menu to Size, and create another test render.

FIGURE 12.59
The BSP settings within the Raytracing rollout in the Quality tab

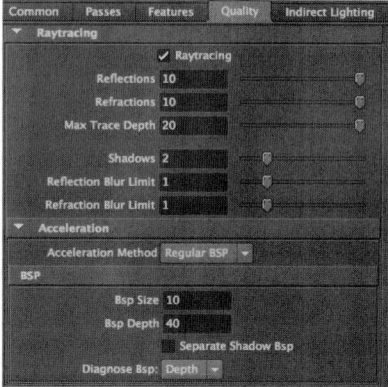

FIGURE 12.60
The Diagnose Bsp option color codes the render based on the voxel depth set in the Acceleration options.

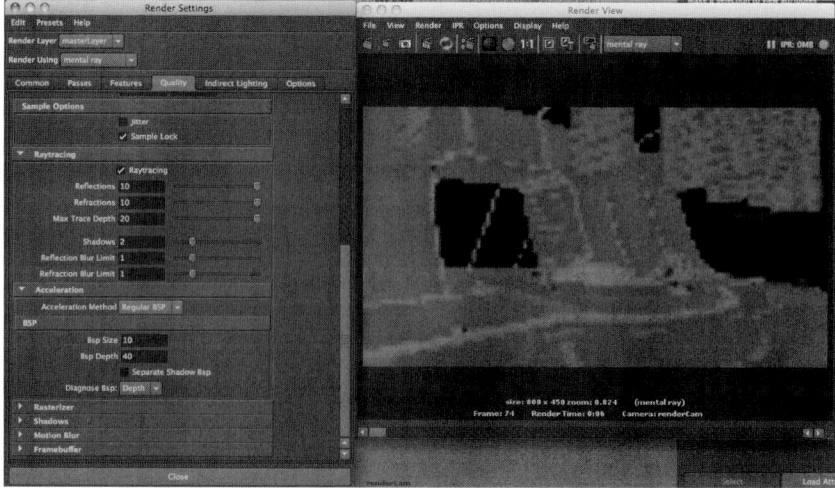

For the most part, the scene appears in blue, indicating that the voxel size is more than adequate. You can try lowering this value, but for this particular scene a size of 10 is fine. If you prefer to have a more detailed report of the impact of the BSP Acceleration settings, set the Verbosity setting of the output messages to Progress Messages (you can do this in Render Current Frame ➤ Options), and observe the report in the Output Window.

Once you have achieved a BSP setting that has little red in the render view, you can increase the anti-aliasing quality, turn Diagnose BSP off, and render the image. If all works well, you should notice a reduced render time without a noticeable loss in quality.

The Bottom Line

Use render layers   Render layers can be used to separate the elements of a single scene into different versions or into different layers of a composite. Each layer can have its own shaders, lights, and settings. Using overrides, you can change the way each layer renders.

> **Master it**   Use render layers to set up alternate versions of the space helmet. Try applying contour rendering on one layer and Final Gathering on another.

Use render passes   Render passes allow you to separate material properties into different images. These passes are derived from calculations stored in the Frame Buffer. Each pass can be used in compositing software to efficiently rebuild the rendered scene. Render pass contribution maps define which objects and lights are included in a render pass.

> **Master it**   Create an Ambient Occlusion pass for the minigun scene.

Perform batch renders   Batch renders automate the process of rendering a sequence of images. You can use Maya's Batch Render options in the Maya interface or choose Batch Render from the command prompt (or Terminal) when Maya is closed. A batch script can be used to render multiple scenes.

> **Master it**   Create a batch script to render five fictional scenes. Each scene uses layers with different render settings. Set the frame range for each scene to render frames 20 through 50. Each scene is named `myScene1.ma` through `myScene5.ma`.

Use mental ray quality settings   The settings on the Quality tab of the Render Settings window allow you to adjust the anti-aliasing quality and the raytrace acceleration of a scene (among other things). Sampling improves the quality of the image by reducing flickering problems. Raytrace acceleration does not affect image quality but improves render times when raytracing is activated in a scene.

> **Master it**   Diagnose both the sampling and the BSP depth of the `helmetComposite_v04.ma` scene.

Chapter 13

Introducing nParticles

This chapter introduces Maya's nParticle dynamics and shows how you can use them creatively to produce a wide variety of visual effects. The example scenes demonstrate the fundamentals of working with and rendering particles. The subsequent chapters on Maya dynamics build on these techniques.

nParticles were introduced in Maya version 2009. These nParticles are connected to the Nucleus solver system, a difference from traditional Maya particles. Nucleus is a unified dynamic system first introduced in Maya 8.5 as part of nCloth. The Nucleus solver is the brain behind the nDynamic systems in Maya.

In this chapter, you will learn to:

♦ Create nParticles

♦ Make nParticles collide

♦ Create liquid simulations

♦ Emit nParticles from a texture

♦ Move nParticles with nucleus wind

♦ Use force fields

Creating nParticles

A *particle* is a point in space that can react to the simulated dynamic forces generated by Maya. These dynamic forces allow you to create animated effects in a way that would be otherwise difficult or impossible to create with standard keyframe animation. When you create a *particle object*, points are created in the scene. You can then attach force fields to the particles to push them around and make them fall, swarm, float, or do any number of other behaviors without the need for keyframes.

Maya particle dynamics have been part of Maya since the earliest versions of the software. In version 2009, Autodesk introduced *nParticles*, which have all the capabilities of the older, traditional particles, plus new attributes, which make them easier to use and at the same time more powerful. Unlike traditional particles, nParticles can collide and influence the behavior of other nParticles. nParticle collisions occur when two or more nParticles come within a specified distance, causing them to bounce off one another or, in some cases, stick together.

Very complex behaviors can be created by adjusting the settings in the nParticle's Attribute Editor. You'll learn how you can create effects by adjusting these settings in this chapter. Since nParticles can do just about everything traditional particles can do plus a lot more, the lessons in this chapter will cover nParticles only and not traditional Maya particles.

An *nCloth object* is a piece of polygon geometry that can also react to dynamic forces. Each vertex in an nCloth object has the properties of an nParticle, and these nParticles are connected by invisible virtual springs, which means nCloth objects can collide with, and influence the behavior of, other nCloth objects and nParticles. In this chapter, you'll get a taste of working with nCloth; Chapter 14 demonstrates more advanced nCloth and nParticle effects.

When you create an nParticle object or an nCloth object, or both, in a scene, a *Nucleus solver* is created. The Nucleus solver is a node in Maya that acts as an engine for all the dynamic effects. The Nucleus solver determines global settings for the dynamics, such as the strength and direction of gravity, the air density, the wind direction, and the quality of the dynamics simulation (for example, how many times per frame the simulation is calculated). The same Nucleus solver is used to calculate the dynamics and interactions within the nParticle system and the nCloth system. A scene can have more than one Nucleus solver, but nDynamic systems using two different solvers can't directly interact. However, two separate nParticle objects using the same Nucleus solver can interact.

Traditional Maya dynamics use a much simpler solver node that does not take into account interactions between different dynamic objects. Traditional particle objects are completely self-contained, so two particle objects in a Maya scene are not aware of each other's existence (so to speak).

The following exercises take you through the process of using the different nParticle creation methods and introduce you to working with the Nucleus solver.

NDYNAMICS

The *Nucleus dynamic systems* (aka nDynamics) are distinguished from the traditional dynamic systems by the letter *n*. So, *nParticles*, *nCloth*, and *nRigids* are part of the nDynamics system, and particles and rigid bodies are part of traditional Maya dynamics.

Drawing nParticles Using the nParticle Tool

You can create nParticles in a scene in a number of ways. You can draw them on the grid, use an emitter to spawn them into a scene, use a surface as an emitter, or fill a volume with nParticles. When you create an nParticle object, you also need to specify the nParticle's style.

Choosing a style activates one of a number of preset settings for the nParticle's attributes, all of which can be altered after you add the nParticle object to the scene. The nParticle styles include balls, points, cloud, thick cloud, and water.

The simplest way to create nParticles is to draw them on the grid using the nParticle tool, as follows:

1. Create a new scene in Maya. Switch to the nDynamics menu set.

2. Choose nParticles ➤ Create nParticles, and set the style to Balls (see Figure 13.1).

3. Choose Create nParticles ➤ nParticle Tool. Click six or seven times on the grid to place individual particles.

FIGURE 13.1
Using the nParticle
menu to specify
the nParticle style.

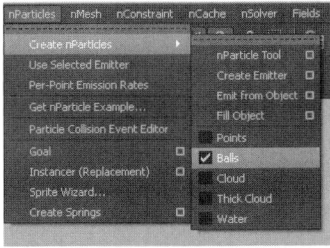

4. Press the Enter key on the numeric keypad to create the particles.

   You'll see several circles on the grid. The ball-type nParticle style automatically creates blobby surface particles. Blobby surfaces are spheres rendered using Maya Software or mental ray. Blobby surfaces use standard Maya shaders when rendered and can be blended together to form a gooey surface.

5. Set the length of the timeline to **600**. Rewind and play the animation. The particles will fall in space.

6. Open the Attribute Editor for the nParticle1 object, and switch to the nucleus1 tab. The settings on this tab control the Nucleus solver, which sets the overall dynamic attributes of the connected nDynamic systems (see Figure 13.2).

FIGURE 13.2
The settings on the
nucleus1 tab define
the behavior of the
environment for
all connected
nDynamic nodes.

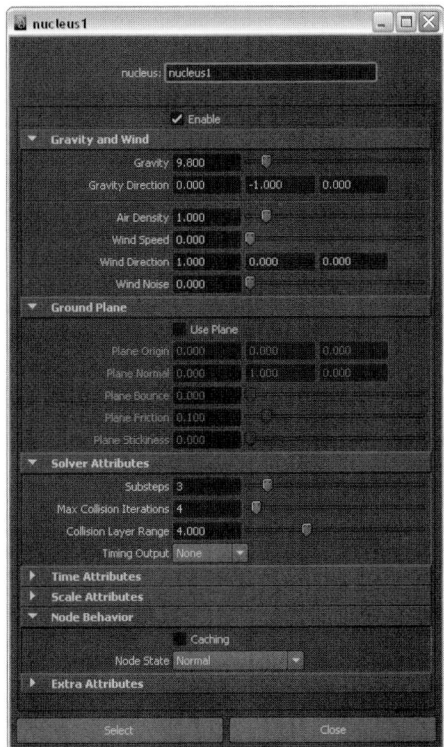

7. By default a Nucleus solver has Gravity enabled. Enable Use Plane in the Ground Plane settings (Figure 13.3). This creates an invisible floor that the nParticles can rest on. Set the Plane Origin's Translate Y to **-1**.

8. The Nucleus solver also has wind settings. Set Wind Speed to **3** and Wind Noise to **4**. By default Wind Direction is set to 1, 0, 0 (Figure 13.4). The fields correspond to the x-, y-, and z-axes, so this means that the nParticles will be blown along the positive x-axis. Rewind and play the animation. Now the nParticles are moving along with the wind, and a small amount of turbulence is applied.

FIGURE 13.3
The ground plane creates an invisible floor that keeps the nParticles from falling.

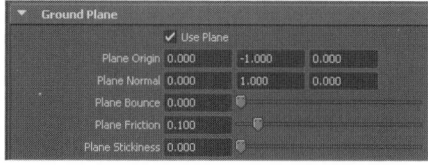

FIGURE 13.4
You can find the settings for Air Density, Wind Speed, Wind Direction, and Wind Noise under the Nucleus solver's attributes.

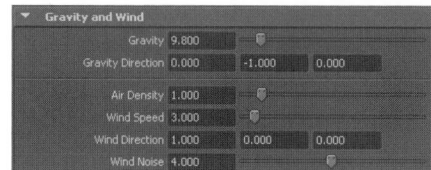

By increasing the Air Density value, you adjust the atmosphere of the environment. A very high setting is a good way to simulate an underwater environment. Using wind in combination with a high air density pushes the nParticles with more force; this makes sense since the air is denser.

The Solver Attributes section sets the quality of the solver. The Substeps setting specifies how many times per frame the solver calculates nDynamics. Higher settings are more accurate but can slow down performance. Increasing the Substeps value may alter some of the ways in which nDynamics behave, such as how they collide with each other and with other objects, so when you increase this value, be aware that you may need to adjust other settings on your nDynamic nodes.

The Scale Attributes section has Time Scale and Space Scale sliders. Use Time Scale to speed up or slow down the solver. Values less than 1 slow down the simulation; higher values speed it up. If you increase Time Scale, you should increase the number of substeps in the Solver Attributes section to ensure that the simulation is still accurate. One creative example of Time Scale would be to keyframe a change in its value to simulate the "bullet time" effect made famous in *The Matrix* movies.

Space Scale scales the environment of the simulation. By default nDynamics are calculated in meters even if the Maya scene unit is set to centimeters. You should set this to 0.1 if you need your nDynamics simulation to behave appropriately when the Maya scene units are set to centimeters. This is more noticeable when working with large simulations. You can also use this setting creatively to exaggerate effects or when using more than one Nucleus solver in a scene. Most of the time it's safe to leave this at the default setting of 1. For the following examples, leave Space Scale set to 1.

Spawning nParticles from an Emitter

An emitter shoots nParticles into the scene, like a sprinkler shooting water onto a lawn. When a particle is emitted into a scene, it is "born" at that moment, and all calculations based on its age begin from the moment it is born.

1. Continue with the scene from the previous section. Add an emitter to the scene by choosing nParticles ➤ Create nParticles ➤ Create Emitter. An emitter appears at the center of the grid.

2. Open the Attribute Editor for the emitter1 object, and set Rate (particles/sec) to **10**. Set Emitter Type to Omni.

3. Rewind and play the scene. The omni emitter spawns particles from a point at the center of the grid. Note that after the particles are born, they collide with the ground plane and are pushed by the nucleus wind in the same direction as the other particles (see Figure 13.5).

   The new nParticles are connected to the same Nucleus solver. If you open the Attribute Editor for the nParticle2 object, you'll see the tabs for nucleus1 and nParticle2, as well as the tab for nParticle1. If you change the settings on the nucleus1 tab, both nParticle1 and nParticle2 are affected.

FIGURE 13.5
A second nParticle system is spawned from an emitter. These nParticles also collide with the ground plane and are pushed by the wind.

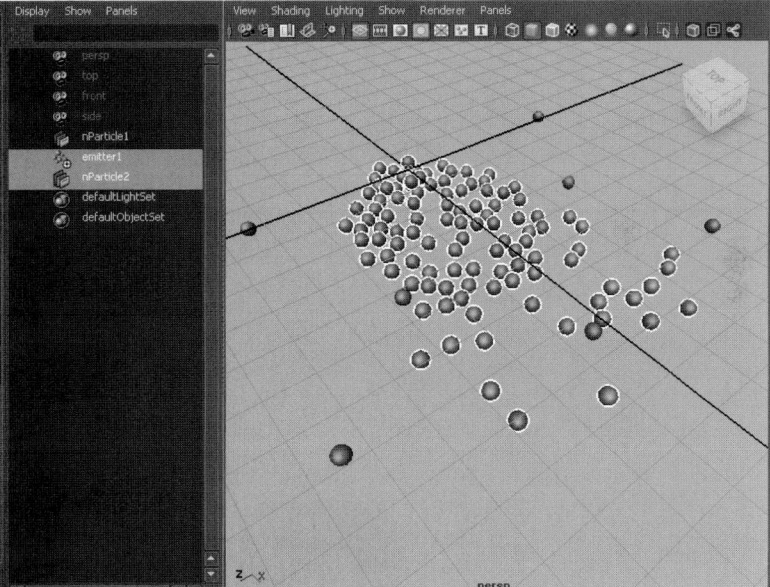

NPARTICLE TABS IN THE ATTRIBUTE EDITOR

The tabs for each nParticle connected to a Nucleus solver appear at the same time at the top of the Attribute Editor. Thus, it is easy to make the mistake of editing the settings for the wrong nParticle object. To avoid this mistake, pay attention to which nParticle object is listed on the tab at the top of the Attribute Editor while you are changing settings!

4. Select nParticle2, and choose nSolver ➤ Assign Solver ➤New Solver. Rewind and play the scene. nParticle2 now falls in space, whereas nParticle1 continues to slide on the ground plane.

5. Open the Outliner, and in the Outliner's Display menu, turn off DAG Objects Only. This allows you to see all the nodes in the scene. If you scroll down, you'll see nucleus1 and nucleus2 nodes (see Figure 13.6).

6. Select nParticle2, and choose nSolver ➤ Assign Solver ➤ nucleus1. This reconnects nParticle2 with nucleus1.

7. Select emitter1, and in the Attribute Editor for emitter1, set Emitter Type to Volume.

8. Set Volume Shape in the Volume Emitter Attributes section to Sphere.

9. Use the Move tool to position the emitter above the ground plane. The emitter is now a volume, which you can scale up in size using the Scale tool (hot key = **r**). nParticles are born from random locations within the sphere (see Figure 13.7).

The directional emitter is another type of emitter similar to the omni and volume emitters in that it shoots nParticles into a scene. The directional emitter emits the nParticles in a straight line. The range of the directional emitter can be altered using the Spread slider, causing it to behave more like a sprinkler or fountain.

FIGURE 13.6
The nucleus nodes are visible in the Outliner.

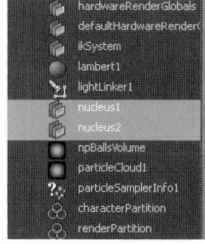

FIGURE 13.7
Volume emitters spawn nParticles from random locations within the volume.

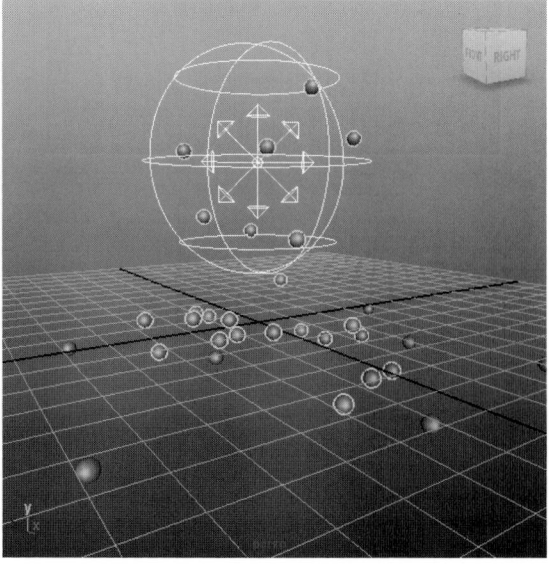

10. Open the Attribute Editor to the nParticleShape1 tab. This is where you'll find the attributes that control particle behavior, and there are a lot of them.

11. As an experiment, expand the Force Field Generation rollout panel, and set the Point Force Field to Worldspace.

12. Rewind and play the animation.

As the emitter spawns particles in the scene, a few nParticles from nParticle2 will bunch up in the space between nParticle1. nParticle1 is emitting a force field that pushes individual nParticles from nParticle2 away. If you set Point Field Magnitude to a negative number, nParticle1 will attract some of the particles from nParticle2. You can also make the nParticles attract themselves by increasing the Self Attract slider (see Figure 13.8).

FIGURE 13.8
The Force Field settings cause one nParticle object to push away other nDynamic systems.

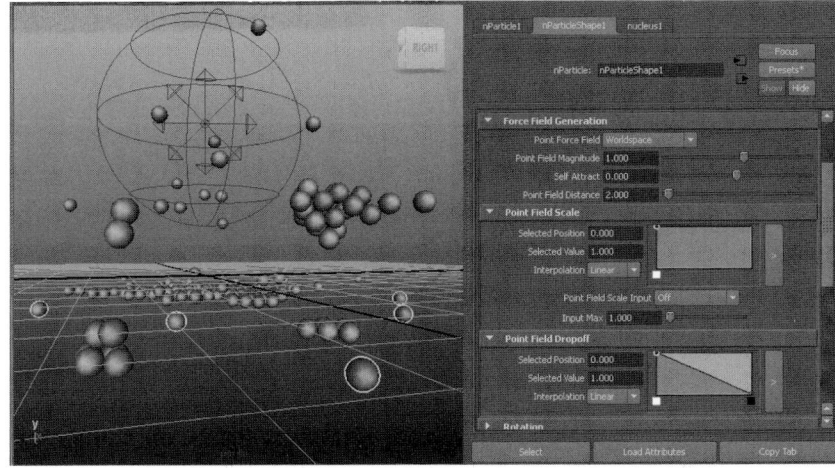

This is an example of how the Nucleus solver allows particles from two different particle objects to interact. The Force Field settings will be further explored in the section "Working with Force Fields" later in this chapter. If you switch nParticle2 to the nucleus2 solver, you will lose this behavior; only nParticles that share a solver can be attracted to each other. Be careful when using force fields on large numbers of nParticles (more than 10,000), because this will slow the performance of Maya significantly. See the nPaticles_v01.ma scene in the chapter13\scenes folder on the DVD for an example of nParticle force fields.

Emitting nParticles from a Surface

You can use polygon and NURBS surfaces to generate nParticles as well.

1. Create a new Maya scene. Create a polygon plane (Create ➢ Polygon Primitives ➢ Plane).

2. Scale the plane 25 units in X and Z.

3. Switch to the nDynamics menu set. Set the nParticle style to Balls (nParticles ➢ Create nParticles ➢ Balls).

4. Select the plane. Choose nParticles ➤ Create nParticles ➤ Emit From Object ➤ Options. In the options, set Emitter Type to Surface and Rate to **10**. Set Speed to **0**. Click Create to make the emitter. Figure 13.9 shows the options for the surface emitter.

FIGURE 13.9
The options for creating a surface emitter

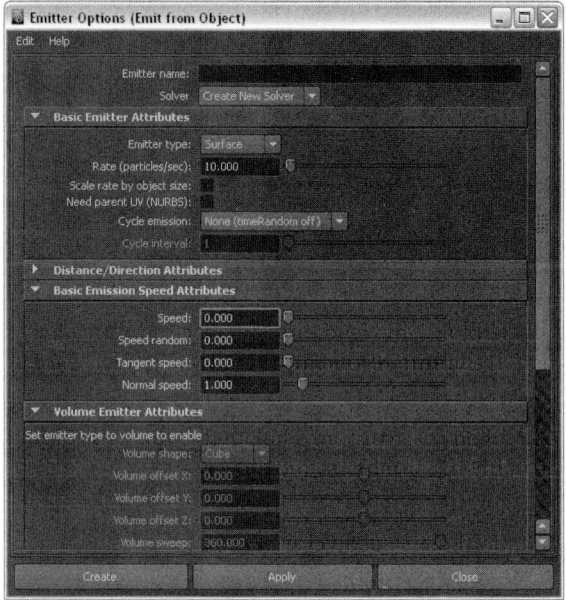

SURFACE EMITTERS

When you create a surface emitter, the emitter node is parented to the emitting geometry in the Outliner.

---

5. Set the timeline to **600**.

6. Open the Attribute Editor to the nucleus1 tab, and set Gravity to **0**.

7. Rewind and play the animation. Particles appear randomly on the surface.

8. Open the Attribute Editor to the nParticle Shape tab. Expand the Particle Size rollout panel. Set Radius to **1**.

9. Click the right side of the Radius Scale ramp to add a point. Adjust the position of the point on the left side of the ramp edit curve for Radius Scale so that it's at 0 on the left side and moves up to 1 on the right side (see Figure 13.10).

FIGURE 13.10
The Radius Scale ramp curve adjusts the radius of the nParticles.

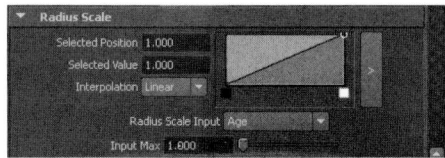

10. Rewind and play the animation. The particles now scale up as they are born (by default Radius Scale Input is set to Age). Notice that adjacent particles push each other as they grow. The ball-style particle has Self Collision on by default, so the particles will bump into each other (see Figure 13.11).

FIGURE 13.11
The balls scale up as they are born and push each other as they grow.

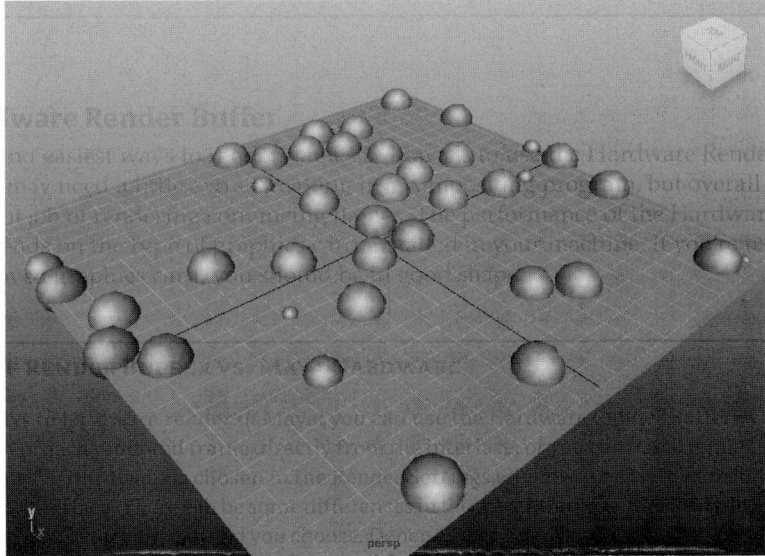

11. Set Radius Scale Randomize to **0.5**. The balls each have a random size. By increasing this slider, you increase the random range for the maximum radius size of each nParticle.

12. Set Input Max to **3**. This sets the maximum range along the x-axis of the Radius Scale ramp. Since Radius Scale Input is set to Time, this means each nParticle takes three seconds to achieve its maximum radius, so they slowly grow in size.

See the nParticles_v02.ma scene in the chapter13\scenes folder on the DVD for an example of nParticles emitted from a surface.

Filling an Object with nParticles

An object can be instantly filled with particles. Any modeled polygon mesh can hold the nParticles as long as it has some kind of depression in it. A flat plane, on the other hand, can't be used.

1. Open the forge_v01.ma scene from the chapter13\scenes folder on the DVD. You'll see a very simple scene consisting of a tub on a stand. A bucket is in front of the tub. The tub will be used to pour molten metal into the bucket.

2. Set the nParticle style to Water by choosing nParticles ➤ Create nParticles ➤ Water.

3. Select the tub object, and choose nParticles ➤ Create nParticles ➤ Fill Object ➤ Options (see Figure 13.12). In the options, turn on Close Packing, and click the Particle Fill button.

FIGURE 13.12
Select the tub
object, and it
will be filled
with nParticles.

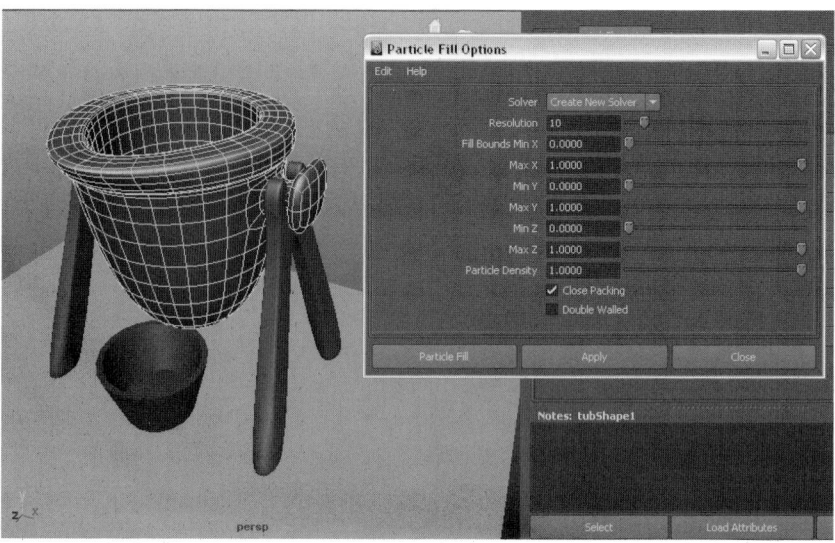

IF NO NPARTICLES ARE CREATED

If no nParticles are created at all, open the options for the Particle Fill command, reset the options, and make sure Close Packing is on. The problem occurs when Maya can't figure out how to fill the surface. You can verify that nParticles do exist by switching to wireframe mode or look for a new nParticle node in the Outliner.

---

4. Set the display to Wireframe. You'll see a few particles stuck in the rim of the tub. If you play the scene, the particles fall through space.

There are two problems:

◆ The object has been built with a thick wall, so Maya is trying to fill the inside of the surface with particles rather than the well in the tub.

◆ The tub is not set as a collision surface (see Figure 13.13).

5. Select the nParticle1 object in the Outliner, and delete it. Note that this does not delete the nucleus1 solver created with the particle, and that's okay; the next nParticle object you create will be automatically connected to this same solver.

This problem has a couple of solutions. When you create the nParticle object, you can choose Double Walled in the Fill Object options, which in many cases solves the problem for objects that have a simple shape, such as a glass. For more convoluted shapes, the nParticles may try to fill different parts of the object. For instance, in the case of the tub, as long as the Resolution setting in the options is at 10 or less, the tub will fill with nParticles just fine (increasing Resolution increases the number of nParticles that will fill the volume). However, if you create a higher-resolution nParticle, you'll find that nParticles are placed within the walls of the tub and inside the handles where the tub is held by the frame.

FIGURE 13.13
The nParticles lodge within the thick walls of the tub.

Another solution is to split the polygons that make up the object so that only the parts of the tub that actually collide with the nParticles are used to calculate how the nParticles fill the object:

1. Switch to shaded view. Select the tub object, and move the view so you can see the bottom of its interior.

2. Choose the Paint Selection tool, right-click the tub, and choose Face to switch to face selection. Use the Paint Selection tool to select the faces at the very bottom of the tub (see Figure 13.14).

FIGURE 13.14
Select the faces at the bottom of the tub with the Paint Selection tool.

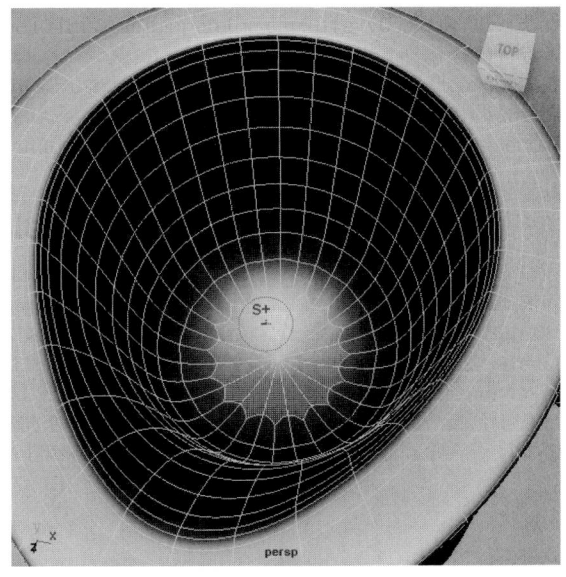

3. Hold the Shift key, and press the > key on the keyboard to expand the selection. Keep holding the Shift key while repeatedly pressing the > key until all the interior polygons are selected up to the edge of the tub's rim (see Figure 13.15).

4. Switch to wireframe mode, and make sure none of the polygons on the outside of the tub has been selected by accident. Hold the Ctrl key, and select any unwanted polygons to deselect them.

5. Switch to the Polygon menu set, and choose Mesh ➢ Extract. This splits the model into two parts. The selected polygon becomes a separate mesh from the deselected polygons. In the Outliner, you'll see that the tub1 object is now a group with two nodes: polySurface1 and polySurface2 (see Figure 13.16).

FIGURE 13.15
Expand the selection to include all the faces up to the rim of the tub.

FIGURE 13.16
Split the tub into two separate mesh objects using the Extract command.

6. Select the polysurface1 and polysurface2 nodes, and choose Edit ➢ Delete By Type ➢ History.

7. Name the interior mesh **insideTub** and the exterior mesh **outsideTub**.

8. Switch to the nDynamics menu set. Select the insideTub mesh, and choose nParticles ➢ Create nParticles ➢ Fill Object ➢ Options.

9. In the options, set Solver to nucleus1, and set Resolution to **15**.

   The Fill Bounds settings determine the minimum and maximum boundaries within the volume that will be filled. In other words, if you want to fill a glass from the middle of the glass to the top, leaving the bottom half of the glass empty, set the minimum in Y to 0.5 and the maximum to 1. (The nParticles would still drop to the bottom of the glass if Gravity were enabled, but for a split second you would confuse both optimists and pessimists.)

10. Leave all the Fill Bounds settings at the default. Turn off Double Walled and Close Packing. Click Particle Fill to apply it. After a couple seconds, you'll see the tub filled with little blue spheres (see Figure 13.17).

11. Rewind and play the animation. The spheres drop through the bottom of the tub. To make them stay within the tub, you'll need to create a collision surface.

FIGURE 13.17
The inside of the tub is filled with nParticles.

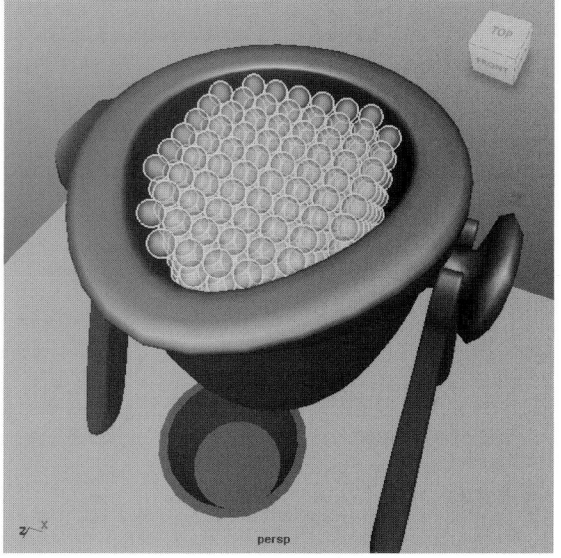

Making nParticles Collide with nCloth Surfaces

nParticles collide with nCloth objects, passive collision surfaces, and other nParticle objects. They can also be made to self-collide; in fact, when the ball-style nParticle is chosen, Self Collision is on by default. To make an nParticle collide with an ordinary rigid object, you need to convert the collision surface into a passive collider. The passive collider can be animated as well.

Passive Collision Objects

Passive collision objects, also known as *nRigids*, are automatically connected to the current Nucleus solver when they are created.

1. Rewind the animation, and select the insideTub mesh.

2. Choose nMesh ➤ Create Passive Collider. By default the object is assigned to the current Nucleus solver. If you want to assign a different solver, use the options for Create Passive Collider.

3. Play the animation. You'll see the nParticles drop down and collide with the bottom of the tub. They'll slosh around for a while and eventually settle.

CREATING NRIGID OBJECTS

When you create a passive collider object (aka nRigid object), any new nDynamic system you add to the scene that is connected to the same Nucleus solver will collide with the nRigid, as long as the new nDynamic node has Collisions enabled.

When creating a collision between an nParticle and a passive collision surface, there are two sets of controls you can tune to adjust the way the collision happens:

◆ Collision settings on the nParticle shape control how the nParticle reacts when colliding with surfaces.

◆ Collision settings on the passive object control how objects react when they collide with it.

For example, if you dumped a bunch of basketballs and Ping-Pong balls on a granite table and a sofa, you would see that the table and the sofa have their own collision behavior based on their physical properties, and the Ping-Pong balls and basketballs also have their own collision behavior based on their physical properties. When a collision event occurs between a Ping-Pong ball and the sofa, the physical properties of both objects are factored together to determine the behavior of the Ping-Pong ball at the moment of collision. Likewise, a basketball has its own physical properties that are factored in with the same sofa properties when a collision occurs between the sofa and a basketball.

The nDynamics systems have a variety of ways to calculate collisions as well as ways to visualize and control the collisions between elements in the system:

1. Select the nRigid node in the Outliner, and switch to the nRigidShape1 tab in the Attribute Editor. Expand the Collisions rollout panel.

   The Collide option turns collisions on or off for the surface. It's sometimes useful to temporarily disable collisions when working on animating objects in a scene using nDynamics. Likewise, the Enable option above the Collisions rollout panel disables all nDynamics for the surface when it is deselected. It's possible to keyframe this attribute by switching to the Channel Box and to keyframe the Is Dynamic channel for the rigidShape node.

2. Set the Solver Display option to Collision Thickness. Turning this option on creates an interactive display so you can see how the collisions for this surface are calculated (see Figure 13.18).

FIGURE 13.18
You can display the collision surface thickness using the controls in the nRigid body shape node.

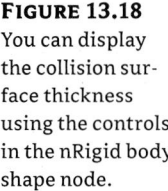

3. Switch to wireframe view (hot key = **4**). Move the Thickness slider back and forth, and the envelope grows and shrinks, indicating how thick the surface will seem when the dynamics are calculated.

   The thickness will not change its appearance when rendered, only how the nParticles will collide with the object. A very high Thickness value makes it seem as though there is an invisible force field around the object.

4. Switch back to smooth shaded view (hot key = **5**). Collision Flag is set to Face by default, meaning that collisions are calculated based on the faces of the collision object. This is the most accurate but slowest way to calculate collisions.

5. Set Collision Flag to Vertex. Rewind and play the animation. You'll see the thickness envelope drawn around each vertex of the collision surface.

   The nParticles fall through the bottom of the surface, and some may collide with the envelopes around the vertices on their way through the bottom. The calculation of the dynamics is faster, though. This setting may work well for dense meshes, and it will calculate much faster than the Face method.

6. Set Collision Flag to Edge; rewind and play the animation. The envelope is now drawn around each edge of the collision surface, creating a wireframe network (see Figure 13.19).

COLLISION FLAG: FACE VS. EDGE

The calculation is much faster than when Collision Flag is set to Face, but the nParticles stay within the tub. You may notice some bumping as the nParticles collide with the wireframe. Many times this may not be noticeable at all, which makes the Edge method useful for calculating collisions.

FIGURE 13.19
When Collision Flag is set to Vertex, the nParticles collide with each vertex of the collision surface, allowing some to fall through the bottom. When the flag is set to Edge, the nParticles collide with the edges, and the calculation speed improves.

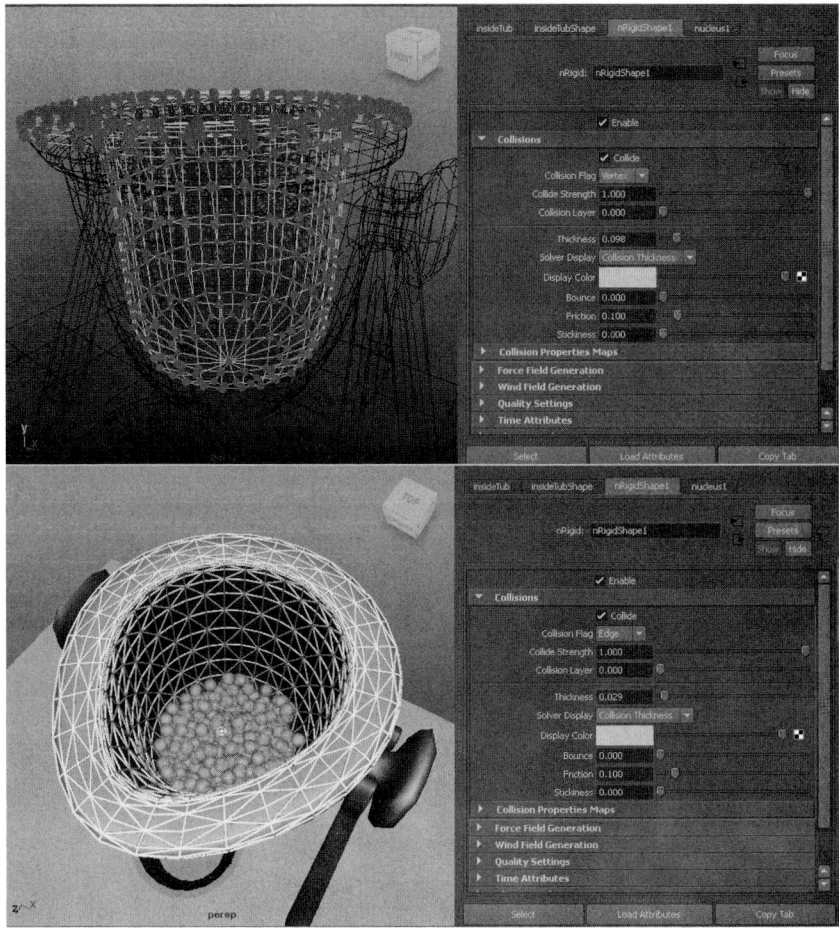

The other settings in the Collisions section include the following:

Bounce   This controls how high the nParticles bounce off the surface. Think of the Ping-Pong balls hitting the granite table and the sofa. The sofa would have a much lower Bounce setting than the granite table.

Friction   A smooth surface has a much lower Friction setting than a rough one. nParticles will slide off a smooth surface more easily. If the sofa were made of suede, the friction would be higher than for the smooth granite table.

Stickiness   This is pretty self-explanatory—if the granite table were covered in honey, the Ping-Pong balls would stick to it more than to the sofa, even if the friction is lower on the granite table. The behavior of the nParticles sticking to the surface may be different if Collision Flag is set to Face than if it is set to Edge or Vertex.

You can use the display settings within the nParticle's Attribute Editor to visualize the collision width of each nParticle; this can help you determine the best collision width setting for your nParticles.

1. Make sure that Collision Flag is set to Edge and that Bounce, Friction, and Stickiness are set to 0. Set Collision Thickness to **0.05**.

2. Select the nParticle1 object, and open the Attribute Editor to the nParticleShape1 tab. Expand the Collisions rollout panel for the nParticle1 object. These control how the nParticles collide with collision objects in the scene.

3. Click the Display Color swatch to open the Color Chooser, and pick a red color. Set Solver Display to Collision Thickness. Now each nParticle has a red envelope around it. Changing the color of the display makes it easier to distinguish from the nRigid collision surface display.

4. Set Collide Width Scale to **0.25**. The envelope becomes a dot inside each nParticle. The nParticles have not changed size, but if you play the animation, you'll see that they fall through the space between the edges of the collision surface (see Figure 13.20).

FIGURE 13.20
Reducing the Collide Width Scale value of the nParticles causes them to fall through the spaces between the edges of the nRigid object.

5. Scroll down to the Liquid Simulation tab, and deselect Enable Liquid Simulation. This makes it easier to see how the nParticles behave when self-collision is on. The Liquid Simulation settings alter the behavior of nParticles; this is covered later in the chapter.

6. Turn on Self Collide, and set Solver Display to Self Collision Thickness.

7. Set Collide Width Scale to **1** and Self Collide Width Scale to **0.1**. Turn on wireframe view (hot key = **4**), and play the animation; watch it from a side view.

   The nParticles have separate Collision Thickness settings for collision surfaces and self-collisions. Self Collide Width Scale is relative to Collide Width Scale. Increasing Collide Width Scale also increases Self Collide Width Scale (see Figure 13.21).

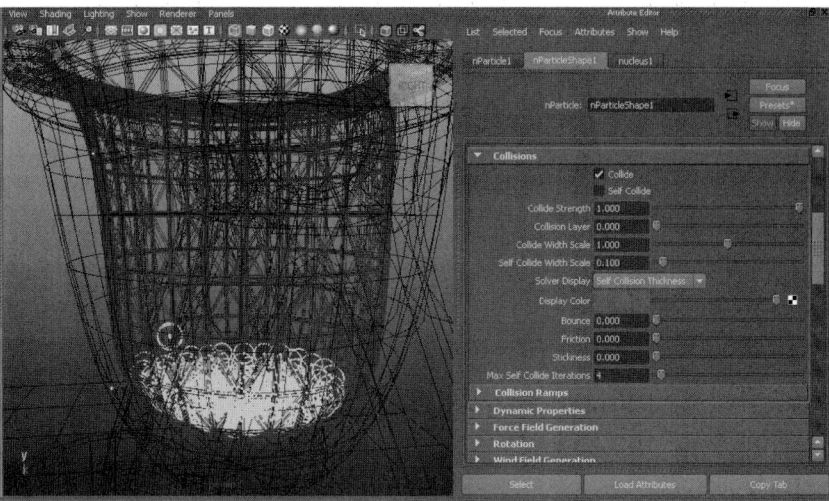

FIGURE 13.21
Reducing the Self Collide Width Scale value causes the nParticles to overlap as they collide.

8. Scroll up to the Particle Size settings, and adjust the Radius; set it to **0.8**. Both Collide Width Scale and Self Collide Width Scale are relative to the radius of the nParticles. Increasing the radius can cause the nParticles to pop out of the top of the tub.

9. Set Radius to **0.4** and Collide Width Scale to **1**, and turn off Self Collide. Turn Enable Liquid Simulation back on.

10. Save the scene as **forge_v02.ma**.

To see a version of the scene so far, open forge_v02.ma from the chapter13\scenes folder on the DVD.

The nParticles also have their own Bounce, Friction, and Stickiness settings. The Max Self Collide Iterations slider sets a limit on the number of calculated self-collisions per substep when Self Collide is on. This keeps the nParticles from locking up or the system from slowing down too much. If you have a lot of self-colliding nParticles in a simulation, lowering this value can increase performance.

The Collision Layer setting sets a priority for collision events. If two nDynamic objects using the same Nucleus solver are set to the same Collision Layer value, they will collide normally. If they have different layer settings, those with lower values will receive higher priority. In other words, they will be calculated first in a chain of collision events. Both nCloth and passive objects will collide with nParticles in the same or higher collision layers. So if the passive collision object has a Collision Layer setting of 10, an nParticle with a Collision Layer setting of 3 will pass right through it, but an nParticle with a Collision Layer value of 12 won't.

Collide Strength and Collision Ramps

New! Maya 2011 introduces several additional ways to control how nParticles collide with rigid surfaces and other nParticles. You can use the Collide Strength attribute to dampen the collision effect between nParticles or nParticles and other surfaces. At a strength of 1, collisions will be at 100 percent, meaning nParticles will collide at full force. A setting of 0 turns off collisions completely for the nParticle object. Values between 0 and 1 create a dampening effect for the collision.

Utilizing Collision Strength becomes more interesting when you modify Collide Strength using the Collide Strength Scale ramp. The ramp allows you to determine the strength of collisions on a per-particle basis using a number of attributes such as Age, Randomized ID, Speed, and others as the input for the ramp. Try this exercise to see how this works:

1. Open the collisionStrength.ma scene from the chapter13\scenes directory on the DVD. This scene has a spherical volume emitter shooting out ball-type nParticles. There is a simple polygon object named pSolid1 within the scene as well.

2. Select the pSolid1 polygon object, and turn it into a collision object by switching to the nDynamics menu and choosing nMesh ➢ Create Passive Collider.

3. Rewind and play the scene; the nParticles collide with the pSolid object as you might expect.

4. Select the nParticle1 node, and open its Attribute Editor.

5. Play the scene, and try adjusting the Collision Strength slider back and forth while the scene is playing. Observe the behavior of the nParticles. Try setting the slider to a value of **10**. The collisions then become very strong.

6. Set Collision Strength to **8**.

7. Expand the Collide Strength Scale ramp in the Collision Ramps rollout panel.

8. Edit the ramp so that the value on the left side is at **0.1** and the value on the right is at **1**, and set Collide Strength Scale Input to Randomized ID (see Figure 13.22).

FIGURE 13.22
Adjusting the Collide Strength Scale setting adds randomness and variety to the strength of the collisions in the simulation.

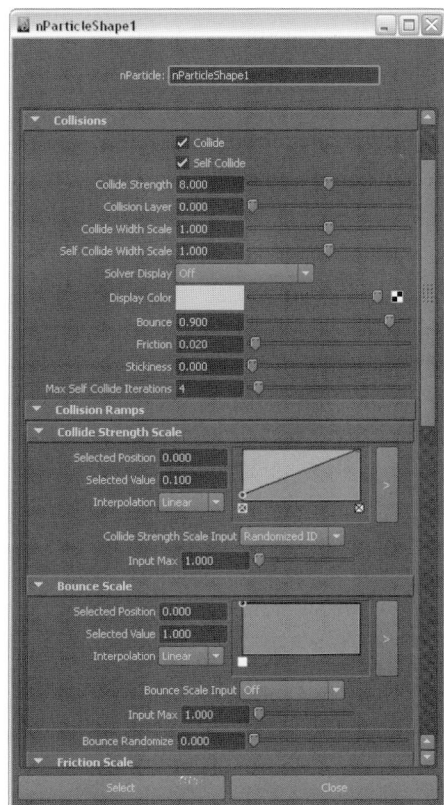

9. Rewind and play the animation. You'll see the strength of collisions is randomized; some collisions are weak, while others are exaggerated.

   Other collision attributes can also be controlled with ramps. These include Bounce, Scale, and Stickiness. Remember that these scales act as multipliers for the values that are set in the Collisions section.

   nRigid objects also have a Collision Strength setting; however, they do not have a collision ramp.

10. In the Collisions section, set Collide Strength to **1**. Set Stickiness to **50**.

11. Expand the Stickiness Scale ramp.

12. Set the input to Age and Input Max to **3**. Adjust the ramp so that it slopes down from the left to the right (see Figure 13.23).

13. Increase the emitter rate to **50**. Rewind and play the scene. The nParticles stick to the wall and gradually lose their stickiness over time (see Figure 13.24).

14. Scroll to the top, and expand the Particle Size section. Try setting the Radius Scale Input option of the nParticles to Randomized ID. Adjust the radius scale to create random variation in the size of the nParticles. Then set an attribute such as Friction to use Radius as the scale input. See whether you can make larger nParticles have more friction than smaller ones. Remember to set the Friction attribute in the Collision section to a high value such as **100** (see Figure 13.25).

FIGURE 13.23
The ramp for Stickiness Scale uses the nParticle's age as an input for controlling stickiness over time.

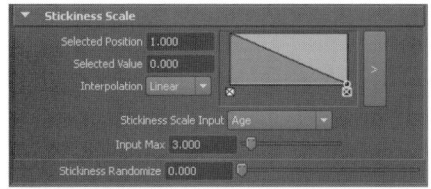

FIGURE 13.24
The nParticles lose stickiness over time and slide down the walls of the collision object.

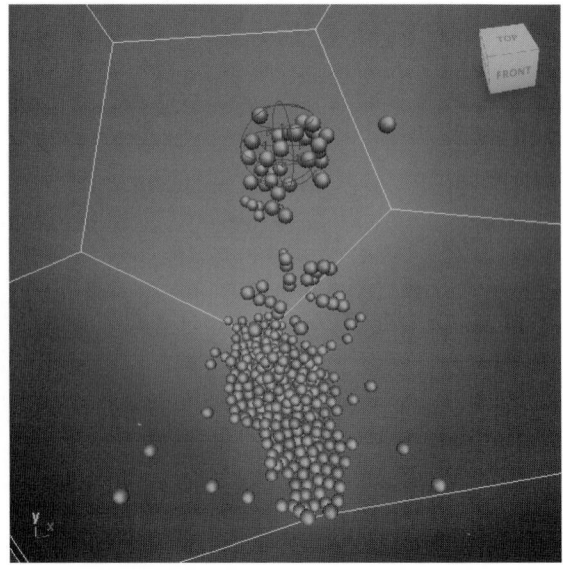

FIGURE 13.25
The Friction Scale Input option is set to Radius, and the ramp is adjusted so that larger nParticles have more friction than smaller ones.

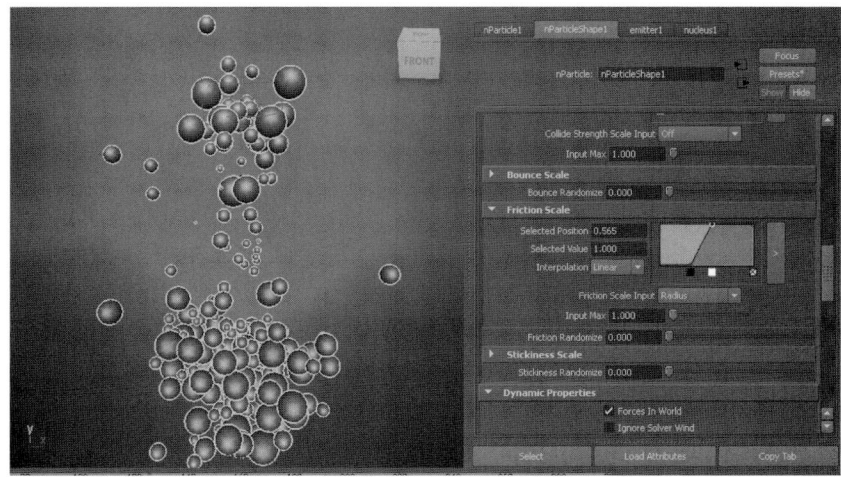

Using nParticles to Simulate Liquids

You can make nParticles simulate the behavior of fluids by enabling the Liquid Simulation attribute in the particle's shape node or by creating the nParticle as a water object. In this exercise, you'll use a tub filled with nParticles. The tub will be animated to pour out the nParticles, and their behavior will be modified to resemble hot molten metal.

Creating Liquid Behavior

Liquid simulations have unique properties that differ from other styles of nParticle behavior. This behavior is actually amazingly easy to set up and control.

1. Continue with the scene from the previous section, or open the forge_v02.ma scene from the chapter13\scenes folder on the DVD. In this scene, the tub has already been filled with particles, and collisions have been enabled.

2. Select nParticle1 in the Outliner, and name it **moltenMetal**.

3. Open its Attribute Editor to the moltenMetalShape tab, and expand the Liquid Simulation rollout panel (Figure 13.26).

    Liquid simulation has already been enabled because the nParticle style was set to Water when the nParticles were created. If you need to remove the liquid behavior from the nParticle, you can deselect the Enable Liquid Simulation check box; for the moment, leave the box selected.

FIGURE 13.26
Turning on Enable Liquid Simulation causes the nParticles to behave like water.

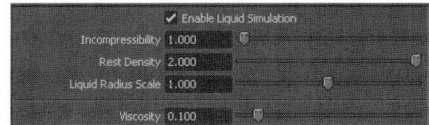

4. Switch to a side view, and turn on wireframe mode.

5. Play the animation, and observe the behavior of the nParticles.

If you look at the Collisions settings for moltenMetal, you'll see that the Self Collide attribute is off, but the nParticles are clearly colliding with each other. This type of collision is part of the liquid behavior defined by the Incompressibility attribute (this is discussed a little later in the chapter).

6. Play the animation back several times; notice the behavior when

A. Enable Liquid Behavior is off.

B. Self Collide is on (set Self Collide Width Scale to **0.7**).

C. Both Liquid Behavior and Self Collide are enabled.

7. Turn Liquid Behavior back on, and turn Self Collide off.

8. Open the Particle Size rollout panel, and set Radius to **0.25**; play the animation. There seems to be much less fluid for the same number of particles when the radius size is lowered.

9. Play the animation for about 140 frames until all the nParticles settle.

10. With the moltenMetal shape selected, choose nSolvers ➢ Initial State ➢ Set From Current.

11. Rewind and play the animation; the particles start out as settled in the well of the tub (see Figure 13.27).

FIGURE 13.27
Setting Initial
State makes the
nParticles start out
from their settled
position.

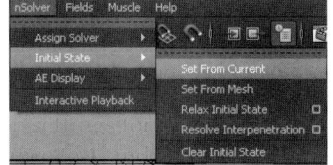

12. Select moltenMetal. At the top of the Attribute Editor, deselect Enable to temporarily disable the nParticle simulation so you can easily animate the tub.

13. Select the tub1 group in the Outliner, and switch to the side view.

14. Select the Move tool (hot key = **w**). Hold the **d** key on the keyboard, and move the pivot for tub1 so it's aligned with the center of the handles that hold it in the frame (see Figure 13.28).

15. Set the timeline to frame 20.

16. In the Channel Box, select the Rotate X channel for the tub1 group node, right-click, and set a keyframe.

17. Set the timeline to frame 100.

18. Set the value of tub1's Rotate X channel to **85**, and set another key.

FIGURE 13.28
Align the pivot point for the tub group with the handles from the side view.

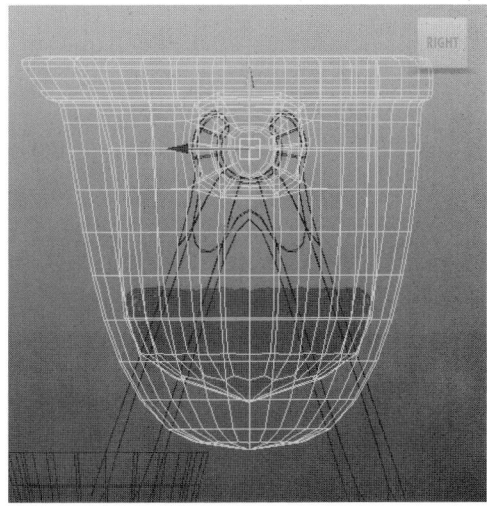

19. Move the timeline to frame 250, and set another keyframe.

20. Set the timeline to 330, set Rotate X to **0**, and set a fourth key.

21. Select moltenMetal, and in the Attribute Editor, select the Enable check box.

22. Rewind the animation, and play it. The nParticles pour out of the tub like water (see Figure 13.29).

FIGURE 13.29
When you animate the tub, the nParticles pour out of it like water.

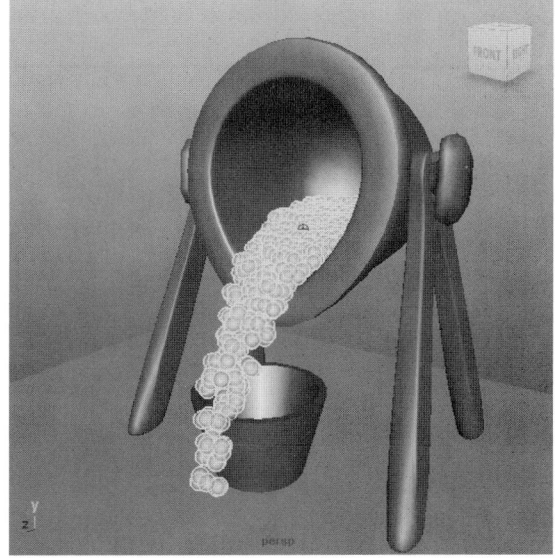

23. Switch to the perspective view. When you play the animation, the water goes through the bucket and the floor.

24. Select the bucket, and choose nMesh ➤ Create Passive Collider.

25. Switch to the nucleus1 tab, and turn on Use Plane.

26. Set the PlaneOrigin's Translate Y to **-4.11** to match the position of the floor. Now when you play the animation, the nParticles land in the bucket and on the floor.

SET THE COLLISION FLAG TO EDGE

You can improve the performance speed of the playback by selecting the nRigid node connected to the bucket and setting Collision Flag to Edge instead of Face.

---

27. By default the liquid simulation settings approximate the behavior of water. To create a more molten metal–like quality, increase Viscosity to **10**. Viscosity sets the liquid's resistance to flow. Sticky, gooey, or oily substances have a higher viscosity.

VISCOSITY AND SOLVER SUBSTEPS

Increasing the number of substeps on the Nucleus solver will magnify viscosity.

---

28. Set Liquid Radius Scale to **0.5**. This sets the amount of overlap between nParticles when Liquid Simulation is enabled. Lower values create more overlap. By lowering this setting, the fluid looks more like a cohesive surface.

You can use the other settings in the Liquid Simulation rollout panel to alter the behavior of the liquid:

Incompressibility   This setting determines the degree to which the nParticles resist compression. Most fluids use a low value (between 0.1 and 0.5). If you set this value to 0, all the nParticles will lie at the bottom of the tub in the same area, much like a nonliquid nParticle with Self Collide turned off.

Rest Density   This sets the overlapping arrangement of the nParticles when they are at rest. It can affect how "chunky" the nParticles look when the simulation is running. The default value of 2 works well for most liquids, but compare a setting of 1 to a setting of 5. At 1 fewer nParticles overlap, and they flow out of the tub more easily than when Rest Density is set to 5.

New!

Surface Tension   The Liquid Simulation settings now have a Surface Tension slider in Maya 2011. Surface tension simulates the attractive force within fluids that tends to hold them together. Think of how a drop of water forms a surface as it rests on wax paper or how beads of water form when condensing on a cold pipe.

29. To complete the behavior of molten metal, set Rest Density to **2**, and set Incompressibility to **0.5**.

30. In the Collisions rollout panel, set Friction to **0.5** and Stickiness to **0.25**.

31. Expand the Dynamic Properties rollout panel, and increase Mass to **6**. Note that you may want to reset the initial state after changing the settings because the nParticles will now collapse into a smaller area (see Figure 13.30).

32. Save the scene as **forge_v03.ma**.

To see a version of the scene to this point, open forge_v03.ma from the chapter13\scenes folder.

FIGURE 13.30
Adjusting the settings under Liquid Simulation, Collisions, and Dynamic Properties makes the nParticles behave like a heavy, slow-moving liquid.

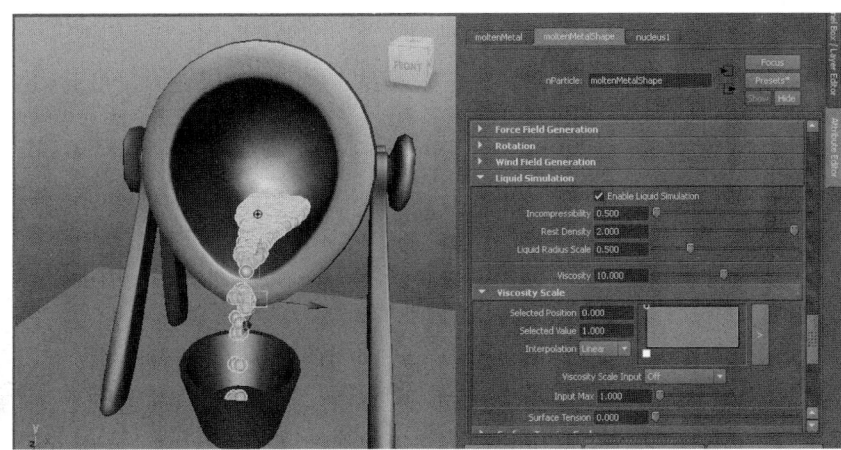

New!

VISCOSITY SCALE AND SURFACE TENSION RAMP

In Maya 2011, you can now fine-tune the behavior of your liquid simulations using Viscosity Scale and Surface Tension ramps.

You can use the viscosity scale to modify the viscosity over time. To do this, set Viscosity Scale Input to Age, and adjust the ramp. You can also use other inputs such as Randomized ID and Radius to determine how viscosity is applied to the liquid.

The Surface Tension Scale Ramp setting allows you to scale the surface tension value based on an input such as the age of the particle, a randomized ID, the radius, and more using settings similar to the other ramps.

Converting nParticles to Polygons

You can convert nParticles into a polygon mesh. The mesh updates with the particle motion to create a smooth blob or liquid-like appearance, which is perfect for rendering fluids. In this section, you'll convert the liquid nParticles created in the previous section into a mesh to make a more convincing molten metal effect.

1. Continue with the scene from the previous section, or open the `forge_v03.ma` scene from the `chapter13\scenes` folder on the DVD.

2. Play the animation to about frame 230.

3. Select the moltenMetal object in the Outliner, and choose Modify ➤ Convert ➤ nParticle To Polygons.

The nParticles have disappeared, and a polygon mesh has been added to the scene. You'll notice that the mesh is a lot smaller than the original nParticle simulation; this can be changed after converting the nParticle to a mesh. You can adjust the quality of this mesh in the Attribute Editor of the nParticle object used to generate the mesh.

4. Select the new polySurface1 object in the Outliner, and open the Attribute Editor to the moltenMetalShape tab.

5. Expand the Output Mesh section. Set Threshold to **0.8** and Blobby Radius Scale to **2.1**.

FINE-TUNING THE MESH

The settings in step 5 smooth the converted mesh. Higher Threshold settings create a smoother but thinner mesh; increasing Blobby Radius Scale does not affect the radius of the original nParticles. Rather, it uses this value as a multiple to determine the size of the enveloping mesh around each nParticle. Using the Threshold and Blobby Radius Scale settings together, you can fine-tune the look of the converted mesh.

---

6. Set Motion Streak to **0.5**. This stretches the moving areas of the mesh in the direction of the motion to create a more fluid-like behavior.

7. Mesh Triangle Size determines the resolution of the mesh. Lowering this value increases the smoothness of the mesh but also slows down the simulation. Set this value to **0.3** for now, as shown in Figure 13.31. Once you're happy with the overall look of the animation, you can set it to a lower value. This way, the animation continues to update at a reasonable pace.

FIGURE 13.31
Adjust the quality of the mesh in the Output Mesh section of the nParticle's shape node attributes.

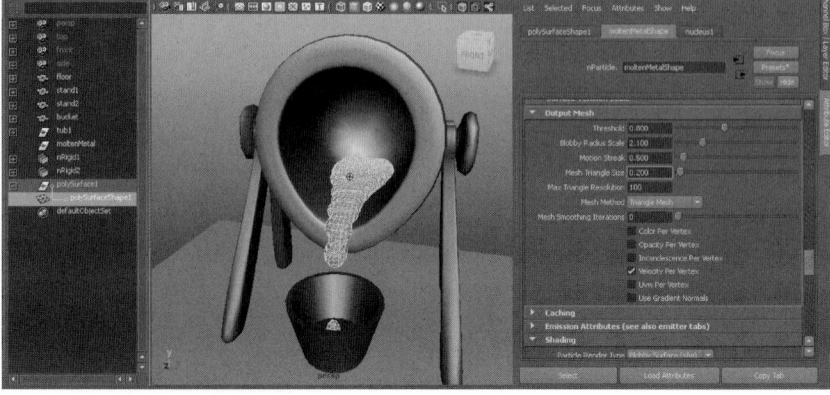

Max Triangle Resolution sets a limit on the number of triangles used in the nParticle mesh. If the number is exceeded during the simulation, Max Triangle Size is raised automatically to compensate.

ADJUST MAX TRIANGLE SIZE NUMERICALLY

Be careful when using the slider for Mesh Triangle Size. It's easy to move the slider to a low value by accident, and then you'll have to wait for Maya to update, which can be frustrating. Use numeric input for this attribute, and reduce the value by 0.05 at a time until you're happy with the look of the mesh.

Use Gradient Normals smoothes the normals of the mesh.

Mesh Method determines the shape of the polygons that make up the surface of the mesh. The choices are Cubes, Tetrahedra, Acute Tetrahedra, and Quad Mesh. After setting the Mesh Method option, you can create a smoother mesh around the nParticles by increasing the Max Smoothing Iterations slider. For example, if you want to create a smoother mesh that uses four-sided polygons, set Mesh Method to Quads, and increase the Max Smoothing Iterations slider. By default, the slider goes up to 10. If a value of 10 is not high enough, you can type values greater than 10 into the field.

Shading the nParticle Mesh

To create the look of molten metal, you can use a simple Ramp shader as a starting point.

1. Select the polySurface1 node in the Outliner. Rename it **metalMesh**.

2. Right-click the metalMesh object in the viewport. Use the pop-up menu to assign a ramp material. Choose Assign New Material. A pop-up window will appear; choose Ramp Shader from the list (see Figure 13.32).

FIGURE 13.32
Assign a Ramp shader to the metalMesh object.

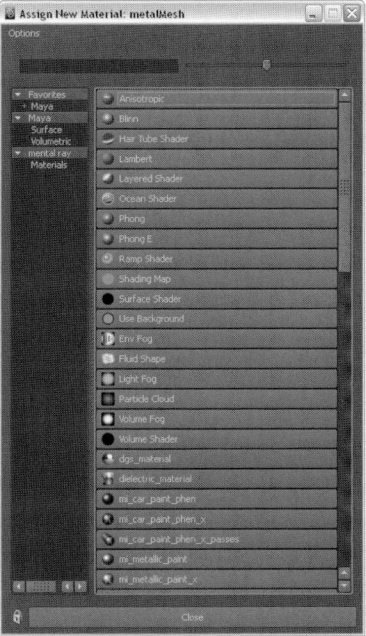

3. Open the Attribute Editor for the new Ramp shader. In the Common Materials Attributes section, set Color Input to Facing Angle.

4. Click the color swatch, and use the Color Chooser to pick a bright orange color.

5. Click the right side of the ramp to add a second color. Make it a reddish orange.

6. Create a similar but darker ramp for the Incandescence channel.

RAMP SHADER COLOR INPUT SETTINGS

Each of the color channels that uses a ramp will use the same Color Input setting as the Color rollout panel. So, in the case of this ramp, Incandescence will also use Facing Angle as the input.

---

7. Set Specularity to **0.24** and the specular color to a bright yellow.

8. Increase the Glow intensity in the Special Effects rollout panel to **0.15**.

9. Back in the moltenMetal particle Attribute Editor, decrease the Mesh Triangle Size to **0.1** (it will take a couple minutes to update), and render a test frame using mental ray. Set the Quality preset on the Quality tab to Production.

10. Save the scene as **forge_v04.ma**.

To see a version of the finished scene, open forge_v04.ma from the chapter13\scenes folder on the DVD (see Figure 13.33).

FIGURE 13.33
Render the molten metal in mental ray.

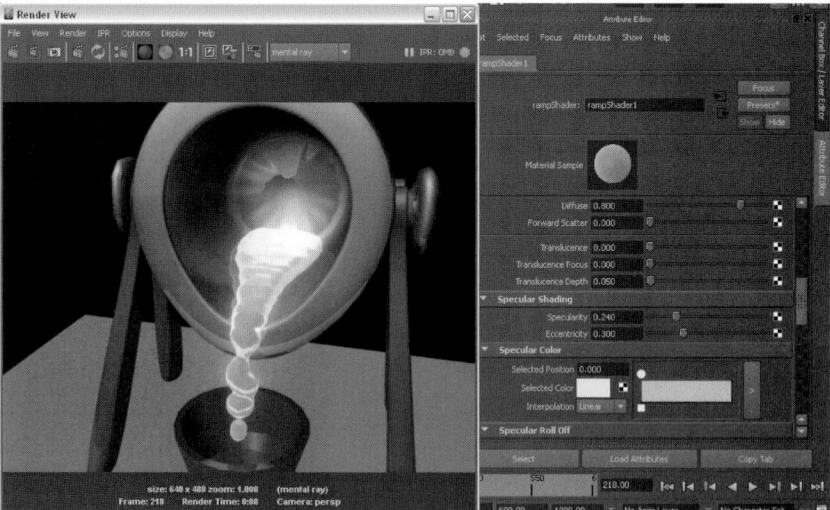

Emit nParticles Using a Texture

The behavior of nParticles is often determined by their many dynamic properties. These control how the nParticles react to the settings in the Nucleus solver as well as fields, collision objects, and other nParticle systems. In the following section, you'll get more practice working with these settings.

If you have used standard particle systems in previous versions of Maya, you'll be pleased to see how, since 2009, Maya has streamlined the workflow for creating particle effects. Many of the attributes that required custom connections, expressions, and ramps are now automated.

Surface Emission

In this exercise, you'll use nParticles to create the effect of flames licking the base of a space capsule as it reenters the atmosphere. You'll start by emitting nParticles from the base of the capsule and use a texture to randomize the generation of the nParticles on the surface.

1. Open the `capsule_v01.ma` scene from the `chapter13\scenes` directory on the DVD. You'll see a simple polygon capsule model. The capsule is contained in a group named spaceCapsule. In the group there is another surface named *capsule emitter*. This will serve as the surface emitter for the flames (see Figure 13.34).

FIGURE 13.34
The capsule group consists of two polygon meshes. The base of the capsule has been duplicated to serve as an emitter surface.

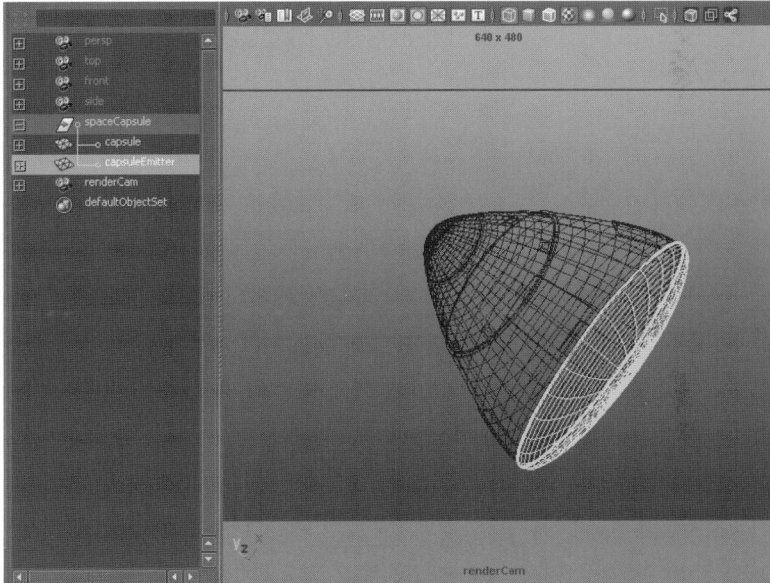

CREATING AN EMITTER SURFACE FROM A MODEL

The capsule emitter geometry was created by selecting the faces on the base of the capsule and duplicating them (Edit Mesh ➢ Duplicate Face). A slight offset was added to the duplicate face operation to move it away from the capsule surface. The idea is to have the nParticles generated by the bottom of the capsule. By creating an object separate from the bottom of the model, you can make the process much easier and faster.

2. Play the animation. The capsule has expressions that randomize the movement of the capsule to make it vibrate. The expressions are applied to the Translate channels of the group node. To see the Expressions, do the following:

   A. Open the Expression Editor (Window ➢ Animation Editors ➢ Expression Editor).

   B. Choose Select Filter ➢ By Expression Name.

   C. Select expression1, expression2, or expression3.

   You'll see the expression in the box at the bottom of the editor (see Figure 13.35).

FIGURE 13.35
Create the vibration of the capsule using random function expressions applied to each of the translation channels of the capsule.

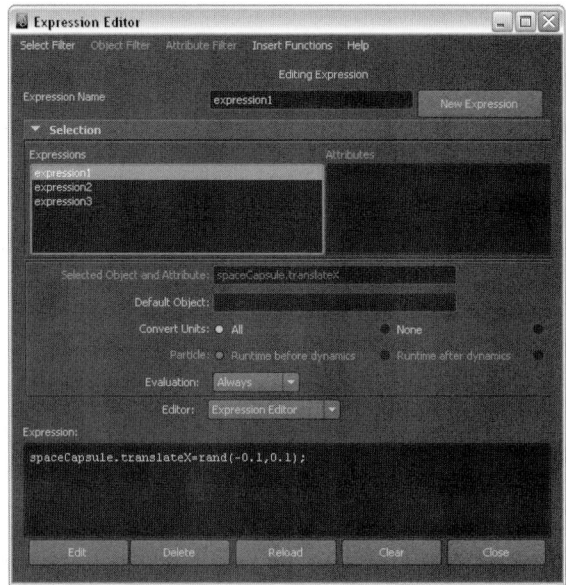

3. In the viewport, choose to look through the renderCam. The camera has been set up so the capsule looks as though it's entering the atmosphere at an angle.

4. In the Outliner, expand the spaceCapsule, and choose the capsuleEmitter object.

5. Switch to the nDynamics menu set, and choose nParticles ➢ Create nParticles ➢ Points to set the nParticle style to Points.

6. Select the capsuleEmitter, and choose nParticles ➢ Create nParticles ➢ Emit From Object ➢ Options.

7. In the options, choose Edit ➢ Reset to clear any settings that remain from previous Maya sessions.

8. Set Emitter Name to flameGenerator. Set Emitter Type to Surface and Rate (particles/sec) to **150**. Leave the rest of the settings at the default, and click the Apply button to create the emitter.

9. Rewind and play the animation. The nParticles are born on the emitter and then start falling through the air. This is because the Nucleus solver has Gravity activated by default. For now this is fine; leave the settings on the Nucleus solver where they are.

To randomize the generation of the nParticles, you can use a texture. To help visualize how the texture creates the particles, you can apply the texture to the surface emitter:

1. Select the capsuleEmitter, and open the UV Texture Editor (Window ➤ UV Texture Editor). The base already has UVs projected on the surface.

2. Select the capsuleEmitter, right-click the surface in the viewport, and use the pop-up menu to create a new Lambert texture for the capsuleEmitter surface. Name the shader **flameGenShader**.

3. Open the Attribute Editor for flameGenShader, and click the checkered box to the right of the Color channel to create a new render node for color.

4. In the Create Render Node window, click Ramp to create a ramp texture.

5. In the Attribute Editor for the ramp (it should open automatically when you create the ramp), name the ramp **flameRamp**. Make sure texture view is on in the viewport so you can see the ramp on the capsuleEmitter surface (hot key = **6**).

6. Set the ramp's Type to Circular Ramp, and set Interpolation to None.

7. Remove the blue color from the top of the ramp by clicking the blue box at the right side at the top of the ramp. Click the color swatch, and use the Color Chooser to change the green color to white and then the red color to black.

8. Set Noise to **0.5** and Noise Freq to **0.3** to add some variation to the pattern (see Figure 13.36).

9. In the Outliner, select the nParticle node and hide it (hot key = **Ctrl+h**) so you can animate the ramp without having the nParticle simulation slow down the playback. Set the renderer to High Quality display.

FIGURE 13.36
Apply the ramp to the shader on the base capsuleEmitter object.

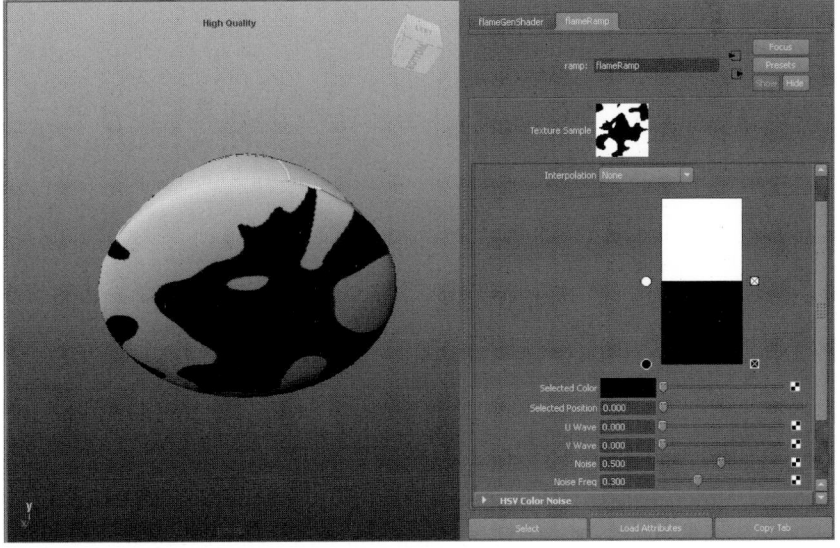

10. Select the flameRamp node, and open it in the Attribute Editor (select the node by choosing it from the Textures area of the Hypershade).

11. Rewind the animation, and drag the white color marker on the ramp down toward the bottom. Its Selected Position should be at .05.

12. Right-click Selected Position, and choose Set Key (see Figure 13.37).

13. Set the timeline to frame 100, move the white color marker to the top of the ramp, and set another key for the Selected Position.

14. Play the animation; you'll see the dark areas on the ramp grow over the course of 100 frames.

15. Open the Graph Editor (Window ➢ Animation Editors ➢ Graph Editor). Click the Select button at the bottom of the ramp's Attribute Editor to select the node; you'll see the animation curve appear in the Graph Editor.

16. Select the curve, switch to the Insert Keys tool, and add some keyframes to the curve.

17. Use the Move tool to reposition the keys to create an erratic motion to the ramp's animation (see Figure 13.38).

FIGURE 13.37
Position the white color marker at the bottom of the ramp and keyframe it.

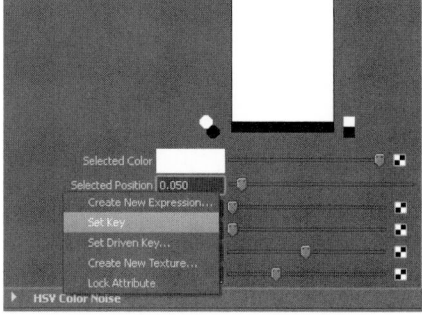

FIGURE 13.38
Add keyframes to the ramp's animation on the Graph Editor to make a more erratic motion.

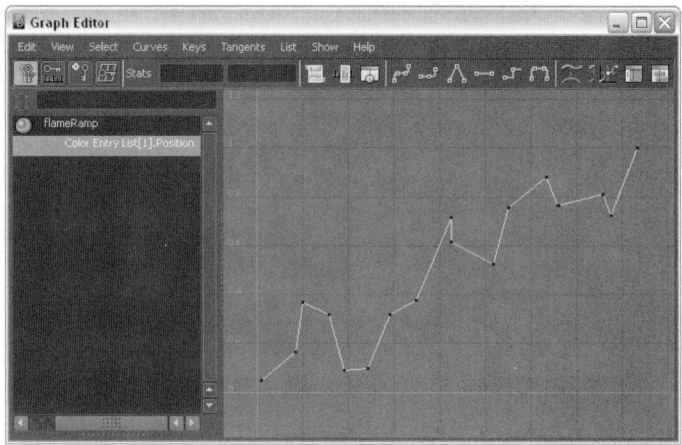

ANIMATE U WAVE AND V WAVE WITH EXPRESSIONS

To add some variation to the ramp's animation, you can animate the U and V Wave values or create an expression. In the U Wave field, type =0.5+(0.5*noise(time));, as shown here. The noise(time) part of the expression creates a random set of values between -1 and 1 over time. Noise creates a smooth curve of randomness values as opposed to the rand function, which creates a discontinuous string of random values (as seen in the vibration of the capsule). By dividing the result in half and then adding 0.5, the range of values is kept between 0 and 1. To speed up the rate of the noise, multiply time by 5 so the expression is =0.5+(0.5*noise(time*5));. You can use an expression to make the V Wave the same as the U Wave; just type =flameRamp.uWave in the field for the V Wave attribute. When you play the animation, you'll see a more varied growth of the color over the course of the animation.

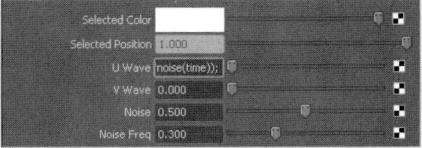

18. In the Outliner, select the capsuleEmitter node, and expand it.

19. Select the flameGenerator emitter node, and open its Attribute Editor.

20. Scroll to the bottom of the editor, and expand Texture Emission Attributes.

21. Open the Hypershade to the Textures tab.

22. MMB-drag flameRamp from the Textures area onto the color swatch for Texture Rate to connect the ramp to the emitter (see Figure 13.39).

23. Select Enable Texture Rate and Emit From Dark.

24. Increase Rate to **2400**, unhide the nParticle1 node, and play the animation. You'll see that the nParticles are now emitted from the dark part of the ramp.

25. Select the capsuleEmitter node, and hide it. Save the scene as **capsule_v02.ma**.

    To see a version of the scene to this point, open capsule_v02.ma from the chapter13\scenes folder on the DVD.

FIGURE 13.39
Drag the ramp texture with the middle mouse button from the Hypershade onto the Texture Rate color swatch to make a connection.

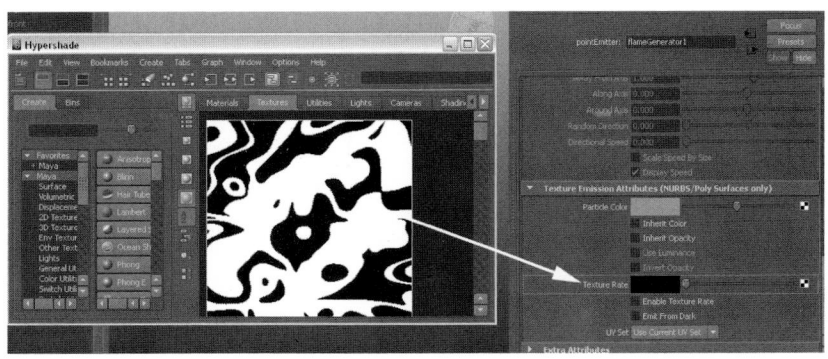

INHERIT COLOR AND OPACITY

You can make the particles inherit the color of the texture or use the color to control opacity. To do this, first switch to the particle's shape node attributes, expand the Add Dynamic Attributes rollout panel in the particle's shape tab, and click Opacity or Color. Then choose Add Per Particle from the pop-up window. Switch to the emitter's attributes, place the texture in the Particle Color swatch in the Texture Emission Attributes, and then enable Inherit Color or Inherit Opacity or both.

Using Wind

The Nucleus solver contains settings to create wind and turbulence. You can use these settings with nParticles to create snow blowing in the air, bubbles rising in water, or flames flying from a careening spacecraft.

The Wind Settings

Now that you have the basic settings for the particle emission, the next task is to make the particles flow upward rather than fall. You can do this using either an air field or the Wind settings on the Nucleus solver. Using the Wind settings on the Nucleus solver applies wind to all nDynamic nodes (nCloth, nRigid, nParticles) connected to the solver. For this section, you'll use the Nucleus solver. Fields will be discussed later in this chapter.

1. Continue with the scene from the previous section, or open the `capsule_v02.ma` file from the `chapter13\scenes` directory. Set Renderer to Default Render Quality in the viewport's menu bar in order to improve playback speed (nParticles should be enabled in the viewport's Show menu as well). Select the capsule emitter and hide it; this also improves performance.

2. Select the nParticle1 object in the Outliner. Rename it **flames**.

3. Open the Attribute Editor, and choose the nucleus1 tab.

4. Set Gravity to **0**, and play the animation. The particles emerge from the base of the capsule and stop after a short distance. This is because by default the nParticles have a Drag value of 0.01 set in their Dynamic Properties settings.

5. Switch to the flamesShape tab, expand the Dynamic Properties rollout panel, and set Drag to **0**. Play the animation, and the nParticles emerge and continue to travel at a steady rate.

6. Switch back to the nucleus1 tab:

   A. Set the Wind Direction fields to 0, 1, 0 so the wind is blowing straight up along the y-axis.

   B. Set Wind Speed to **5** (see Figure 13.40).

   C. Play the animation.

   There's no change; the nParticles don't seem affected by the wind.

FIGURE 13.40
The settings for
the wind on the
nucleus tab

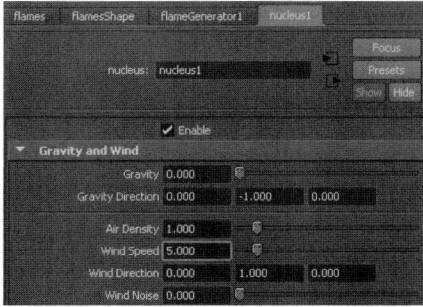

For the Wind settings in the Nucleus solver to work, the nParticle needs to have a Drag value, even a small one. This is why all the nParticle styles except Water have drag applied by default. If you create a Water-style particle and add a Wind setting, it won't affect the water until you set the Drag field above 0. Think of drag as a friction setting for the wind. In fact, the higher the Drag setting, the more the wind can grab the particle and push it along, so it actually has a stronger pull on the nParticle.

7. Switch to the tab for the flamesShape, set the Drag value to **0.01**, and play the animation. The particles now emerge and then move upward through the capsule.

8. Switch to the nucleus1 tab; set Air Density to **5** and Wind Speed to **25**. The Air Density setting also controls, among other things, how much influence the wind has on the particles.

A very high air density acts like a liquid, and a high wind speed acts like a current in the water. It depends on what you're trying to achieve in your particular effect, but you can use drag or air density or a combination to set how much influence the Wind settings have on the nParticle. And of course another attribute to consider is the particle's mass. Since these are flames, presumably the mass will be very low.

9. Set Air Density to **1**. Play the animation. The particles start out slowly but gain speed as the wind pushes them along.

10. Set the Mass attribute in the Dynamic Properties section to **0.01**. The particles are again moving quickly through the capsule (see Figure 13.41).

FIGURE 13.41
Set the Mass and
Drag attributes
to a low value,
enabling the
nParticle flames
to be pushed by
the wind on the
Nucleus solver.

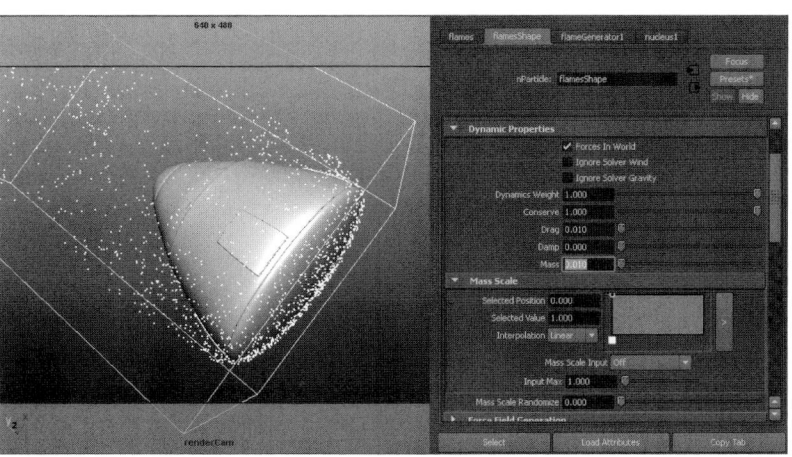

11. Switch to the nucleus1 tab, and set Wind Noise to **10**. Because the particles are moving fast, Wind Noise needs to be set to a high value before there's any noticeable difference in the movement. Wind Noise adds turbulence to the movement of the particles as they are pushed by the wind.

SOLVER SUBSTEPS

The Substeps setting on the Nucleus tab sets the number of times, per frame, the nDynamics are calculated. Increasing this value increases the accuracy of the simulation but also slows down performance. It can also change how some aspects of nDynamics behave. If you change the Substeps setting, you may need to adjust Wind Speed, Noise, Mass, and other settings.

---

12. To make the nParticles collide with the capsule, select the capsule node, and choose nMesh ➤ Create Passive Collider. The nParticles now move around the capsule.

13. Select the nRigid1 node in the Outliner, and name it **flameCollide**.

14. Expand the Wind Field Generation settings in the flameCollideShape node. Set Air Push Distance to **0.5** and Air Push Vorticity to **1.5** (see Figure 13.42).

15. Save the scene as **capsule_v03.ma**.

FIGURE 13.42
The Wind Field Generation settings on the flameCollide-Shape node

To see a version of the scene to this point, open `capsule_v03.ma` from the `chapter13\scenes` folder on the DVD.

A passive object can generate wind as it moves through particles or nCloth objects to create the effect of air displacement. In this case, the capsule is just bouncing around, so the Air Push Distance setting helps jostle the particles once they have been created. If you were creating the look of a submarine moving through murky waters with particulate matter, the Air Push Distance setting could help create the look of the particles being pushed away by the submarine, and the Air Push Vorticity setting could create a swirling motion in the particles that have been pushed aside. In the case of the capsule animation, it adds more turbulence to the nParticle flames.

The Wind Shadow Distance and Diffusion settings block the effect of the Nucleus solver's Wind setting on nParticles or nCloth objects on the side of the passive object opposite the direction of the wind. The Wind Shadow Diffusion attribute sets the amount at which the wind curls around the passive object.

Air Push Distance is more processor intensive than Wind Shadow Distance, and the Maya documentation recommends that you do not combine Air Push Distance and Wind Shadow Distance.

nParticles have these settings as well. You can make an nParticle system influence an nCloth object using the Air Push Distance setting.

Shading nParticles and Using Hardware Rendering to Create Flame Effects

Once you have created your nParticle simulation, you'll have to decide how to render the nParticles in order to best achieve the effect you want. The first decision you'll have to make is how to shade the nParticles—meaning, how they will be colored and what rendering style will best suit your needs. Maya makes this process fairly easy, because there are several rendering styles to choose from, including Point, MultiPoint, Blobby Surface, Streak, MultiStreak, and Cloud. Any one of these styles will change the appearance of the individual nParticles and thus influence the way the nParticle effect looks in the final rendered image.

To make coloring the nParticles easy, Maya provides you with a number of colored ramps that control the nParticles' color, opacity, and incandescence over time. You can choose different attributes, such as Age, Acceleration, Randomized ID, and so on, to control the way the color ramps are applied to the nParticles. You can find all of these attributes in the Shading section of the nParticle's Attribute Editor.

Most of the time, you'll want to render nParticles as a separate pass from the rest of the scene and then composite the rendered nParticle image sequence together with the rest of the rendered scene in your compositing program. This is so that you can easily isolate the nParticles and apply effects such as blurring, glows, and color correction separately from the other elements of the scene. You have a choice how you can render the nParticles. This can be done using mental ray, Maya Software, Maya Hardware, or the Hardware Render Buffer. This section demonstrates how to render using the Hardware Render Buffer. Later in the chapter you'll learn how to render nParticles using mental ray.

Shading nParticles to Simulate Flames

Shading nParticles has been made much easier since Maya version 2009. Many of the color and opacity attributes that required manual connections are now automatically set up and can easily be edited using the ramp in the nParticle's Attribute Editor. In this section, you'll use these ramps to make the nParticles look more like flames.

1. Continue with the same scene from the previous section, or open `capsule_v03.ma` from the `chapter13\scenes` folder on the DVD.

2. Select the flames nParticle node in the Outliner, and open the Attribute Editor to the flamesShape node. Expand the Lifespan Attributes rollout panel, and set Lifespan to Random Range. Set Lifespan to **3** and Lifespan Random to **3**.

   This setting makes the average life span for each nParticle three seconds with a variation of half the Lifespan Random setting in either direction. In this case, the nParticles will live anywhere between 0.5 and 4.5 seconds.

3. Scroll down to the Shading rollout panel, and expand it; set Particle Render Type to MultiStreak. This makes each nParticle a group of streaks and activates attributes specific to this render type.

4. Set Multi Count to **5**, Multi Radius to **0.8**, and Tail Size to **0.5** (see Figure 13.43).

5. In the Opacity Scale section, set Opacity Scale Input to Age. Click the right side of the Opacity Scale ramp curve to add an edit point. Drag this point down. This creates a ramp where the nParticle fades out over the course of its life (see Figure 13.44).

FIGURE 13.43
Change Particle
Render Type to
MultiStreak to
better simulate
flames.

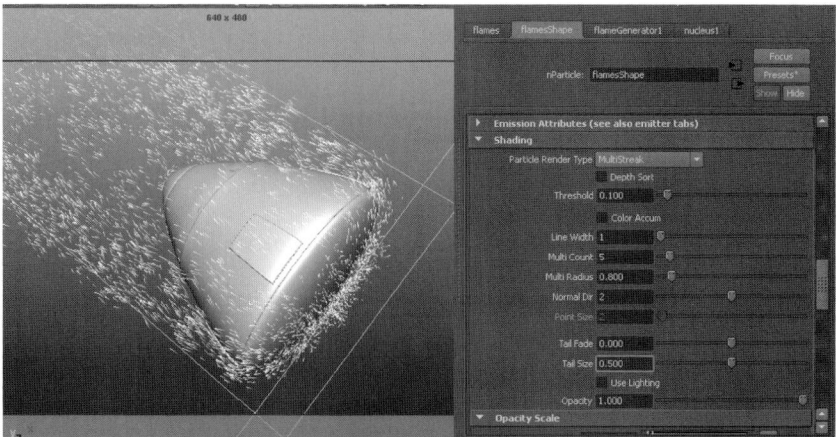

FIGURE 13.44
The opacity and
color ramps in the
nParticle's attri-
bute replace the
need to connect
ramps manually.

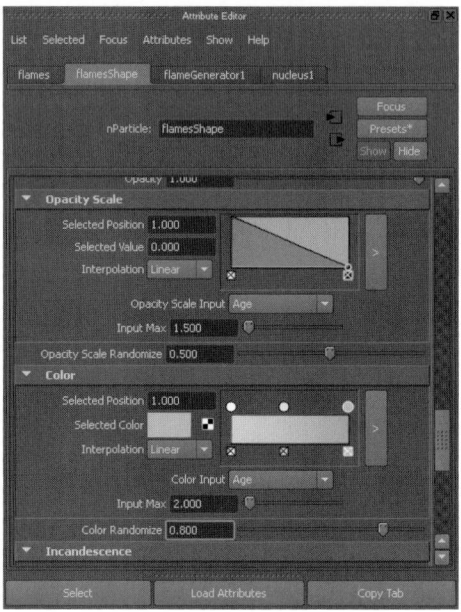

If you've used standard particles in older versions of Maya, you know that you normally
have to create a per-particle Opacity attribute and connect it to a ramp. If you scroll down
to the Per Particle Array Attributes section, you'll see that Maya has automatically added
the Opacity attribute and connected it to the ramp curve.

FLASHING nPARTICLE COLORS

If the opacity of your nParticles seems to be behaving strangely or the nParticles are flashing different colors, make sure that the renderer in the viewport is not set to High Quality Rendering. Setting
it to Default Quality Rendering should fix the problem.

6. Set Input Max to **1.5**. This sets the maximum range along the x-axis of the Opacity Scale ramp. Since Opacity Scale Input is set to Age, this means that each nParticle takes 1.5 seconds to become transparent, so the nParticles are visible for a longer period of time.

INPUT MAX VALUE

If the Input Max value is larger than the particle's life span, it will die before it reaches zero opacity, making it disappear rather than fade out. This is fine for flame effects, but you should be aware of this behavior when creating an effect. If Opacity Scale Input is set to Normalized Age, then Input Max has no effect.

---

7. To randomize the opacity scale for the opacity, set Opacity Scale Randomize to **0.5**.

8. Expand the Color rollout panel. Set Color Input to Age. Click the ramp just to the right of the color marker to add a new color to the ramp. Click the color swatch, and change the color to yellow.

9. Add a third color marker to the right end of the ramp, and set its color to orange.

10. Set Input Max to **2** and Color Randomize to **0.8**. See Figure 13.44.

11. In the Shading section, enable Color Accum. This creates an additive color effect, where denser areas of overlapping particles appear brighter.

12. Save the scene as **capsule_v04.ma**.

To see a version of the scene to this point, open `capsule_v04.ma` from the `chapter13\scenes` folder on the DVD.

Creating an nCache

Before rendering, it's always a good idea to create a cache to ensure that the scene renders correctly.

1. Continue with the scene from the previous section, or open the `capsule_v04.ma` file from the `chapter13\scenes` folder on the DVD.

2. Set the timeline to 200 frames.

3. In the Outliner, expand the capsuleEmitter section, and select the flameGenerator emitter. Increase Rate (particle/sec) to **25,000**. This will create a much more believable flame effect.

4. Select the flames node in the Outliner. Switch to the nDynamics menu set, and choose nCache ➢ Create New Cache ➢ Options. In the options, you can choose a name for the cache or use the default, which is the name of the selected node (flameShape in this example). You can also specify the directory for the cache, which is usually the project's data directory. Leave File Distribution set to One File Per Frame and Cache Time Range to Time Slider. Click Create to make the cache (see Figure 13.45).

FIGURE 13.45
The options for
creating an nCache

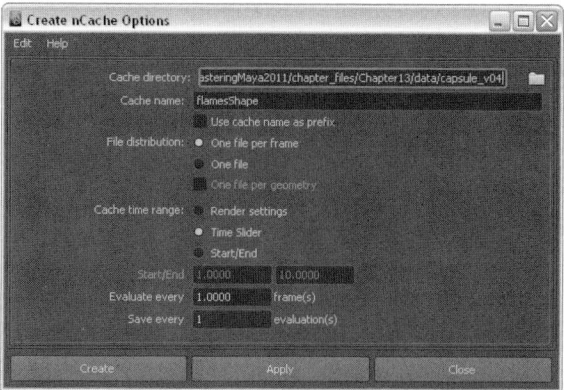

The scene will play through, and the cache file will be written to disk. It will take a fair amount of time to create the cache, anywhere from 5 to 10 minutes depending on the speed of your machine.

5. Open the Attribute Editor for the flameShape tab, and turn off the Enable button so that the nParticle is disabled. This prevents Maya from calculating the nParticle dynamics while using an nCache at the same time.

6. Play the animation, and you'll see the nParticles play back even though they have been disabled.

The playback is much faster now since the dynamics do not have to be calculated.

If you make any changes to the dynamics of the nParticles, you'll have to delete or disable the existing cache before you'll see the changes take effect.

By default, only the position and velocity attributes of the nParticle are stored when you create an nCache. If you have a more complex simulation in which other attributes change over time (such as mass, stickiness, rotation, and so on), then open the Caching rollout panel in the nParticle's Attribute Editor, set Cacheable Attributes to All, and then create a new nCache (see Figure 13.46). It is a fairly common mistake to forget to do this, and if this is not set properly, you'll notice that the nParticles do not behave as expected when you play back from the nCache or when you render the animation. The nCache file will be much larger when you change the Cacheable Attributes setting.

You can use the options in the nCache menu to attach an existing cache file to an nParticle or to delete, append, merge, or replace caches.

FIGURE 13.46
Set the Cacheable
Attributes menu to
All when you want
to cache attributes
other than just
Position and
Velocity.

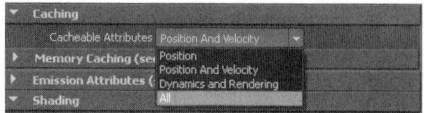

PARTICLE DISK CACHE

nParticles do not use the Particle Disk Cache settings in the Dynamics menu set. A normal Particle Disk Cache works only for standard particles. Create an nCache for nParticles and any other nDynamic system.

Using the Hardware Render Buffer

One of the fastest and easiest ways to render flames in Maya is to use the Hardware Render Buffer. The results may need a little extra tweaking in a compositing program, but overall it does a very decent job of rendering convincing flames. The performance of the Hardware Render Buffer depends on the type of graphics card installed in your machine. If you're using an Autodesk-approved graphics card, you should be in good shape.

THE HARDWARE RENDER BUFFER VS. MAYA HARDWARE

There are two ways to hardware render in Maya: you can use the Hardware Render Buffer, which takes a screenshot of each rendered frame directly from the interface, or you can batch render with Maya Hardware. Maya Hardware is chosen in the Render Settings window. The Hardware Render Buffer uses its own interface. There can be some differences in the way the final render looks depending on which hardware rendering method you choose. Depending on the effect you want to achieve, you may want to test each method to see which one produces the best results.

The Blobby Surface, Cloud, and Tube nParticle render styles can only be rendered using software (Maya Software or mental ray). All nParticle types can be rendered in mental ray, although the results may be different than those rendered using the Hardware Render Buffer or Maya Hardware.

NETWORK RENDERING WITH HARDWARE

If you are rendering using a farm, the render nodes on the farm may not have graphics cards, so using either the Hardware Render Buffer or Maya Hardware won't actually work. You'll have to render the scene locally.

---

1. To render using the Hardware Render Buffer, choose Window ➤ Rendering Editors ➤ Hardware Render Buffer. A new window opens showing a wireframe display of the scene. Use the Cameras menu in the buffer to switch to the renderCam.

2. To set the render attributes in the Hardware Render Buffer, choose Render ➤ Attributes. The settings for the buffer appear in the Attribute Editor.

The render buffer renders each frame of the sequence and then takes a screenshot of the screen. It's important to deactivate screen savers and keep other interface or application windows from overlapping the render buffer.

3. Set Filename to **capsuleFlameRender** and Extension to **name.0001.ext**.

4. Set Start Frame to **1** and End Frame to **200**. Keep By Frame set to 1.

   Keep Image Format set to Maya IFF. This file format is compatible with compositing programs such as Adobe After Effects.

5. To change the resolution, you can manually replace the numbers in the Resolution field or click the Select button to choose a preset. Click this button, and choose the 640×480 preset.

6. In the viewport window, you may want to turn off the display of the resolution or film gate. The view in the Hardware Render Buffer updates automatically.

7. Under Render Modes, turn on Full Image Resolution and Geometry Mask. Geometry Mask renders all the geometry as a solid black mask so only the nParticles will render. You can composite the rendered particles over a separate pass of the software-rendered version of the geometry.

8. To create the soft look of the frames, expand the Multi-Pass Render Options rollout panel. Enable Multi-Pass Rendering, and set Render Passes to **36**. This means the buffer will take 36 snapshots of the frame and slightly jitter the position of the nParticles in each pass. The passes will then be blended together to create the look of the flame. For flame effects, this actually works better than the buffer's Motion Blur option. Leave Motion Blur at 0 (see Figure 13.47).

FIGURE 13.47
The settings for the Hardware Render Buffer

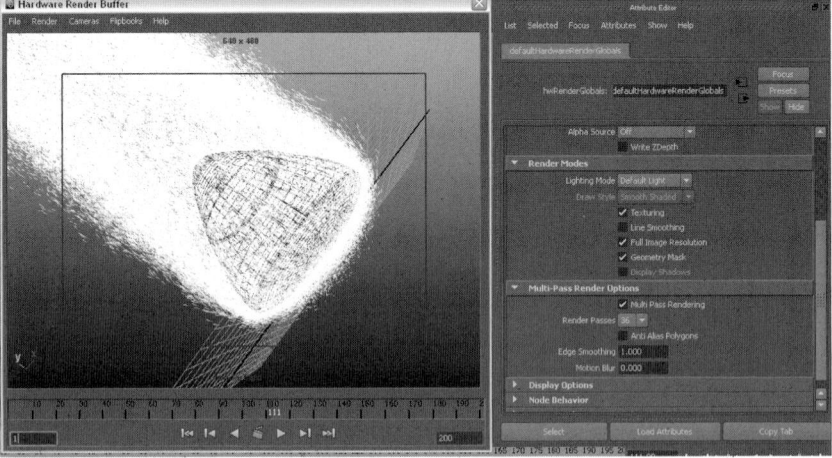

9. Play the animation to about frame 45.

10. In the Hardware Render Buffer, click the clapboard icon to see a preview of how the render will look (see Figure 13.48).

FIGURE 13.48
When Geometry
Mask is enabled,
the Hardware
Render Buffer
renders only the
nParticles.

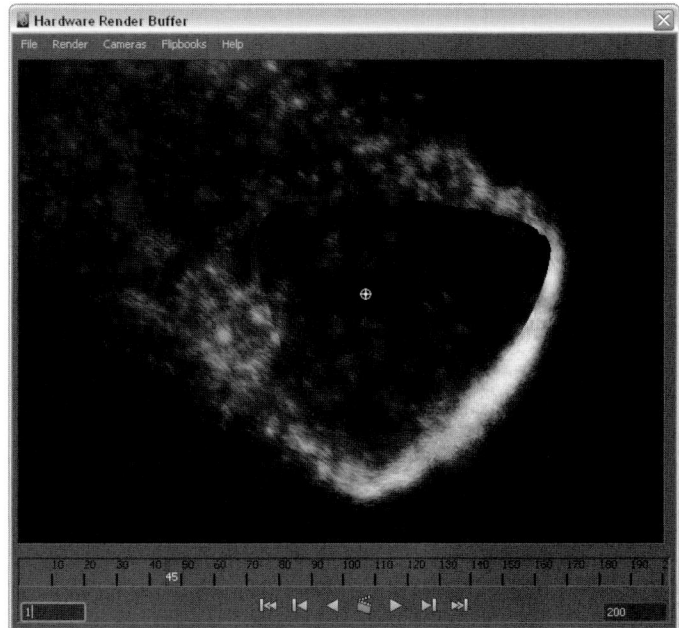

11. If you're happy with the look, choose Render ➢ Render Sequence to render the 200-frame sequence. It should take 5 to 10 minutes depending on your machine. You'll see the buffer render each frame.

12. When the sequence is finished, choose Flipbooks ➢ capsuleFlameRender1-200 to see the sequence play in FCheck.

13. Save the scene as **capsule_v05.ma**.

To see a version of the scene to this point, open the capsule_v05.ma scene from the chapter13\ scenes directory on the DVD.

To finalize the look of flames, you can apply additional effects such as glow and blur in your compositing program. Take a look at the capsuleReentry movie in the chapter13 folder of the DVD to see a finished movie made using the techniques described in this section.

nParticles and Fields

The behavior of nParticles is most often controlled by using fields. There are three ways to generate a field for an nParticles system. First, you can connect one or more of the many fields listed in the Fields menu. These include Air, Gravity, Newton, Turbulence, Vortex, and Volume Axis Curve. Second, you can use the fields built into the Nucleus solver—these are the Gravity and Wind forces that are applied to all nDynamic systems connected to the solver. Finally, you can use the Force field and the Air Push fields that are built into nDynamic objects. In this section, you'll experiment using all of these types of fields to control nParticles.

Using Multiple Emitters

When you create the emitter, an nParticle object is added and connected to the emitter. An nParticle can actually be connected to more than one emitter.

1. Open the generator_v01.ma scene in the chapter13\scenes folder on the DVD. You'll see a device built out of polygons. This will act as your experimental lab as you learn how to control nParticles with fields.

2. Switch to the nDynamics menu set, and choose nParticles ➤ Create nParticles ➤ Cloud to set the nParticle style to Cloud.

3. Choose nParticles ➤ Create nParticles ➤ Create Emitter ➤ Options.

4. In the options, set Emitter Name to **energyGenerator**. Leave Solver set to Create New Solver. Set Emitter Type to Volume and Rate (particles/sec) to **200.**

5. In the Volume Emitter Attributes rollout panel, set Volume Shape to Sphere. You can leave the rest of the settings at the defaults. Click Create to make the emitter (see Figure 13.49).

FIGURE 13.49
The settings for the volume emitter

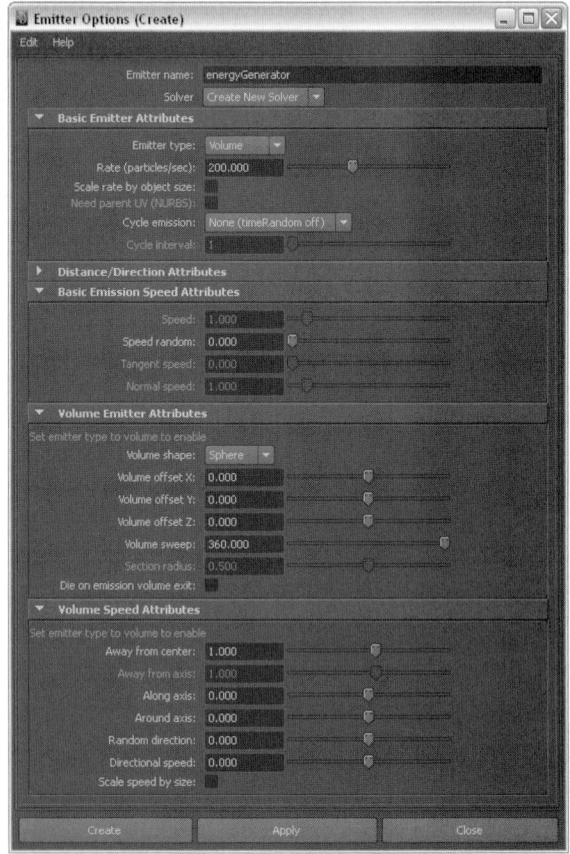

6. Select the energyGenerator1 emitter in the Outliner. Use the Move tool (hot key = **w**) to position the emitter around one of the balls at the end of the generators in the glass chamber. You may want to scale it up to about 1.25 (Figure 13.50).

FIGURE 13.50

Place the volume emitter over one of the balls inside the generator device.

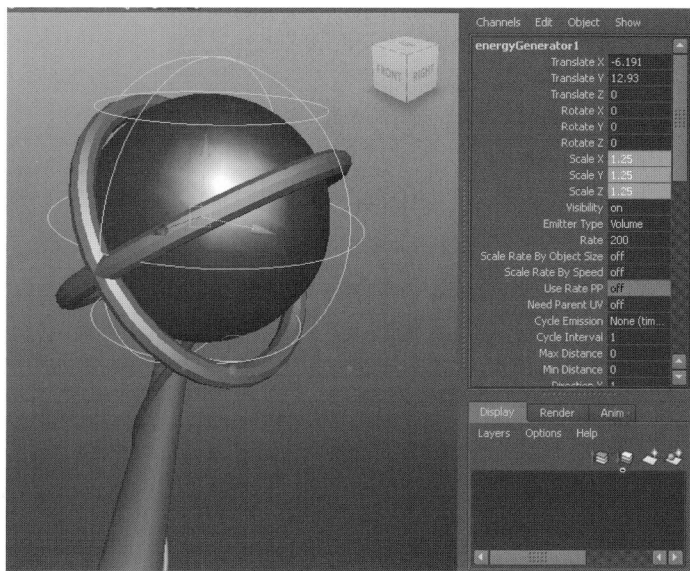

7. Set the timeline to **800**, and play the animation. The nParticles are born and fly out of the emitter.

   Notice that the nParticles do not fall even though Gravity is enabled in the Nucleus solver and the nParticle has a mass of 1. This is because in the Dynamic properties for the Cloud style of nParticle, the Ignore Solver Gravity check box is enabled.

8. Select the energyGenerator1 emitter, and duplicate it (hot key = **Ctrl+d**). Use the Move tool to position this second emitter over the ball on the opposite generator.

   If you play the animation, the second emitter creates no nParticles. This is because duplicating the emitter did not create a second nParticle object, but that's okay; you're going to connect the same nParticle object to both emitters.

9. Select nParticle1 in the Outliner, and rename it **energy**.

10. Select energy, and choose Window ➢ Relationship Editors ➢ Dynamic Relationships. A window opens showing the objects in the scene; energy is selected on the left side.

11. On the right side, click the Emitters radio button to switch to a list of the emitters in the scene. EnergyGenerator1 is highlighted, indicating that the energy nParticle is connected to it.

12. Select energyGenerator2 so both emitters are highlighted (see Figure 13.51).

FIGURE 13.51
Use the Dynamic Relationships Editor to connect the energy nParticle to both emitters.

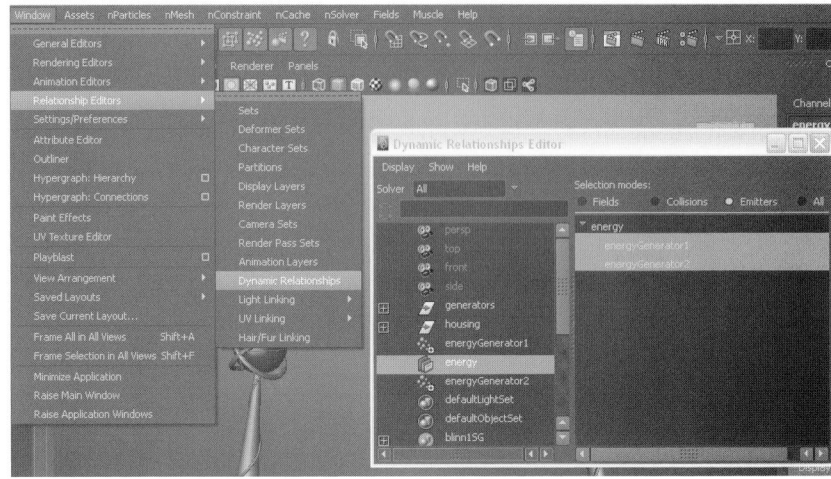

13. Close the Dynamic Relationships Editor, and rewind and play the animation. You'll see both emitters now generate nParticles—the same nParticle object actually.

14. Select the energy object, and open the Attribute Editor. Switch to the nucleus tab, and set Gravity to **1**.

15. In the energyShape tab, expand the Dynamic Properties rollout panel, and turn off Ignore Solver Gravity so the energy nParticles slowly fall after they are emitted from the two generator poles (see Figure 13.52).

FIGURE 13.52
The energy nParticles are emitted from both emitters. Gravity is set to a low value, causing the nParticles to slowly fall.

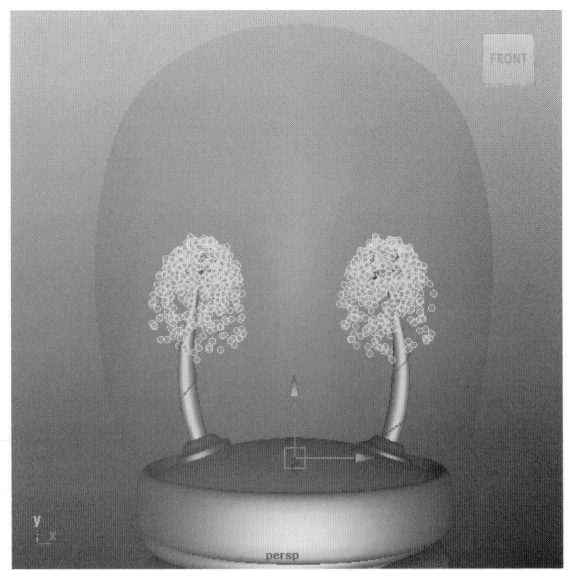

Volume Axis Curve

Volume Axis Curve is a versatile dynamic field that can be controlled using a NURBS curve. You can use this field with any of the dynamic systems (traditional and nDynamic) in Maya. In this section, you'll perform some tricks using the field inside a model of an experimental vacuum chamber.

1. Select the energy nParticle node in the Outliner. In the Attribute Editor, open the Lifespan rollout panel, and set the Lifespan mode to Random Range.

2. Set Lifespan to **6** and Lifespan Random to **4**. The nParticles will now live between 4 and 8 seconds each.

3. With the energy nParticle selected, choose Fields ➢ Volume Curve. By creating the field with the nParticle selected, the field is automatically connected.

DYNAMIC RELATIONSHIP EDITOR

You can use the Dynamic Relationship Editor to connect fields to nParticles and other dynamic systems. Review the previous section on using multiple emitters to see how the Dynamic Relationship Editor works.

---

4. Select curve1 in the Outliner, and use the Move tool to position it between the generators. The field consists of a curve surrounded by a tubular field.

5. Use the Show menu to disable the display of polygons so the glass case is not in the way.

6. Select curve1 in the Outliner, and right-click the curve; choose CVs to edit the curve's control vertices.

7. Use the Move tool to position the CVs at the end of the curve inside each generator ball, and then add some bends to the curve (see Figure 13.53).

FIGURE 13.53
Position the CVs of the Volume Axis curve to add bends to the curve. The field surrounds the curve, forming a tube.

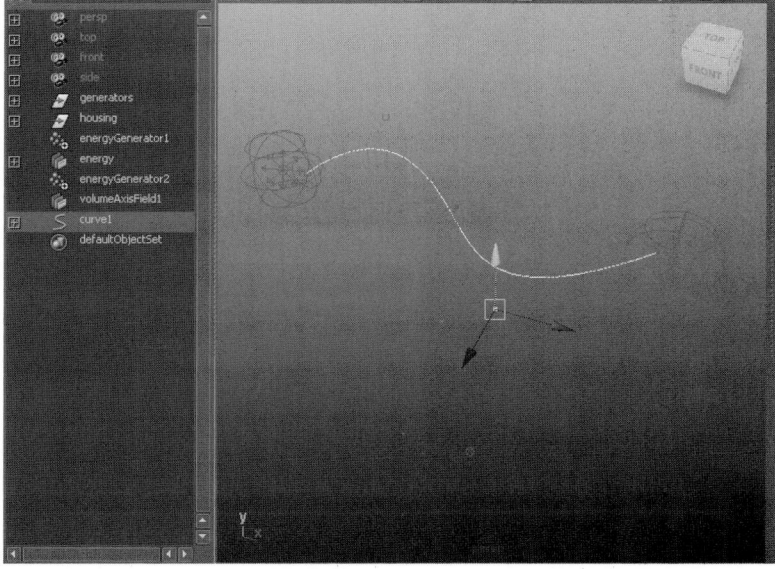

8. Rewind and play the animation. A few of the nParticles will be pushed along the curve. So far, it's not very exciting.

9. Select the volumeAxisField1 node in the Outliner, and open its Attribute Editor. Use the following settings:

   A. The default Magnitude and Attenuation settings (5 and 0) are fine for the moment.

   B. In the Distance rollout panel, leave Use Max Distance off.

   C. In the Volume Control Attributes rollout panel, set Section Radius to **3**.

   D. Set Trap Inside to **0.8**. This keeps most of the nParticles inside the area defined by the volume radius (the Trap Inside attribute is available for other types of fields such as the Radial field).

   E. Leave Trap Radius set to 2. This defines the radius around the field within which the nParticles are trapped.

   F. Edit the Axial Magnitude ramp so each end is at about 0.5 and the middle is at 1, as in Figure 13.54. Set the interpolation of each point to Spline. This means that the area at the center of the curve has a stronger influence on the nParticles than the areas at either end of the curve.

FIGURE 13.54
The settings for the Volume Axis Curve field

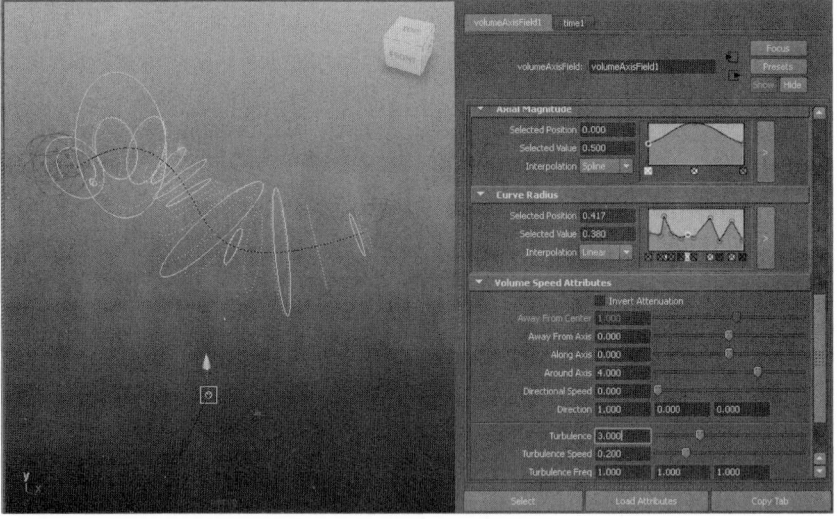

   G. Edit the Curve Radius ramp: add some points to the curve, and drag them up and down in a random jagged pattern. You'll see the display of the field update; this creates an interesting shape for the curve.

   H. In the Volume Speed Attributes rollout panel, set Away From Axis and Along Axis to **0**, and set Around Axis to **4**. This means that the nParticles are pushed in a circular motion around the curve rather than along or away from it. If you zoom into the field, you'll see an arrow icon at the end of the field indicating its direction. Positive numbers make the field go clockwise; negative numbers make it go counterclockwise.

1. Set Turbulence to **3**, and leave Turbulence Speed at 0.2. This adds noise to the field, causing some nParticles to fly off (see Figure 13.54).

10. Play the animation. You'll see the nParticles move around within the field. Faster-moving particles fly out of the field.

    This is interesting, but it can be improved to create a more dynamic look.

11. In the Attribute Editor for the Volume Axis Curve field, remove the edit points from the Curve Radius ramp.

12. Edit the curve so it has three points. The points at either end should have a value of 1; the point at the center should have a value of 0.1.

13. Select the edit point at the center, and in the Selected Position field type **=0.5+(0.5* (noise(time*4)));**. This is similar to the expression that was applied to the ramp in the "Surface Emission" section of this chapter. In this case, it moves the center point back and forth along the curve, creating a moving shape for the field (see Figure 13.55).

14. Save the scene as **generator_v02.ma**.

To see a version of the scene to this point, open the generator_v02.ma scene from the chapter13\scenes folder on the DVD. This version uses a dynamic hair to control the field. To learn how to use this technique, refer to "Using a Dynamic Hair Curve with a Volume Axis Curve."

FIGURE 13.55
Create an expression to control the Selected Position attribute of the Curve Radius ramp's center point. The numeric field is not large enough to display the entire expression.

USING A DYNAMIC HAIR CURVE WITH A VOLUME AXIS CURVE

For an even more dynamic look, you can animate the curve itself using hair dynamics (as shown here). Hair is discussed in Chapter 15, but here is a quick walk-through of how to set this up. In addition to making the volume curve dynamic, this workflow demonstrates how to change the input curve source for the volume curve.

(CONTINUES)

USING A DYNAMIC HAIR CURVE WITH A VOLUME AXIS CURVE *(CONTINUED)*

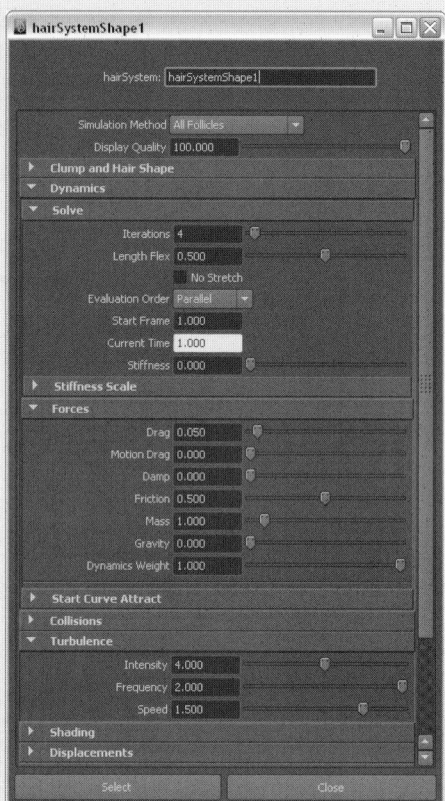

1. Select the curve1 object in the Outliner. Switch to the Dynamics menu set, and choose Hair ➤ Make Selected Curves Dynamic.

2. Open the Attribute Editor for the hairsystem1 node, and switch to the hairSystemShape1 tab.

3. In the Dynamics rollout panel, set Stiffness to **0** and Length Flex to **0.5**.

4. In the Forces rollout panel, set Gravity to **0**.

5. In the Turbulence rollout panel, set Intensity to **4**, Turbulence Frequency to **2**, and Turbulence Speed to **1.5**.

    If you play the animation, you'll see two curves; the original Volume Axis curve is unchanged, but a second curve is now moving dynamically. You need to switch the input curve for the Volume Axis curve from the original curve to the Dynamic Hair curve.

6. In the Outliner, expand the hairSystem1OutputCurves group, and select the curveShape2 node. Open the Connection Editor (Window ➤ General Editors ➤ Connection Editor), as shown here. The curveShape2 node should be loaded on the left side.

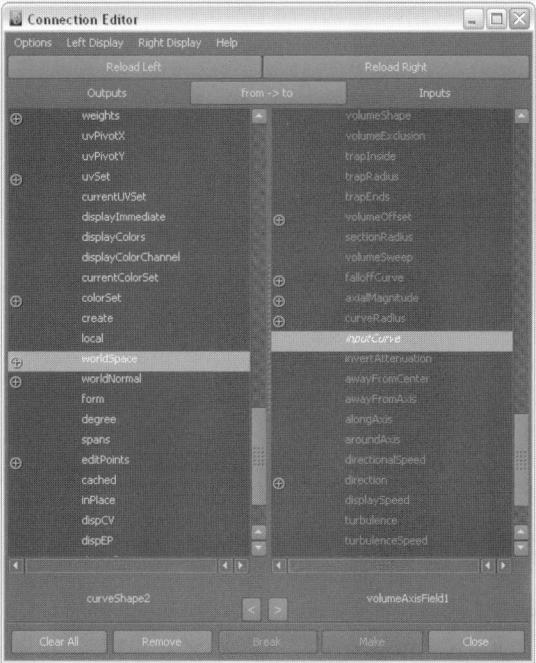

7. In the Outliner, select the VolumeAxisField1, and click Reload Right in the Connection Editor.

8. Select worldSpace from the list on the left and inputCurve from the list on the right to connect the Dynamic Hair curve to the Volume Axis field.

9. Play the animation; the Volume Axis field now animates in a very dynamic way.

You can use this technique to swap any curve you create for the input of the Volume Axis field.

You can use the Hypergraph to view connections between nodes (as shown here). In your own animations, you may need to do some detective work to figure out how to make connections like this. If you graph the Volume Axis field in the Hypergraph, you can hold your mouse over the connection between curveShape2 and the Volume Axis field to see how the worldSpace attribute of the curve is connected to the input curve of the field. It's a simple matter of making the same connection between the shape node of a different curve to the Volume Axis field to replace the input curve for the field.

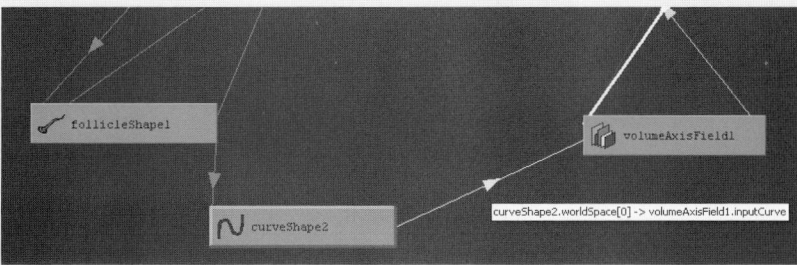

Working with hair curves is discussed in detail in Chapter 15.

ANIMATING BLOOD CELLS

Blood cells flowing through a tubular-shaped blood vessel are a common challenge facing many animators. In early versions of Maya, the solution has been to use the Curve Flow Effect, which uses a series of goals, or emitters, placed along the length of a curve. With the introduction of the Volume Axis curve in Maya 2009, the solution to this animation problem is much easier to set up and edit.

To create this effect, follow these steps:

1. Add an omni emitter and an nParticle to a scene using the Water nParticle style.
2. Draw a curve that defines the shape of the blood vessel.
3. Extrude a NURBS circle along the length of the curve to form the outside walls of the vessel.
4. Place the emitter inside the blood vessel at one end of the curve.
5. Select the nParticle, and add a Volume Axis Curve field.
6. Use the Connection Editor to attach the worldSpace attribute of the blood vessel curve's shape node to the inputCurve attribute of the Volume Axis Curve field.
7. In the Volume Axis Curve field's attributes, set Trapped to 1, and define the trapped radius so it fits within the radius of the vessel.
8. Adjust the Along Axis and Around Axis attributes until the nParticles start to flow along the length of the curve.
9. Adjust the Drag attribute of the nParticles to adjust the speed of the flow.
10. Set the life span of the nParticles so they die just before reaching the end of the blood vessel.

You can use the Blobby Surface render type to make the nParticles look like globular surfaces or try instancing modeled blood cells to the nParticles. Instancing is covered in Chapter 14.

Working with Force Fields

nParticles, nCloth, and passive collision objects (also known as *nRigids*) can all emit force fields that affect themselves and other nDynamic systems attached to the same nucleus node. In this example, the surface of the glass that contains the particle emitters will create a field that controls the nParticle's behavior.

1. Continue with the scene from the previous section, or open the generator_v02.ma scene from the chapter13\scenes folder on the DVD.
2. Expand the Housing group in the Outliner. Select the dome object, and choose nMesh ➤ Create Passive Collider.
3. In the Outliner, rename the nRigid1 node to **domeCollider**.
4. To keep the particles from escaping the chamber, you'll also need to convert the seal and base objects to passive collision objects:
   A. Select the seal object, and choose nMesh ➤ Create Passive Collider.
   B. Name the new nRigid node to **sealCollide**.
   C. Do the same for the base, and name it **baseCollide**.

5. Play the animation. Because some of the nParticles are thrown from the Volume Axis Curve field, they are now contained within the glass chamber (see Figure 13.56).

6. Open the settings for the energyShape node in the Attribute Editor. In the Particle Size rollout panel, make sure Radius Scale Input is set to Age.

7. Edit the Radius Scale ramp so it slopes up from 0 on the left to 1 in the middle and back down to 0 on the left.

8. Set Interpolation to Spline for all points along the curve.

9. Set Input Max to **3** and Radius Scale Randomize to **0.5** (see Figure 13.57).

10. Select the domeCollider node, and open the Attribute Editor to the domeColliderShape tab.

11. Expand the Force Field Generation settings, and set Force Field to Single Sided. This generates a force field based on the positive normal direction of the collision surface.

    Along Normal generates the field along the surface normals of the collision object. In this case, the difference between Along Normal and Single Sided is not noticeable. Double Sided generates the field based on both sides of the collision surface.

FIGURE 13.56
Parts of the generator device are converted to collision objects, trapping the nParticles inside.

FIGURE 13.57
Edit the Radius Scale settings to create a more randomized radius for the nParticles.

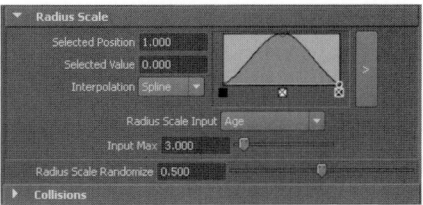

12. The normals for the dome shape are actually pointing outward. You can see this if you choose Display ➢ Polygons ➢ Face Normals. To reverse the surface, switch to the Polygons menu set, and choose Normals ➢ Reverse (see Figure 13.58).

FIGURE 13.58
Reverse the normals for the dome surface so they point inward.

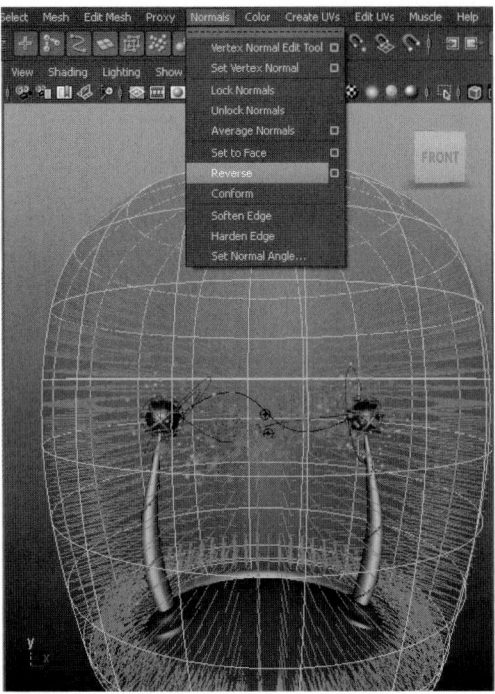

13. Back in the Force Field Generation settings for the domeColliderShape node, set Field Magnitude to **100** and Field Distance to **4**, and play the animation. The particles are repelled from the sides of the dome when they are within 4 field units of the collision surface. A lower field magnitude will repel the particles with a weaker force, allowing them to collide with the dome before being pushed back to the center. If you set Magnitude to **1000**, the nParticles never reach the collision surface.

14. Set Field Magnitude to **-100**. The nParticles are now pulled to the sides of the dome when they are within 4 field units of the collision surface, much like a magnet. Setting a negative value of -1000 causes them to stick to the sides.

The Field Scale Edit ramp controls the strength of the field within the distance set by the Field Distance value. The right side of the ramp is the leading edge of the field—in this case 4 field units in from the surface of the dome. The left side represents the scale of the force field on the actual collision surface.

You can create some interesting effects by editing this curve. If Field Magnitude is at a value of -100 and you reverse the curve, the nParticles are sucked to the dome quickly when they are within 4 units of the surface. However, they do not stick very strongly to the side, so they bounce around a little within the 4-unit area. Experiment creating different shapes for the curve, and see how it affects the behavior of the nParticles. By adding variation to the center of the curve, you get more of a wobble as the nParticles are attracted to the surface.

15. Save the scene as **generator_v03.ma**.

To see a version of the scene to this point, open the generator_v03.ma scene from the chapter13\scenes folder on the DVD.

Painting Field Maps

The strength of the force field can be controlled by a texture. The texture itself can be painted onto the collision surface.

1. Continue with the scene from the previous section, or open the generator_v03.ma scene from the chapter13\scenes folder on the DVD.

2. In the Attribute Editor for domeCollider, set the Field Scale ramp so it's a straight line across the top of the curve editor. Set Field Magnitude to **1**.

3. Select the dome object, and choose nMesh ➤ Paint Texture Properties ➤ Field Magnitude. The dome turns white, and the Artisan Brush tool is activated. If the Dome turns black, open the Flood controls in the Artisan Tool options, and click the Flood button to fill the surface with a value of 1 for the Field Strength attribute.

4. Open the tools options for the Artisan Brush. The color should be set to black, and Paint Operation should be set to Paint.

5. Use the brush to paint a pattern on the surface of the dome. Make large, solid lines on the surface; avoid blurring the edges so the end result is clear (see Figure 13.59).

FIGURE 13.59
Use the Artisan Brush tool to paint a pattern for the field magnitude on the collision surface.

6. When you've finished, click the Select tool in the toolbox to close the Artisan Brush options.

7. Open the Hypershade. On the Textures tab, you'll see the texture map you just created. You can also use file textures or even animated sequences for the map source.

8. Select the dome in the scene. In the Work Area of the Hypershade, right-click, and choose Graph ➢ Graph Materials On Selected Objects.

9. MMB-drag the file1 texture from the texture area of the Hypershade down onto the shader, and choose Color. Connecting the texture to the color does not affect how the field works, but it will help you visualize how the map works (see Figure 13.60).

FIGURE 13.60
Connect the newly painted texture to the color of the dome shader.

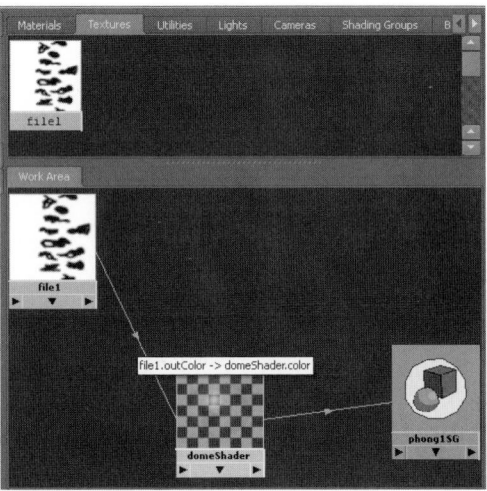

If you play the animation, you won't see much of a result. The reason is that the values of the map are too weak and the movement of the nParticles is too fast to be affected by the field.

10. In the Hypershade, select the file1 texture, and open its Attribute Editor. The outAlpha of the texture is connected to the field magnitude of the collision surface. You can see this when you graph the network in the Hypershade.

11. To increase the strength of the map, expand the Color Balance section. Set Alpha Gain to **1000** and Alpha Offset to **-500**. Chapter 2 has a detailed explanation of how the Alpha Gain and Alpha Offset attributes work. Essentially this means that the light areas of the texture cause the force field magnitude to be at a value of 500, and the dark areas cause it to be at -500.

12. Play the animation. You'll see that most of the nParticles stay in the center of the dome, but occasionally one or two nParticles will fly out and stick to the side. They stick to the areas where the texture is dark (see Figure 13.61).

Vertex maps assign values to the vertices of the surface using the colors painted by the brush; texture maps use a file texture. One may work better than the other depending on the situation. You can paint vertex maps by choosing nMesh ➤ Paint Vertex Properties. In the Map properties, set Map Type to Vertex or Texture, depending on which one you are using.

FIGURE 13.61
The painted force field texture causes most of the nParticles to remain hovering around the center, but a few manage to stick to the dark areas.

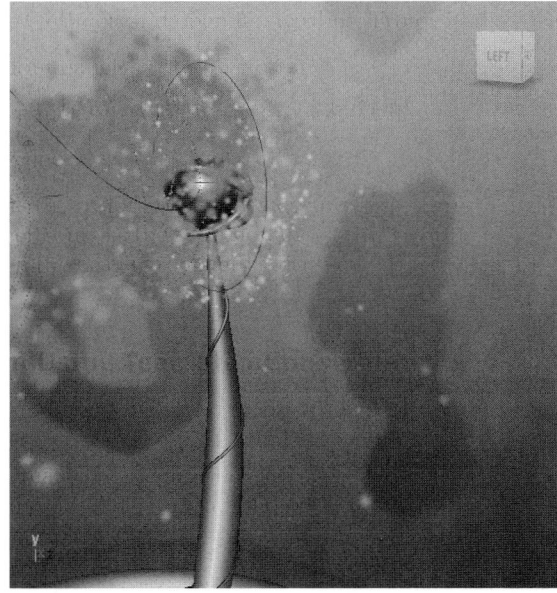

When using a texture or vertex map for the force field, the Force Field Magnitude setting acts as a multiplier for the strength of the map.

TEXTURE MAPS FOR DYNAMIC ATTRIBUTES

You can create texture maps for other attributes of the collision surface, including stickiness, friction, bounce, and collision thickness.

---

13. Back in the domeCollider node, set Field Magnitude to **10**, and play the animation. You'll see more nParticles stick to the surface where the texture has been painted. To smooth their motion, you can adjust the Field Scale ramp.

14. Save the scene as `generator_v04.ma`.

To see a version of the scene to this point, open `generator_v04.ma` from the `chapter13\ scenes` folder on the DVD.

Using Dynamic Fields

The traditional set of dynamic fields is found in the Fields menu. They have been included as part of Maya since version 1.

Fields such as Air and Gravity are similar to the wind and gravity forces that are part of the Nucleus system. But that is not to say you can't use them in combination with the Nucleus forces to create a specific effect.

Drag is similar to the Drag attribute of nParticles; it applies a force that in some cases slows an nParticle down; in other cases, it actually pulls the nParticle in a direction determined by the force. You can use the Inherit Transform slider on the Drag field to create wakelike effects in a cloud of particles, similar to the wind field generation on nDynamic objects.

Radial fields are similar to force fields emitted by nRigids and nParticles; they push or pull particles, depending on their Magnitude settings.

A Uniform force is similar to Gravity because it pushes a particle in a particular direction. The Volume Axis field is similar to the Volume Axis curve used earlier in the chapter. It has a built-in turbulence and affects particles within a given volume shape (by default).

ATTENUATION AND MAX DISTANCE IN DYNAMIC FIELDS

Attenuation with dynamic fields can be a little difficult to wrap your head around when you start using fields with dynamic simulations because many fields have both Attenuation and a Max Distance falloff curve, which, at first glance, appear to do very similar things.

The Maya documentation defines Attenuation with regard to an air field as a value that "sets how much the strength of the field diminishes as distance to the affected object increases. The rate of change is exponential with distance; the Attenuation is the exponent. If you set Attenuation to 0, the force remains constant over distance. Negative numbers are not valid." Before you break out the calculator, you can get a visual guide of how Attenuation affects the application of a field by using the Show Manipulators tool on a field. Try this experiment:

1. Start a new scene in Maya.

2. Switch to the nDynamics menu, and set the nParticle type to Balls.

3. Choose Create nParticles ➤ nParticle Tool ➤ Options.

4. In the options, select the Create Particle Grid check box and With Text Fields under Placement.

5. In the Placement options, set the Minimum Corner X, Y, and Z values to -10, 0, -10 and the Maximum Corner X, Y, and Z to 10, 0,10, as shown here. Press Enter on the numeric keypad to make the grid.

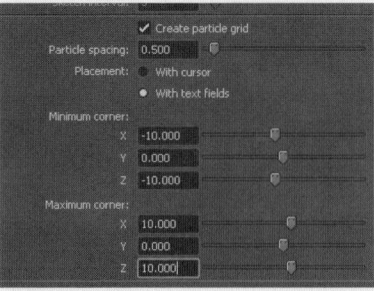

6. Select the nParticle grid, and choose Fields ➤ Air. An air field is placed at the center of the grid. On the Nucleus tab, set Gravity to 0.

7. Select the air field, and open the Attribute Editor (as shown here). You'll see that the air field is at the default settings where Magnitude is 4, the air field is applied along the y-axis (Direction = 0, 1, 0), and Attenuation is set to 1. Under the Distance settings, Use Max Distance is on, and Max Distance is set to 20.

8. Play the animation, and you'll see the grid move upward; the strength of the air field is stronger at the center than at the edges, creating a semispherical shape as the particles move up. You may need to extend the length of the timeline to something like 500 frames to see the motion of the particles.

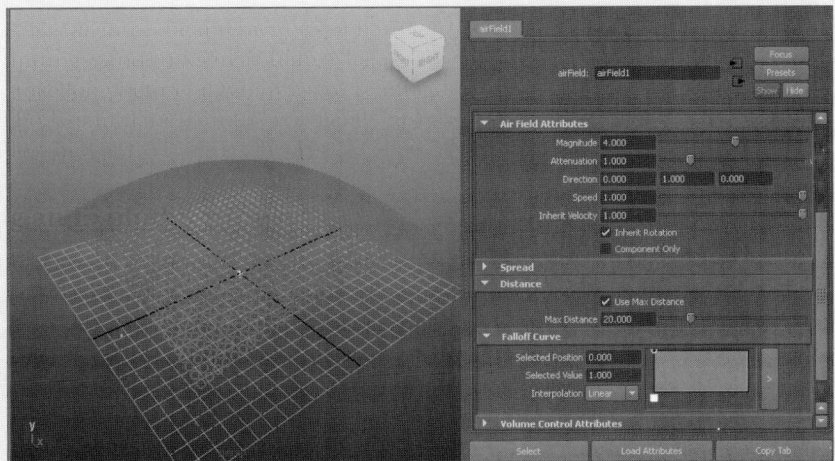

9. Rewind the animation, turn Use Max Distance off, and play the animation again. Now the entire grid moves uniformly. For air fields, Attenuation has no effect when Use Max Distance is off.

10. Rewind the animation. Turn Use Max Distance back on.

11. Select the air field, and choose the Show Manipulators tool from the toolbox.

12. Drag the blue dot connected to the attenuation manipulator handle in toward the center of the manipulator, and play the animation. You'll see that the shape of the field resembles the attenuation curve on the manipulator (see the following illustration).

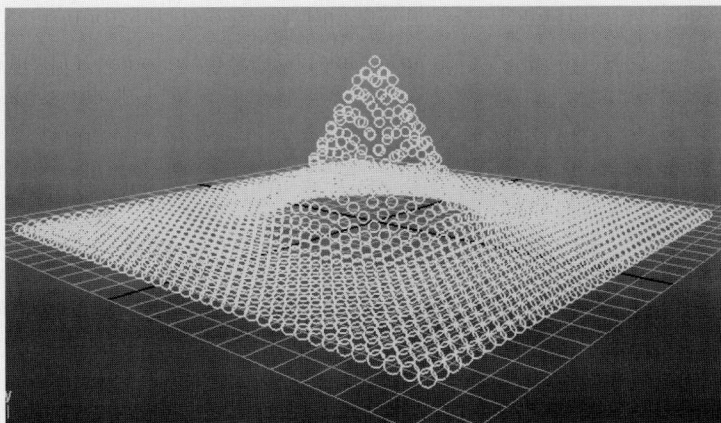

(CONTINUES)

ATTENUATION AND MAX DISTANCE IN DYNAMIC FIELDS *(CONTINUED)*

13. If you turn off Use Max Distance, you'll see the Attenuation slider flatten out because it no longer affects the field.

14. Turn Use Max Distance on, and set Attenuation to **0**.

15. In the Attribute Editor, find the falloff curve for the air field. Click at the top-left corner of the falloff curve to add a control point.

16. Drag the new control point downward, and play the animation. The falloff curve appears to work much like Attenuation. You can create interesting shapes in the field motion by adding and moving points on the falloff curve, and you can also change the interpolation of the points on the curve (as shown here).

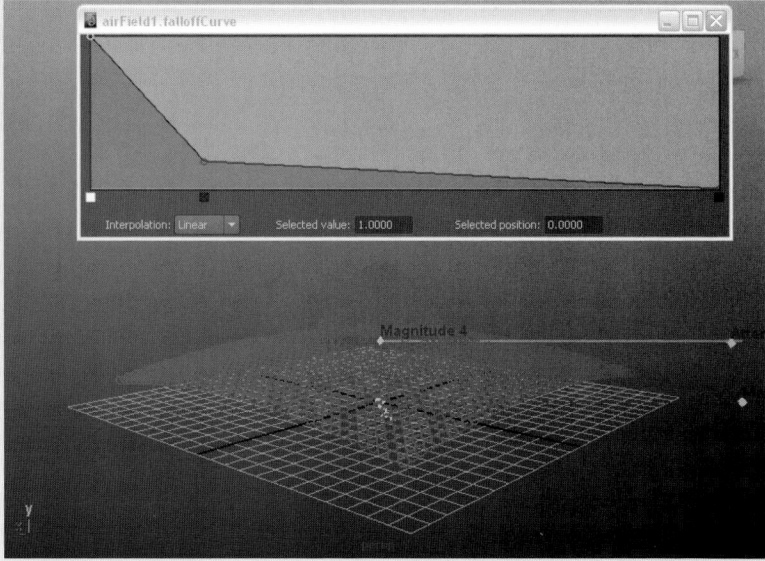

The difference between Attenuation and the Max Distance falloff curve is often subtle in practice. Think of it this way: attenuation affects how the force of the field is applied; the falloff curve defines how the maximum distance is applied to the force. It's a little easier to see when you lower the Conserve value of the nParticle. By default Conserve is at 1, meaning that particles do not lose any energy or momentum as they travel. Lowering Conserve even a little (say to a value of 0.95) causes the nParticle to lose energy or momentum as it travels; the effect is that the nParticle slows down when it reaches the boundary of the force. In practice, the best approach is to set Attenuation to 0 when you first apply the field to a particle system and then adjust Attenuation and/or the Max Distance setting and falloff until you get the behavior you want.

Some fields have unique properties that affect how they react to Attenuation settings. With some fields, such as Turbulence, the Attenuation attribute will affect the dynamic simulation even when Use Max Distance is off. Once again, it's a good idea to start with Attenuation at 0 and then add it if needed.

The behavior of Attenuation and Max Distance is the same for both nDynamic systems and traditional Maya dynamics.

The Turbulence field creates a noise pattern, and the Vortex field creates a swirling motion. Newton fields create a Newtonian attraction to dynamic objects.

1. Open the `generator_v04.ma` scene from the `chapter13\scenes` folder on the DVD.

2. Select the energy nParticle object, and choose Fields ➢ Turbulence to connect a Turbulence field to the nParticle.

3. In the Attribute Editor for the Turbulence field, set Magnitude to **100**, Attenuation to **0**, and Frequency to **0.5**.

4. In the Dynamic Properties section of the nParticle's Attribute Editor, set Drag to **0.1**. This can help tone down the movement of the nParticles if they get a little too crazy. An alternative technique would be to lower the conserve a little.

5. To see the particles behave properly, you'll probably want to create a playblast. Set the timeline to **300**, and choose Window ➢ Playblast. A flip book will be created and played in FCheck. For more about creating playblasts, consult Chapter 4.

6. Save the scene as **`generator_v05.ma`**.

To see a version of the scene to this point, open `generator_v05.ma` from the `chapter13\scenes` folder on the DVD.

Rendering Particles with mental ray

All particle types can be rendered using mental ray software rendering, and particles will appear in reflections and refractions. In this section, you'll see how easy it is to render different nParticle types using mental ray.

Setting nParticle Shading Attributes

In this exercise, you'll render the nParticles created in the generator scene:

1. Open the `generator_v05.ma` scene from the `chapter13\scenes` folder on the DVD.

2. Select the energy nParticle node in the Outliner, and open its Attribute Editor to the energyShape tab.

3. Expand the Shading attributes in the bottom of the editor. Set Opacity to **0.8**.

4. Set Color Input to Age. Make the left side of the ramp bright green and the right side a slightly dimmer green.

5. Set Incandescence Input to Age. Edit the ramp so the far-left side is white followed closely by bright green. Make the center a dimmer green and the right side completely black (see Figure 13.62).

6. Select each of the emitter nodes, and raise the Rate value to **1000**.

7. Select the domeShader node in the Hypershade, and break the connection between the color and the file texture (don't delete the file texture—it still controls the force field magnitude).

8. Set the color of the domeShader to a dark gray.

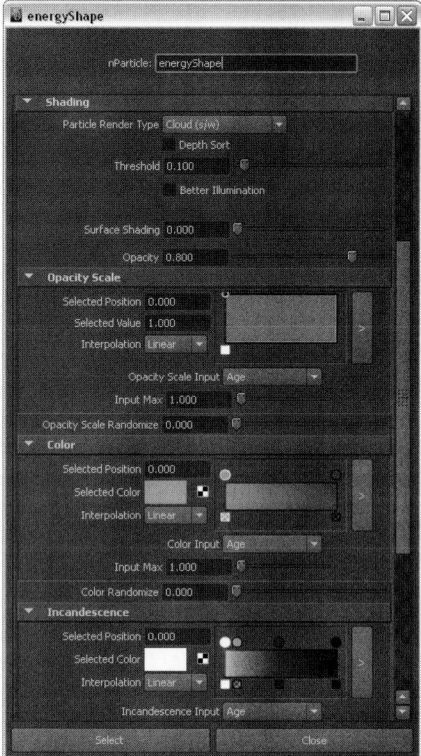

FIGURE 13.62
The shading attributes for the energy nParticle

9. Play the animation for about 80 frames.

10. Open the render settings, and set the renderer to mental ray.

11. On the Quality tab, set the Quality preset to Production.

12. Select the energy nParticle, and in the Render Stats section of the energyShape tab, select the boxes for Visible in Reflections and Refractions.

13. Create a test render of the scene. You can see in the glass of the chamber and the metal base that the nParticles are reflected.

14. Open the Hypershade, and select the metal shader. Increase Reflectivity in the Attribute Editor to **0.8**. The nParticles are more visible in the reflection on the base.

15. Select the dome shader, and in its Attribute Editor under Raytrace Options, activate Refractions, and set the Refractive Index to **1.2**.

16. Under the Specular Shading rollout panel, increase Reflectivity to **0.8**.

17. Create another test render. You can see the effect refraction has on the nParticles (see Figure 13.63).

    You can render the point, multipoint, streak, and multistreak render types using mental ray. They will appear in reflections and refractions as well; however, you'll notice that in the Render Stats section for these nParticle types, the options for Reflections and Refractions are unavailable.

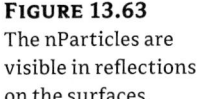

FIGURE 13.63
The nParticles are visible in reflections on the surfaces.

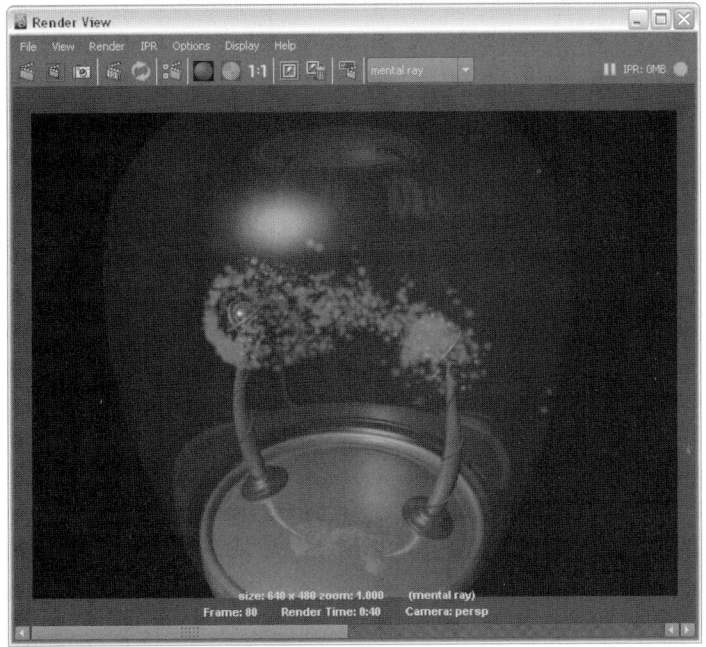

18. In the Hypershade, select the npCloudVolume shader. This shader is created with the nParticle. Graph the network in the Hypershade Work Area (see Figure 13.64).

You can see that a particleSampler node is automatically connected to the volume shader. This node transfers the settings you create in the nParticle's Attribute Editor for color, opacity, and transparency to the shader. An npCloudBlinn shader is also created. This shader is applied when you switch Particle Type to Points. You can further refine the look of the nParticles by adjusting the settings in the npCloudVolume shader's Attribute Editor.

FIGURE 13.64
Shaders are automatically created for the nParticles. The particleSamplerInfo node connects the attributes of the nParticle to the shader.

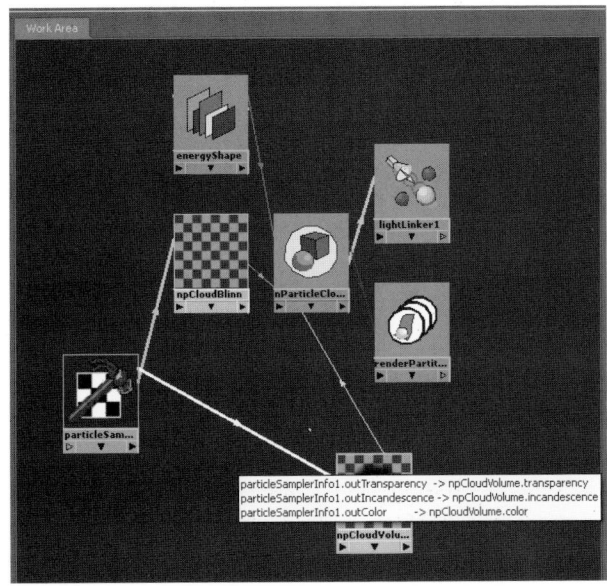

You can add a shader glow to the particles by increasing Glow Intensity in the npCloud-Volume shader; however, the glow does not appear behind refractive surfaces with standard Maya shaders.

19. When you are happy with the look of the render, you can create an nCache for the energy nParticle and render the sequence using mental ray.

20. Save the scene as `generator_v06.ma`.

To see a finished version of the scene, open the `generator_v06.ma` file from the `chapter13\ scenes` directory.

FURTHER READING

There is no limit to the number of creative effects you can create using nParticles. This chapter is but a brief introduction. If you have enjoyed working through these examples, you can continue your nParticle education by reading Todd Palamar's *Maya Studio Projects: Dynamics* (Sybex, 2009), which covers a variety of effects using many of Maya's dynamic tools.

The Bottom Line

Create nParticles   nParticles can be added to a scene in a number of ways. They can be drawn using the tool or spawned from an emitter, or they can fill an object.

> **Master it**   Create a spiral shape using nParticles.

Make nParticles collide   NParticles can collide with themselves, other nParticles, and polygon surfaces.

> **Master it**   Make nParticles pop out of the top of an animated volume.

Create liquid simulations   Enabling Liquid Simulations changes the behavior of nParticles so they act like water or other fluids.

> **Master it**   Create a flowing stream of nParticles that ends in a waterfall.

Emit nParticles from a texture   The emission rate of an nParticle can be controlled using a texture.

> **Master it**   Create your own name in nParticles.

Move nParticles with nucleus wind   The wind force on the nucleus node can be used to push nParticles.

> **Master it**   Create the effect of bubbles pushed back and forth under water.

Use force fields   Force fields can be emitted by nParticles and collision objects, creating interesting types of behavior in your scenes.

> **Master it**   Add a second nParticle object emitted from the base of the generator. Enable its force field so that it attracts a few of the original nParticles.

Chapter 14

Dynamic Effects

Maya's nCloth system was originally designed to make dynamic cloth simulation for characters easier to create and animate. The Nucleus dynamics solver, which you learned about in Chapter 13, is at the heart of nCloth simulations (the *n* in *nCloth* stands for "nucleus"). nCloth has evolved into a dynamic system that goes well beyond simply simulating clothing. Creative use of nCloth in combination with nParticles yields nearly limitless possibilities for interesting effects, as you'll see as you go through the exercises in this chapter.

In this chapter, you'll delve deeper into Maya dynamics to understand how the various dynamic systems, such as nCloth, nParticles, and rigid bodies, can be used together to create spectacular effects. You'll also use particle expressions to control the motion of particle instances.

In this chapter, you will learn to:

◆ Use nCloth

◆ Combine nCloth and nParticles

◆ Use Maya rigid body dynamics

◆ Instance geometry to nParticles

◆ Create nParticle expressions

◆ Create smoke trails

Creating nCloth Objects

Typically nCloth is used to make polygon geometry behave like clothing, but nCloth can actually be used to simulate the behavior of a wide variety of materials. Everything from concrete to water balloons can be achieved by adjusting the attributes of the nCloth object. nCloth uses the same dynamic system as nParticles and applies it to the vertices of a piece of geometry. An nCloth object is simply a polygon object that has had its vertices converted to nParticles. A system of virtual springs connects the nParticles and helps maintain the shape of nCloth objects. nCloth objects automatically collide with other nDynamic systems (such as nParticles and nRigids) that are connected to the same Nucleus solver, and an nCloth object collides with itself.

In this section, you'll see how to get up and running fast with nCloth using the presets that ship with Maya as well as get some background on how the Nucleus solver works. The examples in this chapter illustrate a few of the ways nCloth and nParticles can be used together to create interesting effects. These examples are only the beginning; there are so many possible applications and uses for nCloth that a single chapter barely scratches the surface. The goal of this chapter is to give you a starting place so you feel comfortable designing your own unique effects. Chapter 15 demonstrates techniques for using nCloth to make clothing for an animated character.

Making a Polygon Mesh Dynamic

Any polygon mesh you model in Maya can be converted into a dynamic nCloth object (also known as an *nDynamic object*); there's nothing special about the way the polygon object needs to be prepared. The only restriction is that only polygon objects can be used. NURBS and subdivision surfaces can't be converted to nCloth.

There are essentially two types of nCloth objects: active and passive. *Active* nCloth objects are the ones that behave like cloth. They are the soft, squishy, or bouncy objects. *Passive* objects are solid pieces of geometry that react with active objects. For example, to simulate a tablecloth sliding off a table, the tablecloth would be the active nCloth object, and the table would be the passive nCloth object. The table prevents the tablecloth from falling in space. You can animate a passive object, and the active object will react to the animation. So, you can keyframe the table tilting, and the tablecloth will slide off the table based on its dynamic settings.

The first lesson in this chapter shows how to create the effect of a dividing cell using two nCloth objects:

1. Create a new scene in Maya.

2. Create a polygon cube at the center of the grid. The cube should have one subdivision in width, height, and depth.

3. Scale the cube up eight units in each axis.

4. Select the cube, switch to the Polygon menu set, and choose Mesh ➤ Smooth.

5. In the Channel Box, select the polySmoothFace1 node, and set Divisions to **3**. This creates a sphere. Unlike a regular polygon sphere, the smoothed cube has no poles at the end, which prevent unwanted pinching when the cube is converted to an nCloth object (Figure 14.1).

FIGURE 14.1
Create a sphere by smoothing a polygon cube.

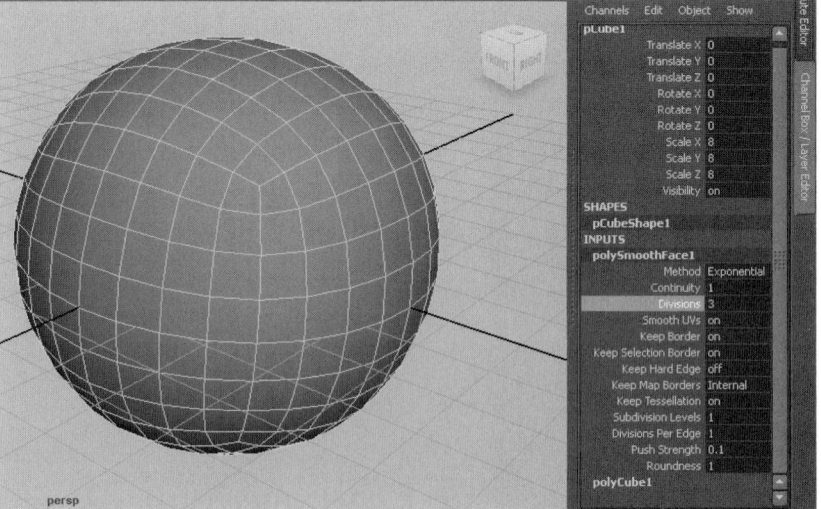

6. Switch to a side view. Right-click the cube, and choose Vertices to switch to component mode.

7. Switch to wireframe view (hot key = **4**). Select all the vertices on the right-side centerline of the grid but not the vertices on the centerline.

8. Select the Scale tool (hot key = **r**), and scale the vertices along the z-axis so they are flat.

9. Turn on Grid Snapping, and use the Move tool (hot key = **w**) to snap these vertices on the centerline. You should end up with a rounded cube with one flattened side (Figure 14.2).

FIGURE 14.2
Select, scale, and snap the vertices of the right half of the cube along the centerline in the side view.

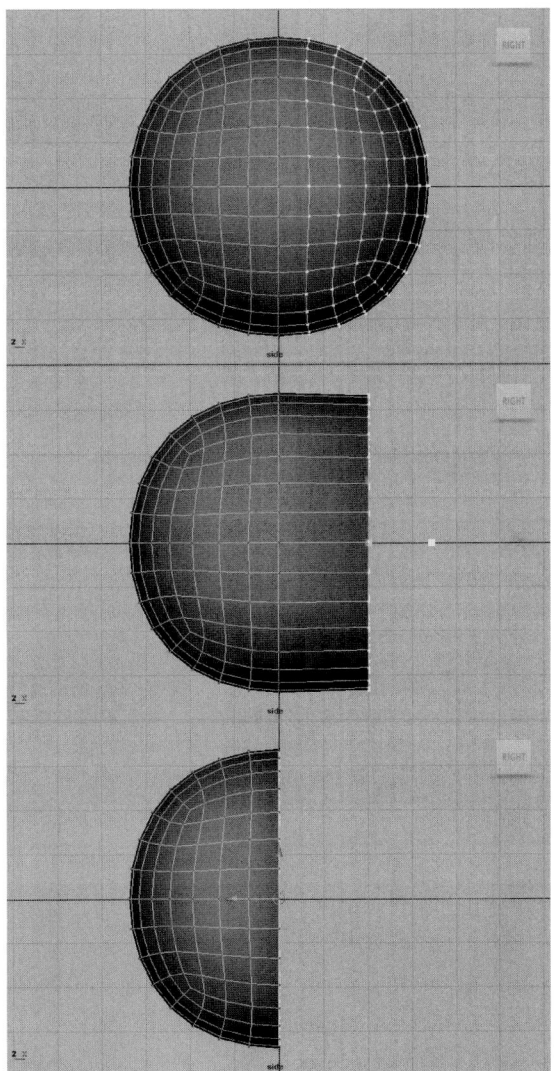

10. Name the cube **cellLeft**.

11. Turn off Grid Snapping. Select cellLeft, and move it just to the left of the centerline; set the Translate Z channel to **0.08**.

12. Turn Grid Snapping on; hold the **d** key, and use the Move tool to position the pivot point at the center of the grid. Be careful not to move the geometry, only the pivot point.

MOVING THE PIVOT POINT

You can also press the **Insert** key on your Windows keyboard (or the **Home** key on a Mac keyboard) while the Move tool is active. This switches to pivot point editing mode. You can then reposition the pivot point without holding the **d** key. To exit the mode, just press the Insert key again.

---

13. Select cellLeft, and choose Modify ➤ Freeze Transformations. The Translate and Rotate channels should now be at 0 and the Scale channels at 1.

14. Select cellLeft, and duplicate it (hot key = **Ctrl+d**).

15. Set the Scale Z channel of the duplicate to **-1**.

16. Choose Modify ➤ Freeze Transformations. A warning appears in the Script Editor that says "Freeze transform with negative scale will set the 'opposite' attributes for these nodes." You can safely ignore this warning.

17. Name the duplicate **cellRight** (see Figure 14.3). Select both sides, and delete the history (Edit ➤ Delete By Type ➤ History).

FIGURE 14.3
Create the second half of the cell by duplicating and scaling the first.

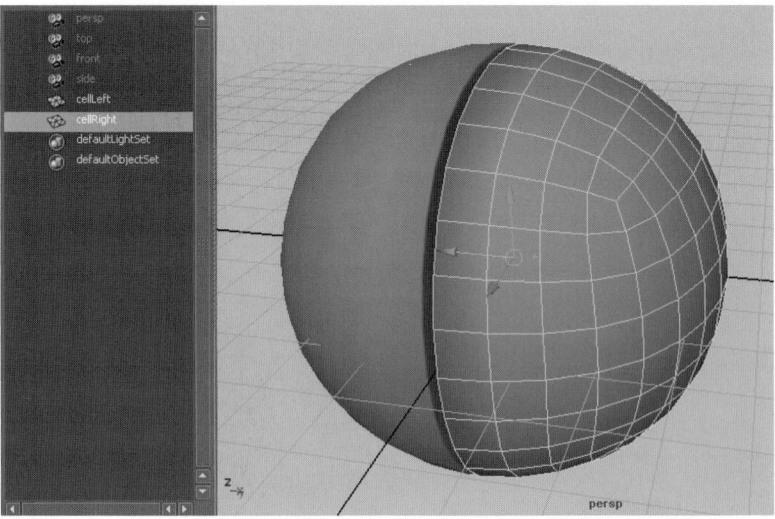

18. Switch to the nDynamics menu set. Select both objects, and choose nMesh ➤ Create nCloth. In the Outliner, you'll see that two nCloth nodes have been added.

19. Switch to the wireframe mode, and select nCloth1. One of the cell halves turns purple, indicating the nCloth node is an input connection to that particular piece of geometry.

20. Rename the nCloth1 and nCloth2 nodes **cellLeftCloth** and **cellRightCloth** according to which piece of geometry they are connected to (Figure 14.4).

FIGURE 14.4
Add two nCloth nodes to the Outliner, one for each side of the cell, and rename them cellLeftCloth and cellRightCloth.

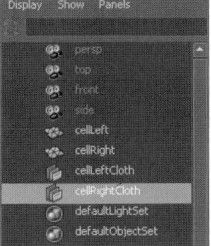

21. Set the timeline to 400 frames, and play the scene. You'll see both pieces of geometry fall in space. This is because Gravity is turned on by default in the Nucleus solver.

22. Save the scene as `cellDivide_v01.ma`.

To see a version of the scene to this point, open `cellDivide_v01.ma` from the `chapter14\ scenes` directory on the DVD.

Understanding nCloth Nodes

When you create an nCloth object or any nCloth dynamic system (nParticles, nRigids), several additional nodes are created and connected. You can see this when you graph the cellLeft shape on the Hypergraph, as shown in Figure 14.5.

FIGURE 14.5
The input and output connections for the cellLeft shape are graphed on the Hypergraph.

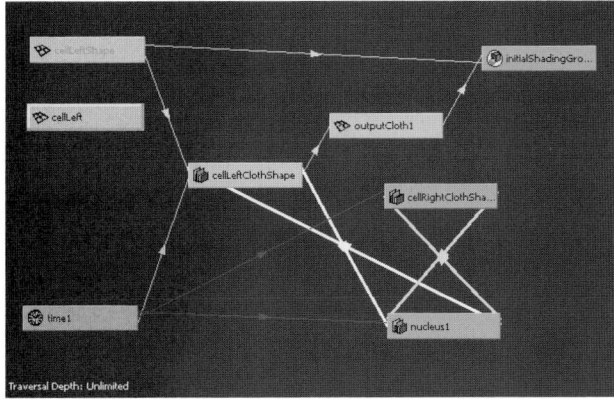

Each nCloth object consists of the original geometry, the nCloth node, and the Nucleus solver. By default, any additional nDynamic objects you create are attached to the same Nucleus solver. Additional nodes include the original cellLeftShape node, which is connected as the inputMesh to the cellLeftClothShape node. This determines the original starting shape of the nCloth object.

1. Continue with the scene from the previous section, or open `cellDivide_v01.ma` from the `chapter14\scenes` folder on the DVD.

2. Select the cellLeftCloth node, and open the Attribute Editor.

3. Switch to the cellLeftClothShape tab, as shown in Figure 14.6. This node was originally named nCloth1. The tabs found here include the following:

   cellLeftCloth   This tab contains the settings for the nCloth1 transform node. Most of the time you won't have a reason to change these settings.

   cellLeftClothShape   This tab contains the settings that control the dynamics of the nCloth object. There are a lot of settings on this tab, and this is where you will spend most of your time adjusting the settings for this particular nCloth object.

   nucleus1   This tab contains all the global settings for the Nucleus solver. These include the overall solver quality settings but also the Gravity and Air Density settings. If you select the cellRightCloth node in the Outliner, you'll notice it also has a nucleus1 tab. In fact, this is the same node as attached to the cellLeftCloth object.

FIGURE 14.6
The Attribute Editor for the cellLeftCloth-Shape node has tabs for the transform and shape nodes as well as the nucleus1 solver.

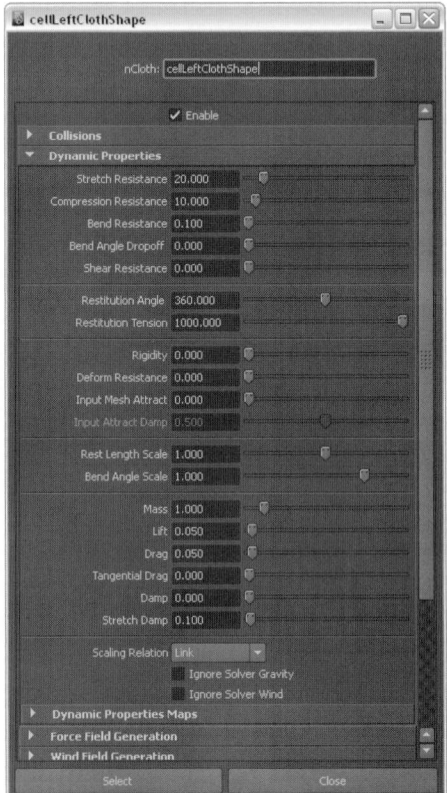

It's possible to create different Nucleus solvers for different nDynamic objects, but unless the nDynamic objects are connected to the same Nucleus solver, they will not directly interact.

NAME YOUR NCLOTH NODES

Because the nCloth objects are connected to the same Nucleus solver, when you open the Attribute Editor for the nucleus node, you'll see tabs for each node that's connected to the solver. To reduce confusion over which nCloth object is being edited, always give each nCloth node a descriptive name as soon as the node is created.

---

4. Select the nucleus1 tab, and set Gravity to **0**.

When you rewind and play the scene, nothing happens because there are no forces acting on the cells.

Applying nCloth Presets

The concept behind this particular example is that both halves of the cell together form a single circular spherical shape. To make the cells separate, you'll adjust the nDynamic settings so that each half of the cell inflates and pushes against the other half, moving them in opposite directions. Creating the correct settings to achieve this action can be daunting simply because there is a bewildering array of available settings on each nCloth shape node. To help you get started, Maya includes a number of presets that can act as a template. You can apply a preset to the nCloth objects and then adjust a few settings until you get the effect you want.

1. Continue with the scene from the previous section.

MAYA PRESETS

You can create a preset and save it for any Maya node. For instance, you can change the settings on the nucleus1 node to simulate dynamic interactions on the moon and then save those settings as a preset named moonGravity. This preset will be available for any Maya session. Some nodes, such as nCloth and fur nodes, have presets already built in when you start Maya. These presets are created by Autodesk and other Maya users and can be shared between users. You'll often find new presets available on the Autodesk Area website (http://area.autodesk.com).

To apply a preset to more than one object, select all the objects, select the preset from the list by holding down the Presets button, and choose Replace All Selected.

---

2. Select the cellLeftCloth node, and open the Attribute Editor to the cellLeftClothShape node.

3. At the top of the editor, click and hold the Presets button in the upper right. The asterisk by the button label means that there are saved presets available for use.

4. From the list of presets, scroll down to find the waterBalloon preset. A small pop-up appears; from this pop-up choose Replace (see Figure 14.7). You'll see the settings in the Attribute Editor change, indicating the preset has been loaded.

FIGURE 14.7
Using a preset
selected from the
Presets list is a
quick way to start
a custom nCloth
material.

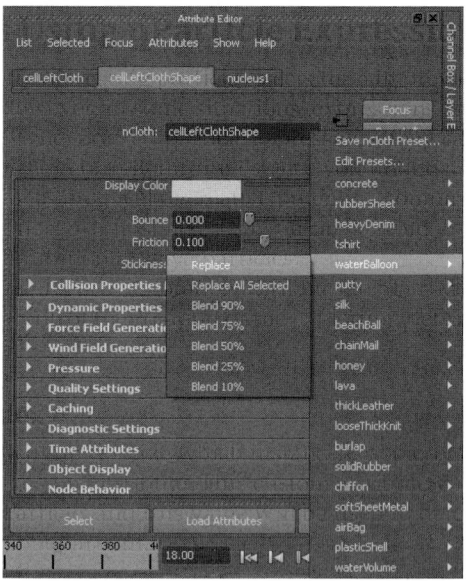

5. Repeat step 2 for the cellRightCloth node.

6. Rewind and play the animation. Immediately you have a decent cell division.

OVERLAPPING NCLOTH OBJECTS

Initially it might seem like a good idea to have two overlapping nCloth objects that push out from the center. However, if the geometry of the two nCloth objects overlaps, it can confuse the Nucleus solver and make it harder to achieve a predictable result.

The next task is to create a more realistic behavior by adjusting the setting on the nCloth objects:

1. Switch to the nucleus1 tab, and set Air Density to **35**. This makes the cells look like they are in a thick medium, such as water (see Figure 14.8).

FIGURE 14.8
Increasing the Air
Density setting on
the nucleus1 tab
makes it appear as
though the cells are
in a thick medium.

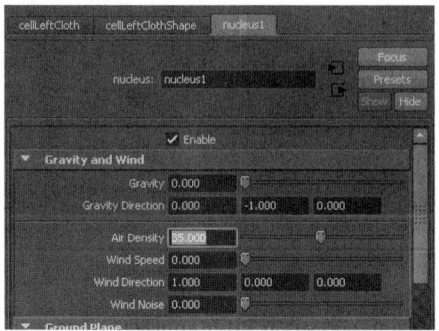

2. You can blend settings from other presets together to create your own unique look. Select cellLeftCloth, and in its shape node tab click and hold the Presets button in the upper right.

3. Choose Honey ➢ Blend 10%. Do the same for the cellRightCloth.

4. Play the animation. The two cells separate more slowly.

5. You can save these settings as your own preset so it will be available in other Maya sessions. From the Presets menu, choose Save nCloth Preset. In the dialog box, name the preset **Cell** (see Figure 14.9).

6. Save the scene as **cellDivide_v02.ma**.

FIGURE 14.9
You can save your own custom presets to the Presets list so they will be available in other Maya sessions.

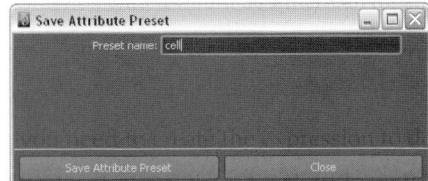

SAVING MAYA PRESETS

When you save a Maya preset, it is stored in a subfolder of maya\2011\presets\attrPresets. Your custom nCloth presets will appear in the nCloth subfolder as a MEL script file. You can save nCloth presets created by other users to this folder, and they will appear in the Presets list. If you save a preset using the same name as an existing preset, Maya will ask you if you want to overwrite the existing preset.

Making Surfaces Sticky

At this point, you can start to adjust some of the settings on the nCloth tabs to create a more interesting effect. To make the cells stick together as they divide, you can increase the Stickiness attribute.

1. Continue with the scene from the previous section, or open the cellDivide_v02.ma scene from the chapter14\scenes directory on the DVD.

2. Select the cellLeftCloth node, and open the Attribute Editor to its shape node tab.

3. Expand the Collisions rollout panel, and set Stickiness to 1 (see Figure 14.10). Do the same for the cellRight object.

   Notice that many of the settings in the Collision rollout panel are the same as the nParticle Collision settings. For a more detailed discussion of how nucleus collisions work, consult Chapter 13.

4. Play the animation; the cells remain stuck as they inflate. By adjusting the strength of the Stickiness attribute, you can tune the effect so the cells do eventually come apart. Try a setting of 0.1 for both cells.

FIGURE 14.10
Increase the Stickiness attribute in the cellLeftCloth-Shape tab of the Attribute Editor.

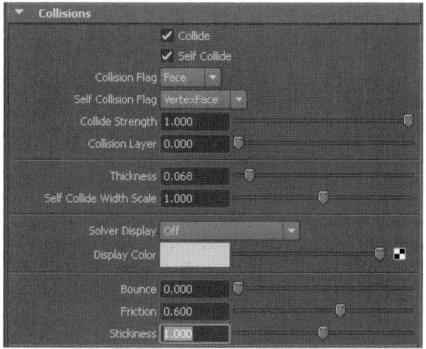

USE PRESETS TO COPY ATTRIBUTES

To save time when working with two identical nCloth objects, you can overwrite the nCloth preset and then apply it to the other nCloth object. To do this, just save the nCloth preset using the Presets menu in the Attribute Editor, and use the same preset name to overwrite older presets. This has the advantage of saving your settings so that if your computer crashes before you save the scene, you won't need to re-create the settings from scratch.

5. Save the nCloth settings as **stickyCell**. Save the scene as **cellDivide_v03.ma**.

CREATE PLAYBLASTS OFTEN

It's difficult to gauge how the dynamics in the scene work using just the playback in Maya. You may want to create a playblast of the scene after you make adjustments to the dynamics so you can see how effective your changes are. For more information on creating playblasts, consult Chapter 5.

Creating nConstraints

nConstraints can be used to attach nCloth objects together. The constraints themselves can be broken depending on how much force is applied. In this example, nConstraints will be used as an alternative technique to the Stickiness attribute. There are some unique properties of nConstraints that can allow for more creativity in this effect.

1. Continue with the scene from the previous section, or open the cellDivide_v03.ma scene from the chapter14\scenes directory on the DVD.

2. Shift+click both the cellLeftCloth and cellRightCloth nodes in the Outliner. Open the Channel Box, and, with both nodes selected, set Stickiness to **0** to turn off this attribute.

> ### EDIT MULTIPLE OBJECTS USING THE CHANNEL BOX
>
> By using the Channel Box, you can set the value for the same attribute on multiple objects at the same time. This can't be done using the Attribute Editor.

3. Switch to the side view. In the Outliner, Shift+click the cellLeft and cellRight polygon nodes. Set the selection mode to Component. By default the vertices on both objects should appear.

4. Drag a selection down the middle of the two objects so the vertices along the centerline are selected (see Figure 14.11).

FIGURE 14.11
Create nConstraints between the vertices along the flattened side of each cell.

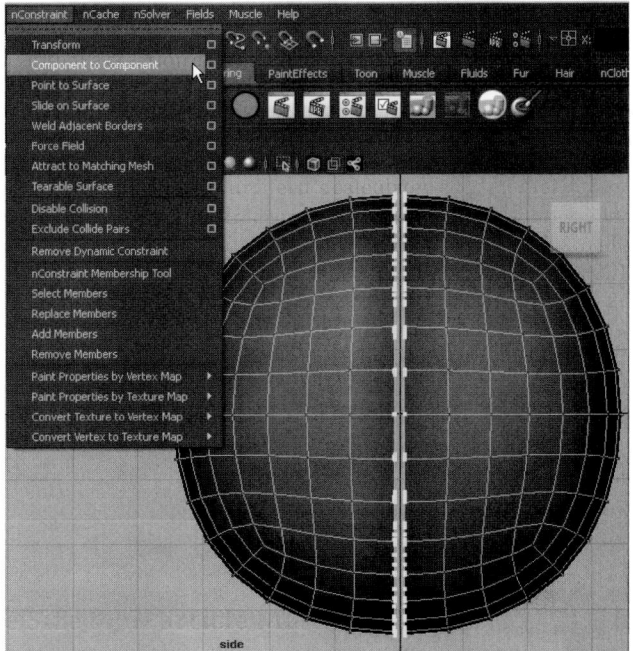

5. In the nDynamics menu set, choose nConstraint ➤ Component To Component. This creates a series of springs that connect the two objects.

6. Rewind and play the scene. The two sides of the cell are stuck together.

7. In the Outliner, a new node named dynamicConstraint1 has been created. Select this node, and open the Attribute Editor.

A wide variety of settings are available in the Attribute Editor for the dynamicConstraint node; each one is described in detail in the Maya documentation. For the moment, your main concern is adjusting the constraint strength.

> **TRANSFORM CONSTRAINTS**
>
> A transform node can be created between nCloth objects and the transform node of a piece of geometry. You can create the constraint between the vertices and another object such as a locator. Then you can animate the locator and have it drag the nCloth objects around in the scene by the nConstraint attached to the selected vertices.

8. Strength determines the overall strength of the constraint. Tangent Strength creates a resistance to the tangential motion of the constraint. In this example, you can leave Strength at 20 and set Tangent Strength to **0**.

9. Glue Strength is the setting that determines whether the constraint will break when force is applied. It is calculated in world space based on the size of the objects. A value of 1 means the constraint can't be broken; a value of 0 turns the constraint off altogether. Set this attribute to **0.25**.

10. Glue Strength Scale modifies the Glue Strength based on the world space distance between the constraints. Set this value to **0.6**.

11. Rewind and play the animation. The two sides of the cell start to separate but fail to part completely.

    The Force attribute determines the level of attraction between the constraints. Positive values cause the constraints to repel each other after they break; negative values cause the constraints to attract each other. In this scene, very small values can create a big difference.

12. Set the Force attribute on the dynamic constraint node to **0.01**. Rewind and play the scene.

13. The cells now push each other apart and keep going. To halt their motion after separation, adjust the Dropoff Distance value. Set this to **3**.

14. Adjust the Strength Dropoff curve so that there is a sharp decline to 0 on the left side of the curve. The strength of the force drops to 0 as the distance between the constraints approaches 3 units (Figure 14.12).

15. You can fine-tune the effect by adding a small amount of motion drag. Set Motion Drag to **0.01**. If the cells can't quite separate, try raising Force by small increments until you get a result you like.

> **THE CONSTRAINT FORCE ATTRIBUTE**
>
> Using the Force attribute, you can make constraints repel each other after they break. This would work well for a situation like a shirt splitting under pressure as buttons fly off. Setting the Force attribute to a small negative value causes the constraints to attract each other. This works well for gelatinous or gooey substances that reform after being sliced by a passive collision object.

FIGURE 14.12
Add a small value to the Force attribute, and lower the Dropoff Distance to a value of 3. By adjusting the Strength Dropoff ramp, you can fine-tune the field.

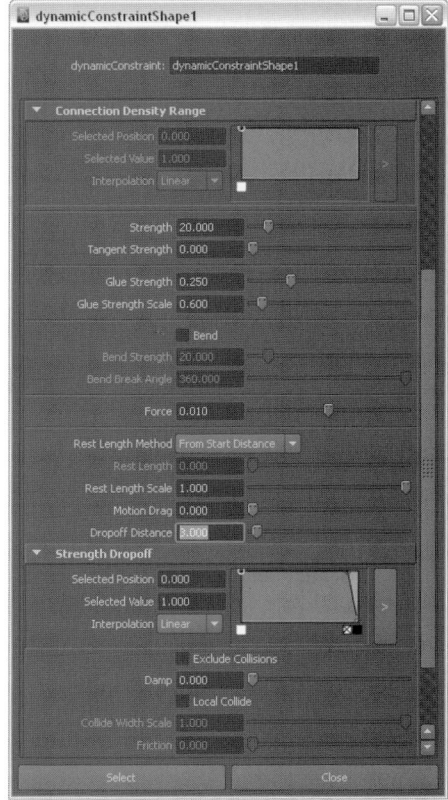

Working with nDynamics becomes a very experimental process much like cooking; you adjust the sliders and season to taste until the effect looks like what you want. Since many of the attributes are interconnected, it's best to adjust one at a time and test as you go. You can move an nCloth object after it has been constrained. However, the results of the simulation might not behave the way you expect. It's usually best to make sure your nCloth objects and their constraints are positioned where you want them. Avoid setting keyframes on the translation or rotation of the nCloth object.

Rest Length attributes significantly affect how the simulation behaves. *Rest length* refers to the length of each constraint when no tension is applied (imagine an unattached spring sitting on a table; its length at rest is its rest length). If Rest Length Method is set to Start Frame, then the rest length of each constraint is equal to its length at the first frame of the animation. If this is set to Constant, then the rest length is determined using the Rest Length numeric input.

Rest Length Scale applies a scaling factor to the constraints. If this is set to 1 and Rest Length Method is set to From Start Distance, then the constraints have no initial tension. In other words, at frame 1 the scale is equal to the rest length. Lowering this value increases the tension on the constraint and makes it harder to break.

1. Rewind the animation, and set Rest Length Scale to **0.5**.

2. Play the animation to frame 40, and set a keyframe on Rest Length Scale.

3. Play the animation to 50, and set Rest Length Scale to **1**.

4. Set another keyframe. Rewind and play the animation. This is one way in which you can control the timing of the cell division. You can also control this attribute using an expression or set-driven key. The cells may not separate completely at this point—that's OK, because in the next section you'll add pressure to complete the division effect.

REST LENGTH SCALE

The nCloth nodes also have a Rest Length Scale attribute that can be adjusted to alter the behavior of the cells. The stickyCell preset created by blending the waterBalloon and Honey presets has a Rest Length Scale of 0.73. Lowering this value causes the cells to push against each other with more force. Setting this value to 1 reduces the tension, making the cells more relaxed and less likely to divide.

---

5. Save the scene as **cellDivide_v04.ma**.

To see a version of the scene to this point, open the **cellDivide_v04.ma** scene from the **chapter14\scenes** folder on the DVD.

CONNECTING NCLOTH OBJECTS TO DYNAMIC CURVES

In a recent scientific animation I created for Harvard Medical School, I attached a chromosome made of an nCloth object to a spindle fiber created from a dynamic curve. The technique I used involved these steps:

1. Create a standard CV curve. This will be used to drag the nCloth chromosome around the scene.

2. Select the curve, and switch to the Dynamics menu set.

3. Choose Hair ➤ Make Selected Curves Dynamic. When you convert a curve to a dynamic curve, a duplicate of the original curve is created. This curve is contained within a group named hairSystem1OutputCurves. Dynamic Curves are discussed in detail in Chapter 15.

4. Attach a locator to the output curve of the hair system using a motion path.

5. In the options for the motion path, set Time Range to Start.

6. Delete the keyframes on the motion path's U Value, and set the U Value so the locator is at one end of the curve. This way, the locator is attached to the curve.

7. Use a transform nConstraint to attach the vertices at the center of the nCloth chromosome (known in biology circles as the *centromere* of the chromosome) to the locator.

Once this setup is complete, you can use the hair curve to drag the nCloth object all over the scene.

Making nCloth Objects Expand Using Pressure

Using pressure, you can inflate a piece of geometry like a balloon or, in the case of this example, make it appear as though the geometry is filled with fluid.

There are two ways to calculate pressure: Manual Pressure Setting and Volume Tracking Model.

Manual Pressure Setting   Manual Pressure Setting is very simple—the Pressure slider and Pressure Damping slider are the only two controls (see Figure 14.13). These can be keyframed to make it appear as though the nCloth object is being filled with air. If you set Pressure at 0 and create a keyframe, then play the animation to frame 100, set Pressure to 1, and set another keyframe, the nCloth object will grow in size over those frames as if it were being inflated.

Volume Tracking Model   Volume Tracking Model, which is used by the waterBalloon preset originally applied to the cell geometry, is a more accurate method for calculating volume and has more controls (see Figure 14.14).

FIGURE 14.13

Manual Pressure Setting has very simple controls for adding internal pressure to nCloth objects.

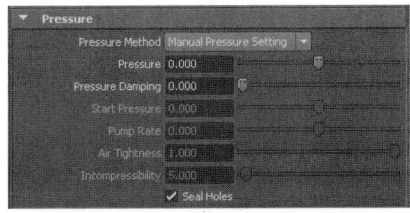

FIGURE 14.14

Volume Tracking Model has more controls and produces a more accurate internal pressure simulation for nCloth objects.

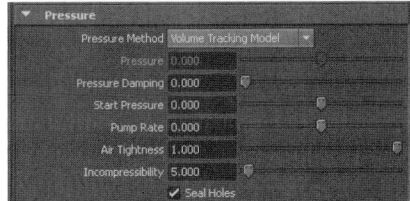

When Volume Tracking Model is selected as the pressure method, you have access to additional controls, such as Pump Rate, Air Tightness, and Incompressibility. The Pump Rate value determines the rate at which air is added within the volume. Positive values continue to pump air into the volume; negative values suck the air out. The Start Pressure value sets the initial pressure of the air inside the volume at the start of the animation.

The Air Tightness value determines the permeability of the nCloth object. Lower settings allow the air to escape the volume. The Incompressibility setting refers to the air within the volume. A lower value means the air is more compressible, which slows down the inflation effect of the cell. Activating Seal Holes causes the solver to ignore openings in the geometry.

As you may have noticed, after the cells divide in the example scene, they don't quite return to the size of the original dividing cell. You can use the Pump Rate attribute to inflate the cells.

1. Continue with the scene from the previous section, or open the `cellDivide_v04.ma` scene from the `chapter14\scenes` directory on the DVD.

2. Select the cellLeftCloth shape, and open its Attribute Editor.

3. Expand the Pressure settings. Note that Pressure Method is already set to Volume Tracking Model. These settings were determined by the waterBalloon preset originally used to create the effect.

4. Set Pump Rate to **50** for each cell, and play the animation (Figure 14.15). Each cell starts to grow immediately and continues to grow after the cell divides.

5. Try setting keyframes on the start Pump Rate of both cells so that at frame 15 Pump Rate is 0, at frame 50 it's 50, and at frame 100 it's 0.

6. To give an additional kick at the start of the animation, set Start Pressure to **0.25**.

FIGURE 14.15
Setting Pump Rate to 50 on the cellLeftCloth object causes it to grow as it separates from the right side.

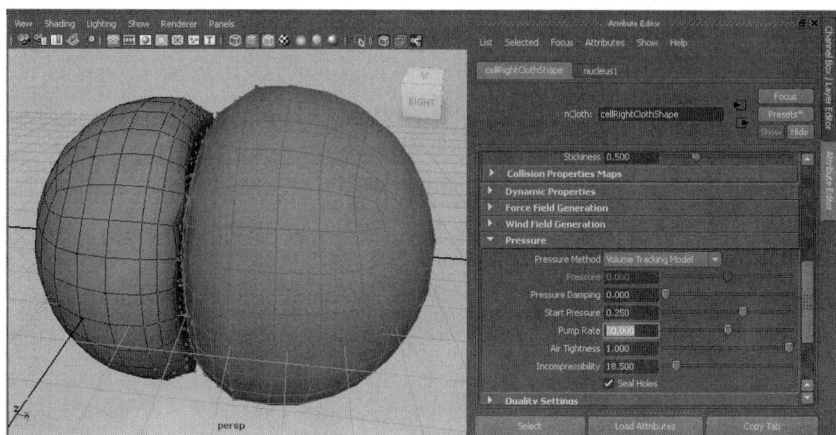

CONNECT ATTRIBUTES USING THE CONNECTION EDITOR

You can save some time by using the Connection Editor to connect the Pressure attributes of one of the cells to the same attributes of the other. This way you need only keyframe the attributes of the first cell. For more information on using the Connection Editor, consult Chapter 1.

Additional Techniques

To finish the animation, here are some additional techniques you can use to add some style to the behavior of the cells:

1. In the Collisions rollout panel, increase the Stickiness attribute of each cell to a value of **0.5**. You can also try painting a Stickiness texture map. To do this, select the cells, and choose nMesh ➢ Paint Texture Properties ➢ Stickiness. This activates the Artisan Brush, which allows you to paint specific areas of stickiness on the cell surface (refer to Chapter 13 to see how a similar technique is used to paint the strength of a force field on geometry).

2. If you want the objects to start out solid and become soft at a certain point in time, set keyframes on each cell's Input Mesh Attract attribute. The input mesh is the original geometry that was converted into the nCloth object. Setting the Input Mesh Attract attribute to 1 or higher causes the nCloth objects to assume the shape of the original geometry. As this value is lowered, the influence of the nucleus dynamics increases, causing the objects to become soft.

To see a finished version of the scene, open the `cellDivide_v05.ma` scene from the `chapter14\` `scenes` folder on the DVD.

COMBINE TECHNIQUES

In practice, you'll most likely find that the best solution when creating a complex effect is to combine techniques as much as possible. Use Dynamic Fields, Force, Wind, nConstraints, Air Density, Stickiness, and Pressure together to make a really spectacular nCloth effect.

Creating an nCache

At this point, you'll want to cache the dynamics so that playback speed is improved and the motion of the cells is the same every time you play the animation. This also ensures that when you render the scene, the dynamics are consistent when using multiple processors.

1. Shift+click the cellLeft and cellRight objects in the Outliner.

2. Choose nCache ➢ Create New Cache ➢ Options.

    In the options, you can specify where the cache will be placed. By default the cache is created in a subfolder of the current project's `Data` folder. If the scene is going to be rendered on a network, make sure the cache is in a subfolder that can be accessed by all the computers on the network.

    In the options, you can specify whether you want to create a separate cache file for each frame or a single cache file. You can also create a separate cache for each geometry object; this is not always necessary when you have more than one nCloth object in a scene (Figure 14.16).

FIGURE 14.16
The options for creating an nCache

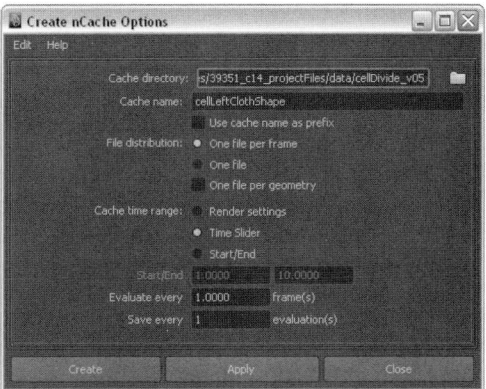

3. The default settings should work well for this scene. Click the Create button to create the cache. Maya will play through the scene.

DELETE NCACHE BEFORE MAKING CHANGES

When the cache is complete, the scene will play much faster. If you make changes to the nCloth settings, you won't see the changes reflected in the animation until you delete or disable the nCache (nCache ➤ Delete nCache). Even though the geometry is using a cache, you should not delete the nCloth nodes. This would disable the animation.

After the nCache has been created, it is important that you disable the nCloth objects so that Maya does not calculate dynamics for objects that are cached. This is especially important for large scenes with complex nDynamics.

4. In the Attribute Editor for cellLeftClothShape, scroll to the top, and deselect the Enable button to disable the nCloth calculation. Do the same for cellRightClothShape.

5. You can select the cellLeft and cellRight objects and move them so they overlap at the center at the start of the scene. This removes the seam in the middle and makes it look as though there is a single object dividing into two copies.

6. You can also select the cellLeft and cellRight objects and smooth them using the Smooth operation in the Polygon ➤ Mesh menu, or you can simply select the nCloth object and activate Smooth Mesh Preview by pressing the **3** key on the keyboard.

CACHEABLE ATTRIBUTES

New!

The specific attributes that are included in the nCache are set using the Cacheable Attributes menu in the Caching rollout panel found in the Attribute Editor for each nCloth object. You can use this menu to cache just the position or the position and velocity of each vertex from frame to frame. New to Maya 2011, you now also have the choice to cache the dynamic state of the nCloth object from frame to frame.

Caching the dynamic state means that the internal dynamic properties of the nCloth object are stored in the cache along with the position and velocity of each vertex. This means that if you decide to add more frames to the cache using the Append To Cache option in the nCache menu, you're more likely to get an accurate simulation. This is because Maya will have more information about what's going on inside the nCloth object (things such as pressure, collision settings, and so on) and will do a better job of picking up from where the original cache left off. This does mean that Maya will require more space on your hard drive to store this extra information.

Creating nCloth and nParticle Interactions

Creating dynamic interaction between nParticles and nCloth objects is quite easy because both systems can share the same Nucleus solver. The collision properties of nDynamics make effects that were extremely difficult to create in previous versions of Maya very simple to create. Before continuing this section, review Chapter 13 so you understand the basics of working with nParticles.

In this section, you'll see how you can use nParticles to affect the behavior of nCloth objects. nCloth objects can be used to attract nParticles, nParticles can fill nCloth objects and cause them to tear open, and many interesting effects can be created by using nParticles and nCloth objects together.

Creating an nParticle Goal

Goal objects attract nParticles like a magnet. A goal can be a locator, a piece of geometry, or even another nParticle. In Chapter 13 you worked with force fields, which are similar to goals in some respects in that they attract nParticles dynamically. Deciding whether you need to use a goal or a force field generated by an nDynamic object (or a combination of the two) depends on the effect you want to create and usually involves some experimentation. This section will demonstrate some uses of goal objects with some simple examples.

1. Create a new, empty scene in Maya.

2. Create a locator (Create ➢ Locator).

3. Switch to the nDynamics menu set, and choose nParticles ➢ Create nParticles ➢ Balls to set the nParticle style to Balls.

4. Choose nParticles ➢ Create nParticles ➢ Create Emitter. By default an omni emitter is created at the center of the scene.

5. Use the Move tool to position the emitter away from the locator (set Translate X, Y, and Z to **20**).

6. Set the length of the timeline to 300.

7. Play the animation. Balls are emitted and fall through space because of the Gravity settings on the nucleus node.

8. Select the nParticle object, and Ctrl+click locator1. Choose nParticles ➢ Goal ➢ Options.

9. In the options, set Goal Weight to **1** (see Figure 14.17).

10. Rewind and play the scene.

    The nParticles appear on the locator and bunch up over time. Since Goal Weight is set to 1, the goal is at maximum strength, and the nParticles move so quickly between the emitter and the goal object that they cannot be seen until they land on the goal. Since the Balls-style nParticles have Collision on by default, they stack up as they land on the goal.

11. Select the nParticle object. In the Channel Box, set Goal Weight to **0.25**. Play the animation. You can see the nParticles drawn toward the locator. They move past the goal and then move back toward it, where they bunch up and start to collide, creating a swarm (see Figure 14.18).

FIGURE 14.17
Convert the locator into a goal for the nParticles.

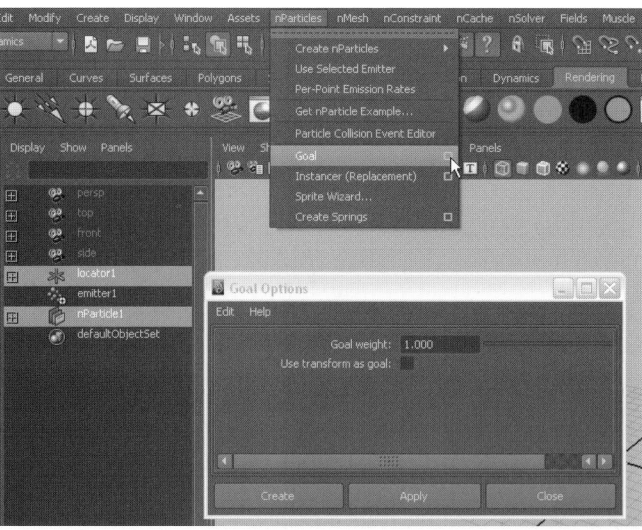

FIGURE 14.18
Lower the Goal Weight for the nParticle in the Channel Box, causing the nParticles to swarm around the locator.

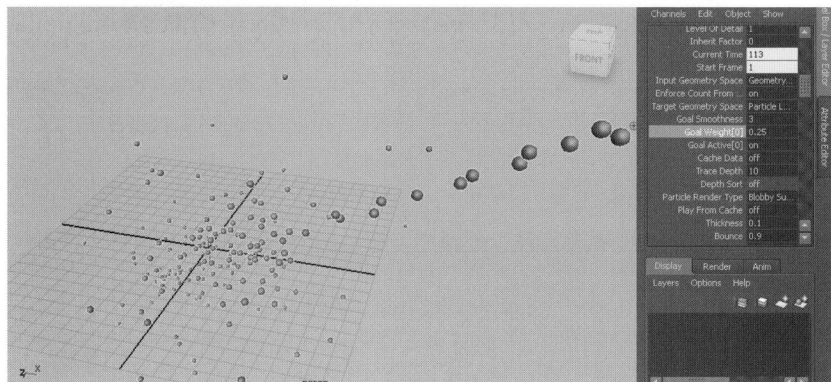

12. Create a second locator. Position locator2 10 units above locator1.

13. Select the nParticle and Ctrl+click locator2. Make it a goal with a weight of **0.25** as well.

14. Play the scene. The nParticles swarm between the two goals.

MULTIPLE GOALS

As goals are added to an nParticle, they are numbered according to the order in which they are added. The numbering starts at 0, so the first goal is referred to as Goal Weight[0], the second goal is referred to as Goal Weight[1], and so on. It's a little confusing; sometimes it's best to name the goal objects themselves using the same numbering convention. Name the first goal locator **locatorGoal0**, and name the second **locatorGoal1**. When adding expressions or when creating MEL scripts, this technique will help you keep everything clear.

15. Select one of the locators, and choose nSolver ➢ Interactive Playback. You can move the locator in the scene while it's playing and watch the nParticles follow. They are always drawn to the midpoint between the two goals (Figure 14.19).

FIGURE 14.19
Using Interactive Playback, you can move the goals around and watch the nParticles follow.

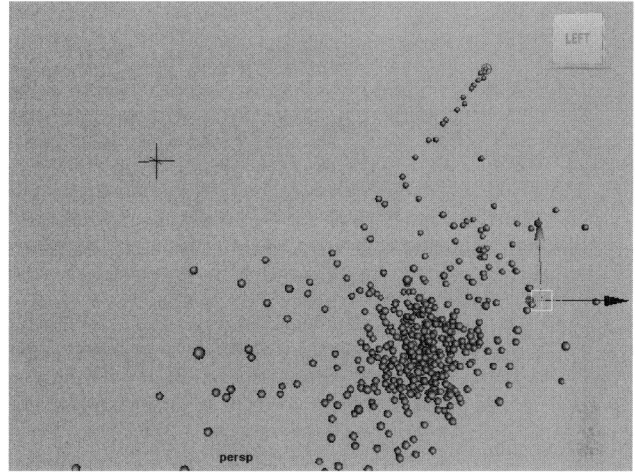

16. Open the Attribute Editor for the nParticle, and switch to the nParticleShape1 tab. Try lowering the Conserve value on the nParticles. This causes the nParticles to lose energy as they fly through the scene.

17. Try these settings:

Conserve: **0.98**

Drag: **0.05**

Wind Speed on the nucleus tab: **8**

Wind Noise: **25**

You can edit these settings in the Attribute Editor or in the Channel Box for the nParticleShape1 node. Suddenly a swarm of particles buzzes between the goal. By animating the position of the goals, you control where the swarm goes.

18. Enter the following settings:

Point Force Field on the nParticle node: World Space

Self Attract: **-10**

Point Field Distance: **10**

Now the motion of the nParticles is controlled by the goals, gravity, wind, wind noise, and a force field generated by the nParticles themselves. You can quickly create complex behavior without the need for a single expression (see Figure 14.20).

To see an example version of this scene, open the swarm.ma file from the chapter14\scenes folder on the DVD.

FIGURE 14.20
Combining goals, forces, dynamic attributes, and wind noise creates some very complex nParticle behaviors.

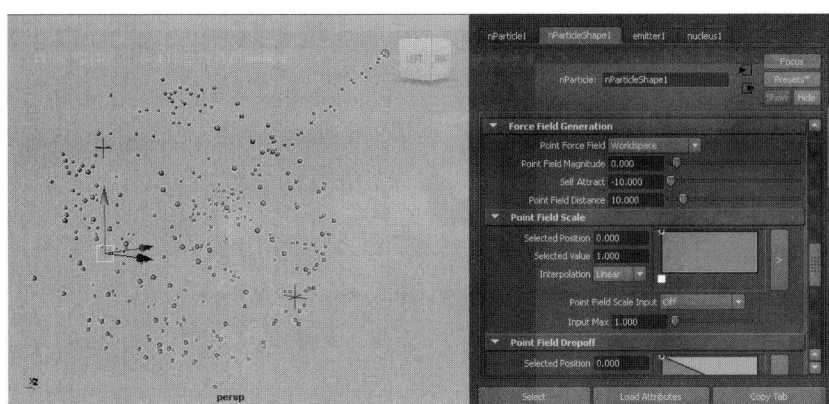

Using nCloth as a Goal

In this example, an nCloth object will be used as a goal. The nParticles will be attracted to the nCloth surface and collide with it at the same time to create a very interesting effect.

1. Create a new, empty Maya scene.

2. Create a polygon cube at the center of the grid. The cube should have one subdivision in width, height, and depth.

3. Scale the cube up eight units in each axis.

4. Select the cube, switch to the Polygon menu set, and choose Mesh ➢ Smooth.

5. In the Channel Box, select the polySmoothFace1 node, and set Divisions to **3**.

6 Select the cube, and switch to the nDynamics menu set.

7. Choose nMesh ➢ Create nCloth to make the object an nCloth.

8. Open the Attribute Editor for the nCloth object, and use the Presets menu to apply the solidRubber preset to the nCloth object (see Figure 14.21).

FIGURE 14.21
Apply the solidRubber preset to the nCloth object.

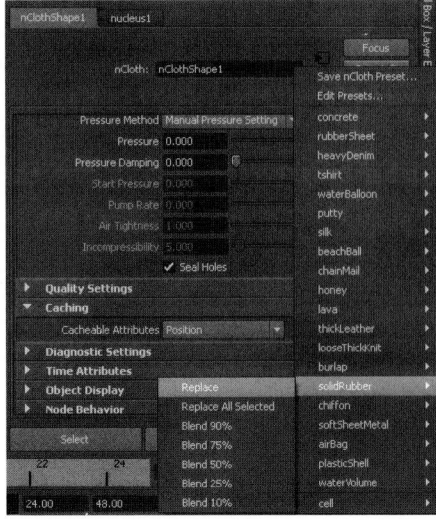

9. Set the length of the timeline to 500 frames.

10. Switch to the nucleus tab, and activate the Use Plane option under the Ground Plane roll-out panel to create an invisible ground plane. Set the Plane Origin's y-axis to **-4**.

11. Play the animation. The nCloth object falls and then bounces on the invisible floor.

12. Choose nParticles ➢ Create nParticles ➢ Balls to set the nParticle style to Balls.

13. Choose nParticles ➢ Create nParticles ➢ Create Emitter to create an emitter. By default the emitter should be set to Omni, and the rate should be at 100.

14. Select the nParticle, and Ctrl+click the nCloth object. Choose nParticles ➢ Goal ➢ Options.

15. In the options, set Goal Weight to **0.5**. Click Create to make the goal.

16. Position the emitter away from the nCloth object. Rewind and play the scene. The nParticles fly toward the nCloth object and attack it. Each nParticle is attracted to a vertex on the nCloth object. The nParticles will stack up when they can't reach a vertex.

17. Set the Mass option of the nParticles to **10**. The attack is much more violent (see Figure 14.22).

To see an example of the scene described, open the `nClothGoal.ma` scene from the `chapter14\scenes` directory.

FIGURE 14.22
When an nCloth object is used as a goal, the nParticles are attracted to the nCloth object and collide with it at the same time, making it appear as though the nParticles are attacking the nCloth object.

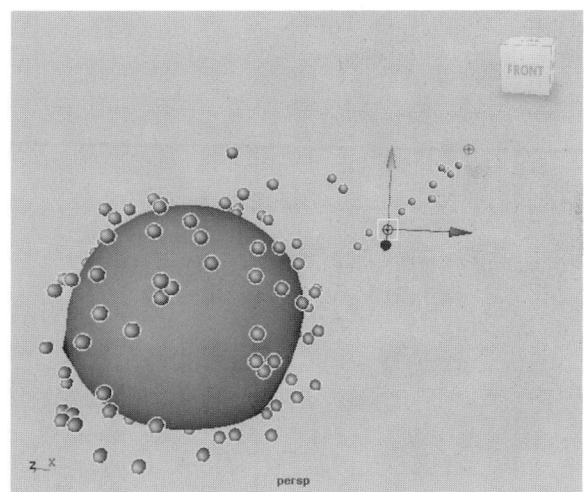

Controlling Collision Events

Using the Collision Event Editor, you can specify what happens when a collision between an nParticle and a goal object occurs.

1. Continue with the scene from the previous section, or open the `nClothGoal.ma` scene from the `chapter14\scenes` directory.

2. Select the nParticle, and choose nParticles ➤ Particle Collision Event Editor.

3. In the Editor window, select the nParticle. Leave the All Collisions check box enabled.

4. Set Event Type to Emit.

SPLIT VS. EMIT

The difference between Emit and Split is fairly subtle, but when Emit is selected, new particles are emitted from the point of collision, and you can specify that the original colliding nParticle dies. When you choose Split, the option for killing the original nParticle is unavailable.

---

5. Enter the following settings:

Num Particles: **5**

Spread: **0.5**

Inherit Velocity to **0.5**

Check the Original Particle Dies option. Click Create Event to make the event (Figure 14.23).

Note that the collision event will create a new nParticle object.

FIGURE 14.23
The Collision Event Editor allows you to create an event wherever the nParticle collides with a surface.

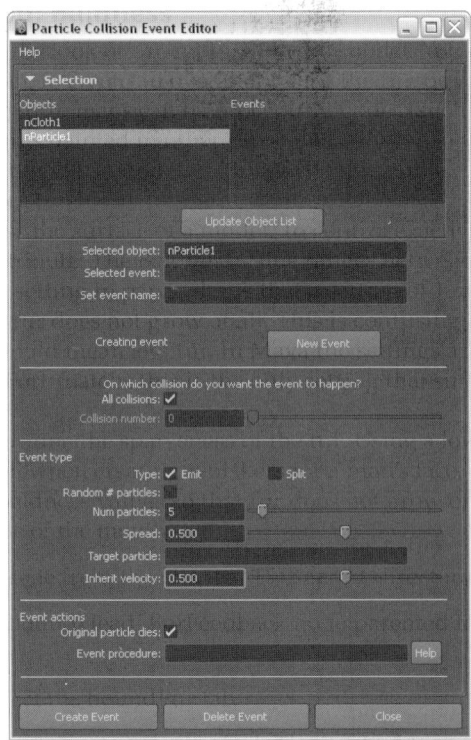

6. Rewind and play the scene.

It may be difficult to distinguish the new nParticles that are created by the collision event from the original colliding nParticles. To fix this, continue with these steps:

7. Select nParticle2 in the Outliner, and open its Attribute Editor.

8. In the Particle Size rollout panel, set Radius to **0.05**.

9. In the Shading rollout panel, set Color Ramp to a solid yellow.

10. Rewind and play the scene.

Each time an nParticle hits the nCloth object, it dies and emits three new nParticles. The nParticle2 node in the Outliner controls the behavior and settings for the new nParticles. To see an example of this scene, open the `collisionEvents.ma` scene from the `chapter14\scenes` folder on the DVD.

Ripping an Object Open Using Tearable nConstraints

This short example demonstrates how to create a bursting surface using nParticles and an nCloth surface.

1. In a new Maya scene, create a polygon cube at the center of the grid. The cube should have one subdivision in width, height, and depth.

2. Scale the cube up eight units in each axis.

3. Select the cube; switch to the Polygon menu set; and choose Mesh ➢ Smooth.

4. In the Channel Box, select the polySmoothFace1 node, and set Divisions to 3.

5. Select the cube, and switch to the nDynamics menu set.

6. Choose nMesh ➢ Create nCloth to make the object an nCloth.

7. Open the Attribute Editor for the nCloth object, and use the Presets menu to apply the rubberSheet preset to the nCloth object.

8. Switch to the nucleus1 tab, and set Gravity to **0**.

9. Choose nParticles ➢ Create nParticles ➢ Balls to set the nParticle style to Balls.

10. Choose nParticles ➢ Create nParticles ➢ Create Emitter to create a new emitter. By default the emitter is placed at the origin inside the nCloth object.

11. Select the nParticles; in the Attribute Editor for the nParticleShape1 tab, expand the Particle Size rollout panel, and set Radius to **0.5**.

12. Set the length of the Timeline to 800.

13. Rewind and play the animation. The nParticles start to fill up the surface, causing it to expand (see Figure 14.24). If some nParticles are passing through the surface, switch to the Nucleus solver, and raise the Substeps value to 8.

14. Create a new shader, and apply it to the nCloth object.

FIGURE 14.24
Placing the emitter inside the nCloth object causes it to fill with nParticles.

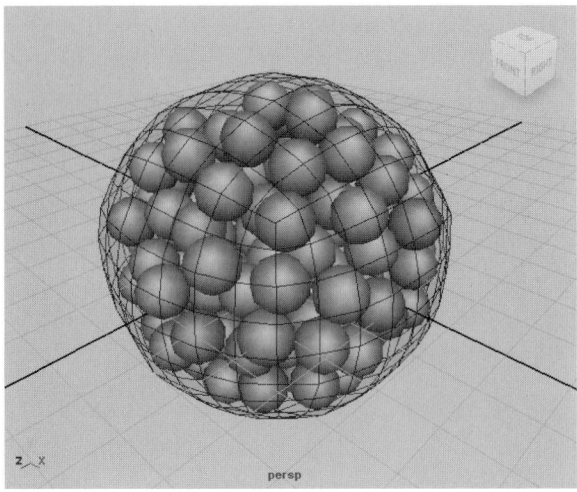

15. Set the transparency of the shader to a light gray so that you can see the nParticles inside the nCloth object.

16. Select the pCube1 object in the Outliner.

17. Choose nConstraint ➤ Tearable Surface. This applies a new nConstraint to the surface.

18. If you play the scene, you'll see the surface burst open (Figure 14.25). Open the Attribute Editor for the nDynamic constraint. Set Glue Strength to **0.3** and Glue Strength Scale to **0.8**; this will make the nConstraint more difficult to tear, so the bursting will not occur until around frame 500.

To see two examples of Tearable Surface nConstraints, open `burst.ma` and `burst2.ma` from the `chapter14\scenes` directory on the DVD.

FIGURE 14.25
Adding a Tearable Surface nConstraint allows the surface to rip when a certain amount of force is applied.

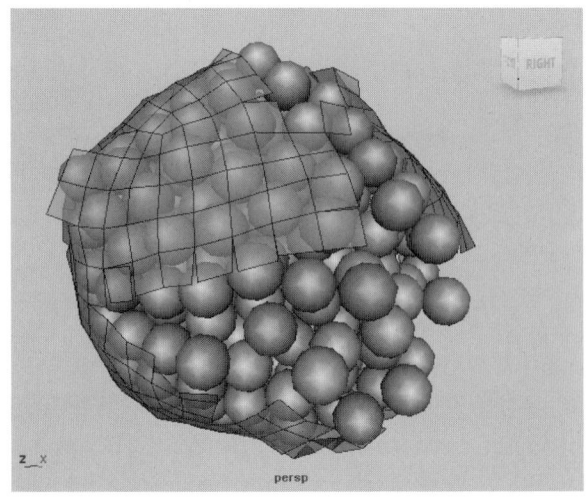

DESIGNING TEARING SURFACES

You can specify exactly where you'd like the tearing to occur on a surface by selecting specific vertices before applying the Tearable Surface nConstraint.

Rigid Body Dynamics

Rigid body dynamics are the interactions of hard surfaces such as the balls on a pool table, collapsing buildings, and links in a chain. Maya's rigid body dynamic system has been part of the software since long before nDynamics were introduced. In this section, you'll learn how to set up a rigid body simulation and how it can be used with nParticles to create the effect of a small tower exploding.

Creating an Exploding Tower

The example scene has a small tower of bricks on a hill. You'll use a rigid body simulation to make the bricks of the tower explode outward on one side. Later you'll add nParticles to the simulation to create an explosion.

The scene is designed so only one side of the tower will explode. Only a few stone bricks will be pushed out from the explosion; these bricks have been placed in the active group. The bricks in the passive group will be converted to passive colliders; they won't move, but they will support the active brick. The bricks in the static group will be left alone. Since they won't participate in the explosion, they won't be active or passive, just plain geometry. This will increase the efficiency and performance of the scene.

1. Open the `tower_v01.ma` scene in the `chapter14\scenes` directory, expand the active group that's inside the tower node, and select all the brick nodes in this group.

2. Switch to the Dynamics menu set (not the nDynamics menu set), and choose Soft/Rigid Bodies ➢ Create Active Rigid Body.

3. Expand the passive group, Shift+click all the bricks in this group, and choose Soft/Rigid Bodies ➢ Create Passive Rigid Body.

4. Select the ground, and choose Soft/Rigid Bodies ➢ Create Passive Rigid Body.

   By default, there is no gravity attached to the active rigid bodies; to add gravity, you need to create a gravity field.

5. Shift+click all the members of the active group, and choose Fields ➢ Gravity.

   If you play the scene, you'll see the active bricks sag slightly. You actually don't want them to move until the explosion occurs. To fix this, you can keyframe their dynamic state.

6. To animate their dynamic state, rewind the scene, Shift+click the members of the active group, and set the Active attribute in the Channel Box to Off.

7. Move the Time Slider to frame 19, right-click the Active channel, and choose Key Selected from the pop-up (see Figure 14.26).

FIGURE 14.26
You can keyframe the Active state of the rigid bodies.

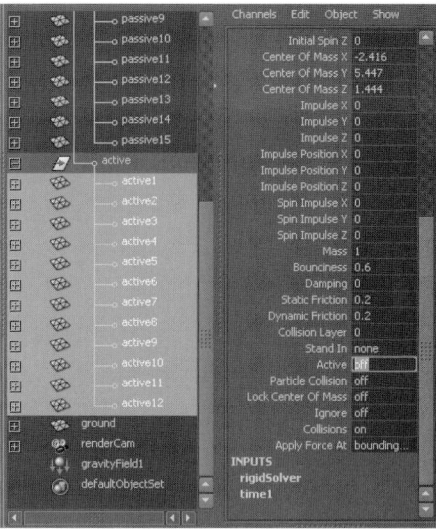

8. Move the timeline to frame 20, set Active to On, and set another keyframe.

9. To make the bricks explode, select the members of the active group, and add a radial field.

10. Position the radial field behind the active bricks, and enter the following settings:

    Magnitude: **400**

    Attenuation: **0.5**

    Max Distance: **5**

11. Select the active bricks, and set their Mass value to **20** (see Figure 14.27).

    When you play the scene, the bricks fly out at frame 20.

FIGURE 14.27
Increase the Mass value of the rigid bodies to make the bricks appear heavier.

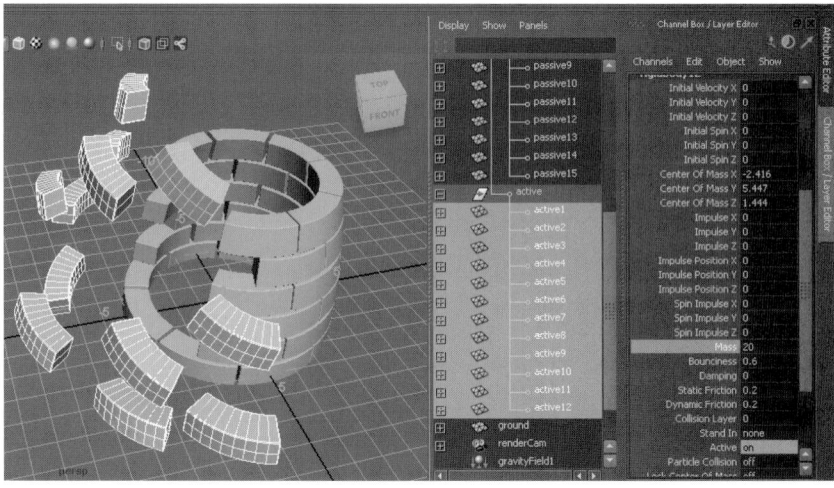

INTERPENETRATION ERRORS

Interpenetration errors occur when the geometry of the rigid body objects pass through each other in such a way as to confuse Maya. Only one side of the surface is actually used in the calculation based on the direction of the surface normals—there are no double-sided rigid bodies. The surface of two colliding rigid bodies (active + active or active + passive) need to have their normals pointing at each other to calculate correctly.

To fix these errors, you can increase the Tessellation Factor value in the Performance Attributes rollout panel of each of the rigid body objects.

Tuning the Rigid Body Simulation

You can tune the simulation by editing the settings on the active rigid bodies. The easiest way to do this for multiple objects is to select them all in the Outliner and then edit the settings in the Channel Box. For this example, you can decrease the amount of bouncing and sliding in the motion of the bricks by adjusting the friction and bounciness settings. There are two kinds of friction: Static Friction and Dynamic Friction.

Static Friction Static Friction sets the level of resistance for a resting dynamic object against another dynamic object. In other words, if an object is stationary, this means how much it resists movement once a force is applied.

Dynamic Friction Dynamic Friction sets how much a moving dynamic object resists another dynamic object, such as a book sliding across a table.

Other settings to take note of include Damping and Collision Layer. Damping slows down the movement of dynamic objects. If the simulation takes place under water, you can raise this setting to make it look as though the objects are being slowed down by the density of the environment.

The collision layer specifies which objects collide with other objects. By default, all rigid bodies are on collision layer 0. However, if you set just the active bricks to collision layer 1, they react only with each other and not the ground or the passive bricks, which would still be on collision layer 0.

1. Select the ground plane, and set both the Static and Dynamic Friction attributes in the Channel Box to **1**.

2. Shift+click the active bricks and, in the Channel Box, set Dynamic Friction to **0.5**. Lower Bounciness to **0.1**.

3. Save the scene as **rigidBodyTower_v01.ma**.

To see a version of the scene to this point, open rigidBodyTower_v01.ma from the chapter14\ scenes directory.

RIGID BODY SOLVING METHODS

Rigid bodies use a rigid solver node to calculate dynamics. This node is called the Rigid Solver and appears as a tab in the Attribute Editor when you select one of the rigid body objects such as the bricks in the active group. The rigid solver uses one of three types of methods to calculate the dynamics. The three rigid solver methods are Mid-Point, Runge Kutta, and Runge Kutta Adaptive. Mid-Point is the fastest but least accurate type, Runge Kutta is more accurate and slower, and Runge Kutta Adaptive is the most accurate and slowest method. For most cases, you can leave the setting on Runge Kutta Adaptive.

NCLOTH RIGID BODIES

You can use nCloth objects to create rigid body effects as well. Try creating an nCloth Cube, and use the Concrete Preset to simulate a solid object. Using a high value for the Rigidity settings in the nCloth objects attributes is key to creating hard surfaces out of nCloth. You may find that for more complex scenes involving rigid body dynamics, traditional rigid body dynamics are faster to work with than nCloth.

Baking the Simulation

It's common practice to bake the motion of traditional rigid bodies into keyframes once you're satisfied that the simulation is working the way you want. This improves the performance of the scene as well as allows you to adjust parts of the animation by tweaking the keyframes on the Graph Editor.

1. In the Outliner, Shift+click the active bricks, and choose Edit ➤ Keys ➤ Bake Simulation ➤ Options.

2. In the Channel Box, Shift+click the Translate and Rotate channels.

3. In the Bake Simulation Options section, set Time Range to Time Slider.

4. Set the Channels option to From Channel Box. Keyframes are created for just the channels currently selected in the Channel Box. This eliminates the creation of extra, unnecessary keys.

5. Turn on Smart Bake. This setting tells Maya to create keyframes only where the animation requires it instead of creating a keyframe on every frame of the animation.

   The Increase Fidelity option improves the accuracy of the smart bake. Fidelity Keys Tolerance specifies the baking tolerance in terms of a percentage. Higher percentages produce fewer keyframes but also allow for more deviation from the original simulation.

   Other important options include the following:

   Keep Unbaked Keys   Keeps any key outside the baked range.

   Sparse Curve Bake   Keeps the shape of connected animation curves when baking. Since the bricks are using dynamics, this option does not apply.

   Disable Implicit Control   This is useful when the object's animation is being driven by Inverse Kinematic handles and other controls. Again, this is not necessary when baking rigid body dynamics.

6. Activate Increase Fidelity, and set Fidelity Keys Tolerance to **1** percent. See Figure 14.28.

7. Click the Bake button to bake the simulation into keyframes. The animation will play through as the keys are baked.

8. When the animation is finished, select Edit ➤ Delete All By Type ➤ Rigid Bodies to remove the rigid body nodes.

9. Select the active bricks, and open the Graph Editor (Window ➤ Animation Editors ➤ Graph Editor) to see the baked animation curves for the bricks (see Figure 14.29).

FIGURE 14.28
The options for baking keyframes

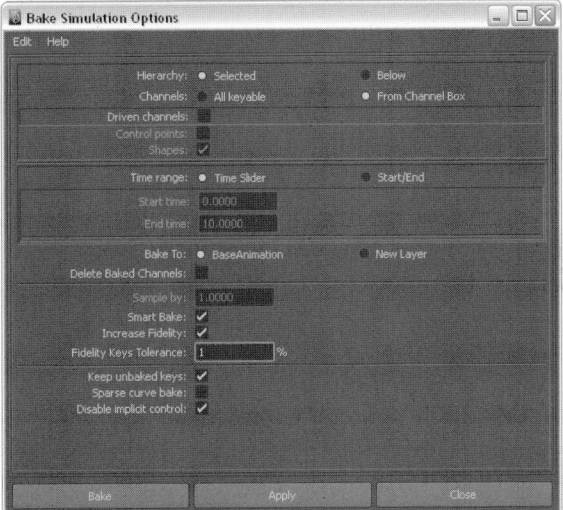

FIGURE 14.29
The Graph Editor shows the animation curves for the baked simulation of the active bricks.

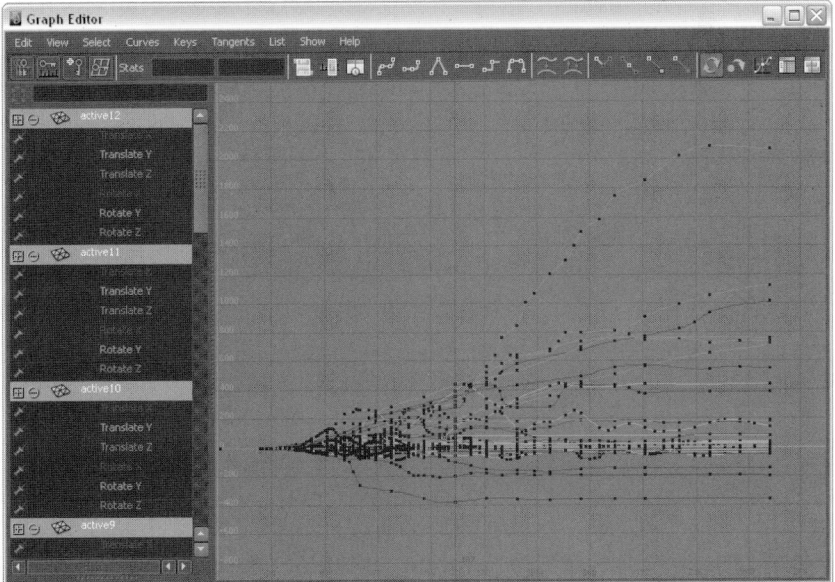

10. If any of the bricks continue to wobble after landing on the ground, you can edit their motion on the Graph Editor by deleting the "wobbly" keyframes.

11. Save the scene as `rigidBodyTower_v02.ma`.

To see an example of the scene that uses traditional rigid bodies, open the `rigidBodyTower_v02.ma` scene from the `chapter14\scenes` folder on the DVD.

DUPLICATING TRADITIONAL RIGID BODIES

When duplicating rigid bodies that have fields connected, do not use Duplicate Special ➤ Duplicate Input Connections or Duplicate Input Graph. These options do not work well with rigid bodies. Instead, duplicate the object, convert it to an active rigid body, and then use the Relationship Editor to make the connection between the rigid bodies and the fields.

Creating Flying Debris Using nParticle Instancing

nParticle instancing attaches one or more specified pieces of geometry to a particle system. The instanced geometry then inherits the motion and much of the behavior of the particle system. For this example, you'll instance debris and shrapnel to a particle system and add it to the current explosion animation. In addition, you'll control how the instance geometry behaves through expressions and fields.

The goal for the exercises in this section is to add bits of flying debris to the explosion that behave realistically. This means you'll want debris of various sizes flying at different speeds and rotating as the particles move through the air. The first step is to add an nParticle system to the scene that behaves like debris flying through the air.

Adding nParticles to the Scene

The first step in creating the explosion effect is to add nParticles to the scene and make sure they are interacting with the ground and the bricks of the tower. It's a good idea to try to be efficient in your approach to doing this so that Maya is not bogged down in unnecessary calculations. To begin with, you'll add a volume emitter at the center of the tower.

1. Open the `rigidBodyTower_v02.ma` scene from the `chapter14\scenes` directory. In this scene, the rigid body simulation has been baked into keyframes.

2. Switch to the nDynamics menu set, choose nParticles ➤ Create nParticles ➤ Balls to set the nParticle style to Balls.

3. Choose nParticles ➤ Create nParticles ➤ Create Emitter ➤ Options.

4. In the Options, set Emitter Type to Volume and Rate to **800**.

5. In the Distance/Direction Attributes rollout panel, set Direction X and Direction Z to **0** and Direction Y to **1** so the nParticles initially move upward.

6. In the Volume Emitter Attributes rollout panel, set Volume Shape to Cylinder.

7. In the Volume Speed Attributes rollout panel, enter the following settings:

   Away From Axis: **1**

   Along Axis: **0.5**

   Random Direction: **1**

   Directional Speed: **4**

8. Click Create to make the emitter (see Figure 14.30).

FIGURE 14.30
The options for the
volume emitter

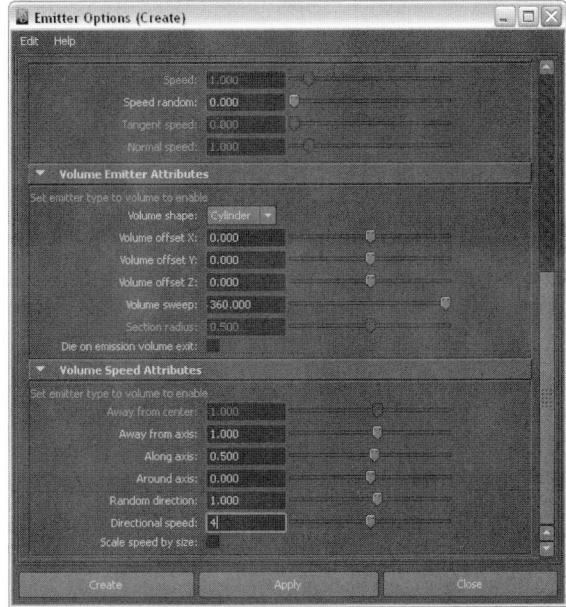

9. Switch to wireframe mode. Select emitter1 in the Outliner, and use the Move and Scale tools to position the emitter at the center of the stone tower.

10. Set Translate Y to **3.1** and all three Scale channels to **2**.

11. Rewind and play the animation.

    The nParticles start pouring out of the emitter. They pass through the bricks and the ground.

12. Select the ground, and choose nMesh ➢ Create Passive Collider.

13. Shift+click the bricks in the passive group, and convert them to passive colliders; do the same for the bricks in the active group.

    The nParticles still pass through the static bricks at the back of the tower. You can convert the static bricks to passive colliders; however, this adds a large number of new nRigid nodes to the scene, which may slow down the performance of the scene. You can conserve some of the energy Maya spends on collision detection by creating a single, simple collider object to interact with the nParticles that hit the back of the tower. This object can be hidden in the render.

14. Switch to the Polygon menu set, and choose Create ➢ Polygon Primitives ➢ Cylinder.

15. Select the nParticle1 node, and in the Attribute Editor for the shape nodes, set Enable to Off to temporarily disable the calculations of the nParticle while you create the collision object.

16. Set the timeline to frame 100 so you can easily see the opening in the exploded tower.

17. Set the scale and position of the cylinder so it blocks the nParticles from passing through the back of the tower. Set the following:

Translate Y: **2.639**

Scale X and Scale Z: **2.34**

Scale Y: **3.5**

18. Select the cylinder, and switch to face selection mode; delete the faces on the top and bottom of the cylinder and in the opening of the exploded tower (Figure 14.31).

19. Rename the cylinder **collider**. Switch to the nDynamics menu set, and choose nMesh ➢ Create Passive Collider.

20. Select the nParticles, and turn Enable back on.

21. Rewind and play the animation; the nParticles now spill out of the front of the tower once it breaks open (Figure 14.32).

22. Save the scene as **explodingTower_v01.ma**.

To see a version of the scene up to this point, open the explodingTower_v01.ma scene from the chapter14\scenes folder on the DVD.

FIGURE 14.31
Delete the faces on the top and bottom of the cylinder. Select the faces near the opening of the exploded tower and delete them.

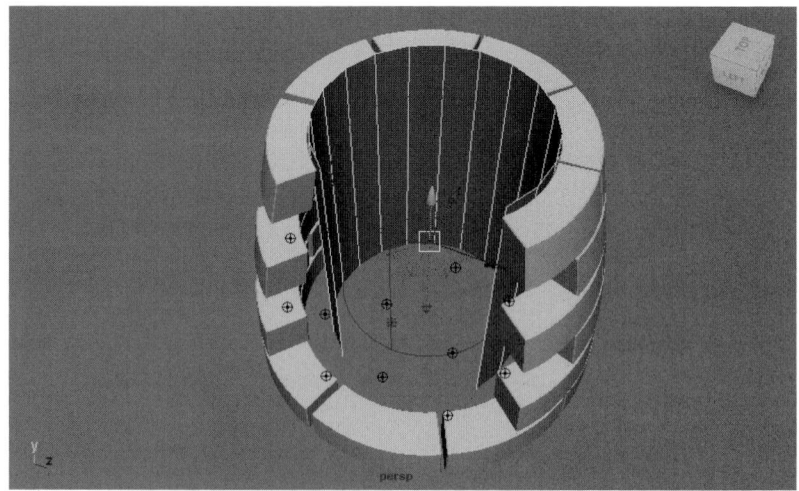

FIGURE 14.32
With the collision surface in place, the nParticles pour out of the opening in the front of the stone tower.

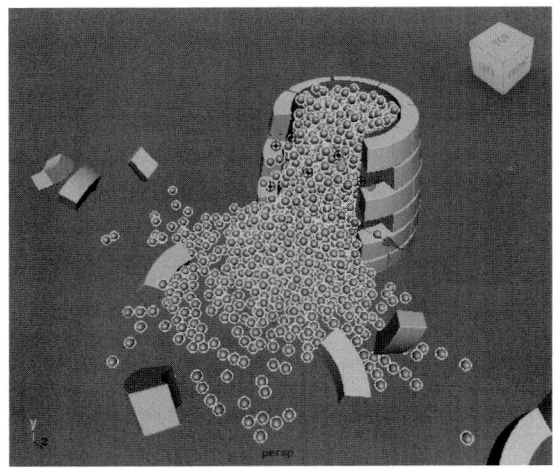

Sending the Debris Flying Using a Field

The effects so far look like a popcorn popper gone bad. To make it look as though the nParticles are expelled from the source of the explosion, you can connect the radial field to the nParticle.

1. Continue with the scene from the previous section, or open the explodingTower_v01. ma from the chpater14\scenes folder on the DVD. Select nParticle1, and rename it **particleDebris**.

2. Open the Attribute Editor for particleDebris. Switch to the nucleus1 tab.

3. In the Time Attributes rollout panel, set Start Frame to 20 so that the emission of the nParticles is in sync with the exploding brick.

   It's not necessary to have the debris continually spewing from the tower. You need only a certain number of nParticles. You can either set keyframes on the emitter's rate or set a limit to the number of nParticles created by the emitter. The latter method is easier to do and to edit later.

4. In the Attribute Editor for particleDebris, expand the Emission Attributes rollout panel. Max Count is set to -1 by default, meaning that the emitter can produce an infinite number of nParticles. Set this value to **1200** (see Figure 14.33).

FIGURE 14.33
Set Max Count to 1200, limiting the number of nParticles created by the emitter.

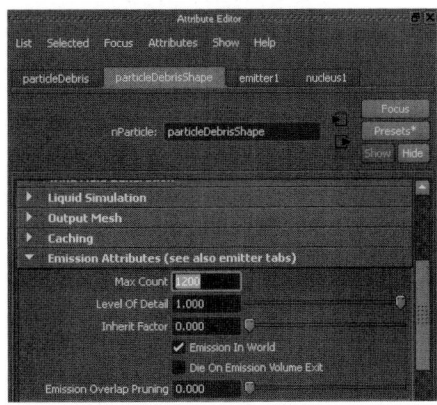

5. After the number of nParticles reaches 1200, the emitter stops creating new nParticles. Select the emitter, and set the rate to **2400**. This means that the emitter will create 1,200 nParticles in half a second, making the explosion faster and more realistic.

MAX COUNT AND nPARTICLE DEATH

This method works well as long as the nParticles do not have a finite life span. If there is a life span set for the nParticles or if they die from a collision event, the emitter creates new nParticles to make up the difference.

---

6. You can connect the particleDebris node to the existing radial field that was used to push out the bricks. To connect the radial field to the particleDebris node, select the particleDebris node, and Ctrl+click radialField1 in the Outliner. Choose Fields ➤ Affect Selected Object(s).

MAKING CONNECTIONS WITH THE RELATIONSHIP EDITOR

You can also connect the field to the nParticle using the Dynamic Relationship Editor. This is discussed in Chapter 13.

---

7. Rewind and play the animation. Not all the nParticles make it out of the tower; many of the nParticles are pushed down on the ground and toward the back of the collider object. To fix this, reposition the radial field.

8. Set the Translate X of the field to **1.347** and the Translate Y to **0.364**. (See Figure 14.34.)

9. Save the scene as **explodingTower_v02.ma**.

To see a version of the scene to this point, open the explodingTower_v02.ma scene from the chapter14\scenes folder on the DVD.

FIGURE 14.34
Once you reposition the radial field, the nParticles are sent flying out of the tower.

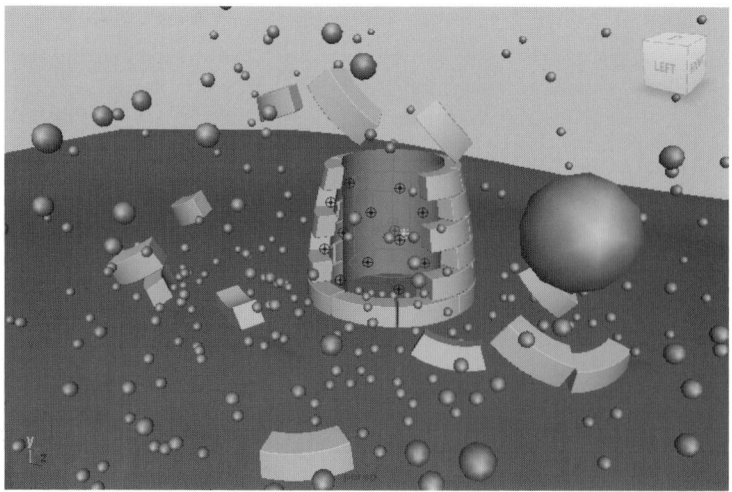

Creating a More Convincing Explosion by Adjusting nParticle Mass

Next, to create a more convincing behavior for the nParticles, you can randomize the mass. This means that there will be random variation in how the nParticles move through the air as they are launched by the radial field.

1. Select the particleDebris node in the Outliner, and open its Attribute Editor.

2. Under the Dynamic Properties rollout panel, you can leave Mass at a value of 1. In the Mass Scale settings, set Mass Scale Input to Randomize ID. This randomizes the mass of each nParticle using its ID number as a seed value to generate the random value.

3. If you play the animation, the mass does not seem all that random. To create a range of values, add a point to the Mass Scale ramp on the right side, and bring it down to a value of **0.1**.

   When Mass Scale Input is set to Randomize ID, you can alter the range of variation by adjusting the Input Max slider. If you think of the Mass Scale ramp as representing possible random ranges, lowering Input Max shrinks the number of random values available to the randomize function, thus forcing the randomizer to have more "contrast" between values. Increasing Input Max makes more data points available to the randomize function, making a smoother variation between random values and producing less contrast (see Figure 14.35).

4. Set the Input Max slider to **0.5**.

   The Mass Scale Randomizer slider is an additional randomization value that is multiplied against the initial mass value, such as if you set Mass Scale Input to speed or age or acceleration, or you can use the slider to add some random variation to the mass. You don't need to use this slider if the Mass Scale input is set to Randomize ID, and sometimes it can result in creating random values so close to zero that the nParticles end up getting stuck in the air.

5. Create a playblast of the scene so that you can see how the simulation is working so far.

   The nParticles are sliding along the ground in a strange way. To make them stop, you can increase the stickiness and friction of the ground.

6. Select the ground geometry, and open its Attribute Editor.

7. Switch to the nRigidShape1 tab. Under the Collisions rollout panel, set Stickiness to **1** and Friction to **0.2**.

8. Save the scene as **explodingTower_v03.ma**.

To see a version of the scene, open explodingTower_v03.ma from the chapter14\scenes folder on the DVD.

FIGURE 14.35

Mass Scale sets a range for the mass for each nParticle. The Input Max value is used to add contrast to the values generated by the ramp.

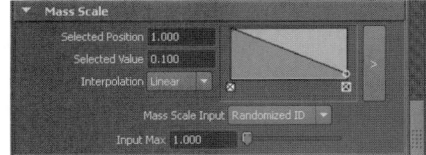

Instancing Geometry

The debris is currently in the shape of round balls, which is not very realistic. To create the effect of flying shrapnel, you'll need to instance some premade geometry to each nParticle. This means that a copy of each piece of geometry will follow the motion of each nParticle.

1. Continue using the scene from the previous section, or open the explodingTower_v03.ma scene from the chapter14\scenes directory.

2. The debris is contained in a separate file, which will be imported into the scene. Choose File ➤ Import, and select the debris.ma scene from the chapter14\scenes directory on the DVD.

   The debris scene is simply a group of seven polygon objects in the shape of shards.

3. Expand the debris:debris group in the Outliner, Shift+click all the members of the group, and choose nParticles ➤ Instancer (Replacement) ➤ Options.

   In the Options window, all the debris objects are listed in the order in which they were selected in the Outliner. Notice that each one has a number to the left in the list. This number is the index value of the instance. The numbering starts with 0.

4. In the Particle Object To Instance drop-down menu, choose the particleDebrisShape object. This sets the instance to the correct nDynamic object (see Figure 14.36).

5. Leave the rest of the settings at the default, and choose Create to instance the nParticles. In the Outliner, a new node named instance1 has been created.

6. Play the scene. Switch to wireframe mode, and zoom in closely to the nParticles so you can see what's going on.

7. Save the scene as **explodingTower_v04.ma**.

To see a version of the scene up to this point, open the explodingTower_v04.ma scene from the chapter14\scenes folder on the DVD.

FIGURE 14.36
The selected objects appear in the Instanced Objects list. Select the particleDebris-Shape node in the Particle Object To Instance options.

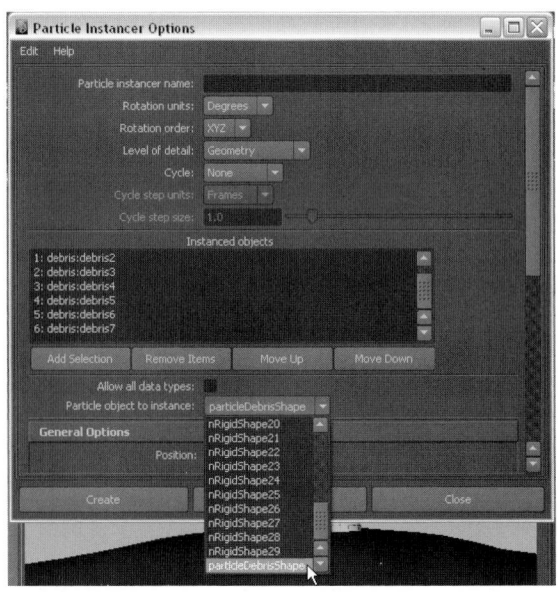

When playing the scene, you'll notice that each nParticle has the same piece of geometry instanced to it, and they are all oriented the same way (see Figure 14.37). To randomize which objects are instanced to the nParticles and their size and orientation, you'll need to create some expressions. In the next section, you'll learn how to randomly assign the different objects in the imported debris group to each nParticle as well as how to make them rotate as they fly through the air, and you will learn how to use each nParticle's mass to determine the size of the instanced geometry. All of this leads to a much more realistic-looking explosion.

FIGURE 14.37
Each nParticle has the same piece of geometry instanced to it.

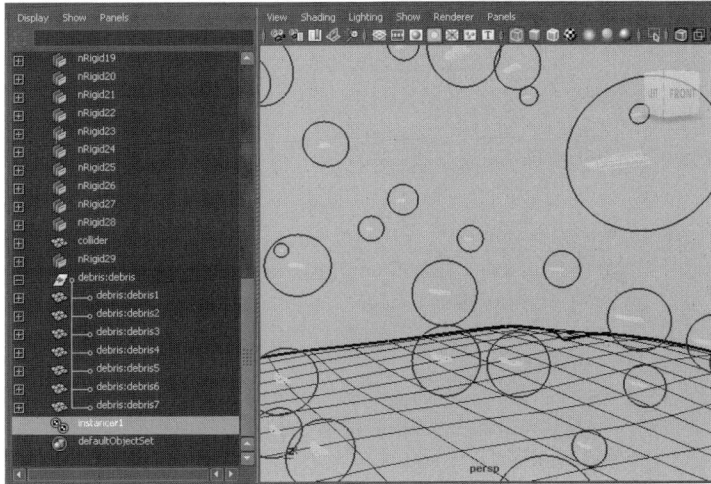

TIPS FOR WORKING WITH NPARTICLE INSTANCES

Geometry that is instanced to nParticles inherits the position and orientation of the original geometry. If you place keyframes on the original geometry, this is inherited by the instanced copies.

If you're animating flying debris, it's a better idea to animate the motion of the instances using expressions and the dynamics of the nParticles rather than setting keyframes of the rotation or translation of the original instanced geometry. This makes animation simpler and allows for more control when editing the effect.

It's also best to place the geometry you want to instance at the center of the grid and place its pivot at the center of the geometry. You'll also want to freeze transformations on the geometry to initialize its translation, rotation, and scale attributes.

In some special cases, you may want to offset the pivot of the instanced geometry. To do this, position the geometry away from the origin of the grid, place the pivot at the center of the grid, and freeze transformations.

If you are animating crawling bugs or the flapping wings of an insect, you can animate the original geometry you want to instance, or you can create a sequence of objects and use the Cycle feature in the instance options. The Cycle feature causes the instance to progress through a sequence of geometry based on the index number assigned to the instanced geometry. The Cycle feature offers more flexibility than simply animating the instanced geometry. You can use expressions to randomize the start point of the cycle on a per-particle basis. Particle expressions are covered in the next section.

You can add more objects to the Instanced Objects list after creating the instance using the options in the Attribute Editor for the instance node.

Animating Instances Using nParticle Expressions

nParticles allow you to create more interesting particle effects than in previous versions of Maya without relying on expressions. However, in some situations, expressions are still required to achieve a believable effect. If you've never used particle expressions, they can be a little intimidating at first, and the workflow is not entirely intuitive. Once you understand how to create expressions, you can unleash an amazing level of creative potential; combine them with the power of the Nucleus solver, and there's almost no effect you can't create. Expressions work the same way for both nParticles and traditional Maya particles.

Maya 2011 has also added new per-particle rotation attributes to nParticles. In this section, you'll use these new attributes to control the rotation of the exploding debris as it flies through the air.

Randomizing Instance Index

The first expression you'll create will randomize which instance is copied to which nParticle. To do this, you'll need to create a custom attribute. This custom attribute will assign a random value between 0 and 6 for each nParticle, and this value will be used to determine the index number of the instance copied to that particular particle.

1. Select the particleDebris node in the Outliner, and open its Attribute Editor to the particleDebrisShape tab.

2. Scroll down and expand the Add Dynamic Attributes rollout panel.

3. Click the General button (see Figure 14.38); a pop-up dialog box appears. This dialog box offers you options to determine what type of attribute will be added to the particle shape.

4. In the Long Name field, type **debrisIndex**. This is the name of the attribute that will be added to the nParticle.

FIGURE 14.38
The General button in the Add Dynamic Attributes section allows you to create your own custom attributes.

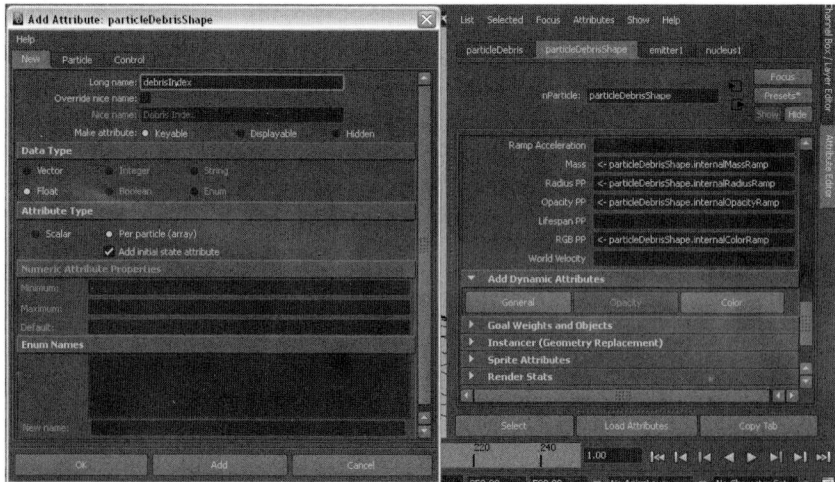

NAMING AN ATTRIBUTE

You can name an attribute anything you want (as long as the name does not conflict with a preexisting attribute name). It's best to use concise names that make it obvious what the attribute does.

5. Set Data Type to Float. A float is a single numeric value that can have a decimal. Numbers like 3, 18.7, and -0.314 are examples of floats.

6. Set Attribute Type to Per Particle (Array).

PER PARTICLE VS. SCALAR ATTRIBUTES

A Per Particle attribute contains a different value for each particle in the particle object. This is opposed to a Scalar attribute, which applies the same value for all the particles in the particle object. For example, if an nParticle object represented an American president, a per-particle attribute would be something like the age of each president when elected. A scalar attribute would be something like the nationality of the presidents, which would be American for all of them.

---

7. Click OK to add the attribute.

Now that you have an attribute, you need to create the expression to determine its value:

1. Expand the Per Particle (Array) Attributes rollout panel, and you'll see Debris Index listed.

2. Right-click the field next to Debris Index, and choose Creation Expression (see Figure 14.39).

FIGURE 14.39
The new Debris Index attribute appears in the Per Particle (Array) Attributes list. To create an expression, right-click and choose Creation Expression.

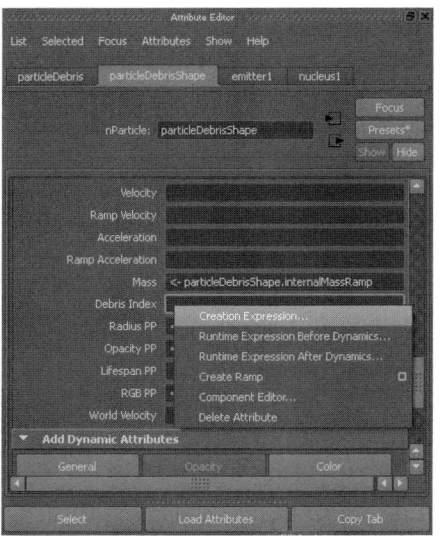

The Expression Editor opens, and debrisIndex is selected in the Attributes list. Notice that the Particle mode is automatically set to Creation.

3. In the Expression field, type **debrisIndex=rand(0,6);**. Remember that the list of instanced objects contains seven objects, but the index list starts with 0 and goes to 6 (see Figure 14.40).

This adds a random function that assigns a number between 0 and 6 to the debrisIndex attribute of each nParticle. The semicolon at the end of the expression is typical scripting syntax and acts like a period at the end of a sentence.

FIGURE 14.40
Add an expression to randomize the value of the debrisIndex attribute for each nParticle.

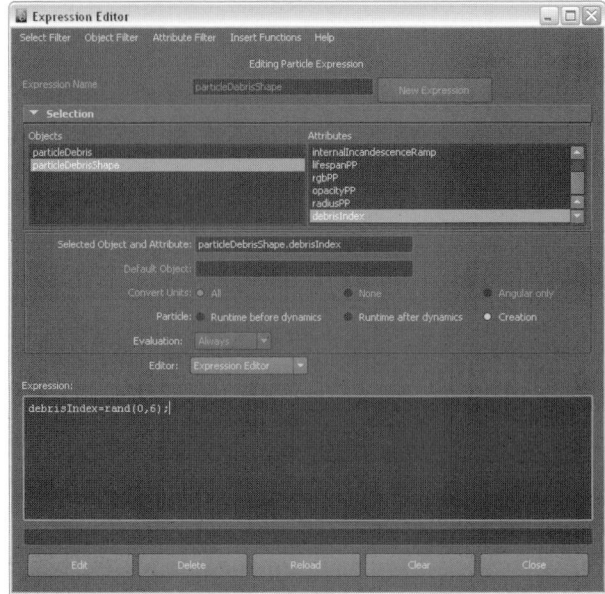

4. Click the Create button to create the expression.

5. Rewind and play the animation.

Nothing has changed at this point—the same piece of debris is assigned to all the nParticles. This is because even though you have a custom attribute with a random value, you haven't told Maya how to apply the attribute to the particle.

6. Expand the Instancer (Geometry Replacement) rollout panel in the Attribute Editor.

7. In the General Options section, expand the Object Index menu, and choose debrisIndex from the list (see Figure 14.41).

FIGURE 14.41
Assign the new debrisIndex attribute as the input for the Object Index attribute in the Instancer section of the nParticle's Attribute Editor.

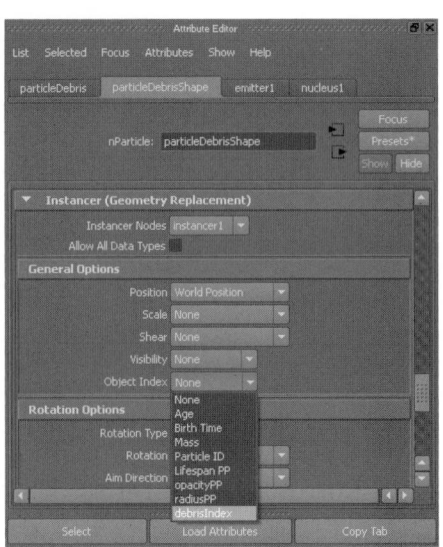

Now when you rewind and play the animation, you'll see a different piece of geometry assigned to each nParticle.

8. Save the scene as **explodingTower_v05.ma**.

To see a version of the scene up to this point, open the explodingTower_v05.ma scene from the chapter14\scenes folder on the DVD.

CREATION VS. RUNTIME EXPRESSIONS

There are two types of expressions you can create for a particle object: creation and runtime. The difference between creation and runtime is that creation expressions evaluate once when the particles are created (or at the start of the animation for particles that are not spawned from an emitter), and runtime expressions evaluate on each frame of the animation for as long as they are in the scene.

A good way to think of this is that a creation expression is like a trait determined by your DNA. When you're born, your DNA may state something like "Your maximum height will be 6 feet 4 inches." So, your creation expression for height would be maximum height = 6 feet 4 inches. This has been set at the moment you are created and will remain so throughout your life unless something changes.

Think of a runtime expression as an event in your life. It's calculated each moment of your life. If for some reason during the course of your life your legs were replaced with bionic extend-o-legs that give you the ability to automatically change your height whenever you want, this would be enabled using a runtime expression. It happens after you have been born and can override the creation expression. Thus, at any given moment (or frame in the case of particles), your height could be 5 feet or 25 feet, thanks to your bionic extend-o-legs.

If you write a creation expression for the particles that says radius = 2, each particle will have a radius of 2, unless something changes. If you then add a runtime expression that says something like "If the Y position of a particle is greater than 10, then radius = 4," then any particle that goes beyond 10 units in Y will instantly grow to four units. The runtime expression overrides the creation expression and is calculated at least once per frame as long as the animation is playing.

Connecting Instance Size to nParticle Mass

Next you'll create an expression that determines the size of each nParticle based on its mass. Small pieces of debris that have a low mass will float down through the air. Larger pieces that have a higher mass will be shot through the air with greater force. The size of instances is determined by their Scale X, Scale Y, and Scale Z attributes, much like a typical piece of geometry that you work with when modeling in Maya. This is different from a Balls-type nParticle that uses a single radius value to determine its size.

The size attributes for instanced geometry are contained in a vector. A vector is an attribute with a three-dimensional value, as opposed to an integer or a float, which has only a single-dimensional value.

1. Select the particleDebris object, and in the Attribute Editor, under Add Dynamic Attributes, click the General button to create a new attribute.

2. Set the Long Name value to **debrisScale**.

3. Set Data Type to Vector and Attribute Type to Per Particle (Array). See Figure 14.42.

FIGURE 14.42
Create another attribute and name it debrisScale; this time set Data Type to Vector.

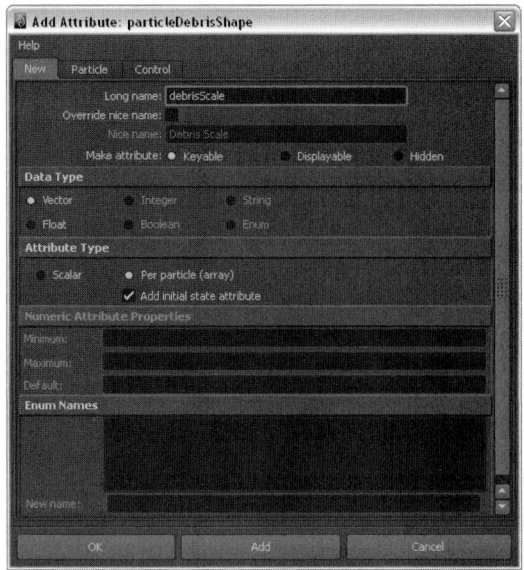

4. In the Per Particle (Array) Attributes section, right-click the field next to debrisScale, and choose to create a creation expression.

REFRESH THE ATTRIBUTE LIST

If the new attribute does not appear in the list, click the Load Attributes button at the bottom of the Attribute Editor to refresh the list.

In the Expression field of the Expression Editor, you'll see the debrisIndex expression (note that the name debrisIndex has been expanded; it now says `particleDebrisShape.debrisIndex=rand(0,6);`). Maya does this automatically when you create the expression.

5. Below the debrisIndex expression, type **debrisScale=<<mass,mass,mass>>;**. Click Edit to add this to the expression (see Figure 14.43).

The double brackets are the syntax used when specifying vector values. Using mass as the input value for each dimension of the vector ensures that the pieces of debris are uniformly scaled.

6. In the Instancer (Geometry Replacement) attributes of the particleDebris object, set the Scale menu to debrisScale (see Figure 14.44).

7. Rewind and play the animation.

FIGURE 14.43
Set the debrisScale attribute to be equivalent to the mass of each nParticle. Add the expression in the Expression Editor.

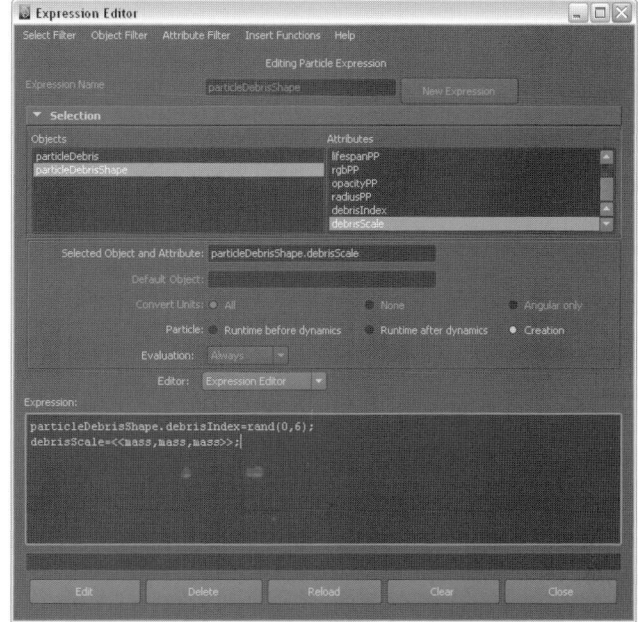

FIGURE 14.44
The size of the debris is determined by the mass of each nParticle. In some cases the mass is so small the instanced geometry can't be seen.

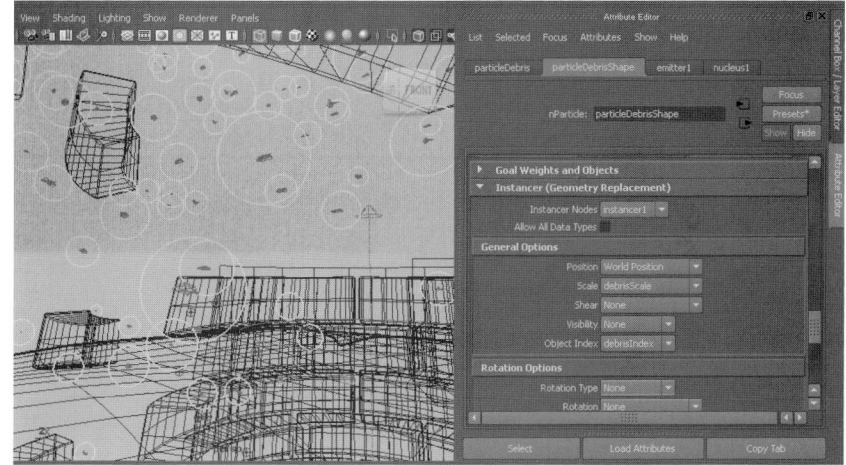

The pieces of debris are now sized based on the mass of the nParticles, but of course the mass of some of the particles is so small that the instanced particles are invisible. To fix this, you can edit the expression, as follows:

1. In the Per-Particle (Array) Attributes section, right-click debrisScale, and choose Creation Expression to open the Expression Editor.

2. In the Expression field, add the following text above the debris scale expression:

```
float $massScale = mass*3;
```

3. Now edit the original debrisScale expression, as shown in Figure 14.45, so it reads as follows:

```
debrisScale = <<$massScale, $massScale, $massScale>>;
```

By using the `float` command in the Expression Editor, you're creating a local variable that is available to be used only in the creation expressions used by the nParticle. This variable is local, meaning that, since it was created in the Creation expression box, it's available only for creation expressions. If you use this variable in a runtime expression, Maya gives you an error message. The variable is preceded by a dollar sign. The `$massScale` variable is assigned the mass multiplied by three.

FIGURE 14.45
Edit the expression so the size of each nParticle is equal to the mass multiplied by three.

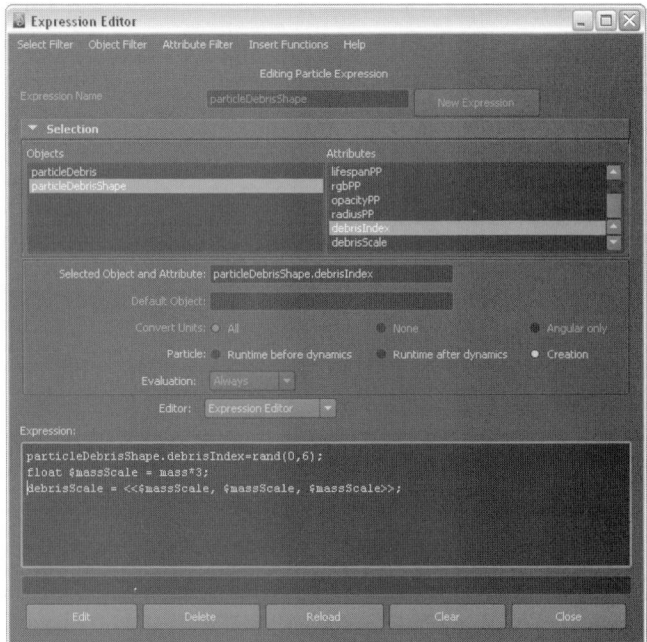

4. Click Edit to implement the changes to the expression.

5. Rewind and play the animation.

It's an improvement; some debris pieces are definitely much bigger, but some are still too small. You can fix this by adding a `clamp` function. Make sure you click the Edit button in the editor after typing the expression.

A clamp sets an upper and lower limit to the values generated by the expression. The syntax is `clamp(lower limit, upper limit, input);`.

6. Edit the expression for the `massScale` variable so it reads `float $massScale=clamp (1,5,mass*5);`. Make sure you click the Edit button in the editor after typing the expression (Figure 14.46).

7. Play the animation.

Now you have a reasonable range of sizes for the debris, and they are all based on the mass on the particles.

FIGURE 14.46
After you add the
clamp expression,
the range of size
for the debris is
more reasonable.

8. In the Attribute Editor for the particleDebris, scroll to the Shading section, and set Particle Render Type to Points so you can see the instanced geometry more easily.

9. Save the scene as **explodingTower_v06.ma**.

To see a version of the scene, open the explodingTower_v06.ma scene from the chapter14\ scenes folder on the DVD.

Controlling the Rotation of nParticles

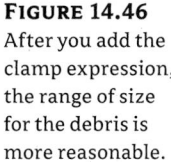
New!

Adding rotation to the flying instances is much easier in Maya 2011 and no longer requires complex expressions. The new Rotation Attributes are calculated per particle and can be used to control the rotation of geometry instanced to the nParticles. In addition, the Rotation Friction and Rotation Damp attributes can be used to fine-tune the quality of the rotation. In this section, you'll add rotation to the debris using these new features.

1. Continue with the scene from the previous section, or open the explodingTower_v06.ma scene from the chapter14\scenes folder on the DVD.

2. Select the particleDebris node in the Outliner, and open its Attribute Editor to the particleDebrisShape tab.

3. Expand the Rotation tab, and turn on Compute Rotation (Figure 14.47). This automatically adds a new attribute to the Per Particle Array Attributes list. However, you won't need to create any expressions in order to make the nParticle rotate.

4. Scroll down to the Instancer (Geometry Replacement) settings. In the Rotation Options, set the Rotation menu to rotationPP.

5. Create a playblast of the scene.

FIGURE 14.47
Turn on Compute Rotation in order to add per-particle rotation attributes to the nParticles.

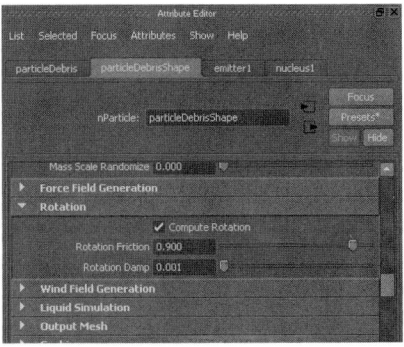

6. You may notice that some of the debris rotates a bit too quickly as it falls to Earth. To adjust this, scroll up to the Rotation section, and set Rotation Damp to **0.01**. Try making another playblast.

7. Save the scene as `explodingTower_v07.ma`.

Rotation Friction and Rotation Damp are per-particle attributes, which can be used in per-particle expressions to drive other attributes:

Rotation Friction This determines how much an nParticle will rotate based on its collision with other nDynamic objects and self-collisions (inter-particle collisions within the same nParticle shape). Setting Rotation Friction to 0 turns off rotation.

Rotation Damp This causes the rotation of nParticles to slow down after collisions with other nDynamic objects and self-collisions.

To see a version of the scene, open the `explodingTower_v07.ma` scene from the `chapter14\scenes` folder on the DVD.

Creating Smoke Trails

To complete the look of the explosion, you can use the cloud nParticle type to add a smoke trail to each of the pieces of debris. The cloud nParticle type uses a special shader to create the look of smoke in a software render.

Using the Cloud nParticle Style

It's possible to turn individual nParticles into an emitter for a second nParticle object. This works very well for creating smoke trails left by flying debris, and a number of other interesting effects.

1. Continue with the scene from the precious section, or open the `explodingTower_v07.ma` scene from the `chapter14\scenes` directory.

2. From the nParticle menu set, choose nParticles ➤ Create nParticles ➤ Cloud to set the nParticle style to Cloud.

3. In the Outliner, select the particleDebris object. Choose nParticles ➤ Create nParticles ➤ Emit From Object ➤ Options.

4. In the options, set Emitter Type to Omni and Rate to **40**. You can leave the other settings at their default.

5. Click Create to add the emitter.

6. In the Outliner, a new nParticle node has been added to the scene. Rename this node **smokeParticle**. If you expand the particleDebris object, you'll see that an emitter has been parented. This is the emitter for the smokeParticle (Figure 14.48).

Since there are a total of 1,200 particleDebris objects that will be emitted in the scene, each one of these will emit 40 cloud nParticles per second. This quickly adds up to a lot of nParticles. To avoid bogging the scene down, set a short life span on the smokeParticles.

7. Select the smokeParticle object, and open its Attribute Editor to the smokeParticleShape tab.

8. Open the Lifespan rollout panel, and enter the following settings (Figure 14.49):

Lifespan mode: Random range

Lifespan: **2**

Lifespan Random: **2**

This means each cloud particle lasts between one and three seconds. Lifespan attributes are covered in Chapter 13.

9. Set Radius in the Particle Size rollout panel to **1.3**.

10. Expand the Radius Scale attributes, and set Radius Scale Input to Age.

FIGURE 14.48
The emitter for the smokeParticle object is automatically parented to the debrisParticle.

FIGURE 14.49
Set the lifespan and particle size attributes for the smokeParticle.

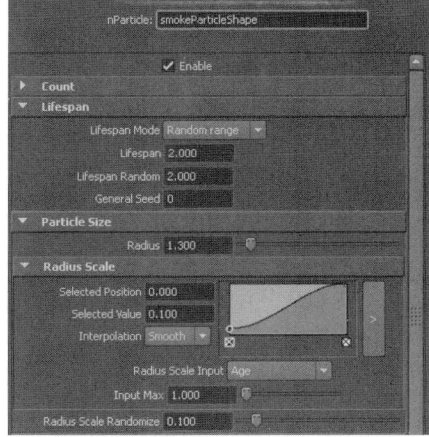

11. Add two control points to the Radius Scale ramp, and edit the position of the points so that the ramp starts at 0.1 and slopes up smoothly to the right.

12. Set Radius Scale Randomize to **0.1**.

DOUBLE-CHECK YOUR SELECTED NPARTICLE

Since both the debrisParticle and the smokeParticle are connected through the nucleus1 solver, it's very easy to accidentally edit the attributes for the wrong particle while working in the Attribute Editor. Make sure you double-check which tab is selected when working in the Attribute Editor!

---

13. In the Dynamic Properties section, set Drag to **0.1**, and make sure Ignore Solver Gravity is activated. This will ensure that the smoke particles do not fall to the ground.

14. Scroll down to the Emission Attributes section, and set Inherit Factor to **0.5**. This causes the smoke particle to inherit some of the motion of the particleDebris object, giving it a more believable motion as it flies out from each piece of debris.

15. Scroll down to the Opacity Scale attributes in the Shading rollout panel. Set Opacity Scale Input to Age.

16. Edit the Opacity Scale ramp so it starts at 0.7 on the left and slopes down to 0 on the right, as shown in Figure 14.50.

17. Expand the Color attributes. Set Color Input to Age.

18. Edit the Color ramp so it is bright yellow on the left side, fading quickly to light gray and then gradually to dark gray on the right of the ramp. This makes each smoke trail bright yellow on the end closest to the flying debris, fading to dark gray over time.

19. Expand the Incandescence section. Set Incandescence Input to Age.

20. Edit the ramp so there is a small sliver of bright yellow on the left side that quickly fades to black (see Figure 14.50).

21. Select the emitter2 node that is parented under the debris particle. Set a keyframe on the Rate attribute on frame 90. Move the timeline to frame 120, and set Rate to **0**; set another keyframe.

22. To create the effect of the smoke drifting upward, add some wind to the Nucleus solver. First select the particleDebris object, and activate the Ignore Solver Wind option in the Dynamic Properties rollout panel so that the debris is not affected by the wind.

23. Open the Nucleus solver, and set Wind Speed to **3**. Set Wind Direction to **0, 1, 0** so it pushes upward. Set Wind Noise to **0.5** to add some turbulence.

24. Save your scene.

25. Rewind the animation, and create a playblast to see the explosion in action (Figure 14.51). It should take anywhere from 5 to 10 minutes to create the playblast.

26. Save the scene as **explodingTower_v08.ma**.

To see a finished version of the scene, open explodingTower_v08.ma from the chapter14\ scenes folder on the DVD.

FIGURE 14.50
The shading settings for the smokeParticle

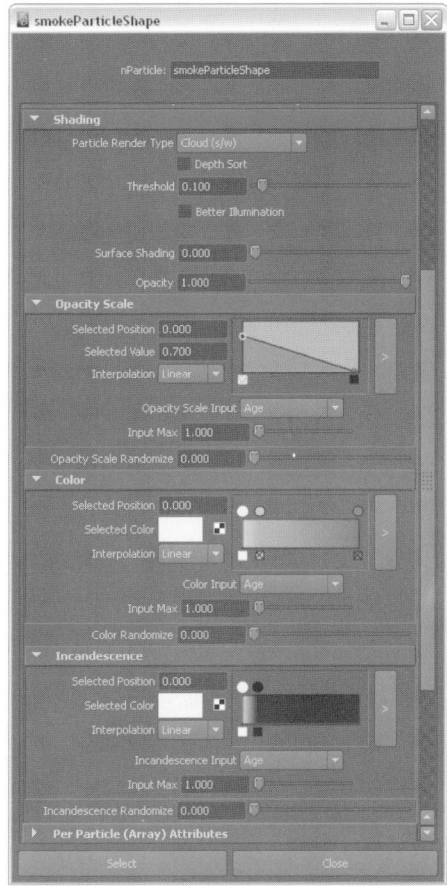

FIGURE 14.51
A playblast of the animation reveals a very dramatic explosion worthy of an episode of *Mythbusters*.

CACHING INSTANCED NPARTICLES

When creating an nCache for nParticles that have geometry instanced to them or any nParticle with custom attributes and expressions, be sure to set the Cacheable Attributes menu in the Caching roll-out panel of the nParticle's Attribute Editor to All. Otherwise, the cache will store only position and velocity data, and the motion of the nParticles will not look correct when you render the scene.

The Bottom Line

Use nCloth   nCloth can be used to make polygon geometry behave dynamically to simulate a wide variety of materials. Using the presets that come with Maya, you can design your own materials and create your own presets for use in your animations.

> **Master it**   Create the effect of a cube of gelatinous material rolling down the stairs.

Combine nCloth and nParticles   Because nCloth and nParticles use the same dynamic systems, they can be easily combined to create amazing simulations.

> **Master it**   Make a water balloon burst as it hits the ground.

Use Maya rigid body dynamics   Rigid body dynamics are not quite as powerful as nCloth objects, but they do calculate much faster and work better for simulations involving a large number of interacting pieces.

> **Master it**   Animate a series of dominoes falling over.

Instance geometry to nParticles   Modeled geometry can be instanced to nParticles to create a wide variety of effects.

> **Master it**   Create the effect of a swarm of insects attacking a beach ball.

Create nParticle expressions   nParticle expressions can be used to further extend the power of nParticles. Using expressions to automate instanced geometry simulations is just one of the ways in which expressions can be used.

> **Master it**   Improve the animation of the insects attacking the beach ball by adding different types of insects to the swarm. Randomize their size, and create expressions so that larger insects move more slowly.

Create smoke trails   Using the cloud nParticle type, smoke can be added to a simulation. nCloth objects and nParticles can be turned into emitters to emit the smoke.

> **Master it**   In the explosion scene from this chapter, make the nCloth bricks emit a smoke trail as they fly out from the tower.

Chapter 15

Fur, Hair, and Clothing

Maya offers a number of tools for adding fur, hair, and clothing to characters. Creative use of these tools adds believability and originality to your animated characters. In addition, many of these tools can be used to create engaging visual effects. This chapter takes you through a number of techniques that you can use to add fur, hair, and clothing to characters.

In this chapter, you will learn to:

◆ Add fur to characters

◆ Add dynamic motion to fur

◆ Create dynamic curves

◆ Add hair to characters

◆ Style hair

◆ Use hair constraints

◆ Paint nCloth properties

Adding Fur to Characters

In this section, you'll add Maya Fur to a model of a hound dog's head. Maya Fur can be used on NURBS, polygon, and subdivision surfaces. There are some limitations when using NURBS and subdivision surfaces. For instance, rendering fur on trimmed NURBS surfaces can add to render time, and many of the paintable fur attributes do not work when using subdivision surfaces. For this reason, it's recommended that you use polygon geometry whenever possible.

Maya Fur works best for short-haired characters or characteristics such as eyebrows and facial hair. Think about using fur for hair that would be 2 inches or shorter in the real world. If your character's hair is longer than that, then consider using Maya Hair or Paint Effects.

Preparing Polygons for Maya Fur

Polygon models need to have properly mapped UV coordinates that lie within a 0 to 1 range in texture space. You should make sure that there are no overlapping UVs. This can cause problems and may even crash Maya when rendering.

Try as best as you can to maintain consistency in texture space as you create UV coordinates. Seams between separate UV shells and between parts of the model's texture coordinates are easily seen in the distribution of fur across the surface, and they can be very difficult to eliminate. Figure 15.1 shows an example of a visible seam in the fur attached to the hound dog model. This seam appears because the end of the nose is a separate shell from the rest of the hound's head. In some cases, it may be impossible to eliminate all seams.

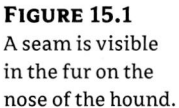

FIGURE 15.1
A seam is visible in the fur on the nose of the hound.

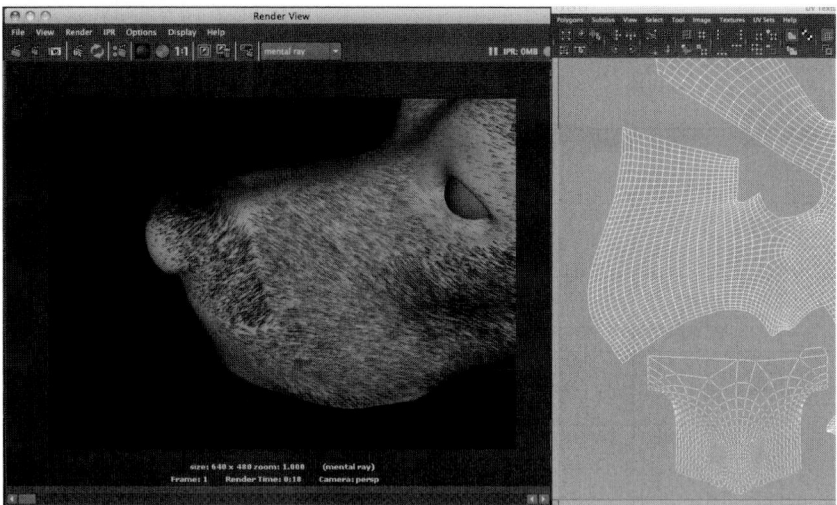

The best strategy is to place UV seams on parts of the surface that are less noticeable than others. Once you have an understanding of how fur works after completing this chapter, you should test a simple fur preset (such as the duckling preset) on your models as you map the UV texture coordinates. You'll see where the problem areas are before you spend a great amount of time perfecting the fur itself. Props, such as clothing, can also be used strategically to hide UV seams.

Chapter 11 has detailed information on how to create UV texture coordinates for polygon models.

USING THE EXAMPLE SCENES

Maya Fur relies heavily on file textures that are saved in the Fur subfolders of the current project. If you intend to use the example scenes in this chapter, you should copy the entire Chapter 15 project folder from the DVD to your local disk. This should ensure that the results you get when you test the example scenes are consistent with what is presented in the figures in this book.

In this example, the hound model has been created, and the UVs have been properly prepared.

1. Open the hound_v01.ma scene from the chapter15\scenes folder.

2. Select the houndHead model, and choose Window ➤ UV Texture Editor.

The UVs for the houndHead model are displayed in the UV Texture Editor (see Figure 15.2). If you are applying fur to a subdivision surface, you may want to convert the model to polygons first and prepare the UVs before applying the fur. You can convert the model to subdivision surfaces after the fur has been applied. Working with subdivision surfaces and polygons is covered in Chapter 4.

FIGURE 15.2
The UV texture coordinates have already been created for the houndHead model.

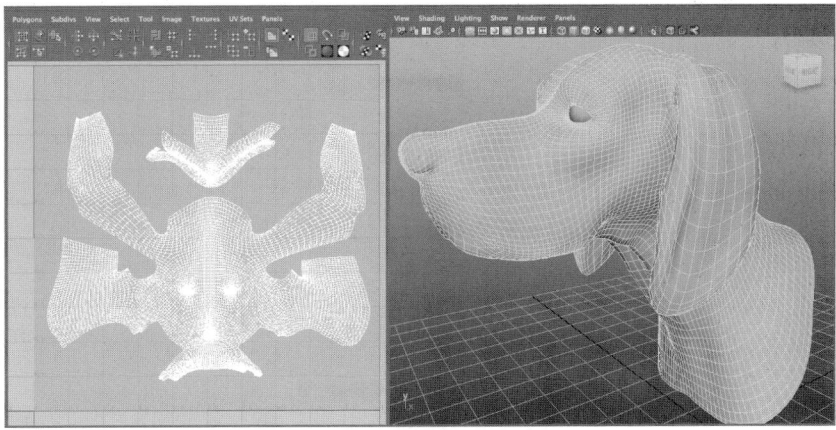

Creating a Fur Description

The fur description node contains all the settings for the fur, such as length, color, width, density, and so on. A single fur description node can be applied to more than one surface.

A number of preset fur descriptions are available on the Fur shelf or by clicking the Presets button in the Attribute Editor for the fur description node. You can use a preset as a starting point. In this exercise, you'll build the fur description from the default fur settings.

1. Select the houndHead model. Switch to the Rendering menu set, and choose Fur ➤ Attach Fur Description ➤ New.

   The houndHead surface is covered in long spikes. These spikes are a preview that approximates how the fur will look on the surface. This approximation is a visual aid you can use while editing the fur. If you do not see the spikes (Figure 15.3), the display of locators may have been disabled in the Viewport window. To fix this, choose Show ➤ Locators from the menu in the Viewport window.

FIGURE 15.3
The fur is displayed as long spikes on the surface. Locators must be visible in the perspective view in order to display the spikes.

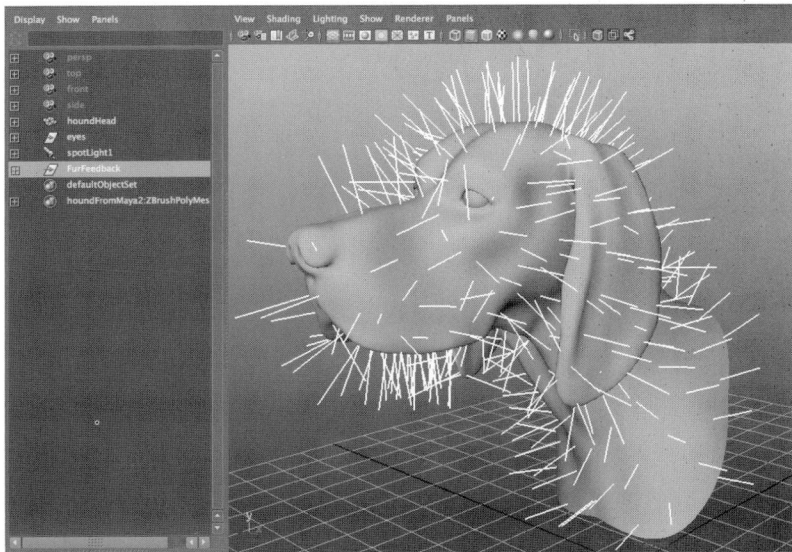

You can find the controls for the fur preview in the Attribute Editor for the houndHead_FurFeedbackShape node. This node is parented under the FurFeedback node in the Outliner.

2. In the Outliner, expand the FurFeedback group, and select the houndHead_FurFeedback node.

3. Open the Attribute Editor, and click the houndHead_FurFeedbackShape tab.

4. To increase the number of fur strands displayed in the viewport, set U Samples and V Samples to **128**.

   You can set these values higher for a more accurate display; however, higher settings will slow the performance of Maya on your computer. The U and V Samples affect only how the fur is displayed in Maya; they do not affect how it will look when rendered.

5. Switch to the FurDescription1 tab in the Attribute Editor. Here you'll find the settings that determine how the fur will look when rendered.

6. In the Fur Description field, rename FurDescription1 to **houndFur**.

7. Save the scene as **hound_v02.ma**.

To see a version of the scene to this point, open the hound_v02.ma scene from the chapter15\scenes folder on the DVD.

Editing the Fur Description: Baldness

There are several ways to design the look of fur applied to your model. You can adjust the slider settings in the fur description node to create an overall look for the fur, or you can apply texture maps to the fur settings. These texture maps can be procedural nodes (such as ramp, fractal, checker), or they can be file textures painted in other programs. You can also use the Artisan Brush tool to paint settings directly on the model. In this section, you'll use Artisan to determine where fur grows on the model.

Fur is applied uniformly across the surface of a model. To control exactly where the fur grows, you'll use the Baldness attribute. The Baldness value ranges between 1 and 0. The confusing aspect about the Baldness setting in particular is that a setting of 1 means fur covers the surface. A setting of 0 means the fur does not grow at all. This is confusing because intuitively more baldness (higher values) should mean less fur. In Maya the settings are reversed, so higher Baldness values mean more fur. Fortunately, this is the only setting that suffers from this counterintuitive behavior.

Settings between 0 and 1 determine the sparseness of the fur. Using a low Baldness setting, such as 0.1 or 0.2, might work well when creating whiskers for a man's face.

In this exercise, you'll apply Baldness values so that fur does not grow on the end of the nose, in the eye sockets, or on the inside of the mouth.

1. Open the hound_v02.ma scene from the chapter15\scenes directory.

2. In the Outliner, select the houndHead_FurFeedback node parented to the FurFeedback group.

3. In the Attribute Editor, select the houndFur tab.

4. Set the Base and Tip Color attributes to bright red. This makes it easier to see the fur as you paint attribute maps. If the fur does not turn red when you adjust the sliders, make sure Color Feedback Enabled is turned on in the houndHead_FurFeedbackShape node.

5. Switch to the houndFur tab. To make it easier to see what's going on, set the Length slider to **0.1**. This reduces the overall length of the fur. Later you'll fine-tune the length of the fur on the model using Artisan.

6. Move the Baldness slider back and forth between a value of 1 and 0. You'll see the fur become sparser when the value is lower.

FUR GLOBAL SCALE

You can also reduce the length of the fur by reducing the Global Scale value (as shown here). However, refrain from adjusting this slider when you first edit a new fur description because the slider should be used to keep all the fur settings consistent when the model itself is scaled. For example, if this model and its fur are imported into a scene that requires the model to be resized, you can adjust the Global Scale of the fur based on the scaling values applied to the model, and the look of the fur should remain consistent when rendered. If you adjust Global Scale before designing the fur, it may make it hard to adjust the settings properly if the model is scaled.

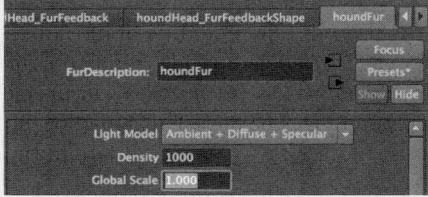

The slider works well to establish an overall value. For precise control, you'll paint Baldness values directly on the model.

7. Set the Baldness slider to 1 so that the fur covers the entire model evenly.

8. In the Outliner, select the houndHead object. Choose Fur ➤ Paint Fur Attributes Tool ➤ Options. The tool options open on the left side of the screen by default at the same time a small pop-up menu appears. If Maya stops for a moment, don't be alarmed; it is preparing the model for painting.

9. In the Paint Fur Attributes Tool Settings pop-up, make sure Fur Attribute is set to Baldness and Fur Description is set to houndFur.

10. Set Attribute Map Width and Height to **1024**.

11. In the options for the Artisan Brush, set Paint Operation to Replace and Value to **0**. Wherever you paint on the surface of the model, fur will be removed.

ATTRIBUTE MAP RESOLUTION

The Attribute Map Width and Height determine the resolution of the baldness map that will be created when you use the Paint Fur Attributes tool. In the case of the hound model, you'll need a higher resolution so that you can more precisely paint Baldness values around the tight areas of the eyes, nose, and lips. If the attribute you are painting does not require precision, you can use lower values for Height and Width.

---

12. In the Tool Options section, under the Display rollout panel, activate Color Feedback. This colors the model according to the values you paint on the fur. The colors act as a guide as you paint.

13. Zoom in on the nose of the model. Hold the cursor over the nose of the hound. Hold the **b** key, and drag left or right to interactively adjust the width of the brush.

14. Start painting in the nose; you'll see the spikes start to disappear as you paint. The area where you paint also turns black (see Figure 15.4).

    Sometimes you need to paint over a spike a couple times to get it to update. If you need more detail in the Fur Feedback, you can increase the U and V Samples values on the houndHead_FurFeedbackShape tab.

FIGURE 15.4
The surface of the hound turns black as you paint the Baldness value on the model. The fur spikes disappear in the black areas.

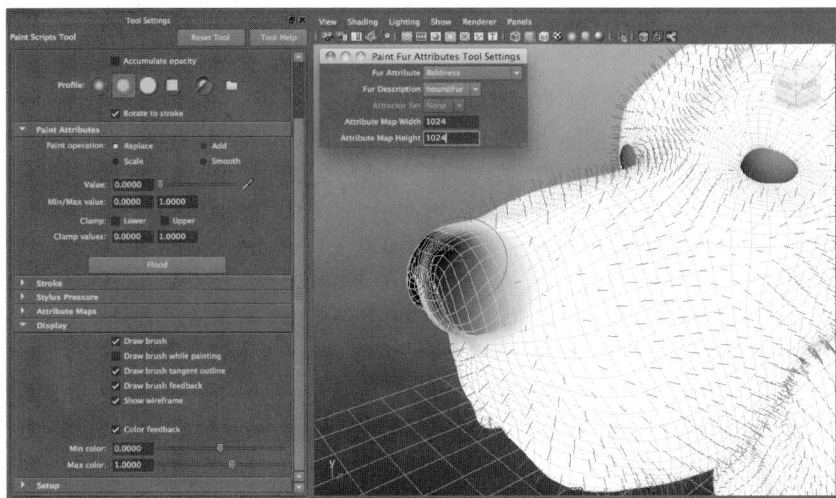

MAP FILE UPDATE

As you paint, Maya creates a temporary map file for the Baldness attributes. Occasionally Maya pauses as it updates the file. Ideally this should not happen too often. If Maya appears to freeze while working, don't be alarmed. Give it a few moments to think while it's updating the fur file.

If you get no reaction from the Paint Fur Attributes tool at all, try unselecting and reselecting the houndHead surface in the Outliner. The Paint Fur Attributes tool works only when the surface object is currently selected, so it won't work if just the fur nodes are selected.

---

15. Paint on the nose and the inside folds of the nose until all the fur spikes are gone. You'll edit the Baldness values more later, so don't stress out if it's not absolutely perfect.

16. When you have finished the nose, use the Show menu in the perspective view to turn off the visibility for NURBS surfaces. The eyes disappear. Paint inside the eye sockets to remove the fur from inside of the eye (see Figure 15.5).

17. To remove fur from the lips, you can move the perspective view inside the model and paint on the backside of the surface (Figure 15.6).

FIGURE 15.5
Use the Paint Fur Attributes tool to remove fur from inside the eye sockets.

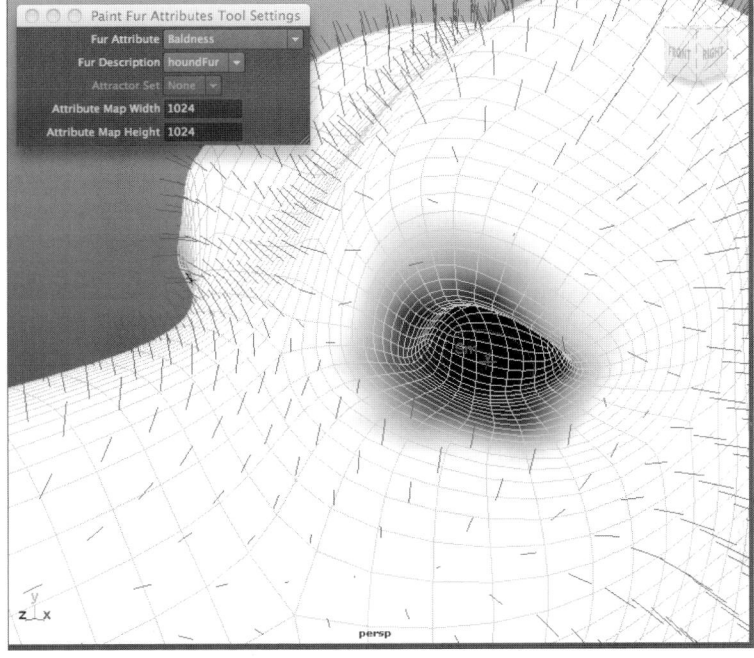

FIGURE 15.6
Remove fur from the lips by painting from the inside of the model.

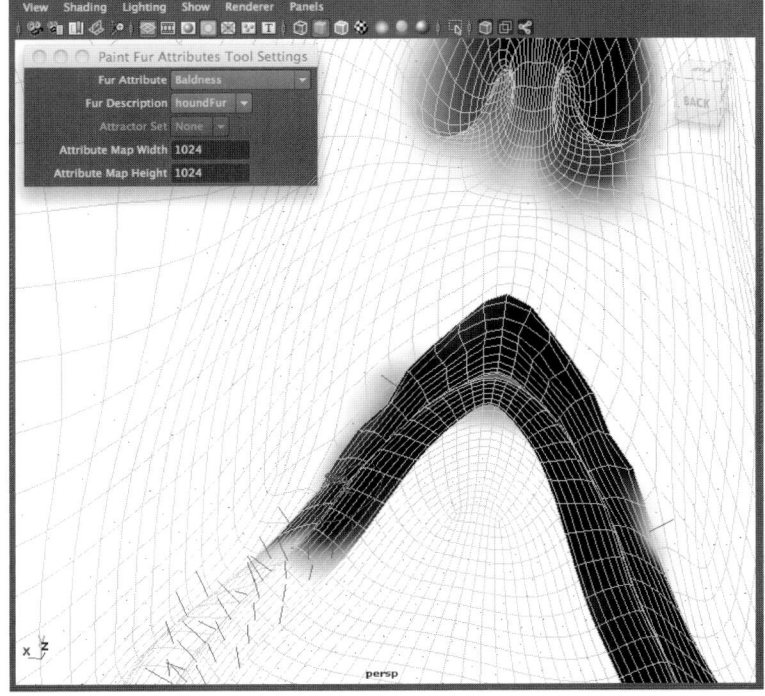

18. In the Attribute Editor for the houndFur node, scroll down and expand the Details section.

19. Find the Baldness rollout panel, and expand the Maps section. This lists the maps painted for the houndHeadShape. Currently the baldness map is listed as UNNAMED. This refers to the map you have been painting on the hound. It exists as a temporary file until you save the scene (see Figure 15.7).

20. Save the scene as **hound_v03.ma**.

When you save the scene, the maps that you have painted for the fur attributes are saved to disk. You can find them in the current project's fur\furAttrMap directory. The maps are saved in the Maya .iff format (see Figure 15.8).

FIGURE 15.7
An unnamed map is listed in the Maps section for the Baldness attribute.

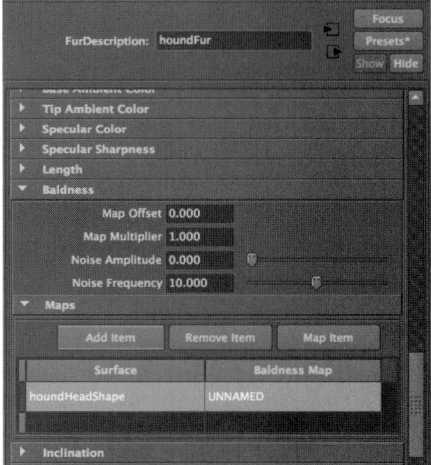

FIGURE 15.8
When you save the scene, the baldness map is written to disk.

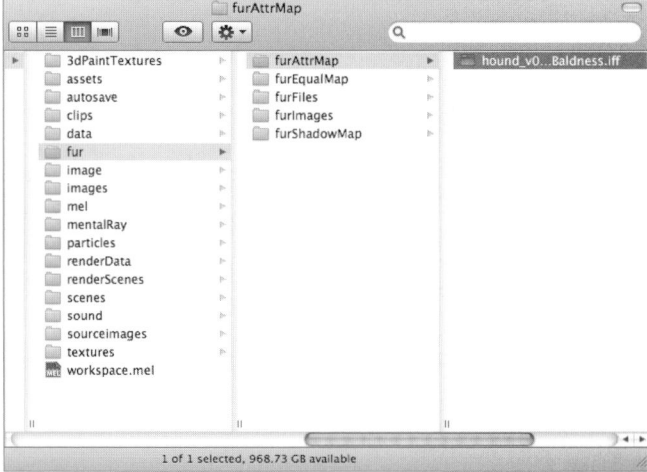

If you reopen the scene, the UNNAMED label is replaced in the Maps section of the Attribute Editor for the houndFur node with the path to the baldness map that has been saved to disk (Figure 15.9).

FIGURE 15.9
When you reopen the scene, the UNNAMED label is replaced with the path to the baldness map that has been written to disk.

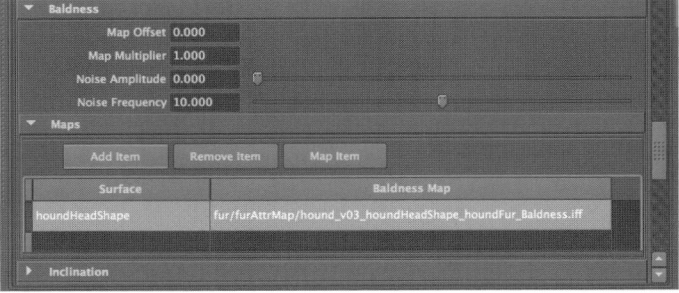

EDITING MAP FILES

Maps listed in the Details section of the fur node are always image files (as opposed to procedural textures such as ramp, fractal, or checker). You can edit these images in other programs such as Photoshop.

To edit a map in Photoshop, follow these steps:

1. Open FCheck. Choose File ➤ View Image, browse to the fur\furAttrMap folder in the current project, and open the image.

2. Use FCheck to save the image in a format Photoshop can read; a TIFF image should work fine. From the File menu in FCheck, choose Save Image. Save the image as **houndBaldnessMap .tif**, as shown here.

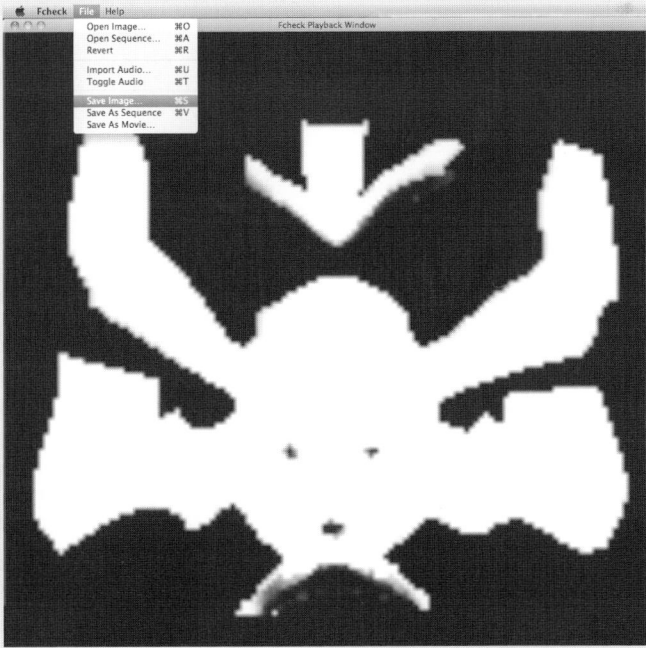

(CONTINUES)

EDITING MAP FILES *(CONTINUED)*

3. Open the houndBaldness.tif map in Photoshop, and edit the image with the standard Photoshop paint tools. Make sure you paint only grayscale values on the map. Lighter colors mean more fur; darker colors mean less fur.

4. When you have finished editing the file, save the image with no compression.

5. In Maya, open the Attribute Editor for the houndFur node.

6. In the Details section under Baldness, expand the Maps section.

7. Select the label under the Surface heading, click the Map Item button, and use the dialog box to select the image edited in Photoshop.

You can activate the Paint Fur Attributes tool to continue editing the map in Maya, as shown here. You'll see the changes made to the map appear on the model if Color Feedback is enabled in the Artisan options. Remember that Maya may take a few moments to update the display on the model.

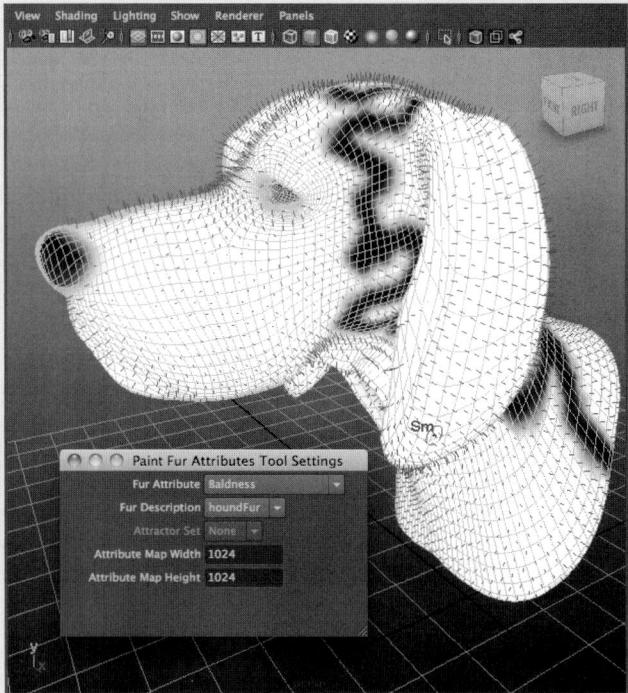

Other programs that have advanced 3D texturing tools, such as BodyPaint, ZBrush, or Mudbox, can be used to paint and edit maps for fur attributes. Save the image (shown here) as a TIFF format file, and apply it to the model using the instructions in step 5. Some programs such as ZBrush invert the vertical dimensions of the texture map. You may need to flip the vertical scaling of texture maps painted in ZBrush before applying them to a fur attribute in Maya.

I prefer doing much of my texture map painting in Pixologic's ZBrush because of its intuitive poly-gon painting workflow. I like to use ZBrush to carefully paint the baldness and other fur attribute maps, especially when doing something such as creating whiskers for a character's face. You can just as easily use Mudbox to paint these maps as well.

Editing the Fur Description: Direction

You can use the Artisan Brush interface to comb the fur by painting the Direction attribute.

1. Continue with the scene from the previous section, or open the hound_v03.ma scene from the chapter15\scenes directory on the DVD.

   You'll notice that there is no Direction or Comb attribute listed in the attributes for the houndFur node. Painting the Direction attribute is the same as painting the Polar attribute.

2. In the houndFur node's Attribute Editor, set Inclination to **1**, and move the Polar slider back and forth. The Polar slider determines the direction in which the fur strands face, but you'll notice that the direction is not uniform across the surface.

   Inclination Sets the angle at which the hair stands from the surface. A value of 0 is per-pendicular to the surface; a value of 1 causes the fur to lie flat against the surface. If the value is 0, then the fur strand sticks straight up, so changing its direction has no visible effect.

   Roll Rotates the fur around its root. A value of 0 is -90 degrees; a value of 1 is 90 degrees.

   Base Curl and Tip Curl Determine the amount of curling applied to the base and tip of the hair. A value of 0.5 produces straight hair; a value of 0 or 1 curls the hair from one side or the other.

The change in direction created by the Polar attribute is based on the direction of the UV texture coordinates. This means that a value applied to fur on one part of the model has a different result than a value applied on another part of the model. To comb the hair correctly, you use the Direction attribute in the Paint Fur Attributes tool to apply a Polar value based on the direction that you drag across the surface. So when you choose to paint the Direction attribute in the Paint Fur Tool options, you're really painting values for the Polar attribute but in a way that is a bit more intuitive.

When painting the direction, set Inclination to a value other than 0, and the Roll value must be something other than 0.5. The Base Curl and Tip Curl values must be something other than 0.5 as well. If these values are not set properly, painting the Direction has no effect. In addition, Color Feedback has no bearing on the direction of the fur, so you can turn this option off in the options for the Artisan tool.

3. Open the Attribute Editor for the houndFur node, and use the following settings:

   Inclination: **0.8**

   Roll: **0.2**

   Base Curl: **0.7**

   Tip Curl: **0.3**

4. Select the houndHead surface. Choose Fur ➤ Paint Fur Attributes Tool ➤ Options. Wait a few moments for Maya to update.

5. In the Options box for the Artisan tool, scroll to the bottom. In the Display options, turn off Color Feedback.

6. In the pop-up options for the Paint Fur Attributes Tool settings, set Fur Attribute to Direction. Make sure Fur Description is set to houndFur and Attribute Map Width and Height are set to **1024**. The Paint Operation or Value settings in the Artisan options do not affect how the fur is combed.

7. Drag across the surface to push the fur in the general direction you want it to go. Use Figure 15.10 for reference. Figure 15.11 shows how the paint stroke influences the direction of the fur on the model.

   Paint lightly and slowly using repeated strokes to make the fur point in the desired direction. Combing the fur requires some patience and practice. It's helpful to increase the U and V samples on the FurFeedback node so that you can see more fur as you are painting. It can be difficult to maintain a consistent direction across UV seams. The fewer seams you have in your UV texture coordinates, the easier it will be to paint the direction of the fur.

   The Direction attribute responds to the direction in which you move the cursor over the surface.

8. Save the scene as **hound_v04.ma**.

To see a version of the scene to this point, open the hound_v04.ma scene from the chapter15\ scenes directory.

FIGURE 15.10
Observe the direction of the fur in this photo of an American foxhound.

FIGURE 15.11
Paint the direction of the fur on the surface of the hound. Increase the U and V Samples in the fur feedback node to 256 to make it easier to see details in the fur direction.

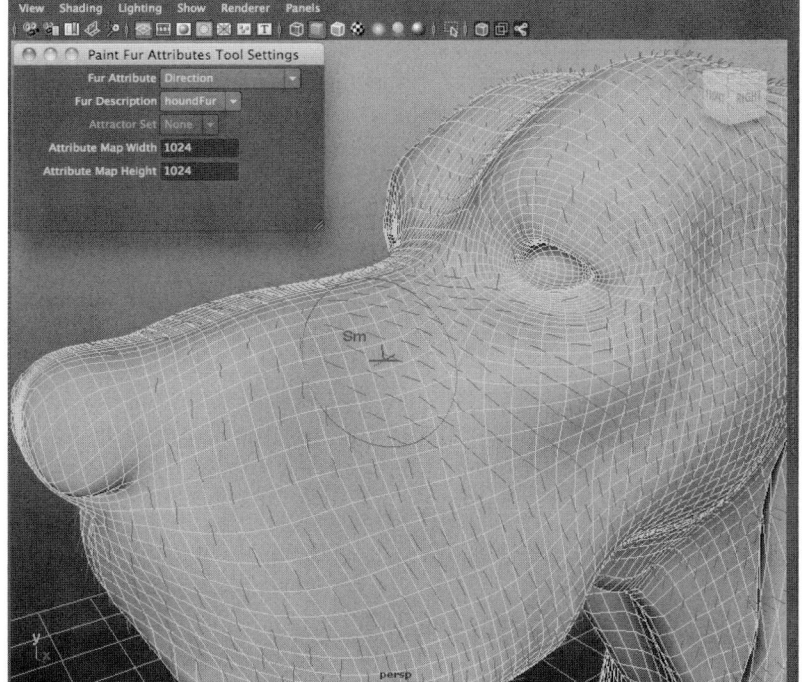

PAINTING ACROSS UV TEXTURE BORDERS

As you paint across UV borders on the model, you'll see the hair suddenly flip around. Since fur relies on UV texture coordinates to determine how the Polar attribute affects direction, as you move from one part of the texture space to another, the polarity of the fur can suddenly change (a good example of this occurs on the back of the hound's head). This may drive you crazy. To help deal with these problems, select the model, and choose Display ➤ Polygons ➤ Texture Border Edges. This makes the border edges of the UV coordinates visible as bold lines on the surface of the model. You can also reduce the size of the brush so that you can more easily paint specific areas along the border. With some patience and work, you'll be able to make the direction of the fur consistent across the UV texture border.

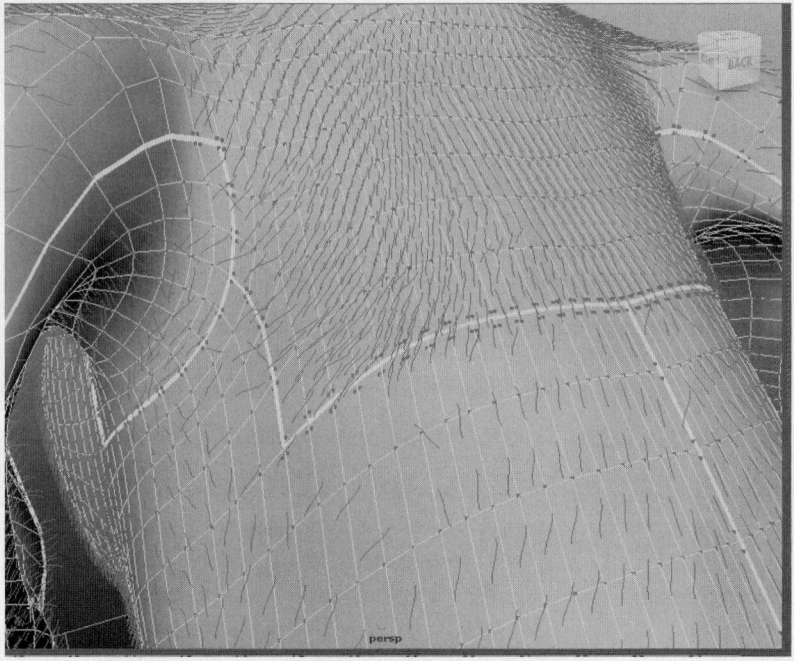

Editing the Fur Description: Length

You can edit the Length attribute using the Paint Attributes tool as well. When editing lengths, you need to pay attention to the values used in the options for the Artisan Brush. For the hound, the fur is shorter near the end of the nose, is medium length on the face, and is long on the back of the head and neck.

1. Continue with the scene from the previous section, or open the hound_v04.ma scene from the chapter15\scenes directory.

2. In the houndHead_furFeedbackShape tab, set U and V Samples to **128**.

3. Select the houndHead object, and choose Fur ➤ Paint Fur Attributes Tool.

4. In the pop-up menu for the Paint Fur Attributes Tool settings, set Fur Attribute to Length. Make sure Fur Description is set to houndFur and Attribute Map Width and Height are set to **1024**.

5. In the options for the Artisan Brush, set Paint Operation to Replace and Value to **0.5**.

6. Paint around the area of the neck. You'll see the fur become longer as you paint (Figure 15.12).

FIGURE 15.12
Edit the length of the hair by painting on areas of the houndHead surface.

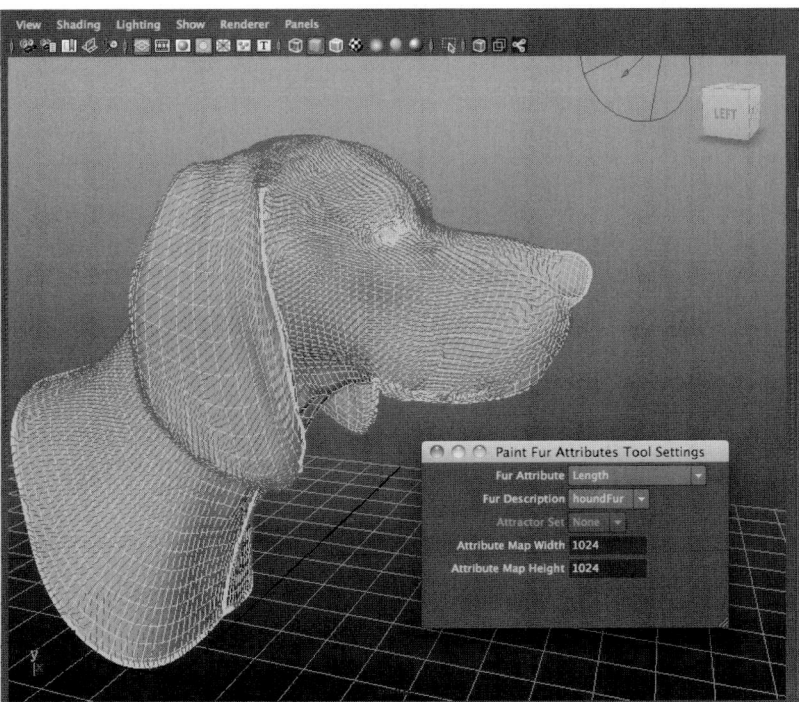

7. Set Value to **0.25**, and paint on the ears, under the ears, the top of the head, and the upper part of the throat.

8. Set Value to **0.1**, and paint the area near the nose and the front of the snout near the lips.

9. To even out the transition between the fur lengths, set Paint Operation to Smooth, and paint the areas on the border between the different lengths of fur.

10. Save the scene as **hound_v05.ma**.

To see a version of the scene to this point, open the hound_v05.ma scene from the chapter15\ scenes directory.

After painting fur lengths you may decide to touch up the Direction attribute of the fur as well. You can change the paint operation mode (from Length to Direction, for example) in the Paint Fur Attributes Tool Settings pop-up whenever you need to, but remember that Maya may pause for a few moments to update the maps when you change attributes.

BAKING TEXTURES INTO MAPS

You can use a procedural texture node (such as a ramp, fractal, or checker) as a starting place for a fur attribute map, as shown here. This works well when you are painting fur applied to a NURBS surface, since the UV texture coordinates are based on the parameterization of the surface itself. The following steps demonstrate how to do this.

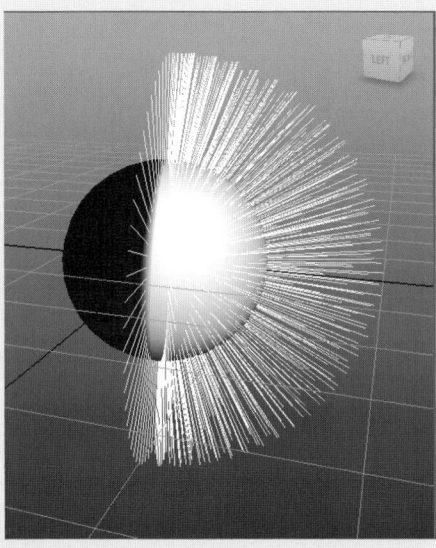

1. Create a new scene in Maya.

2. Create a NURBS sphere.

3. Select the sphere, and choose Fur Attach ➤ Fur Description ➤ New.

4. Open the Attribute Editor for the FurDescription1 node.

5. Right-click the field next to Baldness, and choose Create New Texture.

6. From the Create Texture Node window, choose the ramp texture. The fur on the sphere disappears.

7. Open the Attribute Editor for the ramp texture. Change the colors of the ramp so that the top is black and the bottom is white. Delete the color marker in the center. The fur display returns.

    If you move the markers on the ramp up and down, you'll notice that the fur display does not change. In order to use the ramp values to affect the Baldness setting, you need to bake the ramp.

8. Move the black marker halfway down the ramp, and set Interpolation to None.

9. In the Attribute Editor for the FurDescription node, set Bake Attribute to Baldness, and leave Map Width and Height set to 256. Click the Bake button.

    The fur becomes sparse on part of the sphere. This sparse area corresponds to the black part of the ramp. You can select the ramp texture in the Hypershade and connect it to the Color channel of the sphere's shader if you'd like to see a visual representation of the placement of the ramp on the sphere.

10. Move the Black color marker down. The fur on the sphere will not update until you bake the texture again.

11. In the Attribute Editor for Fur Description, click the Bake button. The fur on the sphere updates.

To see this example, open the rampBaldness.ma scene from the chapter15\scenes directory on the DVD.

A good use for this technique would be for applying fur as grass to a NURBS plane. You can use a fractal texture to create procedural variation in baldness or length to make the grass appear patchy.

Test Render Fur

Now that you have the basic fur description created for the houndHead, you may want to see what it looks like when rendered. You can render the scene using either mental ray or Maya Software. The results should be fairly similar. In this example, you'll use mental ray.

1. Continue using the scene from the previous section, or open the hound_v05.ma scene from the chapter15\scenes folder.

2. Open the Render Settings window, and set the Render Using menu to mental ray.

3. On the Quality tab, set Quality Presets to Production: Rapid Fur (see Figure 15.13). This preset uses the Rasterizer as the primary renderer instead of raytracing. For more information on rendering with mental ray, consult Chapter 12.

FIGURE 15.13
Choose the Rapid Fur preset on the Quality tab of the Render Settings window.

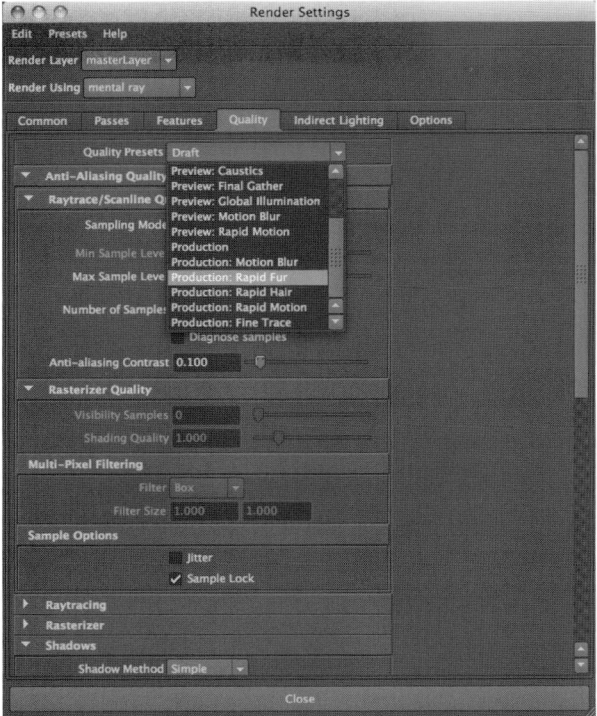

4. Open the Render View window, and create a test render using the perspective camera.

You'll notice immediately that the fur does not look very realistic (see the upper-left image in Figure 15.14). It is very sparse and bright red. You need to increase the Density setting of the fur so that enough hair covers the surface of the model.

FIGURE 15.14
Create test renders of the fur as you adjust the settings.

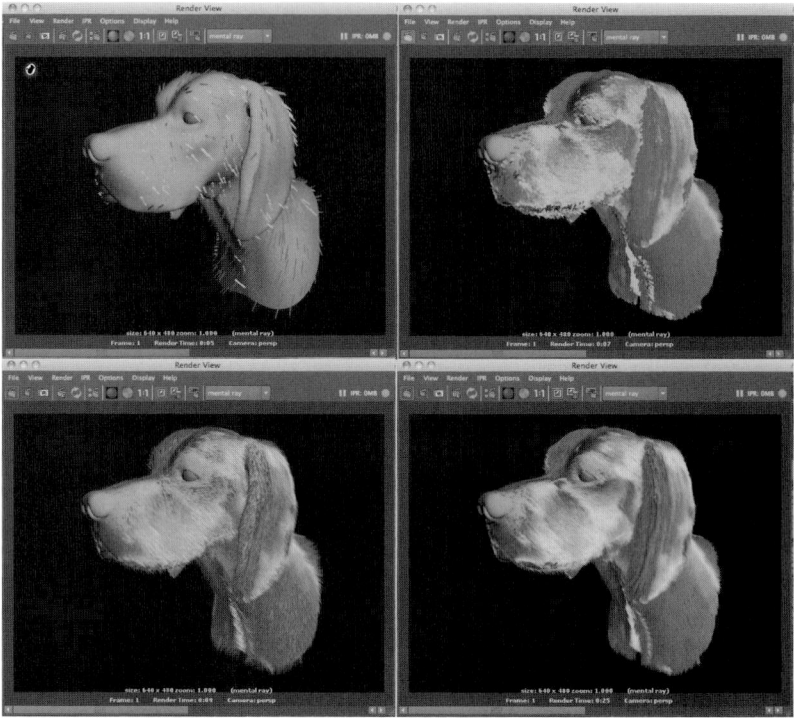

5. Set Density in the houndFur tab to **100,000**, and create another test render (see the upper-right image in Figure 15.14).

The fur is much denser without adding too much to the render time. To improve the look of the fur, you can edit the base and tip widths as well as the basic color.

6. In the houndFur tab in the Attribute Editor, click the color swatch next to Base Color, and use the Color Chooser to set the color to a dark brown.

7. Set Tip Color to a light brown.

8. Make sure Base Opacity is set to **1**, and use the following settings:

Tip Opacity: **0.1**

Base Width: **0.01**

Tip Width: **0.005**

9. Create another test render (see the lower-left image in Figure 15.14).

10. Raise Density to **500,000**, and create another test render (see the lower-right image in Figure 5.14).

11. Save the scene as **hound_v06.ma**.

To see a version of the scene, open the hound_v06.ma scene from the chapter15\scenes directory.

The fur should cover the model completely; however, you will notice that some attributes, such as the baldness map and the direction, may require further editing.

Applying a Color Map

Adding a texture map to the color greatly helps the realism of the fur. You can increase the efficiency of the render by applying the same file texture to the fur color and the shader as applied to the model. This technique should work as long as the model does not get extremely close to the camera.

A texture map that has been carefully painted in Photoshop or in a 3D texturing program works better than a map created by painting color on the fur. In this case, ZBrush was used to create the color texture map for the hound model.

1. Continue with the scene from the previous section, or open the hound_v06.ma scene from the chapter15\scenes directory on the DVD.

2. Open the Hypershade, select the houndShader material, and open its Attribute Editor.

3. Click the checkered button next to the Color channel to open the Create Texture Node window.

4. Click the File button to create a file texture node.

5. In the Attribute Editor for the file node, click the folder icon next to File Name.

6. Use the browser to select the houndBaseColor file texture from the chapter15\ sourceimages directory on the DVD.

7. Press the **6** key to switch to textured view so you can see how the color is placed on the model.

8. Keep the Hypershade window open. In the Outliner, expand the FurFeedback group, and select the houndHead_FurFeedback node.

9. In the Attribute Editor, select the houndFur tab.

10. In the Hypershade, switch to the Textures tab. MMB-drag the file1 texture onto the Base Color swatch in the Attribute Editor for houndFur (see Figure 15.15).

11. In the Hypershade, create a second file texture node (Create 2D Texture ➢ File).

12. In the Attribute Editor for file2, load the houndTipColor texture. This is a lighter, less-saturated version of the base color.

13. Attach this file to the Tip Color channel in the houndFur node.

FIGURE 15.15
Drag the file1 node from the Textures tab of the Hypershade onto the Base Color channel of the houndFur node.

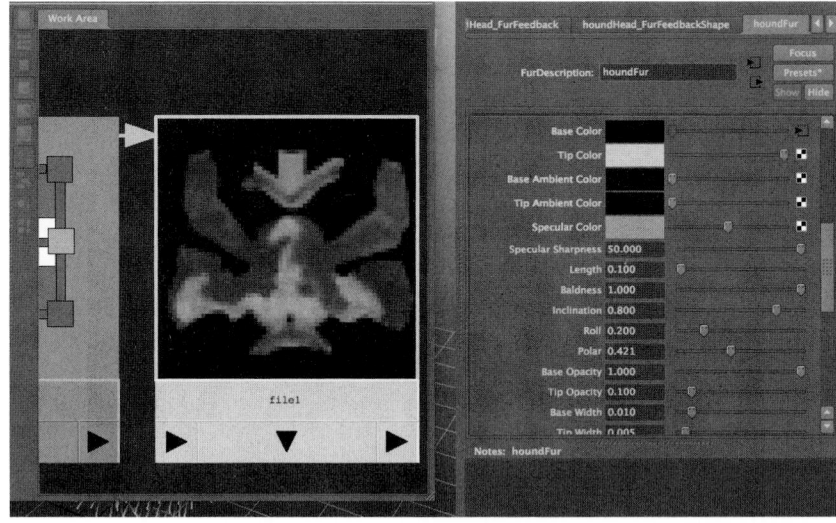

14. Lower Specular Color to a dark gray, and set Specular Sharpness to **80**. This makes the specular highlight on the fur smaller and less reflective.

15. Set the Density value of the fur to **250,000** in the houndFur tab, and create a test render (see the left image in Figure 15.16).

16. To increase the realism of the fur, turn on shadows for the scene lights:

    A. Select the spotlight1 object, and open its Attribute Editor.

    B. Under Shadows, turn on Use Depth Map Shadows.

    C. Set Resolution to **1024**, and turn off Use Auto Focus.

    D. Create another test render (see the right image in Figure 15.16).

17. Save the scene as **hound_v07.ma**.

To see a version of the scene, open the hound_v07.ma scene from the chapter15\scenes directory.

FIGURE 15.16
Add a color map to the fur description (left image), and render the scene shadows (right image).

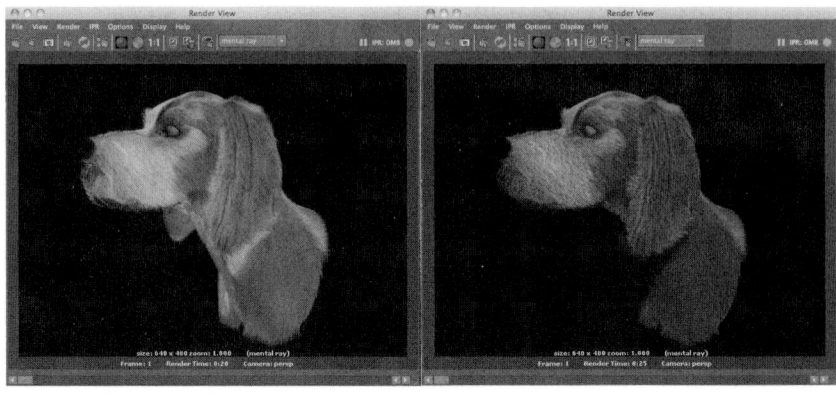

Applying Map Offsets and Multipliers

In the Details section of the houndFur node, you'll notice each attribute has Map Offset, Map Multiplier, Noise Amplitude, and Noise Frequency settings. These sliders can apply an additional adjustment to the fur map attributes.

The Map Offset and Multiplier attributes are used to change the range of values for any of the attributes. Most of the attributes are limited to a range between 0 and 1, which corresponds to the grayscale values painted on the surface with the Paint Fur Attributes brush. If you would like to change the range so that it can go beyond 1, you can use Map Offset or Map Multiplier.

Offset adds a number to the overall range. If you want to offset the range for an attribute so that instead of a range of 0 to 1 the range becomes 2 to 3, set Offset to **2**.

If you want to expand or diminish the range of values, use Multiplier. For example, if you want the range of a value to be between 0 and 10 instead of 0 to 1, set Multiplier to **10**.

The Noise Amplitude and Frequency sliders add randomness to the map values.

1. Continue with the scene from the previous section, or open the hound_v07.ma scene from the chapter15\scenes directory.

    The fur for the hound is a little too long to be appropriate for a typical foxhound. Rather than repaint the Length values, you can simply adjust Multiplier for the Length attribute.

2. Open the Attribute Editor for the houndFur node, and expand the Details ➢ Length rollout panel.

3. Set Map Multiplier to **0.5**.

4. Expand the Tip Ambient Color attribute, and set Noise Amplitude to **0.5** and Noise Frequency to **25**. This adds variation to the brightness of the fur tips.

5. Make sure the texture maps are properly connected in the houndFur tab and on the shader.

6. Create a test render from the perspective camera (Figure 15.17).

7. Save the scene as **hound_v08.ma**.

To see a version of the scene, open the hound_v08.ma scene from the chapter15\scenes directory.

FIGURE 15.17
Shorten the overall length of the hair by reducing the Multiplier value for the Length attribute. Add variation to the tip color by adding noise to the Tip Ambient Color attribute.

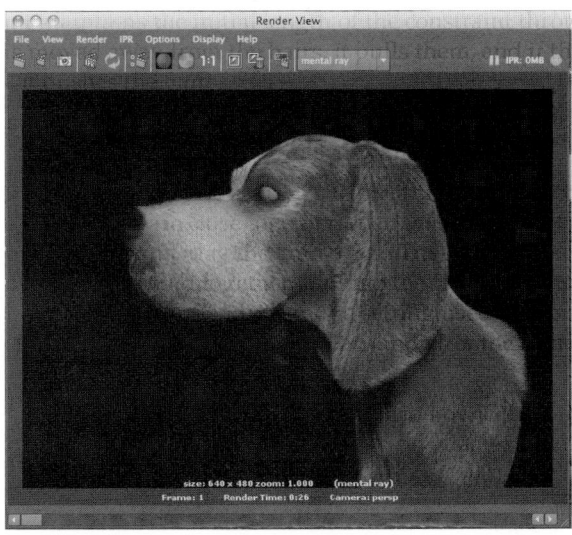

Enhancing the Realism of Fur

The basic fur description for the hound has been created, but to make it look realistic, a fair amount of editing still needs to be done. There are many additional attributes you can use to help accomplish this. This section describes how these attributes work. As with the Baldness, Length, Direction, and Color attributes, you can use a single value to determine the overall setting for each attribute, paint values for the attribute on selected areas, or use a texture map to determine the strength of the selected values.

Inclination, Roll, and Polar are attributes that determine the direction the fur is pointing along the surface of the model. As noted, Inclination determines whether the hair points straight up from the surface (at values closer to 0) or lies along the surface (at values closer to 1). The Roll setting rotates each hair around the base, and the Polar attribute determines the direction the fur points along the surface. Roll and Polar can be used together to fine-tune the direction of the hair. If you have painted a map for the Direction attribute using the Paint Fur Attributes tool, changing the Polar setting has no effect.

After painting a map for the Direction attribute using the Paint Fur Attributes tool, you may want to paint values for the Inclination and Roll attributes. This can help define more exactly the direction in which the fur points along the surface. You may find yourself switching back and forth among Direction, Inclination, and Roll as you edit the fur on the surface. If you need precise control over the styling of the fur, be prepared to spend some time working with these attributes.

Base Opacity and Tip Opacity are self-explanatory attributes. The base of the fur is the part of the fur strands closest to the surface; the tip is the part of the fur farthest from the surface. Opacity is applied as a gradient across the length of the fur. To create the look of soft, fine fur, set Base Opacity to **1** and Tip Opacity to a very low setting or even **0**. You can experiment with these values to create special effects; try a low Base Opacity and a high Tip Opacity.

Base Width and Tip Width establish the shape of the fur strands. A small Tip Width coupled with a large Base Width produces a pointy shape for the fur. A very low Tip Width helps create the look of soft, fine fur.

The Base Curl and Tip Curl attributes add curl to the fur strands at the base or tip. A value of 0.5 produces no curling. A value of 1 or 0 produces curling in one direction or the other.

The Scraggle, Scraggle Frequency, and Scraggle Correlation attributes add random kinks to the hair to create a messy appearance. The Scraggle setting determines the strength of the scraggle. Scraggle Frequency determines how many kinks appear in each strand of fur. Scraggle Correlation determines how the Scraggle value of one strand affects another. A setting of 0 for Scraggle Correlation creates random kinks throughout the fur strands, and a Scraggle Correlation of 1 means all the fur strands kink the same way, creating a wavy appearance for the fur.

The Clumping, Clumping Frequency, and Clump Shape settings cause the fur strands to attract each other into bunches on the surface. This is useful for making a surface appear wet or matted. The Clumping setting sets the strength of the clumping, and Clumping Frequency determines the number of clumps created across the surface. Clumping Frequency ranges between 0 and 100; higher values take longer to render. Clump Shape determines whether the clumps themselves are convex or concave. Settings closer to -10 produce concave clump shapes, while settings closer to 10 produce convex clumps (Figure 15.18).

FIGURE 15.18
Clumping is demonstrated on two planes. The plane on the left has a Clump Shape value of -10; the plane on the right has a Clump Shape value of 10.

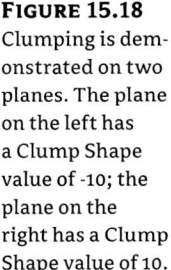

FIGURE 15.18
Clumping is demonstrated on two planes. The plane on the left has a Clump Shape value of -10; the plane on the right has a Clump Shape value of 10.

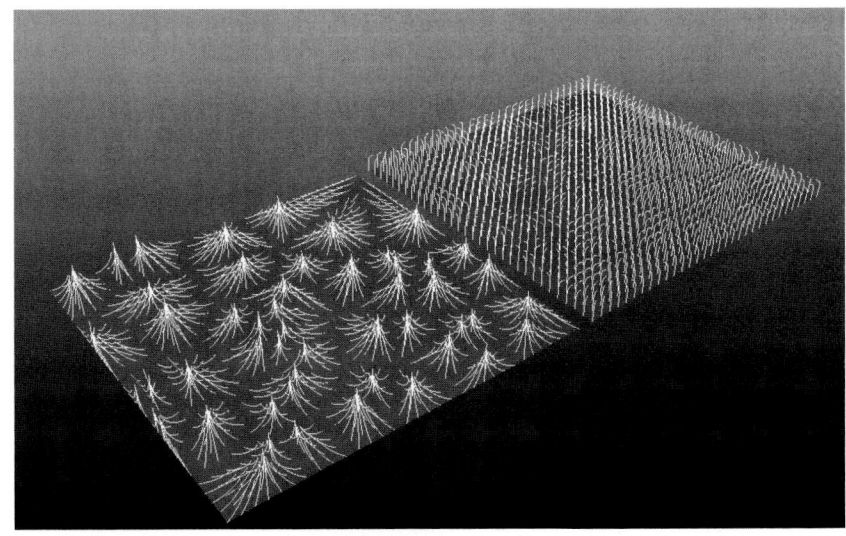

Adding Dynamic Motion to Fur

Creating dynamic motion for fur is actually quite easy. A fur description node uses dynamic hair curves to control the movement of the fur.

Attaching a Fur Description to Hair Curves

In this example, you'll add a hair system to a simple NURBS sphere that already has fur applied. The hair curves will then be used to add dynamic motion to the fur.

1. Open the furBall_v01.ma scene from the chapter15\scenes directory on the DVD.

    The Baldness attribute of the fur has been created using a ramp texture that has been baked into the fur description.

2. Right-click the sphere, and choose Surface Point.

3. Hold the Shift key, and select 10 or 12 surface points at the top of the sphere (see Figure 15.19).

4. Switch to the Dynamics menu set, and choose Hair ➤ Create Hair ➤ Options.

5. In the Create Hair Options box, set Output to NURBS Curves, and choose At Selected Points Faces. Leave the other settings at their default values.

ADDING HAIRS TO POLYGONS

If fur is applied to a polygon surface, select the faces of the surface before adding the hair curves. If you want to add hair curves all over the surface rather than at specific points/faces, choose the Grid option on the Create Hair Option box.

FIGURE 15.19
Select surface
points at the top
of the sphere.

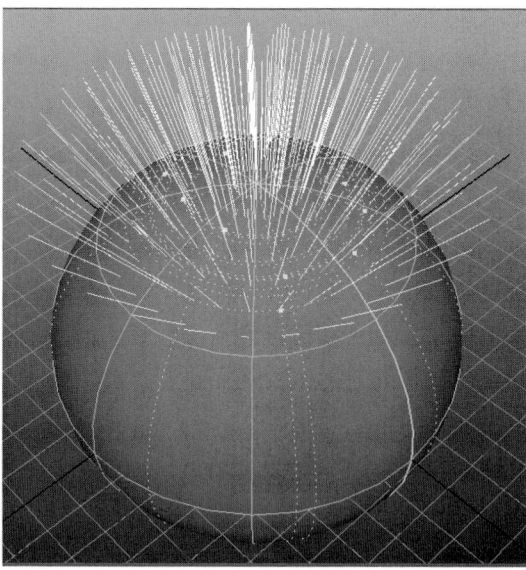

6. Click the Create Hairs button to make the hairs. The hair curves appear as longer curves coming out of the surface of the sphere.

7. Open the Outliner, and select the hairSystem1 node.

8. Switch to the Rendering menu set, and choose Fur ➢ Attach Hairsystem To Fur ➢ FurDescription1.

9. Set the timeline to 200, and play the scene. As the hair curves fall, the strands of fur follow. Try animating the sphere so that it moves around the scene (see Figure 15.20).

10. Save the scene as **furBall_v02.ma**.

FIGURE 15.20
The strands of fur
follow the motion
of the hair curves.

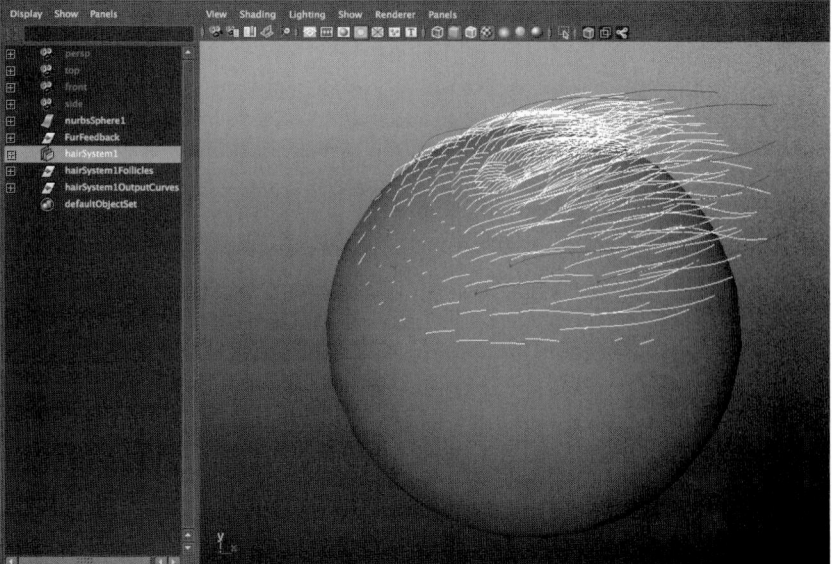

To see a version of the scene, open the `furBall_v02.ma` scene from the `chapter15\scenes` folder on the DVD.

To keep the hair from penetrating the NURBS sphere, you need to make the sphere a collision object for the hair curves. This along with other dynamic properties of hair curves is discussed later in the chapter. Essentially, any dynamics added to the hair curves are inherited by the fur.

Rendering Fur Using mental ray

You can render fur using mental ray or Maya Software. When rendering with Maya Software, you'll need to add a fur shadowing node to the lights in the scene. In this section, you'll learn how to render fur with mental ray, which generally produces a more realistic result than Maya Software.

If you plan to use depth map shadows, use the Production: Rapid Fur preset. If you plan to use ray trace shadows, use the Production: Fine Trace Render preset. If you need the fur to appear in reflections or refractions, use raytracing.

Fur renders use indirect lighting techniques such as Final Gathering. Be aware that the render times for dense fur descriptions when Final Gathering is enabled can be quite long.

Rendering Fur Using Raytracing

To create a realistic render of the hound using raytracing, follow these steps:

1. Open the `hound_v08.ma` scene from the `chapter15\scenes` directory.

2. Open the Hypershade, and select the houndShader material.

3. In the attributes for the material, set the Diffuse attribute to **1**. Increasing the Diffuse quality of the shader can sometimes help blend the surface material with the color of the fur.

4. Open the Render Settings window, and select the Quality tab. Set Quality Presets to Production: Fine Trace.

5. In the Outliner, select the spotlight, and open its Attribute Editor.

6. Under Shadows, turn on Use Ray Trace Shadows.

   The Fur/Shadowing attributes listed below the Use Ray Trace Shadows settings are used specifically when rendering with Maya Software, which requires that the shadow-casting lights be connected to the fur description. This is not necessary when rendering with mental ray.

7. Create a directional light. Rotate the light so that it is shining toward the camera. This creates nice fill lighting as well as a fringe of light along the edge of the fur.

8. In the settings for the directional light, turn off Emit Specular, and set Intensity to **0.8**.

9. In the Outliner, expand the FurFeedback group, and select the houndHead_FurFeedback node. In the Attribute Editor, click the houndFur node.

10. Set Density to **500,000**. Scroll down to the list of Attributes. Set Tip Opacity to **0** and Base Opacity to **0.5**. This helps soften the look of the fur.

11. Set Base Width to **0.008** and Tip Width to **0.001**.

12. Create a test render from the perspective camera. The scene takes between five and eight minutes to render depending on your machine (see Figure 15.21).

13. Save the scene as **hound_v09.ma**.

To see a finished version of the scene, open the hound_v09.ma scene from the chapter15\ scenes directory on the DVD.

You can continue to improve the look of the fur by improving the texture maps applied to the fur description as well as by improving the lighting in the scene.

Maya Fur does a pretty good job creating fur effects for many typical situations. For truly stunning fur and hair effects, you may want to consider using the Shave and a Haircut plug-in developed for Maya by Joe Alter. This plug-in has been used for many feature films and television shows. For more information, visit www.joealter.com.

FIGURE 15.21
Render the hound using ray trace shadows.

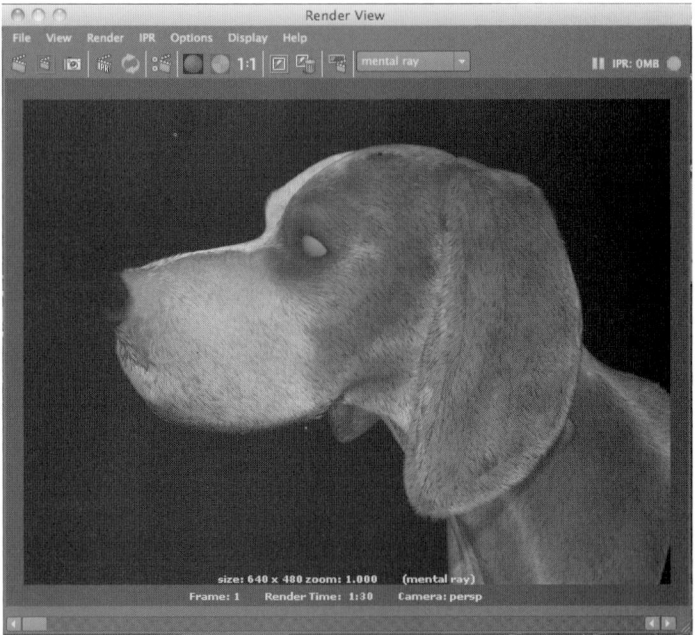

Animating Using Dynamic Curves

Dynamic curves are NURBS curves that have dynamic properties. The primary use of dynamic curves is to drive the dynamics of hair systems applied to characters. However, the usefulness of dynamic curves goes far beyond creating hair motion. Curves used to loft or extrude surfaces, curves used for Paint Effects strokes, curves projected on NURBS surfaces, curves used as IK splines, curves used as particle emitters, and so on, can be made dynamic, thus opening up a large number of possibilities for creating additional dynamic effects in Maya. Furthermore, dynamic curves calculate fairly quickly compared to nCloth, making surfaces created from lofted dynamic curves a useful alternative to nCloth for some situations.

While working through the scenes in this chapter, you may want to set the timeline preferences to loop so that you can see the hair update continuously as you adjust its settings. To do this, follow these steps:

1. Choose Window ➢ Settings/Preferences ➢ Preferences.

2. Choose the Time Slider category in the Preferences box.

3. Set Looping to Continuous.

DYNAMIC CURVES VS. NUCLEUS

As you learn about dynamic curves, you'll immediately notice many similarities between the interfaces for dynamic curves and Nucleus, yet dynamic curves are not part of nDynamics. This is because the introduction of dynamic curves predates the introduction of nDynamics and the Nucleus solver.

Using Dynamic Curves with IK Splines

In Chapter 7, you learned about the IK Spline tool, which uses a curve to control the Inverse Kinematics (IK) of a joint chain. The curve itself can be converted into a dynamic curve that can be used to drive the IK Spline tool. This is a great way to add dynamic motion to a rig used for tails or tentacles.

In this example, you'll use a dynamic curve to control a segmented armored tail. The armored tail consists of polygon pieces, each of which has been parent-constrained to a joint in a chain. The first step is to create a curve (see Figure 15.22).

1. Open the armoredTail_v01.ma scene from the chapter15\scenes folder on the DVD.

2. Switch to a side view, and turn on Point Snapping.

FIGURE 15.22
The armored tail consists of polygon pieces constrained to a joint chain.

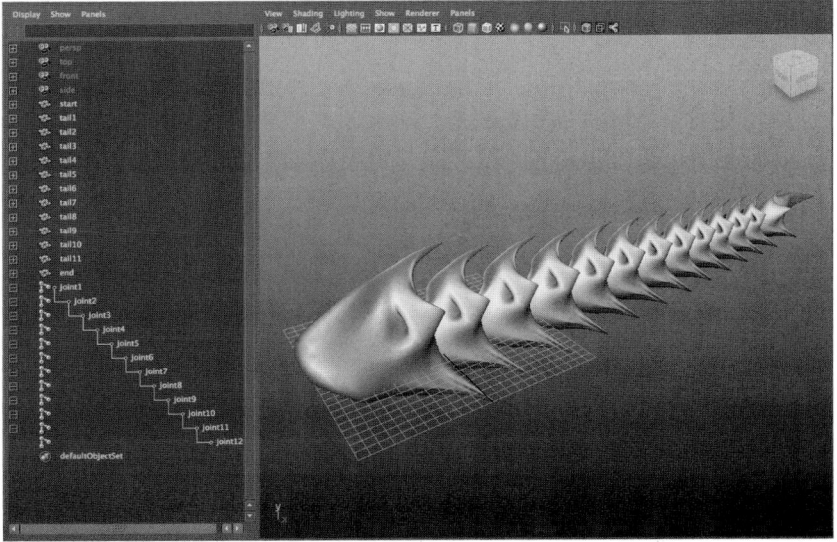

3. In the viewport's Show menu, turn off the visibility of polygons so only the joints are visible.

4. Choose Create ➤ EP Curve Tool. Click the first joint in the chain on the far left and the last joint in the chain on the far right.

5. Press the Enter key to complete the curve.

   The EP Curve tool creates a curve that has four CVs. Using the EP Curve tool is an easy way to create a straight curve. If you want to add more vertices, you can use the Edit Curves ➤ Rebuild Curve command. In the options, specify how many spans you want to add to the curve. In this example, the curve should work fine with only four CVs.

6. Switch to the perspective view. Turn off the visibility of Joints in the Show menu so only the curve is visible.

7. Switch to the Dynamics menu set. Select curve1, and choose Hair ➤ Make Selected Curves Dynamic. In the Outliner, a new hairSystem1 node is created as well as two groups: hairSystem1Follicles and hairSystem1OutputCurves (see Figure 15.23).

FIGURE 15.23
A number of nodes are added to the scene when a curve is made dynamic.

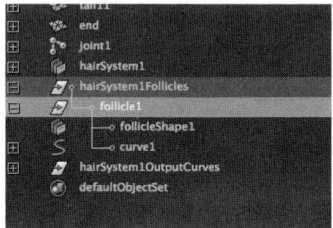

UNDERSTANDING DYNAMIC HAIR CURVE NODES

The hairSystem1 node controls the dynamics of the curve; it is similar to the Nucleus solver when using nDynamics.

The hairSystem1Follicles group contains the follicle1 node and the original curve1. The follicle node contains settings to control the dynamics of the individual follicles. Some of these settings can override the hairSystem settings. If you selected a number of curves before issuing the Make Selected Curves Dynamic command, the hairSystem1Follicles group would contain a follicle node for each curve. This is explored later on when creating hair for a character.

The hairSystem1OutputCurves group creates a duplicate curve named curve2. This curve is a duplicate of the original curve. The output curve is the dynamic curve; the curve in the follicle group is the original, nondynamic curve. The purpose of the nondynamic curve is to serve as an attractor for the dynamic curve if needed. The dynamic curve gets its shape from the follicle curve.

8. Set the timeline to **200**, and click the Play button. You'll see the dynamic curve move a little (it can be a little hard to see; this will be more obvious in the next step).

9. Stop the playback, and switch to the hairSystem1 tab.

10. In the Dynamics rollout panel, set the Stiffness value to **0**, and play the scene. You'll see the dynamic curve droop a little. As the scene is playing, increase Length Flex.

The Stiffness setting controls the rigidity of the curve. A higher Stiffness setting makes the curve less flexible. Lowering the Stiffness value makes the curve bend easily.

As you increase the Length Flex value, the curve stretches as much as it needs to in order to accommodate the dynamic forces applied to the curve. You'll notice the curve droop downward, indicating that it has weight. The hairSystem1 shape has a Gravity setting built in, much like the Nucleus solver discussed in Chapter 13.

You'll notice that both ends of the curve appear to be attached to the original curve (Figure 15.24).

FIGURE 15.24
The dynamic curve droops as if it is attached at both ends to the original curve.

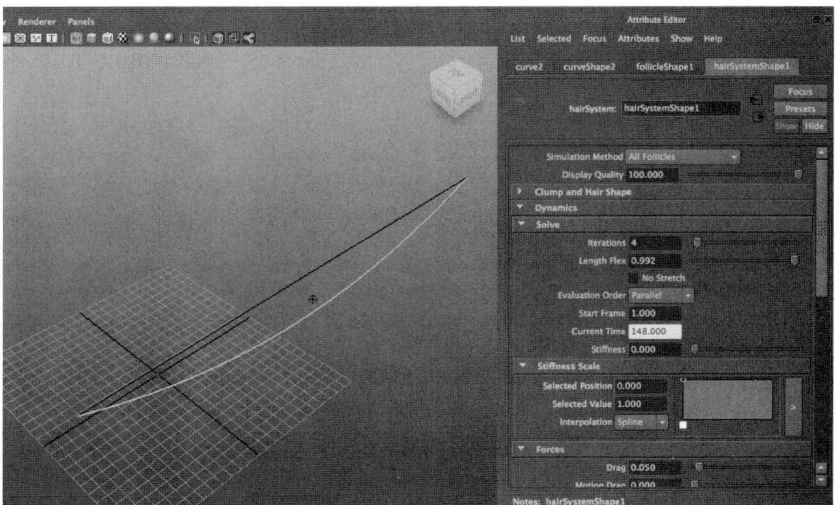

11. Stop the playback, and rewind the animation.

12. Set Length Flex to **0.5** and Stiffness to **0.1**.

13. Select the follicle1 node in the Outliner, and switch to the Move tool (turn off Grid or Point Snapping if it is still on).

14. Choose Solvers ➢ Interactive Playback. The animation starts playing automatically. As it is playing, move the follicle around in the scene; you'll see the dynamic curve follow the movements.

15. Stop the animation, and switch to the follicleShape1 tab in the Attribute Editor.

16. Set the Point Lock menu to Base. Turn on Interactive Playback, and move the follicle around again. You'll see that the dynamic curve is attached at only one end.

    If you wanted the curve to be attached to the other end, you'd set Point Lock to Tip. To detach the curve entirely, set Point Lock to No Attach.

17. Stop the animation, and rewind the playback.

KEYFRAME POINT LOCK

The Point Lock attribute can be keyframed in the Channel Box for the follicle node. To animate a dynamic curve detaching from one end, follow these steps:

1. Set Point Lock to Both Ends.
2. Create a keyframe by right-clicking the Point Lock channel in the Channel Box and choosing Key Selected.
3. Change the current frame on the timeline.
4. Set Point Lock to Tip or Base (the opposite end will become detached).
5. Set another keyframe.

This is a good way to create the effect of a cable or rope snapping.

---

18. Select the follicle node, and set the Translate channels to **0** to return the curve to its start position.
19. With the follicle selected, turn on Point Snapping.
20. Hold the **d** key, and use the Move tool to move the pivot point of the follicle to the end of the curve on the side where the dynamic curve is still attached, as shown in Figure 15.25.

FIGURE 15.25
Move the pivot point of the follicle to the end of the curve.

TIPS FOR MOVING THE PIVOT POINT

As you move the pivot point, the curve should not move; sometimes it takes a couple of tries to get Maya to properly switch to move pivot mode. An alternative to the **d** hotkey is to press the Insert key on a PC or the Home key on a Mac on the keyboard while the Move tool is activated—not every keyboard has an Insert key, however.

21. When the pivot point is repositioned, Shift+click the Translate and Rotate channels in the Channel Box, right-click, and choose Key Selected from the pop-up menu.

22. Turn on Auto Keyframe; go to various points in the animation, and move and rotate the follicle.

While Auto Keyframe is on, a keyframe is placed on all the Translate and Rotate channels as you make changes to the position of the follicle. The dynamic curve may not update correctly as you make changes; don't worry about that at the moment.

You want to create an animation where the curve moves around in the scene like a sword slashing through the air.

23. Rewind and play the animation; you'll see the dynamic curve follow the movements of the follicle as it moves through the air.

24. Save the scene as `armoredTail_v02.ma`.

To see a version of the scene, open the `armoredTail_v02.ma` scene from the `chapter15\scenes` directory.

Creating an IK Spline Handle from the Dynamic Curve

In this section, you'll create an IK spline handle for the armored tail and attach it to the dynamic curve. The dynamics of the curve will be edited to change the behavior of the tail.

1. Continue with the scene from the previous section, or open the `armoredTail_v02.ma` scene from the `chapter15\scenes` directory.

2. In the perspective view, turn on the visibility of joints in the Show menu.

3. In the Outliner, select and hide the follicle1 node. This prevents you from selecting the wrong curve when creating the IK spline handle.

4. Switch to the Animation menu set, and choose Skeleton ➤ IK Spline Handle Tool ➤ Options.

5. In the options, make sure Auto Create Curve and Snap Curve To Root are both off.

6. With the IK Spline Handle tool active, select the first joint in the chain and the last joint in the chain.

7. Zoom in closely, and carefully select the blue curve that runs down the center of the chain.

If the operation is successful, you'll see the ikHandle1 node appear in the Outliner. The Dynamic curve (curve2) will move out of the hairSystem1OutputCurves group. That should not affect how the curve behaves.

8. Rewind and play the scene. The joints follow the motion of the curves.

9. In the Show menu of the perspective view, turn the visibility of polygons back on, and play the scene. The armored tail thrashes around when you play the animation.

10. In the Outliner, select the hairSystem1 node, and open its Attribute Editor to the hairSystemShape1 tab.

11. Scroll down, and expand the Dynamics section.

    The Stiffness Scale edit curve changes the stiffness of the curve along the length of the curve. The left side of the curve corresponds to the stiffness at the base; the right side of the curve corresponds to the stiffness at the tip.

12. Add a point to the Stiffness Scale edit curve by clicking the left side of the curve and dragging downward.

13. Play the animation, and you'll see the end of the tail lag behind the motion more than the front of the tail. You should be able to edit the curve while the animation is playing and observe the changes (see Figure 15.26).

14. Save the scene as **armoredTail_v03.ma**.

FIGURE 15.26
Editing the Stiffness Scale curve changes the stiffness along the length of the dynamic hair.

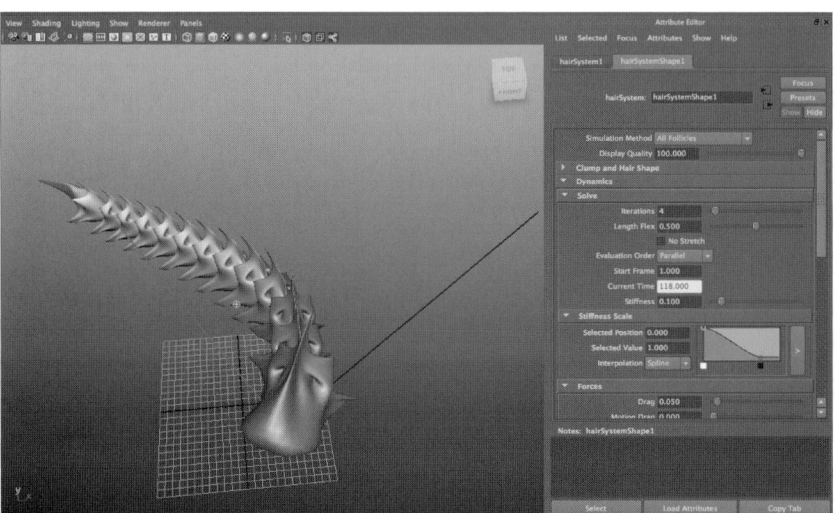

The Stiffness setting creates the overall stiffness value for the dynamic curve. Stiffness Scale modifies that value along the length of the curve. Both settings, like almost all of the dynamic curve settings, can be animated.

To see a version of the scene, open the armoredTail_v03.ma file from the chapter15\scenes directory.

Using Forces

The settings in the Forces section add levels of control for the curve's motion. Play the animation in the armoredTail_v03.ma scene, and adjust these settings while the scene loops so you can see how they affect the motion of the tail.

The Iterations setting affects how the hair responds to stiffness and dynamics. *Iterations* refers to the number of times the hair solver calculates per time step, similar to the Substeps setting on the Nucleus node. Increase it to improve the accuracy of the hair motion; higher values slow down Maya's playback.

Drag   Creates friction between the dynamic curve and the air. Increasing this is a good way to simulate the motion of hair in thick fluids.

Motion Drag   Similar to Drag. However, Motion Drag is affected by the Stiffness Scale attribute. In other words, the Drag setting creates a drag in the motion across the length of the dynamic curve, whereas Motion Drag creates a drag along the length of the curve that is influenced by the Stiffness Scale curve. This can be used to fine-tune the motion of the dynamic curve.

Damp   Used most often to control erratic motion of dynamic curves. Higher Damp values decrease the momentum of the curve as it follows the motion of the follicle.

Friction   Reduces the motion of dynamic curves when they collide with surfaces. This won't produce a visible effect unless the curve comes in contact with a collision surface. Collisions are discussed in more detail later in the chapter.

Mass   Affects the motion of the curve only when additional fields (created from the Dynamics menu set) are applied to the curve, for example, a Turbulence or a Drag field. Mass does not change how the curve responds to forces created in the hairSystem1 shape node. Increasing Mass increases the simulated weight of each CV on the curve as the curve moves through a dynamic field.

Dynamics Weight   Controls the amount of overall influence external dynamic fields (such as Turbulence and Drag) have over the dynamic curve. It does not affect how the Forces settings in the hairSystem node affect the dynamic curve.

Start Curve Attract   Creates an attraction between the original curve (curve1 in the armoredTail example) and the dynamic curve. This can be used to blend between the dynamic curve and animation created through the use of deformers on the original curve. The Attraction Scale curve can be used to edit the strength of the attraction along the length of the curve, similar to the Stiffness Scale.

Adding Hair to a Character

Hair is created by attaching follicle nodes to a surface. Each follicle node controls a number of hairs. The follicles themselves are styled using a combination of control curves and forces. Follicles and control curves are connected to a hair system node. A single hair system node can control hair connected to any number of surfaces, and a single surface can be attached to multiple hair systems.

When you create hair, you have to consider how you plan to render it. You have the choice of creating Paint Effects strokes for the hair or curves that can be used to render in third-party rendering engines such as Render Man, or you can create both Paint Effects strokes and curves. Even though hair uses Paint Effects, it renders using mental ray without the need to convert the hair to polygons.

In this section, you'll create and style hair for a character.

Applying Hair to a Surface

When you want to apply hair to a character, you can either apply the hair uniformly to the entire surface or paint the hair selectively on parts of the surface.

It is common practice to create a nonrendering scalp surface that can be parented to a character's head and then apply the hair to the scalp surface rather than directly to the character's head. This allows flexibility because scalp surfaces and their attached hair can easily be swapped between characters. It also speeds up playback in the animation because the hair dynamics are not factored into the calculations required to deform the character's surface if it has been skinned to a skeleton or to other deformers.

Some animators like to apply separate hair systems to each part of the scalp to control the various sections of a particular hairstyle. For instance, one hair system may be applied to the bangs that hang over the character's forehead, while another system is used for the hair on the back of the head. In this exercise, you'll keep things simple by using a single hair system for the character's hairstyle. Both methods are valid, and as you become comfortable working with hair, you may want to experiment with different techniques to see which approach works best for you.

The following procedure uses the Nancy Hair scene, which contains the rigged nancy character used in Chapter 6. The head is rigged to a series of joints. You can select and rotate the headCtrl curves above the head to change the position of the head. A scalp surface has been created by duplicating part of the head geometry. This scalp geometry is parent-constrained to one of the joints in the head rig.

You can apply hair to NURBS or polygon surfaces. When using polygon surfaces, the UV texture coordinates must be mapped so that none of the UVs overlap and the coordinates fit within the 0 to 1 range in the UV Texture Editor. As with fur, you'll get better results from your hair system if the UV coordinates have been carefully mapped. Remember to delete history for the surface once you have created UV texture coordinates to keep the coordinates (and attached hair) from moving unpredictably during animation.

1. Open the nancyHair_v01.ma scene from the chapter15\scenes directory.

2. In the Outliner, select the scalp surface, and open its Attribute Editor.

3. In the scalpShape tab, expand the Render Stats section; then turn off Casts Shadows, Receive Shadows, Motion Blur, and Primary Visibility so the surface will not render or affect any other geometry in the render.

ADDING HAIR TO A SURFACE

You can add hair to a surface in a number of ways. You can paint hair on the surface using the Artisan Brush interface, you can select faces on polygons or surface points on NURBS surfaces and apply hair to the selected components, or you can create a uniform grid of follicles on a surface. Once you attach follicles to a surface, you can add more follicles later to fill in blank areas by painting them on the surface.

For the scalp you'll create a simple grid and then add follicles if needed later.

4. Select the scalp surface, switch to the Dynamics menu set, and choose Hair ➤ Create Hair ➤ Options.

5. In the Create Hair Options box, choose Edit ➢ Reset to reset the options to the default settings.

6. Set the Output to Paint Effects, and choose the Grid option. Use the following settings:

   U and V Count: **24**

   Points Per Hair: **20**

   Passive Fill: **1**

   Randomization: **0.1**

UNDERSTANDING FOLLICLE TYPES

Follicles can be dynamic, passive, or static:

Dynamic follicles   Dynamic follicles react to forces and dynamic fields based on the settings in the hairSystem node or on any dynamic overrides created in the follicle shape node. Dynamic follicles can collide with surfaces.

Passive follicles   Passive follicles inherit the dynamic motion of nearby dynamic follicles, which can reduce computational overhead, especially when collisions are involved.

Static follicles   Static follicles have no dynamic motion but can be used to style parts of the hair. You can change the mode of a follicle after creating the hair system if you decide to make a passive follicle dynamic, make a dynamic follicle static, or use any other of the three modes.

The Randomization setting randomizes the arrangement of the grid to make the hair placement look less even.

By increasing the Passive Fill option, a number of the follicles created when the hair is attached to the surface will be passive rather than dynamic. If the Passive Fill option is set to 1, every other row and column of the follicles based on the settings for U and V Count will be passive follicles. If the setting is 2, every two rows and every two columns of follicles will be passive.

When you first create a hair system, you can create a number of passive follicles using this setting. This speeds up the dynamics as you create the initial hairstyle. Later you can convert the follicles to dynamic or static follicles as needed.

---

7. Turn on the Edge Bounded and Equalize options.

   When the Grid method is used, the follicles are placed uniformly on the surface based on the U and V coordinates. If Edge Bounded is on, the follicles are placed up to and including the edge of the UV coordinates. In the case of the example, this means hairs are placed along the edge of the scalp surface. The Equalize option evens out the spacing of the follicle placement to compensate for areas of the U and V coordinates that may be stretched or squashed.

8. Set Points Per Hair to **20** and Length to **5**.

   Hairs that have more points per curve are more flexible and have more detail in their motion as they respond to dynamics; they also slow down the playback speed of Maya in the scene. The Length attribute can be modified after creation.

The Place Hairs Into option should be set to New Hair System. If a hair system exists in the scene already, you can use this option to add the newly created hairs into the existing system by selecting it from the list. Figure 15.27 shows the settings for the new hair.

FIGURE 15.27
The Create Hair Options area

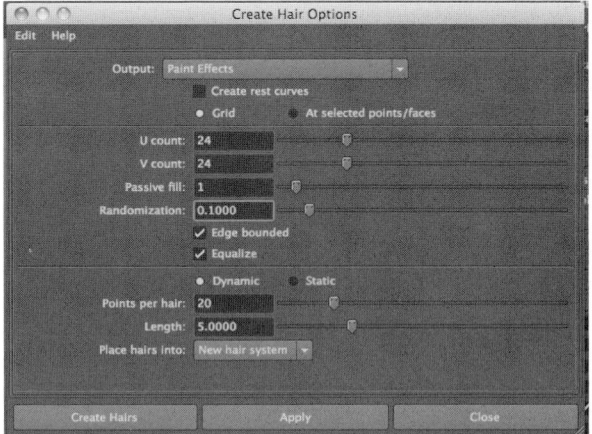

9. Click Create Hairs to make the hair. The hairs appear as long spikes coming out of the head (see Figure 15.28).

10. Click Play on the scene, and the hairs start to fall. After a few moments, the hairs start to settle.

11. Save the scene as **nancyHair_v02.ma**.

To see a version of the scene, open the nancyHair_v02.ma scene from the chapter15\scenes directory.

In the next section, you'll learn how to style the hair.

FIGURE 15.28
The hairs appear as long spikes on the top of the head. When you click the Play button, the hairs fall and settle into a basic hair shape.

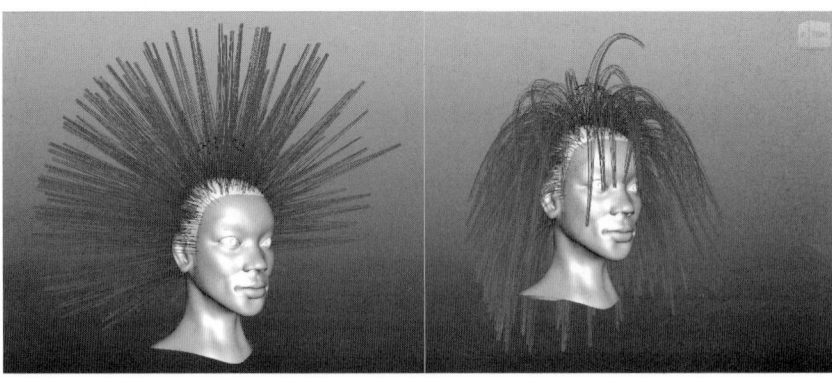

HAIR TRANSPLANTS

You can move an existing hair system from one surface to another surface using the Transplant command. To use this command, follow these steps:

1. Select the hair system you want to move.

2. Ctrl+click the destination surface.

3. From the Dynamics menu set, choose Hair ➤ Transplant Hair.

If the surfaces have very similar UV texture coordinates, you can choose to move the hair based on the UV coordinates in the Transplant options. Otherwise, you can choose to move the hair based on the closest points in the surface. In this case, make sure the destination surface is placed and scaled to match the existing hair system and its source.

Creating Hair Collisions

Polygon and NURBS surfaces can collide with hair, and there are a number of settings on the hairSystemShape node that can affect how the collisions are calculated as well as how the hair behaves when it collides with a surface.

To understand how to create collisions between surfaces and hair, you'll follow an example that is a slight detour from working with characters:

1. Open the underseaPlants_v01.ma scene from the chapter15\scenes directory. This scene contains a very simple NURBS plane that has been sculpted to look like the floor of the ocean.

2. Select the floor surface. Switch to the Dynamics menu set, and choose Hair ➤ Paint Hair Follicles. The Options box for the Artisan Brush interface opens along with a pop-up box for the Paint Hair Follicles settings.

3. In the Paint Hair Follicles Settings box, make sure Hair System is set to Create New, and set Output to NURBS Curves. Use the following settings:

   Follicle Density U and V: **6**

   Leave Points Per Hair at **6**

   Hair Length: **3**

4. Paint on the surface to add a few follicles. The interaction may be faster if the shaded mode is set to wireframe or if Color Feedback is turned off in the Display section of the Artisan Tool options.

5. When you have 15 to 20 curves painted on the surface, close the Paint Hair Follicle Settings box, and switch to the Select tool.

6. In the Outliner, select the hairSystem1 node, and open its Attribute Editor.

7. On the hairSystemShape1 tab, enter the following settings:

   Stiffness: **0.03**

   Drag: **0.7**

   Gravity: **0**

8. In the Turbulence settings, enter the following settings:

   Intensity: **0.8**

   Frequency: **1**

   Speed: **1**

9. Set the timeline to **300**, and play the scene. The curves appear to move a bit like some undersea plant life (see Figure 15.29).

FIGURE 15.29
Paint a hair system on a model of the ocean floor. Set the dynamics to simulate undersea plant life.

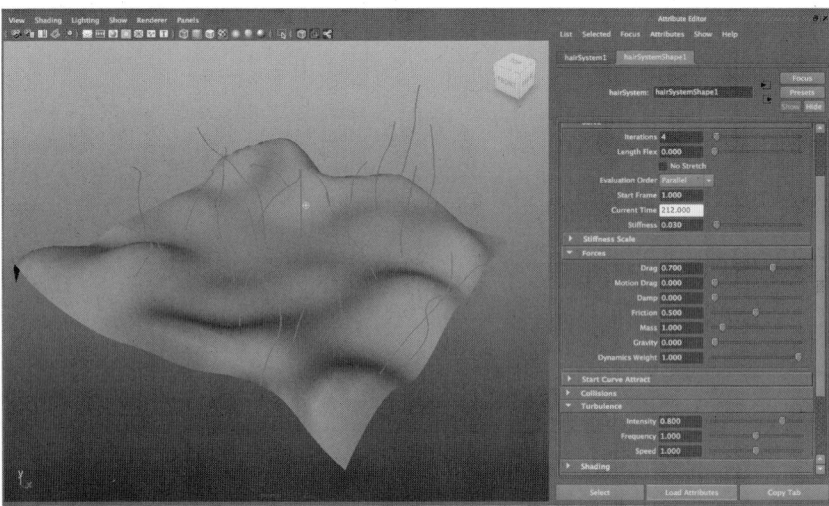

HAIR CURVE DISPLAY SETTINGS

You may see two curves per each hair, one that moves and one that stays still. This is because the display is set to start curves and current curves. If you just want to see the dynamic/moving curves, choose Hair ➤ Display ➤ Current Position.

---

10. Create a polygon sphere. Animate the sphere moving around randomly through the hair curves in such a way that the sphere contacts the hair curves.

11. When you are happy with the animation, select the polySphere, and Ctrl+click the hairSystem node in the Outliner. Choose Hair ➤ Make Collide.

12. Play the scene.

   You may not see much of a collision just yet, or the sphere may appear to collide with some but not all of the hairs.

13. Select the hairSystem node, and open its Attribute Editor. Scroll down to the Collisions section.

14. Play the animation. As the animation is playing, increase the Collide Over Sample value. This setting adjusts how often collisions are calculated per time step. Higher values increase accuracy but slow down playback in Maya. Set the value to **6**.

You'll notice that the hair sticks to the sphere as it passes. This is a common problem when using geometry to collide with hair. There are some techniques you can use to reduce this problem.

15. Turn on Draw Collide Width, and increase the Collide Width Offset value.

The Draw Collide Width setting creates circles around the hair curve that represent the collision width. Increasing Collide Width Offset increases the collision boundary, making the collision thickness of each hair larger (Figure 15.30).

FIGURE 15.30
The collision width of the hair is displayed as circles around each hair.

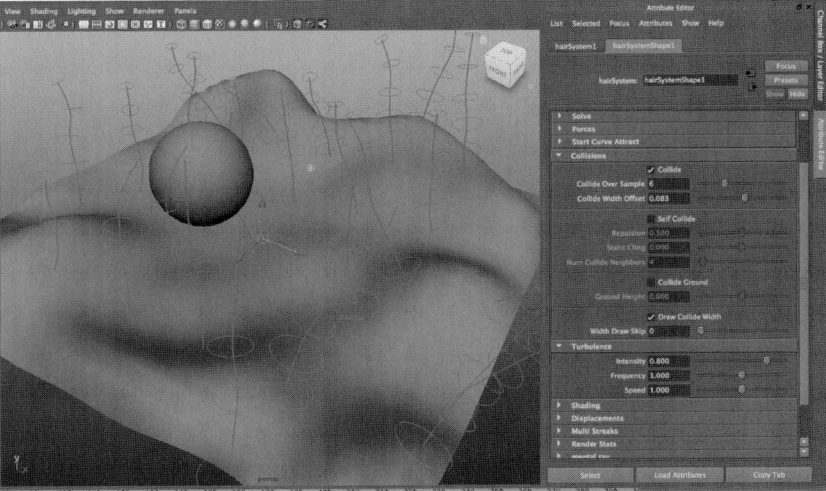

To reduce the stickiness of the hair, you can lower the Friction setting in the hairSystem's Dynamics settings as well as increase the Iterations value and lower the Stiffness value. Increasing Friction makes the hair stick to the surface longer, which may work well when animating the tendrils of a jellyfish.

Ultimately, if you are unable to eliminate the hair sticking to the collision surface, you may need to consider some alternative techniques. Some models experience more or fewer sticking problems than others.

One technique for eliminating the stickiness is to attach a radial field to the hair and parent the field to the collision object. The max distance of the field can be adjusted to reach just beyond the edge of the sphere.

The best way to eliminate the sticking problem is to use hair collision constraint primitives. This is a special type of hair constraint that uses simple primitives as collision objects. The collision constraints can be parented to objects, and collisions between the hairs and the constraints are faster and more accurate than collisions between geometry and hair. In addition, a collision constraint can be made to collide only with specific follicles. Collision geometry, on the other hand, collides with all the hairs in a hair system.

In the next section, you'll use collision constraints to control how the hair interacts with the character's head. The collision example used in this section is available in the chapter15\ scenes directory as the underseaPlants_v02.ma scene.

ADDITIONAL COLLISION PROPERTIES

Additional hair collision options include Self-Collide, which enables collisions between the hair follicles of a system. You can use the Static Cling option to make the hairs stick together when they collide, while the Repulsion option increases the tendency for hairs to repulse each other.

An invisible collision plane can be created by enabling the Collide Ground option. This setting creates an infinite plane parallel to the x- and z-axes in the scene. The height of the ground is set using the Ground Height slider.

Hair Collision Constraints

Hair collision constraints are simple spherical and cubical primitives that can be used to collide with dynamic hair. The accuracy and speed of collision constraints is superior to collision geometry. Multiple collision constraints can be added to a hair system and scaled to approximate the surface of colliding objects in the scene. In this section, you'll add collision constraints to the nancy character's hair.

1. Open the nancyHair_v02.ma scene from the chapter15\scenes directory.

2. In the Outliner, select the hairSystem1 node, and open its Attribute Editor.

3. To improve the playback of simulations during animation, set Display Quality at the top of the editor to **1**, and set Simulation Method to Dynamic Follicles Only.

4. In the Outliner, expand the hairSystemFollicles group. Select the top node in the group, hold the Shift key, scroll down, and select the bottom node in the group.

5. From the Dynamics menu set, choose Hair ➤ Create Constraint ➤ Collide Sphere.

6. In the Perspective window, switch to wireframe mode. Select the hairConstraint1 node, represented by a wire sphere, and position it roughly in the center of the head.

7. Use the Scale tool to scale the sphere to match the size of the cranium (see Figure 15.31).

8. Switch to the front view, and scale the constraint in a little to match the head.

9. Repeat steps 3 through 5 to create additional collide spheres. Position these to match the jaw, neck, and ears.

10. When you have positioned the collide spheres to match the basic shape of the head, turn off the visibility of polygons in the perspective view, and turn on the visibility of joints.

11. Use a parent constraint to connect the collide sphere in the head, jaw, and ears to the large joint that runs down the center of the head:

    A. Select the joint.

    B. Select the collide sphere to be constrained.

    C. In the options for the parent constraint, make sure the Translate and Rotate channels are selected as well as Maintain Offset.

12. Use a parent constraint to connect the collide sphere in the neck to the middle neck joints.

FIGURE 15.31
Scale the collision constraint to match the size of the cranium.

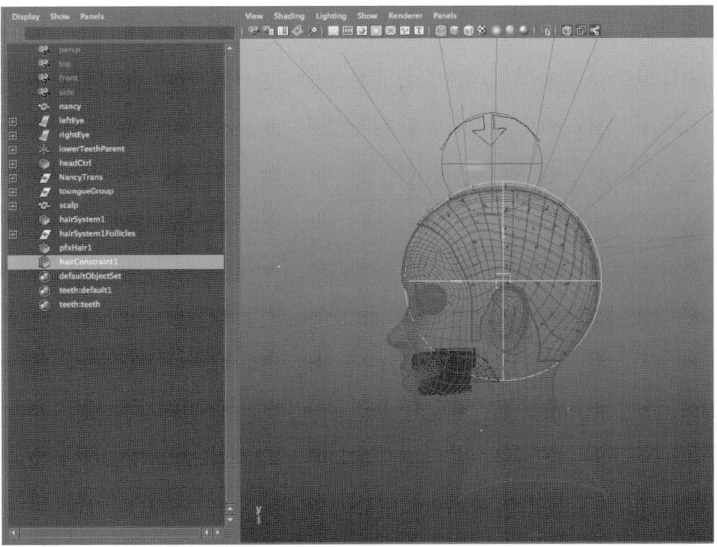

13. Play the scene. The hairs should not penetrate the head, thanks to the constraints. This is more obvious if you lower the Stiffness attribute to a low value such as 0.03 in the hair shape node so that the hairs droop more (see Figure 15.32).

14. Save the scene as **nancyHair_v03.ma**.

To see a version of the scene, open the nancyHair_v03.ma scene from the chapter15\scenes directory.

FIGURE 15.32
Parent constrain the collide spheres to the joints in the head rig. When you lower the Stiffness value and play the scene, the hairs are prevented from moving through the collide spheres.

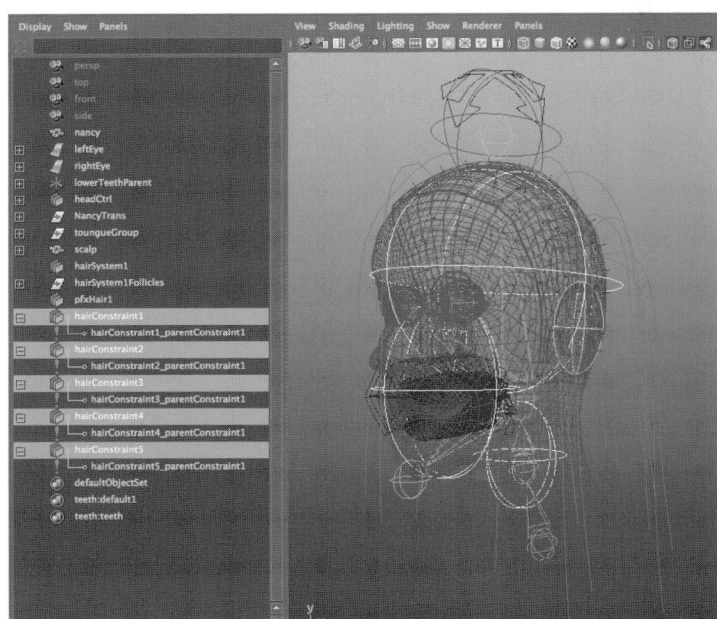

Determining Hair Shape

A number of settings in the hair system node determine the look of the hair. These are found in the Clump and Hair Shape section of the hair system's attributes.

1. Open the nancyHair_v03.ma scene from the chapter15\scenes directory.

2. Select hairSystem1, and open its Attribute Editor to the hairSystemShape1 tab.

3. Set Display Quality to **100** so you get a more accurate preview of the hair. Leave Simulation Method set to Dynamic Follicles Only.

   This improves performance while working in the scene. Keep in mind, though, that you are viewing about half the hair that is actually on the head. If you look at the scalp surface, you'll see the small colored spikes indicating the position of the follicles. Red follicles indicate dynamic follicles; blue follicles indicate passive follicles. The passive follicles are hidden until you switch Simulation Method to All Follicles.

   The hair appears as groups bunched around long spikes that shoot out from the scalp. Each group of hairs is a clump. The movement of each clump of hair is driven by the movement of the follicles. This way, Maya can create dynamics for thousands of hairs using a much smaller number of follicles.

4. The hair remains as long spikes until you play the simulation and let the hair fall down. For the moment, leave the animation at frame 1. It's easier to see how the clumps work when the hair is in its spiky state.

5. In the Clump and Hair Shape section, increase the Hairs Per Clump number to **60** to increase the fullness of the hair.

6. Play the animation until frame 20, and then stop the animation.

7. Zoom in to the end of a clump, and move the Bend Follow slider back and forth.

   When Bend Follow is at 0, the end of the clump appears flat if the follicle is curved. When Bend Follow is 1, the clump shape is more tubular toward the end of the clump. This attribute should be used to fine-tune the look of your hair as you develop the overall shape.

8. Rewind the animation, and set Clump Width to **0.7**. This expands the overall width of the clumps, which helps fill out the hairstyle without the need to add more follicles.

   In the Clump and Hair Shape rollout, you can use the following settings to determine the look of the hair:

   Baldness Map The Baldness Map field allows you to apply a texture to control where the hair grows on the head. The texture must be a black-and-white 2D texture. The texture itself does not need to be baked as it does with fur. Just like with fur, black areas of the map indicate no hair (or baldness), and white areas indicate places where the hair grows. Texture maps can also be used, much like the texture maps created for fur baldness.

The Sub Segments attribute   This improves the details of the hair (such as curls and kinks) when rendered. Increasing this setting does not affect the dynamics of the hair.

Thinning   Higher values shorten the number of hairs per clump to create a thin and wispy look to the hair.

Clump Twist   This rotates each clump around the base of the follicle. Positive values rotate the clump in one direction; negative values rotate it in the opposite direction.

Bend Follow   This determines how closely the rotation of the clump affects the shape of the hair clumps. This is most noticeable at the end of each clump.

Hair Width   Hair Width adjusts the width of the hairs. This can be used to thicken or thin the hair. The effect of changing hair width is seen when the hair is rendered. This is a setting you'll probably want to return to when you are setting up your hair for a render.

Below the Clump and Hair Shape setting sliders are a number of edit curves that can be used to further refine the hair shape. The left side of each curve represents the area of the clump closest to the root; the right side represents the area closest to the tip. Each scale uses the setting in the sliders in the Clump And Hair Shape section as a starting point, so each scale is a modifier for the settings you have already created. The following describes how each ramp affects the look of the hair:

Clump and Hair Width Scale   You can exaggerate or reduce the amount of tapering in the clumps by changing the Clump Width Scale edit curve. Hair Width Scale modifies the width of the hairs based on the setting in the Hair Width slider.

Clump Curl   The Clump Curl edit curve can be used to twist the clumps around the central axis of the follicle. By default the graph is set so that the value of the curling is at 0.5. By moving a point on the curve up (moving up creates values closer to 1; moving down creates values closer to 0) or down, the curling twists in one direction or the other (see Figure 15.33).

FIGURE 15.33
Adding and moving points along the various edit curves can shape the overall look of the hair.

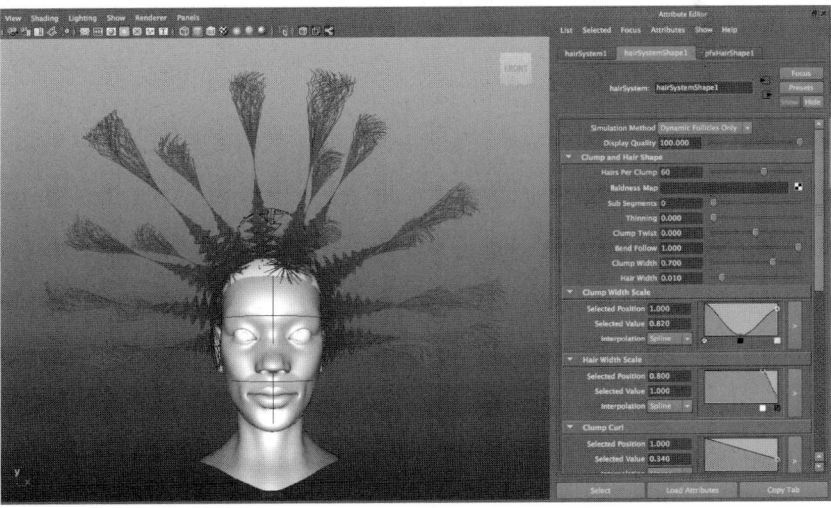

Clump Flatness   The Clump Flatness scale can be used to make the clumps appear as flat planks of hair. Higher values along the curve flatten out the clumps. This setting works well for creating the shape of wet hair.

The final two settings in this section are sliders labeled Clump Interpolation and Interpolation Range:

Clump Interpolation   Increasing the Clump Interpolation slider spreads the hair out between clumps. This can be used to even out the shape of the hair so that the clumping is much less obvious. Dynamics are calculated based on the position of each clump. If you set a high Clump Interpolation value, you may find that hairs do not appear to collide correctly. This is because the interpolation can push hairs outside the boundary of the original clump width, and thus their placement exceeds the collision width of their clump.

Interpolation Range   Interpolation Range sets the limits for how far a hair can move out of the width of the clump when Clump Interpolation is increased. The value set in Interpolation Range is multiplied against the Clump Width setting.

9. Play the animation to frame 50, and stop.

10. Remove any extra points you may have placed on the Clump Width Scale and Clump Curl so that there are only two points on the scales, one on the far right and one on the far left.

11. Set the value of the point on the left side of the Clump Width Scale to **1**; set the point on the far right to **0.32**.

12. Set the point on the far right of the Clump Curl curve to **0.6**.

13. Set the point on the far left of the Clump Flatness scale to **0.5**. Add a point to the far right side of Clump Flatness, and move it to **0.7**. This helps the roots of the hair to lie closer to the head, creating less of a "poufy" shape.

14. Set Clump Interpolation to **0.3**. Leave Interpolation Range set to the default value of **8**.

15. Rewind and play the animation, and make any changes you'd like to the shape of the hair. The length, color, and other properties are further defined in the next section.

16. To get a better sense of the overall look of the hair, set Simulation Method to All Follicles; then rewind and play the animation (see Figure 15.34).

17. Save the scene as **nancyHair_v04.ma**.

To see a version of the scene, open the nancyHair_v04.ma scene from the chapter15/scenes folder.

FOLLICLE OVERRIDES

Many of the settings found in the hairSystemShape node are also found on the nodes for individual follicles in the Per Follicle Overrides section of each follicle's Attribute Editor. You can use these overrides to refine the hair shape for individual follicles. Dynamic overrides are available only for dynamic follicles; these settings are grayed out for passive or static follicles.

FIGURE 15.34
Establish the basic shape of the hair using the settings in the hairSystem1 node.

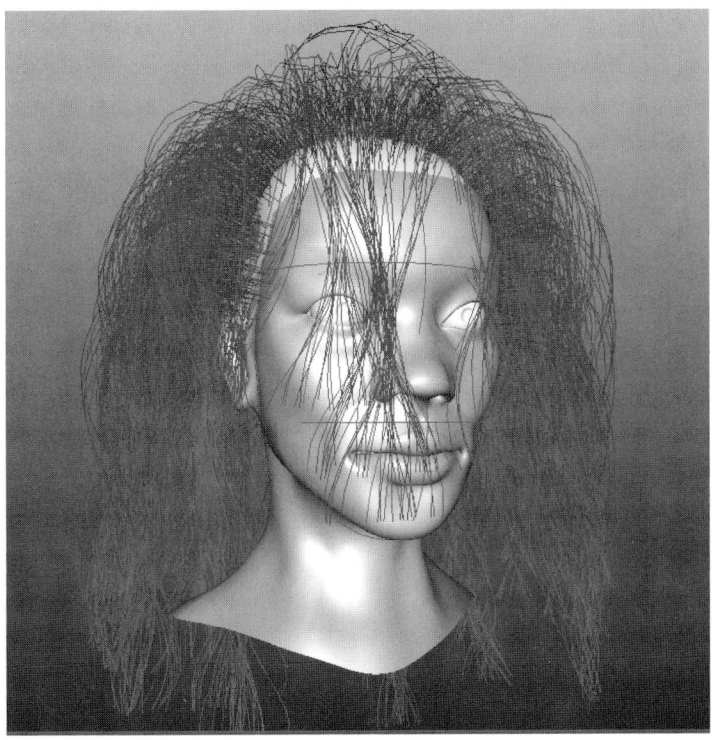

Styling Hair

Once the hair has been set up, you can use a number of tools to style the hair. You can use dynamic fields as a hair styling tool, paint follicle properties on the hair, or even manipulate the CVs of control curves.

Start and Rest Positions

Before styling the hair properly, you should create a start position for the hair so that the animation does not start with the hair sticking straight out of the head. This makes styling much easier.

The start position represents the shape of the hair at the start of the simulation. The rest position represents the hair's shape when no forces are acting upon it. These are very similar, but you can distinguish between the two by thinking of it like this: Imagine an animation where a character is jumping up and down and then stops. The animation starts with the character in midair. You want to set the start position to represent what the hair looks like when the character is in midair. Once the character stops jumping and the hair settles, the hair assumes its rest position. For some animations the start and rest positions may look exactly the same; other times, such as in the example described, the start and rest positions look different.

1. Continue using the scene from the previous section, or open the nancyHair_v04.ma scene from the chapter15\scenes directory.

2. Select the hairSystem1 node, and open its Attribute Editor to the hairSystemShape1 node.

3. Set Simulation Method to Dynamic Follicles Only and Display Quality to **50**.

4. Play the animation until the hair has completely settled.

5. Once the hair has settled, expand the hairSystem1Follicles group in the Outliner, and Shift+click all of the follicle nodes.

6. Choose Hair ➤ Set Start Position ➤ From Current.

7. Set the rest position by choosing Hair ➤ Set Rest Position ➤ From Current.

8. Rewind the animation. The hair should now be down and relatively motionless at the start of the animation.

The start and rest positions are actually determined by two sets of curves that drive the follicles. You can activate the visibility of these curves in the Perspective window.

HAIRSTYLE PRESETS

Maya comes with a number of preset hairstyles in the Visor, as shown here. You can open these by choosing (from the Dynamics menu set) Hair ➤ Get Hair Example. To use a hairstyle, right-click one of the icons, and choose to import the file into your scene. Each preset style comes with hairline geometry that can be parented to your character's head. Or you can copy the style using the Transplant Hair option.

SETTING THE START AND REST POSITIONS

Notice that you can set the start position from the rest position, and vice versa. You can change these positions at any time as you continue to work on the hair and any animations. Notice also that the start and rest positions are applied to the follicles themselves rather than to the hair system. This means you can set start and rest positions for individual follicles if needed.

9. In the Viewport menu, use the Show menu to turn off the visibility of Strokes. This hides the Paint Effects hair.

10. Select the hairSystem1 node, and choose Hair ➤ Display ➤ Start Position. A series of curves appears in blue, representing the hair's start position.

11. Choose Hair ➤ Display ➤ Rest Position. The rest position curves appear in red. If the start and rest positions for the hair system are different, each set of curves will have a different shape.

12. Save the scene as **nancyHair_v05.ma**.

To see a version of the scene, open the nancyHair_v05.ma scene from the chapter15\scenes directory on the DVD.

Painting Follicle Attributes

Using the Artisan Brush interface, you can paint follicle attributes. Before doing this, you must make sure that the hair is in its rest or start position. Some attributes, such as Inclination, require that the animation be on frame1.

1. Continue with the scene from the previous section, or open the nancyHair_v05.ma scene from the chapter 15\scenes directory.

2. Select the hairSystem1 node, and open its Attribute Editor.

3. Switch to the hairSystemShape1 tab, and set Simulation Method to All Follicles. The Display Quality value can be raised to **50**.

4. In the Outliner, select the hairSystem1 node (or the scalp surface).

5. From the Dynamics menu set, choose Hair ➤ Paint Hair Follicles.

   The Tool Options area for the Artisan Brush interface opens as well as the Paint Hair Follicles Settings pop-up box.

6. Set Paint Mode to Trim Hairs. This setting allows you to reduce the length of the hair as you paint across the follicles.

   For the dynamics to remain consistent, you must adjust the number of points on the hair as you paint. When you created the hair originally, the Points Per Hair attribute was set to 10, so to trim the length of a hair to half, set Points Per Hair to 5. The Points Per Hair setting is the setting that actually determines how the hair will be trimmed. Whether you set Hair Length to **1,000** or **0.1** and set Points Per Hair to **5**, the hair will be trimmed to half the original length regardless of the Hair Length setting.

7. Set Points Per Hair to **5**, and paint across the follicles in the front of the scalp to create bangs for the nancy character (Figure 15.35).

8. Once you have trimmed the hair, select the follicles in the Outliner (it's easiest just to Shift+click all the follicles rather than figure out which ones were painted), and choose Hair ➤ Set Rest Position ➤ From Current. You may want to reset the start position as well.

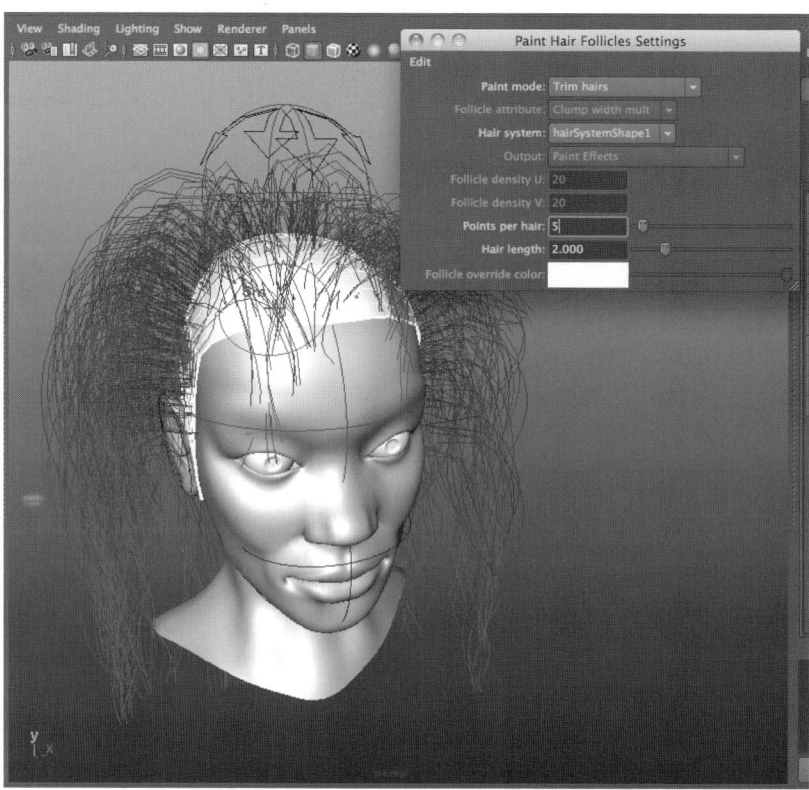

FIGURE 15.35
Trim the hair at the front of the head using the Paint Hair Follicles tool.

QUICK SELECT FOLLICLES

Repeatedly selecting all the follicles or certain follicles whenever you need to set the rest or start position gets tedious rather quickly. You can speed up the process by creating a quick select set for the follicles.

1. Shift+click the follicles in the Outliner.

2. Choose Create ➢ Sets ➢ Quick Select Set.

3. Name the set **NancyFolliclesAll**.

4. You have the option to create a shelf button for this set. To do this, click Add Shelf Button.

   The button appears in the shelf. Every time you need to select all the follicles, just click the button.

5. If you want the button to appear on the shelf the next time you start Maya, click the downward-facing black triangle next to the shelf, and choose Shelf ➢ Save All Shelves.

Be aware that this selection set is specific to this scene. If you click the button in another scene, you will get an error.

If you want to take it a step further, try writing a MEL script that selects the follicles and sets the rest and/or start position all in one click. Creating MEL scripts is discussed in Chapter 17.

9. To extend the hair, set Paint Mode to Extend Hair, and increase Points Per Hair to a number larger than 10. Remember to reset the rest and start positions after extending the hair.

You can use the Hair ➤ Scale Hair tool to apply global scaling to the hair. To use this tool, select it from the Hair menu, and drag left or right. This tool will scale all aspects of the hair, so some adjustment to the shape and dynamics settings maybe required after using the tool.

To paint other attributes, set Paint Mode to Edit Follicle Attributes, and choose an attribute from the Follicle Attribute menu. When painting these attributes, the Value setting in the Brush Options area determines the value painted on the follicles.

10. Save the scene as **nancyHair_v06.ma**.

To see a version of the scene, open the nancyHair_v06.ma scene from the chapter15\scenes directory.

Styling Hair with Fields

You can use dynamic fields to style hair. To do this, simply apply a field to a hair system, run the simulation, and then set the rest and/or start position once the hair assumes the desired shape. Follow these steps to create a unique hairstyle for the nancy character:

1. Continue with the scene from the previous section, or open the nancyHair_v06.ma scene from the chapter15\scenes directory.

2. In the Outliner, select hairSystem1.

3. From the Dynamics menu set, choose Fields ➤ Newton.

4. Move the icon for the Newton field above the head, and open its Attribute Editor.

5. In the Attribute Editor, set Magnitude to **100** and Attenuation to **0** (Figure 15.36).

FIGURE 15.36
Style the hair using a Newton field.

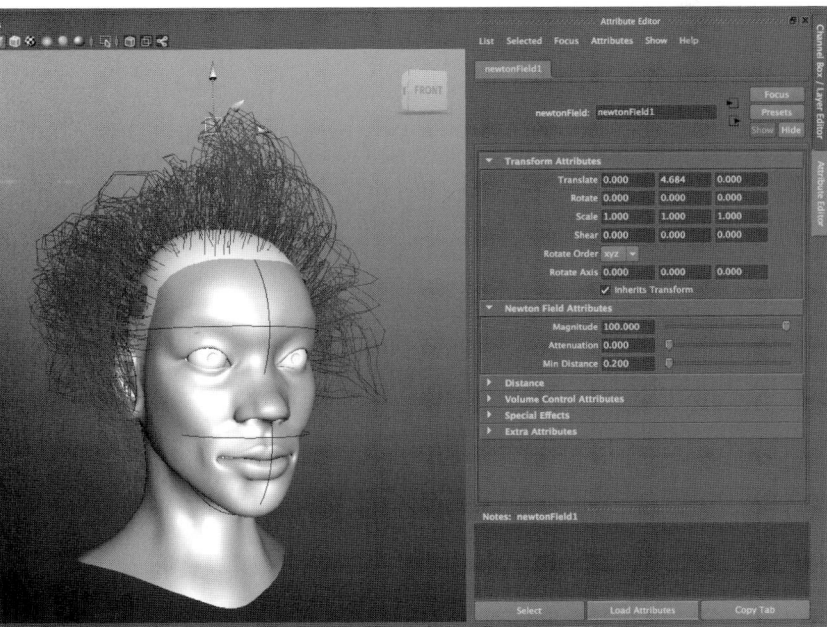

6. Play the animation. The hair should be sucked up into the field.

7. After about 100 frames or so, stop the animation.

8. Shift+click the follicles in the Outliner, and choose Hair ➢ Set Rest Position ➢ From Current. Then choose Hair ➢ Set Start Position ➢ From Current.

9. Delete the Newton field, and rewind the scene.

10. Select the hairSystem1 node, and open its Attribute Editor.

11. In the Dynamics section, set the Start Curve Attract attribute to **0.3**. This helps the hair maintain its shape when the scene is played.

    If motion continues in some of the hairs after the field has been deleted and the start and rest positions have been set, try decreasing the Stiffness value and increasing Iterations. Also changing the Attraction Scale for specific follicles in the Dynamics Override section of the follicle's Attribute Editor can help fix problem areas.

12. Save the scene as **nancyHair_v07.ma**.

To see a version of the scene, open the nancyHair_v07.ma scene from the chapter15\scenes directory on the DVD.

Modifying Curves

You can modify curves directly by moving their CVs or by using the tools in the Hair ➢ Modify Curves menu. By modifying curves directly, you can fine-tune a style.

You can modify only start or rest curves. To do this, use the Show menu in the viewport window to disable the visibility of strokes in the scene, and choose Hair ➢ Display Rest Position (or Start Position). Select the curve (or right-click the curve, and choose Control Vertex to work just on selected CVs), and apply one of the actions listed in the Hair ➢ Modify Curves menu. You can also edit the shape of the curve directly using the Move tool to change the position of CVs on the curve (see Figure 15.37).

FIGURE 15.37
Modify the CVs of a start curve using the Move tool.

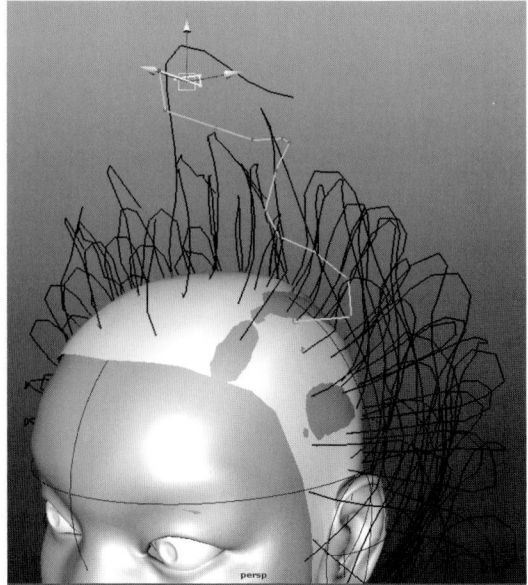

As you are editing the curve, you can lock the length so that the changes you make do not stretch the curve beyond its original length. Select the curve, and choose Hair ➢ Lock Length (or use the l hot key). Conversely, you can unlock the curve if you want to change its length.

Curling, Noise, Sub Clumping, and Braids

Curling, Noise, and Braids all work best when the Sub Segments attribute in the Clump and Hair Shape section of the hair system node is increased. You can find the Curling and Noise settings in the Displacement section of the hair system node.

The Sub Clumping setting causes the hair within clumps to bunch together. This helps when creating wet or kinky hair.

The Braid option is available as an attribute for individual hair follicle nodes. For a braid to work successfully, you may need to alter the clump shape and the hairs per clump. Often it may be a good idea to use a separate hair system to create a detailed braid.

Creating Hair Constraints

Hair constraints are another way to shape hair and are a useful tool for making hair follow other objects in the scene, such as rubber bands or ribbons.

Constraints are applied to selected follicles, and they work only with active follicles. If you try to apply a constraint to a passive follicle, you get a warning that says no hair curves have been selected for the constraint.

You've already used the collision constraint. When you create a constraint, the position of the constraint is indicated by a locator. The locator's position at the start of the animation determines the constraint's starting position. The position of the constraint on subsequent frames of the animation determines how it pulls the hair relative to its position at the start of the animation.

This exercise demonstrates how to add a constraint to a hair system. The example demonstrates the constraint in a simplified scene, making it easier to see how the different types of constraints affect a hair system. This scene has a simple hair system applied to the top of a polygon sphere. The output of the system is curves.

1. Open the constraintsStart_v01.ma scene from the chapter15\scenes directory.

2. Play the scene until about frame 60. The hair curves at the center of the bunch should be visible and easy to select.

3. Select all the curves at the center, as shown in Figure 15.38.

4. Rewind the animation while the curves are still selected.

5. Choose Hair ➢ Create Constraint ➢ Rubber Band to create a constraint. A locator appears at the center of the bunch.

6. Use the Move tool to move the locator above the top of the hair.

   When you move the locator, blue lines appear connecting the hairs to the locator. Since the animation is at frame1, the current position of the locator is the start position of the constraint.

7. With the Move tool still active, choose Solvers ➢ Interactive Playback.

8. While the scene plays, move the locator around, and watch how the hairs react (see Figure 15.39).

FIGURE 15.38
You can easily select the hair curves at the center of the bunch when the animation is played.

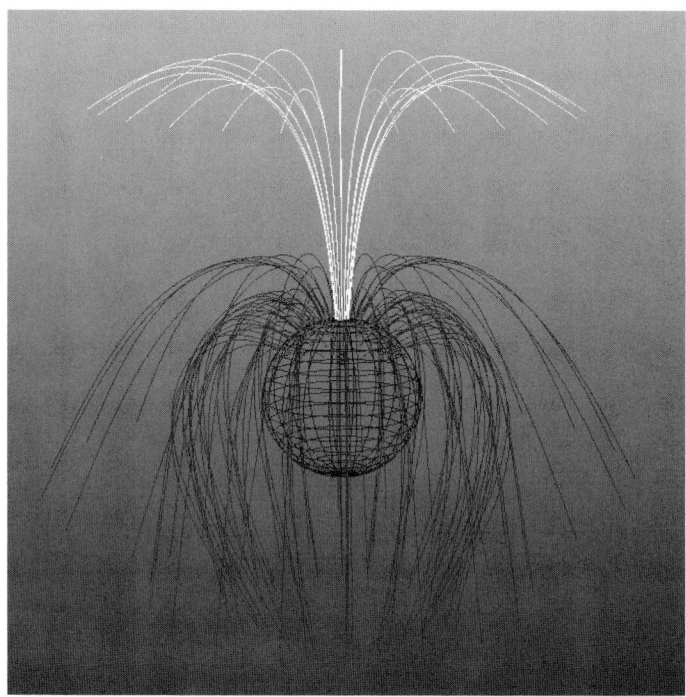

FIGURE 15.39
As you move the locator, the hairs react to its new position.

9. Rewind the animation, and change the position of the locator. Start Interactive Playback again. The position of the locator at the start frame affects how the blue lines are attached to the hairs as well as how the constraint pulls the hairs on subsequent frames.

10. Save the scene as `constraintsStart_v02.ma`.

11. Select the hairConstraint1 node in the Outliner, and open its Attribute Editor.

You can change how the constraint is attached to the hairs (the position of the blue lines that attach the constraint to the hairs) by changing the Point Method setting:

Nearest   The Nearest setting uses the closest distance along the hair to the locator at the start frame of the animation to determine where the constraint is connected to the hairs.

U Parameter   The U Parameter setting allows you to specify the precise U parameter along the length of the curve as the connection point between the constraint and the hairs. The U parameter of the curve ranges between 0 and 1.

U Distance   The U Distance setting defines the distance between the start of the curve and the connection point in U space. So if the curve is 6 units long, the U distance ranges between 0 and 6.

Glue Strength   The two primary controls for hair constraints are Glue Strength and Stiffness. Setting Glue Strength to a value less than 1 allows the constraint to be broken depending on the amount of force applied to it during the simulation.

Stiffness   The Stiffness value can be used to determine the amount of influence the constraint has over the hair curves.

You can add as many constraints as you need to a hair system. You can also change which curves are connected by selecting the curves, Ctrl+clicking the constraint, and choosing Hair ➢ Assign Hair Constraint. You can change the type of constraint after you create it. Here is a brief description of the different constraint types:

Rubber band   Rubber band constraints are somewhat stretchy. The distance between the constraint and the hair on the first frame of the animation establishes the length of the rubber band. If the constraint is moved beyond this length later in the animation, the hairs are pulled toward the constraint.

Stick   The stick constraint maintains the initial length of the constraint throughout the animation. If the constraint is moved away from the hairs, it pulls them, and if the constraint is moved closer to the hairs, it pushes the hairs.

Transform   Transform is similar to the stick constraint in that the constraint both pulls and pushes the hairs. The rotation of transform constraints also affects the hairs.

Hair-to-hair   Hair-to-hair constraints create a clump. To use this constraint properly, play the simulation until some of the hairs are close together; then select the hair curves, and create a hair-to-hair constraint. Rewind and play the animation. The hairs are connected by blue lines and should react as if they are bound together. Moving the locator changes the position of the constraints along the hair curves depending on the setting used for Point Method in the constraint properties. Moving the constraint locator around after the initial frame has no effect on how the constraint behaves (see Figure 15.40).

Hair bunch   Hair bunch is a method of simulating self-collision between hairs that is more computationally efficient than the built-in Self Collide feature available in the Collision section of the hairSystem node. This constraint is meant to keep hairs from intersecting one another.

To see a version of the scene with an attached hair constraint, open the constraintsStart_v02.ma scene from the chapter15\scenes directory on the DVD.

FIGURE 15.40
Use a hair-to-hair constraint to bind the ends of selected hairs together.

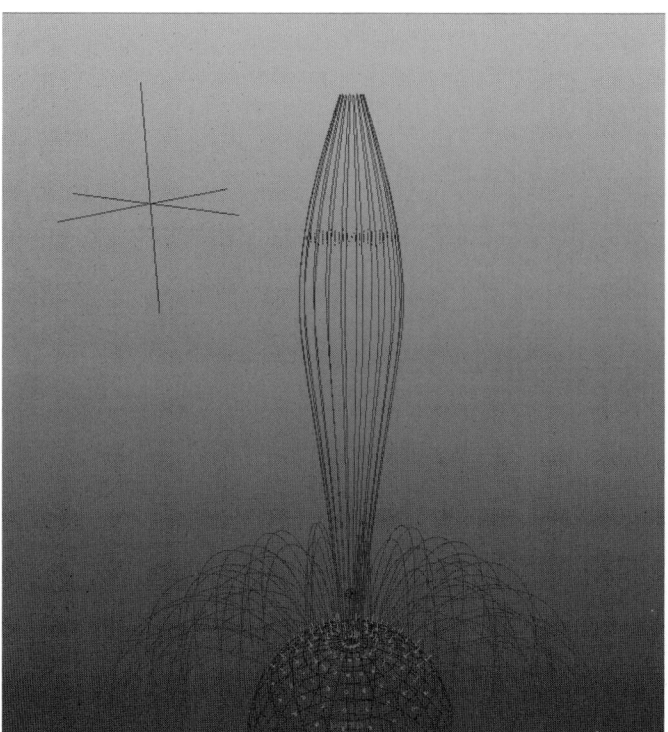

Rendering Hair

Rendering hair can be done using Maya Software or mental ray. The hair should be either Paint Effects strokes or Paint Effects strokes converted to geometry. Paint Effects strokes are discussed in detail in Chapter 7.

COLORING HAIR

If you decide to render hair as Paint Effects strokes, you can change the Hair Color, Translucence, and Specular properties using the settings in the hairSystemShape tab's Shading section.

Rendering hair is a very straightforward process. If you're not familiar with Paint Effects, you should review Chapter 8 before reading this section.

When you convert hair to geometry, the Hair Tube shader is automatically applied. You can render Paint Effects hair using mental ray without the need to convert the hair to geometry.

When you are ready to render the hair, you'll want to increase the Hair Sub Segments setting in the hairSystem's Attribute Editor, as well as Hairs Per Clump, Hair Width, and Hair Width Scale, in order to create fuller hair. You can always add follicles as well using the Paint Follicles tool.

In the Render Stats section of the hairSystem node, you can enable Receive Shadows, Visible In Reflections, and Visible In Refractions when rendering with mental ray. On the Quality tab of the mental ray render settings, you can use the Rapid Motion Hair preset to render hair without raytracing or the Production: Fine Trace preset for rendering with raytracing. If the hair will not render using mental ray, make sure the Render Fur/Hair setting is activated on the Features tab of the mental ray Rendering section.

In this scene, the dreads.mel preset, found on the Hair Examples tab of the Visor, is applied to the nancy model. The hairLights.mel file has also been imported from the Visor and applied to the scene.

1. Open the renderHair.ma scene from the chapter15\scenes folder on the DVD.

2. Switch to the quarterSide camera, and create a test render in the Render View window.

The scene is set up to render using mental ray. The render will take a couple minutes. Figure 15.41 shows the results (shadows have been enabled for the lights in the image).

Most standard lights will render hair nicely. When you're testing the look of the hair, using the hairLights.mel preset makes it easy to see how the hair will look when rendered.

FIGURE 15.41
Apply the dreadlocks preset hair to the nancy model, and render it with mental ray.

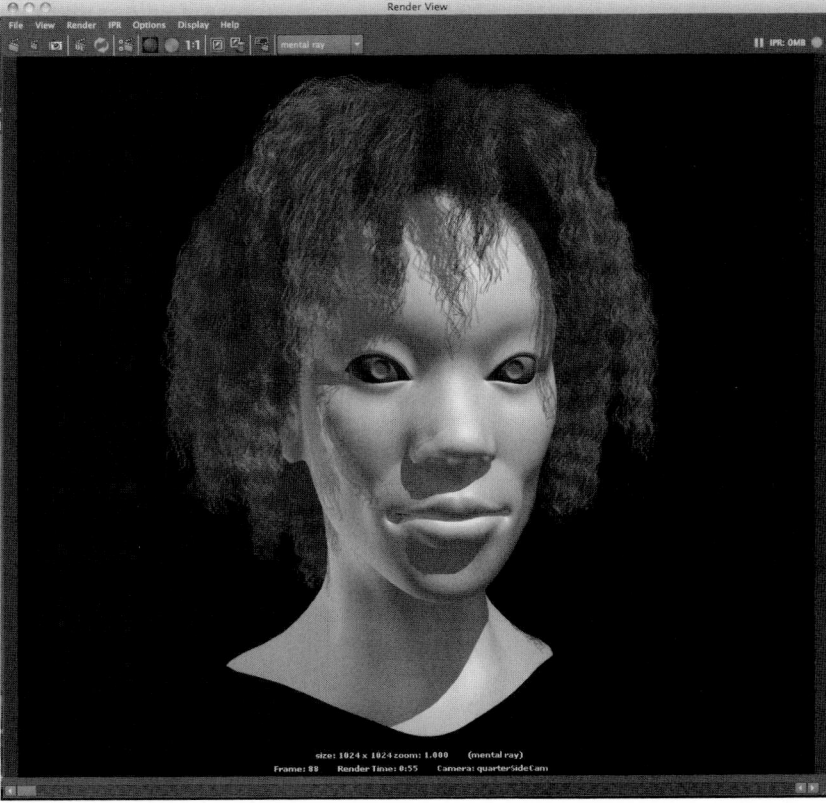

Creating Clothing for Characters

Chapter 14 introduced the nCloth dynamic simulation tools in the context of creating advanced simulations with nParticles. As the name suggests, nCloth was originally developed to simulate the dynamic properties of clothing. In this section, you'll explore techniques for using nCloth to add dynamic motion to a character's clothes. The example files are simple, but you can use the same techniques for more complex characters and models.

Before starting this section, you should review Chapters 13 and 14 so that you understand how nDynamics and the Nucleus solver work.

Modeling Clothes for nCloth

The models you create for use with nCloth must be polygon meshes. Beyond that, there is nothing special about how you model your clothing. Smooth mesh polygons work just as well as standard polygons. You'll start by taking a look at an example scene.

This scene has a very simple cartoon character that has been rigged and animated. The character has a shirt and pants that have both been created using standard polygon modeling techniques. Both objects are currently smooth mesh polygons. The scene has been arranged so that the display layers contain the major components of the model and the animation rig.

1. Open the simpleMan_v01.ma scene from the chapter15\scenes directory on the DVD (see Figure 15.42).

FIGURE 15.42
The simpleMan_ v01.ma scene contains a simple cartoon character. Clothes have been modeled using polygons.

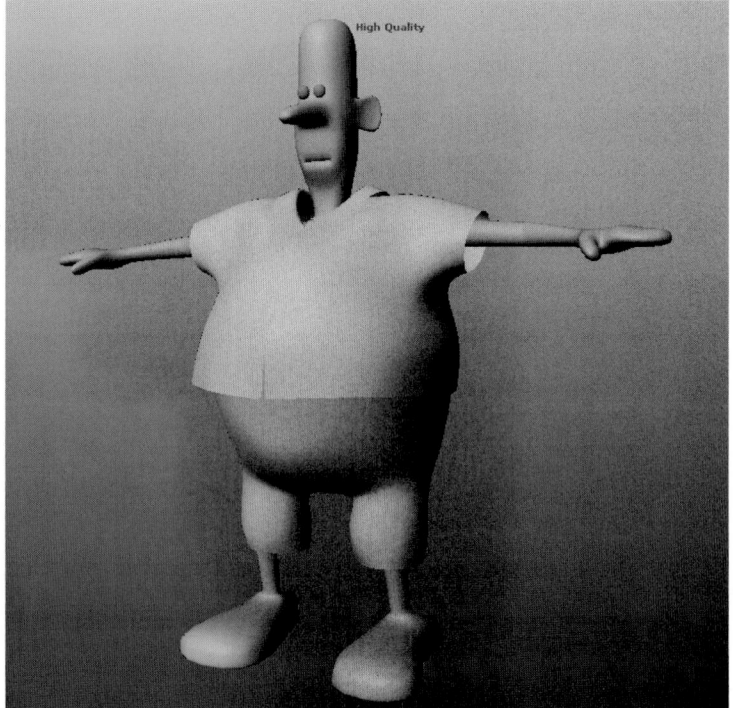

2. Turn off the visibility of the SHIRT and PANTS layers, and play the scene. Starting at frame 50, you'll see the man has been animated so that he moves up and down. This is just a simple animation cycle suitable for testing basic nCloth properties.

3. Rewind and restore the visibility of the PANTS layer. If you select the pants geometry, you'll see it's a basic polygon mesh. Press the **1** key, and you'll see the pants as standard nonsmoothed polygons.

Converting Smooth Mesh Polygons to nCloth

You can convert smooth mesh polygons to nCloth objects. When you do this, the smooth mesh polygons switch to standard polygon mode automatically. You can then switch them back to smooth mesh polygons.

1. Continue with the `simpleMan_v01.ma` scene from the previous section.

2. Switch to the nDynamics menu set.

3. Select the pants, and choose nMesh ➤ Create nCloth. The pants switch to standard polygon mode.

4. Select the pants, and press the **3** key to switch back to smooth mesh polygons.

5. Play the scene. You'll see the pants fall down. (This kind of thing can be embarrassing, but it happens a lot to cartoon characters; see Figure 15.43.)

FIGURE 15.43
When you play the scene, the character's pants fall down.

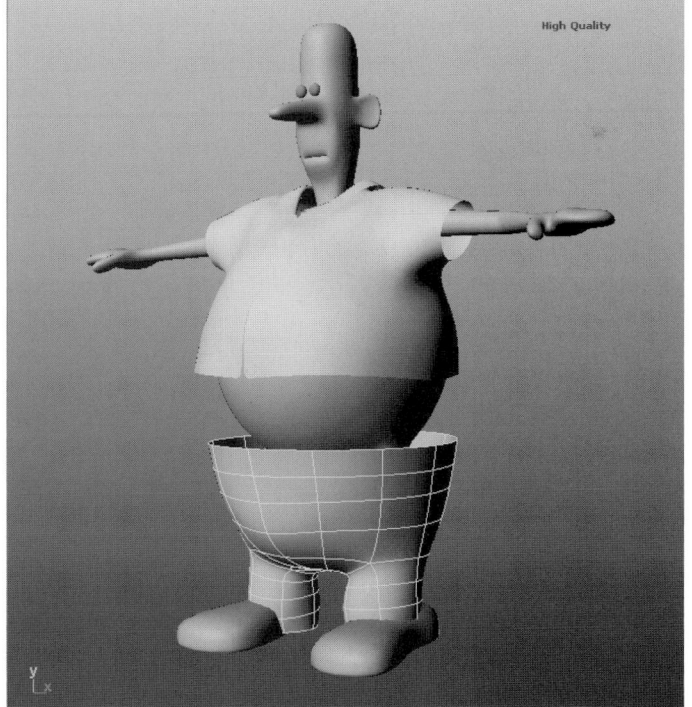

The first step in preventing the pants from falling is to make the character's body a Passive Collider object. It does not matter that the character is already rigged and animated. However, it's a good idea to convert the polygons to nCloth objects (both nCloth and Passive Collider objects) when the character is in the default pose and there are no intersections between the nCloth and Passive Collider geometry.

1. Rewind the animation.

2. In the Display Layer Editor, click the R next to the MAN layer to turn off Reference mode so you can directly select the man geometry.

3. Select the man geometry, and choose nMesh ➢ Create Passive Collider.

SIMPLE VS. COMPLEX GEOMETRY

The geometry used for the man is fairly simple. If you have a very complex character, you may want to use a lower-resolution copy of the geometry as a collision object. This lower-resolution copy should have its Primary Visibility setting turned off in the Render Stats section of its Attribute Editor, and the geometry should be skinned to joints or deformers in a way that matches the deformations of the higher-resolution objects.

---

4. Rewind and play the scene. The pants still fall down, but they are stopped from falling indefinitely by the character's feet.

5. Save the scene as **simpleMan_v02.ma**.

To see a version of the scene, open the `simpleMan_v02.ma` scene from the `chapter15\scenes` directory.

In the next section, you'll create a constraint that will keep a character's pants from falling down.

Adding a Transform Constraint

The simplest way to keep the character's pants on is to create a transform constraint. A transform constraint attaches the selected vertices on an nCloth object to the pivot point of another object without affecting the position of the nCloth vertices. When the constraining object is translated or rotated, the vertices follow along, dragging the rest of the nCloth object with them.

1. Continue with the scene from the previous section, or open the `simpleMan_v02.ma` scene from the `chapter15\scenes` directory on the DVD.

2. Turn off the visibility of the MAN layer, and turn on the visibility of the JOINTS layer.

   At the center of the pelvis you'll see a locator. This is the rootControl locator used to animate the character's skeleton. You can use this locator as the constraining object for the nCloth pants.

3. Right-click the pants, and choose Edges to switch to edge selection mode.

4. Double-click one of the edges at the top of the pants. This selects all the edges that run around the top of the pants (left image, Figure 15.44).

FIGURE 15.44
Select the edges at the top of the pants (left image). Convert the edge selection to vertices (center image). When you constrain the vertices to the rootCtrl locator, the pants stay up and collide with the animated character (right image).

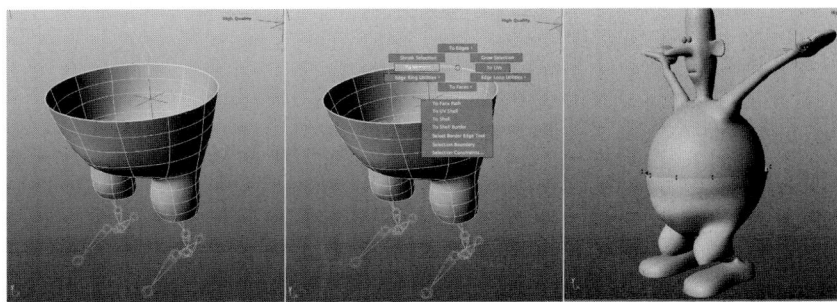

5. Hold the mouse over the selected edges, press the Ctrl key, and RMB-drag to the left.

6. Select the To Vertices label from the marking menu. This converts the selection to vertices (center image, Figure 15.44).

7. With the vertices selected (they should be highlighted in yellow) in the Outliner, Ctrl+click the rootCtrl locator, and choose nConstraint ➤ Transform. The vertices should turn green, indicating that they are constrained. In the Outliner, you'll see a new dynamicConstraint1 node has been created.

8. Turn the visibility of the MAN layer back on, and play the animation. The pants should now stay in place, and when the man starts moving, they should collide with the character's legs (right image, Figure 15.44).

9. Save the scene as `simpleMan_v03.ma`.

To see a version of the scene, open the `simpleMan_v03.ma` scene from the `chapter15\scenes` directory on the DVD.

Using Component Constraints

Components of nCloth objects, such as vertices, can be used as constraints. Using this technique, you can easily simulate the effect of buttons holding a shirt together.

1. Continue with the scene from the previous section, or open the `simpleMan_v03.ma` scene from the `chapter15\scenes` directory.

2. In the Display Layer Editor, turn on the visibility of the SHIRT layer.

3. Before converting the shirt to an nCloth object, make sure it does not intersect with the pants. Rotate the view so you can see the back of the character; here you can see that the shirt is intersecting the pants (left image, Figure 15.45).

4. Right-click the faces near the intersection, and choose Faces.

5. Use the Move tool to move the faces outward just enough that they do not intersect the pants (right image, Figure 15.45).

FIGURE 15.45
The surface of the shirt intersects the pants in the back of the character. Use the Move tool to move the faces of the shirt outward to fix the problem.

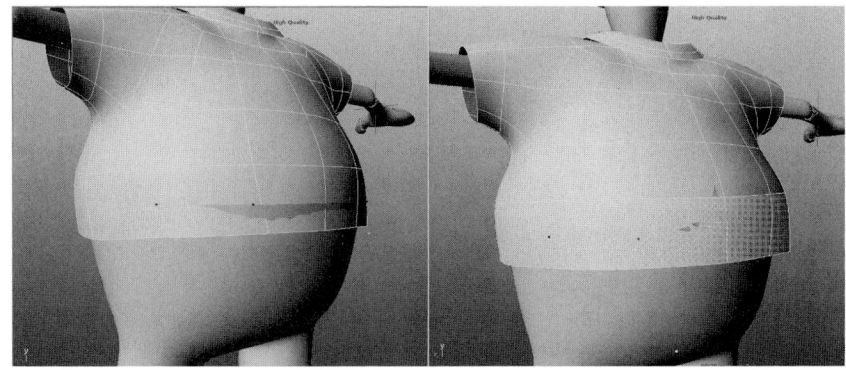

6. Select the shirt, and choose nMesh ➤ Create nCloth. The shirt switches back to standard polygon mode; select the shirt, and press the **3** key to return to smooth mesh.

7. Rewind and play the animation. The shirt falls until it collides with the character geometry. It moves as the character moves; however, you can see the front of the shirt fly open (see Figure 15.46).

8. Zoom in to the front of the shirt, and turn off the visibility of the MAN and PANTS display layers.

9. Right-click the shirt, and choose Vertices.

FIGURE 15.46
As the character moves, the front of the shirt flies open.

10. Switch to wireframe mode. Select the two vertices at the top of the shirt close to the collar (Figure 15.47, left image).

11. Choose nConstraints ➢ Component To Component. This creates a constraint between the two vertices.

12. Repeat step 8 and 9 to create constraints for the other three pairs of vertices running down the shirt. You don't need to constrain the two at the very bottom. You should end up with four constraints running down the front of the shirt (Figure 15.47, right image).

13. Switch to shaded mode, turn on the MAN and PANTS layers, and rewind and play the scene. The front of the shirt is now bound as if it has buttons (see Figure 15.48).

14. Save the scene as **simpleMan_v04.ma**.

FIGURE 15.47
Select vertices near the collar, and turn them into a con- straint (left image). Then create four pairs of constraints on the front of the shirt (right image).

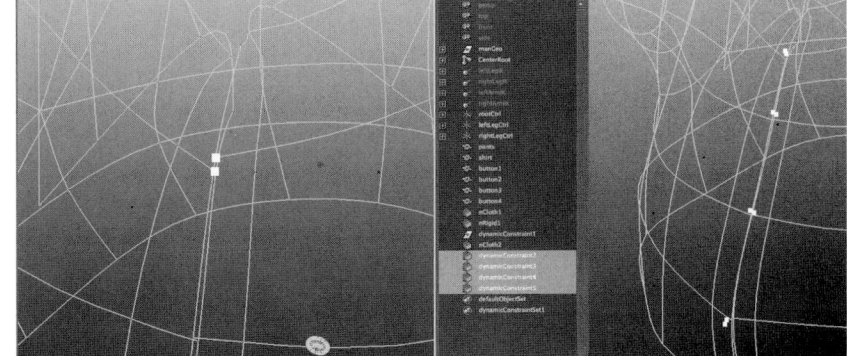

FIGURE 15.48
When you play the animation, the shirt stays closed as if it has buttons.

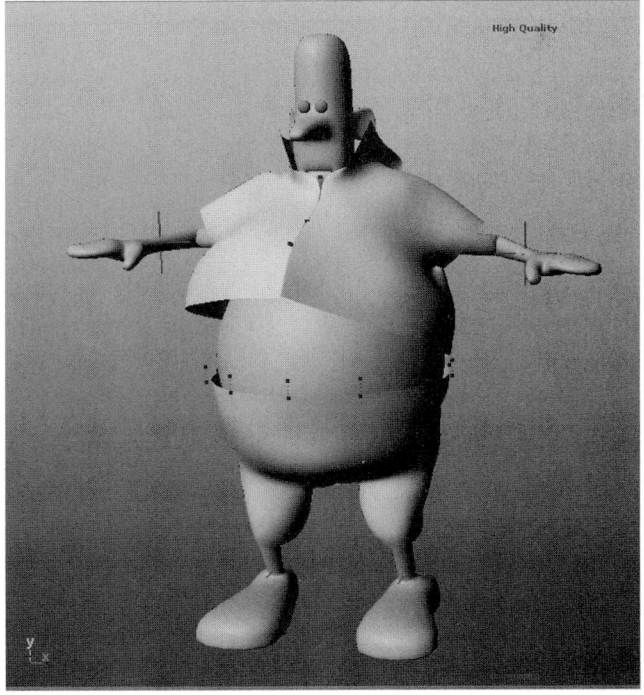

To see a version of the scene, open the `simpleMan_v04.ma` scene from the `chapter15\scenes` directory on the DVD.

Connecting Buttons to the Shirt

You can connect buttons to the shirt geometry using the Point On Poly constraint, which is new to Maya 2011.

New!

1. Continue with the scene from the previous section, or open the `simpleMan_v04.ma` scene from the `chapter15\scenes` directory on the DVD.

2. In the Outliner, select button1. The button is located at the origin, so currently it is in the center of the character. Use the Move tool to move the button close to the top of the shirt. Enter the following settings:

   Translate X: **0.115**

   Translate Y: **3.576**

   Translate Z: **2.295**

3. Right-click the shirt geometry, and choose Vertex to switch to vertex selection mode.

4. Select one of the vertices toward the top of the shirt on the inside edge (See Figure 15.49). Shift+click the button1 node.

5. Switch to the Animation menu set, and choose Constrain ➢ PointonPoly. The button will snap to the geometry. Most likely, the position and the rotation will be off.

6. In the Outliner, select the button1 object, expand it, and select the button1_pointOnPolyConstraint1 node.

7. Open the Channel Box, and MMB-drag the field for Offset Rotate X to rotate the button to a better position; try a value of **75**. You can use the other Offset fields to fine-tune the rotation and position of the button (Figure 15.50).

FIGURE 15.49
The vertices toward the top of the shirt are selected, and then the button is Shift+clicked.

Figure 15.50
The Offset fields are used to rotate and translate the constrained button into the correct position.

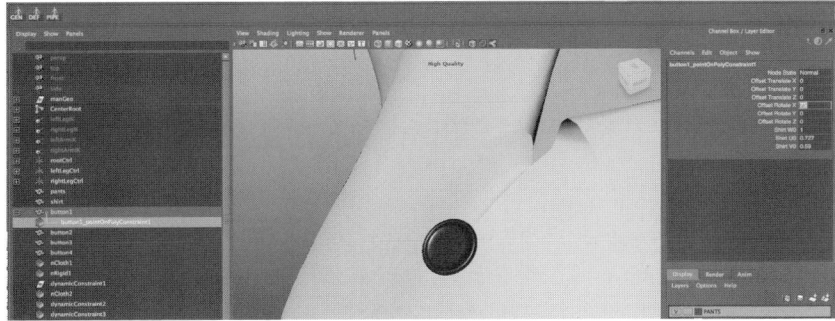

8. Repeat the process to constrain the other three buttons in the Outliner to the shirt.

9. Save the scene as `simpleMan_v05.ma`.

To see a version of the scene, open the `simpleMan_v05.ma` scene from the `chapter15` folder on the DVD.

You can also select a face of a polygon object and use the Point On Poly constraint to attach an object to a polygon face.

Painting nCloth Properties

nCloth properties, such as Bounce, Stretch, and Wrinkle, can be painted onto an nCloth object. There are two ways to do this: vertex property maps and texture property maps.

When you paint a vertex property map, you paint property values directly onto the vertices of the object, similar to painting smooth skin weights for joints. The more vertices you have in your object, the more detail you can create for your vertex property map. The vertex map values are saved with the object, so you do not need to link to external map files.

Texture property maps are independent of the number of vertices in the object, but they do require that UVs are properly created for the object, meaning that the UVs do not overlap and remain within the 0 to 1 range in the UV Texture Editor. Texture property maps for nCloth objects are very similar to texture property maps created for fur (this was demonstrated earlier in the chapter). However, you do not need to bake the maps after applying them.

When you paint a vertex or texture map, the map is listed in the Attribute field in the Dynamic Properties section of the nCloth shape node's Attribute Editor.

Painting a Vertex Property Map

In this example, you'll paint Wrinkle attributes for the simple man character's pants. A wrinkle map displaces an nCloth object to create folds in the surface. You can paint detailed wrinkles into objects with a lot of vertices. In this example, you'll use the wrinkle map to add cartoonish embellishments to the pants, which have a fairly low number of vertices.

When applying a Wrinkle attribute, positive values push the nCloth outward, while negative values push inward. There are a few peculiarities about painting Wrinkle values, which you'll explore in this lesson.

1. Continue with the scene from the previous section, or open the `simpleMan_v05.ma` scene from the `chapter15\scenes` directory.

2. Turn off the visibility of the SHIRT and JOINTS layers.

3. Rewind and play the animation. The pants maintain their shape until they start to collide.

4. Rewind the animation again; select the pants object, and choose (from the nDynamics menu set) nMesh ➤ Paint Vertex Properties ➤ Wrinkle ➤ Options.

   The pants turn white, indicating that a value of 1 is applied to the vertices of the pants for the Wrinkle property. Make sure the Renderer in the Viewport menu is set to Default Render Quality so that you can see the color values painted onto the pants geometry.

5. Rewind and play the animation. The pants suddenly bloat outward, even though you have not made any changes. What just happened (top image, Figure 15.51)?

FIGURE 15.51
When you create the wrinkle map and play the animation, the pants bloat outward. When you apply the value 0 to all the vertices, the pants turn black and the shape returns to normal.

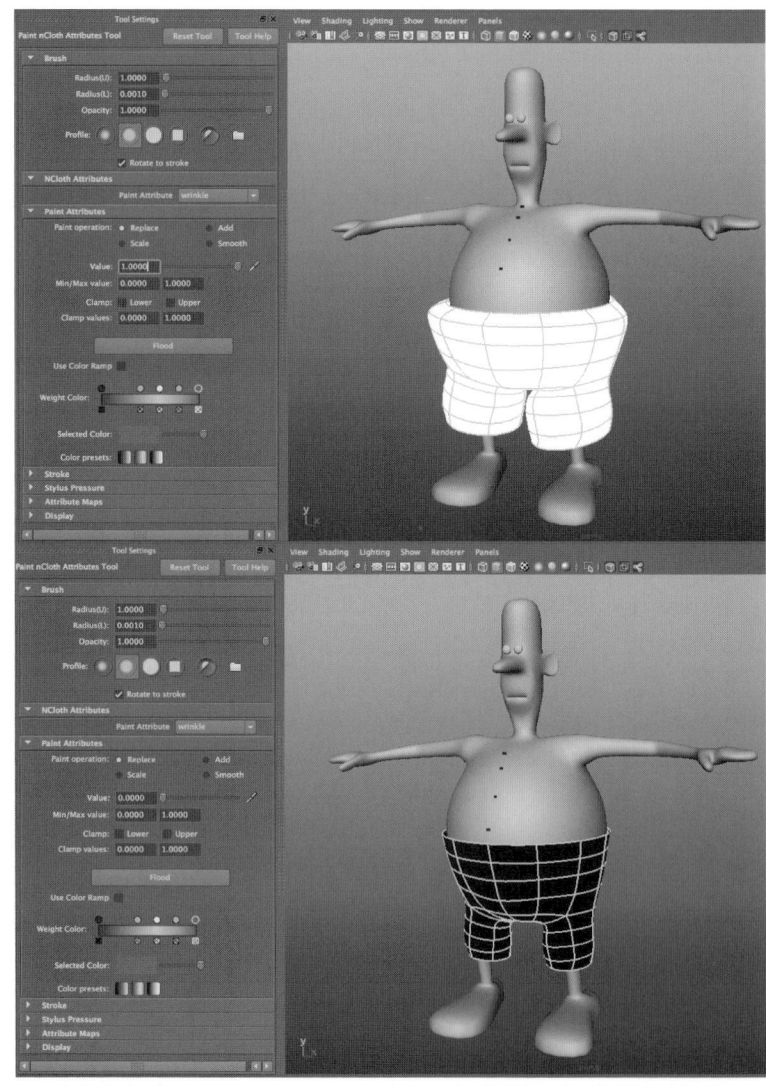

When you start to create the wrinkle map, Maya applies a value of 1 to all the vertices of the object at the moment the map is created. Prior to creating the wrinkle map, no Wrinkle value is applied to the pants, so they do not bloat outward until the map is made. This behavior is specific to the wrinkle map.

6. Open the Tool Options box, and set the value to **0**. Make sure the Paint Attributes menu in the nCloth Attributes rollout panel of the Tool settings is set to Wrinkle.

7. Click the Flood button, and rewind the animation.

   The pants turn black, and the bloating disappears. The wrinkle values are now set to 0 for all the vertices of the pants geometry (bottom image, Figure 15.51).

   At this point, you'll paint the area where the pant legs emerge from the pants with a value of -0.2 so that the pant legs shrink inward. Notice, however, that the Value slider in the Artisan Tool options only goes from 0 to 1.

8. In the Tool Options box, look at the Min/Max value fields. Set the first field, which is the Min Value, to **-1**, and the second field, which is the Max Value, to **1**.

   Now it is possible to paint negative numbers, but you'll notice that since the black color on the pants indicates a value of 0, there is no color feedback for negative numbers. This can be changed as well.

9. Scroll down to the bottom of the Tool Options box, and expand the Display rollout panel. Make sure Color Feedback is on. Set Min Color to **-1** and Max Color to **1** (see Figure 15.52).

   The pants turn gray, indicating that the current value applied to the vertices (0) is in the middle range of colors between black and white. As you paint negative values on the pants, you'll see darker areas appear.

FIGURE 15.52

You can adjust the Min/Max value fields to allow for a wider range of values for the Paint nCloth Attributes tool. Adjusting the Min Color and Max Color sliders allows you to visualize the new values painted on the surface.

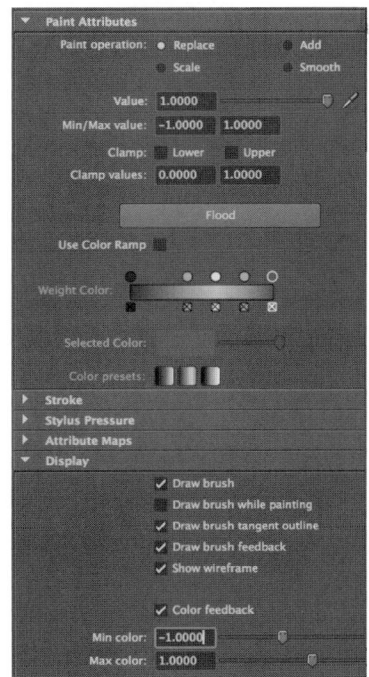

10. Set the Value slider to **-0.2**, and paint around the area where the pant legs meet the pants.

11. Rewind and play the scene. You'll see the tops of the pant legs shrink in a little.

12. To create flares (flares on shorts are apparently all the rage now), set the value to **0.4**, and paint the cuffs of the pants (see Figure 15.53).

13. To create the impression of a drawstring, paint a value of **-1** around the area of the pants where a belt would go.

14. Press the **q** hot key to switch to the Select tool. Doing this will close the Artisan tool; the pants return to green.

15. Rewind and play the animation. Experiment making more changes by painting various Wrinkle values on the pants.

16. Save the scene as `simpleMan_v06.ma`.

To see a version of the scene, open the `simpleMan_v06.ma` scene from the `chapter15\scenes` directory.

FIGURE 15.53
Paint a value of -0.2 around the belt area of the pants. Paint positive values near the pant cuffs to create flares.

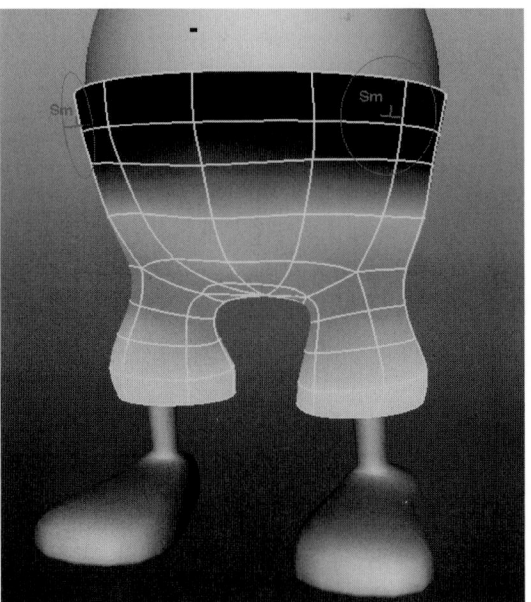

The Bottom Line

Add fur to characters   Maya Fur is a rendering module that adds realistic short hairs to the surface of characters to simulate fur. Fur can be rendered using both Maya Software and mental ray. The placement, length, and other attributes of fur can be controlled by painting on the surface with the Artisan tool interface. When adding fur to polygons, the success of the fur is largely dependent on how well the UV texture coordinates have been mapped.

Master it   Create Fur for the giraffe model used in Chapter 11.

Add dynamic motion to fur   Using hair curves as a control, fur can be made to react to dynamic forces.

Master it   Create a field of grass that blows in the wind.

Create dynamic curves   A standard Maya curve can be made dynamic by using the Make Dynamic Curves action in the Hair menu. A copy of the curve is created that will respond to dynamic motion and forces. The curve can be used in skeletons for IK Spline tools, as a source for Paint Effects strokes, as a modeling tool, or for any other effect that requires curves.

Master it   Create a flag using dynamic curves.

Add hair to characters   Hair is created using Paint Effects strokes that are controlled by follicles. The follicles are dynamic curves that respond to forces and movement. Follicles can be applied to polygon or NURBS surfaces as a grid or by painting on the surface. The Visor contains a number of hair presets that can be imported into a scene.

Master it   Add hair to the old man character from Chapter 9.

Style hair   Hair can be styled by painting attribute values on follicles, by using dynamic fields, or by directly editing the CVs of start or rest curves.

Master it   Create an avant-garde hairdo for the nancy character using fields.

Use hair constraints   Hair constraints can be used to control the motion of hair or to connect the hair to props, such as hair ties and scrunchies.

Master it   Use a constraint to create a ponytail for a character.

Paint nCloth properties   Properties such as Bounce, Stretch, and Wrinkle can be painted onto nCloth objects using either texture or vertex painting techniques. When painting properties, the Min and Max Value ranges in the Artisan interface may need to be altered to allow for values beyond the range of 0 to 1. Vertex maps have the advantage that the values are not stored in an external texture file.

Master it   Add starch to the simple man's shirt by painting a Rigidity value on the shirt geometry.

Chapter 16

Maya Fluids

Maya Fluids is a suite of tools designed to create a number of fluid-based effects. The tools available in Maya Fluids consist of containers and emitters, which are designed to simulate gaseous effects such as clouds, smoke, flames, explosions, galactic nebulae, and so on, as well as dynamic geometry deformers and shaders, which can be used to simulate rolling ocean waves, ripples in ponds, and wakes created by boats. Maya 2011 has added new controls and features that enhance the realism of the effects you can create using fluids.

In this chapter, you will learn to:

◆ Use fluid containers

◆ Create a reaction

◆ Render fluid containers

◆ Use fluids with nParticles

◆ Create an ocean

Using Fluid Containers

Fluid containers can be thought of as mini scenes within a Maya scene. Fluid containers are best used for gaseous and plasma effects such as clouds, flames, and explosions. The effect itself can exist only within the container. Fluids can be generated inside the container by using an emitter or by painting the fluid inside the container. Dynamic forces then act on the fluid within the container to create the effect.

There are two types of containers: 2D and 3D. They work the same way. Two-dimensional containers are flat planes that generally calculate faster than 3D containers, which are cubical volumes. If you do not need an object to fly through a fluid effect or if the camera angle does not change in relation to the fluid, you might want to try a 2D container instead of a 3D container. Using a 2D container can save a lot of calculation and render time. Two-dimensional containers are also a great way to generate an image sequence that can be used as a texture on a surface.

FLUIDS VS. NPARTICLES

When should you use fluids, and when should you use nParticles? There's no hard-and-fast rule for choosing one over the other. However, if you need to create a dense cloud and you find yourself setting the rate of an nParticle emitter greater than 100,000 nParticles per second, you should really consider switching to Fluids. Fluids and nParticles can work together as well, as you'll see later in the chapter.

Fluids are not part of the Nucleus system, so they are not influenced by settings on the Nucleus solver. nParticles and the Nucleus solver are covered in Chapters 13 and 14.

Using 2D Containers

In this first exercise, you'll work with fluid basics to create a simple but interesting effect using 2D containers. When you set up a container, you can choose to add an emitter that generates the fluid within the container, or you can place the fluid inside the container using the Artisan Brush interface. You'll start your experimentation using the latter method.

1. Create a new scene in Maya. Switch to the Dynamics menu set.

2. Choose Fluid Effects ➢ Create 2D Container. A simple plane appears on the scene.

   The simple plane is the 2D container. If you play the scene, nothing happens because currently there are no fluids within the container. In the Outliner you'll see a new node named fluid1. The fluid1 object, like many Maya objects, consists of a transform node (named fluid1) and a shape node (fluidShape1).

3. Select fluid1, and choose Fluid Effects ➢ Add/Edit Contents ➢ Paint Fluids Tool.

4. Click the Tool settings icon in the upper right of the interface to open the settings for the Artisan Brush interface.

5. Open the Tool options, and make sure Paintable Attributes is set to Density and Value is set to 1.

6. Paint a few strokes on the container. Clumps of green dots appear if you are in wireframe mode.

7. Press the **5** key on the keyboard to switch to shaded mode. The clumps appear as soft, blurry blobs (see Figure 16.1).

8. Set the length of the timeline to **200**.

9. Rewind and play the scene. The fuzzy blobs rise and distort like small clouds. They mix together and appear trapped by the edges of the container.

FIGURE 16.1
Use the Artisan Brush to paint areas of density in the 2D fluid container.

PLAYING FLUID SIMULATIONS

Like many of Maya's dynamics modules, Fluids evaluates each frame based on what occurs in the previous frame. Therefore, you need to have your playback preferences set to Every Frame in order for Fluids to calculate correctly.

The properties that govern how the fluid exists within the container and how it behaves are controlled using the settings on the fluidShape1 node. When you painted in the container using the Paint Fluid tools, you painted the density of the fluid. By creating areas of density, you position the fluid in an otherwise empty container.

The list of attributes that can be painted in a container using Artisan also include Density and Color, Density and Fuel, Velocity, Temperature, Fuel, Color, and Falloff. As you work through the exercises in this chapter, you'll learn how each of these attributes affect fluid simulations.

Adding an Emitter

Another way to generate a fluid within a fluid container is to use a *fluid emitter*. Fluid emitters are similar to particle emitters in that they consist of a point or area in 3D space that generates fluids at a rate you can control. The main difference between fluids and particles is that the fluids created by an emitter can exist only within the confines of the fluid container.

Fluid emitter types include omni, volume, surface, and curve:

◆ An omni emitter is a point in space that emits in all directions.

◆ A volume emitter creates fluids within a predefined area that can be in the form of a simple primitive such as a sphere or a cube.

◆ Surface emitters create fluids from the surface of a 3D object.

◆ Curve emitters create fluids along the length of a NURBS curve.

New! Maya 2011 has added fluid emission maps that can control the emission of a fluid's density, heat, and fuel using a texture. This opens up a lot of creative possibilities for creating some interesting effects. In this exercise, you'll map a file texture to the fluid's density attribute.

1. Continue with the scene from the previous section. Rewind the scene. In the options for the Artisan Brush, set Value to **0**, and click the Flood button. This clears the container of any existing fluid density.

2. Create a NURBS plane (choose Create ➢ NURBS Primitives ➢ Plane). Rotate the plane 90 degrees on the x-axis, and scale the plane so that it fits within the 2D container (see Figure 16.2).

3. Select the plane, and then Shift+click the fluid1 node. Choose Fluid Effects ➢ Add/Edit Contents ➢ Emit From Object ➢ Options. In the options, make sure Emitter Type is set to Surface. You can leave the rest of the settings at their default values (see Figure 16.3).

4. Rewind and play the animation; you'll see a cloud appear around the plane. To get a better idea of what's going on, use the Show menu in the viewport to disable the display of NURBS surfaces. This should not affect the simulation.

FIGURE 16.2
A NURBS plane is placed within the 2D fluid container.

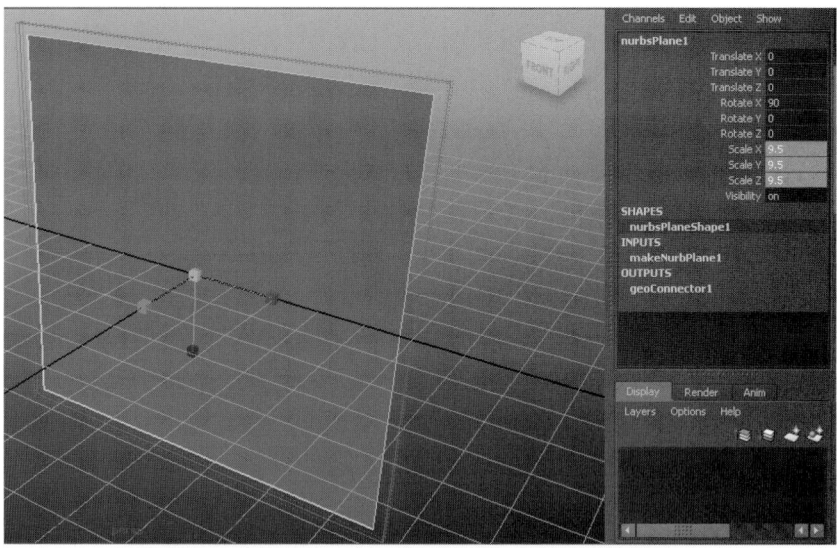

FIGURE 16.3
The options for the fluid emitter

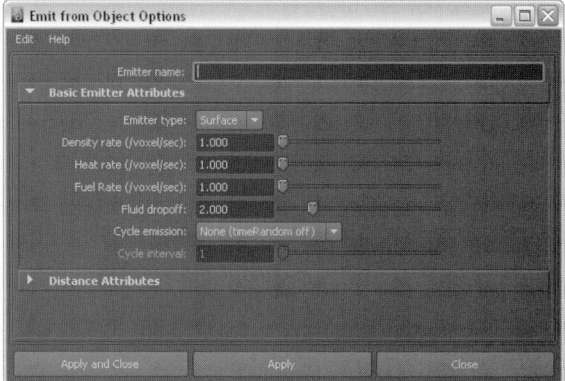

5. In the Outliner, expand the nurbsPlane1 object, and select fluidEmitter1.

6. Open its Attribute Editor, and expand the Fluid Attributes rollout panel.

7. Click the checkered icon to the right of Density Emission Map (see Figure 16.4). This opens the Create Texture Node window. Select File from the 2D Textures section.

8. When you select the File texture type, a new node called file1 is added. The Attribute Editor for file1 should open automatically when you create the node; if it does not, open it now.

9. Click the folder icon to the right of the Image Name field. Browse your computer, and find the jollyRoger.tif file in the chapter16\sourceimages folder of the DVD.

10. Rewind and play the scene. You'll see a cloud appear in the form of the skull and cross-bones. After a few moments, it will rise to the top of the fluid container.

FIGURE 16.4
You can find the
Density Emission
Map settings in the
Attribute Editor
for the Fluid
Emitter node.

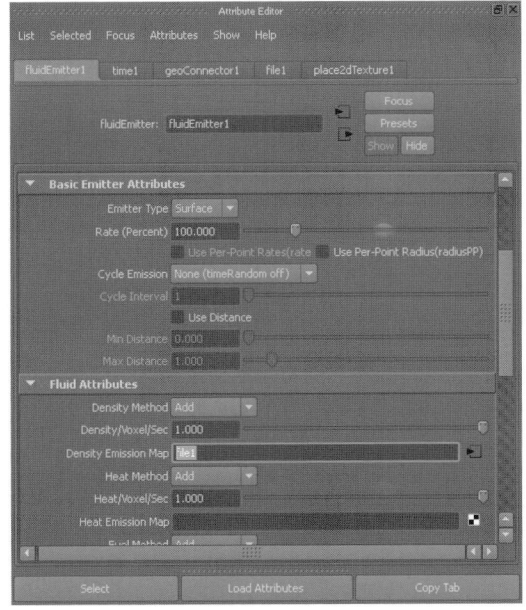

11. In the Outliner, select fluid1, and open its Attribute Editor.

12. To improve the look of the cloud, you can increase the Base Resolution setting of the fluid container. Set Base Resolution to **120**. This will slow down the playback of the scene, but the image will be much clearer (see Figure 16.5).

13. Save the scene as **jollyRoger_v01.ma**.

FIGURE 16.5
Increasing the
Base Resolution
setting will result
in a clearer image
created from the
texture map.

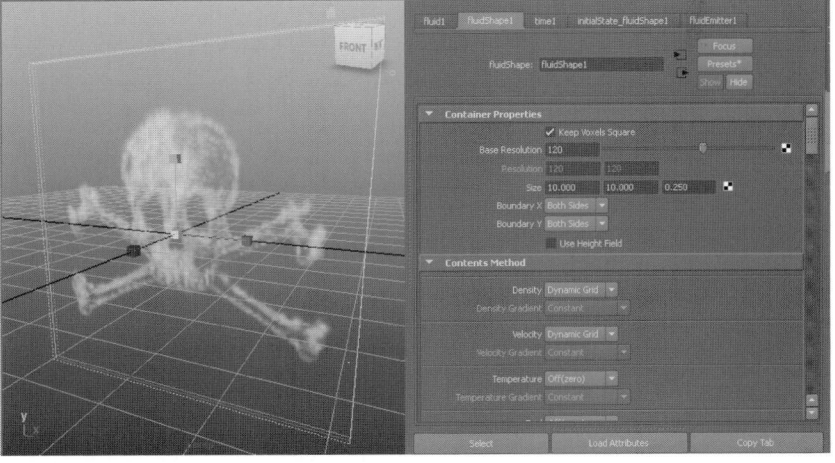

To see a version of the scene, open the `jollyRoger_v01.ma` scene from the `chapter16\` `scenes` directory on the DVD. Create a playblast of the animation to see how the image acts as an emitter for the fluid.

Fluid containers are subdivided into a grid. Each subdivision is known as a *voxel*. When Maya calculates fluids, it looks at each voxel and how the fluid particles in one voxel affect the particles in the next voxel. As you increase the resolution of a fluid container, you increase the number of voxels and the number of calculations Maya has to perform in the simulation.

The Base Resolution slider is a single control that you can use to adjust the resolution of the fluid container along both the x- and y-axes as long as the Keep Voxels Square option is selected. If you decide you want to create rectangular voxels, you can deselect this option and then set the X and Y resolution independently. This can result in a stretched appearance for the fluid voxels. Generally speaking, square voxels will result in a better appearance for your fluid simulations.

The nice thing about 2D containers is that you can use a fairly high resolution setting (such as 120) and get decent playback results. 3D containers take much longer to calculate because of the added dimension, so higher settings can result in really slow playback. When using 2D or 3D containers, it's a good idea to start with the default Base Resolution setting and then move the resolution upward incrementally as you work on refining the effect.

EMISSION TEXTURE MAPS

Emission texture maps only work with surface and volume fluid emitters.

Using Fields with Fluids

Fluids can be controlled using dynamic fields such as Turbulence, Volume Axis, Drag, and Vortex. In this section, you'll distort the image of the Jolly Roger using a Volume Axis field.

As demonstrated in the previous section, when you play the Jolly Roger scene, the image forms and then starts to rise to the top of the container like a gas that is lighter than air. In this exercise, you want the image to remain motionless until a dynamic field is applied to the fluid. To do this, you'll need to change the Buoyancy property of the fluid and then set the initial state of the fluid container so that the image of the skull and crossbones is present when the animation starts.

1. Continue with the scene from the previous section, or open the `jollyRoger_v01.ma` scene from the `chapter16\scenes` folder on the DVD.

2. In the Outliner, select the fluidShape1 node, and open the Attribute Editor.

3. Scroll down to the Content Details rollout panel, and expand the Density section.

4. Set Buoyancy to **0**. Set Density Scale to **2**. This can create a clearer image from the smoke without having to increase the fluid resolution (see Figure 16.6).

5. Rewind and play the animation. The image of the Jolly Roger should remain motionless as it forms.

6. Play the animation to frame 30, at which point you should see the image fairly clearly.

7. Select Fluid1, and choose Fluid Effects ➤ Set Initial State.

FIGURE 16.6
You set the Buoyancy option of the fluid so that the gas will not rise when the simulation is played.

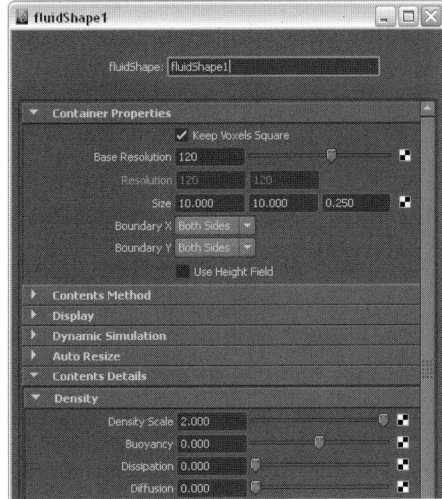

8. Switch to the fluidEmitter1 tab in the Attribute Editor, and set Rate (percent) to **0** so that the emitter is no longer adding fluid to the container.

9. Rewind and play the animation.

   You should see the image of the skull and crossbones clearly at the start of the animation, and it should remain motionless as the animation plays.

CHANGING THE DYNAMIC PROPERTIES OF A SIMULATION

If you set the initial state of a fluid but then decide to make changes to the dynamic properties of the simulation, first delete the initial state (Fluid Effects ➢ Clear Initial State) and then make your changes. Otherwise, the simulation may not update properly.

---

10. Select Fluid1, and choose Fields ➢ Volume Axis. By selecting Fluid1 before creating a field, the field and the fluid are automatically connected.

    In this exercise, imagine that the field is a cannonball moving through the ghostly image of the skull and crossbones.

11. Open the Attribute Editor for volumeAxisField1. Use the following settings:

    Magnitude: **100**

    Attenuation: **0**

    Use Max Distance: **on**

    Max Distance: **0.5**

    Volume Shape: **Sphere**

    Away From Center: **10**

12. On frame 1 of the animation, set the Translate Z of the Volume Axis field to **5**, and set a keyframe.

13. Set the timeline to frame 50. Set the Translate Z of the Volume Axis field to **-5**, and set another keyframe.

14. Set Translate X to **1.3** and Translate Y to **2**.

15. Rewind and play the animation (or create a playblast). As the Volume Axis field passes through the container, it pushes the fluid outward like a cannonball moving through smoke (see Figure 16.7).

FIGURE 16.7
The Volume Axis field pushes the smoke as it moves through the field.

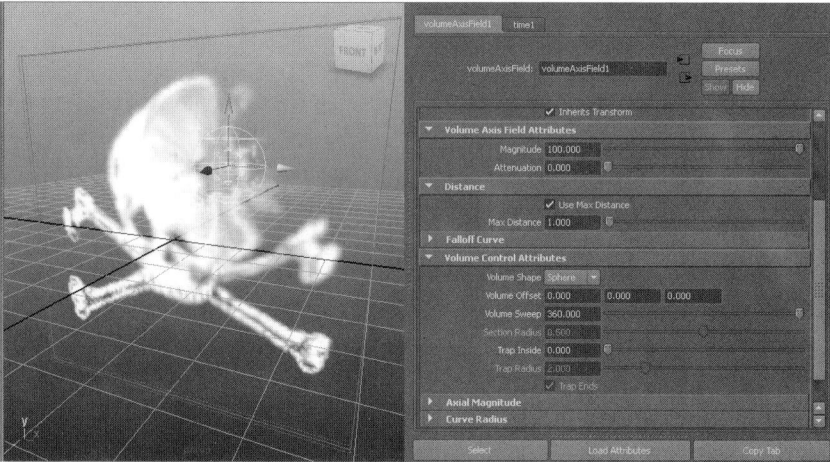

16. Add two more Volume Axis fields to the container with the same settings. Position them so they pass through the image at different locations and at different frames on the timeline.

17. Create a playblast of the scene. Watch it forward and backward in FCheck.

18. Save the scene as `jollyRoger_v02.ma`.

To see a version of the scene, open the `jollyRoger_v02.ma` scene from the `chapter16\` `scenes` directory on the DVD. You will need to create a new cache for this scene in order to see the effect.

If you decide to try rendering this scene, make sure the Primary Visibility setting of the NURBS plane is turned off in Render Stats of the plane's Attribute Editor; otherwise, the plane will be visible in the render.

Now that you have had a little experience working with containers, the next section explores some of the settings more deeply as you create an effect using 3D fluid containers and emitters.

FLUID EXAMPLES

Maya comes with a number of Fluid examples located in the Visor. To use one of these examples, choose Fluid Effects ➤ Get Fluid Example. You can find the Fluid examples on the Ocean Examples, Fluid Examples, and Fluid Initial States tabs (as shown here). To use an example, right-click the example icon and choose Import Into Maya Scene. Information about the examples is stored in the Notes section of the fluid shape node's Attribute Editor. These notes explain how the example was created and how it can be edited. Much of the information in the notes will make more sense after you have some experience using Fluids.

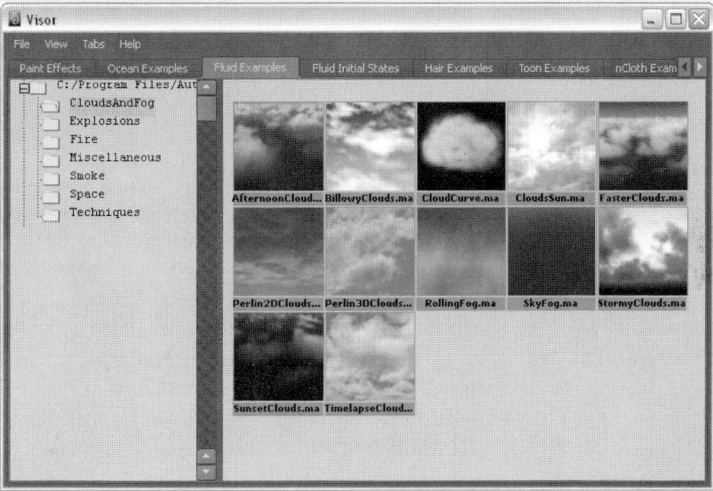

Using 3D Containers

Three-dimensional fluid containers work just like 2D containers except they have depth as well as width and height. Therefore, they are computationally much more expensive. If you double the resolution in X and Y for a 2D container, the number of voxels increases by a factor of 4 (2×2); if you double the resolution of a 3D container, the number of voxels increases by a factor of 8 ($2 \times 2 \times 2$). A good practice for working with 3D containers is to start at a low resolution, such as $20 \times 20 \times 20$, and increase the resolution gradually as you develop the effect.

1. Start a new Maya scene, and switch to the Dynamics menu set.

2. Choose Fluid Effects ➤ Create 3D Container.

   You'll see the 3D container appear in the scene. On the bottom of the container you'll see a small grid. The size of the squares in the grid indicates the resolution (in X and Z) of the container.

3. Select the fluidShape1 node in the Outliner, and open its Attribute Editor.

4. Expand the Display section on the fluidShape1 tab. Set Boundary Draw to Reduced. This shows the voxel grid along the x-, y-, and z-axes (see Figure 16.8). The grid is not drawn on the parts of the container closest to the camera, so it's easier to see what's going on in the container.

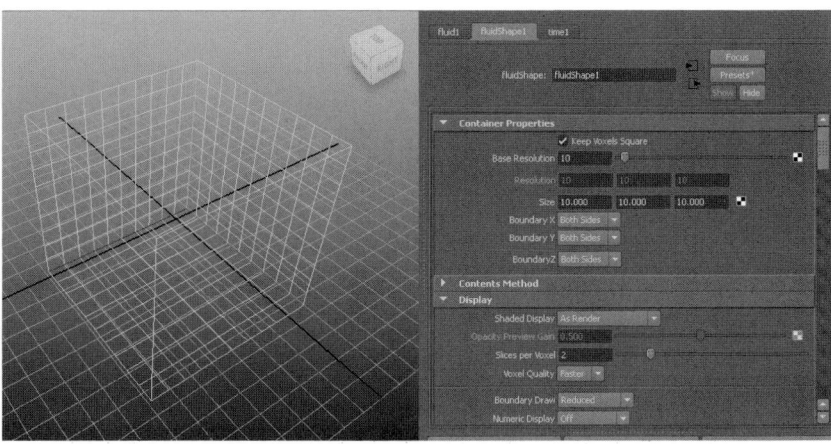

At the top of the Attribute Editor for the fluidShape1 node, you'll see the Keep Square Voxels option is selected. As long as this is on, you can change the resolution of the 3D grid for all three axes using the Base Resolution slider. If Keep Voxels Square is off, you can use the Resolution fields to set the resolution along each axis independently.

You'll also see three fields that can be used to determine the size of the 3D grid. You can use the Scale tool to resize the fluid container, but it's a better idea to use the Size setting in the fluid's shape node. This Size setting affects how dynamic properties (such as Mass and Gravity) are calculated within the fluid. Using the Scale tool does not affect these calculations, so increasing the scale of the fluid using the Scale tool may not give you the results you want. It depends on what you're trying to accomplish, of course. If you look at the Blast.ma example in the Visor, the explosion effect is actually created by animating the Scale X, Y, and Z channels of the fluid container.

Creating a Reaction

There's no better way to gain an understanding of how fluids work than by directly designing an effect. In this section, you'll learn how emitters and fluid settings work together to create flame and smoke. You can actually simulate a reaction within the 3D container as if it were a miniature chemistry lab.

Emitting Fluids from a Surface

In this example, you'll use an animated surface to emit temperature into a container that will appear as a flame. The simplest way to create flames or explosions is to add temperature. However, as you'll see later, more interesting effects result when fuel and density are combined with temperature.

1. Open the reaction_v01.ma scene from the chapter16/scenes directory on the DVD.

2. This scene contains a spiral curve. Play the animation. You'll see a tube animate along the length of the curve.

   The surface was created by converting an animated Paint Effects stroke into a NURBS surface. The surface is named emitterSurface (see Figure 16.9).

USING MULTIPLE EMITTERS

The contents that you can inject into a container by a fluid emitter are density, fuel, and temperature. You can use an emitter to inject any combination of the three. The settings on the fluid container's shape node determine how these contents behave within the container. You can use more than one emitter within a container and can create reactions by the interaction of anything within the container. For instance, you can use one emitter to add fuel and another to add temperature. Note that the contents of two separate fluid containers can't interact.

FIGURE 16.9
An animated tube is created by converting a Paint Effects stroke into a NURBS surface.

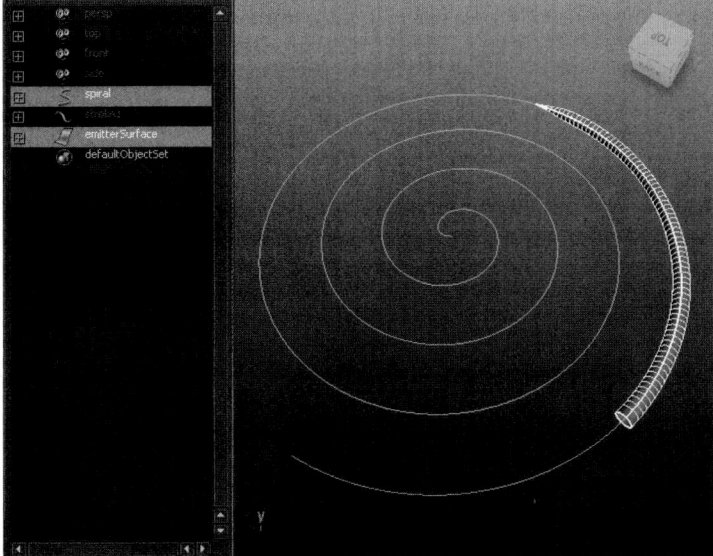

3. Switch to the Dynamics menu set, and choose Fluid Effects ➢ Create 3D Container. A 3D grid appears in the scene.

4. Select fluid1 in the Outliner, and open its Attribute Editor.

5. Switch to the fluidShape1 tab. Set Base Resolution to **40**, and set all three Size fields to **20**.

6. Select fluid1, and use the Move tool to reposition it so that the animated spiral is near the bottom of the container. Set the Translate Y of fluid1 to **9**.

7. In the Outliner, select the emitterSurface, and Ctrl+click fluid1. Choose Fluid Effects ➢ Add/Edit Contents ➢ Emit From Object ➢ Options.

8. In the Emit From Object Options window, choose Edit ➢ Reset to set the options to their default values. Set Emitter Type to Surface.

9. Set Density Rate (/Voxel/Sec) to **0**. Set Heat Rate (/Voxel/Sec) to **5**. Set Fuel Rate (/Voxel/Sec) to **0** (see Figure 16.10). This emitter emits only temperature (heat) into the container and nothing else.

FIGURE 16.10
The options for the
fluid emitter

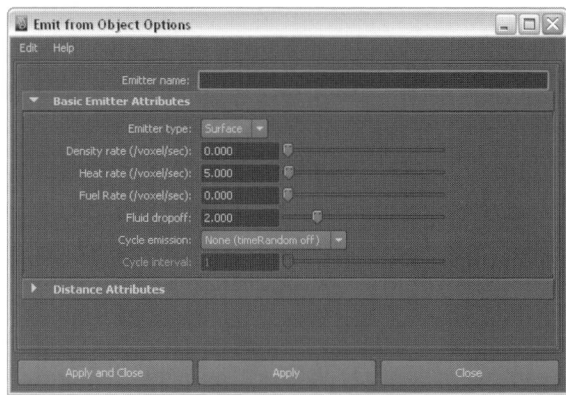

10. Click Apply and Close to create the emitter.

    In the Outliner you'll see that the emitter node is parented to the emitterSurface node. If you play the animation, you'll see no change. You need to edit the fluid container itself so that it can properly display the temperature emitted by the surface.

11. Select the fluid container (fluid1), and open the Attribute Editor to the fluidShape1 tab.

12. In the Contents Method section, set Temperature to Dynamic Grid.

THREE OPTIONS FOR ADDING TEMPERATURE

There are several options for adding temperature (as well as velocity, density, or fuel) to a 3D container. These are Static Grid, Dynamic Grid, and Gradient. If you don't need to calculate a particular content, you can set these to Off.

Static Grid   This is used for elements of the simulation that are placed within the container using the Paint tool or emitters. The values created for these elements are not changed by the simulation. For example, if you wanted to create a simple cloud, you could set Density to Static Grid, paint the cloud in the container, and then animate the container moving across the sky.

Dynamic Grid   This is used when the element and its values will change over time as a result of the simulation. Most of the examples in this section use dynamic grids.

Gradients   This creates a static range of values between 0 and 1. The values affect the simulation but are not changed by it. For example, a container can be set so that the velocity at one end is higher than the velocity at the other end, which causes the fluid to move steadily faster as it approaches the higher range of values in the gradient. When you choose the Gradient option, a menu becomes available that allows you to determine the direction of the gradient.

---

13. Scroll down to the Shading section. Set Transparency to a very light gray color, almost white. In the Color section, click the color swatch, and choose a black color.

14. The Incandescence ramp is already set to Temperature. By setting Color to black, you'll be able to see how the colors of the Incandescence ramp represent the temperature of the fluid.

15. In the Opacity section, set Opacity Input to Temperature.

16. Expand the Display section, and set the Shaded Display option to As Render.

17. Press the **6** key to switch to shaded mode. Rewind and play the animation. The animation will play more slowly, but you'll see some yellow flames start to rise from the emitter surface (see Figure 16.11).

18. Save the scene as `reaction_v02.ma`.

To see a version of the scene, open the `reaction_v02.ma` scene from the `chapter16\scenes` folder on the DVD.

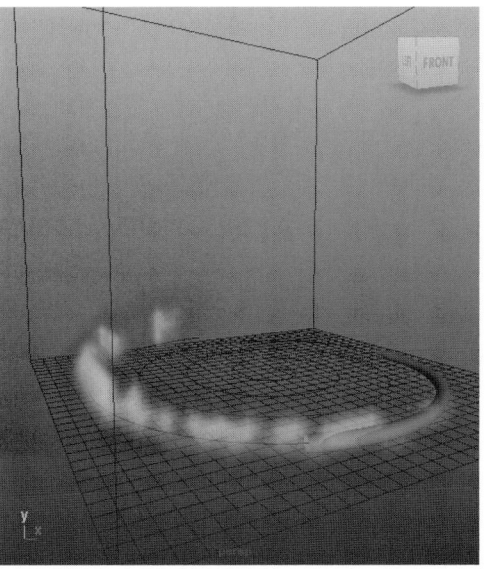

FIGURE 16.11
When you play the animation, yellow flames rise from the animated surface.

Adding Velocity

Velocity is used to push fluids around within a container. You can add velocity as a constant force to push fluids in a particular direction, or you can use an emitter. The Swirl setting adds rolling and swirling motion to the contents of a container. In the current example, the flames are already rising to the top of the container because of the Buoyancy setting, so you'll use Velocity to add swirl.

1. Continue with the scene from the previous section, or open the `reaction_v02.ma` scene from the `chapter16\scenes` folder on the DVD.

2. In the Contents Method section, make sure Velocity is set to Dynamic Grid.

3. Expand the Contents Details rollout panel and the Velocity subsection. Raise Swirl to **10**.

4. Rewind and play the animation. The fluid looks more like a swirl; however, the fluid does not last very long before disappearing.

5. Expand Temperature, and set Temperature Scale to **3**. Stop the animation at frame 80.

   Temperature Scale is a global control for increasing the overall temperature of the container. This increases the size of the flame and keeps it around a little longer.

VELOCITY DRAW

You can activate the Velocity Draw option in the Display rollout panel of the fluid shape node. This creates a number of arrows within the container that indicate the direction of the fluid velocity, as shown here. Longer arrows indicate areas of faster motion.

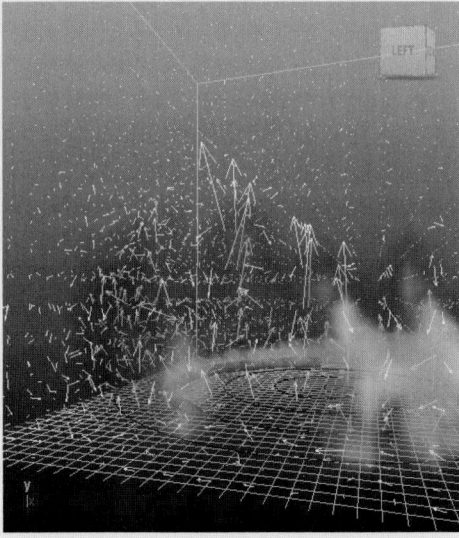

---

6. Scroll down to the Shading section. Move the orange color marker to the left slightly, and move the yellow color marker also slightly to the left. The left side of the Incandescence ramp is used to color lower temperatures; the right side colors higher temperatures.

7. Click the right side of the Incandescence ramp to add another color marker. Set the color of the new marker to a light bluish white.

8. Set Input Bias to **0.4**. This moves the bias of the incandescence so that more of the fluid receives more color.

9. Edit the Opacity ramp by adding points to the curve. Just like the Incandescence ramp, the left side of the curve controls opacity based on lower temperatures, while the right side controls the opacity of higher temperatures.

You can experiment with this ramp to shape the way the flames look (see Figure 16.12).

10. Save the scene as `reaction_v03.ma`.

To see a version of the scene, open the `reaction_v03.ma` scene from the `chapter16\scenes` directory on the DVD.

Figure 16.12

The flame is colored and shaped using the Incandescence and Opacity ramps based on temperature.

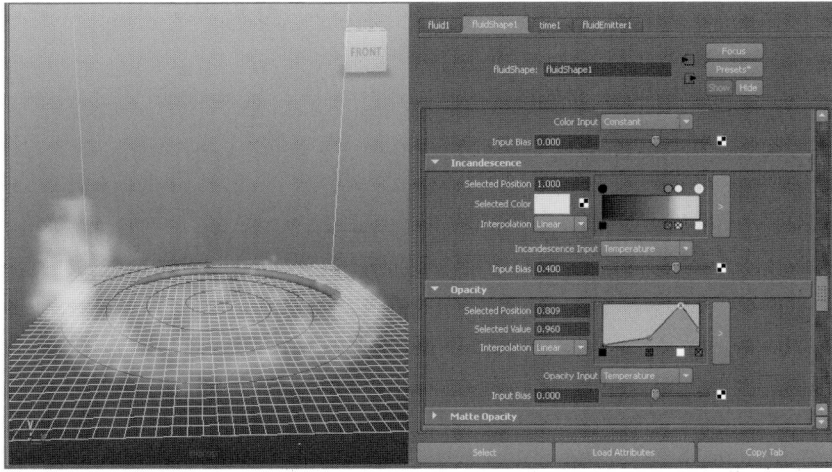

Adding Fuel

Once you have a flame in your container, you can create a dramatic reaction by adding fuel. As with velocity, density, and temperature, you can add fuel by using an emitter, by painting fuel with Artisan, or by using a gradient. In this exercise, you'll use a second emitter to add fuel:

1. Continue with the scene from the previous section, or open the reaction_v03.ma scene from the chapter16\scenes directory on the DVD.

2. Select fluid1, and choose Fluid Effects ➤ Add/Edit Contents ➤ Emitter ➤ Options.

3. In the Options, use the following settings:

   Emitter Type: **Volume**

   Density Rate and Heat Rate: **0**

   Fuel Rate: **10**

4. In the Volume Emitter Attributes section, set Volume Shape to Sphere.

5. Click Apply and Close to create the emitter. The emitter appears as a sphere at the center of fluid1.

6. In the Outliner, expand fluid1, and select fluidEmitter2.

7. Use the Move tool to move the emitter down closer to the bottom of fluid1. Set its Translate Y to **-8**.

   You can think of the fuel emitter as a gas leak inside the container. As the temperature and the fuel come within close proximity of each other, a reaction takes place. The fuel burns until the fuel is exhausted or the temperature is lowered. Since the fuel is injected into the container, the flame keeps burning. If you play the scene at this point, no reaction will take place. You must set the fuel to Dynamic Grid in the fluid shape node before the temperature can react with the fuel in the emitter.

8. Open the fluidShape1 node in the Attribute Editor, and set Fuel in the Contents Method section to Dynamic Grid.

9. Scroll down to the Contents Details section, and expand Fuel. Use the following settings:

   Reaction Speed: **1**

   Ignition Temperature: **0.1**

   Max Temperature: **100**

   Heat Released: **100**

   Light Released: **1**

10. Rewind and create a playblast of the scene.

    The emitter surface acts like a fuse—when the temperature it emits gets close to the fuel emitter, a reaction takes place, and suddenly a plume of flame and gas rises dramatically from the center. You'll also notice that after the initial reaction the fuel coming from the emitter continues to burn. This is because a small piece of the emitter surface continues to emit heat below the fuel emitter.

    Reaction Speed Determines how fast the reaction takes place once the heat ignites the fuel. Higher values produce faster reactions.

    Ignition Temperature Sets the minimum temperature required to ignite the fuel. If you want to create a reaction that occurs regardless of temperature, set this value to a negative number such as -0.1.

    Heat Released Causes the reaction to add more temperature to the fluid container.

    Light Released Adds value to the current Incandescent value of the fluid, which causes the fluid to glow brightly when rendered.

    You'll notice that as the simulation plays, the flame and smoke appear trapped within the walls of the 3D container. This is because, by default, containers have boundaries on all sides. You can remove these boundaries to let the contents escape. Be aware that as the contents leave the container, they will disappear, since fluid simulations cannot exist outside the fluid container (2D or 3D).

11. Select the fluid1 node, and open its Attribute Editor.

12. In the Container Properties section at the top of the fluidShape1 tab, set the Boundary Y option to -Y Side. This means that there is a boundary on the bottom of the container but not on the top (see Figure 16.13).

13. Create another playblast of the simulation. The explosion is no longer trapped at the top of the container.

14. Save the scene as **reaction_v04.ma**.

To see a version of the scene, open the reaction_v04.ma scene from the chapter16\scenes directory on the DVD.

FIGURE 16.13
Boundaries keep the simulation within the container (left image). When you set the Y boundary to -Y Side, the explosion can escape out the top (right image).

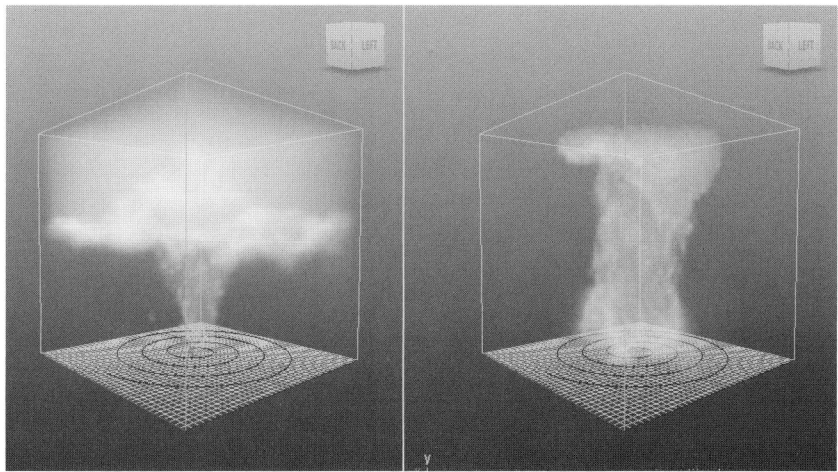

Rendering Fluid Containers

Fluid simulations can be rendered using Maya Software or mental ray, and they will be identical for the most part. Since fluids have an incandescent value, they can be used as light-emitting objects when rendering with Final Gather. If you want the fluid to appear in reflections and refractions, you need to turn on the Visible In Reflections and Visible In Refractions options in the Render Stats section of the fluid's shape node.

This section demonstrates some ways in which the detail and the shading of fluids can be improved when rendered.

Texturing Fluids

You can add more detail to a fluid simulation by increasing the resolution of the fluid container; however, this makes playback of the scene slower as well as increases render times. Fluids have a set of built-in procedural texturing options that can help add more detail to the fluid without the need to change the resolution of the fluid container.

1. Continue with the scene from the previous section, or open the `reaction_v04.ma` scene from the `chapter16\scenes` directory on the DVD.

2. Play the scene to about frame 200, and stop the animation.

3. Open the Render Settings window, and set Renderer to mental ray.

4. On the Quality tab, set Quality Preset to Production.

5. Open the Render View window, and create a render from the perspective camera. Store the render in the Render View window.

6. Select fluid1, and open the Attribute Editor to the fluidShape1 tab.

7. In the Shading section, set Dropoff Shape to Y Gradient and Edge Dropoff to **0.1**.

DROPOFF VALUES

Dropoff Shape fades the edges of the simulation as the contents approach the edge of the container. Choosing Y Gradient means that the top of the simulation fades out as it leaves the top of the container. The Edge Dropoff value sets the range of the fading effect.

---

8. Scroll down and expand the Textures section. Turn on Texture Opacity and Texture Incandescence. Notice that the cloud appears to have more detail even in the perspective view.

9. By default, Texture Type should be set to Perlin Noise. You can also choose Billow, Volume Wave, Wispy, or Space Time. Perlin Noise is good for creating random detail in the cloud.

   The settings for Perlin Noise are very similar to the settings found in the 3D noise texture that you create in the Hypershade.

10. Set Frequency to 4 to add more detail.

11. Create a test render, and compare this with the previously saved render.

    The fluid now looks as though it is more detailed. This can help add a sense that the fluid simulation is much larger (see Figure 16.14).

12. You can animate the texture using the Texture Time attribute. In the field next to Texture Time, type `= time*0.1;`. This creates an expression where the texture is animated based on the current time of the animation.

13. Save the scene as `reaction_v05.ma`.

To see a version of the scene, open the `reaction_v05.ma` scene from the `chapter16\scenes` directory on the DVD.

FIGURE 16.14
Render the simulation using mental ray (left image). Adding a Perlin Noise texture adds detail to the simulation without changing the fluid resolution (right image).

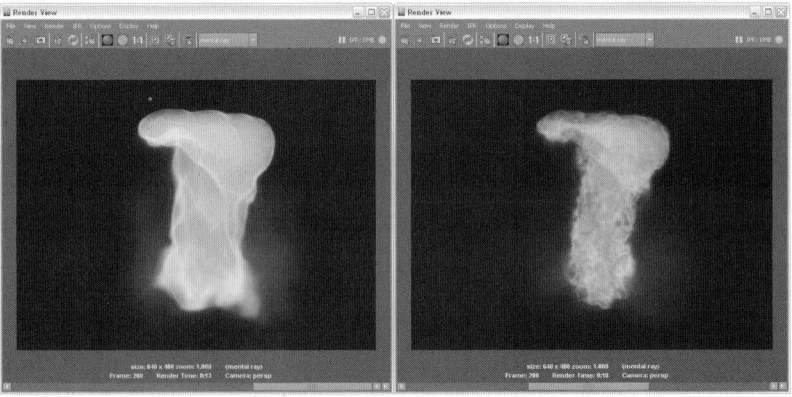

THICK CLOUD NPARTICLES

When you create an nParticle using the Thick Cloud particle style, a fluid node is created. This fluid node does not contain a simulation but is used to determine how the nParticles will look when rendered. Using the texturing and shading settings on the fluid node, you can change the look of the nParticle. For more information on using nParticles, consult Chapters 13 and 14.

Glowing Fluids

Fluid simulations can benefit from using shader glow. This creates the impression that the bright parts of the fluid are emitting light in the scene.

1. Continue with the scene from the previous section, or open the `reaction_v05.ma` scene from the `chapter16\scenes` directory on the DVD.

2. Rewind and play the scene to about frame 200.

3. Select fluid1, and open the Attribute Editor to the fluidShape1 tab.

4. In the Shading section, set Glow Intensity to **0.15**.

GLOW INTENSITY

The Glow Intensity attribute works exactly like the Glow Intensity slider found in the Special Effects section of the standard Maya shaders. This boosts the incandescent values of the fluid as a post-render effect, making the fluid appear to glow. Just like all glow effects in the scene, the quality of the glow is controlled using the shader glow node found in the Hypershade.

When rendering a sequence using a glow, you should always turn off the Auto Exposure setting in the shader glow node to eliminate flickering that may occur when the animation is rendered.

5. Open the Hypershade, select shaderGlow1, and open its Attribute Editor.

6. Turn off Auto Exposure.

Whenever Auto Exposure is disabled, the glows become much more intense in the render. To fix this, you can adjust the Glow Intensity value in the Glow Attributes section of the shader glow node.

7. In the Common Shader Glow Attributes area, set Threshold to **0.1**.

8. In the Glow Attributes section, set Glow Intensity to **0.1** (Figure 16.15).

FIGURE 16.15
Edit the Shader Glow settings to reduce flickering and overexposure in the render.

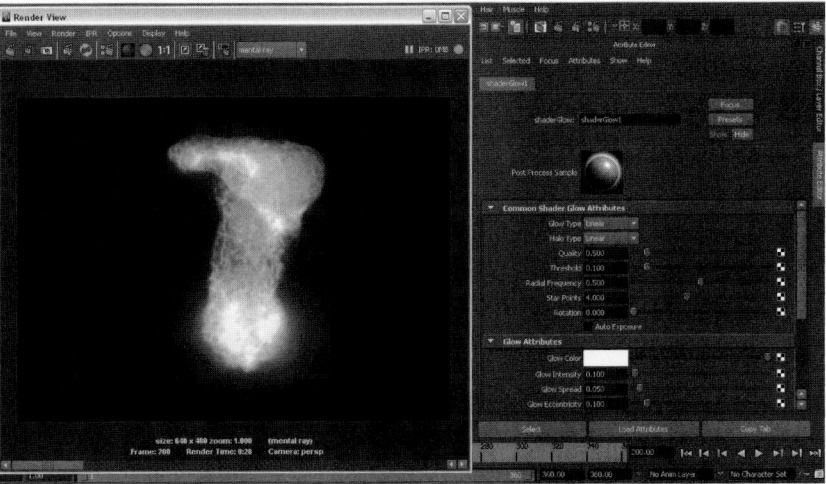

GLOW AND THRESHOLD VALUE

The Threshold setting sets the minimum value required to create a glow effect in the final image. In other words, if Threshold is 0, then the glow is applied to all the visible pixels in the image, although black pixels do not produce much of a glow. When you raise Threshold to a value such as 0.1, then very dim pixels will not glow; only pixels above the Threshold value will glow in the final render. The higher the Threshold value, the less glow you'll see, and the glow itself will be localized to the brighter areas of the image.

9. Create a test render to see the fluid with the glow applied.

10. Save the scene as **reaction_v06.ma**.

To see a version of the scene, open the reaction_v06.ma scene from the chapter16\scenes directory on the DVD.

GLOW SETTINGS IN THE OUTPUT WINDOW

Auto Exposure is used to control the exposure for any particular frame in the scene. As the camera and objects in the scene move, Auto Exposure adjusts the shader glow to prevent overexposure. This is what leads to flickering when Auto Exposure is enabled on the shader glow node in rendered sequences. The glow settings appear in the Output window (as shown here) when you render a test frame (as long as Verbosity is set to Progress Messages in Render Current Frame ➤ Options). If you want to match the settings used by Auto Exposure, you can render a test frame with Auto Exposure on, note the values in the Output Window, turn Auto Exposure off, and then adjust the other settings in the shader glow node based on the values listed in the Output window. Set Glow Intensity to the Glow: Normalization value listed in the Output window. Set Halo Intensity to the Halo: Normalization value.

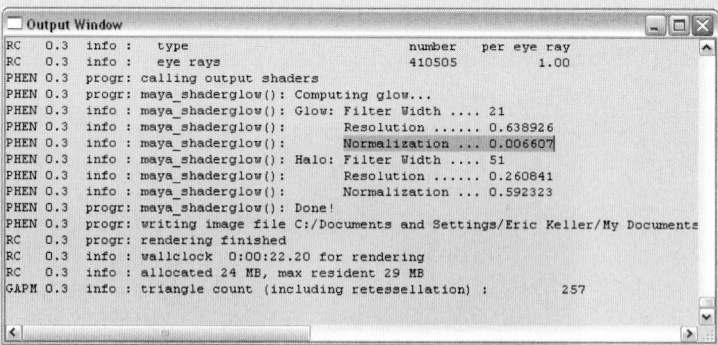

Lighting Fluids

Fluids can react to lighting in the scene, and you can apply self-shadowing to increase the realism. As an example of how to light fluids, a scene with simple clouds has been created for you to experiment with.

1. Open the `simpleCloud_v01.ma` scene from the `chapter16\scenes` directory on the DVD.

2. Play the animation to frame 100. A simple cloud appears in the center of the scene.

   The scene contains a fluid container, an emitter, a plane, and a light. The scene is already set to render using mental ray at production quality.

3. Open the Render View window, and render the scene from the perspective camera. A puffy white cloud appears in the render. Store the render in the Render View window (Figure 16.16, left image).

FIGURE 16.16
Render the cloud with built-in lights (left image). Enable Self Shadows (center image). Then render the cloud using a directional light that casts ray trace shadows (right image).

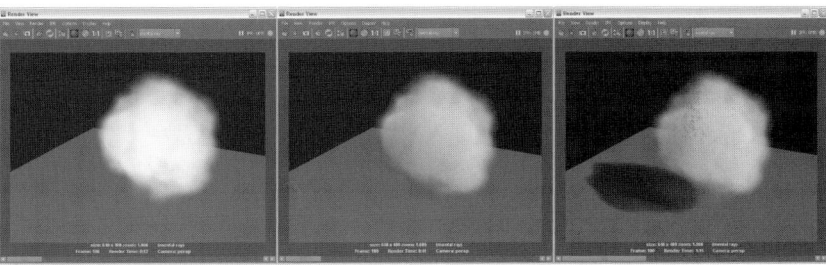

4. Select the fluid1 node, and open the Attribute Editor to the fluidShape1 tab. Scroll down to the Lighting section at the bottom of the editor.

New!

   The Lighting section contains two main settings: Self Shadow and Real Lights. When Real Lights is off, the fluids are lit from a built-in light. Maya 2011 now has three Light Type options when using an internal light: Directional, Point, and Diagonal. Using an internal light will make rendering faster than using a real light.

   When using a Directional internal light type, you can use the three fields labeled Directional Light to aim the light. The Diagonal internal light is the simplest option; it creates lighting that moves diagonally through the x- and y-axes of the fluid. The Point internal light is similar to using an actual point light; it even lets you specify the position of the light and has options for Light Decay just like a regular point light. These options are No Decay, Linear, Quadratic, and Cubic. For more information on light decay, consult Chapter 9.

   You can use the options for Light Color, Brightness, and Ambient Brightness to modify the look of the light. Ambient Diffusion will affect the look of the cloud regardless of whether you use internal or real lights and will be visible only when rendering with mental ray. Ambient Diffusion controls how the light spreads through the fluid and can add detail to shadowed areas.

5. Turn on Self Shadowing. You'll see that the cloud now has dark areas at the bottom in the perspective view. The Shadow Opacity slider controls the darkness of the shadows.

6. Create a test render, and store the render in the Render View window (Figure 16.16, middle image).

   Shadow Diffusion controls the softness of self-shadowing, simulating light scattering. Unfortunately, it can be seen only in the viewport. This effect will not appear when rendering with software (Maya Software or mental ray). The documentation recommends that if you'd like to use Shadow Diffusion, you can render a playblast and then composite the results with the rest of your rendered images using your compositing program.

7. In the Outliner, select the directional light, and open its Attribute Editor. Under Shadows, turn on Use Ray Trace Shadows.

8. Select fluid1, and in the Lighting section under the fluidShape1 tab, turn off Self Shadows. Turn on Real Lights.

9. In the Render Stats section, make sure Casts and Receive Shadows are on.

10. Create another test render from the perspective camera (Figure 16.16, right image).

When rendering using Real Lights, the fluid casts shadows onto other objects as well as itself. When rendering using real shadow casting lights, make sure that Self Shadow is disabled to avoid calculating the shadows twice. You can see that rendering with Real Lights does take significantly longer than using the built-in lighting and shadowing. Take this into consideration when rendering fluid simulations.

Create Fluids and nParticle Interactions

Fluids and nParticles can work together in combination to create a near limitless number of interesting effects. New in Maya 2011, you can now use nParticles as fluid emitters, and you can also use a fluid to affect the movement of nParticles as if it were a field. In this section, you'll find two quick examples that show you how to make the systems work together.

Emitting Fluids from nParticles

In this section, you'll see how you can emit fluids into a 3D container using nParticles, and you'll also learn about the Auto Resize feature that can help you optimize calculations for fluids.

1. Open the rockWall.ma scene from the chapter16 folder on the DVD. Rewind and play the scene.

   In this scene, nParticles are emitted from a volume emitter. A rock wall has been modeled and turned into a collision object. If you watch the animation from camera1, you'll see that the scene resembles the wall of a volcanic mountain during an eruption.

2. Stop the animation, and switch to the perspective camera.

3. Switch to the Dynamics menu set, and choose Fluid Effects ➤ Create 3D container to add a container to the scene.

4. Set Translate Y of the container to **1.26** and Translate Z to **1.97** (see Figure 16.17).

5. Open the Attribute Editor for the fluid1 node. Switch to the fluidShape1 tab, and set the base resolution to **30**.

6. In the Outliner, select the nParticle1 node, and Ctrl+click the fluid1 node.

FIGURE 16.17
A 3D fluid container is added to the scene and positioned over the polygon wall.

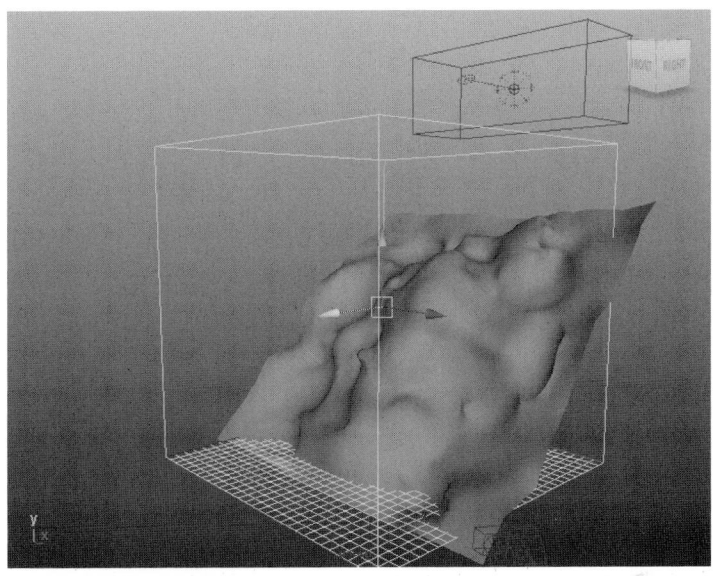

7. Choose Fluid Effects ➤ Add/Edit Contents ➤ Emit From Object ➤ Options.

8. In the Options, use the following settings:

   Emitter Type: **Surface**

   Density: **10**

   Heat Rate and Fuel Rate: **0**

9. Click Apply to create the emitter. The new fluid emitter is parented to the nParticle1 node.

10. Rewind and play the scene. As the nParticles enter the fluid container, they leave a trail of smoke that rises and gathers at the top of the container (Figure 16.18).

FIGURE 16.18
The nParticles emit fluids as they enter the container.

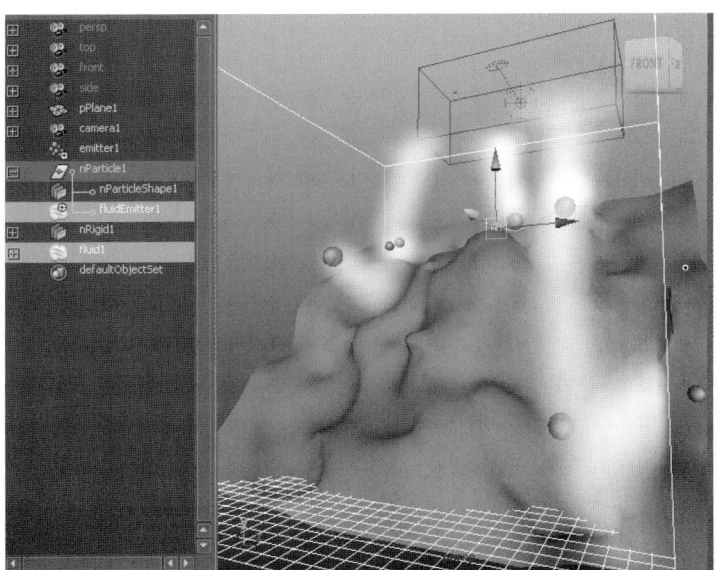

11. Open the Attribute Editor for the fluid1 node. Set Boundary X, Boundary Y, and Boundary Z to None. This will keep the fluid from becoming trapped at the sides of the container.

12. Scroll down to the Auto Resize rollout panel. Expand this, and turn on Auto Resize.

13. Rewind and play the simulation.

Auto Resize causes the fluid container to automatically change its shape to accommodate the fluid (see Figure 16.19). The Max Resolution slider sets a limit to the resolution. When you use Auto Resize, be mindful of the maximum size of the entire simulation; think about what will be within the rendered frame and what will be outside of it. You don't want to waste resources calculating fluid dynamics that will never be seen in the final render.

FIGURE 16.19
The fluid container automatically resizes to accommodate the emitted density.

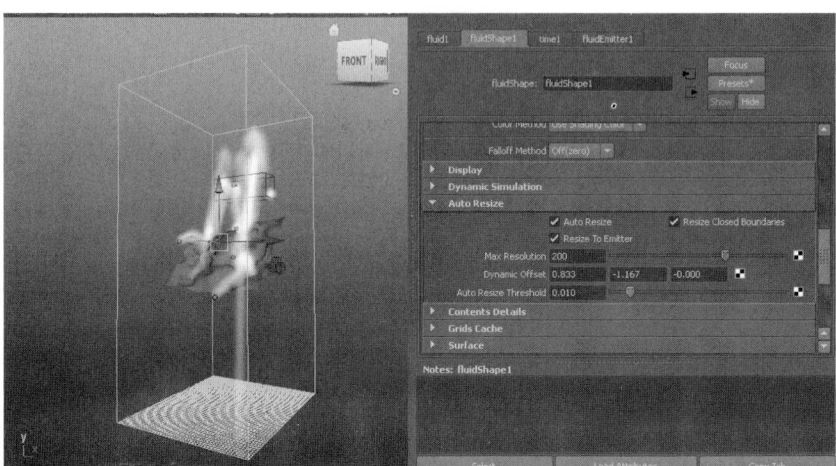

AUTO RESIZE AND DENSITY

Auto Resize for fluid containers is calculated based on the density of the fluid within the container. If none of the emitters within a container emits fluid density, the Auto Resize feature will not function correctly.

The problem with this setup is that as the nParticles fall off the bottom edge of the rockWall collision object, the fluid container stretches downward to accommodate their position. Also, as the fluid rises, the container stretches upward to contain the fluid. There are a couple strategies you can use so that the Auto Resize feature does not stretch the container too far.

14. Open the Attribute Editor for the fluid1 node. In the Contents Detail section, expand the Density rollout panel.

15. Set Buoyancy to **0.25** and Dissipation to **1**.

This will keep the fluid from rising indefinitely, which will limit stretching of the fluid in the upward direction. It also helps to keep the smoke trails left by the bouncing nParticles a little more defined.

To keep the fluid1 container from stretching downward forever, you can kill the nParticles as they fall off the bottom edge of the rockWall collision object. One way to do this is to lower the life span; however, this strategy can backfire because some of the nParticles that take longer to bounce down the wall may disappear within the camera view, which can ruin the effect. A better solution is to write an expression that kills the nParticles when they fall below a certain point on the y-axis.

16. Select the nParticle1 object in the Outliner, and open its Attribute Editor.

17. In the Lifespan rollout panel toward the top, set Lifespan Mode to lifespanPP only.

18. Scroll down to the Per Particle (Array) Attributes section. Right-click the field next to Lifespan PP, and choose Creation Expression.

19. In the Expression field, type `lifespanPP=8;`.

This creation expression creates an overall lifespanPP, so each nParticle that is born will have a maximum life span of eight seconds. This should be enough time so that slower-moving nParticles don't die before leaving the frame.

20. In the Expression Editor, click the Runtime Before Dynamics radio button next to switch to expression mode. Runtime expressions calculate every frame of the simulation and can override the settings established by the creation expression.

21. Type the following into the Expression field:

```
vector $pPos = position;
float $yPos = $pPos.y;

if($yPos<-4)
{
lifespanPP=0;
}
```

This expression says that if the Y position of the nParticle is less than -4, then the nParticle's life span is 0 and the nParticle dies. You need to jump through a few small hoops to get this to work properly. First, you need to access the Y position of the nParticle, which, because of Maya's expression syntax, cannot be done directly. In other words, you can't just say `if(position.y<-4)`. Instead, you have to set up some variables to get to the Y position. That's just a quirk of Maya's expression syntax. So, the first line of the expression creates a vector variable called `$pPos` that holds the position of the nParticle. The second line creates a float variable called `$yPos` that retrieves the Y value of the `$pPos` vector variable. Now you can use `$yPos` in the `if` statement as a way to access the Y position of each nParticle (see Figure 16.20). For more information on nParticle expressions, consult Chapter 14.

FIGURE 16.20
Per-particle
expressions are
created to kill the
nParticles when
they fall below -4
units on the y-axis.

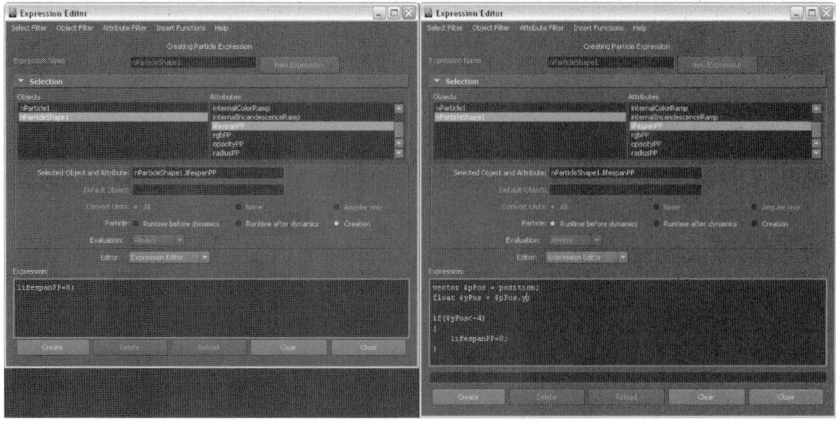

22. Click Create to make the expression. If there are no syntax errors, rewind and play the scene. The nParticles should die off as they leave the bottom of the rockWall.

23. Save the scene as rockWall_v02.ma.

To see a version of the scene, open rockWall_v02.ma from the chapter16\scenes folder on the DVD.

Creating Flaming Trails

To finish the look, you can edit the fluid settings so that the trails left by the nParticles look like flames.

1. Continue with the scene from the previous section, or open the rockWall_v02.ma scene from the chapter16\scenes folder on the DVD.

2. Play the scene for about 40 frames.

3 Select the fluid1 node, and open its Attribute Editor.

4. In the Contents Method section, set Temperature and Fuel to Dynamic Grid.

5. Scroll down to the Content Details section, and in Temperature section, set Buoyancy to **0.25** and Dissipation to **0.5**.

6. In the Fuel section, use the following settings:

   Reaction Speed: **0**

   Ignition Temperature: **–1**

   Max Temperature: **1**

   Heat Released: **1**

   Since Ignition Temperature is at -1, a reaction should occur regardless of how much temperature is released.

7. In the Shading section, set Transparency to a dark gray, and set Glow Intensity to **0.1**.

8. In the Color section, click the color swatch, and set the color to black.

9. The Incandescence ramp should be set to Temperature already. If not, choose Temperature from the menu next to Incandescence Input.

10. In the Outliner, expand the nParticle1 node, select the fluidEmitter1 node, and open its Attribute Editor.

11. Under Fluid Attributes, use the following settings:

    Heat Method: **Add**

    Heat/Voxels/Sec slider: **100**

    Fuel Method: **Add**

    Fuel/Voxels/Sec: **100**

12. Rewind and play the animation. You should see flaming trails left behind each nParticle.

    You can improve the look by experimenting with the settings as well as increasing the Base Resolution and Max Resolution settings in the Auto Resize section (see Figure 16.21).

13. Save the scene as **rockWall_v03.ma**.

To see a version of the scene, open the rockWall_v03.ma scene from the chapter16\scenes folder on the DVD.

FIGURE 16.21
The nParticles leave flaming trails as they bounce down the side of the rock wall.

Adding Sparks to a Flame

In this section, you'll create sparks using nParticles. This exercise demonstrates how the motion of nParticles can be affected by a fluid object. The motion of the sparks will be controlled using a flame within a 3D container. To keep things simple, you'll use one of the flame examples in the Visor.

1. Create a new scene in Maya. Choose Window ➤ General Editors ➤ Visor.

2. Click the Fluid Examples tab in the Visor window, and choose the Fire folder.

3. Right-click the Flame.ma example, and choose Import Maya File Flame.ma. This imports the 3D container, emitter, and all of its settings into the scene.

4. Select the flame container, and open its Attribute Editor to the flameShape tab.

5. In the display options, set Shaded Display to Temperature. This does not affect how the flame looks when rendered, but it makes it easier to see the simulation in the perspective view.

6. Press the **6** key to switch to shaded view. Set the timeline to **800**, and play the scene. You'll see the flame simulation play at the center of the 3D container (see Figure 16.22).

FIGURE 16.22
Import the flame example into the scene. A flame burns at the center of the container when you play the scene.

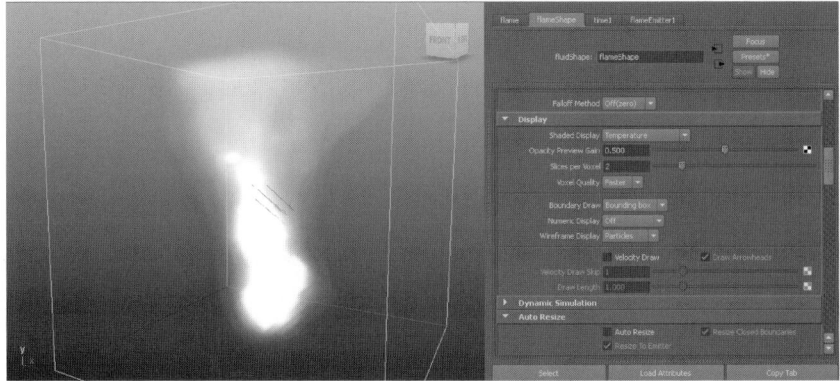

7. Switch the menu set to nDynamics. Choose nParticles ➤ Create nParticles ➤ Points to set the nParticle style to Points.

8. Choose nParticles ➤ Create nParticles ➤ Create Emitter ➤ Options.

9. In the options, set Emitter Type to Volume and Rate to **40**.

10. In the Volume Emitter Attributes section, set Volume Shape to Cylinder. Click Create to make the emitter.

11. Select the emitter, and use the Move tool to position the emitter at the base of the flame.

12. When you play the scene, the nParticles fall out of the emitter. Select nParticle1 in the Outliner, open its Attribute Editor, and switch to the Nucleus1 tab.

13. Set Gravity in the Gravity And Wind section to **0**.

14. In the Outliner, select nParticle1, and Ctrl+click the flame shape.

15. Choose Fields ➢ Affect Selected Objects. This connects the fluid simulation to the nParticles.

16. Rewind and play the scene. You'll see the nParticles that are closest to the center of the flame shoot out of the top of the simulation. This may be easier to see if you set the Display option in the flameShape tab to As Render.

Once the nParticles leave the fluid container, they continue to move at a constant rate. You can edit the settings on the nParticle shape node to make the movement more interesting:

1. Select nParticle1, and open its Attribute Editor to the nParticleShape1 tab.

2. In the Lifespan section, set Lifespan Mode to Random Range. Set Lifespan to **2** and Lifespan Random to **1**. As explained in Chapter 13, this means that the nParticles have a life span between one and three seconds.

3. In the Dynamic Properties section, set Drag to **0.3**. This causes the nParticles to slow down as they move away from the flame.

4. Rewind and play the animation.

The nParticles follow the movement of the flame fairly well, but they stop outside the fluid container, which looks rather odd. You can use the opacity settings to make slower-moving particles fade out and disappear, which really helps them to look like sparks.

5. Scroll down and expand the Shading rollout panel.

6. Set Opacity Scale Input to Speed.

7. Click the ramp to add a new point. Edit the ramp so it looks like Figure 16.23. This causes slower-moving particles to become completely transparent.

FIGURE 16.23
Edit the Opacity Scale edit curve so slower-moving particles disappear.

8. In the Color section, set Color Input to Speed.

9. Edit the Color ramp so that the left side is black, the center is orange, and the right side is yellow. Create a similar ramp and input for Incandescence.

10. In the Shading section, use the following settings:

Particle Render Type: **Streak**

Tail Size: **0.2**

Tail Fade: **–1**

Opacity : **0.5**

11. Rewind and play the animation. You should have some nice-looking sparks that fly upward with the motion of the flame. If the scene is rendered using mental ray, the sparks and the flame appear together (Figure 16.24).

12. Save the scene as **sparkingFlame.ma**.

To see a version of the scene, open the sparkingFlame.ma file from the chapter16\scenes directory on the DVD.

FIGURE 16.24
When you render the scene with mental ray, the sparks and the flame appear to interact.

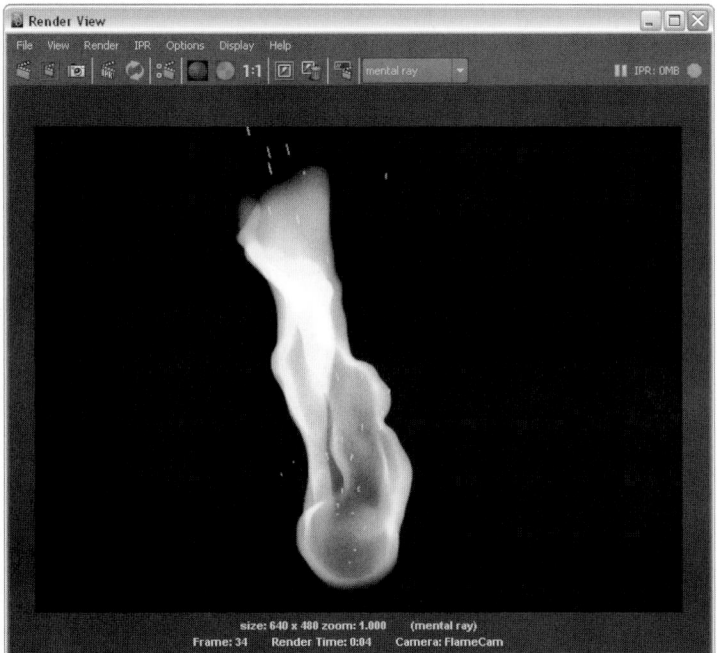

Creating an Ocean

The ocean fluid effect uses a surface and a special Ocean shader to create a realistic ocean surface that can behave dynamically. The Ocean shader uses an animated displacement map to create the water surface. Ocean surfaces can take a while to render, so you should consider this when planning your scene.

You can find all the controls needed to create the ocean on the Ocean shader node. This node is created and applied automatically when you make an ocean. In this example, you'll create the effect of a space capsule floating on the surface of the ocean:

1. Open the capsule_v01.ma scene from the chapter16\scenes directory on the DVD. This scene has the simple space capsule model used in Chapter 13.

2. Switch to the Dynamics menu set, and choose Fluid Effects ➢ Ocean ➢ Create Ocean.

When you create an ocean, you'll see a large NURBS surface appear. This represents the surface of the ocean. At the center is a preview plane, which approximates how the ocean will behave when the scene is played.

FILL AN OBJECT WITH A FLUID

You can use NURBS and polygon surfaces as collision objects in fluid containers, as shown here.

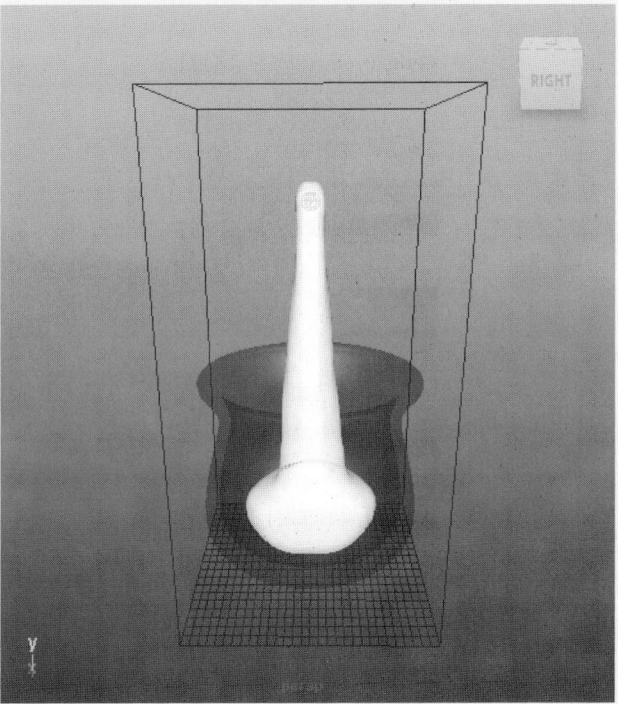

You can fill an object with a fluid using these steps:

1. Create a 3D fluid container with an emitter.

2. Set the buoyancy of the fluid to a negative value so that it falls.

3. Create a NURBS or polygon surface in the shape of a cup.

4. Place the geometry below the emitter.

5. Select the geometry, and choose Fluid Effects ➢ Make Collide.

6. Run the simulation, and edit the fluid to generate the desired behavior.

Filling an object like this can take some time. In some cases, you may get better results using nParticles, as demonstrated in Chapter 13. To make the object appear like a solid, set Surface to a Hard Surface render type in the fluid shape node. For an example scene, open the fluidCollision.ma scene in the chapter16\scenes directory on the DVD. I've used this technique to create clouds of heavy smoke coming out of a bubbling cauldron for a commercial. The emitter is placed inside the cauldron and as the fluid fills the geometry, the heavy cloud will crawl up the sides of the cauldron and spill over the top creating a spooky effect.

3. Rewind and play the scene. You'll see the preview plane move up and down. This demonstrates the default behavior of the ocean (Figure 16.25).

FIGURE 16.25
The ocean effect uses a preview plane to indicate the behavior of the ocean.

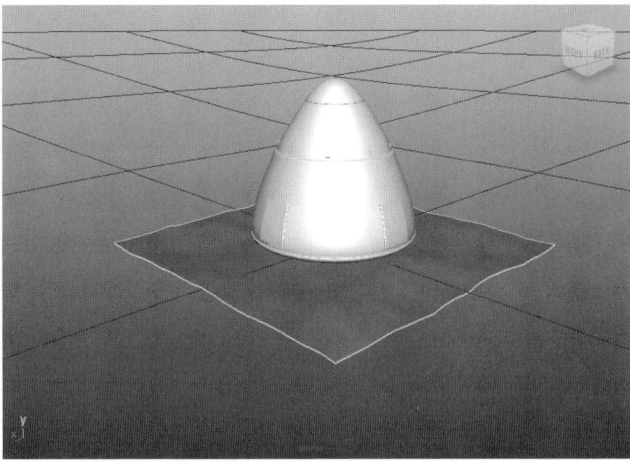

4. In the Outliner, select the Transform1 node, and open the Attribute Editor. Switch to the Ocean Shader tab.

You'll find all the controls you need to change the way the ocean looks and behaves in the Ocean Shader controls. Each control is described in the Maya documentation, but many of the controls are actually self-explanatory (possibly a first for Maya).

5. Expand the Ocean Attributes rollout panel. To slow down the ocean, set Wave Speed to **0.8**. You can use Observer Speed to simulate the effect of the ocean moving past the camera without the need to animate the ocean or the camera. Leave this at 0.

6. To make the ocean waves seem larger, increase Wave Length Max to **6**. The wave length units are measured in meters.

To make the ocean seem a little rougher, you can adjust the Wave Height edit curve. The Wave Height edit curve changes the wave height relative to the wave length. If you edit the curve so that it slopes up to the right, then the waves with longer wavelengths will be proportionally taller than the waves with shorter wavelengths. A value of 1 means that the wave is half as tall as it is long. When you edit this curve, you can see the results in the preview plane.

Wave Turbulence works the same way, so by making the curve slope up to the right, longer waves will have a higher turbulence frequency.

Wave Peaking creates crests on top of areas that have more turbulence. Turbulence must be a non-zero value for wave peaking to have an effect.

7. Experiment with different settings for the Wave Height, Wave Turbulence, and Wave Peaking edit curves (Figure 16.26). Create a test render from the perspective camera to see how these changes affect the look of the ocean.

8. To make the capsule float in the water, select the capsule, and choose Fluid Effects ➤ Ocean ➤ Float Selected Objects.

FIGURE 16.26
You can shape the ocean by editing the Wave Height, Wave Turbulence, and Wave Peaking edit curves.

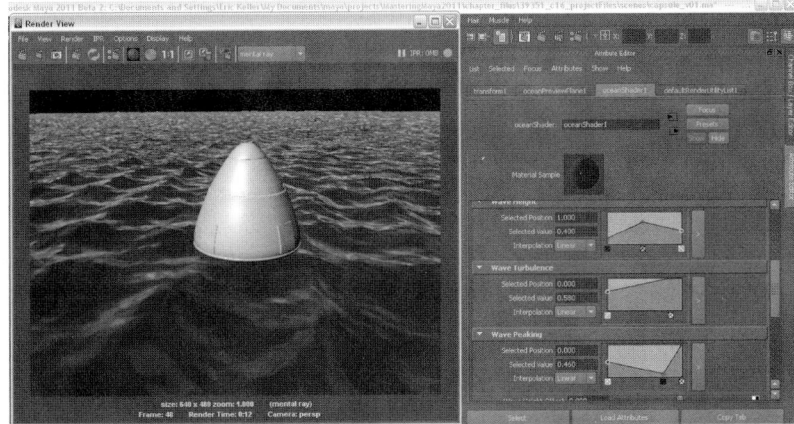

9. In the Outliner, select Locator1, and open its Attribute Editor.

10. In the Extra Attributes section, set Buoyancy to **0.01** and Start Y to **-3**.

11. Select the capsule, and rotate it a little so that it does not bob straight up and down.

12. Select the transform1 node, and open the Attribute Editor to the Ocean Shader tab.

13. In the Common Material Attributes section, set Transparency to a dark gray color. This allows you to see some of the submerged parts of the capsule through the water. The oceanShader already has a refraction index of 1.3, so the water will refract light.

14. Set Foam Emission to **0.355**. This shades the peaks of the ocean with a light color, suggesting whitecaps.

15. Create a test render of the scene from the perspective camera (see Figure 16.27).

16. Save the scene as **capsule_v02.ma**.

FIGURE 16.27
Render the capsule floating in the water.

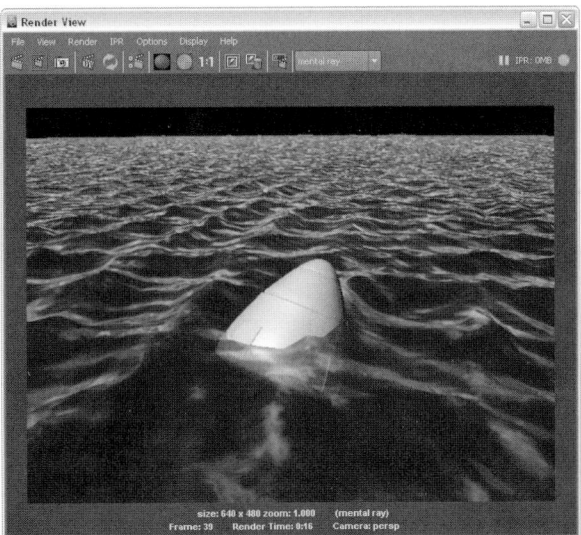

To see a finished version of the scene, open the `capsule_v02.ma` scene from the `chapter16\` `scenes` directory on the DVD.

This is a good start to creating a realistic ocean. Take a look at some of the ocean examples in the Visor to see more advanced effects.

The Bottom Line

Use fluid containers   Fluid containers are used to create self-contained fluid effects. Fluid simulations use a special type of particle that is generated in the small subunits (called *voxels*) of a fluid container. Fluid containers can be 2D or 3D. 2D containers take less time to calculate and can be used in many cases to generate realistic fluid effects.

> **Master it**   Create a logo animation that dissolves like ink in water.

Create a reaction   A reaction can be simulated in a 3D container by combining temperature with fuel. Surfaces can be used as emitters within a fluid container.

> **Master it**   Create a chain reaction of explosions using the Paint Fluids tool.

Render fluid containers   Fluid containers can be rendered using Maya Software or mental ray. The fluids can react to lighting, cast shadows, and self-shadow.

> **Master it**   Render the `TurbulentFlame.ma` example in the Visor so that it emits light onto nearby surfaces.

Use fluids with nParticles   Fluid simulations can interact with nParticles to create a large array of interesting effects.

> **Master it**   nCloth objects use nParticles and springs to simulate the behavior of cloth. If fluids can affect nParticles, it stands to reason that they can also affect nCloth objects. Test this by creating a simulation where a fluid emitter pushes around an nCloth object.

Create an ocean   Ocean effects are created and edited using the Ocean shader. Objects can float in the ocean using locators.

> **Master it**   Create an ocean effect that resembles stormy seas. Add the capsule geometry as a floating object.

Chapter 17

MEL Scripting

MEL is a powerful scripting language that can be used to automate many tasks within Maya. Using MEL, you can create your own scripts, which can save you time and labor and extend the capabilities of Maya. MEL has developed over the years into a powerful tool embraced by many artists and technical directors. Much of the tedium of working in Maya can be eliminated with even just a few simple scripts. Maya users from around the world share their MEL scripts online; these scripts can be downloaded and installed as part of Maya, allowing you to customize your workflow.

In addition to the MEL scripting language, you can also use Python; this gives you a second option for automating tasks. In this chapter, you'll learn how to write simple MEL scripts to automate tasks that would otherwise be repetitive and time-consuming. You'll also get an introduction to the Python scripting interface.

In this chapter, you will learn to:

◆ Use a MEL command

◆ Use MEL scripting techniques

◆ Create a procedure

◆ Use the Python scripting interface

Using a MEL Command

MEL stands for Maya Embedded Language. MEL is a scripting language similar to a programming language such as C++ or Java. An important difference between a programming language such as Java and a scripting language such as MEL is that a programming language must be compiled into an executable program, whereas a scripting language already resides within a program and does not need to be compiled. Programming languages tend to be more powerful, but scripting languages such as MEL are easy to learn and use. Since there is no compiling when using MEL, you can see the results, or errors, in the script instantly.

A scripting language uses a series of commands that tell a running program what to do. What you may not realize is that you already use MEL all the time. The entire Maya interface is created using MEL commands. When you choose an option from a menu in Maya, Maya actually executes a command. To demonstrate this, try the following exercise.

MEL Interfaces

There are a number of ways to enter MEL commands. You can use the command shell, the command line, or the Script Editor.

1. Open Maya to a new, empty scene. Choose Window ➢ General Editors ➢ Command Shell. The command shell opens as a blank window. The word mel: appears in the upper left. This is the command prompt.

2. Type **sphere**, and press the Enter key on the keyboard.

   A NURBS sphere appears at the center of the grid; you'll also see some text in the command shell describing the result of the command. This text includes the nurbsSphere1 node and the history node named makeNurbsSphere1 (see Figure 17.1).

FIGURE 17.1
Entering the sphere command in the command shell creates a sphere on the grid.

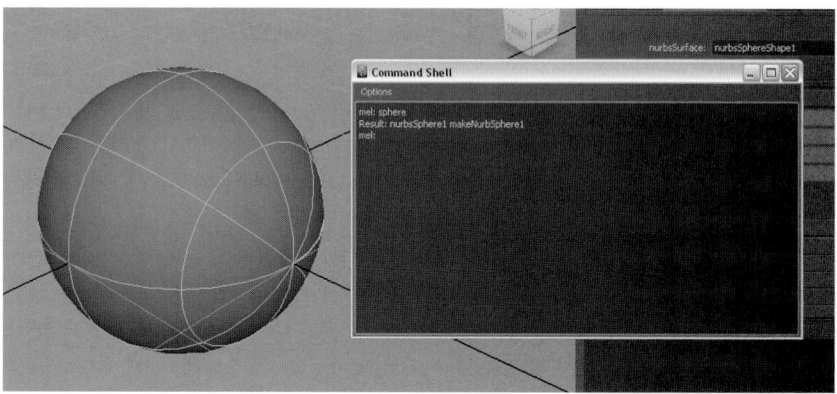

3. With the sphere selected, type **delete** in the command shell, and press the Enter key; the sphere disappears. Close the command shell.

   At the bottom of the Maya interface on the left side, you should see the label MEL and a blank line. This is the command line; it is another place where you can enter MEL commands. If you don't see this, choose Display ➢ UI Elements ➢ Command Line. If the label reads Python instead of MEL, click the label to switch to MEL.

4. Type **sphere** in the command line, and press the Enter key (Figure 17.2). Once again, a new sphere appears on the grid.

5. With the sphere selected, type **delete** and press the Enter key to delete the sphere.

6. On the bottom, far-right side of the Maya interface, click the Script Editor button to open the Script Editor. This is yet another interface you can use to enter MEL commands.

FIGURE 17.2
Enter the **sphere** command in the command line at the bottom left of the Maya interface.

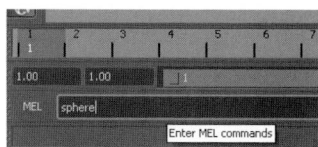

The Script Editor has two stacked windows. The top half of the editor shows the history of the commands entered and executed while Maya is open. This persists even when you close the scene file and open a new one. The bottom half of the Script Editor is the area where you can enter and edit MEL scripts. The two tabs in the bottom half of the editor allow you to switch between MEL and Python (see Figure 17.3).

FIGURE 17.3
The Script Editor is divided into the upper area, which lists the command history, and the lower area, where you can enter multiline scripts.

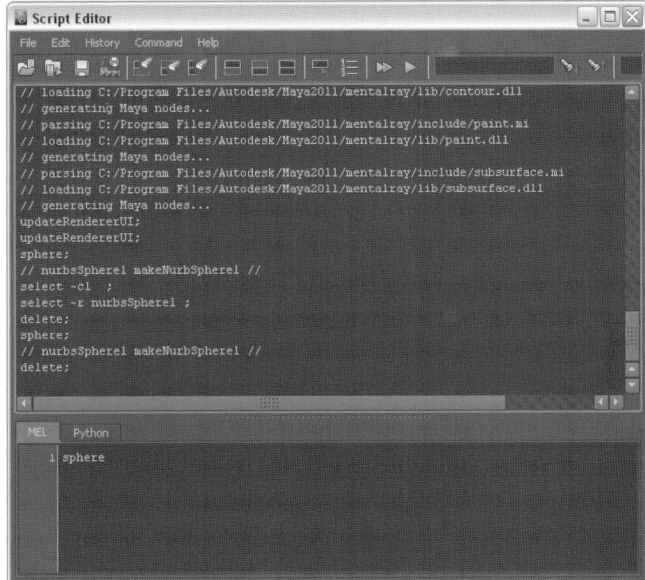

7. Make sure the MEL tab is active in the bottom half of the Script Editor. Type **sphere** and press the Enter key on the keyboard.

When you press the Enter key on the keyboard, instead of executing the command, the Script Editor moves to a new line. This may be confusing at first. The Script Editor is designed to allow you to create multiline scripts. The Enter key on the keyboard starts a new line. To execute the commands in the Script Editor, press the Enter key on the numeric keypad of the keyboard. Some computers, such as laptops, do not have numeric keypads. If this is the case, use the Ctrl+Return key combination, or look to see whether there is a smaller, separate Enter key on another part of the keyboard.

8. Press the Enter key on the numeric keypad to execute the script. A sphere should appear on the grid once again.

ENTER VS. RETURN

For the remainder of this chapter, when the instruction "Press the Enter key" is given, press the Enter key on the numeric keypad (or use Ctrl+Return if your computer keyboard does not have a numeric keypad). If the instruction "Press the Return key" is given, press the Return/Enter key on the main part of the keyboard.

You'll notice in the history of the Script Editor that a semicolon is appended at the end of the sphere command. In practice, you should always place a semicolon at the end of each command. This lets Maya know that the command should be executed and, if the Script Editor contains a second line of commands, Maya needs to move on to execute the next line of the script. A semicolon in MEL is analogous to a period at the end of a sentence in English. Get into the habit of adding a semicolon to the end of each command or line in your scripts. In most cases, if you leave the semicolon off the end of a line, you'll get an error message, and the script will not execute.

The Script Editor has a number of features available in the Script Editor menu bar. You can save selected lines of code to the shelf as a button. The buttons execute the lines of code whenever you click them, which is useful for commands that you repeat a lot. You can use the File menu to load MEL scripts that have been saved to text files. Any plain-text file saved using the .mel extension can be loaded as a MEL script. You can also save selected lines of code in the Script Editor as a MEL script.

The File ➤ Source Script menu option in the Script Editor window is used to load a MEL script into current memory so it is available as a command in the current Maya session. This is explained later in this chapter.

The options in the Edit menu can be used to copy and paste MEL commands as well as to clear the history visible in the top section of the Script Editor. Search and replace features are also available here.

The Command menu lets you create new tabs in the Script Editor in case you want to enter new commands without disturbing any of the commands entered in another tab. This is useful as a testing area.

To keep things simple, you'll use the Script Editor for most of this chapter as opposed to the command shell or the command line. Many of the common features found in the Script Editor menus, such as creating shelf buttons, loading scripts, and sourcing scripts, are used in the examples in this chapter.

MEL Scripting Techniques

You can become an accomplished Maya animator without ever writing a single MEL script. If this is the case, why should you concern yourself with learning MEL? MEL is a way to save time and labor. You may not be interested in advanced MEL scripting features, such as creating custom plug-ins or your own Maya interfaces, which are certainly possible using MEL. But sooner or later you'll run into a situation in which you need to perform the same complex task multiple times, which can quickly become tedious and time-consuming.

Consider the following scenario, which is very common in a production environment. You just spent the better part of a week setting up a complex nParticle simulation. Variations of this simulation are used in ten different shots, each shot has its own scene, and each scene contains five or six separate nParticle objects that have similar attributes. The particle motion has been approved, but suddenly the client requests that, instead of simple colored spheres, all the shots now need to use animated logos. The client also wants to see the new version using the logos first thing Monday morning. It's now Friday, and you have planned a weekend getaway with your friends. You realize that the best way to turn the colored nParticle balls into animated logos is to use sprites.

A *sprite* is a special type of particle that places a flat, rectangular plane at the position of each particle (sprites can be used with traditional Maya particles or nParticles; in this example you'll use nParticles). The plane is always oriented so it is perpendicular to the camera. Using a shader and expressions, an image is mapped to the plane. The images can be animated to create nParticle effects that would be difficult to generate using the other nParticle types. For instance, an animated sequence of flames can be mapped to the sprites to generate realistic fire. Since sprites are two-dimensional planes, they do not have a Radius attribute. Instead, they use Scale X and Scale Y. Likewise, sprites rotate only around the z-axis. This rotation is controlled using the Sprite Twist attribute. Custom attributes and expressions need to be created for each of the nParticle objects so the sprite images animate correctly.

You can choose to go into each scene and manually add attributes and expressions for each nParticle object, which will most likely destroy your weekend plans, or you can create a MEL script that automates the conversion of all particle objects in each scene, which may take only a few hours. In this situation, having even a basic understanding of simple MEL commands can save your weekend and your sanity.

In this section of the chapter, you'll add custom attributes and expressions to an nParticle object so it renders as sprites as the basis for creating your own MEL script. You'll save this script as a shelf button and also as a separate MEL file. You'll gain an understanding of some useful MEL tricks and we hope an appreciation for MEL that inspires you to learn more about MEL scripting.

Learning from the Script Editor

One of the best MEL scripting learning resources available is the Script Editor. As you execute commands in Maya using the menu, the Script Editor prints a history of the commands and their results in the history section of the Script Editor. By observing the feedback in the history section, you can learn common commands, and you can then use these commands in your scripts.

You need to be aware of two important concerns about the way Maya lists the command history:

◆ The first is that, by default, Maya does not list every single command in the history section. If you'd like to see every command executed during a Maya session, go to the Script Editor window, and choose History ➤ Echo All Commands. The resulting history list becomes very long very quickly, but in some cases this is the best way to find out how Maya executes certain commands that are otherwise hidden from view.

◆ Second, the commands that Maya uses to perform a task are not always phrased the same way as the commands you use in the scripts that you write. Experimentation and experience teach you how to translate commands listed in the history into commands you can use in your scripts.

The example used in this chapter is a hypothetical commercial spot. Your task is to create a script that makes converting the existing particles into sprites easier so you can simply select one or more of the existing nParticle systems, run a script, and automatically create the necessary attributes and expressions.

The scene starts with dark blue nParticle spheres appearing inside a cylindrical volume emitter. A vortex field pushes the nParticles along in circular motion. The dark blue nParticles are sucked into a volume axis curve field, which spirals upward. As the camera tracks upward, a second set of pink nParticles is being born. They are sucked into a second spiraling volume axis curve field (see Figure 17.4).

The script you will write automates the process of converting the nParticle spheres into sprites and attaching attributes and expressions to alter their behavior. To learn how to create the script, you'll perform actions as you normally would. In this case, you'll convert the blue_ nParticle into sprites, and then you'll observe what happens in the Script Editor and use this to build a script. You'll then use the script to convert the pink_nParticle into sprites.

FIGURE 17.4
Pink and blue
nParticles follow
along the spiral
paths created by
two volume axis
curve fields.

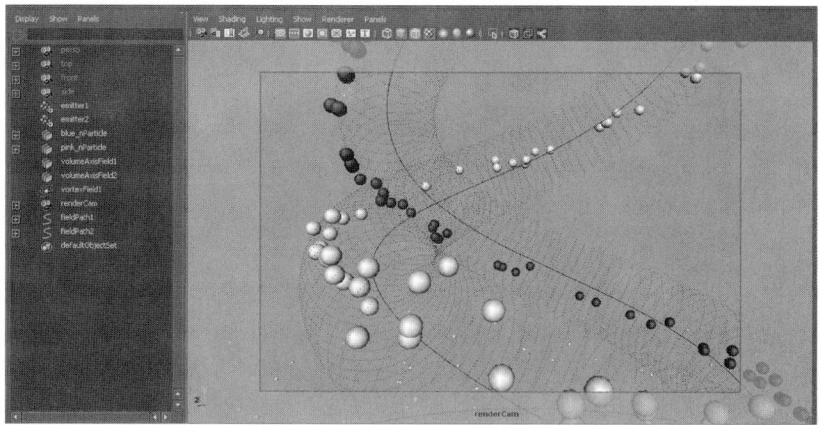

Let's look at the first shot in the commercial.

1. Open the shot1_v01.ma scene from the chapter17\scenes directory on the DVD.

2. Switch to the renderCam camera in the perspective view, and rewind and play the scene.

3. Open the Script Editor window (Window ➤ General Editors ➤ Script Editor), and move it off to the side so you can see it and the Attribute Editor.

4. Choose Edit ➤ Clear All from the Script Editor menu. This clears both parts of the Script Editor so you have a fresh view of what's going on. Make sure Echo All Commands is not selected in the History menu.

5. Select the blue_nParticle node in the Outliner, and open its Attribute Editor to the blue_nParticleShape tab.

6. Scroll to the Shading section, and set the Particle Render Type menu to Sprites.

The Script Editor displays a number of lines in the history section. The first line says `select -r blue_nParticle ;`. This is the command that was executed when you selected the blue_nParticle object in the first part of step 5. The command is followed by many additional commands, each of which sets up the basic sprite nParticle type attributes (see Figure 17.5).

FIGURE 17.5
Changing the
nParticle type to
sprites produces a
number of lines of
code in the Script
Editor.

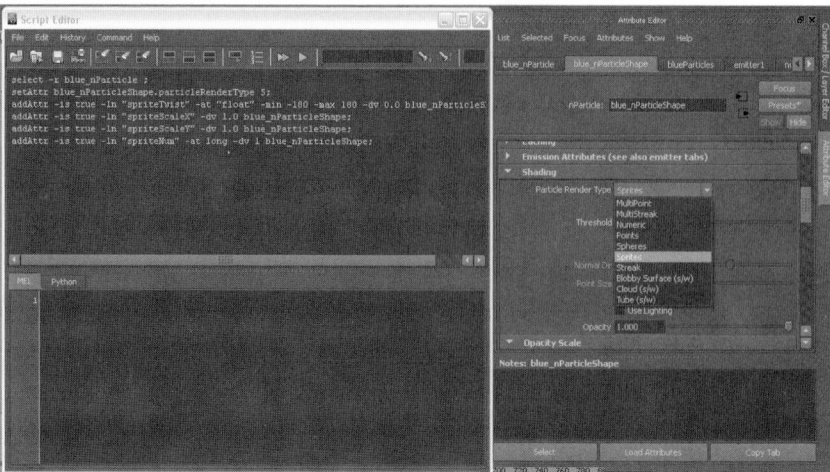

THE SELECT COMMAND

The `select` command is one of the most frequently used commands in a MEL script. If you Shift+click a number of objects in the Outliner, the command as listed in the history of the Script Editor looks like this:

```
select -r object1 object2 object3;
```

In this case, the `select` command syntax replaces the current selection with the objects listed after the `-r` flag. What is interesting is that if you Shift+click objects in the perspective view instead of in the Outliner, then the commands listed in the Script Editor history consist of several lines that look like this:

```
select -r object1;
select -tgl object2;
select -tgl object3;
```

Here the first line replaces the current selection with the newly selected object (`object1` in this example), and then the toggle flag is used to add more selected objects to the list (`object2` and `object3`).

However, if you Ctrl+click objects in the Outliner, the list of commands in the Script Editor history looks like this:

```
select -r object1;
select -add object2;
select -add object3;
```

In this case, the `-add` flag is used instead of the `-tgl` flag. The first line replaces the current selection with `object1`, and then each subsequent `select` command uses the `-add` flag to add another object to the selection (`object2` and `object3`).

This demonstrates that the context in which commands are executed often affects which flags are used.

The command syntax for many commands is `command flag nodeName;`, so the command in this case is `select`. The flag is `-r`, the node is `blue_nParticle`, and the command is ended using a semicolon. Most of this is fairly straightforward except for the command flag. What does `-r` mean? Flags are preceded by a hyphen and often abbreviated, so you have to find out what the r flag stands for. You can find out what a flag does by opening the help files and doing a search for the particular command in question, or you can type **help** and the name of the command directly in the Script Editor.

Type **help select;** in the lower half of the Script Editor, and press the Enter key. In the history section of the Script Editor, you'll see a list of flags (see Figure 17.6).

According to the help on the `select` command, the `-r` flag stands for *replace*. The `-r` flag tells the `select` command to replace the current selection with the object specified in the command. So, as you select objects in the scene, the `-r` flag is used each time the selection is changed. The other flags listed in the Script Editor can be used with the `select` command as well. For example, if you wanted to create a script in which all directed acyclic graph (DAG) objects are selected, you can use the `-ado` flag. The command looks like this: `select -ado;`. Executing this command using this syntax selects all DAG nodes in the scene at once.

FIGURE 17.6
Typing help and
the name of the
command you
need help with into
the Script Editor
displays a list of
available flags.

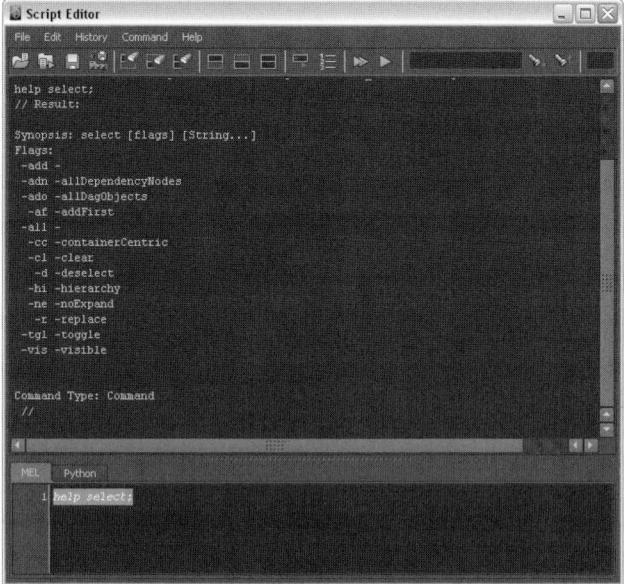

The second line in the Script Editor history reads setAttr blue_nParticleShape.particle RenderType 5;. In this line, the command being executed is setAttr, which sets an attribute for a particular node. The node receiving the setAttr command is the blue_nParticleShape node, which was selected in the first line of the Script Editor history. The attribute being set on the blue_nParticleShape is the particleRenderType, and the value applied to the particle RenderType is 5. So, what does this mean?

When accessing a node's attribute, the dot syntax is used. To set the particle render type of the blue_nParticle shape node, you must specify the syntax using nodeName.attributeName. Hence, you have blue_nParticleShape.particleRenderType specified in the setAttr command. The value of the setting depends on the attribute. In this case, particleRenderType requires a numeric setting to convert the nParticle from a sphere into a sprite.

Maya uses a numbered sequence for some attributes, such as particleRenderType. The way in which an attribute setting is listed in a menu in the Maya interface gives a clue as to how Maya numbers the attribute's settings. Take a look at the Particle Render Type menu in the shading section of the particle shape node. The menu options are MultiPoint, MultiStreak, Numeric, Points, Spheres, Sprites, Streak, BlobbySurface, Cloud, and Tube. The numbers Maya uses in the command are not listed, but if you change the particle render type to one of the choices in the menu and observe the script history, you'll see a different number applied at the end of the setAttr blue_ nParticleShape.particleRenderType line. The particleRenderType attribute uses 0 for MultiPoint, 1 for MultiStreak, 2 for Numeric, 3 for Points, and so on. Hence, to change the particle render type to sprites, the command is setAttr blue_nParticleShape.particleRenderType 5;.

The next few lines in the Script Editor use the addAttr command. This command adds attributes to the selected node. The syntax is the same as the setAttr command; however, in this case, there are a few flags as well. These flags specify the settings that will be used for the added attribute. In the history section of the Script Editor, the third line says this:

```
addAttr -is true -ln "spriteTwist" -at "float" -min -180 -max 180 -dv 0.0
    blue_nParticleShape;
```

In this case, the attribute being added is the `spriteTwist` command, which is used only by the sprite particle type (and not by any of the other types such as sphere, blobby surface, or point). The -`is` flag means "internal set." This is an internal flag used for updating the user interface. This is not something you need to specify every time you use this command. In fact, many flags that Maya lists in the history section can be left out when you use them in your own scripts. This is another aspect of scripting that you'll understand more with experience.

To find out what's going on with the four `addAttr` commands and their various flags that appear in the Script Editor, you can do a little detective work. The lines read as follows:

```
addAttr -is true -ln "spriteTwist" -at "float" -min -180 -max 180 -dv 0.0
    blue_nParticleShape;
addAttr -is true -ln "spriteScaleX" -dv 1.0 blue_nParticleShape;
addAttr -is true -ln "spriteScaleY" -dv 1.0 blue_nParticleShape;
addAttr -is true -ln "spriteNum" -at long -dv 1 blue_nParticleShape;
```

Take a look at the Attribute Editor for the blue_nparticleShape node. If you scroll down to the Sprite Attributes rollout and expand this section, you'll see there are Sprite Num, Sprite Scale X, Sprite Scale Y, and Sprite Twist attributes.

Rewind the animation; then play it for 50 frames and click Stop. Experiment with changing the values for the Sprite Twist, Sprite Scale X, and Sprite Scale Y settings in the Attribute Editor, and observe the results in the camera view (see Figure 17.7).

FIGURE 17.7
The four attributes listed in the Sprite Attributes section of the Attribute Editor were added using the `addAttr` command. These settings change the behavior of the sprites.

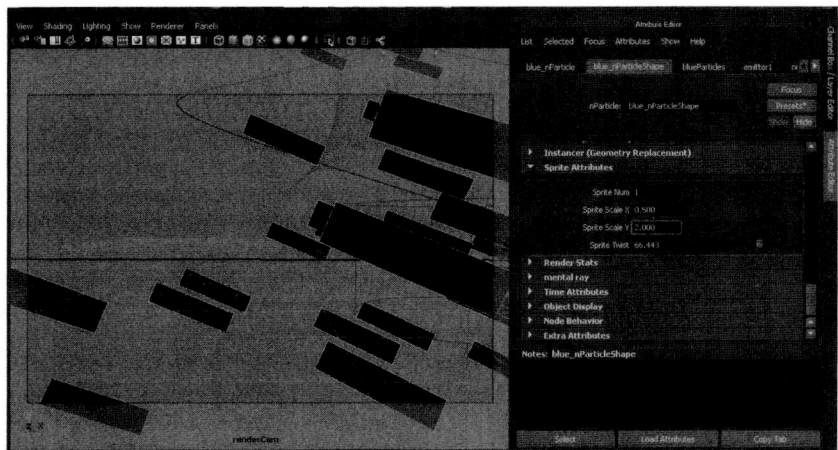

Sprite Num changes the image used for the sprite itself. Since no image is assigned, currently this attribute has no effect. Sprite Twist changes the rotation of the sprites around the sprite's local z-axis. Sprite Scale X changes the horizontal size of the sprites, and Sprite Scale Y changes the vertical size.

Select the pink_nParticle object in the Outliner, and open its Attribute Editor. You'll notice that under Sprite Attributes these settings do not exist. Therefore, you can surmise that these attributes were added to the blue_nParticle shape when Maya executed the four `addAttr` commands when the particle render type was changed to sprites in step 4.

The point of this example is to give you an understanding of what happens behind the scenes when you change settings for various node attributes in Maya. What you've learned from these observations is that changing the particle render type to sprites in the Attribute Editor not only sets the particle type to sprites but also executes several lines of code, which adds several attributes specific to sprites.

The Sprite Num, Sprite Twist, Sprite Scale X, and Sprite Scale Y attributes added to the blue_nparticleShape node affect all blue nParticles equally. In the animation you're creating, you'll want to override these settings with Per Particle, Num, Twist, and Scale attributes so each individual nParticle has its own behavior. This means that in the script you're creating, you won't need to use the four `addAttr` commands listed in the Attribute Editor.

Undo any changes made to the Sprite Attributes settings for blue_nParticle. Save the scene as **shot1_v02.ma**. To see a version of the scene so far, open the shot1_v02.ma scene from the chapter17\scenes directory on the DVD.

COMMAND REFERENCE

The Maya documentation includes a searchable command reference. Perusing these descriptions of commands will help you understand MEL and solve problems you may be experiencing in your scripts. Open the help files and choose Commands from the Technical Documentation section on the left side of the Maya Help interface. If you don't see the link to the Technical Documentation on the right side of the Help window, click the Show/Hide Quick links button toward the bottom; then click the MEL commands.

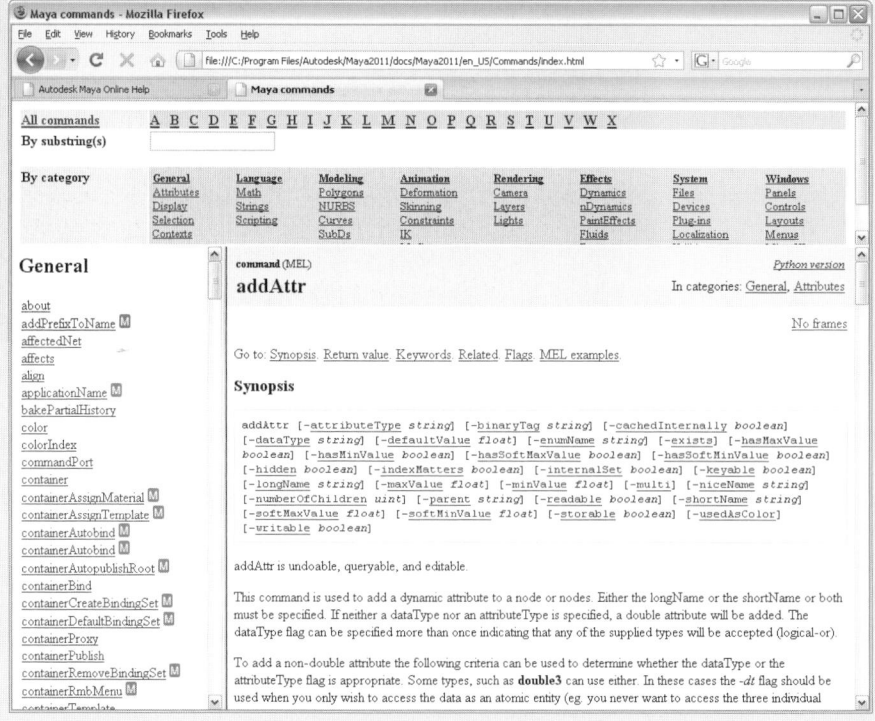

Creating a MEL Script File

The term *MEL script* refers to the lines of commands typed and executed in the Script Editor or a series of commands saved in a text file that uses the `.mel` extension. You can create MEL scripts in the Script Editor, but it is often a better idea to create your scripts in a separate text editor program. Keeping the script open in a separate text editor prevents you from losing your work if Maya crashes. As you work, you can copy and paste text from your text editor into the Maya Script Editor.

COMMAND HISTORY IN THE SCRIPT EDITOR

If you select text in the work area of the Script Editor and then press the Enter key while the text is still selected, the command is executed, but the text will remain in the work area, allowing you to repeat the command again without having to retype the text. This is a good way to test individual commands embedded within a long script without running the whole script.

When creating a MEL script file, use a standard text editor such as Notepad or WordPad (in Windows, or use TextEdit on the Mac), and make sure the encoding is set to plain text. If you use a word processor such as Microsoft Word, hidden characters copied and pasted from Word into the Script Editor can cause errors in your script, so do not use Microsoft Word to create MEL scripts!

Continue with the scene from the previous section, or open the `shot1_v02.ma` scene from the `chapter17\scenes` directory on the DVD. Open a text editor, such as Notepad or TextEdit, and in a blank text file type the following:

```
//set the particle render type of the current selection to sprite
setAttr blue_nParticleShape.particleRenderType 5;
```

These are the first two lines of your first MEL script, the script that will convert a selected nParticle's render type from spheres to sprites. The first line of the script starts with the double slash followed by some descriptive text. This is a comment line. Maya ignores everything on this line of the script that follows the double slash. The text is a comment that tells you what the next line in the script does. It's a good practice to use comment lines as much as possible to help you keep track of what's going on in the script, especially if you may be returning to the script later and might forget what the script does.

The second line is the command that sets the particle render type to sprites. This line is copied from the Script Editor. You may have seen a potential problem in the way this line is written. Since the command specifies that the particle render type of blue_nParticleShape will be set to 5, only nodes named exactly blue_nParticleShape will be affected by the command. You'll need to edit the script so any nParticleshape that is selected will be affected by the `setAttr` command. To accomplish this, you'll use an array.

An *array* is a list contained within a variable. Array variables are often used to hold a list of the currently selected nodes in a scene.

Edit the script so it says the following:

```
//create an array containing the current selection
string $mySelection[] = `ls -selection`;

//set the particle render type of the current selection to sprite
//setAttr blue_nParticleShape.particleRenderType 5;
```

Notice that the double slash has been added to the `setAttr` command. This turns this line into a comment so it is ignored when the script is run. This is a way to save the commands you know you'll be using later in the script.

The command that creates the array is the second line, which reads `string $mySelection[]` `= `ls -selection`;`. The first part of the command to the left of the equal sign creates the array variable. The variable type is a string. String variable types contain letters as opposed to float or integer variable types, which contain numeric values. The variable is named `$mySelection[]`. Variables are preceded by dollar signs. You can name a variable anything you want, but it's best to make the name descriptive of what the variable contains. The square brackets indicate that the variable is an array. Think of the double brackets as a box that holds the list.

The equal sign is used to assign data to the variable. Notice the slanted accent (`) marks. This symbol is created using the key below the Esc key and to the left of the number keys on most keyboards known as the *tilde key*; programmers like to call it a *backtick*. It is not an apostrophe. If you used an apostrophe in your script, change it to the backtick; otherwise, you'll get an error when you run the script. The text between the two backticks is the `list` command. In this case, the selection flag (`-selection`) is added to the `list` command (`ls`), so the list that will be created is the currently selected objects in the scene. Hence, the command is written as `ls -selection;`. The `-selection` flag is often abbreviated as `sl`. At the start of many scripts, you'll see a line that reads `ls -sl;`. This means "list selected objects."

So, why is the `list` command contained within the backticks? The second line of the script creates a variable array named `$mySelection[]`, and then, using the `list` command, it places all the selected objects in the scene into `$mySelection[]`. The backticks are used to assign the results of an executed command to a variable. The order of the selected objects in the list is based on the order in which they were selected before the script is executed.

Edit the script so that it says the following:

```
//create an array containing the current selection
string $mySelection[] = `ls -selection`;

//set the particle render type of the current selection to sprite
setAttr ($mySelection[0]+".particleRenderType") 5;
```

It may look as though the `setAttr` command has been drastically changed, but in reality it has been edited only slightly. The text has been changed, so `blue_nParticleShape` has been replaced with the variable `$mySelection[0]`. The 0 contained in the square brackets of `$mySelection[]` refers to the first item listed in the `$mySelection[]` array. The numbering of lists in Maya always begins with 0, not 1.

Since a variable is being used instead of a specific node name, the syntax must be changed so Maya does not search for a node named `$mySelection[0]`. The proper syntax for accessing the attribute of a node contained within a variable requires that the variable name is placed within parentheses and that the attribute name is appended with a plus sign and surrounded by quotes. So, instead of `$mySelection[0].particleRenderType`, you have to type `($mySelection +` `".particleRenderType")`.

At this point, you can test the code. Select the code in the text editor, and copy it. Switch to Maya. In the Outliner, select the pink_nParticle object. Paste the copied text into the work area of the Script Editor, and press the Enter key (Figure 17.8).

If all goes well, you'll see no error messages and the pink_nParticle node will display as sprites. If there are error messages, double-check your script for typos, and make sure only pink_nParticle is selected when the script is run.

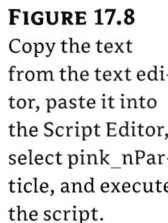

FIGURE 17.8
Copy the text from the text editor, paste it into the Script Editor, select pink_nParticle, and execute the script.

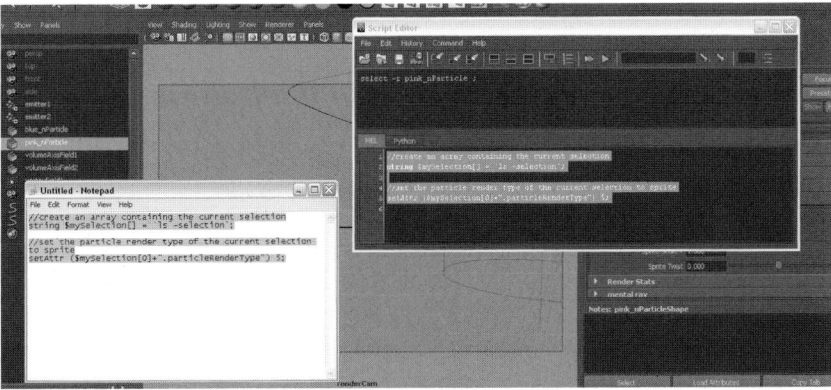

Notice that if you select the pink_nParticleShape node, Maya also adds the four `addAttr` lines to the script, which you can see in the history section in the top half of the Script Editor. These lines create the spriteTwist, spriteScaleX, spriteScaleY, and spriteNum attributes automatically.

Save the text file as **mySpriteScript.mel**. Make sure the encoding is plain text and that the extension is `.mel`. Some text editors will ask you whether you want to append `.txt` to the end of the filename; do not do this.

Save the scene as **shot1_v03.ma**. To see a version of the scene, open the `shot1_v03.ma` scene from the `chapter17\scenes` directory on the DVD.

COLOR CODING

When you paste the lines of code into the Script Editor, you'll notice that Maya color codes parts of the script. Comments are in red, variable types are in green, commands are in blue (and italicized), and attributes are in yellow. As you write more scripts, you'll be able to spot syntax errors more easily thanks to the color coding.

Adding Attributes with MEL

If you recall from the section on nParticle expressions in Chapter 14, expressions can be used to control the behavior of individual nParticles within an nParticle object. In the simulation you are editing, you need to create a random rotation and size for the nParticles (based on the hypothetical client's request). To do this, you'll create a per-particle twist attribute and per-particle Scale X and Scale Y attributes.

1. Continue with the scene from the previous section, or open the `shot1_v03.ma` scene from the `chapter17\scenes` directory on the DVD. Continue editing the `mySpriteScript.mel` file in your text editor.

   Once again, you can use the Script Editor to find out the precise syntax for adding these attributes.

2. In the Outliner, select the blue_nParticle object, and open its Attribute Editor to the blue_nParticleShape tab.

3. Scroll down and expand the Add Dynamic Attributes section below the Per Particle Array Attributes list.

4. Click the General button to open the Add Attribute window.

5. In the Add Attribute window, switch to the Particle tab.

6. Scroll toward the bottom of the list, and Ctrl+click spriteNumPP, spriteScaleXPP, spriteScaleYPP, and spriteTwistPP. The *PP* indicates that each attribute is a per-particle attribute (see Figure 17.9).

FIGURE 17.9
Select the per-particle sprite attributes in the Add Attribute menu.

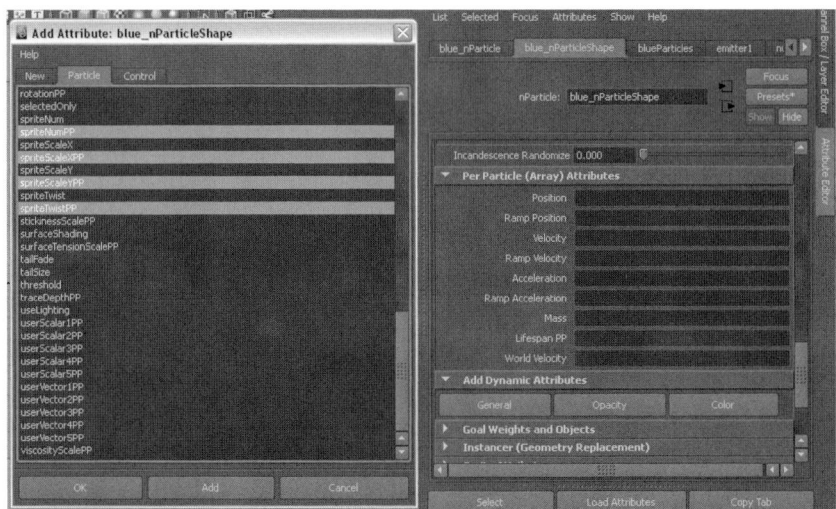

7. Click the Add button to add these attributes. The new attributes should appear in the Per Particle (Array) Attributes list. If they do not, click the Load Attributes button at the bottom of the Attribute Editor to refresh the window.

8. Open the Script Editor, and take a look at the history. At the top you'll see that the addAttr command is used to add the attributes to the blue_nParticleShape object. Notice that each attribute uses two addAttr commands to add the attribute (see Figure 17.10).

   You can copy these lines of code and adapt them to the script based on what you've learned so far.

FIGURE 17.10
The Script Editor reveals the syntax for adding the per-particle array attributes.

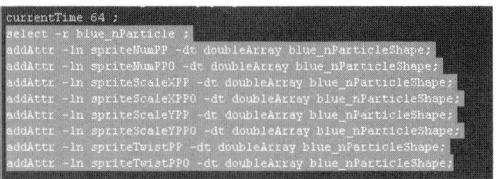

9. Edit the mySpriteScript.mel file so it reads as follows:

```
//create an array containing the current selection
string $mySelection[] = `ls -selection`;

//set the particle render type of the current selection to sprite
setAttr ($mySelection[0]+".particleRenderType") 5;

//add per-particle spriteNum, scale, and twist attributes

addAttr -ln spriteNumPP -dt doubleArray $mySelection[0];
addAttr -ln spriteNumPP0 -dt doubleArray $mySelection[0];

addAttr -ln spriteScaleXPP -dt doubleArray $mySelection[0];
addAttr -ln spriteScaleXPP0 -dt doubleArray $mySelection[0];

addAttr -ln spriteScaleYPP -dt doubleArray $mySelection[0];
addAttr -ln spriteScaleYPP0 -dt doubleArray $mySelection[0];

addAttr -ln spriteTwistPP -dt doubleArray $mySelection[0];
addAttr -ln spriteTwistPP0 -dt doubleArray $mySelection[0];
```

In this case, the pasted code from the Script Editor was changed so that blue_nParticleShape is now the variable $mySelection[0];.

10. Test the script. First, save the mySpriteScript.mel file in the text editor. Save the Maya scene as **shot1_v04.ma**.

11. Go back to an earlier version of the Maya scene, before pink_nParticle was converted to a sprite, so you can test the entire script. Open the shot_v02.ma scene for the chapter17\ scenes folder on the DVD.

12. In the Outliner, select pink_nParticle. Copy all the text in the mySpriteScript.mel file, and paste it into the work area of the Script Editor.

13. Press the Enter key to run the script.

When you run the script, you should have no error messages. If you do see an error in the Script Editor, double-check the text of the script, and make sure there are no mistakes.

Even though there are no errors, you may have noticed that something is not quite right. Select pink_nParticle, and open its Attribute Editor to the pink_nParticleShape tab. In the Per Particle (Array) Attributes section, you'll notice that the per-particle attributes do not appear, even when you click the Load Attributes button at the bottom of the Attribute Editor. What happened?

14. In the Attribute Editor, click the pink_nParticle tab to switch to the nParticle's transform node.

15. Expand the Extra Attributes section. Here you'll find the per-particle attributes. They have been added to the wrong node (see Figure 17.11).

FIGURE 17.11
The per-particle
array attributes
have been added to
the transform node
by mistake.

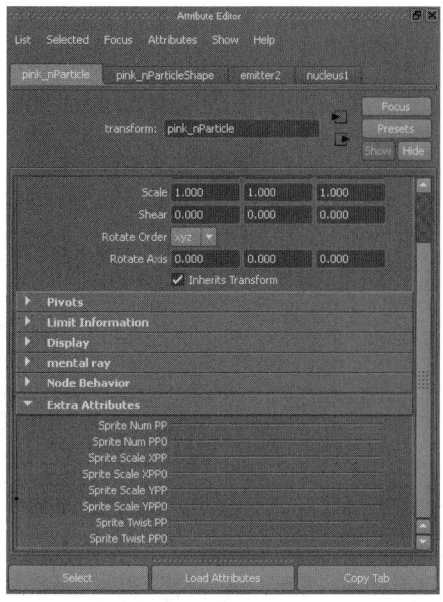

This is a common mistake that is easy to make. When you write a MEL script, you must keep in mind the potential problems that can occur when you or another user applies the script in a scene. In this case, the MEL script did exactly what you asked it to: it added per-particle attributes to the selected node, which in this case is the pink_nParticle node.

Your intent is to add the attributes to the shape node. You have two options:

◆ You can make sure that you—and anyone else who uses the script—remember to always select the shape nodes of the nParticles every time you use the script.

◆ You can build in a command that ensures that the attributes are applied to the shape node.

The second option is more desirable and actually involves little coding.

16. Edit the text at the top of the script in the mySpriteScript.mel file so it reads as follows:

```
//create an array containing the shape nodes of the current selection
pickWalk -d down;
string $mySelection[] = `ls -selection`;
```

A new line has been added to the top of the script using the pickWalk command. This command moves the current selection down one node (notice the –d flag, which stands for direction, and that the flag is set to down) in the node hierarchy, which means that if a user selects the nParticle node, the pickWalk command at the top of the script will move the selection down to the shape node and then load the selected shape node into the $mySelection[] array variable.

If the user has already selected the shape node before running the script, it will still function properly since there are almost always no other nodes below the shape node in the node hierarchy. Later you'll see how to add a conditional statement so the user will get an error if they pick anything other than an nParticle object. Anticipating user errors is a big part of becoming an accomplished MEL script author.

Repeat steps 10–12 to test the script. This time the new attributes should appear in the Per Particle (Array) Attributes list of the pink_nParticleShape node, as shown in Figure 17.12.

Save the `mySpriteScript.mel` file.

FIGURE 17.12

When you correct the script, the new attributes are added to the Per Particle (Array) Attributes section of the pink_nParticleShape tab.

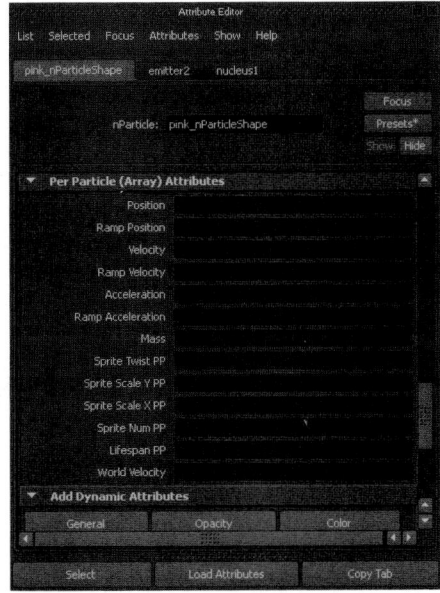

Adding an Image Sequence to the Sprites

At this point, you can apply the animated image sequence of the logos to the blue_nParticle sprites:

1. Open the `shot1_v04.ma` scene from the `chapter17\scenes` folder on the DVD.

2. Open the Hypershade window, and create a new Lambert shader. Name the shader **spriteShade**.

3. Select blue_nParticle in the Outliner.

4. In the Hypershade, right-click spriteShade, and choose Assign Material To Selection.

5. Rewind and play the animation to frame 50. The sprites appear as blue squares.

6. Open the Attribute Editor for spriteShade.

7. Add a file texture node to the Color channel by clicking the checkered box next to Color and choosing File from the 2D Textures category under the Maya heading.

8. In the options for the file node, click the folder next to Image Name, and select the `logo.1.iff` file from the `chapter17\sourceimages` folder on the DVD.

The image appears as a small pentagon with a hole in it. When you rewind and play the scene, each of the blue_nParticles should look like the small pentagon. The image has an alpha channel that is automatically used in the Transparency channel of spriteShade. This image is actually the first in an animated sequence of 60 frames. The process for adding image sequences to sprites is a little odd. The next steps explain how this is done:

1. Open the Attribute Editor for the file1 node that has been applied to the Color channel of spriteShade.

2. Expand the Interactive Sequence Caching options.

3. Turn on Use Interactive Sequence Caching, and use the following settings:

   Sequence Start: **1**

   Sequence End: **60**

   Sequence Increment: **1**

4. Turn on the Use Image Sequence option above the Interactive Sequence options (Figure 17.13 shows this).

5. Rewind and play the scene. The sprites don't look any different, and you'll see a warning in the Script Editor complaining that images cannot be found once the animation passes frame 60.

   The spriteNumPP attribute controls how the image sequence is applied to each sprite. Until you create an expression for this attribute, you won't see the image sequence properly on the sprites.

6. Open the Attribute Editor for the blue_nParticleShape node.

7. In the Per Particle (Array) Attributes section, right-click the field next to spriteNumPP, and choose Creation Expression to open the Expression Editor.

FIGURE 17.13
Turn on Use Interactive Sequence Caching and Use Image Sequence to apply the animated images to the spriteShade material.

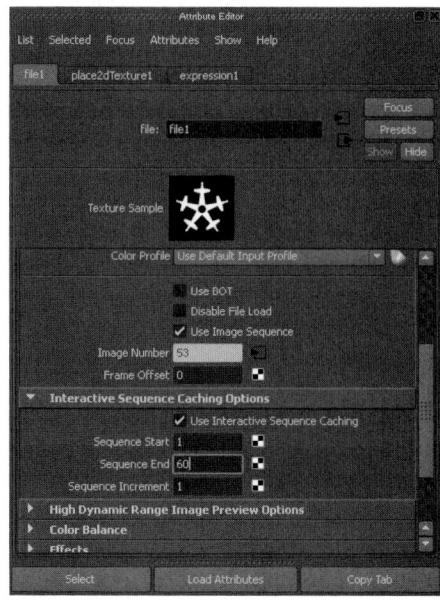

8. In the Expression section of the Expression Editor, type the following:

   `spriteNumPP=1;`

9. Click the Create button to make the expression.

10. In the Expression Editor, click the Runtime Before Dynamics button to switch to runtime expression mode.

11. Type the following:

    `spriteNumPP=spriteNumPP+1;`

12. Click the Create button to make the expression.

13. Rewind and play the animation. Now you'll see each of the blue logos appears as a small pentagon that grows into the snowflake logo as it is born (see Figure 17.14).

14. Save the scene as **shot1_v05.ma**.

To see a version of the scene to this point, open the shot1_v05.ma scene from the chapter17\ scenes folder on the DVD.

FIGURE 17.14
The snowflake logo is animated as each sprite nParticle is born into the scene.

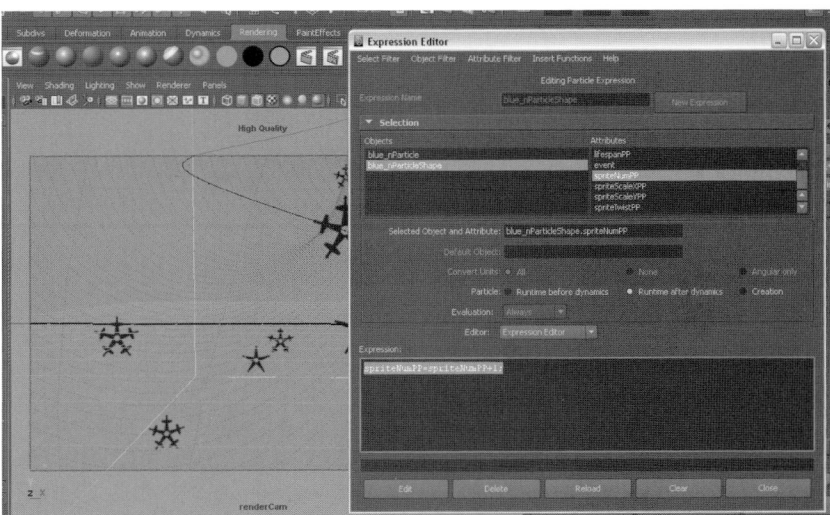

Adding Expressions Using MEL

The previous section described the standard manner in which the spriteNumPP attribute is used to animate sprite images. Imagine going through that whole process for multiple nParticle objects. This is where scripting with MEL can take much of the tedium out of working in Maya. In this section, you'll add commands to your MEL script that will apply the same expressions to all selected nParticles in a scene. In addition, you'll add expressions to control the twist and scale of the nParticles.

1. Continue with the scene from the previous section, or open the shot1_v05.ma scene from the chapter17\scenes directory on the DVD. Open the mySpriteScript.mel file in a text editor.

If you look in the Script Editor when you add the creation expression for blue_nParticle's spriteNumPP, you'll see the following command:

```
dynExpression -s "blue_nParticleShape.spriteNumPP=1;" -c blue_nParticleShape;
```

The runtime expression looks like this:

```
dynExpression -s "blue_nParticleShape.spriteNumPP=blue_nParticleShape.
spriteNumPP+1;"
    -rbd blue_nParticleShape
```

The expression is added using the dynExpression command. The -s flag specifies a string that is the expression itself surrounded by quotes. You'll see that the creation expression uses the -c flag, and the runtime before dynamics expression uses the -rbd flag.

2. Edit the text in the mySpriteScript.mel file so it reads as follows:

```
//create an array containing the shape nodes of the current selection
pickWalk -d down;
string $mySelection[] = `ls -selection`;

//set the particle render type of the current selection to sprite
setAttr ($mySelection[0]+".particleRenderType") 5;

//add per-particle twist, scale, and spriteNum attributes

addAttr -ln spriteNumPP -dt doubleArray $mySelection[0];
addAttr -ln spriteNumPP0 -dt doubleArray $mySelection[0];

addAttr -ln spriteScaleXPP -dt doubleArray $mySelection[0];
addAttr -ln spriteScaleXPP0 -dt doubleArray $mySelection[0];

addAttr -ln spriteScaleYPP -dt doubleArray $mySelection[0];
addAttr -ln spriteScaleYPP0 -dt doubleArray $mySelection[0];

addAttr -ln spriteTwistPP -dt doubleArray $mySelection[0];
addAttr -ln spriteTwistPP0 -dt doubleArray $mySelection[0];

//add expressions for per-particle attributes

dynExpression -s "spriteNumPP=1;" -c $mySelection[0];
dynExpression -s "spriteNumPP=spriteNumPP+1;" -rbd $mySelection[0];
```

You'll notice that in the expression text itself, within the quotes, you can print just the name of the attribute spriteNumPP without adding the array variable. Maya understands that the expression will be added to the selected nParticle object.

3. Test the script by selecting the pink_nParticle object in the Outliner.

4. Copy all the text in the text file, and paste it into the work area of the Script Editor. Press the Enter key.

5. In the Hypershade, select spriteShade, and apply it to the pink_nParticle object.

6. If there are no error messages, rewind and play the scene.

You'll see the pink_nParticle object now has the animated sprites applied. The sprites are pink thanks to the pink color that was originally applied to the spheres in the first version of the scene.

7. Select the blue_nParticle object, and edit the creation expression. Add the following, and click the Edit button (see Figure 17.15):

```
spriteTwistPP=rand(360);

spriteScaleXPP=rand(0.5,2);
spriteScaleYPP=spriteScaleXPP;
```

FIGURE 17.15
Edit the creation expression for the blue_nParticleShape in the Expression Editor.

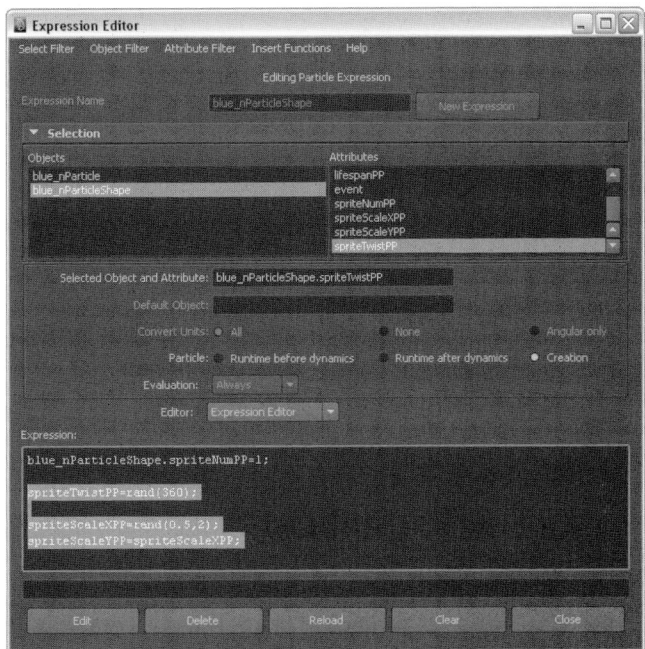

8. Edit the runtime before dynamics expression. Add the following line, and click the Edit button:

```
spriteTwistPP=spriteTwistPP+1;
```

9. Rewind and play the scene. The blue_nParticles are rotated randomly as they fly through the scene. They are also sized randomly.

Note that when you set a scaleXPP value for a sprite, you should then set the scaleYPP attribute equal to the scaleXPP attribute. This way, the sprites are scaled uniformly and remain square shaped.

10. To add these changes to the script, edit the text in the `mySpriteScript.mel` file so the expressions look like this (the expressions printed in this book span more than one line; when you place them in your script, you should paste them onto a single line without adding returns):

```
//add expressions for per-particle attributes

dynExpression -s "spriteNumPP=1; \r\n\r\nspriteTwistPP=rand(360);
     \r\n\r\nspriteScaleXPP=rand(.5,2);
     \r\nspriteScaleYPP=spriteScaleXPP;" -c $mySelection[0];

dynExpression -s "spriteNumPP=spriteNumPP+1;
     \r\n\r\nspriteTwistPP=spriteTwistPP+1;"
     -rbd $mySelection[0];
```

Figure 17.16 shows the script text in a text editor. The `\r` and `\n` that you see in the expression stand for "return" (`\r`) and "newline" (`\n`). Adding these to the expressions in your MEL script creates spaces between the expressions in the Expression Editor, which makes the expressions organized and easy to read.

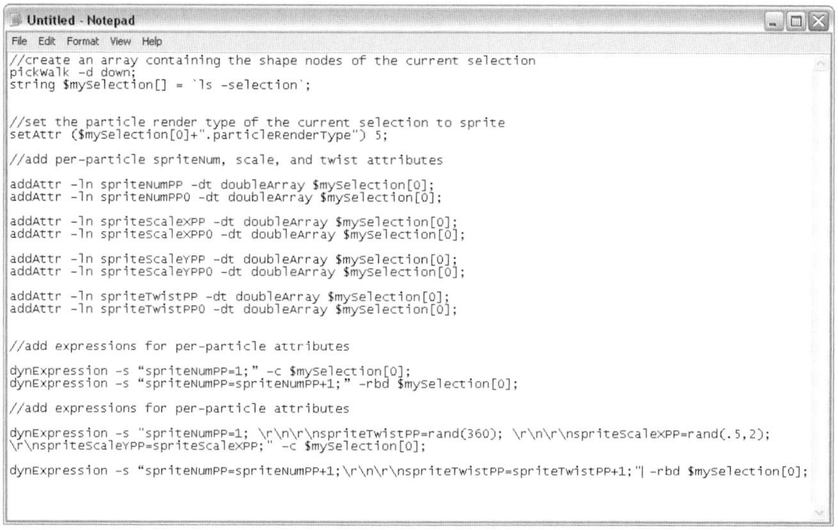


```
//create an array containing the shape nodes of the current selection
pickWalk -d down;
string $mySelection[] = `ls -selection`;


//set the particle render type of the current selection to sprite
setAttr ($mySelection[0]+".particleRenderType") 5;

//add per-particle spriteNum, scale, and twist attributes

addAttr -ln spriteNumPP -dt doubleArray $mySelection[0];
addAttr -ln spriteNumPP0 -dt doubleArray $mySelection[0];

addAttr -ln spriteScaleXPP -dt doubleArray $mySelection[0];
addAttr -ln spriteScaleXPP0 -dt doubleArray $mySelection[0];

addAttr -ln spriteScaleYPP -dt doubleArray $mySelection[0];
addAttr -ln spriteScaleYPP0 -dt doubleArray $mySelection[0];

addAttr -ln spriteTwistPP -dt doubleArray $mySelection[0];
addAttr -ln spriteTwistPP0 -dt doubleArray $mySelection[0];


//add expressions for per-particle attributes

dynExpression -s "spriteNumPP=1;" -c $mySelection[0];
dynExpression -s "spriteNumPP=spriteNumPP+1;" -rbd $mySelection[0];

//add expressions for per-particle attributes

dynExpression -s "spriteNumPP=1; \r\n\r\nspriteTwistPP=rand(360); \r\n\r\nspriteScaleXPP=rand(.5,2);
\r\nspriteScaleYPP=spriteScaleXPP;" -c $mySelection[0];

dynExpression -s "spriteNumPP=spriteNumPP+1;\r\n\r\nspriteTwistPP=spriteTwistPP+1;"| -rbd $mySelection[0];
```

FIGURE 17.16 Edit the text in the MEL script to update the expressions.

11. Edit the text, and save the `mySpriteScript.mel` file. Select pink_nParticle. Copy and paste the text from the text file into the work area of the Script Editor.

12. Select the last lines that add the expressions in the Script Editor, and press the Enter key (see Figure 17.17).

By selecting just the last few lines and pressing Enter, you will execute only those lines that add the expressions. At this point, the other lines in the script have already been applied to the pink_nParticle object.

To see a version of the scene, open the `shot1_v06.ma` scene from the `chapter17\scenes` folder on the DVD.

FIGURE 17.17
The lines that add the expression commands are highlighted in the Script Editor. Pressing the Enter key executes just the selected lines of code.

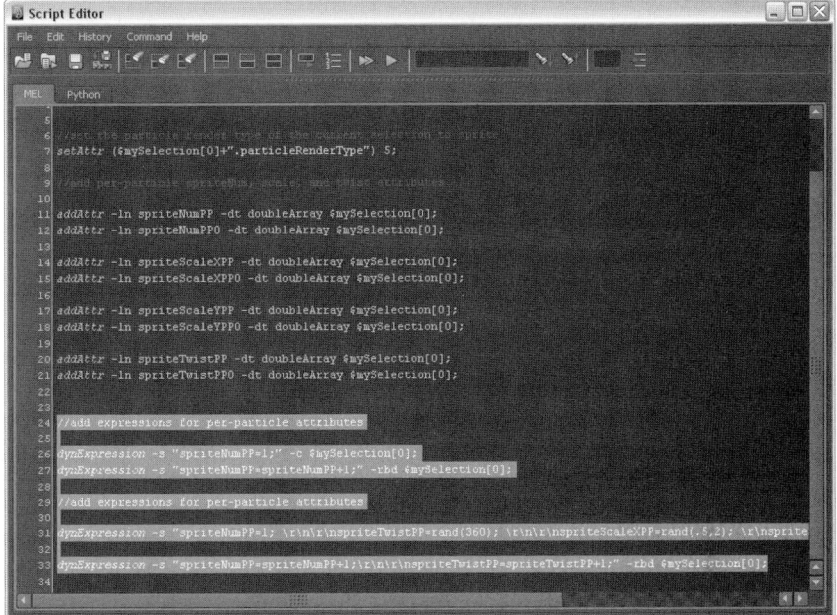

Creating a Conditional Statement

Conditional statements are used to direct the commands of a script toward one action or another. If a certain condition is met, then the script performs an action; if not, the script does something else. Conditional statements work very well for error detection. In the case of the current example, you'll use a conditional statement to make sure the script works only when an nParticle object is selected. This can prevent errors from occurring in the script or in the scene.

You will add a conditional statement to the mySpriteScript.mel file that tests to make sure the selected object is an nParticle object. If it is, then the script will run and perform all the commands you've created in the previous section. If it is not, the script will print an error message that says that the selected object is not an nParticle.

There are several types of conditional statements. In this example, you'll use the most common if/then conditional. The syntax for this type of conditional looks like this:

```
If (condition to test is true)
    {
    Execute commands;
    }
else
    {
    Print error message or execute a different set of commands;
    }
```

The statement within the parentheses at the start of the conditional is the statement that needs to be tested. If this statement is true, then the commands within the first set of curly braces are executed. Notice that these commands are indented. Using indentation in your script makes the script appear organized and legible.

If the statement within the parentheses is false, then Maya skips down to the `else` statement and executes the set of commands in the second set of curly braces. This can be an error message or even additional conditional statements. In this section, you'll add a conditional statement that uses the `objectType` command to test whether the selected object is an nParticle.

1. Open your most recent version of the `mySpriteScript.mel` file.

2. At the top of the script, edit the text so that it says the following:

```
//create an array containing the shape nodes of the current selection
pickWalk -d down;
string $mySelection[] = `ls -selection`;

//make sure selected object is an nParticle
if (`objectType -isType "nParticle" $mySelection[0]`){
```

The `objectType` command uses the `isType` flag to test whether `$mySelection[0]` is an nParticle. Notice that this command is surrounded by the backtick marks within the parentheses. These backtick marks are used whenever one command is nested within another. Compare this line with the line that creates the `$mySelection[]` array variable and assigns it to a list of the selected objects. How is the use of the backtick marks similar in these two lines?

When you use the `if` statement, the condition within the parentheses is tested to be either true or false. If the statement is true, a value of 1 is returned. If the statement is false, a value of 0 is returned.

3. Use the Tab key to indent the commands you created in the previous section.

4. Add the `else` statement and the error message at the bottom. The entire script should look like this:

```
//create an array containing the shape nodes of the current selection
pickWalk -d down;
string $mySelection[] = `ls -selection`;

//make sure selected object is an nParticle
if (`objectType -isType "nParticle" $mySelection[0]`){

    //set the particle render type of the current selection to sprite
    setAttr ($mySelection[0]+".particleRenderType") 5;

    //add per-particle twist, scale, and spriteNum attributes

    addAttr -ln spriteNumPP -dt doubleArray $mySelection[0];
    addAttr -ln spriteNumPP0 -dt doubleArray $mySelection[0];

    addAttr -ln spriteScaleXPP -dt doubleArray $mySelection[0];
    addAttr -ln spriteScaleXPP0 -dt doubleArray $mySelection[0];

    addAttr -ln spriteScaleYPP -dt doubleArray $mySelection[0];
    addAttr -ln spriteScaleYPP0 -dt doubleArray $mySelection[0];
```

```
        addAttr -ln spriteTwistPP -dt doubleArray $mySelection[0];
        addAttr -ln spriteTwistPP0 -dt doubleArray $mySelection[0];

        //add expressions for per-particle attributes

        dynExpression -s "spriteNumPP=1;\r\n\r\nspriteTwistPP=rand(360);
            \r\n\r\nspriteScaleXPP=rand(.5,2);
            \r\nspriteScaleYPP=spriteScaleXPP;" -c $mySelection[0];

        dynExpression -s "spriteNumPP=spriteNumPP+1;
            \r\n\r\nspriteTwistPP=spriteTwistPP+1;"
            -rbd $mySelection[0];

    }
    else
    {
        error "Sorry, you must select an nParticle to use this script";
    }
```

5. To test the script, open the shot2_v01.ma scene from the chapter17\scenes directory on the DVD. This is the second shot in the commercial spot. It uses five nParticle objects.

6. Select the orange_nParticle object in the Outliner.

7. Select and copy all the text in the mySpriteScript.mel file, and paste it into the Script Editor.

8. Press the Enter key to run the script. If there are no errors, the orange_nParticle object will turn into a sprite.

9. Select the emitter1 object in the Outliner. Copy and paste the script into the Script Editor, and run the script again. This time you should see an error message that says, Sorry, you must select an nParticle to use this script.

10. Save the mySpriteScript.mel file in your text editor.

Remember to assign the spriteShade shader to the orange_nParticle and turn on Hardware Texturing in the Shading menu of the viewport; otherwise, you will not see the image on the sprites applied to the orange_nParticle.

Creating a Loop

As it stands, the script is designed to convert one nParticle object at a time. By adding a simple loop to the script, running the script a single time will convert all of the selected nParticles at the same time.

There are many types of loop statements you can use in MEL. One of the most common and easiest to create is the for loop. It uses the following syntax:

```
for ($i=0;$i<length of loop;$i++){ loop commands }
```

There are three commands within the parentheses separated by semicolons:

◆ The first command creates a variable named $i. The new $i variable is set to equal 0, which is the starting value of the loop.

◆ The second command in the parentheses sets the limit of the loop. So long as the variable $i is less than a particular value, the loop continues to run.

◆ The third statement in the parentheses increases the variable $i by increments of 1. Another way of saying $i = $i + 1 is to use $i++.

The commands that will be executed each time the loop runs are contained within curly braces, just like the conditional statement. Once again, using the Tab key to indent statements within the braces can help you keep the script visually organized, especially if multiple nested loops are used.

Open the mySpriteScript.mel file in your text editor. Add the text to create the loop in the script. The following shows where this text is placed within the script:

```
//create an array containing the shape nodes of the current selection
pickWalk -d down;
string $mySelection[] = `ls -selection`;

//create a loop based on the number of selected object
for ($i=0;$i<size($mySelection);$i++){

    //make sure selected object is an nParticle
    if (`objectType -isType "nParticle" $mySelection[$i]`){

        //set the particle render type of the current selection to sprite
        setAttr ($mySelection[$i]+".particleRenderType") 5;

        //add per-particle twist, scale, and spriteNum attributes

        addAttr -ln spriteNumPP -dt doubleArray $mySelection[$i];
        addAttr -ln spriteNumPP0 -dt doubleArray $mySelection[$i];

        addAttr -ln spriteScaleXPP -dt doubleArray $mySelection[$i];
        addAttr -ln spriteScaleXPP0 -dt doubleArray $mySelection[$i];

        addAttr -ln spriteScaleYPP -dt doubleArray $mySelection[$i];
        addAttr -ln spriteScaleYPP0 -dt doubleArray $mySelection[$i];

        addAttr -ln spriteTwistPP -dt doubleArray $mySelection[$i];
        addAttr -ln spriteTwistPP0 -dt doubleArray $mySelection[$i];

        //add expressions for per-particle attributes

        dynExpression -s "spriteNumPP=1;\r\n\r\nspriteTwistPP=rand(360);
            \r\n\r\nspriteScaleXPP=rand(.5,2);
            \r\nspriteScaleYPP=spriteScaleXPP;" -c $mySelection[$i];

        dynExpression -s "spriteNumPP=spriteNumPP+1;
            \r\n\r\nspriteTwistPP=spriteTwistPP+1;"
```

```
                    -rbd $mySelection[$i];


          }
          else
          {
               error "Sorry, you must select an nParticle to use this script";
          }
     }
```

The loop is set to run as long as $i is less than the size of $mySelection. The size of $mySelection is based on the number of items selected before the script is run. For each iteration of the loop, $i is increased by an increment of 1.

The first time the loop runs, $i is equal to 0; the second time the loop runs, $i is equal to 1; the third time the loop runs, $i is equal to 2; and so on, until $i is equal to the number of items selected in the scene.

Notice that the 0 in the brackets of the $mySelection variable is now changed to the $i variable throughout the script. Recall that the items in the list contained in the $mySelection array variable are numbered based on the order in which they are selected and that this numbering starts with 0. By changing the code so that $mySelection[0] is now $mySelection[$i], the commands are run on each of the objects contained in the array variable.

Before completing the script, there is one final line of code you can add to the loop. This line simply turns on the Depth Sort option for sprites, which is usually off by default. Depth Sort ensures that the sprites closest to the camera appear in front of the sprites farthest from the camera.

In the script, add a line after the command that sets the particle render type to sprites but before the lines that add the per-particle render attributes. The new line should read as follows:

```
//Turn on Depth Sort
setAttr ($mySelection[$i]+".depthSort") 1;
```

Figure 17.18 shows the final script as it appears in Notepad.

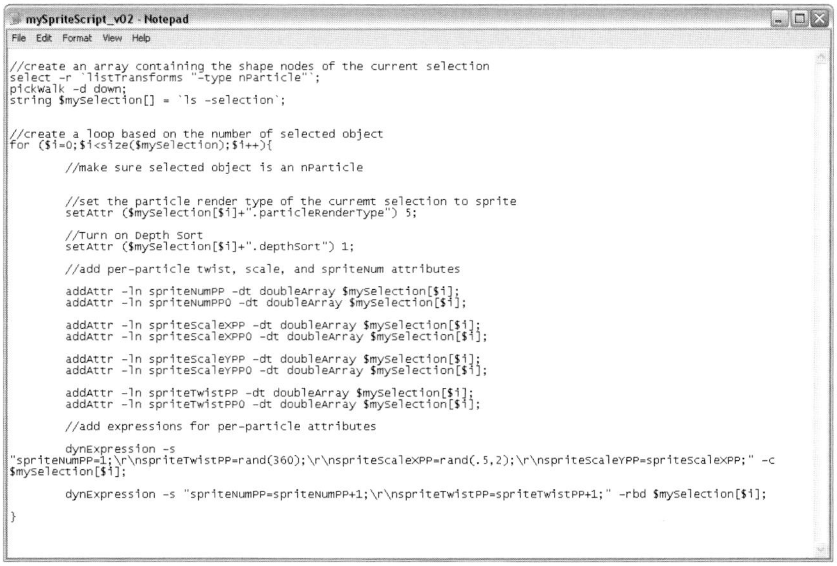

FIGURE 17.18
The final script as it appears in Notepad

Save the mySpriteScript.mel file to your local directory. Save the script in the Maya\scripts directory found in the My Documents folder.

Scripts are usually saved in the My Documents\Maya\scripts folder on your local drive. You may also save scripts to the My Documents\Maya\2010\scripts directory (Mac users can place their scripts in the Users\Shared\Autodesk\maya\2011-x64\scripts folder), or if they are specific to your project, you can save them in the mel folder of the current project.

You can compare your version of the script with the mySpriteScript.mel file in the chapter17\mel directory on the DVD.

1. To test the script, open the shot2_v01.ma scene from the chapter17\scenes folder on the DVD. If it is already open, reload the scene.

2. In the Outliner, Shift+click the green_nParticle, red_nParticle, yellow_nParticle, purple_nParticle, and orange_nParticle objects.

3. Open the Script Editor, and choose File ➤ Load Script.

4. Find the script on your local drive, and choose it.

5. The script loads in the work area of the Script Editor window. Press the Enter key to run the script. If there are errors, open the mySpriteScript.mel file from the chapter17\mel folder on the DVD. Compare your code with the code in this file; keep a sharp eye for typos, because even the smallest mistake can cause an error. Unfortunately, debugging scripts for small errors is a rite of passage for beginning MEL scripters.

6. Select the nParticle objects, open the Hypershade, and apply the spriteShade material to the selected nParticle objects.

7. Save the scene as **shot2_v02.ma**.

To see a finished version of the scene, open the shot2_v02.ma scene from the chapter17\scenes folder on the DVD. Make sure Hardware Texturing is on so that you can see the images on the sprites.

If everything works, congratulations on creating your first MEL script. With more practice and study, you'll find that creating scripts saves you a great deal of time and labor.

CREATE A SHELF BUTTON FOR A SCRIPT

You can create a shelf button from selected code in the Script Editor. If the script is something you think you'll use fairly often in a scene, a shelf button can save even more time. Whenever you need to run the script, you simply click the shelf button. To create a shelf button, switch to the Custom Shelf tab, select the code you want to make into a button, and choose File ➤ Save Script To Shelf. Give the shelf a name as descriptive as you can within the six-character limit. Remember to save the shelves before quitting Maya so that the buttons appear the next time you open Maya. To do this, click the black down-arrow button to the left of the shelves, and choose Save All Shelves.

Procedures

A complex MEL script often consists of procedures. A *procedure* is a small section of code that may be called upon by the script one or more times. You can think of a procedure as a mini-MEL script within a script. Procedures are a useful and efficient way to organize a script.

Making a Procedure from a Script

In this example, you'll create a procedure from a script:

1. In your text editor, open the shakeMe.mel file from the chapter17\mel folder on the DVD.

   The shakeMe.mel script is a very simple loop that attaches an expression to the Translate channels of selected objects. Take a look at the code:

   ```
   string $mySel[] = `ls -sl`;

   for ($i=0;$i<size($mySel);$i++){

       makeIdentity -apply true -t 1 -r 1 -s 1 -n 0 $mySel[$i];

       expression -s "translateX=rand(-1,1);"   -o $mySel[$i] -ae 1 -uc all ;
       expression -s "translateY=rand(-1,1);"   -o $mySel[$i] -ae 1 -uc all ;
       expression -s "translateZ=rand(-1,1);"   -o $mySel[$i] -ae 1 -uc all ;

   };
   ```

   The script starts by making an array of the selected objects in the scene (the -sl flag is an abbreviation for *selection*). The loop then uses the makeIdentity command to freeze all the transformations for the selected objects. The three expression commands attach an expression to each of the Translate channels, which randomizes the position of the translation between -1 and 1.

   The flags in the expression command are -s (string), -o (object), -ae (always evaluate), and -uc (unit conversion).

2. To test the script, make a new blank scene in Maya.

3. Create a number of polygon cubes, and place them randomly in the scene.

4. Select the cubes, and open the Script Editor. Copy and paste the code from the shakeMe.mel file into the work area of the Script Editor; then press the Enter key.

5. Rewind and play the scene. The cubes should shake randomly around their original location.

6. To turn the script into a procedure, edit the text file so it looks like the following:

   ```
   proc shakeMe(){

       string $mySel[] = `ls -sl`;

       for ($i=0;$i<size($mySel);$i++){

           makeIdentity -apply true -t 1 -r 1 -s 1 -n 0 $mySel[$i];

           expression -s "translateX=rand(-1,1);"   -o $mySel[$i] -ae 1 -uc all
   ;
           expression -s "translateY=rand(-1,1);"   -o $mySel[$i] -ae 1 -uc all
   ;
   ```

```
                        expression -s "translateZ=rand(-1,1);"  -o $mySel[$i] -ae 1 -uc all
     ;


          }
     }
```

At the start of the script, the text `proc shakeMe()` is added. This creates a new procedure named `shakeMe`. The procedure is contained within the set of curly braces.

7. Create a new scene in Maya.

8. Create a number of randomly placed polygon cubes.

9. Copy and paste the edited text into the Script Editor. Select the cubes, and press the Enter key. Nothing happens.

   Nothing happens because instead of executing a script, you've actually *sourced* the procedure. In other words, you've made this snippet of code available as part of Maya.

10. With the cubes selected, type **shakeMe** into the command line, and press the Enter key. The script is now applied to the selected cubes.

    This is useful because you can run the script any number of times on any number of selected objects by selecting the objects and then typing shakeMe into the command line.

11. Save this file as **shakeMeProc.mel**.

To see a version, open the `shakeMeProc.mel` file from the `chapter17\mel` folder on the DVD.

Using a Procedure Within a Script

The real usefulness of a procedure is when it is contained as part of a script. The procedure can be called on within the script at any time, which is a way of reusing the same bit of code whenever it is needed. Procedures should always appear at the start of the script so that, when the script is run, the procedures are sourced into Maya's memory before the rest of the script executes.

As a simple example, suppose that instead of randomly moving the selected objects between a value of -1 and 1, you wanted to create a range for the expression that itself is based on a random value.

1. Open a text editor to a new file, and type the following:

   ```
   //create a random number between 0 and 3
   float $randVal = rand(3);
   ```

   This is an extremely simple script that generates a random number between 0 and 3.

2. Copy the text shakeMe proc from the `shakeMeProc.mel` file in the `chapter17\mel` folder.

3. Paste this text before the lines you have typed in the text editor so the script looks like the following:

   ```
   proc shakeMe(){
   ```

```
string $mySel[] = `ls -sl`;

for ($i=0;$i<size($mySel);$i++){

        makeIdentity -apply true -t 1 -r 1 -s 1 -n 0 $mySel[$i];

        expression -s "translateX=rand(-1,1);"  -o $mySel[$i] -ae 1 -uc all
;
        expression -s "translateY=rand(-1,1);"  -o $mySel[$i] -ae 1 -uc all
;
        expression -s "translateZ=rand(-1,1);"  -o $mySel[$i] -ae 1 -uc all
;

    }
}

//Create a random number between 0 and 3
float $randVal = rand(3);
```

4. Edit the first line of the script to read **proc shakeMe($num){**. This adds a variable that allows the script to pass information to the procedure.

5. Even though the variable is stated in the procedure, you still need to declare its type as a float. Edit the first three lines of the script like this:

```
proc shakeMe(float $num){

    float $num;

    string $mySel[] = `ls -sl`;
```

6. Within the loop, below the makeIdentity command, add two new lines:

```
        float $lowRange = -0.5*$num;
        float $highRange = 0.5*$num;
```

These lines create two new variables that represent the low and high ranges of the random value that will be used in the next lines of the script. So if the initial $num is equal to 3, the low range will be -1.5, and the high range will be 1.5. Thus, the object will move randomly within a total range of three units when the expression is applied.

7. Edit the expression lines of the script:

```
expression -s ("translateX=rand(" + $lowRange + "," + $highRange +");")
  -o $mySel[$i] -ae 1 -uc all ;
expression -s ("translateY=rand(" + $lowRange + "," + $highRange +");")
  -o $mySel[$i] -ae 1 -uc all ;
expression -s ("translateZ=rand(" + $lowRange + "," + $highRange +");")
  -o $mySel[$i] -ae 1 -uc all ;
```

It is very important to pay attention to how these lines are written because it illustrates an important aspect of using MEL to create expressions. On the surface it may seem logical to place the $lowRange and $highRange variables directly into the expression so that the line looks like this:

```
expression -s "translateX=rand($lowRange, $highRange );"
    -o $mySel[$i] -ae 1 -uc all ;
```

But this will not work. If you run the script using this syntax, you will get an error that says that $lowRange and $highRange have not been declared as variables. At first this makes no sense—clearly you declared the variables in the two lines added before the expression lines. So, why is Maya complaining about undeclared variables?

You have to understand what the expression command actually does. When you use the expression command, it is like you are telling MEL to write the expression for you in the Expression Editor. Variables within the Expression Editor are local. They have no relationship or connection to the variables created within MEL scripts (one alternative is to declare the variables as global variables; however, for the sake of understanding how to write expressions with MEL, let's pretend global variables do not exist).

When you run the script, MEL creates the expressions exactly as they appear between the quotes in the expression command. Therefore, if you place variables within these quotes that have not been declared *in the expression itself*, Maya won't understand where these variables came from. To work around this, you concatenate the expression using the plus sign. This is the same syntax you used earlier in the chapter when you set an attribute for an object contained within a variable. The syntax looks like this:

```
Expression -string "The first part of the expression text" +
    the variable created in mel +
    "the second part of the expression text";
```

Finally, at the very end of the script, add a line that calls the procedure so the entire script, with procedure, looks like this:

```
proc shakeMe(float $num){

    float $num;

    string $mySel[] = `ls -sl`;

    for ($i=0;$i<size($mySel);$i++){

        makeIdentity -apply true -t 1 -r 1 -s 1 -n 0 $mySel[$i];

        float $lowRange = -0.5*(0.5+$num);
        float $highRange = 0.5*(0.5+$num);


        expression -s ("translateX=rand(" + $lowRange + "," + $highRange
+");")
            -o $mySel[$i] -ae 1 -uc all ;
```

```
            expression -s ("translateY=rand(" + $lowRange + "," + $highRange
+");")
                -o $mySel[$i] -ae 1 -uc all ;
            expression -s ("translateZ=rand(" + $lowRange + "," + $highRange
+");")
                -o $mySel[$i] -ae 1 -uc all ;


    }
};

//Create a random number between 0 and 3
float $randVal = rand(3);
shakeMe($randVal);
```

When you select objects in a scene and run the script, the shakeMe procedure is loaded into memory. This is everything within the curly braces. Then the variable $randVal is created and assigned a number between 0 and 3 randomly. The last line of the script calls the shakeMe procedure and passes the procedure the random value held in the $randVal variable. In the procedure, the $num variable is set to be equivalent to the $randVal value, and the procedure is executed.

To see a finished version of the script, open the shakeMeProc_v02.mel file from the chapter17\mel folder on the DVD.

Global Procedures

The procedure created in the previous section is a *local* procedure. The procedure is available only within the script that uses it. A *global* procedure is one that can be called upon by any script in Maya. Maya uses global procedures to create the interface and perform the tasks necessary to make Maya functional. To make a procedure global, you simply start the procedure using the text global proc instead of just proc.

You should be very careful when creating your own global procedures. It is possible to overwrite one of Maya's own global procedures, which can disrupt the way Maya works. The safest bet is to name the global procedure using your own name or initials in a way that will most likely not interfere with one of Maya's global procedures.

Scripts containing global procedures can be saved in the My Documents\Maya\Scripts folder on your local drive directory (Mac users can place their scripts in the Users\Shared\Autodesk\maya\2011-x64\scripts folder). These scripts should load automatically when Maya starts, making the procedures available for use within a Maya session.

You can source a procedure using the File menu in the Script Editor. This loads the procedures contained within a MEL script file into memory so they are available when working in Maya. You can then run the procedure by typing the name of the procedure on the command line. The author of the procedure will usually include instructions on how to use the procedure within comment tags at the top of the procedure. When you source a procedure, you won't notice an immediate change in Maya until you actually call the procedure in a script or on the command line. It's usually a good idea to open the script file that contains the procedure and read the instructions at the top before trying to source and run the procedure.

Using Maya Commands Within Python

Python is a scripting language developed independently of Maya. Python is used for a wide variety of computing tasks well beyond 3D animation and modeling. In recent years, Python has been incorporated into a number of 3D animation packages, making it easier for the various software programs to work together within a studio pipeline.

If you are familiar with Python, you can use Python to run MEL commands within a Python script. To run or write a Python script within Maya, switch to the Python tab in the Script Editor. This tells Maya to interpret any commands as Python and not MEL. Likewise, you can switch the command line and the command shell to Python mode.

Before you can use Maya commands within Python scripts, you must first import the Maya commands into Python. To do this, switch to the Python tab in the Script Editor, and type the following:

```
import maya.cmds
```

Press the Enter key to execute the command.
You can test a Maya command by typing the following:

```
maya.cmds.sphere (radius=1, name='myBall')
```

Note that the syntax for the Python command is different from the MEL syntax. Apostrophes are used around the myBall variable instead of quotes or accent marks, and the line does not end in a semicolon.

 **Real World Scenario**

MEL AND PYTHON IN ACTION: MOLECULAR MAYA

Maya has a huge reputation as the industry standard for creating visual effects for film, commercials, and television. Most studios in Hollywood use Maya as its primary 3D application. But did you know that scientists, specifically molecular biologists, are starting to use Maya to help them visualize their own research in life processes?

For many years, scientists using Maya's animation, dynamic, and rendering capabilities to as a visualization tool, struggled with trying to accurately represent the molecular structures and interactions of proteins within the living cell. This involved using a number of scripts and other types of visualization software and a lot of tedious hard work. Most of the time was spent on getting structures of molecules such as DNA into Maya, and then we were limited by how we could display the structure itself to spheres or particles.

In the past year, this has all changed thanks to the efforts of Harvard Medical School scientist Gaël McGill and extremely talented Python programmer and biologist Campbell Strong. Together they have created a free plug-in for Maya called Molecular Maya (or mMaya). This plug-in was created using MEL and Python scripting, and it makes many of the tasks that used to be overwhelmingly time-consuming as easy as clicking a button.

Using MEL and Python, McGill and Strong have created a customized interface that appears whenever Maya starts. The interface consists of a number of panels with tabs and settings, very similar to the Attribute Editor. Through the interface you can load the protein structure that you need directly into Maya. The protein structures are contained in a specially formatted text file known as a Protein Data Bank (PDB) file. What's more, if you don't have the file on your computer, the Molecular Maya interface can connect directly to the online Protein Data Bank at www.pdb.org, and if you know the specific protein ID number, you can type this into molecular Maya, and, without having to leave Maya, the protein will be downloaded and appear in the viewport within just a few seconds. Beyond just acquiring the protein, Molecular Maya allows you to easily switch between various representational styles so you can view the structure as ribbons, as ball and stick, or as a mesh. Molecular Maya automatically creates these various representations and puts them in a group. The heart of the structure uses nParticles, and currently a system is being developed to take advantage of Maya's nDynamics so that interactions between molecular structures can be accurately simulated.

The goal of this plug-in is to allow scientists to take advantage of the animation and dynamic capabilities of Maya so that they can, even with limited experience using Maya, import whatever protein they may be working on and create and render very simple animations. Artists like myself can spend more time creating visualizations of molecular processes for scientists and less time struggling with importing the structures.

All of this is made possible thanks to MEL and Python. Everything from the interface to the web connectivity to the modeling and dynamics is handled with well-written MEL and Python scripts and allows Maya to be utilized for amazing purposes beyond the entertainment industry.

As an artist, you may be interested only in creating simple time-saving scripts; however, it's important to understand that the power of MEL and Python can allow you to accomplish almost anything in Maya.

The Molecular Maya plug-in is available as a free download from www.molecularmovies.org.

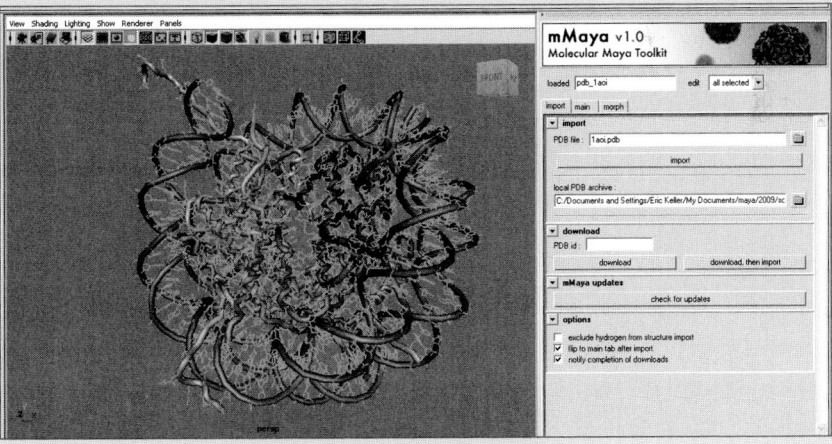

The Bottom Line

Use a MEL command   MEL commands are used to perform many tasks within Maya. There are numerous ways to enter MEL commands in the Maya interface. These include the command shell, the command line, and the Script Editor.

Master it   Create a polygon cube using the command shell. Create a NURBS cone using the command line. Create a polygonSphere using the Script Editor.

Use MEL scripting techniques   Many basic MEL techniques can be used to reduce the number of repetitive tasks performed during a Maya session. Using commands, conditional statements, and loops, you can create simple scripts that make working in Maya faster and more efficient.

Master it   Write a more efficient version of the `mySpriteScript` file that automatically selects all the nParticle objects in a scene without the need for a conditional statement to test the type of the selected nodes.

Create a procedure   Procedures are sections of code that can be called upon at any time within a script. Procedures can help make longer scripts more efficient by eliminating the need to repeat sections of code.

Master it   Write a procedure that adds an expression to selected objects that use the `noise` function to randomly scale objects over time.

Use the Python scripting interface   Python can be used within the Script Editor to execute Python commands or to execute MEL commands within a Python script. The Maya commands must be imported at the start of Python script if you want to incorporate MEL into the Python code.

Master it   Use Python to make a NURBS torus.

The Bottom Line

Chapter 1: Working in Maya

Understand transform and shape nodes   DAG nodes have both a transform node and a shape node. The transform node tells where an object is located; the shape node describes how it is made. Nodes can be parented to each other to form a hierarchy.

> **Master it**   Arrange the nodes in the `miniGun_v03.ma` file in a hierarchical structure so the barrels of the guns can rotate on their z-axis, the guns can be aimed independently, and the guns rotate with the turret.

> **Solution**   In the Outliner, MMB-drag the left_gunBarrels node onto the left_housing node. MMB-drag the left housing node onto left_mount, and then MMB-drag the left mount onto the turret node. Do the same for the right gunBarrels, housing, and mount nodes. Graph the node structure on the Hypergraph, and examine the network.

Create a project   Creating a project directory structure keeps Maya scene files and connected external files organized to ensure the animation project is efficient.

> **Master it**   Create a new project named Test, but make sure the project has only the scene, source images, and data subfolders.

> **Solution**   Use the Options box in the Create New Project command to make a new project named Test; leave all the fields blank except for scenes, source images, and data. Name the folders in these fields `scenes`, `sourceImages`, and `data`, respectively.

Use assets   An asset is a way to organize the attributes of any number of specified nodes so that their attributes are easily accessible in the Channel Box. This means that members of each team in a pipeline only need to see and edit the attributes they need to get their job done, thus streamlining production.

> **Master it**   Create an asset from the nodes in the `miniGun_v04.ma` scene in the `chapter1\ scenes` folder. Make sure that only the Y rotation of the turret, the X rotation of the guns, and the Z rotation of the gun barrels are available to the animator.

> **Solution**   Create a container that holds the turretAim curve and turret nodes (and their child nodes). Use the Asset Editor to publish the Rotate Y, Rotate X, and Barrel Spin attributes of the turretAim curve node to the container. Set the container to black box mode so the animator can't access any of the attributes of the contained nodes.

Create file references File references can be used so that as part of the team works on a model, the other members of the team can use it in the scene. As changes to the original file are made, the referenced file in other scenes will update automatically.

Master it Create a file reference for the miniGun_v04.ma scene; create a proxy from the miniGun_loRes.ma scene.

Solution Create a new scene, and reference the miniGun_v04.ma file in the chapter1\ scenes directory. Use the Reference Editor to make a proxy from the miniGun_loRes .ma scene in the same folder on the DVD.

Chapter 2: Virtual Film Making with Maya Cameras

Determine the image size and film speed of the camera You should determine the final image size of your render at the earliest possible stage in a project. The size will affect everything from texture resolution to render time. Maya has a number of presets that you can use to set the image resolution.

Master it Set up an animation that will be rendered to be displayed on a high-definition progressive-scan television.

Solution Open the Render settings, and choose the HD 1080 preset under the Image Size presets on the Common tab. Progressive scan means the image will not be interlaced (rendered as alternating fields), so you can render at 24 frames per second. Open the Preferences/Settings window, and set the Time setting under Settings to Film (24 FPS).

Create and animate cameras The settings in the Attribute Editor for a camera enable you to replicate real-world cameras as well as add effects such as camera shaking.

Master it Create a camera setting where the film shakes back and forth in the camera. Set up a system where the amount of shaking can be animated over time.

Solution Enable the Shake Overscan attribute on a camera. Attach a fractal texture to the Shake Overscan attribute, and edit its amplitude settings. Create an expression that sets the Alpha Offset to minus one-half the Alpha Gain setting. Set keyframes on Alpha Gain to animate the shaking of the Shake Overscan attribute over time.

Create custom camera rigs Dramatic camera moves are easier to create and animate when you build a custom camera rig.

Master it Create a camera in the car chase scene that films from the point of view of chopperAnim3 but tracks the car as it moves along the road.

Solution Create a two-node camera (Camera and Aim). Attach the camera to a NURBS curve using a motion path, and parent the curve to chopperAnim3. Parent the aim of the camera to the vehicleAnim group. Create an asset for the camera so that the position of the camera around the helicopter can be changed as well as the position of the aim node relative to the vehicleAnim group.

Use depth of field and motion blur Depth of field and motion blur replicate real-world camera effects and can add a lot of drama to a scene. Both are very expensive to render and therefore should be applied with care.

Master it Create a camera asset with a built-in focus distance control.

Solution   Create the same camera and focus distance control as shown in this chapter. Select the camera, camera shape node, and distance controls, and place them within a container. Publish the Z Translation of the distToCam locator to the container. Publish the F Stop and Focus Region Scale attributes as well.

Create orthographic and stereoscopic cameras   Orthographic cameras are used primarily for modeling because they lack a sense of depth or a vanishing point. A stereoscopic rig uses three cameras and special parallax controls that enable you to render 3D movies from Maya.

Master it   Create a 3D movie from the point of view of the driver in the chase scene.

Solution   Create a stereo camera rig, and parent it to the car in the chase scene. Use the center camera to position the rig above the car's cockpit.

Chapter 3: NURBS Modeling in Maya

Use image planes   Image planes can be used to position images for use as a modeling guide.

Master it   Create image planes for side, front, and top views for use as a model guide.

Solution   Create reference drawings or use photographs taken from each view. Save the images to your local disk. Create image planes for the front, side, and top views, and apply the corresponding reference images to each image plane. Use the settings in each image plane's Attribute Editor to position the image planes in the scene. Use display layers for each plane so their visibility can be turned on and off easily.

Apply NURBS curves and surfaces   NURBS surfaces are created by lofting a surface across a series of curves. The curve and surface degree and parameterization affect the shape of the resulting surface.

Master it   What is the difference between a one-degree (linear) surface, a three-degree (cubic) surface, and a five-degree surface?

Solution   The degree of the surface is determined by the number of CVs per span minus one, so a one-degree surface has two CVs per span, a three-degree surface has four CVs per span, and a five-degree surface has six CVs per span. Linear and cubic surfaces are the ones used most frequently.

Model with NURBS surfaces   A variety of tools and techniques can be used to model surfaces with NURBS. Hard-surface/mechanical objects are well-suited subjects for NURBS surfaces.

Master it   Create a NURBS model of a common object you own such as a cell phone, a computer monitor, or a particle accelerator.

Solution   Start with drawings or photographs of the object, and place them on image planes. Use whichever techniques described in this chapter work best for you to create the object. Remember to combine tools and techniques and use the construction history to your advantage.

Create realistic surfaces   Manufactured objects usually have visible seams and parting lines that reveal how they are put together. Adding these details to your surfaces greatly increases the realism of your objects.

Master it Examine a manufactured object closely, and pay attention to the seams and parting lines. Look at weather stripping on the windows of vehicles; look at the trim around tail lights and openings in the surface. Look at the panels on the underside of electronic products such as a cell phone. Try to imitate these in your models even if the object does not exist in the real world.

Solution Use intersecting surfaces, curves projected or drawn on a surface, and the Trim tool to create parting lines and seams around panels. Use lofts and freeform fillets to bridge gaps between surfaces. Manipulate the hulls on the lofts and fillets to change the shape of the surfaces.

Adjust NURBS render tessellation You can change how the rendering engine converts a NURBS surface into triangles at render time by adjusting the tessellation of the objects. This can impact render times and increase efficiency in heavy scenes.

Master it Test the tessellation settings on a row of NURBS columns. Compare render times and image quality using different tessellation settings.

Solution Create a row of identical NURBS Greek columns using a revolve surface. Place a camera in the scene that looks down the row of columns. Compare render times and quality when you lower or raise the tessellation of surfaces far away and close to the camera. Use the Display Render Tessellation feature, the Attribute Editor, or the surfaces so that you can visualize the difference in tessellation.

Chapter 4: Polygon Modeling

Understand polygon geometry Polygon geometry consists of flat faces connected and shaped to form three-dimensional objects. You can edit the geometry by transforming the vertices, edges, and faces that make up the surface of the model.

Master it Examine the polygon primitives in the Create ➤ Polygon Primitives menu.

Solution Create an example of each primitive shown in the menu. Adjust their settings in the INPUTS section of the Channel Box. Switch to vertex selection mode, and move the vertices of each primitive to create unique shapes.

Work with smooth mesh polygons The smooth mesh preview display allows you to work on a smoothed version of the polygon model while limiting the number of components needed to shape the model. You can use creasing to create hard edges in selected areas.

Master it Create a backpack for the space suit.

Solution Create a polygon cube, and activate smooth mesh preview. Use the Insert Edge Loop tool, extrude faces, and crease edges to create a backpack that fits on the back of the space suit.

Model using deformers Deformers such as the lattice, nonlinear deformers, and the Soft Modification tool can be used to help shape geometry and groups of objects.

Master it Create a number of small-detail objects for the belt of the space suit. Shape the details so that they conform to the belt.

Solution Create a number of small objects suitable for detailing the belt. Line up the objects in the front view. Group the objects, and use a combination of lattices and bend deformers to shape the objects so they conform to the circular shape of the belt.

Combine meshes   Multiple meshes can be combined under a single shape node. When this is done, you can edit the components of the combined meshes as a single mesh.

> **Master it**   Combine two polygon spheres, and use the polygon-editing tools to join the faces of the spheres.
>
> **Solution**   Create two polygon spheres. Combine the spheres (Mesh ➤ Combine). Use the Bridge tool to connect faces between the spheres. Select a face on each sphere, and choose Edit Mesh ➤ Bridge.

Model polygons with Paint Effects   Paint Effects strokes can be converted to NURBS and Polygon geometry. Using the default brush, you can quickly create hoses and wires. Because construction history connects the converted objects to the strokes, you can use the stroke settings to edit the shape of the converted objects.

> **Master it**   Add additional hoses and wires to the space suit.
>
> **Solution**   Make the torso object live, and draw curves directly on the surface. Select the curves, and choose Paint Effects ➤ Curve Utilities ➤ Attach Brush To Curves. Open the Attribute Editor for the stroke nodes, and edit the settings to shape the wire detail. Choose Modify ➤ Convert Paint Effects To Polygons to turn the strokes into polygons.

Convert NURBS surfaces to polygons   NURBS surfaces are frequently used as a starting place to create polygon objects, giving you the power of both types of models.

> **Master it**   Convert the helmet object into polygons.
>
> **Solution**   Select the NURBS objects, and convert each to polygons. You will need to adjust the conversion options for many of the surfaces as you create them. Once you have converted all the objects, combine them into a single surface.

Sculpt polygons using Artisan   The Artisan toolset is a brush-based modeling and editing tool. Using Artisan, you can sculpt directly on the surface of geometry.

> **Master it**   Use Artisan to sculpt dents into a surface.
>
> **Solution**   Create a polygon surface with fairly dense geometry. Choose Polygons ➤ Sculpt Geometry to activate Artisan. Open the options for the tool while working, and then use the brush to make small dents in the surface of the geometry. Try this technique on parts of the space suit.

Use subdivision surfaces   Subdivision surfaces are similar to smooth mesh preview polygons except that specific parts of the model can be subdivided and edited as needed. You can traverse the subdivision levels while you work.

> **Master it**   Add wrinkles, seams, and other details to the glove model.
>
> **Solution**   Convert the subdivision surface version of the glove into polygons, and insert edge loops to create lines around the perimeter of the glove. Convert the glove back into subdivision surfaces. Add creasing to the inserted edge loops, and use the Move tool in tweak mode to add detail to the model. Move up to higher subdivision levels to create finer detail.

Chapter 5: Animation Techniques

Use Inverse Kinematics   Inverse Kinematics creates a goal object, known as an End Effector, for joints in a chain. The joints in the chain orient themselves based on the translation of the goal. The IK Handle tool is used to position the End Effector.

Master it   Create an Inverse Kinematic control for a simple arm.

Solution   Create a simple arm using three joints—one for the upper arm, one for the forearm, and one for the wrist. Rotate the forearm slightly so the Inverse Kinematic solver understands which direction the joint should rotate. Freeze transformations on the joints. Activate the IK Handle tool, click the first joint (known as the root), and then click the wrist joint. Move around the IK Handle to bend the joint.

Animate with keyframes   A keyframe marks the state of a particular attribute at a point in time on the timeline. When a second keyframe is added to the attribute at a different point in time, Maya interpolates the values between the two keyframes, creating animation. There are a number of ways to edit keyframes using the timeline and the Channel Box.

Master it   Create a number of keyframes for the Translate channels of a simple object. Copy the keyframes to a different point in time for the object. Try copying the keyframes to the Scale channels. Try copying the keys to the Translate channels of another object.

Solution   After creating keys for the object, Shift-drag a selection on the timeline. Use the arrows in the selection box to move or scale the keys. Right-click the keys, and choose Copy. Move to a different point in time on the timeline, and paste the keys. Copying, pasting, and duplicating keys to another object can be accomplished by selecting the channels in the Channel Box and using the options that appear when you right-click the channels.

Use the Graph Editor   More sophisticated animation editing is available using the animation curve editing tools on the Graph Editor.

Master it   Create a looping animation for the mechanical bug model using as few keys as possible. The bug should leap up repeatedly and move forward with each leap.

Solution   Create keyframes on the bug's Translate Y and Translate Z channels. Set four keys on the Translate Y channel so the bug is stationary, then moves up along the y-axis, moves back down to zero, and then holds for a number of frames. In the Graph Editor, set the Post-Infinity option for the Translate Y channel to Cycle. Create a similar set of keyframes for the Translate Z channel on the same frames. Set the Post-Infinity option for Translate Z to Cycle With Offset.

Preview animations with a playblast   A playblast is a tool for viewing the animation as a flip book without having to actually render the animation. FCheck is a utility program that is included with Maya. Playblasts can be viewed in FCheck.

Master it   Create a playblast of the mechBugLayers_v04.ma scene.

Solution   Open the mechBugLayers_v04.ma scene from the chapter5\scenes directory on the DVD. Rewind the animation and create a playblast by choosing Windows ➢ Playblast. Watch the playblast in FCheck.

Animate with expressions   Expressions are a powerful way to automate the movement of an object. Using conditional statements, you can create an expression that causes the animation to react to changes in the scene automatically.

Master it   Create an expression to randomly rotate the bug's eyes up and down. Make the rotation faster based on the height of the bodyCtrl curve.

Solution   Create an expression on the Translate Y channel of the eyeAimLoc locator in the mechanicalBug rig. The expression should read as follows:

```
eyeAimLoc.translateY = (bodyCtrl.translateY*noise(time));
```

Animate with motion paths   Motion paths allow you to attach an object to a curve. Over the course of the animation, the object slides along the curve based on the keyframes set on the motion path's U Value.

Master it   Make the bug walk along a motion path. See whether you can automate a walk cycle based on the position along the path.

Solution   Draw a curve in a scene with the fully rigged mechanical bug. Attach the bodyCtrl curve to the curve using Animate ➤ Attach To Motion Path. Create set driven keys for the leg animation, but instead of using the Translate Z of the bodyCtrl curve, use the U Value of the motion path node.

Use animation layers   Using animation layers, you can add new motion that can override existing animation or be combined with it.

Master it   Create animation layers for the flying bug in the `mechBug_v08.ma` scene in the `chapter5\scenes` directory on the DVD. Create two layers: one for the bodyCtrl curve and one for the legsCtrl curve. Use layers to make the animation of the wings start with small movements and then flap at full strength.

Solution   Open the `mechBug_v08.ma` scene. Select the bodyCtrl curve. In the animation layers, create an empty layer. Select the BaseAnimation layer, select the bodyCtrl curve, and choose Layers ➤ Extract Selected. Do the same for the legsCtrl curve and the wing motors. Set keyframes on the weight of the layer that contains the wing motors. Keyframe the weight from a value of 0 to a value of 1 over 20 frames.

Chapter 6: Animating with Deformers

Animate facial expressions   Animated facial expressions are a big part of character animation. It's common practice to use a blend shape deformer to create expressions from a large number of blend shape targets. The changes created in the targets can be mixed and matched by the deformer to create expressions and speech for a character.

Master it   Create blend shape targets for the nancy character. Make an expression where the brows are up and the brows are down. Create a rig that animates each brow independently.

Solution   Create two duplicates of the neutral nancy character. Use the modeling tools to model raised eyebrows on one copy and lowered eyebrows on the other. Add these targets to the nancy model. Use the Paint Blend Shape tool to make four additional targets: leftBrowUp, leftBrowDown, rightBrowUp, and rightBrowDown. Add these new targets to the nancy model. Create a custom slider using the Curve tool. Connect the slider to the Blend Shape controls using driven keys.

Create blend shape sequences   Blend shapes can be applied in a sequential order to animate a sequence of changes over time.

Master it   Create a blend shape sequence of a mushroom growing.

Solution   Create a model of a mushroom. Create a duplicate of the model, and edit each duplicate to represent stages in the growth of the mushroom. Work backward from the formed mushroom to the very beginning. Select the mushroom stage models in order of their growth stages, and apply them to the first stage of the mushroom group as a blend shape. Select the In-between setting in Blend Shape Options.

Deform a 3D object   Lattices are free-form deformers that create a 3D cage around an object. The differences between the lattice and the lattice base are used to deform geometry.

Master it   Animate a cube of jelly squishing along a path.

Solution   Create a polygon cube with a lot of divisions. Apply a lattice deformer to the cube. Scale the lattice and the base node together so they encompass the path of the cube. Use the Move tool to select and move the lattice points. Animate the cube moving through the lattice.

Animate nonlinear deformers   Nonlinear deformers apply simple changes to geometry. The deformers are controlled by animating the attributes of the deformer.

Master it   Animate an eel swimming past the jellyfish you created in this chapter.

Solution   Model a simple eel using your favorite tools and techniques. Apply a sine deformer to the eel. Create an expression that animates the offset of the sine wave. Group the eel and the deformer, and animate the group moving past the jellyfish.

Add jiggle movement to an animation   Jiggle deformers add a simple jiggling motion to animated objects.

Master it   Add a jiggling motion to the belly of a character.

Solution   Create a rotund character. Animate the character moving. Add a jiggle deformer to the character. Use the Paint Jiggle Weights tool to mask the jiggle weights on the entire character except for the belly.

Chapter 7: Rigging and Muscle Systems

Create and organize joint hierarchies   A joint hierarchy is a series of joint chains. Each joint in a chain is parented to another joint, back to the root of the chain. Each joint inherits the motion of its parent joint. Organizing the joint chains is accomplished through naming and labeling the joints. Proper orientation of the joints is essential for the joints to work properly.

Master it   Create a joint hierarchy for a giraffe character. Orient the joints so the x-axis points down the length of the joints.

Solution   Draw joint chains to fit inside the giraffe's geometry. Parent the chains together to create a complete skeleton. Use Orient Joint to force the x-axis down the length of each bone.

Use Inverse Kinematics rigs A joint chain that uses Inverse Kinematics uses a goal called an End Effector to orient the joints in the chain. A number of solvers are available in Maya.

> **Master it** Create an Inverse Kinematic rig for a character's leg. Use a separate control to position the knee of the character.
>
> **Solution** Open the IK Handle tool options. Set it to use an RP solver. Select the root joint of the leg, and Shift-select the ankle joint. Press Enter to complete the IK Handle. Create a NURBS curve control handle, and snap its position to the IK Handle. Parent the IK Handle to the NURBS control handle.

Apply skin geometry Skinning geometry refers to the process in which geometry is bound to joints so that it deforms as the joints are moved and rotated. Each vertex of the geometry receives a certain amount of influence from the joints in the hierarchy. This can be controlled by painting the weights of the geometry on the skin.

> **Master it** Paint weights on the giraffe model to get smooth-looking deformations on one side of the model. Mirror the weights to the other side.
>
> **Solution** Select the giraffe geometry. Open the Paint Weights tool. Pin the joints you want to paint. Use Replace and Smooth to paint the correct deformation weight values.

Use Maya Muscle Maya Muscle is a series of tools designed to create more believable deformations and movement for objects skinned to joints. Capsules are used to replace Maya joints. Muscles are NURBS surfaces that squash, stretch, and jiggle as they deform geometry.

> **Master it** Use Maya Muscle to create muscles for the hind leg of the giraffe. Use the muscle system to cause skin bulging and sliding.
>
> **Solution** Convert all the joints to capsules. Open the Muscle Builder interface. Add the L_upperleg_jnt to the Attach Obj 1 field. Add L_lowerleg_jnt to the Attach Obj 2 field. Choose Build/Update. Shape the muscle by manipulating its cross sections. Finalize the muscle. Convert the smooth skin to a muscle system. Select your muscles, and choose Connect Selected Muscle Objects. Paint weights for the skin to make the muscles slide or stick.

Chapter 8: Paint Effects and Toon Shading

Use the Paint Effects canvas The Paint Effects canvas can be used to test Paint Effects strokes or as a 2D paint program for creating images.

> **Master it** Create a tiling texture map using the Paint Effects canvas.
>
> **Solution** Choose a brush from the Visor, such as the `downRedFeathers.mel` brush from the `feathers` folder. On the canvas toolbar, enable the Horizontal and Vertical Wrap options. Paint feathers across the canvas; strokes that go off the top or sides will wrap around to the opposite side. Save the image in the Maya IFF format, and try applying it to an object in a 3D scene.

Paint on 3D objects Paint Effects brushes can be used to paint directly on 3D objects as long as the objects are either NURBS or polygon geometry. Paint Effects brushes require that all polygon geometry have mapped UV texture coordinates.

Master it   Create a small garden or jungle using Paint Effects brushes.

Solution   Model a simple landscape using a polygon or NURBS plane. Create some small hills and valleys in the surface. Make the object paintable, and then experiment using the Brush presets available in the Visor. The `plants`, `plantsMesh`, `trees`, `treesMesh`, `flowers`, and `flowersMesh` folders all have presets that work well in a garden or jungle setting.

Design a brush   Custom Paint Effects brushes can be created by using a preset brush as a starting place. You can alter the settings on the brush node to produce the desired look for the brush.

Master it   Design a brush to look like a laser beam.

Solution   Use one of the neonGlow brushes found in the `glows` folder in the Visor. Paint the brush in a 3D scene, paint as straight a line as possible, or attach the stroke to a straight curve using the options in the Paint Effects ➢ Curve Utilities menu. Open the Attribute Editor for the neon brush, and adjust the Color and Glow settings in the Shading section of the Brush attributes. Set the Stamp Density in the Brush Profile to a low value to create a series of glowing dots.

Shape strokes with behaviors   Behaviors are settings that can be used to shape strokes and tubes, giving them wiggling, curling, and spiraling qualities. You can animate behaviors to bring strokes to life.

Master it   Add tendrils to a squashed sphere to create a simple jellyfish.

Solution   Use the slimeWeed brush in the `grasses` folder of the Visor. Paint on the bottom of the sphere. Adjust the look of the tendrils by modifying the Noise, Curl, Wiggle, and Gravity forces in the Behavior section of the Brush attributes.

Animate strokes   Paint Effects strokes can be animated by applying keyframes, expressions, or animated textures directly to stroke attributes. You can animate the growth of strokes by using the Time Clip settings in the Flow Animation section of the Brush attributes.

Master it   Animate blood vessels growing across a surface. Animate the movement of blood within the vessels.

Solution   Use any of the Branching Tree presets as a starting point for the blood vessels. Use the Shading attributes to add a red color. Animate the growth of the vessels by activating Time Clip in the Flow Animation attributes. To animate the blood in the vessels, set the Texture type to Fractal for the color in the Texturing section and activate Texture Flow in the Flow Animation attributes.

Render Paint Effects strokes   Paint Effects strokes are rendered as a post process using Maya software. To render with mental ray, you should convert the strokes to geometry.

Master it   Render an animated Paint Effects tree in mental ray.

Solution   Choose the Tree Sparse stroke from the `Trees` folder of the Visor. Draw the tree in the scene, and add animation using the Turbulence controls (choose Tree Wind turbulence). Convert the tree to polygons and render with mental ray.

Use Toon Shading   Toon Shading uses Paint Effects to create lines around the contours of an object and a ramp shader to color the surface of the object to replicate the look of a hand-drawn cartoon.

> **Master it**   Add glowing contour lines to a futuristic vehicle to imitate the look of a vector-style rendering in a computer display.

> **Solution**   Add Paint Effects outlines to a vehicle. Select one of the neon brush strokes from the Glows folder of the Visor, and apply it to the toon lines (Toon ➢ Apply Paint Effects Brush To Toon Lines).

Chapter 9: Lighting With Mental Ray

Use shadow-casting lights   Lights can cast either depth map or ray trace shadows. Depth map shadows are created from an image projected from the shadow-casting light, which reads the depth information of the scene. Ray trace shadows are calculated by tracing rays from the light source to the rendering camera.

> **Master it**   Compare mental ray depth map shadows to ray trace shadows. Render the crystalGlobe.ma scene using soft ray trace shadows.

> **Solution**   Depth map shadows render faster and are softer than ray trace shadows. Ray trace shadows are more physically accurate. Create a light and aim it at the crystalGlobe. Enable Ray Trace Shadows, and increase the Shadow Rays and the Light Radius settings.

Render with Global Illumination   Global Illumination simulates indirect lighting by emitting photons into a scene. Global Illumination photons react with surfaces that have diffuse shaders. Caustics use photons that react to surfaces with reflective shaders. Global Illumination works particularly well in indoor lighting situations.

> **Master it**   Render the rotunda_v01.ma scene using Global Illumination.

> **Solution**   Create a photon-emitting area light, and place it near the opening in the top of the structure. Set its Intensity to 0. Create a shadow-casting direct light, and place it outside the opening in the ceiling. Turn on Emit Photons for the area light, and enable Global Illumination in the Render Settings window. Increase Photon Intensity and the number of photons emitted as needed.

Render with Final Gathering   Final Gathering is another method for creating indirect lighting. Final Gathering points are shot into the scene from the rendering camera. Final Gathering includes color bleeding and ambient occlusion shadowing as part of the indirect lighting. Final Gathering can be used on its own or in combination with Global Illumination.

> **Master it**   Create a fluorescent lightbulb from geometry that can light a room.

> **Solution**   Model a fluorescent lightbulb from a polygon cylinder. Position it above objects in a scene. Apply a Lambert shader to the bulb, and set the incandescent channel to white. Enable Final Gathering in the Render Settings window, increase the Scale value, and render the scene. Adjust the settings to increase the quality of the render.

Use Image-Based Lighting   Image-Based Lighting (IBL) uses an image to create lighting in a scene. High Dynamic Range Images (HDRI) are usually the most effective source for IBL.

There are three ways to render with IBL: Final Gathering, Global Illumination, and with the light shader. These can also be combined if needed.

Master it Render the car scene using the Uffizi Gallery probe HDR image available at `www.debevec.org/Probes/`.

Solution Create an Image-Based Lighting node in the car scene using the settings in the Render Settings window. Download the Uffizi Gallery light probe image from `www.debevec.org/Probes/`. Apply the image to the IBL node in the scene (use Angular mapping). Experiment using Final Gathering, Global Illumination, and the IBL light shader. Use these in combination to create a high-quality render.

Render using the Physical Sun and Sky network The Physical Sun and Sky network creates realistic sunlight that's ideal for outdoor rendering.

Master it Render a short animation showing the car at different times of day.

Solution Add the Physical Sun and Sky network to the car scene using the settings in the Render Settings window. Make sure Final Gathering is enabled. Keyframe the sunDirection light rotating on its x-axis over 100 frames. Render a sequence of the animation.

Understand mental ray area lights mental ray area lights are activated in the mental ray section of an area light's shape node when the Use Light Shape option is enabled. mental ray area lights render realistic, soft ray trace shadows. The light created from mental ray area lights is emitted from a three-dimensional array of lights as opposed to an infinitely small point in space.

Master it Build a lamp model that realistically lights a scene using an area light.

Solution Build a small lamp with a round bulb. Create an area light, and place it at the center of the bulb. In the area light's shape node settings, enable Use Shape in the mental ray settings, and set the shape Type to Sphere. Scale down the light to fit within the bulb. Enable Ray Trace Shadows, and render the scene.

Chapter 10: Mental Ray Shading Techniques

Understand shading concepts Light rays are reflected, absorbed by, or transmitted through a surface. A rough surface diffuses the reflection of light by bouncing light rays in nearly random directions. Specular reflections occur on smooth surfaces; the angle at which rays bounce off a smooth surface is equivalent to the angle at which they strike the surface. Refraction occurs when light rays are bent as they are transmitted through the surface. A specular highlight is the reflection of a light source on a surface. In CG rendering, this effect is often controlled separately from reflection; in the real world, specular reflection and highlights are intrinsically related.

Master it Make a standard Blinn shader appear like glass refracting light in the `jellybeans_v01.ma` scene in the `chapter10\scenes` folder of the DVD.

Solution Open the `jellyBeans_v01.ma` scene in the `chapter10\scenes` folder of the DVD. Open the Hypershade, and select the glass material—this is a standard Maya Blinn shader. In the Raytrace Options of the glass shader's Attribute Editor, turn on Refractions, and set Refractive Index to 1.1. Create a test render.

Apply reflection and refraction blur   Reflection and Refraction Blur are special mental ray options available on many standard Maya shading nodes. You can use these settings to create glossy reflections when rendering standard Maya shading nodes with mental ray.

Master it   Create the look of translucent plastic using a standard Maya Blinn shader.

Solution   Apply a Blinn shader to an object. Increase transparency and reflectivity. Enable Refractions in the Raytrace Options settings. In the mental ray section, increase the Mi Reflection and Mi Refractions settings. Render with mental ray.

Use basic mental ray shaders   The DGS and Dielectric shaders offer numerous options for creating realistic reflections and transparency. The mib (mental images base) shader library has a number of shaders that can be combined to create realistic materials.

Master it   Create a realistic CD surface using the mib shaders.

Solution   Attach a mib_illum_ward_deriv shader to the base shader slot of the mib_glossy_reflection node. Apply this material to the top of a disc. Use the settings on the mib_illum_ward_deriv shader to create anisotropic specular highlights.

Apply the car paint shader   Car paint consists of several layers, which creates the special quality seen in the reflections on car paint. The mi_carpaint_phen shader can realistically simulate the interaction of light on the surface of a car model. The diffuse, reflection, and metallic flakes layers all work together to create a convincing render.

Master it   Design a shader for a new and an old car finish.

Solution   Apply the mi_carpaint_phen_x shader to a model, and add lighting to the scene (using a Physical Sun and Sky network is a fast way to create realistic lighting). For the new car, make sure that the reflections have a Glossy setting of 1, and increase the strength of the flakes. For the older car, lower the Glossy setting on the reflections and the strength of the flakes; add a dirt layer to the shader.

Use the MIA materials   The MIA materials and nodes can be used together to create realistic materials that are always physically accurate. The MIA materials come with a number of presets that can be used as a starting point for your own materials.

Master it   Create a realistic polished-wood material.

Solution   Create a mia_material_x shader for an object in a scene that uses physical sky and sun lighting. Use the Glossy finish as a starting place to create the material. In the Color channel of the Diffuse settings, add the Wood 3D texture from the standard Maya 3D texture nodes. Add glossiness to the reflections and the highlight (remember that lower settings spread out the reflection, whereas higher settings create a more defined reflection).

Render contours   mental ray has the ability to render contours of your models to create a cartoon drawing look for your animations. Rendering contours requires that options in the Render Settings window and in the shading group for the object are activated.

Master it   Render the space suit helmet using contours.

Solution   Open one of the versions of the helmet scene in the chapter10\scenes directory. Apply a material to the helmet geometry. Enable Contour Rendering in the material's shading group node and on the Features tab of the Render Settings window.

Chapter 11: Texture Mapping

Create UV texture coordinates   UV texture coordinates are a crucial element of any polygon or subdivision surface model. If a model has well-organized UVs, painting texture and displacement maps is easy and error free.

Master it   Map UV texture coordinates on a giraffe's leg; then try a complete figure.

Solution   Match your selection to your projection. Only select faces that make a cylindrical shape. Use cylindrical mapping to lay out the UVs.

Create bump and normal maps   Bump and normal maps are two ways to add detail to a model. Bump maps are great for fine detail, such as pores; normal maps allow you to transfer detail from a high-resolution mesh to a low-resolution version of the same model as well as offer superior shading and faster rendering than bump maps.

Master it   Create high-resolution and low-resolution versions of the model, and try creating a normal map using the Transfer Maps tool. See whether you can bake the bump map into the normal map.

Solution   Using the `girafferTransferMaps_v01.ma` scene file, open the Transfer Maps interface. Add the low-resolution giraffe to the Target Mesh rollout. Add the high-resolution giraffe to the Source Mesh rollout. Click the Normal button to add a normal map. Select Bake and Close to complete the tool.

Create a misss_fast_skin shader   The misss_fast_skin shader can create extremely realistic-looking skin. The secret is using painted texture maps for the Subsurface and Specularity channels.

Master it   Change the look of the giraffe by going from Blinn shaders to Subsurface scattering.

Solution   From the Materials section, create a miss_fast_skin_shader. Assign the material to selected faces on the character. Add painted textures to the Overall, Diffuse, and Epidermal color channels.

Chapter 12: Rendering for Compositing

Use render layers   Render layers can be used to separate the elements of a single scene into different versions or into different layers of a composite. Each layer can have its own shaders, lights, and settings. Using overrides, you can change the way each layer renders.

Master it   Use render layers to set up alternate versions of the space helmet. Try applying contour rendering on one layer and Final Gathering on another.

Solution   Open the `helmetComposite_v01.ma` scene from the `chapter12\scenes` directory on the DVD. Add a second render layer by copying the helmet layer. In the render settings for the helmet layer, create a layer override for the Enable Contours setting, and turn this on (remember to activate one of the Draw By Property Difference options). Create a Layer Override for the Final Gathering option in the Indirect Illumination tab, and turn Final Gathering off. Apply a Lambert texture to all the helmet surfaces while in the helmet layer, and activate Contours in the Lambert's shading group node attributes. The helmet2 layer should still have Final Gathering activated. Test render both layers, and see whether contours render correctly on the helmet layer and whether Final Gathering renders on the helmet2 layer.

Use render passes   Render passes allow you to separate material properties into different images. These passes are derived from calculations stored in the Frame Buffer. Each pass can be used in compositing software to efficiently rebuild the rendered scene. Render pass contribution maps define which objects and lights are included in a render pass.

Master it   Create an Ambient Occlusion pass for the minigun scene.

Solution   Open the `minGunComposite_v01.ma` scene. On the Passes tab of the Render Settings window, create an Ambient Occlusion pass. Move the AO (Ambient Occlusion) pass from the Scene Passes section to the Associated Passes section. On the Features tab, enable Ambient Occlusion. Open the Attribute Editor for the AO pass, and turn on Use Local Settings. Set Maximum Distance to 5. Use the File menu in the Render View window to load the Ambient Occlusion pass (if the Load Render Pass option is not available, use the File menu to browse to the `images` directory of the current project; you'll find the pass in a folder called `miniGun/AO`).

Perform batch renders   Batch renders automate the process of rendering a sequence of images. You can use Maya's Batch Render options in the Maya interface or choose Batch Render from the command prompt (or Terminal) when Maya is closed. A batch script can be used to render multiple scenes.

Master it   Create a batch script to render five fictional scenes. Each scene uses layers with different render settings. Set the frame range for each scene to render frames 20 through 50. Each scene is named `myScene1.ma` through `myScene5.ma`.

Solution   Create a text file in plain-text format. Each line should be a command-line render script that looks like this:

```
Render -r file -s 20 -e 50 myScene1.ma
```

Save the text file as **batchRender.bat** (or .batch on a Mac) in the same directory as the scenes. On a Windows machine, you can double-click the .bat file. On a Mac, you need to use the Terminal to change the mode of the file into an executable (chmod 777). On the Mac, type **./batchRender.batch** to start the render.

Use mental ray quality settings   The settings on the Quality tab of the Render Settings window allow you to adjust the anti-aliasing quality and the raytrace acceleration of a scene (among other things). Sampling improves the quality of the image by reducing flickering problems. Raytrace acceleration does not affect image quality but improves render times when raytracing is activated in a scene.

Master it   Diagnose both the sampling and the BSP depth of the `helmetComposite_v04` `.ma` scene.

Solution   Open the `helmetComposite_v04.ma` scene on the `chapter12\scenes` directory on the DVD. In the Render Settings window, activate Diagnose Samples, and perform a test render (turn off Final Gathering). The areas of light gray and white indicate the areas where most of the sampling occurs. Turn off Diagnose Sampling, and in the Acceleration options, set the Diagnose Bsp option to Depth. Set the sampling of the scene to -3, and perform a test render. The orange and red portions of the test render indicate areas where BSP voxels are approaching or have reached maximum depth.

Chapter 13: Introducing nParticles

Create nParticles   nParticles can be added to a scene in a number of ways. They can be drawn using the tool or spawned from an emitter, or they can fill an object.

Master it   Create a spiral shape using nParticles.

Solution   Create a polygon helix, and fill it with nParticles. Make the surface transparent, and set Gravity to **0** in the Nucleus solver.

Make nParticles collide   NParticles can collide with themselves, other nParticles, and polygon surfaces.

Master it   Make nParticles pop out of the top of an animated volume.

Solution   Create a polygon cube, and remove the top. Animate the cube shrinking along the x- or z-axis. Fill the cube with nParticles (make the nParticle style Balls or Water with an Incompressibility value of 1), and make the cube a collision surface.

Create liquid simulations   Enabling Liquid Simulations changes the behavior of nParticles so they act like water or other fluids.

Master it   Create a flowing stream of nParticles that ends in a waterfall.

Solution   Model a trough in a polygon plane that slopes downward and ends at a cliff. Create a volume emitter set to the water nParticle style. Set Incompressibility to **0.5**.

Emit nParticles from a texture   The emission rate of an nParticle can be controlled using a texture.

Master it   Create your own name in nParticles.

Solution   Use a digital paint program to create a texture using your name (black letters on a white surface work best). Import the texture into Maya using a file texture node. Create a surface emitter using a plane. Attach the file node to the Texture Emission Rate attribute of the emitter, and select Emit From Dark.

Move nParticles with nucleus wind   The wind force on the nucleus node can be used to push nParticles.

Master it   Create the effect of bubbles pushed back and forth under water.

Solution   Create an emitter using the ball-style nParticles. Set Gravity Direction to **1** in the y-axis field so the nParticles are pulled upward. Set Air Density to greater than **20**. Create an expression that randomizes the wind speed using the `noise` function, such as `nucleus1.windSpeed=2*(noise(time));`, and set the Wind Noise attribute to **5**.

Use force fields   Force fields can be emitted by nParticles and collision objects, creating interesting types of behavior in your scenes.

Master it   Add a second nParticle object emitted from the base of the generator. Enable its force field so that it attracts a few of the original nParticles.

Solution   Create a surface emitter from the base object in the generator. In the options, set Min Distance to **1** and Max Distance to **1.5**; this ensures that the new particle is not trapped by the base surface (it is a collision object). Set Emission Rate to **10**, and lower the emission rates on the other emitters so the scene plays at a reasonable rate. Set the Point Force field to Worlds pace. Set Magnitude to **10**.

Chapter 14: Dynamic Effects

Use nCloth   nCloth can be used to make polygon geometry behave dynamically to simulate a wide variety of materials. Using the presets that come with Maya, you can design your own materials and create your own presets for use in your animations.

Master it   Create the effect of a cube of gelatinous material rolling down the stairs.

Solution   Model a cube and some stairs. Position the cube above the stairs, and convert it into an nCloth object. Apply the Putty preset and try blending Water Balloon, Solid Rubber, and other presets until you get a nice gelatinous motion. Try raising the stickiness on the material to counteract some of the bounciness.

Combine nCloth and nParticles   Because nCloth and nParticles use the same dynamic systems, they can be easily combined to create amazing simulations.

Master it   Make a water balloon burst as it hits the ground.

Solution   Create a polygon balloon, and convert it to an nCloth object. Place it above a floor object. Apply the Water Balloon preset to the nCloth. Fill the nCloth balloon with water nParticles. Add a tearable constraint to the nCloth balloon. Play the animation, and adjust the settings until you get the effect you want.

Use Maya rigid body dynamics   Rigid body dynamics are not quite as powerful as nCloth objects, but they do calculate much faster and work better for simulations involving a large number of interacting pieces.

Master it   Animate a series of dominoes falling over.

Solution   Create a large number of polygon cubes, and arrange them in a line on a floor that is a passive rigid body. Convert the cubes into active rigid bodies. Add a gravity field to all of the active bodies. Apply a small radial field to the first rigid body so it falls over and collides with the second rigid body, creating a chain reaction of toppling dominoes.

Instance geometry to nParticles   Modeled geometry can be instanced to nParticles to create a wide variety of effects.

Master it   Create the effect of a swarm of insects attacking a beach ball.

Solution   Model a single insect. Place the model at the origin of the grid, and freeze transformations on the model. Animate the insect's wings flapping at a high rate of speed. Add an nCloth sphere and an nParticle emitter to the scene. Instance the insect to the nParticles, and make the nCloth sphere a goal for the nParticles. To make the insects face the correct direction, set the aim direction in the nParticles' Instance attributes to Velocity.

Create nParticle expressions   nParticle expressions can be used to further extend the power of nParticles. Using expressions to automate instanced geometry simulations is just one of the ways in which expressions can be used.

Master it   Improve the animation of the insects attacking the beach ball by adding different types of insects to the swarm. Randomize their size, and create expressions so that larger insects move more slowly.

Solution   Model several types of insects; place them all at the origin. Add the new geometry to the instance node in the swarm scene. Make a creation expression to randomize the index number of the instances so more than one type of insect is included in the swarm. Use the Mass Scale ramp to randomize the mass of the insect nParticles. Create an expression that bases the scale in X, Y, and Z of each instance on the mass of each nParticle.

Create smoke trails   Using the cloud nParticle type, smoke can be added to a simulation. nCloth objects and nParticles can be turned into emitters to emit the smoke.

Master it   In the explosion scene from this chapter, make the nCloth bricks emit a smoke trail as they fly out from the tower.

Solution   Select the active bricks and convert them to surface emitters. Set the nParticle type to Cloud. Use the nParticle ramps to make the cloud nParticles grow and fade in opacity as they are emitted from the nCloth bricks. Make sure the nParticles have a defined life span.

Chapter 15: Fur, Hair, and Clothing

Add fur to characters   Maya Fur is a rendering module that adds realistic short hairs to the surface of characters to simulate fur. Fur can be rendered using both Maya Software and mental ray. The placement, length, and other attributes of fur can be controlled by painting on the surface with the Artisan tool interface. When adding fur to polygons, the success of the fur is largely dependent on how well the UV texture coordinates have been mapped.

Master it   Create furry whiskers for the old man model used in Chapter 11.

Solution   Open the UVMap_v06.ma scene from the chapter11\scenes directory on the DVD. Attach fur to the model, and paint a baldness map so that nonwhiskered areas are at a value of 0 and whiskered areas have a low value, such as 0.3, to create sparse whiskers.

Add dynamic motion to fur   Using hair curves as a control, fur can be made to react to dynamic forces.

Master it   Create a field of grass that blows in the wind.

Solution   Model some rolling hills, and apply the Grass Fur preset to the hills. Make the length of the grass fairly long. Apply a grid of hair follicles to the field, and apply forces to the hair follicles (you may want to lower the gravity in the hairSystem node). Attach the hairSystem to the grass fur description.

Create dynamic curves   A standard Maya curve can be made dynamic by using the Make Dynamic Curves action in the Hair menu. A copy of the curve is created that will respond to dynamic motion and forces. The curve can be used in skeletons for IK Spline tools, as a source for Paint Effects strokes, as a modeling tool, or for any other effect that requires curves.

Master it   Create a flag using dynamic curves.

Solution   Create two parallel curves, and make both dynamic. Set the Point Lock attribute on both curves to Base. Loft a NURBS surface between the dynamic curves. Edit the dynamic properties of the curves, and apply fields to the curves to create a flapping motion for the flag.

Add hair to characters   Hair is created using Paint Effects strokes that are controlled by follicles. The follicles are dynamic curves that respond to forces and movement. Follicles can be applied to polygon or NURBS surfaces as a grid or by painting on the surface. The Visor contains a number of hair presets that can be imported into a scene.

Master it   Add hair to the old man character from Chapter 9.

Solution   Open the UVMap_v06.ma scene from the chapter11\scenes folder on the DVD. Create a scalp surface for the old man by duplicating selected faces on the head. Paint follicles on the head to suggest hair growing from the sides and back of the head. Use Thinning and other hair properties to create the look of long and wispy hair.

Style hair   Hair can be styled by painting attribute values on follicles, by using dynamic fields, or by directly editing the CVs of start or rest curves.

Master it   Create an avant-garde hairdo for the nancy character using fields.

Solution   Open the nancyHair_v06.ma scene. Apply a turbulence field to the hairSystem1 node. Set Magnitude to a high value (**10** to **20**), and set Attenuation to **0**. Play the animation. When the hair achieves an interesting state, select the follicles, and set the state as the hair's rest position (and start position). Delete the field, and increase the hair's start curve Attract attribute.

Use hair constraints   Hair constraints can be used to control the motion of hair or to connect the hair to props, such as hair ties and scrunchies.

Master it   Use a constraint to create a ponytail for a character.

Solution   Create hair for a character. Select a number of the start curves, and apply a hair-to-hair constraint. Play the simulation, and adjust the properties of the constraint to create a ponytail at the back of the head. The effect of the motion of the constraint is visible in the hair strokes.

Paint nCloth properties   Properties such as Bounce, Stretch, and Wrinkle can be painted onto nCloth objects using either texture or vertex painting techniques. When painting properties, the Min and Max Value ranges in the Artisan interface may need to be altered to allow for values beyond the range of 0 to 1. Vertex maps have the advantage that the values are not stored in an external texture file.

Master it   Add starch to the simple man's shirt by painting a Rigidity value on the shirt geometry.

Solution   Open the simpleMan_v06.ma scene from the chapter15\scenes directory. Select the surface, and paint a vertex map. Choose Rigidity as the property you want to paint. Set Max Value in the Artisan Tool options to **30**. Set the Max Color slider in the Artisan Display options to **30**. Set the Paint value to somewhere between **20** and **30**, and paint on the surface where you want the shirt to be stiff. Adjust the values as needed.

Chapter 16: Maya Fluids

Use fluid containers Fluid containers are used to create self-contained fluid effects. Fluid simulations use a special type of particle that is generated in the small subunits (called *voxels*) of a fluid container. Fluid containers can be 2D or 3D. 2D containers take less time to calculate and can be used in many cases to generate realistic fluid effects.

Master It Create a logo animation that dissolves like ink in water.

Solution Create a 2D fluid container. Add a surface emitter using a NURBS plane, and add an emission map for the diffusion attribute of the emitter. Use a file texture created from a logo. Set the Buoyancy of the fluid to **0**. Use dynamic fields to push the logo to create the dissolving motion. Try using Turbulence, Drag, and Vortex fields on the logo.

Create a reaction A reaction can be simulated in a 3D container by combining temperature with fuel. Surfaces can be used as emitters within a fluid container.

Master It Create a chain reaction of explosions using the Paint Fluids tool.

Solution Create a 3D fluid container. Use the Paint Fluids tool to paint small blobs of fuel separated by short distances. The painted fuel blobs should be arranged so that they create a chain reaction when lit. Add an emitter that emits temperature, and place it below the first fuel blob in the container. Set the Ignition Temperature, Reaction Speed, and Heat Released attributes in the Fuel section of the container so the fuel burns and emits heat when a certain temperature is reached. Set Shading to Temperature so that you can see the reaction.

Render fluid containers Fluid containers can be rendered using Maya Software or mental ray. The fluids can react to lighting, cast shadows, and self-shadow.

Master It Render the `TurbulentFlame.ma` example in the Visor so that it emits light onto nearby surfaces.

Solution Create a scene that has simple modeled surfaces such as a floor and some logs. Import the `TurbulentFlame.ma` scene from the `Fire` folder of the Visor (on the Fluid Examples tab). Set the renderer to mental ray. In the Indirect Lighting section, turn on Final Gathering. Increase Final Gathering Scale to **4**. Turn off Default Light on the Common Attributes tab of the Render Settings window. Play the animation, and render a test frame when the fire is burning.

Use fluids with nParticles Fluid simulations can interact with nParticles to create a large array of interesting effects.

Master It nCloth objects use nParticles and springs to simulate the behavior of cloth. If fluids can affect nParticles, it stands to reason that they can also affect nCloth objects. Test this by creating a simulation where a fluid emitter pushes around an nCloth object.

Solution Create a 3D fluid container and an emitter that emits density and temperature. The fluid should rise in the container, and the Swirl attribute in Velocity should be set to **10** so that there is a turbulent motion. Create a polygon sphere, and place it inside the fluid container above the emitter. Convert the sphere to an nCloth object. Use the Silk preset for the nCloth object, and set Gravity in the Nucleus tab to **0.1**. Play the animation, and experiment with the settings in the fluid container and on the nCloth object until the fluid pushes the nCloth object around.

Create an ocean   Ocean effects are created and edited using the Ocean shader. Objects can float in the ocean using locators.

> **Master It**   Create an ocean effect that resembles stormy seas. Add the capsule geometry as a floating object.

> **Solution**   Import the WhiteCaps.ma scene from the Ocean Examples tab of the Visor. Import the capsule_v01.ma scene from the chapter16\scenes directory on the DVD. Use the Float Selected Objects command to make the capsule float on the surface of the water. Look at the settings in the ocean shader node to see how the stormy sea effect was created.

Chapter 17: MEL Scripting

Use a MEL command   MEL commands are used to perform many tasks within Maya. There are numerous ways to enter MEL commands in the Maya interface. These include the command shell, the command line, and the Script Editor.

> **Master it**   Create a polygon cube using the command shell. Create a NURBS cone using the command line. Create a polygonSphere using the Script Editor.

> **Solution**   Open the command shell, and type **polyCube**. In the command line, type **cone**. In the work area of the Script Editor, type **polySphere**.

Use MEL scripting techniques   Many basic MEL techniques can be used to reduce the number of repetitive tasks performed during a Maya session. Using commands, conditional statements, and loops, you can create simple scripts that make working in Maya faster and more efficient.

> **Master it**   Write a more efficient version of the mySpriteScript file that automatically selects all the nParticle objects in a scene without the need for a conditional statement to test the type of the selected nodes.

> **Solution**   In the Script Editor, choose History ➤ Echo All Commands. In a scene that contains nParticles, choose Edit ➤ Select All By Type ➤ nParticles. Observe the text in the history section of the Script Editor. The line that reads select -r `listTransforms "-type nParticle"`; can be used in the script to automatically select all the nParticles in the scene, which means the conditional statement that tests the selection type is no longer needed. Edit the first few lines of mySpriteScript.mel to include the listTransforms command; then remove the conditional statement from the script. For an example of this alternate version, look at the mySpriteScript_v02.mel script in the chapter17\mel folder on the DVD.

Create a procedure   Procedures are sections of code that can be called upon at any time within a script. Procedures can help make longer scripts more efficient by eliminating the need to repeat sections of code.

> **Master it**   Write a procedure that adds an expression to selected objects that use the noise function to randomly scale objects over time.

> **Solution**   Edit the shakeMeProc.mel file. Replace the text translateX=rand(-1,1); with **scaleX=noise(time);**. Repeat this for TranslateY and TranslateZ.

Use the Python scripting interface Python can be used within the Script Editor to execute Python commands or to execute MEL commands within a Python script. The Maya commands must be imported at the start of Python script if you want to incorporate MEL into the Python code.

Master it Use Python to make a NURBS torus.

Solution Switch the Script Editor tab to Python mode. Import MEL commands by typing **maya.cmds**. Type **maya.cmds.torus()** to create the torus using default settings. Flags can be used to specify attributes of the torus. Look up Python commands in the Technical Documentation section of the Maya help files for more information.

Appendix B

About the Companion DVD

What you'll find on the DVD:

◆ System requirements

◆ Using the DVD

◆ Troubleshooting

This appendix summarizes the content you'll find on the DVD. If you need help with copying the items provided on the DVD, refer to the installation instructions in the "Using the DVD" section of this appendix.

What You'll Find on the DVD

In the Chapter Files directory, you will find all the files for completing the tutorials and understanding concepts in this book.

Many of the files can be found in Maya Project folders. Each folder contains all the scene and support files for that project.

Working with files directly from the DVD is not encouraged, because Maya scenes link to external files such as texture maps and dynamic caches. Copy the entire project for each chapter to your local drive, including the empty folders, to ensure that the example scenes function properly.

System Requirements

This DVD does not include the Maya 2011 software. You will need to have Maya 2011 installed on your computer to complete the exercises in the book.

You will need to be running Maya 2011 to fully use all the files on the DVD (the software is not included on the DVD). Make sure your computer meets the minimum system requirements shown in the following list. If your computer doesn't match up to these requirements, you may have problems using the files on the companion DVD. For the latest information, please refer to the ReadMe file located at the root of the DVD-ROM.

◆ A computer running Microsoft Windows XP (SP2 or newer) or Windows Vista, or Apple OS X 10.5.2 or newer

◆ An Internet connection

◆ A CD-ROM drive

For the latest information on the system requirements for Maya, go to www.autodesk.com/maya. Although you can find specific hardware recommendations there, there is some general information that will help you determine whether you're already set up to run Maya: you need a fast processor, a minimum 2GB of RAM, and a "workstation graphics card" (rather than a consumer-grade gaming video card) for the best compatibility.

Using the DVD

For best results, you'll want to copy the files from your DVD to your computer. To copy the items from the DVD to your hard drive, follow these steps:

1. Insert the DVD into your computer's DVD-ROM drive. The license agreement appears.

   Windows users: The interface won't launch if Autorun is disabled. In that case, choose Start ➤ Run (for Windows Vista, choose Start ➤ All Programs ➤ Accessories ➤ Run). In the dialog box that appears, type **D:\Start.exe**. (Replace D with the proper letter if your DVD drive uses a different letter. If you don't know the letter, see how your DVD drive is listed under My Computer.) Click OK.

2. Read through the license agreement, and then click the Accept button if you want to use the DVD.

The DVD interface appears. The interface allows you to access the content with just one or two clicks. Alternately, you can access the files at the root directory of your hard drive.

Mac users: The DVD icon will appear on your desktop; double-click the icon to open the DVD, and then navigate to the files you want.

Troubleshooting

Wiley has attempted to provide programs that work on most computers with the minimum system requirements. Alas, your computer may differ, and some programs may not work properly for some reason.

The two likeliest problems are that you don't have enough memory (RAM) for the programs you want to use or that you have other programs running that are affecting the installation or running of a program. If you get an error message such as "Not enough memory" or "Setup cannot continue," try one or more of the following suggestions, and then try using the software again:

Turn off any antivirus software running on your computer. Installation programs sometimes mimic virus activity and may make your computer incorrectly believe that it's being infected by a virus.

Close all running programs. The more programs you have running, the less memory is available to other programs. Installation programs typically update files and programs; so if you keep other programs running, installation may not work properly.

Add more RAM to your computer. This is, admittedly, a drastic and somewhat expensive step. However, adding more memory can really help the speed of your computer and allow more programs to run at the same time.

Customer Care

If you have trouble with the book's companion DVD, please call the Wiley Product Technical Support phone number at (800) 762-2974. Outside the United States, call +1 (317) 572-3994. You can also contact Wiley Product Technical Support at `http://sybex.custhelp.com`. John Wiley & Sons will provide technical support only for installation and other general quality control items. For technical support on the applications themselves, consult the program's vendor or author.

To place additional orders or to request information about other Wiley products, please call (877) 762-2974.

Please check the book's website at `www.sybex.com/go/masteringmaya2011`, where we'll post additional content and updates that supplement this book should the need arise.

Index

WILEY PUBLISHING, INC. END-USER LICENSE AGREEMENT

READ THIS. You should carefully read these terms and conditions before opening the software packet(s) included with this book "Book". This is a license agreement "Agreement" between you and Wiley Publishing, Inc. "WPI". By opening the accompanying software packet(s), you acknowledge that you have read and accept the following terms and conditions. If you do not agree and do not want to be bound by such terms and conditions, promptly return the Book and the unopened software packet(s) to the place you obtained them for a full refund.

1. License Grant. WPI grants to you (either an individual or entity) a nonexclusive license to use one copy of the enclosed software program(s) (collectively, the "Software") solely for your own personal or business purposes on a single computer (whether a standard computer or a workstation component of a multi-user network). The Software is in use on a computer when it is loaded into temporary memory (RAM) or installed into permanent memory (hard disk, CD-ROM, or other storage device). WPI reserves all rights not expressly granted herein.

2. Ownership. WPI is the owner of all right, title, and interest, including copyright, in and to the compilation of the Software recorded on the physical packet included with this Book "Software Media". Copyright to the individual programs recorded on the Software Media is owned by the author or other authorized copyright owner of each program. Ownership of the Software and all proprietary rights relating thereto remain with WPI and its licensers.

3. **Restrictions on Use and Transfer.**

(a) You may only (i) make one copy of the Software for backup or archival purposes, or (ii) transfer the Software to a single hard disk, provided that you keep the original for backup or archival purposes. You may not (i) rent or lease the Software, (ii) copy or reproduce the Software through a LAN or other network system or through any computer subscriber system or bulletin-board system, or (iii) modify, adapt, or create derivative works based on the Software.

(b) You may not reverse engineer, decompile, or disassemble the Software. You may transfer the Software and user documentation on a permanent basis, provided that the transferee agrees to accept the terms and conditions of this Agreement and you retain no copies. If the Software is an update or has been updated, any transfer must include the most recent update and all prior versions.

4. Restrictions on Use of Individual Programs. You must follow the individual requirements and restrictions detailed for each individual program in the "About the DVD" appendix of this Book or on the Software Media. These limitations are also contained in the individual license agreements recorded on the Software Media. These limitations may include a requirement that after using the program for a specified period of time, the user must pay a registration fee or discontinue use. By opening the Software packet(s), you agree to abide by the licenses and restrictions for these individual programs that are detailed in the "About the DVD" appendix and/or on the Software Media. None of the material on this Software Media or listed in this Book may ever be redistributed, in original or modified form, for commercial purposes.

5. Limited Warranty.

(a) WPI warrants that the Software and Software Media are free from defects in materials and workmanship under normal use for a period of sixty (60) days from the date of purchase of this Book. If WPI receives notification within the warranty period of defects in materials or workmanship, WPI will replace the defective Software Media.

(b) WPI AND THE AUTHOR(S) OF THE BOOK DISCLAIM ALL OTHER WARRANTIES, EXPRESS OR IMPLIED, INCLUDING WITHOUT LIMITATION IMPLIED WARRANTIES OF MERCHANTABILITY AND FITNESS FOR A PARTICULAR PURPOSE, WITH RESPECT TO THE SOFTWARE, THE PROGRAMS, THE SOURCE CODE CONTAINED THEREIN, AND/OR THE TECHNIQUES DESCRIBED IN THIS BOOK. WPI DOES NOT WARRANT THAT THE FUNCTIONS CONTAINED IN THE SOFTWARE WILL MEET YOUR REQUIREMENTS OR THAT THE OPERATION OF THE SOFTWARE WILL BE ERROR FREE.

(c) This limited warranty gives you specific legal rights, and you may have other rights that vary from jurisdiction to jurisdiction.

6. Remedies.

(a) WPI's entire liability and your exclusive remedy for defects in materials and workmanship shall be limited to replacement of the Software Media, which may be returned to WPI with a copy of your receipt at the following address: Software Media Fulfillment Department, Attn.: *Mastering Autodesk Maya 2011*, Wiley Publishing, Inc., 10475 Crosspoint Blvd., Indianapolis, IN 46256, or call 1-800-762-2974. Please allow four to six weeks for delivery. This Limited Warranty is void if failure of the Software Media has resulted from accident, abuse, or misapplication. Any replacement Software Media will be warranted for the remainder of the original warranty period or thirty (30) days, whichever is longer.

(b) In no event shall WPI or the author be liable for any damages whatsoever (including without limitation damages for loss of business profits, business interruption, loss of business information, or any other pecuniary loss) arising from the use of or inability to use the Book or the Software, even if WPI has been advised of the possibility of such damages.

(c) Because some jurisdictions do not allow the exclusion or limitation of liability for consequential or incidental damages, the above limitation or exclusion may not apply to you.

7. U.S. Government Restricted Rights. Use, duplication, or disclosure of the Software for or on behalf of the United States of America, its agencies and/or instrumentalities "U.S. Government" is subject to restrictions as stated in paragraph (c)(1)(ii) of the Rights in Technical Data and Computer Software clause of DFARS 252.227-7013, or subparagraphs (c) (1) and (2) of the Commercial Computer Software - Restricted Rights clause at FAR 52.227-19, and in similar clauses in the NASA FAR supplement, as applicable.

8. General. This Agreement constitutes the entire understanding of the parties and revokes and supersedes all prior agreements, oral or written, between them and may not be modified or amended except in a writing signed by both parties hereto that specifically refers to this Agreement. This Agreement shall take precedence over any other documents that may be in conflict herewith. If any one or more provisions contained in this Agreement are held by any court or tribunal to be invalid, illegal, or otherwise unenforceable, each and every other provision shall remain in full force and effect.